D0640540

Federal Income Taxation
of Corporate Enterprise

Editorial Advisory Board
Little, Brown and Company
Law Book Division

Richard A. Epstein
James Parker Hall Distinguished Service Professor of Law
University of Chicago

E. Allan Farnsworth
Alfred McCormack Professor of Law
Columbia University

Ronald J. Gilson
Professor of Law
Stanford University

Geoffrey C. Hazard, Jr.
Sterling Professor of Law
Yale University

James E. Krier
Earl Warren DeLano Professor of Law
University of Michigan

Elizabeth Warren
Professor of Law
University of Pennsylvania

Bernard Wolfman
Fessenden Professor of Law
Harvard University

Federal Income Taxation
of Corporate Enterprise
Third Edition

Bernard Wolfman

**Fessenden Professor of Law
Harvard University**

Little, Brown and Company
Boston   Toronto   London

Copyright © 1990 by William D. Andrews, Trustee
All rights reserved. No part of this book may be reproduced in any
form or by any electronic or mechanical means including information
storage and retrieval systems without permission in writing from the
publisher, except by a reviewer who may quote brief passages
in a review.

Library of Congress Catalog Card No. 89-85736

ISBN 0-316-95093-9

Third Edition

MV NY

Published simultaneously in Canada
by Little, Brown & Company (Canada) Limited
Printed in the United States of America

To my grandchildren
Audrey, Avi,
and
Graham

Summary of Contents

Contents

2
The Shareholder Income Tax — Corporate Distributions and Disposition of Investor Interests (Not in Reorganization) 109

4
Reorganizations and Related Transactions   429

5
The Corporate Identity — Special Problems   877

6
The Accumulated Earnings Tax —
§§531-537   **1063**

7
Personal Holding Companies — §§541-547   1115

8
Subchapter S — §§1361-1379   1179

Preface

This is the third edition of the book that first appeared in 1971. It deals with the federal income taxation of corporate enterprise. I have dropped the chapter on partnership taxation, leaving it to books for which it is the main subject. This book has benefitted from the comments of the many who have taught and studied from the earlier editions.* Like those earlier, this edition is for students who have completed a basic course in federal income taxation, one that covers the pervasive concepts affecting corporate and noncorporate transactions alike.

The principal (but not the only) focus of this book is Subchapter C of the Internal Revenue Code, the source of most of the federal income tax law governing corporations and their shareholders. The included cases and rulings and the excerpts from legislative history give direction and wholeness to the subject while at the same time exposing the difficulties of interpretation and the policy tensions that inhere in it. The materials offer abundant opportunities to understand and to build upon the underlying statutory structure and to evaluate it from a critical perspective as well.

Although the taxation of corporations and shareholders has never been a static subject — always quite dynamic in fact — the congressional changes of 1986 were fundamental. More than any other factors, they precipitated this new edition. The organization of the book also has changed. The order in which the chapters appear is altered, and there is a rearrangement of subject matter within some of the chapters as well. The educational theme that underlies the book as a whole, and particularly the first four chapters, is one I want to spell out.

The predicate of Subchapter C is a classical, double tax system, with the corporation taxed on *its* income, and the shareholders taxed on *their* income (including the corporate dividends they receive and the profits they realize when they sell their stock). The first thing to study, then, is what constitutes the *taxable income* of the fictitious entity we call a corporation, and so Chapter 1 is devoted to that subject.

Chapter 2, picking up on the double tax theme, explores the income tax issues that attend the shareholder's receipt of corporate distributions and the proceeds of the sale of corporate stock and the relief from the limitations on capital loss deductions that §1244 provides.

Having studied the special attributes of corporate and shareholder income, the student is now at the point where it is sensible to address

*They are titled *Federal Income Taxation of Business Enterprise*.

the question *whether* to incorporate and to study the income tax consequences to both shareholder and corporation of the incorporation
transaction itself. Chapter 3, affected in a very important dimension by
legislation enacted late in 1989, focuses on the taxfree (and taxable)
incorporation of assets. It analyzes the concept and consequences of
nonrecognition. Let me say, however, that despite my reasons for deferring
the consideration of incorporation until after the student learns about
the corporate tax base and the tax impact of distributions to shareholders, it is quite reasonable for a teacher to begin a corporate tax course
with Chapter 3, with the birth of the corporation, and there are professors who do so.

Chapter 4, covering the "reorganization" of corporations — e.g., recapitalizations, mergers, stock-for-stock swaps, and spinoffs — goes
further into the subject of nonrecognition and related concepts, and it
will occupy a substantial part of the course. Chapters 1 and 2 will have
helped the student to understand and weigh the considerations in so-
called taxable corporate acquisitions. Chapter 4 does the same with respect to so-called taxfree acquisitions, and the student will learn when
to choose and when not to choose the taxfree over the taxable transaction.
In both settings students will come to appreciate the financial world's
recent preoccupation with leveraged buyouts and other forms of corporate restructuring, and they will learn about the role net operating
loss carryovers tend to play in some of them.

For most professors and students, Chapters 1 through 4 will comprise
the corporate tax course, four credits for many, three for others. Chapter
5, however, has material which, in part, the professor can bring into the
earlier chapters where it seems desirable, and in a five-credit course can
cover it in full. It deals with problems of corporate identity, with the
issue of when an unincorporated enterprise will be taxed as a corporation, when consolidated corporate returns are appropriate and the
questions such returns present, and when the Commissioner may allocate
the income of one corporation to another under §482.

Chapters 6 and 7 examine the penalty taxes to which C corporations
may be subject, the §531 tax on unreasonable accumulations of corporate
earnings, and the §541 tax on personal holding company income. Some
professors will include materials from these chapters when they teach
the subjects covered in the first four. Others will cover them separately,
either in a discrete follow-up course or in a five-credit corporate tax
course.

Chapter 8, the final chapter, introduces Subchapter S, developing its
structural framework and dealing with the more important questions of
interpretation and application. The opportunity for closely held corporations to operate without incurring a corporate tax has been
significant since Subchapter S was first enacted in 1958, but the 1986
legislation has increased its importance. Subchapter S is worth studying

both in its own right and as a form of integration in competing contrast with Subchapter C.

This book takes account of a number of the provisions in the Revenue Reconciliation Act of 1989, signed by the President in December. It also deals with several cases and rulings that came down late in 1989. As professors know, however, the principal changes that have affected corporate-shareholder taxation happened in 1986 when the *General Utilities* doctrine was repealed, the capital gains tax preference was eliminated, and the maximum corporate tax rate was set 21 percent higher than the maximum individual rate. The effects of these changes permeate this book and present new challenges for student and professor just as they do for practitioner, taxpayer, and policymaker. The subject is more intriguing than ever before.

The book has excerpts from committee reports and articles and it has considerable text, much in the form of questions and comment, but it is essentially a casebook. My experience as both practitioner and teacher suggests that the case method, with its painstaking concern for judicial extrapolation of the statute, is the most successful in guiding students to the points of inquiry and understanding that make for sophistication, broad perspective, a sense of organic legal development, and a critical, even skeptical, view of accepted policy and dogma. Sometimes the cases reveal or conceal the difficult ethical questions that the tax lawyer faces, but these are largely beyond the scope of this work. For a book devoted to that subject, see B. Wolfman and J. Holden, Ethical Problems in Federal Tax Practice (2d ed. 1985).

The liberties I have taken are many. I have omitted footnotes freely without renumbering those that remain. Citations to the Internal Revenue Code of 1986 substitute for provisions of earlier statutes where substitution seems helpful. Brackets will indicate this change. Where the original statutory language is important, it is preserved; sometimes the corresponding provision of current law is noted for comparative purposes.

The prefaces to my first and second editions express my debt to those who helped me with them. For this edition I acknowledge with gratitude the excellent research assistance of C. William Baxley and Anthony P. Polito and the help with the index which Cynthia D. Mann provided. Finally, I thank all of my students past for not allowing my focus to blur too much.

Bernard Wolfman

Cambridge, Massachusetts
January 24, 1990

Federal Income Taxation
of Corporate Enterprise

1

The Corporation Income Tax

I. HISTORY AND DESCRIPTION

Ever since 1909 Congress has imposed a tax on the income of business corporations. Although the earlier federal tax on corporate income imposed in 1894 fell with the tax on individual income in Pollock v. Farmers' Loan & Trust Co., 158 U.S. 601 (1895), the Supreme Court sustained the constitutionality of the 1909 corporate impost in Flint v. Stone Tracy Co., 220 U.S. 107 (1911), as an "indirect" or "excise" tax, not requiring apportionment, on the corporation's "exercise of the privilege" of engaging in business as a corporation. The federal income tax enacted during the Civil War treated corporate income as the income of its shareholders and taxed the individual shareholders accordingly. Today partnership income is treated as the income of the partners and taxed to them, but corporate income is taxed to the corporation, and its shareholders are taxed only on the distributions which the corporation makes to them and on the gains realized when they dispose of their stock.

Ordinarily corporations may not deduct the dividends they pay to their shareholders. As a result, corporate income is said to be subject to a "double tax," to a tax at the corporate level and then, when the income is distributed to shareholders, to a tax as income in the hands of the shareholders. However, to mitigate the burden of more than one corporate level tax on the same income, §243 provides that corporate shareholders are generally entitled to a "dividends received" deduction. Individual shareholders, however, are not entitled to a dividends received deduction or exclusion.

Corporate tax rates have fluctuated widely since Congress imposed a one percent tax on corporate income in excess of $5,000 in 1909. As recently as 1963 the corporate rate on income over $25,000 was 52 percent, and the rate applicable to income up to $25,000 was 30 percent. During wartime Congress often imposed corporate excess profits taxes that exacted levies at extraordinarily high rates on the income remaining after imposition of the ordinary corporate tax to the extent that it exceeded the income of a specified prewar period or exceeded a "normal" return on invested capital.

The tax on corporate income is imposed by §11 of the Internal

1

Revenue Code of 1986. Today, it consists of a three-level series of rates rising from 15 percent on the first $50,000 of taxable income, to 25 percent on the next $25,000, and to 34 percent on taxable income above $75,000. Taxable incomes between $100,000 and $335,000 are subject to a surcharge of 5 percent, the result of which is to phase out the graduated rates otherwise applicable to the first $75,000 of income. In effect, corporations with taxable incomes of $335,000 or more are taxed at a flat rate of 34 percent. The Code also provides a corporate "alternative minimum tax" of 20 percent on items of "tax preference." See §§55-59.

The changes in the rate structures made by the Tax Reform Act of 1986 were designed to shift a substantial amount of the total income tax burden from the individual sector to the corporate. In 1986, the corporate income tax produced 8.5 percent of federal revenues, and the individual income tax produced 46.9 percent. By contrast, budget estimates indicate that for 1988 the corporate income tax accounted for 13.1 percent of federal revenues, while the individual income tax accounted for 43.9 percent.

There are a number of special types of corporations that the Code treats discretely, some tax-exempt, like universities, others, like insurance companies, taxable under special formulae. This chapter is concerned with the ordinary business corporation whose taxable income is subject to tax under §11. Chapter 8 deals with Subchapter S of the Code, which enables certain closely held corporations to free themselves of the corporate income tax.

II. THE CORPORATION'S INCOME — ITS SPECIAL ASPECTS

"Taxable income" is the base on which the corporation income tax is levied. For the most part "taxable income" is computed for the corporation as it is for the individual proprietor. The makeup of gross income and the allowable business deductions are substantially the same for corporations and individuals. For example, like individual proprietors, corporations are generally permitted by §163 to deduct the interest they pay. However, the so-called personal deductions, dependency exemptions, and the standard deduction are not allowed to corporations. The charitable deduction is available, but with limitations and conditions that are inapplicable to individuals.

Some transactions, peculiar to business corporations, have generated problems in determining or refining a corporation's gross income, problems that do not arise in the case of an individual. Others have generated unique issues with respect to deductions. As the manot income. Just as "borrowed money" is not treated as income in the case of an individual, so borrowed money is not regarded as income in the case of a corporation. No tax issue has arisen in connection with a corporation's resale of its bonds for a price higher than the price it paid to buy them on the open market. Why not?

2. Reduction of Outstanding Capital

a. Debt — §§108, 1017

UNITED STATES v. KIRBY LUMBER CO.
284 U.S. 1 (1931)

Mr. Justice HOLMES delivered the opinion of the Court.

In July, 1923, the plaintiff, the Kirby Lumber Company, issued its own bonds for $12,126,800 for which it received their par value. Later in the same year it purchased in the open market some of the same bonds at less than par, the difference of price being $137,521.30. The question is whether this difference is a taxable gain or income of the plaintiff for the year 1923. By [§61] gross income includes "gains or profits and income derived from any source whatever," and by the Treasury Regulations . . . that have been in force through repeated reenactments, "If the corporation purchases and retires any of such bonds at a price less than the issuing price or face value, the excess of the issuing price or face value over the purchase price is gain or income for the taxable year." . . . We see no reason why the Regulations should not be accepted as a correct statement of the law.

In Bowers v. Kerbaugh-Empire Co., 271 U.S. 170, the defendant in error owned the stock of another company that had borrowed money repayable in marks or their equivalent for an enterprise that failed. At the time of payment the marks had fallen in value, which so far as it went was a gain for the defendant in error, and it was contended by the plaintiff in error that the gain was taxable income. But the transaction as a whole was a loss, and the contention was denied. Here there was no shrinkage of assets and the taxpayer made a clear gain. As a result of its dealings it made available $137,521.30 assets previously offset by the obligation of bonds now extinct. We see nothing to be gained by the discussion of judicial definitions. The defendant in error has realized within the year an accession to income, if we take words in their plain popular meaning, as they should be taken here. Burnet v. Sanford & Brooks Co., 282 U.S. 359, 364.

Judgment reversed.

NOTES

1. If Kirby Lumber Co.'s wholly owned subsidiary had purchased the parent's outstanding bonds, would the result in the case have been avoided? See §108(e)(4), adopted as part of the Bankruptcy Tax Act of 1980.

2. Suppose that an insolvent corporation with total assets, all depreciable, worth $1,000 and liabilities of $5,000 was released from $4,500 of its debt by agreement with its creditors. Suppose, too, that the corporation had a net operating loss carryover of $2,000 and that the adjusted basis of its assets was $1,000. What do §§108(a) and (b) and 1017(a) provide for in such a case? See Pollack and Goldring, Filing for Bankruptcy Can Alter Tax Consequences of Numerous Transactions, 66 J. Taxn. 330 (1987).

3. If shareholders are also creditors of a corporation and they reduce or cancel the indebtedness, does the corporation have income? Cf. *Fender Sales*, page 507 infra. Does it matter whether the shareholders held the corporate debt in proportion to their stockholdings and whether they all agreed to a proportionate debt reduction or cancellation? See §108(e)(6), added to the Code by the Bankruptcy Tax Act of 1980, and Rev. Rul. 76-316, 1976-2 C.B. 22 (forgiveness of principal by shareholder is contribution to capital, but forgiveness of interest already deducted by accrual basis corporation is taxable income to the corporation on tax benefit principles). Prior to the Bankruptcy Tax Act of 1980, several cases relying on §118 held that the forgiveness by a shareholder of interest already deducted by a corporation was not taxable income to the corporation. See, e.g., Putoma Corp. v. Commissioner, 601 F.2d 734 (5th Cir. 1979); Hartland Associates, 54 T.C. 1580 (1970).

4. The law is now settled that a taxpayer has recognized gain when its creditor forecloses on property securing a nonrecourse loan even if the fair market value of the property is less than the amount of the outstanding nonrecourse liability. See Commissioner v. Tufts, 461 U.S. 300 (1982), rejecting the possible contrary implications of Crane v. Commissioner, 331 U.S. 1, n.37 (1947).

5. In the past a corporation could avoid recognition of cancellation of indebtedness income by issuing stock in exchange for its debt. See Commissioner v. Motor Mart Trust, 156 F.2d 122 (1st Cir. 1946). The Bankruptcy Tax Act of 1980 limited the applicability of this exception to corporations that are either insolvent or in bankruptcy. See §108(e)(10).

UNITED STATES STEEL CORP. v. UNITED STATES
848 F.2d 1232 (Fed. Cir. 1988)

Before Friedman and Rich, Circuit Judges, and Bennett, Senior Circuit Judge.

FRIEDMAN, Circuit Judge. This is an appeal from a decision of the United States Claims Court that United States Steel Corporation (U.S. Steel) realized taxable income when it repurchased its outstanding bonds for less than their face amount. United States Steel Corp. v. United States, 11 Cl. Ct. 375 (1986), opinion on reconsideration, 11 Cl. Ct. 541 (1987). We reverse and remand.

I

Upon the organization of U.S. Steel's predecessor in 1901, the company issued $100 par value preferred stock. We assume, as the parties have done throughout this case, that the company received that amount for the preferred shares.

In 1966, U.S. Steel merged with its subsidiary in a tax-free reorganization in which the company issued 4⅝ percent debentures with a face value of $175 in exchange for each share of preferred stock. The market price of the debentures and the preferred stock was each approximately $165.

In 1972, U.S. Steel repurchased $12,500,000 face amount of the debentures for $8,437,500. This amount reflected a price equivalent to $118.13 for each $175 (face value) debenture. The corporation reported the difference between the face value ($175) and the repurchase price ($118) as income in 1972.

In 1982, U.S. Steel filed a timely claim for a refund of the tax paid on that amount. When the Internal Revenue Service failed to act on the claim within six months, U.S. Steel filed this refund suit in the Claims Court. It asserted that it had not realized any income from the cancellation of the indebtedness reflected in the debentures because the company paid more for them in 1972 ($118.13) than it originally received for the preferred stock in 1901 ($100).

On cross-motions for summary judgment, the Claims Court held that U.S. Steel had realized taxable income when it acquired the debentures in 1972 for less than their face value, but in an amount less than the Service had asserted.

Relying upon United States v. Kirby Lumber Co., 284 U.S. 1 (1931), the Claims Court held that

> the consideration received by USS in the 1966 bonds-for-stock exchange determines the issue price of those bonds. Thus, the value of the preferred shares USS received in exchange for issuing its debentures in 1966 (about $165 per share) is to be considered

the issue price of those debentures for purposes of computing taxable gain on repurchase of the debentures in 1972 pursuant to the Treasury regulations.

United States Steel Corp., 11 Cl. Ct. at 385.
The court further held:

> However, the amount of taxable gain cannot exceed the difference between the issue price, which in this case is the value of the consideration the company received when it issued its bonds, and the repurchase price of those bonds. . . . In other words, under the decision herein, the plaintiff should have included in income only the difference between the value of the preferred stock in 1966 (the issue price of the bonds) and the repurchase price of the bonds in 1972.

Id. (citation omitted). The government has not challenged this ruling.

II

Section 61(a)(12) of the Internal Revenue Code of 1954 provides:

> Except as otherwise provided in this subtitle, gross income means all income from whatever source derived, including (but not limited to) the following items: . . .
> (12) Income from discharge of indebtedness[.]

The Treasury Regulations in effect when U.S. Steel acquired the debentures in 1972 provided:

> If bonds are issued by a corporation and are subsequently repurchased by the corporation at a price which is exceeded by the issue price plus any amount of discount already deducted, or (in the case of bonds issued subsequent to Feb. 28, 1913) minus any amount of premium already returned as income, the amount of such excess is income for the taxable year.

Treas. Reg. §1.61-12(c)(3) (1972).

The question in this case, which is one of first impression in this court, is whether the "issue price" of the debentures in 1966 was the fair market value at that time of the stock for which the debentures were exchanged ($165), as the government contends and the Claims Court held, or the amount the company received for the preferred stock at its original issuance in 1901 ($100). With respect to bonds issued on or before May 12, 1969, neither the Internal Revenue Code nor the Regulations provided rules for determining the issue price of bonds exchanged for property.

A. The starting point for our analysis is the Supreme Court decision in United States v. Kirby Lumber, 284 U.S. 1 (1931). Apparently that was the first case in which the Court recognized and applied the cancellation-of-indebtedness doctrine to hold that a corporation realized income upon redeeming its bonds for less than face value.

In that case the Court stated that the corporation in July issued bonds "for which it received their par value." Id. at 2. Later the same year, the corporation purchased some of those bonds in the open market for less than par. The Court held that the difference between the purchase price and the par value of the bonds constituted taxable income to the corporation. The Court applied the predecessor to Treas. Reg. 1.61-12(c)(3), quoted above, which in substance was the same, as "a correct statement of the law." Id. at 3. The Court stated that as a result of the purchase of its bonds at less than par, the corporation made "a clear gain" because "[a]s a result of its dealings it made available $137,521.30 assets previously offset by the obligation of the bonds now extinct." Id.

Kirby Lumber sheds little light on the question before us regarding the "issue price" of the U.S. Steel debentures. In *Kirby Lumber,* the Court stated that the corporation had received the par value of the bonds upon their issuance, which therefore was their issue price. The question in *Kirby Lumber* was whether, upon the repurchase of the bonds for less than their issue price, the corporation realized taxable income. In contrast, the issue in the present case is whether the issue price of the debentures was the market value of the preferred stock at the time it was exchanged for the debentures or the amount the company received when the stock originally was issued.

The Tax Court dealt with this issue in the reviewed decision in Fashion Park, Inc. v. Commissioner, 21 T.C. 600 (1954). There the company had issued for $5-a-share $50 par preferred stock. In a tax-free reorganization, the company issued $50 face value bonds in an exchange for the preferred stock. Subsequently the company repurchased some of the bonds at a price less than the $50 face value but more than the $5 issue price of the preferred.

The court held that the company had not realized any taxable gain on the repurchase of the debentures. The court stated that

> [t]he amount received originally as the basis of the obligation must be considered as $5 for each bond, and although the bonds represented a corporate obligation in their face amount, the retirement of that obligation for a lesser amount by a payment far in excess of the amount received upon the assumption of the liability does not in fact leave the petitioner with an increase in assets over what it had before.

21 T.C. at 605. . . .

The government attempts to distinguish Fashion Park on the ground that since there it conceded that the issue price of the bonds was the $5 the company received upon issuance of the preferred stock, the Tax Court never had to determine the issue price of the bonds. The government's concession, however, itself constituted a recognition that the proper basis for determining the issue was the amount the company had received for the preferred stock for which it exchanged the bonds. The rationale of the decision in Fashion Park that the company had no gain upon the purchase of the bonds for less than their face value was that the transaction did not increase the company's assets, and the latter conclusion assumed the correctness of the government's concession.

The Court of Claims, the decisions of which are binding precedent, . . . held that in determining gain on cancellation of indebtedness, the "issue price" of the debentures was the amount the corporation had received on the issuance of preferred stock, in exchange for which it issued the debentures. St. Louis-S.F. Ry. Co. v. United States, 444 F.2d 1102 (1971), *cert. denied*, 404 U.S. 1017 (1972). There in a 1947 reorganization the company had issued preferred stock. In 1954, it issued debentures for the preferred on the basis of $100 maturity value of debentures for each $100 par value share of preferred. The market value of each share of preferred at the time of exchange was $69.14. Subsequently the company reacquired some of the debentures for an amount less than their maturity value. The Court of Claims held:

> The actual issue price, the value of what plaintiff received for the debentures, controls any determination of gain on the cancellation of indebtedness. Treas. Reg. 1.61-12(c); United States v. Kirby Lumber Co., 284 U.S. 1, 52 S. Ct. 4, 76 L. Ed. 131 (1931); Fashion Park, Inc., 21 T.C. 600 (1954). However, we have already found that the issues [sic] price of the bonds was their maturity value. The value of the stock received by the plaintiff was equivalent to the maturity value of the bonds. Therefore, the Service properly computed the gain on the cancellation of indebtedness.

444 F.2d at 1107-08.

In Commissioner v. Rail Joint Co., [61 F.2d 751 (2d Cir. 1932),] the Second Circuit affirmed the Tax Court determination that a corporation did not realize taxable gain when it repurchased bonds it originally issued as dividends to common shareholders. The court of appeals noted that "the purchase and retirement of the bonds in the two years in question resulted in decreasing the corporation's liabilities without a corresponding decrease in its assets, and the petitioner contends that the difference should be deemed income. . . ." 61 F.2d at 752. The court pointed out, however, that the corporation "never received any increment to its assets, either at the time the bonds were delivered or at the time they were retired. . . . [T]he corporation received no asset which it did not possess prior to the opening and closing of the bond transaction, and it is impossible to see wherein it has realized any taxable income. In such circumstances the Kirby Case cannot be regarded as controlling." Id.

The principle these cases establish is that in determining whether a corporation's cancellation of indebtedness results in taxable income, the critical inquiry is whether the effect of the cancellation is to increase the corporation's assets.

The "issue price" of the debentures must be ascertained in the light of that standard. Applying that principle, we conclude that the "issue price" of U.S. Steel's debentures was the amount the company received when it originally issued the preferred stock in 1901 and not the market value of the preferred when the debentures were issued in exchange for the stock in 1966.

Like the exchange of bonds for preferred stock in *Fashion Park*, U.S. Steel's 1966 exchange of debentures for stock did not increase the company's assets. The capital the company obtained through the issue of the preferred stock was acquired when the company issued the stock in 1901. As a result of the restructuring of U.S. Steel's corporate structure following the 1966 issuance of debentures in exchange for the preferred stock, "there has been no new capital acquired and no additional cost incurred in retaining the old capital." Commissioner v. National Alfalfa Dehydrating & Milling Co., 417 U.S. 134, 152 (1974).

As noted, the governing regulation treats as income the difference between the "issue price" of the debentures and their repurchase price. The purpose of that calculation is to determine whether the corporation received income from discharge of indebtedness. Since the exchange by U.S. Steel of its debentures for preferred stock did not increase the company's assets, the issue price of the debentures was the capital the company received for the preferred stock for which the debentures were exchanged.

The fact that the substitution of preferred stock for debentures reduced U.S. Steel's liability by the amount of the retired debentures did not increase the company's assets or result in income to the company. . . .

Indeed, it is the elimination of U.S. Steel's liability on the redeemed debentures that the government primarily relies upon to support its claim that the company realized income upon the purchase of the debentures for less than their face amount. The government points to the statement in *Kirby Lumber* that "[a]s a result of its dealings it made available $137,521.30 assets previously offset by the obligation of the bonds now expired." 284 U.S. at 3. That statement, however, cannot properly be read as announcing a general rule that any reduction of debt liability through an exchange of stock for debentures necessarily and automatically constitutes income to the extent of the reduction, and should not be extended to cover the significantly different situation involved in the present case.

The government argues that "at no point has the taxpayer adequately explained why it would issue an obligation worth $165 to receive consideration that it claims is only equal to approximately $100." The obvious answer is that the interest on the debentures was deductible but the dividends on the preferred stock were not. Apparently U.S. Steel made the business judgment that it was better off financially to be able to deduct the interest on the debentures despite the fact that the face amount of the debentures exceeded the par value of the preferred stock.

B. The government points out that the issue price of debentures also is involved in deciding the question of original issue debt discount where debt is issued in exchange for stock, the market value of which is less than the face value of the debt. When bonds are issued at less than their face value, the result is a discount (deduction) representing the increased interest cost to the issuing corporation, which may be amortized and deducted over the life of the bonds. The government relies on cases holding that in that situation the issue price of the debentures is the market value at the time of the exchange of the stock for which the debentures were exchanged.

The leading case dealing with bond discount arising upon the issuance of bonds in exchange for preferred stock is Commissioner v. National Alfalfa Dehydrating & Milling Co., 417 U.S. 134 (1974). There the company (NAD) had issued $50 par preferred stock. In a reorganization the company issued debentures in exchange for the preferred. One $50 debenture was exchanged for each outstanding share of preferred. In the over-the-counter market, which was "thin," the stock price was approximately $33 per share at the time of the exchange. The corporation claimed a bond discount (deduction) for the difference between the face value of the debenture ($50) and the market value of the preferred stock ($33). The Court held that no discount was allowed.

The Court stated the issue as "whether debt discount arises where a corporate taxpayer issues an obligation in exchange for its own outstanding preferred shares." 417 U.S. at 147. The Court ruled that the "relevant inquiry in each case must be whether the issuer-taxpayer has incurred, as a result of the transaction, some cost or expense of acquiring the use of capital." Id.

The Court pointed out:

> It has not been demonstrated that NAD, by the exchange, incurred any additional cost for the use of capital. NAD merely replaced that portion of its paid-in capital represented by its preferred with paid-in capital represented by its debentures. From

the perspective of the corporation, the transaction was the exchange of one form of interest or participation in the corporation for another. But the corporate assets were neither increased nor diminished. . . .

. . . But again, when viewed from the corporation's perspective, and regardless of the income tax effect upon the former preferred shareholder, which we deem to be irrelevant, there has been no new capital acquired and no additional cost incurred in retaining the old capital. . . .

. . . Upon the exchange, the corporation canceled the preferred, and thus eliminated the preferred stock account upon its books, together with the preferred's attendant obligations. The market value of the preferred at that moment bore no direct relationship to the amount of funds on hand. The capital "freed" by the cancellation of the preferred was merely transferred to the liability account for the debentures. No new capital was involved.

417 U.S. at 151–53 (citations and footnotes omitted).

The focus of the inquiry is different in bond discount and cancellation-of-indebtedness cases. In the former, it is on the cost of capital borrowed by the corporation—whether there was bond discount because the issuer received less than the face amount of the debt. The answer to that question necessarily depends upon the value to the issuer of the preferred stock it acquired in exchange for the debt, since if the preferred stock is worth less than the debt, the difference represents an additional cost of borrowing, which is treated as interest. In cancellation-of-indebtedness cases, however, the focus is on whether the corporation increased its capital as a result of eliminating its indebtedness. Accordingly, the bond discount cases are not necessarily applicable to cancellation-of-indebtedness cases.

The decision in *National Alfalfa* nevertheless is helpful in determining whether U.S. Steel increased its assets in replacing its preferred stock with its debentures. In holding that National Alfalfa had not "incurred any additional cost for the use of capital" by exchanging its debentures for preferred stock, the Court pointed out that in the exchange "the corporate assets were neither increased nor diminished," and that "[n]o new capital was involved." 417 U.S. at 151–53. As we have explained in Part IIA, that is precisely the situation that existed in connection with U.S. Steel's issuance of its debentures in exchange for its preferred stock. There is no reason to believe that in this respect the Supreme Court would view the situation in the present case any differently from that in *National Alfalfa*.

The government attempts to distinguish *National Alfalfa* on the ground that because there the market for the preferred stock was "thin," it would have been highly speculative, as the Court recognized, to attempt to determine the market price of the number of shares of preferred stock that were acquired. The Court relied on the thinness of the market for the preferred stock, however, as a reason for rejecting the company's contention that the "economic realities" of the transaction were the same as if the company had actually sold its $50 debentures for $33 in cash and then used that cash to purchase the preferred at $33 a share. 417 U.S. at 148. The portion of *National Alfalfa* upon which we have relied, holding that the company did not acquire any additional capital through the exchange, was not dependent upon the discussion of the market thinness point, but constituted a separate portion of the opinion. . . .

Reversed and remanded.

NOTE

For a lively debate over the merits of the *United States Steel* decision, see Gunn, Reconciling *United States Steel* and *Kirby Lumber*, Tax Notes, February 13, 1989, p. 851; Shakow, *United States Steel* and *Kirby Lumber*: Another View, Tax Notes, March 13, 1989, p. 1371; and Gunn, *United States Steel* and the Functional Approach to Legal Problems, Tax Notes, April 10, 1989, p. 213 (replying to Shakow), and for their respective last words see Tax Notes, May 29, 1989, pp. 1173-1175.

b. Equity

Corporation M issued its $100 par value preferred stock for $100 per share. Years later, the stock is selling at $85 per share in the open market. Sensing a bargain, Corporation M, acting at the direction of its Board, which is controlled by a shareholder who owns 40 percent of the outstanding stock, offers to buy at $90 per share all of its stock that is tendered. Twenty percent of the outstanding stock is tendered, for which Corporation M pays the offered price. Upon delivery of the shares the acquired stock is cancelled, and Corporation M reduces its authorized and outstanding capital by the par value of the shares. Corporation M does not realize income in the transaction. Why? Cf. J. A. Maurer, Inc., 30 T.C. 1273 (1958). If a reduction in equity capital does not result in corporate income, why should *Kirby Lumber* hold to the contrary in the case of debt capital?

3. *Receipt of a Dividend — §§243, 301(b)*

Section 301(c)(1) requires that the "portion of [a corporate] distribution which is a dividend (as defined in section 316)" be "included in gross income." The "portion of a distribution" that is not a dividend is first applied against the basis of the shareholder's stock, and after the basis is exhausted the excess of the distribution is treated as "gain from the sale or exchange" of the stock. See §301(c)(2) and (3).

Section 301(b)(1) provides that the "amount of any distribution" shall be the amount of cash plus the fair market value of other property received. But note the provisions of §243. It is a three-tiered provision that permits corporate shareholders to deduct a percentage of the dividends they receive. A corporation that owns at least 80 percent of the voting power and value of the payor corporation may deduct 100 percent of the dividends received if it makes an election under §243. If a corporation owns 20 percent or more of the payor corporation (by vote and value), the corporation may deduct 80 percent. Finally, a corporation owning less than 20 percent of the payor corporation's stock may deduct only 70 percent of the dividends received. §§243(a) and (c).

Should there be a dividends received deduction at all? If so, why (and when) should it be less than 100 percent? See American Law Institute—Federal Income Tax Project—Subchapter C (Supplemental Study), Reporter's Draft Study at 97-101 (June 1, 1989); Mundstock, Taxation of Intercorporate Dividends Under an Unintegrated Regime, 44 Tax. L. Rev. 1 (1988); Francis, The Taxation of Intercorporate Dividends: Current Problems and Proposed Reforms, 64 Taxes 427 (1986); Seligman, Issues in the Taxation of Intercorporate Investment Income, 2 Am. J. Tax Pol. 253 (1983).

Read §246A. Why does it have a special limitation in the case of "debt-financed portfolio stock"? By way of analogy, consider the relationship among §§103(a), 163(a), and 265(a)(2). The extent of the limitation in §246A turns on how much indebtedness is "directly attributable to investment in the portfolio stock." §246A(d)(3)(A). See Rev. Rul. 88-66, 1988-2 C.B. 34, for the Service's reading of this provision.

Corporation S, a Pennsylvania corporation, distributes to its parent, Corporation P, a dividend consisting of 1,000 shares of General Motors common stock. The shares had an adjusted basis of $50 per share in Corporation S's hands and are worth $85 per share at the time of distribution. What are the tax consequences of the distribution to Corporation P? Why? For the tax consequences to Corporation S, see page 27 et seq. When Corporation P, one year after receipt, sells the stock for $90 per share, what will the tax consequences be? Why? See §301(d). How would each of the tax consequences be varied if the General Motors stock had been subject to a $30 per share liability which Corporation P assumed?

Section 1059, expanded as recently as 1989, is an unduly elaborate provision dealing with "extraordinary dividend[s]." You can gain an understanding of its general purpose by reading subsections (a) through (c). What does subsection (a)(2) do to subsection (a)(1)? Why were they written that way?

TSN LIQUIDATING CORP., INC. v. UNITED STATES
624 F.2d 1328 (5th Cir. 1980)

Before Fay, Kravitch and Randall, JJ.

RANDALL, J. This case presents the question whether assets distributed to a corporation by its subsidiary, immediately prior to the sale by such corporation of all the capital stock of such subsidiary, should be treated, for federal income tax purposes, as a dividend or, as the district court held, as part of the consideration received from the sale of such capital stock. We hold that on the facts of this case, the assets so distributed constituted a dividend and we reverse the judgment of the district court.

In 1969, TSN Liquidating Corporation, Inc. ("TSN"), which was then named "Texas State Network, Inc." owned over 90% of the capital stock of Community Life Insurance Company ("CLIC"), an insurance company chartered under the laws of the State of Maine. In early 1969, negotiations began for the purchase of CLIC by Union Mutual Life Insurance Company ("Union Mutual"). On May 5, 1969, TSN and the other CLIC stockholders entered into an Agreement of Stock Purchase (the "Stock Purchase Agreement") with Union Mutual for the sale of the capital stock of CLIC to Union Mutual. The Stock Purchase Agreement provided that there would be no material adverse change in the business or assets of CLIC prior to the closing "except that as of closing certain shares and capital notes as provided in Section 4.(i) above will not be a part of the assets of [CLIC]." Since the purchase price of the capital stock of CLIC under the Stock Purchase Agreement was based primarily on the book value (or, in some instances, market value) of those assets owned by CLIC on the closing date, the purchase price would be automatically reduced by the elimination of such shares and notes from the assets of CLIC. On May 14, 1969, as contemplated by the Stock Purchase Agreement, the Board of Directors of CLIC declared a dividend in kind, payable to stockholders of record as of May 19, 1969, consisting primarily of capital stock in small, public companies traded infrequently and in small quantities in the over-the-counter market. On May 20, 1969, the closing was held and Union Mutual purchased substantially all the outstanding capital stock of CLIC, including the shares held by TSN. The final purchase price paid by Union Mutual to the selling stockholders of CLIC was $823,822, of which TSN's share was $747,436. Union Mutual thereupon contributed to the capital of CLIC $1,120,000 in municipal bonds and purchased from CLIC additional capital stock of CLIC for $824,598 in cash paid to CLIC.

In its income tax return for the fiscal year ended July 31, 1969,

TSN reported its receipt of assets from CLIC as a dividend and claimed the 85% dividends received deduction available to corporate stockholders pursuant to §243(a)(1) of the Internal Revenue Code of 1954. TSN also reported its gain on the sale of the capital stock of CLIC on the installment method pursuant to §453 of the Code. On audit, the Internal Revenue Service treated the distribution of the assets from CLIC to TSN as having been an integral part of the sale by TSN of capital stock of CLIC to Union Mutual, added its estimate ($1,677,082) of the fair market value of the assets received by TSN to the cash ($747,436) received by TSN on the sale, and disallowed the use by TSN of the installment method for reporting the gain on the sale of the capital stock of CLIC since aggregating the fair market value of the distributed assets and the cash resulted in more than 30% of the proceeds from the sale being received in the year of sale. TSN paid the additional tax due as a result of such treatment by the Internal Revenue Service, filed a claim for a refund and subsequently instituted this action against the Internal Revenue Service.

The district court made the following findings of fact in part II of its opinion:

> With regard to the negotiations between CLIC and Union Mutual in early 1969, the Court finds that Union Mutual was interested in purchasing CLIC and proposed a formula for valuing the assets, liabilities, and insurance in force, which, together with an additional amount, would be the price paid for the CLIC stock.
>
> The investment portfolio of CLIC was heavily oriented toward equity investments in closely held over-the-counter securities. At least in the mind of CLIC's officers, the makeup of CLIC's investment portfolio was affecting its ability to obtain licenses in various states. As early as the Spring of 1968, the management and principal stockholders of CLIC had begun to seek a solution to the investment portfolio problem. The Court finds, however, that CLIC had never formulated a definite plan on how to solve its investment portfolio problem.
>
> Union Mutual did not like CLIC's investment portfolio but considered bonds to be more in keeping with insurance industry responsibilities. The management of CLIC regarded the Union Mutual offer as a good one, and tried without success to get Union Mutual to take the entire investment portfolio.
>
> Accordingly, the [Stock Purchase Agreement] required CLIC to dispose some of the investment portfolio assets. Thus, the price that would be paid for the CLIC stock was based upon a formula which valued the assets after excluding certain stocks. . . .
>
> Plaintiff's disposition of the undesirable over-the-counter stock was necessitated by its sale arrangements with Union Mutual. Plaintiff had no definite plans prior to its negotiations with Union Mutual as to how to get rid of the undesirable stock, when it was

to get rid of the undesirable stock, or even that it would definitely get rid of the undesirable stock. Accordingly, the Court finds that the dividend in kind of 14 May 1969 was part and parcel of the purchase agreement with Union Mutual. . . .

In part III of its opinion, the district court made the following additional findings:

> Union Mutual was interested in purchasing the stock of an approximately $2 million corporation in order that that corporation might be licensed to do business in other states. Tr. 92. As of 30 April 1969, CLIC had assets of $2,115,138. DX 2. On 14 May 1969, CLIC declared a dividend valued at approximately $1.8 million. As a result of this dividend, CLIC was left with assets totaling approximately $300,000. The final purchase price paid by Union Mutual to the selling shareholders of CLIC was $823,822. In addition, Union Mutual contributed $1,120,000 of municipal bonds to the capital of CLIC and purchased additional shares of stock of CLIC for $824,598. DX 3. Thus, subsequent to closing on 20 May 1969, CLIC was worth $2,400,000. DX 3. Thus, CLIC was worth $2 million when the [Stock Purchase Agreement] was signed on 5 May 1969 and worth over $2 million immediately after closing.
>
> There was no business purpose served in this case by the dividend declared by CLIC prior to the sale of all its stock to Union Mutual. It is evident that the dividend benefitted the shareholders of CLIC and not CLIC itself. There was no benefit or business purpose in CLIC's declaration of the dividend separate and apart from the sale. The Court finds that the dividend would not, and could not, have been made without the sale. . . .
>
> What actually happened in the period 5 through 20 May 1969 was that the stockholders received $1.8 million in virtually tax-free stocks, as well as over $800,000 in cash, for a total of approximately $2.6 million. This was certainly a fair price for a corporation valued at the time of sale at $2,115,138, and reflects a premium paid for good will and policies in force, as well as the fact that CLIC was an existing business with licenses in eight or nine states. Hence, a $2 million corporation was sold for $2.6 million including the dividend and the cash. . . .

After noting the time-honored principle that the incidence of taxation is to be determined by the substance of the transaction rather than by its form and the related principle that the transaction is generally to be viewed as a whole and not to be separated into its component parts, the district court held:

> The distribution of assets to [TSN] from its subsidiary, CLIC, immediately prior to [TSN's] disposition of its entire stock interest in CLIC should be treated as a part of the gain from the sale of the stock. Thus, the Court concludes that the in-kind distribution of 14 May 1969 to the stockholders of CLIC is taxable to [TSN]

as gain from the sale of its stock. The alleged dividend was merely intented [sic] to be part of the purchase price paid by Union Mutual to CLIC for its stock. . . .

The district court relied for its holding primarily on the cases of Waterman Steamship Corp. v. Commissioner, 430 F.2d 1185 (5th Cir. 1970), *cert. denied* 401 U.S. 939, 91 S. Ct. 936, 28 L. Ed. 2d 219 (1971), and Basic, Inc. v. United States, 549 F.2d 740 (Ct. Cl. 1977), all discussed infra.

On appeal, TSN argues that the cases relied upon by the district court are exceptions to what TSN characterizes as the established rule, namely, that assets removed from a corporation by a dividend made in contemplation of a sale of the stock of that corporation, when those assets are in good faith to be retained by the selling stockholders and not thereafter transferred to the buyer, are taxable as a dividend and not as a part of the price paid for the stock for the reason that, in economic reality and in substance, the selling stockholders did not sell and the buyer did not purchase or pay for the excluded assets. The principal cases cited by TSN for its position are Gilmore v. Commissioner, 25 T.C. 1321 (1956), Coffey et al. v. Commissioner, 14 T.C. 1410 (1950), and Rosenbloom Finance Corp. v. Commissioner, 24 B.T.A. 763 (1931). According to TSN, the controlling distinction between the *Coffey* line of cases relied upon by TSN and the *Waterman* line of cases relied upon by the district court is whether the buyer negotiated to acquire and pay for the stock, exclusive of the assets distributed out as a dividend, on the one hand, or whether the buyer negotiated to acquire and pay for the stock, including the assets which were then the subject of a sham distribution designed to evade taxes, on the other hand. In the former case, according to TSN, there is a taxable dividend; in the latter case there is not.

We begin by noting that the district court was certainly correct in its position that the substance of the transaction controls over the form and that the transaction should be viewed as a whole, rather than being separated into its parts. Further, having reviewed the record, we are of the view that the operative facts found so carefully by the district court are entirely accurate (except for the valuation of the distributed assets, as to which we express no opinion). We differ with the district court only in the legal characterization of those facts and in the conclusion to be drawn therefrom. We agree with TSN that this case is controlled by the *Coffey, Gilmore* and *Rosenbloom* cases rather than by the *Waterman* and *Basic* cases relied upon by the district court.

In *Coffey,* the principal case relied upon by TSN, the taxpayers owned the stock of Smith Brothers Refinery Co., Inc. and were negotiating for the sale of such stock. Representatives of the purchasers and representatives of the sellers examined and discussed the various assets owned by Smith Brothers Refinery Co., Inc., and the liabilities of the company, with a view to reaching an agreement upon the fair market value of the stock. During these negotiations, the representatives of the purchasers and of the sellers could not agree upon the value of certain assets (including a contingent receivable referred to as the Cabot payment). The representatives of the purchasers informed the representatives of the sellers that the sellers could withdraw those assets from the assets of the company and that they would buy the stock without those assets being a part of the sale, thereby eliminating the necessity for arriving at a valuation of those assets in determining the value of the stock on a net worth basis. The contract of sale provided that the unwanted assets would be distributed by the corporation as a dividend prior to the sale of the stock. The selling stockholders contended before the tax court, as the Internal Revenue Service does in the case before this court, that the Cabot payment distributed to them as a dividend in kind was "part of the consideration for stock sold and that any profit resulting from its receipt by them is taxable as a capital gain." The tax court rejected that contention because it was contrary to the substance of the transaction. . . . [It] held the distribution to be a dividend.

In *Gilmore,* the purchasers of corporate stock did not wish to pay for quick assets owned by the corporation, namely cash on hand and United States bonds, and the parties provided for a presale dividend to exclude them from the assets to be transferred to the purchaser by means of the sale of the corporate stock. The tax court held that the assets distributed to the stockholders by means of a dividend were taxable as a dividend and not as a part of the sales proceeds for the corporate stock. . . .

In *Rosenbloom,* the sole stockholder of Joseph S. Finch Company was Rosenbloom Finance Corporation. Rosenbloom entered into a contract for the sale of all the capital stock of Joseph S. Finch Company to Shenley Products Company. With respect to the unwanted assets, the contract provided:

> All other assets of every character whatsoever owned by the Finch Company at the time of the transfer of said shares of stock, as herein provided, shall be transferred to the party of the first part (petitioner) by dividend distribution, prior to the consummation of the sale of said shares of stock herein provided for. . . .

The board of tax appeals held that the assets distributed to Rosenbloom Finance Corporation by Joseph S. Finch Company should be treated as an ordinary dividend and not as an amount distributed in partial liquidation. . . .

The Internal Revenue Service states that it does not disagree with the holdings in *Coffey*, *Gilmore* and *Rosenbloom*, but it takes the position that they do not apply in the circumstances of this case. The Internal Revenue Service focuses on the receipt by the selling stockholders of CLIC of investment assets, followed immediately by an infusion by Union Mutual of a like amount of investment assets into CLIC, and says that the reinfusion of assets brings the case before the court within the "conduit rationale" of *Waterman*. In *Waterman*, Waterman Steamship Corporation ("Waterman") was the owner of all the outstanding capital stock of Pan-Atlantic Steamship Corporation ("Pan-Atlantic") and Gulf Florida Terminal Company, Incorporated ("Gulf Florida"). Malcolm P. McLean made an offer to Waterman to purchase all the outstanding capital stock of Pan-Atlantic and Gulf Florida for $3,500,000. Since Waterman's tax basis for the stock of the subsidiaries totaled $700,000, a sale of the capital stock of the subsidiaries for $3,500,000 would have produced a taxable gain of approximately $2,800,000. Because the treasury regulations on consolidated returns provided that the dividends received from an affiliated corporation are exempt from tax, a sale of capital stock of the subsidiaries for $700,000, after a dividend payment to Waterman by the subsidiaries of $2,800,000, would, at least in theory, have produced no taxable gain. The Board of Directors of Waterman rejected McLean's offer, but authorized Waterman's president to submit a counter proposal providing for the sale of all the capital stock in the subsidiaries for $700,000, but only after the subsidiaries paid dividends to Waterman in the aggregate amount of $2,800,000. As finally consummated, the dividends and the sale of the capital stock of the subsidiaries took the following form:

(1) Pan-Atlantic gave a promissory note to Waterman for $2,800,000 payable in 30 days as a "dividend."

(2) One hour later, Waterman agreed to sell all of the capital stock of Pan-Atlantic and Gulf Florida for $700,000.

(3) Thirty minutes later, after the closing of the sale of the capital stock of the subsidiaries had occurred, Pan-Atlantic held a special meeting of its new Board of Directors, and the Board authorized Pan-Atlantic to borrow $2,800,000 from McLean and a corporation controlled by McLean. Those funds were used by Pan-Atlantic promptly to pay off the $2,800,000 note to Waterman (which was not yet due).

In its tax return for the fiscal year involved, Waterman eliminated from income the $2,800,000 received as a dividend from Pan-Atlantic and reported $700,000 as the sales price of the capital stock of the two subsidiaries. Since Waterman's tax basis for the stock was the same as the sales price therefor, no taxable gain was realized on the sale. On audit, the Internal Revenue Service took the position that Waterman had realized a long-term capital gain of $2,800,000 on the sale of the capital stock of the subsidiaries and increased its taxable income accordingly. On appeal from a judgment by the tax court in favor of the taxpayer, the Internal Revenue Service contended that the rules applicable to situations where a regular dividend has been declared are not applicable when the parties contemplate that a purported dividend is to be inextricably tied to the purchase price and where, as was the case before the court, the amount of the dividend is not a true distribution of corporate profits. The Internal Revenue Service argued that the funds were supplied by the buyer of the stock, with the corporation acting as a mere conduit for passing the payment through to the seller. This court agreed with the Internal Revenue Service:

> The so-called dividend and sale were one transaction. The note was but one transitory step in a total, pre-arranged plan to sell the stock. We hold that in substance Pan-Atlantic neither declared nor paid a dividend to Waterman, but rather acted as a mere conduit for the payment of the purchase price to Waterman.

Waterman, 430 F.2d at 1192. The opinion of this court began with this sentence:

> This case involves another attempt by a taxpayer to ward off tax blows with paper armor.

Id. at 1185. The opinion stressed the sham, tax motivated aspects of the transaction:

> Here, McLean originally offered Waterman $3,500,000 for the stock of Pan-Atlantic and Gulf Florida. Waterman recognized that since its basis for tax purposes in the stock was $700,180, a taxable gain of approximately $2,800,000 would result from the sale. It declined the original offer and proposed to cast the sale of the stock in a two step transaction. Waterman proposed to McLean that it would sell the stock of the two subsidiaries for $700,180 after it had extracted $2,800,000 of the subsidiaries' earnings and profits. It is undisputed that Waterman intended to sell the two subsidiaries for the original offering price — with $2,800,000 of the amount disguised as a dividend which would be eliminated from income under Section 1502. Waterman also intended that none of the assets owned by the subsidiaries would be removed prior to the sale. Although the distribution was cast in the form of a dividend, the distribution was to be financed by McLean with payment being made to Waterman through Pan-Atlantic. To inject substance into the form of the transaction, Pan-Atlantic issued its note to Waterman before the closing agreement was signed. The creation of a valid indebtedness however, cannot change the true nature of the transaction. . . . The form of the transaction used by the parties is relatively unimportant, for the true substance and effect of their agreement was that McLean

would pay $3,500,000 for all of the assets, rights and liabilities represented by the stock of Pan-Atlantic and Gulf Florida.

Id. at 1194, 1195. This court concluded its opinion in *Waterman* by cautioning against "giving force to 'a purported [dividend] which gives off an unmistakably hollow sound when it is tapped.' " Id. at .1196 (quoting United States v. General Geophysical Co., 296 F.2d 86, 89 (5th Cir. 1961), *cert. denied,* 369 U.S. 849 (1962) [page 41 supra]. A final footnote to the opinion stated that the decision should not be interpreted as standing for the proposition that a corporation which is contemplating a sale of its subsidiary's stock would not under any circumstances distribute its subsidiaries' profits prior to the sale without having such distribution deemed part of the purchase price. Id. at 1196 n.21.

In summary, in *Waterman,* the substance of the transaction, and the way in which it was originally negotiated, was that the purchaser would pay $3,500,000 of its money to the seller in exchange for all the stock of the two subsidiaries and none of the assets of those subsidiaries was to be removed and retained by the sellers. In the case before the court, the district court found that Union Mutual did not want and would not pay for the assets of CLIC which were distributed to TSN and the other stockholders of CLIC. Those assets were retained by the selling stockholders. The fact that bonds and cash were reinfused into CLIC after the closing, in lieu of the unwanted capital stock of small, publicly held corporations, does not convert this case from a *Coffey* situation, in which admittedly unwanted assets were distributed by the corporation to its stockholders and retained by them, into a *Waterman* situation, in which the distribution of assets was clearly a sham, designed solely to achieve a tax free distribution of assets ultimately funded by the purchaser. Indeed, the Internal Revenue Service does not argue, in the case before the court, that the transaction was in any respect a sham. Instead, the Service would have us hold that the mere infusion of assets into the acquired company after the closing, assets which are markedly different in kind from the assets that were distributed prior to the closing, should result in the disallowance of dividend treatment for the distribution of the unwanted assets, and the Service cites *Waterman* as authority for that proposition. We view the sham aspect — the hollow sound — of the transaction described in *Waterman* as one of the critical aspects of that decision, and we decline to extend the *Waterman* rule to a case which admittedly does not involve a sham and which, in other important respects, is factually different from *Waterman.*

The Internal Revenue Service also cites *Basic* as authority for the disallowance of dividend treatment for the distribution of the unwanted assets in this case. Basic Incorporated ("Basic") owned all the capital stock of Falls Industries Incorporated ("Falls"), which in turn owned all the stock of Basic Carbon Corporation ("Carbon"). Carborundum Company ("Carborundum") made an initial offer to acquire all the assets of Falls and Carbon. This offer failed to gel when Basic demanded that Carborundum agree to indemnify Basic for any tax assessments that might become payable on the transaction in excess of those which Basic could anticipate and compute in advance, a proposal that was unacceptable to Carborundum. Carborundum then made a second proposal to acquire directly from Basic the capital stock of Falls and the capital stock of Carbon and requested that Basic transfer the ownership of the capital stock of Carbon from Falls to Basic prior to the transaction. In order to achieve that, Falls distributed the capital stock of Carbon to Basic as a dividend, which put Basic in the position of owning the capital stock of both Falls and Carbon. The sale of such capital stock to Carborundum was then consummated. In its federal income tax return for the year involved, Basic reported dividend income from Falls in the amount of $500,000 as a result of its receipt of the capital stock of Carbon. It thereupon claimed a dividends received deduction in the amount of 85% of the dividend pursuant to §243(a)(1) of the Code. Finally, it reported a long-term capital gain of $2,300,000 from the sale to Carborundum of the shares of Falls and Carbon. On audit, the Internal Revenue Service determined that the gain from the sale of the shares of capital stock of Falls and Carbon should be increased by the amount of the purported dividend. On those facts, the court of claims held that the distribution of the capital stock of Carbon by Falls to Basic was not a true dividend but was part of the total transaction by which Basic, in substance, sold the capital stock of Falls and Carbon to Carborundum:

> Under the facts and circumstances presented here, plaintiff has not shown that there was a reason for the transfer of the Carbon stock from Falls to Basic aside from the tax consequences attributable to that move. Accordingly, for purposes of taxation, the transfer was not a dividend within the meaning of Section 316(a)(1). Instead, it should be regarded as a transfer that avoided part of the gain to be expected from the sale of the business to Carborundum, and should, therefore, be now taxed accordingly.

Basic, 549 F.2d at 749. Basic was a conduit through which an asset, the capital stock of Carbon, was passed to the buyer. The substance of the transaction was a brief removal of the "dividend" asset (the Carbon stock) on the way to the hands of the waiting buyer. In the case before the court, unlike the situation that obtained in *Basic,* the distributed assets were retained by the stockholders to whom they were distributed, rather than being immediately transferred to the purchaser.

As additional support for its position, the court in *Basic* focused on the absence of a business purpose, viewed from the standpoint of Falls, for the payment of a dividend of a valuable corporate asset, i.e., the capital stock of Carbon, by Falls to Basic. The district court, in the case before this court, applied the same test to the payment of the dividend of the unwanted assets by CLIC to TSN, the controlling stockholder of CLIC, and found that, strictly from the standpoint of CLIC, the dividend was lacking in business purpose and, indeed, could not have taken place apart from the sale and the subsequent infusion of investment assets into CLIC by Union Mutual. However, it seems to us to be inconsistent to take the position that substance must control over form and that a transaction must be viewed as a whole, rather than in parts, and at the same time to state that the business purpose of one participant in a multi-party transaction (particularly where the participant is a corporation controlled by the taxpayer and is not itself a party to the sale transaction) is to be viewed in isolation from the over-all business purpose for the entire transaction. We agree that the transaction must be viewed as a whole and we accept the district court's finding of fact that the dividend of the unwanted assets was "part and parcel of the purchase arrangement with Union Mutual," motivated specifically by Union Mutual's unwillingness to take and pay for such assets. That being the case, we decline to focus on the business purpose of one participant in the transaction — a corporation controlled by the taxpayer — and instead find that the business purpose for the transaction as a whole, viewed from the standpoint of the taxpayer, controls. The facts found by the district court clearly demonstrate a business purpose for the presale dividend of the unwanted assets which fully explains that dividend. We note that there is no suggestion in the district court's opinion of any tax avoidance motivation on the part of the taxpayer TSN. The fact that the dividend may have had incidental tax benefit to the taxpayer, without more, does not necessitate the disallowance of dividend treatment.

Having concluded that the pre-sale distribution by CLIC to its stockholders (including TSN) of assets which Union Mutual did not want, would not pay for and did not ultimately receive is a dividend for tax purposes, and not part of the purchase price of the capital stock of CLIC, we reverse the judgment of the district court and remand for proceedings consistent with this opinion.

Reversed and remanded.

NOTES

1. When the shareholder is an individual, not a corporation, she is not entitled to a dividends received deduction under §243(a). Typ-

ically, such a shareholder prefers characterization of a pre-sale distribution as part of the proceeds she receives from the sale of her stock, taxable as capital gain rather than ordinary income. In Casner v. Commissioner, 450 F.2d 379 (5th Cir. 1971), a case not mentioned in *TSN Liquidating Corporation, Inc.*, the Fifth Circuit held that a pre-sale cash distribution to an individual was part of the proceeds of sale. In Rev. Rul. 75-493, 1975-2 C.B. 109, the Service announced its refusal to follow *Casner* and, distinguishing *Waterman Steamship Corporation*, discussed in *TSN Liquidating Corporation, Inc.*, ruled that a pre-sale cash distribution to an individual was a dividend, not to be treated as part of the proceeds of sale.

2. In Litton Industries., Inc. v. Commissioner, 89 T.C. 1086 (1987), the Tax Court held that the distribution of a promissory note by a subsidiary to its parent was a dividend and not a part of the subsequent sales price of the subsidiary. In so holding, the court distinguished *Waterman Steamship Corporation* on the ground that the dividend was complete even before Litton attempted to sell its subsidiary. As in *TSN Liquidating Corporation, Inc.*, the transaction was not considered a sham. For a discussion of the tax planning aspects of the case, see Bloom, Minimizing the Federal Income Tax Liability on the Sale of a Subsidiary — Presale Dividends After *Litton Industries, Inc. v. Commissioner*, 15 J. Corp. Taxn. 195 (1988).

Might the "consent dividend" procedures of §565 be used to effect an intercorporate dividend prior to sale of the stock of the "distributing" corporation? Cf. Sheppard, Informed Consent: IRS Tries to Correct Section 565 Mistake, Tax Notes, March 28, 1988, p. 1439.

3. The reporter for the American Law Institute Federal Income Tax Project on Subchapter C has proposed a resolution to the problem posed by *TSN Liquidating Corporation, Inc.* and *Waterman Steamship Corporation*. Under the proposal, a parent's basis in its subsidiary's shares would generally reflect the subsidiary's undistributed earnings. As a result, such a parent corporation's gain from the sale of the shares of the subsidiary corporation would not include its subsidiary's undistributed earnings. Thus, the *TSN Liquidating* problem would not arise. See American Law Institute — Federal Income Tax Project — Subchapter C (Supplemental Study), Reporter's Study Draft (June 1, 1989). Cf. Treas. Reg. §1.1502-32, which requires the parent corporation of a group filing consolidated returns to make annual adjustments to the basis of the stock in each of its subsidiaries to reflect the economic results of each subsidiary's operations during the year.

4. ·Although stock exchange rules set the ex-dividend date after the record date, the owner of stock on the record date is the recipient of dividend income for federal income tax purposes. Accordingly, a corporation that receives dividends on stock that it purchased before

the ex-dividend date but after the record date should not include the dividends in its gross income, and it is not entitled to the dividends received deduction under §243. See Rev. Rul. 82-11, 1982-1 C.B. 51.

5. In Lastarmco v. Commissioner, 79 T.C. 810 (1982), *aff'd*, 737 F.2d 1440 (5th Cir. 1984), the Tax Court had to provide a rank order for both the dividends received deduction (§243(a)(1)) and the percentage depletion deduction (§613A(c)), both of which are limited to a percentage of the taxpayer's taxable income. Deciding for the taxpayer, it held that the §613A(c) deduction should be taken before the §243(a)(1) deduction.

4. *Gain or Loss on the Disposition of Property — The Rise and Demise of* General Utilities

a. The Evolution of the *General Utilities* Doctrine

Section 336 now provides that a corporation generally recognizes gain or loss upon the distribution of appreciated or depreciated property to its shareholders in a complete liquidation. Similarly, under §311, a corporation recognizes gain, but not loss, upon the disposition of property in a nonliquidating distribution of property that is not in complete liquidation.

One might expect these rules to flow ineluctably from the principle of double taxation of corporate profits. If a corporation were able to avoid tax on the distribution of appreciated property to its shareholders, a substantial amount of income would go untaxed at the corporate level. Yet for more than 50 years the law sanctioned such a result. Under the *General Utilities* doctrine, a corporation could distribute appreciated assets to its shareholders without recognizing any gain. Moreover, after the passage of the 1954 Code, a corporation that sold appreciated property pursuant to a plan of complete liquidation was not taxed on the gain. The following materials trace the development and consequences of the *General Utilities* doctrine.

GENERAL UTILITIES & OPERATING CO. v. HELVERING
296 U.S. 200 (1935)

Mr. Justice McREYNOLDS delivered the opinion of the Court. January 1st, 1927, petitioner — General Utilities, a Delaware corporation — acquired 20,000 shares (one-half of total outstanding) common stock Islands Edison Company, for which it paid $2,000. Gillet & Company owned the remainder.

During January, 1928, Whetstone, President of Southern Cities Utilities Company, contemplated acquisition by his company of all Islands Edison common stock. He discussed the matter with Lucas, petitioner's president, also with Gillet & Company. The latter concern agreed to sell its holdings upon terms acceptable to all. But Lucas pointed out that the shares which his company held could only be purchased after distribution of them among stockholders, since a sale by it would subject the realized profit to taxation, and when the proceeds passed to the stockholders there would be further exaction. Lucas had no power to sell, but he, Gillet and Whetstone were in accord concerning the terms and conditions under which purchase of all stock might become possible — "it being understood and agreed between them that petitioner would make distribution of the stock of the Islands Edison Company to its stockholders and that counsel would prepare a written agreement embodying the terms and conditions of the said sale, agreement to be submitted for approval to the stockholders of the Islands Edison Company after the distribution of said stock by the petitioner."

Petitioner's directors, March 22, 1928, considered the disposition of the Islands Edison shares. Officers reported they were worth $1,122,500, and recommended an appreciation on the books to that figure. Thereupon a resolution directed this change; also "that a dividend in the amount of $1,071,426.25 be and it is hereby declared on the Common Stock of this Company payable in Common Stock of The Islands Edison Company at a valuation of $56.12 ½ a share, out of the surplus of the Company arising from the appreciation in the value of the Common Stock of The Islands Edison Company held by this Company, viz., $1,120,500.00, the payment of the dividend to be made by the delivery to the stockholders of this Company, pro rata, of certificates for the Common Stock of The Islands Edison Company held by this Company at the rate of two shares of such stock for each share of Company Stock of this Corporation."

Accordingly, 19,090 shares were distributed amongst petitioner's 33 stockholders and proper transfers to them were made upon the issuing corporation's books. It retained 910 shares.

After this transfer, all holders of Islands Edison stock sold to Southern Cities Utilities Company at $56.12 ½ per share. Petitioner realized $46,346.30 net profit on 910 shares and this was duly returned for taxation. There was no report of gain upon the 19,090 shares distributed to stockholders.

The Commissioner of Internal Revenue declared a taxable gain upon distribution of the stock in payment of the dividend declared March 22nd, and made the questioned deficiency assessment. Seeking redetermination by the Board of Tax Appeals, petitioner alleged, "The Commissioner of Internal Revenue has erroneously held that the petitioner corporation made a profit of $1,069,517.25 by distributing to its own stockholders certain capital stock of another corporation which it had theretofore owned." And it asked a ruling that no taxable gain resulted from the appreciation upon its books and subsequent distribution of the shares. Answering, the Commissioner denied that his action was erroneous, but advanced no new basis of support. A stipulation concerning the facts followed; and upon this and the pleadings, the Board heard the cause.

It found "The respondent has determined a deficiency in income tax in the amount of $128,342.07 for the calendar year 1928. The only question presented in this proceeding for redetermination is whether petitioner realized taxable gain in declaring a dividend and paying it in the stock of another company at an agreed value per share, which value was in excess of the cost of the stock to petitioner." Also, "On March 26, 1928, the stockholders of the Islands Edison Company (one of which was petitioner, owning 910 shares) and the Southern Cities Utilities' Company, entered into a written contract of sale of the Islands Edison Company stock. At no time did petitioner agree with Whetstone or the Southern Cities Utilities Company, verbally or in writing, to make sale to him or to the Southern Cities Utilities Company of any of said stock except the aforesaid 910 shares of the Islands Edison Company."

The opinion recites — The Commissioner's "theory is that upon the declaration of the dividend on March 22, 1928, petitioner became indebted to its stockholders in the amount of $1,071,426.25, and that the discharge of that liability by the delivery of property costing less than the amount of the debt constituted income, citing United States v. Kirby Lumber Co., 284 U.S. 1." "The intent of the directors of petitioner was to declare a dividend payable in Islands Edison stock; their intent was expressed in that way in the resolution formally adopted; and the dividend was paid in the way intended and declared. We so construe the transaction and on authority of First Utah Savings Bank, supra [17 B.T.A. 804; aff'd, 60 App. D.C. 307; 53 F.(2d) 919 (1931)], we hold that the declaration and payment of the dividend resulted in no taxable income."

The Commissioner asked the Circuit Court of Appeals, 4th Circuit, to review the Board's determination. He alleged, "The only question to be decided is whether the petitioner [taxpayer] realized taxable income in declaring a dividend and paying it in stock of another company at an agreed value per share, which value was in excess of the cost of the stock."

The court stated: "There are two grounds upon which the petitioner urges that the action of the Board of Tax Appeals was wrong: First, that the dividend declared was in effect a cash dividend and that the respondent realized a taxable income by the distribution of the Islands Edison Company stock to its stockholders equal to the difference between the amount of the dividend declared and the cost of the stock; second, that the sale made of the Islands Edison Company stock was in reality a sale by the respondent (with all the terms agreed upon before the declaration of the dividend), through its stockholders who were virtually acting as agents of the respondent, the real vendor."

Upon the first ground, it sustained the Board. Concerning the second, it held that, although not raised before the Board, the point should be ruled upon. "When we come to consider the sale of the stock of the Islands Edison Company, we cannot escape the conclusion that the transaction was deliberately planned and carried out for the sole purpose of escaping taxation. The purchaser was found by the officers of the respondent; the exact terms of the sale as finally consummated were agreed to by the same officers; the purchaser of the stock stated that the delivery of all the stock was essential and that the delivery of a part thereof would not suffice; the details were worked out for the express and admitted purpose of avoiding the payment of the tax and for the reason that the attorneys for the respondent had advised that, unless some such plan was adopted, the tax would have to be paid; and a written agreement was to be prepared by counsel for the respondent which was to be submitted to the stockholders — all this without the stockholders, or any of them, who were ostensibly making the sale, being informed, advised, or consulted. Such admitted facts plainly constituted a plan, not to use the harsher terms of scheme, artifice or conspiracy, to evade the payment of the tax. For the purposes of this decision, it is not necessary to consider whether such a course as is here shown constituted a fraud, it is sufficient if we conclude that the object was to evade the payment of a tax justly due the government.

"The sale of the stock in question was, in substance, made by the respondent company, through the stockholders as agents or conduits through whom the transfer of the title was effected. The stockholders, even in their character as agents, had little or no option in the matter and in no sense exercised any independent judgment. They automatically ratified the agreement prepared and submitted to them."

A judgment of reversal followed.

Both tribunals below rightly decided that petitioner derived no taxable gain from the distribution among its stockholders of the Islands Edison shares as a dividend. This was no sale; assets were not used to discharge indebtedness.

The second ground of objection, although sustained by the court, was not presented to or ruled upon by the Board. The petition for review relied wholly upon the first point; and, in the circumstances, we think the court should have considered no other. Always a taxpayer is entitled to know with fair certainty the basis of the claim against him. Stipulations concerning facts and any other evidence properly are accommodated to issues adequately raised.

Recently (April, 1935) this court pointed out: "The Court of Appeals is without power on review of proceedings of the Board of Tax Appeals to make any findings of fact." "The function of the court is to decide whether the correct rule of law was applied to the facts found; and whether there was substantial evidence before the Board to support the findings made." "If the Board has failed to make an essential finding and the record on review is insufficient to provide the basis for a final determination, the proper procedure is to remand the case for further proceedings before the Board." "And the same procedure is appropriate even when the findings omitted by the Board might be supplied from examination of the records." Helvering v. Rankin, 295 U.S. 123, 131, 132.

Here the court undertook to decide a question not properly raised. Also it made an inference of fact directly in conflict with the stipulation of the parties and the findings, for which we think the record affords no support whatever. To remand the cause for further findings would be futile. The Board could not properly find anything which would assist the Commissioner's cause.

The judgment of the court below must be reversed. The action of the Board of Tax Appeals is approved.

Reversed.

NOTES

1. The Supreme Court rejected on procedural grounds the Government's argument that the shareholder's sale of the stock should be attributed to the corporation. Implicit in this Government contention was the twofold proposition that a sale by a corporation triggers realization of gain, but that absent a sale (and an "amount realized") by the corporation there is no realization. See §1001(a). Ten years later the Government succeeded in an "attribution of sale" approach in Commissioner v. Court Holding Co., page 33 infra.

The Supreme Court rejected on its merits the Government's contention that distribution of the stock was the equivalent of a sale in that it satisfied a corporate debt that the corporation owed to its shareholders as a result of the dividend declaration. The Board of Tax Appeals and the Court of Appeals had also rejected this contention. The Supreme Court (page 30 supra) said "this was no sale;

assets were not used to discharge indebtedness." Why is "sale" so crucial? Was there no "indebtedness," or was it that assets were not used to "discharge" it?

The Supreme Court's opinion ignored a third contention advanced by the Government. The Government argued that "in making it available to its own stockholders the corporation is realizing the appreciation, and nothing more is necessary. It . . . is incomprehensible how a corporation can distribute to its stockholders something which it has not itself received." Brief for Commissioner at 18-19, Commissioner v. Court Holding Co., 324 U.S. 331 (1945). In essence the Government contended that the distribution of the stock, if not a "sale," was nevertheless a "disposition," and that in distributing the appreciation to its shareholders the "amount" was "realized." §1001(a). The Court's failure to deal with this contention is not explained. The Government's failure to raise the argument in either of the lower courts may be the reason. Nevertheless, the *General Utilities* decision was widely regarded as standing for the proposition that a corporation realized no income (or loss) on the distribution of appreciated (or depreciated) assets to its shareholders. For many years prior to *General Utilities* the Regulations had stated that a liquidating distribution of appreciated (or depreciated) property does not trigger a realization of gain (or loss) (Treas. Reg. 118, §39.22(a)-20 (1939 Code)), and *General Utilities* seemed to many to confirm that "rule" in the case of nonliquidating distributions by operating corporations. (In tax parlance a corporation is "liquidating" when it distributes its assets to its shareholders in retirement of their stock. Liquidation does not connote the mere conversion of non-cash assets into cash.)

How important to your evaluation of the Court's decision in *General Utilities* is the fact that the distributed property was immediately sold by the shareholders, and that the purpose of the distribution before sale was to avoid taxation of gain to the corporation? In a similar situation, the tax avoidance purpose loomed large in the decision under §482 to attribute the shareholder's gain on sale to the distributing corporation. See Southern Bancorporation, 67 T.C. 1022 (1977).

2. Why had the Commissioner conceded in the Regulations that no corporate gain or loss was to be recognized in liquidating distributions? On what basis might the tax treatment of interim distributions by an ongoing corporation be differentiated? Should they be differentiated? Might the Commissioner have fared better in *General Utilities* if he had first revoked the provisions of the Regulations as to liquidating distributions and then had promulgated one that asserted that any distribution of an asset to its shareholders would result in corporate realization of gain or loss to the same extent as

It is urged that respondent corporation never executed a written agreement, and that an oral agreement to sell land cannot be enforced in Florida because of the Statute of Frauds, Comp. Gen. Laws of Florida, 1927, vol. 3, §5779. But the fact that respondent corporation itself never executed a written contract is unimportant, since the Tax Court found from the facts of the entire transaction that the executed sale was in substance the sale of the corporation. The decision of the Circuit Court of Appeals is reversed, and that of the Tax Court affirmed.

It is so ordered.

UNITED STATES v. CUMBERLAND PUBLIC
SERVICE CO.
338 U.S. 451 (1950)

Mr. Justice BLACK delivered the opinion of the Court. A corporation selling its physical properties is taxed on capital gains resulting from the sale. There is no corporate tax, however, on distribution of assets in kind to shareholders as part of a genuine liquidation.[2] The respondent corporation transferred property to its shareholders as a liquidating dividend in kind. The shareholders transferred it to a purchaser. The question is whether, despite contrary findings by the Court of Claims, this record requires a holding that the transaction was in fact a sale by the corporation subjecting the corporation to a capital gains tax.

Details of the transaction are as follows. The respondent, a closely held corporation, was long engaged in the business of generating and distributing electric power in three Kentucky counties. In 1936 a local cooperative began to distribute Tennessee Valley Authority power in the area served by respondent. It soon became obvious that respondent's Diesel-generated power could not compete with TVA power, which respondent had been unable to obtain. Respondent's shareholders, realizing that the corporation must get out of the power business unless it obtained TVA power, accordingly offered to sell all the corporate stock to the cooperative, which was receiving such power. The cooperative refused to buy the stock, but countered with an offer to buy from the corporation its transmission and distribution equipment. The corporation rejected the offer because it would have been compelled to pay a heavy capital gains tax. At the same time the shareholders, desiring to save payment of the corporate capital gains tax, offered to acquire the transmission and distribution equip-

2. "No gain or loss is realized by a corporation from the mere distribution of its assets in kind in partial or complete liquidation, however they may have appreciated or depreciated in value since their acquisition. . . ." Treas. Reg. 103, §19.22(a)-21. [1939 Code.]

ment and then sell to the cooperative. The cooperative accepted. The corporation transferred the transmission and distribution systems to its shareholders in partial liquidation. The remaining assets were sold and the corporation dissolved. The shareholders then executed the previously contemplated sale to the cooperative.

Upon this sale by the shareholders, the Commissioner assessed and collected a $17,000 tax from the corporation on the theory that the shareholders had been used as a mere conduit for effectuating what was really a corporate sale. Respondent corporation brought this action to recover the amount of the tax. The Court of Claims found that the method by which the stockholders disposed of the properties was avowedly chosen in order to reduce taxes, but that the liquidation and dissolution genuinely ended the corporation's activities and existence. The court also found that at no time did the corporation plan to make the sale itself. Accordingly it found as a fact that the sale was made by the shareholders rather than the corporation, and entered judgment for respondent. One judge dissented, believing that our opinion in Commissioner v. Court Holding Co., 324 U.S. 331, required a finding that the sale had been made by the corporation. Certiorari was granted, 338 U.S. 846, to clear up doubts arising out of the *Court Holding Co.* case.

Our *Court Holding Co.* decision rested on findings of fact by the Tax Court that a sale had been made and gains realized by the taxpayer corporation. There the corporation had negotiated for the sale of its assets and had reached an oral agreement of sale. When the tax consequences of the corporate sale were belatedly recognized, the corporation purported to "call off" the sale at the last minute and distributed the physical properties in kind to the stockholders. They promptly conveyed these properties to the same persons who had negotiated with the corporation. The terms of purchase were substantially those of the previous oral agreement. One thousand dollars already paid to the corporation was applied as part payment of the purchase price. The Tax Court found that the corporation never really abandoned its sales negotiations, that it never did dissolve, and that the sole purpose of the so-called liquidation was to disguise a corporate sale through use of mere formalisms in order to avoid tax liability. The Circuit Court of Appeals took a different view of the evidence. In this Court the Government contended that whether a liquidation distribution was genuine or merely a sham was traditionally a question of fact. We agreed with this contention, and reinstated the Tax Court's findings and judgment. Discussing the evidence which supported the findings of fact, we went on to say that "the incidence of taxation depends upon the substance of a transaction" regardless of "mere formalisms," and that taxes on a corporate sale cannot be avoided by using the shareholders as a "conduit through which to pass title."

This language does not mean that a corporation can be taxed even when the sale has been made by its stockholders following a genuine liquidation and dissolution.[3] While the distinction between sales by a corporation as compared with distribution in kind followed by shareholder sales may be particularly shadowy and artificial when the corporation is closely held, Congress has chosen to recognize such a distinction for tax purposes. The corporate tax is thus aimed primarily at the profits of a going concern. This is true despite the fact that gains realized from corporate sales are taxed, perhaps to prevent tax evasions, even where the cash proceeds are at once distributed in liquidation.[4] But Congress has imposed no tax on liquidating distributions in kind or on dissolution, whatever may be the motive for such liquidation. Consequently, a corporation may liquidate or dissolve without subjecting itself to the corporate gains tax, even though a primary motive is to avoid the burden of corporate taxation.

Here, on the basis of adequate subsidiary findings, the Court of Claims has found that the sale in question was made by the stockholders rather than the corporation. The Government's argument that the shareholders acted as a mere "conduit" for a sale by respondent corporation must fall before this finding. The subsidiary finding that a major motive of the shareholders was to reduce taxes does not bar this conclusion. Whatever the motive and however relevant it may be in determining whether the transaction was real or a sham, sales of physical properties by shareholders following a genuine liquidation distribution cannot be attributed to the corporation for tax purposes.

The oddities in tax consequences that emerge from the tax provisions here controlling appear to be inherent in the present tax pattern. For a corporation is taxed if it sells all its physical properties and distributes the cash proceeds as liquidating dividends, yet is not taxed if that property is distributed in kind and is then sold by the shareholders. In both instances the interest of the shareholders in the business has been transferred to the purchaser. Again, if these stockholders had succeeded in their original effort to sell all their stock, their interest would have been transferred to the purchasers just as effectively. Yet on such a transaction the corporation would have realized no taxable gain.

3. What we said in the *Court Holding Co.* case was an approval of the action of the Tax Court in looking beyond the papers executed by the corporation and shareholders in order to determine whether the sale there had actually been made by the corporation. We were but emphasizing the established principle that in resolving such questions as who made a sale, fact-finding tribunals in tax cases can consider motives, intent, and conduct in addition to what appears in written instruments used by parties to control rights as among themselves. . . .

4. It has also been held that where corporate liquidations are effected through trustees or agents, gains from sales are taxable to the corporation as though it were a going concern. See, e.g., First National Bank [of Greeley] v. United States, 86 F.2d 938, 941; Treas. Reg. 103, §19.22(a)-21. [1939 Code.]

Congress having determined that different tax consequences shall flow from different methods by which the shareholders of a closely held corporation may dispose of corporate property, we accept its mandate. It is for the trial court, upon consideration of an entire transaction, to determine the factual category in which a particular transaction belongs. Here as in the *Court Holding Co.* case we accept the ultimate findings of fact of the trial tribunal. Accordingly the judgment of the Court of Claims is affirmed.

Mr. Justice Douglas took no part in the consideration or decision of this case.

NOTES

1. Would you have expected the Tax Court to draw the same conclusions from the evidence in *Cumberland* as the Court of Claims did? Why? What evidence in *Cumberland* led the Court of Claims to reach a conclusion different from the one the Tax Court reached in *Court Holding Co.*? In the context of the two cases, in what sense is the inquiry as to who made the sale a factual one? What guidance did the Supreme Court provide for trial courts charged with determining "the factual category in which a particular transaction belongs?"

2. If *General Utilities* had been decided for the Government (on which theory?), might *Court Holding Co.* and *Cumberland* have arisen anyhow? The Supreme Court did not cite *General Utilities* in either case. Why not? In *Cumberland* the Court said that the "corporate tax . . . aimed primarily at the profits of a going concern," page 37 supra. *Court Holding Co.* did not involve a "going concern"; *General Utilities* did. In *Court Holding Co.* the corporate tax was imposed; in *General Utilities* it was not.

b. Codification and Narrowing of the *General Utilities* Doctrine — 1954 to 1986

In 1954, the *General Utilities* doctrine was codified in §311(a) to provide that as to nonliquidating distributions, a distributing corporation would not recognize gain or loss on a distribution "with respect to its stock." Section 336(a) provided similar treatment for distributions in complete or partial liquidations. But there were exceptions. Section 311(a) excepted the distribution of installment obligations from corporate tax immunity, and §311(b) and (c) provided exceptions to the general nonrecognition rule in the case of distributions of LIFO inventory and property subject to liabilities in excess of basis. Section 336 had an exception for the distribution of installment obligations.

Congress also resolved the imputation problem posed by the *Court Holding* case, at least in the context of a complete liquidation. In old §337 (pre-1986 Code), Congress provided generally that a corporation would not recognize gain or loss on the sale of property pursuant to a complete liquidation.

The period from 1954 to 1986 saw a gradual narrowing of the *General Utilities* doctrine. In 1969 Congress added §311(d), which provided that distributions of appreciated property in redemption of the distributing corporation's stock would result in recognition of the gain to the distributing corporation, except in certain specified situations. In 1982, Congress narrowed the exceptions to §311(d). The 1984 Act further narrowed the exceptions to §311(d), so much so that, with few exceptions, distributions of appreciated property, whether by way of dividend or redemption, were made subject to the corporate income tax. Under §336, however, distributions in complete liquidation remained generally immune from the corporate tax.

c.   Repeal of *General Utilities* — The Tax Reform Act of 1986

The 1986 Act repealed what was left of the *General Utilities* doctrine, but with provisions applicable in particular circumstances requiring nonrecognition of loss. Specifically, in a nonliquidating distribution the corporation recognizes gain, but not loss. See §311. In a complete liquidation, gain on the disposition of property to shareholders generally is recognized without limitation, but losses must run the gauntlet of §336(d) in order to be recognized. See §336(a) and (d). Congress repealed old §337; therefore, gain or loss on the sale of property pursuant to a complete liquidation must be recognized. There is no exception for either goodwill or land, although some proponents of *General Utilities* repeal had recommended it. See generally Wolfman, Subchapter C and the 100th Congress, Tax Notes, Nov. 17, 1986, p. 669, excerpted page 862 infra.

Section 336(b) provides that if distributed property is subject to liabilities the fair market value is treated as though it were at least equal to the liabilities. This follows the principle set out in Crane v. Commissioner, 331 U.S. 1 (1947), and the holding in Tufts v. Commissioner, 461 U.S. 300 (1983), which resolved the question of how much gain must be recognized by a taxpayer who transfers property in exchange for the assumption of liabilities that exceed the fair market value of the property. Cf. Crane, Toward a Theory of the Corporate Tax Base: The Effect of a Corporate Distribution of Encumbered Property to Shareholders, 44 Tax L. Rev. 13 (1988).

New §337 defers the recognition of gain on property distributed in a complete liquidation if the property is distributed to an "80-percent distributee." Why is it appropriate to grant nonrecognition treatment upon the liquidation of a subsidiary into its parent? See Chapter 4, infra, pages 541–542.

All gain is recognized on an S corporation's distribution of appreciated assets, unless nonrecognition is called for by §§354, 355, or 356 (provisions dealt with in Chapter 4). See §1363(d) and (e). In the case of a newly formed S corporation, the gain ordinarily will be subject to only a single-level tax, this at the shareholder level. If a C corporation converts to an S corporation, however, the liquidating distribution will be subject to a corporate-level tax on appreciation that antedates the conversion but with relief from the corporate tax if the corporation holds the property for at least 10 years after it attains its S status. See §1374.

Although the *General Utilities* doctrine has been repealed (§§311 and 336), the *Court Holding* and *Cumberland* opinions have remaining important significance. They are frequently cited for their treatment of the pervasive "substance-over-form" problem, one that occurs often. A court will sometimes ignore the form of a transaction and delve into its underlying "substance" when determining its tax consequences. See, e.g., Stewart v. Commissioner, 714 F.2d 977 (9th Cir. 1983), in which the court held that a corporation's sale of its assets to a third party immediately after the sole shareholder had transferred them to the corporation was, in reality, a sale by the shareholder and not by the corporation — *Court Holding* is flipped! For a case in which a taxpayer utilized the *Court Holding* doctrine effectively, see Anderson, 92 T.C. No. 9 (1989).

In repealing the *General Utilities* doctrine Congress had the benefit of a number of studies and proposals. See, e.g., ALI Federal Income Tax Project — Subchapter C — Proposals on Corporate Acquisitions and Dispositions and Reporter's Study on Corporate Distributions (1982); The Subchapter C Revision Act of 1985: A Final Report Prepared by the Staff, S. Prt. 99-47, 99th Cong., 1st Sess. 42, 53, 59-72 (Comm. Print, May 1985); Shube, Corporate Income or Loss on Distributions of Property: An Analysis of *General Utilities*, 12 J. Corp. Taxn. 3 (1985); Wolfman, Taxing Corporate Distributions of Appreciated Property: The Case for Repeal of the *General Utilities* Doctrine, 22 San Diego L. Rev. 81 (1985); Yin, *General Utilities* Repeal: Is Tax Reform Really Going to Pass It By?, Tax Notes, June 16, 1986, p. 1111. But cf. Beck, Distributions in Kind in Corporate Liquidations: A Defense of *General Utilities*, 38 Tax Law. 663 (1985).

d. The Current Law — Illustrative Problems

The intricacies of §§311, 336, and 337 are illustrated by the following problems:

1. Suppose X Corporation in a nonliquidating distribution distributes to its sole shareholder, A, property with a basis of 100 and a fair market value of 200. What are the tax consequences to X Corporation? Suppose instead that the fair market value of the distributed property is 50. What consequences to X Corporation? Why did Congress choose to disallow recognition of loss upon the distribution of property in a nonliquidating distribution?

2. Pursuant to a plan of complete liquidation, Y Corporation distributes property with a basis of 100 and a fair market value of 90. The property is subject to liabilities of 150. What are the tax consequences to Y Corporation? For the consequences of the transaction to the shareholders, see Chapter 2, infra, page 148 et seq.

3. Eighty percent of T Corporation's stock is owned by P Corporation, and the remaining 20 percent is owned by an individual, B. In a complete liquidation, T Corporation makes a pro rata distribution to its shareholders of property with a basis of 100 and a fair market value of 200. What are the tax consequences to T Corporation? Suppose instead that the distributed property has a fair market value of 50. Does T Corporation recognize loss on the distribution?

4. C, an individual who is the sole shareholder of Z Corporation, contributes property to Z Corporation that has a basis of 100 and a fair market value of 50. As you will learn in Chapter 3, the basis of the property in Z Corporation's hands will be 100. See §362(a). Six months later, when the property has a value of 10, Z Corporation distributes the property to C in a complete liquidation. Does Z Corporation recognize loss on the distribution?

e. Computation of Gain — Question of Basis — §§1012, 334, and 338

UNITED STATES v. GENERAL GEOPHYSICAL CO.
296 F.2d 86 (5th Cir. 1961), *cert. denied,* 369 U.S. 849 (1962)

Before Rives and Wisdom, Circuit Judges, and Dawkins, Jr., District Judge.

WISDOM, Circuit Judge. February 25, 1954 General Geophysical Company, the taxpayer, transferred certain depreciable assets having a tax basis of $169,290 and a market value of $746,525 to two of its major stockholders in the redemption of their stock. Later that day the taxpayer reacquired the same assets from the former stockholders in exchange for corporate notes in the amount of $746,525. In its 1954 income tax return the corporation claimed depreciation deductions using as the cost basis the market value of the assets at the time of the transaction. The sole question this litigation presents is whether the corporation's reacquisition of the assets stepped up the basis. We hold that it did not and reverse the decision below.

Earl W. Johnson founded General Geophysical Company in 1933 to engage in oil exploration, and managed its operations until his sudden death in 1953. At his death his estate, his wife, his mother, and a friend Paul L. Davis owned 77% of the corporation's total stock and 94% of its voting shares. The major portion of the remaining shares was owned by Chester Sappington, T.O. Hall, and Albert B. Gruff, who were also officers in the corporation. The Johnson stock was community property: half belonged to the widow and the other half was held by the Second National Bank of Houston as executor and trustee for Johnson's estate. The testimony shows that the bank and Mrs. Johnson soon realized that neither of them could contribute anything of value to running the corporate business, and that they should not attempt it. They realized also that if the corporation were liquidated and its properties sold, they would receive less than the value of their stock in a going concern. Sappington, Hall, and Grubb believed that they could run the corporation successfully and if so, they should receive its future profits. Accordingly, the corporation agreed to retire the stock held by the bank, the two Mrs. Johnsons, and Davis. After long negotiations the parties settled on a valuation of the stock at $245 a share, payable partly in cash and partly in notes. The attorney for the retiring stockholders advised against this proposal for fear that it would leave the stockholders without sufficient protection in case the corporation should be forced into bankruptcy. He based this legitimate business fear on Robinson v. Wangemann, 5 Cir., 1935, 75 F.2d 756, 758, which holds that when a former shareholder owns notes of a bankrupt corporation, received in the redemption of his stock, he "cannot be permitted to share with the other unsecured creditors in the distribution of the assets of the bankrupt estate." To avoid exposure to this risk, the stockholders proposed that the Johnson stock be retired in exchange for cash and corporate property having a market value equal to that of the stock. The redemption was carried out in accordance with this proposal. A few hours later, the corporation repurchased the property for corporate notes, giving the former stockholders a mortgage on certain of its properties.

Witnesses for the taxpayer insisted that there was no agreement between the corporation and the stockholders to reexchange the corporate properties transferred to the stockholders in the redemption of their shares. The trial judge so found, and it seems clear that there was no legally binding agreement to that effect. The attorney for the stockholders did testify, however, that he had discussed the possibility of such a resale and before February 25, 1954 had prepared the documents for a resale in case that was decided upon after the initial transfer.

Under Section 1012 of the Internal Revenue Code of 1954, 26 U.S.C.A. §1012, "the basis of property shall be the cost of such property." This requires a determination of when the taxpayer acquired the property and the price he paid for it. Our decision depends on whether or not the transactions in question created an interruption in the ownership of the property, producing a new basis on its reacquisition. The Government asserts that we should disregard the form of the transfer and recognize that the substance of the transactions was a redemption of the corporate stock for cash and notes, leaving the ownership and basis of the depreciable assets undisturbed. The taxpayer answers that there was no fraud or subterfuge in these transactions, that the stockholders acquired complete and unfettered ownership of the properties, and that the trial judge's finding of two separate and independent transactions cannot be overturned on appeal.

The solution of hard tax cases requires something more than the easy generalization that the substance rather than the form of a transaction is determinative of its tax effect, since in numerous situations the form by which a transaction is effected does influence or control its tax consequences. This generalization does, however, reflect the truth that courts will, on occasion, look beyond the superficial formalities of a transaction to determine the proper tax treatment.

In the landmark case of Gregory v. Helvering, 1935, 293 U.S. 465 . . ., the Supreme Court refused to give effect to corporate transactions which complied precisely with the formal requirements for nontaxable corporate reorganizations, on the ground that the transactions had served no function other than that of a contrivance to bail out corporate earnings to the sole shareholder at capital gains tax rates. In Commissioner v. Court Holding Co. [page 33 supra] the Supreme Court taxed a corporation on the gain from the sale of an apartment house notwithstanding a transfer of the house to the corporation's two shareholders before the sale, since it found that the transfer was made solely to set in a more favorable tax form a sale which in reality was made by the corporation. Similarly, in Helvering v. Clifford, 1940, 309 U.S. 331 . . . , the Supreme Court taxed a trust grantor on the income of the trust property since the formal transfer of the property by the grantor was lacking in substance. The Court found that the dilution in his control seemed insignificant and immaterial and that "since the husband retains control over the investment, he has rather complete assurance that the trust will not effect any substantial change in his economic position." 309 U.S. at pages 335-336. . . . Each case must be decided on its own merits by examining the form and substance of the transactions and the purpose of the relevant tax provisions to determine whether recognition of the form of the transaction would defeat the statutory purpose.

The case at bar presents an unusual tax question created by the conjunction of two parts of the tax code not frequently brought together by a single transaction: the provisions governing basis and capital gains, and the rule that no gain is recognized by a corporation when it distributes property with respect to its stock. The basis of property is determined by its cost; when the property is sold the owner realizes a taxable gain equal to the difference between the basis and the proceeds received in the sale. There is no danger that a taxpayer could effect an artificial sale and repurchase to raise the basis of appreciated property, since such a transaction would subject him to a tax on the step-up in the basis. There are, therefore, no provisions to prevent tax avoidance by such a device, and the question whether a transfer and reacquisition should be recognized as independent transactions creating tax consequences would generally affect only the *timing* of the imposition of a tax rather than its *amount*. The twist here comes from the fact that the corporation did not incur a tax on the difference between basis and current market value when it transferred the assets to its shareholders in redemption of their stock. Section 311(a) . . . provides that "no gain or loss shall be recognized to a corporation on the distribution, with respect to its stock, of . . . property." This provision is expressly made applicable to stock redemption distributions by the Treasury Regulations.[2] The rule may be easily justified by the fact that when a corporation transfers appreciated property to its shareholders, as a dividend or in exchange for their shares, the gain created by the appreciation has not accrued to the corporation and should not be taxed to it.[3]

A new horizon of tax avoidance opportunities would be opened by allowing a stepped-up basis to result from the transaction here effected. Corporations would be enabled without difficulty to raise the basis of their assets whenever it fell below the market value by transferring the assets to shareholders by a dividend or stock redemption and then buying back the same assets for the cash that they otherwise would have distributed directly. Since market values are often pushed up by inflation and the basis is frequently reduced under the liberal depreciation rules far faster than the assets actually depreciate, this possibility would have enormous practical significance. These tax avoidance implications do not constitute a license

2. Treas. Reg. 1.311-1(a) (1955).

3. If the corporation in effect does realize the gain by handling the sale of the property after its distribution to the shareholders, the gain probably would be attributed to the corporation. See United States v. Lynch, 9 Cir., 1951, 192 F.2d 718, certiorari denied 1952, 343 U.S. 934 . . . ; Commissioner v. Transport Trading & Terminal Corp., 2 Cir., 1949, 176 F.2d 570, certiorari denied 1950, 338 U.S. 955. These cases were decided before enactment of Section 311, but since that section is largely a codification of the rule laid down by General Utilities & Operating Co. v. Helvering, 1935, 296 U.S. 200 . . . , which did precede these cases their validity is probably not undercut by the statute. Mintz and Plumb, Dividends in Kind — The Thunderbolts and the New Look, 10 Tax L. Rev. 41, 45-48 (1954). . . .

to courts to distort the laws or to write in new provisions; they do mean that we should guard against giving force to a purported transfer which gives off an unmistakably hollow sound when it is tapped. It is a hollow sound for tax purposes; here, we are not concerned with business purposes or the legal effectiveness of the transaction under the law of Texas. Under the tax law, it is of course open to a corporation making a dividend distribution or a stock redemption to distribute appreciated assets rather than cash and to use its cash to purchase similar assets for replacement at a stepped-up basis. Such transactions are however limited by their costs. Moreover, in such a case it would be clear that the corporation had disposed of its former assets and acquired new ones. When, however, a corporation contends that it stepped up the basis by transferring assets to its shareholders and then reacquiring them, we must scrutinize the transactions to make sure that the alleged divestiture did occur. The transactions should be recognized as creating an interruption in the ownership of the assets sufficient to produce a new basis *only* when the corporation has made a clear and distinct severance of its ownership prior to the reacquisition.

The facts of these transactions will not support a holding that the corporation had terminated its ownership for these purposes. It parted with bare legal title to the property for a few short hours. It made no physical delivery of any of the assets. Its control and use of the property were never interrupted. Even the surrender of its legal title was made under circumstances creating a strong expectation that it would be returned shortly. True, the stockholders may have had complete legal freedom to refuse to resell the assets to the corporation, but there was almost no likelihood that they would do so. It was a foregone conclusion that they would resell the assets to someone, since the very reason for the original redemption was that the stockholders did not wish to continue ownership of the assets and management of the business. And since the assets were already integrated into the operations of the taxpayer and represented 47% of its assets,[4] the taxpayer was the logical, and as a practical matter, the only possible purchaser. That the stockholders had already drawn up papers for the resale, in case they decided to make one, undoubtedly strengthened the confidence with which the taxpayer could look forward to the reacquisition of the properties. There was never the whisper of a suggestion that the company was to cut down on its operation, as would be inevitable if it permanently parted with 47% of its assets, including three rigs. The most that can be said is that the taxpayer gave to the bank and Mrs. Johnson the power to divest

---

4. The assets transferred were valued by the parties at $746,525. At the rate of $245 per share, that total would represent 3047 shares, or slightly over 47% of the 6461 shares then outstanding.

it of its ownership of certain properties; they held that power for a few hours and then returned it. The transactions, from the corporation's standpoint, were more like an option than a sale, and the option expired quickly without having been exercised.

The taxpayer asserts that the transactions were prompted by a valid business purpose and were effected without a motive of tax avoidance. We accept these assertions, which are supported by the trial judge's findings, as true. They lend support to the taxpayer's case, but they do not control the disposition of the case. Intent often is relevant in questions of taxation, particularly where the bona fides of a transaction is called into question, but in most cases tax treatment depends on what was done, not why it was done. And our decision in this case rests not on the motivation of the transactions in question but rather on our conclusion that the admitted facts of the two transfers preclude a finding of a sufficient hiatus in the corporate ownership of the assets to justify bestowal of a new basis on them after the reacquisition.[5]

To determine the basis of the assets we look backward to ascertain when the corporation acquired them. We note the transactions here in question, but we can scarcely say that the corporation's ownership dates from that occasion. These transactions, whatever their effect on other legal questions, did not create an interruption in the ownership sufficient to produce a new basis. The basis must be found from the original purchase price and the adjustments made to it. The district court's findings may be correct; his conclusions are in error.

The judgment is reversed.

ON PETITION FOR REHEARING

PER CURIAM. The petition for rehearing in this case expresses strongly the petitioner's conviction that this Court failed to recognize the bona fides of the transaction. In denying this petition we wish, again, to make clear that we did not base the decision on a lack of good faith in the parties to the transaction. It is true that we said, "we should guard against giving force to a purported transfer which gives off an unmistakably hollow sound when it is tapped." But this statement was set off (in the same sentence) against the other extreme: "These tax avoidance implications do not constitute a license to courts

5. If these transactions could not have been explained by valid nontax reasons, they obviously would have been only a subterfuge which could not have been effective to change the basis of the assets. . . .

to distort the laws or to write in new provisions." Throughout the opinion we were careful to say that our decision was not based on any lack of good faith in the parties to the transaction, and that we did not pass on the legal effect of the transaction outside of the tax frame of reference. We do not question the integrity of the parties or suggest that there was any flimflam. We do not doubt the business purposes of the transaction. The decision does not purport to question the effectiveness of the transaction in protecting the stockholders against the holding in Robinson v. Wangeman, 5 Cir., 1935, 75 F.2d 756. But we hold and reaffirm that for *tax purposes* there was not a sufficient severance of the corporation's ownership over the assets for the transaction to create the tax consequence that when the corporation reacquired the assets it took them with a stepped-up basis. The transaction is analogous to a *Clifford* trust, valid under state law but ineffective for *tax purposes* to remove the trust income from the settlor's taxable income. Helvering v. Clifford, 1940, 309 U.S. 331. . . . It is ordered that the petition for rehearing filed in the above styled and numbered cause be, and the same is hereby denied.

NOTES

1. The court said (page 46 supra) that its "decision depends on whether or not the transactions in question created an interruption in the ownership of the property. . . ." What is the source of the court's premise? Is it a fair premise for determining "cost" under §1012? The court also said (page 44 supra) that the "twist [in this case] comes from the fact that the corporation did not incur a tax on the difference between basis and current market value when it transferred the assets to its shareholders in redemption of their stock. Section 311(a). . . ." In light of §311(b) today, the "twist" would be absent. Should that change the result in the case?

2. Consider this case: Corporation M would like to step up the $500,000 basis of its manufacturing plant (building, not land) to its $1 million dollar value in order to increase its depreciation deductions. It would also like to increase its cash position. It therefore sells its plant to a bank for $1 million dollars in cash and immediately thereafter buys it back, paying for it with its 10-year, 15 percent note, secured by a first mortgage on the plant and the land under it. As taxpayer's counsel, what would you argue to the Fifth Circuit as your principal ground for distinguishing *General Geophysical*? What additional facts would you like to find in the record to buttress your position? What would you expect that court to decide was Corporation M's basis?

KIMBELL-DIAMOND MILLING CO. v.
COMMISSIONER
14 T.C. 74 (1950), *aff'd per curiam*, 187 F.2d 718 (5th Cir. 1950), *cert. denied*, 342 U.S. 827 (1951)

BLACK, Judge. This proceeding involves deficiencies in income, declared value excess profits, and excess profits taxes for the fiscal years ended May 31, 1945 and 1946. . . . The deficiencies are primarily due to respondent's reduction of petitioner's basis in assets acquired by it in December, 1942, through the liquidation of another corporation known as Whaley Mill & Elevator Co. (sometimes hereinafter referred to as Whaley). By reason of this reduction respondent has adjusted petitioner's allowable depreciation. . . . By appropriate assignments of error petitioner contests these adjustments. . . .

This leaves for our consideration the determination of petitioner's basis in the assets acquired from Whaley.

The facts have been stipulated and are adopted as our findings of fact. They may be summarized as follows:

Petitioner is a Texas corporation, engaged primarily in the business of milling, processing, and selling grain products, and has its principal office in Fort Worth, Texas. Petitioner maintained its books and records and filed its corporation tax returns on an accrual basis for fiscal years ended May 31 of each year. . . .

On or about August 13, 1942, petitioner sustained a fire casualty at its Wolfe City, Texas, plant which resulted in the destruction of its mill property at that location. The assets so destroyed [had an aggregate adjusted basis of $18,921.90]. . . . This property was covered by insurance, and on or about November 14, 1942, petitioner collected insurance in the amount of $124,551.10 ($118,200.16 as a reimbursement for the loss sustained by the fire and $6,350.94 as a premium refund). On December 26, 1942, petitioner's directors approved the transaction set forth in the minutes below:

> THAT, WHEREAS, on or about August 1, 1942, the flour mill and milling plant of Kimbell-Diamond Milling Company located at Wolfe City, Texas was destroyed by fire; and
>
> WHEREAS, Kimbell-Diamond Milling Company collected from the insurance companies carrying the insurance on the said destroyed properties the sum of $125,000.00 as indemnification for the loss sustained, which said insurance proceeds were by the proper officers of this corporation promptly deposited in a special account in the Fort Worth National Bank of Fort Worth, Texas, where they have since been kept intact in order to have the same available for replacing, as nearly as might be, the destroyed properties; and
>
> WHEREAS, it has at all times been the intention and desire of Kimbell-Diamond Milling Company to replace its burned mill

either by constructing a new mill or by purchasing facilities of substantially similar kind and use; and

WHEREAS, due to existing building restrictions and other causes, it has been found impractical and impossible to replace the destroyed facilities by new construction, but it has come to the attention of the officers of this corporation that the stock of Whaley Mill & Elevator Company, a Texas corporation, which, among its other assets, owns physical properties substantially comparable to the destroyed Wolfe City Milling plant, can be purchased;

NOW, THEREFORE, BE IT RESOLVED:

1. That the proper officers of Kimbell-Diamond Milling Company be, and they are hereby, authorized, empowered and directed to purchase the entire authorized, issued and outstanding capital stock of Whaley Mill & Elevator Company, a Texas corporation, consisting of 4,000 shares of the face or par value of $100.00 per share, for a sum not in excess of $210,000.00; that payment for the said stock of Whaley Mill & Elevator Company be made, to the extent possible, from the insurance proceeds deposited in a special account in the Fort Worth National Bank, and that the balance of the agreed consideration for the stock of Whaley Mill & Elevator Company be paid out of the general funds of Kimbell-Diamond Milling Company.

2. That as soon as practicable after the purchase of the Whaley Mill & Elevator Company stock hereby authorized has been consummated, all necessary steps be taken to completely liquidate the said corporation by transferring its entire assets, particularly its mill and milling equipment, to Kimbell-Diamond Milling Company in cancellation and redemption of the entire issued and outstanding capital stock of Whaley Mill & Elevator Company, and that the charter of said corporation be forthwith surrendered and cancelled.

On December 26, 1942, petitioner acquired 100 percent of the stock of Whaley Mill & Elevator Co. of Gainesville, Texas, paying therefor $210,000 in cash which payment, to the extent of $118,200.16, was made with the insurance proceeds received by petitioner as a result of the fire on or about August 13, 1942.

On December 29, 1942, the stockholders of Whaley assented to the dissolution and distribution of assets thereof. On the same date an "Agreement and Program of Complete Liquidation" was entered into between petitioner and Whaley, which provided, inter alia:

THAT, WHEREAS, KIMBELL-DIAMOND owns the entire authorized issued and outstanding capital stock of WHALEY, consisting of 4000 shares of a par value of $100.00 per share, which said stock was acquired by KIMBELL-DIAMOND primarily for the purpose of enabling it to secure possession and ownership of the flour mill and milling plant owned by WHALEY, the parties herewith agree that the said mill and milling plant shall forthwith be conveyed to KIMBELL-DIAMOND by WHALEY under the following program for the complete liquidation of WHALEY viz.:

(1) KIMBELL-DIAMOND shall cause the 4000 shares of the capital stock of WHALEY owned by it to be surrendered to WHALEY for cancellation and retirement, whereupon WHALEY shall forthwith convey, transfer and assign unto KIMBELL-DIA-MOND all property of every kind and character owned or claimed by it, particularly its flour mill and milling plant, located at Gainesville, Texas, and all machinery and equipment appurtenant thereto, or used in connection therewith, in full and complete liquidation of all of the outstanding stock of WHALEY. The aforesaid distribution in complete liquidation shall be fully consummated by not later than midnight, December 31, 1942.

(2) When the entire assets of every kind and character, owned by WHALEY, have been transferred to KIMBELL-DIAMOND in full and complete liquidation of the capital stock of WHALEY, owned by KIMBELL-DIAMOND, WHALEY shall forthwith make application to the Secretary of State of the State of Texas for its dissolution as a corporation and surrender its corporate charter.

On December 31, 1942, the Secretary of State of the State of Texas certified that the Whaley Mill & Elevator Co. was dissolved as of that date. . . .

There is no dispute that the petitioner's adjusted basis in its depreciable assets which were destroyed by fire was $18,921.90; nor that the depreciable assets which it received from Whaley had an adjusted basis in the hands of Whaley of $139,521.62. Petitioner, in the years herein involved, proceeded under the theory that it was entitled to Whaley's basis. Respondent takes the position that petitioner's cost is its basis in the assets acquired from Whaley. . . . The petitioner does not controvert the allocation of cost made by respondent to the various assets acquired from Whaley, both depreciable and nondepreciable property. As to the depreciable assets purchased to replace those involuntarily converted, respondent contends that petitioner's basis is limited by [§1033(b)] of the Internal Revenue Code. . . . Petitioner argues that the acquisition of Whaley's assets and the subsequent liquidation of Whaley brings petitioner within the provisions of [§332] and, therefore, by reason of [§334(b)(1)*] petitioner's basis in these assets is the same as the basis in Whaley's hands. In so contending, petitioner asks that we treat the acquisition of Whaley's stock and the subsequent liquidation of Whaley as separate transactions. It is well settled that the incidence of taxation depends upon the substance of a transaction. Commissioner v. Court Holding Co., 324 U.S. 331. It is inescapable from petitioner's minutes set out above and from the "Agreement and Program of Complete Liquidation" entered into between petitioner

*There was no counterpart to §334(b)(2) in the 1939 Code. — ED.

and Whaley, that the only intention petitioner ever had was to acquire Whaley's assets.

We think that this proceeding is governed by the principles of Commissioner v. Ashland Oil & Refining Co., 99 Fed. (2d) 588, certiorari denied, 306 U.S. 661. In that case the stock was retained for almost a year before liquidation. Ruling on the question of whether the stock or the assets of the corporation were purchased, the court stated:

> The question remains, however, whether if the entire transaction, whatever its form, was essentially in intent, purpose and result, a purchase by Swiss of property, its several steps may be treated separately and each be given an effect for tax purposes as though each constituted a distinct transaction. . . . And without regard to whether the result is imposition or relief from taxation, the courts have recognized that where the essential nature of a transaction is the acquisition of property, it will be viewed as a whole, and closely related steps will not be separated either at the instance of the taxpayer or the taxing authority.

See also Koppers Coal Co., 6 T.C. 1209 and cases there cited.

We hold that the purchase of Whaley's stock and its subsequent liquidation must be considered as one transaction, namely, the purchase of Whaley's assets which was petitioner's sole intention. This was not a reorganization within [§332], and petitioner's basis in these assets, both depreciable and nondepreciable, is, therefore, its cost, or $110,721.74 ($18,921.90, the basis of petitioner's assets destroyed by fire plus $91,799.84, the amount expended over the insurance proceeds). Since petitioner does not controvert respondent's allocation of cost to the individual assets acquired from Whaley, both depreciable and nondepreciable, respondent's allocation is sustained. . . .

Decision will be entered for the respondent.

. . . Reviewed by the Court.

NOTE

Kimbell-Diamond led to great uncertainty. It was impossible to be sure when a taxpayer would succeed in bringing its apparent purchase of stock within the doctrine. Where a taxpayer wished to avoid application of the doctrine, however, it could readily do so by delaying the liquidation until a considerable period after the purchase of its stock had elapsed. To bring certainty to this area, Congress codified and expanded the *Kimbell-Diamond* rule. Its most recent incarnation is found in §338, enacted as part of the Tax Equity and Fiscal Responsibility Act of 1982 (TEFRA), prior to the repeal of the *General Utilities* doctrine. A "general explanation" of §338 follows.

STAFF OF THE JOINT COMMITTEE ON
TAXATION, GENERAL EXPLANATION OF THE
REVENUE PROVISIONS OF THE TAX EQUITY
AND FISCAL RESPONSIBILITY ACT OF 1982
131-139 (Dec. 31, 1982)

PRIOR LAW

Upon the complete liquidation of a subsidiary corporation, 80 percent of the voting power and 80 percent of the total number of shares of all other classes of stock (other than nonvoting preferred stock) of which is owned by the parent corporation, gain or loss is generally not recognized and the basis of the subsidiary's assets and its other tax attributes are carried over (secs. 332, 334(b)(1), and 381(a)).

Under prior law, however, if the controlling stock interest was acquired by purchase within a 12-month period and the subsidiary was liquidated pursuant to a plan of liquidation adopted within 2 years after the qualifying stock purchase was completed, the transaction was treated as in substance a purchase of the subsidiary's assets (sec. 334(b)(2)). The acquiring corporation's basis in the "purchased" assets was the cost of the stock purchased as adjusted for items such as liabilities assumed, certain cash or dividend distributions to the acquiring corporation, and postacquisition earnings and profits of the subsidiary. The liquidating distributions could be made over a 3-year period beginning with the close of the taxable year during which the first of a series of distributions occurs (sec. 332(b)(3)). Thus, this treatment applied even though the liquidation could extend over a 5-year period after control had been acquired.

In these cases, when the assets were treated as purchased by the acquiring corporation, recapture income was taxed to the liquidating corporation, the investment tax credit recapture provisions were applicable, and tax attributes, including carryovers, of the liquidated corporation were terminated.

Cases interpreting the law applicable before the rules in section 334(b)(2) were adopted treated the purchase of stock and prompt liquidation in some cases as a purchase of assets (Kimbell-Diamond Milling Co. v. Commissioner 14 T.C. 74, aff'd per curiam, 187 F.2d 718 (5th Cir.), cert. denied, 342 U.S. 827 (1951)). It is not clear whether such treatment still applied after the enactment of section 334(b)(2) in cases where the requirements of that provision were not met.

A stock purchase and liquidation was treated as a purchase of all the assets of the acquired corporation under prior law if section 334(b)(2) applied. Revision of the special treatment of partial liquidations under the Act restricts the options of a corporate purchaser seeking to treat a purchase of a corporation as a purchase of assets in part combined with a continuation of the tax attributes of the acquired entity. Neither prior law nor the Act's revision of the treatment of partial liquidations restrict a corporate purchaser from achieving such selectivity by purchasing assets directly from a corporation while concurrently purchasing the corporation's stock. Selectivity could also be achieved if an acquired corporation, prior to the acquisition, dispersed its assets in tax-free transactions among several corporations which could be separately purchased. The corporate purchaser then through selective qualifying liquidations could obtain asset purchase treatment for one or more acquired corporations while preserving the tax attributes of one or more other corporations. . . .

EXPLANATION OF PROVISIONS

GENERAL TREATMENT OF STOCK PURCHASE AS ASSET
PURCHASE

The Act repeals the provision of prior law (sec. 334(b)(2)) that treated a purchase and liquidation of a subsidiary as an asset purchase. The amendments made by the Act were also intended to replace any nonstatutory treatment of a stock purchase as an asset purchase under the *Kimbell-Diamond* doctrine. Instead, an acquiring corporation, within 75 days after a qualified stock purchase, except as regulations may provide for a later election, may elect to treat an acquired subsidiary (target corporation) as if it sold all its assets pursuant to a plan of complete liquidation at the close of the stock acquisition date. The target corporation will be treated as a new corporation that purchased the assets on the day following such date. Gain or loss will not be recognized to the target corporation except for gain or loss attributable to stock held by minority shareholders as described below, to the same extent gain or loss is not recognized (sec. 337) when a corporation sells all its assets in the course of a complete liquidation. This provision was intended to provide nonrecognition of gain or loss to the same extent that gain or loss would not be recognized under section 336 if there were an actual liquidation of the target corporation on the acquisition date to which prior law section 334(b)(2) applied.

If, because of the application of other provisions of the Internal Revenue Code, the rules of section 337 providing for nonrecognition of gain or loss on the disposition of assets are made inapplicable, gain or loss is recognized under section 338. For example, section 337 does not apply to a sale or exchange of a United States real property interest by a foreign corporation (sec. 897(d)(2)). Thus, if the target corporation is a foreign corporation holding an interest in U.S. real property, gain or loss allocable to such interest is recognized if the acquiring corporation makes an election to which section 338(a) applies. . . .

A qualified stock purchase occurs if 80 percent or more of the voting power and 80 percent of the total number of shares of other classes of stock (except nonvoting, preferred stock) is acquired by purchase during a 12-month period (the acquisition period). The acquisition date is the date within such acquisition period on which the 80-percent purchase requirement (the qualified stock purchase) is satisfied. Generally, the 80-percent purchase requirement may be satisfied through the combination of stock purchases and redemptions. However, it is expected that the regulations will provide rules to prevent selective asset distributions.

The election is to be made in the manner prescribed by regulations, and once made, will be irrevocable.

TREATMENT OF TARGET CORPORATION AS A NEW
CORPORATION

The assets of the target corporation will be treated as sold (and purchased) for an amount equal to the grossed up basis of the acquiring corporation in the stock of the target corporation on the acquisition date. The amount is to be adjusted under regulations for liabilities of the target corporation and other relevant items. It was anticipated that recapture tax liability of the target corporation attributable to the deemed sale of its assets is an item which may result in an adjustment under the regulations.

Under the gross-up formula, if the acquiring corporation owns less than 100 percent by value of the target corporation's stock on the acquisition date, the deemed purchase price is grossed up [as provided in §338(b) — Ed]. It was not intended that minority shareholders in the target corporation be treated as having exchanged their shares for stock in the new corporation. However, nonrecognition of gain or loss to the target corporation is limited, unless the target corporation is liquidated within one year after the acquisition date, to the highest actual percentage by value of target corporation stock held by the acquiring corporation during the one-year period beginning on the acquisition date. . . .

The Act provides that the deemed sale (and purchase) of all its assets by the target corporation applies for purposes of subtitle A of the Internal Revenue Code and is deemed to occur at the close of the acquisition date in a single transaction. Under these rules, the provisions of subtitle F of the Code relating to assessment, collection, refunds, statutes of limitations, and other procedural matters apply without regard to the status of the target corporation as a new corporation. The target corporation thus remains liable for any tax liabilities incurred by it for any period prior to the election. The target corporation is required to file an income tax return for its taxable year ending as of the close of the acquisition date. . . .

DEFINITION OF PURCHASE

The term "purchase" is defined as it was under prior law (sec. 334(b)(3)) to exclude acquisitions of stock with a carryover basis or from a decedent, acquisitions in an exchange to which section 351 applies, and acquisitions from a person whose ownership is attributed to the acquiring person under section 318(a). Attribution under section 381(a)(4) relating to options will be disregarded for this purpose. However, if, as a result of a stock purchase, the purchasing corporation is treated under section 318(a) as owning stock in a third corporation, the purchasing corporation will be treated as having purchased stock in such third corporation but not until the first day on which ownership of such stock is considered as owned by the purchasing corporation under section 318(a). This rule may be illustrated by the following example:

Assume a target corporation and a third corporation each have only one class of stock outstanding and that the target corporation owns 50 percent of the stock of the third corporation. The purchasing corporation purchases 20 percent of the target corporation on each of five separate dates, January 1, April 1, July 1, October 1, and December 31, 1983. Under section 318(a), no portion of the stock of the third corporation is constructively owned by the purchasing corporation until July 1, 1983, the date on which its ownership of the target corporation first exceeds 50 percent (sec. 318(a)(2)(C)). On that date, the purchasing corporation is treated as purchasing 30 percent (60 percent of 50 percent) of the third corporation. By virtue of the remaining purchases of the target corporation stock, the purchasing corporation will be treated as having purchased 50 percent of the third corporation's stock by December 31, 1983. If, by June 30, 1984 (the end of the 12-month acquisition period applicable to the third corporation), either the purchasing corporation or the target corporation purchases an additional 30 percent of the third corporation, an election, if made for the target corporation, would also apply to the third corporation.

In the above example, the amount for which the assets of the third corporation are treated as sold (and purchased) is determined by reference to the portion of the price paid for the target corporation's stock allocable to the 50-percent interest in the third corporation's stock owned by the target corporation plus any amount paid to purchase an additional 30 percent of such stock after December 31, 1983, and within the remaining portion of the acquisition period applicable to the third corporation. If ownership of the third corporation is less than 100 percent on the acquisition date, the basis so determined is grossed up pursuant to section 338(b)(2).

A purchase of over 80 percent but less than 100 percent of the stock of a target corporation which in turn owns 80 percent of the stock of a third corporation is not a qualified stock purchase with respect to the third corporation because the purchasing corporation has not acquired by purchase the requisite 80 percent of the third corporation's stock. This is so, even though the purchasing corporation, the target corporation, and the third corporation constitute an affiliated group as defined in section 1504(a).

CONSISTENCY REQUIREMENT

The rules require consistency where the purchasing corporation makes qualified stock purchases of two or more corporations that are members of the same affiliated group. For this purpose, purchases by a member of the purchasing corporation's affiliated group, except as regulations provide otherwise, are treated as purchases by the purchasing corporation.[1] The consistency requirement applies as well to a combination of a direct asset acquisition and qualified stock purchase.

The consistency requirement applies with respect to purchases over a defined "consistency period" determined by reference to the acquisition date applicable to the target corporation. The "consistency period" is the one-year period preceding the target corporation acquisition period plus the portion of the acquisition period up to and including the acquisition date, and the one-year period following the acquisition date. Thus, if all the target corporation's stock is purchased on the same day by the purchasing corporation, the one-year period immediately preceding and the one-year period immediately following such day are included in the consistency period. If, within such period, there is a direct purchase of assets from the target corporation or a target affiliate by the purchasing corporation, the rules require that the acquisition of the target corporation be treated as an asset purchase.

The consistency period may be expanded in appropriate cases by the Secretary where there is in effect a plan to make several qualified stock purchases or any such purchase and asset acquisition with respect to a target corporation and its target affiliates.

The consistency requirement is applied to an affiliated group

1. Transfer of target corporation stock within the purchasing corporation's affiliated group will not disqualify a section 338 election (cf. Chrome Plate Inc. v. U.S., 614 F.2d 990 (5th Cir.1980)).

with reference to a target corporation and any "target affiliate." A corporation is defined as a "target affiliate" of the target corporation if each was, at any time during that portion of the consistency period ending on the acquisition date of the target corporation, a member of an affiliated group that had the same common parent. An affiliated group has the same meaning given to such term by section 1504(a) (without regard to the exceptions in sec. 1504(b)). This definition also applies in determining whether a purchase is made by a member of the same affiliated group as the purchasing corporation.

An acquisition of assets from the target corporation or a target affiliate during the consistency period applicable to the target corporation will require the qualified stock purchase of the target corporation to be treated as a purchase of assets. In applying these rules, stock in a target affiliate is not to be treated as an asset of any other target affiliate or of the target corporation.

In applying these rules, acquisitions of assets pursuant to sales by the target corporation or a target affiliate in the ordinary course of its trade or business and acquisitions in which the basis of assets is carried over will not cause the consistency requirement to apply. The sale by a target corporation will be considered as a sale in the ordinary course of business for this purpose even though it is not customary in the course of the selling corporation's business provided it is a transaction that is a normal incident to the conduct of a trade or business, such as a sale of used machinery that was employed in the seller's trade or business.

Where there are, within a consistency period, only qualified stock purchases of the target corporation and one or more target affiliates by the purchasing corporation, an election with respect to the first purchase will apply to the later purchases. A failure to make the election for the first purchase will preclude any election for later purchases.

To prevent avoidance of the consistency requirements, the Act authorizes the Secretary to treat stock acquisitions which are pursuant to a plan and which satisfy the 80-percent requirement to be treated as qualified stock purchases even though they are not otherwise so defined. For example, an acquiring corporation may acquire 79 percent of the stock of a target corporation and, within a year, purchase assets from such corporation or a target affiliate planning to purchase the remaining target corporation stock more than one year after the original stock purchase. The Secretary may under these circumstances treat the purchase of the target corporation's stock as a deemed sale of its assets by the target corporation. The Act also authorizes such regulations as may be necessary to ensure that the requirements of consistency of treatment of stock and asset purchases with respect to a target corporation and its target affiliates are not circumvented through the use of other provisions of the law or regulations, including the consolidated return regulations. . . . [See §338(i) — ED.]

The application of the consistency requirements is illustrated in the following examples. . . .

> *Example 1.* The acquiring corporation makes a qualified stock purchase of T's stock and within a one-year period purchases assets from T or a target affiliate of T. The acquiring corporation is deemed to have made an election with respect to T as of the acquisition date applicable to T.
>
> *Example 2.* The acquiring corporation makes a qualified stock purchase of T's stock and makes the election within 75 days of the acquisition date. The acquiring corporation is treated as having acquired by purchase the stock of any other corporation owned by T actually or constructively which is attributed to the acquiring corporation under section 318(a) (other than sec. 318(a)(4)). To the extent that such treatment results in qualified stock purchases by the acquiring corporation of other corporations actually or constructively owned by T, the election with respect to T applies to all such corporations. Each such corporation will be treated as having sold (and as having purchased as a "new" corporation) its assets on the acquisition date with respect to T. Gain or loss will not be recognized to the extent gain or loss is not recognized under section 337. The deemed sale price of the assets will be determined by reference to the grossed-up amount allocated to the stock of each selling corporation as a result of the qualified stock purchase and election with respect to T.
>
> *Example 3.* P, an acquiring corporation, makes a qualified stock purchase of all the stock of corporation T on February 1, 1983. No election is made. On December 1, 1983, P makes a qualified stock purchase of all the stock of corporation U, a target affiliate of corporation T. No election may be made with respect to corporation U. . . .

NOTES

1. The 1986 Act's main impact on §338 comes from its repeal of the "old" §337. Under that provision, a corporation about to completely liquidate could sell its assets and avoid corporate tax on the appreciation (with a few exceptions, such as for recapture under §§1245 and 1250). Now that a corporate sale of assets, like a distribution in kind, produces taxable gain, §338 has been amended to conform. Many people believe that with the repeal of *General Utilities,* the consistency requirements of §338 should also be repealed. What do you think? Given that the target will generally recognize gain now

that the *General Utilities* doctrine has been repealed, are there any situations left in which it would make sense to make a §338 election?

2. Section 338(h)(10) provides an alternative election to the conventional §338 election. If a selling consolidated group makes an (h)(10) election, the selling corporation recognizes no gain or loss on the sale of the target's stock, but the target must recognize gain or loss as if it had sold its assets. The following excerpt from the 1986 Conference Report explains the important changes that the 1986 Act made to §338(h)(10):

> (ELECTION TO TREAT SALES OR DISTRIBUTIONS OF CERTAIN SUBSIDIARY STOCK AS ASSET TRANSFERS)
>
> The conference agreement generally conforms the treatment of liquidating sales and distributions of subsidiary stock to the present law treatment of nonliquidating sales or distributions of such stock; thus, such liquidating sales or distributions are generally taxable at the corporate level. The conferees believe it is appropriate to conform the treatment of liquidating and nonliquidating sales or distributions and to require recognition when appreciated property, including stock of a subsidiary, is transferred to a corporate or an individual recipient outside the economic unit of the selling or distributing affiliated group.
>
> Section 338(h)(10) of the present law, in certain circumstances, permits a corporate purchaser and a seller of an 80-percent-controlled subsidiary to elect to treat the sale of the subsidiary stock as if it had been a sale of the underlying assets. Among the requirements for the filing of an election under section 338(h)(10) are that the selling corporation and its target subsidiary are members of an affiliated group filing a consolidated return for the taxable year that includes the acquisition date. If an election is made, the underlying assets of the company that was sold receive a stepped-up, fair market value basis; the selling consolidated group recognizes the gain or loss attributable to the assets; and there is no separate tax on the seller's gain attributable to the stock. This provision offers taxpayers relief from a potential multiple taxation at the corporate level of the same economic gain, which may result when a transfer of appreciated corporate stock is taxed without providing a corresponding step-up in basis of the assets of the corporation. The conference agreement, following the House bill, retains this provision.
>
> In addition, the conference agreement permits the expansion of the section 338(h)(10) concept, to the extent provided in regulations, to situations in which the selling corporation owns 80 percent of the value and voting power of the subsidiary, but does not file a consolidated return. Moreover, the conference agreement provides that, under regulations, principles similar to those of section 338(h)(10) may be applied to taxable sales or distributions of controlled corporation stock. . . .

The conferees do not intend this election to affect the manner in which a corporation's distribution to its shareholders will be characterized for purposes of determining the shareholder level income tax consequences.

H.R. Conf. Rep. No. 841, 99th Cong., 2d Sess., pt. 2, at 203 (1986).

3. Compare §338(h)(10) with §336(e). Section 338(h)(10) allows a parent corporation owning 80 percent or more of a subsidiary's shares to avoid recognition of gain or loss upon the *sale* of its subsidiary. Section 336(e) expands the nonrecognition treatment of the parent to include not only sales but also exchanges and distributions of the stock of the subsidiary. Like §338(h)(10), the price of the §336(e) election is the immediate recognition of gain as if the subsidiary's assets had been sold, exchanged, or distributed.

4. Since the repeal of the *General Utilities* doctrine and "old" §337, the parties to an acquisition more often than not want to avoid making a §338 election, either intentionally or inadvertantly. To be sure no such election is deemed made, a protective carryover basis election may be filed pursuant to Reg. §1.338-4T(f)(6)(i)(A). See Rev. Proc. 89-40, 1989-27 I.R.B. 15. But one commentator has proposed that a corporate level tax should always be imposed when stock sales effect a transfer of "control" of the target corporation. In effect this would make §338 a mandatory provision rather than an elective one. See Lewis, A Proposal for a Corporate Level Tax on Major Stock Sales, Tax Notes, December 7, 1987, p. 1041. But cf. Wolfman, Whither "C"?, page 869 infra.

B. DEDUCTIONS

1. *Distributions of Property (Including Cash)*

a. Dividend vs. Interest — §163

FIN HAY REALTY CO. v. UNITED STATES
398 F.2d 694 (3d Cir. 1968)

Before Hastie, Chief Judge, Freedman and Van Dusen, Circuit Judges.

FREEDMAN, Circuit Judge. We are presented in this case with the recurrent problem whether funds paid to a close corporation by its shareholders were additional contributions to capital or loans on which the corporation's payment of interest was deductible under §163 of the Internal Revenue Code of 1954.

The problem necessarily calls for an evaluation of the facts, which we therefore detail.

Fin Hay Realty Co., the taxpayer, was organized on February 14, 1934, by Frank L. Finlaw and J. Louis Hay. Each of them contributed $10,000 for which he received one-half of the corporation's stock and at the same time each advanced an additional $15,000 for which the corporation issued to him its unsecured promissory note payable on demand and bearing interest at the rate of six percent per annum. The corporation immediately purchased an apartment house in Newark, New Jersey, for $39,000 in cash. About a month later the two shareholders each advanced an additional $35,000 to the corporation in return for six percent demand promissory notes and the next day the corporation purchased two apartment buildings in East Orange, New Jersey, for which it paid $75,000 in cash and gave the seller a six percent, five year purchase money mortgage for the balance of $100,000.

Three years later, in October, 1937, the corporation created a new mortgage on all three properties and from the proceeds paid off the old mortgage on the East Orange property, which had been partially amortized. The new mortgage was for a five year term in the amount of $82,000 with interest at four and one-half percent. In the following three years each of the shareholders advanced an additional $3,000 to the corporation, bringing the total advanced by each shareholder to $53,000, in addition to their acknowledged stock subscriptions of $10,000 each.

Finlaw died in 1941 and his stock and notes passed to his two daughters in equal shares. A year later the mortgage, which was about to fall due, was extended for a further period of five years interest at four percent. From the record it appears that it was subsequently extended until 1951. In 1949 Hay died and in 1951 his executor requested the retirement of his stock and the payment of his notes. The corporation thereupon refinanced its real estate for $125,000 and sold one of the buildings. With the net proceeds it paid Hay's estate $24,000 in redemption of his stock and $53,000 in retirement of his notes.[4] Finlaw's daughters then became and still remain the sole shareholders of the corporation.

Thereafter the corporation continued to pay and deduct interest on Finlaw's notes, now held by his two daughters. In 1962 the Internal Revenue Service for the first time declared the payments on the notes

---

4. The record is fragmentary and provides no clear basis from which to reconstruct the events of 1951. It may perhaps be inferred from it that Hay's estate received the total of $77,000 solely for the redemption of his stock and that the notes of $53,000 were retired either from the proceeds of the sale of real estate or in some other manner during the same year. In such event the total paid in redemption of Hay's stock and the retirement of his notes would be $130,000 rather than $77,000.

not allowable as interest deductions and disallowed them for the tax years 1959 and 1960. The corporation thereupon repaid a total of $6,000 on account of the outstanding notes and in the following year after refinancing the mortgage on its real estate repaid the balance of $47,000. A short time later the Internal Revenue Service disallowed the interest deductions for the years 1961 and 1962. When the corporation failed to obtain refunds it brought this refund action in the district court. After a nonjury trial the court denied the claims and entered judgment for the United States. 261 F. Supp. 823 (D.N.J. 1967). From this judgment the corporation appeals.

This case arose in a factual setting where it is the corporation which is the party concerned that its obligations be deemed to represent a debt and not a stock interest. In the long run in cases of this kind it is also important to the shareholder that his advance be deemed a loan rather than a capital contribution, for in such a case his receipt of repayment may be treated as the retirement of a loan rather than a taxable dividend.[6] There are other instances in which it is in the shareholder's interest that his advance to the corporation be considered a debt rather than an increase in his equity. A loss resulting from the worthlessness of stock is a capital loss under §165(g), whereas a bad debt may be treated as an ordinary loss if it qualifies as a business bad debt under §166. Similarly, it is only if a taxpayer receives debt obligations of a controlled corporation[7] that he can avoid the provision for nonrecognition of gains or losses on transfers of property to such a corporation under §351.[8] These advantages in having the funds entrusted to a corporation treated as corporate obligations instead of contributions to capital have required the courts to look beyond the literal terms in which the parties have cast the transaction in order to determine its substantive nature.

In attempting to deal with this problem courts and commentators have isolated a number of criteria by which to judge the true nature of an investment which is in form a debt: (1) the intent of the parties; (2) the identity between creditors and shareholders; (3) the extent of participation in management by the holder of the instrument; (4) the ability of the corporation to obtain funds from outside sources; (5) the "thinness" of the capital structure in relation to debt; (6) the risk involved; (7) the formal indicia of the arrangement; (8) the relative

6. The partial retirement of an equity interest may be considered as essentially equivalent to a dividend under §302, while the repayment of even a debt whose principal has appreciated is taxed only as a capital gain under §1232.

7. While not all debt obligations qualify for the desired tax treatment, equity interests can never qualify.

8. A taxpayer might wish to avoid §351 when he transfers depreciated property to the corporation and seeks to recognize the loss immediately and also when the transferred property is to be resold by the corporation but will not qualify for capital gains treatment in the hands of the corporation.

position of the obligees as to other creditors regarding the payment of interest and principal; (9) the voting power of the holder of the instrument; (10) the provision of a fixed rate of interest; (11) a contingency on the obligation to repay; (12) the source of the interest payments; (13) the presence or absence of a fixed maturity date; (14) a provision for redemption by the corporation; (15) a provision for redemption at the option of the holder; and (16) the timing of the advance with reference to the organization of the corporation.

While the Internal Revenue Code of 1954 was under consideration, and after its adoption, Congress sought to identify the criteria which would determine whether an investment represents a debt or equity, but these and similar efforts have not found acceptance. It still remains true that neither any single criterion nor any series of criteria can provide a conclusive answer in the kaleidoscopic circumstances which individual cases present. See John Kelley Co. v. Commissioner of Internal Revenue, 326 U.S. 521, 530 . . . (1946).

The various factors which have been identified in the cases are only aids in answering the ultimate question whether the investment, analyzed in terms of its economic reality, constitutes risk capital entirely subject to the fortunes of the corporate venture or represents a strict debtor-creditor relationship. Since there is often an element of risk in a loan, just as there is an element of risk in an equity interest, the conflicting elements do not end at a clear line in all cases.

In a corporation which has numerous shareholders with varying interests, the arm's-length relationship between the corporation and a shareholder who supplies funds to it inevitably results in a transaction whose form mirrors its substance. Where the corporation is closely held, however, and the same persons occupy both sides of the bargaining table, form does not necessarily correspond to the intrinsic economic nature of the transaction, for the parties may mold it at their will with no countervailing pull. This is particularly so where a shareholder can have the funds he advances to a corporation treated as corporate obligations instead of contributions to capital without affecting his proportionate equity interest. Labels, which are perhaps the best expression of the subjective intention of parties to a transaction, thus lose their meaningfulness.

To seek economic reality in objective terms of course disregards the personal interest which a shareholder may have in the welfare of the corporation in which he is a dominant force. But an objective standard is one imposed by the very fact of his dominant position and is much fairer than one which would presumptively construe all such transactions against the shareholder's interest. Under an objective test of economic reality it is useful to compare the form which a similar transaction would have taken had it been between the corporation and an outside lender, and if the shareholder's advance is far more speculative than what an outsider would make, it is obviously a loan in name only.

In the present case all the formal indicia of an obligation were meticulously made to appear. The corporation, however, was the complete creature of the two shareholders who had the power to create whatever appearance would be of tax benefit to them despite the economic reality of the transaction. Each shareholder owned an equal proportion of stock and was making an equal additional contribution, so that whether Finlaw and Hay designated any part of their additional contributions as debt or as stock would not dilute their proportionate equity interests. There was no restriction because of the possible excessive debt structure, for the corporation had been created to acquire real estate and had no outside creditors except mortgagees who, of course, would have no concern for general creditors because they had priority in the security of the real estate. The position of the mortgagees also rendered of no significance the possible subordination of the notes to other debts of the corporation, a matter which in some cases this Court has deemed significant.

The shareholders here, moreover, lacked one of the principal advantages of creditors. Although the corporation issued demand notes for the advances, nevertheless, as the court below found, it could not have repaid them for a number of years. The economic reality was that the corporation used the proceeds of the notes to purchase its original assets, and the advances represented a long-term commitment dependent on the future value of the real estate and the ability of the corporation to sell or refinance it. Only because such an entwining of interest existed between the two shareholders and the corporation, so different from the arm's-length relationship between a corporation and an outside creditor, were they willing to invest in the notes and allow them to go unpaid for so many years while the corporation continued to enjoy the advantages of uninterrupted ownership of its real estate.

It is true that real estate values rose steadily with a consequent improvement in the mortgage market, so that looking back the investment now appears to have been a good one. As events unfolded, the corporation reached a point at which it could have repaid the notes through refinancing, but this does not obliterate the uncontradicted testimony that in 1934 it was impossible to obtain any outside mortgage financing for real estate of this kind except through the device of a purchase money mortgage taken back by the seller.

It is argued that the rate of interest at six percent per annum was far more than the shareholders could have obtained from other investments. This argument, however, is self-defeating, for it implies that the shareholders would damage their own corporation by an overcharge for interest. There was, moreover, enough objective evidence to neutralize this contention. The outside mortgage obtained at the time the corporation purchased the East Orange property bore interest at the rate of six percent even though the mortgagee was protected by an equity in excess of forty percent of the value of the property.[14] In any event, to compare the six percent interest rate of the notes with other 1934 rates ignores the most salient feature of the notes — their risk. It is difficult to escape the inference that a prudent outside businessman would not have risked his capital in six percent unsecured demand notes in Fin Hay Realty Co. in 1934. The evidence therefore amply justifies the conclusion of the district court that the form which the parties gave to their transaction did not match its economic reality.

It is argued that even if the advances may be deemed to have been contributions to capital when they were originally made in 1934, a decisive change occurred when the original shareholder, Finlaw, died and his heirs continued to hold the notes without demanding payment. This, it is said, could be construed as a decision to reinvest, and if by 1941 the notes were sufficiently secure to be considered bona fide debt, they should now be so treated for tax purposes. Such a conclusion, however, does not inevitably follow. Indeed, the weight of the circumstances leads to the opposite conclusion.

First, there is nothing in the record to indicate that the corporation could have readily raised the cash with which to pay off Finlaw's notes on his death in 1941. When Hay, the other shareholder, died in 1949 and his executor two years later requested the retirement of his interest, the corporation in order to carry this out sold one of its properties and refinanced the others. Again, when in 1963 the corporation paid off the notes held by Finlaw's daughters after the Internal Revenue Service had disallowed the interest deductions for 1961 and 1962 it again refinanced its real estate. There is nothing in the record which would sustain a finding that the corporation could have readily undertaken a similar financing in 1941, when Finlaw died, even if we assume that the corporation was able to undertake the appropriate refinancing ten years later to liquidate Hay's interest. Moreover, there was no objective evidence to indicate that in 1941 Finlaw's daughters viewed the notes as changed in character or in security, or indeed that they viewed the stock and notes as separate and distinct investments. To indulge in a theoretical conversion of equity contributions into a debt obligation in 1941 when Finlaw died would be to ignore what such a conversion might have entailed. For Finlaw's estate might then have been chargeable with the receipt of dividends at the time the equity was redeemed and

14. The corporation purchased the property for $175,000 and the sellers took back a purchase money mortgage of $100,000.

converted into a debt. To recognize retrospectively such a change in the character of the obligation would be to assume a conclusion with consequences unfavorable to the parties, which they themselves never acknowledged.

The burden was on the taxpayer to prove that the determination by the Internal Revenue Service that the advances represented capital contributions was incorrect. The district court was justified in holding that the taxpayer had not met this burden.

This judgment of the district court will be affirmed.

VAN DUSEN, Circuit Judge (dissenting). I respectfully dissent on the ground that the "entire evidence," in light of appellate court decision discussing the often-presented problem of corporate debt versus equity, does not permit the conclusion reached by the District Court.

When the parties holding debt of the taxpayer corporation have a formal debt obligation and it is clear that all parties intended the investment to take the form of debt, a series of considerations such as those mentioned by the District Court should be used to determine whether the form and intent should be disregarded for federal tax purposes. Tomlinson v. 1661 Corporation, 337 F.2d 291 (5th Cir. 1967); J.S. Biritz Construction Co. v. C.I.R., 387 F.2d 451, 455-56 (8th Cir. 1967). As I read the District Court's opinion, the focus was entirely on inferring "the intent of the taxpayer's only two stock-holders" at the time the debt was created. To that end, the District Court drew certain inferences which are largely immaterial to the proper decision, and which are clearly erroneous in light of the stipulated facts and uncontroverted evidence.

Whether or not the corporate taxpayer is entitled to an interest deduction turns in this case on the "real nature of the transaction in question" or on whether "the degree of risk may be said to be reasonably equivalent to that which equity capital would bear had an investor, under similar circumstances, made the advances. . . ." Diamond Bros. Company v. C.I.R., 322 F.2d 725, 732 (3rd Cir. 1963); Tomlinson v. 1661 Corporation, supra, at 295. When this test is used, the entire history of the corporate taxpayer becomes relevant and a focus solely on the year of incorporation or investment of the debt is not sufficient.

Turning within this framework to the facts, the record does not justify the conclusion that the form of the debt should be disregarded for purposes of federal taxation. The debt was evidenced by written notes, carried 6% interest which was paid every year, and was not subordinated in any way to similar debt of general creditors. It was carried on the corporate books and tax returns as debt, being payable on demand, it was always listed as a debt maturing in less than one year,[10] and on Mr. Finlaw's estate tax return was listed as promissory notes payable on demand.[11] The parties clearly intended the advances as debt and unfailingly treated them as such. The only testimony on the usual capitalization of real estate companies in the Newark area was that:

> The usual capitalization is a thousand dollar investment in capital and then the rest of the monies are loaned either . . . by individuals or stockholders of the corporation to the corporation, which in turn the individuals lending the money expect a return for their loans. . . .
>
> [Of the real estate corporations that] I have dealt with, at least ninety-five percent and more have had a thousand capitalization and, of course, loans from the various lenders would depend upon the size of the transaction, monies that were required.

On this record, Conclusions of Law 3-8 as worded are not justified. The District Court placed heavy reliance on the fact that the stockholders' debt was in the same proportion as their equity holdings. This fact without more is not controlling since there is no doubt that investors can have a dual status. The inferences that "more" was involved in this case are not justified by this record. The fact that the loans were used to begin the corporate life and buy the income-producing assets must be placed in proper perspective. Without any basis in the record, the District Court assumed that the loans were advanced to prevent a sudden corporate deficit that was created by the Wainwright Street property investment's unexpectedly requiring more funds than the corporation had. Real estate cases, however, and uncontroverted testimony in this case show that corporations owning and operating buildings frequently and traditionally borrow the substantial part of money needed to secure their principal assets and that this was contemplated by a corporate resolution passed in the month of organization at the original directors' meeting. Cases denying the validity of debt because it is contemporaneously ad-

---

10. Apparently the District Court regarded demand notes as having no fixed maturity, see Conclusion of Law 4. This seems incorrect since demand paper means that the debt is "mature" at the holder's option. The better characterization would seem to be that demand notes held by someone with a voice in management are a type of long-term investment. See, e.g., Taft v. C.I.R., 314 F.2d 620 (9th Cir. 1963).

11. This consistent treatment does not, of course, estop either the Commissioner or the taxpayer any more than the decision in this case controls the tax status of repaid principal on these loans in the hands of the remaining Fin Hay shareholders. The Government may well have sought to challenge these corporate interest deductions before challenging the individuals' returns as a matter of tactics, but this, and the question of the tax consequences of the liquidation of the remaining loans in 1962-1963, should not influence the decision in the present case, see Budd Company v. United States, 252 F.2d 456, 458 (3rd Cir. 1957).

vanced with the start of corporate life generally involve other industries or a partnership becoming a corporation.

The loans were denied debt status because there was no intent to seek repayment within a "reasonable time," because the corporation had no retirement provision (or fund) for the principal and because the debt had no maturity date (Conclusions 3 and 4). To the contrary, demand notes have a maturity date at the discretion of the holder (or of his transferee when the notes are freely negotiable, as were the Fin Hay notes). And failure to transfer the notes or demand payment is irrelevant when, as here, the evidence shows that the 6% rate made the debt a good investment. In addition, when a corporation holds appreciating real estate and contemplates recourse to refinancing, the lack of a sinking fund assumes little, if any, significance. There was no evidence and no discussion of what constitutes a "reasonable time" for refraining from making a demand on such a promissory note.

The loans were also found to be equity because redemption was expected only out of future earnings or surplus and because they were unsecured and subordinate to prior secured loans (Conclusions 6 and 8). To the contrary, the evidence shows that the parties contemplated redemption out of "refinancing" as well if a demand were made when surplus was deficient; and this in fact was what happened in 1951 and 1962-1963. Corporate debt does not become equity because it is contemplated that principal will be retired by refinancing. In addition, a review of the "subordination" cases shows that there was no "subordination" in this case as that term is used in other cases where the challenged debt was subordinated to all other debt of similar type or otherwise subordinated by agreement.

The District Court also placed emphasis on the fact that at the end of 1935 the shareholders' salaries were accrued but unpaid in the amount of $2400 and that in 1938 through 1940 the shareholders advanced an additional $6000 as loans. The corporate tax returns and books, however, show that the salaries could have been paid at the end of 1935 from $4,340.21 in cash on deposit, and that during the period of the additional loans of $6000 the shareholders received $6800 in dividends from the corporation. These additional facts, unexplained by the District Court, negate the implication that Fin Hay Realty Company was in serious financial trouble at the outset of its existence, at least to any such degree that all the challenged loans were made "at a risk" similar to that of venture capital. It is noted, in addition, that by 1938, when the original purchase money mortgage was refinanced, $18,000 of principal had been paid.

Although appellate decisions on the debt-equity problem constantly reiterate the maxim that each instance of definition turns on the particular facts of each case, a reading of many of these cases,

including all those cited above, indicates two rather distinct conclusions concerning the assessment of the severity of the "risk" attached
to alleged debt transactions. First, when the problem of definition
arises under 26 U.S.C. §§165, 166 (worthless stock, bad debt), the
risk of failure has already been realized and the party seeking to
minimize the degree of such risk must show more "factors" than
otherwise clearly argue for a debt classification. Secondly, regardless
of the end purpose for defining indebtedness, fewer factors need be
present (such as subordination, no interest, etc.) to allow a conclusion
of "equity" when, as a matter of common knowledge, the economic
enterprise has a higher chance of commercial failure. Consequently,
few cases (and particularly few where taxpayers holding formal debt
lose) deny debt status or even raise the question where the enterprise
risk, as in this case, involves the mere holding and operation of real
estate. As the risks increase, involving in addition construction of the
real estate, or non-real estate operations subject to more immediate
risk-creating problems of marketing, labor, advertisement, supplies,
etc., the frequency of cases challenging debt and of decisions finding
equity increase. The uncontradicted testimony (without finding of
lack of credibility) of the universal practice in the Newark area in
conformity to the course followed by taxpayer . . . is entitled to consideration. Also, the subsequent successful history of this corporate
taxpayer cannot be disregarded and militates strongly against denying an interest deduction on this record. The Fin Hay Realty Co.
did not go bankrupt, was not unable to refinance or extend its purchase money mortgage due in 1939, and has never failed to meet a
demanded purchase of the notes.

On this record, these loans were bona fide loans, "at risk" in this
enterprise in no different way than any debt investment is "at risk"
for a general creditor of a real estate holding and operating corporation. The District Court pointedly took judicial notice, both of the
bargain real estate purchases possible in 1934 and of the steadily
rising real estate values in Essex County, New Jersey. Subsequent
refinancings by the taxpayer, as well as the entire course of its history,
demonstrate that this investment in this particular venture was not
a "risk capital" investment of the type that should compel disregarding the clear intent of the parties and form of the transaction. Two
recent "real estate" decisions (involving, moreover, construction as
well as holding of real estate) suggest the proper result for the present
case. As stated in Tomlinson v. 1661 Corporation, supra, at 300:

> We cannot by manipulation of tax law, preclude the parties
> from exercising sound business judgment in obtaining needed in-
> vestment funds at the most favorable rate possible, whether it be
> a commercial loan, or, more likely and as is the case here, a loan
> from private interested sources with sufficient faith in the success

of the venture and their ultimate repayment to delete or minimize the "risk factor" in their rate of return.

Similarly, in J.S. Biritz Construction Co. v. C.L.R., supra, at 459, the court said:

> There is actually no evidence that this was not a loan, was not intended to be a loan, or that Biritz actually intended to make a capital investment rather than a loan.
> We think the Tax Court has painted with too broad a brush in limiting the permissible activities of an entrepreneur in personally financing his business. Financing embraces both equity and debt transactions and we do not think the courts should enunciate a rule of law that a sole stockholder may not loan money or transfer assets to a corporation in a loan transaction. If this is to be the law, Congress should so declare it. We feel the controlling principle should be that any transaction which is intrinsically clear upon its face should be accorded its legal due unless the transaction is a mere sham or subterfuge set up solely or principally for tax-avoidance purposes.

I would reverse and enter judgment for the corporate taxpayer.

NOTES

1. *Fin Hay Realty*'s objective test may sometimes be used by the taxpayer for his own benefit. See Segel v. Commissioner, 89 T.C. 816 (1987), in which the Tax Court followed *Fin Hay Realty* in holding that because the terms of cash advances were more speculative than an outside creditor would have accepted, the apparent debt constituted equity, a result advantageous to the taxpayer in the context of an S corporation. See also Hardman v. United States, 827 F.2d 1409 (9th Cir. 1987); Scriptomatic, Inc. v. United States, 555 F.2d 364, 368 (3d Cir. 1977).

2. The debt-equity problem raised in *Fin Hay Realty* is hoary and thorny. The Supreme Court faced the issue in companion cases, John Kelley Co. v. Commissioner and Talbot Mills v. Commissioner, 326 U.S. 521 (1946). Whether the corporations in those cases could deduct "interest" payments depended upon the classification of the "hybrid" securities on which the payments had been made. The instruments in *John Kelley Co.* were 20-year, 8-percent, noncumulative income debenture bonds, some of which were issued to the shareholders (all members of a family group) in exchange for stock and others of which had been sold to these shareholders for cash. Payment of the interest was conditioned on sufficient net income to meet the obligation. Although the debentures were subordinated to all other creditors, they contained acceleration provisions in the event of de-

faults. The terms of the indenture excluded the holders from management. The Tax Court had held that the payments were interest on indebtedness, deductible under §163; the Court of Appeals for the Seventh Circuit reversed.

In the companion case (*Talbot Mills*) 25-year registered notes were issued to the shareholders — once again a family group — in exchange for four-fifths of their stock. The annual interest was not to exceed 10 percent nor to be less than 2 percent; it was computed by a formula that took into account the annual earnings of the corporation. Although the interest could be deferred until maturity when "necessary by reason of the condition of the corporation," it was cumulative, and dividends could not be paid until interest arrearages were met. The corporation's right to mortgage its real property was limited, and the board of directors was given power to subordinate the notes. Emphasizing the fluctuating payments and the fact that all the notes were issued in exchange for stock, the Tax Court had distinguished its decision in *Kelley*, holding the payments to be dividends; the First Circuit affirmed.

After hearing both cases together, the Supreme Court held that the debt vs. equity issue was, under the *Dobson* (320 U.S. 489 (1943)) doctrine, one for the Tax Court to resolve. Stating that no one characteristic could be decisive, the Supreme Court affirmed the Tax Court's very nearly inconsistent holdings.

In light of the Supreme Court's deference, the factors deemed significant by the Tax Court in *Kelley* and *Talbot Mills* became the seeds for the growth of "tests" to distinguish debt from equity. The Tax Court's seeming reliance on the formal structure of ordinary debt instruments soon led most taxpayers to abandon hybrid securities and to adopt formal, fixed interest, fixed maturity, unconditional debt instruments; it is around these formal debt instruments that most of today's battles are fought.

3. One of the important early tests was the so-called debt to equity ratio. The Supreme Court had cautioned against an "obviously excessive debt structure" (326 U.S. at 526), but since the 4:1 ratio of debt to equity in *Talbot Mills* had not been labelled "obviously excessive," many tax planners concluded that 4:1 was a "safe" ratio. The courts held that interest was deductible in a number of cases where the ratio was less than 4:1; the Commissioner's acquiescences seemed to confirm the margin of safety. See, e.g., Gazette Telegraph Co., 19 T.C. 692 (1953) (acq.), *aff'd on other grounds*, 209 F.2d 926 (10th Cir. 1954); Ruspyn Corp., 18 T.C. 769 (1952) (acq.).

Concurrently, capital structures with high debt to equity ratios were struck down. See, e.g., Alfred R. Bachrack, 18 T.C. 479 (1952), *aff'd per curiam*, 205 F.2d 151 (2d Cir. 1953); Isidor Dobkin, 15 T.C. 31 (1950), *aff'd per curiam*, 192 F.2d 392 (2d Cir. 1951). For a com-

pilation of the cases in tabular form with their ratios computed, see
Caplin, The Caloric Count of a Thin Corporation, 17 N.Y.U. Inst.
Fed. Taxn. 771 (1959).

The great reliance placed on the debt to equity ratio received a
jarring blow in Gooding Amusement Co., 23 T.C. 408 (1954), *aff'd*,
236 F.2d 159 (6th Cir. 1956), where formal debt instruments were
classified as equity despite a ratio of 1:1. The court held the "real
intention" of the parties was never to enforce the notes or otherwise
to assert the rights of bona fide creditors.

Although in *Gooding* itself equity classification was the result, that
case ironically paved the way for debt classification in cases where a
high debt to equity ratio existed. Since the ratio was no longer tal-
ismanic, taxpayers with increasing frequency urged the courts to
ignore it just as the Commissioner had done in *Gooding*. Where sufficient justification was found, the courts passed over a high debt to
equity ratio and ruled in favor of the taxpayers. See Baker Commodities, Inc., 48 T.C. 374 (1967) (700:1 ratio not fatal; cash flow
of business adequate to cover debt payments), *aff'd on other grounds*,
415 F.2d 519 (9th Cir. 1969); Arthur M. Rosenthal, 24 T.C.M. (CCH)
1373 (1965) (14:1 ratio not significant in view of substantial cash
invested and fact that notes were issued for property which corporation could have rented instead of buying — a "non-essential" asset);
Charles E. Curry, 43 T.C. 667 (1965) (30:1 ratio not unreasonable
in light of substantial disproportion between holdings of stock and
notes, substantial cash contribution, and commercially reasonable indenture terms). Several courts have abandoned the ratio test entirely.
See Gloucester Ice & Cold Storage Co. v. Commissioner, 298 F.2d
183, 185 (1st Cir. 1962); Rowan v. United States, 219 F.2d 51, 55
(5th Cir. 1955).

4. Some of the justifications for ignoring the debt to equity ratio
have assumed the status of independent tests.

(a) Whether "substantial capital" had been contributed has become an important question. See, e.g., Sheldon Tauber, 24 T.C. 179
(1955). In Murphy Logging Co. v. United States, 378 F.2d 222 (9th
Cir. 1967), a corporation with a debt to equity ratio of 160:1 was
permitted to deduct interest payments on loans where the shareholders "contributed" their ability to procure contracts and "their
own integrity and reputation for getting things done."

(b) Whether debt and equity are held pro rata by the shareholders has also become an important question. Pro rata holdings
have been a formidable barrier when not insuperable to taxpayer
successes. See Gilbert v. Commissioner, 248 F.2d 399 (2d Cir. 1957).
Conversely, disproportionate holdings may be helpful to the taxpayer
(see Bauer v. Commissioner, 748 F.2d 1365 (9th Cir. 1984)), although
they may not be a guarantee of success. See P.M. Finance Corp. v.

Commissioner, 302 F.2d 786 (3d Cir. 1962). Might "disproportion" lead to no more than the conclusion that the corporation "had issued disproportionate amounts of common and preferred stock"? See The Colony, Inc., 26 T.C. 30, 43 (1956), *aff'd on other grounds*, 244 F.2d 75 (6th Cir. 1957), *rev'd on other grounds*, 357 U.S. 28 (1958). As to alleged indebtedness owing to a corporation's sole shareholder, see, e.g., Alma deB. Spreckles, 8 T.C.M. (CCH) 1113 (1949), and Maloney v. Spencer, 172 F.2d 638 (9th Cir. 1949), instances in which the debt classification was sustained. Many "sole shareholders" are easier targets for the opposite result.

(c) Some courts purport to resolve the debt vs. equity question according to the "intent of the parties" to the transaction. See, e.g., Marathon Oil Co. v. Commissioner, 838 F.2d 1114 (10th Cir. 1987). What is meant by the "intent of the parties" when the parties are in fact dealing with themselves? In the absence of an arm's length transaction, isn't it impossible to ascertain the "intent of the parties"?

(d) Some cases emphasize the question whether the funds were placed at the "risk of the business." See Schine Chain Theaters, 22 T.C.M. (CCH) 488 (1963), *aff'd,* 331 F.2d 849 (2d Cir. 1964). Is that an adequate test?

5. How would you articulate a test to distinguish debt from equity? Two opinions are useful for their discussion of the difficulties involved and their canvass of the relevant criteria. See Texas Farm Bureau v. United States, 725 F.2d 307, *as modified on denial of reh'g,* 732 F.2d 437 (5th Cir. 1984), *cert. denied,* 469 U.S. 1106 (1985); Stinnett's Pontiac Serv., Inc. v. Commissioner, 730 F.2d 1634 (11th Cir. 1984).

6. May loans granted by a nonshareholder be classified as equity, preferred stock, for example? See Foresun, Inc. v. Commissioner, 348 F.2d 1006 (6th Cir. 1965) (lender related to shareholders); Motel Co. v. Commissioner, 340 F.2d 445 (2d Cir. 1965) (lender related to shareholders); Merlo Builders, 23 T.C.M. (CCH) 185 (1964) (lender unrelated to shareholders).

7. In Samuel G. Miller, 57 T.C.M. 46 (CCH) (1989), page 309 infra, the taxpayer formed a corporation to which he contributed $150,000 in exchange for 150 shares of common stock and a $135,000 promissory note. The taxpayer subsequently made additional advances of $395,740 to the corporation which were recorded on the books of the corporation as loans. After the business failed, the taxpayer sought to recharacterize the debt as equity so that he would be entitled to an ordinary loss under §1244 (see Chapter 2, pages 301-317 infra). The court rejected this attempt, stating that "taxpayers have little freedom to ignore the form of their own transactions and are ordinarily bound by the tax consequences that flow from the form of transactions they use."

Should the initial characterization of a debt instrument as equity continue after the instrument is sold by the shareholder-creditor to a nonshareholder? See Texoma Supply Co., 17 T.C.M. (CCH) 147 (1958). Might "debt" become "equity" when the debt instrument is sold by the creditor to a shareholder whose investment in stock is small vis-à-vis his investment in debt? *Compare* Edwards v. Commissioner, 415 F.2d 578 (10th Cir. 1969), *with* Jewell Ridge Coal Corp., 21 T.C.M. (CCH) 1048 (1962), *aff'd,* 318 F.2d 695 (4th Cir. 1963).

8. Three shareholders form a new corporation, contributing $1,500 to its capital. Then a bank lends $240,000 to the corporation but does so only because the individual shareholders guarantee the loan. May the corporation deduct the interest paid to the bank? See Murphy Logging Co. v. United States, 239 F. Supp. 794 (D. Ore. 1965), *rev'd,* 378 F.2d 222 (9th Cir. 1967). You should read both the District Court's and the Court of Appeals' opinions. *Compare* General Alloy Casting Co., 23 T.C.M. (CCH) 887 (1964), *aff'd per curiam,* 345 F.2d 794 (3d Cir. 1965), where the deductibility of interest on a shareholder-guaranteed bank loan went unchallenged notwithstanding the fact that the deductibility of alleged interest payments on a direct $200,000 "loan" from shareholders was denied, *with* Plantations Patterns, Inc. v. Commissioner, 462 F.2d 712 (5th Cir.), *cert. denied,* 409 U.S. 1076 (1972), in which the court treated a shareholder's guarantee as a substitute for a capital contribution, thus denying a corporate interest deduction. And *compare* Selfe v. United States, 778 F.2d 769 (11th Cir. 1985) *with* Daniel Leavitt Estate v. Commissioner, 875 F.2d 420 (4th Cir. 1989).

9. Ought the corporate income tax treat "interest" differently from "dividends"? The Code treats equity holders as the "owners" of the corporation. The relationship between a corporation and its debt holders, on the other hand, is treated as though it were the same as between an individual and his creditors. Is this a sensible view? Are debt and equity securities merely different claims against a stream of earnings? If they were to be treated identically, should dividends and interest both be deductible or nondeductible? See B. Bittker and J. Eustice, Federal Income Taxation of Corporations and Shareholders 4-2 to 4-5 (5th ed. 1987); Warren, The Corporate Interest Deduction: A Policy Evaluation, 83 Yale L.J. 1585 (1974).

Section 247 provides that a public utility may deduct the dividends it pays on certain of its preferred stock. Why?

10. The classification of an investment as "debt" or "equity" has direct tax significance to the investor, apart from the question whether the corporation has made a deductible interest payment or a nondeductible dividend payment. In the investor's case the classification of an investment as "equity" as opposed to "debt" has no impact on the taxability of the alleged "interest" payment he has

received. When the alleged "debt" is repaid, however, its classification as "equity" will have major impact. If the investment proves worthless the tax deduction will usually be of greater tax benefit if the debt stands up as such and is not reclassified as stock. Why might Finlaw's estate in *Fin Hay Realty* have been "chargeable with the receipt of dividends" if the equity had been treated as redeemed and converted into debt (page 65 supra)?

If the investor is a corporation, the classification of an investment as "equity" rather than "debt" should result in the allowance of a dividends received deduction under §243 as to the "interest" payments the investor receives. See, e.g., §164 (e)(5)(B), added to the Code in 1989.

Footnote 8 of the majority opinion in *Fin Hay Realty* (page 62 supra), and the sentence of text at footnotes 7 and 8 were written, of course, before enactment of the 1989 tax legislation which denies nonrecognition under §351 as to property transferred to a corporation in exchange for debt, whether or not it is evidenced by a security.

11. Section 279 disallows interest due on corporate debt issued in connection with particular types of corporate acquisitions. The Code creates the term *corporate acquisition indebtedness* for this purpose. Seemingly intended to discourage acquisitions of businesses by large corporations that are financed significantly through debt, the interest deduction is disallowed where the debt, although accepted generally as debt and not equity, has certain of the characteristics of equity. Because the section was designed in light of the financing methods of the 1960s, it has been easily avoided by the corporate acquisitions taking place in more recent years. See B. Bittker and J. Eustice, Federal Income Taxation of Corporations and Shareholders 4-49 to 4-50 (5th ed. 1987). For a general background and analysis of §279, see Canellos, The Overleveraged Acquisition, 39 Tax Law. 91 (1985).

In cases covered by §267(a)(2), interest deductions will be deferred because of the relationship and different accounting methods of the particular creditor and debtor, although the debt may be unassailably debt and not equity. In its 1989 tax legislation Congress added §163(j) to the Code, further curtailing the deduction for interest paid by corporations to certain related persons. Why do you think this provision was enacted, and why were its reach and limits tailored as they are? In the same Act, Congress also added §163 (e)(5), disallowing (or deferring) the interest deduction with respect to certain "high yield" original issue discount obligations. Why?

12. The debt vs. equity issue was given exhaustive consideration in Plumb, The Federal Income Tax Significance of Corporate Debt: A Critical Analysis and a Proposal, 26 Tax L. Rev. 369 (1971). The Service announced in Rev. Proc. 80-22, 1980-1 C.B. 654, and again

in Rev. Proc. 81-10, 1981-1 C.B. 647, that it would not ordinarily rule on the question whether a particular interest in a corporation constitutes stock or debt.

REVENUE RULING 83-98
1983-2 C.B. 40

For federal income tax purposes, should the adjustable rate convertible notes (ARCNs) described below be treated as debt, so that amounts paid periodically with respect thereto are deductible as interest under section 163 of the Internal Revenue Code, or should they be treated as equity?

FACTS

X corporation has outstanding one class of common stock that is traded on a national securities exchange. This stock has traded recently at about $20 per share; its current dividend rate is $.78 per share, or about 3.9 percent, annually.

X proposes to issue $10 million worth of ARCNs. An ARCN will be offered at a price of $1000 cash or 50 shares of X common stock (worth $1000). The terms of the ARCNs will be as follows. They will mature in 20 years, and on maturity the holder will be entitled to elect to receive either $600 cash or 50 shares of X common stock. Each ARCN will be convertible at any time into 50 shares of X common stock. X will have no right to compel redemption of ("call") an ARCN until two years after issuance, after which it will have the right to call any ARCN at a price of $600 cash. Upon call, the holder may exercise his conversion right.

An amount designated as interest will be paid on the ARCNs quarterly at a rate based upon dividends paid on X common stock. More specifically, the annual amount payable with respect to an ARCN will be equal to the dividends paid on 50 shares of X common stock, plus an amount ($20) equal to two percent of the issue price ($1,000) of the note. However, such payments may not be less than $60, or more than $175, per ARCN. The current yield for nonconvertible, non-contingent debt instruments of corporations similar to X is 12 percent.

The ARCNs will be subordinated to all present and future senior and general creditors of X. In the event of bankruptcy, the holder of an ARCN will be treated as a creditor in the amount of $600.

LAW AND ANALYSIS

Whether an instrument represents indebtedness or an equity investment for federal income tax purposes depends on the facts and circumstances of each case. No particular fact is conclusive in making such a determination. John Kelley Co. v. Commissioner, 326 U.S. 521 (1946), 1946-1 C.B. 191. Among the factors that may be considered in making such a determination are: (a) whether there is a written unconditional promise to pay on demand or on a specific date a sum certain in money in return for an adequate consideration in money or money's worth, and to pay a fixed rate of interest; and (b) the intent of the parties in creating the instrument. See Fin Hay Realty Co. v. United States, 398 F.2d 694 (3d Cir. 1968); Dobkin v. Commissioner, 15 T.C. 31 (1950), *affirmed*, 192 F.2d 392 (2d Cir. 1951).

The ARCNs in this case are structured so that under most likely eventualities they will be converted into X common stock. At maturity the holder of an ARCN will convert the ARCN to stock rather than take cash if the stock can be sold for more than $600 in the aggregate. Because the X stock is worth $1,000 when the ARCNs are issued, redemption for cash at maturity will occur only if the stock drops in price by more than 40 percent. Further, as long as the 50 shares of X common stock are trading at more than $600 in the aggregate (i.e., for more than $12 per share), it would be economically disadvantageous for the holder of an ARCN to permit X to redeem it for $600. Thus, in such a situation, X may in effect force conversion at any time beginning two years after issuance by calling the ARCN.

Moreover, in many circumstances it will be to X's advantage to force conversion because by doing so it would avoid having to pay out cash. Redemption for cash may cause it to recognize ordinary income in the amount of the difference between the issue price of the ARCN and the cash redemption price (less the amount, if any, already returned as income). Section 1.61-12(c)(3) of the Income Tax Regulations. But see sections 108 and 1017, permitting deferral of recognition under some circumstances if the corporation foregoes certain tax benefits. Thus, there is a significant income tax cost that increases the net cost of a cash retirement well above $600. On the other hand, if X issues stock upon the conversion of an ARCN, it will recognize no gain or loss. See Rev. Rul. 59-222, 1959-1 C.B. 80. If the value of the stock into which ARCNs are convertible is less than the after-tax cost of a cash retirement, X benefits from conversion of ARCNs into stock. Conversion can be forced by X as long as the value of 50 shares of X stock exceeds $600.

Because of the very high probability that all of the ARCNs issued will be converted into stock, the ARCNs do not in reality represent a promise to pay a sum certain. Rather, the $600 face value is a figure calculated primarily to ensure conversion into stock; its only other function is to provide a floor for purposes of loss that will become material only if the price of X common stock declines by more than 40 percent from its price at the time the ARCNs are issued.

Other factors in this case that support a conclusion that the ARCNs constitute equity rather than debt include (i) the guaranteed annual return of $60 with respect to the $1,000 investment is unreasonably low in comparison to the annual return on comparable non-convertible, non-contingent instruments at the time the ARCNs are issued, (ii) under the terms of the ARCNs, more than 65 percent of the future annual yield may be discretionary based on the level of discretionary dividends paid on X common stock, and (iii) the ARCNs are subordinated to X's general creditors.

The fixed principal and fixed minimum interest payable on the ARCNs are insufficient factors to support their classification as debt. It is apparent that neither X nor the purchasers of ARCNs ascribe any economic value or practical significance to the fixed debt features of the ARCNs since the ARCNs will be sold for a price approximately equal to the value of the common stock into which the ARCNs can be converted, rather than at a substantial premium.

The ARCNs in this case are fundamentally different from the instruments classified as debt in Rev. Rul. 68-54, 1968-1 C.B. 69, because the instruments considered there were intended to create and did create a fixed obligation to pay money on a given date; the interest rate, although to some extent dependent on earnings, was determinable according to a formula and did not float in tandem with discretionary common stock dividends; and the notes were not convertible into stock. These factors outweighed the subordination of the debentures.

Rev. Rul. 73-122, 1973-1 C.B. 66, is also distinguishable because the instruments considered there, although subordinated, gave rise to a right to be repaid a sum certain at some time within ten years; interest was to be paid at a fixed rate; and there was no conversion feature.

In both Rev. Rul. 68-54 and Rev. Rul. 73-122, unlike the present case, a consideration of the entire transaction revealed that true indebtedness was intended to be created; that is, unrelated parties dealing at arm's length contemplated a cash repayment of the obligation within a fixed period of time. Here the parties contemplate that the ARCNs will not be redeemed for cash but will at some point be converted into stock of X.

HOLDING

The ARCNs constitute an equity interest in X and will be treated as stock for Federal income tax purposes. Accordingly, the periodic distributions with respect to the ARCNs, although denominated as interest, are distributions subject to section 301 of the Code, and are not deductible by X.

EFFECT ON OTHER REVENUE RULINGS

Rev. Ruls. 68-54 and 73-122 are distinguished.

NOTES

1. The Commissioner issued Rev. Rul. 83-98 after several transactions like the one it describes were consummated and publicized in the financial press. Some of the transactions were blessed by the formal opinions of tax counsel whose view of the law is quite opposed to that expressed in the ruling. If there were to be litigation over this issue, who should prevail?

2. Section 385 gives the Treasury the authority to issue regulations setting forth the factors to be considered in deciding debt vs. equity questions. In 1980 the Treasury used that authority to promulgate final regulations, but delayed their effectiveness. The regulations proved very controversial, and in 1983 they were withdrawn. What regulations would you write if you were in Treasury? Is it even possible to draft rules that will satisfactorily decide every case? For a thorough explanation of the now withdrawn §385 regulations, see Weiss and McCarty, A Summary of the Final Regulations on the Treatment of Certain Interests in Corporations as Stock or Indebtedness, Tax Notes, March 30, 1981, p. 700.

In its 1989 legislation Congress amended §385(a) to authorize the Treasury to treat an apparent debt instrument "as in part stock and in part indebtedness." It remains to be seen whether this will stimulate the Treasury once again to attempt drafting a set of comprehensive Regulations under §385.

3. The reporter for the American Law Institute Federal Income Tax Project on Subchapter C has recommended that the difference between debt and equity be reduced by allowing a corporation to deduct the dividends it pays on newly contributed capital. The proposal would permit a corporation to deduct the dividends it pays in an amount not in excess of (a) 2 percentage points plus the federal long-term interest rates times (b) the corporation's "qualified contributed capital." The term *qualified contributed capital* includes only shareholder contributions to capital after the effective date of the proposal and does not include accumulated earnings or contributions to capital made before the proposal takes effect. See American Law Institute — Federal Income Tax Project — Subchapter C (Supplemental Study), Reporter's Study Draft at 88-97 (June 1, 1989).

b. Dividend vs. Business Expense — §162

SAFWAY STEEL SCAFFOLDS CO. OF GEORGIA v.
UNITED STATES
590 F.2d 1360 (5th Cir. 1979)

Before Brown, Chief Judge, and Tuttle and Thornberry, Circuit
Judges.

THORNBERRY, Circuit Judge. This is a tax refund suit. The question presented is how much of $21,600 paid by the taxpayer, Safway
Steel Scaffolds Company of Georgia, to Charles and Richard Werner
is deductible under 26 U.S.C. §162(a)(3) as rent. The Commissioner
disallowed $9,720 of the claimed deduction and the district court
sustained the government's position. The taxpayer, claiming that the
entire amount is deductible, brings this appeal. For the reasons stated,
we affirm.

Charles and Richard Werner are the sole stockholders of the
taxpayer. In 1947, the brothers purchased four parcels of land in
downtown Atlanta for $9,500 and assembled a single commercially
useable parcel. On January 1, 1948, they leased the property to the
plaintiff. The lease was for twenty years and was to expire on December 31, 1967. Among other things, the lease provided: (1) that
the taxpayer was to pay an annual rent of $2,400 in monthly install-
ments of $200; (2) that the taxpayer was to pay all taxes and utility
charges; and (3) that the taxpayer could erect improvements on the
vacant lot, but on expiration of the lease all attached improvements
would become the property of the lessors (Werner brothers). The
lease contained no option for renewal.

In January 1948, the Board of Directors of the plaintiff selected
an architect to design a building for the taxpayer. On April 3, 1948,
construction of the building began and the taxpayer moved into the
new structure on December 3, 1948. The building had 18,433 square
feet and the total cost of the building was $128,025. The district court
found, and we will not disturb his finding here, that the structure
had a useful life of approximately thirty-four years.

At the expiration of the 1948 lease, the land and improvements
reverted to the Werner brothers. However, the taxpayer and its own-
ers-lessors entered into a new lease. This lease provided for a three
year rental term and a net rental of $1,800 per month ($21,600
yearly). The parties have stipulated that this amount is a fair rental
amount for the improvements and the ground rent. The taxpayer
contends that the entire amount is deductible as rent while the government contends that the amount of rent allocable to the
improvements is not deductible under §162(a)(3).[4]

4. The district court found that the value of the land plus the improvements
was $200,000 in 1968, with $110,000 allocated to the land and $90,000 allocated to

It is ordinarily inappropriate to inquire into the reasonableness of the rent paid, however, this case presents an exception to the general rule. That exception is the case of a close relationship between the lessor and the lessee . . . or if the contract arises "between persons having an interest on both sides of a transaction." . . . In case of a close relationship between the lessor and the lessee the inquiry becomes, "If, viewing the circumstances in which the lease is made, it is such a lease as reasonable [persons] dealing at arm's length would make, then it is valid and binding . . . for tax purposes." . . .

The taxpayer argues that the court should look only to the reasonableness of the stated rental amount under the 1968 rent to determine the deductibility of the rent. The district court, however, concluded that it should examine all of the circumstances of the case and view the entire history between the taxpayer and the Werner brothers as a series of transactions to determine the tax consequences.

We agree that the district court correctly identified the test and justifiedly inquired into the reasonableness of all the transactions made between Safway and the Werner brothers. The district court concluded that the ground rental of $2,400 per year was not unreasonable, but that parties dealing at arm's length would not have allowed an improvement with a thirty-four year useful life to revert at the end of a twenty year lease period without some economic benefit being given for the improvement such as a renewal option.[6] Therefore, the district court concluded that the payment attributable to the value of the improvements was really in the nature of a nondeductible dividend made to the Werner brothers and not a deductible rent expense.[7]

. . . We have concluded that the district court properly applied the facts and made correct determinations of law. It is our opinion that the district court should be affirmed.

Affirmed.

---

the improvements. Since the value of the improvements is 45% of the total value, the Commissioner disallowed 45% of the $21,600 claimed as a rental deduction [21,600 x .45 = $9,720].

6. Or as suggested by the government, a concomitant reduction in rent attributable to the taxpayer for a period of the reasonable life of the improvements could be given.

7. The taxpayer also argues that the government is estopped from asserting the nondeductibility of the rent because the government audited the taxpayer's returns in 1959 and made no objection about the reasonableness of the rent. We think the cases conclusively demonstrate that no estoppel arises from these facts. See Union Equity Cooperative Exchange v. C.I.R., 481 F.2d 812, 817 (10 Cir. 1973). We also note that the taxpayer's argument rests on the implication that the Commissioner approved its rental deduction during the audit. We think another plausible inference is that the question simply never arose. A different question might arise were the Commissioner to affirmatively mislead the taxpayer as to a mistake of fact. (The government is never estopped as to a matter of law, Automobile Club v. Commissioner, 353 U.S. 180 (1957).)

NOTES

1. A closely held corporation may incur an expense that it seeks to deduct under §162 but that the Commissioner will disallow because it benefits the shareholders personally and is not meaningful in terms of the corporation's conduct of its business or income producing activities. Such expenses are frequently called "constructive" or "disguised" dividends. (Disallowance of the deduction is often accompanied by taxation of the payment to the shareholders as a dividend. See pages 144-145 infra.) See, e.g., American Properties, Inc. v. Commissioner, 262 F.2d 150 (9th Cir. 1958), in which the court sustained the disallowance of a corporate payment for the construction and upkeep of a boat that bore a direct relationship to the shareholder's hobby but none to the corporation's business. On what grounds would you expect a corporation to claim the right to a §162 deduction of the payments made to cover the expenses of the wedding of the majority shareholder's daughter? See Haverhill Shoe Novelty Co., 15 T.C. 517 (1950); cf. Warren Brekke, 40 T.C. 789 (1963) (corporate payments not actually for the use of property despite the tag of "rent"). But see Sanitary Farm's Dairy, Inc., 25 T.C. 463 (1955), acq. 1956-2 C.B. 8 (costs of an African safari allowed). The latter case was part of the Treasury's weaponry in its battle to secure the 1962 amendments that make up §274. For a case where the court disallowed a corporate deduction under §274(d) for travel and entertainment expenses, but held no constructive dividend to the shareholder who incurred the expenses on the corporation's behalf, see Henry Schwartz Corp., 60 T.C. 728 (1973), acq. 1974-2 C.B. 4.

2. What of a corporate payment that is of little significance to the corporation's business activity but benefits only some, but not all, of its shareholders? Can it be disallowed? Can it be characterized as a dividend? Cf. Paramount-Richards Theatres, Inc. v. Commissioner, 153 F.2d 602 (5th Cir. 1946). This issue can be closely related to that of distinguishing debt from equity. See, e.g., Mills v. I.R.S., 840 F.2d 229 (4th Cir. 1987) (holding that a payment by a corporation to a related corporation was a bona fide repayment of debt and therefore did not constitute a constructive dividend to a major shareholder of both corporations). Compare the situation involving an alleged interest payment where the "debt" is not held by an avowed shareholder (Note 6, page 73 supra).

3. As to alleged "salary" that may be disallowed as a dividend, see Treas. Reg. §1.162-7(b)(1); Cannon, Reasonable Compensation and Accumulated Earnings, 39 N.Y.U. Inst. Fed. Taxn. 11-1, 11-3 to 11-11 (1981). For a recent discussion of the factors considered in determining whether compensation will be disallowed as a "disguised" dividend, see Owensby & Kritikos v. Commissioner, 819 F.2d

1315 (5th Cir. 1987). As to accrued salary owing to a cash basis employee-shareholder owning more than 50 percent in value of the corporation's stock, see §§267(a)(2) and (b)(2).

4. For the notion that even "reasonable" salaries may contain a nondeductible dividend element to the extent of a "reasonable" return on equity capital, see Charles McCandless Tile Service v. United States, 422 F.2d 1336 (Ct. Cl. 1970). But see George R. Laure, 70 T.C. 1087 (1978), acq. partially in result, 1979-1 C.B. 1, *aff'd and rev'd in part on other issues*, 653 F.2d 253 (6th Cir. 1981); Rev. Rul. 79-8, 1979-1 C.B. 92 (dividend history relevant to determination of reasonableness, but once found reasonable, salaries are deductible despite failure to pay substantial dividends); Coggin, The Status of the *McCandless* Doctrine, 55 Taxes 720 (1977).

5. For circumstances in which a corporate charitable contribution will be treated as a constructive dividend to the corporation's shareholders, see Henry J. Knott, 67 T.C. 681 (1977), acq. 1979-1 C.B. 1, and Rev. Rul. 79-9, 1979-1 C.B. 125.

c. Dividend vs. Purchase

Corporation M purchased a yacht and a seashore residence. The yacht is used half the time to entertain corporate customers and half the time for the pleasure of the sole shareholder and his family. The seashore residence is used exclusively for the pleasure of the shareholder and his family. What are the tax consequences to Corporation M of the purchases it has made? What are the tax consequences to the shareholder? See pages 139-144 infra.

d. Retirement of Shares vs. Business Expense

In Five Star Mfg. Co. v. Commissioner, 355 F.2d 724 (5th Cir. 1966), the court permitted a corporation to deduct as an ordinary and necessary business expense the amount paid to a 50-percent shareholder and director in redemption of all of his stock. In the court's view, the redemption was an absolute business necessity, since the stockholder-director had been looting the corporation and his removal was the only hope the corporation had for continued viability. The decision is extremely difficult to justify. Although a "necessary" payment, it was a capital expenditure, not an "expense." What, after all, is the function of §162(a) in the context of the corporate income tax? *Five Star Mfg. Co.* has been held applicable at best to cases of "life or death" business exigency, and its authority is questionable. See Harder Services Inc., 67 T.C. 585 (1977), *aff'd without published opinion*, 573 F.2d 1290 (2d Cir. 1977); H & G In-

dustries, Inc. v. Commissioner, 495 F.2d 653 (3d Cir. 1974); Jim
Walter Corp. v. United States, 498 F.2d 631 (5th Cir. 1974).

Section 162(k), added by the 1986 Act, generally disallows any
amounts paid by a corporation "in connection with the redemption
of its stock." Its enactment was a response to the rise of so-called
"greenmail" payments by corporate takeover targets. Should any corporate payment in redemption of stock ever have been allowed as a
current business expense even in the absence of §162(l)? Would it
matter, as with greenmail, that some of the redemption payment
exceeded the fair market value of the redeemed stock?

e. Incorporation Expense — §248

Prior to the enactment of §248 in 1954, a corporation's organizational expenses (e.g., lawyers' fees, fees to the state upon filing
of Articles of Incorporation, etc.) were not deductible under §162
because they were regarded as capital expenditures. If the corporation did not have a limited life, the intangible assets the
expenditures produced were treated as having an indefinite life, and
thus no amortization was permitted under §167. Ultimately, on complete liquidation of the corporation, a loss might be allowed under
§165(a). Cf. Canal-Randolph Corp. v. United States, 568 F.2d 28 (7th
Cir. 1977) (per curiam), denying a deduction for the pre-1954 organization expenses of a 79-percent-owned subsidiary corporation
on the occasion of its merger into its parent.

Section 248 authorizes corporations to elect ratable amortization
of their organizational expenses over any period selected as long as
it is not less than 60 months. When and how must an election be
made? When must the period for amortization begin? See §248;
Treas. Reg. §1.248-1.

Should organizational expenses be deductible in full when incurred or paid? Should they not be deductible at all? Not until
liquidation? Is the approach of §248 sensible? Why?

Section 248 is not applicable to reorganization expenses. See
McCrory Corp. v. United States, 651 F.2d 828 (2d Cir. 1981). See,
also, Affiliated Capital Corp., 88 T.C. 1157 (1987) (expenses of a
posteffective amendment to registration statement not a recurring
business expense but rather a capital expenditure).

In National Starch & Chem. Corp., 93 T.C. No. 7 (1989), the
court held that an acquiring corporation may not deduct currently,
but must capitalize the expenses it incurred in connection with the
friendly takeover of a target corporation. Revoking an earlier letter
ruling to the contrary, and following the reasoning in *National Starch*,
the Service has ruled that the costs a target corporation incurred to

fend off a *hostile* takeover are capital expenditures, not deductible under §162. Ltr. Rul. 8945003.

2. Distributions of Stock

a. To Pay an Expense—§162

Compensation—§§83, 162, 421-424. Corporation M pays a reasonable bonus to one of its salesmen by issuing to him Corporation M common stock having a fair market value of $5000. What are the tax consequences to Corporation M? What is the authority for your conclusion? Would the result be different if the salesman were also the sole shareholder?

REVENUE RULING 62-217
1962-2 C.B. 59

A corporation distributed shares of its treasury stock to its employees as compensation for services rendered. The cost basis of the treasury stock to the corporation was less than its fair market value on the date of the distribution to the employees. In filing its Federal income tax return for the taxable year, the corporation deducted the fair market value of the stock on the date of the distribution as a business expense.

In accordance with the nonrecognition of gain or loss provisions of section 1032(a) of the Internal Revenue Code of 1954 and section 1.1032-1(a) of the Income Tax Regulations, relating to the receipt by a corporation of money or other property in exchange for its own stock (including a transfer of shares as compensation for services), the corporation did not report gain upon the distribution of treasury stock.

Held, the fair market value of the treasury stock on the date of the distribution is deductible as a business expense in accordance with the provisions of section 162(a) of the Code. The nonrecognition of gain or loss provisions of section 1032(a) of the Code have no effect upon a business expense deduction that is otherwise allowable under section 162(a) of the Code.

NOTES

1. In addition to its holding as to the business expense deduction, consider the §1032 aspect of Rev. Rul. 62-217 in connection with the materials on pages 3-4 supra. The ruling refers to the "cost

basis" of treasury stock, but Rev. Rul. 74-503, 1974-2 C.B. 117, 118, modified Rev. Rul. 62-217 "to remove any implication that . . . a corporation's treasury stock held by it has a cost basis rather than a zero basis."

2. The majority shareholder of P Corporation transfers ten shares of P stock to B, who is an employee of P's subsidiary, Corporation S, as reasonable compensation for services performed by B for S. Does the majority shareholder of P recognize gain or loss on the transaction? Does Corporation S recognize gain or loss? Is S entitled to a deduction? In what amount? See Rev. Rul. 80-76, 1980-1 C.B. 15.

3. A, the controlling shareholder of X Corporation, transfers several shares of stock to B, an employee of X Corporation, in order to induce B to remain in X's employ. What are the tax consequences to A, B, and X? See Rev. Rul. 80-196, 1980-2 C.B. 32.

In Alves v. Commissioner, 79 T.C. 864 (1982), aff'd, 734 F.2d 478 (9th Cir. 1984), the Tax Court, with five judges dissenting, held that even if an employee pays fair market value for restricted stock, he is taxable under §83(b). In part the decision rested on the court's interpretation of Treas. Reg. §1.83-2(a). The Ninth Circuit's opinion is set forth at page 520 infra.

4. Treas. Reg. §1.83-6(d) treats the transfer of shares by a shareholder to corporate employees as a contribution to capital. The validity of this regulation was recently upheld by the Sixth Circuit. See Tilford v. Commissioner, 705 F.2d 825 (6th Cir.), cert. denied, 464 U.S. 992 (1983).

5. For an important effect of an election under §83(b), see Rev. Rul. 83-22, 1983-1 C.B. 17. See Estate of Gresham, 79 T.C. 322 (1982), aff'd, 752 F.2d 518 (10th Cir. 1985), with respect to the interplay of §83 and the alternative minimum tax on "items of tax preference" defined in §57.

6. Corporation X grants its executives options to buy from it Corporation X common stock at $10 per share. At the time of the grant the stock is worth $10 a share. Two years later, when one of the executives exercises the option, the stock is worth $15 per share. What is the tax consequence to Corporation X? Why? See §83(h) and Treas. Reg. §1.83-6; cf. §422A and Note 4, page 525 infra.

7. Assume that salary to sole shareholder-employees is deducted in the year accrued by an accrual basis corporation and is paid in a subsequent year by issuance of the corporation's stock. Assume too that §267 is inapplicable. What is the tax consequence to the corporation when the stock is issued? See Fender Sales, page 507 infra.

Interest — §§162, 163. Corporation N, a manufacturing company, orders raw materials from its supplier and is billed in the amount of $10,000. Wishing to conserve cash, Corporation N offers to satisfy the bill by issuing shares of its common stock fairly valued at $11,000, although the shares are not readily marketable because of a thin market. The supplier accepts the stock. What are the tax consequences to Corporation N? Why?

b. To Buy an Asset — §§1032, 1012, 362, 334

Corporation A uses Treasury shares worth $50,000 (acquired a year earlier for $40,000) to purchase needed machinery. What are the tax consequences to Corporation A at the time of purchase? What is Corporation A's basis in the machinery?

If Corporation A purchased stock in Corporation Z, paying for it with its own common stock, there would be no immediate tax consequence to Corporation A. §1032. The basis of the Z stock acquired would depend in part on whether the acquisition was a "reorganization" as defined in §368(a). See Chapter 4.

c. To Acquire Cash — §§162, 1032

Newly issued stock distributed in exchange for cash equal to the stock's value gives rise to no corporate deduction. What is the result if a valued employee is permitted to buy stock worth $10,000 for $8,000? *Compare* page 85 supra. If the corporation had used Treasury stock that had cost it $8000 would the result be different? See page 3-4 supra.

d. To Pay a Dividend

Corporation M pays its common shareholders dividends consisting of ten shares of newly issued Corporation M common stock for each share of stock held. What are the tax consequences to Corporation M? As to the consequences to the shareholders see Chapter 4, pages 431-459 infra.

III. THE INCIDENCE OF THE CORPORATION INCOME TAX

J. PECHMAN, FEDERAL TAX POLICY*
141-148 (5th ed. 1987)

... There is no more controversial issue in taxation than the question, "who bears the corporation income tax?" On this question,

*Copyright © 1987 by the Brookings Institution. Reprinted by permission. First edition reviewed, Wolfman, 76 Yale L.J. 1036 (1967). — Ed.

economists and businessmen alike differ among themselves. The following quotations are representative of these divergent views:

> Corporate taxes are simply costs, and the method of their assessment does not change this fact. Costs must be paid by the public in prices, and corporate taxes are thus, in effect, concealed sales taxes. (Enders M. Voorhees, chairman of the Finance Committee, U.S. Steel Corporation, address before the Controllers' Institute of America, New York, September 21, 1943.)

> The initial or short-run incidence of the corporate income tax seems to be largely on corporations and their stockholders. . . . There seems to be little foundation for the belief that a large part of the corporate tax comes out of wages or is passed on to consumers in the same way that a selective excise [tax] tends to be shifted to buyers. (Richard Goode, *The Corporation Income Tax,* Wiley, 1951, pp. 71-72.)

> . . . The corporation profits tax is almost entirely shifted; the government simply uses the corporation as a tax collector. (Kenneth E. Boulding, *The Organizational Revolution,* Harper, 1953, p. 277.)

> It is hard to avoid the conclusion that plausible alternative sets of assumptions about the relevant elasticities all yield results in which capital bears very close to 100 percent of the [corporate] tax burden. (Arnold C. Harberger, "The Incidence of the Corporation Income Tax," *Journal of Political Economy,* vol. 70, June 1962, p. 234.)

> . . . An increase in the [corporate] tax is shifted fully through short run adjustments to prevent a decline in the net rate of return [on corporate investment], and . . . these adjustments are maintained subsequently. (Marian Krzyzaniak and Richard A. Musgrave, *The Shifting of the Corporation Income Tax,* Johns Hopkins Press, 1963, p. 65.)

> . . . There is no inter-sector inefficiency resulting from the imposition of the corporate profits tax with the interest deductibility provision. Nor is there any misallocation between safe and risky industries. From an efficiency point of view, the whole corporate profits tax structure is just like a lump sum tax on corporations. (Joseph E. Stiglitz, "Taxation, Corporate Financial Policy, and the Cost of Capital," *Journal of Public Economics,* vol. 2, 1973, p. 33.)

> . . . If the net rate of return is given in the international market place, the burden of a tax on the income from capital in one country will not (in the middle or long run) end up being borne by capital (which can flee) but by other factors of production (land, labor, and to a degree, old fixed capital). (Arnold C. Harberger, "The State of the Corporate Tax: Who Pays It? Should It Be

Replaced?" in Charles E. Walker and Mark A. Bloomfield, eds., *New Directions in Federal Tax Policy for the 1980s,,* Ballinger, 1983.)

Unfortunately, economics has not yet provided a scientific basis for accepting or rejecting one side or the other. This section presents the logic of each view and summarizes the evidence.

THE SHIFTING MECHANISM

One reason for the sharply divergent views is that the opponents frequently do not refer to the same type of shifting. It is important to distinguish between short- and long-run shifting and the mechanisms through which they operate. The "short run" is defined by economists as a period too short for firms to adjust their capital to changing demand and supply conditions. The "long run" is a period in which capital can be adjusted.

THE SHORT RUN

The classical view in economics is that the corporation income tax cannot be shifted in the short run. The argument is as follows: all business firms, whether they are competitive or monopolistic, seek to maximize net profits. This maximum occurs when output and prices are set at the point where the cost of producing an additional unit is exactly equal to the additional revenue obtained from the sale of that unit. In the short run, a tax on economic profit should make no difference in this decision. The output and price that maximized the firm's profits before the tax will continue to maximize profits after the tax is imposed. (This follows from simple arithmetic. If a series of figures is reduced by the same percentage, the figure that was highest before will be the highest after.)

The opposite view is that today's markets are characterized neither by perfect competition nor by monopoly; instead, they show considerable imperfection and mutual interdependence or oligopoly. In such markets, business firms may set their prices at the level that covers their full costs *plus* a margin for profits. Alternatively, the firms are described as aiming at an after-tax target rate of return on their invested capital. Under the cost-plus behavior, the firm treats the tax as an element of cost and raises its price to recover the tax. (Public utilities are usually able to shift the tax in this way, because state rate-making agencies treat the corporation tax as a cost.) Similarly, if the firm's objective is the after-tax target rate of return, imposition of a tax or an increase in the tax rate — by reducing the rate of return on invested capital — will have to be accounted for in making output and price decisions. To preserve the target rate of return, the tax must be shifted forward to consumers or backward to the workers or partly forward and partly backward.

It is also argued that economists' models are irrelevant in most markets where one or a few large firms exercise a substantial degree of leadership. In such markets, efficient producers raise their prices to recover the tax, and the tax merely forms an "umbrella" that permits less efficient or marginal producers to survive.

When business managers are asked about their pricing policies, they often say that they shift the corporation income tax. However, even if business firms intend to shift the tax, there is some doubt about their ability to shift it fully in the short run. In the first place, the tax depends on the outcome of business operations during an entire year. Businessmen can only guess the ratio of the tax to their gross receipts, and it is hard to conceive of their setting a price that would recover the precise amount of tax they will eventually pay. (If shifting were possible, there would be some instances of firms shifting more than 100 percent of the tax, but few economists believe that overshifting actually occurs.)

Second, businessmen know that should they attempt to recover the corporation income tax through higher prices (or lower wages), other firms would not necessarily do the same. Some firms make no profit or have large loss carry-overs and thus pay no tax; among other firms, the ratio of tax to gross receipts differs. In multiproduct firms, the producer has even less basis for judging the ratio of tax to gross receipts for each product. All these possibilities increase the uncertainty of response by other firms and make the attempt to shift part or all of the corporation income tax hazardous.

THE LONG RUN

In the long run, the corporation income tax influences investment by reducing the rate of return on corporate equity. If the corporation income tax is not shifted in the short run, new after-tax rates of return are depressed, and the incentive to undertake corporate investment is thereby reduced. After-tax rates of return tend to be equalized with those in the noncorporate sector, but in the process corporate capital and output will have been permanently reduced. Thus, if there is no short-run shifting and if the supply of capital is fixed, the burden of the tax falls on the owners of capital in general. If the depressed rate of return on capital reduces investment, productivity of labor decreases and at least part of the tax may be borne by workers.

Where investment is financed by borrowing, the corporation tax cannot affect investment decisions because interest on debt is a deductible expense. If the marginal investment of a firm is fully

Figure 1-1. Percentage of Business Income Originating in the Corporate
Sector, 1929–86[a]

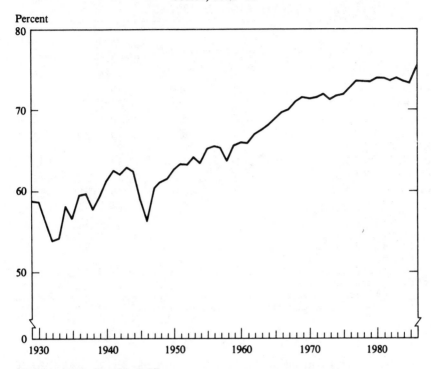

Source: Appendix table D-17.
a. Business income is national income originating in business enterprises.

financed by debt, the corporation tax becomes a lump-sum tax on
profits generated by previous investments and is borne entirely by
the owners of the corporation, the stockholders. In view of the recent
large increase in debt financing (see the section on equity and debt
finance below), a substantial proportion of the corporation income
tax may now rest on stockholders and not be diffused to owners of
capital in general through the shifting process just described.

The Corporation Tax in an Open Economy

The foregoing analysis assumed that the corporation tax was
imposed in a close economy. In an open economy, the rate of return
on capital is set in the international marketplace. If the tax in one
country is higher than it is elsewhere, capital will move to other
countries until the rate of return is raised to the international level.
Thus the burden of the tax would not be borne by capital but by

Table 1-1
Rates of Return and Debt-Capital Ratio, Manufacturing Corporations, Selected Periods, 1927-83

Period	Return on equity[a]		Return on total capital[a,b]		Ratio of debt to total capital[c]	General corporation tax rate[d]
	Before tax	After tax	Before tax	After tax		
1927-29	8.8	7.8[e]	8.7	7.8[e]	15.2	12.2
1936-39	7.8	6.4[e]	7.3	6.2[e]	15.0	17.0
1953-56	18.4	9.2	15.7	8.2	19.0	52.0
1957-61	14.1	7.3	12.2	6.8	20.5	52.0
1964-67	17.8	10.1	14.9	9.1	25.1	48.5
1968-71	13.5	6.8	11.6	7.0	32.7	50.7
1977-80	19.4	13.9	16.4	12.8	35.8	47.0
1981-83	11.2	8.2	12.7	10.8	36.5	46.0

Source: Appendix table D-18.
a. Equity and debt capital are averages of book values for the beginning and end of the year.
b. Profits plus interest paid as a percentage of total capital
c. End of year.
d. Statutory rate of federal corporation income tax applicable to large corporations (average of annual figures).
e. Rates of return are slightly understated (probably by 0.3 percentage point or less) because no allowance has been made for the foreign tax credit.

other factors of production (land, labor, and old fixed capital) that cannot move. Since labor is the largest input into corporate products, wage earners would bear most of the burden of the corporation tax through lower real wages.

In the years immediately after World War II, most countries imposed tight capital controls and currencies were not convertible. As capital controls were dismantled and many foreign currencies other than the U.S. dollar became acceptable in international transactions, the open economy model became more realistic. During this later period, the effective corporation tax rates have been declining in the United States. It follows that recent U.S. tax policy has probably reduced any adverse effect of the corporation income tax on real wages, not increased it as some allege.

The Evidence

The evidence on the incidence of the corporation income tax is inconclusive. The data do not permit a clear determination of the factors affecting price and wage decisions. Different authors examining the same set of facts have come to diametrically opposite conclusions.

Figure 1-2. Property Income Share in Corporate Gross Product Less
Indirect Taxes, 1929–1986ª

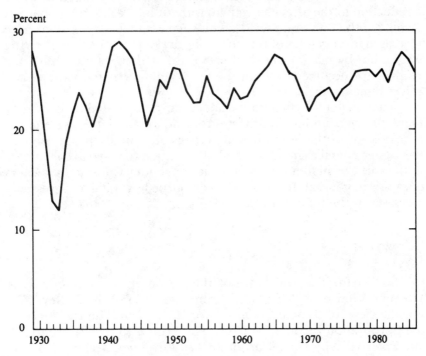

Percent

Source: Appendix table D-17.
a. Property income includes corporate profits before taxes after capital-consumption
and inventory valuation adjustments, and net interest.

Over the long run, unincorporated business has not grown at
the expense of incorporated business. Corporations accounted for
58.7 percent of the national income originating in the business sector
in 1929; their share reached 75.6 percent in 1986. [Figure 1-1.] Much
of the increase came from the relative decline in industries, particularly farming, in which corporations are not important; but even in
the rest of the economy, there is no indication of a shift away from
the corporate form of organization. The advantages of doing business
in the corporate form far outweigh whatever deterrent effects the
corporation tax might have on corporate investment.

Beyond this, the data are conflicting. On the one hand, before-
and after-tax rates of return reported by corporations after tax have
been higher since the end of World War II than in the late 1920s,
when the corporation income tax was much lower. [Table 1-1.] On
the other hand, except for recession years, the share of pre-tax property income (profits, interest, and capital consumption allowances) in

corporate gross product changed little. [Figure 1-2.] Corporations
have been able to increase their before-tax profits enough to avoid
a reduction in the after-tax return, without increasing their share of
income in the corporate sector. This suggests that corporations have
increased pre-tax rates of return not by marking up prices or lowering
wages, but by making more efficient use of their capital. But what
might have occurred without the tax is unknown, and its long-run
effect remains unclear.

The burden of corporate taxation borne by individuals is strikingly different under the different incidence assumptions. The tax
is regressive in the lower income classes and mildly progressive in
the higher ones if as much as one-half is shifted forward to consumers
in the form of higher prices and the remainder is borne by owners
of capital in general. If the entire tax is borne by capital, progressivity
increases in the higher income classes. . . .

NOTE

See Klein, The Incidence of the Corporation Income Tax: A
Lawyer's View of a Problem in Economics, 1965 Wis. L. Rev. 576.
For the views of some economists, see Harberger, The Incidence of
the Corporation Income Tax, 70 J. Pol. Econ. 215 (1962); Auerbach
and Poterba, Why Have Corporate Tax Revenues Declined?, 1 Tax
Policy and the Economy 1 (1987).

REPORT OF THE STAFF OF THE JOINT
COMMITTEE ON TAXATION, TAX POLICY, AND
CAPITAL FORMATION
95th Cong., 1st Sess. 9 (Comm. Print 1977)

. . . A necessary step in increasing the rate of capital accumulation
is to make the private sector of the economy more willing to invest
in plant, equipment and other types of capital. Several tax changes
have been suggested to accomplish this goal [including] integration
of the individual and corporate income taxes. . . .

INTEGRATION OF CORPORATE AND INDIVIDUAL INCOME TAXES

EXISTING LAW

1. Under existing law, corporate income is taxed differently than
other sources of income. That part of corporate earnings which is

paid out to individual shareholders as dividends has been taxed first under the corporate income tax and then is taxed under the individual income tax. Earnings which are retained by the corporation, however, are taxed once at the corporate level, and not at all at the shareholder level except to the extent that they raise the value of the stock and result in recognized capital gains. Thus, there is double taxation of corporate income paid out as dividends, and the tax burden on retained earnings is much different than would be true if the tax rate were equal to the shareholder's individual tax bracket.

2. An exception to these general rules exists for so-called "subchapter S" corporations. If a corporation has fifteen or fewer shareholders and meets certain other requirements, it may elect to be treated generally as a partnership, so that there is no corporate income tax and retained earnings are subject to the individual income tax. This represents total integration of the corporate and individual income taxes.

3. Business income earned by partnerships and sole proprietorships is taxed at the individual income tax rates applicable to the owners of the business.

PROBLEMS WITH THE EXISTING SYSTEM OF TAXING
CORPORATE INCOME

1. *Cost of capital.* — The double tax on dividends significantly increases the cost of funds for corporate investment financed by new issues of stock. As a result, the before-tax rate of return on such investment projects must be higher for them to be profitable, and corporations, therefore, undertake fewer investments than they otherwise would.

2. *Allocation of capital between corporate and noncorporate business.* — Because the double taxation of dividends raises the cost of funds to corporate business relative to noncorporate business, it leads to an inefficient allocation of capital. Corporate investments need to be more profitable than noncorporate investments if they are to yield a sufficiently large after-tax return to make it worthwhile for a business to undertake them. From the standpoint of economic efficiency, there is too little capital in the corporate sector.

On the other hand, in some cases capital is invested in corporate business because the corporate tax rate is lower than the shareholder's individual tax rate. . . . In such situations, the second tax on retained earnings (either when they are subsequently paid out as dividends or lead to recognized capital gains) is sufficiently unimportant that the business is carried on in corporate form even though nontax considerations might otherwise have caused the business to be carried on in noncorporate form.

3. *Corporate financial structures.* — There is now a strong tax in-

centive for corporations to use certain sources of funds and to avoid others. Retained earnings are the cheapest source of funds, because they are exempt from the individual income tax until realized as a capital gain. Current law also encourages the use of debt finance relative to new stock issues, since interest payments are deductible and dividends are not. More debt increases the risk associated with corporate financial structures because firms must meet higher fixed charges for interest and face greater risk of bankruptcy. This causes corporations to undertake too few risky investment projects. By encouraging the use of retained earnings as a source of equity financing rather than new issues of stock, the double taxation of dividends also biases the allocation of capital in favor of those firms that are already earning income and against new businesses. The tax incentive for earnings retention may be a major cause of corporate mergers and takeovers.

4. *Tax equity.* — A basic principle of tax equity is that a person's tax burden should not depend on the source of his income. The existing method of taxing corporate income violates this principle in two ways. First, dividends in excess of the $100 dividend exclusion ($200 for joint returns) are taxed twice.* Second, retained earnings are taxed proportionately at corporate tax rates, which because of various deductions, exclusions, preferential tax rates and credits effectively average below 30 percent on income earned within the U.S., rather than at progressive individual tax rates, which range from 14 to 70 percent. While there is a tax on any capital gains that result from retained earnings, this burden is usually relatively modest because only a fraction of accrued capital gains are realized each year and because of the 50-percent exclusion for realized long-term capital gains.** Thus, for many individual shareholders, present law imposes a lighter over-all tax burden on retained earnings than would taxing them currently under the individual income tax.

ALTERNATIVE PROPOSALS FOR CORPORATE INTEGRATION

There are many possible ways to integrate the individual and corporate income taxes. Some of these involve sizable losses of revenue, but it is possible to integrate in ways that increase revenue.

Corporate integration would be a major legislative undertaking. In effect, it would rewrite the corporate income tax. What follows are three possible ways to achieve corporate integration. Many variations on these basic proposals are possible.

*Before the repeal of §116, noncorporate shareholders could exclude up to $200 of combined dividend and interest income ($400 for joint returns). — ED.

**The Tax Reform Act of 1986 eliminated the preferential rate for capital gains. — ED.

INTEGRATION FOR DIVIDENDS — WITHHOLDING APPROACH

1. Integrating the corporate and individual income taxes just for dividends involves eliminating the double taxation of dividends but keeping the existing treatment of retained earnings. This can be done through the "withholding approach," under which the corporate tax allocable to dividends would be transformed into a withholding tax similar to the withholding tax on wage and salary income. An alternative approach would be to allow corporations to deduct their dividends in computing their taxable income under the corporate income tax.

2. Under the withholding approach, corporations would have an incentive to raise a larger percentage of their funds from new issues of stock and a smaller percentage from debt and retained earnings than under existing law. Because the tax burden on corporate investments would be lower, more potential investment projects would have an after-tax profitability sufficiently high for them to be undertaken, which should increase corporate investment.

3. Instead of including in their taxable income their dividends received in excess of the $100 dividend exclusion, shareholders would include in taxable income the before-tax income of the corporation attributable to dividends (that is, the dividends "grossed up" by the corporate tax attributable to the dividends). Shareholders would then claim a tax credit for the amount of the corporate tax attributable to the dividend. This credit could exceed the shareholder's tax liability, and in that sense would be treated the same as overwithholding on wages and salaries. Corporations would report to each shareholder the amount of his grossed-up dividend and his tax credit.

4. *Treatment of corporate tax preferences.* — A major issue in designing an integration plan is whether shareholders should be able to claim a tax credit for the amount of U.S. tax the corporation actually pays (the "exact" or "pro-rata" method) or whether they should assume that the corporation paid the 48-percent maximum statutory rate (the "48-percent" method).* Because the U.S. corporate tax after credits is only about 25 percent of the so-called "book income" that corporations report to shareholders, the revenue effect of eliminating the double taxation of dividends is very sensitive to whether the exact method or the 48-percent method is used. Use of the 48-percent method almost triples the revenue loss from eliminating the double taxation of dividends.

(a) There are three reasons for the gap between the 25-percent effective rate of U.S. tax on worldwide book income and the 48-percent maximum statutory corporate tax rate: (1) tax credits, such

*The Tax Reform Act of 1986 lowered the maximum statutory rate to 34 percent. — ED.

as the foreign tax and investment credits; (2) deductions and exclusions arising from such tax preferences as DISC and accelerated depreciation, which cause "book income" to be greater than taxable income; and (3) preferential tax rates applying to certain amounts or sources of income, such as the surtax exemption or the alternative capital gains rate.

(b) The 48-percent method, in effect, passes through the benefits of these tax preferences to shareholders, even though the corporate tax itself is being effectively eliminated with respect to income paid out as dividends. The exact method, in contrast, denies the corporation and its shareholders the benefit of the tax preferences to the extent that the preferences are allocable to dividends. (This is why the exact method can also be termed the pro-rata method: it prorates the tax preferences between dividends and retained earnings and retains the preferences only with respect to retained earnings.) The 48-percent method, in effect, allocates all preferences to retained earnings.

(c) Apart from the revenue loss involved in using the 48-percent method, the main issue in choosing between the exact method and the 48-percent method is whether Congress desires to maintain the existing tax incentives for corporations to engage in particular activities and to make particular types of investments or whether these incentives should be scaled down in the same proportion that the corporate tax is being scaled down as a result of integration.

(d) The foreign tax credit presents a special issue. Passing through the foreign tax credit to shareholders by allowing them to claim a credit for the corporation's tax before it subtracts the foreign tax credit would promote neutrality between U.S. and foreign investment by U.S. corporations; however, it would involve a sizable revenue loss and would do nothing to encourage capital formation in the United States. Under the exact method, shareholders would not claim a credit for their corporations' foreign tax credits on their individual tax returns, but the corporation would deduct foreign taxes in computing book income.

5. *Shareholders eligible for integration.* — Another issue with significant revenue effects is whether tax-exempt shareholders should be made eligible for integration. Tax-exempt organizations, pension funds and foreigners receive about 20 percent of all dividends (net of intercorporate dividends), but making them eligible for integration would increase the revenue loss by about 50 percent (that is, the tax-exempt shareholders would receive one-third of the tax reduction from integration). The reason the tax-exempt shareholders benefit disproportionately from integration is that for taxable shareholders, some of the shareholder credit is "recaptured" by the gross-up, but

there would be no gross-up for tax-exempt shareholders. However, excluding tax-exempt shareholders from integration would reduce the beneficial effects of integration on corporate financial structures and resource allocation. Whether foreign shareholders in U.S. corporations should be eligible for integration is an appropriate subject for tax treaty negotiations.

6. *Intercorporate dividends.* — Corporations who own shares in other corporations could be eligible for the shareholder credit, although it would then be appropriate to repeal the deduction for intercorporate dividends received.

7. *Revenue effects.* — Under the exact or pro-rata method without eligibility for tax-exempt shareholders, integration for dividends would involve a revenue loss of about $5 billion at 1976 levels of income and profits. (The estimate includes the revenue gain of $0.4 billion from repeal of the dividend exclusion.) Extending eligibility to tax-exempt shareholders would increase the revenue loss to between $7 and $8 billion. Using the 48-percent method rather than the exact method would increase the revenue loss to about $14 billion if tax-exempt shareholders are excluded and to about $21 billion if they are included.

INTEGRATION FOR BOTH DIVIDENDS AND RETAINED EARNINGS

1. Conceptually, integrating the corporate and individual income taxes for both dividends and retained earnings involves taxing all corporate income under the individual income tax and eliminating the double taxation of dividends. The corporate income tax would, in effect, be eliminated, except as a withholding device, for shareholders made eligible for integration. Shareholders would include in their taxable income their pro rata share of the corporation's pretax earnings. Corporations would continue to pay the corporate income tax, largely as under existing law, but shareholders would obtain a tax credit (which could exceed their tax liability) for the corporate tax paid on those earnings. The relevant information could be communicated to shareholders along with their dividend checks or their information returns (form 1099).

2. Under this proposal, the tax structure would be neutral with respect to a corporation's financial structure, since all corporate-source income, whether it be dividends, interest or retained earnings, would be taxed at the income tax rates applicable to the shareholders or bondholders.

3. The issues concerning treatment of tax preferences and tax-exempt shareholders apply also to integration for both dividends and retained earnings. Making tax-exempt shareholders eligible for in-

tegration under this proposal, even under the exact method, would involve a revenue loss of about $10 billion; and the cost would be prohibitively large under the 48-percent method.

4. *Treatment of corporate losses.* — Treating corporations like partnerships would imply allowing shareholders to deduct the corporation's losses on their individual income tax returns. However, unless all corporate tax preferences were repealed, this would create possibilities for tax shelters similar to those that have been used in recent years through the use of limited partnerships. One solution might be to not allow shareholders to deduct these losses but rather to allow corporations to carry them forward for (say) ten years. There could be no net operating loss of capital loss carrybacks under integration for both dividends and retained earnings, because they would require a shareholder's recomputing his individual tax each time one of the corporations whose stock he owned used such a carryback.

5. *Redeterminations of tax.* — When there is a redetermination either of corporate earnings or of tax liability as a result of an amended return or an audit, the adjustment would be made for the year in which the redetermination occurs, not for the taxable year for which the redetermination is made. This rule also would be necessary to prevent cumbersome recomputations of tax for prior years by shareholders.

6. *Basis adjustment.* — Shareholders who have included corporate retained earnings in income would be permitted to adjust the cost or other basis of their stock upward by the amount of those retained earnings. This basis adjustment is needed to prevent double taxation — once as the earnings are reported and again as a capital gain. The basis adjustment would be the main complexity for the shareholders that would result from integration for retained earnings.

7. There could be objections to integration for retained earnings by taxpayers in higher tax brackets. Some shareholders would be subject to a tax on retained earnings in excess of the amount withheld by the corporation. Because integration would probably cause a significant increase in dividend payout, this may not be a significant problem except in the case of corporations with very low effective tax rates which retain a large fraction of their earnings. The problem could be alleviated by any reduction in high individual tax brackets that could accompany a broadening of the individual tax base.

8. *Revenue effect.* — The revenue effect of integration for both dividends and retained earnings would vary widely depending on whether the exact method or the 48-percent method is used, whether shareholders would be allowed to deduct corporate losses on their own tax returns, and whether tax-exempt shareholders would be made eligible for integration.

(a) At one extreme, an integration plan which excluded tax-exempt shareholders, used the exact method and did not allow shareholders to deduct corporate losses would increase revenues by about $8–$9 billion at 1976 income levels (taking into account the effect of the basis adjustment in reducing future capital gains taxes). The reason for this revenue gain is that integration for retained earnings involves taxing such income at shareholder's tax rates (which would average about 48 percent for individual shareholders once grossed up corporate-source income is included in taxable income) rather than the 25-percent effective U.S. corporate tax rate on worldwide book income. The revenue gain from integration for retained earnings under this approach would be more than enough to offset the revenue loss from eliminating the double taxation of dividends. An integration proposal that gains revenue would not encourage business investment, although it would have beneficial effects on corporate financial structures and the allocation of capital.

(b) It is possible to design an integration proposal for both dividends and retained earnings with approximately the same revenue effect as the proposal for integration for just dividends discussed above. For example, there could be integration for both dividends and retained earnings and a cut in the top bracket individual income tax rate to 50 percent, and corporations could be allowed to use accelerated depreciation on equipment in computing book income. This would involve a revenue loss of about $5 billion.

DIVIDEND DEDUCTION

1. The administratively easiest way to eliminate the double tax on dividends is to allow corporations to deduct dividends paid in computing the corporate income tax. This method requires no change at all in the individual income tax. A result similar to a deduction for a portion of dividends paid would be achieved by applying a higher tax rate to retained earnings (the "split-rate" approach).

2. The dividend deduction would have similar effects on capital accumulation as the withholding approach applied to dividends if the two were designed to have the same revenue effect. Possibly, corporate managers would consider a dividend deduction under the corporate tax to be a stronger stimulus than the same tax reduction on dividends for the shareholder, but there are unlikely to be significant differences.

3. There are, however, several disadvantages to the dividend deduction relative to the withholding method. It would automatically give tax-exempt and foreign shareholders the benefits of integration, which increases the revenue loss. Also, the dividend deduction is taken at the corporation's marginal tax rate (generally 48 percent), while the withholding approach outlined above gives shareholders

credit only for the lower average effective tax rate paid by corporations. This feature also increases the revenue loss from the dividend deduction. Under a dividend deduction, retained earnings would become the most expensive source of funds and new stock issues the cheapest.

4. The intercorporate dividends received deduction would be eliminated if there were a dividend deduction, since the paying corporation would already have received a deduction for the dividend.

5. A dividend deduction for all dividends, along with repeal of the dividend exclusion, would lose about $15 billion. This revenue loss could be offset by repeal of other corporate tax incentives. The principal such incentives, in terms of revenue involved, and the revenue gain from repealing them for corporations are the investment credit ($8.6 billion), ADR ($1.6 billion), the surtax exemption ($4.7 billion), percentage depletion ($1.0 billion) and DISC ($1.0 billion).

EXAMPLES OF INTEGRATION PROPOSALS

Consider a corporation with $300 of book income. Under existing law, assume its corporate tax liability is $100. Further assume that it now pays $150 in dividends out of its $200 in after-tax income and retains $50. If the shareholders are in the 40-percent bracket, they pay $60 in tax on their dividend, so that the total tax burden — corporate plus individual — is $160. If the retained earnings lead to an equivalent increase in stock prices, there will be a capital gains tax in the future of $10, assuming the gain is long-term. Examples of the three general approaches to integration are displayed in [Table 1-2].

INTEGRATION FOR DIVIDENDS — WITHHOLDING APPROACH

Assume that the corporation continues to pay a $150 dividend. Since this is three-fourths of after-tax income, the corporate tax attributable to the dividend would be $75 out of the $100 in overall corporate tax liability. The shareholders would report income of $225 (the $150 dividend "grossed up" by the $75 in corporate tax attributable to the dividend). The individual tax on this amount at a 40-percent rate is $90. The shareholders would claim a tax credit of $75 for the corporate tax attributable to the dividends, so that their net individual tax would be $15. The total tax burden would be $115 ($100 corporate tax plus $15 individual tax), a reduction of $45 from existing law.

Assume now that, in response to the elimination of the double tax on dividends, the corporation raises its dividend from $150 to $180, so that retained earnings fall to $20. Now, the corporate tax

Table 1-2
Examples of Integration Proposals[5]

Corporation	Present law	Integration for dividends — withholding approach (a)	(b)[1]	Integration for dividends and retained earnings	Dividend deduction (a)	(b)[1]
Pretax income	$300	$300	$300	$300	$300	$300.0
Corporate tax[2]	100	100	100	100	28	13.6
After-tax income	200	200	200	200	272	286.4
Dividends	150	150	180	150	150	180.0
Retained earnings	50	50	20	50	122	106.4
Shareholder						
Dividend	150	150	180.	—	150	180.0
Gross-up[4]	—	75	90	—	—	—
Increase in taxable income	150	225	270	300	150	180.0
Individual tax[3]	60	90	108	120	60	72.0
Shareholder credit	—	75	90	100	—	—
Tax after credit	60	15	18	20	60	72.0
Total tax liability, corporate and individual	160	115	118	120	88	85.6

1. Assumes increase in dividend payment to $180.
2. Assumes average effective rate of 33⅓ percent but marginal rate of 48 percent.
3. Assumes tax rate of 40 percent.
4. The gross-up under the withholding approach for dividends equals the corporate tax times the ratio of dividends to after-tax corporate income.
5. These examples are discussed in the text.

attributable to the dividend is $90. Shareholders would report income of $270 ($180 in dividends grossed up by $90 in corporate tax attributable to the dividends), on which the individual tax is $108. Since they would get a tax credit of $90, the net individual tax would be $18, and the total tax burden would be $118, a tax cut of $42 from present law.

INTEGRATION FOR BOTH DIVIDENDS AND RETAINED EARNINGS

The shareholders would report $300 in income. At their 40-percent bracket, this would involve income tax liability of $120. There would be a tax credit for the $100 of corporate income tax paid, so that their individual tax liability would be $20 (compared to

$60 under existing law). The total tax burden would be $120, so that the overall tax reduction would be $40 relative to present law. Shareholders would increase the basis of their stockholdings by the grossed-up retained earnings, or by $75. This basis adjustment would reduce the future capital gains tax on the stock by $15 for a long-term gain. These results are independent of whether corporations change their dividend payout policies in response to integration.

DIVIDEND DEDUCTION

Assume that the corporation pays a $150 dividend. If its marginal tax bracket is 48 percent (which is consistent with an average effective rate of 33⅓ percent on "book income"), the dividend deduction would reduce its tax from $100 to $28. The individual shareholders would continue to pay $60 of tax on their dividend, so the total tax burden would be $88, a reduction of $72 from present law.

More likely, the corporation would increase its dividend payout. If the dividend increases to $180, the corporate tax would be $13.60 and the individual tax would be $72 for a total tax burden of $85.60, a reduction of $74.40 from present law. . . .

DISTRIBUTIONAL EFFECTS OF BUSINESS TAX CHANGES

1. Most of the alternative investment incentives outlined above involve a cut in the tax on corporate-source income. There is considerable disagreement among the economists on who benefits from such a tax cut. The most common view of the "incidence" of a corporate tax rate cut is as follows:[8]

(a) The immediate beneficiaries of a corporate rate cut are shareholders, who benefit from the higher after-tax earnings of the corporation. To the extent that the additional after-tax profits are paid out as dividends, low-bracket shareholders will derive a larger after-tax benefit per share of stock than shareholders in high individual tax brackets. However, to the extent the additional corporate after-tax profits are retained, in which case the only individual income tax is a capital gains tax upon sale of the stock, there will be a looser link between the benefit per share to individual shareholders and their individual income tax bracket. In either case, the benefits will be highly concentrated, since the one percent of taxpayers with the largest incomes own half of all corporate stock, and the 5 percent with the highest income own two-thirds of all stock. All current share-

---

8. The "incidence" of a tax refers to what persons or sources of income bear the burden of that tax. The analysis of the incidence of a corporate tax rate change presented here also applies to changes in corporate taxes resulting from accelerated depreciation, the investment credit, or more liberal deduction of losses.

holders will benefit to the extent that a lower tax burden on corporate-source income raises stock prices.

(b) These higher after-tax returns in the corporate sector cannot persist for very long, since they will encourage additional investment in those industries. This shift in investment from the noncorporate sector to the corporate sector should reduce before-tax rates of return in the corporate sector and raise them in the noncorporate sector until the after-tax rates of return in the two sectors assume approximately the same relationship they had before the corporate tax reduction. Thus, the benefits of the corporate tax reduction will be partly shifted to owners of wealth other than corporate stock. This shifting makes the tax cut more progressive since wealth in general is more equally distributed than corporate stock: the wealthiest 1 percent of families own about one-fourth of all wealth, compared to one-half of all corporate stock.

(c) The incidence of a corporate tax cut also depends on the extent to which it increases investment. An increase in investment would increase worker productivity and raise wages, thereby passing through some or all of the benefit of the tax cut to workers.

2. The incidence of corporate integration will be more progressive than that of other corporate tax cuts, especially if integration applied to retained earnings as well as dividends. There should be the same general pattern — an immediate benefit to shareholders and an eventual benefit to other wealthholders and to workers; but there are major differences between integration and general corporate tax cuts.

(a) Eliminating the double taxation of dividends confers more benefit per share to shareholders in lower brackets than to those in higher brackets. Because of the gross-up in the withholding approach, the Treasury recovers 70 percent of the shareholder tax credit from a shareholder in the 70-percent bracket and only 14 percent from a shareholder in the 14-percent bracket. Taxpayers with adjusted gross income over $50,000, slightly less than 1 percent of the total, receive 27 percent of the tax cut from eliminating the double tax on dividends, even though this group owns about one-half of corporate stock owned by individuals. (Eliminating the double tax on dividends, thus, has the same distributional effect as a corporate rate cut in which 100 percent of the additional corporate cash flow is paid out as dividends.)

(b) To the extent that eliminating the double tax on dividends causes corporations to increase their dividend payout, its incidence will be more progressive. Without double taxation, dividends would be taxed at the progressive individual tax rates (14 to 70 percent) while, except for the capital gains tax upon sale of the stock, retained earnings are taxed at a flat corporate rate. Thus any tendency by corporations to reduce retained earnings and increase dividends helps low-bracket shareholders and hurts high-bracket shareholders.

(c) Integrating the individual and corporate income taxes for retained earnings is a progressive tax change, since it leads to an actual tax increase for shareholders in individual tax brackets higher than the corporate tax rate and a tax cut for those in lower brackets.

NOTES

1. For the Ford administration's proposal for integrating the corporate and individual taxes, a "model plan," see U.S. Dept. of the Treasury, Blueprints for Basic Tax Reform 4-5, 69-75, 133-134, 194-200 (1977). See also Polito, A Proposal for an Integrated Income Tax, 12 Harv. J.L. & Pub. Poly. 1009 (1989); C. McLure, Jr., Must Corporate Income Be Taxed Twice? (1979); Feldstein, Corporate Tax Integration: The Estimated Effects on Capital Accumulation and Tax Distribution of Two Integration Proposals, in Capital Taxation 156-79 (1983); NTA-TIA Symposium, The Taxation of Income from Corporate Shareholding, 28 Natl. Tax J. No. 3 (Sept. 1975); Klein, Income Taxation and Legal Entities, 2 UCLA L. Rev. 13 (1972).

In Canellos, Corporate Tax Integration: By Design or By Default, Tax Notes, June 8, 1987, p. 999, the author describes various forms of integration including "do-it-yourself" methods. The latter consisted of highly leveraged capital structures and the use of master limited partnerships. The Revenue Act of 1987, however, has made it more difficult to escape the corporation income tax by organizing as a master limited partnership. See §7704.

2. In recent years economists have tried anew to determine whether the corporate income tax and the individual income tax on dividends combine to subject corporate income to a "double tax." They remain in disagreement. *Compare* Poterba and Summers, The Economics Effects of Dividend Taxation in Taxes and Corporate Financial Management 227 (1985) (" 'double taxation' view is most consistent with the . . . evidence"), *with* Auerbach, Wealth Maximization and the Cost of Capital, 93 Q.J. of Econ. 443 (1979), Bradford, The Incidence and Allocation Effects of a Tax on Corporate Distributions, 15 J. Pub. Econ. 1 (1981), and King, Public Policy and the Corporation (1977) (taxes are "capitalized" and "have no impact on a firm's *marginal* incentive to invest"). See also Miller and Scholes, Dividends and Taxes, 6 J. Fin. Econ. 333 (1978); Miller and Scholes, Dividends and Taxes: Some Empirical Evidence, 90 J. Pol. Econ. 1182 (1982) ("dividend-paying firms are not penalized in the marketplace . . . dividend taxes are therefore nondistortionary").

GENERAL REFERENCES

See American Law Institute, Federal Income Tax Project — Subchapter C — Proposals on Corporate Acquisitions and Dispositions and Reporter's Study on Corporate Distributions (1982); American Law Institute — Federal Income Tax Project — Subchapter C (Supplemental Study), Reporter's Study Draft (June 1, 1989); Bryan, Leveraged Buyouts and Tax Policy, 65 N.C. L. Rev. 1039 (1987); Beghe, The American Law Institute Subchapter C Study: Acquisitions and Distributions, 33 Tax Law. 743 (1980); Warren, The Relation and Integration of Individual and Corporate Income Taxes, 94 Harv. L. Rev. 717 (1981). See also Clark, The Morphogenesis of Subchapter C: An Essay in Statutory Evolution and Reform, 87 Yale L.J. 90 (1977).

2

The Shareholder Income Tax—
Corporate Distributions and
Disposition of Investor Interests
(Not in Reorganization)

I. HISTORY—RATE STRUCTURE—
CORRELATION WITH CORPORATION
INCOME TAX

From 1913 to 1954, the personal income tax consisted of two parts,
a "normal" tax and an "additional" tax.

> The personal income tax act of 1913 exempted dividends from
> normal tax. Both the tax rate on corporate income and the normal
> rate on personal income were set at 1 percent; thus, for distributed
> earnings, the corporate tax operated as a withholding feature of
> the personal levy.* This treatment continued through 1918, as
> increases in the personal normal rate were matched by increases
> in the corporate rate. [Author's footnote: "With these exceptions:
> a corporate rate greater than the personal normal rate in 1917,
> and greater than the rate applicable to the first $4000 of normal
> tax income in 1918."] But from 1919 on, the corporate rate ex-
> ceeded the personal normal rate and thus the corporate tax
> became, in part, a separate and distinct levy on distributed cor-
> porate earnings. The rate gap widened gradually until 1936 when
> the bridge between the two taxes was removed completely by the
> abolition of the dividend exemption. A return to something like
> the 1919-36 procedure was instituted by the Internal Revenue
> Code of 1954 in the form of a tax credit based on dividends re-
> ceived. But here, too, a substantial gap exists between the personal
> income tax credit and the rate of corporate tax. Therefore, since
> 1919, the distributed earnings of corporate enterprises have been
> treated differently from the other sources of income for Federal
> income-tax purposes: from 1919 to 1936, because the corporate
> rate was higher than the personal normal rate; from 1936 through

*The personal income tax consisted of both a "normal" and an "additional" tax from
1913 to 1954. Dividends were not exempted from the additional tax. — Ed.

1953, because corporate earnings were taxed at the corporate level when earned with no allowance at the personal level when distributed; and from 1954 on, because the personal income-tax relief accorded distributed earnings falls short of the corporate tax rate.*

Although there has been congressional vacillation over the years as to the extent to which corporate earnings are to be subjected to both a corporate and an individual tax, Congress has imposed a "double tax" on distributed earnings since 1913. For many years, however, under the now-repealed §116 the double tax was mitigated to a very limited extent, as shareholders were permitted to exclude $100 of dividends ($200 on a joint return) from gross income.

The taxation of dividends is not dependent alone on the statutory word *income*. The Code is explicit in providing that "dividends" are includable in a taxpayer's gross income. See §§61(a)(7) and 301(c)(1). As defined in §316(a), a "dividend" for income tax purposes is "any distribution of property made by a corporation to its shareholders (1) out of its earnings and profits accumulated after February 28, 1913, or (2) out of its earnings and profits" of the current taxable year. A distribution that does not constitute a "dividend" is treated as a tax-free return of capital to the extent of the taxpayer's stock basis (§301(c)(2)), but to the extent that the distribution exceeds the taxpayer's basis, the excess is treated as "gain from the sale or exchange of" the stock (§301(c)(3)(A)). Usually, but not always, the taxable gain is a capital gain, long-term if the stock has been held for the requisite holding period.

The Tax Reform Act of 1986, however, repealed the 60 percent deduction for long-term capital gains. As a result, capital gains are now subject to the same tax rates as ordinary income. This repeal of the capital gains preference has a profound and pervasive impact on the taxation of shareholders. It substantially lowers the financial stake in many of the issues that the essentially unchanged structure of Subchapter C continues to pose. Yet despite the reduced dollar significance to a number of the statutory questions, the issues themselves remain.

Although the law no longer provides a deduction for long-term capital gains, it has not abolished the category of *capital gains and capital losses*. It preserves the capital gain/ordinary income dichotomy, and it continues to limit the deductibility of capital losses. Capital losses are allowed in full against capital gains, but only to the extent of $3,000 against ordinary income. Therefore, even though a capital gain will be subject to tax at the same rate as ordinary income, capital losses will have an offset value against capital gains that will often be far greater than their offset value against ordinary income. The un-

*D. Holland, Differential Taxation and Tax Relief, 3 Tax Revision Compendium 1551, 1552 (House Ways and Means Comm. 1959).

limited carryover for unused capital losses remains in the law.

The concept of "earnings and profits," the first subject in this chapter, is quite important. In many respects it is similar to, and sometimes — but only sometimes — identical with, "earned surplus" or "retained earnings" as those terms are used in financial accounting. A case in which the earned surplus figure on a corporation's balance sheet may not reflect the accumulated earnings and profits occurs when the corporation has distributed a dividend in its own stock, thereby capitalizing all or part of its earned surplus. Despite the reduction in earned surplus, there is no reduction in the corporation's earnings and profits, since no corporate assets have been distributed.

Section 312 describes the impact on earnings and profits that results from various corporate transactions, but the Code itself does not define the term *earnings and profits*. The process of definition has been left to a common-law type of judicial development and, in part, to the Treasury. See Treas. Reg. §1.312-6. It is important to recognize that the concept of a corporation's earnings and profits is not relevant to the corporation's income tax liability. Its relevance is in determining whether a corporate distribution constitutes dividend income to the shareholders within the definition of "dividend" in §316(a).

The statute did not always limit taxation to earnings and profits accumulated after March 1, 1913. See Lynch v. Hornby, 247 U.S. 339, 344 (1918), in which the Supreme Court said:

> Dividends are the appropriate fruit of stock ownership, are commonly reckoned as income, and are expended as such by the stockholder without regard to whether they are declared from the most recent earnings, or from a surplus accumulated from the earnings of the past, or are based upon the increased value of the property of the corporation. The stockholder is, in the ordinary case, a different entity from the corporation, and Congress was at liberty to treat the dividends as coming to him as extra, and as constituting a part of his income when they came to hand.
>
> Hence we construe the provisions of the Act that "the net income of a taxable person, shall include gains, profits, and income derived from . . . interest, rent, dividends, . . . or gains or profits and income derived from any source whatever" as including . . . all dividends declared and paid in the ordinary course of business by a corporation to its stockholders after the taking effect of the Act (March 1, 1913), whether from current earnings, or from the accumulated surplus made up of past earnings or increase in value of corporate assets, notwithstanding it accrued to the corporation in whole or in part prior to March 1, 1913.

Before the *Hornby* decision came down Congress amended the statute prospectively to define "the term 'dividends' . . . [as] any distribution made or ordered to be made by a corporation . . . out of its earnings or profits accrued since March first, nineteen hundred and thirteen." In 1936 the law was amended again, this time to broaden the source for dividends to include current earnings even if there are no accumulated earnings and profits (i.e., the "nimble dividend").

Prior to the 1986 Act, the lack of adequate earnings and profits to cover a distribution meant that the taxpayer would be able to recover stock basis tax-free and would very likely have capital gain on the amount of distribution in excess of basis. With the repeal of the long-term capital gains preference, however, amounts received in excess of basis no longer enjoy favored status. Because the only issue now is the taxability or not of the stock basis, this considerably reduces the importance of the concept of earnings and profits. Moreover, when stock basis is low, it is unlikely that it will be worthwhile for taxpayers to incur the cost of determining the corporation's earnings and profits account. Of course, stock received from a decedent's estate, with a basis determined under §1014, is likely to be relatively high.

Later in this chapter we address corporate distributions made to shareholders in redemption of all or part of their stock. In the past, the main issue was whether a particular redemption distribution would be treated as a dividend. In that event, typically, the entire amount distributed would be ordinary income. If not characterized as a dividend, the distribution would be treated as one made "in exchange" for the stock. In the latter case the stockholder would usually enjoy tax-free recovery of the stock basis and capital gain as to the excess. Here, too, the 1986 Act reduced the stakes. The question now is limited to whether there is to be tax-free basis recovery, because all taxable amounts — capital gain or dividend — are subject to the same rate.

This chapter also addresses §1244 of the Code. Under certain circumstances, §1244 provides that shareholders of "small business corporations" recognize ordinary loss rather than capital loss on the sale or exchange of their stock, removing the §1211 limitation on deductibility.

The chapter concludes with "collapsible corporations" and §341, a provision of extraordinary intricacy. Although the 1986 Code preserves §341, it minimizes its role. When applicable, §341(a) taxes gain on stock transactions as though it were ordinary income. This was a significant penalty when tax rates on ordinary income were considerably higher than those on long-term capital gains, but with the elimination of the capital gains preference the sting of §341 is much less. Moreover, because of the repeal of *General Utilities,* the reach of §341 is limited. The main continuing significance to collapsibility is that income made ordinary by §341(a) will not provide the same valuable offset for capital losses as capital gains will. As you will see when we reach the subject, however, §341(f) may provide a way to avoid even that limitation.

Finally, no discussion of the 1986 Act's effect on capital gains is complete without your speculating whether Congress will see fit to reinstate the preferential rate in the near future. The Conference Committee Report provides:

> The current statutory structure for capital gains is retained in the Code to facilitate reinstatement of a capital gains rate differential if there is a future tax increase.

H.R. Rep. No. 841, 99th Cong., 2d Sess., pt. 2, at 106 (1986).

II.   CORPORATE DISTRIBUTIONS OF PROPERTY (INCLUDING CASH)

A.   DISTRIBUTIONS

1.   Earnings and Profits — §312

a.   Relevance and Computation

BANGOR & AROOSTOOK R.R. v. COMMISSIONER
193 F.2d 827 (1st Cir. 1951), *cert. denied*, 343 U.S. 934 (1952)

Before Magruder, Chief Judge, and Woodbury and Hartigan, Circuit Judges.

MAGRUDER, Chief Judge. Bangor and Aroostook Railroad Company petitions for review of a decision of the Tax Court of the United States determining that there is a deficiency in petitioner's excess profits tax in the sum of $3,677.45 for the calendar year 1943.

The applicable statute is the Excess Profits Act of 1940 . . . ; Internal Revenue Code §710 et seq. . . . Speaking generally, the "excess profits credit" is the statutory measure of normal profits exempt from the excess profits tax; the credit is deducted from the "excess profits net income" to obtain the "adjusted excess profits net income" upon which the tax is laid. The excess profits credit could be computed in either of two ways, by the average earnings method, I.R.C. §713, or by the invested capital method, I.R.C. §714. Petitioner elected the latter method, under which eight percent of its "invested capital" became its excess profits credit. One component entering into the calculation of the "invested capital" was the "accumulated earnings and profits as of the beginning of such taxable year" I.R.C. §718(a)(4).

In 1942 petitioner purchased in the open market for retirement and cancellation certain of its bonds of an aggregate par value of $634,000. The total purchase price was $497,553.30; and the difference between these two sums, or $136,446.70, is referred to hereinafter as petitioner's "bond profit" for the calendar year 1942. It is undisputed that this bond profit was realized income within the general definition of I.R.C. §22(a).*... United States v. Kirby Lumber Co., 1931, 284 U.S. 1.... Petitioner would have been taxable upon the whole amount of the bond profit in 1942, except for the fact that it elected to take advantage of the option provided under I.R.C. §[108] and §[1017] and thus was permitted to exclude the bond profit from the computation of its normal tax net income and surtax net income in its return for 1942.

Notwithstanding this treatment of the bond profit in its 1942 return, petitioner sought to diminish its excess profits tax for the calendar year 1943 by including $136,446.70, or the whole amount of the so-called bond profit, in the item "accumulated earnings and profits" as of January 1, 1943. Such inclusion enhanced the figure for petitioner's "invested capital" and its "excess profits credit," with a resultant reduction in petitioner's excess profits tax for 1943. The Tax Court ruled that the bond profit, not having been "recognized" though "realized" in 1942, should be excluded from "accumulated earnings and profits" as of January 1, 1943. This exclusion produced the deficiency found in the decision now under review.

We think the ruling of the Tax Court was correct....

It is important to observe the distinction between (1) income which is exempt from tax and (2) income which, though "realized" in a constitutional sense and thus within the power of Congress to tax, is not at the outset "recognized," the incidence of the tax being merely postponed.

As to (1), exempt income, such for instance as interest on tax-free bonds, if income of this sort is to be taken into "earnings or profits," the only logical time to do so is when the income is realized. It is so provided by regulation. Section [1.312-6(b)] on the subject of corporate dividends out of "earnings or profits," states that among the items "entering into the computation of corporate earnings or profits for a particular period are all income exempted by statute, income not taxable by the Federal Government under the Constitution, as well as all items includible in gross income under section [61] or corresponding provisions of prior Revenue Acts.... Interest on State bonds and certain other obligations, although not taxable when received by a corporation, is taxable to the same extent as other dividends when distributed to shareholders in the form of dividends."

It is not in express terms provided that tax-exempt income, when realized, is also taken into "accumulated earnings and profits" under

---

*Section 61(a) is the 1986 Code counterpart of §22(a) of the 1939 Code, but §22(a) did not have the equivalent of §61(a)(12). — Ed.

I.R.C. §718(a)(4). That term is not defined in the Code. But §35.718-
2 of Reg. 112 refers back to §[312] of the Code and the regulations
prescribed thereunder, and states that in general "the concept of
'accumulated earnings and profits' for the purpose of the excess
profits tax is the same as for the purpose of the income tax. . . ." . . .
The clear inference from the regulations that truly exempted income
may be carried into "accumulated earnings and profits," is evidently
in accordance with the congressional purpose. . . . If therefore a corporation receives during a given year income which is exempt from
taxation, such as interest on tax-free bonds, and such income is left
in the business to be available as working capital, it is reasonable and
proper that such income, though not taxable to the corporation receiving it, should be included in the item "accumulated earnings and
profits" as of the beginning of the following year, §718(a)(4) of the
Code, in the computation of the corporation's excess profits tax for
that year.

But as to (2), income which, though "realized," is not at the outset
"recognized," the problem is quite different. This concept in perhaps
its most familiar instances appears in [the nonrecognition provisions
of the Code]. The thought behind the nonrecognition provisions . . .
is that, in certain transactions involving "the sale or exchange of
property," though a gain may have been realized in a constitutional
sense, it is unfair or inappropriate to tax the gain at the outset in
view of the fact that in a popular and economic sense there has been
a mere change in the form of ownership and the taxpayer has not
yet really "cashed in" on the more or less theoretical gain. As expressed by the Supreme Court in Commissioner of Internal Revenue
v. Wheeler, 1945, 324 U.S. 542, 546 . . . : "Congress has determined
that in certain types of transaction the economic changes are not
definitive enough to be given tax consequences, and has clearly provided that gains and losses on such transactions shall not be
recognized for income-tax liability but shall be taken account of
later. . . . *It is sensible to carry through the theory in determining the tax
effect of such transactions on earnings and profits.*" [Italics added.]

In Commissioner of Internal Revenue v. F.J. Young Corp., 1939,
103 F.2d 137, the third circuit had held that a gain which resulted
from a tax-free exchange of securities under §[351] of the Revenue
Act of 1928 must be considered "earnings or profits" out of which
a "dividend" might be declared within the meaning of §[316] of the
Act. But the court ignored or overlooked a provision of . . . Reg. 94
. . . [Treas. Reg. §1.312-6(b)] which explicitly stated: "Gains and losses
within the purview of §11001(c)] *or corresponding provisions of prior
Acts* are brought into the earnings and profits at the time and to the
extent such gains and losses are recognized under that section." [Ital-
ics added.] . . . In Commissioner of Internal Revenue v. Wheeler,

1945, 324 U.S. 542 . . . supra, the Supreme Court expressly upheld the regulation as a reasonable and valid exercise of the rule-making power. It follows that Commissioner of Internal Revenue v. F.J. Young Corp., supra, and cases like it, cannot be taken as authorities in support of the position urged by the taxpayer in the case at bar.

Congress itself has indicated approval of the foregoing regulation by writing it expressly into the law. Section [312(f) provides:] "Gain or loss so realized shall increase or decrease the earnings and profits to, but not beyond, the extent to which such a realized gain or loss was recognized in computing net income under the law applicable to the year in which such sale or disposition was made." This evidently was regarded as not a change in existing law but only in the nature of a clarifying amendment. The House committee stated that the provision of [§312(f)] merely enacted the rule which had been applied by the Treasury under existing law. It was pointed out that while taxpayers generally had concurred in the Treasury rule, the Board of Tax Appeals and some court decisions, mentioning specifically Commissioner of Internal Revenue v. F.J. Young Corp., 3 Cir., 103 F.2d 137, had followed the contrary theory "that gain or loss, even though not recognized in computing net income, nevertheless affects earnings and profits." The report further stated: "The purpose of this amendment is to clarify the law with respect to what constitutes earnings and profits of a corporation. This is important not only for the purpose of determining whether distributions are taxable dividends but also in determining equity invested capital for excess-profits-tax purposes." H.R. Rep. No. 2894, 76th Cong., 3d Sess., p. 41.

It is true enough that the result reached here by the Tax Court is not directly commanded by §[312(f)] of the Code, for that subsection by its terms deals with the delayed recognition of gain or loss realized from the "sale or other disposition of property by a corporation," whereas the nonrecognized gain in the present case resulted from the taxpayer's reacquisition of its own bonds. But it does not follow that the underlined principle exemplified by the specific instances covered by the literal language of §[312(f)] should not be applied in other analogous nonrecognition situations. . . .

Congress sought in §[312(f)] to "clarify" the law in particular instances where the law had been muddied by court decisions like Commissioner of Internal Revenue v. F.J. Young Corp., 3 Cir., 1939, 103 F.2d 137. But when §[312(f)] was enacted, there had been no similar court decisions dealing with the effect on earnings and profits of gains from the discharge of indebtedness realized but not at the same time recognized; so that particular problem did not receive the attention of Congress when §[312(f)] was in process of enactment. The Tax Court properly observed in the case at bar: "Surely, by taking pains to make certain that unrecognized gains or losses from sales or other dispositions of property would not be reflected in earnings and profits, Congress could not have intended thereby to produce a different result with respect to other unrecognized gains or losses, merely by failing to mention them."

The underlying principle, of which §[312(f)] is but an illustration, is that "earnings and profits" must be computed on the same basis as that employed in computing income subject to the income tax; in other words, that gains ought to be reflected in earnings and profits at the time they are "recognized" and taken into account for income tax purposes. . . .

. . . The taxpayer having technically realized its so-called bond profit in 1942, elected under an optional method of accounting permitted by the statute to postpone recognition of such gain and to exclude the amount thereof from its gross income reported for 1942. It cannot then shift its method of accounting, and treat that gain as both realized and recognized in 1942, for the purpose of enhancing a deduction (the excess profits credit) used in the computation of its excess profits tax liability for 1943.

The rule in United States v. Kirby Lumber Co., 1931, 284 U.S. 1, . . . has been criticized both on theoretical and practical grounds, and doubtless in many cases it worked a hardship. Congress took account of these criticisms in 1939, when it amended the Internal Revenue Code by adding [§108]. . . .

It appears, then, that when the provision of §[108] for delayed recognition of gain is compared with the . . . delayed recognition situations, the . . . sections stem from a common legislative conviction that it is fairer not to impose the income tax forthwith upon the theoretical gains realized from certain transactions, but to postpone the recognition of the gain, and the incidence of the tax, until the occurrence of an economically more significant event.

. . . The Commissioner, in auditing the taxpayer's 1942 return, reduced the basis of its depreciable property pursuant to the applicable regulations under §[1017]. As a result, the taxpayer's depreciation deduction for 1942 was reduced in the amount of $1,736.69. This adjustment correspondingly increased the taxpayer's taxable income for 1942. Such increased income in the sum of $1,736.69 was therefore added by the Commissioner to the taxpayer's "accumulated earnings and profits" as of January 1, 1943, for the purpose of computing the taxpayer's excess profits credit in determining the excess profits tax for 1943. The Commissioner and the Tax Court agree that, to that extent, the bond profit having been reflected in 1942 income should be reflected also in the item of accumulated earnings and profits as of January 1, 1943. The taxpayer's basis having been reduced, by command of the statute, depreciation to be taken by the taxpayer for income tax purposes in the succeeding years will necessarily be lower, and taxable gains correspondingly higher; and as the bond profit is thus gradually recognized and reflected in income, it will at the same time be reflected in earnings and profits. If and when the taxpayer sells the property the basis of which has thus been reduced, the whole of the bond profit will have been recognized and reflected both in income and in earnings and profits. . . . Such treatment of the bond profit seems to be clearly required by the statute and the applicable regulations. It would necessarily follow that the Tax Court properly rejected the taxpayer's contention that the whole amount of the bond profit should be taken into "accumulated earnings and profits" as of January 1, 1943; for otherwise, the bond profit would be doing double duty in reducing taxpayer's excess profits tax liability for 1943 and subsequent years. . . .

The decision of the Tax Court is affirmed.

NOTES

1. In January 1987, Corporation Y is formed, and it has no earnings for that year. In 1989, Y loses $10,000. In 1990, Y earns $10,000. What is the tax consequence to the shareholders if a dividend is paid at the end of 1989? At the beginning of 1990? See §316(a). Is the difference in result appropriate? Why?

2. X Corporation distributes to its shareholders as a dividend a building with an adjusted basis of $50,000 and a fair market value of $100,000. What impact does that distribution have on the corporation's earnings and profits? Why? What would be the effect on X Corporation's earnings and profits if it gave the building to charity? See Rev. Rul. 78-123, 1978-1 C.B. 87 (reduction limited to property's adjusted basis); see also Antoginini, The Impact on Earnings and Profits of Distributions of Appreciated Property, 14 J. Corp. Taxn. 227 (1987).

3. Corporation M computes its taxable income with the benefit of percentage depletion. Its taxable income for 1990 so computed is $225,000. On a cost depletion basis its taxable income would be $250,000. By what sum (approximately) is the corporation's earnings and profits account increased as a result of the year's operations? See Treas. Reg. §1.312-6; cf. §312(k).

4. Why should tax-deferred income (such as that involved in *Bangor & Aroostook R.R.*) augment the earnings and profits account for purposes of §316(a) only if and as it is recognized? Cf. Treas. Reg. §1.312-6.

5. Suppose Corporation X's only 1990 income is the interest it

receives on its municipal bond holdings. X receives $10,000 in interest and distributes $10,000 to its shareholders. Do the shareholders have dividend income? What is the effect of §103?

6. Corporation X, owning stock in Corporation Y, receives a distribution from Corporation Y which was not taxable as a dividend. What is the impact on Corporation X's earnings and profits? What happens to the basis of the stock Corporation X holds in Corporation Y? See §312(f)(2). Compare Rev. Rul. 76-239, 1976-1 C.B. 90 (under §312(f)(1), gain not recognized under now-repealed §333 does not increase earnings and profits) with Rev. Rul. 76-175, 1976-1 C.B. 92 (pursuant to Treas. Reg. §1.312-7(b)(1), losses disallowed under §267 decrease earnings and profits).

7. Mr. Able buys ten shares of Corporation Z's stock on September 30, 1989. On October 1, 1989, a dividend is declared to all holders. What are the income tax consequences to Able? Why? Ought a shareholder be required to treat a distribution as a dividend if the covering earnings and profits all antedate his stock purchase and if his stock basis exceeds the amount of his distribution? See United States v. Phellis, 257 U.S. 156, 171-172 (1922); Powell, Income from Corporate Dividends, 35 Harv. L. Rev. 363 (1922). Ought distributions by an ongoing corporation be treated as dividends whether or not there are earnings or profits to cover? See Andrews, "Out of Its Earnings and Profits": Some Reflections on the Taxation of Dividends, 69 Harv. L. Rev. 1403 (1956); Colby, Blackburn, and Trier, Elimination of Earnings and Profits From the Internal Revenue Code, 39 Tax Law. 285 (1986). For extensive treatment of the problems of "earnings and profits," see B. Bittker and J. Eustice, Federal Income Taxation of Corporations and Shareholders 7-9 to 7-21 (5th ed. 1987).

8. X, the sole shareholder of Corporation Y, withdraws sums from the Corporation in 1980. The Corporation and X characterize the withdrawals as loans. Thereafter the Commissioner contends successfully that the withdrawals were dividends. In determining whether a 1990 distribution is a dividend, are accumulated earnings and profits reduced by the 1980 withdrawals? Suppose the withdrawals were really dividends, but the Commissioner awakened to the fact after the statute of limitations barred deficiency assessments for the year 1980? See Jacob M. Kaplan, 43 T.C. 580 (1965), *acq. on another issue,* 1978-2 C.B. 2, *nonacq. on another issue,* 1978-2 C.B. 3. See generally Rev. Proc. 75-17, 1975-1 C.B. 677, issued by the Commissioner "to provide stockholders more certainty as to the taxable status of distributions."

9. Does the income from the adjustment of indebtedness in bankruptcy increase earnings and profits to the extent that the adjustment exceeds required reductions in asset basis? See §312(l); S.

Rep. No. 1035, 96th Cong., 2d Sess. 44-45 (1980). For a case decided
before the passage of §312(l), see Meyer v. Commissioner, 383 F.2d
883 (8th Cir. 1967). There, the court distinguished *Bangor and Aroostook R.R.* on the ground that it involved what was concededly realized
income, though unrecognized, while the Bankruptcy Act specifically
provided that the debtor corporation had no income from the debt
cancellation, leading to a "statutorily declared absence of income."
Consequently, earnings and profits were unchanged. Understandably, the IRS refused to follow *Meyer.* See Rev. Rul. 75-515, 1975-2
C.B. 117.

10. In Sid Luckman, 50 T.C. 619 (1968), a corporation had
granted "restricted stock options" under §421 to employees who exercised the options at prices below the market value of the stock. The
Tax Court held that under §§421(a)(2) and (3) there was no deductible expense for the corporation and so no reduction in earnings
and profits. The Seventh Circuit reversed, 418 F.2d 381 (1969).
Which is the more persuasive, the Tax Court or the Seventh Circuit?
The Tax Court has held to its *Luckman* position. See Harold S. Devine,
59 T.C. 152 (1972), *rev'd on this issue,* 500 F.2d 1041 (2d Cir. 1974).

11. Corporation X has outstanding 10,000 shares of $1 par value
common stock. In addition to X's stated capital of $10,000, it has
$70,000 of paid-in capital. X's accumulated earnings and profits were
$800,000 immediately before it redeemed 1,700 shares of common
stock for $510,000. What effect will the redemption have on earnings
and profits? See §312(n)(8) and Rev. Rul. 70-531, 1970-2 C.B. 76.

12. The IRS will not issue an advance ruling as to the amount
of a corporation's earnings and profits. See Rev. Proc. 80-22, 1980-
1 C.B. 654. For illustrative earnings and profits computations, see
Rev. Rul. 74-164, 1974-1 C.B. 74.

JOSEPH B. FERGUSON v. COMMISSIONER
47 T.C. 11 (1966), *acq.,* 1970-2 C.B. xix

Hoyt, Judge. [The taxpayer was the sole shareholder in a corporation called "444," which was on the cash basis. In 1959 it
expended $75,000 which the Commissioner characterized as a "con-
structive dividend" to the taxpayer. As of the beginning of 1959, 444
had a deficit in its earnings and profits account. Its current earnings
in 1959 were sufficient to cover the "constructive dividend" unless,
as taxpayer contended, the current earnings and profits account were
to be charged with 444's income tax liability for 1959. The Commissioner contended that the corporate tax liability was an improper
charge because the cash basis taxpayer had not paid the tax during
the year 1959.]

This [case] brings us face-to-face with one of the classic unre-solved problems in the area of earnings and profits: Are current year's earnings and profits of a cash basis corporation reduced by Federal income tax on current year's income although such tax is not paid until the following year (or years)? The regulations under section 312, I.R.C. 1954, provide (in sec. 1.312-6):

> (a) In determining the amount of earnings and profits (whether of the taxable year, or accumulated since February 28, 1913, or accumulated before March 1, 1913) due consideration must be given to the facts, and, while mere bookkeeping entries increasing or decreasing surplus will not be conclusive, the amount of the earnings and profits in any case will be dependent upon the method of accounting properly employed in computing taxable income (or net income, as the case may be). For instance, a cor-poration keeping its books and filing its income tax returns under subchapter E, chapter 1 of the Code, on the cash receipts and disbursements basis may not use the accrual basis in determining earnings and profits; . . .

Despite the unambiguous language of this regulation, the courts have had considerable difficulty coping with the effect of Federal income taxes on the earnings and profits of a cash basis corporation.[3] Leading text writers have noted the split of authority which exists in the cases today. Bittker, Federal Income Taxation of Corporations and Shareholders 145, fn. 9; Surrey and Warren, Federal Income Taxation 1238 (1960). This Court has played an integral role in the turbulent history of this problem, a history which must be reviewed and understood in order to adequately analyze and decide the issue in this particular case.

This question was first decided in Hadden v. Commissioner, 49 F.2d 709 (C.A. 2, 1931), in which it was held that earnings and profits of a cash basis corporation *are* reduced by income tax on current year's income. Our first encounter with the problem arose in M.H. Alworth Trust, 46 B.T.A. 1045 (1942), revd. 136 F.2d 812 (C.A. 8, 1943), certiorari denied 320 U.S. 784, in which we held that earnings and profits *are* reduced. We relied on the *Hadden* case but did not discuss it. Our decision was based upon corporate law and accounting concepts of dividends and impairment of capital. We reasoned that earnings and profits must take into account "outstanding liabilities" or else a distribution would leave such liabilities "as a charge on capital, regardless of the method by which the corporation keeps its

3. Although no one ever seems to have questioned the regulation insofar as it prohibits the reduction of earnings and profits of a cash basis corporation by accrued expenses *other than Federal income taxes* (and penalties related thereto).

books and to the extent thereof the distribution would impair capital and would not be a dividend." (46 B.T.A. at 1048). The language used was broad enough to cover all accrued liabilities—not just income taxes.

The decision in *Alworth* was reviewed by the Eighth Circuit, Helvering v. Alworth Trust, 136 F.2d 812 (C.A. 8, 1943), which rejected our reliance on corporate and accounting principles. The Court of Appeals pointed out that the *Hadden* case suffered from a marked lack of reasoning to support its result and that the tax rules prescribed by the internal revenue laws regarding dividends do not necessarily conform to standard corporate law concepts; that a distribution may be taxable as a dividend under the tax law even though the corporation making the distribution may have been barred by local corporate statutes (by reason of capital impairment, etc.) from distributing earnings. It was held that it would be an unwarranted extension of the tax statute to require that earnings and profits must be reduced by Federal taxes for the current year of a cash basis corporation.

This Court has followed the rule of the Eighth Circuit in *Alworth* in subsequent cases in which we have considered the issue. Paulina duPont Dean, 9 T.C. 256 (1947), acq. 1947-2 C.B. 2, appeal dismissed nolle prosequi (C.A. 3, 1949); United Mercantile Agencies, Inc., 23 T.C. 1105 (1955). Our opinion in United Mercantile Agencies, Inc., supra, was reversed by the Sixth Circuit sub nom. Drybrough v. Commissioner, 238 F.2d 735 (C.A. 6, 1956), and the *Drybrough* case has become established as the leading case taking what is generally regarded as the polar position to *Alworth*. The reversal of our opinion in *United Mercantile* by *Drybrough* has been followed in Thompson v. United States, 214 F. Supp. 97 (N.D. Ohio 1962); and Demmon v. United States, 321 F.2d 203 (C.A. 7, 1963).

There can be no quarrel with the fact that current year's earnings and profits are not necessarily synonymous with current year's taxable income. For example, interest received on tax-exempt bonds is not included in taxable income, yet must be included in earnings and profits, sec. 1.312-6(b), Income Tax Regs.; the reduction of earnings and profits for depletion is limited to depletion computed on the cost method even though the deduction from taxable income may be based on the more liberal percentage method. Ibid. sec. 1.312-6(c)(1). This absence of synonymity between earnings and profits and taxable income has been emphasized by the cases which adhere to the *Drybrough* view. Thus, one of the principal arguments raised has been: Since earnings and profits are determined for another purpose and are not necessarily the same as taxable income, there is no good reason why a strict cash basis must be adhered to for earnings and profits purposes even though the cash basis is used in accounting for taxable income.

This position is correct only in that there is no statute or inescapable rule of logic which *requires* strict adherence to the cash basis for earnings and profits purposes. However, there *is* a long-standing regulation which establishes such a requirement, sec. 1.312-6(a), Income Tax Regs.; such a regulation has a sound basis in administrative policy and there are no persuasive reasons why any departure from the cash basis used for reporting income *should be* permitted for purposes of computing earnings and profits and why the Commissioner's regulations should be ignored.

The rationale which appears to underlie *Drybrough* and its progeny is traceable all the way back to the Board of Tax Appeal's opinion in *Alworth* which was subsequently reversed in the Eighth Circuit. On page 739 of 238 F.2d the court in *Drybrough* expressly states that it is persuaded by the reasoning of the Board in *Alworth*. After being reversed in *Alworth* this Court has consistently followed the reversal, and we see no reason why we should not adhere to the same view here. The quoted regulations have been in existence for many years and should be upheld.

We hold that the current earnings and profits of 444, a cash basis taxpayer, for the year 1959 are not to be reduced by any unpaid 1959 Federal income tax liability of 444. Helvering v. Alworth Trust, supra; Paulina duPont Dean, supra. Sec. 1.312-6(a), Income Tax Regs. Hence, the petitioner is chargeable with constructive dividend income. . . .

NOTES

1. The Tax Court has amplified and reaffirmed its position in Joseph B. Ferguson. See William C. Webb, 69 T.C. 1008 (1977).

2. A corporation incurs fraud penalties that are disallowed as deductions for income tax purposes on "public policy" grounds. Do the penalties, when accrued or paid, reduce earnings and profits? See Estate of Stein, 25 T.C. 940, 965-967 (1956), *acq. on this issue,* 1957-2 C.B. 7, *aff'd per curiam on another issue sub nom.* Levine v. Commissioner, 250 F.2d 798 (2d Cir. 1958); Rev. Rul. 57-332, 1957-2 C.B. 231. *Compare* §964(a) *with* Rev. Rul. 77-442, 1977-2 C.B. 264.

3. An accrual method taxpayer properly elects to defer payments received in the current taxable year for services to be performed in the succeeding taxable year. Does this give rise to current earnings and profits? See Rev. Rul. 79-68, 1979-1 C.B. 133.

4. Corporation Y, a 75-percent subsidiary of Corporation X, pays Corporation X a $1,000 dividend. As a result of §243 Corporation X's taxable income is increased by $200. What is the effect on Corporation X's earnings and profits? Are more facts needed? See R. M. Weyerhaeuser, 33 B.T.A. 594, 597 (1935); cf. Zarky and Biblin,

The Role of Earnings and Profits in the Tax Law, 1966 S. Calif. Tax
Inst. 145, 154.

b. Effect of "Inadequacy"

TRUESDELL v. COMMISSIONER
89 T.C. 1280 (1987)

NIMS, Judge. . . . Respondent issued a statutory notice of deficiency . . . for the taxable year[s] 1977 . . . 1978 and 1979. . . .

After concessions, the issues for decision are: (1) whether petitioner failed to report $22,231.86 in taxable income for the taxable
year 1977; (2) whether petitioner . . . failed to report $46,083.48 and
$45,659.71 in taxable income for the taxable years 1978 and 1979,
respectively; and (3) whether the resulting deficiencies are due to
fraud.

FINDINGS OF FACT

. . . During the taxable years 1977 and 1978, petitioner was the
president and sole shareholder of Asphalt Patch Company, Inc.
(hereinafter referred to as Asphalt Patch).

On January 1, 1979, Jim T. Enterprises, Inc. (hereinafter referred to as Jim T. Enterprises), was incorporated. Petitioner's son,
Robert Truesdell (hereinafter referred to as Robert), was named
president of the corporation. In 1979 Robert was the sole shareholder
of Jim T. Enterprises. Robert was 17 years old in 1979. . . . Petitioner
has conceded that although Robert was the record shareholder of
Jim T. Enterprises, petitioner was actually the sole shareholder of
the corporation.

Asphalt Patch [and Jim. T Enterprises both] engaged in three
lines of business: asphalt bagging, trucking or hauling and installing
asphalt paving. . . . Petitioner directed and controlled the activities
of Asphalt Patch and Jim T. Enterprises. Petitioner and his son were
the only persons authorized to sign corporate checks. Petitioner authorized all corporate bank deposits. Petitioner arranged all the
deliveries of bagged asphalt and supervised the recording and billing
of bagged asphalt sales for both corporations. Checks received in
payment for bagged asphalt sales were placed on petitioner's desk.

Petitioner also managed all the trucking work, keeping all the
records relating to the trucking aspects of the business of the corporations and handling all the billing for trucking work. All checks
received in payment for trucking work were placed on petitioner's

desk. The asphalt bagging business was the primary business of both corporations. Purchasers who contracted for large quantities of bagged asphalt used charge accounts. An order for bagged asphalt was written on an invoice that was later sent as a bill to the customer. Payments received for bagged asphalt were recorded in a ledger book by invoice number, number of bags sold and amount of payment received. Some of the invoices were numbered, and some were not. Customers who purchased bagged asphalt "off the street" would pay cash and take the materials with them. "Off the street" purchases were recorded on unnumbered invoices. Unnumbered invoices were placed on petitioner's desk. Trucking customers placed orders by telephone. Trucking work was not recorded on invoices. Unnumbered bills were sent to trucking customers. Petitioner handled all the billing for trucking work and kept the trucking records himself.

Petitioner had a special book in which he recorded trucking income. It was necessary to keep records of trucking income so that they would be available to the various trucking broker-customers and their bookkeepers. Nevertheless, paperwork relating to trucking work was frequently thrown away.

Paving job inquiries were received by telephone, recorded in a telephone logbook and referred to an estimator. . . . Estimate forms were not numbered. Petitioner personally supervised the paving work. Because paving customers usually paid petitioner upon completion of the job, they usually were not billed. Petitioner frequently threw the contract away after a customer paid for a paving job. . . .

During the years in issue petitioner used corporate funds for personal expenditures or deposited checks made payable to Asphalt Patch or Jim T. Enterprises into his personal checking and savings accounts. During the calendar year 1977 petitioner deposited checks totaling $10,530.78 made payable to Asphalt Patch into his personal checking account at the Brea office of the National Bank of Whittier and deposited checks totaling $1,244.50 made payable to Asphalt Patch into his personal savings account at Crocker National Bank in Covina, California. These checks were drawn in payment for paving and trucking work done by the corporation. During the calendar year 1977 petitioner endorsed and cashed or deposited into a personal account $7,231.63 worth of checks made payable to Asphalt Patch in payment for trucking and paving work performed by the corporation. . . .

[The court's recitation of similar transactions in both 1978 and 1979 has been omitted.]

Petitioner did not report as income on his individual Federal income tax returns for the taxable years 1977, 1978 and 1979 any of the checks issued to Asphalt Patch or Jim T. Enterprises that were cashed or deposited into [his] personal accounts. . . .

ULTIMATE FINDINGS OF FACT

Petitioner controlled the activities of Asphalt Patch and Jim T. Enterprises. Although most of the income from the corporations' sales of bagged asphalt was accurately recorded on the books and reported on the tax returns of the corporations, income from trucking and paving work was not accurately recorded on the books or reported on the tax returns of the corporations for the years in issue. Petitioner kept records of trucking and paving work in such a manner that the corporations' bookkeepers and accountants were unaware of much of the income from trucking and paving.

During the years 1977 and 1978, petitioner diverted to himself $22,231.86 and $46,083.48, respectively, from the income of Asphalt Patch. During the year 1979 petitioner diverted to himself $44,234.71 from income of Jim T. Enterprises. This diverted income was not recorded on the corporations' books or reported on the corporations' income tax returns. Nor was it reported as income on petitioner's income tax returns for the years in issue.

Petitioner also failed to report income from sales of bagged asphalt to "off the street" customers. . . .

OPINION

. . . Respondent takes the position that the entire amounts diverted by petitioner from Asphalt Patch and Jim T. Enterprises during the taxable years 1977 and 1978 are includable in petitioner's income. Petitioner argues that he did not divert any corporate funds to his own use. . . . The evidence does not support this assertion. . . .

Petitioner's most cogent argument, however, is that the funds he diverted constitute constructive dividends to him, and therefore, are taxable as income to him only to the extent of the earnings and profits of the corporations. Under sections 301(c) and 316(a), dividends are taxable to the shareholder as ordinary income to the extent of the earnings and profits of the corporation, and any amount received by the shareholder in excess of earnings and profits is considered as a nontaxable return of capital to the extent of the shareholder's basis in his stock. Any amount received in excess of both the earnings and profits of the corporation and the shareholder's basis in his stock is treated as gain from the sale or exchange of property.

Dividends may be formally declared or they may be constructive. The fact that no dividends are formally declared does not foreclose the finding of a dividend-in-fact. . . . The crucial concept in a finding that there is a constructive dividend is that the corporation has conferred a benefit on the shareholder in order to distribute available earnings and profits without expectation of repayment. Noble v. Commissioner, 368 F.2d at 443. We find that the diverted funds in this case constitute constructive dividends to petitioner.

Respondent himself determined that the earnings and profits of Asphalt Patch were $23,540 and $4,594 in the taxable years 1978 and 1979, respectively, and that the earnings and profits of Jim T. Enterprises were $16,127.69 in the taxable year 1979. Petitioner failed to introduce any evidence that the earnings and profits of either corporation for any of the years in issue were less than the amounts determined by respondent. Accordingly, we find that the earnings and profits of Asphalt Patch were $23,540 and $4,594 in the taxable years 1978 and 1979, respectively, and that the earnings and profits of Jim T. Enterprises were $16,127.69 in the taxable year 1979.

Because neither party introduced evidence as to the earnings and profits of Asphalt Patch for the taxable year 1977, petitioner has failed his burden of proving that there were not sufficient earnings and profits to support the deficiency determined in respondent's notice of deficiency for that year. However, respondent has failed his burden of proving that Asphalt Patch had sufficient earnings and profits to support the increase in deficiency for that year asserted in his amended answers.

Respondent has failed to prove that the earnings and profits of the corporations were sufficient to permit the full amount of the funds diverted by petitioner during the taxable years 1977 and 1978 to be taxed as ordinary income under a constructive dividend theory. Deficiencies in excess of the earnings and profits of the corporations were asserted in respondent's amended answers. Respondent bears the burden of proving the amounts in excess of the deficiencies determined in the notices of deficiency. Rule 142(a). Respondent maintains, nevertheless, that it is unnecessary to characterize the diverted funds as constructive dividends and that therefore the full amount diverted is taxable to petitioner as ordinary income.

Respondent does not attempt to describe the diverted funds as additional salary, illicit bonuses, commissions or anything more than diversions. Instead, respondent argues that any diversions from a corporation by its sole shareholder are taxable to the shareholder as ordinary income.

Respondent relies on Leaf v. Commissioner, 33 T.C. 1093 (1960), *affd. per curiam* 295 F.2d 503 (6th Cir. 1961), in which we held that the taxpayer, who unlawfully had diverted funds from his insolvent corporation with the intention of defrauding creditors, was liable for taxes on the full amount of the diverted funds regardless of the lack of earnings and profits of the corporation. In *Leaf* we based our holding on . . . the predecessor of section 61(a), which defines gross income as "all income from whatever source derived," and on the following language in Rutkin v. United States, 343 U.S. 130, 137 (1952):

> An unlawful gain, as well as a lawful one, constitutes taxable income when its recipient has such control over it that, as a practical matter, he derives readily realizable economic value from it. . . . That occurs when cash, as here, is delivered by its owner to the taxpayer in a manner which allows the recipient freedom to dispose of it at will, even though it may have been obtained by fraud and his freedom to use it may be assailable by someone with a better title to it.
>
> Such gains are taxable in the yearly period during which they are realized. . . .

Leaf and *Rutkin* are distinguishable from the instant case. *Leaf* and *Rutkin* both involved an unlawful receipt of funds by the taxpayer. The taxpayer in *Rutkin* had extorted funds from another individual, and the issue was whether extorted money was taxable to the extortionist. . . .

In *Leaf* corporate funds that should have been available to creditors were fraudulently transferred to the taxpayer in contemplation of bankruptcy. We need not and do not express an opinion on the need to apply a constructive dividend analysis in a situation where the shareholder utilized the corporation to steal from, embezzle from, or otherwise defraud other stockholders or third parties dealing with the corporation or shareholder. The taxpayer in *Leaf* had argued that the diverted funds were loans and therefore not taxable as income to him. We refused to adopt the taxpayer's characterization in the absence of any evidence of an intention to make repayment at the time of the taking. The issue in *Leaf* was whether the taxpayer's obligation to repay the diverted funds and his actual restitution of some of those funds in a later year precluded his liability for tax on their receipt. We held that the taxpayer had such control over the funds that they represented taxable income to him for the year in which they were taken. Although the taxpayer in *Leaf* was the sole shareholder of the corporation, he did not argue that the diverted funds constituted constructive dividends, and therefore, this issue was not before the Court. . . .

In this case petitioner's diversions of income from Asphalt Patch and Jim T. Enterprises were not per se unlawful. The diverted funds were not, at least on their face, stolen, embezzled or diverted in fraud of creditors. There has been no suggestion that the diversions were improper as a matter of corporate law. They are most appropriately described as distributions made by the corporations to their sole shareholder. DiZenzo v. Commissioner, 348 F.2d 122 (2d Cir. 1965), revg. T.C. Memo. 1964-121; Simon v. Commissioner, 248 F.2d 869 (8th Cir. 1957), revg. a Memorandum Opinion of this Court. . . .

Respondent relies on Davis v. United States, 226 F.2d 331 (6th Cir. 1955), and Weir v. Commissioner, 283 F.2d 675, 684 (6th Cir. 1960), revg. a Memorandum Opinion of this Court, in which the Sixth Circuit held that it is not necessary to classify a sole shareholder's diversions of corporate income as constructive dividends. The Sixth Circuit reasoned in both cases that the taxpayer's dominion and control over the diverted funds warranted taxation of the diverted funds as ordinary income.

We respectfully disagree with the the analysis of the Sixth Circuit. As a general proposition, where a taxpayer has dominion and control over diverted funds, they are includable in his gross income under section 61(a), Commissioner v. Glenshaw Glass Co., 348 U.S. 426, 431 (1955), unless some other modifying Code section applies. The latter is the situation here since Congress has provided that funds (or other property) distributed by a corporation to its shareholders over which the shareholders have dominion and control are to be taxed under the provisions of section 301(c). . . .

Respondent relies on United States v. Miller, 545 F.2d 1204 (9th Cir. 1976), in which the Ninth Circuit refused, in a criminal proceeding, to apply the constructive distribution rules automatically to shareholder diversions of corporate funds. . . . The Ninth Circuit ultimately agreed with the trial court's holding that the diversions in question constituted salary to the defendant. Respondent does not claim nor has he introduced evidence that the diversions were in the nature of salary to the petitioner. In concluding our discussion of the constructive dividend issue, we would emphasize that in a case such as this diverted amounts taxed to a shareholder as constructive dividends also remain fully taxable to the corporation to which attributable. The record indicates that the corporations in question did not report the diverted funds. But respondent's agents became well aware of the existence of Asphalt Patch and Jim T. Enterprises, and the fact that taxable income had been diverted from them, during the examination of petitioner's tax affairs. We know of nothing which would have prevented a parallel examination of the corporate tax affairs and a determination of the correct taxable income reportable by the corporations.

For the foregoing reasons, we hold that the amounts diverted by petitioner from his corporations constitute constructive dividends and are taxable to him under the provisions of section 301(c). . . . To the extent that this Court's decision in Benes v. Commissioner, 42 T.C. 358 (1964), aff'd 355 F.2d 929 (6th Cir. 1966), reaches a contrary result, it will no longer be followed. . . .

Reviewed by the Court.

NOTE

Corporation M, an accrual basis taxpayer, has an accumulated and a current deficit in earnings and profits. Its sales manager, who owns 10 percent of the corporation's stock, pockets a customer's $10,000 cash payment for previously billed merchandise. The payment does not go through the corporation's bank account or books, and no other shareholder or corporate officer knows of the payment. Does the sales manager have $10,000 in ordinary income? What is the impact of James v. United States, 366 U.S. 213 (1961), in this context? Would the result be different if the sales manager's wife owned 90 percent of the stock? Would the result be different if the sales manager (with no wife) owned 50 percent of the stock? Ninety percent of the stock?

2.   *Constructive Dividends — §316*

a.   Dividend vs. Loan

ALTERMAN FOODS, INC. v. UNITED STATES
611 F.2d 866 (Ct. Cl. 1979)

Before Kashiwa, Kunzig and Bennet, Judges.
PER CURIAM. This case comes before the court on plaintiff's exceptions. . . .
Upon consideration of the trial judge's decision, the briefs and oral argument of counsel, and [the court's conclusion that sufficient earnings and profits were available to constitute constructive dividends] the court hereby affirms and adopts the decision as the basis for its judgment in this case. Accordingly, as set forth in the following conclusion of law, plaintiff's petition is dismissed.

OPINION OF TRIAL JUDGE

SCHWARTZ, Trial Judge. This is a suit for refund of income taxes. The question, familiar in the law of tax liabilities of stockholders in controlled corporations, is whether advances by corporate subsidiaries to their sole stockholder, the plaintiff-taxpayer, were loans to the taxpayer, as alleged by it, or constructive dividends and thus taxable income, as maintained by the Commissioner.
In 1966-74, plaintiff Alterman Foods, Inc., owned all the stock of some 57 subsidiaries engaged in the operation of a chain of retail grocery supermarkets in the Atlanta area. . . .

Each subsidiary signed a management agreement, under which the plaintiff sold to it, at cost, merchandise, fixtures, remodeling and construction and insurance. All other needed services — warehousing, advertising management and supervision, legal, accounting and office services and supplies, as well as licenses for the use of store and product tradenames — were provided for a fee of 2½ percent of gross sales. In addition, and this provision is the source of the present case, the subsidiaries were required to advance to the plaintiff their gross receipts, from which the plaintiff would pay itself the amounts due for merchandise, repairs and the other services provided.

Accounts of the advances and expenditures were kept by both parent and subsidiary. The balances fluctuated on a periodic and annual basis as advances were received by the parent and expenditures made by it and debited against the advances. The net advances, i.e., the excess of advances by the subsidiary over expenditures by plaintiff on behalf of the subsidiary, were in plaintiff's financial and tax returns treated as accounts payable, under liabilities, and in the books of the subsidiary as accounts receivable, under assets.

Not all subsidiaries in all the tax years added to their net advances. Advances might decline as against expenditures by the parent, resulting in a decrease in the year-end balance of net advances or even a reversal from a balance of net advances to one in which plaintiff's expenditures on behalf of the subsidiary exceeded the advances. This occurred in years in which a subsidiary was operating an unprofitable market, in years in which plaintiff made substantial capital expenditures for remodeling of a market, or in years of both such characteristics.

Nevertheless, the aggregate of net advances from all subsidiaries grew as the years continued to be profitable in the overall. . . .

In computing the amounts of advances to be taxed as dividends, the Commissioner . . . treated each subsidiary as a separate entity and, generally speaking, assessed deficiencies to the extent of the increase in a tax year of the net advances by a subsidiary to the plaintiff. He did not, however, assess a deficiency in cases of advances in a year which merely reduced the prior year's excess of expenditures over advances. He treated as a constructive dividend only an increase from a beginning annual balance of net advances to a greater year-end such balance. And where the beginning balance showed an excess of expenditures over advances, the Commissioner treated as a constructive dividend only the increase from a zero balance to the year-end balance of net advances. The annual increases in net advances thus treated by the Commissioner as constructive dividends was $9.4 million.

The same case was presented as is here presented and the same contentions were made in plaintiff's suit for a refund with respect to the tax year 1965, the year immediately preceding the years now in suit. In that case, the Court of Appeals for the Fifth Circuit affirmed the action of the district court in setting aside a verdict for the plaintiff and entering judgment for the Government. Alterman Foods, Inc. v. United States, 505 F.2d 873 (5th Cir. 1974). . . . The decision by the Fifth Circuit is both persuasive and confirmatory of the decision made on the record here.

The inquiry whether corporate funds have passed to a shareholder as bona fide loans, creating a creditor-debtor relationship, depends on whether the parties definitely intended that the sums advanced would be repaid. Alterman Foods, Inc. v. United States, supra, 505 F.2d 873, 875-76 (5th Cir. 1974); . . . Clark v. Commissioner, 266 F.2d 698, 710-11 (9th Cir. 1959).

Intent is to be determined on consideration of all the circumstances. These include, the Fifth Circuit noted, the extent to which the shareholder controls the corporation; the earnings and dividend history of the corporation; the magnitude of the advances; and presence or absence of conventional indicia of debt such as the giving of a note or security, a maturity date, a ceiling on the advances and effort and ability to repay or to require repayment. 505 F.2d at 877, n.7.

To these factors might be added the treatment of the advances in corporate financial statements and tax returns; whether interest was charged or paid on the balances; and in some instances, the use to which the shareholder put the advances. . . . No single factor is, of course, determinative. Together all the factors may convey whether repayment or indefinite retention was intended. Koufman v. Commissioner, 35 T.C.M. (CCH) 1509, 1523 (1976). . . .

The setting and the controlling relationships are perhaps the first circumstance to be considered. All the factors must be assessed in the context, here, of the 100 percent ownership by the shareholder of the stock of the subsidiaries. Members of the founding family were the owners of approximately 50 percent of the stock of the parent and were also the directors and officers of both the parent and subsidiaries.

No doubt an advance by [a] corporation to a controlling shareholder can constitute a loan. . . . But a relationship between shareholder and corporation of total control and identity of interest creates obvious difficulties to thinking of the shareholder and corporation as debtor and creditor. A withdrawal of corporate funds may be used as a means of giving a controlling stockholder permanent use of the funds, in effect a dividend, without payment of the tax due on payment of a dividend. The possible tax evasion motive invites most careful scrutiny. . . .

The advances here came about under the rigorous discipline of a management contract between parent and each subsidiary which . . . provided that the subsidiary would "advance to us [plaintiff] from time to time, upon our request, such funds as we may require, which will be credited to your [the subsidiary's] account. Accountings shall be made and had between us from time to time, at such times as we may mutually agree upon." Apparently the funds "required" to be advanced were all the funds available. . . .

Plaintiff points to the terms of the management agreement and to the consistent treatment of year-end balances as accounts payable or receivable as evidence of a bona fide debtor-creditor relationship and an intent on the part of the creditor to repay the advances in the future. The terms of the agreement, however, neither characterize the balance in the intercompany account as a loan or debt or specify any repayment schedule or time for settlement of an outstanding balance. The vague reference to accountings "between us from time to time, at such times as we may mutually agree upon" is insufficient either to give the putative creditor the right to demand repayment of an outstanding balance or to show an intent on the part of the parent to repay. Actually, accountings never took place. The management contract thus gives little weight to plaintiff's argument that repayment was intended.

The consistent treatment of year-end balances as accounts payable, in the plaintiff's financial statements and annual reports and in tax returns, provides some small support for plaintiff's position. Creditors and bankers rely on financials. . . . But the cases are frequent in which treatment as loans on the books of the taxpayer is held unavailable to forestall the contrary conclusion. Regensburg v. Commissioner, 144 F.2d 41, 44 (2d Cir. 1944), cert. denied, 323 U.S. 783 . . . (1944); Electric & Neon, Inc., 56 T.C. . . . [1324, 1329, 1339-40 (1971), aff'd, 496 F.2d 876 (5th Cir. 1974)]. The Fifth Circuit in its decision on the same issue for this plaintiff's 1965 tax year denied the plaintiff's tax returns and financial reports status as "objective economic indicia of debt," . . . 505 F.2d at 879. In a case of complete identity between corporation and stockholder the books are a self-serving arrangement by the taxpayer calling for scrutiny for possible evasion of taxes. The court of appeals was of the view — here shared — that the careful scrutiny appropriate in such cases required emphasis on the objective indicia of plaintiff's intent rather than on the formal statements of that intent on the books of the plaintiff.

One of these indicia may be the payment or nonpayment of formal dividends. Nonpayment of formal dividends may be strong evidence that concurrent advances to stockholders are disguised dividends. Koufman v. Commissioner, supra. Here the subsidiaries, entirely apart from the advances under consideration, paid formal

134

dividends to a total of $4,508,485 during the years in question. While these are substantial sums, they are inconclusive as showing that the additional sums advanced were not also dividends, in view of the relative size of those advances and particularly the very substantial and growing retained earnings of the subsidiaries — $18.6 million by the last of the tax years. The pattern suggests that . . . the advances were actually disguised dividends. . . . The increases in advances, formal dividends paid by the subsidiaries and their retained earnings were as follows:

Tax Years	Increases in Advances Taxed as Dividends	Formal Dividends	Retained Earnings
1966	884,139.27	647,400	6,546,967
1967	1,281,150.99	479,300	8,108,114
1968	1,388,841.99	640,535	9,515,650
1969	968,772.82	666,750	10,707,826
1970	1,333,227.00	685,500	11,922,157
1971	498,031.00	685,250	13,148,979
1972	597,479.00	703,750	14,360,352
1973	1,418,745.35	none	16,597,817
1974	982,683.07	none	18,571,235
	$9,353,070.49	$4,508,485	

Another set of figures confirm[s] the doubts. Of the 57 subsidiaries, 18 were profitable in each of the successive tax years, earning more than $25,000 annually. Profits actually ranged up to $200,000 annually; the average was $92,000. Advances by these subsidiaries increased in almost 9 out of 10 of these years. The constant parallel between substantial income and increasing advances, again, suggests dividends. . . .

There are other factors of context and degree suggesting that the advances were economic dividends as much as the formal dividends.

There was no ceiling on the balance of advances which could be accumulated in plaintiff's hands. Plaintiff offered testimony that a market would require a substantial capital expenditure for remodeling every 5 to 8 years, and thus a "repayment" of advances. Yet advances from some subsidiaries increased in each tax year, and the general trend was constantly upwards. The need for remodeling, then, did not impose an effective ceiling on an outstanding debit balance and did not produce a predictable repayment of the outstanding balance of net advances. Both the absence of a ceiling and the trend of increasing balances weigh heavily against a conclusion that the advances were loans. See *Koufman,* supra; George Blood Enterprises, Inc., 35 T.C.M. (CCH) 436, 446 (1976).

Inability to pay advances from a controlled corporation is a mark of a distribution rather than a loan. Edward M. Wrenn, Jr. v. United States, 78-1 U.S.T.C. ¶9484 (D.C.W.D. Tenn. 1978); Al Goodman Inc. v. Commissioner, 23 T.C. 288, 301 (1954). Plaintiff was in a liquid position and had excellent credit during the years in suit. It would have been able, had it been necessary, to borrow enough to pay the net advances. To this extent the objective indicia are consistent with an intent to repay.

The use by the plaintiff of the net advances presents a mixed picture on the issue of intent to repay. On the one hand, indicia contradicting a loan are that plaintiff had no urgent need for the sums involved and was under the management agreements unrestricted in its use of the sums advanced. Plaintiff could and presumably did use the advances throughout its business, for dividends or purchases or other of its needs. Some of the advances were invested in interest-bearing short-term certificates of deposit. On the other hand it is urged that with the cash advanced plaintiff obtained volume and cash discounts on its wholesale grocery purchases which it could pass on to the subsidiaries. Cases on this factor, as might be expected, are inconclusive. Compare White v. Commissioner, 17 T.C. 1562, 1568 (1952) (finding that loans were intended despite the shareholder's personal use of the funds) with George Blood Enterprises, Inc. v. Commissioner, supra, (shareholder's use of the funds to purchase a lake house indicative of constructive dividends).

Absent were customary indications of loan such as the payment of interest, the giving of a promissory note, a limit on the amount involved, the presence of security or collateral for the loan or restriction on the use of the sums. There was neither reserve or sinking fund for repayment of the advances nor fixed maturity date or schedule for repayment. True, payment by plaintiff of the subsidiaries' expenses had the same effect as a partial repayment of a debit balance, but there was never a transfer of cash to a subsidiary solely for the purpose of offsetting a debit balance. Other than the demands implicit in the subsidiaries' submission of their bills to plaintiff for payment, the subsidiaries which had made advances demanded neither a formal accounting of the balances nor a transfer of cash by way of repayment. In other words, there was no attempted collections of the purported loans, and, indeed, little objective evidence of loan except the books created by the parties.

. . . A certain degree of informality may be expected in dealings between a controlling shareholder and his corporation. . . . In this case, however, the informalities make clear the crucial fact that there was no way of knowing that the advances by a particular subsidiary would be repaid either at a set time or at any time in the foreseeable future. Repayment could take place only if future events required greater expenditures on behalf of a subsidiary than the sums it could advance. Though such events — reduced profitability or a need for large capital expenditures — were largely, but not completely, beyond plaintiff's control, there was a substantial possibility that they would not occur within a reasonable or even a foreseeable period of time. In many cases, net advances increased in all 9 tax years in question, and in other cases decreases did not reduce the balance even close to zero. The pattern over the years is one in which profits were steadily made and steadily transferred to the plaintiff.

What happened in the later years may shed full light on the earlier years. As was said in Estate of Taschler v. United States, 440 F.2d 72, 77 (3rd Cir. 1971): "What may appear to be a debtor-creditor relationship from dealings viewed within a certain span of time may turn out to be a mirage when later transactions are taken into account. The circumstances surrounding disbursements in later years and their cumulative effect may be considered in determining a taxpayer's intent prior to those years." The continuation of large and growing balances of net advances indicates that plaintiff did not have a definite intent to repay the advances; it had only a contingent intent to repay should circumstances so require. If the circumstances did not materialize, plaintiff would continue to hold and use the debit balances free and clear of any responsibility to repay the sums to the subsidiaries, as if dividends had been paid. The fact that in some instances net advances were significantly reduced or even reversed is not indicative of more than a contingent intent to repay. Future events created a definite intent to repay — only the part expended for the benefit of the subsidiary.

It is firmly established that a contingent intent to repay, or an intent to repay only if and when the sums are needed by the corporation, is legally insufficient to render advances to shareholders bona fide loans. Alterman Foods, Inc. v. Commissioner, supra, 505 F.2d at 879; General Aggregates Corp. v. Commissioner, 313 F.2d 25, 28 (1st Cir. 1963), cert. denied, 375 U.S. 815 ... (1963); ... O'Reilly v. Commissioner, 27 T.C.M. (CCH) 1543, 1547 (1968); cf. Kaplan v. Commissioner, 43 T.C. 580 (1965) (repayment upon shareholder's death legally insufficient to show advances to be loans). Plaintiff's contingent intent to repay in this case, then, was insufficient to render the net advances to it loans; such advances were therefore taxable dividends.

Cases relied upon by plaintiff as holding advances to be a loan involved only one or two running accounts created by a shareholder's withdrawals from a corporation. Here there were more than 50 accounts created by a large corporate shareholder withdrawing sums from 57 subsidiaries. The number, consistency and increasing amounts of the withdrawals create a pattern indicating no intent to repay, except fortuitously and in small part. Moreover, the cases relied upon by plaintiff contained factual indicators of an intent to repay which are here absent. For instance, there were attempts to settle the outstanding balance by transfer of property to the corporation; . . . reversals or zero balances in all the accounts in question in prior or subsequent years . . . ; the shareholder's payment of capital gains tax on the account upon the dissolution of the corporation. . . . Also, in some of those cases there were attempts by the corporation or its agents to collect the balance from the shareholder . . . ; payment by shareholder to corporation of substantial amounts of interest included by the latter in its taxable income . . . ; and a pledge of stock as collateral security for the note given the corporation. . . .

Each of the cases turns on its own facts. In these foregoing cases, the finder of the facts concluded, on all the evidence and on an evaluation of witnesses' credibility, that definite repayment was intended. By the same method, the conclusion reached in the instant case is that definite repayment was not intended. The only possible deterrent to this conclusion is that taxation of both the dividends claimed by the Commissioner and the formal dividends declared and paid during the years in question will mean the treatment as dividends of an unusually high level of the subsidiaries' annual earnings. But the taxpayer offers the taxing system no choice. The subsidiaries did in fact transfer virtually their entire receipts to plaintiff, their sole shareholder, and the parties chose not to file consolidated returns which might have permitted a tax-free transfer of dividends. Plaintiff chose its method of doing business, and it cannot now avoid the tax consequences of its choice. See *Alterman Foods, Inc.,* supra, 505 F.2d at 878; Wiseman v. United States, 371 F.2d 816, 818 (1st Cir. 1967). It may be noted, finally, that plaintiff was allowed the 85 percent dividends-received deduction under section 243(a)(1) of the 1954 Code.

Plaintiff's case fails for lack of proof by a preponderance of the evidence that the annual increases in net advances from its individual subsidiaries in the tax years 1966-74 were bona fide loans or otherwise nontaxable.

NOTES

1. A and B, who together owned all of the outstanding shares of Corporations X, Y, and Z, had open-account, interest-free loans from each of those corporations. At the same time, A and B were guarantors of certain large loans made by third parties to Corporation

Z. Do the interest-free loans from these corporations to their share-holders constitute constructive dividends? See Joseph Creel, 72 T.C. 1173 (1979), *aff'd on other grounds sub nom.* Martin v. Commissioner, 649 F.2d 1133 (5th Cir. 1981). Does the fact that in order to make interest-free loans to its shareholders Corporation Z had to carry interest-bearing obligations to third parties distinguish that corpo-ration's loans to A and B from the loans made by the other two corporations? *Compare Creel* (shareholders treated as actual borrowers on loans from third parties so that interest payments by corporation are constructive dividends) *with* Falkoff v. Commissioner, 604 F.2d 1045 (7th Cir. 1979), *rev'g* 36 T.C.M. (CCH) 417 (1977) (corporation rather than shareholder treated as actual borrower; no constructive dividend) (alternative holding).

2. A owns 100 percent of the outstanding stock of both X Cor-poration and Y Corporation. Y forgives a loan to X. Has A received a constructive dividend? Does it matter that X and Y, both contrac-tors, pooled their resources to obtain larger bonds and to increase their range of services? See Raymond Magnon, 73 T.C. 980 (1980) (holding no constructive dividend because the court inferred from the cooperation of X and Y that the payment was not made "primarily for the benefit of" A and A received no "direct or tangible benefit"). When a transfer of cash is made between commonly held corpora-tions, a finding of no real indebtedness between the corporations, though it would result in a denial of the interest deduction, will not always result in a finding of a constructive dividend to the share-holder. If there is a real corporate business objective or only an indirect benefit to the common owner, the payment may not consti-tute a constructive dividend. See Gilbert L. Gilbert, 74 T.C. 60 (1980). But see Johnson v. Commissioner, 652 F.2d 615 (6th Cir. 1981), where the court held that funds transferred from one corporation to another constituted a constructive dividend to the common share-holder, not an intercorporate loan.

In Stinnett's Pontiac Service, Inc. v. Commissioner, 730 F.2d 634 (11th Cir. 1984), an advance from one corporation to its sibling cor-poration was treated as a constructive dividend to the corporations' common shareholder and as a capital contribution from the share-holder to the sibling corporation. The court reached its conclusion because it found that the advance was designed primarily to benefit the shareholder rather than the advancing corporation. Compare, however, Mills v. Commissioner, 840 F.2d 229 (4th Cir. 1988), where the court ruled that a payment "is not a constructive dividend unless it benefits the shareholder in some direct way quite apart from his strictly derivative interest as a shareholder." Id. at 235. An advance by one corporation to a related corporation for the purpose of remedying the latter's perceived undercapitalization was not a constructive dividend to the common shareholder because the common shareholder was under no obligation to remedy the undercapitalization.

b.   Dividend vs. Corporate Investment

PRUNIER v. COMMISSIONER

248 F.2d 818 (1st Cir. 1957)

Before Magruder, Chief Judge, and Woodbury and Hartigan, Circuit Judges.

MAGRUDER, Chief Judge. There is now before us a joint petition for review of two decisions of the Tax Court entered on April 12, 1957 — one determining that there is a deficiency in income tax of Henry E. Prunier and wife for the taxable year 1950 in the amount of $1,080.88, the other determining that there is a deficiency in income tax of Joseph E. Prunier and wife for the same taxable year in the amount of $1,348.98. The Tax Court . . . sustained a determination by the Commissioner that certain premiums paid by the corporation J. S. Prunier & Sons, Inc., on insurance policies on the lives of Henry and Joseph Prunier constituted taxable income to the taxpayers under the general language of §[61(a)].

Of the 450 shares of stock of J. S. Prunier & Sons, Inc., outstanding, Henry Prunier and his brother Joseph each owned [220 shares]. Henry held the offices of president and treasurer, and Joseph was vice-president of the corporation.

As not infrequently happens in these closely held family corporations, the corporate books and records were kept in so sketchy and messy a fashion as to make it difficult to determine what was corporate action and what was the individual action of the two dominant stockholders.

Beginning in 1942 and running up to and including 1950, the brothers took out a total of eight life insurance policies. Four were purchased by Henry on his own life, naming his brother Joseph as beneficiary, in a total face amount of $45,000. Four were taken out by Joseph on his own life, naming his brother Henry as beneficiary, in a total amount of $45,000.

During the taxable year 1950 there was nothing in the terms of the policies, nor in the endorsements thereon, to indicate that the corporation had become their beneficial owner. Some question having been raised by the taxing authorities about this, it appears that at various dates in 1952 (which was subsequent to the tax year in question) endorsements were placed on each of the eight policies naming the corporation J. S. Prunier & Sons, Inc., beneficiary, but inexplicably containing the reservation, in all eight policies, of a right in Henry to change the beneficiary.

From at least as far back as 1946 the corporation has paid the premiums due on the various policies. It was testified on behalf of the taxpayers, and found as a fact by the Tax Court, as follows:

> When the policies were written, Henry and Joseph informed the agent of the substance of the written agreements which the policies were intended to carry out. They intended that in the event of the death of either the corporation should be the owner of the proceeds of the policies on the life of the deceased party for a single specific purpose, namely, use the proceeds to purchase the stock interest of the deceased party in the corporation at a price agreed upon by them prior to the death of either.

The tax treatment given to these transactions by the corporation was consistent with this found intention of the parties. Thus, in the agreed stipulation of facts the following statements appear:

> The corporation did not claim a deduction for the premiums paid on the above-mentioned insurance policies on its income tax return for the taxable year 1950, but did include the amount thereof in the adjustment made to surplus on Schedule M of its said return as follows:
>
> "8. Insurance premiums paid on the life of any officer or employee where the corporation is directly or indirectly a beneficiary . . . $8,081.44."
>
> Similar adjustments were made by the corporation on its income tax returns for the taxable years 1946 and 1949, inclusive, for the premiums paid on those of the above-mentioned policies in effect during those years.

The aforesaid understanding that the corporation was to become the owner of the policies was first reflected on the books of the corporation, sometime toward the end of 1946, by the following entry in the minute book of the corporation describing a meeting of the directors:

> It is understood and agreed that any policies that Henry E. Prunier has on Joseph E. Prunier and any policies that Joseph E. Prunier has on Henry E. Prunier shall go to the corporation in the event of the death of either of them and this money is to be used by the corporation to buy out the interest of the party that dies.
>
> These policies are the ones that the corporation pays the premiums on.
>
> This will apply to any policies that may be bought in the future.
>
>   (s)   Henry E. Prunier
>
> Witness   (s)   Joseph E. Prunier
>
> (s)   Irene M. Prunier

. . . Petitioners place their reliance upon the settled ruling that where a corporation is the beneficiary and owner of a policy of insurance on the life of an employee or stockholder, the payment of premiums by the corporation does not constitute income to the insured individual. Casale v. Commissioner, 2 Cir., 1957, 247 F.2d 440. . . .

On the other hand, the Commissioner thinks the present case falls within the equally settled ruling that where a corporate employee or stockholder, or someone related to him, is beneficiary, and not the corporation, on a policy of life insurance on such employee or stockholder, payment of the premiums on such policy by the corporation constitutes income to the insured individual. Paramount-Richards Theatres, Inc. v. Commissioner, 5 Cir., 1946, 153 F.2d 602. . . .

We think the present case is more nearly like the type of case relied upon by petitioners. Despite the informality of the transactions, it seems to us that, in view of the facts in the record and of the findings by the Tax Court, the corporation would have been held to be the beneficial owner of the eight insurance policies under controlling Massachusetts law, and thus could have obtained the help of a court of equity to recover the proceeds of the insurance policies if one of the brothers had died in 1950. . . . We suspect also that in that event the corporation, on some theory of "ratification" or of "adoption," would have been held contractually bound to apply the proceeds of the policies to buy out the stock interest of the deceased stockholder, and that the deceased stockholder's legal representative would have been contractually bound to sell. . . .

Whether the corporation would have been legally obliged to continue paying the premiums in 1950 we do not need to say. The fact is that the corporation did pay the premiums. Also we do not have to decide what would have been the respective legal obligations of the parties, and what would have been the tax consequences, if one of the insured brothers had died in 1950. The fact is that neither brother died in 1950, and so far as appears both are still alive. It is sufficient for the purposes of the present case to say that neither brother realized any taxable gain in 1950 from the payment of the life insurance premiums by the corporation.

We do not understand that the majority of the Tax Court reached the conclusion they did on any notion of "disregarding the corporation fiction." Human beings take advantage of laws permitting incorporation because they think it will be economically advantageous to them individually. That is so whether the corporation is a "closely held" company owned by two stockholders, or one having two thousand stockholders. In a loose manner of speaking, it can be said that any corporate gain is a benefit, indirectly, to the stockholders, so that if a corporation becomes the beneficial owner of insurance policies, the stockholders receive the benefit thereof. Of course this argument proves too much, for it would lead to the conclusion that profits made by a corporation in its business are automatically taxable income to the stockholders. This is contrary to the taxation scheme of the Internal Revenue Code. And the government is only contending in this case that it was the payment of premiums by the corporation which constituted income to the insured employees and stockholders, which in itself is a recognition of the corporation as a separate legal entity.

The gist of the Tax Court's argument is contained in the following excerpt from the majority opinion:

> In view of what has been said above, it appears that if Joseph or Henry had died during the taxable year, the corporation would not have been enriched by receiving the proceeds from insurance policies on the life of the deceased and using them to purchase stock he had owned in the corporation. The corporation's indebtedness to creditors would have remained undiminished, and while the corporation would have eliminated at least the greater part of the deceased's ownership interest in it, represented by his stock, the proportional interest of the surviving stockholder, or stockholders, thereby would have been greatly increased. In this situation and since the record does not otherwise indicate any benefit which might flow to the corporation from the purchase of a deceased insured's stock interest, we conclude that during the taxable year the corporation was neither the beneficial owner nor the beneficiary of the insurance policies on the lives of Joseph and Henry involved here.

Certainly the fact that the corporation may have contractually bound to apply any proceeds of the policies, had they matured in 1950, to buy out the stock interest of a deceased stockholder, does not mean that the corporation would not have been "enriched" by collecting the face amount of the policies. All that would then have been involved would have been a change in the form of the assets from cash to treasury stock. We have hitherto pointed out the limited utility of the concept of corporate purpose as distinguished from stockholder purpose. See Lewis v. Commissioner, 1 Cir., 1949, 176 F.2d 646, 649-650. But if it were necessary to look for a corporate business purpose in the present case, we could refer to the arguments in Mannheimer & Friedman, "Stock-Retirement Agreements," 28 Taxes 423, 425 (1950), as follows:

> Even while the decedent is still alive, the agreement and insurance benefit the corporation because they tend to stabilize the corporation's business. If the bank knows about the agreement, it may well be inclined to extend credit more liberally to the cor-

poration because the possibility of inexperienced shareholders injecting themselves into the management is eliminated. If the key employees are informed of the agreement, it will be an inducement to them to remain with the corporation because they realize that the continuation of the business in the hands of the survivor is assured — and with it their jobs.

If there is no stock-retirement agreement when the decedent dies, often his family will ask a high price for his stock, or demand dividends without regard to the needs of the corporation, or even press for dissolution. So far as the survivor is concerned, he may very well be unwilling to work indirectly for the benefit of his former "partner's" family or directly with the second husband of his former "partner's" widow.

In the present case the government has not made any real effort to controvert the argument that under the Massachusetts decisions a court of equity would treat the corporation as the equitable owner of the policies of insurance. That being so, and having in mind the statutory scheme whereby the corporation J. S. Prunier & Sons, Inc., is dealt with as a separate legal entity and a separate taxable unit, and disregarding the loose sense in which it could be said that a benefit to J. S. Prunier & Sons, Inc., is a benefit to its controlling stockholders, it is sufficiently evident that the payment of premiums by the corporation in 1950 did not constitute, in that taxable year, reportable income to Henry and Joseph Prunier. See generally Casale v. Commissioner, 2 Cir., 1957, 247 F.2d 440. What will happen when one of the brothers dies is not before us.

A judgment will be entered vacating the decisions of the Tax Court and remanding the case to that Court for further proceedings not inconsistent with this opinion.

NOTES

1. If a corporation owns an insurance policy on the life of a principal shareholder and designates (revocably) the shareholder's estate as the beneficiary, what is the tax consequence to the estate when the proceeds are paid to the insured's estate after he dies? Why? The answer given in Ducros v. Commissioner, 272 F.2d 49 (6th Cir. 1959), is one which the Commissioner has announced he will not follow. See Rev. Rul. 61-134, 1961-2 C.B. 250. The *Ducros* court held that the estate did not recognize income upon the receipt of the proceeds. Is the result in *Ducros* consistent with the logic of *Prunier?*

Husband (H) and Wife (W) are both substantial shareholders in a closely held corporation. The corporation owns and pays premiums on insurance policies on the life of H, a corporate officer, revocably designating W as the beneficiary. W receives the policy proceeds on H's death. Is this a constructive dividend? To whom? See Estate of J. E. Horne, 64 T.C. 1020 (1975), *acq. in result* 1980-1 C.B. 1.

For the tax consequences to the shareholder of a "split-dollar" arrangement pursuant to which the shareholder and the corporation share the costs and benefits of a life insurance policy, see Howard Johnson, T.C. 1316 (1980); Rev. Rul. 79-50, 1979-1 C.B. 138.

If a corporation makes an irrevocable designation of its shareholder insured's estate as beneficiary, would premium payments made after the designation constitute dividends? Why?

See Goldstein, Tax Aspects of Corporate Business Use of Life Insurance, 18 Tax L. Rev. 133 (1963); Sneed, A Defense of the Tax Court's Result in *Prunier* and *Casale,* 43 Cornell L.Q. 339 (1958).

2. Section 264(a)(1) governs the tax consequences to the corporation of paying the premium. It provides that the premiums on a policy on the life of an officer, employee, or person financially interested in the business are not deductible if the corporation is a direct or indirect beneficiary. Thus, payments will be deductible only if the payment is in the nature of compensation and the employer is not, directly or indirectly, a beneficiary. (Of course, the compensation must be "reasonable" if it is to be deductible. See §162(a)(1).)

c. Dividend vs. "Unreasonable" Expense

1. A payment by a corporation, though not made directly to the shareholder, may satisfy an obligation of the shareholder or confer some type of personal benefit upon him. Payment of that benefit may therefore constitute a constructive dividend. In John L. Ashby, 50 T.C. 409 (1968), the Tax Court held that the corporate taxpayer was not entitled to deduct club and entertainment expenses or depreciation, maintenance, and repairs on a boat that it owned. The corporation failed to prove error in the amount of entertainment expense the Commissioner had allowed and failed to prove the club or boat was used primarily for business, as was then required by §274. The Commissioner also sought to tax the majority shareholder with the disallowed expenses as a dividend. The court sustained the Commissioner in full as to the entertainment and club items. As to the boat, however, the shareholder was taxed only on 48/68ths of the costs involved, since the court found that only that percentage of the boat use benefitted the individual. Section 274 does not prevent partial allocation to the individual shareholder, although it may require disallowance in full as to the corporation.

In general, as the Tax Court said in *Ashby,* 50 T.C. at 417, "[i]t is well established that any expenditure made by a corporation for the personal benefit of its stockholders or the making available of corporate owned facilities to stockholders for their personal benefit may result in the receipt by the stockholders of constructive dividends. See Challenge Manufacturing Co., 37 T.C. 650 [(1962)], and cases cited therein." Cf. Rapid Electric Co., 61 T.C. 232 (1973), *acq.*, 1974-2 C.B. 4; Sparks Nugget, Inc. v. Commissioner, 458 F.2d 631 (9th Cir. 1972), *cert. denied,* 410 U.S. 928 (1973) (excessive rental payments between two corporations were constructive dividends to sole shareholder of both); Sammons v. United States, 433 F.2d 728 (5th Cir. 1970), *cert. denied,* 402 U.S. 945 (1971) (constructive dividend on bargain sale between brother-sister corporations). But cf. Henry J. Knott, 67 T.C. 681 (1977), *acq.,* 1979-1 C.B. 1, announced in Rev. Rul. 79-9, 1979-1 C.B. 125 (bargain sale of property to family foundation by family-owned corporation was a corporate charitable contribution, not a constructive dividend; family members received no property or other benefit). Is this a way to avoid the percentage limitations provided in §170(b)(1) on charitable deductions by individuals?

2. When a corporate payment for entertaining undertaken by a shareholder is disallowed, must it be taxed as a constructive dividend to the shareholder if there are sufficient earnings and profits? See Henry Schwartz Corp., 60 T.C. 728 (1973), *acq.,* 1974-2 C.B. 4 (corporate taxpayer denied deduction for failure to meet substantiation requirements of §274(d); shareholder taxpayer taxed on receipt of constructive dividend only to the extent expenditure not allocable to ordinary and necessary business expenses).

3.   Waiver of Dividend — §61

REVENUE PROCEDURE 67-14
1967-1 C.B. 591

§1.   PURPOSE

The purpose of this Revenue Procedure is to specify the conditions which must be present before the Internal Revenue Service will consider issuing a ruling on a proposed waiver of dividends transaction.

§2.   BACKGROUND

The Service has published two Revenue Rulings involving a waiver by a majority stockholder of his right to future undeclared dividends.

.01 Revenue Ruling 45, C.B. 1953-1, 178, described a fact situation under which no family or direct business relationship existed between the majority and minority stockholders, and the waiver was executed for a valid business purpose. The Revenue Ruling concluded that any dividend payments to the minority stockholders would not result in income to the waiving stockholder.

.02 On the other hand, Revenue Ruling 56-431, C.B. 1956-2, 171, involved a waiver by a majority stockholder whose relatives owned 25 percent of the stock of the corporation. Because of the existence of the significant family interest, the alleged business purpose was considered incidental and the waiver was considered as having been executed primarily for the benefit of the related stockholders. The Revenue Ruling concluded that the waiving stockholder would be taxed on the increased distribution to the related stockholders resulting from the waiver.

.03 Revenue Ruling 65-256, C.B. 1965-2, 85, although not involving an explicit waiver of dividends, did involve a merger under the terms of which the majority stockholder of one of the corporations agreed to accept a separate class of stock in the successor corporation subject to certain dividend limitations. In that ruling, members of the majority stockholder's family owned only 0.06 percent of the total capital stock of the surviving corporation and there were bona fide business reasons for the majority stockholder's acceptance of a class of stock with dividend restrictions. The ruling concluded that the majority stockholder would not be in constructive receipt of income when dividends are paid on a second class of stock.

§3. Requests for Rulings

Based upon the Revenue Rulings described above, the Service will consider a request for a ruling on a proposed waiver of dividends transaction under the following conditions:

.01 A bona fide business reason must exist for the proposed waiver of dividends.

.02 The relatives of the stockholder proposing to waive his right to future dividends must not be in a position to receive more than 20 percent of the total dividends distributed to the nonwaiving shareholders. For this purpose the relatives of a waiving stockholder include his brother and sister (whether by the whole or half blood), spouse, ancestors, and lineal descendants, the spouses of his brothers and sisters (whether by the whole or half blood) and the spouses of his lineal descendants.

.03 A ruling issued on a proposed waiver of dividends transaction will clearly indicate that the ruling will no longer be applicable if any change in the stock ownership during the waiver period enables nonwaiving relatives to receive more than 20 percent of a dividend, unless the change occurs because of death.

.04 A ruling issued on a proposed waiver of dividends transaction will not be effective for a period longer than three years from the date of the ruling.

.05 A request for a ruling on a proposed waiver of dividends transaction must be submitted to the National Office in accordance with Revenue Procedure 67-1 [1967-1 C.B. 544].

NOTES

1. What is meant by a "bona fide business reason" in the context of a dividend waiver? What is an example of such a "business reason"? On what theory is a "waived" dividend taxed to a shareholder who does not receive an actual distribution? Why is family relationship with other shareholders relevant? If shareholders neglect to "waive" before receipt, may they return a dividend distribution and be free of tax on the dividend if they could have waived on a tax-free basis before the distribution? Why?

2. Suppose a corporation declares a pro rata dividend on November 1, 1988, payable on January 10, 1989, to shareholders of record on December 30, 1988. On December 30, 1988, all shareholders ask the Board of Directors to rescind the dividend declaration and the Board does so. Do the shareholders have income and, if so, when? Why? Would your answer be different if the shareholders made their request and the Board acted on January 5, 1989? On January 10, 1989? Why?

3. See Rev. Rul. 71-164, 1971-1 C.B. 108, in which a national bank director owned bank stock totaling $1,000 par value, as required by federal law. The remaining shares were owned by the bank's corporate parent. The director waived all dividends in excess of $.50 per share, and was held not taxable on the amounts waived.

In Bagley v. United States, 348 F. Supp. 418 (D. Minn. 1972), a waiving stockholder was taxed on his pro rata (49.9 percent) share of dividends paid. His waiver benefitted his sister and the children of his first marriage. His second wife, owning over 11 percent of the stock, was held not taxable although she made an identical waiver. The court determined that she lacked control over dividend policy and did not have a close family relationship to the nonwaiving stockholders, so that she should not be considered to have received her share of dividends and then made a gift of them to the beneficiaries of the waiver. See also Green v. United States, 460 F.2d 412 (5th Cir. 1972).

4. A shareholder who chooses to accept less than his pro rata

portion of assets distributed by a liquidating corporation will be treated as if he received a pro rata distribution, and then made transfers to the other shareholders. See Rev. Rul. 79-10, 1979-1 C.B. 140.

5. When you study §305(b), page 475 infra, consider what impact it may have on Rev. Proc. 67-14.

6. See Note, Income and Gift Tax Treatment of a Waiver of Rights to Future, Undeclared Dividends by a Corporate Shareholder, 32 Vand. L. Rev. 889 (1979).

B. DISTRIBUTIONS IN RETIREMENT OF INVESTOR INTEREST

1. Debt Retirement vs. Dividend or Redemption of Stock

If a sole shareholder lends money to his corporation and that corporation repays the loan, the shareholder-lender typically has a tax-free recovery of capital or, perhaps, a capital gain. See §1271. But suppose the loan is properly regarded as equity. What might the tax consequences be? Most of the materials that follow in this chapter involve the tax consequences to a shareholder whose equity interest is retired. It is well to remember that an apparent "debt" may be reclassified and treated as "equity." Review the "thinness" issues posed in the materials in Chapter 1 at pages 60-79 supra.

2. Liquidating Distributions and Redemptions

a. Complete Liquidations — §331

COMMISSIONER v. CARTER
170 F.2d 911 (2d Cir. 1948)

Before L. Hand, Chief Judge, and Swan and Chase, Circuit Judges. SWAN, Circuit Judge. This appeal presents the question whether income received by the taxpayer in 1943 is taxable as long-term capital gain, as the Tax Court ruled, or as ordinary income as the Commissioner contends. The facts are not in dispute. The taxpayer, Mrs. Carter, had owned for ten years all the stock of a corporation which was dissolved on December 31, 1942. Upon its dissolution all of its assets were distributed to her in kind, subject to all its liabilities which she assumed. In the distribution she received property having a fair market value exceeding by about $20,000 the cost basis of her stock, and she reported such excess as a capital gain in her 1942 return and paid the tax thereon. In the corporate liquidation she also received 32 oil brokerage contracts which the parties stipulated had no ascertainable fair market value when distributed. Each contract provided for payment to the corporation of commissions on future deliveries of oil by a named seller to a named buyer. The contracts required no additional services to be performed by the corporation or its distributee, and the future commissions were conditioned on contingencies which made uncertain the amount and time of payment. In 1943 the taxpayer collected commissions of $34,992.20 under these contracts. She reported this sum as a long-term capital gain; the Commissioner determined it to be ordinary income. The Tax Court held it taxable as capital gain. The correctness of this decision is the sole question presented by the Commissioner's appeal.

Mrs. Carter's stock was a "capital asset" as defined by [§1221]. In exchange for her stock, she received the assets of the corporation upon its dissolution. The tax consequences of such a transaction are controlled by [§331(a) which calls for liquidating distribution to be "treated as in full payment in exchange for stock," §1001(a) which defines gain or loss as the spread between "adjusted basis" and "amount realized," §1001(b) which defines "amount realized" as "the sum of any money received plus the fair market value of . . . property . . . received," and §1001(c) which provides that all gain or loss is to be recognized unless otherwise provided in the statute]. . . . From the foregoing statutory provisions, it is obvious that if the oil brokerage contracts distributed to the taxpayer had then had a "fair market value," such value would have increased correspondingly the "amount realized" by her in exchange for her stock and would have been taxable as long-term capital gain, not as ordinary income. . . . Fleming v. Commissioner of Internal Revenue, 5 Cir., 153 F.2d 361. The question presented by the present appeal is whether a different result is required when contract obligations having no ascertainable fair market value are distributed in liquidation of a corporation and collections thereunder are made by the distributee in later years.

In answering this question in the negative, the Tax Court relied primarily upon Burnet v. Logan, 283 U.S. 404. . . .*

The Commissioner argues that the Logan case is inapplicable because there the taxpayer had not recovered the cost basis of her stock while here she had. The Tax Court thought the distinction immaterial. We agree. The Supreme Court spoke of the annual payments as constituting "profit" after the seller's capital investment

*Burnet v. Logan involved a year when capital gains and ordinary income were taxed at the same rate. — ED.

should be returned. Until such return it cannot be known whether gain or loss will result from a sale; thereafter it becomes certain that future payments will result in gain. No reason is apparent for taxing them as ordinary income. As this court said in Commissioner of Internal Revenue v. Hopkinson, 2 Cir., 126 F.2d 406, 410, "payments received by the seller after his basis had been extinguished would have been taxable to him as capital gains from the sale of the property," citing Burnet v. Logan as authority.

The Commissioner also urges that the *Logan* case is distinguishable because it dealt with a sale of stock rather than exchange of stock for assets distributed in a corporate liquidation. This contention is answered by White v. United States, 305 U.S. 281, 288, . . . and Helvering v. Chester N. Weaver Co., 305 U.S. 293, 295, . . . where the court held that the recognition required . . . of gains and losses on liquidations must for purposes of computation of the tax, be taken to be the same as that accorded to gains and losses on sales of property.* Consequently we agree with the Tax Court's ruling that the principle of the *Logan* case is applicable to a corporate liquidation where stock is exchanged in part for contracts having no ascertainable market value, and that future collections under such contracts are taxable as capital gain in the year when received if the distributee has previously recovered the cost basis for the stock.

The Commissioner's argument that such collections are analogous to the receipt of interest or rent upon bonds or real estate distributed in a corporate liquidation overlooks a significant distinction. Payment of interest or rent does not impair the value of the bond or real estate since each remains as a capital asset regardless of the number of payments. See Helvering v. Manhattan Life Ins. Co., 2 Cir., 71 F.2d 292, 293. But with respect to the oil brokerage contracts, under which no additional services were to be rendered by the payee, each payment decreases their value until, with the final payment it will be completely exhausted; and, if the payments be treated as income, the distributee has no way to recoup his capital investment, since concededly he has no economic interest in the oil producing properties and therefore no right to depletion deductions.[2] Hence to consider the brokerage payments as ordinary income

---

*See cross-reference provisions of §331(c). — ED.

2. It is true, in the case at bar, the taxpayer had no capital investment in the brokerage contracts because from other assets distributed she had already recovered the cost basis of her stock and the oil brokerage contracts had no ascertainable fair market value. But the Commissioner's analogy argument would be equally applicable if the brokerage contracts had been the only corporate assets distributed and it had been possible to ascribe to them a fair market value of $21,000. In that case, the distributee's capital investment in the brokerage contracts would have been $20,000, the cost basis of her stock being $1,000. She would be entitled to recover her capital investment before she could be charged with receiving either gain or ordinary income,

would produce a most unjust result and one quite unlike the result which follows the distribution of bonds or real estate in a corporate liquidation.

For the foregoing reasons we think the decision of the Tax Court correct. It is affirmed.

NOTES

1. In Rev. Rul. 58-402, 1958-2 C.B. 15, the Service reviewed *Carter*, Burnet v. Logan, 283 U.S. 404 (1931), and other cases and concluded that it "will continue to require valuation of contracts and claims to receive indefinite amounts of income, such as those acquired with respect to stock in liquidation of a corporation, except in rare and extraordinary cases." What is a "rare and extraordinary" case in this context? Under what circumstances might it be to the taxpayer's advantage to have a "contracts right" distribution in liquidation valued at time of liquidation?

2. Suppose Mr. Baker forms a corporation of which he is the sole shareholder, making an initial contribution to capital of $50,000. The corporation is very successful and in three years has retained earnings and profits of $450,000. Baker liquidates the corporation, distributing all the assets to himself in one liquidating distribution. What are the tax consequences to Baker? See §331. Suppose instead that after the corporation accumulates earnings and profits of $450,000, Baker dies, and Charlie inherits all of the corporation's stock. What are the tax consequences to Charlie if he immediately liquidates the corporation? See §§1014 and 331. What are the arguable justifications for §331? For a contrary rule?

3. In *Carter*, what would the result have been if the brokerage contracts had had an ascertainable fair market value of $10 in 1942? If the transaction were to take place today, the result might well be different. See §1271(a)(1) and (a)(2)(A).

4. Note that under §346(a), a distribution is treated as part of a complete liquidation if the distribution is one of a series of distributions pursuant to a plan of liquidation. If a corporation makes such a series of liquidating distributions and has a number of shareholders, the distributions must be allocated among the various blocks of shares. For the method of allocation required by the Service, see Rev. Rul. 85-48, 1985-1 C.B. 126, amplifying Rev. Rul. 68-348, 1968-2 C.B. 141.

---

and the only source of recovery would be the payments which would ultimately exhaust the value of the contracts. Hence the answer given above to the analogy argument is apposite.

ESTATE OF MEADE v. COMMISSIONER
489 F.2d 161 (5th Cir.), *cert. denied,* 419 U.S. 882 (1974)

Before Gewin, Ainsworth and Morgan, Circuit Judges.

AINSWORTH, Circuit Judge. Taxpayers incurred legal expenses in connection with the settlement of a civil antitrust claim that had been assigned to them in pro rata shares as distributees in a corporate liquidation. These cases present the question whether the legal expenses are deductible from ordinary income under section 212 of the Internal Revenue Code of 1954, or whether, under section 263 of the Code, they must be capitalized and offset against long-term capital gain realized by taxpayers from the settlement.

. . . Joseph M. Meade and William S. King were the sole shareholders of the Alabama Wire Company, Inc. In 1963, that corporation and its wholly owned subsidiary employed an Atlanta, Georgia, law firm to advise whether Kaiser Aluminum and Chemical Corporation, in connection with its dealings with Alabama Wire and its subsidiary, had violated the federal antitrust laws. For this initial employment, which ceased in early 1964, the Atlanta firm was paid legal fees by Alabama Wire and its subsidiary.

The name of Alabama Wire was thereafter changed to Terrace Corporation, and, on February 15, 1965, the corporation was liquidated. Among the proceeds of the liquidation was the potential claim against Kaiser Aluminum, which, the parties have stipulated, had no ascertainable value at that time. Meade and King, individually, thus acquired ownership of the potential antitrust claim. Meade received a one-third interest in the claim, and King received a two-thirds interest, in accordance with their proportionate ownership of the distributing corporation.

Based upon a later opinion of Atlanta counsel, Meade and King, in 1965, retained the firm to pursue the antitrust claim on their personal behalf. An agreement was entered whereby the firm would be paid a monthly retainer fee plus 20 percent of any amount recovered. When it was subsequently determined that San Francisco counsel should be employed to bring the suit against Kaiser Aluminum in California, the agreement was modified to provide that a retainer of $10,000 would be paid to San Francisco counsel (which amount was to be credited against future retainer charges due Atlanta counsel), and that both counsel would share a 33 percent participation in any amount recovered.

Suit was brought against Kaiser Aluminum in 1965 in the names of Meade and King, individually, as assignees of the cause of action of Alabama Wire and its subsidiary. Treble damages of $9,000,000 were sought. The case was settled in 1966 for $900,000, of which Meade received $300,000 and King, $600,000. On his respective 1966 income tax return, each reported the proceeds of the settlement as additional long-term capital gain from the liquidation of Terrace Corporation.

. . . Meade and King, in 1966, paid legal fees and litigation expenses totaling $320,993.67. Meade paid one third of that amount, and King paid two thirds. Each claimed the full amount so paid by him as a deduction against ordinary income on his 1966 tax return. The Commissioner disallowed these deductions and treated the entire amount of legal expenses as an offset against the long-term capital gain realized by taxpayers from their antitrust claim. . . . [T]he Tax Court held that the attorneys' fees and expenses are properly deductible under section 212(1) as payments for the production of income. . . . We reverse the decision of the Tax Court.

The stock of Terrace Corporation constituted a capital asset in the hands of the taxpayers of Terrace Corporation. Thus, the proceeds of the liquidation of Terrace Corporation, received in exchange for their Terrace stock, constituted capital gain to taxpayers. Since the antitrust claim was included as part of the proceeds of the liquidation, the fair market value of the claim ordinarily would have entered into the computation — made at that time — of taxpayers' capital gain from the liquidation. . . . In this instance, however, the potential claim had no ascertainable fair market value at the time of distribution, and no value was assigned to it for purposes of computing taxpayers' capital gain from the liquidation. The liquidation therefore remained an "open transaction," and, for tax purposes, the amounts subsequently received from the antitrust claim related back to the initial exchange. See Burnet v. Logan, 283 U.S. 404 [(1931)]. . . . It being undisputed that the Terrace stock was a capital asset in taxpayers' hands, taxpayers and the Commissioner agree that taxpayers had long-term capital gain upon the settlement with Kaiser Aluminum in 1966.

This appeal involves the treatment of taxpayers' legal expenses in connection with the settlement of the antitrust claim. Taxpayers contend that these legal expenses are deductible from ordinary income as expenses incurred "for the collection of income" under section 212(1). The Commissioner argues that the legal expenses must be capitalized and offset against taxpayers' capital gain because they were incurred in connection with the disposition of a capital asset, the Terrace Corporation stock, within the meaning of section 263.

. . . Although section 263, which deals with capital expenditures, explicitly denies a deduction only for certain types of expenditures, it is clear that the section does not provide an exclusive list. C.I.R. v. Lincoln Savings and Loan Association, 403 U.S. 345, 358 . . . (1971). The limits of nondeductibility for capital expenditures are found in the case law. Here, we are guided by fundamental doctrine recently noted by the Supreme Court in Woodward v. C.I.R., 397 U.S. 572, 575 . . . (1970): "It has long been recognized, as a general matter, that costs incurred in the acquisition or disposition of a capital asset are to be treated as capital expenditures." More specifically, expenses incurred by shareholders in effecting the liquidation of their corporation — our concern in this case — ordinarily constitute capital expenditures, which enter into the computation of gain or loss arising from the distribution. . . .

The Supreme Court's recent decisions in Woodward v. C.I.R., supra, and its companion case, United States v. Hilton Hotels Corporation, 397 U.S. 580 . . . (1970), shed further light on the principles applicable to this appeal. In those cases, the Court unanimously held that expenses of litigation that arise out of the acquisition of a capital asset are capital expenses. The cases presented two substantially identical situations. Taxpayers incurred legal expenses in appraisal proceedings in connection with a purchase of dissenting shareholders' stock that was required under local law. Taxpayers argued that the "primary purpose" test should be applied in determining the deductibility of the costs of acquiring or disposing of property. That rule, developed in the context of expenditures to defend or perfect title to property, provides that such expenditures are capital in nature only where the taxpayer's primary purpose in incurring them is to defend or perfect title. . . . The primary purpose of their expenditures in the appraisal proceedings, taxpayers argued, related not to the acquisition of title, but to the price to be paid for the stock, and, therefore, their expenditures should not be characterized as acquisition costs.

In rejecting the taxpayers' claims in *Woodward* and *Hilton Hotels*, the Supreme Court found the primary purpose test inapplicable to the situations before it: "A test based upon the taxpayer's 'purpose' in undertaking or defending a particular piece of litigation would encourage resort to formalisms and artificial distinctions." Woodward v. C.I.R., 397 U.S. at 577. . . . Instead, the Court adopted the "origin" test, choosing to consider the origin and character of the claim for which the expenditures were made. On the basis of that test, the Court held that the determination of a purchase price by litigation is clearly part of the process of acquisition and should be treated as part of the cost of the stock that the taxpayers acquired. In so holding, the Court noted that "ancillary expenses incurred in acquiring or disposing of an asset are as much part of the cost of that asset as is the price paid for it." Woodward v. C.I.R., 397 U.S. at 576. . . . We find the Court's reasoning compelling in its application to the facts before us.

As we noted above, the exchange in the liquidation of taxpayers' stock for the Terrace assets resulted in capital gain treatment to the taxpayers. The exchange remained an open transaction until the proceeds of the antitrust claim were collected by taxpayers. Since the open transaction event qualified for capital gain treatment, the amounts ultimately collected from the settlement do also. In effect, the proceeds of the settlement constituted additional consideration for taxpayers' stock in Terrace Corporation. While taxpayers have agreed with the Commissioner that the liquidation should be kept open in order to include the proceeds of the settlement as capital gains, taxpayers seek to close that transaction for the purpose of characterizing the legal expenses involved as deductible expenses for the collection of income. The Supreme Court's "origin of the claim" test prevents us from agreeing with taxpayers.

The "origin" test was first set forth by the Court in United States v. Gilmore, 372 U.S. 39 . . . (1963). There it was held that legal expenses incurred by a taxpayer in defending a divorce suit were nondeductible personal expenses even though taxpayers' securities holdings, and possibly his business reputation, would be affected by the outcome of the case. The Court sustained the Government's position that deductibility depended on the "origin and nature" of the claim against the taxpayer, and found that the claim arose out of the personal relationship of marriage. The Court stated the proper test as follows: "[T]he origin and character of the claim with respect to which an expense was incurred, rather than its potential consequences upon the fortunes of the taxpayer, is the controlling basic test of whether the expense was 'business' or 'personal' and hence whether it is deductible or not under §23(a)(2) [section 212 of the 1954 Code]." 372 U.S. at 49. . . . It was this test that the Court adopted in *Woodward* in determining that the origin of the particular litigation involved was found in the process of the acquisition of a capital asset, and that therefore the expenses of the litigation were nondeductible capital expenses.

Although there is admittedly a distinction between the two situations, we think it clear that the Court adopted this test, not only with respect to the acquisition of a capital asset, but also for determining whether legal expenses are incurred in the process of *disposition* of property. . . . Substantially the same problems arise in each determination. In both the disposition and acquisition of property, a determination must be made of the tax consequences of monetary outlays in connection with contesting the value of certain capital assets. The uncertainty and difficulty of considering the taxpayer's motive in incurring expenses are present in both situations. For the deductibility of payments to depend upon such subjective considerations would, as the Court noted in *Woodward*, encourage resort to "formalisms and artificial distinctions."

Applying the "origin" standard to the facts before us, we are convinced that the antitrust claim against Kaiser Aluminum — as it rested in the hands of these taxpayers — had its origin in the process of the disposition of their stock in Terrace Corporation. The claim was part of the Terrace assets received by taxpayers in the liquidation of the corporation, and taxpayers' disposition of their stock was an open transaction for purposes of the collection of the proceeds of the settlement. Thus, the valuation of the claim against Kaiser Aluminum was vital to the disposition of taxpayers' stock, and the litigation necessary for this determination was an integral part of the overall transaction. Hence, the expenses incurred in the litigation that led to the settlement are properly treated as part of the cost of the stock that the taxpayers exchanged in the liquidation.

Taxpayers have directed our attention to two circuit court decisions, Naylor v. C.I.R., 5 Cir., 1953, 203 F.2d 346, and C.I.R. v. Doering, 2 Cir., 1964, 335 F.2d 738, which presented problems similar to the one before us. In *Naylor,* taxpayer gave an option to purchase certain stock, which was a capital asset in his hands, at a price based on the stock's net asset value shown on the books of the company on a certain date. The purchaser exercised his option, but thereafter a dispute arose over the valuation, and taxpayer hired an attorney to negotiate with the purchaser concerning the value of the shares. Taxpayer's expenses in connection with the valuation were held deductible under the predecessor of section 212(1).

Doering involved a fact pattern slightly different from *Naylor.* In *Doering,* taxpayer owned stock in Argosy Pictures Corporation, which had contracted to produce certain films for distribution by Republic Pictures Corporation. A dispute arose between the corporations as to the amount of Argosy's participation in the proceeds under the contract, but Argosy liquidated before a settlement was effected. Because the claim had no ascertainable fair market value at the time, the transaction remained "open" for tax purposes. In redemption of his stock, a capital asset, taxpayer received cash and a pro rata portion of Argosy's claim against Republic. Thereafter, in effecting a settlement of the dispute over the terms of Argosy's contract with Republic, taxpayer incurred legal expenses. The full Tax Court, four judges dissenting, allowed him to deduct the expenses under section 212 because they were incurred for the "collection of income." A divided panel of the Second Circuit affirmed.

We think that the *Naylor* and *Doering* decisions have been considerably eroded by *Woodward* and *Hilton Hotels,* which arrived at results different from *Naylor* and *Doering,* though all four cases presented similar fact situations. . . . *Naylor* and *Doering* are, however, distinguishable from the Supreme Court decisions and from the cases before us.

We see *Naylor* as holding that if a disposition of a capital asset has been consummated, and subsequent controversy concerns no more than enforcement of the terms of the agreement, then the problem is one of collection of income under section 212. . . . As the Court noted in *Naylor*, "[T]he situation called for the services of an attorney to collect the proceeds of a sale of a capital asset. Petitioner's attorney was employed after an enforceable contract of sale existed." . . . Similarly, *Doering* involved legal expenses that were found to be a cost of collecting sums due the taxpayer under "a fully executed and enforceable contract." . . .

In *Woodward* and *Hilton Hotels*, on the other hand, the problem was treated as one of the establishment of a purchase price in the acquisition of a capital asset. The transactions there were clearly considered incomplete until the litigation to set a purchase price had concluded. "The whole process of acquisition required both legal operations — fixing the price, and conveying title to the [stock]." . . . So also in the cases before us, we are concerned with transactions not consummated until the claim against Kaiser Aluminum had been settled. Establishment of the value of the antitrust claim was a contingency on which the finality of taxpayers' stock disposition depended. By contrast, in *Naylor* and *Doering*, fully enforceable agreements existed, and litigation involved only the interpretation and enforcement of those agreements. Accordingly, the legal expenses involved in those cases may more easily fit within the concept of expenses incurred for the collection of income than taxpayers' expenses in the cases before us.

Reversed.

NOTES

1. Should a shareholder's gain on liquidation be recognized at all and, if so, to what extent? If it should be recognized, how should it be taxed? Should a shareholder be taxed to the extent of his allocable share of earnings and profits even if he has no gain, and if so, how? Should a shareholder's loss be recognized on complete liquidation? Cf. §267(a)(1).

2. Section 332 provides for the nonrecognition of a parent corporation's gain on the liquidation of its subsidiary in certain circumstances. Functionally, an intercorporate liquidation (at least where the shareholder corporation is in control of the subsidiary) may be very similar to a merger. For that reason, §332 will be studied with "reorganizations" in Chapter 4, infra.

3. See B. Bittker and J. Eustice, Federal Income Taxation of Corporations and Shareholders 11-1 to 11-41 (5th ed. 1987).

b. Redemptions — §§301, 302, 303, 304, 318

i. Distributions in Complete Termination of Interest

BLEILY & COLLISHAW, INC. v. COMMISSIONER
72 T.C. 751 (1979), *aff'd without opinion*, 647 F.2d 169 (9th Cir. 1981)

IRWIN, Judge. Respondent determined a deficiency of $6,573 in petitioner's income tax for the taxable year 1973.

The only issue in this case is whether redemptions by Maxdon Construction, Inc. (Maxdon), of its stock held by petitioner constituted dividends taxable as ordinary income under sections 301 and 316 or constituted distributions in exchange for its stock pursuant to section 302 and, therefore, taxable as capital gains.

FINDINGS OF FACT

. . . Petitioner Bleily & Collishaw, Inc. (B & C), is a California corporation which was originally engaged in the construction business but gradually became a landholding company. . . . Ray Collishaw is B & C's president and owns all its shares.

In 1969, B & C bought 225 shares of Maxdon's stock. Maxdon's remaining 525 shares were held by its president, Donald J. Neumann. In 1969, a close business relationship existed between B & C and Maxdon and Maxdon did subcontracting for B & C. As B & C stopped its contracting work, however, it no longer had any use for Maxdon's subcontracting work. Since Neumann felt there was no advantage to Maxdon in B & C's continuing ownership of its stock, he wanted sole control and ownership of Maxdon.

Sometime prior to August 17, 1973, Neumann met with Collishaw to discuss the purchase of B & C's shares. Collishaw agreed to sell all of B & C's Maxdon stock at $200 per share and was willing to do so at that time. However, because Neumann had problems obtaining enough cash for an immediate purchase of all B & C's Maxdon stock, he offered to buy only a portion of the stock. Nonetheless, Collishaw intended at all times to sell the shares if and when Neumann offered to buy them, although he was not under any contractual or legal obligation to do so.

Neumann expected to, and in fact did, receive or earn enough money every month to make additional purchases of stock. Each month prior to each transaction, Collishaw contacted his accountant who then determined the proper number of shares to be redeemed that month. Each sale was supported by a separate written redemption agreement executed by Maxdon and B & C providing a redemption price of $200 per share and reciting the number of shares Maxdon then had outstanding, the number then owned by B & C, and the number of shares B & C was to sell. Maxdon redeemed all of B & C's stock during the 23-week period August 17, 1973 — February 22, 1974, thereby terminating B & C's interest in Maxdon. . . .

During 1973, Maxdon redeemed a total of 166 shares of stock for a total of $33,200. Petitioner claimed this amount on its 1973 corporate income tax return as a dividend, subject to the 85-percent deduction allowed by section 243. Respondent determined that the redemptions constituted an exchange of stock, thereby taxing the redemptions as capital gains.

OPINION

The issue before us is whether section 302(b) applies to the redemptions, thereby taxing the transaction under section 302(a). If section 302(a) does not apply, then the redemptions are taxable under sections 301 and 316 as dividends. . . .

Respondent contends that sections 302(b)(1), 302(b)(2), and 302(b)(3) all apply whereas petitioner contends that none of these sections apply.

We deal first with section 302(b)(3). For section 302(b)(3) to apply there must be a complete redemption of all of the stock owned by a shareholder. Where several redemptions have been executed pursuant to a plan to terminate a shareholder's interest, the individual redemptions constitute, in substance, the component parts of a single sale or exchange of the entire stock interest. We have refused, however, to treat a series of redemptions as a single plan unless the redemptions are pursuant to a firm and fixed plan to eliminate the stockholder from the corporation. . . . .

Generally, a gentleman's agreement lacking written embodiment, communication, and contractual obligations will not suffice to show a fixed and firm plan. Leleux v. Commissioner, supra. On the other hand, a plan need not be in writing, absolutely binding, or communicated to others to be fixed and firm although these factors all tend to indicate that such is the case. Niedermeyer v. Commissioner, supra.

Each case is necessarily a factual determination and based upon the record we are convinced Maxdon planned to eliminate B & C as a shareholder. The initiative for the redemption came from Neumann, not Collishaw. It is undisputed that Neumann wanted sole ownership of Maxdon and desired to buy B & C's interest as fast as his cash position would allow. It was only because Neumann did not have enough cash for an immediate purchase that B & C's entire block of Maxdon stock was not purchased on August 17, 1972. As Neumann obtained cash he made purchases every month for 6 con-

secutive months of a number of shares[5] until B & C's interest was
liquidated. Collishaw had agreed to the sale of all its shares and to
the purchase price. As noted before, the fact that the agreement was
not binding is not dispositive. Cf. Himmel v. Commissioner, supra
(no fixed plan where the agreement read that so long as petitioner
lives the corporation may redeem his preferred shares at par, provided that it is "financially able to redeem same," if its other
shareholders desire that this be done), and Benjamin v. Commissioner, supra ("vague anticipation is not a firm plan with fixed
conditions"). Here, both shareholders agreed to the redemption, and
Maxdon planned to purchase B & C's Maxdon stock over the course
of a few months as funds became available.

Because we have found that there was an integrated plan, we
do not need to determine whether each redemption considered separately meets the "essentially equivalent to a dividend test" under
section 302(b)(1), or whether section 302(b)(2) applies to the redemption.[6]

Decision will be entered for the respondent.

NOTES

1. Compare Benjamin v. Commissioner, 592 F.2d 1259 (5th Cir.
1979), in which the court held that a redemption of a portion of a
stockholder's shares did not qualify for capital gains treatment as part
of a plan to terminate completely the shareholder's interest since
there was no time framework for the redemption and the taxpayer
as a director had wide discretion in determining when the redemption
would be completed. To the same effect, see Mary G. Roebling, 77
T.C. 30 (1981); Mary Johnston, 77 T.C. 679 (1981).

5. It seems that the precise amount of shares to be redeemed each month was
agreed upon by both parties at least in part to avoid the 80-percent test of sec.
302(b)(2):

	(i) Ratio that B & C's (voting) stock in Maxdon immediately after the redemption bears to all voting stock at such time	(ii) Ratio that B & C's (voting) stock in Maxdon immediately before the redemption bears to all voting stock at such time	80% of (ii)
8/17/73	24.02	30.00	24.00
9/23/73	19.23	24.02	19.21
10/19/73	15.46	19.23	15.38
11/23/73	12.50	15.46	12.36
12/21/73	10.10	12.50	10.00
1/18/74	8.22	10.10	8.08
2/22/74	—	8.22	—

6. It is clear that no individual redemption meets the "substantially disproportionate" test of sec. 302(b)(2); it is respondent's position that the redemptions must
be considered together, thereby meeting that test.

2. See also Estate of Mathis, 47 T.C. 248 (1966), *acq.*, 1967-1 C.B. 2. There, the corporation contracted to purchase preferred stock for a cash payment of $26,130, followed by monthly payments of $500 for 13 to 20 months, and a final payment of $100,000. Since all but the final payment equalled the accrued but undeclared and unpaid dividends, the Commissioner argued that all payments preceding the $100,000 were taxable as dividends and not as part of the purchase price. According to the court, however (at 255):

> The evidence of record has convinced us that $36,130 of the $136,130 received under the preferred stock redemption agreement was measured by an allowance for accrued and unpaid dividends, although no formal declaration of dividends had ever occurred. However, this does not mean that the $36,130 should be treated as ordinary dividend income. On the contrary, accrued dividends on preferred stock paid in connection with a stock redemption are properly treated as part of the payment in exchange for the stock. . . . The problem with [the Commissioner's] argument is that it fails to distinguish an obligation arising under a purchase contract from an intangible right to dividends which have never been declared.

What would have been the result in *Mathis* if the dividend had been declared prior to the redemption? See Arie S. Crown, 58 T.C. 825 (1972), *aff'd mem.*, 487 F.2d 1404 (7th Cir. 1973), in which a portion of the amount received by preferred stockholders on redemption of their shares was taxed as a dividend. No dividend had been declared, but the court concluded that the corporation had incurred a legal obligation to pay a dividend on the preferred by its prior declaration and payment of a dividend on its common stock. See also Victor E. Gidwitz Family Trust, 61 T.C. 664 (1974), *acq.*, 1974-2 C.B. 2; Rev. Rul. 75-320, 1975-2 C.B. 105; Rev. Rul. 69-131, 1969-1 C.B. 94; Rev. Rul. 69-130, 1969-1 C.B. 93 (superseding G.C.M. 5180, cited in *Mathis*).

If beneficiaries of the Mathis estate had owned 90 percent of the remaining stock in the corporation, might the result in the case have been different? Consider the effect of §318.

3. A buys a $1,000, 15-percent corporate bond at par. More than a year after the purchase, between interest dates, A, a cash basis taxpayer, sells the bond to B for a lump sum equal to par plus accrued interest. What are A's tax consequences? See Treas. Reg. §1.61-7(d); Charles T. Fisher, 19 T.C. 384 (1952), *aff'd,* 209 F.2d 513 (6th Cir.), *cert. denied,* 347 U.S. 1014 (1954). Cf. Jaglom v. Commissioner, 303 F.2d 847 (2d Cir. 1962) (bond with defaulted interest purchased "flat"; on resale, sale price allocable to interest accrued since taxpayer's purchase).

A corporate bond bearing 9-percent interest, issued in 1988 for its $1,000 face value, changes hands in the market. B buys it on the open market for $900. More than six months thereafter the corporation retires the bond, paying B $1,000 plus accrued interest of $30. What is the tax consequence to B? What is your authority?

Corporation M in 1976 issued a face amount $1,000 bond, due 1989, bearing interest at 8 percent, for $900. A bought the bond in 1980 in the open market for $850. In 1989 the corporation retired the bond, paying A $1,000 plus $30 accrued interest. What is the tax consequence to A? See §1271.

4. Should the tax treatment on the sale or retirement of preferred stock with cumulative dividend arrearages differ from that accorded bonds with defaulted interest? Why?

LYNCH v. COMMISSIONER
801 F.2d 1176 (9th Cir. 1986), *rev'g* 83 T.C. 597 (1984)

Before Farris, Hall and Kozinski, Circuit Judges.

HALL, Circuit Judge. The Commissioner . . . petitions for review of a Tax Court decision holding that a corporate redemption of a taxpayer's stock was a sale or exchange subject to capital gains treatment. The Commissioner argues that the taxpayer held a prohibited interest in the corporation after the redemption and therefore the transaction should be characterized as a dividend distribution taxable as ordinary income. We agree with the Commissioner and reverse the Tax Court.

I

Taxpayers, William and Mima Lynch, formed the W. M. Lynch Co. on April 1, 1960. The corporation issued all of its outstanding stock to William Lynch (taxpayer). The taxpayer specialized in leasing cast-in-place concrete pipe machines. He owned the machines individually but leased them to the corporation which in turn subleased the equipment to independent contractors.

On December 17, 1975 the taxpayer sold 50 shares of the corporation's stock to his son, Gilbert Lynch (Gilbert), for $17,170. Gilbert paid for the stock with a $16,000 check given to him by the taxpayer and $1,170 from his own savings. The taxpayer and his wife also resigned as directors and officers of the corporation on the same day.

On December 31, 1975 the corporation redeemed all 2300 shares of the taxpayer's stock. In exchange for his stock, the taxpayer received $17,900 of property and a promissory note for $771,920. Gilbert, as the sole remaining shareholder, pledged his 50 shares as a guarantee for the note. In the event that the corporation defaulted on any of the note payments, the taxpayer would have the right to vote or sell Gilbert's 50 shares.

In the years immediately preceding the redemption, Gilbert had assumed greater managerial responsibility in the corporation. He wished, however, to retain the taxpayer's technical expertise with cast-in-place concrete pipe machines. On the date of the redemption, the taxpayer also entered into a consulting agreement with the corporation. The consulting agreement provided the taxpayer with payments of $500 per month for five years, plus reimbursement for business related travel, entertainment, and automobile expenses.[1] In February 1977, the corporation and the taxpayer mutually agreed to reduce the monthly payments to $250. The corporation never withheld payroll taxes from payments made to the taxpayer.

After the redemption, the taxpayer shared his former office with Gilbert. The taxpayer came to the office daily for approximately one year; thereafter his appearances dwindled to about once or twice per week. When the corporation moved to a new building in 1979, the taxpayer received a private office.

In addition to the consulting agreement, the taxpayer had other ties to the corporation. He remained covered by the corporation's group medical insurance policy until 1980. When his coverage ended, the taxpayer had received the benefit of $4,487.54 in premiums paid by the corporation. He was also covered by a medical reimbursement plan, created the day of the redemption, which provided a maximum annual payment of $1,000 per member. Payments to the taxpayer under the plan totaled $96.05.

II

We must decide whether the redemption of the taxpayer's stock in this case is taxable as a dividend distribution under §301 or as long-term capital gain under §302(a). [On the date of the redemption, W. M. Lynch Co. had accumulated earnings and profits of $315,863 and had never paid a dividend.]

Section 302(b)(3) provides that a shareholder is entitled to sale or exchange treatment if the corporation redeems all of the shareholder's stock. In order to determine whether there is a complete redemption for purposes of section 302(b)(3), the family attribution rules of section 318(a) must be applied unless the requirements of section 302(c)(2) are satisfied. Here, if the family attribution rules

1. The corporation leased or purchased a pickup truck for the taxpayer's use in 1977. If someone at the corporation needed the truck, the taxpayer would make it available to him.

apply, the taxpayer will be deemed to own constructively the 50 shares held by Gilbert (100% of the corporation's stock) and the transaction would not qualify as a complete redemption within the meaning of section 302(b)(3).

Section 302(c)(2)(A) states in relevant part:

> In the case of a distribution described in subsection (b)(3), [the family attribution rules in] section 318(a)(1) shall not apply if—
>> (i) immediately after the distribution the distributee has no interest in the corporation (including an interest as officer, director, or employee), other than an interest as a creditor. . . .

The Commissioner argues that in every case the performance of post-redemption services is a prohibited interest under section 302(c)(2)(A)(i), regardless of whether the taxpayer is an officer, director, employee, or independent contractor.

The Tax Court rejected the Commissioner's argument, finding that the services rendered by the taxpayer did not amount to a prohibited interest in the corporation. . . . In reaching this conclusion, the Tax Court relied on a test derived from Lewis v. Commissioner, 47 T.C. 129, 136 (1966) (Simpson, J., concurring):

> Immediately after the enactment of the 1954 Code, it was recognized that section 302(c)(2)(A)(i) did not prohibit office holding per se, but was concerned with a retained financial stake in the corporation, such as a profit-sharing plan, or in the creation of an ostensible sale that really changed nothing so far as corporate management was concerned. Thus, in determining whether a prohibited interest has been retained under section 302(c)(2)(A)(i), we must look to whether the former stockholder has either retained a financial stake in the corporation or continued to control the corporation and benefit by its operations. In particular, where the interest retained is not that of an officer, director, or employee, we must examine the facts and circumstances to determine whether a prohibited interest has been retained under section 302(c)(2)(A)(i). Lynch v. Commissioner, 83 T.C. 597, 605 (1984).

After citing the "control or financial stake" standard, the Tax Court engaged in a two-step analysis. First, the court concluded that the taxpayer was an independent contractor rather than an employee because the corporation had no right under the consulting agreement to control his actions. Second, the court undertook a "facts and circumstances" analysis to determine whether the taxpayer had a financial stake in the corporation or managerial control after the redemption. Because the consulting agreement was not linked to the future profitability of the corporation, the court found that the taxpayer had no financial stake. Id. at 606-07. The court also found no evidence that the taxpayer exerted control over the corporation. Id. at 607. Thus, the Tax Court determined that the taxpayer held no interest prohibited by section 302(c)(2)(A)(i). [Finding that the tax-payer was not an employee obviated the need for the Tax Court to decide whether the parenthetical language in section 302(c)(2)(A)(i) prohibited employment relationships per se. Seda v. Commissioner, 82 T.C. 484, 488 (1984) (court stated that "section 302(c)(2)(A)(i) may not prohibit the retention of all employment relationships").]

III

. . . The Tax Court's interpretation of what constitutes a pro-hibited interest under section 302(c)(2)(A)(i) is a question of law reviewed de novo. . . . We reject the Tax Court's interpretation of section 302(c)(2)(A)(i). An individualized determination of whether a taxpayer has retained a financial stake or continued to control the corporation after the redemption is inconsistent with Congress' desire to bring a measure of certainty to the tax consequences of a corporate redemption. We hold that a taxpayer who provides post-redemption services, either as an employee or an independent contractor, holds a prohibited interest in the corporation because he is not a creditor.

The legislative history of section 302 states that Congress in-tended to provide "definite standards in order to provide certainty in specific instances." S. Rep. No. 1622, 83d Cong. 2d Sess. 233, reprinted in 1954 U.S. Code Cong. & Ad. News 4621, 4870. "In lieu of a factual inquiry in every case, [section 302] is intended to prescribe specific conditions from which the taxpayer may ascertain whether a given redemption" will qualify as a sale or be treated as a dividend distribution. H.R. Rep. No. 1337, 83d Cong. 2d Sess. 35, reprinted in 1954 U.S. Code Cong. & Ad. News 4017, 4210. The facts and circumstances approach created by the Tax Court undermines the ability of taxpayers to execute a redemption and know the tax con-sequences with certainty.

The taxpayer's claim that the Senate rejected the mechanical operation of the House's version of section 302 is misleading. The Senate did reject the House bill because the "definitive conditions" were "unnecessarily restrictive." S. Rep. No. 1622, 83d Cong., 2d Sess. 44, reprinted in 1954 U.S. Code Cong. & Ad. News 4621, 4675. However, the Senate's response was to add paragraph (b)(1) to section 301, which reestablished the flexible, but notoriously vague, "not essentially equivalent to a dividend" test. This test provided that all payments from a corporation that were not essentially equivalent to a dividend should be taxed as capital gains. The confusion that stemmed from a case-by-case inquiry into "dividend equivalence" prompted the Congress to enact definite standards for the safe har-bors in section 302(b)(2) and (b)(3). The Tax Court's failure to recognize that section 302(c)(2)(A)(i) prohibits all noncreditor interests in the corporation creates the same uncertainty as the "dividend equivalence" test.

The problem with the Tax Court's approach is apparent when this case is compared with Seda v. Commissioner, 82 T.C. 484 (1984). In *Seda*, a former shareholder, at his son's insistence, continued working for the corporation for two years after the redemption. He received a salary of $1,000 per month. The Tax Court refused to hold that section 302(c)(2)(A)(i) prohibits the retention of employment relations per se, despite the unequivocal language in the statute. Id. at 488. Instead, the court applied the facts and circumstances approach to determine whether the former shareholder retained a financial stake or continued to control the corporation. The Tax Court found that the monthly payments of $1,000 constituted a financial stake in the corporation. Id. This result is at odds with the holding in *Lynch* that payments of $500 per month do not constitute a financial stake in the corporation. . . . The court also found in *Seda* no evidence that the former shareholder had ceased to manage the corporation. 82 T.C. at 488. Again, this finding is contrary to the holding in *Lynch* that the taxpayer exercised no control over the corporation after the redemption, even though he worked daily for a year and shared his old office with his son. Compare *Lynch*, 83 T.C. at 607 with *Seda*, 82 T.C. 488. *Seda* and *Lynch* thus vividly demonstrate the perils of making an ad hoc determination of "control" or "financial stake."

A recent Tax Court opinion further illustrates the imprecision of the facts and circumstances approach. In Cerone v. Commissioner, [87 T.C. 1 (1986)], a father and son owned all the shares of a corporation formed to operate their restaurant. The corporation agreed to redeem all of the father's shares in order to resolve certain disagreements between the father and son concerning the management of the business. However, the father remained an employee of the corporation for at least five years after the redemption, drawing a salary of $14,400 for the first three years and less thereafter. The father claimed that he was entitled to capital gains treatment on the redemption because he had terminated his interest in the corporation within the meaning of section 302(b)(3).

Even on the facts of *Cerone*, the Tax Court refused to find that the father held a prohibited employment interest per se. Instead, the Tax Court engaged in a lengthy analysis, citing both *Seda* and *Lynch*. The court proclaimed that *Lynch* reaffirmed the rationale of *Seda*, even though *Lynch* involved an independent contractor rather than an employee. After comparing the facts of *Seda* and *Cerone*, the Tax Court eventually concluded that the father in *Cerone* held a financial stake in the corporation because he had drawn a salary that was $2,400 per year more than the taxpayer in *Seda* and had been employed by the corporation for a longer period after the redemption. . . . However, the Tax Court was still concerned that the prohibited interest in *Seda* might have been based on the finding in that case that the taxpayer had both a financial stake and continued control of the corporation. The Tax Court, citing *Lynch,* held that the "test is whether he retained a financial stake or continued to control the corporation." Cerone, slip op. at 54. Thus, the Tax Court found that the father in *Cerone* held a prohibited interest because he had a financial stake as defined by *Seda.*

Although the Tax Court reached the correct result in *Cerone,* its approach undermines the definite contours of the safe harbor Congress intended to create with sections 302(b)(3) and 302(c)(2)(A)(i). Whether a taxpayer has a financial stake according to the Tax Court seems to depend on two factors, length of employment and the amount of salary. Length of employment after the redemption is irrelevant because Congress wanted taxpayers to know whether they were entitled to capital gains treatment on the date their shares were redeemed. See S. Rep. No. 1622, 83d Cong., 2d Sess. 235-36, reprinted in 1954 U.S. Code Cong. & Ad. News 4621, 4872-73. See also Treas. Reg. §1.302-4(a)(1) (taxpayer must attach a statement disclaiming any interest in the corporation with the first tax return filed after the distribution). As for the amount of annual salary, the Tax Court's present benchmark appears to be the $12,000 figure in *Seda.* Salary at or above this level will be deemed to be a financial stake in the enterprise, though the $6,000 annual payments in this case were held not to be a financial stake. There is no support in the legislative history of section 302 for the idea that Congress meant only to prohibit service contracts of a certain worth, and taxpayers should not be left to speculate as to what income level will give rise to a financial stake.

In this case, the taxpayer points to the fact that the taxpayers in *Seda* and *Cerone* were employees, while he was an independent contractor. On appeal, the Commissioner concedes the taxpayer's independent contractor status. We fail to see, however, any meaningful way to distinguish *Seda* and *Cerone* from *Lynch* by differentiating between employees and independent contractors. All of the taxpayers performed services for their corporations following the redemption. To hold that only the employee taxpayers held a prohibited interest would elevate form over substance. The parenthetical language in section 302(c)(2)(A)(i) merely provides a subset of prohibited interests from the universe of such interests, and in no way limits us from finding that an independent contractor retains a prohibited interest. Furthermore, the Tax Court has in effect come to ignore the parenthetical language. If employment relationships are not prohibited interests per se, then the taxpayer's status as an

employee or independent contractor is irrelevant. What really matters under the Tax Court's approach is how the taxpayer fares under
a facts and circumstances review of whether he has a financial stake
in the corporation or managerial control. Tax planners are left to
guess where along the continuum of monthly payments from $500
to $1000 capital gains treatment ends and ordinary income tax begins.

Our holding today that taxpayers who provide post-redemption
services have a prohibited interest under section 302(c)(2)(A)(i) is
inconsistent with the Tax Court's decision in Estate of Lennard v.
Commissioner, 61 T.C. 554 (1974). That case held that a former
shareholder who, as an independent contractor, provided post-redemption accounting services for a corporation did not have a
prohibited interest. The Tax Court found that "Congress did not
intend to include independent contractors possessing no financial
stake in the corporation among those who are considered as retaining
an interest in the corporation for purposes of the attribution waiver
rules." Id. at 561. We disagree. In the context of Lennard, the Tax
Court appears to be using financial stake in the sense of having an
equity interest or some other claim linked to the future profit of the
corporation. Yet, in cases such as Seda and Cerone, the Tax Court has
found that fixed salaries of $12,000 and $14,400, respectively, constitute a financial stake. Fees for accounting services could easily
exceed these amounts, and it would be irrational to argue that the
definition of financial stake varies depending on whether the taxpayer
is an employee or an independent contractor. In order to avoid these
inconsistencies, we conclude that those who provide post-redemption
services, whether as independent contractors or employees, hold an
interest prohibited by section 302(c)(2)(A)(i) because they are more
than merely creditors.

In addition, both the Tax Court and the Commissioner have
agreed that taxpayers who enter into management consulting contracts after the redemption possess prohibited interests. Chertkof v.
Commissioner, 72 T.C. 1113, 1124-25 (1979), aff'd, 649 F.2d 264 (4th
Cir. 1981); Rev. Ruling 70-104, 1970-1 C.B. 66 (1970). Taxpayers
who provide such services are, of course, independent contractors.
However, unlike the Commissioner's opinion in Rev. Ruling 70-104
that all management consulting agreements are prohibited interests,
the Tax Court applies the financial stake or managerial control test.
In Chertkof, the court found that because the services provided under
the contract "went to the essence" of the corporation's existence, the
taxpayer had not effectively ceded control. 72 T.C. at 1124. Here,
the Tax Court distinguished Chertkof on the ground that the taxpayer
did not retain control of the corporation, but instead provided only
limited consulting services. Lynch, 83 T.C. at 608. We believe that
any attempt to define prohibited interests based on the level of control

leads to the same difficulties inherent in making a case-by-case determination of what constitutes a financial stake.

IV

Our decision today comports with the plain language of section 302 and its legislative history.... Taxpayers who wish to receive capital gains treatment upon the redemption of their shares must completely sever all noncreditor interests in the corporation.[2] See, e.g., Treas. Reg. §1.302-4(d) (a creditor's claim must not be subordinate to the claims of general creditors or in any other sense proprietary, i.e., principal payments or interest rates must not be contingent on the earnings of the corporation). We hold that the taxpayer, as an independent contractor, held such a noncreditor interest, and so cannot find shelter in the safe harbor of section 302(c)(2)(A)(i). Accordingly, the family attribution rules of section 318 apply and the taxpayer fails to qualify for a complete redemption under section 302(b)(3). The payments from the corporation in redemption of the taxpayer's shares must be characterized as a dividend distribution taxable as ordinary income under section 301.

The taxpayer argues that some creditor relationships might result in an "opportunity to influence" as great or greater than any officer, director, or employee relationship. He cites Rev. Ruling 77-467, 1977-2 C.B. 92, which concluded that a taxpayer who leased real property to a corporation, after the corporation redeemed his shares, held a creditor's interest under section 302(c)(2)(A)(i). While the taxpayer here may be correct in his assessment of a creditor's "opportunity to influence" a corporation, he overlooks the fact that Congress specifically allowed the right to retain such an interest.

Reversed.

DUNN v. COMMISSIONER
615 F.2d 578 (2d Cir. 1980)

Before Van Graafeiland and Kearse, Circuit Judges, and Dooling, District Judge.

DOOLING, District Judge. The Commissioner appeals from a decision of the Tax Court... holding that amounts received by appellee taxpayer, Georgia Dunn, in 1970 and 1971 from Bresee Chevrolet Co., Inc. ... were received in complete redemption of all her stock in Bresee, and that immediately after the distribution she had no

---

2. Our definition of a prohibited interest still leaves an open question as to the permissible scope of a creditor's interest under section 302(c)(2)(A)(i).

interest in Bresee as an officer, director, employee or otherwise, other than an interest as a creditor. In consequence, the Tax Court held, the amounts the taxpayer received were capital gains and not dividends, as the Commissioner contended.

When the redemption transaction was entered into the taxpayer owned 249 of the 500 shares of Bresee, her son William Dunn owned 149 shares and each of her married daughters owned 51 shares. In May 1970 taxpayer contracted to "sell or redeem from" Bresee her 249 shares of the company's stock for $335,154 payable $100,000 on June 1, 1970, and the balance with 5 percent interest over a period of ten years. Bresee redeemed the taxpayer's stock on the June 1, 1970, closing date; she was then paid the $100,000, and in 1971 was paid $45,260.34.

. . . Section 302 treats redemptions as exchanges within Section 302(a) if they qualify under one of the [three] subsections of Section 302(b): the subsection under which the taxpayer's transaction has been held to qualify is subsection (b)(3) which provides —

(3) TERMINATION OF SHAREHOLDER'S INTEREST —

> Subsection (a) shall apply if the redemption is in complete redemption of all of the stock of the corporation owned by the shareholder.

And Section 302(a) applies, through Section 302(b)(3), when, as Section 302(c)(2)(A)(i) requires,

> (i) immediately after the distribution the distributee has no interest in the corporation (including an interest as officer, director, or employee), other than an interest as a creditor. . . .

Thus, if after the redemption the taxpayer retained an interest in Bresee other than as a creditor, the 1970 and 1971 payments to her would be treated as taxable dividends — to the extent of Bresee's earnings. . . . §302(d).

I

. . . The appellee Herbert A. Dunn was never a director or stockholder of Bresee; he had been in the automobile business since 1925 essentially as a salesman, and he had been general manager and for a time, until 1951, president of Bresee. In about 1951, however, taxpayer's son William B. Dunn became president of Bresee, and, at about the same time, apparently with the encouragement of General Motors Corporation ("GM"), the grantor of the Bresee franchise, the taxpayer transferred 125 shares of her stock to her son, and, following that, made yearly gifts of stock to her three children until they owned a majority of the stock.

There was testimony that GM wanted William Dunn to own a majority of the stock. By 1970 appellee Herbert Dunn was seventy-seven years old and taxpayer was seventy-three. The taxpayer wished to spend most of her time in Florida, and she did not want to have any business responsibilities. Appellee Herbert Dunn, while continuing as a salesman with Bresee, also planned to spend part of each winter in Florida.

Judge Tannenwald found on ample evidence that the taxpayer wished to dispose of her stock because she had been advised that it created a liquidity problem from an estate planning point of view, and because she and her husband wanted additional income, as they advanced in age, and Bresee had not paid any dividends except in one year. In the negotiations between the taxpayer and Bresee each party was represented by separate counsel.

Such were the general circumstances when the taxpayer entered into the May 27, 1970, Stock Purchase Agreement (the "Agreement") with Bresee. . . . The Agreement recited that Bresee operated as a Chevrolet franchise subject to all of the terms of the franchise agreement with GM, and that among the franchise terms was one requiring Bresee to maintain a certain "Owned Net Working Capital" in order to retain the dealership. The Stock Purchase Agreement stated that the parties understood that the Owned Net Working Capital requirement would prohibit Bresee's paying any principal or interest under the Agreement if payment would reduce Owned Net Working Capital to an amount less than required by the franchise agreement or unless payment permitted the dealer to retain at least 50 percent of net after tax profits to be added to surplus. It was then agreed, with respect to payment of principal or interest under the Agreement, or on the accompanying ten year promissory note, that

> . . . if . . . the making of and payment thereunder would result in a violation of both said requirements, then and in such event, the due date of such payment or the part thereof which would result in such violation, shall be postponed until such date as when said payments or a part thereof can be made and still meet either the requirement in regard to "Owned Net Working Capital" or the requirement in regard to retention of 50% of net profits after taxes.

On June 1, 1970, Bresee redeemed all 249 of taxpayer's shares and paid taxpayer $100,000. After the redemption the taxpayer was not an officer, director, or employee of Bresee and through the date of trial had not acquired any stock in Bresee. After the redemption Bresee had 221 shares of stock outstanding, 143 of which were owned by William Dunn; each of his two married sisters owned 39 shares. . . .

On June 1, 1971, Bresee's financial condition was such that payment of the $55,154 and interest would have violated the GM

Minimum Capital Standard Agreement, and, accordingly, the payments were in part "postponed" under the above quoted terms of the Stock Purchase Agreement. The taxpayer received only $45,260.34 in principal, and she received no interest in June 1971. The balance of the principal payment due on June 1, 1971, was paid in June 1972, and the interest of $11,757.70 due on June 1, 1971, was paid in September 1974. After June 1, 1971, no payments on principal were either timely made or made during the taxable year when due. Payments of $23,311.80, the agreed annual payment amount, were made about a year or more late, on June 18, 1973, May 29, 1974, October 15, 1975, and July 27, 1976. At the time each payment was made, Bresee was in violation of the Minimum Capital Standard Agreement, although its net working capital was increasing each year.

While GM was not advised of each payment as it was made, it did receive monthly balance sheets and profit and loss statements; it did not object to Bresee's payments to the taxpayer. There was testimony, but Judge Tannenwald made no finding on this point, that before the redemption transaction Bresee never met the working capital requirement.

The "Termination of shareholder's interest" provision Section 302(b)(3), which accords sale or exchange treatment to redemptions of the stock of one shareholder if there is a complete redemption of all of the stock owned by that shareholder, applies to family corporations, not as some narrow and grudging exception to some otherwise general rule, but as a sensible and evident, explicit and appropriate definition of a type of capital transaction. The statute says simply that the capital transaction analysis applies if the retiring stockholder genuinely quits the company except to retain an interest as a creditor. Where a stockholder whose shares are purportedly redeemed in their entirety retains in some form the substance of stock ownership, then, as the Court put it in United States v. Davis, 397 U.S. 301, 307, . . . (1970), "such a redemption is always 'essentially equivalent to a dividend' within the meaning of that phrase in §302(b)(1)."

Judge Tannenwald found on the evidence that the taxpayer was not an officer, director or employee of Bresee after the redemption, that up to the date of trial she had not acquired any stock in Bresee and that she had filed with the tax return the required agreement to notify the Secretary of the Treasury of any acquisition of interest in the company. Hence the sole question is whether immediately after the distribution the taxpayer was anything more than a creditor of Bresee.

The Commissioner argues that the Treasury regulation, 26 C.F.R. §1.302-4(d), defining the term creditor in the context of

§302(b)(3) stock redemptions, is decisive of the case when it is applied to the postponement of payment provision of the Agreement. The regulation reads (as it has read since 1955):

> For the purpose of Section 302(c)(2)(A)(i), a person will be considered to be a creditor only if the rights of such person with respect to the corporation are not greater or broader in scope than necessary for the enforcement of his claim. Such claim must not in any sense be proprietary and must not be subordinate to the claims of general creditors. An obligation in the form of a debt may thus constitute a proprietary interest. For example, if under the terms of the instrument the corporation may discharge the principal amount of its obligation to a person by payments, the amount or certainty of which are dependent upon the earnings of the corporation, such a person is not a creditor of the corporation. Furthermore, if under the terms of the instrument the rate of purported interest is dependent upon earnings, the holder of such instrument may not, in some cases, be a creditor.

The Commissioner's contentions rest upon the fact that under the Stock Purchase Agreement if the making of any of the installment payments to the taxpayer would result in Bresee's failing to meet the net owned working capital requirement and the 50 percent of net profit retention clause, then payment of all or part of the installment is postponed until the payment can be made in whole or part without transgressing the GM agreement.

The Commissioner's confidence that the terms of the regulation require the conclusion that the taxpayer was not simply a creditor is not supported by the facts in the case. The regulation is concerned with the redeeming stockholder's status in two directions. First, that the redeeming stockholder does not remain someone with rights greater or broader than those of an ordinary creditor, for example, having the right to convert the claim into stock, or the right to vote as a stockholder in the event of a default in paying interest or principal, or a right to inspect the books or the stockholders list. As the regulation says, the claim must not be in any sense proprietary. None of these indicia of proprietary interest is claimed to be present in the taxpayer's case. She retained no office, no vote, no right to resume her position as stockholder in the event of default, or to convert her claim into stock, or any other right which would return to her a measure of control and of proprietary interest.

The regulation then turns to a second aspect of proprietorship — equity ownership — that is, that the redeeming stockholder's claim as creditor must not be subordinate to the claims of general creditors. The Commissioner appears to assume in part of his argument that the Agreement did subordinate the taxpayer's claim to those of general creditors. Nothing in the Agreement affects the rank of the taxpayer's claim as against general creditors, and there is nothing in the Agreement that, if Bresee had been put into liquidation, would have given any creditor a basis for arguing that he should be paid before the taxpayer was paid. It is certainly true that Bresee could not stay in business unless it paid its operating expenses as they came due, and that, in that sense, an ordinary trade creditor, with a right to insist on payment of his bill when due, stood in a different position than the taxpayer. But that is just the difference between any trade creditor selling on current account and a long-term creditor, secured or unsecured. Nothing in the Agreement gave trade creditors any standing whatever to insist upon Bresee's observance of GM's owned net working capital requirement. Indeed, in practical reality Bresee's general creditors were just as subject as the taxpayer to the invocation of the only sanction which GM had for enforcing the owned net working capital requirement, that is, termination of Bresee's Chevrolet franchise: the owned net working capital requirement could as easily be breached by incurring operating expenses as by paying the taxpayer.

The regulation then asserts that a person is not a creditor of the corporation if under the terms of the instrument the corporation may discharge the principal amount of its obligation by payments "the amount or certainty of which are dependent upon the earnings of the corporation." The Commissioner relies on this sentence ultimately, but it is not applicable. Only the time when the payments were made might be influenced by Bresee's owned net working capital position or rate of net profits after taxes, but neither the amount of the payments to be made nor the duty to make the payments was dependent on the existence of earnings. Neither the owned net working capital, nor the profit limitation aspect of the postponement clause in the Agreement defines the amount Bresee must pay under the Agreement or makes Bresee's earnings either the source or the measure of Bresee's obligation to the taxpayer. Bresee could pay the taxpayer from the proceeds of a mortgage on the dealership premises, or from capital contributed by the shareholders or raised on a new issue. The obligation to pay was unconditional and certain in its amount.[6]

The Tax Court did appear to accept as correct the Commissioner's argument that Bresee could discharge the obligation by payments the amount or certainty of which was dependent upon Bresee's earnings, a contention that must be rejected as an incorrect

---

6. The final sentence in the regulation states that if the rate of "purported interest is dependent upon earnings, the holder . . . may not, in some cases, be a creditor." The interest rate under the Agreement is not made dependent upon earnings. Rather, the Agreement simply reflects recognition of the owned net working capital provision as excusing timely performance.

reading of the Agreement. The court's view was that the restriction on time of payment was not an arrangement voluntarily agreed upon between the taxpayer and Bresee as a means of enabling her to perpetuate a stockholder-like interest in Bresee but was a GM exaction to which the taxpayer and Bresee alike had to bow. Nothing in that submission to the realities of Bresee's business life reflected a retention of a proprietary interest in Bresee by the taxpayer; the court analogized the situation to one in which a payment restriction was imposed by law.

The regulation, then, does not support the Commissioner's position, for the instrument under review does not exhibit a single one of the characteristics given significance by the regulation. . . .

The distinction between deferment of payability and contingency of obligation is familiar, Pierce Estates, Inc. v. Commissioner, 195 F.2d 475, 477-478 (3d Cir. 1952), and does indeed mark a difference between true debt and obligations that are presently something less than debt, but which become debt when the contingency occurs and fixes the obligation to pay. See generally American Bemberg Corp. v. United States, 253 F.2d 691 (3d Cir.), *cert. denied,* 358 U.S. 827 . . . (1958); cf. Island Petroleum Co. v. Commissioner, 57 F.2d 992, 994 (4th Cir.) (taxpayer to lose advances only if operations unsuccessful; if successful, to receive its advances back; the advances were, therefore, loans), *cert. denied,* 287 U.S. 646 . . . (1932).

II

. . . Section 385 of the Code, added in 1969, in authorizing the Secretary to prescribe regulations for determining whether a corporate interest is to be treated for purposes of the Code as stock or indebtedness, sets forth five "factors" — including subordination — which the Secretary may include in his regulations. No regulations have been promulgated under Section 385, although regulations issued under Section 385 might carry more weight than the current regulation because considered "legislative." See Chrysler Corp. v. Brown, 441 U.S. 281 . . . (1979). . . . The case law presents the background for reading such an interpretive regulation as is here involved.

It has not been doubted since John Kelley Co. v. Commissioner, 326 U.S. 521, 526, 530 . . . (1946), that the question whether an interest is truly a stock or debt interest, and whether the payments made upon it are truly deductible interest or are non-deductible dividends, is determined typically on the total facts surrounding the creation and use of the instrument and not by its possession of some single characteristic. In *Kelley* the Court held that amounts paid as "interest" on noncumulative income debentures that were subordinated to general creditors but preferred over common stock could properly be held by the Tax Court to constitute interest on indebtedness and deductible. . . . See also Scriptomatic, Inc. v. United States, 555 F.2d 364, 373 (3d Cir. 1977). . . . See also Lisle v. Commissioner, 35 T.C.M. (CCH) 627 (1976) (although corporation had twenty years to pay for shares, the shares were pledged to secure payment, and selling stockholders retained the right to vote, transaction held an exchange within §302(a)). . . .

Neither under the language of the regulation relied upon nor under the cases which have dealt with the "debt or equity" question is there any basis in the present case for holding that the taxpayer had any interest in Bresee other than an interest as a creditor after the closing under the Stock Purchase Agreement.

Affirmed.

NOTES

1. The Service has ruled that retention of an interest as a voting trustee of a voting trust following redemption of one's own shares is sufficient to prevent waiver of family attribution because of the degree of control that is retained. See Rev. Rul. 71-426, 1971-2 C.B. 173. But see Rev. Rul. 79-334, 1979-2 C.B. 127, which holds that if, pursuant to the terms of a will, the redeemed shareholder accepts appointment as trustee of a trust holding stock in the distributing corporation, there is no violation of the requirements of §302(c)(2)(A), even though the trust instrument empowers its trustees to vote any stock held by the trust. See also Rev. Rul. 72-380, 1972-2 C.B. 201 (qualification as executor of estate with power to vote stock not a forbidden "interest"), amplified by Rev. Rul. 75-2, 1975-1 C.B. 99 (executor who became president of corporation controlled by estate acquired a forbidden "interest").

In Rev. Rul. 81-233, 1981-2 C.B. 83, the Service held that the requirements of §302(c)(2)(A) are violated if, within 10 years after a redemption, the distributee becomes the custodian of stock of the distributing corporation under the Uniform Gifts to Minors Act.

See generally Rose, The Prohibited Interest of §302(c)(2)(A), 36 Tax L. Rev. 131 (1981).

2. What is the purpose of §302(c)(2)(B)? A was the president and sole shareholder of X Corporation; his son, B, was vice president. A retired from the business, gave half his X stock to B, and sold the remainder to X, taking steps to comply with §302(c)(2)(A). How should the redemption be treated? See Rev. Rul. 77-293, 1977-2 C.B. 91.

In Rev. Rul. 85-19, 1985-1 C.B. 94, a transfer of stock back to the donor within 10 years of its acquisition was not considered to have been made for tax avoidance purposes under §302(c)(2) because the transaction merely returned the stock to its original owner. Should the fact of retransfer, by itself, always be enough?

3. A, her husband B, and their children C and D own stock in X corporation. On A's death X redeems all of the shares held by A's estate and by B. Can the estate effect a waiver of the §318(a)(1) family attribution rules? See §302(c)(2)(C); but cf. Lillian N. Crawford, 59 T.C. 830 (1973), *nonacq.* 1974-2 C.B. 5, which was decided before the enactment of §302(c)(2)(C).

> *ii. Substantially Disproportionate Redemptions —*
> *§302(b)(2)*

REVENUE RULING 81-41
1981-1 C.B. 12

. . . A domestic corporation, X, had outstanding 5,100 shares of voting common stock and 4,900 shares of voting preferred stock. Except for minor limitations of local law, the common and preferred stock have equal voting rights. . . . All the preferred stock is owned by A, who is the founder of X and the board chairman. The preferred stock is not section 306 stock within the meaning of section 306(c) of the Code. A holds no common stock in X, either directly or constructively. . . . The common stock in X is widely held by persons unrelated to A.

In accord with a request from A, X redeemed 2,000 shares of the preferred stock for cash. Thus, A's vote in X was reduced from 49 percent immediately before the redemption to 36.25 percent immediately after the redemption (2,900 shares still held by A divided by 8,000 shares then outstanding). There was no plan or intent for X to redeem any of the stock held by shareholders other than A.

LAW AND ANALYSIS

Section 302(a) of the Code provides that if a corporation redeems its stock and if paragraph (1), (2), (3), or (4) of section 302(b) applies to the redemption the redemption shall be treated as a distribution in part or full payment in exchange for the stock. Section 302(b)(2) states as a general rule that section 302(a) shall apply to a redemption if the distribution is substantially disproportionate with respect to the shareholder. Under section 302(b)(2)(C) a distribution is substantially disproportionate if:

> (i) the ratio which the voting stock of the corporation owned
> by the shareholder immediately after the redemption bears to all

of the voting stock of the corporation at such time, is less than 80 percent of

(ii) the ratio which the voting stock of the corporation owned by the shareholder immediately before the redemption bears to all of the voting stock of the corporation at such time.

For purposes of this paragraph, no distribution shall be treated as substantially disproportionate unless the shareholder's ownership of the common stock of the corporation (whether voting or nonvoting) after and before redemption also meets the 80 percent requirement of the preceding sentence. . . .

. . . In the present case, A owned 49 percent of the voting stock of X prior to the redemption. Eighty percent of 49 percent is 39.2 percent. Because A owned 36.25 percent of the voting stock of X after the redemption, the first "80 percent test" of section 302(b)(2)(C) is satisfied. In addition, because A owned only 36.25 percent of the voting stock of X after the redemption, the limitation of section 302(b)(2)(B) is met. Also, because this redemption was not part of a plan to redeem other stock of X, the provisions of section 302(b)(2)(D) are not violated. The question remaining is whether the second "80 percent test" of section 302(b)(2)(C), which concerns the ownership of common stock, has to be satisfied even though A owned no common stock either directly or constructively.

The Senate Finance Committee Report accompanying the enactment of section 302 states:

Paragraph (2) of subsection (b) sets forth a general rule that if the redemption is substantially disproportionate, it will be treated as a sale under subsection (a), if the other conditions described in the paragraph are met. *It is intended that the general rule shall apply with respect to a redemption of preferred stock (other than section 306 stock) as well as common stock.* S. Rep. No. 1622, 83d Cong., 2d Sess. 234 (1954). (Emphasis added.)

Morever, section 1.302-3 of the Income Tax Regulations states that section 302(b)(2) of the Code only applies to a redemption of voting stock or to a redemption of both voting stock and other stock, but does not apply to the redemption solely of nonvoting stock. Therefore, both the legislative history and the regulations accompanying section 302(b)(2) indicate that the provision should apply to the redemption of voting preferred stock.

In the same report, the Senate Finance Committee does make two statements that a substantially disproportionate redemption requires a reduction in the redeemed shareholder's ownership of common stock in the redeeming corporation. However, the context of the first of these statements (S. Rep. No. 1622 at 44-45) indicates that this requirement is a safeguard against abuse where the redeeming shareholder holds common stock. Similarly, the second statement

(S. Rep. No. 1622 at 234) views this requirement as meaning, "it is necessary that the shareholder's ownership of voting or nonvoting common stock (that is, his participating interest) in the corporation also be reduced by the percentage required with respect to voting stock." These statements indicate that in the case of a redeeming shareholder owning two or more classes of stock, one of which is common stock, the shareholder may not retain or improve his or her "participating" interest in the corporation (while having a substantially disproportionate reduction in his or her voting interest) and still claim the protection of the section 302(b)(2) safe harbor. To conclude otherwise would permit a "bail-out" of corporate earnings at capital gains rates without a sacrifice of the shareholder's economic interest in the corporation. See United States v. Davis, 397 U.S. 301, 313 (1970). . . . Thus, these statements (indicating that section 302(b)(2) requires a reduction in common stock ownership) are addressed to situations where the redeeming shareholder owns common stock, and are not addressed to situations where the redeeming shareholder does not own any common stock.

. . . Therefore, the additional "safeguard" provided by the second "80 percent test" of section 302(b)(2)(C) is inapplicable to A. . . .

REVENUE RULING 87-88
1987-2 C.B. 81

ISSUE

If shares of both voting and nonvoting common stock are redeemed from a shareholder in one transaction, are the two classes aggregated for purposes of applying the substantially disproportionate requirement in section 302(b)(2)(C) of the Internal Revenue Code?

FACTS

X corporation had outstanding 10 shares of voting common stock and 30 shares of nonvoting common stock. The fair market values of a share of voting common stock and a share of nonvoting common stock are approximately equal. A owned 6 shares of X voting common stock and all the nonvoting common stock. The remaining 4 shares of the X voting common stock were held by persons unrelated to A within the meaning of section 318(a) of the Code.

X redeemed 3 shares of voting common stock and 27 shares of nonvoting common stock from A in a single transaction. Thereafter, A owned 3 shares of X voting common stock and 3 shares of nonvoting common stock. The ownership of the remaining 4 shares of X voting common stock was unchanged.

LAW AND ANALYSIS

If a distribution in redemption of stock qualifies under section 302(b)(2) of the Code as substantially disproportionate, the distribution is treated under section 302(a) as a payment in exchange for the stock redeemed.

Under section 302(b)(2)(B) and (C) of the Code, a distribution is substantially disproportionate if (i) the shareholder owns less than 50 percent of the total combined voting power of the corporation immediately after the redemption, (ii) immediately after the redemption the ratio of voting stock owned by the shareholder to all the voting stock of the corporation is less than 80 percent of the same ratio immediately before the redemption, and (iii) immediately after the redemption the ratio of common stock owned by the shareholder to all of the common stock of the corporation (whether voting or nonvoting) is less than 80 percent of the same ratio immediately before the redemption.

Under section 302(b)(2)(C) of the Code, if more than one class of common stock is outstanding, the determination in (iii) above is made by reference to fair market value. Section 302(b)(2) applies to a redemption of both voting stock and other stock (although not to the redemption solely of nonvoting stock). Section 1.302-3(a) of the Income Tax Regulations.

With regard to requirements (i) and (ii) described above, after the redemption, A owned less than 50 percent of the voting power of X (43 percent), and A's voting power was reduced to less than 80 percent of the percentage of voting power in X that A owned before the redemption (from 60 percent to 43 percent for a reduction to 72 percent of the preredemption level).

With regard to requirement (iii) above, section 302(b)(2)(C) of the Code provides that, if there is more than one class of common stock outstanding, the fair market value of all of the common stock (voting and nonvoting) will govern the determination of whether there has been the requisite reduction in common stock ownership. The fact that this test is based on fair market value and is applied by reference to all of the common stock of the corporation suggests that the requirement concerning reduction in common stock ownership is to be applied on an aggregate basis rather than on a class-by-class basis. Thus, the fact that A has no reduction in interest with regard to the nonvoting common stock and continues to own 100 percent of this stock does not prevent the redemption of this class of stock from qualifying under section 302(b)(2) when the whole transaction meets section 302(b)(2) requirements. To conclude otherwise would require that, notwithstanding a redemption of one class of common stock in an amount sufficient to reduce the shareholder's aggregate common stock ownership by more than 20 percent in value, every other class of common stock owned by the shareholder must be subject to a redemption.

Prior to the redemption, A owned 90 percent of the total fair market value of all the outstanding X common stock (36 out of the 40 shares of voting and nonvoting common stock). After the redemption, A owned 60 percent of the total fair market value of all the X common stock (6 out of 10 shares). The reduction in ownership (from 90 percent to 60 percent) was a reduction to less than 80 percent of the fraction that A previously owned of the total fair market value of all the X common stock.

HOLDING

If more than one class of common stock is outstanding, the provisions of section 302(b)(2)(C) of the Code are applied in an aggregate and not a class-by-class manner. Accordingly, the redemption by X of 3 shares of voting common stock and 27 shares of nonvoting common stock qualifies as substantially disproportionate within the meaning of section 302(b)(2), even though A continues to own 100 percent of the outstanding nonvoting common stock.

NOTES

1. Section 302(b)(2)(D) provides that §302(b)(2) is not applicable to any redemption made pursuant to a plan that has the purpose or effect of using a series of redemptions to result in an aggregate distribution not substantially disproportionate to the shareholder. In Rev. Rul. 85-14, 1985-1 C.B. 92, §302(b)(2)(D) was held to deny the §302(b)(2) safe harbor to the majority shareholder where a second redemption of another shareholder restored the majority shareholder's control.

2. See B. Bittker & J. Eustice, Federal Income Taxation of Corporations and Shareholders, 9-13 to 9-17 (5th ed. 1987).

iii. *Distributions Not Essentially Equivalent to a Dividend — §302(b)(1)*

HIMMEL v. COMMISSIONER
338 F.2d 815 (2d Cir. 1964)

Before Moore, Smith and Kaufman, Circuit Judges.

MOORE, Circuit Judge. Isidore and Lillian Himmel (collectively referred to as the taxpayer) petition for review of a decision of the Tax Court, 41 T.C. 62 (1963), upholding the Commissioner of Internal Revenue's determination of deficiency in taxpayer's income tax for the years 1957 and 1958 in the amount of $2,346.11 and $3,287.45, respectively. In both years, taxpayer received from the H. A. Leed Co. in redemption of certain shares of stock held by him, payments which he did not report in his tax returns for those years. The Commissioner and the Tax Court found the payments to be essentially equivalent to dividends, which, under the Internal Revenue Code of 1954, Section 302, should have been treated as ordinary income. We disagree with that finding and, accordingly, reverse the judgment.

Whether a redemption "is 'essentially equivalent to' a dividend, involving as it does application of a statutory rule to found facts, is a question of law. . . ."[2]

In 1946 taxpayer with Leonard Goldfarb and Edward G. Schenfield incorporated the H. A. Leed Co. to process aluminum. The original capital was $8,100 and each shareholder received 27 shares of $100 par common stock. . . . From the beginning until late 1948 taxpayer made advances to the company which were carried on the books as "Loans Payable." He expected to be repaid when the company was able to do so. In a recapitalization in late 1948 to improve the company's credit position, each shareholder received 5 more shares of common in cancellation of $500 notes to each. Taxpayer also received 266 shares of $100 par Class A 2% cumulative nonvoting preferred and 110 shares of $100 par Class B 2% cumulative voting preferred, in cancellation of the then outstanding indebtedness to him of $37,600. Both classes of preferred stock were created at that time and both were redeemable, but the Class B stock could not be redeemed until all the Class A stock had been redeemed. In 1950 taxpayer gave his 32 shares of common to his two sons, 16 to each. In 1954 on the death of Schenfield, the company purchased his 32 shares from his estate. By corporate action in February 1956 a special account was set up into which $3,000 per year was to be deposited solely for the retirement of the company's outstanding preferred stock of the total par value of $37,600. In late 1956 the shareholders voted to redeem 50 shares of Class A at par and the taxpayer agreed to waive all accrued but unpaid dividends on the redeemed shares. Similar provision was made for redemption at taxpayer's death and for other redemptions during taxpayer's life. In January 1957, 50 shares of Class A were redeemed for $5,000, and in 1958 70 shares of Class A were redeemed for $7,000. No dividends had been paid through December 31, 1958, and in both 1957 and 1958 earnings and profits exceeded the amounts distributed.

---

2. Though equivalence depends upon the facts, see Treas. Reg. §1.302-2(b), it is not itself a fact.

Distributions of property by a corporation to a shareholder to the extent they are made out of earnings and profits, section 316, are generally to be included in the gross income of the shareholder. Section 301(a), (c). The ordinary income tax rates would thus be applicable. However, if a corporation redeems its stock, section 317(b), the redemption may be treated as a distribution in part or in full payment in exchange for the stock, section 302(a), thus subjecting the distribution to tax only in the event of capital gains. But this preferential treatment may be availed of only in certain circumstances, one of which is that "the redemption is not essentially equivalent to a dividend." Sections 302(b)(1), 302(d). Primarily the problem is to determine and apply the appropriate tests of dividend equivalence. But the relevance of each of the possible criteria depends largely upon the particular capital structure-distribution pattern.

Ownership of stock can involve three important rights: (1) to vote, and thereby exercise control, (2) to participate in current earnings and accumulated surplus, and (3) to share in net assets on liquidation. Ownership of common stock generally involves all of these. Ownership of preferred stock generally involves the last two, but only to limited extents, unless otherwise provided. Payments to a shareholder with respect to his stock can be of three general sorts: (1) distribution of earnings and profits which effects no change in basic relationships between the shareholder and either the corporation or the other shareholders — i.e., a dividend; (2) payments to a shareholder by a third party in exchange for ownership of the stock and its attendant rights, which accordingly eliminates or contracts pro tanto the shareholder's rights — i.e., a sale; and (3) payments to a shareholder by the corporation in exchange for ownership of the stock. With the last, which can often formally be called a redemption, the effect on the shareholder's basic rights vis-à-vis the corporation and other shareholders depends upon many facts. It is possible for such a transaction to resemble, exactly or substantially, either a dividend or a sale. For tax purposes the payment is considered ordinary income if, by its "net effect," it is "essentially equivalent to a dividend."

The hallmarks of a dividend, then, are pro rata distribution of earnings and profits *and* no change in basic shareholder relationships. Too frequently the inquiry in §302(b) cases does not keep this sufficiently in mind. Existence of a pro rata distribution may be determined by comparing the patterns of distribution to see whether the shareholders received the same amount as they would have received had the total distribution been a dividend on the common stock outstanding. But, aside from a single-shareholder corporation, it is not enough merely that the taxpayer received the same amount as he would have received with a dividend, for that could be the result of a sale of some stock to a third party. Rather, pro rata distribution indicates also, at least in a one-class capital structure, the extent to which — if any — the basic rights of ownership have been affected. Where there is only common those rights would exist in proportion to shares held. Therefore, quite often the net effect of a distribution may adequately be gauged by determining what would have been the pattern with a dividend.[4]

Additional and more difficult problems are raised when a corporation has more than one class of stock. The additional class will often be a preferred, which typically has no voting rights, has preferential though limited rights to participate in earnings, and has rights to share in liquidation only to the extent of capital contributed, and perhaps accrued but unpaid dividends. Redemption of some preferred stock consequently may cause different changes in a shareholder's total rights than would redemption of common. Even more is this so when the preferred and common are not held in the same proportions by the same shareholders. Shares of different classes should therefore not casually be lumped together. For example, redemption of a nonvoting preferred can have no effect on relative voting rights, and can never meet the "substantially disproportionate" tests of section 302(b)(2). Rights to earnings will depend upon the exact preference given the preferred, e.g., whether it participates beyond its dividend, whether the dividend is cumulative, etc. Rights on liquidation may vary similarly.

These problems are all well illustrated by this case. In the two years in question, taxpayer received from the corporation $5,000 and $7,000, in redemption of 50 and 70 of the 266 shares of Class A nonvoting preferred, all held by him. Other shareholders received nothing. Had the same funds been distributed as a dividend on the 64 shares of common outstanding, Goldfarb would have received $2,500 and $3,500 and taxpayer would actually have received nothing, as he held no common. However, by dint of the attribution rules, section 318(a)(1)(A)(ii), he would be deemed to have owned his sons' shares and therefore to have received the $2,500 and $3,500 actually received by them. Thus he would have received 50% of what he

---

4. In stressing the importance of the "substantially pro rata" tests, we are not unmindful of the more specific provision of §302(b)(2). The pro rata test, quite assuredly, developed under §115(g) whose only provision was for distributions "essentially equivalent to a dividend." While the 1954 revision added specific "safe harbors" for redemptions that completely terminate a shareholder's interest in the corporation, §302(b)(3), and for distributions that are substantially disproportionate according to certain precise quantitative standards, §302(b)(2), it also kept the 1939 Code provision for distributions not "essentially equivalent to a dividend." Moreover, it stated that failure to meet any one of the more specific tests should not be taken into account in applying the old test. §302(b)(5). And since 302(b)(2) is keyed only to changes in voting power, it is obvious that without 302(b)(1) a substantially disproportionate redemption of nonvoting stock could never qualify for capital gain treatment.

actually did receive. Even if the funds had first gone to pay accumulated but unpaid dividends on the two classes of preferred, taxpayer would have received, according to the Commissioner's calculations, only 82.5% of what he actually did receive.[5]

With a multi-class capitalization, the amount of a hypothetical dividend that would have been received can reflect the shareholder's right to participate in current and accumulated earnings, though it is a less accurate index of the effects on voting power or rights on liquidation. Here, an alteration in rights to earnings of 17.5% (waiver of dividends) or 50% (nonwaiver of dividends) is substantial enough in itself to bar treatment of the redemption as "essentially equivalent to a dividend." In no other case has a comparable difference apparently been considered otherwise. . . .

The Tax Court acknowledged the difference in result between the distribution here and a dividend but thought it unimportant because taxpayer was "the owner of such a heavy percentage of the distributing corporation's stock. . . ." 41 T.C. at 71. But the cases relied on by the Tax Court are very different from the one before us. In [Bradbury v. Commissioner, 298 F.2d 111 (1st Cir. 1962)], only 8.7% of the distribution would have gone to the other shareholders were it a dividend, and 91.3% of all shares were considered owned by the taxpayer. Moreover, even without attribution taxpayer was the controlling shareholder. And in Keefe v. Cote, 213 F.2d 651 (1st Cir. 1954), taxpayer owned over 99% of all shares and would have received all of any dividend save a fraction of 1%. Indeed, there a "legitimate business purpose" was found adequate to bar dividend equivalency. Lastly, in both cases only common stock existed so that all essential shareholder relationships existed pro rata with dividend rights.

The Tax Court also stressed the fact that the redemption effected no change in voting power. Of course, this could be relevant if only common stock existed; but where nonvoting stock exists redemption even of all of it cannot affect voting power. Since nonvoting preferred was redeemed here we do not think such weight should have been given to the absence of any change in voting power. However, were voting shares redeemed we think that the Tax Court's lumping together of common and voting preferred would have been justifiable, if only to gauge the impact on voting power.

However, the Tax Court also stressed the fact that taxpayer's total ownership of all shares was reduced only 2.74% by the redemption, a change not thought substantial. But this figure was obtained by lumping together all shares outstanding — common, vot-

---

5. We do not consider what might have been the proper tax treatment for the amount of dividends actually waived as neither party raised the issue.

ing preferred, and nonvoting preferred. We think that such a figure
is not particularly helpful. It cannot stand in the abstract, but must
be related to some significant aspect of the complex of shareholder
rights. The Tax Court did not indicate any such relationship and we
are not convinced that necessarily there is any in a corporation having
several differently defined classes of stock. The figure does not relate
to voting power. It does not relate to rights to share in earnings. It
might be thought to relate to rights on liquidation, but it does not
accurately do that either.

Taxpayer urges us to consider the changes in relative shares of
net worth attributable to each shareholder. Some courts have looked
to these changes in book value of a shareholder's total holdings in
order to assess the effect of the distribution on liquidation rights.
See, e.g., Abraham Frisch, [18 T.C.M. (CCH) 358 (1959)]. We agree
that it is a proper inquiry. The test has not been extensively developed, however, perhaps because relatively few of the cases have
involved even two classes of stock, and none that we have found has
involved three classes, as are present here. Of course with only one
class there is no need to turn to a net worth test since liquidation
rights, like the other basic shareholder rights, will exist in direct
proportion to shares held.

Taxpayer asserts, and the Commissioner did not contend otherwise, that the effect of the distributions was to reduce his share of
net worth from 62% to 57% — a difference of 5%. We cannot say
that this difference is so insubstantial as to make the redemptions
"essentially equivalent to a dividend." To place the changes in context
we note that with redemption of the last shares held by taxpayer —
either in one complete redemption or as the culmination of a series
the last of which would perforce be a "complete" redemption — his
sons' shares would no longer be attributed to him since on these facts
his interest in the company would be terminated. Sections 302(b)(3),
302(c)(2). Prior to any redemption, the preferred itself represented
only 22% of the net worth as of December 31, 1957. Thus, for taxpayer, the maximum possible share of net worth that could be
affected by a redemption was 22%, not the 62% attributed to him
through section 318. A change of 5% should be compared with this
lesser figure.[7]

In fact, taxpayer would also have us support our conclusion by
finding, contrary to the Tax Court, that the redemptions were part

7. We think it quite proper to be aware of the effect of a distribution on significant corporate interests without strict regard to the attribution rules. Cf. Moore,
Dividend Equivalency — Taxation of Distributions in Redemption of Stock, 19 Tax
L. Rev. 249, 252-255 (1964); Note, Stock Redemptions from Close Family Corporations Under Section 302, 47 Minn. L. Rev. 853, 867-870 (1963).

of an overall plan to terminate his interest in the corporation. However, we do not feel compelled to reach the question. . . .

The decision of the Tax Court is reversed.

LEVIN v. COMMISSIONER
385 F.2d 521 (2d Cir. 1967)

Before Moore, Smith and Kaufman, Circuit Judges.

KAUFMAN, Circuit Judge. The perils of acting without competent tax advice are demonstrated anew, if further evidence be needed, by this petition to review a decision of the Tax Court, 47 T.C. 258 (1966), holding that distributions in 1960, 1961, 1962, and 1963 to the taxpayer in redemption of her stock in a family corporation were "essentially equivalent to a dividend" within the meaning of section 302(b)(1) of the Internal Revenue Code of 1954, and hence taxable at ordinary rates. We affirm the decision of the Tax Court.

The evidence, as found by the Tax Court,[3] established that Mrs. Levin's family corporation, the Connecticut Novelty Corporation, Inc., commenced operations as a partnership between her husband and her brother, Joseph Levine. . . . Taxpayer succeeded to her husband's interest in the business upon his death in 1940. Thereafter, her brother Joseph came to live with her and her son Jerome, and became a "second father" to him. She relied heavily on Joseph's advice in business matters.

Following incorporation of the business in 1948, its 1300 outstanding single class common shares were held as follows: Joseph Levine, 650 shares; Mrs. Levin, 649 shares; Jerome Levin, 1 share.[4] The three stockholders also constituted the board of directors and officers of the corporation until Joseph Levine's death in April 1962, when Jerome's wife became a director. Taxpayer was secretary and treasurer until 1959, when she limited her office in the company to secretary.

Jerome was employed full time in the business since graduating from high school in 1944. In 1957 he contemplated marriage and discussed his status in the company with his mother and uncle in order to learn "where he stood" in the business. He insisted on this so that if it became necessary he could embark on another career while still young. Thereafter, Joseph and the taxpayer agreed to give

---

3. The facts were largely stipulated. The only significant factual dispute is whether a shift in control over the corporation actually occurred as a result of the redemption. In the view we take of the case, it is unnecessary to decide this question; nor need we consider whether, as taxpayer urges, the clearly erroneous rule has any application to §302(b)(1) cases. . . .

4. Jerome paid no consideration for his one share.

him a greater participation in the business ownership and management. As a result the existing stock was cancelled and 1300 new shares of common stock were issued and distributed in this manner: Joseph, 485 shares; taxpayer, 484 shares; Jerome, 331 shares. Jerome gave no consideration for the 330 additional shares.

Within a few years Jerome sought outright ownership of the business and to retire his uncle and mother. But he desired to accomplish this by a method which would make provision for them during the balance of their lives. Accordingly, on January 19, 1960, a plan was devised whereby the corporation would redeem the stock of taxpayer and Joseph at $200 per share. Pursuant to this plan Joseph and taxpayer executed identical agreements with the corporation. She was to receive $7000 per year without interest beginning April 1, 1960 until $96,800[5] was paid. Upon default the unpaid balance would become due upon the "seller's" election. As an alternative, the corporation was given the option to pay the entire or any part of the purchase price at any time. After the plan was consummated, Jerome conducted the business with "a greater freedom of action." But out of "respect and sentiment," as we are told, Joseph and taxpayer were retained as directors and officers of the corporation. . . .

[T]hey continued to perform services for the corporation and to receive salaries while at the same time taxpayer accepted a cut in her salary to $1200 per year, the maximum amount then permitted to be earned without a reduction in her social security benefits. . . .

The dispute before us arises from taxpayer's treatment of the $7000 payments. In the taxable years in question, 1960 through 1963, she reported the compensation from the corporation under the 1960 agreement as long-term capital gains. The Commissioner treated the payments as essentially equivalent to dividends and accordingly determined deficiencies for all the years in question.[7]

I

The difference between a stock redemption that is essentially equivalent to a dividend and one that is not is grounded on a long history in the tax law. The distinction was essential because without it the tax on dividends at ordinary income rates could easily be defeated by the simple expedient of issuing more stock to the

5. This was computed by multiplying the number of shares taxpayer actually owned, 484, by the purchase price per share, $200.

7. The Commissioner also treated as essentially equivalent to dividends credits which the corporation allowed taxpayer against her obligation to pay for a cottage transferred to her in 1962. The Tax Court's valuation of this cottage at $19,000 is not challenged here.

shareholders, who then would "sell" back their new shares to the corporation. It would then be asserted that the proceeds of this alleged sale were taxable at capital gains rates because they represented proceeds from the "sale" of a capital asset. To eliminate this patent loophole, Congress early provided that such distributions would receive capital gain treatment only if they were "not essentially equivalent to a dividend." See generally 1 Mertens, Law of Federal Income Taxation §9.99 (Oliver ed. 1962).

But this simplistic formula created more problems than it solved for the courts were then called upon to answer the elusive question as to when a distribution was or was not "essentially equivalent to a dividend." At first it was generally believed that, in view of its history, the provision was aimed only at distributions motivated by a tax avoidance purpose. Accordingly, if a distribution served a "business purpose," the courts held it was not essentially equivalent to a dividend. This rationale was becoming increasingly difficult to apply, however, and it came to its demise in 1945 when, in interpreting an analogous statutory provision, the Supreme Court ruled that motive had little relevancy. The Court then adopted a more objective "net effect" test, under which the question of dividend equivalency depended on whether the distribution in redemption of stock had the same economic effect as a distribution of a dividend would have had. Commissioner v. Estate of Bedford, 325 U.S. 283 (1945). In time this test also proved ephemeral; some courts developed many criteria to determine the "net effect" of a distribution, while in determining "net effect" we differed and relied primarily on changes in "basic rights of ownership."[10] However, most cases have been resolved on their own facts and circumstances.

Until 1954 the "not essentially equivalent to a dividend" test, with all its perplexing problems, had been the sole statutory guide in this area. But the draftsmen of the 1954 Internal Revenue Code, faced with "the morass created by the decisions,"[12] attempted to clarify the standards and thus to make more precise the dividing line between stock redemptions that qualified for capital gains treatment and those that did not by adding objective tests, see §302(b)(2)-(4),* and rules defining constructive ownership, see §318.

Since the "not essentially equivalent to a dividend" test is no longer applied in a vacuum, it is impossible to interpret it without examining the statutory scheme of which it is now a part. Section

10. See, e.g., Himmel v. Commissioner, 338 F.2d 815, 817 (2d Cir. 1964).

12. Ballenger v. United States, 301 F.2d 192, 196 (4th Cir. 1962).

*Section 302(b)(4), dealing with certain stock issued by railroads, was repealed by the Bankruptcy Tax Act of 1980. The current §302(b)(4) (dealing with partial liquidations) was moved from §346 by Congress in 1982. — ED.

302(a) provides that a stock redemption[13] shall be treated as an "exchange" if it falls into any one of the categories of §302(b).[14] These categories are: (1) a redemption that is "not essentially equivalent to a dividend" under §302(b)(1); (2) a "substantially disproportionate" redemption under §302(b)(2); (3) a complete redemption terminating the shareholder's interest in the corporation under §302(b)(3). Section 302(b)(2) contains an exact mathematical formula to determine whether the disproportion is "substantial." The test in §302(b)(3) is not mathematical, but it is stated with equal clarity. The shareholder must redeem all of his actually and constructively owned stock to qualify for capital gain treatment under this provision, and §302(c)(2) provides that if certain clear-cut conditions are met the family attribution rules of §318(a) will not apply in determining whether the shareholder has disposed of all his stock.

Mrs. Levin concedes that she fails to meet the requirements of either §302(b)(2) or §302(b)(3),[16] and so she relies on §302(b)(1).[17] Our task of interpretation and reasoned elaboration cannot be adequately performed if we examine each provision as if it existed in a vacuum. The Code draftsmen hopefully expected that the preciseness of the tests set out in the new provisions, §302(b)(2) and §302(b)(3), would serve to relieve the pressure on the "not essentially equivalent to a dividend" test reenacted as §302(b)(1). The new requirements, if carefully observed, provided safe harbors for taxpayers seeking capital gain treatment. As a result, their enactment permitted more accurate and long-range tax planning.

The legislative history of §302(b)(1) supports the view that it was designed to play a modest role in the statutory scheme. As originally passed by the House of Representatives, no provision was made for the "not essentially equivalent to a dividend" test; reliance was placed entirely on provisions similar to §302(b)(2)and §302(b)(3). Thereafter

13. Section 317(b) defines redemption for purposes of §§301-395 as a corporation's acquisition in its stock from a shareholder in exchange for property, whether or not the stock is cancelled, retired, or held as a treasury stock. This definition settled the question whether there could be dividend equivalence if the redeemed stock was held as treasury stock rather than being cancelled. See Kirschenbaum v. Commissioner, 155 F.2d 23, 25 (2d Cir.), *cert. denied*, 329 U.S. 726, 67 S. Ct. 75, 91 L. Ed. 628 (1946).

14. A redemption that does not fall within one of these categories is treated, by virtue of §302(d), as a distribution under §301, i.e., as a dividend to the extent of current and post 1913 earnings and profits.

16. Taxpayer fails to meet the test of §302(b)(3) because she remained a director, an officer, and an employee of the corporation after the redemption. Moreover, she failed to file the proper notification with the Secretary of the Treasury.

17. In determining whether the redemption satisfies §302(b)(1), we are directed by §302(b)(5) not to take into account that the redemption fails to meet the requirements of §302(b)(2) or §302(b)(3); but a discussion and understanding of these provisions are useful in interpreting §302(b)(1).

the Senate Finance Committee added §302(b)(1) and explained its action as follows:[18]

> While the House bill set forth definite conditions under which stock may be redeemed at capital-gain rates, these rules appeared unnecessarily restrictive, particularly in the case of redemptions of preferred stock which might be called by the corporation without the shareholder having any control over when the redemption may take place. Accordingly, your committee follows existing law by reinserting the general language indicating that a redemption shall be treated as a distribution in part or full payment in exchange for stock if the redemption is not essentially equivalent to a dividend.

As a leading commentator observed, "It is not easy to give §302(b)(1) an expansive construction in view of this indication that its major function was the narrow one of immunizing redemptions of minority holdings of preferred stock."[19]

II

The 1954 Code also adopted a number of constructive ownership rules that provided for the attribution of stock owned by one person or legal entity to another. These provisions overruled the prior case law which unrealistically had not viewed the family as a unit unless other family members were "dummy stockholders." Lukens v. Commissioner, 246 F.2d 403, 407-408 (3d Cir. 1957). By providing a "reasonable rule of thumb,"[20] these rules reduced the difficulties necessarily involved in determining in each case the extent of actual control in a family corporation, in which informal influence over relatives, often impossible of proof, was more important than formal control through voting rights based on actual stock ownership. Like §302(b)(2) and §302(b)(3), these rules represented an attempt to make the law more predictable, and thereby to serve as aids to the tax or estate planner.

Section 318(a) [(1)], the family attribution rule[, is] applicable here. . . .

In this case, then, the taxpayer must be deemed the owner of her son's shares since §302(c)(1) provides in part: "section 318(a) shall apply in determining the ownership of stock for purposes of this section."[21]

---

18. S. Rep. No. 1622, 83d Cong., 2d Sess., 44-45 (1954).

19. Bittker & Eustice, Federal Income Taxation of Corporation and Shareholders (2d ed.) 291.

20. Bittker & Eustice, op. cit., 288.

21. Although some commentators have argued that the attribution rules are not applicable to §302(b)(1) because it does not expressly refer to the "ownership" of stock, Bittker & Eustice, op. cit., 292, correctly point out that it is reasonable to apply

III

Taxpayer argues that the family attribution rules should not be determinative in this §302(b)(1) case. But the definitive language of the statute gives her small comfort despite the three cases upon which she relies so heavily.

In Perry S. Lewis, 47 T.C. 129 (1966), the Tax Court ignored the stock attribution rules in deciding a §302(b)(1) case. Lewis and his sons owned an automobile dealer franchise, and Lewis' shares were redeemed after the automobile manufacturer put heavy pressure on older men like Lewis to yield franchises to younger men. Lewis severed all relations with the corporation other than remaining as an apparently honorary director and officer. The Tax Court held that distributions to Lewis over a period of five years in exchange for his stock were not essentially equivalent to a dividend, because the stock redemption served a substantial "business purpose." While the majority ignored altogether the family attribution rules, Judge Simpson, in a separate concurrence, pointed out that they required that Lewis be treated as owning his sons' shares, and hence as owning 100% of the corporation's outstanding stock. He concurred, however, on the ground that there was a complete termination of Lewis' interest in the corporation which satisfied §302(b)(3). *Lewis* does not aid the taxpayer[22] because this court has not looked with favor upon the "business purpose" test. Even if we were to consider it, the Tax Court failed to articulate any reason for ignoring §318. But, taxpayer argues that the Tax Court in *Lewis* simply considered the "bona fides" of the change in ownership with special care because of the attribution rules, and suggests we do the same. We have already stated that the core of the changes made by the 1954 Code in this not uncommon reticulate fashion for a tax statute was to shift from uncertainty and impreciseness to objective tests; "tax administration would be severely handicapped if the rules applied only as presumptions . . ." Ringel, Surrey & Warren, Attribution of Stock Ownership in the Internal Revenue Code, 72 Harv. L. Rev. 209 (1958). Acceptance of taxpayer's argument would eviscerate the attribution rules and all that Congress hoped to achieve thereby.

Mrs. Levin also refers us to the footnote dictum in Ballenger v. United States, 301 F.2d 192, 199 (4th Cir. 1962), indicating that some

---

the attribution rules whenever ownership of stock is relevant, whether by statutory direction or otherwise. Indeed, the Treasury Regulations initially made the application of the attribution rules to §302(b)(1) mandatory, 19 Fed. Reg. 8240 (1954), although they now provide only that the attribution rules "must be considered," Treas. Regs. §1.302-2(b), thus allowing some play in the joints for cases hereinafter discussed, e.g., situations involving family estrangement.

22. Of course the concurring opinion in *Lewis* does not support taxpayer's position here because she makes no claim that there was a complete redemption under §302(b)(3).

commentators have "suggested that the attribution rules should not be too literally applied to §302(b)(1)." It is interesting, however, that the attribution rules were applied in *Ballenger*, and the quoted dictum lends feeble support to taxpayer's claim that the attribution rules should be ignored here as they were in *Lewis*.

Finally, taxpayer relies on another footnote observation in Himmel v. Commissioner, 338 F.2d 815, 820 (2d Cir. 1964), stating that "[w]e think it quite proper to be aware of the effect of a distribution on significant corporate interest without strict regard to the attribution rules." The reliance is misplaced. In *Himmel* we *applied* the attribution rules in determining that if there had been a dividend on the common stock rather than a redemption of the non-voting cumulative preferred taxpayer *constructively* would have received significantly *less* than he did as a result of the redemption. This alteration in rights to earnings was "substantial enough in itself to bar treatment of the redemption as 'essentially equivalent to a dividend.' In no other case has a comparable difference apparently been considered otherwise." *Himmel*, at 818. In the case before us, if there had been $14,000 annual dividends (the amount of the annual distributions to taxpayer and Joseph) instead of a stock redemption, taxpayer would have received constructively about $8,778[24] or *more* than she received from the stock redemption. The Tax Court correctly stated that the comparative dividend test is designed to test "whether the distributions *equal or exceed* the amounts that would be received as a cash dividend," and that accordingly *Himmel* "is not analogous."

Moreover, *Himmel* involved a corporation with three classes of stock which were not held proportionately. This situation created "additional and more difficult problems;"[25] compliance with §302(b)(2) was impossible,[26] and immediate compliance with §302(b)(3) was impractical.[27] By contrast, in the present case taxpayer easily could have complied with §302(b)(3) by simply resigning as a director, officer, and employee of the corporation and notifying the Secretary of the Treasury.[28] She simply could not have her cake and eat it too.

We do not hold that there may not be cases in which strict application of the attribution rules may be inappropriate. In addition

---

24. Taxpayer actually owned 37.2 percent of the stock, and constructively owned another 25.5 percent (Jerome's) or 62.7 percent in all; 62.7 per cent of $14,000 is $8,778.

25. *Himmel,* supra, 338 F.2d at 818.

26. The test of §302(b)(2) depends on a reduction in the amount of voting stock held; in *Himmel,* non-voting stock was redeemed.

27. The corporation lacked the funds to redeem all the taxpayer's stock.

28. See §302(c)(2)(A). In addition, taxpayer would have had to satisfy the requirement of the last sentence of §302(c)(2)(B).

to the preferred stock situations referred to in the Senate Report quoted supra, family estrangement may render the application of the family attribution rules unwise. See Bittker, The Taxation of Stock Redemptions and Partial Liquidations, 44 Cornell L.Q. 299, 324 (1959); Moore, Dividend Equivalency — Taxation of Distributions in Redemption of Stock, 19 Tax L. Rev. 249, 252-55 (1964). But in the case before us taxpayer has offered no valid reason for ignoring the family attribution rules, and we perceive none.

IV

Accordingly, we must attribute Jerome's shares to his mother. As a result, before the redemption she constructively owned her 484 shares and her son's 331 shares, or about 63 percent of the 1300 outstanding shares. After the redemption she still constructively owned her son's shares. Thus, after the redemption of the stock owned by her and her brother, by the rule of attribution she became the constructive owner of 100 percent of the outstanding stock. It is apparent therefore that her constructive ownership actually increased as a result of the redemptions. As the Tax Court said, this "is most unlike a sale." For when a taxpayer's (constructive) ownership decreases by a significant amount, we are justified in concluding that a substantial reduction in taxpayer's interest in the corporation has occurred warranting capital gain treatment as a sale or exchange. But when only a small reduction in control occurs, the distribution has been held to be essentially equivalent to a dividend; a fortiori, when no reduction, but rather an increase, in control occurs, taxpayer has not parted with anything justifying capital gain treatment.

The Tax Court correctly noted that in this case control in the sense of access to corporate benefits was more important than any legal right to direct the destiny of the corporation. In reality, taxpayer's benefits from the corporation changed little as a result of the redemption. Before 1960 she received a salary of $7800 per year; after 1960 she received $8200 per year, composed of annual distributions of $7000 and salary of $1200. While in form taxpayer redeemed her stock, in substance she parted with nothing justifying capital gain treatment.

The judgment is affirmed.

NOTE

What is the significance of the "comparative dividend" test in *Himmel* in determining dividend equivalency? Which is the preferable test, "net effect" or "comparative dividend"? Are they mutually exclusive? Would a shareholder be more likely to have dividend income if the redemption proceeds provide him with more or with less than an outright dividend distribution would give him? Why?

UNITED STATES v. DAVIS
397 U.S. 301 (1970)

Mr. Justice MARSHALL delivered the opinion of the Court. In 1945, taxpayer and E. B. Bradley organized a corporation. In exchange for property transferred to the new company, Bradley received 500 shares of common stock, and taxpayer and his wife similarly each received 250 such shares. Shortly thereafter, taxpayer made an additional contribution to the corporation, purchasing 1,000 shares of preferred stock at a par value of $25 per share.

The purpose of this latter transaction was to increase the company's working capital and thereby to qualify for a loan previously negotiated through the Reconstruction Finance Corporation. It was understood that the corporation would redeem the preferred stock when the RFC loan had been repaid. Although in the interim taxpayer bought Bradley's 500 shares and divided them between his son and daughter, the total capitalization of the company remained the same until 1963. That year, after the loan was fully repaid and in accordance with the original understanding, the company redeemed taxpayer's preferred stock.

In his 1963 personal income tax return taxpayer did not report the $25,000 received by him upon the redemption of his preferred stock as income. Rather, taxpayer considered the redemption as a sale of his preferred stock to the company — a capital gains transaction under §302 of the Internal Revenue Code of 1954 resulting in no tax since taxpayer's basis in the stock equaled the amount he received for it. The Commissioner of Internal Revenue, however, did not approve this tax treatment. According to the Commissioner, the redemption of taxpayer's stock was essentially equivalent to a dividend and was thus taxable as ordinary income under §§301 and 316 of the Code. Taxpayer paid the resulting deficiency and brought this suit for a refund. The District Court ruled in his favor, 274 F. Supp. 466 (D.C.M.D. Tenn. 1967), and on appeal the Court of Appeals affirmed. 408 F.2d 1139 (C.A. 6th Cir. 1969).

The Court of Appeals held that the $25,000 received by taxpayer was "not essentially equivalent to a dividend" within the meaning of that phrase in §302(b)(1) of the Code because the redemption was the final step in a course of action that had a legitimate business (as opposed to a tax avoidance) purpose. That holding represents only one of a variety of treatments accorded similar transactions under

§302(b)(1) in the circuit courts of appeals.[2] We granted certiorari, 396 U.S. 815 (1969), in order to resolve this recurring tax question involving stock redemptions by closely held corporations. We reverse.

I

The Internal Revenue Code of 1954 provides generally in §§301 and 316 for the tax treatment of distributions by a corporation to its shareholders; under those provisions, a distribution is includable in a taxpayer's gross income as a dividend out of earnings and profits to the extent such earnings exist.[3] There are exceptions to the application of these general provisions, however, and among them are those found in §302 involving certain distributions for redeemed stock. The basic question in this case is whether the $25,000 distribution by the corporation to taxpayer falls under that section — more specifically, whether its legitimate business motivation qualifies the distribution under §302(b)(1) of the Code. Preliminarily, however, we must consider the relationship between §302(b)(1) and the rules regarding the attribution of stock ownership found in §318(a) of the Code.

Under subsection (a) of §302, a distribution is treated as "payment in exchange for the stock," thus qualifying for capital gains rather than ordinary income treatment, if the conditions contained in any one of the four paragraphs of subsection (b) are met. In addition to paragraph (1)'s "not essentially equivalent to a dividend" test, capital gains treatment is available where (2) the taxpayer's voting strength is substantially diminished, [or] (3) his interest in the company is completely terminated. . . . [T]axpayer admits that paragraphs (2) and (3) do not apply. Moreover, taxpayer agrees that for the purposes of §§302(b)(2) and (3) the attribution rules of §318(a)

---

2. Only the Second Circuit has unequivocally adopted the Commissioner's view and held irrelevant the motivation of the redemption. See Levin v. Commissioner, 385 F.2d 521 (1967); Hasbrook v. United States, 343 F.2d 811 (1965). The First Circuit, however, seems almost to have come to that conclusion, too. *Compare* Wiseman v. United States, 371 F.2d 816 (1967), *with* Bradbury v. Commissioner, 298 F.2d 111 (1962).

The other courts of appeals that have passed on the question are apparently willing to give at least some weight under §302(b)(1) to the business motivation of a distribution and redemption. See, e.g., Commissioner v. Berenbaum, 369 F.2d 337 (C.A. 10th Cir. 1966); Kerr v. Commissioner, 326 F.2d 225 (C.A. 9th Cir. 1964); Ballenger v. United States, 301 F.2d 192 (C.A. 4th Cir. 1962); Heman v. Commissioner, 283 F.2d 227 (C.A. 8th Cir. 1960); United States v. Fewell, 255 F.2d 496 (C.A. 5th Cir. 1958). See also Neff v. United States, 157 Ct. Cl. 322, 305 F.2d 455 (1962). Even among those courts that consider business purpose, however, it is generally required that the business purpose be related, not to the issuance of the stock, but to the redemption of it. See Commissioner v. Berenbaum, supra; Ballenger v. United States, supra.

3. . . . Taxpayer makes no contention that the corporation did not have $25,000 in accumulated earnings and profits.

apply and he is considered to own the 750 outstanding shares of common stock held by his wife and children in addition to the 250 shares in his own name.

Taxpayer, however, argues that the attribution rules do not apply in considering whether a distribution is essentially equivalent to a dividend under §302(b)(1). According to taxpayer, he should thus be considered to own only 25 percent of the corporation's common stock, and the distribution would then qualify under §302(b)(1) since it was not pro rata or proportionate to his stock interest, the fundamental test of dividend equivalency. See Treas. Reg. 1.302-2(b). However, the plain language of the statute compels rejection of the argument. In subsection (c) of §302, the attribution rules are made specifically applicable "in determining the ownership of stock for purposes of this section." Applying this language, both courts below held that §318(a) applies to all of §302, including §302(b)(1) — a view in accord with the decisions of the other courts of appeals, a long-standing treasury regulation,[6] and the opinion of the leading commentators.

Against this weight of authority, taxpayer argues that the result under paragraph (1) should be different because there is no explicit reference to stock ownership as there is in paragraphs (2) and (3). Neither that fact, however, nor the purpose and history of §302(b)(1) support taxpayer's argument. The attribution rules — designed to provide a clear answer to what would otherwise be a difficult tax question — formed part of the tax bill that was subsequently enacted as the 1954 Code. As is discussed further, infra, the bill as passed by the House of Representatives contained no provision comparable to §302(b)(1). When that provision was added in the Senate, no purpose was evidenced to restrict the applicability of §318(a). Rather, the attribution rules continued to be made specifically applicable to the entire section, and we believe that Congress intended that they be taken into account wherever ownership of stock was relevant.

Indeed, it was necessary that the attribution rules apply to §302(b)(1) unless they were to be effectively eliminated from consideration with regard to §§302(b)(2) and (3) also. For if a transaction failed to qualify under one of those sections solely because of the attribution rules, it would according to taxpayer's argument nonetheless qualify under §302(b)(1). We cannot agree that Congress intended so to nullify its explicit directive. We conclude, therefore, that the attribution rules of §318(a) do apply; and, for the purposes of deciding whether a distribution is "not essentially equivalent to a dividend" under §302(b)(1), taxpayer must be deemed the owner of all 1,000 shares of the company's common stock.

6. See Treas. Reg. 1.302-2(b).

II

After application of the stock ownership attribution rules, this case viewed most simply involves a sole stockholder who causes part of his shares to be redeemed by the corporation. We conclude that such a redemption is always "essentially equivalent to a dividend" within the meaning of that phrase in §302(b)(1)[8] and therefore do not reach the Government's alternative argument that in any event the distribution should not on the facts of this case qualify for capital gains treatment.[9]

The predecessor of §302(b)(1) came into the tax law as §201(d) of the Revenue Act of 1921, 42 Stat. 228:

> A stock dividend shall not be subject to tax but if after the distribution of any such dividend the corporation proceeds to cancel or redeem its stock at such time and in such manner as to make the distribution and cancellation or redemption essentially equivalent to the distribution of a taxable dividend, the amount received in redemption or cancellation of the stock shall be treated as a taxable dividend. . . .

Enacted in response to this court's decision that pro rata stock dividends do not constitute taxable income, Eisner v. Macomber, 252 U.S. 189 (1920), the provision had the obvious purpose of preventing a corporation from avoiding dividend tax treatment by distributing earnings to its shareholders in two transactions — a pro rata stock dividend followed by a pro rata redemption — that would have the same economic consequences as a simple dividend. Congress, however, soon recognized that even without a prior stock dividend essentially the same result could be effected whereby any corporation, "especially one which has only a few stockholders, might be able to make a distribution to its stockholders which would have the same effect as a taxable dividend." H.R. Rep. No. 1, 69th Cong., 1st Sess., 5. In order to cover this situation, the law was amended to apply "(whether or not such stock was issued as a stock dividend)" whenever a distribution in redemption of stock was made "at such time and in such manner" that it was essentially equivalent to a taxable dividend. Revenue Act of 1926, §201(g), 44 Stat. 11.

This provision of the 1926 Act was carried forward in each subsequent revenue act and finally became §115(g)(1) of the Internal

---

8. Of course, this just means that a distribution in redemption to a sole shareholder will be treated under the general provisions of §301, and it will only be taxed as a dividend under §316 to the extent that there are earnings and profits.

9. The Government argues that even if business purpose were relevant under §302(b)(1), the business purpose present here related only to the original investment and not at all to the necessity for redemption. See cases cited, n.2, supra. Under either view, taxpayer does not lose his basis in the preferred stock. Under Treas. Reg. 1.302-2(c) that basis is applied to taxpayers' common stock.

Revenue Code of 1939. Unfortunately, however, the policies encompassed within the general language of §115(g)(1) and its predecessors were not clear, and there resulted much confusion in the tax law. At first, courts assumed that the provision was aimed at tax avoidance schemes and sought only to determine whether such a scheme existed. See, e.g., Commissioner v. Quackenbos, 78 F.2d 156 (C.A. 2d Cir. 1935). Although later the emphasis changed and the focus was more on the effect of the distribution, many courts continued to find that distributions otherwise like a dividend were not "essentially equivalent" if, for example, they were motivated by a sufficiently strong nontax business purpose. See cases cited n.2, supra. There was general disagreement, however, about what would qualify as such a purpose, and the result was a case-by-case determination with each case decided "on the basis of the particular facts of the transaction in question." Bains v. United States, . . . 289 F.2d 644, 646 (1961).

By the time of the general revision resulting in the Internal Revenue Code of 1954, the draftsmen were faced with what has aptly been described as "the morass created by the decisions." Ballenger v. United States, 301 F.2d 192, 196 (C.A. 4th Cir. 1962). In an effort to eliminate "the considerable confusion which exists in this area" and thereby to facilitate tax planning, H.R. Rep. No. 1337, 83d Cong., 2d Sess., 35, the authors of the new Code sought to provide objective tests to govern the tax consequences of stock redemptions. Thus, the tax bill passed by the House of Representatives contained no "essentially equivalent" language. Rather, it provided for "safe harbors" where capital gains treatment would be accorded to corporate redemptions that met the conditions now found in §§302(b)(2) and (3) of the Code.

It was in the Senate Finance Committee's consideration of the tax bill that §302(b)(1) was added, and Congress thereby provided that capital gains treatment should be available "if the redemption is not essentially equivalent to a dividend." Taxpayer argues that the purpose was to continue "existing law," and there is support in the legislative history that §302(b)(1) reverted "in part" or "in general" to the "essentially equivalent" provision of §115(g)(1) of the 1939 Code. According to the Government, even under the old law it would have been improper for the Court of Appeals to rely on "a business purpose for the redemption" and "an absence of the proscribed tax avoidance purpose to bail out dividends at favorable tax rates." See Northup v. United States, 240 F.2d 304, 307 (C.A. 2d Cir. 1957); Smith v. United States, 121 F.2d 692, 695 (C.A. 3d Cir. 1941); cf. Commissioner v. Estate of Bedford, 325 U.S. 283 (1945). However, we need not decide that question, for we find from the history of the 1954 revisions and the purpose of §302(b)(1) that Congress intended more than merely to re-enact the prior law.

In explaining the reason for adding the "essentially equivalent" test, the Senate Committee stated that the House provisions "appeared unnecessarily restrictive, particularly, in the case of redemptions of preferred stock which might be called by the corporation without the shareholder having any control over when the redemption may take place." S. Rep. No. 1622, 83d Cong., 2d Sess., 44. This explanation gives no indication that the purpose behind the redemption should affect the result.[10] Rather, in its more detailed technical evaluation of §302(b)(1), the Senate Committee reported as follows:

> The test intended to be incorporated in the interpretation of paragraph (1) is in general that currently employed under section 115(g)(1) of the 1939 Code. Your committee further intends that in applying this test for the future that the inquiry will be devoted solely to the question of whether or not the transaction by its nature may properly be characterized as a sale of stock by the redeeming shareholder to the corporation. For this purpose the presence or absence of earnings and profits of the corporation is not material. Example: X, the sole shareholder of a corporation having no earnings or profits causes the corporation to redeem half of its stock. Paragraph (1) does not apply to such redemption notwithstanding the absence of earnings and profits. [S. Rep. No. 1622, supra, at 234.]

The intended scope of §302(b)(1) as revealed by this legislative history is certainly not free from doubt. However, we agree with the Government that by making the sole inquiry relevant for the future the narrow one whether the redemption could be characterized as a sale, Congress was apparently rejecting past court decisions that had also considered factors indicating the presence or absence of a tax-avoidance motive.[11] At least that is the implication of the example given. Congress clearly mandated that pro rata distributions be treated under the general rules laid down in §§301 and 316 rather than under §302, and nothing suggests that there should be a dif-

10. See Bittker & Eustice, [Federal Income Taxation of Corporation and Shareholders], at 291: "It is not easy to give §302(b)(1) an expansive construction in view of this indication that its major function was the narrow one of immunizing redemptions of minority holdings of preferred stock."

11. This rejection is confirmed by the Committee's acceptance of the House treatment of distributions involving corporate contractions — a factor present in many of the earlier "business purpose" redemptions. In describing its action, the Committee stated as follows:

"Your committee, as did the House bill, separates into their significant elements the kind of transactions now incoherently aggregated in the definition of a partial liquidation. Those distributions which may have capital-gain characteristics *because they are not made pro rata* among the various shareholders would be subjected, at the shareholder level, to the separate tests described in [§§301 to 318]. On the other hand, those distributions characterized by what happens solely at the corporate level by reason of the assets distributed would be included as within the concept of a partial liquidation." S. Rep. No. 1622, supra, at 49. (Emphasis added.)

ferent result if there were a "business purpose" for the redemption. Indeed, just the opposite inference must be drawn since there would not likely be a tax-avoidance purpose in a situation where there were no earnings or profits. We conclude that the Court of Appeals was therefore wrong in looking for a business purpose and considering it in deciding whether the redemption was equivalent to a dividend. Rather, we agree with the Court of Appeals for the Second Circuit that "the business purpose of a transaction is irrelevant in determining dividend equivalence" under §302(b)(1). Hasbrook v. United States, 343 F.2d 811, 814 (1965).

Taxpayer strongly argues that to treat the redemption involved here as essentially equivalent to a dividend is to elevate form over substance. Thus, taxpayer argues, had he not bought Bradley's shares or had he made a subordinated loan to the company instead of buying preferred stock, he could have gotten back his $25,000 with favorable tax treatment. However, the difference between form and substance in the tax law is largely problematical, and taxpayer's complaints have little to do with whether a business purpose is relevant under §302(b)(1). It was clearly proper for Congress to treat distributions generally as taxable dividends when made out of earnings and profits and then to prevent avoidance of that result without regard to motivation where the distribution is in exchange for redeemed stock.

We conclude that that is what Congress did when enacting §302(b)(1). If a corporation distributes property as a simple dividend, the effect is to transfer the property from the company to its shareholders without a change in the relative economic interests or rights of the stockholders. Where a redemption has that same effect, it cannot be said to have satisfied the "not essentially equivalent to a dividend" requirement of §302(b)(1). Rather, to qualify for preferred treatment under that section, a redemption must result in a meaningful reduction of the shareholder's proportionate interest in the corporation. Clearly, taxpayer here, who (after application of the attribution rules) was the sole shareholder of the corporation both before and after the redemption, did not qualify under this test. The decision of the Court of Appeals must therefore be reversed and the case remanded to the District Court for dismissal of the complaint.

It is so ordered.

Mr. Justice DOUGLAS, with whom The Chief Justice and Mr. Justice Brennan concur, dissenting.

I agree with the District Court, 274 F. Supp. 466, and with the Court of Appeals, 408 F.2d 1139, that respondent's contribution of working capital in the amount of $25,000 in exchange for 1,000 shares of preferred stock with a par value of $25 was made in order for the corporation to obtain a loan from the RFC and that the preferred stock was to be redeemed when the loan was repaid. For the reasons stated by the two lower courts, this redemption was not "essentially equivalent to a dividend," for the bona fide business purpose of the redemption belies the payment of a dividend. As stated by the Court of Appeals:

> Although closely-held corporations call for close scrutiny under the tax law, we will not, under the facts and circumstances of this case, allow mechanical attribution rules to transform a legitimate corporate transaction into a tax avoidance scheme. [408 F.2d, at 1143-1144.]

When the Court holds it was a dividend, it effectively cancels §302(b)(1) from the Code. This result is not a matter of conjecture, for the Court says that in case of closely held or one-man corporations a redemption of stock is "always" equivalent to a dividend. I would leave such revision to the Congress.

ALBERS v. COMMISSIONER
414 U.S. 982 (1973), *denying cert. to* Miele v. Commissioner, 474 F.2d 1338 (3d Cir. 1973), *aff'g mem.* 56 T.C. 556 (1971)

Mr. Justice POWELL, with whom Mr. Justice Douglas and Mr. Justice Blackmun join, dissenting. The five petitioners in this case own virtually all the outstanding stock of a small corporation, A & S Transportation Co. (A & S). The company operates a barge. The barge fell into such disrepair as to require replacement, but A & S lacked the necessary resources and credit. A & S requested the Federal Maritime Commission to guarantee, as it is empowered by law to do, a proposed first mortgage loan from a bank. Before the Commission would extend its guarantee, it required of A & S at least $150,000 of additional private capital. The Commission presented A & S with two options. A & S could resort either to subordinated debt or to the issuance of nonvoting, nondividend paying, noncumulative preferred stock unredeemable until full payment of the desired loan.

A & S chose the latter course. In proportion to their holdings of A & S common, petitioners in 1959 purchased $150,000 of preferred stock possessing all the attributes required by the Commission. The loan was then consummated with the Commission's guarantee, and A & S purchased a replacement vessel. By 1964 the loan was paid off in full. Having no further need for the $150,000, and in accord with the wishes of petitioners, A & S redeemed the preferred stock in 1965 and 1966 in two equal installments. No premium was paid, and *petitioners received precisely the amount each had previously invested.* The Commissioner of Internal Revenue treated the redemptions as the receipt of ordinary income, taking the view that they were "essentially equivalent to a dividend" within the meaning of §301(b)(1) of the Internal Revenue Code of 1954, 26 U.S.C. §302(b)(1). Citing United States v. Davis, 397 U.S. 301 (1970), the Tax Court agreed. . . . The Court of Appeals for the Third Circuit affirmed without published opinions. . . .

On the above facts it seems plain that the redemption of preferred stock provided petitioners nothing more than a return of the capital they were compelled by the Commission to pay into A & S to obtain the additional financing the corporation needed to remain in business. To tax that return of capital at ordinary income rates is an extraordinary result, yet one that I recognize to be mandated by the full sweep of United States v. Davis, supra. Because of strong doubts as to the correctness of any decision that produces such a bizarre result, I would grant certiorari to reconsider *Davis*.

Section 302(b)(1) of the Code shelters from dividend treatment, and accompanying potential ordinary income consequences, any stock redemption that "is not essentially equivalent to a dividend." A majority of the Court in *Davis* read that provision to mean that a stock redemption by a small, closely held corporation is "*always* 'essentially equivalent to a dividend' " where there is no "change in the relative economic interests or rights of the stockholders." 397 U.S., at 307, 313 (emphasis added). Undoubtedly the Court sought to promote ease of administration through adoption of a simplistic, per se rule. Yet the Court explicitly recognized that the weight of authority in the lower federal courts was contrary to its mechanical approach. Id., at 303 n.2. Furthermore, the Court conceded that the "legislative history is certainly not free from doubt." Id., at 311.

In my view, the result produced by *Davis* in this case is justified neither by the language of the Code nor by the legislative history, and certainly not by precedent prior to *Davis*. In these circumstances, ease of administration is too high a price to pay for the presumably unforeseen and undeniably harsh consequences visited on these and similarly situated taxpayers.

The Tax Court noted petitioners' position "that the preferred stock was no longer needed after the loan had been paid in full and that redemption of the stock was consistent with the business purpose for which the stock was issued." . . . The Tax Court did not refute the factual correctness of this position, or consider whether there had been a tax evasion motivation.[4] Rather, that court simply disregarded all factual considerations as immaterial to an application of the *Davis* per se rule:

> We consider [petitioners'] argument as having been foreclosed
> and the issue determined by the case of United States v. Davis,

---

4. No finding was made by the Tax Court, for example, that any earned surplus was available from which ordinary dividends could have been paid.

397 U.S. 301 (1970). In *Davis*, the United States Supreme Court held that a redemption without a change in the relative economic interests or rights of the stockholders is always essentially equivalent to a dividend under §302(b)(1). It is the effect of the redemption and not the purpose behind it which is determinative of dividend equivalence. [Ibid. (Citations omitted.)]

Mr. Justice Douglas, dissenting in *Davis* with the concurrence of the Chief Justice and Mr. Justice Brennan, viewed the majority opinion as reading §302(b)(1) out of the Code:

> When the Court holds it [the redemption under consideration in *Davis*] was a dividend, it effectively cancels §302(b)(1) from the Code. This result is not a matter of conjecture, for the Court says that in the case of closely held or one-man corporations a redemption of stock is "always" equivalent to a dividend. [397 U.S., at 314.]

The Tax Court's decision in this case abundantly bears out Mr. Justice Douglas' view. In light of the deliberate retention of the "essentially equivalent to a dividend" language in the 1954 revision of the Code, most courts prior to *Davis* had assumed that §302(b)(1) required a factual determination as to the business purpose of the stock redemption. Had such a factual inquiry been made in this case, it is evident that the result would have been different.

In addition to the presence of a legitimate business purpose and the absence of any evidence of tax evasion, the preferred stock in question here was nondividend paying — a highly unusual provision for a preferred stock. Thus petitioners, having been induced by the Commission to advance additional private capital to A & S, found themselves either locked in without income on their investment or compelled, as the price of recouping it, to pay taxes at ordinary income rates on a nonexistent gain. It is difficult to think of a more unjust result, and yet this is the inevitable consequence of the sweeping *Davis* requirement that a redemption "always" be deemed " 'essentially equivalent to a dividend' " in the absence of "a change in the relative economic interests or rights of the stockholders." 397 U.S., at 307, 313.[6]

---

6. This one qualification (namely, a change in the relative economic interests or rights of stockholders) may immunize from *Davis* consequences the larger corporations, where a congruity of interest between common and preferred stockholders is found far less frequently than in the family type of small corporations. But even where it can fairly be said (and often the facts as to this are ambiguous) that there has been no such change, this does not mean that minority stockholders are not severely penalized by the *Davis* rule. In this case, the Tax Court noted that the redemption was made at the insistence of petitioners, who were in the unhappy position of holding nondividend preferred stock. But nothing in *Davis* protects a minority stockholder in a close corporation (and their number is legion) who may have little or no influence as to whether or when preferred stock is redeemed. If the

One may recognize the tax-avoidance concern underlying the Court's opinion in *Davis* without concluding that the only remedy with respect to closely held corporations is "always" to tax stock redemptions as dividends without regard to facts and circumstances. It may indeed have been reasonable to create a rebuttable presumption in favor of the Government, but it is difficult to see a justification for a result as harsh and inequitable as that often produced by the *Davis* rule. Moreover, if Congress' purpose was to enact the *Davis* per se rule, it could have been expressed in the simplest language.[8] As the Court notes in *Davis*, the Senate Finance Committee deliberately chose not to take that option. 397 U.S., at 310-311.

In my view the *Davis* rule, often a trap for unwary investors in small businesses and facially contrary to the relevant Code provision, should be reconsidered.

NOTES

1. In Blanco v. Commissioner, 602 F.2d 324 (Ct. Cl. 1979), *cert. denied* 444 U.S. 1072 (1980), a sole shareholder who, upon discovering that a distribution in redemption of a portion of his shares in the corporation would be taxed as a dividend under *Davis*, tried to rescind the transaction by issuing an interest-bearing note to the corporation and having the corporation return his shares to him. The court declined to decide the effect of a successful rescission, finding that the facts simply did not support the taxpayer claim of rescission, for he did not return the proceeds of the redemption in exchange for the

---

majority shareholders in such a corporation effect a pro rata redemption, a minority shareholder has no means to avoid *Davis* consequences. In this connection, the language of the Senate Finance Committee in restoring the "essentially equivalent" language to §302 of the Code is relevant. The Senate Committee stated that the House bill, which had deleted this language, "appeared unnecessarily restrictive, particularly, in the case of redemptions of preferred stock which might be called by the corporation without the shareholder having any control over when the redemption may take place." S. Rep. No. 1622, 83d Cong., 2d Sess., 44 (1954). See United States v. Davis, supra. . . . The truth is that minority shareholders, even in close corporations, frequently have no such control.

8. It has been suggested that since *Davis* was decided March 23, 1970, Congress has had more than three years to repudiate or ameliorate the *Davis* per se rule. With all respect, this suggestion seems unrealistic. Congress has had under consideration during this period a general revision of the Code as well as a broad re-examination of many of the fundamental assumptions underlying the present Code. It is unlikely that piecemeal adjustments would have been made during this period of study and re-examination. Furthermore, the *Davis* rule falls most heavily on small family corporations unlikely to have specialized tax counsel capable of warning that *Davis* has converted §302(b)(1) into "a treacherous route to be employed only as a last resort." B. Bittker & J. Eustice, supra n.7, at 9-9. It is these very corporations that are least likely to make their voices heard in Congress, since they have limited "lobbying" capabilities.

return of his shares. Thus, he was taxable on the redemption as a dividend, and his payments on the note were treated as contributions to capital.

2. Can (should) *Himmel* survive *Davis?* Consider Rev. Rul. 85-106, page 210 infra, for an indication of the Commissioner's thinking. Compare Morris v. United States, 441 F. Supp. 76 (N.D. Tex. 1977) (redemption of 35 percent of preferred stock from owner of 50 percent of common, as part of redemption of all outstanding preferred, was meaningful reduction of proportionate interest because of loss of dividend priority).

3. A owns all of the outstanding stock of Corporation X and Corporation Y, a supplier of X. In order to make a public offering of X stock possible, the underwriter recommends that common ownership be ended. A sells his Y stock to X under an arrangement requiring installment payments by X. The payments are made out of the proceeds of the public offering. The IRS argued that this transaction was a §304(a)(1) redemption (see page 270 et seq. infra), and was to be treated as a distribution under §302(d). Is it an indirect sale to the public and therefore not essentially equivalent to a dividend? Can the changed relationship of A to Y — now subject to SEC rules and regulations — result in a "meaningful reduction" of interest? See Jack Paparo, 71 T.C. 692 (1979) (treating payments as dividends).

REVENUE RULING 76-385
1976-2 C.B. 92

Advice has been requested whether, under the circumstances described below, a redemption of stock was a redemption that was not essentially equivalent to a dividend under section 302(b)(1) of the Internal Revenue Code of 1954.

Corporation X, a family corporation, owned all of the stock of corporation Y. X and Y both owned a small number of shares of stock of corporation Z. Z's stock is listed on the New York Stock Exchange. It has outstanding one class of stock consisting of 28 million shares of common stock.

Pursuant to a settlement of Federal antitrust litigation, Z agreed to divest itself of certain property owned by it. In accordance with this agreement, Z offered to distribute the property to its shareholders in redemption of shares of their Z stock. The offer was accepted by a portion of the Z shareholders, including Y. However, X did not accept the offer. In redemption of Y's stock in Z, Z distributed to Y a portion of the property required to be divested with a fair market value equal to the fair market value of the Z stock surrendered by

Y. Although the redemption terminated Y's actual ownership of stock of Z, Y still is considered as owning the Z stock owned by X after the redemption through the application of the constructive ownership of stock rules of section 318(a)(3)(C) of the Code, which section 302(c) makes applicable to section 302. Thus, when the stock constructively owned by Y is considered, calculations indicate that the redemption reduced Y's percentage of ownership of the stock of Z from .0001118 percent to .0001081 percent. Based on this reduction, the percentage of stock of Z owned by Y after the redemption was 96.7 percent of the percentage of stock owned by Y before the redemption. . . .

The redemption of Z's stock held by Y was not a termination of interest under section 302(b)(3) of the Code because Y continued to own, through the application of section 318(a)(3)(C), the Z stock held by X. Furthermore, the redemption of Z's stock held by Y was not substantially disproportionate within the meaning of section 302(b)(2) because the reduction in Y's percentage ownership in Z did not meet the percentage requirement of section 302(b)(2)(C). . . .

One purpose for the enactment of section 302(b)(1) of the Code was to provide capital gain treatment for redemptions of stock held by certain minority shareholders, especially minority holders of preferred stock who exercise no control over corporate affairs. See S. Rep. No. 1622, 83rd Cong., 2d Sess., 44-45 (1954).

The redemption in the instant case falls within the category of redemptions Congress intended to exclude from dividend treatment through the enactment of section 302(b)(1) of the Code since the redemption involves a minority shareholder whose relative stock interest in Z is minimal and who exercises no control over the affairs of Z. In addition, as a result of the redemption, Y experienced a reduction of its voting rights, its right to participate in current earnings and accumulated surplus, and its right to share in net assets on liquidation. Thus, under the facts and circumstances of the instant case, the redemption qualifies under section 302(b)(1).

Accordingly, the redemption was not essentially equivalent to a dividend within the meaning of section 302(b)(1) of the Code and, therefore, qualified as an exchange under section 302(a). . . .

NOTE

See Wright v. United States, 482 F.2d 600 (8th Cir. 1973) (meaningful reduction where shareholder's ownership of the corporation was reduced from 85 to 61.7 percent, eliminating the two-thirds voting control required by state law for certain corporate actions); Rev. Rul. 78-401, 1978-2 C.B. 127 (reduction from 90 percent to 60 percent not meaningful where no action requiring two-thirds vote was contemplated); Rev. Rul. 75-502, 1976-2 C.B. 92 (redemption that resulted in a reduction of an estate's voting rights from 57 to 50 percent not essentially equivalent to a dividend). See also Agway, Inc. v. United States, 524 F.2d 1194 (Ct. Cl. 1975) (cooperative periodically issued and redeemed preferred stock, redeeming oldest first; non-pro rata redemptions are not substantially equivalent to dividends); Rev. Rul. 77-426, 1977-2 C.B. 87 (redemption of 5 percent of preferred stock, from shareholder who owned 100 percent of preferred but no common, not essentially equivalent to a dividend); Rev. Rul. 76-364, 1976-2 C.B. 91 (reduction from 27 to 22.27 percent ownership, plus loss of ability to control the corporation in concert with any one of the other three shareholders, was a meaningful reduction).

REVENUE RULING 81-289
1981-2 C.B. 82

ISSUE

Whether a redemption of stock pursuant to an isolated tender offer is taxable as an exchange under section 302(a) and (b)(1) of the Internal Revenue Code.

FACTS

X corporation has outstanding 1,000,000x shares of voting common stock which are widely held and publicly traded. X has approximately 1,000x shareholders, none of whom owns a significant amount of the X common stock. In an isolated transaction and not as part of a periodic redemption plan, X offered to purchase from its shareholders 25,000x shares of common stock at the rate of $20x per share. Approximately 10 percent of X's shareholders tendered stock for redemption. X redeemed a total of 20,000x shares of its stock pursuant to the tender offer. Individual A, who owned 2,000x shares of X stock at the time of the tender offer, surrendered 40x shares for redemption. Accordingly, A's proportionate interest in X was .2 percent (2,000x shares divided by 1,000,000x shares) before the tender offer and remained .2 percent (1,960x shares divided by 980,000x shares) after the tender offer. A was not related to any other shareholder of X within the meaning of section 318.

LAW AND ANALYSIS

Section 302(a) of the Code provides, in part, that a redemption of stock will be treated as a distribution in part or full payment in exchange for the stock redeemed if section 302(b)(1), (2), or (3) applies. Section 302(b)(1) will apply if the redemption is "not essentially equivalent to a dividend." Section 302(b)(2) will apply if the distribution is "substantially disproportionate" with respect to the shareholder. Section 302(b)(3) will apply if all of the shareholder's stock of the corporation is redeemed. Section 302(c)(1) provides that the constructive ownership of stock rules of section 318 will apply in determining ownership of stock for purposes of section 302.

Section 302(b)(2) of the Code does not apply because A did not experience a more than 20-percent reduction in proportionate interest in X, as required by section 302(b)(2)(C). Section 302(b)(3) does not apply because A continues to own stock of X. The question, therefore, is whether A's redemption was "not essentially equivalent to a dividend" under section 302(b)(1).

Section 1.302-2(b) of the Income Tax Regulations provides, with respect to section 302(b)(1) of the Code, that the question of whether a distribution in redemption of stock of a shareholder is not essentially equivalent to a dividend depends on the facts and circumstances of each case, and that all distributions in pro rata redemptions generally will be treated as distributions under section 301 if the corporation has only one class of stock outstanding.

In United States v. Davis, 397 U.S. 301 (1970), the Supreme Court of the United States held that (1) the constructive ownership of stock rules of section 318(a) of the Code apply to redemptions under section 302(b)(1); (2) the business purpose of a redemption is irrelevant under section 302(b)(1); and (3) a redemption of stock from a sole shareholder (which is necessarily pro rata) will always have the effect of a dividend. In so holding, the Court stated, at page 313, that in order for a redemption to qualify under section 302(b)(1), it must result in a "meaningful reduction in the shareholder's proportionate interest in the corporation." The Court, by using singular possessive language, indicated that a shareholder-by-shareholder analysis is the requisite procedure for determining dividend equivalence. The existence and size of a reduction in proportionate interest that results from a redemption is important because the relationships of the shareholders and the continued exercise of control and participation in the earnings and assets by those shareholders whose stock is redeemed may render essentially meaningless any differences between the redemption and an ordinary dividend distribution. For example, after applying the constructive ownership of stock rules of section 318 of the Code in *Davis*, the taxpayer owned all of the redeeming corporation's stock both before and after the redemption with the result that the distribution was precisely pro rata and, thus, essentially equivalent to a dividend.

Subsequent to the *Davis* decision in 1970, lower courts have established a pattern of applying the meaningful reduction standard to the facts of the case, focusing on the criteria set forth earlier in

Himmel v. Commissioner, 338 F.2d 815 (2d Cir. 1964). In *Himmel*, the Second Circuit emphasized that stock ownership involves these important rights: (1) the right to vote and thereby exercise control; (2) the right to participate in current earnings and accumulated surplus; and (3) the right to share in net assets on liquidation. In Rev. Rul. 75-502, 1975-2 C.B. 111, and Rev. Rul. 75-512, 1975-2 C.B. 112, the *Davis* meaningful reduction standard was applied to these three criteria on a shareholder-by-shareholder basis in situations involving closely held corporations.

The United States Tax Court applied the meaningful reduction standard in a situation involving a publicly held corporation, stating that the " 'meaningful reduction' test deserves wider application since the reasoning behind the *Davis* decision transcends the narrow facts of the case." Sawelson v. Commissioner, 61 T.C. 109, 117 (1973). See also Brown v. United States, 345 F. Supp. 241 (S.D. Ohio 1972), *aff'd without opinion*, 477 F.2d 599 (6th Cir.), *cert. denied*, 414 U.S. 1011 (1973), in which it was held that the meaningful reduction standard applied, notwithstanding that some of the corporation's stock was held by the public. Moreover, the meaningful reduction standard was applied to a redemption by a publicly traded corporation in Rev. Rul. 76-385, 1976-2 C.B. 92. In that revenue ruling, the Internal Revenue Service took the position that a redemption that resulted in a reduction of a minority shareholder's proportionate interest from .0001118 percent to .0001081 percent was not essentially equivalent to a dividend, since the minority shareholder experienced a reduction of its voting rights, its right to participate in current earnings and accumulated surplus, and its right to share in net assets on liquidation.

HOLDING

In the present situation the redemption did not result in any reduction of A's right to vote, to participate in current earnings and accumulated surplus, or to share in the corporation's net assets on liquidation. Thus, this redemption with regard to A does not satisfy the meaningful reduction standard and does not qualify as an exchange within the meaning of section 302(a) and (b)(1) of the Code.

REVENUE RULING 85-106
1985-2 C.B. 116

ISSUE

Is a redemption of nonvoting preferred stock not essentially equivalent to a dividend within the meaning of section 302(b)(1) of the Internal Revenue Code when there is no reduction in the percentage of voting and nonvoting common stock owned by the

redeemed shareholder, and when the redeemed shareholder continues to have an undiminished opportunity to act in concert with other
shareholders as a control group, under the circumstances described
below?

FACTS

Corporation X had outstanding three classes of stock consisting
of 100 shares of voting common stock, 100 shares of nonvoting common stock, and 50 shares of nonvoting 9 percent cumulative
preferred stock. The fair market value of each share of common
stock was approximately half the fair market value of each share of
preferred stock. The voting common stock was held as follows:

Shareholders	Shares
A	19
B	19
C	18
Minority shareholders	44
Total	100

None of the minority shareholders owned more than five shares.
None of the holders of the voting common stock were related within
the meaning of section 318(a) of the Code. The combined voting
power of A, B, and C was sufficient to elect a majority of the board
of directors of X.

The nonvoting common stock and the preferred stock were held
(directly and indirectly) in approximately the same proportions as
the common stock. C held no nonvoting common stock or preferred
stock directly, but was the sole remaining beneficiary of a trust, T,
which owned 18 percent of both the nonvoting common stock and
the preferred stock.

The trustees of T decided that it would be in the best interests
of that trust if most of the X preferred stock held by T could be
converted into cash. After negotiation, X redeemed six shares of
preferred stock for its fair market value of 6x dollars. Following this
redemption, T continued to hold three shares of preferred stock,
and 18 percent of the nonvoting common stock. Under section
318(a)(3)(B) of the Code, T is also considered to own the voting
common stock owned by its sole beneficiary, C.

LAW AND ANALYSIS

Section 302(a) of the Code provides, in part, that if a corporation
redeems its stock, and if section 302(b)(1), (2), (3), or (4) applies, such

redemption will be treated as a distribution in part or full payment in exchange for the stock.

Section 302(b)(1) of the Code provides that section 302(a) will apply if the redemption is not essentially equivalent to a dividend. Section 302(b)(2) provides that section 302(a) will apply if (in addition to other requirements) the redemption substantially reduces the voting power of the shareholder. Section 302(b)(3) provides that section 302(a) will apply if the redemption completely terminates the shareholder's interest in the corporation. Section 302(b)(4) does not deal with the type of redemption under consideration. Section 302(c)(1) provides, with an exception not here relevant, that the constructive ownership rules of section 318(a) apply in determining the ownership of stock for purposes of section 302.

The lack of any reduction in T's 18 percent vote prevented this redemption from qualifying under section 302(b)(2) of the Code, and the lack of complete termination of interest prevented it from qualifying under section 302(b)(3). The question remains whether the redemption should be considered not essentially equivalent to a dividend so as to qualify under section 302(b)(1). Under section 1.302-2(b) of the Income Tax Regulations, this determination depends upon the facts and circumstances of each case.

In United States v. Davis, 397 U.S. 301 (1970), 1970-1 C.B. 62, the Supreme Court of the United States held that in order to qualify under section 302(b)(1) of the Code, a redemption must result in a meaningful reduction of the shareholder's proportionate interest in the corporation, and that, for this purpose, the attribution rules of section 318 apply.

In determining whether a reduction in interest is "meaningful," the rights inherent in a shareholder's interest must be examined. The three elements of a shareholder's interest that are generally considered most significant are: (1) the right to vote and thereby exercise control; (2) the right to participate in current earnings and accumulated surplus; and (3) the right to share in net assets on liquidation. Rev. Rul. 81-289, 1981-2 C.B. 82.

In applying the above principles, it is significant that (as a result of section 318(a)(3)(B) of the Code) the redemption did not reduce T's percentage of the vote in X. It is true that T reduced its percentage interest in current earnings, accumulated surplus, and net assets upon liquidation, and reduced the fair market value of its ownership in X. However, when the redeemed shareholder has a voting interest (either directly or by attribution), a reduction in voting power is a key factor in determining the applicability of section 302(b)(1) of the Code. Johnson Trust v. Commissioner, 71 T.C. 941, 947, 948 (1979). Rev. Rul. 78-401, 1978-2 C.B. 127; Rev. Rul. 77-218, 1977-1 C.B. 81; Rev. Rul. 75-502, 1975-2 C.B. 111; Rev. Rul. 75-512, 1975-2 C.B. 112.

It is also true that T was not the largest shareholder. A and B each held slightly larger voting interests, and larger interests measured by fair market value. T, however, was not in the position of a minority shareholder isolated from corporate management and control. Compare Rev. Rev. 75-512, where the majority of the redeeming corporation's voting stock was held by a shareholder unrelated (within the meaning of section 318(a)) to the redeemed trust. Also compare Rev. Rul. 76-385, 1976-2 C.B. 92, where the redeemed shareholder's total interest was de minimis.

In the present situation, a significant aspect of T's failure to reduce voting power is the fact that the redemption leaves unchanged T's potential (by attribution from C) for participating in a control group by acting in concert with A and B. Compare Rev. Rul. 76-364, 1976-2 C.B. 91, where a reduction in voting interest was found meaningful in itself when it caused the redeemed shareholder to give up a potential for control by acting in concert with one other shareholder. In addition, the Tax Court has indicated significance for this factor of potential group control (*Johnson Trust*, at 947). See also Bloch v. United States, 261 F. Supp. 597, 611-612 (S.D. Tex. 1966), *aff'd per curiam*, 386 F.2d 839 (5th Cir. 1967), where, in finding that "the distributions in question were essentially equivalent to a dividend," the court noted that there was no change in the redeemed shareholder's potential for exercising control "by aligning himself with one or more of the other stockholders."

Although there was a reduction of T's economic interest in X, such reduction was not sufficiently large to result in a meaningful reduction of T's interest. The absence of any reduction of T's voting interest in X (through C) and T's potential (through C) for control group participation are compelling factors in this situation.

In Himmel v. Commissioner, 338 F.2d 815 (2d Cir. 1964), dealing with a similar question, a decision was reached permitting the applicability of section 302(b)(1) of the Code. That case, however, was decided prior to the decision of the Supreme Court in *Davis*. Thus, *Himmel* fails to reflect the development in the law represented by the *Davis* limitation on section 302(b)(1) applicability where there is no meaningful reduction of the shareholder's proportionate interest in the corporation. Thus, pursuant to *Davis*, it is proper to view *Himmel* as incorrect to the extent it conflicts with the position contained in this revenue ruling.

HOLDING

The redemption of nonvoting preferred stock held by T does not qualify as a redemption under section 302(b)(1) of the Code, under the facts of this ruling when there is no reduction in the percentage of voting and nonvoting common stock owned by T, and when T continues to have an undiminished opportunity to act in concert with other shareholders as a control group. Since the redemption does not otherwise qualify under section 302(b), it is not a distribution in part or full payment for the stock under section 302(a). Consequently, under section 302(d), the redemption will be treated as a distribution of property to which section 301 applies.

NOTES

1. See also Letter Rul. 8848062 (Sept. 9, 1988) (redemption resulting in a reduction of taxpayer's constructive ownership of nonvoting common stock from 48.9 percent to 45.62 percent essentially equivalent to a dividend; taxpayer owned 50 percent of the corporation's voting common stock both before and after the redemption). Compare Letter Rul. 8540074 (July 10, 1985), which concluded that a sole shareholder who redeems most of his stock (90%) and simultaneously sells half of the remaining shares to an employee qualifies as a redemption not essentially equivalent to a dividend.

2. If the "control group" and potential for action in "concert" were sensible concerns for the Commissioner to address, as he did in Rev. Rul. 85-106, should he not reconsider and revoke Rev. Rul. 75-502, 1975-2 C.B. 111, in which he found a "meaningful reduction" although the redemption reduced the shareholder's voting interest from 57 percent to only 50 percent?

For a critical comment on Rev. Rul. 85-106, see Karlin, Rev. Rul. 85-106: An Unsupported Attack on Section 302(b)(1) Redemptions, 64 Taxes 529 (1986).

DAVID METZGER TRUST v. COMMISSIONER
693 F.2d 459 (5th Cir. 1982), *cert. denied*, 463 U.S. 1207 (1983)

Before Thornberry, Johnson and Higginbotham, Circuit Judges.
HIGGINBOTHAM, Circuit Judge. . . . In reviewing this decision of the Tax Court . . . we face three questions: (1) whether the attribution rules of I.R.C. §318(a) must be applied despite family discord in determining whether a redemption meets the "not essentially equivalent to a dividend test" of §302(b)(1); (2) whether a trust may waive the attribution rules of §318(a) by filing a waiver agreement pursuant to §302(c)(2)(A)(iii); (3) whether the attribution rules of §267(c) must be applied to interest payments between family members in discord. Governed by the plain language of the Code, a goal of a coherent tax policy, and the relevant Supreme Court precedents, we affirm the decision of the Tax Court. . . .

Appellant David Metzger Trust was created by David Metzger in 1942 to benefit his wife as life income beneficiary and his three children, Jacob, Catherine, and Cecelia, as one-third remaindermen each. Jacob, the eldest son, was named trustee of the Trust. Four years later, David incorporated the family business as Metzger Dairies, Inc., the other appellant. The Trust became a shareholder of Metzger Dairies.

On David's death in 1953 Jacob Metzger assumed control of Metzger Dairies. Catherine and Cecelia were directors. In the years following the father's death the sibling quarrel grew in intensity. By the 1960s, open animosity developed among Jacob, Catherine, and Cecelia. Whatever the source of their alienation, a downturn in the success of the dairy only exacerbated the problem. Catherine and Cecelia became angry when the corporation stopped paying dividends. Catherine resented what she considered to be Jacob's interference in the management of Metzger Dairy of San Antonio, a corporation of which her son was president but whose stock was owned for the most part by the same parties who owned the stock of Metzger Dairies. Cecelia was annoyed at both Jacob and Catherine because both corporations failed to pay dividends. The argument among Jacob, Catherine, and Cecelia over these and other issues unrelated to the business of the corporations continued until 1972, when the acrimony reached the point that Jacob, Catherine, and Cecelia concluded it was necessary to terminate their joint ownership of the corporations.

After lengthy negotiations all agreed that Jacob and his family would own Metzger Dairies, Catherine and her family would own Metzger Dairy of San Antonio, and Cecelia and her family would be cashed out. The plan was for Metzger Dairies to redeem all shares owned by Catherine, Cecelia, the trusts for Catherine and Cecelia, and the David Metzger Trust. It was necessary to include the David Metzger Trust in the redemption because Catherine and Cecelia were due to receive one-third of the Trust corpus on the death of David Metzger's widow.

Immediately before the redemption, the stock of Metzger Dairies was held as follows:

Stockholder	Shares
David Metzger Trust	420
Nora Metzger (David Metzger's widow)	420
Jacob Metzger	600
Trust for Jacob Metzger	120
Catherine	600
Trust for Catherine	120
Cecelia	600
Trust for Cecelia	120

The redemption occurred on January 22, 1973, leaving Metzger Dairies' stock as follows:

Stockholder	Shares
Jacob Metzger	600
Trust for Jacob Metzger	120
Trust for David Metzger, II (son of Jacob)	294
Trust for Nan Metzger (daughter of Jacob)	207

The Commissioner concedes that the principal motivation for the redemption was not to receive undistributed earnings, but to end a business relationship that was characterized by hatred and discord among Jacob, Catherine, and Cecelia. On February 10, 1976, Jacob, as trustee of the David Metzger Trust, delivered to the IRS a waiver agreement, executed pursuant to 26 C.F.R. §1.302-4 and purporting to waive any future interest the trust might have in the corporation.

The deferred obligation of Metzger Dairies to pay for Cecelia's 600 shares was evidenced by a promissory note executed by the corporation and payable to Cecelia in three annual installments of principal, plus interest, beginning January 22, 1974. Interest payments were actually made on January 21, 1974, January 7, 1975, and January 5, 1976. As a cash basis taxpayer, Cecelia reported interest income in 1974, 1975 and 1976, the respective years of receipt. Metzger Dairies was an accrual basis taxpayer and claimed deductions in the fiscal years ending September 30, 1973, September 30, 1974, and September 30, 1975, for the liability for interest as it accrued.

In May 1977 the Commissioner of Internal Revenue assessed deficiencies against the David Metzger Trust for the calendar year 1973 and against Metzger Dairies for the fiscal years ending September 30, 1973, and September 30, 1974.[2] On August 17, 1977, Metzger Dairies and the Trust petitioned the Tax Court for a redetermination of these deficiencies. Later the Commissioner assessed deficiencies against Metzger Dairies for fiscal year 1975 as well.[3] . . . The Tax Court upheld the deficiencies. . . .

Our specific analysis is channeled by the Code's structure: payments to shareholders from accumulated earnings will be treated as

2. The Commissioner assessed a deficiency of $292,977.47 against the Trust on the grounds that the $585,303.25 it received in redemption of the Metzger Dairies stock should have been reported as dividend income. The Commissioner assessed deficiencies against Metzger Dairies of $2,106.86 (F.Y. 1973) and $24,856.38 (F.Y. 1974) mainly after disallowing interest deductions of $32,167.28 (F.Y. 1973) and $31,533.07 (F.Y. 1974) for interest accrued but not paid to Cecelia until more than 2½ months after the close of the fiscal year.

3. The Commissioner disallowed $13,926.46 of the interest deduction claimed by Metzger Dairies for F.Y. 1975 that represented interest accrued but not actually paid to Cecelia until more than 2½ months after the close of the fiscal year. On this basis a deficiency of $6,684.68 was assessed.

dividends unless the payment can be brought under an exception. That is, the controlling premise is that distributions by corporations to stockholders out of the taxable year's earnings or out of accumulated earnings are to be treated as dividends. I.R.C. §316(a). Section 302 provides the exceptions. If the redemption is "not essentially equivalent to a dividend," §302(b)(1), a "substantially disproportionate redemption of stock," §302(b)(2), or a "termination of [the] shareholder's interest," §302(b)(3), it will be treated as a distribution in exchange for the stock. At first glance, all three of these provisions are applicable to the Metzger transaction since the corporation purchased all the stock of Catherine, Cecelia, their trusts, and the David Metzger Trust, while at the same time made no payments to the other stockholders, namely Jacob Metzger and his trust. Yet the attribution rules of the Code pose immediate problems. . . .

[Under the attribution rules, an] individual is considered to own the stock owned by his spouse, children, grandchildren, and parents. §318(a)(1). An estate or trust is considered to own the stock owned by a beneficiary of the estate or trust. §318(a)(3). A beneficiary is considered to own proportionately the stock owned by the estate or trust of which he is a beneficiary. §318(a)(2). By these rules the Trust is the owner of the entire stock of Metzger Dairies both before and after the redemption.[6]

The Code provides that, with one exception, these attribution rules "shall apply in determining the ownership of stock for purposes of" §302. §302(c)(1). The one exception is that §318(a)(1), the rules governing attribution of ownership from individuals to individuals, shall not apply in the case of a distribution described in §302(b)(3), that is, a complete termination of a shareholder's interest, *if*:

1. "immediately after the distribution the distributee has no interest in the corporation (including an interest as officer, director, or employee), other than an interest as a creditor" (§302(c)(2)(A)(i));

2. "the distributee does not acquire any such interest (other than stock acquired by bequest or inheritance) within 10 years." (§302(c)(2)(A)(ii));

3. the distributee files an agreement (a "waiver agreement") as prescribed by Treasury regulations (§302(c)(2)(A) (iii)).[7]

---

6. Before redemption the Trust was the constructive owner of Nora, Jacob, Catherine, and Cecelia's shares, because they were its beneficiaries. §318(a)(3)(B). Jacob, Catherine, and Cecelia were the constructive owners of the shares held by their individual trusts. §318(a)(2)(B). Thus, the Trust constructively owned all of Metzger Dairies' stock.

After redemption the Trust remained constructive owner of all the stock because the shares held by the trusts for Jacob's children were attributable to the children, §318(a)(2)(B), thence to Jacob, §318(a)(1)(A), and finally to the Trust, §318(a)(3)(B).

7. Even if these three conditions are met, the attribution rules will not be waived if the distributee acquired any of the redeemed stock within the past ten years from a person whose stock ownership is otherwise attributable to him and tax avoidance

In other words, §302(c)(2)(A) by its terms permits an *individual* to avoid attribution of ownership if he gets out of the corporation and agrees to stay out.

The commands of §§302 and 318 are unambiguous. By their literal language, as an "entity" rather than an individual, the David Metzger Trust does not qualify for the sole statutory exception to the attribution rules. . . .

The Trust argues [however] that family discord may "mitigate" the application of the attribution rules in determining dividend equivalency, especially given the undisputed fact that the purpose of the redemption was not to distribute corporate earnings. From the stipulated fact that the purpose of redemption was to bring peace to a family quarrel, the Trust launches two attacks upon the attribution rules. First, it argues that because it is undisputed here that the family cannot function as an economic unit, the attribution rules, built as they are upon that premise, are inapplicable. Second, the Trust argues that even if the Trust by virtue of attribution is virtually the sole shareholder before and after, the redemption was nonetheless not essentially equivalent to a dividend. The argument continues that this follows from the undisputed purpose of the redemption. That is, the purpose not being to bail out corporate earnings, the central base for application of nonequivalency has been touched.

As will be seen the first argument fails because it is built upon the erroneous assumption that attribution is treated by the Code as a rebuttable presumption rather than a mandated view of familial relationships. The second argument fails because it denies full sway to the decision of the Supreme Court in United States v. Davis, 397 U.S. 301 (1970). Indeed, *Davis* provides much of the answer to the first argument as well. For this reason we will address the arguments together, separating them only when necessary to context.

In *Davis* the Court held that the attribution rules of §318(a) must be applied before determining dividend equivalency. The Court held that regardless of a purpose other than to distribute corporate earnings the after-attribution structure was such that the redemption was in the nature of a dividend. In *Davis*, the taxpayer had purchased the preferred stock of a corporation in 1945 in order to increase the corporation's working capital so that it might qualify for an RFC loan. As originally planned, the loan was fully repaid and the corporation redeemed the taxpayer's preferred stock. By this time, however, the

---

was a primary purpose of the transaction. §302(c)(B)(i). Nor will they be waived if within the past ten years a person whose stock ownership is otherwise attributable to the distributee acquired stock from the distributee and tax avoidance was a primary purpose of that transaction, unless the stock is included in the redemption. §302(c)(2)(B)(ii). These are known as the "look back" provisions; §302(c)(2)(A)(ii) is known as the "look forward" provision.

corporation's common stock was held entirely by the taxpayer, his wife, his son, and his daughter. The Commissioner viewed the redemption as essentially equivalent to a dividend because after application of the attribution rules the taxpayer "owned" 100% of the corporation's common stock. Any distribution to him, therefore, was a pro rata distribution to all the corporation's stockholders, or the essential equivalent of a dividend.

The Supreme Court agreed with the Commissioner's analysis. In its first step it held that the attribution rules had to be applied in determining dividend equivalency under §302(b)(1). "[T]he attribution rules continued to be made specifically applicable to the entire section, and we believe that Congress intended that they be taken into account wherever ownership of stock was relevant." 397 U.S. at 306-307. The taxpayer was deemed the owner of all 1000 shares of the company's common stock.

Second, the Court held that the presence or absence of a tax-avoidance motive could not be considered in determining dividend equivalency under §302(b)(1). Id. 397 U.S. at 311. "[T]he business purpose of a transaction is irrelevant in determining dividend equivalence." Id. 397 U.S. at 312 (quoting Hasbrook v. United States, 343 F.2d 811, 814 (2d Cir. 1965)). The Court therefore concluded that the IRS had properly characterized the redemption of the preferred stock as essentially equivalent to a dividend, regardless of the taxpayer's (and the corporation's) business purpose back in 1945.[8]

In *Davis* the Court reasoned:

> After application of the stock ownership attribution rules, this case viewed most simply involves a sole stockholder who causes part of his shares to be redeemed by the corporation. We conclude that such a redemption is always "essentially equivalent to a dividend" within the meaning of that phrase in §302(b)(1). . . .

Id. 397 U.S. at 307. *Davis* teaches that in applying the "essentially equivalent to a dividend" test after the attribution rules are applied, if the resulting structure has virtually the same incidents of ownership the corporate payments distribute earnings despite an indisputable contrary business purpose.

Confronted by the Supreme Court's holding in *Davis*, the Trust argues that its position nevertheless is supported by Treas. Reg. §1.302-2(b), language in *Davis* interpreting §302(b)(1) as applying whenever there is a "meaningful reduction in the shareholder's proportionate interest," and the legislative history of §302(b)(1).

---

8. It is not totally clear that the attribution rules *had* to be applied in *Davis* to reach the Commissioner's result. Even if the taxpayer were not considered the owner of all the corporation's common stock, redemption of his preferred did not reduce his voting interest in the corporation.

Treas. Reg. §1.302-2(b) provides:

> The question whether a distribution in redemption of stock of
> a shareholder is not essentially equivalent to a dividend under
> section 302(b)(1) depends upon the facts and circumstances of each
> case. One of the facts to be considered in making this determi-
> nation is the constructive stock ownership of such shareholder
> under section 318(a).

Pointing to this language the Trust argues that before and after
structure is only one factor in the dividend equivalency inquiry. The
argument continues that despite the circumstance that after attribution there was no shift in the incidents of control there was no
dividend because indisputably the redemption was for another purpose.

Treas. Reg. §1.302-2(b), however, contained the same language
prior to the *Davis* decision. The regulation is ambiguous. It can be
interpreted as the Trust would have it, namely that attribution is only
a presumption. On the other hand, it can be interpreted as saying
that attribution rules must be given full effect, but are not necessarily
decisive on the ultimate issue of dividend equivalency.

It is true, as the Trust points out, that some commentators and
courts have indicated that *Davis* does not foreclose arguments for
capital gains treatment based on family discord. . . . In Robin Haft
Trust v. Commissioner, 510 F.2d 43 (1st Cir. 1975), the First Circuit
held that family discord might "negate the presumption" of the attribution rules that the taxpayer trusts exercised continuing control
over the corporation after their actual holdings had been redeemed.
Id. at 48. The trusts had been set up to benefit four children and
were funded by shares of the corporation. The father of the children
also owned a large percentage of the corporation's stock. While the
father was going through divorce proceedings and was not even in
contact with the children, the trusts' shares were redeemed as part
of a program to terminate the involvement of the wife's family in the
corporation. The IRS applied the attribution rules. Since the percentage of shares constructively owned by each of the trusts increased
after the redemption, the IRS determined that the payment to the
trusts was ordinary income. The Tax Court upheld the Commissioner. The First Circuit, however, directed the Tax Court "to
reconsider taxpayers' claims in the light of the facts and circumstances
of the case, including the existence of family discord tending to negate
the presumption that taxpayers would exert continuing control over
the corporation despite the redemption." Id. at 48.

For the most part, courts and commentators who urge that *Davis*
leaves open the family discord question have emphasized that the
Davis Court, despite its preference for objective tests, defined the
"essentially equivalent to dividend" test in open-ended terms. "[T]o

qualify for preferred treatment under [§302(b)(1)], a redemption must result in a meaningful reduction of the shareholder's proportionate interest in the corporation." 397 U.S. at 313. In *Robin Haft Trust,* the First Circuit concluded that "[t]his language certainly seems to permit, if it does not mandate, an examination of the facts and circumstances to determine the effect of the transaction transcending a mere mechanical application of the attribution rules." 510 F.2d at 48. . . .

These interpretations are not persuasive. The *Davis* Court was referring to a meaningful reduction in the shareholder's interest *after* application of the attribution rules. It would be strange indeed if what the Court really meant was that the attribution rules are to be applied before determining dividend equivalency, but then in the course of determining dividend equivalency their applicability could be reconsidered. If that were so, the attribution rules would hardly "provide a clear answer to what would otherwise be a difficult tax question. . . ." 397 U.S. at 306.

The Trust also points to the legislative history of §§302 and 318. It is not necessary to traverse a long and complicated history here. Section 302's predecessor was a single dividend equivalency test. It had been interpreted flexibly, so that a redemption with a legitimate business purpose was treated as not "essentially equivalent to a dividend." In 1954 the House version of §302 contained only the safe harbors of §302(b)(2) ("substantially disproportionate redemption") and §302(b)(3) ("termination of shareholder's interest"). The Senate added §302(b)(1), the old essential equivalency test, because the House rules "appeared unnecessarily restrictive." S. Rep. No. 1622, 83d Cong., 2d Sess. 44, reprinted in 1954 U.S. Code Cong. & Ad. News 4621, 4675. Thus, several commentators have argued that Congress meant to reinstate subjective inquiry. In *Davis,* however, while conceding that "[t]he intended scope of §302(b)(1) as revealed by this legislative history is certainly not free from doubt," 397 U.S. at 311, the Court concluded that Congress was rejecting past decisions that looked to motive. Section 302(b)(1) was not intended to be a mechanical test, but it was not intended to be a subjective test, either. Rather, Congress intended "a factual [inquiry]," "devoted solely to the question of whether or not the transaction by its nature may properly be characterized as a sale of stock by the redeeming shareholder to the corporation." S. Rep. No. 1622, 83d Cong., 2d Sess., reprinted in 1954 U.S. Cong. & Ad. News 4621, 4870-4871. The Senate Report adds that "the presence or absence of earnings and profits of the corporation is not material" to dividend equivalency. Id. at 4871. If so, motive could hardly be material since in the absence of earnings there would be no motive to seek capital gain treatment. The issue, as the *Davis* Court said, was not the taxpayer's motive but whether there was "a meaningful reduction of the shareholder's proportionate interest in the corporation." 397 U.S. at 313.

We return to the first level of the Trust argument — that attribution bottomed as it is on assumed family unity ought not to be applied when the assumption is contrary to stipulated fact. Nothing in the legislative history suggests that the attribution rules are to be "mitigated" in special cases. On the contrary, the Senate Report states that "the rules for constructive ownership of stock section 318(a) shall apply for purposes of this section generally." S. Rep. No. 1622, 83d Cong., 2d Sess., reprinted in 1954 U.S. Cong. & Ad. News 4621, 4872. Neither the language of the statute, the Supreme Court's opinion in *Davis*, nor the legislative history supports treating the attribution rules as rebuttable presumptions as the Trust is seeking. Under the Trust's approach the Commissioner and the courts would be forced to highly case specific inquiries into elusive fact patterns. The pattern, intensity, and predicted duration of a family fight are difficult enough for the solomonic justice of our domestic relations courts. It is hardly the basis for soundly administered tax policy. The fixity of the attribution rules then in this sense is not their weakness but their strength.

In summary, we believe that the Commissioner and Tax Court were correct in refusing to take family discord into account in applying the attribution rules.[16] When a question is raised as to the dividend equivalency of a redemption, under §302(b)(1) the correct approach is to apply the attribution *rules* first, then to determine whether there has been "a meaningful reduction of the shareholder's proportionate interest," without regard to whether the interest is actually or constructively held. What is "meaningful" then, to borrow a word, is essentially an inquiry into structure, a structure that applies statutorily dictated rules of economic unity. . . .

[Discussion of the trust waiver-of-attribution issue is omitted.]

Section 267 of the Code disallows deductions for certain transactions between related taxpayers. The underlying philosophy of §267(a)(2), the subsection at issue here, is that related taxpayers should not be able to generate tax deductions in a given year without corresponding income. Metzger Dairies as an accrual basis taxpayer claimed deductions for amounts that were not actually paid to Cecelia until more than 2½ months after the close of its fiscal year. Cecelia, as a cash basis taxpayer, did not report those amounts as income until

16. The Tax Court in its opinion below did suggest that in cases of non-prorata distribution family hostility "can be a relevant fact to be considered in determining whether the reduction in the shareholder's interest is meaningful so as to qualify the distribution as not essentially equivalent to a dividend under section 302(b)(1)." 76 T.C. 42, 62-63 (1981). That notion is inconsistent with our approach. Regardless, such a case was not presented below or here.

the following taxable year. Therefore, if Metzger Dairies and Cecelia were related taxpayers within the meaning of §267, Metzger Dairies was not entitled to certain interest deductions.[25]

Section 267(b) defines the relationships covered by §267(a). These include "[a]n individual and a corporation more than 50 percent in value of the outstanding stock of which is owned, directly or indirectly, by or for such individual." §267(b)(2). Section 267(c), however, provides that "[f]or purposes of determining, in applying subsection (b), the ownership of stock . . . (2) [a]n individual shall be considered as owning the stock owned, directly or indirectly, by or for his family." Section 267(c)(4) defines the family of an individual as including his brothers and sisters. Therefore, putting §267(b), §267(c)(2), and §267(c)(4) together, Cecelia and Metzger Dairies (since Jacob owned a controlling interest in the corporation after the redemption[26]) were related persons within the meaning of §267. If the literal language of §267 is followed, the Commissioner was correct in disallowing the deductions.

Appellant Metzger Dairies, however, argues that the attribution rules of §267 should not apply because of family hostility. Metzger Dairies seeks an exception to §267(c) similar to the family discord exception to §318(a) sought by the David Metzger Trust.

Metzger Dairies cites no case in support of such an exception. In fact, Metzger Dairies cites no case in support of any nonstatutory exception to §267. On the other hand, both the Supreme Court and the Fifth Circuit have read the section in literal terms. In McWilliams v. Commissioner, 331 U.S. 694 (1947), the Supreme Court held that §267's predecessor disallowed losses from sales of stock by a taxpayer when his wife simultaneously bought the same stock on the exchange. Although this was a transparent tax-avoidance transaction, the Court spoke generally about the role of §267's predecessor:

> Section 24(b) states an absolute prohibition — not a presumption — against the allowance of losses on any sales between the members of certain designated groups. The one common characteristic of these groups is that their members, although distinct legal entities, generally have a near-identity of economic interests. It is a fair inference that even legally genuine

25. Section 267(a)(2) sets forth three conditions that must be met for disallowance of the interest deduction. First, the interest otherwise deductible must not have been paid within $2\frac{1}{2}$ months of the close of the taxpayer's taxable year. §267(a)(2)(A). Second, the interest must not, unless paid, be includible in the income of the recipient for the same taxable year. §267(a)(2)(B). Third, the taxpayer and the recipient must be related persons within the meaning of subsection (b). §267(a)(2)(C). Metzger Dairies concedes that the first two conditions were met; the dispute is over the third.

26. After the redemption, Jacob's actual ownership was 600 of the 1221 outstanding shares. Thus, §267(c) has to be applied once more (under §267(c)(1) stock owned by a trust is deemed to be owned proportionately by its beneficiaries) to get Jacob above the 50% figure.

intra-group transfers were not thought to result, usually, in economically genuine realizations of loss, and accordingly that Congress did not deem them to be appropriate occasions for the allowance of deductions.

Id. 331 U.S. at 699.

We recently interpreted §267 in Wyly v. United States, 662 F.2d 397 (5th Cir. 1981). There we held that loss deductions were properly denied to parents who had sold stock to trusts set up to benefit their children. Under Texas law, there was a remote possibility that one (or both) of the parents would benefit under the trusts, if all four of the children died first. This possibility was held sufficient to make the parents and the independent trustee "related persons" under §267(b)(6), which refers to "[a] fiduciary of a trust and a beneficiary of such trust." As we then observed, "There is, in §267, no language to support the taxpayer's claim that a beneficiary who has only a remote chance of sharing in trust property is not a 'beneficiary' of the trust for purposes of §267." Id. at 402. Likewise, there is no language to absolve Cecelia and Jacob from being family members within the meaning of §267(c)(4). The *Wyly* court added, "[I]t does not matter whether the transaction is bona fide, at arm's length, or in good faith with no tax-avoidance motive. Whatever the reason, if the proscribed relationship exists, no loss is recognized for tax purposes." Id. at 401.

Metzger Dairies points out that both *Wyly* and Merritt v. Commissioner, 400 F.2d 417 (5th Cir. 1968), were concerned with §267(a) and §267(b). A literal interpretation of §§267(a) and (b), it contends, does not foreclose a nonliteral interpretation of §267(c). Nevertheless, here, as in *Wyly*, the "proscribed relationship" existed. We see no reason for interpreting §267(c) differently from §267(b) or §267(a). Both §267(b) and §267(c) are attribution rules, in that they define the circumstances under which a shared economic interest will be presumed. Congress cannot have intended one subsection to be interpreted literally and the other flexibly. Only a strict interpretation of both provisions is logically consistent. Only such an interpretation will "relieve[] the taxing authority of many complicated and complex melioristic decisions in family transactions." Merritt v. Commissioner, 400 F.2d at 421.

In sum, §267(c) provides constructive ownership rules which "shall" be applied in determining the relatedness of taxpayers. We see no reason to deviate from this express statutory command. Indeed, by our reading, the Fifth Circuit and Supreme Court precedents forbid it. Accordingly, we hold that Metzger Dairies was not entitled to the interest deductions claimed because it and Cecelia were related persons within the meaning of §267. . . .

Affirmed.

NOTES

1. In *Metzger*, it was discord among *beneficiaries* that the taxpayer urged to preclude application of §318(a)(3). Frequently, however, the hostility argument is made by taxpayers seeking to avoid application of the family attribution rules of §318(a)(1). See, e.g., Blanche S. Benjamin, 66 T.C. 1084 (1976), *aff'd*, 592 F.2d 1259 (5th Cir. 1979); Haft Trust v. Commissioner, 510 F.2d 43 (1st Cir. 1975).

2. The question of a hostility exception to the attribution rules is by no means a dead letter. The Service has taken the position of the *Metzger* court in Rev. Rul. 80-26, 1980-1 C.B. 66, holding that "the facts and circumstances of a particular case cannot contradict the mechanical determination under section 318 of how much stock a shareholder owns." The First Circuit adopted the opposite position in *Haft Trust*. Cf. Niedermeyer v. Commissioner, 535 F.2d 500 (9th Cir.) (per curiam), *cert. denied*, 492 U.S. 1000 (1976) (unnecessary to decide whether *Haft* is correct since facts did not show a genuine family fight). See generally Rickey v. United States, 592 F.2d 1251 (5th Cir. 1979) (rejecting a "mechanical application of the attribution rules"). The Tax Court decisions are not uniformly consistent with its position in *Metzger*. *Compare* Michael N. Cerone, 87 T.C. 1 (1986) (no hostility exception), and Robin Haft Trust, 61 T.C. 398 (1973) (same), *rev'd*, 510 F.2d 43 (1st Cir. 1975), *with* Rodgers P. Johnson Trust, 71 T.C. 941 (1979) (assuming existence of hostility exception), and Estate of Squier, 35 T.C. 950 (1961) (hostility exception applied), *acq.*, 1961-2 C.B. 5, *acq. withdrawn and nonacq. substituted* 1978-2 C.B. 4.

BLOCH v. UNITED STATES
261 F. Supp. 597 (S.D. Tex. 1966), *aff'd per curiam*, 386 F.2d 839
(5th Cir. 1967)

[Southern Elevator and Storage Company, Inc., was a Texas corporation engaged in the operation of grain storage facilities. Immediately before the redemption here in question the corporation had 680 shares of capital stock outstanding which were owned as follows: 306 shares (45 percent) by Bloch, the taxpayer; 306 shares (45 percent) by Bryan; and 68 shares (10 percent) by Harris. In order to give Parrish, the plant manager, an equity interest in the corporation, the corporation had adopted, on June 1, 1956, a resolution whereby the corporation was to redeem 15 percent of the corporation's stock from Bloch and 15 percent from Bryan, or 102 shares from each, which were to be held by the corporation; Parrish was given an option to buy two-thirds of this redeemed stock from the corporation, and Harris was give an option to buy one-third. The option price for both was 85 percent of the redemption price. (This arrangement was adopted in preference to a direct sale from Bloch and Bryan to Parrish and Harris in order to enable them to purchase the stock at a lower price than Bloch and Bryan were to receive for it, while giving Parrish and Harris the benefit of the restricted stock option provisions of the Code.)]

GRAVEN, Senior District Judge. . . . 6. At a meeting of the Board of Directors of Southern on January 2, 1959, a resolution was adopted authorizing an immediate stock redemption from Bryan and Bloch of 15 percent each of their Southern stock. This was in accordance with the resolution and agreement of June 1, 1956, referred to above. Pursuant to the January 2, 1959, resolution, on January 15, 1959, Bloch and Bryan each surrendered to Southern 102 shares of stock. In connection therewith, each of them received a non-negotiable, non-interest bearing note from the corporation in the amount of $35,700, dated January 2, 1959, and payable on or before three years from that date. That sum represented a redemption price of $350 per share. . . .

Southern paid the following amounts to Bloch on the dates indicated in satisfaction of the $35,700 note: $2,700 on April 28, 1960; $1,487.50 on February 3, 1961; $9,371.25 on February 24, 1961; and the remaining $22,141.25 on September 30, 1961. The note held by Bryan was fully paid not later than October 23, 1961.

In his 1960 and 1961 income tax returns Bloch reported the payments above set forth as capital gains. The Internal Revenue Service assessed the deficiency taxes based upon the contention that those payments constituted dividends, taxable as ordinary income. It is the character of those payments to Bloch that is in controversy herein.

7. On January 15, 1959, Bloch and Bryan each surrendered to Southern his certificate for 306 shares of stock and each received a new certificate for 204 shares. The remaining 204 shares were cancelled in redemption by the secretary of the corporation and affixed to the corporate stock records as redeemed shares. Those 204 shares were then held in the corporate treasury for sale pursuant to the option contract to Parrish and Harris until paid for by the opionees. The resolution of January 2, 1959, heretofore noted, had granted Parrish and Harris an option for five years to purchase the redeemed stock at a price of $297.50 per share. Parrish and Harris exercised their options and redeemed shares were issued to them as paid for by them at various intervals subsequent to the redemption of the shares by the corporation.

. . . On May 15, 1956, Bryan, Bloch, Harris and Parrish entered into a partnership to engage in the business of buying, selling, and factoring grain and other products. That partnership will be referred to in more detail later on.

8. It was heretofore noted that the hub of this controversy is whether the stock redemption distributions made by Southern to the taxpayer in 1960 and 1961 should be taxed as ordinary income or as capital gains. In that connection, it is necessary to consider certain statutory provisions and regulations. Section 316(a) . . . sets out the general rule or proposition that distributions by a corporation to its shareholders out of either current earnings and profits or earnings and profits accumulated since February 28, 1913, are dividends. Section 301(c)(1) . . . provides the further general rule that dividend distributions are taxable to the recipient as ordinary income unless they come within certain exceptions. Some of these exceptions are found in Section 302 . . . pertaining to distributions in redemption of stock. Section 302(a) provides that if the transaction constitutes a stock redemption within the definition of Section 302(b), it will be treated as in part or full payment in exchange for the stock and will qualify for capital gains treatment. Section 302(b) sets out [three] categories of stock redemption transactions, each of which will qualify for capital gains treatment. Since the parties agree that two of these four categories are not material under the facts of this case, only the two which the taxpayer contends do apply will be examined. Thus the pertinent points of Section 302 for purposes of this case are [Section 302(b)(1) and (2)]. . . . In the application of the provisions of Section 302 to the facts of this case, Section 318(a) . . . must also be considered since Section 302(c)(1) provides that in determining the ownership of stock for purpose of application of the provisions of Section 302(b) to the facts of a particular case, the attribution rules of Section 318(a) are pertinent. . . .

It will be noted that [§§302(b)(1) and (2)] characterize two types of transactions, either of which will qualify as a capital gains redemption. The first type of transaction is set forth in Subsection (b)(1), i.e., where the redemption is not essentially equivalent to a dividend. The other type of transaction is set forth in Subsection (b)(2), i.e., where the distribution is substantially disproportionate within the meaning of the Section. The parties are in controversy as to whether the redemption in this case falls into either of those categories. The issue as to the matter of the redemption in question being substantially disproportionate will first be considered.

Under the provisions of Section 302 relating to disproportionate distributions, a taxpayer is required to meet two tests, both of which are arithmetical in character. Those tests are as follows:

> (1) Immediately after the redemption, the taxpayer must own less than 50 percent of the total combined voting power of all classes of stock entitled to vote, and
> (2) Immediately after the redemption, the portion of the corporation's voting stock then owned by the taxpayer must be less

than 80 percent of the portion of the stock owned by him before the redemption.

To state these tests another way, after the redemption a taxpayer must own less than 50 percent of the voting stock of the corporation, and the redemption must have reduced the ratio of his voting stock to the total corporate voting stock to an amount less than 80 percent of such ratio before the redemption.

. . . [T]here were originally 680 shares of Southern voting stock, of which the taxpayer owned 306 shares. . . . [O]n January 15, 1959, the taxpayer and Bryan each surrendered his certificate for 306 shares and each was reissued a certificate for 204 shares. The 102 shares surrendered by each were surrendered for the purpose of carrying out the option agreements with Parrish and Harris. If these 204 shares were to be considered as not constituting voting stock of the corporation, then the voting stock consisted of 486* shares. It is clear that whether the voting stock is considered as being 680 shares or 486 shares, the taxpayer meets . . . the 50 percent test. The parties are not in controversy as to the taxpayer meeting that test. They are in controversy as to whether the taxpayer meets . . . the 80 percent test. That controversy revolves, in part, around whether the 204 shares surrendered by the taxpayer and Bryan and held in the treasury for the purpose of meeting the stock purchase options of Parrish and Harris shall be considered as voting stock for the purpose of applying the 80 percent test. The Government contends that those shares are not to be so considered. The taxpayer contends that they are to be so considered. The provisions of Section 302(b)(2) noted above make reference to the "voting stock" or "voting power" of the corporation. Treasury Regulations Section 1.302-3(a) relating thereto provides that the stock to be considered is that "which is issued and outstanding in the hands of the shareholders." Southern was a Texas corporation. A reference to Texas law is made by the taxpayer in his main brief in which he states: "Texas law would not permit the issuance of the shares to Parrish and Harris in exchange for Notes. Therefore the shares were held in the Corporate treasury until paid for in compliance with the law. . . ." It appears that the stock in question was held in the corporate treasury until paid for. The pretrial stipulation of facts reflects that Parrish and Harris participated in corporate dividends only as to the issued shares. The taxpayer relies strongly on the case of Sorem v. Commissioner of Internal Revenue (10th Cir. 1964), 334 F.2d 275, in which a similar question is involved. The Court in that case held that for purposes of applying the constructive ownership or attribution rules of Section 318, employees who held stock options must be considered as owning the stock for

---

*476? — Ed.

which they held options. Under the holding of that case, the shares held in the corporate treasury by Southern for the purpose of meeting the options held by Parrish and Harris would be considered as owned by them in connection with the matter of the taxpayer meeting the 80 percent test. The provisions of Regulations Section 1.318-3(c), when coupled with those of Regulations Section 1.302-3(a), noted above, might be interpreted as requiring a different conclusion. Because of another feature, it is not necessary for the Court to decide whether the holding of the *Sorem* case should or should not be followed. However, if in this case this Court was squarely presented with the question as to whether the holding of the *Sorem* case should or should not be followed, it would be reluctant to follow such holding. It would seem that it would be highly questionable that stock held in the treasury of a corporation which might be issued or might never be issued depending upon whether the optionees of such stock would or would not exercise their options could not properly be considered as being owned by the optionees for the purpose of applying the attribution rules under Section 318.

However, assuming, as contended by the taxpayer, that Parrish and Harris are to be regarded as the owners of the 204 shares of stock in question, there comes into focus Section 318. . . . A portion of that statute pertinent to the facts in this case has since been repealed,* but was in effect during the period of time here involved. It was heretofore noted that in 1956 Bloch, Bryan, Parrish and Harris had entered into a partnership. Because of some confusion and conflict in the briefs as to that partnership, it seems appropriate to set out a portion of the pretrial stipulation of facts relating to such partnership, as follows:

> 14. On May 15, 1956, B. F. Bryan, William H. Bloch, Lee Orr Harris, and William R. Parrish entered into a partnership to engage in the business of brokering, factoring, and buying and selling grain and other products, the profits to be divided equally by said partners as to the first $10,000.00 of net partnership profits and with profits in excess of $10,000.00 to be distributed as follows: 40 percent to B. F. Bryan and 20 percent each to William H. Bloch, Lee Orr Harris and William R. Parrish. Losses were to be divided equally. The partnership made a profit in each and every year of its operation. The partnership actively began conduct of business in late June 1956.

The partnership was known as the Southern Elevator Grain Company. It continued to carry on its business operations through July 1961, when it was dissolved, apparently because of dissension

---

*See §318(a)(5)(C), which was not part of the statute during the years involved. — ED.

between B. F. Bryan and the other partners. The interest of the parties did not change during the existence of the partnership.

Under the provisions of the attribution statute (Section 318) then in effect, stock owned by a partner is deemed to be owned by the partnership, and stock owned by the partnership (including that which it is deemed to own because a partner actually owns it) is deemed to be owned by the partners in their partnership proportions. If, as the taxpayer contends, Parrish and Harris were the owners of the 204 shares of option stock, under the provisions of Section 302(b)(2) it is manifest that they were also to be considered the owners of it under Section 318(a)(2), which is specifically made applicable to Section 302.

If the 680 shares are to be considered as the shares of stock outstanding both before and after redemption, it is then necessary to determine the ownership percentage in the light of the attribution statute. Before the redemption, the taxpayer owned 306 shares in his own right and constructively owned 93.5 shares through the partnership. The total percentage owned (399.5/680) was 58.75 percent. After the redemption, he owned 204 shares in his own right and constructively owned 119 shares through the partnership. The total percentage owned (323/680) was 47.5 percent. The after-redemption ownership was 80.8 + percent of the before-redemption ownership (47.5 to 58.75). Thus the taxpayer does not meet the 80 percent test.

The above conclusions result from application of the constructive ownership rules to the partnership situation, as follows. The ownership of the partnership shares before the redemption was as follows: Bryan's 306 shares and Harris' 68 shares, totalling 374 shares, are deemed to be owned by the partnership and are, in turn, deemed owned to the extent of one- fourth, or 93.5 shares, by the taxpayer as a partner to that extent. The ownership of the partnership shares after the redemption was as follows: Bryan's 204 shares, Parrish's 136 shares and Harris' 136 shares, totalling 476 shares, are deemed to be owned by the partnership and are, in turn, deemed owned to the extent of one-fourth, or 119 shares, by the taxpayer as a partner. The partnership was apparently somewhat related to Southern because of its personnel and business activities. However, in order for Section 318 to be applicable it is not necessary that the partnership be engaged in activities similar to that of the corporation involved.

If the 204 shares of stock held in the treasury are not regarded as voting stock, then the situation would be as follows: prior to the redemption the taxpayer owned 306 shares of the 680 shares outstanding, or 45 percent, and after the redemption he will have owned 204 shares of the 476 shares outstanding, or 42.8 percent. The 42.8 percent ownership percentage after redemption is substantially more than 80 percent of the 45 percent ownership percentage before redemption (being 95+ percent), so the taxpayer would also fail to meet the 80 percent test under this assumption of facts.

By way of summary, it can be stated that if the 204 shares held in the treasury of Southern are to be regarded as not outstanding stock, then the taxpayer would not meet the 80 percent test irrespective of constructive ownership or attribution rules. If those 204 shares are to be regarded as outstanding, then the taxpayer fails to meet the 80 percent test because of the applicability of the attribution statute (Section 318). . . .

9. The next matter for consideration is whether the stock redemption distributions to the taxpayer were within the scope of Section 302(b)(1). As heretofore set out, that Section provides that a redemption is entitled to capital gains treatment "if the redemption is not essentially equivalent to a dividend." Several related issues are involved in a consideration of this question. These have to do with the adequacy of the corporate earnings and profits, whether the claims for refund properly raised such issue, and the proper time at which to measure corporate earnings and profits for purposes of applying the provisions of Section 302(b)(1) to the facts of this case. The taxpayer contends that at the pertinent time in question the corporate earnings and profits were not adequate to cover the redemption distributions. In connection with this contention the Government asserts that the taxpayer did not properly raise such issue in his claims for refund. . . . [The Court decided this issue in the taxpayer's favor.]

The next issue for consideration is whether the corporate earnings and profits and accumulated surplus were adequate to cover the redemption disbursements. This is the subject of vigorous controversy. Considerable evidence was presented on this issue and it was discussed at some length in the briefs. It involves a number of questions. The first question is the proper time to measure the adequacy of corporate earnings and profits. The parties are in agreement that the redemption occurred on January 15, 1959. The parties are also in agreement that the cash disbursements by Southern to the taxpayer took place in 1960 and 1961 when the corporate non-interest bearing note given by Southern to the taxpayer was paid. Both parties seem to be in agreement that the 1960 and 1961 corporate distributions should be taxed to him in those years, i.e., the years of receipt, rather than in 1959 when he received the corporate note. The taxpayer reported the disbursements in his 1960 and 1961 income tax returns and he claimed a refund of the taxes involved for those same years. The taxpayer contends that although the tax impact of the redemption distributions should fall in the years of receipt, the proper point in time for the purpose of measuring the adequacy of corporate earnings and profits on the dividend issue shall have been on January

15, 1959, when the redemption occurred. The taxpayer cites in support of this last contention the case of Estate of James T. Moore, Tax Court Memo Decision 1961-257. That case . . . had to do with when a redemption actually occurred and not when corporate earnings to profits are to be measured. . . . It appears to be well settled that the date of the payment of a note rather than the date of delivery of the note is the dividend date. Emil Stein (1942), 46 B.T.A. 135; Estate of Joseph Nitto (1949), 13 T.C. 858, 867. The Court is of the view and holds that the time payments were made on the note is the proper time for measuring corporate earnings and profits for dividend purposes. . . .

[The court found that there were adequate earnings and profits. It then went on to hold that the distribution was essentially equivalent to a dividend. It held first that there was not a bona fide corporate purpose for casting the transaction in the form of a redemption, since the purpose was to give the sellers a greater amount for their stock than the buyers would have to pay for it, while giving the buyers certain tax benefits. It then relied on the following factors to find dividend equivalency: There were adequate earnings and profits for a dividend in the amount of the distributions; the taxpayer's position vis-à-vis the corporation was not substantially altered by the transaction since he remained a minority stockholder; and the transaction was not part of a contraction of the business. The fact that the distribution was not pro rata was not sufficient to negate the finding of dividend equivalency.

The Commissioner's deficiency assessment with respect to the distributions was upheld.]*

NOTES

1. What does §318(a)(5)(C) accomplish? If it had been applicable to the years involved in this case would it have affected the result?

2. Although treasury shares are not considered in determining the change in stock ownership resulting from a redemption, §318(a)(4) treats a person holding an option to purchase stock as the owner of that stock. There is a conflict in the circuits as to whether §318(a)(4) applies only when the option is held by the person whose shares are redeemed. *Compare* Patterson Trust v. United States, 729 F.2d 1089 (6th Cir. 1984) (option to acquire stock deemed to be ownership even though the option holder was not a redeeming shareholder) *with* Friend v. United States, 345 F.2d 761 (1st Cir. 1965)

---

*In its brief per curiam opinion of affirmance the Fifth Circuit embraced the district court's decision, but said, "it is unnecessary to adopt the opinion of the district court. . . ." 386 F.2d 839. — Ed.

(dictum that §318(a)(4) only applies as to options held by redeeming shareholder). See Bloom and Willens, How to Treat Option Shares Held by Third Parties in Planning for a Redemption, 62 J. Taxn. 80 (1985).

3. See Hellawell, A Computer Program for Legal Planning and Analysis: Taxation of Stock Redemptions, 80 Colum. L. Rev. 1363 (1980).

PROBLEMS

The following problems relate to the preceding materials and to §§302 and 318 generally:

1. Husband (H) and Wife (W) each own 50 percent of the outstanding stock of Corporation C. The parties wish C to redeem all of H's stock for an amount of cash equal to the stock's fair market value. What facts must you know and what must you advise be done as conditions to your giving an opinion that the redemption will be within §302(b)(3)?

2. The facts are the same as in Problem 1, except that H wishes to retain at least a minimal stock interest. Can you suggest the redemption of a sufficient percentage of his shares to permit the redemption to qualify under §302(b)(2)?

3. The facts are the same as in Problem 1, except that H and W also own 50 percent each of Corporation B. Will your opinion as to the applicability of §302(b)(3) on the redemption of H's stock in C have to be altered? What would have been your answer prior to the adoption of §318(a)(5)(C) in 1964?

4. X owns all (100 shares) of the stock of Corporation N. Corporation N redeems 50 of X's shares under circumstances making the distribution essentially equivalent to a dividend. X's basis for his stock was $100 per share. Five years after the redemption X sells his remaining 50 shares for $50,000. What is his gain on the sale? Why?

5. If a corporation without earnings and profits redeems part of a shareholder's stock under circumstances that make the distribution "essentially equivalent to a dividend," might the tax consequences differ from those that would attend a distribution that was not "essentially equivalent to a dividend"? Consider, inter alia, the question whether the basis of the redeemed shares remains identified with those shares or whether the shareholder's aggregate basis for all his shares is to be allocated. If allocated, how? See Englebrecht and Lett, Adjustments and Allocations of Basis of Stock Dispositions Deemed Essentially Equivalent to Dividends Under Secs. 302 and 306, 56 Taxes 288 (1978).

6. Brother (B) and Sister (S) each owned 50 percent of the stock

of P Corporation. S died, bequeathing $10,000 in cash to B. Corporation P wishes to redeem the stock held by S's estate for its fair market value of $500,000. S's estate as a whole is worth $1 million. Except as to the bequest to B, colleges and universities are the sole beneficiaries of S's estate. May the redemption qualify under §302(b)(3)? Why? See Treas. Reg. §1.318(a). Cf. Estate of Webber v. United States, 404 F.2d 411 (6th Cir. 1968). What if B had been left a remainder interest valued at $10,000? *Compare* §318(a)(3)(A) *with* §318(a)(3)(B)(i) and Rev. Rul. 76-213, 1976-1 C.B. 92.

Cf. Rev. Rul. 71-211, 1971-1 C.B. 112 (renunciation of interest in trust by beneficiary prevents attribution of trust's stock to him).

What is an "interest in the corporation" within the meaning of §302(c)(2)(A)(i)? Treas. Reg. §1.302-4(c) states that an interest in a "successor corporation" is a forbidden interest. But see Rev. Rul. 76-496, 1976-2 C.B. 93 (on when a corporation is a "successor").

7. Under the 1939 Code, redemptions were not subject to attribution of ownership rules. Given a congressional purpose to make family and financial relationships relevant, how would you have written §318? Given the congressional view that "essential equivalence" was not a definite enough test to stand by itself, how would you have written what is now §302(b)?

8. See B. Bittker & J. Eustice, Federal Income Taxation of Corporations and Shareholders 9-1 to 9-37 (5th ed. 1987); Goldstein, Stock Redemptions and the Attribution Rules, 27 N.Y.U. Inst. Fed. Taxn. 793 (1969); Wolfman, Some of the Attribution-of-Ownership Problems Involved in the Redemption of Stock Under the 1954 Code, 33 Taxes 382 (1955).

iv. Redemption vs. Sale

ESTATE OF SCHNEIDER v. COMMISSIONER
855 F.2d 435 (7th Cir. 1988)

Before Cummings, Flaum, and Easterbrook, Circuit Judges.

FLAUM, Circuit Judge. Al J. Schneider ("Schneider") was the principal shareholder of American National Corporation ("ANC"), a holding company, which in turn owned 100% of the stock of Schneider Transport, Inc. ("Transport"). In 1974, 1975 and 1976 Schneider sold portions of his ANC stock to certain Transport employees who were participating in an employee stock ownership plan. Schneider reported these transactions on the 1974-76 federal income tax returns he filed jointly with his wife, Agnes Schneider, characterizing them as sales of capital assets which generated long-term capital gains.

The Internal Revenue Service (the "IRS") alleged that these sales actually constituted a redemption of Schneider's stock by ANC followed by a distribution of this stock pursuant to the employee stock ownership plan. The IRS asserted that Schneider should have reported the entire amounts he received from these alleged sales as dividend distributions. The IRS therefore issued deficiency notices for 1975 and 1976. The matter proceeded to trial and the Tax Court entered judgment against Schneider and his wife for $17,046 and $20,716 for the tax years of 1975 and 1976 respectively. We affirm.

I

Transport was founded by Schneider in 1938 and is engaged in the freight transport business. Transport was one of a group of closely held corporations (the "affiliated corporations") owned by Schneider and his immediate relatives. In 1971 Transport adopted an employee stock bonus plan (the "Transport Plan"). Under the plan, Transport's Board of Directors determined in December of each year the total sum to be awarded by Transport to certain of its employees as bonuses for work done in that year. Early in the following year Transport's President selected and notified the employees who would receive bonuses. These employees were given an option to receive their bonus in either cash or Transport nonvoting common stock. Employees who elected stock received previously unissued Transport nonvoting common stock; the number of shares received was based on the "Current Formula Price" (the book value of the stock with some modifications).

A bonus recipient's rights in the stock he or she received under the Plan were subject to a 10%-per-year vesting requirement. If the employee ceased to work for Transport within ten years of receiving the stock, he or she was required to offer to sell the stock to Transport at a price equal to 10% of the Current Formula Price for that year multiplied by the number of years of continued employment since the year the bonus was awarded. In addition, an employee wishing to sell any stock received pursuant to the Transport Plan was required to first offer the stock to Transport at the same price that would govern under the vesting rules. The plan required that notice of these restrictions be stamped on the stock certificates issued to the bonus recipients.

In 1973, the affiliated corporations were substantially reorganized. ANC was formed to act as a holding company for these corporations. Pursuant to the reorganization, former Transport shareholders received ANC stock in exchange for their Transport stock. As of January 1, 1974, the Schneiders and their relatives owned

100% of ANC's class A voting stock and 99.6% of the class B non-voting shares. In addition, on this same day the members of the Schneider family and ANC entered into "the American National Non-Employee Buy-Sell Agreement" (the "Buy-Sell Agreement"). Under the Buy-Sell Agreement ANC was given a right of first refusal at the Current Formula Price before any Schneider family share-holder could sell his or her stock to a third party. Stock received by employees under the Transport Plan or the later adopted ANC Plan was not subject to this agreement.

ANC also substantially adopted the Transport Plan, including the vesting requirements, for its employees and for all employees of its subsidiaries, including Transport. The secretary and president of ANC were authorized to issue the number of class B nonvoting shares necessary to implement what was now called the American National Employee Stock Ownership Plan ("the ANC Plan"). The ANC Plan, as later amended, differed from the Transport Plan in that the stock the bonus recipients would receive pursuant to the plan was not required to be issued directly by ANC in the first instance; rather, in the Board of Directors' discretion the stock could be already out-standing stock that the bonus recipients purchased from existing class shareholders. In addition, ANC waived its right of first refusal under the Buy-Sell Agreement for all shares furnished by Schneider to carry out the needs of the plan.

Schneider sold a small portion of his class B stock to employees pursuant to this arrangement in 1974, 1975, and 1976. The payment of the 1975 bonus, the first year in which the IRS assessed a deficiency, serves to illustrate the mechanics of the plan. On December 28, 1974 Transport's Board of Directors determined that the total amount of bonuses to be awarded for work related to 1974 would be $166,000. On February 20, 1975 certain employees were notified that they would receive a bonus, but were not told the exact amount of their individual bonuses. These employees were then required to elect pursuant to the American National Employee Stock Ownership Plan Undertaking and Agreement ("the Undertaking and Agreement") whether to receive at least 25% of their bonus as ANC class B stock. On April 4, 1975 the bonus recipients were notified of the exact amount of their bonuses. Those employees who had committed to take at least 25% of their bonus in stock were then required to specify the exact percentage that they would take in this form.

Transport paid the bonuses on April 21, 1975. Those employees electing to receive a portion of their bonus in the form of ANC class B stock received two checks. The first check was for the cash portion of the bonus, the second for the amount to be received in stock. On the back of the second check was stamped "pay to the order of Al J. Schneider." Each employee who received two checks was instructed by a supervisor to sign the endorsement on the second check. The checks were collected and then transferred to Schneider. Schneider in turn deposited the checks in the Schneiders' personal account. On May 12, 1975, ANC issued a total of 9,623 shares of class B stock to those employees who elected to receive a portion of their bonus in this form. The certificates these employees received, however, were not subject to the Buy-Sell Agreement but rather were subject to the terms and conditions of the ANC Plan, including the vesting provisions. Notice of these restrictions was stamped on the stock certificates. On the same day, Schneider's class B certificate was cancelled and a new certificate issued representing 9,623 fewer shares. Schneider's stock continued to be subject to the Buy-Sell Agreement.

II

A

On appeal, the issue is how Schneider's sales of his ANC class B nonvoting stock to Transport's employees should be characterized for tax purposes. It is Schneider's position that the transactions which occurred should be respected. He contends that Transport paid cash bonuses to a select number of its employees and these employees decided to purchase the ANC stock from Schneider. Because the shares were capital assets in Schneider's hands and were sold in bona fide sales to Transport's employees, in Schneider's view, he correctly reported as a capital gain each year the sum of the differences between the selling prices and his tax basis in the shares he sold. The Tax Court rejected this view. The court held that the transactions involving the payment of the 1975 and 1976 bonuses and stock sales should be characterized as stock redemptions followed by distributions of the redeemed shares as compensation to the electing bonus recipients.[3] The Tax Court specifically found that the intended employee compensation was the stock, not the preendorsed checks.[4]

---

3. There is some confusion generated by the fact that ANC, the holding company, adopted the ANC Plan for its employees and "employees of all its subsidiary and affiliated corporations." The confusion centers on whether in the Tax Court's view, ANC or Transport distributed the stock to the participants in the ANC Plan. The ANC Plan seems to have originally contemplated that Transport would distribute the ANC stock. The minutes of the January 1, 1974 Board of Directors' meeting state that "[a]s to those employees who choose stock, Transport, or the other subsidiary and affiliated corporations . . . will transfer to [ANC] the cash to buy newly-issued shares from [ANC]." This is corroborated by the fact that the Transport Board, not the ANC Board, voted on the total sum of the bonus that Transport would award each year. In addition, minutes from the March 17, 1974 Board of Directors' meeting state that if ANC issued new stock to meet the requirements of the Plan, "Transport would have to pay cash into [ANC] for the shares to be issued." Although there is some conflicting evidence (and the IRS and the Tax Court often fudge the issue), see, e.g., Schneider, 88 T.C. at 916 n.7, 942, we assume when discussing the IRS's

We . . . review the Tax Court's characterization under a clearly erroneous standard.

B

This case involves a series of transactions structured in a manner which ostensibly achieved preferential tax treatment from the perspective of the taxpayer. The right of a taxpayer to arrange his or her affairs to minimize taxes is well established. The Supreme Court observed long ago that "[t]he legal right of a taxpayer to decrease the amount of what otherwise would be his [or her] taxes, or altogether avoid them, by means which the law permits, cannot be doubted." Gregory v. Helvering, 293 U.S. 465, 469 (1935). But to state this principle is not to decide the case. . . .

[W]e affirm the Tax Court's characterization of Schneider's stock sales as constructive redemptions. As the Tax Court observed, "[a]t the start of each year's stock bonus process, [Schneider] had stock and the corporations had funds. At the end of each year's stock bonus process, [Schneider] had funds that came from the corporations, and the corporations' employees had stock that came from [Schneider]." . . . Our specific focus is on how ANC class B stock which Schneider initially held subject to the restrictions imposed by the Buy-Sell Agreement ended up in the hands of Transport employees subject to the limitations of the ANC Plan. We agree with the explanation arrived at by the Tax Court: a redemption followed by a stock distribution.

Schneider attempts to avoid this characterization by emphasizing that the Tax Court specifically found that he was not in need of cash at the time of the alleged stock sales. In Schneider's view this indicates

---

and the Tax Court's position that Transport administered the employee stock ownership plan in the same manner as it did prior to 1974, only that after this date it used ANC stock, not its own. Accordingly, under this position, Schneider's ANC stock was redeemed by ANC and then issued to Transport in exchange for cash, the amount corresponding to the sum of the second checks. Transport in turn distributed the stock to its employees pursuant to the plan. Further, even if Transport, not ANC, is considered to have redeemed Schneider's stock, under §304 of the Internal Revenue Code, Transport would be deemed to have first distributed the cash to ANC which then used the cash to redeem Schneider's stock.

4. The Tax Court employed the step-transaction doctrine, ruling in part that the employees were mere conduits for the "second check" and therefore the cash flowed directly from Transport to Schneider. We approach the other half of the transaction, focusing on how the stock got from Schneider to the Transport employees. Because we hold that there were more steps — the stock was transferred to ANC, Transport and then to the employees — than Schneider would wish to recognize, we do not speak in terms of the step-transaction doctrine.

Once the transactions are characterized in this manner, the appropriate tax treatment for Schneider's exchange of his stock for cash is determined by the rules governing stock redemptions. Schneider concedes on appeal that if it is determined that his stock was redeemed by ANC, the sum he received is properly taxed as ordinary income to him.

that the arrangement was not an effort to bail money out of the corporation at capital gain rates, but rather was motivated by legitimate business purposes. He claims that the structure of the transaction was designed to facilitate the administration of the ANC Plan. In order to implement the plan, Transport was required to obtain the ANC shares necessary to meet its obligations to those employees who elected to receive ANC stock. The principal operating officer, Schneider's son, testified that it was not desirable to satisfy these obligations by having ANC issue new shares to Transport because it would dilute the ownership interests of ANC's existing shareholders. In addition, the issuance of new ANC stock would have resulted in a troublesome cash build-up in ANC. As the minutes of ANC's board of directors' meeting explain:

> At present, [ANC] is functioning only as a holding company. If newly issued stock of [ANC] is to be used to provide the shares necessary under the [ANC] Plan, *Transport would have to pay the cash into [ANC] for the shares to be issued.* [ANC] would then have little use for this cash and would probably either have to lend it back to Transport or contribute it to Transport capital.
>
> *A simpler method is to merely give the employee the cash and let him buy the stock from [Schneider].* [Schneider] stated that he was willing to accommodate the [ANC] Plan in this manner, at least this year. . . .

(Emphasis added.) The unstated byproduct of this arrangement was that Schneider would allegedly receive capital gains treatment when he relinquished his shares.

The fact that Schneider did not need cash and therefore allegedly did not have a tax motive for participating in this particular arrangement is not dispositive. See . . . Gregory, 293 U.S. at 469 ("the question for determination is whether what was done, apart from the tax motive, was the thing which the statute intended"). . . . Schneider must show that the legal restrictions applicable to the stock can be reconciled with his position that the stock was sold directly to Transport's employees. This he cannot do.

Schneider claims that the cash payment and stock sales must be viewed as independent steps for tax purposes. He asserts that the bonus recipients constructively received their bonus entirely in cash at the time they were required to elect the form their bonus would take. In Schneider's view, cash is the standard form of compensation and the election itself constituted an independent step under which an employee who received cash chose to use a portion of it to purchase stock.

Even if we assume that this characterization of the specific operation of the election feature is correct, it does not indicate whether Transport or Schneider was the direct source of the stock that the electing bonus recipients received. The Transport Plan and the later ANC Plan (American National Employee Stock Ownership Plan) were adopted to attract, retain, and motivate top managerial personnel by providing "an equity position" in the parent holding company. In the typical situation where a bonus plan involves a stock ownership component, the company is the source of the stock. The amount of the bonus represents compensation to the employee; that the employee can opt to receive a portion of the bonus as stock does not usually alter the fact that the bonus, in whatever form, is received directly from the employer. Indeed, this was how the Transport Plan operated from its adoption until 1974.

That bonus plans generally act in this manner, however, does not mean that variations are automatically problematic; a subtler argument seems both possible and implicit in Schneider's position. It can be contended that Transport merely arranged and facilitated the stock sales without actually having acted as a principal in the transactions. Under this position, Transport's stated goal of having its managerial personnel own stock was achieved by making it possible for these employees to purchase stock on attractive terms from a separate source, Schneider, and by assisting the employees in carrying out the sales by pre-endorsing and collecting the checks on Schneider's behalf. If we accept this view, Transport's bonuses to its employees consisted of cash and the value of the service of making ANC class B stock available to employees at the given price. Prior to 1974, employees who received cash bonuses could turn around and purchase stock from Transport. From 1974-76 Transport continued this basic format, but instead of acting as the seller, it arranged to make the stock available through Schneider.

In other circumstances it may be a difficult task to determine whether non-cash property arranged by the employer on an elective basis should be viewed as acquired by the employer from a third-party provider of such property and then distributed by the employer to the employee. The alternative position, that the employer pays only cash to the employee as compensation and then for the employee's convenience, and upon his or her election, transfers the cash to the third-party on behalf of the employee may not be implausible. Generally this distinction will not matter because our focus is on the tax ramifications to the third-party which will typically not vary regardless of whether the property is deemed sold to the corporation or the corporation's employees. For most kinds of property, a third-party seller will usually recognize the same type of gain or loss in either case. The issue becomes critical here only because the property is stock and Schneider is a substantial shareholder in ANC. As previously discussed, in this situation the tax consequences to Schneider vary depending on whether he sold his stock to a third party as opposed to having it redeemed by ANC. Because the documents executed in these transactions indicate that the ANC stock the electing bonus recipients received did not move directly from Schneider to the employees, we hold that Schneider's stock was constructively redeemed.

The stock received by the employees was subject to the restrictions imposed by the ANC Plan, including the vesting provisions. In contrast, this same stock in Schneider's hands, which the electing bonus recipients allegedly purchased directly from him, was subject to the Buy-Sell Agreement, not the ANC Plan. Paragraph 2 of the Buy-Sell Agreement set forth ANC's right of first refusal and provided that "[i]f stock of [ANC] is sold under the terms of [paragraph 2] to a person other than [ANC], such shares shall be free of all further restrictions hereunder." Because ANC had waived its right of first refusal with respect to the stock Schneider sold to the employees, absent other agreements, the employees' stock should not have been subject to any restrictions.

Schneider contended at oral argument that the ANC Plan restrictions were a condition of his offer to sell the class B stock. Although we have not been directed to any documentary evidence of this assertion in the record, if this were so, then ANC was merely the third-party beneficiary of the sales agreement between Schneider and the electing employees. ANC's actions belie such a status. In later years ANC modified the restrictions in the ANC Plan, in particular relaxing some of the vesting provisions applicable to employees over 55 years of age. Schneider's counsel conceded at oral argument that it did so without obtaining the express consent of either Schneider or the employees. A third-party beneficiary, however, cannot modify a contract between Schneider and individual employees without their express consent. Transport acted as if it were a principal to the contract, not a third-party beneficiary.

Transport was in fact a party to the key agreement. The ANC plan restrictions were imposed on the employee's stock as a condition set forth in the Undertaking and Agreement executed by the employee. The agreement was between the employee and the corporation; Schneider was not a party. It provided in part that "in consideration of the receipt of stock under the American National Stock Ownership Plan . . . the employee agrees to all restrictions and undertakes all the obligations set forth in the Plan." The Undertaking and Agreement also accounts for the corporation's ability to unilaterally amend the plan, providing that "[t]he Employee agrees that the Plan may be amended and interpreted in the future by the Board of Directors of the corporation and that he will abide by all such amendments and interpretations." Thus, contrary to Schneider's position at oral argument, the ANC Plan restrictions were applicable because of an agreement executed between the corporation and the bonus recipient. Under these facts and circumstances, we hold that the shares received by the employees were obtained directly from Transport.

Once it is determined that the bonus recipients received their stock from Transport, the rest of the pieces fall into place. In order to administer the ANC Plan, Transport needed to acquire the necessary ANC stock. ANC was the most obvious source, but it was reluctant to issue new stock because of the dilution and cash build-up effects. Both problems were solved by having ANC obtain the stock from Schneider. There was no dilution because the stock was previously outstanding. In addition, ANC suffered no cash build-up because the funds Transport paid to it were used to satisfy the obligations to Schneider it incurred to acquire his stock. ANC's acquisition of Schneider's stock, however, is a redemption under §317 of the Internal Revenue Code.

The decision of the Tax Court is Affirmed.[9]

v.   Redemptions Related to Inter-Shareholder Transfers

COMMISSIONER v. ROBERTS
203 F.2d 304 (4th Cir. 1953)

Before Parker, Chief Judge, and Soper and Dobie, Circuit Judges.

Dobie, Circuit Judge. . . . The Tax Court held that the distribution in connection with the redemption of the stock of the corporation, *under the circumstances of this case*, was not essentially equivalent to, and not taxable as, the distributions of a dividend under [§§302(b)(1) and 302(d)]. . . . We think the decision of the Tax Court was clearly erroneous. It must, therefore, be reversed.

We quote the applicable provisions of the . . . Treasury Regulations: . . .

> The question whether a distribution in connection with a cancellation or redemption of stock is essentially equivalent to the distribution of a taxable dividend depends upon the circumstances of each case. A cancellation or redemption by a corporation of a portion of its stock pro rata among all the shareholders will generally be considered as effecting a distribution essentially equivalent to a dividend distribution to the extent of the earnings and profits accumulated after February 28, 1913. On the other

9. The parties also contest the applicability of §83 of the Internal Revenue Code and in particular Treasury Regulation §1.83-6(d)(1). The Tax Court did not reach this issue. Because we affirm the Tax Court's finding of constructive redemptions, we also do not reach the issue of the application of §83 to this case.

hand, a cancellation or redemption by a corporation of all of the stock of a particular shareholder, so that the shareholder ceases to be interested in the affairs of the corporation, does not effect a distribution of a taxable dividend. A bona fide distribution in complete cancellation or redemption of all of the stock of a corporation, or one of a series of bona fide distributions in complete cancellation or redemption of all of the stock of a corporation, is not essentially equivalent to the distribution of a taxable dividend. If a distribution is made pursuant to a corporate resolution reciting that the distribution is made in liquidation of the corporation, and the corporation is completely liquidated and dissolved within one year after the distribution, the distribution will not be considered essentially equivalent to the distribution of a taxable dividend; in all other cases the facts and circumstances should be reported to the Commissioner for his determination whether the distribution, or any part thereof, is essentially equivalent to the distribution of a taxable dividend. [Treas. Reg. 111, §29.115-9.]

There is little or no dispute about the facts of this case. In March 1932, John T. Roberts, hereinafter called taxpayer, and his brother transferred to a newly created corporation all of the assets of a wholesale plumbing and heating supply business, theretofore conducted by them in partnership, in exchange for all of the stock of the corporation. . . . Fifteen hundred shares were issued to taxpayer, who continued to hold them through the taxable year 1944 here involved. Five hundred shares were issued to taxpayer's brother. Taxpayer's brother died in October 1943, and by his last will made a specific bequest to taxpayer of any shares of stock of the corporation owned by him at the time of his death. Pursuant to an order of the probate court, the executor of the brother's will transferred to taxpayer stock certificates for the 500 shares of the corporation's stock which the brother had owned. These 500 shares were valued for estate tax purposes at $92,000. . . .

On January 1, 1944, total assets amounted to approximately $414,000 (including cash of $160,000 and United States obligations of $96,000), and the earned surplus amounted to approximately $170,000. As of December 31, 1944 (that is, after the distribution in redemption of stock here involved), the corporation's balance sheets showed assets of $320,000 (including cash of $60,000 and United States obligations of $106,000) and an earned surplus of $135,000.

The corporation paid a dividend of $4 a share in 1934; $16 in 1935; $8 in each year 1936 through 1940; $6 in 1941; and no dividends in 1942 and 1943. In 1944, after the stock redemption hereinafter mentioned, a dividend of $2 was distributed. . . .

On December 26, 1944, at a special meeting of the corporation's board of directors, on motion of taxpayer, it was resolved that the corporation purchase from taxpayer for $92,000 the 500 shares of

stock which taxpayer had acquired by bequest from his brother. . . .
On the same day, a special meeting of the stockholders (namely,
taxpayer, for he then owned all the shares of stock in this corporation,) approved; the transaction was completed; and an amendment
to the certificate of incorporation was executed which was later approved by the State Tax Commission. Taxpayer never considered
selling his shares to anyone but the corporation because he wanted
to keep the stock in the family.

The taxpayer did not report the transaction in controversy on
his return, and the Commissioner determined a deficiency on the
ground that the amount of $92,000 paid by the corporation was
taxable as a dividend.

The Tax Court specifically found that the earnings and profits
of the corporation prior to and during 1944 were accumulated for
no definite purpose; that the operations of the corporation were not
impaired by reason of the transaction in controversy, and that the
corporation had never followed a policy of contraction of business;
that the corporation's financial position on December 26, 1944, permitted of a dividend of $92,000, and that the corporation continued
in the same business in subsequent years.

The Tax Court further found that the payment of the $92,000
to taxpayer by the corporation in the taxable year was a distribution
in complete cancellation and redemption of all of that portion of the
corporation's stock bequeathed by taxpayer's brother, constituting a
partial liquidation, and not the essential equivalent of the distribution
of a taxable dividend.

We cannot agree with the holding of the Tax Court that, as of
the time of the stock redemption, the stock acquired by taxpayer
which was redeemed, must be regarded as the stock of the brother.
This runs absolutely counter to reality. This stock had been the brother's; but, months before the redemption, taxpayer's title to this stock
had been completely perfected. . . .

The vital thing here, as we see it, is that, by the redemption of
this stock, the *essential relation* of the taxpayer to the corporation was
not, in any practical aspect, changed. Before the redemption, he
was the sole stockholder in the corporation; after the redemption,
he was still the sole stockholder. Of what real consequence was it that
before the redemption his sole ownership was divided into 2,000
shares, and after the redemption, this same sole ownership was divided into 1,500 shares: He owned the whole corporation before the
redemption; after the redemption, he was still the sole owner.

Here, then, we find a single individual owning all the corporate
stock. . . . The corporation had on hand a large and unnecessary
accumulation of cash, representing "earnings or profits accumulated
after February 28, 1913." . . . The corporation did not then intend
to liquidate or to contract its business. . . . The redemption served

no business purpose of the corporation; it was motivated entirely by the personal considerations of taxpayer. . . . The net effect of the redemption was clearly to distribute to taxpayer the corporate earnings just as if a cash dividend had been declared. . . . Indeed, it is difficult to imagine a more ideal setup for the application of [§§302(b)(1) and 302(d)] than the facts involved in the instant case.

The cases of Flinn v. Commissioner, 37 B.T.A. 1085 and Tiffany v. Commissioner, 16 T.C. 1443, cited by the Tax Court are clearly not in point. There, the corporations purchased all of the stock of a particular stockholder, when there were still other stockholders; here, the corporation merely purchased part of the stock of its sole stockholder. There, the relationship of the stockholder to the corporation was radically changed by the redemption from stockholder to mere ex-stockholder; here, as we have pointed out, there was no such change for, both before and after the redemption, taxpayer was and remained the sole stockholder of the corporation.

The ultimate question of whether, in a particular case, [§§302(b)(1) and 302(d) do or do] not apply, is usually held to be a question of fact. . . .

The Regulations, which have been in effect for many years, provide in part that a redemption by a corporation of a portion of its stock pro rata among all the shareholders would generally be considered as effecting a distribution essentially equivalent to a dividend distribution to the extent of the earnings and profits accumulated after February 28, 1913. That provision of the Regulations is fully met in this case, and likewise other factors which have sometimes been held relevant are also present here.

It might be noted that while dividends were paid by the corporation here prior to 1942, no dividends were paid by the corporation in 1942, 1943, or 1944 prior to redemption, though the corporate earnings in all these years were quite substantial.

Any conclusion other than that which we have reached readily shows how easily the tactics of the taxpayer here could be used as a means of tax evasion. A prosperous corporation, for example, with a single stockholder, earns large sums of money, available for, and which should be paid out as, dividends. This sole stockholder siphons off this money (as was done in the instant case) to himself by selling a portion of his stock to the corporation at a price per share which will just cover these earnings. Surely, this is a redemption "essentially equivalent to the distribution of a taxable dividend." Congress must have had just such a situation in mind when it enacted [§§302(b)(1) and 302(d)]. . . .

The decision of the Tax Court of the United States is reversed and the case is remanded with directions to enter a decision in favor of the Commissioner.

Reversed and remanded with directions.

NOTE

What would the tax consequences have been to the estate and to the taxpayer if, in *Roberts*, (1) the decedent's will had made a bequest of the cash value of the shares, not the shares themselves, (2) the corporation had redeemed the shares in the estate's hands, and (3) the estate turned over to the taxpayer the cash proceeds? Would the result be different if the estate had paid the taxpayer the cash bequest and then had the stock redeemed in its hands? In answering these questions consider §§302(b)(3), 318, 1014, and 102(a). See Treas. Reg. §1.318-3(a).

HOLSEY v. COMMISSIONER
258 F.2d 865 (3d Cir. 1958)

Before Maris, Goodrich and McLaughlin, Circuit Judges.

MARIS, Circuit Judge. . . . J. R. Holsey Sales Company, a New Jersey corporation, was organized on April 28, 1936, as an Oldsmobile dealership. Taxpayer has been president and a director of the company since its organization. Only 20 shares were issued out of the 2,500 shares of no par value stock authorized; these 20 shares were issued to Greenville Auto Sales Company, a Chevrolet dealership, in exchange for all of the latter's right, title, and interest to the Oldsmobile franchise and other assets with respect to the franchise which had been owned and operated by the Greenville Company. The 20 shares issued were assigned a value of $11,000. Taxpayer's father, Charles V. Holsey, in 1936, owned more than two-thirds of the outstanding stock of the Greenville Company, and taxpayer was vice-president and a director of that corporation.

On April 30, 1936, taxpayer acquired from the Greenville Company an option to purchase 50% of the outstanding shares of the Holsey Company for $11,000, and a further option to purchase, within ten years after the exercise of the first option, all the remaining shares for a sum to be agreed upon. The Greenville Company owned all of the outstanding stock of the Holsey Company from its organization in 1936 until November, 1939, when taxpayer exercised his first option and purchased 50% of the outstanding stock of the Holsey Company for $11,000.

On June 28, 1946, the further option in favor of taxpayer was revised. Under the terms of the revised option, taxpayer was granted the right to purchase the remaining outstanding shares of the Holsey Company at any time up to and including June 28, 1951, for $80,000. The revised option was in favor of taxpayer individually and was not assignable by him to anyone other than a corporation in which he owned not less than 50% of the voting stock. On the date of the revision of this option, taxpayer's father owned 76% of the stock of the Greenville Company and taxpayer was a vice-president and director of that corporation. . . .

On January 19, 1951, taxpayer assigned his revised option to the Holsey Company; on the same date the Holsey Company exercised the option and paid the Greenville Company $80,000 for the stock held by it. This transaction resulted in taxpayer becoming the owner of 100% of the outstanding stock of the Holsey Company. In his income tax return for the year 1951, taxpayer gave no effect to this transaction.

The principal officers and only directors of the Holsey Company from April 28, 1936, to December 31, 1951, were taxpayer, his brother, Charles D. Holsey, and their father, Charles V. Holsey. On January 19, 1951, when the revised option was exercised, the earned surplus of the Holsey Company was in excess of $300,000.

The Oldsmobile franchise, under which the Holsey Company operated, was a yearly contract entered into by the Corporation and the manufacturer in reliance upon the personal qualifications and representations of taxpayer as an individual. It was the manufacturer's policy to have its dealers own all of the stock in dealership organizations.

The Commissioner determined that the effect of the transaction of January 19, 1951, wherein the Holsey Company paid $80,000 to the Greenville Company for 50% of the outstanding stock of the Holsey Company, constituted a dividend to taxpayer, the remaining stockholder. The Commissioner therefore asserted a deficiency against taxpayer in the sum of $41,385.34. The Tax Court sustained the Commissioner. 28 T.C. 962.

The question presented for decision in this case is whether the Tax Court erred in holding that the payment by the Holsey Company of $80,000 to the Greenville Company for the purchase from that company of its stock in the Holsey Company was essentially equivalent to the distribution of a taxable dividend to the taxpayer, the remaining stockholder of the Holsey Company. To determine that question we must begin with the applicable statute. . . .

It will be observed that section [316(a)] defines a dividend as a distribution made by a corporation "to its shareholders." Accordingly unless a distribution which is sought to be taxed to a stockholder as a dividend is made to him or for his benefit it may not be regarded as either a dividend or the legal equivalent of a dividend. Here the distribution was made to the Greenville Company, not to the taxpayer. This the Government, of course, concedes but urges that it was made for the benefit of the taxpayer. It is true that it has been held that a distribution by a corporation in redemption of stock which the taxpayer stockholder has a contractual obligation to purchase is essentially the equivalent of a dividend to him since it operates to discharge his obligation. . . . But where, as here, the taxpayer was never under any legal obligation to purchase the stock held by the other stockholder, the Greenville Company, having merely an option to purchase which he did not exercise but instead assigned to the Holsey Company, the distribution did not discharge any obligation of his and did not benefit him in any direct sense.

It is, of course, true that the taxpayer was benefited indirectly by the distribution. The value of his own stock was increased, since the redemption was for less than book value, and he became sole stockholder. But these benefits operated only to increase the value of the taxpayer's stock holdings; they could not give rise to taxable income within the meaning of the Sixteenth Amendment until the corporation makes a distribution to the taxpayer or his stock is sold. Eisner v. Macomber, 1920, 252 U.S. 189 . . . ; Schmitt v. Commissioner of Internal Revenue, 3 Cir., 1954, 208 F.2d 819. In the latter case in a somewhat similar connection this court said (p. 821):

> During these years when Wolverine was buying its own shares it, of course, was subject to income tax as a corporation. Mrs. Green was subject to tax on whatever profit she made by the sale of these shares to the corporation. But what happened to warrant imposing a tax upon Schmitt and Lehren? If one owns a piece of real estate and, because of its favorable location in a city, the land becomes increasingly valuable over a period of years, the owner is not subject to income taxation upon the annual increase in value. In the same way, if a man owns shares in a corporation which gradually become more valuable through the years he is not taxed because of the increase in value even though he is richer at the end of each year than he was at the end of the year before. If he disposes of that which has increased, of course he must pay tax upon his profit. All of this is hornbook law of taxation; nobody denies it.

We think that the principle thus stated is equally applicable here. Indeed the Tax Court itself has so held in essentially similar cases. . . .

The question whether payments made by a corporation in the acquisition and redemption of its stock are essentially equivalent to the distribution of a taxable dividend has been often before the courts and certain criteria have been enunciated. The most significant of these is said to be whether the distribution leaves the proportionate interests of the stockholders unchanged as occurs when a true dividend is paid. Ferro v. Commissioner of Internal Revenue, 3 Cir. 1957, 242 F.2d 838, 841. The application of that criterion to the facts of this case compels the conclusion that in the absence of a direct pecuniary benefit to the taxpayer the Tax Court erred in holding the distribution in question taxable to him. For in his case prior to the distribution the taxpayer and the Greenville Company each had a 50% interest in the Holsey Company whereas after it was over the taxpayer had 100% of the outstanding stock and the Greenville Company none.

The Government urges the lack of a corporate purpose for the distribution and the taxpayer seeks to establish one. But we do not consider this point for, as we have recently held, "It is the effect of the redemption, rather than the purpose which actuated it, which controls the determination of dividend equivalence." Kessner v. Commissioner of Internal Revenue, 3 Cir., 1957, 248 F.2d 943, 944. Nor need we discuss the present position of the Government that the transaction must be treated as a sham and the purchase of the stock as having been made by the taxpayer through his alter ego, the Holsey Company. For the Tax Court made no such finding, doubtless in view of the fact that at the time the taxpayer owned only 50% of the stock and was in a minority on the board of directors. On the contrary, that court based its decision on the benefit which the distribution by the corporation to the Greenville Company conferred upon the taxpayer, which it thought gave rise to taxable income in his hands.

For the reasons stated we think that the Tax Court erred in its decision. The decision will accordingly be reversed and the cause remanded for further proceedings not inconsistent with this opinion.

McLAUGHLIN, Circuit Judge (dissenting). I think that the net effect of the facile operation disclosed in this case amounts to the distribution of a taxable dividend to the taxpayer. I do not think that the *Schmitt* decision controls here. Quite the contrary to the *Schmitt* facts, this taxpayer himself acquired a valuable option to buy the shares and solely on the theory of a gift of the option rights would make the corporation the true purchaser. I agree with the Tax Court that "The assignment of the option contract to J. R. Holsey Sales Co. was clearly for the purpose of having that company pay the $80,000 in exercise of the option that was executed for the petitioner's personal benefit. The payment was intended to secure and did secure for petitioner exactly what it was always intended he should get if he made the payment personally, namely, all of the stock in J. R. Holsey Sales Co."

I would affirm the Tax Court decision.

NOTES

1. What is the factual difference in *Holsey* that may justify a result different from that in *Roberts*, page 242 supra? In your judgment is the factual difference sufficient? If not, which result is preferable?

2. In Rev. Rul. 58-614, 1958-2 C.B. 920, the Service announced

its intention to follow the *Holsey* decision. It distinguished *Holsey* from the case in which the stock "is in reality purchased by a remaining shareholder," and for the latter type of case cited Wall v. United States, 164 F.2d 462 (4th Cir. 1947), and Zipp v. Commissioner, 259 F.2d 119 (6th Cir. 1958), *cert. denied*, 359 U.S. 934 (1959). See also Rev. Rul. 59-286, 1959-2 C.B. 103.

3. *Holsey* holds that benefits which "operated only to increase the value of the taxpayer's stock holdings . . . could not give rise to taxable income within the meaning of the Sixteenth Amendment. . . ." But see §305(b)(2) and (c); cf. Rev. Rul. 77-19, 1977-1 C.B. 83. Section 305 is discussed in Chapter 4, page 459 et seq. infra. The Constitution aside, does *Holsey* reach the sensible result as a matter of statutory construction?

SULLIVAN v. UNITED STATES
363 F.2d 724 (8th Cir. 1966). *cert. denied*, 387 U.S. 905 (1967)

Before Vogel, Chief Judge, Blackmun, Circuit Judge, and Stephenson, District Judge.

STEPHENSON, District Judge. . . . [T]he taxpayer Sullivan purchased the assets of an automobile dealership in Blytheville, Arkansas in 1941. He then formed a corporation to operate the dealership. . . . [I]n September, 1948, Frank Nelson became the resident manager of the dealership under an arrangement which included an agreement permitting Nelson to acquire up to forty (40) percent of the stock and further providing for taxpayer's repurchase of said stock upon Nelson's termination of his employment. After acquiring approximately 38% of the corporation's outstanding stock, Nelson announced his intention to depart from his position in 1956 and offered to sell his stock to taxpayer Sullivan. The corporation's Board of Directors then authorized the redemption of Nelson's stock by the corporation.

The ultimate question before the District Court involved a determination of whether the payment by the corporation in redemption of Nelson's stock constituted a taxable distribution to taxpayer Sullivan, the sole remaining stockholder of the corporation. The District Court found that taxpayer Sullivan was unconditionally and primarily obligated to purchase Nelson's stock in 1956 and that said stock was purchased by the Corporation out of profits distributable as a dividend and therefore held that the taxpayer constructively received income equivalent to a dividend in the amount paid by the Corporation for said stock, ($198,334.58). Initially, an interpretation of the memorandum agreement entered into by Sullivan and Nelson at the time the latter assumed his managerial functions is necessary. The agreement contained the following provisions:

> 6. TRANSFER OF SHARES OF STOCK. It is understood and agreed that Sullivan is permitting Nelson to buy stock in said corporation for the purpose of giving him a working interest only, and said Nelson agrees that said shares of stock cannot and will not be mortgaged, hypothecated or transferred by him, his heirs, executor, administrator or trustee to any person other than William J. Sullivan or such person as said Sullivan directs in writing. Any such sale, delivery or transfer to any other person, firm or corporation shall be null and void. Said Sullivan agrees that he will, within thirty (30) days after such shares have been offered for sale to him, accept the offer to sell, provided always that such shares shall be offered for sale at a price to be determined according to this contract.
>
> 7. TERMINATION OF CONTRACT. Said Nelson agrees that if he should terminate his employment or relationship with William J. Sullivan or employment by the said corporation, and if his connection and association with the corporation should cease or be terminated by Sullivan or the majority owners of the stock of the corporation, then said Nelson agrees to sell and transfer and deliver to Sullivan at the then book value all shares of stock owned by him in the Sullivan-Nelson Chevrolet Co. . . . If said contract is terminated by Nelson or Sullivan as herein provided or by the death of Nelson, the value of the stock owned by Nelson shall be fixed and determined as set up in paragraphs four and five of this agreement. If said Nelson should die or become so disabled by injury or sickness as to become incapable of managing and operating the business, then said Sullivan shall have the immediate and exclusive rights to purchase the stock owned by Nelson or by his heirs, administrators or executors in accordance with the terms of this contract. Title so (sic) said shares of stock shall automatically rest in Sullivan upon Nelson's death and said Sullivan shall be obligated to Nelson's personal representative or representatives for the value thereof as fixed by this agreement.

. . . The District Court was justified in concluding that Sullivan was unconditionally obligated to purchase Nelson's stock.[5]

At this juncture, the payment by the corporation to Nelson presents two basic questions: (1) Was that payment in actuality a dividend and therefore includable in Sullivan's gross income under §§61(a)(7),

---

5. The taxpayer makes an alternative argument to the effect that, even if he was unconditionally obligated to purchase Sullivan's stock, subsequent events constituted a modification or novation of the agreement. Even if this contention is accepted, the court is at a loss as to how the taxpayer is aided. The novation or modification itself would be considered as resulting in an economic benefit and possible constructive dividend taxable against Sullivan. The taxpayer would be left in essentially the same position with respect to his possible tax liability.

316(a) and 301(c)(1), of the Internal Revenue Code? (2) If the payment is considered as a corporate redemption of stock, was the
payment includable in Sullivan's gross income as being essentially
equivalent to a dividend within the meaning of §302(b)(1)? This court
has recognized that both questions are to be resolved as fact issues.
Idol v. Commissioner of Internal Revenue, 319 F.2d 647 (8th Cir.
1963). If a finding is supported by substantial evidence on the record
as a whole and is not against or induced by an erroneous view of the
law, it will not be disturbed on appeal.

When an individual shareholder receives an economic benefit
through a diversion of corporate earnings and profits, such a receipt
may be taxed as a constructive dividend. This court set forth a criteria
for determining whether a payment constitutes a constructive dividend in Sachs v. Commissioner of Internal Revenue, 277 F.2d 879,
882-883 (8th Cir. 1960):

> The motive, or expressed intent of the corporation is not
> determinative, and constructive dividends have been found con-
> trary to the expressed intent of the corporation. The courts, as
> arbiters of the true nature of corporate payments, have consistently
> used as a standard the measure of receipt of economic benefits as
> the proper occasion for taxation.

This court has also adopted criteria for determining whether a
redemption of stock is essentially equivalent to a dividend. . . . While
there is no sole decisive test in this connection, the several guidelines
for the determination include "whether there is a bona fide corporate
business purpose, whether the action was initiated by the corporation
or by the shareholders, whether there was a contraction of the business, and whether there was a substantial change in proportionate
stock ownership." Idol v. Commissioner of Internal Revenue, 319
F.2d 647, 651 (8th Cir. 1963). In addition, the Court has observed
that the "net effect of the transaction is at least an important consideration in determining dividend equivalency." . . .

The general net effect and the purpose of and circumstances
surrounding the transaction involved herein must be carefully scru-
tinized to ascertain whether Sullivan received a taxable dividend.
Prior to the transaction, Sullivan held approximately 62% of the
shares outstanding while Nelson owned the remaining shares. As
previously discussed, Sullivan was unconditionally obligated to purchase Nelson's stock if it was offered to him for sale. After the
transaction was completed, the relevant facts were essentially as follows: (1) Sullivan's personal obligation had been discharged (2)
Sullivan owned all of the outstanding shares of stock of the corporation (3) the corporation's assets were decreased by the amount paid
to Nelson for his stock (4) Nelson's stock was held by the corporation

as treasury stock. It is true that in terms of the financial worth of Sullivan's interest in the corporation, it was the same after the transaction as it was before.[7] The transaction still resulted in an economic benefit to Sullivan, however, because he was relieved of his personal obligation to purchase Nelson's stock. After careful consideration this court concludes that there was no corporate business purpose or other factor which justifies the taxpayer's position that as to him the payment must be considered a stock redemption and not the equivalent of a dividend.[9] On the facts of this case, Sullivan received a taxable dividend as the result of the corporation's purchase of Nelson's stock.

This court is aware that it is often difficult to distinguish true substance from mere form. Tax law places some weight and significance on form and the choice of one alternative rather than another for achieving a desired end is often critical and may be determinative of the tax effect of a transaction. Judge Becker's opinion comprehensively deals with the evidence and the applicable law of this case. The taxpayer has failed to establish grounds for reversal. The judgment of the District Court is affirmed.

NOTES

1. Are *Holsey*, page 246 supra, and *Sullivan* distinguishable? Is it relevant that in *Sullivan* the taxpayer had an obligation to purchase, whereas in *Holsey* there was only an option? Are *Sullivan* and the government's position in *Sullivan* consistent with (as to the government, justifiable in light of) Rev. Rul. 59-286, 1959-2 C.B. 103? In the latter, the surviving shareholder was obligated either to buy the decedent's stock or to vote his stock for liquidation of the corporation. By postmortem agreement the corporation redeemed the decedent's stock at its fair market value. Despite the fact that the remaining shareholder was "personally obligated" to buy the stock and he was "relieved [of his] obligation," he was ruled not to be in receipt of a

---

7. Prior to the transfer of Nelson's stock Sullivan owned 186 shares of the 300 shares outstanding. His stock at this time was worth approximately $323,597.00. After the transfer, his 186 shares were the only outstanding stock of the corporation. Due to the corporate purchase of Nelson's stock, however, the value of the taxpayer's shares remained at approximately $323,597.00.

9. The taxpayer has strongly urged that there was a corporate business purpose motivating the purchase of Nelson's stock because of the valuable services received from him as resident manager of the corporation. The services had already been performed, however, when the stock was purchased. Moreover, it was Sullivan, not the corporation, who was obligated to purchase the stock. Under these circumstances, the District Court properly found that the purchase was not induced by a business purpose. The net effect of the transaction further indicates that a dividend was received by the taxpayer.

dividend since the stock was not "in reality . . . purchased by the remaining shareholder. . . ." The Commissioner's current position is elaborated in Rev. Rul. 69-608, infra.

2. In Daniel T. Jacobs, 41 T.C.M. (CCH) 951 (1981), the Tax Court followed *Sullivan* while acknowledging that the taxpayers "could very easily have avoided dividend treatment . . . had they obtained tax advice from the start." Judge Tannenwald said the court must "leave for another day [the development of] an exception to the now concretized standard of form over substance in [this] area. . . ."

3. For a case involving §304 which distinguishes *Sullivan*, see Citizens Bank & Trust Co. v. United States, page 277 infra.

REVENUE RULING 69-608
1969-2 C.B. 43

Advice has been requested as to the treatment for Federal income tax purposes of the redemption by a corporation of a retiring shareholder's stock where the remaining shareholder of the corporation has entered into a contract to purchase such stock.

Where the stock of a corporation is held by a small group of people, it is often considered necessary to the continuity of the corporation to have the individuals enter into agreements among themselves to provide for the disposition of the stock of the corporation in the event of the resignation, death, or incapacity of one of them. Such agreements are generally reciprocal among the shareholders and usually provide that on the resignation, death, or incapacity of one of the principal shareholders, the remaining shareholders will purchase his stock. Frequently such agreements are assigned to the corporation by the remaining shareholder and the corporation actually redeems its stock from the retiring shareholder.

Where a corporation redeems stock from a retiring shareholder, the fact that the corporation in purchasing the shares satisfies the continuing shareholder's executory contractual obligation to purchase the redeemed shares does not result in a distribution to the continuing shareholder provided that the continuing shareholder is not subject to an existing primary and unconditional obligation to perform the contract and that the corporation pays no more than fair market value for the stock redeemed.

On the other hand, if the continuing shareholder, at the time of the assignment to the corporation of his contract to purchase the retiring shareholder's stock, is subject to an unconditional obligation to purchase the retiring shareholder's stock, the satisfaction by the corporation of his obligation results in a constructive distribution to him. The constructive distribution is taxable as a distribution under section 301 of the Internal Revenue Code of 1954.

If the continuing shareholder assigns his stock purchase contract to the redeeming corporation prior to the time when he incurs a primary and unconditional obligation to pay for the shares of stock, no distribution to him will result. If, on the other hand, the assignment takes place after the time when the continuing shareholder is so obligated, a distribution to him will result. While a pre-existing obligation to perform in the future is a necessary element in establishing a distribution in this type of case, it is not until the obligor's duty to perform becomes unconditional that it can be said a primary and unconditional obligation arises.

The application of the above principles may be illustrated by the situations described below.

SITUATION I

A and B are unrelated individuals who own all of the outstanding stock of corporation X. A and B enter into an agreement that provides in the event B leaves the employ of X, he will sell his X stock to A at a price fixed by the agreement. The agreement provides that within a specified number of days of B's offer to sell, A will purchase at the price fixed by the agreement all of the X stock owned by B. B terminates his employment and tenders the X stock to A. Instead of purchasing the stock himself in accordance with the terms of the agreement, A causes X to assume the contract and to redeem its stock held by B. In this case, A had a primary and unconditional obligation to perform his contract with B at the time the contract was assigned to X. Therefore, the redemption by X of its stock held by B will result in a constructive distribution to A. See William J. and Georgia K. Sullivan v. United States of America, [page 250 supra]. . . .

SITUATION 2

A and B are unrelated individuals who own all of the outstanding stock of corporation X. An agreement between them provides unconditionally that within ninety days of the death of either A or B, the survivor will purchase the decedent's stock of X from his estate. Following the death of B, A causes X to assume the contract and redeem the stock from B's estate.

The assignment of the contract to X followed by the redemption by X of the stock owned by B's estate will result in a constructive distribution to A because immediately on the death of B, A had a primary and unconditional obligation to perform the contract.

SITUATION 3

All of the stock of X corporation was owned by a trust that was to terminate in 1968. Individuals A and B were the beneficiaries of the trust. Since B was the trustee of the trust, he had exclusive management authority over X through his control of the board of directors. In 1966, A paid to B the sum of 25x dollars and promised to pay an additional 20x dollars to B in 1969 for B's interest in the corpus and accumulations of the trust plus B's agreement to resign immediately as supervisor of the trust and release his control over the management of the corporation. The actual transfer of the stock held in trust was to take place on termination of the trust in 1968. In 1969, X reimbursed A for the 25x dollars previously paid to B, paid 20x dollars to B, and received the X stock held by B.

For all practical purposes, A became the owner of B's shares in 1966. Although naked legal title to the shares could not be transferred until the trust terminated in 1968, B did transfer all of his beneficial and equitable ownership of the X stock to A in exchange for an immediate payment by A of 25x dollars and an unconditional promise to pay an additional 20x dollars upon termination of the trust. The payment by X of 20x dollars to B and 25x dollars to A in 1969 constituted a constructive distribution to A in the amount of 45x dollars. See Schalk Chemical Company v. Commissioner, 32 T.C. 879 (1959), *affirmed* 304 F.2d 48(1962).

SITUATION 4

A and B owned all of the outstanding stock of X corporation. A and B entered into a contract under which, if B desired to sell his X stock, A agreed to purchase the stock or to cause such stock to be purchased. If B chose to sell his X stock to any person other than A, he could do so at any time. In accordance with the terms of the contract, A caused X to redeem all of B's stock in X.

At the time of the redemption, B was free to sell his stock to A or to any other person, and A had no unconditional obligation to purchase the stock and no fixed liability to pay for the stock. Accordingly, the redemption by X did not result in a constructive distribution to A. See S. K. Ames, Inc. v. Commissioner, 46 B.T.A. 1020 (1942), *acq.*, C.B. 1942-1, 1.

SITUATION 5

A and B owned all of the outstanding stock of X corporation. An agreement between A and B provided that upon the death of either, X will redeem all of the X stock owned by the decedent at the time of his death. In the event that X does not redeem the shares from the estate, the agreement provided that the surviving share-holder would purchase the unredeemed shares from the decedent's estate. B died and, in accordance with the agreement, X redeemed all of the shares owned by his estate.

In this case A was only secondarily liable under the agreement between A and B. Since A was not primarily obligated to purchase the X stock from the estate of B, he received no constructive distribution when X redeemed the stock.

SITUATION 6

B owned all of the outstanding stock of X corporation. A and B entered into an agreement under which A was to purchase all of the X stock from B. A did not contemplate purchasing the X stock in his own name. Therefore, the contract between A and B specifically provided that it could be assigned by A to a corporation and that, if the corporation agreed to be bound by the terms, A would be released from the contract.

A organized Y corporation and assigned the stock purchase contract to it. Y borrowed funds and purchased all of the X stock from B pursuant to the agreement. Subsequently Y was merged into X and X assumed the liabilities that Y incurred in connection with the purchase of the X stock and subsequently satisfied these liabilities.

The purchase by Y of the stock of X did not result in a constructive distribution to A. Since A did not contemplate purchasing the X stock in his own name, he provided in the contract that it could be assigned to a corporation prior to the closing date. A chose this latter alternative and assigned the contract to Y. A was not personally subject to an unconditional obligation to purchase the X stock from B. See Arthur J. Kobacker and Sara Jo Kobacker, et al. v. Commissioner, 37 T.C. 882 (1962), acq., C.B. 1964-2, 6. Compare Ray Edenfield v. Commissioner, 19 T.C. 13 (1952), acq., C.B. 1953-1, 4.

SITUATION 7

A and B owned all of the outstanding stock of X corporation. An agreement between the shareholders provided that upon the death of either, the survivor would purchase the decedent's shares from his estate at a price provided in the agreement. Subsequently, the agreement was rescinded and a new agreement entered into which provided that upon the death of either A or B, X would redeem all of the decedent's shares of X stock from his estate.

The cancellation of the original contract between the parties in favor of the new contract did not result in a constructive distribution to either A or B. At the time X agreed to purchase the stock pursuant

to the terms of the new agreement, neither A nor B had an unconditional obligation to purchase shares of X stock. The subsequent
redemption of the stock from the estate of either pursuant to the
terms of the new agreement will not constitute a constructive distribution to the surviving shareholder.

NOTES

1. In light of Rev. Rul. 69-608, what is left of Rev. Rul. 59-286,
discussed in the Note following *Sullivan*, page 253 supra?
2. In Richard B. Bennett, 58 T.C. 381 (1972), *acq.*, 1972-2 C.B.
1, a retiring shareholder owned two-thirds of the corporation's stock.
For bona fide nontax reasons he insisted that his shares be purchased
by the remaining shareholder (the taxpayer) rather than redeemed
by the corporation. Immediately after the sale and pursuant to a
plan, the purchased shares were redeemed by the corporation. The
court refused to charge the taxpayer with receipt of a dividend,
holding that he was only a "conduit" or "agent" for the corporation
in acquiring the shares; contra, apparently because the redemption
was planned and executed solely by the purchasing shareholder, John
B. Adams, 69 T.C. 1040 (1978), *aff'd*, 594 F.2d 657 (8th Cir. 1979).
Cf. Casner v. Commissioner, 450 F.2d 379 (5th Cir. 1971) (dividend
distributed as part of a transaction in which all stock of a corporation
is sold, but prior to a binding contract of sale, was a dividend to the
buyer and part of the sales price to the seller); contra: Rev. Rul. 75-
493, 1975-2 C.B. 108 (dividend to seller); Santulli v. United States,
76-2 U.S.T.C. ¶9677 (D. Md. 1976) (distribution to buyer immediately
after sale to provide funds for payment of the purchase price was a
taxable dividend to buyer). See Battle, Dividends, Redemptions and
Stock Purchases in Connection with Reorganizations, 53 Taxes 845
(1975).
See Kuper v. Commissioner, 533 F.2d 152 (5th Cir. 1976), where
brothers X, Y, and Z were equal owners of two corporations, A Corporation and B Corporation. In order to sever X's interest, the
brothers contributed all the B Corporation stock to A Corporation.
A Corporation then transferred cash to B Corporation and redistri-
buted the B Corporation stock to X in complete redemption of his
stock in A Corporation. This series of transactions was held to result
in a taxable exchange of A Corporation stock for B Corporation stock
at the shareholder level, disregarding A's transitory ownership of B
Corporation, and a constructive dividend by A Corporation in the
amount of cash it transferred to B Corporation.
3. In Pulliam v. Commissioner, 48 T.C.M. (CCH) 1019 (1984),
the sole shareholder of a corporation that operated a funeral home

died leaving the corporation stock to several beneficiaries of whom only one was a licensed funeral director. Under state law all shareholders had to be licensed funeral directors. To remedy this, the corporation redeemed the shares of all unlicensed beneficiaries. The court held that this did not result in a dividend to a remaining shareholder, despite the fact that under state law he was obligated to acquire stock, because state law imposed the redemption obligation on the corporation as well.

ZENZ v. QUINLIVAN
213 F.2d 914 (6th Cir. 1954)

Before Miller, Circuit Judge, and Gourley and Starr, District Judges.

GOURLEY, District Judge. The appeal relates to the interpretation of Section [302(b)(1)] . . . and poses the question — Is a distribution of substantially all of the accumulated earnings and surplus of a corporation, which are not necessary to the conduct of the business of the corporation, in redemption of all outstanding shares of stock of said corporation owned by one person *essentially equivalent to the distribution of a taxable dividend under the Internal Revenue Code?*

The District Court answered in the affirmative and sustained a deficiency assessment by the Commissioner of Internal Revenue.

[W]e believe the judgment should be reversed. . . .

Appellant is the widow of the person who was the motivating spirit behind the closed corporation which engaged in the business of excavating and laying of sewers. Through death of her husband she became the owner of all shares of stock issued by the corporation. She operated the business until remarriage, when her second husband assumed the management. As a result of a marital rift, separation, and final divorce, taxpayer sought to dispose of her company to a competitor who was anxious to eliminate competition.

Prospective buyer did not want to assume the tax liabilities which it was believed were inherent in the accumulated earnings and profits of the corporation. To avoid said profits and earnings as a source of future taxable dividends, buyer purchased part of taxpayer's stock for cash. Three weeks later, after corporate reorganization and corporate action, the corporation redeemed the balance of taxpayer's stock, purchasing the same as treasury stock which absorbed substantially all of the accumulated earnings and surplus of the corporation.

Taxpayer, in her tax return, invoked Section [302(a)] of the Internal Revenue Code . . . as constituting a cancellation or redemption by a corporation of all of the stock of a particular shareholder, and therefore was not subject to being treated as a distribution of a taxable dividend.

The District Court sustained the deficiency assessment of the Commissioner that the amount received from accumulated earnings and profits was ordinary income since the stock redeemed by the corporation was "at such time and in such manner as to make the redemption thereof essentially equivalent to the distribution of a taxable dividend" under [§§302(b)(1) and (d)] of the Code.

The District Court's findings were premised upon the view that taxpayer employed a circuitous approach in an attempt to avoid the tax consequences which would have attended the outright distribution of the surplus to the taxpayer by the declaration of a taxable dividend.

Nevertheless, the general principle is well settled that a taxpayer has the legal right to decrease the amount of what otherwise would be his taxes or altogether avoid them, by means which the law permits. . . . The taxpayer's motive to avoid taxation will not establish liability if the transaction does not do so without it. . . .

The question accordingly presented is not whether the overall transaction, admittedly carried out for the purpose of avoiding taxes, actually avoided taxes which would have been incurred if the transaction had taken a different form, but whether the sale constituted a taxable dividend or the sale of a capital asset. . . .

It is a salutary fact that Section [302(a)] is an exception to Section [316] that all distributions of earnings and profits are taxable as a dividend.

The basic precept underlying the capital gains theory of taxation as distinguished from ordinary income tax is the concept that a person who has developed an enterprise in which earnings have been accumulated over a period of years should not be required to expend the ordinary income tax rate in the one year when he withdraws from his enterprise and realizes his gain.

Common logic dictates that a fair basis of measuring income is not determined upon the profits on hand in the year of liquidation but is properly attributable to each year in which the profits were gained.

We cannot concur with the legal proposition enunciated by the District Court that a corporate distribution can be essentially equivalent to a taxable dividend even though that distribution extinguishes the shareholder's interest in the corporation. To the contrary, we are satisfied that where the taxpayer effects a redemption which completely extinguishes the taxpayer's interest in the corporation, and does not retain any beneficial interest whatever, that such transaction is not the equivalent of the distribution of a taxable dividend as to him. . . .

The statutory concept of dividend is a distribution out of earnings and profits, and normally it is proportionate to shares and leaves the shareholder holding his shares as his capital investment. . . .

Complete and partial liquidations are treated for the purpose of the statute, as sales with a consequent measure of gain or loss, even though the proceeds may to some extent be derived from earnings. . . .

[T]he question as to whether the distribution in connection with the cancellation or the redemption of said stock is essentially equivalent to the distribution of a taxable dividend under the Internal Revenue Code and Treasury Regulations must depend upon the circumstances of each case.

Since the intent of the taxpayer was to bring about a complete liquidation of her holdings and to become separated from all interest in the corporation, the conclusion is inevitable that the distribution of the earnings and profits by the corporation in payment for said stock was not made at such time and in such manner as to make the distribution and cancellation or redemption thereof essentially equivalent to the distribution of a taxable dividend.

In view of the fact that the application of [§302(b)(1) and (d)] of the Internal Revenue Code contemplates that the shareholder receiving the distribution will remain in the corporation, the circumstances of this proceeding militate against treating taxpayer's sale as a distribution of a taxable dividend.

We do not feel that a taxpayer should be penalized for exercising legal means to secure a tax advantage. The conduct of this taxpayer does not appear to contravene the purport or congressional intent of the provisions of the Internal Revenue Act which taxpayer invoked.

We conclude that under the facts and circumstances of the present case the District Court was in error, and the taxpayer is not liable as a distributee of a taxable dividend under [§§302(b)(1) and (d)] of the Internal Revenue Code.

The decision and judgment of the District Court is reversed and the case remanded with instruction to enter judgment in accordance with this opinion.

NOTES

1. Suppose Corporation X, wholly owned by Mr. Doe, has a net worth of $1 million, allocated as follows: $600,000 in operating assets needed in the business, $200,000 in securities, and $200,000 in cash. Doe's basis in his stock is $300,000. Buyer Corp. is willing to purchase the operating assets of X, but it has only $700,000. Doe is unwilling

to sell 7/10 of the business to Buyer on the condition that Buyer will later cause X to redeem Doe's remaining shares, and Buyer is unwilling to purchase assets not within the corporate form. How would you design a transaction that would ensure Doe a long-term capital gain of $700,000?

2. *Zenz*, decided under the 1939 Code, was ruled appropriate to the current statutory scheme in Rev. Rul. 55-745, 1955-2 C.B. 223. The *Zenz* approach, combining sales and redemptions in an integrated transaction, may also result in a redemption qualifying under §302(b)(2) as substantially disproportionate with respect to the selling/redeeming shareholder. See Rev. Rul. 75-447, 1975-2 C.B. 113; Rickey v. United States, 427 F. Supp. 484 (W.D. La. 1976), *aff'd on another issue*, 592 F.2d 1251 (5th Cir. 1979) (redemption coupled with gift in following year pursuant to "integrated plan" was substantially disproportionate).

3. Mr. Eagle wishes to dispose of his corporation. A transaction is negotiated under which Mr. Smith purchases half of the stock for $500,000 in cash and the corporation simultaneously redeems the remaining half, paying for it with its ten-year, 6-percent note in the face amount of $500,000 payable only out of the corporation's future income. What are the income tax consequences to Mr. Eagle? Cf. Commissioner v. Brown, 380 U.S. 563 (1965). What are the tax consequences to Mr. Eagle's corporation if it distributes appreciated property to redeem some of Mr. Eagle's shares?

4. The Internal Revenue Service will not rule that a redemption qualifies as a complete termination of interest if the corporation leases property of the former shareholder and the payment for the use is dependent upon earnings or subordinated to general creditors of the corporation. See Rev. Proc. 87-3, 1987-1 C.B. 523; cf. Dunn v. Commissioner, page 169 supra.

5. See Chirelstein, Optional Redemptions and Optional Dividends: Taxing the Repurchase of Common Shares, 78 Yale L.J. 739 (1969); Jassey, The Tax Treatment of Bootstrap Stock Acquisitions: The Redemption Route vs. the Dividend Route, 87 Harv. L. Rev. 1459 (1974); Vernava and Martin, Tax Aspects of the Disposition of Control in a Closely Held Corporation, 58 Iowa L. Rev. 221 (1972).

GROVE v. COMMISSIONER
490 F.2d 241 (2d Cir. 1973)

Before Kaufman, Chief Judge, and Kilkenny* and Oakes, Circuit Judges.

KAUFMAN, Chief Judge. We are called upon, once again, to wres-

*Of the United States Court of Appeals for the Ninth Circuit, sitting by designation.

tle with the tangled web that is the Internal Revenue Code and decipher the often intricate and ingenious strategies devised by tax-payers to minimize their tax burdens. We undertake this effort mindful that taxpayer ingenuity, although channelled into an effort to reduce or eliminate the incidence of taxation, is ground for neither legal nor moral opprobrium. As Learned Hand so eloquently stated, "any one may so arrange his affairs that his taxes shall be as low as possible; he is not bound to choose that pattern which will best pay the Treasury; there is not even a patriotic duty to increase one's taxes. . . ." Helvering v. Gregory, 69 F.2d 809, 810 (2d Cir. 1934), aff'd, 293 U.S. 465 . . . (1935).

The case before us involves charitable contributions to an edu-cational institution. It is becoming increasingly apparent that colleges and universities must engage in extensive fund-raising if they are to continue to exist and provide quality education. In their efforts to induce alumni to make substantial contributions, these institutions have devised interesting gift plans which offer attractive, and legal, tax advantages to the donor. Philip Grove, a successful engineer, was one who responded to the needs of his alma mater, Rensselaer Po-lytechnic Institute ("RPI"). Thus, in 1954, he began making annual donations to RPI of 165 to 250 shares of Grove Shepherd Wilson & Kruge, Inc. ("the Corporation"), a closely held corporation of which he is majority shareholder, vice-president, and a director. In each instance, Grove retained a life interest in any income earned from his gift and limited his charitable contribution deduction to the value of the remainder interest received by RPI. Despite the absence of any prearranged agreement between Grove and RPI, each year be-tween 1954 and 1964 RPI successfully offered individual groups of shares to the Corporation for redemption. RPI then invested the redemption proceeds in income-producing securities and made quarterly disbursements to Grove of any income received. Grove reported any federally taxed items on his personal income tax returns for the year of receipt.

The Commissioner of Internal Revenue refused to approve these arrangements. Instead, he assessed deficiencies in Grove's income taxes for the years 1963 and 1964, contending that Grove had em-ployed RPI as a tax-free conduit for withdrawing funds from the Corporation and that redemption payments by the Corporation to RPI were in reality constructive dividend payments to Grove. Grove successfully challenged the deficiency determinations in the Tax Court, and the Commissioner appealed. We affirm.

I

Philip Grove received an engineering degree in 1924 from Rens-selaer Polytechnic Institute, a private, tax-exempt educational institution. . . . [H]e founded what is now Grove Shepherd Wilson & Kruge, Inc. and at all times since has controlled a majority of its shares. The balance of the Corporation's shares, with the exception of those held by RPI, are owned by officers and employees of the Corporation or their relatives.

The Corporation's business is building airfields, highways, tunnels, canals, and other similar heavy construction projects. . . . These projects usually involve the investment of large sums of money over an extended period of time and involve a high degree of risk. Since, in this industry, contract payments normally are made only after specified levels of progress are achieved, a firm must always commit substantial amounts of its own funds, whether borrowed or internally generated, to a project. Moreover, a company can determine an acceptable contract price based only on its best estimate of the cost to complete the project. A bad "guess" or unforeseen contingency may require a firm to complete a project while incurring a loss. . . . To protect against such adverse developments, successful firms seek to maintain liquidity by holding ample cash or other assets easily converted to cash. One method of conserving cash, adopted by the Corporation, is to retain all earnings and refrain from paying dividends.

As we have noted, RPI, like all universities and colleges, pursued its alumni with a wide variety of contribution plans. One plan employed "life income funds," and its terms were simple. An alumnus would make a gift of securities to RPI and retain a life interest in the income from the donated securities. Whatever dividends and interest were paid during the donor's life would belong to the donor, while any capital appreciation would inure to RPI. Upon the death of the donor, RPI would obtain full title to the securities.

In 1954, Dr. Livingston Houston, RPI's president, suggested to Grove that he make a gift under the "life income funds" plan. Grove explained that his only significant holdings were shares of his own corporation, but expressed a willingness to donate some of these shares under the plan, with certain qualifications. The Corporation, he stated, could not agree to any obligation or understanding to redeem shares held by RPI. This condition, of course, stemmed from a fear that RPI might seek redemption at a time when the Corporation was hard pressed for cash, which, as we have noted, was an asset crucial to a company in the heavy construction business. Moreover, since Grove at that time was unsure of RPI's money-management qualifications, he further conditioned his gift on a requirement that if RPI disposed of the shares, any proceeds would be invested and managed by an established professional firm.

RPI found these terms acceptable and on December 30, 1954, Grove made an initial gift of 200 shares, valued at $25,560. . . .

On the same day, the Corporation and RPI signed a minority shareholder agreement. RPI agreed not . . . "in any way [to] dispose of the whole or any part of the common stock of the Corporation now or hereafter owned . . . until [RPI] shall have first offered the Corporation the opportunity to purchase said shares. . . ." The redemption price was established at book value of the shares as noted on the Corporation's most recent certified financial statement prior to the offer. Pursuant to the contract, the Corporation was "entitled (but not obligated) to purchase all or any part of the shares of stock so offered." If the Corporation did not exercise its option to purchase within sixty days, RPI could transfer the shares to any other party and the Corporation's right of first refusal would not subsequently attach to such transferred shares.[3]

The 1954 gift was the first in a series of annual contributions to RPI by Grove. From 1954 to 1968, Grove donated to RPI between 165 to 250 shares of the Corporation each year, reaching a cumulative total of 2,652 shares, subject to terms substantially similar to those noted earlier.

Generally, RPI offered donated shares to the Corporation for redemption between one and two years after they were donated by Grove. The transactions followed a similar pattern. On each occasion, the Finance Committee of RPI's Board of Trustees first authorized the sale of specific shares of the Corporation. RPI's treasurer or controller would then write to Sidney Houck, the Corporation's treasurer, informing him of RPI's desire to dispose of the shares. Upon receipt of this letter, Houck would call a special meeting of the Corporation's board of directors to consider whether or not to exercise the Corporation's right of first refusal. The Board would adopt a resolution authorizing redemption [,and the shares were redeemed.]

At the time of the first redemption, in December, 1955, RPI opened an investment account at the Albany, New York, office of Merrill Lynch, Pierce, Fenner & Beane ("Merrill Lynch"). The account was captioned "Rensselaer Polytechnic Institute (Philip H. Grove Fund) Account." In accordance with Grove's wishes concerning the management of disposition proceeds, RPI authorized Merrill Lynch to act directly upon investment recommendations made by Scudder, Stevens, & Clark, Grove's personal investment adviser. RPI deposited the proceeds of each redemption transaction into this account which, pursuant to Scudder, Stevens & Clark's instructions, were generally invested in securities of large corporations whose shares traded on organized stock exchanges. . . . RPI made quarterly

3. Other minority shareholders of the Corporation signed similar agreements, which, in effect put in writing the Corporation's practice of redeeming, when financial conditions permitted, any minority-owner shares offered to it, for example, by a departing employee or a deceased employee's widow.

remittances to Grove, accompanied by an analysis of all account transactions.

On his personal income tax return for 1963, Grove reported as taxable income dividends of $4,939.28 and interest of $2,535.73 paid to him by RPI from the Merrill Lynch account. For 1964, Grove reported $6,096.05 in dividends and $3,540.81 in interest. The Commissioner, however, assessed deficiencies in Grove's taxable income for these years, asserting that Grove "realized additional dividends in the amounts of $29,000 and $25,800 in 1963 and 1964, respectively, as the result of the redemption of stock by Grove Shepherd Wilson & Kruge, Inc." . . .

II

The Commissioner's view of this case is relatively simple. In essence, we are urged to disregard the actual form of the Grove-RPI-Corporation donations and redemptions and to rewrite the actual events so that Grove's tax liability is seen in a wholly different light. Support for this position, it is argued, flows from the Supreme Court's decision in Commissioner of Internal Revenue v. Court Holding Co., 324 U.S. 331 . . . (1945), which, in language familiar to law students, cautions that "[t]he incidence of taxation depends upon the substance of a transaction. . . . To permit the true nature of a transaction to be disguised by mere formalisms, which exist solely to alter tax liabilities, would seriously impair the effective administration of the tax policies of Congress." Id. at 334. . . . In an effort to bring the instant case within this language, the Commissioner insists that whatever the appearance of the transactions here under consideration, their "true nature" is quite different. He maintains that Grove, with the cooperation of RPI, withdrew substantial funds from the Corporation and manipulated them in a manner designed to produce income for his benefit. In the Commissioner's view, the transaction is properly characterized as a redemption by the Corporation of Grove's, not RPI's shares, followed by a cash gift to RPI by Grove. This result, it is said, more accurately reflects "economic reality."

The Commissioner's motives for insisting upon this formulation are easily understood once its tax consequences are examined. Although Grove reported taxable dividends and interest received from the Merrill Lynch account on his 1963 and 1964 tax returns, amounts paid by the Corporation to redeem the donated shares from RPI were not taxed upon distribution. If, however, the transactions are viewed in the manner suggested by the Commissioner, the redemption proceeds would be taxable as income to Grove. Moreover, because the redemptions did not in substance alter Grove's relationship to the Corporation—he continued throughout to control a majority of the outstanding shares — the entire proceeds would be taxed as a dividend payment at high, progressive ordinary-income rates, rather than as a sale of shares, at the fixed, and relatively low, capital gains rate. . . .

Clearly, then, the stakes involved are high. We do not quarrel with the maxim that substance must prevail over form, but this proposition marks the beginning, not the end, of our inquiry. . . . Each case requires detailed consideration of its unique facts. Here, our aim is to determine whether Grove's gifts of the Corporation's shares to RPI prior to redemption should be given independent significance or whether they should be regarded as meaningless intervening steps in a single, integrated transaction designed to avoid tax liability by the use of mere formalisms.

The guideposts for our analysis are well marked by earlier judicial encounters with this problem. "The law with respect to gifts of appreciated property is well established. A gift of appreciated property does not result in income to the donor so long as he gives the property away absolutely and parts with title thereto before the property gives rise to income by way of sale." Carrington v. Commissioner of Internal Revenue, 476 F.2d 704, 708 (5th Cir. 1973), quoting Humacid Co., 42 T.C. 894, 913 (1964). As noted below by the Tax Court, the Commissioner here "does not contend that the gifts of stock by [Grove] to RPI in 1961 and 1962 were sham transactions, or that they were not completed gifts when made." If Grove made a valid, binding, and irrevocable gift of the Corporation's shares to RPI, it would be the purest fiction to treat the redemption proceeds as having actually been received by Grove. The Tax Court concluded that the gift was complete and irrevocable when made. The Commissioner conceded as much and we so find.[9]

It is argued, however, that notwithstanding the conceded validity of the gifts, other circumstances establish that Grove employed RPI merely as a convenient conduit for withdrawing funds from the Corporation for his personal use without incurring tax liability. The Commissioner would have us infer from the systematic nature of the gift redemption cycle that Grove and RPI reached a mutually beneficial understanding: RPI would permit Grove to use its tax-exempt status to drain funds from the Corporation in return for a donation of a future interest in such funds.

9. The Commissioner might have argued that at least that portion of the redemption proceeds allocable to Grove's retained life income interest was taxable as a dividend. He chose not to do so and the Tax Court "express[ed] no opinion upon the question, if it were properly presented, whether petitioner derived taxable income upon the redemption of stock to the extent of the life estate which he retained. . . ." Since the Commissioner has bypassed this aspect, it would be inappropriate in our discussions of the gifts to attach any special significance to the retained life interest feature.

We are not persuaded by this argument and the totality of the facts and circumstances lead us to a contrary conclusion. Grove testified before the Tax Court concerning the circumstances of these gifts. The court, based on the evidence and the witnesses' credibility, specifically found that "[t]here was no informal agreement between [Grove] and RPI that RPI would offer the stock in question to the corporation for redemption or that, if offered, the corporation would redeem it." . . . It cannot seriously be contended that the Tax Court's findings here are "clearly erroneous" and no tax liability can be predicated upon a nonexistent agreement between Grove and RPI or by a fictional one created by the Commissioner.

Grove, of course, owned a substantial majority of the Corporation's shares. His vote alone was sufficient to insure redemption of any shares offered by RPI. But such considerations, without more, are insufficient to permit the Commissioner to ride roughshod over the actual understanding found by the Tax Court to exist between the donor and the donee. Behrend v. United States (4th Cir. 1972), 73-1 USTC ¶9123, is particularly instructive. There, two brothers donated preferred shares of a corporation jointly controlled by them to a charitable foundation over which they also exercised control. The preferred shares were subsequently redeemed from the foundation by the corporation and the Commissioner sought to tax the redemption as a corporate dividend payment to the brothers. The court, in denying liability, concluded that although "it was understood that the corporation would at intervals take up the preferred according to its financial ability . . . , this factor did not convert into a constructive dividend the proceeds of the redemption . . . [because] the gifts were absolutely perfected before the corporation redeemed the stock." Id.

. . . Although the Corporation desired a right of first refusal on minority shares — understandably so, in order to reduce the possibility of unrelated, outside ownership interests — it assumed no obligation to redeem any shares so offered. In the absence of such an obligation, the Commissioner's contention that Grove's initial donation was only the first step in a prearranged series of transactions is little more than wishful thinking grounded in a shaky foundation. . . .

We are not so naive as to believe that tax considerations played no role in Grove's planning. But foresight and planning do not transform a non-taxable event into one that is taxable. Were we to adopt the Commissioner's view, we would be required to recast two actual transactions — a gift by Grove to RPI and a redemption from RPI by the Corporation — into two completely fictional transactions — a redemption from Grove by the Corporation and a gift by Grove to RPI. Based upon the facts as found by the Tax Court, we can discover no basis for elevating the Commissioner's "form" over that employed by the taxpayer in good faith. . . . In the absence of any supporting facts in the record we are unable to adopt the Commissioner's view; to do so would be to engage in a process of decision that is arbitrary, capricious and ultimately destructive of traditional notions of judicial review. We decline to embark on such a course.

Accordingly, the judgment of the Tax Court is affirmed.

[Dissenting opinion of Oakes, J., omitted.]

NOTES

1. The court in *Grove* places great importance upon the absence of an agreement by which the corporation would be legally obligated to redeem the shares donated to RPI. Is this importance justifiable? Of what value would the shares be to RPI if they were not redeemed?

2. The Second Circuit may have significantly narrowed the scope of *Grove* in Blake v. Commissioner, 697 F.2d 473 (2d Cir. 1982), written for a unanimous panel by the judge who dissented in *Grove*. See also Letter Rul. 8552009 (Sept. 25, 1985) for further evidence of constriction. But see Daniel D. Palmer, 62 T.C. 684 (1974), *aff'd*, 523 F.2d 1308 (8th Cir. 1975); Rev. Rul. 78-197, 1978-1 C.B. 83.

3. In Jones v. United States, 531 F.2d 1343 (6th Cir. 1976), a shareholder donated stock to a charity after the shareholders had adopted a plan of complete liquidation but before any liquidating distributions had been made. The distributions received by the charity were held taxable to the donor. See Comment, Jones v. United States: Tax Treatment of Gifts of Stock in a Liquidating Corporation, 125 U. Pa. L. Rev. 682 (1977).

4. Corporation X had 180 shares outstanding, owned equally by A and B. A and B each donated 13 shares to charity. The following day, X redeemed 27 shares from each, leaving each with 39.68 percent of the voting stock, less than 80 percent of the proportion each had owned before. The Service held that the transaction qualified as a substantially disproportionate redemption under §302(b)(2). See Letter Rul. 8027027 (Apr. 10, 1980).

5. Compare John D. Gray, 56 T.C. 1032 (1971), where taxpayers controlled two corporations, A and B. The assets of A consisted of cash and preferred stock of B. Taxpayers sold their A stock to outside interests, under an agreement that obligated B to redeem its preferred stock promptly after the sale. The court held that the transaction would be treated as a complete liquidation of A followed by redemption of the B preferred in the taxpayers' hands. The "redemption" proceeds were taxable as dividends. The Court of Appeals

rejected this characterization, but held that the redemption of the B preferred from A occurred prior to the sale of the A stock (possibly resulting in constructive dividends to the taxpayers under §551 because A was a foreign personal holding company). See Gray v. Commissioner, 561 F.2d 753 (9th Cir. 1977), *on remand,* 71 T.C. 719 (1979), *acq.* 1979-2 C.B. (§551 applied).

vi.   Redemptions by Related Corporations — §304

1. Prior to 1950 the Commissioner was unsuccessful in his effort to treat as a distribution essentially equivalent to a dividend the purchase by a subsidiary corporation of a portion of the stock held by the shareholder of its parent corporation. See John Rodman Wanamaker, Trustee, 11 T.C. 365 (1948), *aff'd per curiam,* 178 F.2d 10 (3d Cir. 1949). To meet this problem Congress in 1950 enacted the statutory predecessor of §304(a)(2).

2. Prior to 1954 the Commissioner was unsuccessful in his effort to treat as a distribution essentially equivalent to a dividend the purchase by Corporation A (wholly owned by X) of part of X's stock in Corporation B (wholly owned by X). See, e.g., Emma Cramer, 20 T.C. 679 (1953); Rev. Rul. 59-97, 1959-1 C.B. 684, revoking Rev. Rul. 55-15, 1955-1 C.B. 361. To meet this problem Congress in 1954 enacted §304(a)(1).

3. X owns all the stock of Corporation M, which owns all the stock of Corporation N. Corporation N has no earnings and profits; Corporation M has ample earnings and profits. Corporation N purchases one half of X's stock in M. Might dividend treatment attend the distribution? What would the result be if N had ample earnings and profits and M had none?

4. X owns all the stock of Corporations A and B. B purchases one half of X's stock in A. A has ample earnings and profits; B has none. Might the distribution be treated as a dividend? What would the result be if A had no earnings and profits but B's were ample?

5. Y owns all the stock in Corporations D and E. E buys all Y's stock in D. The distribution is treated as a dividend. What becomes of Y's basis in his D stock? The last sentence of §304(a)(1) suggests a rule by which the basis of the acquired stock in the hands of the acquiring corporation may be determined. Does that rule also apply to §304(a)(2) transactions? See Broadview Lumber Co. v. United States, 561 F.2d 698 (7th Cir. 1977).

6. Under §351 if a person contributes assets to a controlled corporation and receives stock of that corporation in exchange, he realizes no current income. See Chapter 3. Suppose A owns all of the stock in two corporations, X and Y. A contributes all of his X stock to Y in exchange for long-term Y Corp. bonds. Will this be

treated as a redemption for purposes of §302? See §304(b)(3). In a recent case, Camaano v. Commissioner, 1989-2 U.S.T.C. ¶9464 (5th Cir. 1989), *aff'g* Bhada, 89 T.C. 959 (1987), the court held that, because of §317(a), if a corporation takes stock in exchange for its stock, under §304(a) it has not returned "property" for the stock it acquires. As a result, §304 does not apply. What then is the significance of §304(b)(3)?

7. To test an acquisition under §304(a), one applies a modified version of the §318(a) attribution rules (§304(b)(1)). Suppose A, to satisfy §302(b)(3), enters into an agreement under §302(c)(2) not to acquire an interest in a corporation of which he was previously a shareholder. If, by application of the attribution rules to §304, A is considered to have acquired stock in the corporation, will he have violated his agreement? See Rev. Rul. 88-55, 1988-2 C.B. 45.

8. See B. Bittker and J. Eustice, Federal Income Taxation of Corporations and Shareholders 9-53 to 9-60 (5th ed. 1987); Axelrod, Section 304, Excess Loss Accounts and Other Consolidated Return Gallimaufry, Tax Notes, August 17, 1987, p. 279; Tiger, Redemptions Through Use of Related Corporations: New and Old Problems Under Section 304, 39 Tax L. Rev. 77 (1984).

COYLE v. UNITED STATES
415 F.2d 488 (4th Cir. 1968)

Before Sobeloff, Craven and Butzner, Circuit Judges.

SOBELOFF, Circuit Judge. Our task in this tax refund case is . . . to determine whether the proceeds from a transfer of corporate stock are to be taxed as capital gains or ordinary income. The District Court ruled that money which the taxpayer received in exchange for the shares of a corporation he controlled to a corporation wholly owned by his sons should be treated as a capital gain. We disagree and reverse the judgment.

In 1958, taxpayer George L. Coyle, Sr. (now deceased) transferred 66 shares of Coyle & Richardson, Inc. [hereinafter referred to as C & R] to Coyle Realty Company [hereinafter referred to as Realty] for $19,800. Reporting a long-term capital gain on this "sale," Coyle paid a tax computed at that rate on $9,900, which is the difference between the sale price and his basis in the stock. The Internal Revenue Service was of the view that the proceeds should be treated as a dividend and assessed the taxpayer an additional $7,181.90 plus interest. . . .

Before the transaction, the 688 outstanding shares of C & R were distributed in the following manner: taxpayer, 369; taxpayer's three sons, an aggregate of 288; taxpayer's wife, 1; O. M. Buck, 25; Julia

Farley, 5.[1] Thus, taxpayer and his immediate family owned more than 95.6% of the corporation whose shares were sold. Realty, the acquiring corporation, was owned in equal parts by taxpayer's three sons. . . . Although the taxpayer had once held one share of Realty, he had no stock in it when the transaction under inquiry took place.

The initial point of controversy is whether the purchase by Realty is to be treated as a sale or as a redemption. Section 304 of the Internal Revenue Code of 1954, . . . provides in pertinent part:

> (a) Treatment of certain stock purchases.
> (1) Acquisition by related corporation.
> [I]f (A) one or more persons are in control of each of two corporations and (B) in return for property, one of the corporations acquires stock in the other corporation from the person . . . so in control, then . . . such property *shall be treated as a distribution in redemption* of the stock of the corporation acquiring such stock. . . . (Emphasis added.)

Control is defined in §304(c)(1) as at least 50% of the combined voting power of all voting stock or at least 50% of the total value of all classes of stock. For purposes of determining control, §304(c)(2) specifically makes applicable the constructive ownership provisions of §318. . . . Under that section, "an individual shall be considered as owning the stock owned, directly or indirectly, by or for . . . his children. . . ."

Thus, applying the statute literally, taxpayer was in control of both corporations and the acquisition from him by Realty of the C & R stock must be treated as a redemption. His control of C & R results from his actual ownership of 54% of its outstanding stock, not to mention the attribution to him of his sons' 40%. He had 100% control of Realty by virtue of the fact that all of his sons' stock is attributable to him. The District Court recognized and the taxpayer concedes, as he must, that a plain meaning application of Sections 304 and 318 requires this conclusion.

However, the District Court eschewed this direct approach. The court reasoned that since the taxpayer actually owned no shares in Realty, there should be no attribution to him and thus the transaction here was not one between related corporations. Its conclusion then was that the transfer should not be deemed a redemption but a simple sale entitled to long-term capital gain treatment.

This interpretation of the constructive ownership rules is at war with both the language of the statute and legislative purpose of the Congress. The family attribution rules, which are specifically pre-scribed by the statute, were designated to create predictability for the

---

1. Buck and Farley are unrelated to the Coyle family as far as the record shows. Their insignificant holdings in C & R play no part in this case.

tax planner and to obviate the necessity of a court's scrutinizing family arrangements to determine whether every family member is in fact a completely independent financial entity. An authoritative study of the subject begins: "The rules of constructive ownership rest on certain assumptions which are readily supported in the everyday conduct of affairs. . . . Tax administration would be severely handicapped if the rules applied only as presumptions. . . ." Ringel, Surrey & Warren, Attribution of Stock Ownership in the Internal Revenue Code, 72 Harv. L. Rev. 209 (1958). Yet despite the clear congressional judgment and mandate that the shares of a son are to be treated as his father's for certain limited purposes, the court below read the explicit language as no more than a presumption and then disregarded it.

The statute does not require that a person be an actual shareholder in a corporation before shares in that corporation may be attributed to him. In a recent Second Circuit case, Levin v. Commissioner, 385 F.2d 521 (1967), the court attributed 100% ownership to a mother who had redeemed all her shares of a corporation whose sole remaining shareholder was her son. Similarly, an example given in the Federal Tax Regulations unquestionably assumes that one holding no stock in a corporation may nevertheless constructively own 100% of its shares. 26 C.F.R. §1.304-2.[2] Indeed, any other construction would be untenable. Under the District Court's reading, if the taxpayer had retained at the time of the transfer his otherwise insignificant single share in Realty, then 100% of the stock of that corporation could be attributed to him. Clearly such a distinction could not have been proposed by the Congress.

Appellee urges upon us that at least one anomaly will flow from holding the instant transaction subject to §304. Subsection (a)(1) provides that the stock acquired from the person or persons in control shall be treated as a contribution to the capital of the acquiring corporation. It is asserted that since only a shareholder makes contributions to capital and since taxpayer was not an actual shareholder of Realty, the stock acquired from him cannot realistically be so treated. The short answer is that appellee's underlying premise is fallacious. Non-shareholders may and do make contributions to capital, and the Internal Revenue Code recognizes this fact. See §362(c); see also Brown Shoe Co. v. Commissioner of Internal Revenue, 339 U.S. 583 (1950). Moreover, the law requires that the stock only be

---

2. Example [4] in Treas. Reg. §1.304-2[(c)] reads: "Corporation X and corporation Y each have outstanding 100 shares of common stock. H, an individual, W, his wife, S, his son, and G, his grandson, each own 25 shares of stock of each corporation. H sells all of his 25 shares of corporation X to corporation Y. . . . [B]oth before and after the transaction H owned directly and constructively 100 percent of the stock of corporation X. . . ." 26 C.F.R. §1.304-2[(c)].

"treated" for certain tax purposes as a contribution to capital by a person who is "treated" as a shareholder. Just as the transfer is directed by statute to be "treated" like a redemption when in fact the issuing corporation does not get its stock back, so this stock may be "treated" as a capital contribution even though it does not come from an actual shareholder. It should be stressed that appellee raises no specter of adverse effects from treating the shares as a capital contribution either on the non-shareholder or the corporation. The only point made is that the Code's treatment, as applied here is "economically unrealistic." This is simply too thin a reed with which to bring down the clear statutory scheme.

Nor is there merit in appellee's contention that simply because the Treasury Regulations[3] and portions of the legislative history[4] speak interchangeably of the person in control as "taxpayer" or "shareholder," the section may not be applied if the person deemed in control of both corporations is not an actual shareholder in both. It is, of course, true that ordinarily the person transferring stock in a §304 case will be a shareholder in the acquiring corporation. The Regulations and Committee Reports were simply addressing themselves to the commonplace transaction. Merely because these interpretative aids do not envision an insubstantial wrinkle on the same fundamental pattern is no adequate ground for holding uncovered that which is clearly within the statute.

. . . The case before us involves two close corporations owned by the same family and a transfer by the head of that family of stock in one of the corporations to the other. This is precisely the situation which §304 was meant to govern.

Since the District Court held redemption treatment unwarranted, it did not reach the second question to which we now turn: Is the redemption here to be treated as an exchange of stock and thus subject only to a capital gains tax or is it to be treated as a dividend and taxed at ordinary income rates?

Section 302(b) . . . enumerates those categories of redemptions which are to be treated as exchanges. Both sides agree that the only pertinent category in this case is the most general one, (b)(1), which provides that a redemption shall be treated as an exchange if it "is not essentially equivalent to a dividend."

Determination of dividend equivalency requires a factual inquiry into the circumstances of each case. See Ballenger v. United States of America, 301 F.2d 192 (4th Cir. 1962). Ordinarily, then, we would

3. See, e.g. Treas. Reg. §1.304-2 which assumes that the taxpayer is an actual shareholder in the acquiring corporation.
4. See S. Rep. No. 1622 83d Cong. 2d Sess. (1954) 3 U.S. Code Cong. & Ad. News 4876 (1954); H. Rep. No. 1337, 83d Cong., 2d Sess. (1954), 3 U.S. Code Cong. & Ad. News 4062 (1954).

remand for further evidentiary hearings. However, in this case, which was submitted on stipulated facts, both the Government and the taxpayer's estate concur that no remand is necessary. For this reason, as well as the relative simplicity of the facts here, this court proceeds to adjudicate the issue of dividend equivalence.

On this question, appellee's sole contention is that a payment by a corporation to a non-shareholder may not be characterized as a dividend. With this we agree, for §316 defines a "dividend" as "any distribution of property made by a corporation to its *shareholders*" out of earnings and profits. (Emphasis added.) The rub is that §304(b)(1) specifically states: ". . . determinations as to whether the acquisition is, by reason of section 302(b), to be treated as a distribution in part or full payment in exchange for the stock shall be made by reference to the stock of the *issuing corporation*." (Emphasis added.) Thus, in determining whether this redemption was essentially equivalent to a dividend, we must focus attention upon C & R, of which taxpayer was not only a shareholder but by far the major one.[5]

Although several tests have been devised and several factors exalted in determining whether a redemption is not in essence a dividend, we think there is one overriding objective criterion — a significant modification of shareholder interests. See Moore, Dividend Equivalency — Taxation of Distribution in Redemption of Stock, 19 Tax L. Rev. 249 (1964). . . . If the taxpayer's control or ownership of the corporation is basically unaltered by the transaction, then the proceeds he has received as a result of manipulating his corporate stock must be taxed as a dividend. See Commissioner v. Berenbaum, 369 F.2d 337 (10th Cir. 1966).

In examining the respective shareholder interests of C & R before and after the transfer of stock, we must bear in mind that §302(c)(1) explicitly makes applicable to this inquiry the constructive stock ownership rules of §318. Thus, before the transfer, taxpayer is deemed to have owned not only the 369 shares of C & R actually in his name but also the 288 shares owned by his sons and the one share held by his wife. [See §318(a)(1)(A)(ii) and (i).] In all, for purposes of §302, taxpayer before the transaction owned 658 of C & R's 688 outstanding shares. After the transaction, he held only 303 shares in his own name, but in addition, of course, he also is deemed to have owned the 289 shares of his wife and sons. Moreover, the 66 shares now held by Realty must likewise be attributed to him. Section 318(a)(2)(C) provides that stock owned by a corporation will be attributed proportionately to any person owning 50% or more of the corporation. Section 304(b)(1) directs that in applying the construc-

5. Available earnings and profits are to be reckoned by reference to the acquiring corporation. §304(b)(2)(A). Appellee admits that Realty's earnings and profits were adequate to cover the distribution in this case.

tive ownership rules for testing whether a redemption is an exchange or a dividend, the 50% requirement of §318(a)(2)(C) shall not be applicable. In the instant case, this means that the 66 shares held by Realty shall be attributed equally to its owners, taxpayer's sons, and under §318(a)(1)(A)(ii), these shares are attributed from the sons to the taxpayer. Consequently, after the transaction taxpayer owned 658 shares of C & R, precisely the number with which he started.

As noted in Wiseman v. United States, 371 F.2d 816, 818 (1st Cir. 1967), "the real question is what was accomplished by this transaction." The answer here is that while corporate ownership and control remained the same, taxpayer, the major shareholder, had come into possession of $19,800. This was essentially nothing but a dividend and was properly taxed as such.

One tangential difficulty arising from this disposition of the case is the proper allocation of taxpayer's basis in the 66 transferred shares. This potential problem is not before us at this time, but we note in passing that there are at least two reasonable solutions. Ordinarily, when there is an acquisition by a related corporation the controlling person is a shareholder in both, and the basis of his stock in the acquiring corporation is increased by his basis in the stock transferred by him. See Treas. Reg. 26 C.F.R. §1.304-2. In this case, since taxpayer held no shares in Realty, such an approach is not feasible. However, it would be consonant with the underlying rationale of this approach to increase pro rata the basis of the sons' shares in Realty. In Levin v. Commissioner, supra at 528 n.29, where the taxpayer had redeemed all of her shares in the corporation but had not sufficiently severed relations with it to avoid dividend equivalence treatment, the Court said: "Her basis does not disappear; it simply is transferred to her son." As an alternative to increasing the basis of taxpayer's sons in Realty, taxpayer's own basis in his remaining 303 shares of C & R could be augmented by his basis in the 66 transferred shares. In any event, it is clear that taxpayer's basis will not disappear.

To sum up, we construe this transaction as a redemption under §304(a) and find that this redemption was essentially equivalent to a dividend under §302(b). Therefore, we reverse the judgment of the District Court and enter judgment in favor of the Government.

Reversed.

NOTES

1. In Rev. Rul. 70-496, 1970-2 C.B. 74, Corporation X owned 70 percent of Corporation Y and 100 percent of Corporation Z; Y in turn owned 100 percent of Corporation S. Y sold all of its S stock to Z. Y was held to own, directly and by attribution, 100 percent of

both S and Z before and after the sale. By virtue of §§302 and 304, therefore, the sale had the effect of the payment of a dividend from Z to Y and a contribution of capital from Y to Z. Since Y owned no Z stock directly, its basis in the S stock disappeared. The Ruling observes: "However, Y now has additional cash." Is this persuasive support for the disappearance of basis?

2. Section 304(b)(2) states that in an acquisition to which §304(a) applies, "the determination of the amount which is a dividend . . . shall be made as if the property were distributed by the acquiring corporation . . . and then by the issuing corporation." What is the effect of this provision on the issuing corporation? After one or two contrary starts the courts have refused to treat the issuer as having received an actual distribution in order to tax it on receipt of a dividend. *Compare* Union Bankers Insurance Co., 64 T.C. 807 (1975), *acq.*, 1976-2 C.B. 3, *with* Broadview Lumber Co. v. United States, 561 F.2d 698 (7th Cir. 1977). See Rev. Rul. 80-189, 1980-2 C.B. 106 (accepting *Broadview Lumber*).

3. In Rev. Rul. 89-57, 1989-17 I.R.B. 4, the Service ruled that in determining whether the control test of §304(a)(1)(A) is satisfied, the value test of §304(c)(1) will be applied to the aggregate of all classes of a corporation's stock and not on a class-by-class basis.

4. In Rufus K. Cox, 78 T.C. 1021 (1982), taxpayers sold all of their stock in one controlled corporation to another for notes of the latter. The transaction was within §304(a)(1) but produced capital gain, not ordinary income, because there were no earnings and profits in the acquiring corporation, as the then existing §304(b)(2)(A) required. Nevertheless, the taxpayers were denied the right to report their gain on the installment method under §453 because, according to the court, a §304(a)(1) transaction is not a "sale." Accord, Brams v. Commissioner, 734 F.2d 290 (6th Cir. 1984).

CITIZENS BANK & TRUST CO. v. UNITED STATES
580 F.2d 442 (Ct. Cl. 1978)

PER CURIAM [The court adopted the decision of the trial judge.]

MILLER, Trial Judge. This is a suit for refund of $224,849.70 in income taxes and interest paid for the year 1960 as a result of a deficiency assessment. .

Plaintiff, John D. MacArthur (John), has at all pertinent times been the sole shareholder, chairman of the board of directors and chief executive officer of Bankers Life and Casualty Company (Bankers), an insurance company. Telfer MacArthur (Telfer), plaintiff's brother, was experienced in the printing and publishing business and was president of Pioneer Publishing Company (Pioneer).

In its operations Bankers required a considerable amount of

printed materials, such as applications, medical forms, advertising circulars, and policies. Up to 1950 it printed some of such materials itself, in the basement of its home office, and purchased others from various printing companies, including companies owned and operated by Telfer. During 1950, Telfer and plaintiff agreed to form a corporation, Brookshore Company, which they would jointly own and which would supply Bankers' printing needs at standard going rates. Telfer agreed to manage, staff and supervise Brookshore, and John agreed to furnish most of its capital and to have Bankers purchase its printing needs from it. . . .

In 1957, after Telfer had suffered a heart attack, he proposed to John that they enter into a mutual buy-out agreement. This agreement, executed June 29, 1957, acknowledged that they equally owned 2,235 of the outstanding 2,455 shares of Brookshore, and also all of the shares of Mackley Realty Company (Mackley), which they contributed to Brookshore. They agreed that upon the death of either, his estate was to sell his interest in Brookshore to the survivor and the survivor agreed to purchase such interest from the estate, at a stated price which increased with the passage of time prior to the date of death, with a maximum of $200,000 in the event death occurred after January 10, 1960.

Telfer died January 29, 1960. On February 10, 1960, John wrote to Telfer's widow, Elizabeth, —

> As you undoubtedly know, Telfer insisted that I buy his half of Brookshore in the event of his death. I have every intention of keeping faith with him. When you make your final selection of a lawyer and qualify as executrix, let somebody in my office know and I will arrange to make the payment.

. . . While never expressly repudiating its rights and obligations under the 1957 agreement, the representatives of the estate were not receptive to the $200,000 offer. Their reasons included the following:

(a) They believed that one-half of Brookshore . . . was worth a great deal more than $200,000.

(b) They wanted additional idemnity agreements from John against various liabilities which the estate might incur, and they did not want to deal with Bankers because of the belief that an insurance company could not properly enter into an indemnity agreement, and

(c) They also wanted John to purchase from the estate for additional consideration Telfer's stock interest in Pioneer.

On March 24, 1960, an agreement was entered into between Elizabeth, individually and as executrix under Telfer's will, and John. Elizabeth was to deliver all of the shares of Brookshore to John or upon his written direction. In return, John was to pay concurrently to Elizabeth $200,000 and to release, indemnify and hold harmless

Elizabeth and Telfer's estate against any loss arising out of any claims by himself, by the various corporations, and by Telfer's former wife. In addition, Elizabeth agreed forthwith to deliver to John or upon his written direction the remaining shares of Pioneer, which the estate owned, in exchange for an additional $175,000. The agreement was also approved by representatives of Bankers [and] Brookshore . . . to indicate their approval of the releases.

On the same day, pursuant to the agreement, Bankers issued a check in the sum of $375,000 to a bank and the latter in turn issued a cashier's check in the same amount payable to the estate of Telfer. [John's attorney], on behalf of Bankers, delivered the check to Elizabeth's attorneys, and she deposited it in the estate's account. In return, Elizabeth's attorneys delivered the . . . shares to Bankers.

It is stipulated that $200,000 of the $375,000 was for the Brookshore . . . shares and that the fair-market-value of such shares was at least $244,000.

The Commissioner of Internal Revenue determined that because the $200,000 payment satisfied John's obligation in the same amount and because Bankers had earnings and profits in excess of $200,000, Banker's payment in that amount constituted a dividend to John. . . .

In support of its position defendant relies on two cases, Sullivan v. United States, and Wall v. United States, 164 F.2d 462 (4th Cir. 1947). [Summary of *Sullivan* omitted.]

In *Wall*, plaintiff was one of two equal shareholders. Plaintiff purchased the shares of the other shareholder for a cash down payment plus promissory notes payable in 10 successive years, with the stock to be held by trustees as security for the notes but otherwise for the benefit of plaintiff. After only a single year, the corporation assumed payment of the annual liability on the notes. Plaintiff transferred to the corporation his equity in the stock held by the trustees and the corporation entered such stock on its books as treasury stock. The court upheld the Government's position that the annual payments represented dividend income to plaintiff because (at 464) — "[t]he transaction is regarded as the same as if the money had been paid to the taxpayer and transmitted by him to the creditor; and so if a corporation, instead of paying a dividend to a stockholder, pays a debt for him out of its surplus, it is the same for tax purposes as if the corporation pays a dividend to a stockholder, and the stockholder then utilizes it to pay his debt."

Neither of these decisions is authority for the defendant's position herein. They do support the idea that a corporation's satisfaction of its stockholder's debt gives him an economic benefit; but defendant ignores the fact that a payment to or for the benefit of a stockholder is not the only element of a dividend. A dividend also necessitates a distribution of corporate earnings and profits.

I.R.C. §316. Therefore, an exchange of assets of equal value which does not reduce corporate net worth cannot be a distribution of earnings and profits and hence is not a dividend.

This was made clear in Palmer v. Commissioner of Internal Revenue, 302 U.S. 63, 69-70 . . . (1937), wherein the Court stated:

> While a sale of corporate assets to stockholders is, in a literal sense, a distribution of its property, such a transaction does not necessarily fall within the statutory definition of a dividend. For a sale to stockholders may not result in any diminution of its net worth and in that case cannot result in any distribution of its profits.
>
> [T]he bare fact that a transaction, on its face a sale, has resulted in a distribution of some of the corporate assets to stockholders, gives rise to no inference that the distribution is a dividend within the meaning of §[316]. To transfer it from one category to the other, it is at least necessary to make some showing that the transaction is in purpose or effect used as an implement for the distribution of corporate earnings to stockholders.

While the issue in *Palmer* was whether or not a sale of corporate property to stockholders resulted in a dividend to them, the principles underlying the decision are equally applicable to an exchange of property arising out of a purchase by a corporation. Both the courts and the Commissioner of Internal Revenue have ruled that a corporate payment of money or property to a stockholder to acquire corporate assets at a fair price does not reduce earnings and profits and is not a dividend. . . .

For the same reasons, a corporation's assumption and payment of its stockholder's obligation to purchase from a third person an asset of equal or greater value cannot be deemed a dividend to the stockholder if the corporation acquires the asset. Just such a case was presented in Easson v. Commissioner of Internal Revenue, 294 F.2d 653 (9th Cir. 1961). There the taxpayer owned real property which was encumbered by a mortgage with respect to which the taxpayer was personally liable on the underlying notes. He transferred the property subject to the mortgage to a corporation in exchange for all its stock, but remained personally liable on the notes. The Commissioner contended that when the corporation made payments on the mortgage notes the taxpayer in effect received dividend income because such payments discharged taxpayer's legal obligation. The court rejected that contention with the following explanation (at 661):

> While the corporation may incidentally have benefited taxpayer by reducing the mortgage, it is clear that the corporation did not thereby distribute any assets. The corporation owned the apartment subject to the mortgage and as the mortgage decreased its equity in the apartment house increased. Thus when it took money out of cash and applied that amount to the mortgage, its

net worth remained constant. Its total assets were unchanged because the credit to the cash account was offset by a corresponding debit to the fixed assets account.

And see also Stout v. Commissioner of Internal Revenue, 273 F.2d 345 (4th Cir. 1959).

Sullivan and *Wall* are distinguishable from the other cases discussed by the fact that the corporations there received no property in exchange for paying their stockholders' obligations. Because they received only their own stock, their net worth was reduced and they had to deplete their earnings and profits to make the payments. In substance, the transactions were stock redemptions in favor of the plaintiffs which were essentially equivalent to dividends and hence taxable as such. . . . In *Sullivan*, as the extract from the opinion previously quoted shows, the court stated that it was a relevant fact that corporation's assets were decreased by its payment. In *Wall*, the taxpayer argued that because the shares acquired by virtue of the payments were kept in the corporate treasury they remained assets, but the court responded that irrespective of whether or not they were kept in the treasury . . . "[a]s a practical matter, such shares are redeemed in the sense that they no longer constitute any liability of the corporation but represent nothing more than an opportunity to acquire new assets by a reissuance."

Since in return for the $200,000 payment to Telfer's estate Bankers received shares of Brookshore which had an agreed fair-market-value of at least $244,000, it is concluded that Bankers did not distribute any of its earnings and profits by virtue of having satisfied plaintiff's obligation to make such a purchase. . . . Indeed, the undisputed testimony was that Telfer's estate, the sellers, maintained in the negotiations that the $200,000 plaintiff offered was less than the fair value of their Brookshore shares and sought to avoid their agreement to sell them to plaintiff at such price. Thus it can hardly he said that plaintiff was benefited by being relieved of an "obligation," "liability" or "debt" in the onerous sense which those terms ordinarily connote.

Defendant argues alternatively that the $200,000 payment to Telfer's estate was a dividend pursuant to I.R.C. §304. . . .

Plaintiff and defendant agree that subsection 304(a)(1) is designed to prevent a stockholder who controls two corporations from drawing off accumulated corporate earnings through the device of selling part of his stock in one corporation to the other. Plaintiff had controlling interests in both corporations. Defendant contends that the 1960 transaction was the constructive equivalent of plaintiff obtaining the remaining 50 percent of Brookshore shares from Telfer's estate and then selling them to Bankers in return for Bankers assuming and paying plaintiff's obligation for the purchase price.

To apply section 304 in this manner would be to distort rather than to further the statutory purpose. The entire focus of the section is on closing a loophole. Sales proceeds received by a stockholder from a controlled corporation should be treated as dividend income rather than return of capital or capital gain if what the corporation acquires is nothing more than the stock of another corporation the same stockholder controls; for, under such circumstances, the sale is only a transfer from one pocket to another.

An obvious prerequisite for invoking subsection 304(a)(1) is that the stockholder must have received the sales proceeds. Here, however, when the transaction was completed the $200,000 sales proceeds were received by a third person, Telfer's estate, and not by plaintiff. The superseding of plaintiff's obligation to buy the stock at less than fair-market-value was not an assumption of a liability nor a benefit to plaintiff. It was a mere incident to Banker's payment and the estate's receipt of the purchase price.

Another prerequisite for application of the statute is that the stockholder must have owned the stock before the transfer; or else the corporation cannot have acquired it from him, but must have acquired it from a third person. . . . Here, however, plaintiff did not own the additional 50 percent stock interest in Brookshore which was the subject of the acquisition by Bankers. Telfer's estate owned the shares and would not convey them to anyone until it received at least $200,000 in cash for them. Since it was Bankers and not plaintiff which paid the $200,000, there is no basis for imputing to plaintiff acquisition of the shares for himself or ownership at any time. Thus, Bankers necessarily acquired them from a third person and not from plaintiff.

It is concluded, therefore, that plaintiff is entitled to judgment. . . .

vii. Redemptions Following Death — §303

X owned all the stock in Corporation M. On X's death, his stock is worth $1 million. M redeems 30 percent of the stock from X's estate for $300,000. If the distribution is within §303(a), what is the tax consequence to X's estate? Why? What is the tax consequence if the redemption occurs one year after death when 30 percent of the stock is worth and is redeemed for $325,000? Why? What might the tax consequences be in each instance if §303(a) covered only $275,000 of the distribution? In considering these problems under §303, keep in mind the implications of §1014.

What policy objectives does the adoption of §303 probably reflect? Do you support those objectives and the §303 technique for achieving them? Why?

For the interaction of §303 with former §6166 (now §6166A) (allowing election to pay estate taxes in installments), see Rev. Rul. 72-188, 1972-1 C.B. 383.

c. Partial Liquidations — §302(b)(4) and (e)

Until 1982 the tax consequences of partial liquidations were governed by §§331 and 346. In that year Congress moved the rules governing partial liquidations to §302.

ESTATE OF CHANDLER v. COMMISSIONER
22 T.C. 1158 (1954), *aff'd per curiam*, 228 F.2d 909 (6th Cir. 1955)

. . . The issue for decision is whether respondent correctly determined that a pro rata cash distribution in cancellation of half the stock of a corporation was made at such a time and in such manner as to be essentially equivalent to the distribution of a taxable dividend to the extent of accumulated earnings and profits within the purview of section 115(g), Internal Revenue Code of 1939.

FINDINGS OF FACT

. . . All of the petitioners were stockholders of Chandler-Singleton Company. . . . The capital stock of the Company consisted of 500 shares of common stock of $100 par value, all of which were outstanding until November 7, 1946. From its organization until February 28, 1946, the Company was engaged in the operation of a general department store in Maryville, Tennessee. It had a ladies' ready-to-wear department, men's department, children's department, piece goods department, and a bargain basement.

Chandler was the president and manager of the Company. At the beginning of 1944 he was in very poor health. John W. Bush was the secretary of the Company, but until 1944 he had not been particularly active in its affairs. On January 1, 1944, he became assistant manager of the Company. By profession he was a civil engineer, but at that time he was unemployed due to a change in the administration of the City of Knoxville, Tennessee. During 1944 and 1945 Chandler was sick most of the time. In his absence John W. Bush managed the department store.

John W. Bush did not like being a merchant and decided to return to engineering. In November 1945 he informed Chandler that he was resigning as manager at the end of the year. Chandler, feeling unable to manage the department store himself, decided to sell.

At a stockholders' meeting held on February 20, 1946 it was unanimously agreed that the Company should accept an offer to purchase its merchandise, furniture and fixtures, and lease. Chandler was instructed to consummate the deal. The sale was consummated and a bill of sale was executed. . . .

The Company ceased operating the department store on February 28, 1946. McArthur's Incorporated moved in that night and began operating the store the following day.

Chandler had worked hard in the department store and had no outside interest. He wanted something to do and did not want to get out of business entirely. It was planned that a ladies' ready-to-wear store would be opened by the Company to be managed by Clara T. McConnell (now Clara M. Register) who had managed the ladies' ready-to-wear department of the department store. Thirty shares of stock in the Company owned by Chandler's wife were canceled on April 5, 1946. Ten of these shares were issued to Clara McConnell on April 13, 1946, in order that she might have an interest in the Company whose store she was going to manage. A men's store, to be eventually taken over by the eldest son of John and Margaret Bush, was also contemplated. It was thought that approximately half of the assets of the Company would be needed for each of the two stores.

The charter of the Company was amended on May 18, 1946, changing the name of the Company to "Chandler's" pursuant to a resolution passed at a stockholder's meeting held on May 15, 1946.

About the first of June 1946, the Company obtained space for the ladies' ready-to-wear store about one-half block from the old department store now occupied by McArthur's Incorporated. Merchandise was purchased beginning in June; improvements were made; furniture and supplies were acquired; and the store was opened on September 23, 1946. No sales had been made by the Company between February 28, 1946, and September 23, 1946.

The ladies' ready-to-wear store was about the same size as that department in the former department store. The department store had occupied 8,000 to 9,000 square feet of floor space, had employed 10 to 20 persons, and had carried fire insurance in the amount of $65,000 on its stock and fixtures. The new store had approximately 1,800 square feet of floor space, employed 4 to 6 persons, and carried fire insurance in the amount of $10,000.

A special meeting of the stockholders was held on September 28, 1946, the minutes of which read in part as follows:

> The Chairman explained that the purpose of the meeting was to authorize partial liquidation for the following reasons:
> The old business was sold and plans were developed to go back into business, operating two stores, a ladies ready-to-wear

business and a men's store. The ladies ready-to-wear store has been opened and is now operating. Up to now, we have been unable to negotiate a lease for a suitable location, and, after considerable thought, it has been decided to abandon the idea of operating an exclusive men's shop and operate only the one store at the present time. It appears that requirements of the one store will be approximately one-half the capital now invested in Chandler's, Inc.

Upon motion of Margaret Chandler Bush, seconded by J. W. Bush, and unanimously carried, the officials were authorized and instructed to redeem from each shareholder one-half of his stock, paying therefor the book value, which is approximately $269.00 per share. Therefore they are authorized to retire one-half of each shareholder's stock at $269.00 per share and are authorized to apply to the Secretary of State for reduction of the outstanding stock from 500 shares to 250 shares of $100.00 each.

On October 29, 1946, the charter of the Company was amended and its capital stock was reduced from 500 shares of $100 par value common stock, to 250 shares of $100 par value common stock. On November 7, 1946, the 500 shares of outstanding capital stock designated "Chandler-Singleton Company" were called in and canceled. Each stockholder received 1 share of stock designated "Chandler's" and $269 in cash for each 2 shares turned in. The $269 represented the approximate book value of 1 share of Chandler-Singleton Company stock on February 28, 1946. . . .

The comparative balance sheets on December 31, 1945, on February 28, 1946, after the sale to McArthur's Incorporated, and on December 31, 1946, were as follows:

[The balance sheets showed:

	Dec. 31, 1945	Feb. 28, 1946	Dec. 31, 1946
Current Assets	$166,327.09	$150,972.87	$43,810.41
Total Assets	168,735.79	150,972.87	59,090.65
Current Liabilities	61,129.00	16,405.64	12,312.74
Net worth	107,606.79	134,567.23	46,777.91.]

A 10 percent dividend totaling $5,000 was declared on September 24, 1943. The amount of cash and United States bonds possessed by the Company at the beginning of 1946 exceeded the amount required for the current operation of the business by approximately $45,000. Between January 1 and February 28, 1946, the Company's earned surplus increased by $39,460.44, out of which the Company paid dividends in the amount of $12,500. To the extent of at least $58,027.91, the excess cash possessed by the Company prior to the November 7 distribution was not created by a reduction in the amount of capital needed to operate the Company's business.

Petitioners reported the excess of the payments received over the cost of the stock in their individual income tax returns as capital gain. Respondent treated the payments, to the extent of the earned surplus of $58,027.91, as dividends and taxed them to the petitioners as ordinary income.

The acquisition and cancellation of one-half the Company's stock in 1946 was done at such a time and in such a manner as to make the distribution and cancellation essentially equivalent to the distribution of a taxable dividend to the extent of $58,027.91.

OPINION

BRUCE, Judge. Respondent contends that the Company's pro rata distribution in redemption of half its capital stock at book value was made at such a time and in such manner as to make the distribution essentially equivalent to the distribution of a taxable dividend to the extent of earnings and profits. If respondent's contention is correct the distribution to the extent of earnings and profits loses its capital gain status acquired under section 115(c) and (i) and is treated as a taxable dividend under section 115(g)[1] of the Internal Revenue Code of 1939 as it applied in 1946.

A cancellation or redemption by a corporation of all of the stock of a particular shareholder has been held not to be essentially equivalent to the distribution of a taxable dividend. Cf. Carter Tiffany, 16 T.C. 1443; Zenz v. Quinlivan, (C.A. 6) 213 F.2d 914; Regs. 111, sec. 29.115-9. However, "A cancellation or redemption by a corporation of its stock pro rata among all the shareholders will generally be considered as effecting a distribution essentially equivalent to a dividend distribution to the extent of the earnings and profits accumulated after February 28, 1913." Regs. 111, sec. 29.115-9. Such a redemption of stock is generally considered equivalent to a dividend because it does not, as a practical matter, change the essential relationship between the shareholders and the corporation. Cf. Commissioner v. Roberts, (C.A. 4) 203 F.2d 304, *reversing* 17 T.C.

1. SEC. 115. DISTRIBUTIONS BY CORPORATIONS.

(g) REDEMPTION OF STOCK. — If a corporation cancels or redeems its stock (whether or not such stock was issued as a stock dividend) at such time and in such manner as to make the distribution and cancellation or redemption in whole or in part essentially equivalent to the distribution of a taxable dividend, the amount so distributed in redemption or cancellation of the stock, to the extent that it represents a distribution of earnings or profits accumulated after February 28, 1913, shall be treated as a taxable dividend.

1415. But, as pointed out by the regulations, a pro rata distribution is not always "essentially equivalent to the distribution of a taxable dividend" and each case depends upon its own particular circumstances. Commissioner v. Sullivan, (C.A. 5) 210 F.2d 607, *affirming* John L. Sullivan, 17 T.C. 1420. The circumstances in the instant case, however, do not warrant a finding that to the extent of earnings and profits the pro rata distribution was not essentially equivalent to a taxable dividend.

Being a question of fact, the decided cases are not controlling. However, in Joseph W. Imler, 11 T.C. 836, 840, we listed some of the factors which have been considered important, viz., "the presence or absence of a real business purpose, the motives of the corporation at the time of the distribution, the size of the corporate surplus, the past dividend policy, and the presence of any special circumstances relating to the distribution." . . .

An examination of the facts reveals that the Company had a large earned surplus and an unnecessary accumulation of cash from the standpoint of business requirement, both of which could have been reduced to the extent of earnings and profits by the declaration of a true dividend. The only suggested benefit accruing to the business by the distribution in cancellation of half the stock was the elimination of a substantial amount of this excess cash. Ordinarily such cash would be disposed of by the payment of a dividend. Coupled with the fact that the stockholders' proportionate interests in the enterprise remained unchanged, these factors indicate that section 115(g) is applicable. . . .

Petitioners seek to avoid the application of section 115(g) by contending that the cash distribution and redemption of stock did not represent an artifice to disguise the payment of a dividend but was occasioned by a bona fide contraction of business with a resulting decrease in the need for capital. While important, the absence of a plan to avoid taxation is not controlling. A distribution in redemption of stock may be essentially equivalent to a taxable dividend although it does not represent an attempt to camouflage such a dividend. . . . Whether a cancellation or redemption of stock is "essentially equivalent" to a taxable dividend depends primarily upon the net effect of the distribution rather than the motives and plans of the shareholders or the corporation. . . . Moreover, we cannot find from the present record that the reduction of taxes was not the motivating factor causing the stockholders to make a distribution in redemption of stock rather than to declare a dividend to the extent of earnings and profits.

Petitioners' primary contention is that the sale of the department store and the opening of the smaller ladies' ready-to-wear store resulted in a contraction of corporate business. This is a vital factor to be considered, but a contraction of business per se does not render section 115(g) inapplicable. L. M. Lockhart, 8 T.C. 436. Furthermore, even though it is clear that there was a diminution in the size of the Company's business, there was no contraction such as was present in Commissioner v. Sullivan, Joseph W. Imler, and L. M. Lockhart, all supra. In those cases there was a contraction of business with a corresponding reduction in the amount of capital used. Here, although the business was smaller, the amount of capital actually committed to the corporate business was not reduced accordingly. On December 31, 1945, before the sale of the department store to McArthur's Incorporated, the Company had $32,736.53 tied up in fixed assets and inventories. On December 31, 1946, after the ladies' ready-to-wear store was opened, it had $31,504.67 invested in those items. Undoubtedly the department store required larger reserves than the ladies' ready-to-wear store for purchasing inventories and carrying accounts receivable. But to the extent of earnings and profits the excess cash distributed was not created by a reduction in the amount of capital required for the operation of the business. Most of the excess cash had existed since prior to the sale of the department store and did not arise from fortuitous circumstances, as petitioners contend, but from an accumulation of earnings beyond the needs of the business. This excess could have been eliminated by the payment of a taxable dividend, and its distribution in redemption of stock was essentially equivalent to a taxable dividend.

It is true that the entire $67,250 distribution could not have been made in the form of an ordinary dividend and to some extent a redemption of stock was required. But section 115(g) applies if the distribution is only "in part" essentially equivalent to a taxable dividend, and here the distribution was essentially equivalent to a taxable dividend to the extent of earnings and profits.

Decisions will be entered for the respondent.

REVENUE RULING 67-299
1967-2 C.B. 138

Advice has been requested whether the transaction described below involves a distribution resulting from a genuine contraction of the corporate business within the meaning of section 1.346-1(a)(2) of the Income Tax Regulations.

A corporation which is engaged in the business of owning and leasing real estate adopted a plan of partial liquidation. Pursuant to the plan the corporation sold one of its operating parcels of real estate for cash. It used the sales proceeds to remodel some of its remaining parcels of real estate. Shortly thereafter, and within the same taxable year in which the plan was adopted, it distributed an amount of money equal to the sales proceeds to its shareholders in redemption of some of its stock.

Section 346(a)(2) of the Internal Revenue Code of 1954 provides that a distribution will be treated as in partial liquidation of a corporation if the distribution is not essentially equivalent to a dividend, is in redemption of a part of the stock of the corporation pursuant to a plan, and occurs within the taxable year the plan is adopted or within the succeeding taxable year. Section 1.346-1(a)(2) of the regulations states that an example of a distribution which will qualify as a partial liquidation under section 346(a)(2) of the Code is a distribution resulting from a genuine contraction of the corporate business.

In this case, the sale of one parcel of real estate was a potential contraction of the corporate business. However, the remodeling of some of the remaining property was an expansion of the corporation's business offsetting any possible contraction effected by the sale. Thus, the sale of real estate did not result in a genuine contraction of the corporate business, since the net effect of the transactions was to keep the corporate assets at the same level which existed prior to the sale.

Accordingly, the above distribution by the corporation to its shareholders does not qualify as a distribution resulting from a genuine contraction of the corporate business within the meaning of section 1.3461(a)(2) of the regulations.

NOTES

1. What would the result in *Chandler* (page 283 supra) have been if §302(b)(4) and (e) had been applicable?

2. If the corporation involved in Rev. Rul. 67-299 had used excess cash to remodel the real estate it expected to retain before selling the parcel it sold, would the Service's decision have been different? Should it be different? Is Rev. Rul. 67-299 correct? As to the concept of the "active conduct of a trade or business," see Chapter 4, pages 687-708 infra; Treas. Reg. §1.355-3. What if the corporation involved in Rev. Rul. 67-299 had reinvested only a portion of the sales proceeds, and distributed the balance? Gordon v. Commissioner, 424 F.2d 378 (2d Cir.), *cert. denied,* 400 U.S. 848 (1970), relying at least partly on the specific language of old §346(b), held that distribution of less than the entire proceeds prevents the transaction from qualifying as a partial liquidation under that subsection.

3. Corporation M has conducted two separate, active businesses for 10 years. In a distribution qualifying as a partial liquidation under

§302(b)(4), Corporation M distributes the assets of one of the businesses to its shareholders pro rata. Immediately thereafter the shareholders sell the distributed assets to X pursuant to terms negotiated prior to the distribution. What are the tax consequences to Corporation M? What might they have been prior to repeal of the *General Utilities* doctrine?

4. Do the attribution of ownership provisions of §318 apply to §302(b)(4) transactions? Should they?

REVENUE RULING 82-187
1982-2 C.B. 80

ISSUE

Is a distribution by a corporation, in August, 1982, to one of two shareholders that otherwise qualified as a distribution in partial liquidation under section 346(a)(2) of the Internal Revenue Code [predecessor to sections 302(b)(4) and 302(e)(1)] disqualified because it was not pro rata with respect to the shareholders?

FACTS

Corporation X had outstanding 100 shares of a single class of voting common stock, 90 shares of which were owned by A and 10 shares of which were owned by B, an officer of X who is not related to A. For many years X had been engaged in the manufacturing business conducted through three operating divisions of approximately equal size. Upon the discontinuance of one of X's divisions, X immediately sold most of the assets of that division to an unrelated purchaser for cash and the assumption of liabilities that had arisen in connection with the operation of that division. Within the same taxable year of the sale, a plan of partial liquidation was adopted and, in August, 1982, the net proceeds of the sale were distributed solely to A, who surrendered 30 shares of X stock for redemption. Except for the question here at issue with regard to the possible effect of a non pro rata distribution, the distribution met all of the requirements of section 346(a)(2) of the Code and regulations thereunder as a distribution in partial liquidation. Because the redemption was not one described in sections 302(b)(1), 302(b)(2), or 302(b)(3), it would not be treated as a distribution in part or full payment in exchange for the X stock under section 302(a).

LAW AND ANALYSIS

Section 346(a)(2) of the Code provides that a distribution shall be treated as in partial liquidation of a corporation if it is not essentially equivalent to a dividend, is in redemption of a part of the stock of the corporation pursuant to a plan, and occurs within the taxable year in which the plan is adopted or within the succeeding taxable year.

The legislative history of section 346(a)(2) of the Code reflects general congressional intent to apply the "not essentially equivalent to a dividend" language of section 346(a)(2) primarily to the type of then existing cases involving contractions of corporate businesses that are "characterized by what happens solely at the corporate level by reason of the assets distributed. . . ." S. Rep. No. 1622, 83d Cong., 2d Sess. 49 and 261 (1954). Consonant with the legislative history of section 346(a)(2) is section 1.346-1(a) of the Income Tax Regulations, which sets forth, as its only example of a distribution that will qualify as a distribution in partial liquidation under section 346(a)(2), a "distribution resulting from a genuine contraction of the corporate business such as the distribution of unused insurance proceeds recovered as a result of a fire which destroyed part of the business causing a cessation of a part of its activities." Thus, because it is the corporate level characterization of the transaction that is of concern, it is immaterial, for purposes of qualifying under this provision of the Code, whether the distributions made to a corporation's shareholders are or are not made pro rata.

Section 346(c) of the Code specifically contemplates non pro rata distributions qualifying as distributions in partial liquidation under section 346(a)(2) by providing that, with respect to a shareholder, the fact that a distribution qualifies under section 302(a) (relating to redemptions treated as distributions in part or full payment in exchange for stock) by reason of section 302(b) shall not be taken into account in determining whether the distribution, with respect to such shareholder, is also a distribution in partial liquidation of the corporation. For example, a corporation may distribute the net cash proceeds of a corporate contraction (that otherwise qualifies as a partial liquidation) to one of several shareholders in complete redemption of all the stock owned by that shareholder in the corporation, so that the redemption would also qualify as a distribution in full payment in exchange for the stock redeemed as provided in section 302(a) by reason of section 302(b)(3). Although section 346(c) would require that section 302(b)(3) not be taken into account, the distribution will still be treated as a qualifying distribution in partial liquidation described in section 346(a)(2) and the amounts distributed to the shareholder will be treated as in full payment in exchange for the stock redeemed under the provisions of section 331(a)(2). See also sections 1.346-2 and 1.302-l(a) of the regulations, which prescribe the preeminence of section 346 over section 302 in "overlap" cases.

In the present situation, the distribution by X to A was the result of a genuine corporate contraction. Since the distribution neither qualified for treatment as a redemption under section 302(a) of the Code by reason of section 302(b), nor was in excess of the amount available for treatment under section 331(a)(2), the entire amount of the distribution is treated as a distribution in partial liquidation within the meaning of section 346(a)(2). The legislative history of section 346 confirms that only what occurs at the corporate level is relevant in determining whether a transaction qualifies for partial liquidation treatment. Therefore, it is of no consequence, for purposes of qualification of the distribution under section 346(a)(2), that the distribution was non pro rata with respect to the shareholders.

HOLDING

A distribution by X to A that otherwise qualified as a distribution in partial liquidation under section 346(a)(2) of the Code is not disqualified for treatment under section 346(a)(2) because the distribution was made non pro rata.

NOTE

If there is a "genuine corporate contraction" in the post-TEFRA world and a nonpro-rata distribution, will the transaction fail to qualify under §302(b)(4) and (e)(1) because there is no current statutory provision corresponding to §346(c) of the pre-TEFRA era? Was it necessary or wise to hinge the result in Rev. Rul. 82-187 on old §346(c)?

BLASCHKA v. UNITED STATES
393 F.2d 983 (Ct. Cl. 1968)

Before Cowen, Chief Judge, and Laramore, Durfee, Davis, Collins, Skelton, and Nichols, Judges.
. . . Commissioner Hogenson's opinion, as modified by the court, is as follows:
Plaintiff has brought suit to recover income tax and deficiency interest for the year 1959 in the total amount of $74,344.38 plus interest. The sole question is whether a distribution of $115,000 to plaintiff by C. & C. Blaschka, Inc., was a dividend taxable as ordinary income or was a distribution in partial liquidation with the gain realized taxable as long-term capital gain.
The basic facts are not in dispute. Plaintiff and her husband, Carl J. Blaschka, are and were the sole stockholders in C. & C. Blaschka, Inc. (hereinafter referred to as C & C), plaintiff owning

approximately 92.3 percent of the stock and her husband 7.7 percent. The Blaschkas are the executive officers of C & C and, together with their accountant, comprise the board of directors. From 1955 until 1959, both plaintiff and her husband devoted full time to the business activities of C & C.

Until July 1, 1959, C & C was engaged in the wholesaling of popularly priced gloves throughout the United States. This business requires the ability to select popular glove styles, a talent demanding ingenuity and years of experience as well as a great deal of time and travel. Plaintiff and her brother-in-law did the selecting for C & C. In addition, C & C has a wholly owned Canadian subsidiary, Max Mayer & Co., Ltd. (hereinafter called Max Mayer, Ltd.), which is engaged in the wholesale glove business in Canada. C & C keeps tight control over this Canadian corporation and makes every decision of any importance for it. In return for these services, Max Mayer, Ltd. has paid C & C since 1935 an annual "administrative fee" of 3 percent of the net sales of Max Mayer, Ltd.

In 1958, after the loss of two key employees through illness and death, C & C decided to dispose of its United States glove business. By a contract effective July 1, 1959, C & C sold this business to unrelated third parties for $646,442.31, payable in notes and preferred stock. The sale included the name Max Mayer which became the name of the new corporation to which C & C transferred all the assets.

As a result of the sale, C & C had more funds than it needed. After a number of conferences involving the Blaschkas, their accountant and their attorney, it was decided that C & C would enter the real estate rental field. To that end, C & C purchased all the outstanding stock of the Clairette Manufacturing Company, Inc. (hereinafter referred to as Clairette) from its sole stockholder, Mrs. Blaschka, plaintiff herein. Since 1955, Clairette's sole business had been the renting of a building it owned to C & C for warehouse purposes. After the sale, Clairette continued to rent the building to the purchasers of C & C's United States glove business. The transaction was consummated on September 28, 1959, with the transfer by plaintiff of the entire Clairette stock in return for $115,000. It is the tax treatment of this purchase by C & C that is in dispute.

Since plaintiff owned more than 50 percent of the outstanding stock of C & C and Clairette, this sale falls within §304. . . . In essence §304(a)(1) provides that if a person is in control of each of two corporations, and, in return for property, one of the corporations acquires stock in the other corporation from that person, the property is treated as a distribution in redemption of the stock of the acquiring corporation. This provision was enacted in response to a series of unfavorable judicial decisions in which the Treasury attempted unsuccessfully to tax these transactions as distributions essentially equivalent to a dividend and therefore taxable as ordinary income under what is now §§301 and 302. . . .

The function of §304, then, is to complement §302. To that end, §304(b)(1) provides that such a sale is defined as a redemption of the stock of the acquiring corporation, and that for purposes of §302(b), whether such stock acquisition is to be treated as a distribution in exchange for the stock is determined by reference to the stock of the issuing corporation. See also Reg. 1.304-2(a); Ralph L. Humphrey, 39 T.C. 199, 205 (1962). The essential question is whether the distribution has affected the stockholder's proportionate interest and control in the issuing corporation, and for that reason the special rule of §304(b)(1) points to the issuing corporation to apply §304(a) to §302. S. Rep. No. 1622, 83d Cong., 2d Sess. 240 (1954); H.R. Rep. No. 1337, 83d Cong., 2d Sess., A79 (1954); 3 U.S.C. Cong. & Admn. News, pp. 4217, 4877 (1954). The stockholder's sale of his stock in one corporation to a related corporation could substantially change his interest in the issuing corporation, or on the other hand, be a change of form only, with no effect on the stockholder's actual control. . . . Although §304(b)(2) provides that the determination of the amount, paid in the stock redemption as defined in §304(a)(1), which is a dividend shall be made solely with reference to the earnings and profits of the acquiring corporation, no mention is made of §302(b) in that paragraph, nor is there any provision in §304[2] or elsewhere in the 1954 Code, as to which corporation is to be tested to determine whether there has been a partial liquidation in a stock redemption through use of related corporations. It is significant, however, that subsection (e) of §302, by statutory cross reference, points to §331, and this together with the considerations underlying the tax treatment of partial liquidations require that a §304 stock redemption, involving the question of a partial liquidation under §§331(a)(2) and 346, be tested on the level of the acquiring corporation. S. Rep. No. 1622, supra, at 49; U.S.C. Cong. & Admn. News, supra, at p. 4680. The very nature of a partial liquidation, at least as purportedly involved in this case, is a curtailment or contraction of the activities of the acquiring corporation, and the distribution to a stockholder of unneeded funds in exchange for stock in a related corporation. It is concluded that the purported partial liquidation is not to be measured by §302, but that the general rule of §304(a) — that the stock sale is to be treated as a redemption by the acquiring corporation — applies, subject, however, to the statutory definition as to what constitutes a

---

2. For an excellent analysis of the complexities and uncertainties of §304, with special attention to recent cases, and with recommendations for legislative and administrative clarifications, see Marans, Section 304: The Shadowy World of Redemptions Through Related Corporations, 22 N.Y.U. Tax Law Rev. 161 (1967).

partial liquidation under §§331 and 346 of the 1954 Code, applied to the acquiring corporation.

Thus, whether the payment of $115,000 by C & C for the stock of Clairette is a partial liquidation under §§331(a)(2) and 346 must be determined with respect to the activities of C & C. Section 346 provides three tests to determine whether a distribution is to be treated as a payment in partial liquidation. The first dealing with a series of distributions culminating in the complete liquidation of the corporation, is not applicable here since C & C has not and has no intention of completely liquidating. The second, §346(a)(2), provides that a distribution will be considered as a payment in partial liquidation if it is not essentially equivalent to a dividend and is made pursuant to a plan, the payments being made within 2 years of the adoption of the plan. The requirement that the payment be made pursuant to a plan is crucial here, since it is apparent that C & C never adopted a formal plan of partial liquidation. The third test concerns the provisions of §346(b), hereinafter discussed.

That a formal plan of liquidation is not required to qualify under §346 is clear. Fowler Hosiery Co. v. Commissioner, 36 T.C. 201, 218 (1961), aff'd, 301 F.2d 394, 397 (7th Cir. 1962). However, there must be clear evidence of an intention to liquidate if an informal plan is to be established. . . .

In the instant case, C & C had adopted no plan of partial liquidation, either formal or informal, when it paid $115,000 for the Clairette stock. The official minutes of C & C show that there were two special meetings of the stockholders and four special meetings of the board of directors in 1959, and no meetings of either the stockholders or the directors in 1960. Nowhere in these minutes is there any discussion or mention of a plan of partial liquidation of C & C. The corporate resolution dated September 10, 1959, which accepted Mrs. Blaschka's offer of the Clairette stock, likewise makes no mention of any partial liquidation.

Plaintiff contends, however, that the purchase of the Clairette stock was part of a plan of partial liquidation discussed and informally adopted by the directors of C & C, and that the plan was not recorded in the corporate minutes because C & C's accountant and attorney did not think it necessary. But the facts indicate otherwise. Mr. Blaschka admitted that the purchase of Clairette's stock was made only after considering the tax aspects of the transaction. To assert that legal counsel advised a partial liquidation but did not make any written record of the plan is incredulous [sic].

This is all the more so when one considers plaintiff's Notice of Protest of the tax deficiency in controversy in this suit, a nine-page memorandum filed under oath with the Internal Revenue Service. No mention is made in that document of any partial liquidation being carried out by C & C. Furthermore, C & C stated in a memorandum sent to the Internal Revenue Service in 1961 concerning accumulated earnings tax that after its sale of the United States glove business, C & C decided to enter the industrial real estate business rather than liquidate. This is substantiated by Mr. Blaschka's testimony that the purchase of Clairette, whose sole business was the renting of a warehouse, was chosen as C & C's initial entry into this new field because the warehouse was known to be a good rentable building. In view of all this evidence, it is clear that the purchase of the Clairette stock was not pursuant to a plan of partial liquidation and the transaction cannot qualify under §346(a)(2).

Nor does it come under the so-called "safe harbor" of §346(b). Under that subsection, if a corporation has been conducting two or more separate and active businesses for at least 5 years and then ceases one of the businesses, the distribution of the assets of this ceased business or the proceeds from their sale shall be treated as a payment in partial liquidation so long as after the distribution the corporation continues to conduct actively at least one of the preexisting businesses. Just what constitutes "actively engaged in the conduct of a trade or business" for purposes of §346 is defined in §1.346-1(c) of the Regulations, by incorporation of §1.355-1(c):

> [A] trade or business consists of a specific existing group of activities being carried on for the purpose of earning income or profit from only such group of activities, and the activities included in such group must include every operation which forms a part of, or a step in, the process of earning income or profit from such group. Such group of activities ordinarily must include the collection of income and the payment of expenses. [Treas. Reg. §1.355-1(c)]

Plaintiff contends that C & C's management of its wholly owned subsidiary, Max Mayer, Ltd., is a separate trade or business apart from its United States glove business, thereby qualifying the distribution of the proceeds from the sale of the United States business through the purchase of the Clairette stock as a partial liquidation.

Aside from the general definition found in the Regulation, only a few cases have considered the question of what constitutes two separate trades or businesses. What few guidelines exist are found mainly in the 16 examples contained in Reg. §1.355-1(d) and in the more than 25 rulings published by the Treasury. See McDonald, Tax Considerations in Corporate Divisions: Contraction and Liquidation, 39 Taxes (The Tax Magazine of C.C.H.) 994, 1000-1001, nn.60-63 for a complete listing of these rulings through 1961. As a result, the law has developed slowly on an ad hoc basis, with general principles not readily discernible from these factual patterns. However, common threads that run through many of these cases indicate that C

& C was not engaged in the active conduct of two separate businesses in 1959.

One factor that reappears in several of the rulings is whether each business produces a substantial part of the combined income. In Rev. Rul. 57-333, 1957-2 Cum. Bull. 239, a corporation engaged in the food brokerage business also owned an adjacent vacant lot which it leased to a used car dealer. The rental received for the land for each of the last 5 years was less than 2 percent of the total gross income of the entire business. It was ruled that the rental of the lot did not constitute a separate business for purposes of §346(b), with specific mention being made that the rental income received was only a nominal portion of the total gross income. In Rev. Rul. 56-266, 1956-1 Cum. Bull. 184, a corporation operated a retail grocery chain, manufactured and distributed bakery products, and produced and distributed creamery products, as well as owned real estate which it leased to its grocery stores for a rental based on a percentage of gross sales. The real estate activities were ruled not to be a business separate and apart from the grocery business.

Again, in Rev. Rul. 57-464, 1957-2 Cum. Bull. 244, a corporation manufactured heating equipment and owned a modern factory building, an old factory building which it used for storage purposes, and three rental properties. The real estate activities did not constitute a separate business, ruled the Treasury. Once more it was pointed out that the net income received from these properties was "negligible."

Also, in three judicial decisions all holding that two separate businesses did not exist, in which the question was whether the businesses were being *actively* conducted or not, the courts in each instance made reference to the small amount of income produced and lack of adequate record-keeping usually performed in a business. Isabel A. Elliott, 32 T.C. 283, 290-291 (1959); Theodore F. Appleby, 35 T.C. 755, 761 (1961), *aff'd per curiam*, 296 F.2d 925 (3d Cir. 1962), *cert. denied*, 370 U.S. 910 (1962); Bonsall v. Commissioner, 317 F.2d 61, 64 (2d Cir. 1963). Cf. Example (16) in Reg. §1.355-1 (d) involving a corporation that manufactured and sold automobiles and maintained an executive dining room for profit.[4]

That the underlying consideration running throughout these rulings was the sufficiency or insufficiency of income produced rather than some other factor can be seen in those rulings in which two separate businesses were found. Most striking is Rev. Rul. 58-164, 1958-1 Cum. Bull. 184. There, a corporation sold textile products as a commission merchant and owned a valuable building which it leased to outsiders for a substantial net rental. It was ruled that two separate businesses existed. Also, in Rev. Rul. 57-334, 1957-2 Cum. Bull. 240,

---

4. Each "Example" cited will be from Reg. 1.355-1(d).

a corporation rented to others three separate parcels of real estate. It was ruled that rental of one of the three buildings involved constituted a separate business since the remaining real estate accounted for only half the corporation's income. And in Rev. Rul. 56-557, 1956-2 Cum. Bull. 199, the ruling again points to the importance of the fact that the income from the challenged business was substantial, in a determination that there were two separate businesses.

Turning to the income figures in the instant case, they reflect clearly that the services performed for Max Mayer, Ltd., by C & C produced so little income as not to be a business separate and distinct from the United States glove business. In return for these services, Max Mayer, Ltd., paid C & C an "administrative fee" of 3 percent of Max Mayer, Ltd.'s net sales, a figure set in 1935 by plaintiff's uncle. From 1952 through 1958, this *gross* administrative fee was only 1 percent of C & C's *net* sales of $13,893,677.95 for that period. Furthermore, from 1935 to 1962, C & C did not even allocate on its books the expenses attributable to the work performed for Max Mayer, Ltd. — hardly the practice of a corporation in the business of managerial and financial services. Cf. Isabel A. Elliott, supra; Theodore F. Appleby, supra; Bonsall v. Commissioner, supra. Since 1962, the Canadian authorities have required C & C to submit a detailed statement of the specific charges for its services to Max Mayer, Ltd. In 1962, out of a total administrative fee of $24,784.05, C & C earned a profit of only $751.96, or a return of approximately 3 percent. Projecting this profit margin back over the period from 1952 through 1958, C & C's total profits from administrative fees were approximately $4,261, or 1.5 percent of C & C's total net profits before taxes of $283,622 for that period. Such negligible amounts hardly meet the requirement included in Regulation §1.346-1(c) that the activities be carried on "for the purpose of earning income or profit." Treas. Reg. §1.355-1(c), supra.

The Regulations and Treasury Rulings, also, seem to require some form of separation of control and supervision to find separate businesses. In Rev. Rul. 58-54, 1958-1 Cum. Bull. 181, a corporation operated a soft drink bottling and distributing business. All the bottling was done at the main plant although it was distributed through facilities located in four different localities. The Treasury ruled that the distributing facilities did not constitute a separate business or businesses "despite some geographical differences in warehouse locations. They all formed part of one integrated business wherein the product was manufactured in one place, although distributed through several warehouse points." 1958-1 Cum. Bull. 181 at 182.

Rev. Rul. 56-451, 1956-2 Cum. Bull. 208 involved a corporation which published four trade magazines. The metal working magazine had its own editorial staff and advertising space salesmen, who devoted their entire time to this magazine. This publication had separate offices in the same building as the others and kept separate books. The only employees it shared with the others were the general officers of the corporation and certain clerical and production employees. The three other magazines served the electrical industry. The Treasury ruled that the metal working magazine was a separate business.

The Regulations provide still another example. Taxpayer corporation owns and operates two men's retail clothing stores, one in the city and one in the suburbs. The manager of each store directs its operations and makes the necessary purchases. No common warehouse is maintained. Under these circumstances the Regulations state that the activities of each store constitute a trade or business, evidently on the grounds of separate control and operation. (Example (10).)

In short, Max Mayer, Ltd., is a separate and distinct business from C & C in corporate form, but otherwise only in a geographical sense. There is some indication in the Regulations that geographical separation is enough. In Example (8), a corporation which manufactures ice cream at plants in two states is said to operate a trade or business in each state. To the same effect are Examples (13), (14), and (15). Just how these Examples relate to Example (10) supra, where geographical separation existed but where other factors were specifically mentioned, is not clear. Moreover, there is Rev. Rul. 57-190, 1957-1 Cum. Bull. 121. The facts there involved a corporation which sold and serviced cars, carrying on its operations in two buildings located some distance apart in the same city. The Treasury ruled that the separate locations were not sufficient to create separate businesses.

Thus, geographical separation by itself is of questionable significance. Also, all of the above-mentioned Examples (where apparently geographical separation was sufficient) are distinguishable from the instant case. Each Example involved a manufacturing business, manufacturing its products at several locations. Each plant was a viable entity, capable of producing the product from beginning to end. In spite of its separate corporate entity, Max Mayer, Ltd., was in no way viable by itself. Rather did it depend upon the decision of C & C for what it sold and how it sold. Before the Clairette stock sale, plaintiff owned 100 percent of the Clairette stock and 92.3 percent of the C & C stock, and C & C owned 100 percent of Max Mayer, Ltd. This control of all three corporations becomes absolute when the husband's 7.7 percent share of C & C is added. The circumstances strongly infer that in reality the "stock redemption" was equivalent to the declaration of a dividend, especially in view of the large accumulation of earned surplus by the redeeming corporation. When this factor is considered with the negligible amount of income and profits realized, the conclusion is that the management services provided by C & C to Max Mayer, Ltd., were not an "active trade or business" separate and apart from its own operations.

Therefore, the purchase of the Clairette stock by C & C was not a distribution in partial liquidation. The sum of $115,000 is deemed to be paid out of C & C's earnings and profits and taxable at ordinary income rates as a dividend pursuant to §§302 and 301(c)(1). Plaintiff's petition for a refund should be dismissed.

NOTES

1. Should §302(b)(4) and (e) be part of the Code? What justification is there for basis recovery [and capital gains treatment] for a pro rata distribution? What is the relevance of corporate business contraction in deciding at the congressional level whether a distribution should receive capital gains treatment? See Schoettle, Section 346 of the Internal Revenue Code: A Legislative Enigma, 109 U. Pa. L. Rev. 944 (1961). For the Commissioner's ruling policy on partial liquidations, see Rev. Proc. 89-3, 1989-1 I.R.B. 29.

2. In some cases discontinuance of a subsidiary's business and distribution of the subsidiary's assets (or the proceeds of sale of those assets) may result in a genuine contraction of the *parent's* business. See Rev. Rul. 75-223, 1975-1 C.B. 109, *clarified by* Rev. Rul. 77-376, 1977-2 C.B. 107; cf. Rev. Rul. 77-375, 1977-2 C.B. 106. But see Rev. Rul. 79-184, 1979-1 C.B. 143 (sale of all of the shares of a wholly owned subsidiary and pro rata distribution of the proceeds by the parent to its shareholders in redemption of a portion of their stock in the parent does not qualify under §302(b)(4) and (e) because the business "contracted" was conducted by the subsidiary and not by the parent).

Is an actual surrender of stock necessary in order to make §302(b)(4) and (e) applicable? Is it possible for a distribution by a wholly owned subsidiary to its sole corporate shareholder to qualify as a partial liquidation under §302(b)(4) and (e) if there is no redemption of the subsidiary's stock from its parent? See Rev. Rul. 79-257, 1979-2 C.B. 136 (no actual surrender required). See also Rev. Rul. 81-3, 1981-1 C.B. 618 (pro rata distribution to multiple shareholders treated as partial liquidation without actual surrender of shares).

3. For examples of the sort of corporate contraction the Internal Revenue Service considers adequate to satisfy §302(b)(4), see Rev. Rul. 74-296, 1974-1 C.B. 80. See also Rev. Rul. 74-544, 1974-2 C.B. 108; Rev. Rul. 75-3, 1975-1 C.B. 108.

4. Is §302(b)(4) "elective"? See Rev. Rul. 77-468, 1977-2 C.B. 109 (deliberate delay in making distribution, beyond period specified

in §302(e), avoids partial liquidation treatment). Cf. Rev. Rul. 77-150, 1977-1 C.B. 88.

III. SECTION 1244

Section 1244 of the Code was enacted as part of the Small Business Tax Revision Act of 1958. Its purpose is described in H.R. Rep. No. 2198, 85th Cong., 1st Sess., 1959-2 C.B. 711, as follows:

> This section provides ordinary loss rather than capital loss treatment on the sale or exchange of small-business stock. This treatment is available only in the case of an individual and only if he is the original holder of the stock.
>
> This provision is designed to encourage the flow of new funds into small business. The encouragement in this case takes the form of reducing the risk of a loss for these new funds. The ordinary loss treatment which the bill accords shareholders in small corporations in effect is already available to proprietors and partners. They report directly the earnings from these business ventures and thus ordinary losses realized by a proprietorship or partnership presently constitute ordinary losses to the proprietor or partner. As a result, from the standpoint of risk taking, this bill places shareholders in small corporations on a more nearly equal basis with these proprietors and partners.
>
> In accord with your committee's desire to limit the benefit of this provision to small business, the total stock offering of any corporation which is eligible for this ordinary loss treatment is limited to $500,000. Moreover, the total stock offering per corporation plus the equity capital of the corporation may not exceed $1 million. In addition, the maximum loss which a taxpayer can treat as an ordinary loss under this provision is to be $25,000 a year (or $50,000 in the case of a husband and wife filing a joint return).
>
> Your committee also has imposed a restriction designed to limit this tax benefit to companies which are largely operating companies. Thus, the corporation, in the 5 years before the taxpayer incurs the loss on the stock must have derived more than half of its gross receipts from sources other than royalties, rents, dividends, interest, annuities, and the sale of stock or securities. . . .

The Revenue Act of 1978 raised the maximum amount of §1244 stock that can be issued by a single corporation to $1 million, eliminated the need for a "plan" and the "equity capital" limitation of prior law, and raised the maximum amount eligible for ordinary loss treatment to $50,000 ($100,000 on a joint return).

In 1984, Congress amended §1244(c)(1) and (d)(2) by changing "common stock" to "stock." The relevant committee reports make clear that the change was designed to bring preferred stock within the ambit of §1244. See, e.g., H.R. Rep. No. 432, 98th Cong., 2d Sess. 1581 (1984). In the post-1986 world in which there is no capital gains rate preference for individuals, but in which the deductibility of capital losses remains limited, §1244 remains useful to shareholders in providing them with ordinary losses for what, in its absence, would be capital losses. You should consider whether §1244 in theme and structure represents desirable tax policy.

See generally B. Bittker and J. Eustice, Federal Income Taxation of Corporations and Shareholders 4-42 to 4-48 (5th ed. 1987).

MARVIN R. ADAMS v. COMMISSIONER
74 T.C. 4 (1980)

DAWSON, Judge. Respondent determined a deficiency of $22,995 in petitioners' Federal income tax for the year 1975.

At issue is whether petitioners can treat the loss on their corporate stock as an ordinary loss under section 1244 when the stock had been previously issued to a third party, later repurchased by the corporation which returned it to the status of authorized but unissued stock, and then resold it to petitioners.

Marvin R. Adams, Jr. and Jeanne H. Adams [are the petitioners]. . . .

In early 1973, W. Carroll DuBose (DuBose) helped found Adams Plumbing Co., Inc. (Adams Plumbing), whose offices are located in Margate, Florida. Adams Plumbing was incorporated in Florida on July 25, 1973. It had an authorized capital of 100 shares of common stock, with a par value of $1 per share. The corporate minutes show that the stock was issued to DuBose on July 25, 1973. The first officers were William R. Adams (brother of petitioner Marvin R. Adams, Jr.), president, and J. Lucille Adams, secretary.

On August 5, 1974, DuBose was elected chairman of the board of directors of Adams Plumbing and William R. Adams was elected a director. As of that date, William R. Adams was still the president of the corporation, and then also became vice president; Francine Adams was the secretary/treasurer.

On February 10, 1975, Adams Plumbing repurchased the 100 shares from DuBose. On the same day William R. Adams purchased 10 of the 100 shares of Adams Plumbing.

On February 11, 1975, the corporation, pursuant to state law, retired its remaining 90 repurchased shares to the status of authorized but unissued stock. In addition, a written plan complying with the procedural requirements of section 1244 was adopted to issue these 90 shares as section 1244 stock. The corporation at that time was a small business corporation as defined in section 1244.

On March 1, 1975, Adams Plumbing and petitioners (denominated Rodney J. Adams and Jean Adams in the agreement) entered into a sales agreement[2] for 80 of the 90 shares. Pursuant to the terms of the agreement, 80 shares of the corporate stock were issued to petitioners in their joint names on August 1, 1975. They paid $120,000 for the 80 shares. The 80 shares have been held continuously since August 1, 1975.

On August 9, 1975, the remaining 10 shares were sold to Richard F. Wynkoop and his wife, Marlene. Richard Wynkoop was a friend of petitioner Marvin R. Adams, Jr.

2.   AGREEMENT

THIS AGREEMENT made this 1st day of March, 1975, by and between ADAMS PLUMBING COMPANY, INC., a Florida Corporation, (hereinafter referred to as Corporation) and RODNEY J. ADAMS and JEAN ADAMS, husband and wife, (hereinafter referred to as Purchasers).

WHEREAS, the parties mutually agree to sell and purchase stock in the Corporation for sums and amounts and times to be set forth herein.

NOW THEREFORE, the parties mutually agree as follows:

1. The purchasers shall purchase a maximum of 80 shares of common stock in the Corporation for an amount not to exceed a total purchase price of $120,000.

2. Upon receipt of monies by the Corporation, the Directors shall issue stock to RODNEY J. ADAMS, JR. and JEAN ADAMS, husband and wife, in their joint names for $1,000 per each share of stock for the first 60 shares. The remaining 20 shares shall be purchased at $2,700 per share.

3. The Purchasers shall make payments to the Corporation for the purchase of the first 60 shares in various amounts over the next four months and shall have paid in the full purchase price for the 60 shares on or before June 20, 1975.

4. The remaining 20 shares shall be purchased over the subsequent six months at an average purchase price of $2,700 per share and the entire shares must be paid in full on or before December 31, 1975.

5. In further consideration for the sale of said shares of common stock of the Corporation, the purchasers either jointly or individually, shall loan the Corporation various sums to insure the ongoing of the Corporation not to exceed the sums of $60,000 at the prevailing interest rate in Bradenton, Florida for loans of like kind and duration. The term of this loan or any loans made under this paragraph shall not extend for more than five years and shall not be in any balloon payment form. The parties agree that the said loans that shall be made from time to time may be made by demand note or installment note of shorter duration than herein stated.

6. The parties agree that William R. Adams is to be the President of the Corporation and manage all operations of the Corporation for the benefit of the Stockholders involved in the Corporation with full authority to make contracts without restriction except as set forth in the By-Laws of the Corporation and as determined and ratified by the Board of Directors.

7. All shares that are issued to the purchasers under this Agreement shall be voted exclusively by Mr. William R. Adams and this Agreement is to serve as a proxy at any Stockholders meeting whether Special or Annual and shall represent the shares as Attorney-in-fact to act on all matters to come before the Corporation without exception under any and all conditions. This proxy expires upon written notification to the Purchasers of non-representation of shares by Mr. William R. Adams. Otherwise, this proxy shall terminate on December 31, 1975 of each year and from year to year after December 31, 1975. Renewal of this option shall be made by written notice to Mr. William R. Adams by the purchasers that the proxy is to be re-instated for the subsequent year and placed with the Corporate Record Book. . . .

An outline of the stock issued by Adams Plumbing is as follows:

Stock Certificate Number	Number of Shares	Recipient	Date of Transfer
1	100	W. Carroll DuBose*	7/25/73
2	voided	—	—
3	voided	—	—
4	10	William R. Adams	2/10/75
5	voided	—	—
6	10	Richard R. & Marlene B. Wynkoop	8/9/75
7	60	Rodney Adams, Jr. & Jean Adams***	8/1/75
8**	20	Rodney Adams, Jr. & Jean Adams***	8/1/75
9	20	Rodney Adams, Jr. & Jean Adams***	8/1/75

The common stock of Adams Plumbing became worthless in the year 1975. On their joint Federal income tax return for 1975 the petitioners claimed a loss on their investment in Adams Plumbing. They claimed $50,000 as an ordinary loss under the provisions of section 1244, and an additional $70,000 as a capital loss on worthless securities on the Schedule D attached to the return.

On April 20, 1976, Francine Adams tendered her resignation as secretary/treasurer of Adams Plumbing and William R. Adams tendered his resignation as president, vice president, and director of the corporation.

Section 1244 provided during the year involved herein that in the case of an individual a loss on "section 1244 stock" issued to such individual shall be treated as an ordinary loss to the extent of $50,000 for a husband and wife filing a joint return.

One of the elements of the definition of section 1244 stock is that the stock must be issued by the corporation, pursuant to a plan, for money or other property other than stock and securities. Section 1244(c)(1)(D). The regulations promulgated under section 1244 provide that in order to claim a deduction under section 1244 the individual "must have continuously held the stock from the date of

---

*Sold back to Adams Plumbing Co., Inc., on 2/10/75.
**This certificate is missing; joint stock certificate number 9 was issued to replace number 8.
***Rodney Adams Jr. is petitioner Marvin R. Adams, Jr. and Jean Adams is petitioner Jeanne H. Adams.

issuance." Furthermore, an individual who acquires stock from a shareholder by purchase, gift, devise, or in any other manner is not entitled to an ordinary loss under section 1244 with respect to such stock.

The stipulation of facts and the attached exhibits show that petitioners purchased common stock from Adams Plumbing, a corporation qualified as a small business corporation under section 1244. The corporation had initially sold all of its 100 authorized shares of common stock to DuBose in 1973. On February 10, 1975, the corporation repurchased the 100 shares from DuBose, and then sold 10 of the 100 shares to William R. Adams. The remaining 90 shares were retired to the status of authorized but unissued stock. On the next day, February 11, 1975, the corporation adopted a written plan under section 1244 to issue the 90 shares.

On March 1, 1975, petitioners contracted to buy 80 shares of the corporation's common stock with the consideration to be paid before December 31, 1975. The purchase contract provided that the parties agreed that Marvin's brother, William R. Adams, was president of the corporation, managed all operations and that the petitioners' stock was to be voted exclusively by William R. Adams on all matters under any and all conditions.

On August 1, 1975, the corporation issued two certificates of stock to petitioners pursuant to the contract: one certificate for 60 shares and the other for 20 shares. Petitioners held these shares in their joint names continuously from August 1, 1975. The stock became worthless in December, 1975.

On these facts the petitioners argue that they are entitled to ordinary loss treatment under section 1244 on their stock because section 1244(a), section 1244(c)(1)(D) and section 1.1244(a)-1(b), Income Tax Regs. state only that the stock must be issued to an individual and such individual must hold the stock continuously from the date of issuance. Petitioners contend that they have in fact held stock issued by the corporation continuously from the date of issuance to the date of loss. They argue that it is irrelevant that DuBose held all the stock of the corporation prior to its resale back to the corporation and that the corporation retired the stock from treasury stock into authorized but unissued stock.

Because neither the Internal Revenue Code nor the regulations expressly prohibit, or even address, shares which were previously issued to a third party, then reacquired by the corporation, and retired to the status of authorized but issued, from being eligible for section 1244 stock, petitioners contend that the loss incurred qualifies for section 1244 treatment. They assert that to require a corporation to have additional shares authorized, rather than using authorized but unissued shares which have been retired from treasury shares, would be a useless and needless act for section 1244 eligibility and is not specifically required by the law or the regulations.

Stock bought from a stockholder does not qualify as section 1244 stock. Section 1244(c)(1); section 1.1244(a)-1(b), Income Tax Regs. Petitioners argue that a corporation which sells authorized but unissued stock which had been retired from treasury stock is not a shareholder for the purposes of section 1244 because the corporation possessing such stock of its own has none of the powers or duties that the term shareholder or stockholder implies.[6] Moreover, petitioners deny that the corporation served as a conduit for the sale of stock from DuBose to them. They argue that respondent has not alleged that the funds received by DuBose, the prior shareholder, were identical to those paid by petitioners. They point out that on the same day the corporation purchased all its stock from DuBose, William R. Adams purchased 10 shares from the corporation, thus supplying some capital to the corporation. The corporation then adopted a plan to issue section 1244 stock and operated for almost five months before receiving final payment for petitioners' 80 shares.

Respondent contends that because the stock was originally issued to DuBose on July 25, 1973, when he bought all 100 shares of the corporation's authorized stock and DuBose held this stock for over one and one-half years until he sold it back to the corporation on February 10, 1975, petitioners have not "continuously held the stock from the date of issuance" as required by section 1.1244(a)-1(b), Income Tax Regs. In so contending, respondent reads the words of the regulation "date of issuance" to mean "date of *first* issuance."

We think this contention is wide of the mark.[7] When a corporation retires reacquired shares pursuant to state law to the status of authorized but unissued stock, any one purchasing such stock from the corporation in a bona fide transaction will be the original holder of the stock. To hold otherwise would require investors in small businesses to pore over the minutes of every board of directors meeting researching the entire stock issuance history looking for tainted stock. This would create unnecessary complications and confusion, especially where the corporation not only retired repurchased (or

6. Florida Statute 608.13(9)(b) in force at the time of the purchase of shares in 1975 provides that "Shares of its own capital stock owned by the corporation shall not be voted directly or indirectly, or counted as outstanding for the purpose of any stockholders' quorum or vote." 11 Fletcher, Cyclopedia of the Law of Private Corporations (1971 rev.) section 5088 states that "Treasury shares carry no voting rights or rights as to dividends."

7. Compare another provision of section 1.1244(a)-1(b). Income Tax Regs. which states: "Stock acquired through an investment banking firm, or other person, participating in the sale of an issue may qualify for ordinary loss treatment only if the stock is not *first* issued to such firm or person." [Emphasis supplied.]

donated or forfeited or other reacquired) shares to authorized but unissued status but also increased its authorized number of shares.

Respondent also argues that the corporation here acted merely as a conduit for the sale of shares from DuBose to petitioner. He contends that allowance of an ordinary loss in such a situation under section 1244 would run contrary to the legislative purpose of section 1244.

Respondent's support for this argument is found in the following legislative history of the Small Business Tax Revision Act of 1958 which enacted section 1244, Pub. L. 85-866, 72 Stat. 1676:

> This section provides ordinary loss rather than capital loss treatment on the sale or exchange of small-business stock. This treatment is available only in the case of an individual and only if he is the original holder of the stock.
>
> This provision is designed to encourage the flow of *new* funds into small business. The encouragement in this case takes the form of reducing the risk of a loss for these *new* funds. [H. Rep. 2198 85th Cong., 1st Sess. (1958), 1959-2 C.B. 709, 711.] [Emphasis supplied.]

We agree with respondent. Instead of a flow of new funds into a small business, the minimal facts of this case indicate only a substitution of capital. In the situation of an on-going business, we think Congress wanted to encourage the flow of additional funds rather than the substitution of preexisting capital before the benefits of section 1244 could be bestowed. This concern is also reflected in the regulations which deny section 1244 treatment where a stockholder has stock issued to him before the enactment of section 1244 and exchanges such stock for a new issuance of stock after the corporation adopts a valid plan but without the stockholder putting in any new capital. Section 1.1244(c)1(f)(2), Example (i), Income Tax Regs., states:

> A taxpayer owns stock of Corporation X issued to him prior to July 1, 1958. Under a plan adopted after June 30, 1958, he exchanges his stock for a new issuance of stock of Corporation X. The stock received by the taxpayer in the exchange may not qualify as section 1244 stock even if the corporation has adopted a valid plan and is a small business corporation.

Petitioners have the burden of proof here. Welch v. Helvering, 290 U.S. 111 (1933); Rule 142, Tax Court Rules of Practice and Procedure. They have failed to introduce any evidence that there was a net increase in the corporation's capital by virtue of their purchase of stock. They contracted to buy the stock at a set price within three weeks after the corporation had repurchased it from DuBose.

The stock was plainly not "old and cold." Petitioner's brother, William, was at all relevant times president of the corporation and controlled it from February 10, 1975, until August 1, 1975, by being its sole shareholder, and from August 1, 1975, until the stock became worthless in December 1975 by holding petitioners' voting proxies.[8] Despite so close a relationship between the corporation and themselves, petitioners offered no evidence to show a new flow of funds into the corporation. The stipulation of facts is silent on the reasons DuBose wanted to sell, the financial terms of DuBose's sale of the stock back to the corporation and the financial condition of the corporation before and after the sale. We cannot conclude from the stipulated facts that there has been a new and fresh infusion of capital within the legislative purpose of section 1244.

Petitioners appear to contend that such a requirement could easily be circumvented by having the corporation authorize new stock, issue the new stock for new funds and then immediately use the proceeds to redeem the old shareholders. The regulations provide that an individual who acquired stock from a shareholder by purchase, gift, devise, or *in any other manner* is not entitled to an ordinary loss under section 1244. Section 1.1244(a)-1(b), Income Tax Regs. Courts have not closed their eyes to events immediately subsequent to a stock sale. Gregory v. Helvering, 293 U.S. 465 (1935). In Smyers v. Commissioner, 57 T.C. 189 (1971), the taxpayers' controlled corporation issued purported section 1244 stock for cash. The corporation then immediately used a portion of the proceeds to repay the taxpayers for advances they had previously made to the corporation. In holding that the taxpayers were not entitled to ordinary loss treatment under section 1244 when stock was issued for an already existing equity interest, we said:

> The legislative history makes it clear that the congressional intent behind excluding stock or securities of the issuing company as proper consideration for section 1244 stock is that in many cases the equity interest which would be exchanged for the section 1244 stock would be an already existing equity interest in the issuing corporation. In such cases no new capital is being generated. Capital funds already committed are merely being reclassified for tax purposes. . . . [57 T.C. at 196.]

Accordingly, the petitioners must treat the loss on their corporate stock as a capital loss rather than an ordinary loss under section 1244.

Decision will be entered for the respondent.

8. William R. Adams officially tendered his resignation as president, vice-president and director of Adams Plumbing on April 20, 1976.

MILLER v. COMMISSIONER
57 T.C.M. (CCH) 46 (1989)

WRIGHT, Judge. By a notice of deficiency dated November 18, 1985, respondent determined a deficiency in petitioners' Federal income tax in the amount of $41,952.45 for taxable year 1980. After concessions, the sole issue for our consideration is whether [petitioners Samuel G. Miller and his wife] are entitled to claim an ordinary loss with respect to small business stock pursuant to section 1244.

FINDINGS OF FACT

. . . Petitioner Samuel G. Miller (hereafter petitioner) organized a corporation, Sam Miller Enterprises, Inc. (SME or the corporation), under the laws of the State of Kentucky on January 10, 1979. At all times, petitioner was the sole shareholder, the sole director and president of SME. SME was organized to purchase licenses to establish and operate hair cutting salons under a "Command Performance" franchise in Kentucky, Tennessee and South Carolina. Petitioner and two colleagues, William Allen (Allen) and Paul Logsdon (Logsdon) organized three corporations (the subsidiary corporations) to operate the hair salons. SME owned 51 percent of the outstanding stock in each subsidiary corporation with the remaining shares of stock owned equally by SME, Allen and Logsdon. Both Allen and Logsdon had experience managing hair cutting salons although petitioner did not. The parties agreed that when profits exceeded costs SME, Allen and Logsdon would become equal one-third shareholders in each of the three subsidiary corporations. In addition to holding a majority interest in each of the three subsidiary corporations, SME separately owned a hair cutting salon holding a "Command Performance" franchise in Decker Mall (the Decker Mall salon) in Columbia, South Carolina.

On January 23, 1979, petitioner paid $150,000, which he had borrowed from Citizens Fidelity Bank, to SME and was issued 150 shares of the 2,000 shares of common no-par stock which was authorized. SME purchased the franchising licenses for $150,000 and transferred them to the subsidiary corporations. The corporate minutes from the initial organizational meeting indicate that $135,000 of petitioner's first transfer of $150,000 to SME was characterized as a loan to the corporation although there was some evidence that the decision to reclassify the stock purchase was not made until May of 1979. On January 17, 1979, petitioner paid SME with two separate checks, one for $15,000 marked as equity and one for $135,000 marked as promissory note. Well after the actual contribution, petitioner received a promissory note for $135,000.

The working capital necessary to equip and fund the operation of the subsidiary corporations' hair salons and the Decker Mall hair salon was provided, as needed, by payments from petitioner to SME. Over the course of the operation of the salons, petitioner made total payments of $395,740.61. Each transfer was recorded in SME's corporate books as a loan from petitioner and evidenced by a promissory note. Similarly, each time SME advanced cash to the three subsidiary corporations it received promissory notes in exchange. Petitioner believed that he would be unable to obtain outside financing for the necessary working capital because hair cutting salons were considered too risky so he did not try.

The terms of the promissory notes petitioner received were identical. Principal was payable on demand, no collateral was pledged and interest was set at the rate of one percent over prime. SME did not maintain a reserve fund for paying the notes and had no other assets beyond those purchased for the operation of the Decker Mall salon and the stock of the three subsidiary corporations. During 1980, SME paid petitioner $14,612.82 in interest and $5,469.38 in principal. SME also paid $21,243.70 to the Citizens Fidelity Bank as interest on the personal loan of $150,000 that petitioner obtained to purchase the licenses. The three subsidiary corporations paid principal and interest to SME on the advances they had received in the amounts of $30,756.58 and $17,831.99, respectively.

By 1981, petitioner determined that the "Command Performance" hair cutting salons would not be profitable. The salons run by the three subsidiary corporations never produced enough revenue to pay their own expenses, and although the Decker Mall salon produced some revenue, high expenses precluded the realization of profit. All of the proceeds SME received were generated by the Decker Mall salon. SME had no profits in 1979 or 1980.

On September 24, 1980, SME filed a corporate resolution requesting dissolution of the corporation from the State of Kentucky. On December 31, 1980, SME transferred all of its assets and liabilities to petitioner. On March 4, 1981, the promissory notes SME had executed payable to petitioner were reclassified on the corporate books as common stock, increasing the capital stock account from $15,000 to $410,740.61. Dissolution was authorized on April 21, 1981. On his 1980 income tax return, petitioner claimed a loss of $290,606, the excess of the capital account of $410,740.61 over the liquidating distribution of $120,135. The franchise licenses were not resold after the corporation failed.

OPINION

The sole issue for our consideration is whether petitioners were entitled to claim an ordinary loss of $100,000 for their stock in SME under section 1244. Subject to certain limitations, section 1244 allows a taxpayer to treat a loss on section 1244 stock issued to the taxpayer as an ordinary loss rather than a loss from the sale or exchange of a capital asset. Section 1244 stock is defined as common stock issued in exchange for money or other property by a domestic small business corporation, 50 percent of whose income does not come from investment activity. Sec. 1244(c)(1). In order for a transfer to create section 1244 stock, stock must actually be issued to the contributor. If capital is contributed without a corollary transfer of stock, the transferor does not receive section 1244 stock nor does he increase his basis in the section 1244 stock he already owns. Sec. 1244(d)(1)(B); sec. 1.1244(c)-1(b), Income Tax Regs. The technical requirements of section 1244(c)(1) must be satisfied at the time that the alleged section 1244 stock is issued. Kaplan v. Commissioner, 59 T.C. 178, 183 (1972).

Respondent challenges only whether petitioner's interests in SME constituted section 1244 stock. Respondent first argues that almost all of the advances petitioner made to SME in exchange for the promissory notes were not reciprocated with transfers of stock. However, respondent concedes that if the interest petitioner received is stock it qualifies as section 1244 stock. With respect to the single transaction in which petitioner received stock, respondent maintains that because petitioner and SME originally characterized the initial contribution of $150,000 as a payment for stock of $15,000 and a transfer of loan proceeds of $135,000, petitioner cannot now argue that he paid any more than $15,000 for his stock. In the alternative, respondent contends that if the transfers did create an equity interest for petitioner, that interest would be properly characterized as preferred stock or as a contribution to capital rather than as common stock.

Petitioner argues that the promissory notes taken from SME as evidence of each advance payment do not reflect a debt obligation but an equity interest. Although the notes are, on their faces, straightforward debt instruments, petitioner contends that the economic substance of the transactions contains stronger and more compelling indicia of equity than of debt and the instruments should be characterized as stock for tax purposes. Similarly, petitioner contends that his initial contribution to SME of $150,000 should be taken as a full payment for the 150 shares of stock he received rather than as creating a debt of $135,000 which the later attempts to restructure the transaction would indicate. Petitioners bear the burden of proof on all issues. Welch v. Helvering, 290 U.S. 111, 115 (1933); Rule 142(a).

Despite consideration by the Secretary since 1969 and by the courts for decades, there are no uniform standards to resolve the debt-equity issue and each case must depend upon its own individual facts. John Kelley Co. v. Commissioner, 326 U.S. 521 (1946). Debt has been defined as "an unqualified obligation to pay a sum certain at a reasonably close fixed maturity date along with a fixed percentage in interest payable regardless of the debtor's income or the lack thereof." Gilbert v. Commissioner, 248 F.2d 399, 402 (2d Cir. 1957). Equity, on the other hand, reflects the "shareholder's intention . . . to embark upon the corporate adventure, taking the risks of loss attendant upon it, so that he may enjoy the chances of profit." United States v. Title Guarantee & Trust Co., 133 F.2d 990, 993 (6th Cir. 1943).

The fundamental inquiry is whether the parties had a genuine intention to create a debt, with a reasonable expectation of repayment and [whether] that intention [is] reflected in the economic reality surrounding the transaction. Litton Business Systems, Inc. v. Commissioner, 61 T.C. 367, 377 (1973). The Sixth Circuit, to which appeal lies in this case, articulated several factors to be used in evaluating the debt and equity characteristics of a shareholder's interest. Roth Steel Tube Co. v. Commissioner, 800 F.2d 625, 630 (6th Cir. 1986), cert. denied, 481 U.S. 1014 (1987), aff'g a Memorandum Opinion of this Court. These factors are: (1) the names given to the instruments, if any, evidencing the indebtedness; (2) the presence or absence of a fixed maturity date and schedule of payments; (3) the presence or absence of a fixed rate of interest and interest payments; (4) the source of repayments; (5) the adequacy or inadequacy of capitalization; (6) the identity of interest between the creditor and the stockholder; (7) the security, if any, for the advances; (8) the corporation's ability to obtain financing from outside lending institutions; (9) the extent to which the advances were subordinated to the claims of outside creditors; (10) the extent to which the advances were used to acquire capital assets; and (11) the presence or absence of a sinking fund to provide repayments. (Citations to cases omitted.)

No single factor is dispositive and we must consider all of the facts and circumstances of each case. . . .

The first three factors of the Roth Steel Tube analysis all pertain to the terms and conditions of the instruments which evidence the indebtedness. The use of formal notes or debentures is not, by itself, dispositive. Fin Hay Realty Co. v. United States, [page 60 supra]. . . .

A valid debt may be created where no formal writing exists. Byerlite Corp. v. Williams, 286 F.2d 285 (6th Cir. 1960). In the case before us, the instruments which petitioner would have us call stock are clearly marked as promissory notes. The corporate books reflected each advance as a loan and each promissory note as evidence of indebtedness. With the sole exception of the initial transfer of $150,000 which petitioner later attempted to reclassify, petitioner simultaneously received an unambiguous promissory note in exchange for each advance.

The failure to provide for interest payments is another indication of equity rather than debt. . . . Similarly, the absence of a maturity date is strongly indicative of a contribution to capital. . . . Each note issued by SME bears the fixed interest rate of prime plus one percent but does not include a fixed date of maturity. Although the repayments are not scheduled, an ultimate obligation to pay is apparent on the face of these promissory notes. However, it is interesting to note that the interest was not paid when due but only when the salons had generated excess income. In fact, petitioner received only $14,612.82 in interest throughout the time the corporation was in business, in addition to a payment made by SME to Citizens Fidelity Bank on petitioner's behalf. Although petitioner did not demand payment with respect to any of the promissory notes, SME also paid petitioner $5,469.38 in principal. These three Roth Steel Tube factors thus constitute evidence of both debt and equity. . . .

Many of the Roth Steel Tube factors address the different degrees and natures of risk to which the creditor and the shareholder are vulnerable. By his very nature, the shareholder accepts a high proportion of the risk that the business might fail while the creditor's interests are protected, to a greater degree, and his right to recover his investment is greater in the event of business failure. Petitioner's risk of business failure in the SME hair salons equals the risk of any shareholder. SME had no assets other than necessary operating equipment which could provide a source of repayment to petitioner in the event of financial distress, and no collateral was pledged to protect petitioner. Similarly, the corporation did not maintain a sinking fund or reserve to provide repayment. Thus, analysis of the fourth, seventh and eleventh factors indicates characteristics of equity.

Similarly, the corporation was exceedingly undercapitalized. If the amount of equity is limited to $15,000 and the face value of SME's debt is deemed to be $395,740.61 a debt/equity ratio results of 26 to 1. Thin capitalization, or a high debt to equity ratio is indicative of venture capital rather than a loan. . . . The structure of capitalization reflects the extent of risk associated with the questionable instrument because a thinly capitalized corporation has fewer resources with which to repay its debts as well as indicating whether the degree of risk would preclude outside financing. Bauer v. Commissioner, 748 F.2d 1365, 1369 (9th Cir. 1985). The fifth Roth Steel Tube factor demonstrates that the instruments in question had strong aspects of equity.

Where the proceeds of the instruments are devoted exclusively to the purchase of capital assets, the instrument suggests an equity interest. Use of the advances to meet the daily operating needs of the corporation rather than to purchase capital assets is an indication of bona fide indebtedness. Roth Steel Tube Co. v. Commissioner, supra at 632; Raymond v. United States, 511 F.2d 185, 191 (6th Cir. 1975). However, where the infusion of capital is devoted to the purchase of valuable and marketable capital assets there is an indication that repayment of the advance is not strictly limited to the profits of the business. Litton Business Systems, Inc. v. Commissioner, supra at 379; Malone & Hyde, Inc. v. Commissioner, 49 T.C. 575 (1968).

Here, a distinction may be drawn between petitioner's initial contribution of $150,000 and his later advances of varying sums. The entire amount of the first contribution was spent on the purchase of the franchise licenses without which the corporation could not conduct business. However, unlike many capital assets which have a residual value which can be at least partially recovered, the franchise licenses were largely unmarketable. Petitioner testified that any resale of the franchise rights would be subject to conditions and restrictions imposed by the original seller and that a resale fee would be exacted. Thus, even immediately after the purchase the franchise licenses had little residual value.

The remainder of the advances, however, were spent on assets used in the business and daily operating needs. Upon failure of the business, these other assets could be resold, as indeed they were, allowing some of the investment to be recouped. Thus, the tenth Roth Steel Tube factor indicates that the payment of $150,000 contained more equity characteristics and the subsequent payments were symptomatic of both debt and equity. . . .

The sixth, eighth and ninth factors examine whether the purported debt arrangement would have been acceptable to an outside lender. Although we use particular scrutiny in evaluating cases where the shareholders hold debt instruments in proportion to their equity holdings, such direct proportionality does not preclude a finding of a valid debt. J. S. Biritz Construction Co. v. Commissioner, 387 F.2d 451 (8th Cir. 1967). . . .

Where, as here, the shareholder and the creditor are one, the validity of a debt instrument can be gauged by testing whether it would have appealed to an outside lender. The fact that no reasonable outside lender would have extended credit on the terms available to the shareholder/creditor is evidence that the advances were capital contributions rather than loans. Stinnett's Pontiac Service, Inc. v. Commissioner, 730 F.2d 634, 640 (11th Cir. 1984), *aff'g* a Memorandum Opinion of this Court; Georgia-Pacific Corp. v. Commissioner, 63 T.C. 790, 798 (1975).

Petitioner testified that he did not try to obtain outside financing because he knew from prior experience with franchise operations that lending institutions were loathe to make loans to such risky ventures. Instead, he took out a personal loan to fund his initial contribution to SME. He also purchased the Decker Mall salon as a going concern to provide working capital to the newer salons. Although petitioner offered no support for his view, we note that the loans probably might not have appeared very attractive to outside lenders. They were unsecured and the corporation owned no other assets for generating the revenue to provide an alternative source of repayment. Furthermore, the business was not established nor were all the principals experienced. Thus, an analysis of the sixth, eighth and ninth Roth Steel Tube factors also indicates that the instruments bore strong equity characteristics.

Having considered all of these factors, we find that the instruments issued by SME to petitioner in exchange for advances contain characteristics of both debt and equity. On the one hand the risk of business failure was unavoidably associated with the instruments and no protection through collateral, a sinking fund or alternative means of repayment was contemplated. The initial contribution was spent on assets which could not readily be sold although the subsequent advances were spent partly on capital assets and partly on daily operating expenses. The likelihood of repayment rose and fell in perfect synchronization with the fortunes of the business. On the other hand, petitioner himself characterized the instruments he received as promissory notes which strongly indicates that he intended to create a genuine and binding debtor/creditor relationship with the corporation. Similarly, the promissory notes purported to give petitioner an unconditioned right to payment of interest and principal if he chose to enforce it. Finally, SME made payments of both interest and principal during the year in issue. Thus, in classifying these instruments we must weigh the equity characteristics against the debt characteristics to determine the overall economic substance and effect.

Although petitioner himself originally characterized the promissory notes as debt, he invokes the doctrine of substance over form and urges us to adopt the contrary position. The taxpayers have little freedom to ignore the form of their own transactions and are ordinarily bound by the tax consequences that flow from the form of transactions they use. Bolger v. Commissioner, 59 T.C. 760, 767 n.4

(1973). In appropriate circumstances, however, a taxpayer may argue that the substance of the transactions, rather than their form, should control the tax consequences of the transactions. Glacier State Electric Supply Co. v. Commissioner, 80 T.C. 1047 1053 (1983). Where as here, the taxpayers seek to avoid the tax consequences of the form of a transaction, they must present strong proof that the substance of the transaction was different than its form. Landa v. Commissioner, 206 F.2d 431, 432 (D.C. Cir. 1953). . . . The taxpayer's burden is far heavier when his tax reporting positions and other actions did not consistently reflect the substance which he later argues should control the form. . . .

We conclude that petitioner has failed to establish that the promissory notes were erroneously characterized as debt. The form of the notes and the fact that interest and principal payments were actually made clearly indicates indebtedness. Perhaps most persuasive, however, is the fact that it is petitioner himself who chose the form of the transaction and he cannot be allowed to engage in post-transactional tax planning. Petitioner consistently took the position that the notes evidenced indebtedness, and we cannot believe his current contradicting assertions. Thus, we conclude that of the initial investment of $150,000 only $15,000 was a payment of venture capital made in return for 150 shares of stock. The remainder of the payment was originally characterized as debt and will be so considered. In light of the foregoing,

Decision will be entered for the respondent.

NOTES

1. "Small business corporations" A and B, all of the outstanding stock of which is §1244 stock, wish to combine their operations into a single corporate entity. The shareholders of A are not related to the shareholders of B. Can the combination be accomplished without the recognition of gain or loss and so that all the stock of the corporation outstanding exists thereafter will be §1244 stock? See §1244(c)(1)(B) and (d)(2); Theodore Role, 70 T.C. 341 (1978).

2. A, a minority shareholder in a "small business corporation" (Midget), transfers beneficial ownership of shares he owns in a publicly held corporation (Giant) in exchange for Midget common stock. Midget fails, A loses his claim to the Giant stock, and the Midget stock becomes worthless. What type of loss will A realize — ordinary or capital? Would the result be different if A had transferred his Giant stock in exchange for a note from Midget and later exchanged the Midget note for Midget stock? What if cash had changed hands instead of a note? See §1244(c)(1)(B); D.C. Simmons, 72 T.C. 1204 (1979).

3. Treas. Reg. §1.1244(c)-(1)(g)(2), requires a corporation to be "largely an operating company" to qualify under §1244. See Bates v. United States, 581 F.2d 575 (6th Cir. 1978) (sustaining regulation); H. L. Davenport, 70 T.C. 922 (1978) (small loan corporation deriving more than 50 percent of gross receipts from interest had continuous losses but was not largely an operating company).

4. In 1986 Congress enacted §469, which limits the deductibility of passive activity losses. For a discussion of some implications for §1244, see Naples, Section 1244 — Small Business Stock Losses: A Re-Acquaintance That Will Survive Reform and a Proposal for Change, 71 Marq. L. Rev. 283 (1988).

IV. *COLLAPSIBLE CORPORATIONS*

Section 341 of the Code is an extraordinarily intricate provision relating to so-called collapsible corporations. It was enacted by Congress in 1950 to deal with a design for tax avoidance which first developed in the motion picture industry in the 1940s. A producer and several actors would form a corporation to produce a film. After the film was completed, but before public distribution, the corporation would be liquidated. Because of the *General Utilities* doctrine, the corporation would not recognize gain upon making its liquidating distribution. The shareholders (the producer and the actors) would recognize gain on the difference between the value of the film (as determined by previews) and their basis in the stock, but the gain would be taxed at the preferential long-term capital gains rate. In addition, the producer and the actors would receive a stepped-up basis in the film and therefore would not recognize income from sale or exploitation of the film unless and until the proceeds exceeded the new basis. Thus, the device provided two tax benefits. First, a corporate level tax was avoided. Second, the rentals from the exhibition of the film, which would have been taxed as ordinary income to the corporation, were converted into long-term capital gain. See Pat O'Brien, 25 T.C. 376 (1955), for one variety of this general approach to tax planning. Because of the tax benefits, the plan was soon also being used in other industries such as the building industry. Section 341 severely restricted the benefits of such an arrangement by requiring that the gain from the disposition of the stock of a collapsible corporation be treated as ordinary income instead of capital gain.

The 1986 Act undermined the rationale for §341. The repeal of the *General Utilities* doctrine ensures that a corporate level tax cannot be avoided by "collapsing" the corporation. Moreover, the elimination of the preferential rate for capital gains makes the conversion of ordinary income into capital gain far less important than before. For these reasons, many commentators have urged that §341 be repealed. See, e.g., Wolfman, Subchapter C and the 100th Congress, page 862 infra.

Nevertheless, §341 continues in the Code, and therefore a brief description is in order. Section 341(a) provides that a shareholder who disposes of stock in a collapsible corporation (whether in a liquidation or by sale or exchange) recognizes ordinary income even though the transaction ordinarily would produce capital gain. As §341(b) defines the term, a corporation is a "collapsible corporation" if two requirements are met. First, the corporation must be formed or availed of (1) with a view to a sale, liquidation, or distribution before the corporation has realized two thirds of the taxable income to be derived from its property and (2) with a view toward realization by the shareholders of the gain attributable to the property. Section 341(c) then establishes a presumption of collapsibility if the value of the corporation's "section 341 assets" (as defined in §341(b)(3)) is at least 50 percent of the corporation's total assets and at least 120 percent of the basis of the "section 341 assets."

Subsections (d), (e), and (f) provide exceptions to collapsibility treatment. Under subsection (d)(1), a shareholder who owns (actually and constructively) less than 5 percent of the corporation's stock is not subject to §341. Subsection (d)(2) provides that collapsibility treatment is inapplicable to a shareholder gain if not more than 70 percent of the gain is attributable to collapsible property, and (d)(3) insulates gain from such treatment if the gain is realized more than three years after the corporation completes the production or purchase of the collapsible property. Subsection (e) is very complex. Basically, it exempts shareholder gain from collapsibility treatment if the net unrealized appreciation in the corporation's "subsection (e) assets" (property held by the corporation that would produce ordinary income if sold either by the corporation or its shareholders) is not more than 15 percent of the corporation's total net worth.

Perhaps the most important exception to collapsibility treatment is contained in subsection (f). Subsection (f) allows the shareholders of a collapsible corporation to avoid tax on "ordinary income" under §341 if the corporation consents to the recognition of gain upon the distribution of appreciated property to its shareholders. After the repeal of *General Utilities*, with few exceptions a corporation filing a consent under §341(f) is not made subject to any tax to which Congress has not already subjected it, but the shareholders will have capital gain, not ordinary income, and so they can utilize their capital losses against that gain in full.

GENERAL REFERENCES

For a far-reaching examination of many of the problems raised in this chapter and a series of proposals for fundamental legislative revision, see American Law Institute, Federal Income Tax Project — Subchapter C — Proposals on Corporate Acquisitions and Dispositions and Reporter's Study on Corporate Distributions 400-486 (1982); American Law Institute, Federal Income Tax Project — Subchapter C (Supplemental Study), Reporter's Study Draft (July 1, 1989); Bryan, Leveraged Buyouts and Tax Policy, 65 N.C.L. Rev. 1039 (1987); Thurston, The Considerations of Tax Reform: A Study of the Taxation of Nondividend Distributions, 6 Am. J. Tax Pol. 73 (1987); Warren, The Relation and Integration of Individual and Corporate Income Taxes, 94 Harv. L. Rev. 720 (1981).

3

Incorporation of Assets

I. INTRODUCTION

Assume that Smith owns and operates a large and successful retail furniture business in unincorporated form. The assets of her business are reflected below:

	Adjusted Basis	Fair Market Value
Cash	$ 200,000	$ 200,000
Inventory	1,500,000	1,900,000
Accounts Receivable	200,000	200,000
Fixed Assets	250,000	350,000
Goodwill	zero	500,000
	$2,150,000	$3,150,000

If Smith transfers these assets to a corporation in exchange for all of its authorized capital stock, her $1 million gain (asset appreciation) will be "realized" (§1001(b)), but it will not be "recognized" (§351(a)). If Smith had effected the transfer prior to the Revenue Act of 1921, her gain would have been both "realized" and "recognized." Prior to that Act, therefore, her taxable income in the year of incorporation would have included the appreciation in the assets she continued to own in corporate form. By the same process, prior to the Revenue Act of 1921, if her assets had depreciated below their adjusted basis, her realized loss on incorporation would have been recognized (absent a provision such as §267). The Revenue Act of 1921, as with all subsequent enactments, provided for nonrecognition of the loss.

Section 351 and its predecessor provisions are grounded on the thesis that taxation (or deduction of a loss) ought not to occur "where in a popular and economic sense there has been a mere change in the form of ownership and the taxpayer has not really 'cashed in' on the theoretical gain, or closed out a losing venture." Portland Oil Co. v. Commissioner, 109 F.2d 479, 488 (1st Cir. 1940). See also S. Rep. No. 275, 67th Cong., 1st Sess., 1939-1 C.B. (pt. 2) 181, 188-189. The policy is so well ingrained that even the depreciation recapture provisions of §§1245 and 1250 yield to the nonrecognition rule of §351. See §§1245(b)(3) and 1250(d)(3).

Incorporation of the assets of sole proprietorships and partnerships, as well as those of previously unaffiliated investors, is a workaday occurrence in the world of commerce and law. Usually the proposed incorporation transaction and §351 mesh well, and nonrecognition is the result. There are many situations, however, in which only painstaking care will bring a transaction within §351. In fewer but nevertheless important cases the tax lawyer wants to avoid §351; i.e., he wants recognition. Here his role is to tailor the proposed transaction to escape the reach of §351. That provision is not operative merely when the taxpayer elects to have it apply, in contrast to sections like 1033 and 1034. If a transaction fits within §351, there is nonrecognition irrespective of the taxpayer's wishes.

The language of the Code and regulations and the history entwined with their application present a host of intricate questions. This chapter will deal with a number of them. Recognition (or not) of the transferor's gain, however, is only one question in an incorporation transaction. If all the gain is recognized, the transferor's basis for the stock he receives is its fair market value ("tax cost") under §1012. If §351 provides for nonrecognition, the transferor's basis for his stock is determined under §358. The transferee corporation realizes no gain when it issues its stock for assets (§1032), but its basis for the assets received will be determined under §1012 if the transferor recognizes all his gain, and under §362(a) if he does not. If the transferor receives not only stock but cash or other property as well, he may have partial recognition. The measure of recognition and the determination of the basis for both transferor and transferee become more complex in that case. By its terms §351 applies only when the transferor receives stock in exchange for property. Prior to amendment in 1989, however, §351 permitted the receipt of *securities* in addition to stock without recognition of gain or loss. Today, receipt of the transferree corporation's debt, whether or not evidenced by securities, will result in partial recognition, although in some cases even the partially recognized gain may be deferred under the installment sale provisions of §453.

If §351 governs a transaction the "holding period" of the stock received by the transferor will be determined under §1223(1), and the corporation's "holding period" for the property it receives will be determined under §1223(2). With exceptions, "tacking" occurs in both cases. Without the erstwhile long-term capital gains preference, however, the holding period question is of little importance.

Sometimes a corporation may be the transferor, transferring all or part of its assets to another corporation. Section 351 may apply, as in the case of a noncorporate transferor, and §361 (involving "reorganizations," to be studied in Chapter 4) may also apply.

Section 351(e)(1) was added to the Code in 1966 as a response to an ingenious development and a lively administrative controversy involving newly organized, widely held, mutual fund-type investment companies. To what kind of transactions do you think these provisions are addressed? See Rev. Rul. 87-9, page 353 infra; Chirelstein, Tax Pooling and Tax Postponement — The Capital Exchange Funds, 75 Yale L.J. 183 (1965). Treas. Reg. §1.351-1(c) provides the Treasury's interpretation of the 1966 legislation. Since 1976 the problem addressed by §351(e)(1) is dealt with in other contexts by §§368(a)(2)(F), 584(e), 683(a), and 721(b). See Treas. Reg. §1.351-1(c).

As with a number of other nonrecognition provisions, §351 may be inapplicable to gain (but not loss) on a transfer to a foreign corporation. See §367; cf. §§1491 and 1492. This book does not cover the federal income tax problems peculiar to foreign corporations. It leaves them to books dedicated to those issues. See, e.g., J. Isenbergh, International Taxation (1989); P. McDaniel & H. Ault, Introduction to United States International Taxation (3d ed. 1989); M. McIntyre, The International Income Tax Rules of the United States (1989).

Although the Tax Reform Act of 1986 did not directly address the incorporation of assets, the effect of the Act's far-reaching reforms are felt in this chapter, if only indirectly. Because the 1986 Act provides that C corporations will pay tax at a higher top rate than individuals, there has been a reduction in the number of new C corporations formed each year. The Act's repeal of the *General Utilities* doctrine, however, probably reduces the number of C corporation liquidations that would otherwise occur in an effort to secure the benefit of a single tax world that is capped at 28 percent.

Before approaching the knotty tax problems, you should give thought to the mechanics of incorporation. How does a taxpayer incorporate her real estate, her lathe, her accounts receivable, her goodwill? How is stock "issued"? What documents are required, to whom are they delivered, and what assents and acknowledgments are necessary? Do not refer to "incorporating a business" without knowing exactly how it is accomplished. Livery of seisin is out-of-style today, and it was never effective to transfer goodwill.

See B. Bittker and J. Eustice, Federal Income Taxation of Corporations and Shareholders 3-1 to 3-71 (5th ed. 1987); R. Kaplan, Federal Taxation of International Transactions (1988); Jacobs, Something Simple: A Tax-Free Incorporation, 37 Tax Law. 133 (1983).

II.   RECEIPT OF STOCK IN EXCHANGE—
TAX IMPACT ON INVESTOR—§351

A.   QUESTIONS OF "CONTROL" AND "EXCHANGE"

1.   Timing and the "Persons"

AMERICAN BANTAM CAR CO. v. COMMISSIONER
11 T.C. 397 (1948), *aff'd per curiam*, 177 F.2d 513 (3d Cir. 1949), *cert. denied*,
339 U.S. 920 (1950)

[In August 1935, A, B, and C (hereinafter called the associates) acquired the assets of the defunct American Austin Car Co. by purchase from its liquidating trustees. They paid $5,000 in cash; the assets were subject to liabilities of $219,099.83. In May 1936, they decided to form the American Bantam Car Co., the petitioner in this case. Under the plan the associates were to transfer the American Austin assets, subject to the existing liabilities, and $500 in cash to the petitioner in exchange for 300,000 shares of the latter's no par common stock; 90,000 shares of the petitioner's preference stock were to be offered to the public through underwriters. If the underwriters were successful in disposing of the stock they were to receive from the associates 100,000 shares of the common stock in addition to their regular underwriting commissions. All of the interested parties agreed orally to the substance of this plan on June 2, 1936, but no formal written contract was entered into at that time. On the same date petitioner was incorporated with an authorized capital stock of 700,000 shares, consisting of 100,000 shares of $10 par value preferred stock and 600,000 shares of no par common stock. The holders of the preferred stock were entitled to three votes for each share held, and the holders of the common were entitled to one vote per share. On June 3, 1936, the associates transferred the American Austin assets, subject to the aforementioned liabilities, and $500 in cash to the petitioner, and the latter issued 300,000 shares of the common stock to the associates in accordance with their proportionate interests in the assets and money. An appraisal made of the American Austin assets at that time indicated that they were worth $840,800.

[On June 8, 1936, petitioner executed a written agreement with the underwriters for the sale of 90,000 shares of its preferred stock to the public. A selling schedule was established under which the stock was to be disposed of in varying amounts over a period of one year. At the same time the associates and the underwriters executed a written contract under which the former were to transfer a total of 100,000 shares of the petitioner's common stock to the latter as they sold the preferred stock. To facilitate the transfer the associates placed all of the common stock held by them in the custody of a bank. The bank was to hold the common shares until the preferred stock was completely sold; then the common was to be returned to the associates, and they were to deliver 100,000 shares to the underwriters. By October 1937, the underwriters had sold 83,618 shares of the preferred to the public, and at that time they received 87,900 shares of the common from the associates pursuant to the agreement. The underwriters, within one month, sold 1,008 shares of the common to the public.

[For the taxable years 1936 through 1941 the petitioner used $145,000 as its basis for the depreciation of the American Austin assets. In 1942 and 1943, when petitioner showed profit from war production, it used $840,800 as the basis for those assets. The Commissioner contended that the assets had been received in a tax-free exchange and that their basis to the petitioner depended upon their basis in the hands of the associates.]

HILL, Judge. This case requires the determination of the proper basis for the Austin assets acquired by petitioner on June 3, 1936, in exchange for stock. We must decide whether under the facts here section [362(a)] requires petitioner, in computing deductions for depreciation, to take as the basis of the assets so acquired the basis thereof in the hands of the transferors. This section is applicable if the exchange by which petitioner received the Austin assets was one in which gain or loss is not recognized under the provisions of section [351(a)]. . . . We therefore must first consider whether, when the associates turned over the Austin assets to petitioner, subject to liabilities of $219,099.83, plus $500 in cash, and in return petitioner issued to the associates 300,000 shares of its no par common stock, all the requirements of section [351(a)] were satisfied.

At the outset it should be noted that the statute requires for a nontaxable exchange that the property turned over by the transferors be "solely" in exchange for stock or securities of the transferee corporation. The transferors in the instant case actually received from petitioner upon the exchange only 300,000 shares of common stock. Thus, the statutory requirement is met unless it can be said the transferors indirectly received "other property or money" by virtue of the fact the petitioner acquired the transferred property subject to liabilities. Section [357(a)] . . . specifically states that such an acquisition of property subject to liability shall not be considered as "other property or money" received by the transferors. It is clear that a definite business purpose motivated this transaction. Therefore such acquisition by the petitioner does not prevent the exchange from being within the provisions of section [351(a)] and the transferors in exchange for their property did receive "solely" stock from the corporation.

It has been held that money turned over to the transferee corporation by the transferors does not prevent a tax-free exchange, for it is includible within the term "property" in section [351(a)]. [G.C.M. 24415, 1944 C.B. 219]; Haliburton v. Commissioner, 78 Fed. (2d) 265. Therefore, the $500 transfer of cash to petitioner by the associates comes within the terms of section [351(a)].

The first major test of tax-free exchange under section [351(a)] is whether the transferors have "control" of the corporation immediately after the exchange. Section [368(c)] . . . defines "control":

> As used in this section the term "control" means the ownership of stock possessing at least 80 per centum of the total combined voting power of all classes of stock entitled to vote and at least 80 per centum of the total number of shares of all other classes of stock of the corporation.

The first question, then, is whether the associates had such "control" over the petitioner immediately after the exchange on June 3, 1936. Prima facie, when the various steps taken to organize the new corporation and transfer assets to it are considered separately, the associates did have "control" of the petitioner immediately after the exchange within the statutory definition of the word. We think that from June 3 to June 8, 1936, they owned 100 per cent of all the issued stock, and from June 8, 1936, until October 1937 they owned stock possessing at least 80 per cent of the total combined voting power of all classes of stock. On June 3, 1936, the associates were issued absolutely and unconditionally 300,000 shares of no par common stock. The resolution of the board of directors of petitioner accepting the associates' offer of the Austin assets attached no strings whatsoever to the issuance of the stock to them. It is true that on June 2, 1936, petitioner had an authorized capital stock of 700,000 shares, 600,000 common shares and 100,000 preferred shares, but in determining control only stock actually issued is considered. . . . On June 8 no other common stock had been issued, and a contract regarding possible future assignment of those 300,000 shares already issued was not entered into before that date. No preferred stock had been issued on June 3, nor was a contract for its sale provided until June 8. The statutory words "immediately after the exchange" require control for no longer period; in fact, momentary control is sufficient. . . . Certainly, therefore, the associates had absolute control over the corporation from June 3 to June 8, 1936, due to their complete ownership of all outstanding stock.

It is true that, by virtue of their agreement with the associates on June 8, 1936, the underwriters did at that time acquire the right to earn shares of the common stock issued to the associates by the sale of certain percentages of preferred stock, but the ownership of the 300,000 shares remained in the associates until such sales were completed. It is significant to note that this agreement stated that the associates were the owners of the 300,000 shares. On August 16, 1936, the associates deposited all their shares in escrow with the Butler County National Bank & Trust Co., but they only surrendered possession by the terms of their agreement with the bank and retained all other attributes of ownership.

During all of 1936 the associates retained ownership over the 300,000 shares of common stock and during that interval the underwriters sold only 14,757 shares of preferred stock, which did not entitle them to any common stock under the agreement of June 8, 1936. The corporation's bylaws provided that each share of preferred stock should have 3 votes, while each share of common stock should have 1 vote. Therefore, at the end of 1936, out of 344,271 possible stock votes, the total combined voting power of all outstanding stock, the associates owned 300,000, or over 80 per cent. It was not until October 1937, when the underwriter Grant* received 87,900 shares of the associates' common stock in fulfillment of the underwriting agreement, that the associates lost "control" of petitioner within the statutory definition of the word. Retention of "control" for such a duration of time satisfies the governing provision of section [351(a)].

Petitioner, however, contends that the series of steps organizing the new corporation, transferring assets to it, and arranging for the sale of its preference stock must be considered as parts of the integrated plan formulated in May 1936, and, therefore, considered as parts of a single transaction. It argues that this unified transaction started on June 2, 1936, when petitioner was incorporated, and ended in October 1937, when the public offering of the preferred stock by the underwriters ceased and Grant was awarded 87,900 shares of common stock; that the transfer of common stock to Grant in 1937 was the final step of an indivisible operation and must be viewed concurrently with the preceding steps. On this theory the associates did not obtain control of petitioner, for on consummation of this final step in the general plan the associates had only 212,100 shares of common stock, while Grant had 86,892 shares and the public had 1,008 and there were 83,618 shares of outstanding preferred stock owned by the public. The 212,100 stock votes held by the associates in October 1937 fell shy of the required 80 per cent to give the requisite control.

*The factual statement uses the word *underwriters*, while the court's opinion refers to *Grant*. — ED.

In determining whether a series of steps are to be treated as a single indivisible transaction or should retain their separate entity, the courts use a variety of tests. . . . Among the factors considered are the intent of the parties, the time element, and the pragmatic test of the ultimate result. An important test is that of mutual interdependence. Were the steps so interdependent that the legal relations created by one transaction would have been fruitless without a completion of the series?

Using these tests as a basis for their decisions the courts in Hazeltine Corporation v. Commissioner, 89 Fed. (2d) 513, and Bassick v. Commissioner 85 Fed. (2d) 8, treated the series of steps involved in each case as parts of a unified transaction and therefore determined that the transferors of assets to the new corporation did not acquire the requisite control. An analysis of the fact situations involved shows salient distinguishing features from the present facts. In each of the above cases there was a written contract prior both to the organization of the new corporation and the exchange of assets for stock which bound the transferors unconditionally to assign part of the stock acquired to third parties after the exchange. Thus, at the moment of the exchange the recipient of the stock did not own it, but held it subject to a binding contractual obligation to transfer a portion. The court in each case thought that the incorporation and exchange would never have been agreed upon without the supplemental agreement turning over stock to a third party. In such situations it is logical for the courts to say that the exchange and the subsequent transfer are part of one and the same transaction, so that the transferor never actually owned the shares he later assigned.

A close examination of the facts surrounding the exchange in the present case makes it clear that the exchange of assets for stock and the subsequent transfer of a portion of that stock to Grant therein involved should not be considered part of the same transaction so as to deprive the associates of "control" immediately after the exchange. The facts are distinguishable from those existing in the *Hazeltine* and *Bassick* cases on three grounds. First, there was no written contract prior to the exchange binding the associates to transfer stock to the underwriters. At the most, there was an informal oral understanding of a general plan contemplating the organization of a new corporation, the exchange of assets for stock, and marketing of preferred stock of the new corporation to the public. A written contract providing for the transfer of shares from the associates to the underwriters did not come until five days after the exchange. Secondly, when the transfer of shares to the underwriters was embodied specifically in a formal contract, the underwriters received no absolute right to ownership of the common stock, but only when, as, and if, certain percentages of preferred stock were sold. How clearly contingent was the nature of their rights is illustrated by the fact that only one underwriter, Grant, met the terms of the agreement and became entitled to any shares. Thirdly, the necessity of placing the 300,000 shares in escrow with a bank is indicative of complete ownership of such stock by the associates following the exchange.

The standard required by the courts to enable them to say that a series of steps are interdependent and thus should be viewed as a single transaction do not exist here. It is true that all the steps may have been contemplated under the same general plan of May 1936; yet the contemplated arrangement for the sale of preferred stock to the public was entirely secondary and supplemental to the principal goal of the plan to organize the new corporation and exchange its stock for Austin assets. The understanding with the underwriters for disposing of the preferred stock, however important, was not a sine qua non in the general plan, without which no other step would have been taken. While the incorporation and exchange of assets would have been purposeless one without the other, yet both would have been carried out even though the contemplated method of marketing the preferred stock might fail. The very fact that in the contracts of June 8, 1936, the associates retained the right to cancel the marketing order and, consequently the underwriters' mean to own common stock issued to the associates, refutes the proposition that the legal relations resulting from the steps of organizing the corporation and transferring assets to it would have been fruitless without the sale of the preferred stock in the manner contemplated.

Finally, to say that the separate steps should be viewed as one transaction so that ownership of 87,900 shares never passed to the associates has the disadvantage of inferring that the interested parties intended to suspend ownership of 300,000 shares from June 3, 1936, until such time as the underwriters definitely did or did not earn the right to such shares — as it turned out, until October 1937. It is much more logical to say that ownership of all 300,000 shares rested in the associates until the conditions precedent had been fulfilled by the underwriters, and that when the associates turned over the stock to Grant they were exercising their rights of ownership acquired on June 3, 1936. To allow petitioner's contention is to permit a 15-month time lag after the exchange before determining "control immediately after the exchange." Such a proposition defeats the very language of the statute.

A review of decisions encountering this problem under section [351(a)] shows that courts have determined control of the new corporation remained with the transferors of assets following the exchange under circumstances less favorable than in the present case. . . .

Thus we conclude that in the present case the exchange of assets for stock between the associates and petitioner on June 3, 1936, was a separate completed transaction, distinct from the subsequent transfer of common stock to Grant, so that the associates were in control of petitioner immediately after the exchange within the provisions of section [351(a)]. . . .

What then is the basis for depreciation purposes of property acquired by a corporation by a tax-free exchange under section [351(a)]? Section [362(a)] of the code specifically answers this question. The basis is the same as it would be in the hands of the transferor. In the instant case the basis of the Austin assets in the hands of the associates was the cost of those assets to them. They paid $5,000 cash and received the property subject to liabilities of $219,099.83. Thus the basis in their hands was $224,099.83. Therefore, the basis for the Austin assets to the petitioner is also $224,099.83, as contended by the respondent. . . .

NOTE

The original incorporators of American Bantam Car Co. presumably took the position that §351 applied to the incorporation transaction, and that gain was therefore not recognized. Suppose the Commissioner had lost the *American Bantam Car* case, and the court had held that §351 was inapplicable. Would the statute of limitations have prevented the Commissioner from then assessing tax on the original incorporators based on the gain from the incorporation transaction? Today, the Commissioner can rely on §1311, a provision allowing him to reopen a tax year when related parties have taken inconsistent positions and a determination has been made in favor of one of them. See §§1311 and 1312(7).

REVENUE RULING 78-294
1978-2 C.B. 141

Advice has been requested regarding the effect of a sale of stock by an underwriter to the general public on the control requirement of section 351 of the Internal Revenue Code of 1954 in the situations described below.

A is a person who conducted business in a noncorporate form. The business needed additional capital. A decided to incorporate the business to increase its capital through a public offering of stock. Therefore, A sought the assistance of U, an underwriter of corporate stock, in order to engage in the transactions described below. In accordance with the plan, A organized a new corporation, Z. Z had capital stock of 1,000 authorized but unissued shares upon its formation.

Situation 1. Pursuant to an agreement among A, U, and Z, A transferred all of A's business property to Z in exchange for 500 shares of Z stock. U agreed to use its best efforts as Z's agent to sell the 500 unissued shares of Z stock to the general public at $200 per share. U succeeded in selling the 500 shares within two weeks of the initial offering with no change in the terms of the offering. This transaction is considered to fall within the general definition of a "best efforts" underwriting.

Situation 2. Pursuant to an agreement among A, U, and Z, A transferred all of A's business property to Z in exchange for 500 shares of Z stock, and U transferred $100,000 in cash to Z in exchange for the remaining 500 shares. At the time of U's purchase of 500 Z shares U had not entered into a binding contract to dispose of the Z shares. However, U intended to sell its 500 shares of Z stock, but, if unsuccessful, was required to retain them. Following the A-Z and U-Z exchanges, U sold its 500 shares of Z stock to the general public within two weeks of the initial offering. A retained A's 500 shares of Z stock. This transaction is considered to fall within the general definition of a "firm commitment" underwriting. . . .

In a public offering of stock, the function of a best-efforts underwriter is solely to bring the parties together as agent of the corporation. . . . The best-efforts underwriter transfers no property to the corporation and should not be considered a transferor for purposes of section 351 of the Code under these circumstances. On the other hand, in a best-efforts underwriting the movement of property from the public investors to the corporation is direct and uninterrupted so that in appropriate cases the public investors should be deemed to be transferors in testing whether the requirements of section 351 have been met.

Situation 1 — Analysis and Holding. In *Situation 1* the business needed additional capital so that the public stock offering was integral to A's plan to incorporate the going business. In such circumstances it is appropriate to treat the incorporation and subsequent public offering as elements in a single transaction that may be tested for qualification under section 351 of the Code. See Bassick v. Commissioner, 85 F.2d 8 (2d Cir. 1936), *cert. denied,* 299 U.S. 592 (1936).

Furthermore, the charter and bylaws of the issuing corporation as well as various public documents required to be filed with governmental agencies in connection with a public offering of stock set forth the rights of the parties to the offering. Thus, the rights of the parties in *Situation 1* are previously defined as required by section 1.351-1(a)(1) of the regulations.

Finally, the sale of stock to the public in *Situation 1* took place in a short period of time with no change in the terms of the offering. These facts indicate that the transfers in *Situation 1* occurred with an expedition consistent with orderly procedure within the meaning of section 1.351-1(a)(1) of the regulations.

Therefore, the public investors in *Situation 1* should be treated, along with A, as transferors for purposes of section 351 of the Code.

Accordingly, in *Situation 1* the transferors are in control of Z immediately after the exchange within the meaning of section 1.351-1(a)(1) of the regulations. The overall transaction qualifies under section 351 of the Code since the other requirements of that section are also met in *Situation 1*. The determination of whether other public stock offerings involving best-efforts underwriters qualify under section 351 must be made on the basis of an analysis of all the facts and circumstances of those transactions.

Situation 2 — Analysis and Holding. In a firm-commitment underwriting, the underwriter transfers its own property to the issuing corporation in exchange for stock of that corporation. Therefore, such underwriter should be considered a transferor for purposes of section 351 of the Code. Hartman Tobacco Company v. Commissioner, 45 B.T.A. 311, 314 (1941), *acq. in another issue*, 1943 C.B. 11. Furthermore, the firm-commitment underwriter in the instant case assumes the risk of reselling the acquired stock to the general public and in so doing recognizes that it may be forced to retain a portion of that stock for an extended period. Consequently, since the transaction is completed for section 351 purposes with the underwriter's exchange of property for the stock, its subsequent resale of that stock will not violate the control "immediately after" requirement of that Code section. See American Bantam Car Co. v. Commissioner, 11 T.C. 397 (1942), *aff'd per curiam*, 177 F.2d 513 (3rd Cir. 1949), *cert. denied*, 339 U.S. 920 (1950).

Accordingly, under *Situation 2*, since A and the firm-commitment underwriter hold 100 percent of the Z stock at culmination of the incorporation transaction, the transferor group is in control of Z immediately after the exchange. Furthermore, as the other requirements of section 351 of the Code are also satisfied, the transaction is entitled to treatment thereunder.

NOTES

1. The policy theme underlying §351 is that gain or loss should not be recognized where there has been only a change in the form of ownership. Is Rev. Rul. 78-294 consistent with this idea or did more happen than just a change in the form of ownership? Note how A has been able to diversify his investment. Cf. §351(e)(1).

2. A partnership with appreciated assets is interested in expansion. Accordingly, the partners transfer all their partnership interests to a corporation in exchange for its stock. Upon receipt of the stock, pursuant to prior plan, they sell 30 percent of the stock to an underwriter who distributes the stock to the public the same day. Do the partners recognize gain in the amount of the unrealized appreciation of the partnership assets when they form the corporation?

3. Mr. Fox owns a sole proprietorship, the assets of which have substantially appreciated in value since he purchased it. Because he wishes to bring his son into the business, he incorporates under a firm commitment to give 30 percent of the stock to his son immediately. His son has given nothing in return for the stock. Does Fox recognize any income? Why? Would the result be different if there were no firm commitment to his son, but only an understanding that the son would eventually join the business? Cf. Fahs v. Florida Machine and Foundry Co., 168 F.2d 957 (5th Cir. 1948).

4. Suppose A contributes $100,000 in appreciated property in return for 100 percent of the nonvoting preferred stock of Corporation Z, and B contributes $900,000 in cash for 100 percent of the voting common stock. Does A recognize gain?

REVENUE RULING 79-194
1979-1 C.B. 145

ISSUE

Is the control requirement of section 351(a) of the Internal Revenue Code of 1954, which provides for non-recognition of gain or loss on transfers of property to a controlled corporation, satisfied where part of the stock of the controlled corporation received by a transferor in exchange for property is sold to other persons who also transferred property to the corporation in exchange for stock?

FACTS

SITUATION (1)

Corporation Z and a group of investors, pursuant to a binding agreement between them, transferred property to a newly organized corporation, Newco, in exchange for all of Newco's stock (a single class of voting common stock). Z and the investors received 80 percent and 20 percent, respectively, of Newco's stock. Pursuant to the agreement Z sold an amount of its Newco stock for its fair market value to the investors to bring its ownership down to 49 percent. Newco would not have been formed if the investors had not agreed to transfer property to it and their agreement to do so was conditioned on the sale by Z to them of part of Z's Newco stock.

SITUATION (2)

X, a domestic corporation, operates a branch in a foreign country. The foreign country enacted a nationalization law that required that the business that X's branch was engaged in be incorporated in the foreign country and that its citizens be the majority owners of such corporation. A governmental agency in the foreign country directed X to transfer all of the assets of its branch to a newly formed foreign country corporation that is, or will be, at least 51 percent owned by its citizens. Accordingly, X and a group of investors, who were citizens of the foreign country, pursuant to a binding agreement between them, transferred property to Newco, a corporation newly organized in the foreign country, in exchange for all of Newco's stock (a single class of voting common stock). X and the investors received 99 percent and one percent, respectively, of Newco's stock. Pursuant to the agreement, X sold an amount of its Newco stock for its fair market value to the investors to bring its ownership down to 49 percent; the investors would pay X in a series of yearly installments. Newco would not have been formed if the investors had not agreed to transfer property to it and their agreement to do so was conditioned on the sale by X to them of part of X's Newco stock. Further, the investors transferred property to Newco in order to become co-transferors with X, and they purchased X's Newco stock in lieu of the assets of X's branch because of the foreign governmental agency's directive. . . . The fair market value of each asset transferred is in excess of its basis.

LAW AND ANALYSIS

The specific sections of the Code that are applicable are section 351(a), which provides that no gain or loss will be recognized if property is transferred to a corporation by one or more persons solely in exchange for stock or securities in such corporation and immediately after the exchange such person or persons are in control of the corporation, and section 368(c) which defines control for purposes of section 351(a), to mean the ownership of stock possessing at least 80 percent of the total combined voting power of all classes of stock entitled to vote and at least 80 percent of the total number of shares of all other classes of stock of the corporation.

Since the sales of Newco stock by Z to the investors, and of Newco stock by X to the investors, were integral parts of the corporations and pursuant to binding agreements entered into prior to the exchanges, the control requirement of section 351(a) of the Code is determined after the respective sales. See Hazeltine Corp. v. Commissioner, 89 F.2d 513 (3rd Cir. 1937), Intermountain Lumber Co. v. Commissioner, 65 T.C. 1025 (1976) and Rev. Rul. 70-522, 1970-2 C.B. 81.

In Situation (1), after the sales were completed, 49 percent of the Newco stock was owned by Z and 51 percent of the stock was owned by the investors. Therefore, the persons transferring property to Newco in exchange for Newco stock owned 100 percent of the Newco stock "immediately after the exchange" within the meaning of section 351(a). The fact that there was a shift in ownership of stock among the transferors after their exchanges with Newco does not affect the application of section 351(a). See example (1) under section 1.351-1(b) of the Income Tax Regulations in which transfers of property to a new corporation qualify under section 351 even though a shift in the ownership of stock among the transferors is considered to have occurred subsequent to the transfers.

In Situation (2), after the sales were completed, 49 percent of the Newco stock was owned by X and 51 percent of the Newco stock was owned by the investors. Because the amount of stock issued directly to the investors for property is of relatively small value in comparison to the value of all the stock received by them in the transaction, the stock received by the investors is not taken into account in considering whether the transaction qualifies under section 351(a) of the Code. Compare section 1.351-1(a)(1)(ii) of the regulations. Thus, for purposes of determining control under section 351, the investors were not transferors. Therefore, since the person (X) transferring property to Newco in exchange for Newco stock owned only 49 percent of the Newco stock "immediately after the exchange," the control requirement of section 351(a) is not satisfied. The fact that there was a shift in ownership of 49 percent of the Newco stock from a transferor (X) to a non-transferor (the investors) after their exchanges with Newco affects the application of section 351(a). . . .

HOLDING

SITUATION (1)

The control requirement of section 351(a) of the Code is satisfied. No gain or loss is recognized to Z or the investors under section 351(a) on the transfer of property to Newco. Gain or loss to Z upon the sale of the Newco stock will be determined and recognized under section 1001.

SITUATION (2)

The control requirement of section 351(a) of the Code is not satisfied. Gain is recognized to X on the transfer of property to Newco pursuant to section 1001. Gain or loss, if any, to X upon the sale of the Newco stock to the investors will be determined and recognized under section 1001.

NOTES

1. See also Intermountain Lumber Co., 65 T.C. 1025 (1976) (transfer of property to a new corporation in exchange for all its stock, where transferor was committed to assign 50 percent of the new corporation's stock to a third party, was not governed by §351); Rev. Rul. 79-70, 1979-1 C.B. 144 (control requirement of §351 not satisfied where a corporation transferred property to a newly organized corporation in exchange for all its stock and, under a prearranged binding agreement that was an integral part of the incorporation, sold 40 percent of such stock to a third party). Cf. Culligan Water Conditioning of Tri-Cities, Inc. v. United States, 567 F.2d 867 (9th Cir. 1978) (incorporation followed by disposition of control pursuant to plan, whether or not legally binding, would preclude application of §351); D'Angelo Associates, Inc., 70 T.C. 121 (1978), *acq. in result,* 1979-1 C.B. 1 (issuance of shares to family members of individual who transferred property to corporation was a gift of shares pursuant to plan, but did not preclude application of §351).

2. *Compare* Tillinghast and Paully, The Effect of the Collateral Issuance of Stock or Securities on the "Control" Requirement of Section 351, 37 Tax L. Rev. 251 (1982), *with* Keller, The Tax Effects of a Shareholder's Post-Incorporation Sale of Stock: A Reappraisal, 2 Tax L.J. 89 (1985).

REVENUE RULING 84-111
1984-2 C.B. 88

ISSUE

Does Rev. Rul. 70-239, 1970-1 C.B. 74, still represent the Service's position with respect to the three situations described therein?

FACTS

The three situations described in Rev. Rul. 70-239 involve partnerships X, Y, and Z, respectively. Each partnership used the accrual method of accounting and had assets and liabilities consisting of cash, equipment, and accounts payable. The liabilities of each partnership did not exceed the adjusted basis of its assets. The three situations are as follows:

SITUATION 1

X transferred all of its assets to newly formed corporation R in exchange for all the outstanding stock of R and the assumption by R of X's liabilities. X then terminated by distributing all the stock of R to X's partners in proportion to their partnership interests.

SITUATION 2

Y distributed all of its assets and liabilities to its partners in proportion to their partnership interests in a transaction that constituted a termination of Y under section 708(b)(1)(A) of the Code. The partners then transferred all the assets received from Y to newly formed corporation S in exchange for all the outstanding stock of S and the assumption by S of Y's liabilities that had been assumed by the partners.

SITUATION 3

The partners of Z transferred their partnership interests in Z to newly formed corporation T in exchange for all the outstanding stock of T. This exchange terminated Z and all of its assets and liabilities became assets and liabilities of T.

In each situation, the steps taken by X, Y, and Z, and the partners of X, Y, and Z, were parts of a plan to transfer the partnership operations to a corporation organized for valid business reasons in exchange for its stock and were not devices to avoid or evade recognition of gain. Rev. Rul. 70-239 holds that because the federal income tax consequences of the three situations are the same, each partnership is considered to have transferred its assets and liabilities to a corporation in exchange for its stock under section 351 of the Internal Revenue Code, followed by a distribution of the stock to the partners in liquidation of the partnership.

LAW AND ANALYSIS

Section 351(a) of the Code provides that no gain or loss will be recognized if property is transferred to a corporation by one or more persons solely in exchange for stock or securities in such corporation and immediately after the exchange such person or persons are in control (as defined in section 368(c)) of the corporation.

Section 1.351-1(a)(1) of the Income Tax Regulations provides that, as used in section 351 of the Code, the phrase "one or more persons" includes individuals, trusts, estates, partnerships, associations, companies, or corporations. To be in control of the transferee corporation, such person or persons must own immediately after the transfer stock possessing at least 80 percent of the total combined voting power of all classes of stock entitled to vote and at least 80 percent of the total number of shares of all other classes of stock of such corporation.

Section 358(a) of the Code provides that in the case of an exchange to which section 351 applies, the basis of the property permitted to be received under such section without the recognition of gain or loss will be the same as that of the property exchanged, decreased by the amount of any money received by the taxpayer.

Section 358(d) of the Code provides that where, as part of the consideration to the taxpayer, another party to the exchange assumed a liability of the taxpayer or acquired from the taxpayer property subject to a liability, such assumption or acquisition (in the amount of the liability) will, for purposes of section 358, be treated as money received by the taxpayer on the exchange.

Section 362(a) of the Code provides that a corporation's basis in property acquired in a transaction to which section 351 applies will be the same as it would be in the hands of the transferor.

Under section 708(b)(1)(A) of the Code, a partnership is terminated if no part of any business, financial operation, or venture of the partnership continues to be carried on by any of its partners in a partnership. Under section 708(b)(1)(B), a partnership terminates if within a 12-month period there is a sale or exchange of 50 percent or more of the total interest in partnership capital and profits.

Section 732(b) of the Code provides that the basis of property other than money distributed by a partnership in a liquidation of a partner's interest shall be an amount equal to the adjusted basis of the partner's interest in the partnership reduced by any money distributed. Section 732(c) of the Code provides rules for the allocation of a partner's basis in a partnership interest among the assets received in a liquidating distribution.

Section 735(b) of the Code provides that a partner's holding period for property received in a distribution from a partnership (other than with respect to certain inventory items defined in section 751(d)(2)) includes the partnership's holding period, as determined under section 1223, with respect to such property.

Section 1223(1) of the Code provides that where property received in an exchange acquires the same basis, in whole or in part, as the property surrendered in the exchange, the holding period of the property received includes the holding period of the property surrendered to the extent such surrendered property was a capital asset or property described in section 1231. Under section 1223(2), the holding period of a taxpayer's property, however acquired, includes the period during which the property was held by any other person if that property has the same basis, in whole or in part, in the taxpayer's hands as it would have in the hands of such other person.

Section 741 of the Code provides that in the case of a sale or exchange of an interest in a partnership, gain or loss shall be recognized to the transferor partner. Such gain or loss shall be considered as a gain or loss from the sale or exchange of a capital asset, except as otherwise provided in section 751.

Section 751(a) of the Code provides that the amount of money or the fair value of property received by a transferor partner in exchange for all or part of such partner's interest in the partnership attributable to unrealized receivables of the partnership, or to inventory items of the partnership that have appreciated substantially in value, shall be considered as an amount realized from the sale or exchange of property other than a capital asset.

Section 752(a) of the Code provides that any increase in a partner's share of the liabilities of a partnership, or any increase in a partner's individual liabilities by reason of the assumption by the partner of partnership liabilities, will be considered as a contribution of money by such partner to the partnership.

Section 752(b) of the Code provides that any decrease in a partner's share of the liabilities of a partnership, or any decrease in a partner's individual liabilities by reason of the assumption by the partnership of such individual liabilities, will be considered as a distribution of money to the partner by the partnership. Under section 733(1) of the Code, the basis of a partner's interest in the partnership is reduced by the amount of money received in a distribution that is not in liquidation of the partnership.

Section 752(d) of the Code provides that in the case of a sale or exchange of an interest in a partnership, liabilities shall be treated in the same manner as liabilities in connection with the sale or exchange of property not associated with partnerships.

The premise in Rev. Rul. 70-239 that the federal income tax consequences of the three situations described therein would be the same, without regard to which of the three transactions was entered into, is incorrect. As described below, depending on the format chosen for the transfer to a controlled corporation, the basis and holding periods of the various assets received by the corporation and the basis and holding periods of the stock received by the former partners can vary.

Additionally, Rev. Rul. 70-239 raises questions about potential adverse tax consequences to taxpayers in certain cases involving collapsible corporations defined in section 341 of the Code, personal holding companies described in section 542, small business corporations defined in section 1244, and electing small business corporations defined in section 1371. Recognition of the three possible methods to incorporate a partnership will enable taxpayers to avoid the above potential pitfalls and will facilitate flexibility with respect to the basis and holding periods of the assets received in the exchange.

HOLDING

Rev. Rul. 70-239 no longer represents the Service's position. The Service's current position is set forth below, and for each situation, the methods described and the underlying assumptions and purposes must be satisfied for the conclusions of this revenue ruling to be applicable.

SITUATION 1

Under section 351 of the Code, gain or loss is not recognized by X on the transfer by X of all of its assets to R in exchange for R's stock and the assumption by R of X's liabilities.

Under section 362(a) of the Code, R's basis in the assets received from X equals their basis to X immediately before their transfer to R. Under section 358(a), the basis to X of the stock received from R is the same as the basis to X of the assets transferred to R, reduced by the liabilities assumed by R, which assumption is treated as a payment of money to X under section 358(d). In addition, the assumption by R of X's liabilities decreased each partner's share of the partnership liabilities, thus decreasing the basis of each partner's partnership interest pursuant to sections 752 and 733.

On distribution of the stock to X's partners, X terminated under section 708(b)(1)(A) of the Code. Pursuant to section 732(b), the basis of the stock distributed to the partners in liquidation of their partnership interests is, with respect to each partner, equal to the adjusted basis of the partner's interest in the partnership.

Under section 1223(1) of the Code, X's holding period for the stock received in the exchange includes its holding period in the capital assets and section 1231 assets transferred (to the extent that the stock was received in exchange for such assets). To the extent the stock was received in exchange for neither capital nor section 1231 assets, X's holding period for such stock begins on the day following the date of the exchange. See Rev. Rul. 70-598, 1970-2 C.B. 168. Under section 1223(2), R's holding period in the assets transferred to it includes X's holding period. When X distributed the R stock to its partners, under sections 735(b) and 1223, the partners' holding periods included X's holding period of the stock. Furthermore, such distribution will not violate the control requirement of section 368 (c) of the Code.

SITUATION 2

On the transfer of all of Y's assets to its partners, Y terminated under section 708(b)(1)(A) of the Code, and, pursuant to section 732(b), the basis of the assets (other than money) distributed to the partners in liquidation of their partnership interests in Y was, with respect to each partner, equal to the adjusted basis of the partner's interest in Y, reduced by the money distributed. Under section 752, the decrease in Y's liabilities resulting from the transfer to Y's partners was offset by the partners' corresponding assumption of such liabilities so that the net effect on the basis of each partner's interest in Y, with respect to the liabilities transferred, was zero.

Under section 351 of the Code, gain or loss is not recognized by Y's former partners on the transfer to S in exchange for its stock and the assumption of Y's liabilities, of the assets of Y received by Y's partners in liquidation of Y.

Under section 358(a) of the Code, the basis to the former partners of Y in the stock received from S is the same as the section 732(b) basis to the former partners of Y in the assets received in liquidation of Y and transferred to S, reduced by the liabilities assumed by S, which assumption is treated as a payment of money to the partners under section 358(d).

Under section 362(a) of the Code, S's basis in the assets received from Y's former partners equals their basis to the former partners as determined under the section 732(c) immediately before the transfer to S.

Under section 735(b) of the Code, the partners' holding periods for the assets distributed to them by Y includes Y's holding period. Under section 1223(1), the partners' holding periods for the stock received in the exchange includes the partners' holding periods in the capital assets and section 1231 assets transferred to S (to the extent that the stock was received in exchange for such assets). However, to the extent that the stock received was in exchange for neither capital nor section 1231 assets, the holding period of the stock began on the day following the date of the exchange. Under section 1223(2), S's holding period of the Y assets received in the exchange includes the partner's holding periods.

SITUATION 3

Under section 351 of the Code, gain or loss is not recognized by Z's partners on the transfer of the partnership interests to T in exchange for T's stock.

On the transfer of the partnership interests to the corporation, Z terminated under section 708(b)(1)(A) of the Code.

Under section 358(a) of the Code, the basis to the partners of Z of the stock received from T in exchange for their partnership interests equals the basis of their partnership interests transferred to T, reduced by Z's liabilities assumed by T, the release from which is treated as a payment of money to Z's partners under sections 752(d) and 358(d).

T's basis for the assets received in the exchange equals the basis of the partners in their partnership interests allocated in accordance with section 732(c). T's holding period includes Z's holding period in the assets.

Under section 1223(1) of the Code, the holding period of the T stock received by the former partners of Z includes each respective partner's holding period for the partnership interest transferred, except that the holding period of the T stock that was received by the partners of Z in exchange for their interests in section 751 assets of Z that are neither capital assets nor section 1231 assets begins on the day following the date of the exchange. . . .

This revenue ruling supersedes and revokes Rev. Rul. 70-239.

NOTE

With the top corporate rate higher than the top individual rate, incorporation of partnerships is a less common occurrence than it used to be. Nevertheless, some partnerships do and will incorporate, and the tax consequences may well vary according to the form of the transaction used to incorporate the partnership assets and liabilities. See B. Bittker and J. Eustice, Federal Income Taxation of Corporations and Shareholders 3-27 to 3-36 (5th ed. 1987); Kramer and Kramer, Incorporation of a Partnership: IRS's New Position Produces Planning Opportunities and Pitfalls, 64 Taxes 560 (1986).

REVENUE RULING 74-502
1974-2 C.B. 116

Corporation Y wanted to acquire 100-percent control of corporation X, which stock is widely held, in a stock-for-stock exchange intended to be nontaxable to the exchanging shareholders under section 351 of the Internal Revenue Code of 1954. Under the laws of the state involved, subject to approval of the board of directors of each corporation and of the proper State authority, and subject to a favorable vote of at least two-thirds of the outstanding stock of the acquired corporation, the acquiring corporation, by operation of law, becomes the owner of all of the outstanding stock of the acquired corporation, except for stock owned by dissenters, on the effective date of the transaction. At such time, those shareholders of the acquired corporation who do not dissent are entitled to receive shares of stock of the acquiring corporation in exchange for their shares of stock of the acquired corporation. Any shareholder of the acquired corporation who dissents is entitled to receive in cash the appraised value of his shares from the acquired corporation.

At a meeting of the shareholders of X (after prior approval of the plan by the X board of directors and the State authority), 70 percent of the outstanding X stock was voted in favor of a plan of acquisition of the X stock by newly formed corporation Y, and two percent was voted against. The remaining 28 percent of the X stock was not voted. On the effective date of the transaction, Y became the owner of all the outstanding X stock by operation of State law except for two percent of such stock which was owned by those X shareholders who exercised their appraisal rights and who received cash from X for their X stock. In exchange for their X stock, the X shareholders, including those who did not vote on the plan but who participated in the exchange because they did not dissent, received voting common stock and nonvoting preferred stock of Y which represented all of the Y stock outstanding after the transaction.

Held, inasmuch as the identity and rights of all the transferors (the nondissenting X shareholders) were defined by state law and the exchange of their X stock for Y stock was by operation of law simultaneous on the effective date of the transaction, the nondissenting X shareholders were in control of Y immediately after the exchange within the meaning of section 351 of the Code. Therefore, under section 351 no gain or loss is recognized to the former X shareholders who exchanged their X stock for Y stock. Those X shareholders who received cash for their X stock are treated as having had such stock redeemed by X with the redemption being subject to the provisions of section 302.

NOTE

The language of §351 would seem to require an actual exchange, one that is negotiated with the individual transferors. Yet Rev. Rul. 74-502 involved a transaction in which by "operation of law" an ac-

quiring corporation acquired control of a corporation whose shareholders were deemed to be §351 transferors. The state statute
underlying the transaction is Mass. Gen. Laws Ann. Ch. 167A, §4A
(1971), limited to banks and trust companies. Should corporate action
by the acquiring and acquired corporations be sufficient to effect a
§351 exchange, subject only to dissenters' rights? If so, should not
the state law procedure involved in Rev. Rul. 74-502 be applicable
more generally? See Revised Model Bus. Corp. Act §11.02.

REVENUE RULING 76-454
1976-2 C.B. 102

Advice has been requested concerning the Federal income tax
treatment of the transaction described below.

For many years A, an individual, owned all of the stock of X, a
domestic corporation. A organized Y, a domestic corporation, paying
50x dollars in cash for all of its common stock, and subsequently as
part of the plan of incorporation, caused X to purchase from Y all
of Y's 4 percent noncumulative nonvoting preferred stock for 255x
dollars. Upon liquidation, the net assets of Y are distributable 50
percent to the holders of its common stock and 50 percent to the
holders of its preferred stock. Because the right to share in the net
assets upon liquidation for each class of stock is substantially disproportionate to the amounts paid for each class of stock, the 255x dollars
paid by X for the preferred stock exceeds its fair market value. . . .

Section 1.351-1(b)(1) of the regulations provides, in part, as follows:

> Where property is transferred to a corporation by two or more
> persons in exchange for stock or securities . . . it is not required
> that the stock and securities received by each be substantially in
> proportion to his interest in the property immediately prior to the
> transfer. However, where the stock and securities received are
> received in disproportion to such interest, the entire transaction
> will be given tax effect in accordance with its true nature, and in
> appropriate cases the transaction may be treated as if the stock
> and securities had first been received in proportion and then some
> of such stock and securities had been used to make gifts . . . , to
> pay compensation . . . , or to satisfy obligations of the transferor
> of any kind.

In the instant case, after the transfers of cash to Y by A and X,
A and X owned stock possessing 80 percent or more of the total
combined voting power of Y voting stock and 80 percent or more of
all other classes of Y stock. Thus, the control requirement of section
351 of the Code is satisfied.

Furthermore, since A received more stock in Y than A would have received if Y had issued its stock in proportion to the cash transferred by A and X, section 1.351-1(b)(1) of the regulations is applicable.

Accordingly, it is appropriate to treat the transactions in the instant case as transfers by X and A, respectively, of 255x dollars and 50x dollars and the receipt from Y by X and A of stock worth, respectively, 255x dollars and 50x dollars followed by a distribution by X of a sufficient amount of the stock it constructively received to reflect the values of the stocks in the hands of X and A after the transactions. That is, X is treated as having received all of the Y preferred stock and enough of the Y common stock so that the total value of the stock it received equalled the 255x dollar contribution it made to Y. X is then considered to have distributed the Y common stock it constructively received to A to reflect the fact that after the transaction X owned only Y preferred stock and A owned all of Y's common stock. This distribution is subject to the provisions of section 301 of the Code.

KAMBORIAN v. COMMISSIONER
56 T.C. 847 (1971), *aff'd*, 469 F.2d 219 (1st Cir. 1972)

. . . The cases relate to petitioners' transfer of certain securities to International Shoe Machine Corp. in exchange for its common stock. Specifically in question is whether gain realized by petitioners as a result of that transaction qualifies for nonrecognition under section 351. . . .

FINDINGS OF FACT

. . . 1. International Shoe Machine Corp. (International) was incorporated in Massachusetts in 1938 and . . . was engaged in the business of manufacturing and leasing shoe machinery and the sale of related supplies. On April 1, 1964, International's articles of organization were amended to provide for a 20 for 1 split of its common stock into two classes of common stock: Class A, $1 par, voting stock, and class B, $1 par, nonvoting stock. Following an exchange of the preexisting stock for the newly created common stock, International's authorized and issued stock was as follows as of April 1, 1964:

Shares	Class A	Class B
Authorized	100,000	900,000
Issued	37,200	334,800

On September 1, 1965, prior to the transaction here in question, International's capital stock was held as follows:

| | Shares of International | |
Name	Class A common	Class B common
Jacob Kamborian Revocable Trust	20,324	182,916
Jacob Kamborian, Jr.	4,220	37,980
Lisbeth (Kamborian) Godley	3,620	32,580
Michael Becka	60	540
Elizabeth Kamborian Trust	5,000	45,000
Others	3,916	35,244
	37,140	334,260

Jacob S. Kamborian (Jacob) founded International and served as its president at all times relevant herein. Jacob S. Kamborian, Jr., and Lisbeth Kamborian Godley are the children of Jacob and his wife, Elizabeth. Michael Becka (Becka) is not related to the members of the Kamborian family. At the time of the trial herein he had been employed by International or an affiliate since at least 1943 and had served as International's executive vice president and general manager since approximately 1960. . . .

The Elizabeth Kamborian Trust (Elizabeth's trust) was established by Jacob in 1949. At about that time Jacob and Elizabeth experienced domestic difficulties; they separated for a time; and the trust was established on their reconciliation in order to provide financial security for Mrs. Kamborian. The initial trust corpus consisted of 2,500 shares of International stock. . . .

. . . As of September 1, 1956, Becka and Lisbeth K. Godley were the trustees. Jacob had appointed them as successor trustees in 1963 and 1964, respectively. At all times relevant herein, Becka served as the managing trustee; Mrs. Godley did not live in Boston during this period; and periodically Becka informed her of the trust's activities. As of September 1, 1965, the only assets of the trust were 5,000 shares of International's class A common stock and 45,000 shares of its class B common stock.

As of September 1, 1965, International's board of directors consisted of Jacob, Jacob, Jr., Albert Kamborian (Jacob's brother), Becka, Paul Hirsch II, Harold V. Daniels, and Roy S. Flewelling.

Campex Research & Trading Corp. (Campex), a Swiss corporation with its principal place of business in Zug, Switzerland, was a patent holding and licensing company. It held primarily foreign shoe machine patents (i.e., patents not issued by the United States) and granted and administered licenses under them in a number of European countries and in Mexico. On September 1, 1965, and prior to the transaction here in question, the outstanding stock of Campex was held as follows:

Name	Shares of Campex
Jacob Kamborian Revocable Trust	39
Jacob Kamborian, Jr.	4
Lisbeth (Kamborian) Godley	4
Michael Becka	3

On September 1, 1965, the board of directors of International authorized Jacob to enter into an agreement under which (a) the owners of all of the issued and outstanding shares of Campex would exchange their stock for common stock of International and (b) "certain stockholders" of International would purchase for cash additional shares of International's common stock. . . .

As part of the transaction it was contemplated that the Elizabeth Kamborian Trust would purchase additional shares of theretofore unissued International stock for about $5,000, so that the former owners of the Campex stock and the Elizabeth Kamborian Trust, when considered collectively and treated as transferors under section 351(a), . . . would own at least 80 percent of International's stock immediately after the transaction in an attempt to comply with the requirements of section 368(c). . . . If the Elizabeth Kamborian Trust were not taken into account, the International stock held by the former owners of Campex immediately after the transaction amounted to 77.3 percent of each class of outstanding stock of International—an amount that was insufficient to satisfy the requirements of section 368(c). . . .

International acquired Campex stock as part of its program of preparing for a public issue of its stock. . . . As of September 1, 1965, no date had been set for the offering and at the time of the trial herein the public offering had not yet been made. . . .

As trustee of Elizabeth's trust, Becka borrowed approximately $5,000 at an interest rate of 6 percent in order to finance the trust's purchase of the total of 418 shares of International stock on September 1, 1965. The corpus of the trust consisted exclusively of International stock, and Becka anticipated that the loan would be repaid out of dividends paid on the stock. In deciding to acquire additional International stock, Becka also anticipated that International would make a public offering which might enhance the value of the stock.

Prior to the purchase of the International stock on behalf of the trust, Becka discussed his plans with both Jacob and Elizabeth. Jacob, personally and as grantor of the Jacob S. Kamborian Revocable Trust, held a sufficient number of International shares to control the corporation and thus to determine whether it would issue additional shares. In his discussions with Elizabeth, Becka explained that because the $5,000 loan would have to be repaid out of dividends paid on the International stock held by the trust, her income from the trust would be diminished until the loan was repaid. Elizabeth told Becka to go ahead with the transaction. . . .

On their respective Federal income tax returns for 1965, petitioners reported no gain or loss stemming from the exchange of their Campex stock for International stock. In his deficiency notices to petitioners, the Commissioner determined that they realized long-term capital gains. . . .

OPINION

BAUM, Judge. 1. *Exchange of Campex stock for International stock.* Petitioners contend that the gain they realized on their transfer qualifies for nonrecognition under section 351(a). . . . Immediately after the exchange here in issue the stock of International was held as follows:

	Shares of —		
	Class A (voting common)	Class B (nonvoting common)	Percent of total of each class
Jacob S. Kamborian Revocable Trust	22,108	198,971	56.01
Jacob S. Kamborian, Jr.	4,403	39,627	11.16
Lisbeth (Kamborian) Godley	3,803	34,227	9.64
Michael Becka	197	1,775	0.50
Elizabeth Kamborian Trust	5,042	45,376	12.77
Others	3,916	35,244	9.92
Total	39,469	355,220	

Petitioners contend that the transferors of property for purposes of section 351(a) were the five named stockholders listed above and that their percentage stockholdings after the transfer satisfy the 80-percent control requirement imposed by sections 351(a) and 368(c).

The Commissioner's position is that only the first four stockholders listed above — i.e., the former owners of Campex — may be considered as transferors of property here, that the fifth (the Elizabeth Kamborian Trust) may not be taken into account in this connection, and that since there would thus be a failure to satisfy the control requirement, all gain realized on the exchange must be recognized. In particular, he urges that International stock issued to the Elizabeth Kamborian Trust in return for $5,016 does not qualify as stock issued for property within the meaning of section 351(a) and that consequently the persons making qualified transfers of property to International in return for its stock held only 77.3 percent of its stock after the exchange. The Commissioner relies on regulations section 1.351-1(a)(1)(ii). . . .

The Commissioner contends that since the Elizabeth Kamborian Trust purchased only 42 shares of class A common and 376 shares of class B common, the securities issued were "of relatively small value" in relation to the 5,000 shares of class A common and 45,000 shares of class B common which it already held and that the primary purpose of the transfer was to qualify the exchange of Campex stock by the other stockholders for nonrecognition treatment under section 351(a).

Petitioners attack the Commissioner's position on a variety of grounds. They urge (a) that regulations section 1.351-1(a)(1)(ii) is invalid; (b) that even if valid it is inapplicable to the transaction in issue. . . .

(a) *Validity of the regulation.* — Initially we note the well-settled principle that "Treasury regulations must be sustained unless unreasonable and plainly inconsistent with the revenue statutes and that they constitute contemporaneous constructions by those charged with administration of these statutes which should not be overruled except for weighty reasons." Commissioner v. South Texas Lumber Co., 333 U.S. 496, 501. . . .

In arguing that regulations section 1.351-1(a)(1)(ii) is invalid, petitioners point first to the "proportionate interest" test which was included in section 112(b)(5), the predecessor of section 351, under the 1939 Code:

Sec. 112. Recognition of Gain or Loss

(b) Exchanges Solely in Kind.

(5) *Transfer to corporation controlled by transferor.* — No gain or loss shall be recognized if property is transferred to a corporation by one or more persons solely in exchange for stock or securities in such corporation, and immediately after the exchange such person or persons are in control of the corporation; *but in the case of an exchange by two or more persons this paragraph shall apply only if the amount of the stock and securities received by each is substantially in proportion to his interest in the property prior to the exchange.* Where the transferee assumes a liability of a transferor, or where the property of a transferor is transferred subject to a liability, then for the purpose only of determining whether the amount of stock or securities received by each of the transferors is in the proportion

required by this paragraph, the amount of such liability (if under subsection (k) it is not to be considered as "other property or money") shall be considered as stock or securities received by such transferor. [Emphasis supplied.]

The "proportionate interest" test was eliminated when section 351 was enacted in 1954. The committee reports reflect congressional dissatisfaction with the uncertainty which had developed in applying the test (H. Rept. No. 1337, 83 Cong., 2d Sess., pp. A116-A117 (1954)):

> The basic change from present law made by your committee in section 351 is the elimination of the so-called "proportionate interest" test. This requirement, which appears in section 112(b)(5) of the 1939 Code, permits nonrecognition of gain and loss only if the stock and securities received by each transferor are "substantially in proportion" to the interest of such transferor in the property prior to the exchange. This requirement, which, if unsatisfied, serves to vitiate the tax-free nature of the entire transaction, caused considerable uncertainty in its application. In eliminating the proportionate interest test your committee intends that no gain or loss will be recognized to a transferor transferring property to a corporation under section 351 irrespective of any disproportion of the amount of stock or securities received by him as a result of the transfer. Thus, if M and N each owning property having a value of $100 transfers such property to a newly formed corporation X, and M receives all of the stock, such transaction would not be subject to tax under section 351. To the extent, however, that the existing disproportion between the value of the property transferred and the amount of stock or securities received by each of the transferors results in an event taxable under other provisions of this code, your committee intends that such distribution will be taxed in accordance with its true nature. For example, if individuals A and B, father and son, organize a corporation with 100 shares of common stock and A transfers property worth $80 in exchange for 20 shares of stock, while B transfers property worth $20 to the corporation in exchange for 80 shares of stock, no gain or loss will be recognized under section 351. If, however, it is determined that in fact A has made a gift to B, it is your committee's intention that such gift would be subject to tax under the provisions of section 2501 and following. Similarly, if in the preceding example, B had rendered services to A and the disproportion in the amount of stock received constituted, in effect, the payment of compensation by A to B, it is your committee's intention that such compensation will be appropriately taxed. B will be taxable upon the fair market value of the 60 shares of stock received in excess of that received in exchange for his property as an amount received as compensation for services rendered, and A will realize gain or loss upon the difference between the basis of the 60 shares of stock in his hands and its fair market value.

See also id. at 39; S. Rept. No. 1622, 83d Cong., 2d Sess., pp. 50, 264 (1954). Petitioners assert that section 1.351-1(a)(1)(ii) incorporates a proportionate-interest test and that it therefore exceeds the scope of section 351. We disagree. Despite superficial similarities to the "proportionate interest" test, section 1.351-1(a)(1)(ii) is a very different provision.

The "proportionate interest" test was apparently designed to limit the applicability of section 112(b)(5) of the 1939 Code to transactions which did not result in substantial shifts in equity or property interests among the transferor-stockholders. On the other hand, the current regulation appears to be calculated to exclude from the scope of section 351 transactions which would ordinarily fail to meet the 80-percent requirement but which attempt to satisfy it by appending a token exchange of property for stock by one or more persons with stockholdings sufficient to place all of the transferors "in control" of the corporation. We think that the objective of the regulation is considerably narrower than that of the "proportionate interest" test.

The effect of the regulation is also more limited than that of the "proportionate interest" test. Transactions not satisfying the "proportionate interest" test were completely disqualified from nonrecognition treatment under section 112(b)(5) of the 1939 Code. The regulation, on the other hand, disqualifies only particular exchanges by particular stockholders from the scope of section 351 of the 1954 Code; if the remaining transferors can satisfy the 80-percent requirement and otherwise qualify under the statute, the regulation does not prevent them from obtaining nonrecognition treatment.

. . . We conclude that congressional elimination of the "proportionate interest" test in 1954 provides no basis for holding the regulation invalid.

Petitioners also contend that the regulation's reference to "property which is relatively small value in comparison to the value of stock or securities already owned" and its reliance upon the taxpayer's motive find support nowhere in the language of section 351 and that the regulation is for that reason invalid as beyond the scope of the statute. Again, we must disagree. By disqualifying certain token exchanges, the regulation is reasonably designed to exclude from the scope of section 351 transactions which comply with its requirements in form but not in substance. Far from being unreasonable or inconsistent with the statute, the regulation promotes its purpose by helping to ensure substantial compliance with the control requirement before the nonrecognition provisions become operative. In this light the absence of direct support for the regulation in the language of the statute is of minimal significance. . . . We conclude that the regulation is valid.

(b) *Applicability of the regulation.* — Petitioners contend that even if it is valid, the regulation is inapplicable to the transaction here in issue. They argue first that even if Elizabeth's trust had not purchased shares of International stock, the control requirement would have been satisfied, that therefore the purchase was not necessary to meet the control requirement, and that consequently the regulation is by its own terms inapplicable. Petitioners reach this conclusion by asserting that the shares held by Becka and Lisbeth Godley as trustees of Elizabeth's trust should be attributed to them as individuals and added to the shares they held personally in nonfiduciary capacities. On the basis of this premise, petitioners conclude that the 80-percent-control requirement would have been satisfied even if Elizabeth's trust had not participated in the September 1, 1965, transaction: Petitioners' argument is ingenious but unacceptable, for it falters on petitioners' premise that the trust's shares may be attributed to the individual trustees. While legal title to the shares may have been in the names of the trustees, they had no beneficial interest in such shares. The distinction is not one of form but of plain economic reality. In these circumstances we think the trustees' interests in the trust's shares were far too remote to justify attributing the shares to them for purposes of section 351.

Petitioners also contend that the primary purpose for the trust's acquisition of International's stock was not to qualify the other stockholders' exchanges under section 351 and that for this reason the regulation is inapplicable. We note at the outset that the regulation does not make it entirely clear *whose* purpose is to be taken into account. However, both parties have assumed that the purpose of the transferor of property is critical. The language of the regulation (which appears to distinguish between a "transfer" of property and the issuance of stock) supports their assumption, and we shall therefore proceed on this basis. Although Elizabeth's trust was technically the transferor herein, the parties have also assumed that Becka's purpose is critical in this respect — apparently on the ground that as the managing trustee he was primarily responsible for the decision to make the purchase of International stock. We shall proceed on the basis of this assumption as well.

The question of Becka's primary purpose is one of fact, cf. Malat v. Riddell, 383 U.S. 569, and after a review of all the evidence we conclude that his primary purpose was to qualify the other stockholders' exchanges under section 351. We note in particular that at about the time of the transaction, Jacob was ill and Becka was in charge of International's affairs, that in planning the acquisition Becka participated in lengthy discussions with regard to planning the transaction as a tax-free exchange, and that both the vote of International's board of directors and the agreement of September 1, 1965, treated the purchase by Elizabeth's trust and the exchange of Campex stock by the other stockholder as component parts of an integrated transaction avowedly designed to meet the 80-percent control requirement and thereby qualify for nonrecognition treatment under section 351.

At the trial herein, Becka testified that if the trust had not participated in the transaction, the issue of International stock to the other major stockholders would have diluted the trust's percentage interest in International and that he authorized the purchase of International stock in order to minimize such dilution. In particular he testified that the total percentage stock interest held by the trust and the two Kamborian children exceeded 33⅓ percent and that preservation of that interest protected Mrs. Kamborian against the making of certain corporate decisions (requiring a two-thirds majority) without her consent. We do not give his testimony very much weight, however. The record does not establish whether or why the children were regarded as allies of Mrs. Kamborian rather than as allies of her husband. Moreover, the trust's participation in the transaction left them with an aggregate stock interest of 33.57 percent— only 0.08 of 1 percent more than they would have held if the trust had not purchased any additional shares.

Becka also testified that he authorized the purchase of the stock because it was a "good investment." While he may well have taken this into account in making his decision, the record leaves us convinced that the purchase was made primarily to qualify the exchanges by the other stockholders (one of whom was Becka himself) under section 351. We conclude that section 1.351-1(a)(1)(ii) is applicable. . . .

[Other issues omitted.]

NOTE

Under Rev. Proc. 77-37, §3.07, 1977-2 C.B. 568, 570, property will not be considered to be "of relatively small value" within the meaning of Treas. Reg. §1.351-1(a)(1)(ii) if its value equals or exceeds 10 percent of the value of the stock of the transferee which is already owned (or to be received for services) by the transferor.

REVENUE RULING 87-9
1987-1 C.B. 133

ISSUE

Do transfers of marketable stock and cash by different transferors to a newly organized corporation, which is a regulated investment company, constitute transfers to an "investment company" within the meaning of section 351(e)(1) of the Internal Revenue Code?

FACTS

Some of the shareholders of Y corporation transferred their Y stock to X, a newly organized corporation which is a regulated investment company as defined in section 851 of the Code. In addition, other persons transferred cash to X. The Y stock is actively traded on a public stock exchange. The transferors of the Y stock received 89 percent of the stock of X, and the transferors of cash received 11 percent of the stock of X.

LAW AND ANALYSIS

Section 351(a) of the Code provides that no gain or loss will be recognized if property is transferred to a corporation solely in exchange for its stock and immediately after the exchange the transferors are in control (as defined in section 368(c)) of the corporation.

Section 351(e)(1) of the Code and section 1.351-1(c)(1) of the Income Tax Regulations provide that section 351(a) will not apply to transfers to an investment company. Section 1.351-1(c)(1) of the regulations further provides that a transfer will be considered a "transfer to an investment company" if two factors are present. First, the transfer results, directly or indirectly, in diversification of the transferors' interests. Second, the transferee is (i) a regulated investment company, (ii) a real estate investment trust, or (iii) a corporation more than 80 percent of the value of whose assets (excluding cash and nonconvertible debt obligations from consideration) are held for investment and are readily marketable stocks or securities, or interests in regulated investment companies or real estate investment trusts.

Section 1.351-1(c)(5) of the regulations provides that a transfer ordinarily results in the diversification of the transferors' interests if two or more persons transfer nonidentical assets to the corporation in the exchange, unless the portion of assets that are nonidentical to the other assets transferred constitutes an insignificant portion of the total value of the assets transferred. On the other hand, if two or more persons transfer identical assets to a newly organized corporation, the transfer will generally not be treated as resulting in diversification.

In the present situation, the transferors transferred Y stock and cash to X, a regulated investment company within the meaning of section 1.351-1(c)(1)(ii) of the regulations. Further, Y stock and cash are nonidentical assets. A transfer of nonidentical assets ordinarily results in diversification unless the nonidentical assets constitute an insignificant portion of the assets transferred. The question of what is an "insignificant portion" for this purpose is a factual issue. In the present situation, the cash represented a significant part of the value of the property transferred to X; therefore, the transfer of the stock and cash resulted in the diversification of the transferors' interests within the meaning of section 1.351-1(c)(5).

HOLDING

The transfers of Y stock and cash by different transferors to X constitute transfers to an "investment company" within the meaning of section 351(e)(1) of the Code. Consequently, section 351 does not apply to the transaction, and the transferors of the Y stock recognize gain or loss under section 1001 upon the transfer of Y stock to X in exchange for X stock.

NOTE

The principle underlying §351(e)(1) is that recognition of gain is appropriate when the taxpayer has substantially diversified his investment. Should this principle be applied more generally to incorporation transactions? How would you implement such a principle in the Code?

2.   *Effect of "Services"*

MAILLOUX v. COMMISSIONER
320 F.2d 60 (5th Cir. 1963)

Before Rives, Jones and Brown, Circuit Judges.

JONES, Circuit Judge. The petitioners bring to the Court for review a decision of the Tax Court finding income tax deficiencies against them. Joint returns had been filed. Only the husbands, Melvin Mailloux and Robert R. Foley, were participants in the transactions giving rise to the finding of tax liability, and they will be referred to as the taxpayers.

Critchell Parsons was the principal promoter of Rocky Mountain Uranium Corporation. It was incorporated on May 3, 1954.

[In April 1954, Parsons entered into discussions with Mailloux and Foley regarding the financing of a uranium venture, and Mailloux and Foley undertook to perform certain services such as assisting in clearing the issue of stock for sale in Texas, attracting private capital, and securing an underwriter for public financing. On May 18, 1954, the corporation issued a total of 1,450,000 shares to a group of people from whom, in exchange for the shares, the corporation received rights in certain uranium mining claims. Those shares at that time represented 100 percent of the corporation's outstanding stock. Parsons received 900,000 shares. The taxpayers, Mailloux and Foley, did not receive shares directly from the corporation. On May 18, 1954, however, they each received 120,000 shares from Parsons, these coming out of his 900,000 shares.]

The taxpayers were to receive 10 percent of the proceeds of stock sales made prior to a public offering of the stock. The sales were to be at 50 cents a share. The taxpayers received $12,000 from this commission arrangement. The stock was transferred under an agreement that the taxpayers would make no sales without Parsons' approval. This restriction was to permit Parsons to prevent depressing the price by overselling the market. During 1954 Mailloux sold 23,650 shares and Foley sold 24,375 shares. These sales were made at various prices which averaged something over a dollar a share. In the latter part of 1954, some transactions and adjustments between Parsons and the taxpayers were made which resulted in his obtaining and retaining some of their stock certificates. Before the end of the year Parsons and the taxpayers had a disagreement which arose from the failure, which Parsons attributed to the taxpayers, to procure approval from the Securities and Exchange Commission and the Texas Securities Commission of a public offering of the stock. Parsons directed the transfer agent not to make transfers of the taxpayers' certificates. They sued to establish their ownership. The litigation was compromised and settled in 1956. The taxpayers sold a part of their remaining stock in 1956 for ten cents a share and the rest in 1957 for five cents a share.

In their 1954 returns the taxpayers did not report any income on account of the receipt of the stock. The Commissioner made a determination that the stock was compensation for services, and that it had a value of fifty cents a share. A tax deficiency was proposed. [The Tax Court, sustaining the Commissioner, held that the shares received by the taxpayer constituted ordinary income to them in 1954, valuing the shares at 50 cents each. 20 T.C.M. (CCH) 942 (1961).]

Two questions are presented by the taxpayers' petition for review. The contention is made that the stock was received by the taxpayers in a tax-free exchange for property under ... §351. If there was no tax-free exchange and the stock was received for services, the taxpayers contend that it had no market value when received or, in the alternative, the value did not exceed ten cents a share, or at the most, an amount in excess of what they received for it.

Although the taxpayers claimed, and supported the claim with their testimony, that they had an interest in uranium claims which were conveyed to the corporation for shares of its stock, the testimony of Parsons is to the contrary. He testified that they had no interest in the claims. The Tax Court found against the taxpayers on this controverted fact issue, and its findings that the stock was for services and not for property are supported by evidence.

The Tax Court, in fixing the value of the stock, reviewed the sales made by the taxpayers, by Parsons, and by the corporation, and found that the stock, at the time it was transferred to the taxpayers, had a value of not less than fifty cents a share. There was ample evidence before the Tax Court to sustain this finding of the value of the stock issued to the taxpayers unless, as the taxpayers assert, the effect of the restrictive agreement was such as to reduce the value of their stock to an amount less than fifty cents a share. The Tax Court concluded that such restrictions as may have existed had no bearing upon the fair market value of the stock at the time the taxpayers received it. Where a stock is of a highly speculative quality and the terms of a restrictive agreement make a sale impossible, it may be that no fair market value can be attributed to it. Helvering v. Tex-Penn Oil Co., 300 U.S. 481. . . . But where there is no absolute prohibition against a sale, a restriction may reduce but does not destroy fair market value. . . .

We do not think it can be said that where the holder of a highly speculative stock—and speculative Rocky Mountain Uranium Corporation surely was—can carry it into the market place only at the indulgence of another, the fair market value of the stock is the same as it would be if the dominion of the holder was free and unfettered. Parsons prevented the taxpayers from selling a portion of their stock from December 1954 for nearly a year and a half. In December 1954 the national market for the stock was around $3 per share. When the taxpayers were able to sell they realized five and ten cents a share. The inability of the taxpayers to sell between December 1954 and May 1956 may not have been occasioned by the exercise of Parsons' right under the restrictive agreement, but the result would have been no more disastrous if the exercise of the right had been the cause of the inability to sell.

We think the Tax Court should have recognized the effect of impairing the market value of the stock and given effect to that impairment in the ascertainment of fair market value. To permit it to do so, its decision will be reversed and the cause remanded for further proceedings.

Reversed and remanded.

NOTES

1. If the taxpayers had received 150,000 shares each, what tax impact might that have had on Parsons? If, by prearrangement, Parsons had delivered 150,000 shares to Mailloux for his services and 150,000 shares to Foley for cash equal to fair market value, what might the tax impact on Parsons have been? See §351(d)(1). What is the rationale underlying §351(d)(1)?

2. *Mailloux* arose before the enactment of §83. Would that section have any effect on the case if it were to arise today?

3. If A transfers appreciated assets in exchange for Corporation X's entire issue of nonvoting preferred stock and simultaneously B pays cash for the corporation's entire issue of common stock, §351(a) assures A that his gain will go unrecognized. If B had received his common stock in exchange for services, however, the tax impact on both A and B would have been quite different. Why should that be so as to A? As to B? See Herwitz, Allocation of Stock Between Services and Capital in the Organization of a Close Corporation, 75 Harv. L. Rev. 1098 (1962).

4. Services contributed to a corporation in exchange for its stock have never constituted "property" within the nonrecognition provision of §351. The Bankruptcy Tax Act of 1980 restructured §351(d) to provide that, in addition to services, indebtedness of the transferee corporation which is not evidenced by a security, and interest on indebtedness of the transferee corporation that accrued since the time the transferor held the debt, are not to be considered "property" under §351(a).

5. The IRS has ruled that the transfer to a corporation of its own installment obligation, in exchange for stock having a fair market value in excess of the basis of the transferred obligation, is a satisfaction of that obligation at greater than face value, therefore requiring recognition of gain to the transferor under what is now §453B even though §351 would otherwise apply. See Rev. Rul. 73-423, 1973-2 C.B. 161.

3. *Classification of Stock and Computation — §368(c)*

For §351(a) to operate, the transferors of the incorporated assets must be "in control" of the transferee corporation immediately after they effect their exchange. Section 368(c), defining "control," requires the transferors to own stock with at least (1) 80 percent of the total combined voting power of all classes of stock entitled to vote, and (2) 80 percent of the total number of shares of all other classes of outstanding stock.

When is stock with "voting power" "entitled to vote"? Cf. §302(b)(2)(B). Does the "entitled to vote" concept add anything to the "voting power" concept? Cf. §1504(a)(1). Is stock that is not "entitled to vote" different from "nonvoting stock" (§1504(a))? There is no clear-cut answer to these questions, and they arise only infrequently. The language differences may represent only differences in expression of the same ideas, enacted at different times without regard to earlier modes of expression. It is generally accepted that stock has "voting power" and is "entitled to vote" only when it entitles its owner to vote for directors in ordinary course. Stock that permits such voting only after a contingency occurs (e.g., preferred that is permitted to vote only after dividends are in default) probably becomes "entitled to vote" only after the contingency has occurred. Cf. Treas. Reg. §1.302-3(a)(3).

Suppose Mr. T, a transferor, receives 100 percent of a corporation's common (voting) stock in exchange for appreciated property; 10,000 shares of the Class A, 9-percent nonvoting preferred, $1.00 par, for cash of $10,000; and 1,000 shares of the Class B, 8-percent nonvoting preferred, $5.00 par, for cash of $5,000. He has received all of the authorized Class A preferred and half of the authorized Class B preferred. The other half of the authorized Class B preferred (1,000 shares) is issued to Mrs. E in exchange for services worth $5,000. Is Mr. T "in control"? See Rev. Rul. 59-259, 1959-2 C.B. 115.

B. "STOCK" AND/OR SOMETHING ELSE

1. Definitional Criteria

BURR OAKS CORP. v. COMMISSIONER
43 T.C. 635 (1965), aff'd, 365 F.2d 24 (7th Cir. 1966), cert. denied, 385 U.S. 1007 (1967)

FAY, Judge. Respondent . . . determined deficiencies in the income tax of petitioner Burr Oaks Corp. for its taxable years ended September 30, 1958, 1959, and 1960, in the respective amounts of $15,067.26, $52,595.26, and $16,602.61. With regard to the various individual petitioners, respondent determined the following deficiencies in their respective income taxes:

Docket No.	Petitioners	Taxable year ended Dec. 31 —	Deficiency
		1958	$ 499.32
4772-62	A. Aaron and Rosella Elkind	1959	35,520.49
		1960	1,778.90
1581-63	Harold A. and Fannie G. Watkins	1959	30,386.55
1583-63	Maurice and Esther Leah Ritz	1959	37,702.90

Petitioner Burr Oaks Corp. will hereinafter be referred to as the petitioner, and petitioners A. Aaron Elkind, Harold A. Watkins, and Maurice Ritz will hereinafter sometimes be referred to respectively as Elkind, Watkins, and Ritz, or as the individual petitioners.

The only question remaining to be determined insofar as petitioner is concerned is its correct basis in certain unimproved real estate transferred to it by Elkind, Watkins, and Ritz. In order to make this determination, we must first decide whether the transfer by Elkind, Watkins, and Ritz to petitioner constituted a valid sale or a contribution to capital. In the event we find it to be the latter, we must further determine whether it constitutes a transfer to a controlled corporation within the meaning of section 351.

Insofar as petitioners Elkind, Watkins, and Ritz are concerned, we must determine whether certain amounts received by them during 1959 from petitioner were taxable as ordinary income, rather than as long-term capital gain.

Findings of Fact

. . . Petitioner is a corporation formed under the laws of the State of Wisconsin. It maintains its books of account and files its Federal income tax returns on the basis of an accrual method of accounting and a fiscal year ended September 30. . . . [The individual petitioners filed their returns on the basis of a calendar year and the cash method of accounting.]

Elkind, at all times relevant hereto, has been engaged in various aspects of real estate development, with primary emphasis on the development of tracts of one-family houses. These various endeavors were generally conducted through corporations in which Elkind or members of his family were majority stockholders. Elkind also has made a number of investments in real estate, including raw land as well as improved property producing rental income.

Ritz, at all times relevant hereto, was a certified public accountant and the senior partner of an accounting firm of which Elkind was a client. Ritz had made various investments in improved and unimproved real estate prior to the years in issue herein, primarily as a result of opportunities which he came across in connection with his accounting practice.

At all times relevant hereto, Watkins was the president and principal stockholder of a corporation engaged in the manufacture and sale of slippers and other types of casual footwear. Watkins, also, had made several investments in real property over the years, primarily in improved properties producing rental income.

Elkind, Watkins, and Ritz have, at least upon one occasion other than that involved herein, jointly invested in a relatively large tract of unimproved real estate. Thus, on June 4, 1953, they purchased for the sum of $70,124.15 a tract of undeveloped land located just outside the city of Madison, Wis. These individuals held that property (hereinafter referred to as the Gay Farm) jointly until April 20, 1954, at which time it was sold to one of Elkind's development corporations for the sum of $149,650.79. That corporation subdivided the property into 353 lots, constructed one-family homes thereon, and made substantial profits totaling approximately $500,000 upon their sale.

In the fall of 1954 Elkind came across the opportunity to purchase a similar piece of property, this time a tract of land of approximately 70 acres, also located near the outskirts of the city of Madison and theretofore used as a golf course. This property will hereinafter sometimes be referred to as the Burr Oaks property.

Elkind, in December of the same year, contacted Ritz and Watkins in regard to their participation with him in the purchase of that land. Watkins and Ritz agreed to join him in the acquisition upon the understanding that each of them would obtain a one-third interest therein. On December 7 of that year, Elkind tendered to the owner of said property a written offer to purchase the property for the sum of $100,000. The offer provided that $10,000 of the purchase price was payable at the time of acceptance, $10,000 on February 15, 1955, $5,000 on April 1, 1955, with payments of $5,000 due quarterly thereafter until the final balance was paid. The offer was accepted on December 8, 1954.

From the time they acquired the Burr Oaks property through the summer of 1957 Elkind, Watkins, and Ritz attempted to develop said property as a shopping center site or as an industrial park. In furtherance of this plan, they purchased in 1955 an additional 80 feet of frontage on an adjoining thoroughfare for the purpose of providing better access to the Burr Oaks property in the event of its commercial development. This 80 feet of frontage will hereinafter be referred to as the Brinkman property. Their efforts to develop the Burr Oaks property for commercial purposes, however, proved fruitless.

Sometime during 1957 Elkind became convinced that their plans to develop the Burr Oaks property as a shopping center or an industrial park would not materialize. Contemplating that one of his corporations might purchase the property for purposes of subdivision or development, Elkind requested two of his business associates to investigate the zoning and platting possibilities of the Burr Oaks property. On March 11, 1957, a petition was filed with the City Council of Madison, Wis., to change the zoning of the Burr Oaks property. . . .

Elkind then proposed to Watkins and Ritz that the three of them sell the Burr Oaks property to one of Elkind's real estate corporations, as they had done with the Gay Farm property. Watkins and Ritz, recalling the substantial profits made by Elkind's corporation after they had sold the Gay Farm property to it, rejected this proposal. Ritz suggested that the three of them transfer the Burr Oaks property to a corporation which they would form for the purpose of subdividing, developing, and selling the property; that the shareholders thereof would be comprised of his two brothers and the wives of Watkins and Elkind; and that in return for the transfer of the land, the corporation would issue promissory notes to Elkind, Watkins, and Ritz. It was agreed that they would follow Ritz' suggestions.

On September 9, 1957, the City Council of Madison approved a preliminary plat incorporating the zoning proposed for the property in the aforementioned petition filed on March 11, 1957. . . .

Petitioner was incorporated on October 8, 1957, for the purpose of (1) acquiring the Burr Oaks property from Elkind, Watkins, and Ritz; (2) developing and subdividing said property; and (3) selling improved lots therefrom to customers. At the time petitioner was formed, the Burr Oaks property was completely unimproved. Elkind, Watkins, and Ritz were aware of a local ordinance pursuant to which owners of unimproved land could request the city of Madison to make improvements thereon such as streets, sewers, water, and sidewalks. The city would make these improvements and assess the costs incurred in connection therewith against the property. However, it was realized that the cost of some of the improvements to be made, such as grading and supplying crushed stone, would have to be borne directly by the developers. The total cost of such improvements, as estimated by petitioner, was in the amount of $107,243.33.

It was determined by Ritz, Watkins, and Elkind that petitioner's initial capital would be $4,500.

Petitioner issued a total of 450 shares of its common stock to a group composed of Elkind's wife, Watkins' wife, and Ritz' brothers, Philip and Erwin, for an aggregate consideration of $4,500. Elkind's wife received 150 shares of the stock; Watkins' wife also received 150 shares; and Philip and Erwin Ritz each received 75 shares. The record does not indicate the exact date when this stock was issued. Philip and Erwin Ritz paid for their stock by their respective checks, each in the amount of $750 and dated October 9, 1957, Watkins' wife paid for her stock by a check in the amount of $1,500 dated October 14, 1957. Each of the above-mentioned four persons received from petitioner a receipt dated November 1, 1957, evidencing their payment for the stock. At all times relevant hereto, petitioner's stockholders of record and officers and directors were as follows:

Shareholder	Number of Shares Held
Rosella Elkind (Elkind's wife)	150
Fannie G. Watkins (Watkins' wife)	150
Philip M. Ritz (Ritz' brother)	75
Erwin M. Ritz (Ritz' brother)	75

Officers	Position Held	Directors
Watkins	President	Watkins
Philip M. Ritz	Vice president	Ritz
Rosella Elkind	Secretary-treasurer	Elkind
		Fannie G. Watkins
		Philip M. Ritz
		Rosella Elkind

. . . On November 1, 1957, Elkind, Watkins, and Ritz transferred their respective interests in the Burr Oaks property to petitioner. In consideration for this transfer, petitioner assumed the remaining unpaid balance for the property, namely $30,000, and issued to each of Elkind, Watkins, and Ritz what purported on the face thereof to be a promissory note in the principal amount of $110,000. Each of the notes recited that it bore interest at the rate of 6 percent and that it was payable 2 years after the making thereof. The $30,000 obligation for the Burr Oaks property to its original owner, assumed by petitioner from Elkind, Watkins, and Ritz, was entered on petitioner's books under an account captioned "Mortgage Payable." An additional account was set up under the title "Land Contract Payable" in the amount of $330,000 to represent the alleged promissory notes. At the time Elkind, Watkins, and Ritz transferred the Burr Oaks property to petitioner, the fair market value of said property was substantially less than $360,000. The property was not worth more than $165,000 at that time.

Although at the time Elkind, Watkins, and Ritz transferred their interests in said property to petitioner they hoped that petitioner's business would be successful, petitioner's prospects were uncertain. The nature of their investment can best be described by the term "speculative."

Shortly after its incorporation, petitioner found that it did not have sufficient funds on hand with which to commence operations. Therefore, on November 30, 1957, it borrowed $15,000 from Elkind. On February 28, 1958, Elkind loaned petitioner an additional $10,000. These loans, together with interest thereon in the amount of $1,859.78, were repaid on June 30, 1959.

None of petitioner's stockholders of record, namely Watkins' and Elkind's respective wives and Ritz' brothers, took any active interest in the management of petitioner. In fact, none of them had any real idea of the nature of petitioner's business, other than some vague notion that it was engaged in "real estate" in some way or other.

Watkins and Ritz hired Albert McGinnes to manage petitioner. His work included the supervision of the platting, development, and subdivision of the land, as well as taking charge of advertising and sales. McGinnes had known and worked for Elkind and his various corporations for approximately 15 years prior to that time as a lawyer and real estate broker and in various other capacities. McGinnes, moreover, was the person who first interested Elkind in purchasing the Burr Oaks property and checked into the zoning and platting possibilities for the land. During the years in issue, McGinnes continued to work for various Elkind interests.

Ritz' accounting firm, Ritz, Holman & Co., kept petitioner's books and took care of its accounting work. McGinnes was required to account to Ritz, Holman & Co. for the funds which he took in and disbursed in connection with his operation of petitioner's business.

Upon a number of occasions, petitioner transferred various lots or parcels of property to Elkind, Watkins, and Ritz, either at no cost or at a price less than the amount for which such lots could have been sold to third parties. Thus, by deed dated November 3, 1958, petitioner conveyed to Elkind, Watkins, and Ritz a strip of commercial property, 70 feet by 120 feet, located in the southeast corner of the Burr Oaks property. This property was contiguous with another piece of commercial property, the Brinkman property, which Elkind, Watkins, and Ritz had purchased when they were contemplating using Burr Oaks for a shopping center. Nothing was paid to petitioner in consideration for this transfer. The deed by which the transfer was effected purported on its face to correct an erroneous conveyance of the land to petitioner in the first place.

On November 14, 1958, petitioner sold five lots at a price of $3,000 per lot to the Leo Building Corp., which was owned and controlled by Elkind and an associate of his. On the same date petitioner sold an additional five lots for the same price to Carsons, Inc., a corporation owned by Watkins. Petitioner, on May 20, 1960, sold five more lots at $3,000 per lot to M & L Investment, Inc., a corporation in which Ritz owned a substantial interest. . . . The evidence indicates that, at the time they were sold after having been platted, subdivided, and improved, each of these lots could have been sold to outsiders for $500 to $1,000 more than was received from the above corporations. None of petitioner's shareholders of record (Philip and Erwin Ritz, Elkind's wife, or Watkins' wife) was consulted with regard to, or knew of, any of these transfers. Nor was any such transfer authorized by a meeting of petitioner's board of directors.

Although McGinnes was in charge of petitioner's day-to-day operations, Elkind, Watkins, and Ritz controlled and dominated petitioner's affairs.

During its taxable years 1958 through 1963, inclusive, petitioner had gross receipts in the following amounts as a result of its subdivision and sale of the Burr Oaks property:

Taxable year ended Sept. 30 —	Gross sales of lots
1958	$ 86,095
1959	177,200
1960	118,625
1961	68,250
1962	49,400
1963	13,900
Total	513,470

As had been contemplated by Elkind, Watkins, and Ritz at the time of petitioner's incorporation, improvements to the Burr Oaks property, such as streets, sewers, water, and sidewalks, were made by the city of Madison. The city was to recover the cost of these improvements by special assessments against the lots, which assessments were generally payable over a period of 5 to 8 years. To the extent that installments of the special assessments came due prior to the sale of the lots, they were paid by petitioner and added to the price of the lots. To the extent the assessments had not been paid prior to the sale of the lots, they were assumed by the purchaser. Certain costs incurred in connection with the subdivision and improvement of the Burr Oaks property were borne directly by petitioner. . . .

In the latter part of 1959 Elkind, Watkins, and Ritz surrendered to petitioner the original "promissory notes" which they had received from petitioner in connection with their transfer of the Burr Oaks property. In return for the surrender of the notes, each of the individual petitioners received from petitioner a distribution of $23,000 in cash and a promissory note dated November 1, 1959, in the principal amount of $87,000. The new notes recited (1) that they were payable 1 year after the making thereof and (2) that they bore interest at the rate of 6 percent per annum. Later that same year, petitioner paid an additional $8,000 apiece to Elkind, Watkins, and Ritz. Petitioner at that time, in exchange for each of their notes in the principal amount of $87,000, issued to each of them a new promissory note in the principal amount of $79,000.

On December 29, 1959, petitioner purported to repay the outstanding balance on these "new promissory notes." At the close of business on that date petitioner had a bank balance of $5,498.88. The record does not clearly indicate how petitioner purported to repay these notes. However, the record does clearly indicate that petitioner urgently needed as working capital the $237,000 which it claims to have used to repay the three promissory notes. Therefore, immediately after those notes were "repaid," Elkind, Watkins, and Ritz each "loaned" $79,000 to petitioner, and petitioner, in turn, issued to each of the individual petitioners a "new" 1-year promissory note dated December 31, 1959, in the principal amount of $79,000. This transaction did not represent a repayment of the alleged "promissory notes." It was merely an extension of the purported maturity date. The individual petitioners never had any intention of enforcing their "notes" against petitioner.

In addition to the foregoing, petitioner made the following distributions to each of the individual petitioners with regard to the "promissory notes":

Date of distribution	Amount paid to each of the individual petitioners
Aug. 31, 1960	$ 8,000
Jan. 31, 1961	15,000
Dec. 31, 1961	10,000

There was an aggregate balance of $138,000 outstanding upon the three "notes" at the time of the trial in this proceeding, or a total of $46,000 due upon each of said notes.

Petitioner has not distributed any of its earnings to any of the shareholders of record.

Elkind, Watkins, and Ritz treated their transfer of the Burr Oaks property to petitioner in November 1957 as a sale. Petitioner did likewise and set up on its books a cost of $360,000 for said property. Elkind, Watkins, and Ritz, however, did not report any gain with regard to this alleged sale until 1959 when petitioner purportedly paid in full the promissory notes which it had issued to them in connection with said transfer. In their respective income tax returns for 1959, each of them reported long-term capital gain in the amount of $85,729.06 as a result of their transfer of the Burr Oaks property to petitioner in 1957.

Respondent, pursuant to separate notices of deficiency issued to Elkind, Watkins, and Ritz with respect to their taxable year ended December 31, 1959, determined that—"the gain realized from the sale of . . . [the Burr Oaks property] in the total amount of $85,729.06 is taxable as ordinary income rather than as long-term capital gains reported on your income tax return. . . ."

Pursuant to a statutory notice of deficiency issued to petitioner with respect to its taxable years 1958 through 1960, respondent increased petitioner's taxable income for said years by an aggregate amount totaling $192,686.98. This increase was based on respondent's determination that petitioner had understated its income for those years by claiming too high a basis or cost in the land sold by it in that period. The notice of deficiency indicates that, in making his determination, respondent treated petitioner as having a basis of $100,000 in the Burr Oaks property, rather than a basis of $360,000, as petitioner had claimed.

OPINION

There are two issues to be determined in this case. These are (1) petitioner's correct basis in the Burr Oaks property and (2) the proper tax treatment of the amounts received by Elkind, Watkins, and Ritz from petitioner during 1959. In order to resolve these issues, we must classify, for tax purposes, the transaction wherein each of the individual petitioners in November 1957 (1) transferred his respective interest in the Burr Oaks property to petitioner and (2) in return therefor received an instrument purporting to be a promissory note in the principal amount of $110,000.

It is contended by Elkind, Watkins, and Ritz (1) that their transfer of the Burr Oaks property to petitioner constitutes the sale or exchange of a capital asset held in excess of 6 months; (2) that the promissory note received by each of them in return therefor represents a valid indebtedness incurred by petitioner; and (3) that the gain realized by them in connection with said transfer is properly reportable in 1959 when they allege that petitioner "paid in full" the "promissory notes" which had been issued to them.[5]

_____

5. Passing over for the moment the validity of the first two parts of the individual petitioners' argument, we believe it appropriate to point out that the third part of their argument, namely, that the gain realized by them on the transfer of the Burr Oaks property was properly reportable in 1959, is incorrect. Watkins, Elkind, and Ritz at all times relevant hereto were cash basis taxpayers. When cash basis taxpayers sell property, they must include in income the fair market value of any property received in exchange therefor. This would include the fair market value of any notes received. See Pinellas Ice Co. v. Commissioner, 287 U.S. 462 (1933). The individual petitioners have not advanced any of the arguments which would enable them to avoid the applicability of this general rule. Thus, they have made no argument that the "promissory notes" received by them were of indeterminate or unascertainable

It is contended by petitioner that it purchased the Burr Oaks property from Elkin, Watkins, and Ritz at a cost of $360,000 and that such cost is its correct basis in said property.

The plethora of arguments advanced by respondent in his opening statement and on brief indicates to us that the Government had some difficulty in formulating a suitable rationale under which to classify the transfer of the Burr Oaks property to petitioner. It would serve no purpose to set forth at this point the various contentions made by respondent since we believe that the transaction was not a sale, but an equity contribution.[6]

It is true that Elkind, Watkins, and Ritz attempted to cast their transfer of the Burr Oaks property to petitioner in the form of a sale. It is also true that, from a standpoint of form, the alleged promissory notes issued to the individual petitioners are clear evidences of indebtedness. However, it has often been noted in connection with similar issues, the substance of the transaction, rather than its form, is the controlling factor in the determination of the proper tax treatment to be accorded thereto. . . . Whether a transaction such as the one we are now confronted with is in substance, as well as in form, a sale is essentially a question of fact.

As we view the creditable evidence presently before us, the trans-

---

value or that the notes were not received by them in payment for the land. . . . Nor do they contend (1) that the fair market value of the "notes" received by them was less than their respective bases in the land, cf. sec. 1.1001-1, Income Tax Regs., or (2) that the transfer was not a closed transaction, cf. Joseph Marcello, 43 T.C. 168 (1964). There is nothing in the record to show that (1) they elected to report the gain realized by them at the time of the transfer on the installment method or (2) that they were entitled to report their gain on the deferred payment sale method. See sec. 1.453-4(b)(1) and (2) and sec. 1.453-6, Income Tax Regs.

6. The statutory notices issued to the individual petitioners seem to be grounded on the theory that Elkind, Watkins, and Ritz were not entitled to report the sale of the Burr Oaks property as long-term capital gain since they were dealers. The deficiency notices did not raise any question with regard to the proper year for reporting the gain. In view of the fact that respondent, in the deficiency notice to petitioner-corporation, determined that petitioner's basis for the Burr Oaks property was the same as that of the transferors of the property, said statutory notice would seem to be based on the theory that the transfer was governed by sec. 351. This is undoubtedly what caused Elkind, Watkins, and Ritz to raise the following issue by way of amended petition: "In the alternative, in the event the basis of the . . . [Burr Oaks property] in the hands of . . . [petitioner] is determined under section 351 of the Internal Revenue Code, respondent erred in failing to determine that petitioners had no taxable gain for the year 1959 as a result of the transfer of the said real estate to . . . [petitioner]."

We have concluded that the transfer of the Burr Oaks property to petitioner was not a sale on the basis of the clear, uncontroverted facts in the record and without resort to the burden of proof. Nevertheless, we believe it appropriate to point out that the petitioners Elkind, Watkins, and Ritz, as well as the Burr Oaks Corp., have the burden of proof on this issue. For even if we were to regard the issue of whether the transfer of the property constitutes a bona fide sale as new matter insofar as Elkind, Watkins, and Ritz are concerned, they raised that question by way of their amended petition.

fer of the Burr Oaks property to petitioner is so lacking in the essential characteristics of a sale and is replete with so many of the elements normally found in an equity contribution . . . that it appears to us as nothing more than a shabby attempt to withdraw from petitioner, at capital gains rates, the developer's profit normally inherent in the subdivision and sale of raw acreage such as the Burr Oaks property.

This Court has been required upon numerous occasions to determine the true nature of alleged sales or transfers of assets to corporations. In the *Kolkey* case, [27 T.C. 37 (1956)] we listed the following questions as among the relevant criteria for making such a determination:

> Was the capital and credit structure of the new corporation realistic? What was the business purpose, if any, of organizing the new corporation? Were the noteholders the actual promoters and entrepreneurs of the new adventure? Did the noteholders bear the principal risks of loss attendant upon the adventure? Were payments of "principal and interest" on the notes subordinated to dividends and to the claims of creditors? Did the noteholders have substantial control over the business operations; and if so, was such control reserved to them as an integral part of the plan under which the notes were issued? Was the "price" of the properties, for which the notes were issued, disproportionate to the fair market value of such properties? Did the noteholders, when default of the notes occurred, attempt to enforce the obligations? [Emanuel N. (Manny) Kolkey, supra, at 59.]

We have set forth in our Findings of Fact, with some degree of specificity, the various factors which cause us to conclude that the transfer of the Burr Oaks property to petitioner was an equity contribution, rather than a sale. We set forth below some of the more significant factors which led us to this conclusion.

In the first place, petitioner, from the start of its existence, was not only undercapitalized, but, in fact, had no significant capitalization at all. Cf. Hoguet Real Estate Corporation, 30 T.C. 580, 598 (1958). Thus, petitioner was organized in October with a paid-in capital of $4,500. Shortly thereafter, when Elkind, Watkins, and Ritz transferred the Burr Oaks property to petitioner, its books of account reflected liabilities of $360,000. In addition, it was contemplated from the very outset of petitioner's existence that although the city of Madison would initially pay the major portion of the cost of improving the Burr Oaks property, petitioner would, nevertheless, be required to incur substantial development costs. Petitioner estimated that these costs would be in excess of $100,000.

Another factor indicating that petitioner was undercapitalized and did not have sufficient funds with which to commence business is that on November 30, 1957, less than 2 months after it was formed, it borrowed $15,000 from Elkind. On February 28, 1958, it borrowed an additional $10,000 from Elkind.

Moreover, the land transferred to petitioner by Elkind, Watkins, and Ritz was its only asset of significance and, without it, petitioner could not have engaged . . . in business. It was at all times contemplated by Elkind, Watkins, and Ritz that the land would remain at the risk of petitioner's business.

It is generally recognized that one of the crucial factors in determining whether the transfer of property to a thinly capitalized corporation constitutes a bona fide sale, rather than a mere contribution to capital, is the anticipated source of payment to the transferor. Gilbert v. Commissioner, 262 F.2d 512, 514 (C.A. 2, 1959), *affirming* a Memorandum Opinion of this Court, *certiorari denied* 359 U.S. 1002 (1959). If payment to the transferor is dependent solely upon the success of an untried, undercapitalized business, the prospects of which are uncertain, the transfer of property raises a strong inference that it is, in fact, an equity contribution. . . .

At the time of the transfer of the Burr Oaks property to petitioner, its business prospects can only be described as speculative and uncertain. Elkind, Watkins, and Ritz realized that the only way petitioner could raise the $100,000 needed by it for improvements would be from sales of lots. It is obvious that the only hope that Elkind, Watkins, and Ritz had of obtaining repayment of the so-called promissory notes depended upon the successful development and sale of the lots in the Burr Oaks property.

Despite the fact that the respective interests of Elkind, Watkins, and Ritz in petitioner were represented by what purported on their face to be promissory notes in the principal amount of $110,000, the evidence before us indicates that it was the intent of all concerned with the affairs of petitioner that these instruments would give Elkind, Watkins, and Ritz a continuing interest in petitioner's business. The instruments issued by petitioner to Elkind, Watkins, and Ritz recited that they were to mature in 2 years from the date of issuance. However, after a review of the entire record, we believe that it was understood that no payment would be made on the notes, or would ever be demanded by Elkind, Watkins, and Ritz, which in any way would weaken or undermine petitioner's business. See Charter Wire, Inc. v. United States, 309 F.2d 878, 881 (C.A. 7, 1962). It is true that petitioner during 1959 paid $31,000 apiece to Elkind, Watkins, and Ritz with respect to their so-called promissory notes.[8] However, pe-

---

8. On brief, it is argued on behalf of the various petitioners herein that the series of exchanges of notes that occurred at the end of December 1959 between Elkind, Watkins, and Ritz, on the one hand, and petitioner, on the other, constituted a repayment by petitioner of the "unpaid principal balance" in the amount of $79,000

titioner's history with regard to making payments on the alleged promissory notes indicates that the payments thereon came only from gains derived through the sale of lots. Moreover the fact that there was outstanding a substantial principal balance ($46,000) on each of the notes issued to the individual petitioners even as late as the time of the trial herein indicates that the alleged notes were intended to give the individual petitioners a continuing equity interest in petitioner. . . .

The evidence clearly indicates that although Elkind, Watkins, and Ritz were not stockholders of record in petitioner, nevertheless, they completely dominated and controlled petitioner's affairs. Watkins was petitioner's president. Petitioner's board of directors consisted of Elkind, his wife, Ritz, his brother Philip, Watkins, and Watkins' wife. McGinnes, the man who ran petitioner's day-to-day affairs, had been employed by Elkind in one capacity or another for a period of at least 15 years. His activities were generally supervised by Ritz' accounting firm. After listening to his testimony and that of Elkind, Watkins, and Ritz, we are convinced that McGinnes operated petitioner in accordance with their wishes.

Petitioner's shareholders of record consisted of Ritz' brothers Philip and Erwin, Elkind's wife, and Watkins' wife. They knew and understood little, if anything, of the nature of petitioner's business. Moreover, after listening to the testimony at the trial, it was obvious to us that they were subject to the control of Elkind, Watkins, and Ritz.

By virtue of the provision in petitioner's articles of incorporation regarding the issuance of additional shares of common stock at such prices as a majority of the board of directors should determine, Elkind, Watkins, and Ritz were in a position to appropriate to themselves (through the issuance of additional common stock at whatever price they chose) substantially all of the profits that petitioner might realize after repaying its purported indebtedness to them.

The record also indicates that in transferring the Burr Oaks property to petitioner, Elkind, Watkins, and Ritz assigned a highly inflated value to said property. . . . The transfer of the Burr Oaks property to petitioner seems to us an integral part of a plan devised by Ritz whereby Ritz, Watkins, and Elkind could obtain an assured participation in the fruits of the development and subdivision of said property. . . . Watkins and Ritz both admitted that petitioner was

---

on each of the alleged promissory notes, followed immediately by an advance of a similar amount by each of the individual petitioners. This alleged repayment by petitioner of an aggregate of $237,000 took place at a time when petitioner's liquid assets totaled less than $5,500. It is too much to ask this Court to believe that such an obvious sham constituted a repayment of the alleged notes. Cf. Arthur L. Kniffen, 39 T.C. 553, 565-566 (1962).

formed in order to allow them to receive some part of the development profits. The inflation of the "sales price" to petitioner served to extend the period during which Elkind, Watkins, and Ritz could participate in petitioner's business as "creditors" and increased the amount which they could withdraw as "principal" if the venture proved successful.

These are some of the factors which led us to conclude that the promissory notes received by Elkind, Watkins, and Ritz did not represent a true indebtedness. The purported promissory notes issued to the individual petitioners in our opinion constitute preferred stock.[10]

Having decided that for tax purposes the so-called promissory notes issued to Elkind, Watkins, and Ritz constitute an equity interest in petitioner, we must now determine whether the transfer of the Burr Oaks property is governed by section 351. . . .

In contending that section 351 does not govern the transfer of the Burr Oaks property, petitioner has presented three arguments. Two of the arguments (that the transaction was a sale and that no stock or securities were issued to the transferors of the property) have been previously considered and resolved adversely to petitioner. The third argument presented is that Elkind, Watkins, and Ritz, who transferred the Burr Oaks property to petitioner, were not, immediately after that transaction, in control of that corporation within the meaning of the term "control" as defined in section 368(c). Thus, it is contended that even if the promissory notes held by Elkind, Watkins, and Ritz constituted stock, that stock did not carry with it any voting rights. Petitioner further points out (1) that pursuant to its bylaws the right to vote was reserved exclusively to the shareholders of record, namely, Elkind's wife, Watkins' wife, and Ritz' two brothers, and (2) that, for the above reason, the transferors of the Burr Oaks property (Elkind, Watkins, and Ritz) failed to comply with the control requirements set forth in section 368(c) because they did not possess "ownership of stock possessing at least 80 percent of the total combined voting power of all classes of stock entitled to vote." There is a basic fallacy in petitioner's argument in that it is premised on the assumption that Elkind, Watkins, and Ritz were the only transferors of property to petitioner.

As we view the transaction, Elkind, Watkins, and Ritz acted together with Elkind's wife, Watkins' wife, and Ritz' two brothers in

10. Although we have found the purported promissory notes to constitute equity interests in petitioner for tax purposes, we believe that the holders of those instruments occupied a preferred position vis-à-vis the holders of the common stock. In the first place, the purported promissory notes called for the payment of interest at 6 percent a year. This provision constituted a prior charge on the earnings of petitioner in favor of the holders of those instruments, not unlike a preferred dividend. Thus, we regard the purported promissory notes as preferred stock.

forming petitioner. The record clearly indicates that each of them transferred property to petitioner. As we have previously found, Elkind's wife, Watkins' wife, and Philip and Erwin Ritz transferred to petitioner a total of $4,500 shortly after its incorporation. It is settled law that money constitutes property for purposes of section 351. . . . In return therefor, petitioner issued to them an aggregate of 450 shares of its common stock. Shortly thereafter, Elkind, Watkins, and Ritz transferred to petitioner their respective interests in the Burr Oaks property and, in return, received what on its face purported to be promissory notes, but what we have previously determined to be preferred stock.

Although Elkind, Watkins, and Ritz may not have received their preferred stock interests in petitioner at exactly the same time as the common stock was issued to Ritz' brothers and the respective wives of Elkind and Watkins, it seems clear that the transfers of cash and the Burr Oaks property to petitioner were integral parts of a unified transaction. Camp Wolters Enterprises v. Commissioner, 230 F.2d 555, 559 (C.A. 5, 1956), *affirming* 22 T.C. 737 (1954), *certiorari denied* 352 U.S. 826 (1956). See also section 1.351-I(a)(I), Income Tax Regs., which provides:

> The phrase "immediately after the exchange" does not necessarily require simultaneous exchanges by two or more persons, but comprehends a situation where the rights of the parties have been previously defined and the execution of the agreement proceeds with an expedition consistent with orderly procedure. . . .

On the basis of the record before us, it appears to us that Elkind, Watkins, and Ritz, together with Ritz' brothers, Elkind's wife, and Watkins' wife, were in control of petitioner, as defined in section 368(c), immediately after their transfer of property to it. The fact that Elkind, Watkins, and Ritz received no common stock, which according to petitioner's articles of incorporation was the only class of stock entitled to vote, is of no significance; for there is no requirement in section 351 that each transferor receive voting stock for that section to be applicable. See Cyrus S. Eaton, 37 B.T.A. 715 (1938), which involved the transfer of property by two persons to a controlled corporation. One transferor therein received only common stock and the other received only nonvoting preferred. In commenting upon the question of control, we stated: "Inasmuch as the transferors . . . owned all of the stock of the corporation, they have the necessary control required by the statute." See also Gus Russell, Inc., 36 T.C. 965 (1961).

Since the nonrecognition provisions of section 351 apply to the transfer of the Burr Oaks property to petitioner, petitioner's basis in said property is limited to $100,000, which is a carry-over basis from the transferors. Sec. 362(a)(1).

Insofar as the distributions made by petitioner during 1959 to Elkind, Watkins, and Ritz are concerned, we have previously found that, to the extent they purported to be a repayment of the "promissory notes," they were a sham. The net effect of the various payments by petitioner and exchanges of notes was that petitioner distributed $31,000 apiece to Elkind, Watkins, and Ritz in 1959. To this extent, the distributions resemble a redemption of stock in that the respective interests of these three individuals in petitioner were proportionately lessened. However, we are unable to find that said distributions fit within any of the paragraphs of section 302(b). Therefore, the $31,000 distributed by petitioner to Watkins, Elkind, and Ritz is governed by section 302(d) and to the extent of petitioner's earnings and profits is to be treated as a dividend. . . .

NOTES

1. What argument might have been advanced for Ritz, but not for the others, to avoid dividend treatment? Consider the scope of §318(a)(1) in answering this question. Should the argument prevail?

2. Should Ritz have had counsel of his own? Might the one lawyer representing all the taxpayers have had a conflict of interest? See generally B. Wolfman and J. Holden, Ethical Problems in Federal Tax Practice (2d ed. 1985).

STEVENS PASS, INC. v. COMMISSIONER
48 T.C. 532 (1967)

FAY, Judge. . . . The parties have stipulated as to certain items raised in the statutory notice of deficiency so that [one of] the issues remaining for determination [is] as follows:

(1) Whether, upon the liquidation of its subsidiary, petitioner was entitled to the step-up in the basis of depreciable assets pursuant to section 334(b)(2) of the Internal Revenue Code of 1954. . . .

FINDINGS OF FACT

. . . Petitioner, Stevens Pass, Inc., is a Washington corporation which was organized on September 29, 1960. . . . Since December 1, 1960, petitioner has operated the ski area at Stevens Pass. . . .

Petitioner is the survivor by merger, under the laws of the State of Washington with Stevens Pass Company, Inc. (hereinafter referred to as the old company), on December 1, 1960.

The old company was organized in 1946 to operate the ski facilities and area at Stevens Pass, Washington. In 1960 the authorized capital of the old company consisted of 100 shares of Class A voting common stock and 33⅓ shares of Class B nonvoting common stock. The Class A and Class B stocks share in the earnings and capital on the basis of two-thirds to Class A and one-third to Class B. The total authorized and issued shares of the old company on November 30, 1960, were owned as follows:

Name	Class A	Class B
Donald G. Adams*	50	0
Bruce Kehr*	50	0
John H. Caley	0	33⅓

*By agreements dated June 16, 1948, and September 15, 1948, between Adams and Kehr, Adams had 51 percent voting control of the old company.

Sometime during the spring of 1960 an irreparable dispute arose between Donald G. Adams (hereinafter referred to as Adams) and Bruce Kehr (hereinafter referred to as Kehr). It was determined that the dispute could not be settled unless one or the other sold his stock in the old company. However, no agreement was reached that was satisfactory to both parties. Thereafter, Adams, Kehr, and John H. Caley (hereinafter referred to as Caley) attempted to interest outside investors in acquiring stock in a new corporation to be formed to acquire the stock of the old company and then to dissolve it.

On June 10, 1960, Adams, Kehr, and Caley offered to sell all of their shares in the old company to Loren D. Prescott, an agent for undisclosed principals, for the sum of $650,000. Contemporaneously with the execution of the offer to sell, they executed an agreement among themselves concerning the division of the $650,000 sales proceeds as follows: Adams, $250,000; Kehr, $200,000; and Caley, $200,000. This latter agreement also called for the transfer by Kehr of his stock (33⅓ shares) in a corporation known as Trams, Inc., to Adams for the sum of $4,800.

On or about June 30, 1960, a prospectus relevant to the financial condition of the old company was prepared and circulated to various potential investors. The prospectus proposed that a new company (petitioner) be formed to purchase all the shares of the old company and then dissolve it.

On September 2, 1960, a subscription account was set up for investment in petitioner. The subscribers, amount subscribed, and date subscribed were as follows:

Date	Name	Units Subscribed*
Aug. 30, 1960	Melvin R. Whitman	4
Sept. 1, 1960	Mel S. Johnston	3
Sept. 6, 1960	Donald P. Christianson	4
Sept. 8, 1960	Miles W. Tippery	4
Sept. 27, 1960	John M. Shiach	$1\frac{1}{3}$
Sept. 27, 1960	Bernard J. Goiney	$1\frac{1}{3}$
Sept. 27, 1960	Homer V. Hartzell	$1\frac{1}{3}$
Oct. 13, 1960	Reider Tanner	1
Nov. 2, 1960	Vernon O. Lundmark	1
		21

*A unit consisted of 10 shares of no par common stock at $250 per share and one $2,500, 20-year, 6-percent debenture at par for a total investment of $5,000.

The subscribers deposited 10 percent of the subscription price into escrow at a bank located in Seattle, Washington.

On September 9, 1960, the offer to sell made by Adams, Kehr, and Caley was accepted. On September 29, 1960, petitioner was organized. On October 22, 1960, petitioner's stock certificate book reflects the issuance of 400 shares of its no par common stock to the following individuals for a total of $100,000.

Certificate No.	Name	Shares
1	Miles W. or Nellie Tippery	40
2	Bruce Kehr	120*
3	John H. Caley	80
4	Reider Tanner	10
5	Melvin R. Whitman	40
6	Mel S. Johnston	30
7	Vernon O. Lundmark	10
8	Donald P. Christianson	20*
9	John M. Shiach	13.33
10	Homer V. Hartzell	13.33
11	Bernard J. Goiney	13.33
12	Mel S. Johnston	10
		400

*Ten of the shares issued in the name of Bruce Kehr are subject to a trust agreement as the property of Christianson and are held by Kehr as security for a loan of $5,000 made by him to Christianson to enable the latter to purchase an investment unit in petitioner.

On November 4, 1960, petitioner entered into a written agreement with Adams, Kehr, and Caley to purchase their shares in the old company for the sum of $650,000, payment to be made as follows:

(a) $10,000 upon execution of this agreement
(b) $178,500 on closing the transaction
(c) The balance of $461,500 payable in ten equal annual installments of $46,150, plus interest at 5 percent on the declining balance from the date of closing and payable on or before June 30 of each succeeding year beginning with 1961.

This agreement was closed in Seattle, Washington, on November 30, 1960.

In December 1960, petitioner issued 6-percent, 20-year debenture bonds in registered form in the total amount of $100,000. The debentures were dated October 22, 1960, and were issued to the following individuals:

Name	Amount
Miles W. or Nellie Tippery	$ 10,000.00
Bruce Kehr	30,000.00*
John H. Caley	20,000.00
Melvin R. Whitman	10,000.00
Donald P. Christianson	5,000.00*
Vernon O. Lundmark	2,500.00
Reider Tanner	2,500.00
John M. Shiach	3,333.33
Bernard J. Goiney	3,333.33
Homer V. Hartzell	3,333.33
Mel S. Johnston	10,000.00
	$100,000.00

*Of the debentures issued to Kehr, the amount of $2,500 is subject to a trust agreement as the property of Donald Christianson and is held by Kehr as security for a loan of $5,000 by him to Christianson.

On December 1, 1960, the old company and petitioner, through appropriate Board of Directors' and shareholders' action, entered into a joint plan of merger and agreement of merger, whereupon the old company, the wholly owned subsidiary of petitioner, was liquidated pursuant to section 332, and the assets subject to the liabilities were transferred to petitioner.

On December 1, 1960, the old company had assets with a book value of $245,504.83 and liabilities of $125,946.59. Petitioner included the assets received on liquidation at a cost of $775,946.59 (the total of the cost of the stock, $650,000, and the amount of the liabilities assumed, $125,946.59) pursuant to section 334(b)(2). The increase in the book value of assets on the merger was $530,381.76.

The allocation of the step-up in basis is made on the basis of the net fair market values of the assets received (fair market value less applicable liabilities). Petitioner, therefore, estimated the net fair market values of the tram equipment and the other assets and allocated the $650,000 purchase price of the stock to them. Petitioner determined that the old company had had no goodwill and that certain special use permits were without fair market value. It, therefore, did not allocate any portion of the step-up in basis to either item, . . .

Respondent, in his statutory notice of deficiency, determined that section 334(b)(2) was inapplicable in determining the basis of the assets in question and that the basis should be determined under section 334(b)(1). . . .

OPINION

The first issue for determination is whether petitioner may properly compute under section 334(b)(2) the basis of assets received in the liquidation of its wholly owned subsidiary pursuant to section 332. Respondent contends that petitioner must compute the basis of the assets received under section 334(b)(1). . . .

The crux of the present dispute is whether petitioner acquired the stock of the old company by "purchase" as defined by section 334(b)(3). Petitioner contends that it acquired the stock of the old company by the purchase and sale contract closed on November 30, 1960. Respondent at trial took the position that the transfer came within the language of subsection 3(C) of section 334(b). He has, however, failed to pursue this theory[5] and, on brief, argues that the shares acquired from Kehr and Caley were in fact acquired by petitioner in a transaction to which section 351 applied and that the exchange, therefore, falls within subsection 3(B) of section 334(b). The rationale of respondent's contention is that the transaction should be viewed as an exchange by Kehr and Caley of cash and their shares of stock in the old company for stock and debentures in petitioner, plus a cash down payment (an amount unrelated to the cash given by Kehr and Caley) and a 10-year installment obligation. Respondent then states that the cash down payment received should be netted against the cash paid in for the stock and debentures of the petitioner. He further states that the "control" requirement of section 351 is satisfied since the outside investors contributed cash, in effect, simultaneously with the transfer by Kehr and Caley so that they all may be considered as one transferor group.

We cannot agree.

Though at first blush respondent's argument appears to have some merit, on closer inspection we are of the opinion that respon-

---

5. In any event, we are of the opinion that section 334(b)(3)(C) has no application to the factual situation before us. Respondent has urged in his opening statement that Kehr and Caley be treated collectively as one person in order to apply section 318. We can find no authority for such a premise.

dent's position requires an unwarranted extension of the scope of the nonrecognition provisions of section 351. This is the same contention respondent urged us to adopt in the case of Charles E. Curry, 43 T.C. 667 (1965). We declined to do so then, and we decline to do so now. The factual pattern of the *Curry* case is strikingly similar to the case before us. In *Curry*, a family group composed of Charles F. Curry and his wife (Janet), Charles E. Curry, and Carolyn Elbel (daughter of Charles F. and Janet), owned undivided interests in a building, as follows:

Charles F. and Janet Curry	60%
Charles E. Curry	20%
Carolyn Elbel	20%

This group transferred their building to a corporation formed to purchase it for cash and notes. The shares in the purchasing corporation were held as follows:

Charles E. Curry	45%
Donald Elbel (Carolyn's husband)	45%
Charles F. Curry	10%

The corporation took as its basis for depreciation, its cost. Respondent, however, contended that since the transaction should be properly characterized as a section 351 transfer (he argued that the notes were in fact securities), the basis to the purchasing corporation should be the transferor's basis as provided in section 362. We held that section 351 was inapplicable and stated that—

> If respondent's position were adopted, section 351 would apply even where an unrelated third party was the stockholder of the corporation. Assume, for example, a transaction identical to that involved in the instant case except that A.T. & T. was the sole shareholder of [the purchasing corporation]. We cannot believe that Congress intended nonrecognition of gain in such a case. Indeed, respondent would undoubtedly be quick to object if taxpayers tried to prevent recognition by such a device. Yet it is clear that, in a sale effected in this manner, the transfers of cash for stock and property for notes are interdependent steps of a single plan. It is not a ground for distinction that two of the stockholders in the instant case were also transferors of realty, since we have found the parties were capable of independent action and intended a bona fide sale.[6] [43 T.C. at 697]

It is our opinion that this statement is equally applicable to the

6. The instant case, like the case of Charles F. Curry, 43 T.C. 667 (1963), unquestionably involves an arm's-length transaction. . . .

facts before us. We do not believe that this is a proper situation for the application of section 351.

The case of Houck v. Hinds, 215 F.2d 673 (C.A. 10, 1954), which is respondent's sole citation of authority for his contention, is readily distinguishable from the case at bar. In Houck v. Hinds, the members of a partnership sold its assets to a newly formed corporation organized by a third party for installment notes. The third party was unable to interest others in the venture, and members of the partnership then purchased his shares and subscribed for the balance of the corporate shares. The net effect was that the members of the partnership now owned the corporate shares and the corporation's installment notes in the same proportion as their old partnership interests. The Tenth Circuit held that what had occurred was the mere incorporation of the partnership in that the shares were held by the same persons and in the same proportions as the partnership interests.

The case at bar is distinguishable on its facts. We can hardly ignore the facts that, whereas in Houck v. Hinds the ownership remained exactly the same throughout, in this case Adams' 50-percent ownership disappeared, Kehr's 50-percent common-stock interest was reduced to less than 30 percent, Caley's 100-percent nonvoting-stock interest was changed to a 20-percent voting interest, and finally that over 50 percent of the petitioner-corporation is owned by persons who possessed no interest whatever in the old company.

We therefore hold that section 351 is inapplicable and that petitioner may properly compute the basis for the assets received under section 334(b)(2). . . .

NOTES

1. The *Stevens Pass* case posed the question whether the taxpayer had acquired its subsidiary's stock by "purchase," as defined in §334(b)(3) of the pre-TEFRA statute. After TEFRA, the issue would arise as a result of a §338 election, not upon liquidation of the subsidiary, and the question would be whether the acquisition of the subsidiary's stock was effected by "purchase" within the meaning of §338(h)(3) or, as the Commissioner contended, in a §351 transaction. In light of the repeal of the *General Utilities* doctrine in 1986, however, few taxpayers would today make a §338 election.

2. The Second Circuit has recently affirmed a Tax Court decision holding that the "exchange" requirements of §351 are met although a sole proprietor who transfers the assets and liabilities of

his business to a preexisting wholly owned corporation receives no additional stock. Lessinger v. Commissioner, 872 F.2d 519 (2d Cir. 1989), *aff'g on this ground and rev'g in part* 85 T.C. 824 (1985).

A owns all the stock of Corporation X. She contributes to X a piece of real estate worth $100,000 but receives nothing in return. The basis of the real estate before transfer is $50,000. What are the tax consequences to A? To X? What is the basis of the real estate in X's hands? What impact does the transfer have on the basis of A's stock?

Suppose in the above situation that A owns only 50 percent of the stock of X. B and C own the remaining 50 percent. What is the effect on B and C of A's contribution of the real estate?

For a case distinguishing debt from equity in order to decide whether a corporation's note was issued in connection with a "sale" or in a §351 transaction, see Robert W. Adams, 58 T.C. 41 (1972).

3. Prior to the 1989 amendments to §351, a transferor could, in addition to stock, receive debt of the transferee, evidenced by "securities," without recognition of gain. This often enabled the securities holder to withdraw corporate earnings as a tax-free return of basis. In the past, when capital gains were taxed at a preferential rate the securities holder's gain on distributions received in excess of basis was typically capital gain. The law now treats all debt received in a §351 transaction, whether or not evidenced by "securities," as boot. Cf. The Subchapter C Revision Act of 1985, A Final Report Prepared by the Staff, S. Prt. No. 47, 99th Cong., 1st Sess. 46, 57 (Comm. Print, May 1985).

With respect to the definition of "securities" under prior law, see Comment, Section 351 Transfers to Controlled Corporations: The Forgotten Term — "Securities," 114 U. Pa. L. Rev. 314 (1965); Nye v. Commissioner, 50 T.C. 203 (1968).

2.   *Taxation of "Boot"; Basis of Stock Received*

a.   **Taxable Transfer — §§1001, 1012**

Assume that T transfers property with adjusted basis of $10,000 and fair market value of $20,000 to X Corporation in exchange for its common stock worth $20,000. Assume, too, that T is not "in control" after the exchange. As a result, §351 is inapplicable, T's gain is recognized, and §1012 prescribes a cost ($20,000) basis for the stock which T receives.

b. Tax-Free Transfer (in Whole or in Part)

i. Recognition of Gain — §351(b)

If a transferor receives not only the "stock" permitted by §351(a), but "other property or money" to boot, §351(b)(2) provides for non-recognition of loss but §351(b)(1) calls for recognition of gain (the amount realized over basis), to the extent of the "boot" (the money plus the fair market value of the "other property" received). For example, suppose T transfers an asset with adjusted basis of $50,000 and fair market value of $100,000 to a corporation in exchange for its common stock (worth $75,000) and cash in the amount of $25,000. Assume, too, that T is "in control" after the exchange. T's realized gain is $50,000. His recognized gain, however, is $25,000, since §351(b) restricts recognition of the gain to the amount of the boot, here the cash of $25,000.

If two assets are transferred, one at a $50,000 gain and one at a $40,000 loss, and "boot" of $30,000 is received (in addition to stock that qualifies under §351(a)), what is the tax impact? See Rev. Rul. 68-55, 1968-1 C.B. 140.

Suppose the taxpayer receives "boot" of $15,000 for an asset with a basis of $10,000 and a fair market value of $12,000. What is the tax impact on the transferor? Should one be concerned with the earnings and profits account of the corporation? With the relationship between the taxpayer and the other shareholders?

See B. Bittker and J. Eustice, Federal Income Taxation of Corporations and Shareholders 3-15 to 3-19 (5th ed. 1987); Rabinovitz, Allocating Boot in Section 351 Exchanges, 24 Tax. L. Rev. 337 (1969).

ii. Basis of Stock Received — §358

In the hypothetical posed in subsection 2.a., supra, if T had been "in control" after the exchange, and §351(a) had applied, T's gain would not have been recognized. His basis for the stock received would have been $10,000, determined under §358(a)(1).

Assume that T had received stock worth $15,000 and cash of $5,000, that he was "in control," and that his gain of $10,000 was recognized to the extent of $5,000 under §351(b)(1). What is the basis of his stock?

Assume that, instead of cash, T had received an A.T. & T. bond worth $5,000. What would be its basis in T's hands? Consider §358(a)(2); Treas. Reg. §1.358-1.

Suppose that, in a §351 transaction in which T receives stock worth $10,000 and bonds worth $15,000, the asset he transferred had had a basis of $15,000. At what basis does T hold the stock? The bonds? Consider §358(b)(1); Treas. Reg. §1.358-2.

Suppose T, in a §351 transaction, transfers an asset with an adjusted basis of $50,000 and fair market value of $100,000 to X Corporation for common stock worth $75,000 plus X Corporation's assumption of a $25,000 liability that T had incurred when he purchased the asset. What is the basis for the stock in T's hands? Consider §358(a)(1)(A)(ii) and (d); Treas. Reg. §1.358-3. See Rabinovitz, Allocating Boot in §351 Exchanges, 24 Tax L. Rev. 337 (1969).

A transferor may not allocate high basis, long-term property to one block of stock and low basis, short-term property to another, when the properties are transferred as part of a single integrated transaction. See Treas. Reg. §§1.358-1 and 1.358-2(b)(2); Rev. Rul. 85-164, 1985-2 C.B. 117.

iii. Holding Period — §1223(1)

If §358 determines a transferor's basis as to the stock issued him by a corporation (as in a §351 transaction), his holding period for the stock will ordinarily include the period during which he held the assets transferred. This rule for "tacking" and its exceptions are set forth in §1223(1). The holding period rules were important when *long-term* capital gains were taxed at preferential rates.

3. Effect of Liabilities — §357

SIMON v. COMMISSIONER
285 F.2d 422 (3d Cir. 1960)

Before Goodrich, McLaughlin and Staley, Circuit Judges.

STALEY, Circuit Judge. Does a recognizable gain accrue to a taxpayer where pursuant to a prearranged plan he mortgages real estate and receives therefor an amount in excess of the property's adjusted basis under Section [1001(b)] . . . , and shortly thereafter transfers the property without consideration but subject to the mortgage?

The facts as found by the Tax Court, stipulated in part, may be summarized as follows:

In 1941 Joseph B. Simon, petitioner, purchased the RKO Building ("property") in Philadelphia, Pennsylvania, for $104,220.45. On September 28, 1951, he placed a mortgage on it not involving personal liability and received therefor $120,000. On December 27, 1951, the petitioners conveyed the property subject to the mortgage to Exco Corporation ("Exco"), and shortly thereafter, Exco conveyed the same property to Penn-Liberty Insurance Company ("Penn-Liberty").

The petitioners' joint income tax return for the year 1951 did
not show receipt of the mortgaged proceeds or reflect in any way
the conveyance of the property to Exco. The Commissioner determined that these transactions constituted a sale from which the
petitioner realized a long-term capital gain in the amount of
$35,108.33 for the taxable year 1951. A tax deficiency in the amount
of $10,715.94 was assessed against the petitioners. . . . The Tax Court
sustained the Commissioner's determination. . . .

In this court the petitioner does not assail the facts, largely stipulated, as found by the Tax Court, but only its ultimate finding that
a sale took place, asserting that "there are no facts to support the
Court's conclusion that a 'sale,' or any other kind of taxable disposition, took place." . . .

In our evaluation of the evidence before the Tax Court to determine its persuasiveness of that court's conclusion, we are guided
in part by what was said in Commissioner of Internal Revenue v.
Court Holding Co. [page 33 supra] . . . :

> . . . The incidence of taxation depends upon the substance of a
> transaction. The tax consequences which arise from gains from a
> sale of property are not finally to be determined solely by the means
> employed to transfer legal title. Rather, the transaction must be
> viewed as a whole, and each step, from the commencement of
> negotiations to the consummation of the sale, is relevant. A sale
> by one person cannot be transformed for tax purposes into a sale
> by another by using the latter as a conduit through which to pass
> title. To permit the true nature of a transaction to be disguised by
> mere formalisms, which exist solely to alter tax liabilities, would
> seriously impair the effective administration of the tax policies of
> Congress.

During 1951 Penn-Liberty was confronted with a deteriorating
financial condition caused by substantial losses arising from claims
for hurricane damage which had occurred at the end of 1950. The
petitioner Charles Denby and the officers of Penn-Liberty discussed
this situation and agreed to a plan whereby the property in question
would be mortgaged and thereafter conveyed, subject to the mortgage, to Penn-Liberty to help maintain its legal reserves. The interest
shown by petitioner and Denby in Penn-Liberty's plight was understandable. Petitioner was president of Exco and treasurer of Penn-
Liberty, while Denby served as treasurer of Exco. Together, they
owned and controlled Exco, which in turn owned Penn-Liberty.

The petitioner proceeded to execute the plan. Either because
Penn-Liberty did not require a contribution equal to the full value
of the property, or because the petitioner was unwilling to make a
contribution for that amount, he mortgaged the property on September 28, 1951, for $120,000. The petitioner used $79,587.27 of

the mortgage proceeds to satisfy two prior mortgages and pay closing costs, and reduced the principal debt to $119,098.22 by making payments thereon in November and December, 1951, retaining $40,412.73 of the proceeds.

On December 27, 1951, when the property had an adjusted basis of $82,205.17, the petitioners conveyed it to Exco, and immediately thereafter, on December 31, 1951, petitioner, as president of Exco, signed a deed conveying the same property to Penn-Liberty. In both instances the property was conveyed subject to the mortgage for a recited but never paid consideration of $100.

Petitioner testified and he here contends that he intended the conveyance to be a contribution to capital meant to improve Penn-Liberty's financial condition. He also maintains that neither that conveyance nor the placing of the mortgage and retention of part of the proceeds can constitute separately or together a taxable event. However, in determining the true nature of the transaction based on the mortgage and subsequent conveyances, the Tax Court was free to draw its own conclusion from the evidence as a whole, not being bound by the interested though uncontradicted testimony of the taxpayer. . . .

Taxpayer may very well have intended to and probably did improve Penn-Liberty's financial condition by the method employed, for at the time of the conveyance to Penn-Liberty, the property was entered on its books as an asset with an appraised value of $242,800 (less the unpaid principal on the mortgage and $471.43 accrued interest), which was well in excess of the mortgage for $120,000. It thus appears that these transactions served as a means of fulfilling petitioner's intentions while simultaneously returning to him an amount in excess of his then existing investment in the property.

It is immaterial, we think, that in financing the transaction the mortgage was negotiated for and placed by the petitioner prior to the transfer rather than by the purchaser-transferee as is the usual practice. As a matter of fact, when the petitioner gave the mortgage on September 28, 1951, he was at that time president of Exco and treasurer of Penn-Liberty, acting in pursuance of a plan agreed to by both corporations. It would certainly not be untenable to conclude that at the time petitioner gave the mortgage, he was already acting as an agent for both Exco and Penn-Liberty in securing the loan, the proceeds of which would in turn be used to purchase the property from him in his individual capacity.

The time interval between the various steps leading up to the subsequent conveyance to Penn-Liberty and the petitioner's testimony that it was a "Penn-Liberty deal" from the beginning fully support the Tax Court's conclusion that it was a single integrated transaction and constituted a sale. In fact, it seems to us that this conclusion is the only plausible one. . . .

Petitioner relies on Mendham Corp., 1947, 9 T.C. 320, and Woodsam Associates, Inc. v. Commissioner, 2 Cir., 1952, 198 F.2d 357, which we think are not in point. Neither of these cases was concerned with the tax liability of the transferor, for both involved a transfer of property to a corporation for stock under Section [351] ..., whereby no gain or loss was to be recognized. Our conclusion also makes inapplicable Crane v. Commissioner, 1947, 331 U.S. 1, ... and Parker v. Delaney, 1 Cir., 1950, 186 F.2d 455, *certiorari denied* 1951, 341 U.S. 926, ... where the mortgaging of the property and its subsequent disposition by the mortgagor or his successor were unrelated. The Court in *Crane* was faced solely with the question of determining the adjusted basis of real estate. Here there is no dispute as to the property's adjusted basis.

The decision of the Tax Court will be affirmed.

EASSON v. COMMISSIONER
294 F.2d 653 (9th Cir. 1961)

Before Orr, Barnes and Merrill, Circuit Judges.

BARNES, Circuit Judge. . . . In 1952 taxpayer owned and operated an apartment house in Portland, Oregon. On June 19, 1952, taxpayer encumbered the apartment house with a $250,000 mortgage, taxpayer himself signing and assuming personal liability on the notes underlying the mortgage. In October of 1952, taxpayer formed the Envoy Apartments, an Oregon corporation, and transferred the property, subject to the mortgage, to the corporation in exchange for all of its capital stock. Taxpayer, however, remained personally liable on the notes. The Tax Court found that taxpayer had a legitimate business purpose in consummating this transaction and that his principal purpose was not tax avoidance.

At the time of the transfer, the basis of appellant's property was $87,214.86, and its fair market value was $320,000. The principal balance of the mortgage was $247,064.01. Taxpayer and his wife, on their 1952 returns, reported no gain in connection with the transfer of the apartment to the corporation. They claimed that the transfer was tax free under §112(b)(5), Internal Revenue Code of 1939.* . . . The Commissioner, however, determined that taxpayer realized a gain on the transaction and determined further that such gain was taxable at ordinary income tax rates rather than at capital gains rates.

*Section 112(b)(5) of the 1939 Code is the predecessor of §351 of the 1986 Code. — ED.

I.   THE TAX COURT'S DECISION

The Tax Court agreed fully with neither the Commissioner nor the taxpayer. It held that only a portion of the gain should be recognized and taxed in 1952. The taxable portion, the court held, was the difference between taxpayer's basis ($87,214.86) and the principal balance on the mortgage ($247,064.01), viz. $159,849.15. . . .

Section 112(b)(5) provides that no gain or loss is to be recognized when property is transferred to a corporation solely in exchange for stock of the corporation, if immediately after the transfer, the transferor is in control of the corporation. Thus, at first blush, it would appear that taxpayer should prevail; he exchanged the apartment for stock of the corporation and immediately after the exchange he was in control of the corporation. He has met the requirements of §112(b)(5). But there was more to the transaction than just an exchange of an apartment house for stock. The apartment was transferred subject to a mortgage and this circumstance can, in some circumstances, alter the tax consequences of the transaction. Subsection (c) (of §112)* provides that gain will be recognized in a §112(b)(5) transaction to the extent that "boot," i.e., money or property other than stock, is received by the taxpayer. Can the transfer of encumbered property be considered as the receipt of "boot"? Section 112(k)** provides a clear answer to this question.[2] It provides that the transfer of property subject to a liability does *not* constitute the receipt of money or other property within the meaning of §112(c), and the existence of the encumbrance does not disqualify the exchange for tax-free treatment under §112(b)(5) — *unless* the purpose of the taxpayer, in this regard, was tax avoidance or was not a bona fide business purpose. The burden to establish his exemption is on the taxpayer. Here, however, the Tax Court specifically found that taxpayer was not principally motivated by considerations of tax avoidance and that he had a bona fide business purpose. Thus, taxpayer met the test of the specific provisions of §112(k); the provisions of §112(c) are, therefore, inapplicable to this transaction. It would seem, then, that the entire transaction comes within §112(b)(5), and that no gain should yet be recognized. Nevertheless, the Tax Court did not so hold.

The Tax Court noted that a statute must be construed in accordance with its purposes and must not be so interpreted as to lead

---

*Section 351(b) of the 1986 Code. — ED.
**Sections 357(a) and (b) of the 1986 Code. — ED.
2. . . . In 1954, Congress re-enacted §112(k) of the 1939 Code as §357(a) and (b) and added the present §357(c), which for the first time limits §112(k) by declaring that liabilities in excess of basis shall be considered gain. This was characterized in House Report No. 1337 as having "no counterpart under the 1939 Code." Of course, the instant case arose before the passage of §357(c).

to "absurd results." The purpose of §112(b)(5) is not to exempt gain from taxation but to postpone the taxable event to a later time. This postponement is effectuated by adjusting the basis of the stock which the taxpayer receives in the tax free exchange. Under §[358(a)], the basis of the stock is the basis of the property transferred, decreased, however, by the amount of money received, including for purposes of this section the amount of the mortgage, and increased by any gain recognized. Thus, unrecognized gain is retained as a potential liability by reducing the basis of taxpayer's stock.

As an example, if a taxpayer in a §112(b)(5) transaction transfers property worth $10,000 which cost him $1,000, he has an unrecognized gain of $9,000. Since his stock takes the same basis as the property transferred (viz. $1,000), he will recognize the gain when he sells the stock at a later date (presumably at $10,000). If the property transferred were subject to a $500 mortgage, taxpayer would have an additional gain of $500, the gain being currently unrecognized, however, by virtue of §112(k). This additional gain would be postponed by reducing the basis of the stock received by the taxpayer as follows: "Basis of stock received by taxpayer equals the basis of the property transferred, $1,000, less money or property received (including the amount of the mortgage), $500, plus the amount of gain currently recognized (— 0 —), viz. $500." When taxpayer sells the stock, presumably, for $ 10,000, he would realize and pay tax upon a gain of $9,500.

As applied to the facts of this case, the computation prescribed by §[358(a)], would result in a *negative* basis with respect to the stock acquired by taxpayer. Taxpayer's basis on the transferred property was $87,214.86; deducting from this figure the amount of the mortgage ($247,064.01) yields a basis of minus $159,849.15. Holding that property cannot have a negative basis, the court held, further, that the adjusted basis of the stock is zero. This determination, however, would permit the gain of $159,849.15 to escape taxation, unless the nonrecognition provisions of §112(b)(5) are ignored. If petitioner sold his zero basis stock for an amount that equaled the equity in the property transferred, $72,935.99 ($320,000, fair market value, less $247,064.01, mortgage), he would be taxed on that amount and nothing more. Taxpayer would, in effect, have converted the property into cash, realizing a gain of $232,785.14, but never paying a tax on $159,849.15 of it. Since the purpose of §112(b)(5) is not [to] permit a tax avoidance but only to permit postponement, it cannot, consistently with its purpose, be applied without limitation to this transaction. That portion of the gain, which if not presently recognized, will never be recognized, must be taxed now. The Tax Court thus held that $159,849.15 should be currently recognized and taxed. . . . Both the taxpayer and the Commissioner have appealed from the Tax Court's decision.

II.   APPEAL OF JACK EASSON, TAXPAYER

Taxpayer contends that the Tax Court's holding does violence to the clear and unambiguous language of the code sections involved. Section 112(b)(5) states unequivocally that no gain is to be recognized when property is transferred to a corporation in exchange for stock and immediately after the exchange the transferor controls the corporation. Section 112(k) is also clear in providing that the existence of an encumbrance on property exchanged in a §112(b)(5) transaction does not deny the transferor the benefits conferred by §112(b)(5). When a statute is unambiguous, the courts may not look elsewhere for the legislative intent. . . . We believe that the Tax Court did err in failing to adhere to the unambiguous language contained in the statutes in question here. Assuredly, there is authority for departing from the literal meaning of statutory language when literal application would produce absurd results (1 Mertens, Law of Federal Income Taxation, §3.04), but here the Tax Court's interpretation is directly contrary to the language of the statute. Section 112(b)(5) says no gain shall be recognized if certain conditions are fulfilled, yet the Tax Court says gain shall be recognized even though all the conditions enumerated are fulfilled. This is judicial legislation. If absurd results occur by reason of taxing statutes honestly and correctly followed by a taxpayer, it is up to the Congress to remedy the loophole.

Taxpayer's case on this point is bolstered by the fact that the 1954 Code contains a provision specifically covering the situation presented by this case. Section 357(c) of the 1954 Code . . . expressly provides that if the transferred property is subject to liabilities which exceed the transferor's basis in the property then the excess is to be presently recognized as gain. (See note 2, supra.) The court below brushed this aside as a clarification of existing law and not new law (noting dicta to the contrary, however, in W. H. Weaver, 32 T.C. 411, 436). In commenting upon the general effect of the provisions contained in §357(c), the House Ways and Means Committee noted that the provisions are "not found in existing law." H.R. No. 1337 (83d Cong. 2d Sess., p. A129; U.S. Code, Congressional and Administrative News, 1954, v. 3, p. 4066). Thus the existence and history of later legislation tend to indicate that Congress "meant" precisely what it said — and no more — when it adopted §112(b)(5) of the 1939 Code.

In departing from the express language of §112(b)(5), the Tax Court relied upon the fact that a literal interpretation of the section would lead to absurd results. If no such absurd consequences are inherent in a literal application of the section, then no justification for the Tax Court's departure is established. The absurd result feared by the Tax Court was that §112(b)(5) would become an instrument of tax exemption rather than of tax deferment. This conviction stemmed from the Tax Court's belief that there could be no such legal phenomenon as a negative basis. And this is perhaps the most crucial issue in the appeal presented by the taxpayer.

Can property have a negative basis? There is little law on the subject,[3] and we are far from satisfied that the Tax Court's outright rejection of this concept is justifiable. Why, then, did the Tax Court conclude that property cannot have a negative basis? In footnote 8 of its opinion the court explains: . . .

> It is a fundamental concept of income taxation to tax gain when its fruits are available for payment of the tax. If a negative base were allowed then recognition of gain could be deferred until a subsequent loss sale or even an abandonment, and unless taxpayer had other resources the tax would never be collected.

The Tax Court, thus, rejects the negative basis concept on the ground that it may impair the future collectibility of the tax. "We must recognize and collect the tax now, or we may never be able to do so." But such argument is equally applicable to any provision for the deferment of tax; nonrecognition of present gain with a corresponding reduction of basis creates the prospect that tax on the deferred gain may never actually be collected. This prospect is equally real, whether basis is reduced to zero, to a point above zero, or to less than zero.

Judicial hostility to a negative basis is confined to an implication that deductions from a minus basis are undesirable. Crane v. Commissioner, 1947, 331 U.S. 1, 9-10. . . .

There is some judicial support for the concept of negative basis in Parker v. Delaney, 1 Cir., 1950, 186 F.2d 455, 459, *certiorari denied* 341 U.S. 926. . . . There, Chief Judge Magruder in a concurring opinion offered an alternative theory to reach the result obtained by the majority, but "with less strain upon the statutory language." His computation involved the use of a negative basis.

The authority bearing on the question presented here, is, then, inconclusive. The "absurd result" which the Tax Court envisions is by no means the necessary consequence of literally applying §112(b)(5). If the mandate of §112(b)(5) is followed and none of taxpayer's gain is presently recognized, taxpayer's stock can be given

---

3. For an informative and well authenticated argument in support of the recognition of a negative basis, see . . . a thesis . . . written by George Cooper, entitled "Negative Basis," dated April 20th, 1961 [75 Harv. L. Rev. 1352 (1962)], and discussing the instant case, and listing the favorable and unfavorable considerations which might establish the value of recognizing a negative basis, under certain factual conditions, and in some, but not all, cases.

As an aside, it is interesting to note that Mr. Cooper concludes that without the "suggestion" of §357(c) of the 1954 Code, the Tax Court would not have reached the result it did in the instant case.

a negative basis, so that all of his gain will be recognized and taxed when he sells the stock. . . .

III. APPEAL BY COMMISSIONER

This brings us to the appeal by the Commissioner. The Commissioner contends that the Tax Court erred in not holding *all* of taxpayer's gain from the exchange to be presently recognizable and taxable. This is the Commissioner's primary position and his defense of the Tax Court's decision in the appeal brought by taxpayer is only an alternative position, if his position here is rejected.

The Commissioner contends that the transaction is governed by §112(c). This section, it will be recalled, provides that gain will be recognized in a §112(b)(5) transaction to the extent that "boot" (money or property other than stock) is received by taxpayer. The corporation's acquisition of the property subject to the mortgage, the Commissioner contends, constitutes the receipt by taxpayer of "boot." Since the boot so received, $247,064.01, exceeds taxpayer's gain of $232,785.14 (fair market value of the property, $320,000, less taxpayer's basis, $87,214.86), all of the gain must be recognized and taxed. Section 112(k), we have seen, precludes the result contended for by the Commissioner, but §112(k) contains an exception and it is this exception which the Commissioner relies upon now. Section 112(k) provides that

> [if] it appears that the principal purpose of the taxpayer with respect to the assumption or acquisition was a purpose to avoid federal income tax on the exchange, or if not such purpose, was not a bona fide business purpose, such assumption or acquisition (in the amount of the liability) shall, for the purposes of this section, be considered as money received by the taxpayer upon the exchange.

The Tax Court found, however, that taxpayer's "principal purpose in exchanging the property subject to the mortgage for all the capital stock of the new corporation was not to avoid Federal income tax on the exchange, and that he had a bona fide business purpose in so transferring the property." . . . In so finding, the Commissioner contends, the Tax Court erred.

The Tax Court substantiated its ultimate findings by finding further that taxpayer desired to place himself in an extremely liquid position to take advantage of a business downturn which, he believed, would soon occur. In order to achieve this liquid position, taxpayer mortgaged his property, since he was unable to sell it despite efforts to do so. Having decided to retain the apartment for himself, taxpayer also decided to operate the property in corporate form, as he had done for twenty years. For tax reasons, taxpayer had taken the apartment out of the corporation when he had contemplated selling it. After deciding not to sell it, he desired to return it to corporate form in order to secure limited liability and convenience of management should he desire to move elsewhere and to turn the property over to a local real estate organization.

The Commissioner contends (and this is the crux of his appeal) that the Tax Court missed the point of §112(k). The "true question," missed by the Tax Court, the Commissioner contends, is whether the corporation's taking subject to the liability had some bona fide business purpose in connection with the *corporation's* business. Thus, the Commissioner contends, the question was not whether the transfer of the property subject to the liability benefited taxpayer's business interests as an investor; the issue is whether the taking-subject-to-the-liability had any purpose with respect to the business of operating the apartments as rental property. The Tax Court found no such business purpose, and, therefore, the Commissioner claims, it erred in holding that taxpayer met the test of §112(k).

We cannot go along with the Commissioner's interpretation of the statute. We believe it is erroneous. It finds little, if any, support in the case authority cited. The test suggested by the Commissioner looks to the origin of the encumbrance and to the use of the proceeds derived from it. Section 112(k), however, says nothing about the origin of the encumbrance. It says only that if a corporation "acquires from the taxpayer property subject to *a* liability such . . . acquisition shall not be considered as" boot, unless taxpayer's principal purpose regarding the acquisition is tax avoidance or not a bona fide business purpose. Nor is there anything in the section which deals with the reasons for the encumbrance, or the manner in which the mortgage proceeds are used.

If there is a good business purpose for transferring the property without first removing the encumbrance, the requirements of §112(k) are satisfied. Certainly, an investor's desire to remain liquid in order to capitalize on an expected business recession is a good business reason for not discharging the mortgage. . . .

The Commissioner seeks support for his position in Bryan v. Commissioner, 4 Cir., 1960, 281 F.2d 238, *certiorari denied* 364 U.S. 931. . . . The facts of that case, with some simplification, may be readily stated. Taxpayer obtained construction loans of $1,643,500 to build houses. This exceeded his actual cost by $157,798.04. After building the houses taxpayer transferred them to four corporations which in exchange gave him stock and assumed the construction loan. The Tax Court and the Court of Appeals held that taxpayer, under these circumstances, received money or other property and therefore did not meet the requirements of §112(b)(5).

This case, however, provides only weak support for the Commissioner's position here. The Tax Court found in *Bryan*, as it did not find in the instant case, that taxpayer's "principal purpose with respect to the assumption of the liabilities by the four corporations was a purpose to avoid tax," and hence that it was "immaterial . . . whether such purpose might otherwise be considered not a bona fide business purpose." (W. H. Weaver, 32 T.C. 414, 434.) The court of appeals agreed that "his only purpose was to appropriate to himself a major portion of the excess funds . . . and to do it in a form which gave him hope of avoiding federal taxes on the funds with which he enriched himself." Bryan v. Commissioner, supra, 281 F.2d at page 242. There was, therefore, no problem in determining that §112(k) did not apply.

The *Bryan* case does offer some support for the Commissioner's position in stating that the corporation's assumption of the mortgage in excess of taxpayer's basis constituted an indirect payment of cash to taxpayer. "As a cash payment, the nonrecognition sections would have no application." Ibid. These statements must, however, be considered as dicta in view of the court's holding that taxpayer did not meet the requirements of §112(k) and that therefore the assumption of the mortgage constituted the payment of "money or other property." If, on the other hand, the court had held §112(k) applicable, the statements would have been inappropriate. Section 112(k) provides, clearly, that an assumption of liability is not the payment of "other property or money," and to hold that such assumption constitutes a cash payment is a clear contradiction of the words of the statute.

The Tax Court's findings regarding taxpayer's business purpose have not, in our opinion, been shown to be clearly erroneous. And the Commissioner's assertion that taxpayer is a "highly tax conscious person" . . . , as are many citizens these days, is certainly not sufficient to overthrow the Tax Court's further finding that taxpayer's principal motive in *this* transaction was not tax avoidance. The Tax Court fully examined the evidence regarding the exchange before concluding that taxpayer entered this transaction for bona fide business reasons and not to avoid federal taxes.

In concluding his main argument, the Commissioner says, "There is nothing theoretical about Easson's gain. The unencumbered cash is in his hand, and ought to be immediately subject to the payment of income tax." This statement, we believe, lays bare the Commissioner's basic error. The Commissioner believes that taxpayer is in a genuinely different position now than he was before the exchange. This, we believe, is not so. Before the exchange taxpayer owned an apartment house subject to a liability. After the exchange, taxpayer was the sole owner of a corporation which owned the same apartment house subject to the same liability. Where was *any* income?

His stock in the corporation was worth no more than the physical asset which he owned directly before incorporation. Section 112(b)(5) was enacted to deal with this very situation — to permit business reorganizations which, realistically viewed, do not alter the taxpayer's basic position. To use the Commissioner's phraseology, "the unencumbered cash" was in taxpayer's hand as soon as taxpayer had mortgaged the apartment, but the Commissioner does not claim that the hypothecation of the building constituted a taxable event. . . . Taxpayer's transfer of his encumbered apartment house to his wholly owned corporation did not make the cash obtained from the mortgaged transaction any more real or any less encumbered than it was before the transfer. It is our belief that the purpose of the tax laws will best be served by not assessing a tax against taxpayer until he realizes his gain in a transaction in which, realistically speaking, he actually changes his position.

The Commissioner's next contention applies only if the court rejects his positions both as appellee and appellant. In such event, Commissioner contends, taxpayer received dividend income (§115(a), 1954 Code . . .) in 1953 by virtue of the corporation's payments on the mortgage. This contention is based upon the theory that the corporation's payments discharged a legal obligation of taxpayer. While the corporation may incidentally have benefited taxpayer by reducing the mortgage, it is clear that the corporation did not thereby distribute any assets. The corporation owned the apartment subject to the mortgage and as the mortgage decreased its equity in the apartment house increased. Thus when it took money out of cash and applied that amount to the mortgage, its net worth remained constant. Its total assets were unchanged because the credit to the cash account was offset by a corresponding debit to the fixed assets account. The payments of interest on the mortgage cannot, obviously, be analyzed in this way; these payments, it would seem, did constitute income to the taxpayer who would then be entitled to take the deduction for interest paid (1 Mertens, Law of Federal Income Taxation, §9.08, p. 19, n.74). The net effect would be to deny the deduction to the corporation. This interpretation is, however, at variance with the Commissioner's own regulations and should, therefore, be rejected. . . . 1.163-1(b) provides:

> Interest paid by the taxpayer on a mortgage upon real estate of which he is the legal or equitable owner, even though the taxpayer is not directly liable upon the bond or note secured by such mortgage may be deducted as interest on his indebtedness.

And see Mertens, supra, §26.03.

We believe the Commissioner erred in asserting a deficiency against taxpayer based on the 1952 transaction, whereby taxpayer exchanged the apartment house for stock of Envoy Apartments. Furthermore, the Commissioner is in error in his contention that taxpayer received dividend income in 1953 by reason of mortgage and interest payments made by the corporation. We *reverse* the judgment of the Tax Court, and direct that judgment be entered in favor of taxpayer.

NOTES

1. D, owning 100 percent of Corporation W, transfers to W property worth $100,000, with a basis in her hands of $50,000 and subject to a mortgage of $25,000, in exchange for $75,000 worth of stock. What are the tax consequences to D? To W? What is the effect on basis to D and to W? Suppose the stock were worth $75,000, but the mortgage debt was $60,000?

Suppose D owned 80 percent of C, and E owned the remaining 20 percent. D transfers to C property worth $100,000 with a basis in his hands of $50,000 and subject to a mortgage of $25,000, in exchange for stock worth $125,000. What are the tax consequences to D? To C? What is the effect on basis to D and to C? This problem may require an understanding of §305(a), which is considered in Chapter 4, infra page 431 et seq.

2. *Easson* is the only case in which a court has accepted the concept of negative basis. Of what relevance is the fact that the taxpayer is not likely, after incorporation of the asset, to have to repay the obligation he incurred? Is §357(c) a better or worse approach than *Easson*'s as a matter of policy? See Cooper, Negative Basis, 75 Harv. L. Rev. 1352 (1962).

3. When will an assumption of a transferor's liabilities not reached by §357(c)(1) result in taxation under §357(b)? Cf. Rev. Rul. 79-258, 1979-2 C.B. 143. See Greiner, Behling, and Moffety, Assumptions of Liabilities and the Improper Purpose — A Re-Examination of Section 357(b), 32 Tax Law. 111 (1978). Do you think §357(b) should be repealed?

WHAM CONSTRUCTION CO. v. UNITED STATES
600 F.2d 1052 (4th Cir. 1979)

Before Haynsworth, Chief Judge, Bryan, Senior Circuit Judge, and Russell, Circuit Judge.

HAYNSWORTH, Chief Judge. The district court ordered a refund of income taxes paid, and the United States has appealed. It contends that when a subsidiary corporation was formed the parent corporation obtained "other property" which was taxable to it as ordinary income. We agree with the district court that it did not.

For approximately ten years two brothers, Norman and James Wham, were engaged as partners in the operation of a construction business. The business was principally concerned with highway construction, though it did no asphalt work. Late in that period, however, they acquired an asphalt plant and entered into the asphalt paving business. The asphalt paving business, however, was operated as a wholly independent division of the partnership, maintaining separate books of account and separate bank accounts.

In 1959 the brothers incorporated their businesses under one corporate roof, but they continued to operate the two separate businesses as if they were separate entities with a few exceptions noted below. Each continued to have its own bank account, its own separate books. Receipts of each division were deposited only in its bank accounts and purchases of each division were paid for or financed exclusively by it. However, the construction division advanced funds to the asphalt division. This was made particularly necessary because only one capital account was maintained, and that was on the books of the construction company. Thus the books of the asphalt division reflected no net income, all of which was revealed in the capital account on the books of the construction division. This necessitated advances by the construction division to the asphalt division, and these interdivisional transactions were reflected in interdivisional accounts. On the books of the asphalt division an accounts payable item reflected the net balance for the time being of the sums "owed" the construction division, while an accounts receivable item on the books of the construction division reflected the same amount as due it from the asphalt division.

The two brothers decided that they would separate their one corporate house into two, effective at the end of 1966. They organized a new corporation, Wham Asphalt Company, Inc., which issued all of its capital stock to Wham Construction Company in exchange for cash, receivables, inventory and capital assets, which, net of certain stated liabilities, would permit Asphalt to continue its asphalt paving business in its separate corporate home.

Included on the books of the new asphalt corporation was an account payable to the construction company in the amount of $160,402.50. This was the old intra-company account payable after substantial downward adjustment for the depreciated value of certain trucks and equipment which were not transferred to the new asphalt corporation. Several months after its incorporation, Asphalt paid that amount to the construction company.

It was the retention of this receivable when the asphalt subsidiary was created which the Commissioner treated as other property requiring the denial of nonrecognition of gain under §§351(a) and 361(a). . . .

We think the position of the Commissioner entirely too technical and unrealistic. There was not only a retention of the construction company of this "receivable" after the downward adjustments to which we have referred; there was a transfer to the new asphalt corporation of cash and receivables in an amount sufficient to enable the asphalt company to clear its payable within a matter of several months. At the outset, Construction transferred to its new subsidiary over $107,000 in cash and over $54,000 in receivables. For its launching, the new asphalt corporation did need some quick assets, but nothing like the amount with which it was endowed, as the quick payoff demonstrates. To the extent that it did need quick assets for operating purposes in the beginning, the asphalt company could have gotten a bank loan. In that event, without the quick assets received from Construction and the countering account payable, there is no doubt there would have been no recognition of gain in the transaction. Nor is there doubt that, had the asphalt subsidiary been set up with no quick assets and no account payable to the construction company, the construction company itself, a few days after creation of its subsidiary, could have advanced funds to it. If the advance had totaled $160,000 and had been repaid within a few months, as was this payable, there would have been no receipt of "other property" within the meaning of §§351(b) or 361(b). Counsel for the United States conceded as much on oral argument.

Moreover, it is readily apparent that what it got it already owned. What the brothers did was to wrap the asphalt business, close to its reflection on the separate asphalt division books, into a new corporate housing. There was no substantive change, and, had the adjusted intra-company account not been carried forward, the asphalt corporation would not have been provided with the quick assets necessary to its repayment. At least in substantial part the $160,000 which the asphalt corporation paid to the construction company in the summer of 1967 was a derivative of the cash and receivables transferred to the asphalt company by Construction at the time of Asphalt's formation, items upon which the construction company had already been fully taxed once.

The purpose of §351 is to insure that no tax consequence will be recognized when one or more persons transfer property to a corporation solely in exchange for stock or securities in such corporation when the transferor or transferors immediately after the exchange are in control of the corporation. When there has been only a change in form and the transferor has not received anything which, in an economic sense, he did not possess before, he should not suffer the imposition of income tax liability. See Portland Oil Co. v. Commissioner, 109 F.2d 479 (1 Cir. 1946). When there is but one transferor, as here, and the issuing corporation has no assets except those that derived from the transferor, it is difficult to conceive of a concept that the transferor as a result of the transaction received anything which he did not have before unless the exchange was couched in terms of a sale. The exchange here, however, cannot be regarded as a partial sale, for the $160,000 receivable was the same old receivable that had been on the construction division books after adjustment for asphalt division trucks and equipment not transferred. And since its retention necessitated the transfer of quick assets to provide the asphalt corporation with a healthy beginning, it was a giving with one hand what the other hand retained. In short, there was no economic change of substance effected by the exchange, and the construction company received in the exchange no "other property" within the meaning of §§351(b) or 361(b).

We look to the substance of the transactions of the brothers, and not the mere form of their dealings. We conclude that no taxable event occurred in the exchange and that the district court correctly ordered a refund.

Affirmed.

NOTES

1. In Rev. Rul. 80-228, 1980-2 C.B. 115, the Service announced that it would not follow *Wham.* The Service maintains that the account receivable is "other property" for purposes of §351(b) and that the transferor must recognize gain up to fair market value of the account receivable.

2. In Lessinger v. Commissioner, 872 F.2d 519 (2d Cir. 1989), *rev'g* 85 T.C. 824 (1985), the court held that a transferor could avoid gain recognition under §357(c)(1) by giving the transferee corporation his personal note for the excess of liabilities over the basis of the assets transferred. *Contrast* Owen v. Commissioner, 89-2 U.S.T.C. ¶9476 (9th Cir. 1989). See Bogdanski, Shareholder Debt, Corporate Debt: Lessons from Leavitt and Lessinger, 16 J. Corp. Taxn. 348 (1990).

REVENUE RULING 80-199
1980-2 C.B. 122

ISSUE

Whether the term "liabilities" as used in sections 357 and 358(d) of the Internal Revenue Code prior to amendment by the Revenue Act of 1978* includes accounts payable deductible under section 162 of the Code.

FACTS

Individual A conducted a small contracting business as a sole proprietorship, the income of which was reported on the cash receipts and disbursements method of accounting. On January 1, 1978, A transferred to a newly organized corporation all of the assets of the sole proprietorship in exchange for all of the stock of the corporation, plus the assumption by the corporation of all of the liabilities of the sole proprietorship, in a transaction that met the requirements of section 351(a) of the Code. The transactor did not lack a business purpose. The assets transferred were tangible assets having a fair market value of $20,000 and an adjusted basis of $10,000, and accounts receivable having a fair market value of $30,000 and an adjusted basis of zero dollars. The liabilities assumed by the corporation consisted solely of accounts payable of the sole proprietorship in the face amount of $20,000. The accounts would have been deductible by A as ordinary and necessary business expenses under section 162 if A had paid them. The new corporation continued to utilize the cash receipts and disbursements method of accounting.

LAW AND ANALYSIS

The applicable sections of the Code are 351, relating to nonrecognition in a transfer to a corporation controlled by the transferor; 357, relating to assumption of liability; 358, relating to basis to distributees; and 362, relating to basis to corporations.

Section 357(a) provides, in part, as a general rule that the assumption of liabilities on the part of a corporate transferee in connection with a section 351 exchange, or the acquisition by the transferee of property subject to a liability in such an exchange, shall not be treated as a receipt of money or other property by the transferor.

Section 357(c)(1) prior to amendment by the Revenue Act of

*The Revenue Act of 1978 added §357(c)(3). — ED.

1978 provides in part, that in the case of an exchange to which section 351 applies if the sum of the amount of the liabilities assumed, plus the amount of the liabilities to which the property is subject, exceeds the total of the adjusted basis of the property transferred pursuant to such exchange, then such excess shall be considered as a gain from the sale or exchange of a capital asset or of property which is not a capital asset, as the case may be.

Section 358(a)(1) of the Code provides, in part, that in the case of an exchange to which section 351 applies the basis of the property permitted to be received under section 351 without the recognition of gain or loss shall be the same as that of the property exchanged (A) decreased by (i) the fair market value of any other property (except money) received by the taxpayer, (ii) the amount of money received by the taxpayer, and (iii) the amount of loss to the taxpayer which was recognized on such exchange, and (B) increased by (i) the amount which was treated as a dividend, and (ii) the amount of gain to the taxpayer which was recognized on such exchange (not including any portion of such gain which was treated as a dividend).

Section 358(d) of the Code prior to the amendment by the Revenue Act of 1978 provides that if as part of the consideration to the taxpayer, another party to the exchange assumed a liability of the taxpayer, or acquired from the taxpayer property subject to a liability, such assumption or acquisition (in the amount of the liability) shall, for purposes of this section, be treated as money received by the taxpayer on the exchange.

Since the adjusted basis of the assets transferred by A to the corporation was $10,000 and the accounts payable assumed by the corporation was $20,000, the primary question for consideration is whether the transfer of the assets and liabilities of A's sole proprietorship to the corporation results in gain under section 357(c) of the Code. In Raich v. Commissioner, 46 T.C. 604 (1966), the Tax Court of the United States directed its attention to such a question in a case where the taxpayer transferred assets of a business conducted as a sole proprietorship, the income from which was reported on the cash receipts and disbursements method of accounting, to a newly formed corporation in exchange for all of the stock of the corporation plus the assumption by the corporation of all of the liabilities of the sole proprietorship (trade accounts payable and notes payable) in a transaction meeting the requirements of section 351(a). The court held that the trade accounts receivable had a zero basis, and that since the total liabilities, consisting primarily of trade accounts payable, assumed by the corporation were in excess of the adjusted basis of all of the assets transferred, the taxpayer (transferor) incurred a gain under section 357(c) (as it existed prior to the amendment by the Revenue Act of 1978). In Rev. Rul. 69-442, 1969-2 C.B. 53, the

Service indicated that it would follow the decision in Raich v. Commissioner and apply section 357(c) to other situations involving similar facts.

In Focht v. Commissioner, 68 T.C. 223 (1977), *acq.*, page five, this Bulletin, the taxpayer, in 1970, transferred to a newly formed corporation all of the assets of a business conducted as a sole proprietorship, the income of which was reported on the cash receipts and disbursements method of accounting, in exchange for all of the stock of the corporation plus an assumption by the corporation of all the liabilities of the sole proprietorship in a transaction meeting the requirements of section 351(a) of the Code. These liabilities consisted of the liabilities actually assumed by the corporation as well as liabilities to which certain of the property transferred was subject. The liabilities assumed by the corporation consisted primarily of trade accounts payable. The Internal Revenue Service treated all of the liability obligations including the accounts payable as liabilities within the meaning of section 357(c), and determined that the taxpayer incurred a gain, by reason of section 357(c), in the amount by which the liabilities assumed by the corporation exceeded the adjusted basis of the assets transferred. The Tax Court of the United States held that an obligation should not be treated as a liability, under sections 357 and 358(d), to the extent that its payment would have been deductible (under section 162) if made by the transferor. The court held that section 357(c) did not apply to the account payable liabilities for this reason and overruled its prior decision in *Raich* on this point.

The Service will follow the decision in *Focht*.

HOLDING

No gain is realized by A on the exchange of property for stock by reason of section 357(c) of the Code because the accounts payable assumed by the corporation would have been deductible by A as ordinary and necessary business expenses under section 162 in the taxable year paid if A had paid these liabilities prior to the exchange. A's basis in the stock received in the exchange of property for stock under section 358(a)(1) is the $10,000 basis that A had in the property transferred to the corporation. No adjustment to such basis is made under section 358(a)(1)(A)(ii) because of the assumption by the corporation of the $20,000 in accounts payable inasmuch as section 358(d) does not apply to the accounts payable. Likewise, no adjustment to such basis is made under section 358(a)(1)(B)(ii) because section 357(c) does not apply to the accounts payable.

Transactions which occur on or after November 6, 1978 will be governed by sections 357(c) and 358(d) as amended by the Revenue Act of 1978.

COURT DECISIONS THAT THE INTERNAL REVENUE SERVICE
WILL NOT FOLLOW

The Service will not follow the rationale of the decision of the
United States Court of Appeals for the Ninth Circuit in Thatcher v.
Commissioner, 533 F.2d 1114 (9th Cir. 1976) which involved a transaction similar to the facts of this revenue ruling. The court agreed
with the Service that the transferors must recognize gain under section 357(c) of the Code on the incorporation transfer, but the court
also concluded that the transferor should receive a deduction for
trade accounts payable discharged by the transferee corporation to
the extent of the accounts receivable or the gain recognized under
section 357(c), whichever is less.

The Service also will not follow the rationale of the decision of
the United States Court of Appeals for the Second Circuit in Bongiovanni v. Commissioner, 470 F.2d 921 (2d Cir. 1972), involving a
similar transaction and which held that the term "liabilities," as used
in section 357(c) of the Code, did not include all liabilities which are
included for accounting purposes, but was meant to apply only to
what might be called "tax" liabilities, that is, liens in excess of tax
costs, particularly mortgages encumbering property transferred in
an exchange within the meaning of section 351. The above mentioned
language offers no clear guidance as to the meaning of the terms
"accounting" liabilities and "tax" liabilities or to making a distinction
between them. For example, to the extent that the *Bongiovanni* decision could be interpreted as suggested by Footnote 6 in *Thatcher* as
holding that "liabilities" for the purpose of section 357(c) means only
"the excess of *secured* debts over the transferor's adjusted basis in the
assets transferred" (italics supplied), the Service would view such an
interpretation as being unduly restrictive of the term "liabilities."

NOTES

1. For an excellent critique of the problem finally resolved in
Rev. Rul. 80-199 and for a helpful analysis of *Crane* doctrine implications, see Comment, Section 357(c) and the Cash Basis Taxpayer,
115 U. Pa. L. Rev. 1154 (1967). See also Coven, Liabilities in Excess
of Basis: Focht, Section 357(c)(3) and the Assignment of Income, 58
Or. L. Rev. 61 (1979).

2. On incorporation of taxpayer's cash basis proprietorship
under §351, the corporation assumed all of taxpayer's liabilities for
customer deposits. On the ground that customer deposit liabilities
are "akin to loan proceeds obtained by a business," they constitute
"liabilities" under §357(c)(1) and are not excluded under §357(c)(3).
William P. Orr, 78 T.C. 1059 (1982).

3. In Lessinger v. Commissioner, 89-1 U.S.T.C. ¶9254 (2d Cir. 1989), *rev'g* 85 T.C. 824 (1985), the taxpayer transferred the assets and liabilities of a proprietorship he operated to his existing wholly owned corporation. Because the proprietorship had a negative net worth, the taxpayer promised to repay the corporation the amount by which the proprietorship's liabilities exceeded its assets. The Tax Court refused to consider the promise to repay as an asset of the corporation and held that the taxpayer recognized gain under §357(c)(1) to the extent that the liabilities assumed exceeded the basis of the assets transferred. On appeal, the Second Circuit reversed. Despite the fact that the taxpayer's promise to repay was at first not evidenced by a promissory note and that no interest on the debt was paid, the court rejected the Tax Court's conclusion that the promise was "artificial." The court noted that "the creditors of the corporation continued to do business with it on the strength of the taxpayer's personal credit. . . . [W]e have no doubt that any court would enforce [the taxpayer's] promise to protect the corporate creditors if the corporation failed." The Second Circuit also disagreed with the Tax Court's holding that the promise in any case had no basis to the corporation because it had no basis in the hands of the taxpayer. The court concluded that the corporation had a basis in the taxpayer's promise to repay "because it incurred a cost in the transaction involving the the transfer of the obligation by taking on the liabilities of the proprietorship that exceeded its assets." Should §357(c)(1) have applied, or is the appellate court right? See Note 2, page 398 supra.

4. Assignment of Income

HEMPT BROTHERS, INC. v. UNITED STATES
490 F.2d 1172 (3d Cir. 1974), *cert. denied,* 419 U.S. 826 (1974)

Before Aldisert and Weis, Circuit Judges, and Latchum, District Judge.

ALDISERT, Circuit Judge. In this appeal by a corporate taxpayer from a grant of summary judgment in favor of the government in a claim for refund, we are called upon to decide the proper treatment of accounts receivable and of inventory transferred from a cash basis partnership to a corporation organized to continue the business under . . . §351(a). This appeal illustrates the conflict between the statutory purpose of Section 351, postponement of recognition of gain or loss, and the assignment of income [doctrines]. . . .

The facts were wholly stipulated; therefore, they may be summarized as set forth by the government in its brief:

The taxpayer is a Pennsylvania corporation with its principal place of business in Camp Hill, Pennsylvania. It files its federal income tax returns for a fiscal year beginning March 1.

From 1942 until February 28, 1957, a partnership comprised of Loy T. Hempt, J. F. Hempt, Max C. Hempt, and the George L. Hempt Estate was engaged in the business of quarrying and selling stone, sand, gravel, and slag; manufacturing and selling ready-mix concrete and bituminous material; constructing roads, highways, and streets, primarily for the Pennsylvania Department of Highways and various political subdivisions of Pennsylvania, and constructing driveways, parking lots, street and water lines, and related accessories.

The partnership maintained its books and records, and filed its partnership income tax returns, on the basis of a calendar year and on the cash method of accounting, so that no income was reported until actually received in cash. Accordingly, in computing its income for federal income tax purposes, the partnership did not take uncollected receivables into income. . . .

On March 1, 1957, the partnership business and most of its assets were transferred to the taxpayer solely in exchange for taxpayer's capital stock, the 12,000 shares of which were issued to the four members of the partnership. These shares constituted 100% of the issued and outstanding shares of the taxpayer. This transfer was made pursuant to Section 351(a) of the Internal Revenue Code of 1954. . . . Thereafter, the taxpayer conducted the business formerly conducted by the partnership.

Among the assets transferred by the partnership to the taxpayer for taxpayer's shares of stock were accounts receivable in the amount of $662,824.40 arising from performance of construction projects, sales of stone, sand, gravel, etc., and rental of equipment prior to March 1, 1957. . . .

Commencing with its initial fiscal year [which] ended February 28, 1958, taxpayer maintained its books and filed its corporation income tax returns on the cash method of accounting and accordingly, did not take uncollected receivables into income. . . . In its taxable years ending in 1958, 1959, and 1960, taxpayer collected the respective amounts of $533,247.87, $125,326.71 and $4,249.72 of the accounts receivable in the aggregate amount of $662,824.40 (sic) that transferred to it, and included those amounts in income in computing its income for its federal income tax returns for those years, respectively.

As a result of an examination extending over a period of years, it was determined by the Commissioner of Internal Revenue, and agreed to by the taxpayer, that the use of the cash receipts and disbursements method of accounting . . . did not clearly reflect taxpayer's income. Accordingly, taxpayer's income was adjusted . . . to accrue unreported sales [accounts receivable] made during the taxable years in question. . . .

The district court held: (1) taxpayer was properly taxable upon collections made with respect to accounts receivable which were transferred to it in conjunction with the Section 351 incorporation. . . .

I

Taxpayer argues here, as it did in the district court, that because the term "property" as used in Section 351 does not embrace accounts receivable, the Commissioner lacked statutory authority to apply principles associated with Section 351. The district court properly rejected the legal interpretation urged by the taxpayer.

The definition of Section 351 "property" has been extensively treated by the Court of Claims in E.I. Du Pont de Nemours and Co. v. United States, 471 F.2d 1211, 1218-1219 (Ct. Cl. 1973), describing the transfer of a nonexclusive license to make, use and sell area herbicides under French patents:

> Unless there is some special reason intrinsic to . . . [Section 351] . . . the general word "property" has a broad reach in tax law. . . . For section 351, in particular, courts have advocated a generous definition of "property," . . . and it has been suggested in one capital gains case that nonexclusive licenses can be viewed as property though not as capital assets. . . .
> We see no adequate reason for refusing to follow these leads.

We fail to perceive any special reason why a restrictive meaning should be applied to accounts receivables so as to exclude them from the general meaning of "property." Receivables possess the usual capabilities and attributes associated with jurisprudential concepts of property law. They may be identified, valued, and transferred. Moreover, their role in an ongoing business must be viewed in the context of Section 351 application. The presence of accounts receivable is a normal, rather than an exceptional accoutrement of the type of business included by Congress in the transfer to a corporate form. They are "commonly thought of in the commercial world as a positive business asset." Du Pont v. United States, supra, at 1218. As aptly put by the district court: "There is a compelling reason to construe 'property' to include . . . [accounts receivable]: a new corporation needs working capital, and accounts receivable can be an important source of liquidity." . . . In any event, this court had no difficulty in characterizing a sale of receivables as "property" within the purview of the "no gain or loss" provision of Section 337 as a "qualified sale of property within a 12-month period." Citizens Acceptance Corp. v. United States, 462 F.2d 751, 756 (3d Cir. 1972).

The taxpayer next makes a strenuous argument that "[t]he government is seeking to tax the wrong person." It contends that the assignment of income doctrine as developed by the Supreme Court applies to a Section 351 transfer of accounts receivable so that the transferor, not the transferee-corporation, bears the corresponding tax liability. It argues that the assignment of income doctrine dictates that where the right to receive income is transferred to another person in a transaction not giving rise to tax at the time of transfer, the transferor is taxed on the income when it is collected by the transferee; that the only requirement for its application is a transfer of a right to receive ordinary income; and that since the transferred accounts receivable are a present right to future income, the sole requirement for the application of the doctrine is squarely met. In essence, this is a contention that the nonrecognition provision of Section 351 is in conflict with the assignment of income doctrine and that Section 351 should be subordinated thereto. Taxpayer relies on the seminal case of Lucas v. Earl, 281 U.S. 111 . . . (1930), and its progeny for support of its proposition that the application of the doctrine is mandated whenever one transfers a right to receive ordinary income.

On its part, the government concedes that a taxpayer may sell for value a claim to income otherwise his own and he will be taxable upon the proceeds of the sale. Such was the case in Commissioner v. P.G. Lake, Inc., 356 U.S. 260 . . . (1958), in which the taxpayer-corporation assigned its oil payment right to its president in consideration for his cancellation of a $600,000 loan. Viewing the oil payment right as a right to receive future income, the Court applied the reasoning of the assignment of income doctrine, normally applicable to a gratuitous assignment, and held that the consideration received by the taxpayer-corporation was taxable as ordinary income since it essentially was a substitute for that which would otherwise be received at a future time as ordinary income.

Turning to the facts of this case, we note that here there was the transfer of accounts receivable from the partnership to the corporation pursuant to Section 351. We view these accounts receivable as a present right to receive future income. In consideration of the transfer of this right, the members of the partnership received stock—a valid consideration. The consideration, therefore, was essentially a substitute for that which would otherwise be received at a future time as ordinary income to the cash basis partnership. Consequently, the holding in Lake would normally apply, and income would ordinarily be realized, and thereby taxable, by the cash basis partnership-transferor at the time of receipt of the stock.

But the terms and purpose of Section 351 have to be reckoned with. By its explicit terms Section 351 expresses the Congressional intent that transfers of property for stock or securities will not result in recognition. It therefore becomes apparent that this case vividly illustrates how Section 351 sometimes comes into conflict with another provision of the Internal Revenue Code or a judicial doctrine, and requires a determination of which of two conflicting doctrines will control.

As we must, when we try to reconcile conflicting doctrines in the revenue law, we endeavor to ascertain a controlling Congressional mandate. Section 351 has been described as a deliberate attempt by Congress to facilitate the incorporation of ongoing businesses and to eliminate any technical constructions which are economically unsound.

Appellant-taxpayer seems to recognize this and argues that application of the *Lake* rationale when accounts receivable are transferred would not create any undue hardship to an incorporating taxpayer. "All a taxpayer [transferor] need do is withhold the earned income items and collect them, transferring the net proceeds to the Corporation. Indeed . . . the transferor should retain both accounts receivable and accounts payable to avoid income recognition at the time of transfer and to have sufficient funds with which to pay accounts payable. Where the taxpayer [transferor] is on the cash method of accounting [as here], the deduction of the accounts payable would be applied against the income generated by the accounts receivable." . . .

While we cannot fault the general principle "that income be taxed to him who earns it," to adopt taxpayer's argument would be to hamper the incorporation of ongoing businesses; additionally it would impose technical constructions which are economically and practically unsound. None of the cases cited by taxpayer, including *Lake* itself, persuades us otherwise. In *Lake* the Court was required to decide whether the proceeds from the assignment of the oil payment right were taxable as ordinary income or as long term capital gains. Observing that the provision for long term capital gains treatment "has always been narrowly construed so as to protect the revenue against artful devices," 356 U.S. at 265, . . . the Court predicated its holding upon an emphatic distinction between a conversion of a capital investment — "income-producing property" — and an assignment of income per se. "The substance of what was assigned was the right to receive future income. The substance of what was received was the present value of income which the recipient would otherwise obtain in the future." Ibid., at 266. . . . A Section 351 issue was not presented in *Lake*. Therefore the case does not control in weighing the conflict between the general rule of assignment of income and the congressional purpose of nonrecognition upon the incorporation of an ongoing business.

We are persuaded that, on balance, the teachings of *Lake* must give way in this case to the broad congressional interest in facilitating the incorporation of ongoing businesses. As desirable as it is to afford symmetry in revenue law, we do not intend to promulgate a hard and fast rule.[9] We believe that the problems posed by the clash of conflicting internal revenue doctrines are more properly determined by the circumstances of each case. Here we are influenced by the fact that the subject of the assignment was accounts receivable for partnership's goods and services sold in the regular course of business, that the change of business form from partnership to corporation had a basic business purpose and was not designed for the purpose of deliberate tax avoidance, and by the conviction that the totality of circumstances here presented fit the mold of the congressional intent to give nonrecognition to a transfer of a total business from a noncorporate to a corporate form.

But this too must be said. Even though Section 351(a) immunizes the transferor from immediate tax consequences, Section 358 retains for the transferors a potential income tax liability to be realized and recognized upon a subsequent sale or exchange of the stock certificates received. As to the transferee-corporation, the tax basis of the receivables will be governed by Section 362. . . .

[Other issues omitted.]

REVENUE RULING 80-198
1980-2 C.B. 113

ISSUE

Under the circumstances described below, do the nonrecognition of gain or loss provisions of section 351 of the Internal Revenue Code apply to a transfer of the operating assets of an ongoing sole proprietorship (including unrealized accounts receivable) to a corporation in exchange solely for the common stock of a corporation and the assumption by the corporation of the proprietorship liabilities?

FACTS

Individual A conducted a medical practice as a sole proprietorship, the income of which was reported on the cash receipts and

---

9. The Commissioner has apparently taken the position that irrespective of the general principle that income is based upon he who earns it, other considerations should normally control Section 351 transfers. "However, the Service's ruling policy apparently is subject to the proviso that the taxpayer enter into a closing agreement assuring that the corporation will report the income reflected in the receivables upon their collection or other disposition. It would also appear that favorable rulings will not be issued where the timing of the transfer will be such as to result in a distortion of income. For example, such a ruling presumably could not be obtained if a seasonable business were to be incorporated during the portion of the year occurring after sizeable operating expenses had been incurred but before the income attributable thereto was collected." Weiss, [Problems in the Tax-Free Incorporation of a Business, 41 Ind. L.J. 666, 681 (1966)] (footnote omitted).

disbursements method of accounting. A transferred to a newly organized corporation all of the operating assets of the sole proprietorship in exchange for all of the stock of the corporation, plus the assumption by the corporation of all of the liabilities of the sole proprietorship. The purpose of the incorporation was to provide a form of business organization that would be more conducive to the planned expansion of the medical services to be made available by the business enterprise.

The assets transferred were tangible assets having a fair market value of $40,000 and an adjusted basis of $30,000 and unrealized trade accounts receivable having a face amount of $20,000 and an adjusted basis of zero. The liabilities assumed by the corporation consisted of trade accounts payable in the face amount of $10,000. The liabilities assumed by the corporation also included a mortgage liability, related to the tangible property transferred, of $10,000. A had neither accumulated the accounts receivable nor prepaid any of the liabilities of the sole proprietorship in a manner inconsistent with normal business practices in anticipation of the incorporation. If A had paid the trade accounts payable liabilities, the amounts paid would have been deductible by A as ordinary and necessary business expenses under section 162 of the Code. The new corporation continued to utilize the cash receipts and disbursements method of accounting.

LAW AND ANALYSIS

The applicable section of the Code is section 351(a), which provides that no gain or loss shall be recognized when property is transferred to a corporation in exchange solely for stock and securities and the transferor is in control (as defined by section 368(c)) of the transferee corporation immediately after the transfer. . . .

The facts of the instant case are similar to those in *Hempt Bros.* [page 403 supra] in that there was a valid business purpose for the transfer of the accounts receivable along with all of the assets and liabilities of A's proprietorship to a corporate transferee that would continue the business of the transferor. Further, A had neither accumulated the accounts receivable nor prepaid any of the accounts payable liabilities of the sole proprietorship in anticipation of the incorporation, which is an indication that, under the facts and circumstances of the case, the transaction was not designed for tax avoidance.

HOLDING

The transfer by A of the operating assets of the sole proprietorship (including unrealized accounts receivable) to the corporation in exchange solely for the common stock of the corporation and the assumption by the corporation of the proprietorship liabilities (including accounts payable) is an exchange within the meaning of section 351(a) of the Code. Therefore, no gain or loss is recognized to A with respect to the property transferred, including the accounts receivable. For transfers occurring on or after November 6, 1978 (the effective date . . . with respect to sections 357(c)(3) and 358(d)(2) of the Code) the assumption of the trade accounts payable that would give rise to a deduction if A had paid them is not, pursuant to section 357(c)(3), considered as an assumption of a liability for purposes of sections 357(c)(1) and 358(d). See Rev. Rul. 80-199 . . . [page 399 supra] for transfers occurring before November 6, 1978, which holds that trade accounts payable transferred to a corporation in a transaction to which section 351(a) applies are not liabilities for the purposes of sections 357(c) and 358(d) if the transferor of the accounts payable could have deducted the amounts paid in satisfaction thereof under section 162 if the transferor had paid these amounts in satisfaction of the payables prior to the exchange. The corporation, under the cash receipts and disbursements method of accounting, will report in its income the account receivables as collected, and will be allowed deductions under section 162 for the payments it makes to satisfy the assumed trade accounts payable when such payments are made.

A's basis in the stock received in the exchange of property for stock under section 358(a)(1) of the Code is $20,000 which is calculated by decreasing A's $30,000 basis in the assets transferred by the $10,000 mortgage liability under sections 358(a)(1)(A)(ii) and 358(d)(1). No adjustment to such basis is made under section 358(a)(1)(A)(ii) because of the assumption by the corporation of the $10,000 in accounts payable inasmuch as the general rule of section 358(d)(1), which requires the basis in the stock received to be decreased by the liabilities assumed, does not apply by reason of section 358(d)(2), which provides that section 358(d)(1) does not apply to the amount of any liabilities defined in section 357(c)(3) such as accounts payable that would have been deductible by A as ordinary and necessary business expenses under section 162 in the taxable year paid if A had paid these liabilities prior to the exchange. See Rev. Rul. 80-199 [page 399 supra], with respect to transfers which have occurred before November 6, 1978 (the date of the enactment of the Revenue Act of 1978).

LIMITATIONS

Section 351 of the Code does not apply to a transfer of accounts receivable which constitute an assignment of an income right in a case such as Brown v. Commissioner, 40 B.T.A. 565 (1939), *aff'd* 115

F.2d 337 (2d Cir. 1940). In *Brown*, an attorney transferred to a corporation, in which he was the sole owner, a one-half interest in a claim for legal services performed by the attorney and his law partner. In exchange, the attorney received additional stock of the corporation. The claim represented the corporation's only asset. Subsequent to the receipt by the corporation of the proceeds of the claim, the attorney gave all of the stock of the corporation to his wife. The United States Court of Appeals for the Second Circuit found that the transfer of the claim for the fee to the corporation had no purpose other than to avoid taxes and held that in such a case the intervention of the corporation would not prevent the attorney from being liable for the tax on the income which resulted from services under the assignment of income rule of Lucas v. Earl, 281 U.S. 111 (1930). Accordingly, in a case of a transfer to a controlled corporation of an account receivable in respect of services rendered where there is a tax avoidance purpose for the transaction (which might be evidenced by the corporation not conducting an ongoing business), the Internal Revenue Service will continue to apply assignment of income principles and require that the transferor of such a receivable include it in income when received by the transferee corporation.

Likewise, it may be appropriate in certain situations to allocate income, deductions, credits, or allowances to the transferor or transferee under section 482* . . . when the timing of the incorporation improperly separates income from related expenses. See Rooney v. United States, 305 F.2d 681 (9th Cir. 1962), where a farming operation was incorporated in a transaction described in section 351(a) after the expenses of the crop had been incurred but before the crop had been sold and income realized. The transferor's tax return contained all of the expenses but none of the farming income to which the expenses related. The United States Court of Appeals for the Ninth Circuit held that the expenses could be allocated under section 482 to the corporation, to be matched with the income to which the expenses related. Similar adjustments may be appropriate where some assets, liabilities, or both, are retained by the transferor and such retention results in the income of the transferor, transferee, or both, not being clearly reflected.

NOTE

See Keller, The Midstream Incorporation of a Cash-Basis Taxpayer: An Update, 38 Md. L. Rev. 480 (1979). For a cogent argument that the assignment of income doctrine should override §351 with

*See Chapter 5, page 948 infra, for materials on §482. — Ed.

the result that a cash-basis transferor of accounts receivable would generally be taxed, see Coven, Liabilities in Excess of Basis: Focht, Section 357(c)(3) and the Assignment of Income, 58 Or. L. Rev. 61 (1979).

C. CAPITAL CONTRIBUTION vs. CURRENT DEDUCTION

COMMISSIONER v. FINK
483 U.S. 89 (1987)

Justice POWELL delivered the opinion of the Court.

The question in this case is whether a dominant shareholder who voluntarily surrenders a portion of his shares to the corporation, but retains control, may immediately deduct from taxable income his basis in the surrendered shares.

I

Respondents Peter and Karla Fink were the principal share-holders of Travco Corporation, a Michigan manufacturer of motor homes. Travco had one class of common stock outstanding and no preferred stock. Mr. Fink owned 52.2 percent, and Mrs. Fink 20.3 percent, of the outstanding shares. Travco urgently needed new capital as a result of financial difficulties it encountered in the mid-1970s. The Finks voluntarily surrendered some of their shares to Travco in an effort to "increase the attractiveness of the corporation to outside investors." Brief for Respondents 3. Mr. Fink surrendered 116,146 shares in December 1976; Mrs. Fink surrendered 80,000 shares in January 1977. As a result, the Finks' combined percentage ownership of Travco was reduced from 72.5 percent to 68.5 percent. The Finks received no consideration for the surrendered shares, and no other shareholder surrendered any stock. The effort to attract new investors was unsuccessful, and the corporation eventually was liquidated.

On their 1976 and 1977 joint federal income tax returns, the Finks claimed ordinary loss deductions totaling $389,040, the full amount of their adjusted basis in the surrendered shares. The Commissioner of Internal Revenue disallowed the deductions. He concluded that the stock surrendered was a contribution to the corporation's capital. Accordingly, the Commissioner determined that the surrender resulted in no immediate tax consequences, and that the Finks' basis in the surrendered shares should be added to the basis of their remaining shares of Travco stock.

In an unpublished opinion, the Tax Court sustained the Commissioner's determination for the reasons stated in Frantz v. Commissioner, 83 T.C. 162, 174-182 (1984), aff'd, 784 F.2d 119 (CA2 1986), . . . [cert. denied, 107 S. Ct. 3262 (1987).] In *Frantz* the Tax Court held that a stockholder's non pro rata surrender of shares to the corporation does not produce an immediate loss. The court reasoned that "[t]his conclusion . . . necessarily follows from a recognition of the purpose of the transfer, that is, to bolster the financial position of [the corporation] and, hence, to protect and make more valuable [the stockholder's] retained shares." 83 T.C., at 181. Because the purpose of the shareholder's surrender is "to decrease or avoid a loss on his overall investment," the Tax Court in *Frantz* was "unable to conclude that [he] sustained a loss at the time of the transaction." Ibid. "Whether [the shareholder] would sustain a loss, and if so, the amount thereof, could only be determined when he subsequently disposed of the stock that the surrender was intended to protect and make more valuable." Ibid. The Tax Court recognized that it had sustained the taxpayer's position in a series of prior cases. Id., at 174-175. But it concluded that these decisions were incorrect, in part because they "encourage[d] a conversion of eventual capital losses into immediate ordinary losses." Id., at 182.

In this case, a divided panel of the Court of Appeals for the Sixth Circuit reversed the Tax Court. 789 F.2d 427 (1986). . . .

We granted certiorari to resolve a conflict among the circuits . . . and now reverse.

II

A

It is settled that a shareholder's voluntary contribution to the capital of the corporation has no immediate tax consequences. 26 U.S.C. §263; 26 CFR §1.263(a)-2(f) (1986). Instead, the shareholder is entitled to increase the basis of his shares by the amount of his basis in the property transferred to the corporation. . . . When the shareholder later disposes of his shares, his contribution is reflected as a smaller taxable gain or a larger deductible loss. This rule applies not only to transfers of cash or tangible property, but also to a shareholder's forgiveness of a debt owed to him by the corporation. 26 CFR §1.61-12(a) (1986). Such transfers are treated as contributions to capital even if the other shareholders make proportionately smaller contributions, or no contribution at all. See, e.g., Sackstein v. Commissioner, 14 T.C. 566, 569 (1950). The rules governing contributions to capital reflect the general principle that a shareholder may not claim an immediate loss for outlays made to benefit the corporation. Deputy v. du Pont, 308 U.S. 488 (1940); Eskimo Pie Corp. v.

Commissioner, 4 T.C. 669, 676 (1945), *aff'd,* 153 F.2d 301 (CA3 1946). We must decide whether this principle also applies to a controlling shareholder's non pro rata surrender of a portion of his shares.[6]

B

The Finks contend that they sustained an immediate loss upon surrendering some of their shares to the corporation. By parting with the shares, they gave up an ownership interest entitling them to future dividends, future capital appreciation, assets in the event of liquidation, and voting rights.[7] Therefore, the Finks contend, they are entitled to an immediate deduction. See 26 U.S.C. §§165(a) and (c)(2). In addition, the Finks argue that any non pro rata stock transaction "give[s] rise to immediate tax results." Brief for Respondents 13. For example, a non pro rata stock dividend produces income because it increases the recipient's proportionate ownership of the corporation. Koshland v. Helvering, 298 U.S. 441, 445 (1936).[8] By analogy, the Finks argue that a non pro rata surrender of shares should be recognized as an immediate loss because it reduces the surrendering shareholder's proportionate ownership.

Finally, the Finks contend that their stock surrenders were not contributions to the corporation's capital. They note that a typical contribution to capital, unlike a non pro rata stock surrender, has no effect on the contributing shareholder's proportionate interest in the corporation. Moreover, the Finks argue, a contribution of cash or other property increases the net worth of the corporation. For example, a shareholder's forgiveness of a debt owed to him by the corporation decreases the corporation's liabilities. In contrast, when a shareholder surrenders shares of the corporation's own stock, the corporation's net worth is unchanged. This is because the corporation cannot itself exercise the right to vote, receive dividends, or receive a share of assets in the event of liquidation. G. Johnson & J. Gentry, Finney and Miller's Principles of Accounting 538 (7th ed. 1974).

6. The Finks concede that a pro rata stock surrender, that by definition does not change the percentage ownership of any shareholder, is not a taxable event. Cf. Eisner v. Macomber, 252 U.S. 189 (1920) (pro rata stock dividend does not produce taxable income).

7. As a practical matter, however, the Finks did not give up a great deal. Their percentage interest in the corporation declined by only four percent. Because the Finks retained a majority interest, this reduction in their voting power was inconsequential. Moreover, Travco, like many corporations in financial difficulties, was not paying dividends.

8. In most cases, however, stock dividends are not recognized as income until the shares are sold. See [§305].

III

A shareholder who surrenders a portion of his shares to the corporation has parted with an asset, but that alone does not entitle him to an immediate deduction. Indeed, if the shareholder owns less than 100 percent of the corporation's shares, any non pro rata contribution to the corporation's capital will reduce the net worth of the contributing shareholder. A shareholder who surrenders stock thus is similar to one who forgives or surrenders a debt owed to him by the corporation; the latter gives up interest, principal, and also potential voting power in the event of insolvency or bankruptcy. But, as stated above, such forgiveness of corporate debt is treated as a contribution to capital rather than a current deduction. . . . The Finks' voluntary surrender of shares, like a shareholder's voluntary forgiveness of debt owed by the corporation, closely resembles an investment or contribution to capital. See B. Bittker & J. Eustice, Federal Income Taxation of Corporations and Shareholders §3.14, p. 3-59 (4th ed. 1979) ("If the contribution is voluntary, it does not produce gain or loss to the shareholder"). We find the similarity convincing in this case.

The fact that a stock surrender is not recorded as a contribution to capital on the corporation's balance sheet does not compel a different result. Shareholders who forgive a debt owed by the corporation or pay a corporate expense also are denied an immediate deduction, even though neither of these transactions is a contribution to capital in the accounting sense. Nor are we persuaded by the fact that a stock surrender, unlike a typical contribution to capital, reduces the shareholder's proportionate interest in the corporation. This Court has never held that every change in a shareholder's percentage ownership has immediate tax consequences. Of course, a shareholder's receipt of property from the corporation generally is a taxable event. See 26 U.S.C. §§301, 316. In contrast, a shareholder's transfer of property to the corporation usually has no immediate tax consequences. §263.

The Finks concede that the purpose of their stock surrender was to protect or increase the value of their investment in the corporation. Brief for Respondents 3. They hoped to encourage new investors to provide needed capital and in the long run recover the value of the surrendered shares through increased dividends or appreciation in the value of their remaining shares. If the surrender had achieved its purpose, the Finks would not have suffered an economic loss. See Johnson, Tax Models for Nonprorata Shareholder Contributions, 3 Va. Tax. Rev. 81, 104-108 (1983). In this case, as in many cases involving closely-held corporations whose shares are not traded on an open market, there is no reliable method of determining whether the surrender will result in a loss until the shareholder disposes of his remaining shares. Thus, the Finks' stock surrender does not meet the requirement that an immediately deductible loss must be "actually sustained during the taxable year." 26 CFR §1.165-1(b) (1986). . . .[14]

We therefore hold that a dominant shareholder who voluntarily surrenders a portion of his shares to the corporation, but retains control, does not sustain an immediate loss deductible from taxable income. Rather, the surrendering shareholder must reallocate his basis in the surrendered shares to the shares he retains.[15] The shareholder's loss, if any, will be recognized when he disposes of his remaining shares. . . .

IV

For the reasons we have stated, the judgment of the Court of Appeals for the Sixth Circuit is reversed.

It is so ordered.

Justice WHITE, concurring.

14. Our holding today also draws support from two other sections of the Code. First, §83 provides that, if a shareholder makes a "bargain sale" of stock to a corporate officer or employee as compensation, the "bargain" element of the sale must be treated as a contribution to the corporation's capital. S. Rep. No. 91-552, pp. 123-124 (1969), 1969 U.S. Code Cong. & Admin. News 1978, pp. 2027, 2155; 26 C.F.R. §1.83-6(d) (1986). . . . To be sure, Congress was concerned in §83 with transfers of restricted stock to employees as compensation rather than surrenders of stock to improve the corporation's financial condition. In both cases, however, the shareholder's underlying purpose is to increase the value of his investment.

Second, if a shareholder's stock is redeemed — that is, surrendered to the corporation in return for cash or other property — the shareholder is not entitled to an immediate deduction unless the redemption results in a substantial reduction in the shareholder's ownership percentage. §§302(a), (b), (d); 26 C.F.R. §1.302-2(c) (1986). Because the Finks' surrenders resulted in only a slight reduction in their ownership percentage, they would not have been entitled to an immediate loss if they had received consideration for the surrendered shares. 26 U.S.C. §302(b). Although the Finks did not receive a direct payment of cash or other property, they hoped to be compensated by an increase in the value of their remaining shares.

15. The Finks remained the controlling shareholders after their surrender. We therefore have no occasion to decide in this case whether a surrender that causes the shareholder to lose control of the corporation is immediately deductible. In related contexts, the Code distinguishes between minimal reductions in a shareholder's ownership percentage and loss of corporate control. See §302(b)(2) (providing "exchange" rather than dividend treatment for a "substantially disproportionate redemption of stock" that brings the shareholder's ownership percentage below 50 percent); §302(b)(3) (providing similar treatment when the redemption terminates the shareholder's interest in the corporation).

In this case we use the term "control" to mean ownership of more than half of a corporation's voting shares. We recognize, of course, that in larger corporations — especially those whose shares are listed on a national exchange — a person or entity may exercise control in fact while owning less than a majority of the voting shares. See Securities Exchange Act of 1934, §13(d), 48 Stat. 894, 15 U.S.C. §78m(d) (requiring persons to report acquisition of more than 5 percent of a registered equity security).

Although I join the Court's opinion, I suggest that there is little substance in the reservation in footnote 15 of the question whether a surrender of stock that causes the stockholder to lose control of the corporation is immediately deductible as an ordinary loss. Of course, this case does not involve a loss of control; but as I understand the rationale of the Court's opinion, it would also apply to a surrender that results in loss of control. At least I do not find in the opinion any principled ground for distinguishing a loss-of-control case from this one.

[Justice Scalia's opinion, concurring in the judgment, is omitted. Justice Blackmun concurred in the result without an opinion.]

Justice STEVENS, dissenting.

The value of certain and predictable rules of law is often underestimated. Particularly in the field of taxation, there is a strong interest in enabling taxpayers to predict the legal consequences of their proposed actions, and there is an even stronger general interest in ensuring that the responsibility for making changes in settled law rests squarely on the shoulders of Congress. In this case, these interests are of decisive importance for me.

The question of tax law presented by this case was definitively answered by the Board of Tax Appeals in 1941. See Miller v. Commissioner, 45 B.T.A. 292, 299; Budd International Corp. v. Commissioner, 45 B.T.A. 737, 755-756.[1] Those decisions were consistently followed for over 40 years, see, e.g., Smith v. Commissioner, 66 T.C. 622, 648 (1976); Downer v. Commissioner, 48 T.C. 86, 91 (1967); Estate of Foster v. Commissioner, 9 T.C. 930, 934 (1947), and the Internal Revenue Service had announced its acquiescence in the decisions. . . . Although Congress dramatically revamped the tax code in 1954, . . . it did not modify the Tax Court's approach to this issue.

It was only in 1977 (after the Finks had transferred their stock to the corporation), that the Commission retracted its acquiescence in the Tax Court's interpretation. . . .

. . . The Commissioner of Internal Revenue certainly had a right to advocate a change, but in my opinion he should have requested relief from the body that has the authority to amend the Internal Revenue Code. For I firmly believe that "after a statute has been construed, either by this Court or by a consistent course of decision by other federal judges and agencies, it acquires a meaning that should be as clear as if the judicial gloss had been drafted by the Congress itself." Shearson/American Express v. McMahon, 107 S. Ct. 2332 (1987) (Stevens, J., concurring in part and dissenting in part).

---

1. The principle applied in those decisions dates back even further. See Burdick v. Commissioner, 20 B.T.A. 742 (1930), aff'd, 59 F. 2d 395 (1932); Wright v. Commissioner, 18 B.T.A. 471 (1929).

A rule of statutory construction that "has been consistently recognized for more than 35 years" acquires a clarity that "is simply beyond peradventure." Herman & MacLean v. Huddleston, 459 U.S. 375, 380 (1983).

. . . Mr. Fink surrendered his shares in December 1976. Mrs. Fink surrendered hers in January 1977. At that time the law was well settled: the Tax Court had repeatedly reaffirmed the right to deduct such surrenders as ordinary losses, and the Commission had acquiesced in this view for 35 years. . . . It was only on April 11, 1977, that the Commission announced its non-acquiescence. See Internal Revenue Bulletin No. 1977-15, p. 6 (April 11, 1977). "In my view, the retroactive application of the Court's holding in a case like this is unfair to the individual taxpayer as well as unwise judicial administration." Dickman v. Commissioner, 465 U.S. 330, 353 n. 11 (1984) (Powell, J., dissenting).

I respectfully dissent.

III. ISSUANCE OF STOCK — IMPACT ON CORPORATION — §1032

See Chapter 1, pages 3-4, 85-87 supra; Landis, Contributions to Capital of Corporations, 24 Tax. L. Rev. 241 (1969).

IV. PROPERTY RECEIVED BY CORPORATION FOR STOCK — BASIS AND HOLDING PERIOD

A. TAXABLE TRANSFER — §1012

When a corporation issues stock to a shareholder in exchange for property in circumstances that render the transaction wholly taxable to the shareholder, the corporation is treated as a purchaser of the assets and its basis is cost under §1012. See Treas. Reg. §1.1032-1(d) (last sentence).

What is a corporation's "cost" if it issues newly authorized stock in exchange for assets with a fair market value of $1,000? Does it matter that the stock has a fair market value of $1,050? Of $950? Does it matter that the stock represents a minority interest in a closely held corporation and that there is no market for the stock?

Suppose a corporation issues its ten-year, 8-percent bond in exchange for an asset in circumstances that render the bondholder taxable on the asset appreciation. What is the corporation's basis for the asset? Why?

B. TAX-FREE TRANSFER (IN WHOLE OR IN PART) — §362(a)

If a corporation receives assets in a transaction to which §351 applies, the basis is governed by §362(a). See Treas. Reg. §1.1032-1(d); §1.362-1.

Suppose Corporation C issues $10,000 worth of its stock, $5,000 worth of its long-term debentures, and cash of $5,000 to its sole shareholder in exchange for an asset worth $20,000 that had a basis in the shareholder's hands of $10,000. What is the basis of the asset in Corporation C's hands? Why?

Note that in some circumstances "new" §336(d) has the effect of limiting the §362(a) basis of property acquired in a §351 transaction to its *value* at the time it was acquired. Cf. National Securities Corp. v. Commissioner, 137 F.2d 600 (3d Cir. 1943), *cert. denied,* 320 U.S. 794 (1943), page 1002 infra.

C. HOLDING PERIOD — §1223(2)

If a corporation receives property with its basis determined under §362(a), as in a §351 transaction, the corporation's holding period will include the period during which the property was held by the transferor. This "tacking" rule is provided in §1223(2). The rules governing the holding period are, of course, much less important now that the preferential rate for long-term capital gains has been eliminated.

V. ACCOUNTING CONTINUITY

DEARBORN GAGE CO. v. COMMISSIONER
48 T.C. 190 (1967)

TANNENWALD, Judge. Respondent determined deficiencies in petitioner's income tax for the taxable years ended November 30, 1960,

1961, and 1962 in the amounts of $32,962.47, $4,218.02, and $979.78, respectively.

Petitioner having conceded all other items in the deficiency notice, two issues remain for our consideration:

1. Was respondent entitled to require petitioner to include overhead costs in inventory values instead of deducting such costs in the year spent?

2. If so, to what extent, if any, were adjustments properly made under section 481?

Findings of Fact

[The taxpayer was incorporated on May 1, 1957. On that date it received the assets and ongoing business of a partnership in a transaction that qualified under Section 351. The taxpayer, like its predecessor partnership, engaged in manufacturing and maintained substantial inventories. From its inception the taxpayer valued its inventories at cost using the FIFO method and included only the *direct* costs of labor and materials in its valuation. It never included *indirect* costs and administrative expenses (overhead). The taxpayer's predecessor partnership also excluded overhead costs in its inventory valuations but valued its inventories at the lower of cost or market.

[In 1963 the Commissioner examined the taxpayer's returns for fiscal years 1960, 1961, and 1962 and determined that its ending inventories for those years should be increased to reflect overhead costs. The Commissioner made no adjustment to the 1960 opening inventory.

[The Tax Court sustained the Commissioner's judgment that the taxpayer's method of accounting for inventories did not clearly reflect income and that overhead costs should be included. The taxpayer then argued that similar adjustments should be made to the predecessor partnership's inventories for the period since January 1, 1954. Such adjustments would have increased the closing inventories of the partnership on the date it transferred its assets to the taxpayer, and so the taxpayer's opening inventories on May 1, 1957, would have been higher. The Tax Court's opinion with respect to this aspect of the case follows.]

. . . Under section 481, the determination of the petitioner's liability *for the taxable year 1960* must take into account adjustments for prior taxable years to which that section applies. The process of computing these adjustments involves reconstructing petitioner's opening and closing inventories for the taxable years 1957, 1958, and 1959. Unquestionably, overhead costs must be included in petitioner's opening and closing inventories for 1958 and 1959 and the closing inventory for 1957. The critical question which we must resolve is whether such costs must be also included in opening inventory for 1957. In so doing, we must decide which of two general principles applies. The first principle requires that opening inventory be computed on the same basis as closing inventory. . . . The second principle requires that, pursuant to section 362, in a tax-free exchange such as occurred herein when the predecessor partnership transferred its assets to petitioner, the basis of the transferred assets in the hands of the latter is the same as it was in the hands of the former. In implementing this second principle it has been held that the basis of initial opening inventory in the hands of the transferee corporation should not be adjusted in order to correct for an erroneous method of accounting for that inventory by the predecessor transferor. Ezo Products Co., [37 T.C. 385 (1961)] . . . ; but cf. Manhattan Building Co. 27 T.C. 1032 (1957), a case not involving inventories where the taxpayer was permitted to make changes in the basis of property to take into account errors in the tax treatment of prior transactions involving the property. None of these decisions dealt with the inter-relationship of the two principles but this question was discussed in Textile Apron Co., 21 T.C. 147 (1953), where we said that the principle respecting the uniform method of valuing opening and closing inventory for a given taxable year does not apply where the inventory was acquired in a tax-free exchange.

Petitioner argues that, on the basis of the agreed cumulative method utilized in computing petitioner's inventory, the refusal of respondent to make an adjustment based on overhead costs related to its opening inventory for the taxable year 1957 in effect allows respondent to tax $6,643.26 in overhead costs expensed by its predecessor during the period January 1, 1954 to April 30, 1957 and $10,087.47 in such costs thus expensed prior to January 1, 1954. Thus, petitioner insists that it is being taxed on $16,730.73 which is properly attributable to periods to which section 481 does not apply, because of the decisions that that section may only be applied to the petitioner-taxpayer and because that section, by its terms, precludes pre-1954 adjustments where a change of accounting method is made by the respondent, as is the case herein.

The fact of the matter is that these asserted consequences are more apparent than real. In the first place, it can be argued that overhead costs are incurred only after inventory is acquired and that, *as to this petitioner*, there were no overhead costs in its May 1, 1957 opening inventory. See Frank G. Wikstrom & Sons, Inc., supra at p. 361. Such an approach, together with the fact that petitioner acquired the inventory through the issuance of its own shares, justifies the conclusion that petitioner is not being deprived, economically or financially, of the benefit of any actual payment in excess of its predecessor's basis. Secondly, it is not necessarily true that there are any overhead costs actually attributable to closing inventory in the hands of petitioner's predecessor which were incurred by the predecessor prior to January 1, 1954. It seems likely (and the record does not indicate otherwise) that all of the inventory acquired prior to January 1, 1954 was disposed of by the predecessor prior to April 30, 1957 so that the closing inventory on that date represented only acquisitions since January 1, 1954. Indeed, theoretically all of the inventory acquired prior to January 1, 1957 could have been disposed of by petitioner's predecessor prior to April 30, 1957 so that the closing inventory on that date included only acquisitions during the last four month taxable period. See the lucid discussion of Judge Learned Hand as to how inventories are handled in Commissioner v. Dwyer, [203 F.2d 522 (2nd Cir. (1953))] . . . ; see also David W. Hughes, [22 T.C. 1 (1954)] . . . (Judge Opper's dissenting opinion [at page 5]).

We recognize that, if petitioner had never been formed, and the predecessor partnership had continued in business, and the issue before us involved a comparable change in the latter's method of accounting for overhead costs, respondent would have been precluded by the express provisions of section 481 from making any adjustments with respect to periods prior to January 1, 1954 and would, under the applicable decisions, have been required, in making the necessary computations, to include overhead costs both in the opening inventory and closing inventory for the taxable year 1954. Thus, petitioner — a taxpayer separate and distinct from its predecessor — appears to fare worse than its predecessor would have. We also recognize that, in point of fact, the tax benefit of the deductions for overhead costs taken by petitioner's predecessor may not have been as great as the tax burden which our rationale now requires petitioner to bear, e.g., because the partners may have been in lower tax brackets or the partnership may have operated at a loss in some of the prior years. Moreover, if the ownership of petitioner's stock had changed prior to the taxable years herein involved, the economic effect of the tax benefit would not inure to, nor would the tax burden fall upon, the same persons. But these are nothing more than some of the myriad of different consequences which may result from a change to the corporate form of doing business or from the acquisition of stock of a corporation rather than corporate assets. . . .

We do not have before us an attempt by the respondent to impose a tax in 1960 on amounts which had previously been taxed in barred years, with double taxation the result. Cf. John Wanamaker Philadelphia, Inc. v. United States, 359 F.2d 437 (Ct. Cl. 1966). On the contrary, we are confronted with an attempt by petitioner to resist the application of section 481 and the accepted rule as to the basis of inventory acquired in a tax-free exchange in order to obtain our blessing of a double deduction. Under these circumstances and taking into account the progressive legislative design over the years to ameliorate the effects of the statute of limitations through the enactment of section 481, as well as the mitigation provisions of section 1311 et seq., we are not disposed to accept petitioner's arguments and depart from the framework established by the decided cases. To do otherwise would require us to import into section 351 exchanges a concept of continuity of taxpayers which has clearly been rejected. Joseph E. Seagram & Sons, Inc., [46 T.C. 698 (1966)]; Ezo Products Co., supra; ... Textile Apron Co., supra. We conclude, therefore, that, although section 481 is the vehicle by which respondent's adjustments are to be made, he may nevertheless, in computing those adjustments, take advantage of a rule available to him without regard to that section. . . .

Decision will be entered for the respondent.

NOTES

1. Where language of the statute itself is not compelling, one way or the other, should a court resolve the continuity of basis question posed in *Dearborn Gage* restrictively, as the Tax Court did, or should it adopt a broader approach to continuity of basis in view of the general theme underlying §§351(a) and 362(a)(1)? Why?

2. If a partnership incorporates a building under §351(a), and the building had been carried on the partnership's books erroneously at a basis of $50,000 but had an actual basis of $40,000, at what basis will the corporation-transferee take the building?

3. *Dearborn Gage Co.* involved a corporation that valued its inventory by a method different from that used by its predecessor partnership. In Rocco, Inc., 72 T.C. 140 (1979), two corporations on the accrual method of accounting each formed a wholly owned subsidiary. The subsidiaries adopted the cash method of accounting and in their first year recognized a loss primarily because they did not reduce their cost of goods sold by the amount of the ending inventory. Through the filing of a consolidated return, the parent corporations offset their own gains against the subsidiaries' losses. The Commissioner admitted that the subsidiaries' method of accounting and the filing of a consolidated return were proper, but argued that §269 required that the subsidiaries' cost of goods sold be reduced in the amount of their ending inventory. The Tax Court did not find that the tax avoidance purpose required by §269 was present.

4. See also Hempt Brothers, Inc. v. United States, 490 F.2d 1172 (3d Cir. 1974), page 403 supra. There the Third Circuit rejected the corporate taxpayer's contention that tax benefit principles required

that inventory received by it on the incorporation of a sole proprietorship take a fair market value basis.

NASH v. UNITED STATES
398 U.S. 1 (1970)

Mr. Justice Douglas delivered the opinion of the Court.

Petitioners were partners operating eight finance offices in Alabama. The partnership reported its income on the accrual method
of accounting and instead of deducting bad debts within the taxable
year as permitted by §166(a) of the Internal Revenue Code of 1954
it used the reserve method of accounting as permitted by §166(c).
Under the reserve method of accounting a taxpayer includes in his
income the full-face amount of a receivable on its creation and adjusts
at the end of each taxable year the reserve account so that it equals
that portion of current accounts receivable which is estimated to
become worthless in subsequent years. Any additions necessary to
increase the reserve are currently deductible. When an account receivable becomes worthless during the year, the reserve account is
decreased and no additional bad debt deduction is allowed. As of
May 31, 1960, the partnership books showed accounts receivable of
$486,853.69 and a reserve for bad debts of $73,028.05.

On June 1, 1960, petitioners formed eight new corporations and
transferred the assets of the eight partnership offices, including the
accounts receivable, to the corporations in exchange for shares of
the corporations — a transfer which concededly provided no gain or
loss under §351 of the Code.

The Commissioner determined that the partnership should have
included in income the amount of the bad debt reserve ($73,028.05)
applicable to the accounts receivable that had been transferred. Tax
deficiencies were computed; and petitioners, having paid them,
brought this suit for refunds. The District Court allowed recovery
and the Court of Appeals reversed, 414 F.2d 627. We granted the
petition for certiorari to resolve the conflict between the Fifth and
the Ninth Circuits[1] on this question of law. 396 U.S. 1000. . . . We
share the view of the Ninth Circuit and reverse the present judgment.

There is no provision of the Code that deals precisely with this
question. But the Commissioner's basic premise rests on the so-called
tax benefit rule, viz. that a recovery of an item that has produced an
income tax benefit in a prior year is to be added to income in the
year of recovery. The Commissioner argues that that rule, applicable
here, means that unused amounts in a bad debt reserve must be

---

1. Estate of Schmidt v. Commissioner of Internal Revenue, 9 Cir., 355 F.2d 111.

restored to income when the reserve is found to be no longer necessary, as it was here, when the partnership's "need" for the reserves ended with the termination of its business. Congress could make the end of "need" synonymous with "recovery" in the meaning of the tax benefit rule and make the rule read: "a bad debt reserve which has produced an income tax benefit in a prior year is to be added to income in the year when it was recovered or when its need is ended." The semantics would then be honored by the Commissioner's ruling. But we do not feel free to state the tax benefit rule in those terms in the present context. We deal with §351(a) of the Code which provides:

> No gain or loss shall be recognized if property is transferred to a corporation by one or more persons solely in exchange for stock or securities in such corporation and immediately after the exchange such person or persons are in control . . . of the corporation.

All that petitioners received from corporations were securities equal in value to the net worth of the accounts transferred, that is the face value less the amount of the reserve for bad debts. If, as conceded, there is no "gain" or "loss" recognized as a result of the transaction, it seems anomalous to treat the bad debt reserve as "income" to the transferor.

Deduction of the reserve from the face amount of the receivables transferred conforms to the reality of the transaction, as the risk of noncollection was on the transferee. Since the reserve for purposes of this case was deemed to be reasonable and the value of the stock received upon the transfer was equal to the *net value* of the receivables, there does not seem to us to have been any "recovery." A tax benefit was received by the partnership when the bad debt reserve was originally taken as a deduction from income. There would be a double benefit to the partnership if securities were issued covering the face amount of the receivables. We do not, however, understand how there can be a "recovery" of the benefit of the bad debt reserve when the receivables are transferred less the reserve.[5] That merely perpetuates the status quo and does not tinker with it for any double benefit out of the bad debt reserve.

For these reasons, the Court of Appeals in the *Schmidt* case held

---

5. ". . . the infirmities in the accounts receivable which justify the bad debt reserve carry over to those accounts in the hands of the corporation. Presumably the amount that will ultimately be collected by the corporation will not be the gross amount of the receivables, but rather the net amount after deducting the bad debt reserve. Thus, the stock received in exchange for such accounts receivable can only be worth what the receivables themselves are worth, namely, the net collectable amount rather than the gross amount." Arent, Reallocation of Income and Expenses in Connection with Formation and Liquidation of Corporations, 40 Taxes 995, 998 (1962).

that although the "need" for the reserve ended with the transfer, the end of that need did not mark a "recovery" within the meaning of the tax benefit cases, 355 F.2d, at 113. We agree and accordingly reverse the judgment below.

Reversed.

Mr. Justice Black and Mr. Justice Stewart, dissenting.

NOTES

1. How do the transferee corporations in *Nash* determine the basis of each of the accounts receivable they acquired in the §351 transaction? The transferors in *Nash* maintained a bad debt reserve (§166(c), now repealed). Could any or all of the transferee corporations charge off their bad debts as incurred (§166(a)), or would each have to carry over an aliquot portion of the transferors' reserve? How should the basis of the stock received by the transferors in the §351 transaction in *Nash* reflect the accounts receivable they transferred to the corporations? Should Justice Douglas's opinion have dealt with any of these questions? See Raskind, The Tax Treatment of the Reserve for Bad Debts on Incorporation: The Supreme Court Resolution in *Nash*, 31 Ohio St. L.J. 411 (1970).

2. See Philadelphia and Reading Corp. v. United States, 602 F.2d 338 (Ct. Cl. 1979), for a case allowing the transferee corporation in a §351 transaction to continue the transferor's election to amortize §616 development expenses incurred by the transferor. The Court ruled that "in terms of . . . to whom Congress wished to restrict the benefits of §616, transactions covered by section 351 . . . present a much different situation than normal purchase transactions." The §351 transaction merely changed the legal ownership of the mineral property; it did not affect the substance of the transferor's investment.

REVENUE RULING 56-256
1956-1 C.B. 129

Taxpayer, an individual, constructed a building and purchased equipment in 1954 upon which depreciation was computed on the declining balance method as prescribed in section 167(b)(2) of the Internal Revenue Code of 1954. In 1955, the taxpayer transferred the building and equipment to a newly formed corporation in a nontaxable exchange. Held, since the new corporation is a taxable entity separate from that of the individual taxpayer, it follows that the new corporation acquired property, the original use of which did not commence with it as required under section 167(c)(2) of the Code. Accordingly, under the limitations imposed by section 167(c) of the Code, the new corporation may not continue the use of the declining balance method of computing depreciation provided for in section 167(b)(2) of the Code; nor may it use the methods and rates of computing depreciation provided for in section 167(b)(3) of the Code, relating to the sum of the years-digits method, and section 167(b)(4) of the Code, relating to certain other consistent methods, with respect to the property. Depreciation on the building and equipment acquired by the corporation may be computed by using the straight line method or any other method, exclusive of those provided for in paragraphs (2), (3) and (4) of section 167(b) of the Code, which will, based upon existing operating conditions, produce a reasonable allowance therefor within the purview of section 167 of the Code. The above principle is equally applicable in cases where depreciable property is similarly transferred between other separate tax entities. However, see sections 381(a) and 381(c)(6) of the Code, relative to certain acquisitions of assets of a corporation by another corporation; and section 1.1502-46 of the Income Tax Regulations, relative to property received by a member of an affiliated group from another member of the group during a consolidated return period.

NOTE

In Rev. Rul. 67-286, 1967-2 C.B. 101, the Service reaffirmed the position it announced in Rev. Rul. 56-256. In Rev. Rul. 67-286, however, the Service also held that "for purposes of section 167(c) . . . , the useful life of an asset with an estimated useful life of three years or more to the taxpayer [a sole proprietor] at the time of acquisition will not be redetermined merely because the taxpayer [within three years of acquisition] incorporated the . . . business in which the asset was used [under §351]." As a result, the proprietor's election to use one of the depreciation methods permitted by §167(b)(2),(3), or (4) for the less-than-three-year period prior to incorporation was not disturbed.

GENERAL REFERENCE

See American Law Institute, Federal Income Tax Project — Subchapter C 53, 59, 152, 188-195, 314 (1982); The Subchapter C Revision Act of 1985, A Final Report Prepared by the Staff, S. Prt. No. 47, 99th Cong., 1st Sess. (Comm. Print, May 1985).

4

Reorganizations and Related Transactions

I. INTRODUCTION AND HISTORY

As a general rule gain or loss is realized when an asset worth more or less than its adjusted basis is exchanged for another asset. In an arm's length transaction one would expect the asset received to be equal in value to the one surrendered, and the measure of the gain or loss realized would be the difference between the value of the asset received and the adjusted basis of the asset surrendered. See §1001(a) and (b).

Unless the Code provides otherwise, all realized gain or loss is recognized in the computation of a taxpayer's income. Section 1001(c). In many cases, however, Congress has provided for non-recognition, usually on the basis that the exchange has not produced an economically significant change in the nature of the taxpayer's investment or has not brought him close enough to cash or consumable goods to justify taxation in light of the pervasive doctrine that generally prohibits taxation of unrealized appreciation. Section 351, which was studied in detail in Chapter 3, is one example of a non-recognition provision. This chapter will examine other Code provisions that call for nonrecognition in the context of corporate transactions.

If a taxpayer buys a share of General Motors common stock at $50, the doctrine protecting unrealized appreciation prevents the taxation of his appreciation even though the stock has risen in value to $75 and the cash can be realized with a telephone call to a broker. Moreover, if pursuant to a "stock split" or a plan of recapitalization the taxpayer exchanges his single share of General Motors common for two shares of General Motors common, each worth $37.50, his realized gain is not recognized. See §§1036(a); 368(a)(1)(E) and 354(a)(1). But if instead the taxpayer exchanges his General Motors stock for his neighbor's Ford Motor common stock, his $25 gain is both realized and recognized. If the exchange of General Motors stock for Ford Motor stock is not an exchange between shareholders but is one effected directly with Ford Motor Company as a result of

429

a statutory merger of General Motors Company into Ford, the exchanging shareholder's gain is not recognized. See §§368(a)(1)(A) and 354(a)(1). If the plan of merger results in the taxpayer's receiving Ford stock worth $60 and cash of $15 (or a $15 Ford bond), $15 of the gain is recognized. See §356(a) and (d). The recognized gain may be taxable as a dividend (see §356(a)(2)), although a sale to (or exchange with) the neighbor probably would produce capital gain. Transactions like these and the complex tax problems they present to corporations and their investors are the subject of this chapter.

Parts II and III of this chapter deal with stock dividends and recapitalizations, transactions in which the investor's interest in his corporation is reclassified or represented in a new form. The receipt of a new stock certificate (or a bond) in addition to, or in exchange for, the investor's old certificate usually triggers a recognition problem.

Parts IV through VII deal with reorganizations involving more than one corporation: amalgamating reorganizations (mergers and consolidations), divisive reorganizations (spin-offs, split-offs, split-ups, and split-aways), and corporate substitutions (one corporation replacing another). These types of reorganizations raise questions of recognition and basis adjustment for both the investors and the involved corporations. Ordinarily, stock dividends and recapitalizations (involving a single corporation) raise such questions only for the investor.

In Part VIII, this chapter presents issues involving the carryover of tax attributes from one corporation to another, particularly earnings and profits and net operating losses. Usually, but not always, the carryover problems will grow out of a reorganization. It is worth noting at this point that the provision limiting net operating loss carryforwards (§382) was the only provision in the reorganization area that was completely rewritten by the Tax Reform Act of 1986, and the 1989 Act amended §172 to limit the carryback of net operating losses incurred after a "corporate equity reducing transaction."

Finally, there are special problems posed when one or more of the corporations in reorganization is a foreign corporation. See §367. The income taxation of foreign corporations warrants discrete, specialized treatment, and is outside the scope of this book. See, e.g., J. Isenbergh, International Taxation (1989); R. Kaplan, Federal Taxation of International Transactions (1988); P. McDaniel & H. Ault, Introduction to United States International Taxation (3d ed. 1989); M. McIntyre, The International Income Tax Rules of the United States (1989).

II. STOCK DIVIDENDS — RECEIPT AND DISPOSITION

A. HISTORY

1. Taxability of Receipt

EISNER v. MACOMBER
252 U.S. 189 (1920)

Mr. Justice PITNEY delivered the opinion of the court. This case presents the question whether, by virtue of the Sixteenth Amendment, Congress has the power to tax, as income of the stockholder and without apportionment, a stock dividend made lawfully and in good faith against profits accumulated by the corporation since March 1, 1913.

It arises under the Revenue Act of September 8, 1916, c. 463, 39 Stat. 756, et seq., which, in our opinion . . . plainly evinces the purpose of Congress to tax stock dividends as income.[1] . . .

On January 1, 1916, the Standard Oil Company of California, a corporation of that State, out of an authorized capital stock of $100,000,000, had shares of stock outstanding, par value $100 each, amounting in round figures to $50,000,000. In addition, it had surplus and undivided profits invested in plant, property, and business and required for the purposes of the corporation, amounting to about $45,000,000, of which about $20,000,000 had been earned prior to March 1, 1913, the balance thereafter. In January, 1916, in order to readjust the capitalization, the board of directors decided to issue additional shares sufficient to constitute a stock dividend of 50 per cent of the outstanding stock, and to transfer from surplus account to capital stock account an amount equivalent to such issue. Appropriate resolutions were adopted, an amount equivalent to the par value of the proposed new stock was transferred accordingly, and the new stock duly issued against it and divided among the stockholders.

---

1. TITLE I.—INCOME TAX. Part I.—on individuals.

Sec. 2(a) That, subject only to such exemptions and deductions as are hereinafter allowed, the net income of a taxable person shall include gains, profit, or gains or profits and income derived from any source whatever: Provided, That the term "dividends" as used in this title shall be held to mean any distribution made or ordered to be made by a corporation, . . . out of its earnings or profits accrued since March first, nineteen hundred and thirteen, and payable to its shareholders, whether in cash or in stock of the corporation, . . . which stock dividend shall be considered income, to the amount of its cash value.

Defendant in error, being the owner of 2,200 shares of the old stock, received certificates for 1,100 additional shares, of which 18.07 percent, or 198.77 shares, par value $19,877, were treated as representing surplus earned between March 1, 1913, and January 1, 1916. She was called upon to pay, and did pay under protest, a tax imposed under the Revenue Act of 1916, based upon a supposed income of $19,877 because of the new shares; and an appeal to the Commissioner of Internal Revenue having been disallowed, she brought action against the Collector to recover the tax. In her complaint she . . . contended that in imposing such a tax the Revenue Act of 1916 violated Art. I, §2, cl. 3, and Art. I, §9, cl. 4, of the Constitution of the United States, requiring direct taxes to be apportioned according to population, and that the stock dividend was not income within the meaning of the Sixteenth Amendment. A general demurrer to the complaint was overruled upon the authority of Towne v. Eisner, 245 U.S. 418; and, defendant having failed to plead further, final judgment went against him. . . .

We are constrained to hold that the judgment of the District Court must be affirmed: First, because the question at issue is controlled by Towne v. Eisner, supra; secondly, because a re-examination of the question, with the additional light thrown upon it by elaborate arguments, has confirmed the view that the underlying ground of that decision is sound, that it disposes of the question here presented, and that other fundamental considerations lead to the same result.

In Towne v. Eisner, the question was whether a stock dividend made in 1914 against surplus earned prior to January 1, 1913, was taxable against the stockholder under the Act of October 3, 1913, c. 16, 38 Stat. 114, 166, which provided (§B, p. 167) that net income should include "dividends," and also "gains or profits and income derived from any source whatever." Suit having been brought by a stockholder to recover the tax assessed against him by reason of the dividend, the District Court sustained a demurrer to the complaint. 242 Fed. Rep. 702. The court treated the construction of the act as inseparable from the interpretation of the Sixteenth Amendment; and, having referred to Pollock v. Farmers' Loan & Trust Co., 158 U.S. 601, and quoted the Amendment, proceeded very properly to say (p. 704): "It is manifest that the stock dividend in question cannot be reached by the Income Tax Act, and could not, even though Congress expressly declared it to be taxable as income, unless it is in fact income." It declined, however, to accede to the contention that in Gibbons v. Mahon, 136 U.S. 549, "stock dividends" had received a definition sufficiently clear to be controlling, treated the language of this court in that case as obiter dictum in respect of the matter then before it (p. 706), and examined the question as res nova, with the result stated. When the case came here, after overruling a motion to dismiss made by the Government upon the ground that the only question involved was the construction of the statute and not its constitutionality, we dealt upon the merits with the question of construction only, but disposed of it upon consideration of the essential nature of a stock dividend, disregarding the fact that the one in question was based upon surplus earnings that accrued before the Sixteenth Amendment took effect. Not only so, but we rejected the reasoning of the District Court, saying (245 U.S. 426):

> [W]e cannot doubt that the dividend was capital as well for the purposes of the Income Tax Law as for distribution between tenant for life and remainderman. What was said by this court upon the latter question is equally true for the former. "A stock dividend really takes nothing from the property of the corporation, and adds nothing to the interests of the shareholders. Its property is not diminished, and their interests are not increased. . . . The proportional interest of each shareholder remains the same. The only change is in the evidence which represents that interest, the new shares and the original shares together representing the same proportional interest that the original shares represented before the issue of the new ones." Gibbons v. Mahon, 136 U.S. 549, 559, 560. In short, the corporation is no poorer and the stockholder is no richer than they were before. Logan County v. United States, 169 U.S. 255, 261. If the plaintiff gained any small advantage by the change, it certainly was not an advantage of $417,450, the sum upon which he was taxed. . . . What has happened is that the plaintiff's old certificates have been split up in effect and have diminished in value to the extent of the value of the new.

This language aptly answered not only the reasoning of the District Court but the argument of the Solicitor General in this court, which discussed the essential nature of a stock dividend. And if, for the reasons thus expressed, such a dividend is not to be regarded as "income" or "dividends" within the meaning of the Act of 1913, we are unable to see how it can be brought within the meaning of "incomes" in the Sixteenth Amendment; it being very clear that Congress intended in that act to exert its power to the extent permitted by the Amendment. In Towne v. Eisner it was not contended that any construction of the statute could make it narrower than the constitutional grant; rather the contrary.

The fact that the dividend was charged against profits earned before the Act of 1913 took effect, even before the Amendment was adopted, was neither relied upon nor alluded to in our consideration of the merits in that case. Not only so, but had we considered that a stock dividend constituted income in any true sense, it would have been held taxable under the Act of 1913 notwithstanding it was based upon profits earned before the Amendment. We ruled at the same term, in Lynch v. Hornby, 247 U.S. 339, that a cash dividend extraordinary in amount, and in Peabody v. Eisner, 247 U.S. 347, that a dividend paid in stock of another company, were taxable as income although based upon earnings that accrued before adoption of the Amendment. . . .

Therefore, Towne v. Eisner cannot be regarded as turning upon the point that the surplus accrued to the company before the act took effect and before adoption of the Amendment. And what we have quoted from the opinion in that case cannot be regarded as obiter dictum, it having furnished the entire basis for the conclusion reached. We adhere to the view then expressed, and might rest the present case there; not because that case in terms decided the constitutional question, for it did not; but because the conclusion there reached as to the essential nature of a stock dividend necessarily prevents its being regarded as income in any true sense.

Nevertheless, in view of the importance of the matter, and the fact that Congress in the Revenue Act of 1916 declared . . . that a "stock dividend shall be considered income, to the amount of its cash value," we will deal at length with the constitutional question, incidentally testing the soundness of our previous conclusion.

The Sixteenth Amendment must be construed in connection with the taxing clauses of the original Constitution and the effect attributed to them before the Amendment was adopted. In Pollock v. Farmers' Loan & Trust Co., 158 U.S. 601, under the Act of August 27, 1894, c. 349, §27, 28 Stat. 509, 553, it was held that taxes upon rents and profits of real estate and upon returns from investments of personal property were in effect direct taxes upon the property from which such income arose, imposed by reason of ownership; and that Congress could not impose such taxes without apportioning them among the States according to population, as required by Art. I, §2, cl. 3, and §9, cl. 4, of the original Constitution.

Afterwards, and evidently in recognition of the limitation upon the taxing power of Congress thus determined, the Sixteenth Amendment was adopted, in words lucidly expressing the object to be accomplished: "The Congress shall have power to lay and collect taxes on incomes, from whatever source derived, without apportionment among the several States, and without regard to any census or enumeration." As repeatedly held, this did not extend the taxing power to new subjects, but merely removed the necessity which otherwise might exist for an apportionment among the States of taxes laid on income. . . .

A proper regard for its genesis, as well as its very clear language, requires also that this Amendment shall not be extended by loose construction, so as to repeal or modify, except as applied to income, those provisions of the Constitution that require an apportionment according to population for direct taxes upon property, real and

personal. This limitation still has an appropriate and important function, and is not to be overridden by Congress or disregarded by the
courts.

In order, therefore, that the clauses cited from Article I of the
Constitution may have proper force and effect, save only as modified
by the Amendment, and that the latter also may have proper effect,
it becomes essential to distinguish between what is and what is not
"income," as the term is there used; and to apply the distinction, as
cases arise, according to truth and substance, without regard to form.
Congress cannot by any definition it may adopt conclude the matter,
since it cannot by legislation alter the Constitution. . . .

The fundamental relation of "capital" to "income" has been
much discussed by economists, the former being likened to the tree
or the land, the latter to the fruit or the crop; the former depicted
as a reservoir supplied from springs, the latter as the outlet stream,
to be measured by its flow during a period of time. For the present
purpose we require only a clear definition of the term "income," as
used in common speech, in order to determine its meaning in the
Amendment; and, having formed also a correct judgment as to the
nature of a stock dividend, we shall find it easy to decide the matter
at issue.

After examining dictionaries in common use . . . , we find little
to add to the succinct definition adopted in two cases arising under
the Corporation Tax Act of 1909 (Stratton's Independence v. How-
bert, 231 U.S. 399, 415; Doyle v. Mitchell Bros. Co., 247 U.S. 179,
185) — "Income may be defined as the gain derived from capital,
from labor, or from both combined," provided it be understood to
include profit gained through a sale or conversion of capital assets,
to which it was applied in the *Doyle Case* (pp. 183, 185).

Brief as it is, it indicates the characteristic and distinguishing
attribute of income essential for a correct solution of the present
controversy. The Government, although basing its argument upon
the definition as quoted, placed chief emphasis upon the word "gain,"
which was extended to include a variety of meanings; while the significance of the next three words was either overlooked or
misconceived. "*Derived — from — capital,*" — "the *gain — derived —
from — capital,*" etc. Here we have the essential matter: *not* a gain
accruing to capital, not a *growth* or *increment* of value *in* the investment;
but a gain, a profit, something of exchangeable value *proceeding from*
the property, *severed from* the capital however invested or employed,
and *coming in,* being "*derived,*" that is, *received* or *drawn by* the recipient
(the taxpayer) for his *separate* use, benefit and disposal;— *that* is income derived from property. Nothing else answers the description.

The same fundamental conception is clearly set forth in the
Sixteenth Amendment — "incomes, *from* whatever *source derived*" —

the essential thought being expressed with a conciseness and lucidity entirely in harmony with the form and style of the Constitution.

Can a stock dividend, considering its essential character, be brought within the definition? To answer this, regard must be had to the nature of a corporation and the stockholder's relation to it. . . .

Certainly the interest of the stockholder is a capital interest, and his certificates of stock are but the evidence of it. They state the number of shares to which he is entitled and indicate their par value and how the stock may be transferred. They show that he or his assignors, immediate or remote, have contributed capital to the enterprise, that he is entitled to a corresponding interest proportionate to the whole, entitled to have the property and business of the company devoted during the corporate existence to attainment of the common objects, entitled to vote at stockholders' meetings, to receive dividends out of the corporation's profits if and when declared, and, in the event of liquidation, to receive a proportionate share of the net assets, if any, remaining after paying creditors. Short of liquidation, or until dividend declared, he has no right to withdraw any part of either capital or profits from the common enterprise; on the contrary, his interest pertains not to any part, divisible or indivisible, but to the entire assets, business, and affairs of the company. Nor is it the interest of an owner in the assets themselves, since the corporation has full title, legal and equitable, to the whole. . . . If he desires to dissociate himself from the company he can do so only by disposing of his stock.

. . . The dividend normally is payable in money, under exceptional circumstances in some other divisible property; and when so paid, then only (excluding, of course, a possible advantageous sale of his stock or winding-up of the company) does the stockholder realize a profit or gain which becomes his separate property, and thus derive income from the capital that he or his predecessor has invested.

In the present case, the corporation had surplus and undivided profits invested in plant, property, and business, and required for the purposes of the corporation, amounting to about $45,000,000, in addition to outstanding capital stock of $50,000,000. . . . The profits of a corporation, as they appear upon the balance sheet at the end of the year, need not be in the form of money on hand in excess of what is required to meet current liabilities and finance current operations of the company. Often, especially in a growing business, only a part . . . of the year's profits is in property capable of division; the remainder having been absorbed in the acquisition of increased plant, equipment, stock in trade, or accounts receivable, or in decrease of outstanding liabilities. When only a part is available for dividends, the balance of the year's profits is carried to the credit of undivided profits, or surplus, or some other account having like significance. If thereafter the company finds itself in funds beyond current needs it may declare dividends out of such surplus or undivided profits; otherwise it may go on for years conducting a successful business, but requiring more and more working capital because of the extension of its operations, and therefore unable to declare dividends approximating the amount of its profits. Thus the surplus may increase until it equals or even exceeds the par value of the outstanding capital stock. This may be adjusted upon the books in the mode adopted in the case at bar — by declaring a "stock dividend." This, however, is no more than a book adjustment, in essence not a dividend but rather the opposite; no part of the assets of the company is separated from the common fund, nothing distributed except paper certificates that evidence an antecedent increase in the value of the stockholder's capital interest resulting from an accumulation of profits by the company, but profits so far absorbed in the business as to render it impracticable to separate them for withdrawal and distribution. In order to make the adjustment, a charge is made against surplus account with corresponding credit to capital stock account, equal to the proposed "dividend"; the new stock is issued against this and the certificates delivered to the existing stockholders in proportion to their previous holdings. This, however, is merely bookkeeping. . . .

A "stock dividend" shows that the company's accumulated profits have been capitalized, instead of distributed to the stockholders or retained as surplus available for distribution in money or in kind should opportunity offer. Far from being a realization of profits of the stockholder, it tends rather to postpone such realization, in that the fund represented by the new stock has been transferred from surplus to capital, and no longer is available for actual distribution.

The essential and controlling fact is that the stockholder has received nothing out of the company's assets for his separate use and benefit. . . . Having regard . . . to substance and not to form, he has received nothing that answers the definition of income within the meaning of the Sixteenth Amendment. . . .

It is said that a stockholder may sell the new shares acquired in the stock dividend; and so he may, if he can find a buyer. It is equally true that if he does sell, and in doing so realizes a profit, such profit, like any other, is income, and so far as it may have arisen since the Sixteenth Amendment is taxable by Congress without apportionment. The same would be true were he to sell some of his original shares at a profit. But if a shareholder sells dividend stock he necessarily disposes of a part of his capital interest, just as if he should sell a part of his old stock, either before or after the dividend. . . . Yet, without selling, the shareholder, unless possessed of other resources, has not the wherewithal to pay an income tax upon the dividend stock. . . .

We have no doubt of the power or duty of a court to look through the form of the corporation and determine the question of the stock-holder's right, in order to ascertain whether he has received income taxable by Congress without apportionment. But, looking through the form, we cannot disregard the essential truth disclosed; ignore the substantial difference between corporation and stockholder; treat the entire organization as unreal; look upon stockholders as partners, when they are not such; treat them as having in equity a right to a partition of the corporate assets, when they have none; and indulge the fiction that they have received and realized a share of the profits of the company which in truth they have neither received nor realized. We must treat the corporation as a substantial entity separate from the stockholder, not only because such is the practical fact but because it is only by recognizing such separateness that any dividend — even one paid in money or property — can be regarded as income of the stockholder. Did we regard corporation and stockholders as altogether identical, there would be no income except as the corporation acquired it; and while this would be taxable against the corporation as income under appropriate provisions of law, the individual stockholders could not be separately and additionally taxed with respect to their several shares even when divided, since if there were entire identity between them and the company they could not be regarded as receiving anything from it, any more than if one's money were to be removed from one pocket to another.

Conceding that the issue of a stock dividend makes the recipient no richer than before, the Government nevertheless contends that the new certificates measure the extent to which the gains accumulated by the corporation have made him the richer. There are two insuperable difficulties with this: In the first place, it would depend upon how long he had held the stock whether the stock dividend indicated the extent to which he had been enriched by the operations of the company; unless he had held it throughout such operations the measure would not hold true. Secondly, and more important for present purposes, enrichment through increase in value of capital investment is not income in any proper meaning of the term.

The complaint contains averments respecting the market prices of stock such as plaintiff held, based upon sales before and after the stock dividend, tending to show that the receipt of the additional shares did not substantially change the market value of her entire holdings. This tends to show that in this instance market quotations reflected intrinsic values — a thing they do not always do. But we regard the market prices of the securities as an unsafe criterion in an inquiry such as the present, when the question must be, not what will the thing sell for, but what is it in truth and in essence.

It is said there is no difference in principle between a simple stock dividend and a case where stockholders use money received as cash dividends to purchase additional stock contemporaneously issued by the corporation. But an actual cash dividend, with a real option to the stockholder either to keep the money for his own or to reinvest it in new shares, would be as far removed as possible from a true stock dividend, such as the one we have under consideration, where nothing of value is taken from the company's assets and transferred to the individual ownership of the several stockholders and thereby subjected to their disposal.

The Government's reliance upon the supposed analogy between a dividend of the corporation's own shares and one made by distributing shares owned by it in the stock of another company, calls for no comment beyond the statement that the latter distributes assets of the company among the shareholders while the former does not; and for no citation of authority except Peabody v. Eisner, 247 U.S. 347, 349-350. . . .

Upon the second argument, the Government, recognizing the force of the decision in Towne v. Eisner, supra, and virtually abandoning the contention that a stock dividend increases the interest of the stockholder or otherwise enriches him, insisted as an alternative that by the true construction of the Act of 1916 the tax is imposed not upon the stock dividend but rather upon the stockholder's share of the undivided profits previously accumulated by the corporation; the tax being levied as a matter of convenience at the time such profits become manifest through the stock dividend. If so construed, would the act be constitutional?

That Congress has power to tax shareholders upon their property interests in the stock of corporations is beyond question; and that such interests might be valued in view of the condition of the company, including its accumulated and undivided profits, is equally clear. But that this would be taxation of property because of ownership, and hence would require apportionment under the provisions of the Constitution, is settled beyond peradventure by previous decisions of this court.

The Government relies upon Collector v. Hubbard (1870), 12 Wall. 1, 17, which arose under §117 of the Act of June 30, 1864, c. 173, 13 Stat. 223, 282, providing that "the gains and profits of all companies, whether incorporated or partnership, other than the companies specified in this section, shall be included in estimating the annual gains, profits, or income of any person entitled to the same, whether divided or otherwise." The court held an individual taxable upon his proportion of the earnings of a corporation although not declared as dividends and although invested in assets not in their nature divisible. . . . In so far as this seems to uphold the right of Congress to tax without apportionment a stockholder's interest in accumulated earnings prior to dividend declared, it must be regarded as overruled by Pollock v. Farmers' Loan & Trust Co., 158 U.S. 601, 627, 628, 637. Conceding Collector v. Hubbard was inconsistent with the doctrine of that case, because it sustained a direct tax upon property not apportioned among the States, the Government nevertheless insists that the Sixteenth Amendment removed this obstacle, so that now the *Hubbard* Case is authority for the power of Congress to levy a tax on the stockholder's share in the accumulated profits of the corporation even before division by the declaration of a dividend of any kind. Manifestly this argument must be rejected, since the Amendment applies to income only, and what is called the stockholder's share in the accumulated profits of the company is capital, not income. As we have pointed out, a stockholder has no individual share in accumulated profits, nor in any particular part of the assets of the corporation, prior to dividend declared.

Thus, from every point of view, we are brought irresistibly to the conclusion that neither under the Sixteenth Amendment nor otherwise has Congress power to tax without apportionment a true stock dividend made lawfully and in good faith, or the accumulated profits behind it, as income of the stockholder. The Revenue Act of 1916, in so far as it imposes a tax upon the stockholder because of such dividend, contravenes the provisions of Article I, §2, cl. 3, and Article 1, §9, cl. 4, of the Constitution, and to this extent is invalid notwithstanding the Sixteenth Amendment.

Judgment affirmed.

Mr. Justice HOLMES, dissenting. I think that Towne v. Eisner, 245 U.S. 418, was right in its reasoning and result and that on sound principles the stock dividend was not income. But it was clearly intimated in that case that the construction of the statute then before the Court might be different from that of the Constitution. 245 U.S. 425. I think that the word "incomes" in the Sixteenth Amendment should be read in "a sense most obvious to the common understanding at the time of its adoption." . . . For it was for public adoption that it was proposed. McCulloch v. Maryland, 4 Wheat. 316, 407. The known purpose of this Amendment was to get rid of nice questions as to what might be direct taxes, and I cannot doubt that most people not lawyers would suppose when they voted for it that they put a question like the present to rest. I am of opinion that the Amendment justifies the tax. See Tax Commissioner v. Putnam, 227 Massachusetts, 522, 532, 533.

Mr. Justice Day concurs in this opinion.

Mr. Justice BRANDEIS, dissenting, delivered the following opinion, in which Mr. Justice Clarke concurred. Financiers, with the aid of lawyers, devised long ago two different methods by which a corporation can, without increasing its indebtedness, keep for corporate purposes accumulated profits, and yet, in effect, distribute these profits among its stockholders. One method is a simple one. The capital stock is increased; the new stock is paid up with the accumulated profits; and the new shares of paid-up stock are then distributed among the stockholders pro rata as a dividend. If the stockholder prefers ready money to increasing his holding of the stock in the company, he sells the new stock received as a dividend. The other method is slightly more complicated. Arrangements are made for an increase of stock to be offered to stockholders pro rata at par and, at the same time, for the payment of a cash dividend equal to the amount which the stockholder will be required to pay to the company, if he avails himself of the right to subscribe for his pro rata of the new stock. If the stockholder takes the new stock, as is expected, he may endorse the dividend check received to the corporation and thus pay for the new stock. In order to ensure that all the new stock so offered will be taken, the price at which it is offered is fixed far below what it is believed will be its market value. If the stockholder prefers ready money to an increase of his holdings of stock, he may sell his right to take new stock pro rata, which is evidenced by an assignable instrument. In that event the purchaser of the rights repays to the corporation, as the subscription price of the new stock, an amount equal to that which it had paid as a cash dividend to the stockholder.

Both of these methods of retaining accumulated profits while in effect distributing them as a dividend had been in common use in the United States for many years prior to the adoption of the Sixteenth Amendment. They were recognized equivalents. . . . Whichever method was employed the resultant distribution of the new stock was commonly referred to as a stock dividend. . . .

. . . [T]he financial results to the corporation and to the stockholders of the two methods are substantially the same — unless a difference results from the application of the federal income tax law. . . .

It is conceded that if the stock dividend paid to Mrs. Macomber had been made by the more complicated method . . . , that is, issuing rights to take new stock pro rata and paying to each stockholder simultaneously a dividend in cash sufficient in amount to enable him to pay for this pro rata of new stock to be purchased — the dividend so paid to him would have been taxable as income, whether he retained the cash or whether he returned it to the corporation in payment for his pro rata of new stock. But it is contended that, because the simple method was adopted of having the new stock issued direct to the stockholders as paid-up stock, the new stock is not to be deemed income, whether she retained it or converted it into cash by sale. If such a different result can flow merely from the difference in the method pursued, it must be because Congress is without power to tax as income of the stockholder either the stock received under the latter method or the proceeds of its sale; for Congress has, by the provisions in the Revenue Act of 1916, expressly declared its purpose to make stock dividends, by whichever method paid, taxable as income. . . .

Hitherto powers conferred upon Congress by the Constitution have been liberally construed, and have been held to extend to every means appropriate to attain the end sought. In determining the scope of the power the substance of the transaction, not its form, has been regarded. . . . Is there anything in the phraseology of the Sixteenth Amendment or in the nature of corporate dividends which should lead to a departure from these rules of construction and compel this court to hold, that Congress is powerless to prevent a result so extraordinary as that here contended for by the stockholder?

First: The term "income" when applied to the investment of the stockholder in a corporation, had, before the adoption of the Sixteenth Amendment, been commonly understood to mean the returns from time to time received by the stockholder from gains or earnings of the corporation. A dividend received by a stockholder from a corporation may be either in distribution of capital assets or in distribution of profits. Whether it is the one or the other is in no way affected by the medium in which it is paid, nor by the method or means through which the particular thing distributed as a dividend was procured. If the dividend is declared payable in cash, the money with which to pay it is ordinarily taken from surplus cash in the treasury. But (if there are profits legally available for distribution and the law under which the company was incorporated so permits) the company may raise the money by discounting negotiable paper; or by selling bonds, scrip or stock of another corporation then in the treasury; or by selling its own bonds, scrip or stock then in the treasury; or by selling its own bonds, scrip or stock issued expressly for that purpose. How the money shall be raised is wholly a matter of financial management. The manner in which it is raised in no way affects the question whether the dividend received by the stockholder is income or capital; nor can it conceivably affect the question whether it is taxable as income.

Likewise whether a dividend declared payable from profits shall be paid in cash or in some other medium is also wholly a matter of financial management. If some other medium is decided upon, it is also wholly a question of financial management whether the distribution shall be, for instance, in bonds, scrip or stock of another corporation or in issues of its own. . . . If a dividend paid in securities of that nature represents a distribution of profits Congress may, of course, tax it as income of the stockholder. Is the result different where the security distributed is common stock? . . .

Second: It has been said that a dividend payable in bonds or preferred stock created for the purpose of distributing profits may be income and taxable as such, but that the case is different where the distribution is in common stock created for that purpose. Various reasons are assigned for making this distinction. One is that the proportion of the stockholder's ownership to the aggregate number of the shares of the company is not changed by the distribution. But that is equally true where the dividend is paid in its bonds or in its preferred stock. Furthermore, neither maintenance nor change in the proportionate ownership of a stockholder in a corporation has any bearing upon the question here involved. Another reason assigned is that the value of the old stock held is reduced approximately by the value of the new stock received, so that the stockholder after receipt of the stock dividend has no more than he had before it was paid. That is equally true whether the dividend be paid in cash or in other property, for instance, bonds, scrip or preferred stock of the company. The payment from profits of a large cash dividend, and even a small one, customarily lowers the then market value of stock because the undivided property represented by each share has been correspondingly reduced. The argument which appears to be most strongly urged for the stockholders is, that when a stock dividend is made, no portion of the assets of the company is thereby segregated for the stockholder. But does the issue of new bonds or of preferred stock created for use as a dividend result in any segregation of assets for the stockholder? In each case he receives a piece of paper which entitles him to certain rights in the undivided property. Clearly segregation of assets in a physical sense is not an essential of income. The year's gains of a partner are taxable as income, although there, likewise, no segregation of his share in the gains from that of his partners is had.

The objection that there has been no segregation is presented also in another form. It is argued that until there is a segregation, the stockholder cannot know whether he has really received gains; since the gains may be invested in plant or merchandise or other property and perhaps be later lost. But is not this equally true of the share of a partner in the year's profits of the firm or, indeed, of the profits of the individual who is engaged in business alone? And is it not true, also, when dividends are paid in cash? The gains of a business, whether conducted by an individual, by a firm or by a corporation, are ordinarily reinvested in large part. Many a cash dividend honestly declared as a distribution of profits, proves later to have been paid out of capital, because errors in forecast prevent correct ascertainment of values. Until a business adventure has been completely liquidated, it can never be determined with certainty whether there have been profits unless the returns have at least exceeded the capital originally invested. Business men, dealing with the problem practically, fix necessarily periods and rules for determining whether there have been net profits — that is income or gains. They protect themselves from being seriously misled by adopting a system of depreciation charges and reserves. Then, they act upon their own determination, whether profits have been made. Congress in legislating has wisely adopted their practices as its own rules of action.

Third: The Government urges that it would have been within the power of Congress to have taxed as income of the stockholder his pro rata share of undistributed profits earned, even if no stock dividend representing it had been paid. Strong reasons may be assigned for such a view. See Collector v. Hubbard, 12 Wall. 1. The undivided share of a partner in the year's undistributed profits of his firm is taxable as income of the partner, although the share in the gain is not evidenced by any action taken by the firm. Why may not the stockholder's interest in the gains of the company? The law finds no difficulty in disregarding the corporate fiction whenever that is deemed necessary to attain a just result. . . . The stockholder's interest in the property of the corporation differs, not fundamentally but in form only, from the interest of a partner in the property of the firm. There is much authority for the proposition that, under our law, a partnership or joint stock company is just as distinct and palpable an entity in the idea of the law, as distinguished from the individuals composing it, as is a corporation. No reason appears, why Congress, in legislating under a grant of power so comprehensive as that authorizing the levy of an income tax, should be limited by the particular view of the relation of the stockholder to the corporation and its property which may, in the absence of legislation, have been taken by this court. But we have no occasion to decide the question whether Congress might have taxed to the stockholder his undivided share of the corporation's earnings. For Congress has in this act limited the income tax to that share of the stockholder in the earnings which is, in effect, distributed by means of the stock dividend paid. . . .

Sixth: If stock dividends representing profits are held exempt from taxation under the Sixteenth Amendment, the owners of the most successful businesses in America will, as the facts in this case illustrate, be able to escape taxation on a large part of what is actually their income. So far as their profits are represented by stock received as dividends they will pay these taxes not upon their income but only upon the income of their income. That such a result was intended by the people of the United States when adopting the Sixteenth Amendment is inconceivable. Our sole duty is to ascertain their intent as therein expressed. In terse, comprehensive language befitting the Constitution, they empowered Congress "to lay and collect taxes on incomes, from whatever source derived." They intended to include thereby everything which by reasonable understanding can fairly be regarded as income. That stock dividends representing profits are so regarded, not only by the plain people but by investors and financiers, and by most of the courts of the country, is shown, beyond peradventure, by their acts and by their utterances. It seems to me clear, therefore, that Congress possesses the power which it exercised to make dividends representing profits, taxable as income, whether the medium in which the dividend is paid be cash or stock, and that it may define, as it has done, what dividends representing profits shall be deemed income. It surely is not clear that the enactment exceeds the power granted by the Sixteenth Amendment. And, as this court has so often said, the high prerogative of declaring an act of Congress invalid, should never be exercised except in a clear case. "It is but a decent respect due to the wisdom, the integrity and the patriotism of the legislative body, by which any law is passed, to presume in favor of its validity, until its violation of the Constitution is proved beyond all reasonable doubt." Ogden v. Saunders, 12 Wheat. 213, 270.

HELVERING v. GOWRAN
302 U.S. 238 (1937)

Mr. Justice BRANDEIS delivered the opinion of the Court. The questions for decision concern the taxation as income of a dividend in preferred stock and the proceeds received on its sale.

On June 29, 1929, the Hamilton Manufacturing Company . . . had outstanding preferred stock of the par value of $100 a share and common stock without par value. On that day the directors declared from the surplus earnings a dividend of $14 a share on the common stock, payable on July 1, 1929, in preferred stock at its par value. Gowran, as owner of common stock, received as his dividend 533 and a fraction shares of the preferred. On or about October 1, 1929, the company acquired his preferred stock and paid him therefor, at $100 a share, $53,371.50. In his income tax return for the year Gowran did not treat this sum as taxable income, but included $27,262.72 as capital net gain on the shares received and sold, computing the gain under Articles 58 and 600 of Regulations 74, then in force. The Commissioner rejected that treatment of the matter; determined that the $53,371.50 received was income taxable under the Revenue Act of 1928, §115(g), 45 Stat. 791, 822, as a stock dividend redeemed; and assessed a deficiency of $5,831.67.

The taxpayer sought a redetermination by the Board of Tax Appeals. . . . The Commissioner . . . contended that, under the rule declared in Commissioner of Internal Revenue v. Tillotson Mfg. Co., 76 F.(2d) 189, the stock dividend was taxable, because it had resulted in a change of Gowran's proportionate interest in the company. That contention was sustained by the Board; and, on that ground, it affirmed the Commissioner's determination of a deficiency. 32 B.T.A. 820.

The taxpayer sought a review by the Circuit Court of Appeals. The Commissioner again urged that the stock dividend was taxable; and then, for the first time, contended that, even if it was not taxable, the determination of the deficiency should be affirmed, because within the tax year the stock had been sold at its par value and, as its cost had been zero, the entire proceeds constituted income. The Court of Appeals recognized that, since the dividends in preferred stock gave to Gowran an interest different in character from that which his common stock represented, it was constitutionally taxable under Koshland v. Helvering, 298 U.S. 441; but it held that the dividend could not be taxed as income, since by §115(f) Congress had provided: "A stock dividend shall not be subject to tax." And it held further that no part of the proceeds could be taxed as income, since there was no profit on the sale, it being agreed that the fair market value of the stock, both at the date of receipt and at the date of the sale, was $100 a share. 87 F.(2d) 125.

Because of the importance of the questions presented in the administration of the revenue laws, certiorari was granted.

First. The Government contends that §115(f) should be read as prohibiting taxation only of those stock dividends which the Constitution does not permit to be taxed; and that, since by the dividend Gowran acquired an interest in the corporation essentially different from that theretofore represented by his common stock, the dividend was taxable. In support of that construction of §115(f), it is urged that Congress has in income tax legislation manifested generally its intention to use, to the full extent, its constitutional power, Helvering v. Stockholms Bank, 293 U.S. 84, 89; Douglas v. Willcuts, 296 U.S. 1, 9; that this Court holds grants of immunity from taxation should always be strictly construed, Pacific Co. v. Johnson, 285 U.S. 480, 491; and that the only reason for exempting stock dividends was to comply with the Constitution.

This preferred stock had substantially the same attributes as that involved in the *Koshland* case. There the dividend was of common stock to a preferred stockholder, it is true; but we are of opinion that under the rule there declared Congress could have taxed this stock dividend. Nevertheless, by §115(f) it enacted in 1928, as it did in earlier and later Revenue Acts, that "a stock dividend shall not be subject to tax." The prohibition is comprehensive. It is so clearly expressed as to leave no room for construction. It extends to all stock dividends. Such was the construction consistently given to it by the

Treasury Department."[1] The purpose of Congress when enacting §115(f) may have been merely to comply with the requirement of the Constitution as interpreted in Eisner v. Macomber, 252 U.S. 189; and the comprehensive language in §115(f) may have been adopted in the erroneous belief that under the rule declared in that case no stock dividend could be taxed. But such facts would not justify the Court in departing from the unmistakable command embodied in the statute. Congress declared that the preferred stock should not be taxed as a dividend.

Second. The Government contends that, even if §115(f) be construed as prohibiting taxation of the preferred stock dividend, the decision of the Board of Tax Appeals affirming the Commissioner's determination of a deficiency should be sustained, because the gain from sale of the stock within the year was taxable income and the entire proceeds must be deemed income, since the stock had cost Gowran nothing. The Circuit Court of Appeals rejected that contention. It held that there was no income, because, as stipulated, there was no difference between the value of the stock when received and its value when sold. The court likened a non-taxable stock dividend to a tax-free gift or legacy and said: "One who receives a tax-free gift and later sells it, in the absence of statute providing otherwise, is taxed upon the profit arising from the difference in its value at the time he receives it and the sale price. Similarly one who receives a tax-free bequest, when selling it, is taxed upon the profit arising from any excess of the sale price over its fair market value at the time of receipt." [p. 128] Compare Taft v. Bowers, 278 U.S. 470.

The cases are not analogous. Unlike earlier legislation, §113(a)(2) of the Revenue Act of 1928 prescribes specifically the basis for determining the gain on tax-free gifts and legacies. It provides that: "If the property was acquired by gift after December 31, 1920, the basis shall be the same as it would be in the hands of the donor or

---

1. Eisner v. Macomber was decided March 8, 1920. Soon thereafter, the Treasury Department declared in a series of Decisions and Regulations, that no stock dividend was taxable. . . . Then followed legislation in the precise form embodied in §115(f) of the Revenue Act of 1928. . . . Article 628 of the Regulations in force in 1928 provided: "Stock dividends. — The issuance of its own stock by a corporation as a dividend to its shareholders does not result in taxable income to such shareholders, but gain may be derived or loss sustained by the shareholders from the sale of such stock. The amount of gain derived or loss sustained from the sale of such stock, or from the sale of the stock in respect of which it is issued, shall be determined as provided in Articles 561 and 600."

Koshland v. Helvering, 298 U.S. 441, was decided May 18, 1936. On June 22, 1936, Congress, in enacting the Revenue Act of 1936, provided in §115(f): "1. General Rule — A distribution made by a corporation to its shareholders in its stock or in rights to acquire its stock shall not be treated as a dividend to the extent that it does not constitute income to the shareholder within the meaning of the Sixteenth Amendment to the Constitution." 49 Stat. 1648, 1688. See also §115(h).

the last preceding owner by whom it was not acquired by gift." And the basis for the computation on property transmitted at death is provided for in paragraph (5). But the method of computing the income from the sale of stock dividends constitutionally taxable is not specifically provided for. Furthermore, unlike §22(b)(3), excluding from gross income the value of gifts and legacies, §115(f) cannot, in view of its history, be taken as a declaration of congressional intent that the value of all stock dividends shall be immune from tax not only when received but also when converted into money or other property. Gain on them is, therefore, to be computed as provided in §§111 and 113, by the "excess of the amount realized" over "the cost of such property" to the taxpayer. As the cost of the preferred stock to Gowran was zero, the whole of the proceeds is taxable.

Gowran asserts that if this "basis of zero" theory is accepted, the proceeds are taxable not as determined by the Commissioner but as a capital gain at a different rate and under different regulations. This depends upon whether the preferred stock received as a dividend was a "capital asset," defined by §101(c)(8) as "property held by the taxpayer for more than two years." The record is silent as to when Gowran acquired the common stock upon which the preferred was issued as a dividend, but it may be assumed that he had held it for more than two years. For that fact is immaterial since the dividend stock had been held for only three months. Whether taxed by Congress or not, it was income, substantially equivalent for income tax purposes to cash or property, and under §115(b) was presumed to have been made "out of earnings or profits to the extent thereof, and from the most recently accumulated earnings or profits." In no sense, therefore, can it be said to have been "held" by Gowran prior to its declaration. Since the proceeds were therefore not "capital gains," they were taxable at the normal and surtax rates applicable to ordinary income. . . .

Reversed.

2. *Effect of a Disposition*

CHAMBERLIN v. COMMISSIONER
207 F.2d 462 (6th Cir. 1953), *cert. denied*, 347 U.S. 918 (1954)

Before Simons, Chief Judge, and McAllister and Miller, Circuit Judges.

MILLER, Circuit Judge. Petitioner C. P. Chamberlin seeks a review of an income tax deficiency determined by the Respondent for the calendar year 1946, and sustained by the Tax Court. In the Tax

Court the proceeding was consolidated with the proceedings of five other taxpayers similarly situated, all of which proceedings involved the same factual and legal questions. The taxpayers . . . were stockholders of Metal Moulding Corporation, about which this litigation centers. . . .

The Metal Moulding Corporation, hereinafter referred to as the Corporation, is a Michigan corporation engaged in the business of manufacturing metal mouldings and bright work trim used in the manufacture of automobiles. It was incorporated on December 2, 1924 with an authorized common capital stock of $25,000, which was increased in 1935 to $150,000, represented by 1,500 shares of $100 par value voting common stock. From 1940 until December 20, 1946, the issued and outstanding common stock totaled 1,002$\frac{1}{2}$ shares, of which Chamberlin and his wife together owned 83.8%. The directors of the corporation from 1940 to February 12, 1946 consisted of C. P. Chamberlin, Grace A. Chamberlin, and Edward W. Smith. On February 12, 1946, John H. Toner and Raymond H. Berry were added. On October 11, 1946, Smith died and during the remainder of 1946 the board consisted of the four remaining members. From 1940 to the end of 1946, C. P. Chamberlin was president and treasurer, John H. Toner was vice-president and general manager, and Grace Chamberlin was for various periods vice-president, assistant treasurer, and secretary. Benjamin J. Carl was assistant secretary and treasurer until February 12, 1946.

On December 16, 1946, the Corporation's authorized capital stock was increased from $150,000 to $650,000, represented by 6,500 shares of $100 par value common stock. On December 20, 1946, a stock dividend was declared and distributed of five shares of common for each share of common outstanding, and the Corporation's accounts were adjusted by transferring $501,250 from earned surplus to capital account.

On December 26, 1946, the articles of incorporation were amended so as to authorize, in addition to the 6,500 shares of common stock, 8,020 shares of 4$\frac{1}{2}$% cumulative $100 par value preferred stock. On December 28, 1946, a stock dividend was declared of 1$\frac{1}{3}$ shares of the newly authorized preferred stock for each share of common stock outstanding, to be issued pro rata to the holders of common stock as of December 27, 1946, and the Company's accounts were adjusted by transferring $802,000 from earned surplus to capital account. The preferred stock was issued to the stockholders on the same day. Prior to the declaration of the preferred stock dividend, the Corporation at all times had only one class of stock outstanding.

On December 30, 1946, as the result of prior negotiations hereinafter referred to, all of the holders of the preferred stock, except the estate of Edward W. Smith, deceased, which owned 20 shares, signed a "Purchase Agreement," with The Northwestern Mutual Life Insurance Company and The Lincoln National Life Insurance Company, which instrument was also endorsed by the Corporation for the purpose of making certain representations, warranties and agreements. Under the "Purchase Agreement" 4,000 shares of the preferred stock was sold to each of the two insurance companies at a cash price of $100 per share plus accrued dividends from November 1st, 1946 to date of delivery. . . .

In the latter part of 1945, the Corporation's attorney and Chamberlin discussed with an investment firm in Chicago the possibility of selling an issue of preferred stock similar to the stock subsequently issued. The Corporation had such a large accumulated earned surplus it was fearful of being subjected to the surtax provided for by [§531] . . . but at the same time Chamberlin, the majority stockholder, was not willing to have the Corporation distribute any substantial portion of its earned surplus as ordinary dividends because his individual income was taxable at high surtax rates. It was proposed that the issuance of a stock dividend to the stockholders and the sale of it by the stockholders would enable the stockholders to obtain accumulated earnings of the Corporation in the form of capital gains rather than as taxable dividends. The investment counselor contacted The Lincoln National Life Insurance Company of Fort Wayne, Indiana, and during October 1946, furnished the Insurance Company financial information relative to the Corporation. On November 7, 1946, a representative of the Insurance Company came to Detroit and made an inspection of the plant and properties of the Corporation. On November 20, 1946, The Lincoln National Life Insurance Company's finance committee approved the proposed issue and the purchase of one-half thereof. The Northwestern Mutual Life Insurance Company was contacted for the purpose of participating in the purchase of the preferred stock. It made a detailed investigation of the Corporation and of the terms and conditions of the proposed preferred stock issue, and about two weeks before December 30, 1946, its committee on investments approved the purchase of 4,000 shares of the preferred stock to be issued, and passed the matter over to its legal department for the conclusion of the transaction.

The preferred stock contained the following provisions among others: The holders were entitled to cumulative cash dividends at the rate of $4.50 per annum payable quarterly beginning November 1, 1946; the stock was subject to redemption on any quarterly dividend date in whole or in part at par plus specified premiums and accrued dividends; it was subject to mandatory retirement in amounts not exceeding 2,000 shares on May 1, 1948 and 1,000 on May 1st on each succeeding year, depending upon the Corporation's net earnings for the preceding year, until fully retired on May 1, 1954; in the event of certain default of dividend payments or annual retirements, the holders were entitled to elect a majority of the directors; as long as any preferred shares remained outstanding the consent of the holders of at least 75% thereof was required to validate certain actions, including changing the articles of incorporation or capital structure, the sale of the Company's property, or the incurrence of indebtedness for borrowed money in excess of a certain amount; the Corporation could not pay any cash dividend upon any stock junior to the preferred if there was any default in the payment of dividend upon and the annual retirements of the preferred, or if such dividend reduced the net working capital of the Corporation below an amount equal to 150% of the aggregate par value of all outstanding preferred, or $750,000, whichever amount was greater, or reduced the [current] assets of the Company to an amount less than 200% of current liabilities. These provisions had been discussed with the Lincoln National Life Insurance Company and some of them, at least, were included in order to satisfy the investment requirements of the two insurance companies.

No agreement of purchase and sale was entered into between any of the petitioners and either of the two insurance companies prior to the "Purchase Agreement" executed on December 30, 1946, but the stockholders and directors of the Corporation took the necessary actions to put the negotiated plan into effect . . . only after the insurance companies certified their willingness to participate in the purchase. . . .

In reporting this sale of the preferred stock in their 1946 tax returns, each of the stockholders reported his proportion of the proceeds from the sale as a net long-term capital gain from the sale of a capital asset held for more than six months, used a substituted basis as the cost basis of the preferred stock, and in determining the period the preferred stock had been held included the holding period of the common stock upon which the preferred stock dividend was declared.

The Respondent ruled that the preferred stock constituted a dividend taxable as ordinary income, and further determined that the value was the amount received on the sale of the shares against which the expenses incurred in the sale were a valid deduction. . . .

Before considering the ruling of the Tax Court it is well to briefly review some of the Supreme Court decisions involving the taxability of stock dividends. This is well done in Note 5, in the Tax Court's opinion, which, together with the analysis of some of the opinions and the legislative enactments applicable . . . makes a detailed restatement unnecessary in this opinion. In Towne v. Eisner, 245 U.S. 418, . . . and Eisner v. Macomber, 252 U.S. 189, . . . the Court held that a stock dividend of common stock to the holders of the common stock was not income to the stockholder taxable by Congress under the Sixteenth Amendment, in that it did not alter the preexisting proportionate interest of any stockholder or increase the intrinsic value of his holding or of the aggregate holdings of the other stockholders as they stood before. The Court said: "The new certificates simply increase the number of the shares, with consequent dilution of the value of each share" and that a stock dividend "shows that the company's accumulated profits have been capitalized, instead of distributed to the stockholders or retained as surplus available for distribution in money or in kind should opportunity offer." In Koshland v. Helvering, 298 U.S. 441, . . . the Court held that a stock dividend of common stock to the holders of preferred stock was taxable income because it gave the preferred stockholder an interest different from that which his former stockholdings represented. In Helvering v. Gowran, 302 U.S. 238, . . . the Court held that a stock dividend in preferred stock to the holders of common stock, where similar preferred stock was outstanding, was taxable income because it gave the common stockholder an interest essentially different from that theretofore represented by his common stock. In Helvering v. Griffiths [318 U.S. 371], the Court refused to reconsider the ruling in Eisner v. Macomber, supra, holding that legislation subsequent to that ruling did not attempt to make such stock dividends taxable. In Helvering v. Sprouse, 318 U.S. 604, . . . and in Strassburger v. Commissioner of Internal Revenue, 318 U.S. 604, . . . the Court restated the rule that in order to render a stock dividend taxable as income there must be a change brought about by the issue of shares as a dividend whereby the proportional interest of the stockholder after the distribution was essentially different from his former interest. The rule was applied to the facts in the *Strassburger* case where preferred stock was created and distributed as a stock dividend to a stockholder who owned the entire outstanding common stock, the Court holding that the preferred stock dividend did not constitute taxable income.

The Commissioner supported his assessment on the ground that although the preferred stock was issued as a non-taxable dividend, a concerted plan to sell the dividend shares was formulated prior to the distribution of such shares, which, coupled with actual sale immediately after receipt and the payment of the proceeds of sale direct to the stockholders constituted a taxable dividend to the extent of available earnings. He also took the position that the plan and the immediate sale resulted in a change in the proportional interest of the stockholders which was sufficient to exclude it from the rulings in the Supreme Court cases above referred to.

In the Tax Court the petitioner contended that under the rulings in Towne v. Eisner, supra . . . ; Eisner v. Macomber, supra . . . ; Helvering v. Griffiths, supra . . . ; and Strassburger v. Commissioner, supra, . . . and the provisions of Sec. 115(f)(1) . . . ,* the preferred stock dividend was not income within the meaning of the Sixteenth Amendment, and accordingly not taxable as in the case of ordinary dividends under Sec. [61(a)(7)]. . . . Sec. 115 (f)(1) provides: "A distribution made by a corporation to its shareholders in its stock or in rights to acquire its stock shall not be treated as a dividend to the extent that it does not constitute income to the shareholder within the meaning of the Sixteenth Amendment to the Constitution."

The Tax Court held that the issue of whether the stock dividend constituted income to the stockholders should be determined from a consideration of all the facts and circumstances surrounding the issuance of the dividend and not by a consideration limited to the characteristics of the stock declared as a dividend; . . . that such a decision did not rest upon matters of form . . . but rather upon the real substance of the transaction involved; that disregarding the circumstances and terms of the issue it might be said that as a matter of form the stock dividend constituted one which fell within the *Strassburger* case, but that considering the real substance of the transaction it was of the opinion that the stock dividend was not in good faith for any bona fide corporate business purpose, and that the attending circumstances and conditions under which it was issued made it the equivalent of a cash dividend distribution out of available earnings, thus constituting ordinary taxable income in the amount of the value of the preferred shares received. The Court also said that the real purpose of the issuance of the preferred shares was concurrently to place them in the hands of others not then stockholders of the Corporation, thereby substantially altering the common stockholders' pre-existing proportionate interests in the Corporation's net assets and thereby creating an entirely new relationship amongst all the stockholders and the Corporation. . . .

In our opinion, the declaration and distribution of the preferred stock dividend, considered by itself, falls clearly within the principles established in Towne v. Eisner, supra, and Eisner v. Macomber, supra, and is controlled by the ruling in the *Strassburger* case. Accordingly, as a preliminary matter, we do not agree with the Tax Court's statement that the stock dividend is taxable because as a result of the dividend and immediate sale thereafter it substantially altered the common stockholders' pre-existing proportional interests in the Corporation's net assets. The sale to the insurance companies of course resulted in such a change, but the legal effect of the dividend with respect to rights in the corporate assets is determined at the

*Section 115(f) was the 1939 predecessor of §305. Section 305 is more detailed and, in some circumstances, differs in its impact. The 1939 Code contained no counterpart of §306. — Ed.

time of its distribution, not by what the stockholders do with it after its receipt. In Helvering v. Griffiths, supra, 318 U.S. 371, at page 394, . . . the Court pointed out: "at the latest the time of receipt of the dividend is the critical one for determining taxability." In none of the Supreme Court cases referred to above is it suggested that events subsequent to the distribution have any bearing on whether the stockholder's proportional interest is changed. The fact that events occur in quick succession does not by itself change their legal effect. Biddle Avenue Realty Corp. v. Commissioner, 6 Cir., 94 F.2d 435. It seems clear to us that if taxability exists it is not because of the change in pre-existing proportional interests caused by a later sale, but by reason of the other ground relied upon by the Tax Court, namely, that viewed in all its aspects it was a distribution of cash rather than a distribution of stock. That this is the real basis of the ruling appears from the statement in the opinion that "disregarding the circumstances and terms of the issue, it might be said as a matter of form the stock dividend constituted one which fell within the *Sprouse* and *Strassburger* cases. . . . However, . . . not form but the real substance of the transaction is controlling."

The general principle is well settled that a taxpayer has the legal right to decrease the amount of what otherwise would be his taxes, or altogether avoid them, by means which the law permits; . . . and that the taxpayer's motive to avoid taxation will not establish liability if the transaction does not do so without it. . . .

It is equally well settled that this principle does not prevent the Government from going behind the form which the transaction takes and ascertaining the reality and genuineness of the component parts of the transaction in order to determine whether the transaction is really what it purports to be or is merely a formality without substance which for tax purposes can and should be disregarded. . . .

The question accordingly presented is not whether the overall transaction, admittedly carried out for the purpose of avoiding taxes, actually avoided taxes which would have been incurred if the transaction had taken a different form, but whether the stock dividend was a stock dividend in substance as well as in form.

No question is raised about the legality of the declaration of the dividend. Respondent does not contend that proper corporate procedure was not used in creating the preferred stock and in distributing it to the stockholders in the form of a dividend. If the transaction had stopped there we think it is clear that the dividend would not have been taxable in the hands of the stockholders. Strassburger v. Commissioner, supra. Whether the declaration of the dividend was in furtherance of any corporate business purpose or was the result of correct judgment and proper business policy on the part of the management, we believe is immaterial on this phase of the case. The Supreme Court cases in no way suggest that the taxability of a stock dividend depends on the purpose of its issuance or the good or bad judgment of the directors in capitalizing earnings instead of distributing them. The decisions are based squarely upon the proportional interest doctrine. . . . In Dreyfuss v. Manning, D.C.N.J., 44 F. Supp. 383, a stock dividend of preferred stock, declared solely for the purpose of avoiding taxes on undistributed net income, was held non-taxable, which ruling apparently was not appealed by the Commissioner. The presence or absence of a corporate business purpose may play a part in determining whether a stock dividend is a bona fide one, one in substance as well as in form, but it does not by itself change an otherwise valid dividend into an invalid one. A stock dividend, legally created and distributed, which is a dividend in substance as well as in form, does not change from a non-taxable dividend into a taxable one because of the purpose of its issuance or on account of the good or bad judgment of the directors in declaring it. Eisner v. Macomber, supra, 252 U.S. at page 211. . . .

Nor is there any question about the genuineness and unconditional character of the sale of the preferred stock by the stockholders who received it to the two insurance companies. The facts show conclusively that title passed irrevocably from the stockholders to the insurance companies, and that the sellers received in cash without restriction a full consideration, the adequacy of which respondent does not question. But respondent contends that the sale of the stock following immediately upon its receipt resulted in the stockholder acquiring cash instead of stock, thus making it a taxable dividend under Secs. [61(a)(7)] and 115(a). . . . There are two answers to this contention.

A non-taxable stock dividend does not become a taxable cash dividend upon its sale by the recipient. On the contrary, it is a sale of a capital asset. Eisner v. Macomber, 252 U.S. 189, 212 . . . ; Miles v. Safe Deposit & Trust Co., 259 U.S. 247. . . . The rulings in those cases make it clear that its character as a capital asset is in no way dependent upon how long it is held by the taxpayer before its sale. In none of the Supreme Court cases referred to above, dealing with the taxability of stock dividends, was the length of the holding period considered as a factor. Obviously, if the non-taxability of a stock dividend rests solely upon the principle that it does not alter the preexisting proportionate interest of any stockholder or increase the intrinsic value of his holdings, the disposition of the stock dividend by the stockholder thereafter is not a factor in the determination. . . .

The foregoing conclusion is supported by Sec. 117(h)(5), . . .*

*Section 1223(5) of the 1986 Code. — ED.

which provides that for the purpose of determining whether a non-taxable stock dividend which has been sold is a long-term capital gain there shall be included in the holding period the period for which the taxpayer held the stock in the distributing corporation prior to the receipt of the stock dividend. This necessarily recognizes that a stock dividend will often be sold before the expiration of six months after its receipt, and makes no distinction between a stock dividend held one day or for any other period less than six months. Likewise, Sec. 29.113(a)(19)-1, Treasury Regulations III, in establishing the cost basis of a non-taxable stock dividend which has been sold for a gain or loss, makes no distinction between a stock dividend sold immediately after receipt and one held a long period of time before sale.

The other answer to the contention is that although the stockholder *acquired* money in the final analysis, he did not *receive* either money or property *from* the corporation. Sec. 115(a) . . . , in dealing with taxable dividends, defines a dividend as "any distribution *made by a corporation* to its shareholders, whether in money or in other property . . . out of its earnings or profits. . . ." (Emphasis added.) The money he received was received from the insurance companies. It was not a "distribution" by the corporation declaring the dividend, as required by the statute.

We come then to what in our opinion is the dominant and decisive issue in the case, namely, whether the stock dividend, which, by reason of its redemption feature, enabled the Corporation to ultimately distribute its earnings to its stockholders on a taxable basis materially lower than would have been the case by declaring and paying the usual cash dividend, was a bona fide one, one in substance as well as in form. As pointed out in Chisholm v. Commissioner . . . , 2 Cir., 79 F.2d 14, 15, *certiorari denied* Helvering v. Chisholm, 296 U.S. 641, . . . the Court cannot ignore the legal effect of a bona fide transaction on the ground that it avoids taxes, and that "The question always is whether the transaction under scrutiny is in fact what it appears to be in form; a marriage may be a joke; a contract may be intended only to deceive others; an agreement may have a collateral defeasance. In such cases the transaction as a whole is different from its appearance." But if the transaction is actually what it purports to be it must be accepted for its legal results. There are numerous cases, some of which are pressed upon us by the respondent, where the Court, in keeping with the above principle, refused to give effect taxwise to transactions on the part of corporations because the facts and circumstances showed that the so-called corporation was one in form only, incorporated for the sole purpose of avoiding taxes and having no legitimate business purpose, masquerading under the corporate form, and accordingly not a bona fide corporation. See

Gregory v. Helvering . . . , 293 U.S. 465 . . . ; Higgins v. Smith . . . ,
308 U.S. 473. . . . In other cases a valid conveyance has been disregarded taxwise because the purchaser acquired no real interest in
the property conveyed, was a mere conduit in passing title to another,
and the conveyance was in fact a sham. See Minnesota Tea Co. v.
(Helvering) Commissioner . . . , 302 U.S. 609 . . . ; Griffiths v. (Helvering) Commissioner, 308 U.S. 355 . . . ; Commissioner v. Court
Holding Co., 324 U.S. 331. . . .

In our opinion, the stock dividend in this case does not fall within
any of the principles discussed above. It seems clear that it was an
issue of stock in substance as well as in form. According to its terms,
and in the absence of a finding that it was immediately or shortly
thereafter redeemed at a premium, we assume that a large portion
of it has remained outstanding over a period of years with some of
it still unredeemed after nearly seven years. It has been in the hands
of the investing public, free of any control by the corporation over
its owners, whose enforceable rights with respect to operations of the
corporation would not be waived or neglected. Substantial sums have
been paid in dividends. The insurance companies bought it in the
regular course of their business and have held it as approved investments. For the Court to now tell them that they have been holding
a sham issue of stock would be most startling and disturbing news.

It also seems clear that the insurance companies were not purchasers in form only without acquiring any real interest in the
property conveyed. The character of the transaction as a bona fide
investment on the part of the insurance companies is not challenged
by the respondent. The element of a formal conduit without any
business interest is entirely lacking.

If the transaction lacks the good faith necessary to avoid the
assessment it must be because of the redemption feature of the stock,
which, in the final analysis, is what ultimately permitted the distribution of the corporate earnings and is the key factor in the overall
transaction. Redemption features are well known and often used in
corporate financing. If the one in question was a reasonable one, not
violative of the general principles of bona fide corporate financing,
and acceptable to experienced bona fide investors familiar with investment fundamentals and the opportunities afforded by the
investment market, we fail to see how a court can properly classify
the issue, by reason of the redemption feature, as lacking in good
faith or as not being what it purports to be. The insurance companies,
conservative, experienced investors, analyzed the stock issue very
carefully, provisions were required to make it conform to sound
investment requirements, and each of the two companies, acting independently of the other, purchased a very substantial amount in
the regular course of their investment purchases. . . . In our opinion,

the redemption feature, qualified as it was with respect to premiums, amounts subject to redemption in each year, and the length of time the stock would be outstanding, together with the acceptance of the stock as an investment issue, did not destroy the bona fide quality of the issue. We cannot say that the preferred stock was not in fact what it purported to be, namely, an issue of stock in substance as well as in form. . . .

Each case necessarily depends upon its own facts. The facts in this case show tax avoidance, and it is so conceded by petitioner. But they also show a series of legal transactions, no one of which is fictitious or so lacking in substance as to be anything different from what it purports to be. Unless we are to adopt the broad policy of holding taxable any series of transactions, the purpose and result of which is the avoidance of taxes which would otherwise accrue if handled in a different way, regardless of the legality and realities of the component parts, the tax assessed by the Commissioner was successfully avoided in the present case. We do not construe the controlling decisions as having adopted that view. United States v. Isham . . . , 17 Wall. at page 506; Gregory v. Helvering, supra, 293 U.S. at page 469, . . . ; Commissioner v. Tower, supra, 327 U.S. at page 288, . . . ; United States v. Cumberland Public Service Co. . . . , 338 U.S. at page 455. . . .

In deciding this case it must be kept in mind that it does not involve a ruling that the profit derived from the sale of the stock dividend is or is not taxable income. Such profit is conceded to be taxable. The issue is whether it is taxable as income from a cash dividend or as income resulting from a long-term capital gain. Accordingly, it is not the usual case of total tax avoidance. Congress has adopted the policy of taxing long-term capital gains differently from ordinary income. By Sec. 115(g) . . . it has specifically excluded certain transactions with respect to stock dividends from the classification of a capital gain. The present transaction is not within the exclusion. If the profit from a transaction like the one here involved is to be taxed at the same rate as ordinary income, it should be done by appropriate legislation, not court decision.

The judgment is reversed and the case remanded to the Tax Court for proceedings consistent with the views expressed herein.

NOTES

1. Was the result in *Chamberlin* sound? Notwithstanding *Chamberlin*, in Estate of Rosenberg, 36 T.C. 716 (1961), where redeemable preferred stock was issued to the common shareholders who sold it to insurance companies and other corporate investors from whom it

was subsequently redeemed, the Tax Court held that the transaction was a predetermined plan to bail out earnings. The "net effect" was a dividend to the shareholders, taxable at ordinary income rates.

2. Although *Rosenberg* was decided in 1961, the case arose under the 1939 Code. Congress, however, had responded to *Chamberlin* in 1954. It did so by providing generally for the continued exclusion of stock dividends, even when the dividends created disproportionate interests (see §305(a)). But it also provided in §306 for ordinary income on the disposition of the dividend stock in circumstances thought to provide a potential bail-out of corporate earnings at capital gains rates. Section 305(b)(2) et seq., an important modification of §305(a), did not become part of the law until 1969. Sections 306 and 305(b)(2), still intact, are the subjects of the next two divisions of this chapter.

B. CURRENT LAW

1. The §306 Approach: Ordinary Income on Disposition of Stock

The conversion of capital gain income into ordinary income was long considered the principal penalty of §306. The 1986 Act has, of course, greatly reduced the severity of this penalty by removing the preferential rate for capital gains. Absent a resurrection of the capital gains preference, §306 is significant only to the extent that it denies basis recovery and prevents an otherwise available capital loss offset.

FIREOVED v. UNITED STATES
462 F.2d 1281 (3d Cir. 1972)

Before Adams, Rosenn, and Hunter, Circuit Judges.

ADAMS, Circuit Judge. This appeal calls into question the application of section 306 . . . and the "first in–first out rule" to a redemption of preferred stock in a corporation by plaintiff, one of its principal shareholders. In particular we are asked to decide whether the transaction here had "as one of its principal purposes the avoidance of Federal income tax," whether a prior sale of a portion of the underlying common stock immunized a like proportion of the section 306 stock from treatment as a noncapital asset and whether another block of the redeemed stock should be considered to represent stock not subject to section 306.

I. FACTUAL BACKGROUND

On November 24, 1948, Fireoved and Company, Inc. was incorporated. . . . At their first meeting, the incorporators elected Eugene Fireoved, his wife, Marie, the plaintiffs, and a nephew, Robert L. Fireoved, as directors of the corporation. Subsequently, the directors elected Eugene Fireoved as President and Treasurer and Marie Fireoved as Secretary. . . . On December 31, 1948, in consideration for $100 cash, the corporation issued Eugene Fireoved 100 shares of common stock; for $500 cash, it issued him five shares of preferred stock; and in payment for automotive equipment and furniture and fixtures, valued at $6,000, it issued him an additional 60 shares of preferred stock.

In 1954, when Mr. Fireoved learned that his nephew, Robert, was planning to leave the business, he began discussions with Karl Edelmayer and Kenneth Craver concerning the possibility of combining his business with their partnership, Girard Business Forms. . . . Messrs. Fireoved, Edelmayer and Craver agreed that voting control of the new enterprise should be divided equally among the three of them. Because Mr. Fireoved's contribution to capital would be approximately $60,000 whereas the partnership could contribute only $30,000, it was decided that preferred stock should be issued to Mr. Fireoved to compensate for the disparity. In furtherance of this plan, . . . the following corporate changes were accomplished: The name of the company was changed to Girard Business Forms; the authorized common stock was increased from 100 to 300 shares and the authorized preferred stock was increased to 1000 shares; Mr. Fireoved exchanged his 100 shares of common and 65 shares of preferred stock for equal amounts of the new stock; an agreement of purchase was authorized by which the company would buy all the assets of the Edelmayer-Craver partnership in return for 200 shares of common and 298 shares of preferred stock; and Mr. Fireoved was issued 535 shares of the new preferred stock as a dividend[6] on his 100 shares of common stock, thereby bringing his total holding of preferred stock to 600 shares to indicate his $60,000 capital contribution compared to the $29,800 contributed by the former partnership.

As the business progressed, Mr. Edelmayer demanded more control of the company. In response, Mr. Fireoved and Mr. Craver each sold 24 shares of common stock in the corporation to him on February 28, 1958.

On April 30, 1959, the company redeemed 451 of Mr. Fireoved's 600 shares of preferred stock at $105 per share, resulting in net proceeds to him of $47,355.[7] The gain from this transaction was

---

6. At the time Mr. Fireoved received this stock dividend, the company had accumulated earnings and profits of $52,993.06.

7. In 1959, the company had accumulated earnings and profits of $48,235.

reported by Mr. Fireoved . . . as a long term capital gain. Subsequently, the Commissioner . . . assessed a deficiency against the Fireoveds of $15,337.13 based on the Commissioner's view that the proceeds from the redemption of the 451 shares of preferred stock should have been reported as ordinary income and the tax paid at that rate based on section 306. . . .

II. BACKGROUND OF SECTION 306

Because we are the first court of appeals asked to decide questions of law pursuant to section 306, it is appropriate that we first examine the circumstances that led to the inclusion in 1954 of this section in the Code. . . .

A temporarily successful plan for converting ordinary income to long term capital gain is described by the facts of Chamberlin v. C.I.R., 207 F.2d 462 (6th Cir. 1953). There a close corporation had assets of $2.5 million, approximately half of which were in the form of cash and government securities. To have distributed the cash not required in the operation of the business to the shareholders as a dividend would have subjected them to taxation at ordinary income rates. The corporation therefore amended its charter to authorize 8,020 shares of preferred stock to be issued to the shareholders as a dividend on their common stock. The accounts of the corporation were adjusted by transferring $802,000 from earned surplus to the capital account. While these corporate changes were taking place, negotiations occurred between the shareholders and two insurance companies for the purchase of the newly issued preferred stock. In addition, the corporation constructed a timetable for retirement of the preferred stock, which proved satisfactory to the purchasing companies. When the transaction was completed, the selling shareholders reported the gain they realized from the sale of the preferred stock to the insurance companies as a long-term gain from the disposition of a capital asset. The Commissioner contended that the gain should have been reported as ordinary income and accordingly assessed a deficiency against the selling shareholders. The Tax Court agreed with the Commissioner. . . . [T]he Sixth Circuit reversed, . . . thus giving the approval of a federal court to what has been termed "a preferred stock bail-out."

The legislative reaction to the *Chamberlin* decision was almost immediate, resulting in the addition of section 306 to the 1954 Code, in order to prevent shareholders from obtaining the tax advantage of such bail-outs when such shareholders retain their ownership interests in the company.

. . . For tax purposes, Congress created a new type of stock known as section 306 stock. When a corporation having accumulated or retained earnings and profits issues a stock dividend which is not otherwise subject to taxation at the time of issuance (other than common on common), the stock received is section 306 stock. The effect of owning such stock is that on its redemption, if the corporation has sufficient retained earnings at that time, the gain* is taxed at ordinary income rates while any loss resulting may not be recognized for federal tax purposes. Section 306(b) sets forth several exceptions to the general rule which serve to remove the section 306 taint from stock disposed of under those circumstances.

Based on the history of section 306 and its plain meaning evidenced by the provisions, it is not disputed that the 535 shares of preferred stock issued to Mr. Fireoved as a stock dividend in 1954 were section 306 stock. Additionally, it is clear that in 1959, when the company redeemed 451 shares of Mr. Fireoved's preferred stock, the general provisions of section 306 — aside from the exceptions — would require that any amount realized by Mr. Fireoved be taxed at ordinary income rates rather than long-term capital gain rates, because the company had earnings at that time of $48,235 — more than the $47,355 required to redeem the stock at $105 per share.

Thus, the questions to be decided on this appeal are (1) whether certain of the exceptions to section 306 apply to permit the Fireoveds' reporting their gain as a long term capital gain, and (2) whether 65 of the 451 shares redeemed are not section 306 stock because of the first in–first out rule of Treasury Regulation section 1.1012-1(c).

III. WAS THE DISTRIBUTION OF THE STOCK DIVIDEND "IN PURSUANCE OF A PLAN HAVING AS ONE OF ITS PRINCIPAL PURPOSES AVOIDANCE OF FEDERAL INCOME TAX?"

Mr. Fireoved asserts that the entire transaction should fall within the exception established by section 306(b)(4)(A). . . .

As a threshold point on this issue, the Government maintains that because Mr. Fireoved never attempted to obtain a ruling from the "Secretary or his delegate" the redemption should be covered by section 306(a), and the district court should not have reached the question whether the exception applied to Mr. Fireoved. Mr. Fireoved urges that the district court had the power to consider the matter de novo, even without a request by the taxpayer to the Secretary or his delegate. Because the ultimate result we reach would not be altered by whichever of these two courses we choose, we do not resolve this potentially complex procedural problem.

The district court, based on the assumption that it had the power to decide the question, found that although one of the purposes

*Does the court mean "gain" or "proceeds"? — ED.

involved in the issuance of the preferred stock dividend may have been business related, another principal purpose was the avoidance of Federal income tax.

Mr. Fireoved's analysis of the facts presented in the stipulations would reach the conclusion that the *sole* purpose of the stock dividend was business related. He relies heavily on that portion of the stipulation which describes why the decision was made to combine his business with the Edelmayer-Craver partnership: "The partnership could provide the additional manpower which the expected departure of Robert L. Fireoved from the Corporation would require. Additionally, the partnership needed additional working capital which the Corporation had and could provide." Based primarily on the latter sentence, Mr. Fireoved asserts that the district court had no choice but to find that the transition was business related and that it therefore had no avoidance incentive.

In making this argument, however, Mr. Fireoved overlooks the plain import of the language of section 306(b)(4). Whether the section requires the decision to be made by the Secretary or the district court, it is clear that "one of [the] principal purposes" of the stock dividend was for "the avoidance of Federal income tax." The stipulation demonstrates no more than that the reorganized company required more capital than could be supplied by the partnership alone. The stipulation is completely in harmony with the following fact situation: After the partnership was combined with the corporation, the business required the $30,000 contributed by the partnership and all of the $60,000 Mr. Fireoved had in the corporation. Mr. Fireoved decided to take the stock dividend rather than to distribute the cash to himself as a dividend, and then to make a loan to the corporation of the necessary money because if he took the cash, he would subject himself to taxation at ordinary income rates. Therefore "one of the principal purposes" of the stock dividend would be for "the avoidance of Federal income tax."

In a situation such as the one presented in this case, where the facts necessary to determine the motives for the issuance of a stock dividend are peculiarly within the control of the taxpayer, it is reasonable to require the taxpayer to come forward with the facts that would relieve him of his liability. Here the stipulation was equivocal in determining the purpose of the dividend and is quite compatible with the thought that "one of the principal purposes" was motivated by "tax avoidance." We hold then that the district court did not err in refusing to apply the exception created by section 306(b)(4)(A).[11]

---

11. It is important to note that apparently both Mr. Fireoved, in prosecuting this action for a refund, and the Government, in its defense, assumed that if the distribution and redemption of the preferred stock were not controlled by §306(a), the gain would be subject to taxation as a long term capital gain. This is not necessarily

IV. Did the Prior Sale by Mr. Fireoved of 24% of
His Underlying Common Stock Immunize Such
Portion of the Section 306 Stock He Redeemed
in 1959?

. . . The stipulations indicate that, "On February 28, 1958, Fireoved and Craver each sold 24 shares of common stock in the
corporation to Edelmayer," and that appropriate stock certificates
were issued. From this fact, Mr. Fireoved reasons that his sale of 24
of his 100 shares of common stock was undertaken solely for the
business purpose of satisfying Mr. Edelmayer's desire for more control of the corporation, and therefore he should be given the benefit
of section 306(b)(4)(B). In addition, Mr. Fireoved contends that the
disposition of his section 306 stock was related to a business purpose
because he used part of the proceeds to pay off a $20,000 loan that
the company had made to him.

Mr. Fireoved has the same burden here of showing a lack of a
tax avoidance purpose that he had in section 111 supra. It is clear
from the limited facts set forth in the stipulations that he has not
established that the disposition of 24% of the 535 shares of the section
306 preferred stock he owned "was not in pursuance of a plan having
as one of its principal purposes the avoidance of federal income tax."[12]
More important, however, is that an examination of the relevant
legislative history indicates that Congress did not intend to give capital
gains treatment to a portion of the preferred stock redeemed on the
facts presented here.

It is apparent from the reaction evinced by Congress to the
Chamberlin case, supra, that by enacting section 306 Congress was
particularly concerned with the tax advantages available to persons
who controlled corporations and who could, without sacrificing their
control, convert ordinary income to long-term capital gains by the

---

the case at all. Whether or not §306 governs the transaction, it nonetheless involves
a redemption of stock by a corporation to which §302 could apply. Under the tests
set out in §302(b) — the relevant one of which appears to be §302(b)(1) — Mr. Fireoved, who had the burden of proof, may well have been unable to show that the
redemption was not "essentially equivalent to a dividend." . . . We hold, however,
that it is now too late for the Government to raise this issue.

12. Consistent with Mr. Fireoved's sale of 24 shares of common stock in 1958
could have been his knowledge that one year later he would be selling his section
306 stock and a desire on his part to avoid taxation at ordinary income rates. As
noted later in the opinion, the sale of just 24 shares was enough so that he retained
effective control — in the form of veto power — over the corporation. Moreover, the
fact that Mr. Fireoved needed $20,000 of the proceeds to pay off a loan to the
corporation would not meet his burden. The proceeds of the redemption totaled
$47,355. Thus, although $20,000 of the redemption may not have been to avoid
taxes, we can ascribe no purpose other than tax avoidance to the receipt of the
additional $27,355. Therefore, since one of the principal purposes of the redemption
of 451 shares of preferred stock was "the avoidance of Federal income tax," Mr.
Fireoved may not take advantage of §306(b)(4)(B) for any part of the redemption.

device of the preferred stock bail-out. The illustration given in the Senate Report which accompanied section 306(b)(4)(B) is helpful in determining the sort of transactions meant to be exempted by section 306(a):

> Thus if a shareholder received a distribution of 100 shares of section 306 stock on his holdings of 100 shares of voting common stock in a corporation and sells his voting common stock before he disposes of his section 306 stock, the subsequent disposition of his section 306 stock would not ordinarily be considered a tax avoidance disposition *since he has previously parted with the stock which allows him to participate in the ownership of the business.* However, variations of the above example may give rise to tax avoidance possibilities which are not within the exception of subparagraph (B). Thus if a corporation has only one class of common stock outstanding and it issues stock under circumstances that characterize it as section 306 stock, a subsequent issue of a different Class of common having greater voting rights than the original common will not permit a simultaneous disposition of the section 306 stock together with the original common to escape the rules of subsection (a) of section 306. [S. Rep. No. 1622, 83d Cong., 2d Sess., 1954 U.S.C.C.A. News, pp. 4621, 4881 (emphasis added).]

Thus, it is reasonable to assume that Congress realized the general lack of a tax avoidance purpose when a person sells *all* of his control in a corporation and then either simultaneously or subsequently disposes of his section 306 stock. However, when *only a portion* of the underlying common stock is sold, and the taxpayer retains essentially all the control he had previously, it would be unrealistic to conclude that Congress meant to give that taxpayer the advantage of section 306(b)(4)(B) when he ultimately sells his section 306 stock. Cf. United States v. Davis, 397 U.S. 301 . . . (1970).

Shortly after Mr. Fireoved's corporation had been combined with the Edelmayer-Craver partnership, significant changes to the by-laws were made. The by-laws provided that corporate action could be taken only with the unanimous consent of all the directors. In addition, the by-laws provided that they could be amended either by a vote of 76% of the outstanding common shares or a unanimous vote of the directors. When the businesses were combined in late 1954, each of the directors held ⅓ of the voting stock, thereby necessitating a unanimous vote for amendment to the by-laws. After Messrs. Fireoved and Craver each sold 24 shares of common stock to Mr. Edelmayer, Mr. Fireoved held 25⅓% of the common (voting) stock, Mr. Craver 25⅓% and Mr. Edelmayer 49⅓%. It is crucial to note that the by-laws provided for a unanimous vote for corporate action, and after the common stock transfer, the bylaws were capable of amendment only by a unanimous vote because no two shareholders could vote more than 74⅔% of the common stock and 76% of the common stock was necessary for amendment. Thus, although Mr. Fireoved did sell a portion of his voting stock prior to his disposition of the section 306 stock, he retained as much control in the corporation following the sale of his common stock as he had prior to the sale. Under these circumstances it is not consonant with the history of the legislation to conclude that Congress intended such a sale of underlying common stock to exempt the proceeds of the disposition of section 306 stock from treatment as ordinary income. Accordingly, the district court erred when it held that any of the preferred shares Mr. Fireoved redeemed were not subject to section 306(a) by virtue of section 306(b)(4)(B).

V. Does the Rule of First In–First Out Mean That 65 of the 451 Redeemed Shares Were Those Which Mr. Fireoved Acquired When He Incorporated His Business in 1948 and Thus Should Not Be Treated as Section 306 Stock?

. . . Both the district court and Mr. Fireoved reason that the 65 preferred shares he received in 1948 were the first shares owned by him. In 1954, when the corporation was recapitalized, Mr. Fireoved surrendered his certificate for 65 shares, received a 535 share stock dividend and was issued a certificate representing 600 shares of preferred stock. When he disposed of 451 shares in 1959, it was impossible to identify which shares of the 600 share certificate were being sold. By applying the convenient tool of section 1.10 12-1 (c), one might conclude that the 65 original shares were sold first because they were received first.

Superficially, this analysis appears to be correct. However, it overlooks the existence of Section 1223(5) of the Code and the regulations issued pursuant thereto. This section governs the transaction in question because section 307 required Mr. Fireoved to allocate his investment in the underlying common stock between the stock and the preferred stock issued as a dividend. Section 1223(5) is then clear in that it will apply to all situations in which an allocation of basis has occurred pursuant to section 307. These provisions broadly state that the holding period for stock received as a stock dividend is equal to the period for which the underlying stock was held. Applying this test we discover that the preferred stock dividend of 535 shares was issued with respect to the original 100 shares of common received by Mr. Fireoved. Therefore, the holding period for the 535 shares dividend relates back to the date on which the underlying common was issued. Coincidentally, the original 65 shares of preferred stock were issued on the same date as the common. Because the constructive date of issuance for all of the 600 shares of preferred stock owned by Mr. Fireoved is identical, neither the 65 shares nor the 535 shares are first in, but rather are in at the same time.

Since it is impossible adequately to identify which shares were sold when Mr. Fireoved redeemed 451 shares of preferred stock, we hold that a pro rata portion of the 65 shares were redeemed in 1959. In other words, the percentage of the 600 shares of preferred which were not section 306 stock may be represented by the fraction 65/600. That percentage of the 451 shares redeemed in 1959, therefore, would not be section 306 stock.

NOTES

1. See Rev. Rul. 80-33, 1980-1 C.B. 6 (showing that one of the principal purposes of issuance of preferred stock was to prevent adverse impact of issuance of common on a corporation's ability to raise capital from the public does not establish that *none* of the principal purposes was to avoid income tax; if the adverse impact could have been avoided by issuing bonds instead of stock, one of the principal purposes was avoidance of income tax); Rev. Rul. 77-455, 1977-2 C.B. 93 (where shareholder's §306 stock was redeemed in part and sold in part in conjunction with a sale and redemption of the remainder of his interest in the corporation in order to give his son voting control with a smaller investment than would otherwise be necessary, the §306(b)(4)(B) exception protected the shareholder from ordinary income treatment on the disposition); Rev. Rul. 75-247, 1975-1 C.B. 104 (fact that seller of §306 stock simultaneously sold a pro rata portion of common stock in the same corporation did not by itself establish absence of tax avoidance purpose). See Schneider, Internal Revenue Code Section 306 and Tax Avoidance, 4 Va. Tax Rev. 287 (1985).

2. If §306 stock is redeemed in a transaction qualifying under §303(a), the stock loses its §306 taint. See Treas. Reg. §1.303(2)(d).

REVENUE RULING 89-63
1989-18 I.R.B. 4

The Internal Revenue Service has reconsidered Rev. Rul. 56-116, 1956-1 C.B. 164, Rev. Rul. 57-103, 1957-1 C.B. 113, and Rev. Rul. 57-212, 1957-1 C.B. 114. In each of these rulings, certain preferred stock that qualified as section 306 stock within the meaning of section 306(c)(1)(B) of the Internal Revenue Code was held to fall within the exception provided by section 306(b)(4), which renders the provisions of section 306(a) inapplicable. . . .

LAW AND ANALYSIS

Section 306(a) of the Code concerns the treatment of the amount realized on the disposition or redemption of section 306 stock (as defined in section 306(c)). Section 306(b)(4) provides in part that section 306(a) shall not apply if it is established to the satisfaction of the Secretary that the distribution and the disposition or redemption of the section 306 stock was not in pursuance of a plan having as one of its principal purposes the avoidance of federal income tax.

In Rev. Rul. 56-116, two widely held corporations, X and Y, were merged in a reorganization qualifying under section 368(a)(1)(A) of the Code. In the merger, both preferred and common stock of X were issued in exchange for the common stock of Y. There was a business reason for issuing both preferred and common stock of X in exchange for the Y common stock. The management of X had no intention of redeeming any of the preferred stock issued in connection with the merger, except as required under the provisions of purchase fund and sinking fund agreements.

The ruling holds that the X preferred stock issued in connection with the merger is section 306 stock, but it concludes without full explanation that section 306(a)(1) of the Code does not apply to the proceeds of the disposition of such stock, unless the disposition is in anticipation of redemption.

In Rev. Rul. 57-103, 1957-1 C.B. 113, a publicly held corporation acquired all the assets of a closely held corporation with only common stock outstanding in return for voting preferred stock and common stock, constituting 5 percent of the acquiring corporation's outstanding stock, in a reorganization described in section 368(a)(1)(C) of the Code.

Although the preferred stock issued in the reorganization constituted section 306 stock, as defined in section 306(c)(1)(B) of the Code, that ruling holds, citing Rev. Rul. 56-116, that the issuance of such stock was not in pursuance of a plan having as one of its principal purposes the avoidance of federal income tax within the meaning of section 306(b)(4).

In Rev. Rul. 57-212, 1957-1 C.B. 114, publicly held corporation B was merged into publicly held corporation C in a reorganization described in section 368(a)(1)(A) of the Code. Each share of B common stock (the only class of B stock outstanding) was converted into one share of first preferred stock, one-half share of second preferred stock, and three shares of common stock of C. All three classes of C stock were widely held and traded on the New York Stock Exchange. Pursuant to the provisions of a sinking fund, so long as any of the shares of first preferred stock were outstanding, C was required to redeem 3 percent of the outstanding first preferred shares annually.

Rev. Rul. 57-212 reasons that Rev. Rul. 56-116 stands for the proposition that section 306(b)(4) of the Code provides relief from section 306(a)(1) on the disposition of section 306 stock issued by a widely held corporation unless the disposition was in anticipation of redemption. The ruling then considers whether the sinking fund provisions precluded relief under section 306(b)(4) from the operation of section 306(a)(2). It holds that the distribution of the first preferred stock and the subsequent redemption of portions thereof under the sinking fund provisions were not in pursuance of a plan having as one of its principal purposes the avoidance of federal income tax within the meaning of section 306(b)(4). The ruling also states in summary that the provisions of section 306(a)(1) are not applicable to the proceeds of a sale of such shares (whether or not in anticipation of a redemption through the operation of the sinking fund), and the provisions of section 306(a)(2) are not applicable to amounts distributed by C in redemption of such first preferred shares to meet the requirements of its sinking fund provisions.

Upon reconsideration, the Service has concluded that the fact that the section 306 stock is issued by a corporation whose stock is widely held is not sufficient grounds for the application of section 306(b)(4) of the Code. Thus, in such circumstances, relief from the provisions of section 306(a) should not be automatic. Although Rev. Rul. 56-116 does not support its application of section 306(b)(4) by specifically relying on the fact that the section 306 stock was issued by a widely held corporation, Rev. Rul. 56-116 was cited in both Rev. Ruls. 57-103 and 57-212 for that proposition. Both Rev. Ruls. 57-103 and 57-212 use that proposition to support their holdings. Because these rulings conflict with the conclusion that the widely held nature of the issuing corporation's stock is not sufficient grounds for the application of section 306(b)(4), they are revoked. . . .

NOTES

1. See also Rev. Proc. 89-30, 1989-18 I.R.B. 20, which revokes §5 of Rev. Proc. 77-37, 1977-2 C.B. 568, in light of the Service's change of position reflected in Rev. Rul. 89-63. Section 5 of Rev. Proc. 77-37 had laid out the conditions under which a disposition of §306 stock issued by widely held corporations would receive the Service's blessing under §306(b)(4).

2. The Internal Revenue Service will not ordinarily issue an advance ruling on the question whether the distribution, disposition, or redemption of §306 stock in a *closely held corporation* is in pursuance of a tax avoidance plan within the meaning of §306(b)(4). Rev. Proc. 87-3, 1987-1 C.B. 523.

REVENUE RULING 81-91
1981-1 C.B. 123

ISSUE

Is the class B stock described below "section 306 stock" within the meaning of section 306(c) of the Internal Revenue Code?

FACTS

A corporation had outstanding a single class of common stock held by 10 individuals, each of whom owned 20 shares. For valid business reasons the corporation entered into a plan of recapitalization under which each outstanding share of common stock was surrendered to the corporation in exchange for one share of new class A stock plus one share of new class B stock of the corporation.

The recapitalization was a reorganization defined in section 368(a)(1)(E) of the Code* and the exchanges were nontaxable under section 354(a)(1).

Each share of the class A and class B stock had a par value of 10x dollars. The class B shares were entitled to an annual cumulative dividend of 6 percent of par value payable before any dividend was payable on the class A shares, and a prior right to repayment up to par value in the event of liquidation. After the satisfaction of the class B stock's preferences, each share of class A and class B stock shared equally as to dividends and on liquidation. Each class of shares carried equal voting rights and neither class was by its terms redeemable.

LAW AND ANALYSIS

Section 306(c)(1)(B) of the Code provides, in part and in effect, that "section 306 stock" is any stock, except common stock, that is received by a shareholder pursuant to a plan of reorganization under section 368 with respect to the receipt of which gain or loss to the shareholder was to any extent not recognized by reason of section 354, but only to the extent that the effect of the transaction is substantially the same as the receipt of a stock dividend.

The term "common stock" as used in section 306 of the Code is not defined in that section or the related regulations. In determining whether newly issued stock is "common stock" for purposes of section 306, the "preferred stock bailout" abuse Congress sought to prevent

---

*"Recapitalizations" will be studied at page 527 et seq. infra. In general, the Code provides that a shareholder whose stock is retired by the issuing corporation in exchange for another class of its stock does not recognize gain or loss at the time of the exchange. The transaction is treated much like a stock dividend. — ED.

by enactment of that section provides guidance. See S. Rep. No. 1622, 83d Cong., 2d Sess. 26 (1954). See also Chamberlin v. Commissioner, 207 F.2d 462 (6th Cir. 1953), *cert. denied,* 347 U.S. 918 (1954). A bailout occurs if shareholders, through section 306 stock or some other device, withdraw a corporation's earnings and profits at the more favorable tax rates for capital gains. The potential for a preferred stock bailout exists if the shareholders receive a pro rata distribution of two classes of stock in a recapitalization when the corporation has earnings and profits, and the stock of one class, because of its terms, can be disposed of without a surrender by the shareholders of significant interests in corporate growth. Thus, stock is other than "common stock" for purposes of section 306 not because of its preferred position as such, but because the preferred position is limited and the stock does not participate in corporate growth to any significant extent.

The class B stock enjoys voting rights on an equal basis with the class A stock, the only other class of stock outstanding. After satisfaction of its preference as to dividends and as to assets in the event of liquidation, the class B stock shares equally with the class A stock. These rights in the class B stock to participate in corporate growth are significant. Thus, a sale of the class B stock cannot occur without a loss of voting control and interest in the unrestricted growth of the corporation. Therefore, the bailout abuse that Congress sought to prevent by the enactment of section 306 cannot be effected through a sale of the class B stock.

HOLDING

The class B stock is "common stock" and is, therefore, excepted from the definition of section 306 stock under section 306(c)(1)(B) of the Code.

EFFECT ON OTHER REVENUE RULINGS

Rev. Rul. 66-332, 1966-2 C.B. 108, concerns a recapitalization meeting the definition of a reorganization under section 368(a)(1)(E) of the Code. Under the plan the only outstanding stock (common) was reclassified as class A voting stock and the shareholders could continue to hold the class A stock or exchange all or part of such class A stock for units of one share of preferred stock and one share of class B voting stock. The exchange ratio was one share of class A stock for each unit of one share of preferred stock and one share of class B stock.

The question presented in Rev. Rul. 66-332 is whether the class A stock and preferred stock are "section 306 stock" as defined in section 306(c) of the Code.

The preferred stock was entitled to a cumulative dividend of $7 per share before any dividend was paid on either class A or class B stock. The class A stock was entitled to a cumulative dividend of $7 per share before any dividend was paid on class B stock. After all cumulative dividend on the preferred and class A stock had been paid, the class A and class B stock shared equally in all further dividends. The preferred stock was entitled to a preference on any distributions of assets in the amount of its par value. After this preference had been satisfied the class A stock was entitled to a preference on any distribution in the amount of one and one-half times the amount of its par value and thereafter the class A and class B stock shared equally in any further distribution of assets. The class A and class B stock both had voting rights. The preferred stock was nonvoting except in the case of dividend arrearage.

With regard to shareholders who exchanged all of their class A stock for units of preferred and class B stock (situation 1), Rev. Rul. 66-332 concludes that this exchange was substantially the same as the exchange of the old common stock for shares of class B stock and the receipt of a stock dividend in shares of preferred stock. Rev. Rul. 66-332 correctly holds under section 306(c)(1)(B) of the Code that the preferred stock is section 306 stock in the hands of these shareholders.

With regard to shareholders who exchanged only part of their class A stock for units of preferred and class B stock (situation 2), Rev. Rul. 66-332 concludes that since these shareholders still owned class A stock, which was preferred both as to dividends and distributions in liquidation over the class B stock, the class A stock was not common stock for purposes of section 306(c)(1)(B) of the Code. Thus, the effect of the transaction as to them was substantially the same as the exchange of their old common stock for shares of class B stock and the receipt of a stock dividend in shares of class A stock and other preferred stock. Rev. Rul. 66-332 holds that both the class A stock retained and the preferred stock are section 306 stock.

Although the class A stock in situation 2 of Rev. Rul. 66-332 had a preference as to dividends and assets in the event of liquidation, after the satisfaction of these preferences the class A stock and the class B stock shared equally in dividends and the assets of the corporation on liquidation. Thus, a sale of the class A stock could not occur without a loss of an interest in the unrestricted equitable growth of the corporation. Therefore, the class A stock is "common stock" and, thus, is properly excepted from the definition of "section 306 stock" within the meaning of section 306(c)(1)(B) of the Code.

With regard to those shareholders who exchanged none of their class A stock for units of preferred and class B stock (situation 3), Rev. Rul. 66-332 concludes that the transaction as to them was the exchange of their old common stock for participating class A stock, which was not "common stock" because of its preferences as to dividends and distributions in liquidation, but that the effect of the receipt of the class A stock was not the same as the receipt of a stock dividend. Therefore, Rev. Rul. 66-332 holds that the class A stock retained by shareholders in this situation is not "section 306 stock." While this holding is proper, the reason is that the class A stock is "common stock" (since it has an interest in the unrestricted growth of the corporation) and, thus, is excepted from the definition of section 306 stock under section 306(c)(1)(B) of the Code, which makes it unnecessary to consider whether the receipt of the class A stock was the same as the receipt of a stock dividend.

Rev. Rul. 66-332 is modified with regard to situation 2 and situation 3.

NOTES

1. See Rev. Rul. 79-287, 1979-2 C.B. 130, in which the Service ruled that preferred stock received in exchange for identical stock in an "F" reorganization (a mere change of identity, form, or place of incorporation) was not §306 stock. See also Rev. Rul. 82-118, 1982-1 C.B. 56. But cf. Rev. Rul. 82-191, 1982-2 C.B. 78.

2. For the combined effect of §§170(e) and 306, see Rev. Rul. 76-396, 1976-2 C.B. 55. In Walter Bialo, 88 T.C. 1132 (1987), the Tax Court denied a deduction for the fair market value of §306 stock the taxpayer had contributed to a charity. The court's holding was based on the taxpayer's inability to prove a motive other than tax avoidance. What would the result have been in *Grove*, page 262 supra, if the taxpayer had used preferred stock issued to him as a dividend?

3. In Rev. Rul. 76-387, 1976-2 C.B. 96, the Service held that nonvoting stock that could not be disposed of without the shareholder's giving up an interest in the unrestricted equitable growth of the corporation was not "§306 stock." See also Rev. Rul. 79-163, 1979-1 C.B. 131 (stock received in a recapitalization that has either a limited right to dividends or a limited right to assets upon liquidation does not represent an unrestricted right in the equity growth of the corporation and therefore is not common stock within the meaning of §306(c)(1)(B)).

4. In Rev. Rul. 81-81, 1981-1 C.B. 122, the Service ruled that §306(a) will not be applied to the disposition by minority shareholders of the fractional shares of §306 stock they received in a recapitalization, this result by virtue of the application of §306(b)(4). Amplifying its position in Rev. Rul. 66-365, 1966-2 C.B. 116, page 637 infra, the Service ruled that the cash will be treated as though received in a redemption under §302(a).

5. See Rowland, §306: Its History and Function as Bailout Preventer (Including Bailouts That May Never Occur), 39 Tax Law. 121 (1985); Steines, Taxation of Corporate Distributions — Before and After TEFRA, 68 Iowa L. Rev. 937 (1983); Walter, "Preferred Stock" and "Common Stock": The Meaning of the Terms and the Importance of the Distinction for Tax Purposes, 5 J. Corp. Taxn. 211 (1978).

REVENUE RULING 79-274
1979-2 C.B. 131

Is section 306(c)(1)(B) of the Code applicable in a transaction meeting the requirements of sections 351 and 368(a)(1)(B)?

Corporation X had outstanding 3,000x shares of common stock which were owned 1,500x each by individuals A and B. Corporation X is engaged in an ongoing business.

For good business purposes A and B organized corporation Z and transferred all the stock of X to it. In exchange therefor A and B each received 500x shares of Z voting preferred stock and 1,000x shares of Z voting common stock. . . .

. . . [T]he transaction qualified as a transfer of property to a controlled corporation within the meaning of section 351 . . . and as a reorganization as defined in section 368(a)(1)(B). . . .

By its terms, section 306(c)(1)(B) applies only to stock, other than common stock, received in pursuance of a plan of reorganization. Thus, in the instant case, since the transaction qualifies as a nontaxable exchange under section 351 as well as a reorganization defined in section 368(a)(1)(B), the question is whether section 306(c)(1)(B) is applicable. If, for example, the Z stock received by the transferors, A and B, were treated as received in a section 351 exchange only, for purposes of section 306(c)(1)(B), then section 306(c)(1)(B) would not apply to the transaction. The Z voting preferred stock could not be "section 306 stock" since it was not received pursuant to a plan of reorganization.

There is no provision in the Code or regulations that deals with the concurrent application of section 351 and section 368(a)(1)(B) to a transaction.

In Helvering v. Cement Investors, Inc., 316 U.S. 527 (1942), . . . the Supreme Court of the United States recognized that a transaction could meet the requirements of both section 112(b)(5) of the Revenue Act of 1936 (the predecessor of section 351 of the 1954 Code) and the reorganization provisions contained in section 112(a) of the Revenue Act of 1936 (the predecessor of section 368 of the 1954 Code), and that the fact that a transaction was a corporate readjustment or reorganization did not make the reorganization provisions exclusively applicable to the transaction.

Section 306(c)(1)(B) of the Code does not contain an exception for its application where a transaction qualifies as an exchange under section 351 as well as a reorganization under section 368(a)(1)(B). Hence, in the instant case, because the exchange qualifies as a reorganization under section 368(a)(1)(B), section 306(c)(1)(B) applies, notwithstanding that the transaction also qualifies as a section 351 exchange. See Rev. Rul. 76-188, 1976-1 C.B. 99.

Since the transaction qualifies as a reorganization described in section 368(a)(1)(B) of the Code, section 306(c)(1)(B) is applicable to the transaction. If Z has earnings and profits at the end of the tax year in which this transaction was consummated, (1.306-3(a) of the regulations, 301(c)(1) and 316(a) of the Code) the voting preferred stock of Z received by A and B will be "section 306 stock" since it is other than common stock, and because it will be substantially the same as the receipt of a stock dividend under the "cash received in lieu of" test set forth in section 1.306-3(d) of the Income Tax Regulations. (See Example (1) of section 1.306-3(d).)

NOTE

Since the passage of TEFRA in 1982, stock (other than common) issued in certain §351 transactions constitutes §306 stock. See §306(c)(3). The impact of this is limited to situations in which cash received in lieu of preferred stock would have been a taxable dividend (e.g., where §304 might apply). As modified by §304(c)(3)(B), the §318 attribution rules apply in determining whether the stock is §306 stock. See §306(c)(4). Under current law, then, it would appear not to matter in a situation like that in Rev. Rul. 79-274 whether or not Z had earnings and profits so long as X had.

2. The §305(b) Approach: Ordinary Income on Receipt of Stock

HOLDEN, UNRAVELING THE MYSTERIES OF SECTION 305*
36 N.Y.U. Inst. Fed. Taxn. 781 (1978)

INTRODUCTION

Mysteries do indeed abound in Section 305, and they sorely need unraveling. Unfortunately, it will take more than this article to accomplish that task, for many of the mysteries are inherent in the

*Copyright © 1978 by the New York University Institute on Federal Taxation. Excerpts reprinted by permission. — ED.

statutory language rather than the underlying subject matter, and they will be with us until that language is changed.

The current version of Section 305 is a result of Congress' impatience in 1969 with its 1954 resolution of the taxation of stock distributions. However, instead of simply returning to the pre-1954 law, it produced a new legislative wonder. New Section 305 is vastly more complex than was its predecessor, and needlessly so. Despite this complexity, it does little more than to restore the old "shift in proportionate interest" test, which governed before 1954. Unfortunately, one can reach that conclusion only after substantial analysis and the mastery of some very difficult language.

Not only was Section 305 made significantly more complex in 1969, but it was also extended to cover a variety of transactions which do not actually involve stock distributions but which do produce some of the same effects upon corporate ownership. . . .

An Historical Perspective on Section 305

[An extensive survey of the legislative and judicial treatment of stock dividends is omitted.]

DEVELOPMENT OF THE SHIFT-IN-PROPORTIONATE-INTEREST TEST

Congress had, in the 1936 Act, tossed the ball back to the courts, and it remained there until 1954. During the period from 1936 to 1954, they responded, fashioning under the teaching of Eisner v. Macomber a "proportionate interest" test to distinguish taxable from nontaxable stock distributions. Those distributions which did not result in a shift in proportionate interest among shareholders were nontaxable; those which resulted in such a shift were taxable.

Though there were obvious and significant difficulties in applying the rule, given the fact that infinite varieties of stock can be conceived by corporate planners, the rule itself could be simply stated and its fundamental concept was easy enough to grasp. The courts were, during this period, evolving a workable body of law. Their task could have been greatly facilitated had the Treasury Department issued a comprehensive set of Regulations illustrating and explaining the shift-in-proprietary interest test.

THE 1954 REVISION — SECTION 305

Notwithstanding this relatively satisfactory state of affairs, the opportunity to rewrite the law relating to stock distributions as a part of the 1954 overhaul of the tax laws proved too appealing for the Congress to resist. . . .

... Under the 1954 version of Section 305, the general rule was established that stock distributions were nontaxable. There were only two exceptions. First, distributions under which a shareholder could choose to receive either stock or property were to remain, as under the prior law, taxable. Second, if a stock distribution was made to satisfy dividends on preferred stock for the current or prior taxable year, the distribution was to be taxable. . . .

WEAKNESS OF THE 1954 LEGISLATION

Simplicity was both the purpose and the weakness of the 1954 legislation. The rules were easy to enunciate, but they effectively made nontaxable numerous forms of stock distribution by which the proportionate interest among shareholders could be shifted significantly. In these transactions, some kind of compensating payment, in a form other than stock, was generally made to shareholders whose interests were diminished. For example, in the so-called "Citizens Utilities"[16] type transaction, shareholders were offered a choice between ownership of two classes of stock, one paying cash dividends and one paying stock dividends. Shareholders who chose stock dividends could augment their interests in the corporation on a tax-free basis. Those who chose cash experienced a diminution of proprietary interest and were compensated for that by the receipt of cash. The effect was the same as if all shareholders had received a cash dividend and some had reinvested the cash by purchasing more stock. . . .

THE TAX REFORM ACT OF 1969

INTRODUCTORY COMMENT

... Congress . . . conformed to the recent trend in tax legislation by enacting a terribly complex new statute. Not only is revised Section 305 complex, but it is also replete with redundancy and inconsistency. Moreover, despite all of this, it seems to do little more than to restore the old proportionate interest test. . . .

AN OVERVIEW OF AMENDED SECTION 305

Section 305, as amended in 1969, is divided into five subsections, which perform the following functions:

Subsection	*Function*
(a)	States the general rule of nontaxability of stock distributions

16. So called because it originated with Citizens Utilities Company, Stamford, Connecticut. See Journal of Taxation, May 1956, p. 312, September 1956, p. 178.

Subsection	Function
(b)	States five exceptions to the general rule, i.e., five situations in which a stock distribution is taxable
(c)	Authorizes the Treasury to classify certain nondistribution transactions as distributions (i.e., "deemed distributions")
(d)	Defines the terms "stock" and "shareholder"
(e)	Provides cross references

The general rule of nontaxability expressed in subsection (a) is [that] stock dividends are nontaxable unless one of the exceptions stated in subsection (b) applies. The five exceptions of new subsection (b), as is developed more fully below, effectively reintroduce the pre-1954 proportionate interest test and broaden the 1954 rule taxing distributions made in discharge of preferred dividends. Subsection (c) represents an innovation in the 1969 version, in that it creates a "deemed distribution" concept and thus expands significantly the scope of section 305. Subsection (d) carries forward the rule that the term "stock" includes "stock rights" and the rule (at least implicit in prior law) that the term "shareholder" includes a holder of rights. It adds to the prior law by stating that the term "holder" includes a holder of convertible securities.

Any discussion of Section 305 must focus primarily on Section 305(b), containing the five exceptions to the general rule of nontaxability, and on Section 305(c), relating to deemed distributions. . . .

SECTION 305(c) — DEEMED DISTRIBUTIONS

TRANSACTIONS COVERED

Section 305(c) identifies five kinds of transactions which, though they do not actually involve a distribution of stock to shareholders, may have the same effect and may be considered as if they did so. Specifically, these transactions include:

(1) a change in conversion ratio
(2) a change in redemption price
(3) a difference between redemption price and issue price
(4) a redemption having dividend consequences, and
(5) any transaction (including a recapitalization) having a similar effect on the interest of any shareholder.

The Secretary is authorized by Section 305(c) to issue Regulations under which any of the above may be deemed to involve a distribution of stock with respect to any shareholder whose proportionate interest in the corporation is increased by the transaction. . . . A transaction which is so classified as a deemed distribution must then be tested for tax consequences under Section 305(b).

CHANGE IN CONVERSION RATIO

A change in conversion ratio of convertible stock or debt affects the holder's potential equity position vis-à-vis other shareholders and has obvious, though deferred, proportionate interest consequences. . . . Under Section 305(c), the holder may be deemed to have received a distribution of stock, and that deemed distribution may or may not be taxable under the substantive rules of Section 305(b), discussed below. The Committee Reports on Section 305 illustrate the effect of both downward adjustments of conversion ratio (e.g., common stock pays no dividends; convertible preferred pays a cash dividend and the conversion ratio is annually adjusted downward to reflect the dividend; as a result, the interest of common shareholders is increased) and upward adjustments of conversion ratio (common stock pays dividends; convertible preferred does not, but there is a consequent annual increase in the conversion ratio; the interest of the preferred shareholders is thus increased).[21] In the first instance, a distribution would be deemed made to the common shareholders; in the second, it would be deemed made to the preferred shareholders. The taxable character of the deemed distribution would be determined under Section 305(b).

If the conversion ratio of convertible preferred stock or debt is increased or decreased under a bona fide and reasonable adjustment formula in order to prevent dilution resulting from such factors as nontaxable stock distributions to common shareholders or sales of common stock above or below the conversion price, such adjustments will not be deemed to result in a distribution of stock.[22] If, however, an adjustment to the conversion ratio of stock or debt is made to compensate for a taxable dividend distribution on common stock, the adjustment will be deemed to be a distribution of stock.[23] . . .

REDEMPTION HAVING DIVIDEND CONSEQUENCES

Section 305(c) also provides that a redemption which is taxed as a dividend may be treated as resulting in a distribution to any shareholder whose proportionate interest is increased by the transaction. Thus, if a redemption of stock from Shareholder A, which is taxable to A as a dividend, causes the proportionate interest of Shareholder

21. H. Rep. No. 91-413, 91st Cong. 1st Sess. 114 (1969); S. Rep. No. 522, 91st Cong. 1st Sess. 153-54 (1969). . . .
22. Reg. §1.305-7(b).
23. Rev. Rul. 75-513, (C.B. 1975-2, 113), applies this rule to make taxable an adjustment to the conversion ratio of convertible debentures.

B in the corporation to increase, Shareholder B may be deemed to have received a distribution of stock, and the consequences of that deemed distribution must be tested under Section 305(b).

The Committee reports indicate that the target of this provision was the "periodic redemption plan," under which a small amount of stock is from time to time redeemed from some shareholders, with the result that the interests of other shareholders are increased.[25] . . .

In keeping with the Committee Reports, the Regulations state that this rule does not apply in the case of an isolated redemption of stock.[26] . . .

The reason for the solicitude extended to "isolated" dividend-type redemptions is not clear. If a redemption is essentially equivalent to a dividend and results in a reduction of outstanding stock (with a consequent shift in proportionate interest), there is no reason to refrain from classifying the increase in interest to some shareholders as a distribution merely because the transaction is isolated. An actual stock distribution to some shareholders, coupled with a cash distribution to others, cannot escape taxation under Section 305(b)(2) on the grounds of isolation. It is not evident why the redemption variation of the same transaction should enjoy a protected status.

CHANGE IN REDEMPTION PRICE

It is not altogether clear from the statute (which refers merely to a "change in redemption price"), the Committee Reports, or the Regulations, what is intended by this provision.

Presumably, the objective is to insure that an increase in the redemption price of preferred stock, for example, to reflect dividends paid to common shareholders, will be deemed to be a distribution of additional preferred stock, with the result that the deemed distribution will be taxed under Section 305(b)(4), which makes taxable any distribution of stock or preferred stock.

It seems unlikely that this provision will play a major role under Section 305.

DIFFERENCE BETWEEN REDEMPTION PRICE AND ISSUE PRICE

Under Section 305(c), a difference between issue price and redemption price may result in a deemed distribution. Although the

---

25. House Report, p. 114; Senate Report, p. 153.
26. Reg. §1.305-3(e), examples (10), (11). See also, Reg. §1.305-3(b)(3), which applies a similar rule for purposes of §305(b)(2). In Rev. Rul. 77-19, (C.B. 1977-1, 83), the Service ruled that a redemption in which 80 percent of the shareholders, representing holders of less than 200 shares, were eliminated, did not result in a deemed distribution under §305(c).

statute is again not explicit, it seems probable that only preferred stock, as distinguished from debt instruments, is comprehended by this provision. Original issue discount on debt instruments is generally the subject of Section 1232, and it is doubtful that Section 305(c) was intended to interfere with this established statutory pattern. . . . [T]he Regulations[27] . . . refer only to preferred stock in discussing the provision.

Not every spread between issue price and redemption price results in a deemed distribution. The Regulations,[28] in keeping with the Committee Reports,[29] provide that only so much of the difference as exceeds a reasonable call premium will be deemed a distribution. For this purpose, a redemption premium which does not exceed ten percent of the issue price on stock which is not redeemable for five years will be considered reasonable.[30] . . .

The three examples in the Regulations which illustrate the application of this provision establish the principle that the deemed distribution consists of additional preferred stock distributed on the existing preferred stock having the excessive call premium, and hence the distribution is taxable under Section 305(b)(4), relating to distributions of stock on preferred stock.

OTHER TRANSACTIONS (INCLUDING RECAPITALIZATIONS)

The final transaction category which is described as a deemed distribution under Section 305(c) is a catchall, consisting of "any transaction (including a recapitalization) having a similar effect on the interest of any shareholder." The Regulations do not seek to implement the "any transaction" language by describing transactions other than those expressly named in the statute, but this language will doubtless justify the Service and the courts in bringing within Section 305(c) other abusive transactions which do not involve a classical stock distribution.

The Regulations do implement the statutory reference to "recapitalizations" by providing that a deemed distribution will result from any recapitalization

(1) if it is pursuant to a plan to periodically increase a shareholder's proportionate interest, or

(2) if preferred stock with dividends in arrears is exchanged for other stock having either a value or a liquidation preference in excess of the issue price of the preferred stock surrendered.[34]

27. Reg. §1.305-7(a).
28. Reg. §1.305-5(b).
29. Senate Report, p. 154.
30. Reg. §1.305-5(b)(2).
34. Reg. §1.305-7(c).

THE FIVE EXCEPTIONS OF SECTION 305(b)

Section 305(b) provides that five types of stock distribution do not fall within the general rule of Section 305(a) and are thus taxable. These are referred to below . . . as:

(1) disproportionate distribution — Section 305(b)(2)

(2) distribution of common and preferred — Section 305(b)(3)

(3) distribution of convertible preferred — Section 305(b)(5)

(4) distribution with election as to medium of payment — Section 305(b)(1)

(5) distribution made on preferred stock — Section 305(b)(4)

. . . Taken together, these provisions evidence an intent (1) to tax stock distributions which do effect a shift of proportionate interest, and (2) to tax all stock distributions which are made on preferred stock. . . .

DISPROPORTIONATE DISTRIBUTION — SECTION 305(b)(2)

Three elements are required for taxation of a distribution under Section 305(b)(2):

(1) a distribution of stock (which may be actual or deemed)

(2) resulting in the receipt of property by some shareholders, and

(3) resulting in an increase in the proportionate interest of other shareholders.

This is essentially a codification of the old 1936 proportionate interest test, . . . The principal difference between Section 305(b)(2) and the 1936 test is the express requirement in the former that some shareholders receive property. This is referred to below as the "companion distribution" requirement.

Section 305(b)(2) — The Requirement for a Companion Distribution

The companion distribution requirement is largely superfluous. . . . [E]conomic considerations dictate that Shareholder A will not permit the interest of Shareholder B to be increased unless Shareholder A is somehow compensated for the consequent reduction in his own interest. . . . If there is no compensating payment to the shareholders whose interest is diminished, the benefit conferred on the other shareholders probably represents compensation of some kind, or, if the shareholders do not deal at arm's length, a gift. . . .

For these reasons, it is not clear why it was thought necessary to expressly require a companion distribution as a condition for taxable status under Section 305(b)(2). Its inclusion does not appreciably narrow the statute — it simply makes it more complex.

The companion distribution requirement probably resulted from Treasury's preoccupation in 1969 with the so-called "Citizen's

Utilities" type of transaction, where cash dividends are paid on one class of common stock and stock dividends are paid on the other class of common. . . .

As might be expected, the Regulations take a sufficiently expansive view of what constitutes a companion distribution that the requirement is almost eliminated. They state that it is

> not necessary that such [a companion] distribution be pursuant to a plan to distribute cash or property to some shareholders and to increase the proportionate interests of other shareholders.[38]

It is sufficient if that result in fact occurs.

> This is so whether or not the stock distributions and the cash distributions are steps in an overall plan or are independent and unrelated.[39]

It is necessary, however, that the companion distribution (1) be made to a shareholder in his capacity as such, and (2) be taxable to him under Section 301 (or under other specifically identified sections).[40] The Regulations do expressly include as a companion distribution to a shareholder for purposes of Section 305(b)(2) the payment of interest to a holder of a convertible debenture.[41]

The Regulations expressly disqualify as a companion distribution a property distribution which is made (1) pursuant to an isolated redemption of stock, or (2) pursuant to an undertaking to pay [cash] in lieu of fractional shares.[42] A payment of cash in lieu of fractional shares is removed from classification as a companion distribution only if it is made to save the corporation from the trouble and expense of issuing fractional shares and not for the purpose of achieving a shift of proportionate interest. It is conclusively presumed to be for the former purpose if the cash distributed is five percent or less of the value of the stock distributed.

. . . The Regulations also provide that a property distribution will not be treated as a companion distribution under Section 305(b)(2) if it precedes or follows the stock distribution by 36 months or more, unless made pursuant to the same plan.[43]

The companion distribution requirement may also be satisfied by a transaction which is not an actual distribution but which is deemed to be one under Section 305(c). For example, if preferred stock convertible into common stock is issued with an excessive re-

---

38. Reg. §1.305-3(b)(2).
39. Ibid.
40. Reg. §1.305-3(b)(3).
41. Reg. §1.305-3(b)(3).
42. Reg. §§1.305-3(b)(3), 1.305-3(c). See also I.R.S. private ruling No. 7738035, which applies the fractional share rule discussed in the text.
43. Reg. §1.305-3(b)(4).

demption price, a deemed distribution to the preferred shareholders results under Section 305(c). That deemed distribution is taxable under Section 305(b)(4) (relating to distributions on preferred stock), and thus Section 301 applies to it. If the common shareholders receive a distribution of common stock which is not paid also to the holders of convertible preferred, their interest will increase vis-à-vis the interest of the preferred shareholders. There will thus be a conjunction of (1) a distribution of stock (i.e., common stock to common shareholders), (2) resulting in an increase in proportionate interest (of the common shareholders), and (3) a companion distribution to the preferred shareholders (consisting of the deemed distribution, which is taxable under Sections 301 and 305(b)(4). Consequently, the Regulations conclude that the distribution of common stock to common shareholders in this situation is taxable under Section 305(b)(2).[44]

This conclusion in the Regulations does illustrate the point that a deemed distribution will fulfill the companion distribution requirement, but it also illustrates the unrealistic nature of the requirement. Seldom, if ever, will it be feasible for a corporation to ignore convertible preferred shareholders in making a distribution of common stock to common shareholders. If the preferred shareholders do not themselves receive additional common stock, either directly or through adjustment of the conversion ratio, it will.be because they have been compensated in some other way. But the nature and source of their compensation is irrelevant to the question whether the common shareholders have received income — they clearly have to the extent that their proportionate interest has been increased. This increase in interest is alone sufficient to warrant taxation of the distribution, and the need to cast around for and to identify a companion distribution is an unfortunate distraction.

Section 305(b)(2) — The Requirement for an Increase in Proportionate Interest

While the concept of an increase in proportionate interest is easily enunciated, it can in actuality sometimes be difficult to determine whether an increase has occurred, and the Regulations provide helpful examples.[45] . . .

In determining whether an increase in interest has occurred, each class of stock is to be considered separately, and each shareholder within the class is deemed to have an increased interest if his class as a whole has an increased interest.[49] However, a shareholder cannot contend that he did not have an increased interest merely because his class did not, as a whole, have an increased interest. For

44. Reg. §1.305-3(e), example (15).
45. Reg. §1.305-3(e).
49. Reg. §1.305-3(b)(6).

example, if common stock is distributed to one of two common share-holders, the shareholder receiving the distribution clearly has an increased interest even though the common shareholders as a whole do not have an increased interest.

In determining whether an increase in proportionate interest has occurred, there is to be treated as outstanding stock (1) any rights to acquire stock, and (2) any security (i.e., debt) convertible into stock.[50] . . .

[Discussion of the treatment of convertible preferred stock is omitted.]

If a shift in proportionate interest is to be avoided in such cases, the Regulations require that the adjustment to the conversion ratio be a "full adjustment."[52] . . .

The requirement that the conversion ratio of convertible securities be adjusted effectively treats them as if they were fully converted for purposes of measuring a shift in proportionate interest. Accordingly, one would expect to find a general rule, applicable in determining whether a shift in interest has occurred, that convertible preferred is to be placed on a par with common, i.e., it should be treated as fully converted. Thus, a distribution of convertible preferred to holders of common should not result in a shift in proportionate interest regardless whether any or all of the preferred is converted.[54] The Regulations do not, however, clearly take this position and it seems to be an unanswered question.

[Summary of examples omitted. See Treas. Reg. §1.305-3(e).]

Section 305(b)(2) — Summary

Section 305(b)(2) is in substance a reenactment of the pre-1954 shift-in-proportionate interest test. Though it now contains the requirement for a companion distribution, that change is of little consequence because (1) economic realities generally assume that it will always be present, and (2) it is interpreted so broadly in the Regulations that it will seldom be found wanting.

DISTRIBUTION OF COMMON AND PREFERRED — SECTION 305(b)(3)

Section 305(b)(3) provides that a stock distribution is not within the general nontaxability rule of Section 305(a) if some common

50. Reg. §1.305-3(b)(5).
52. [Reg. §1.305-3(d)(1).]
54. If the circumstances indicate that some of the preferred will be promptly converted, the distribution may nonetheless result in some common shareholders receiving (via conversion) common stock while others receive (and retain) preferred stock, making the transaction taxable under §305(b)(3), discussed below. If the circumstances indicate instead that some distributees will promptly and by prearrangement sell their preferred for cash, there will be a shift in proportionate interest and the transaction would be taxable under §305(b)(2) or §305(b)(5), discussed below.

shareholders receive common stock while other common shareholders receive preferred stock. The Regulations contain two examples illustrating this rule.[56]

In the first example, a corporation with two classes of common, A and B, makes a distribution of class A common stock to the holders of class A common stock, and it makes a distribution of newly issued preferred stock to the holders of class B common stock. The Regulations hold that both distributions are taxable.

In the second example, a corporation having one class of common stock distributes to common shareholders a new issue of convertible preferred having a six-month conversion period and a conversion price near the market value of the common stock. The Regulations find that early conversion by some common shareholders is probable, with the result that some common shareholders (those who convert) will, as a consequence of the distribution, hold additional common stock while others (those who do not convert) will hold preferred stock. Consequently, the distribution of the preferred is within Section 305(b)(3) and results in taxable income.

Section 305(b)(3) merely states another aspect of the shift-in-proportionate-interest rule. If some common shareholders receive common stock while others receive preferred, a shift in proportionate interest occurs. If Congress, in stating the disproportionate distribution rule contained in Section 305(b)(2), had simply omitted the companion distribution requirement and had required only a shift in proportionate interest, there would have been no need for Section 305(b)(3). . . .

Distribution of Convertible Preferred — Section 305(b)(5)

Section 305(b)(5) makes a distribution of convertible preferred stock taxable unless it is established, to the satisfaction of the Secretary, that the distribution will not have the effect described in Section 305(b)(2), i.e., that it will not result in a shift in proportionate interest accompanied by a companion distribution.

. . . Section 305(b)(5), like Section 305(b)(3), seems to add little to the statutory framework other than complexity. By its very terms, it can apply only where the distribution will have the result described in Section 305(b)(2), leaving one to wonder exactly what the intended jurisdiction of this provision is. It may be that Section 305(b)(5) was thought to be needed because Section 305(b)(2) applies where there *is* a shift in interest whereas Section 305(b)(5) is phrased to permit consideration of a possible future shift in interest. If this is the jurisdiction, Section 305(b)(2) could easily have been modified to look also to the future. . . .

56. Reg. §1.305-4(b).

ELECTION AS TO MEDIUM OF PAYMENT — SECTION 305(b)(1)

Section 305(b)(1) carries forward from prior law the rule that a distribution which offers the shareholder the option to choose between receiving stock or other property (including cash) is taxable. This rule has been a part of the statutory law since 1936. . . . In 1954 when the shift-in-proportionate-interest test was dropped, the choice-of-medium-of-payment test took on a more significant role. In 1969, when the shift-in-proportionate-interest test returned in the form of Section 305(b)(2), the choice-of-medium-of-payment test necessarily settled again into relative obscurity.

If a stock distribution offers a shareholder the opportunity to choose instead to receive property, and if any shareholder makes that choice, all elements for taxation under Section 305(b)(2) are present, i.e., a distribution of stock, resulting in a shift in proportionate interest and a companion distribution. In this situation, there is obviously no role for Section 305(b)(1).

If the stock distribution offers the election but no shareholder avails himself of it, there is no shift in proportionate interest and no policy reason to make the distribution taxable. It is academic to argue that the mere option to take property, whether or not exercised, is enough to make the distribution taxable. First, such options probably occur only in distributions made by large, publicly held corporations — closely held corporations simply decide such issues by a consensus of shareholders before declaring any distribution. Second, in the case of a large corporation, the prospect that no shareholder will accept the property option is remote, and thus Section 305(b)(2) will virtually always apply. Under these circumstances, there is little room for Section 305(b)(1) to play a significant role.

Despite the prospect for a limited role, Section 305(b)(1) does serve as a handy vehicle for classifying as taxable certain dividend reinvestment plans[58] and distributions from regulated investment companies, which commonly offer the option to take cash or additional stock.[59] And the Service has ruled that a distribution to common shareholders of preferred stock which is immediately redeemable is taxable as offering a choice of stock or cash under Section 305(b)(1).[60] All of these, however, could have been held taxable under Section 305(b)(2). . . .

DISTRIBUTION ON PREFERRED STOCK — SECTION 305(b)(4)

Section 305(b)(4) makes any distribution on preferred stock taxable. It evidences a general policy that stock distributions with respect

58. Rev. Rul. 76-53, C.B. 1976-1, 87. The same result was reached in I.R.S. private ruling No. 7721048.
59. See I.R.S. private ruling No. 7737068.
60. Rev. Rul. 76-258, C.B. 1976-2, 95.

to preferred stock should in all cases be taxable. In the words of the 1969 Senate Report, "Since preferred stock characteristically pays specified cash dividends, stock dividends on preferred stock . . . are a substitute for cash dividends and therefore . . . are taxable."[61]

Section 305(b)(4) thus serves a different policy objective from the four exceptions discussed above, which have in common the concept of disproportionate distribution. . . . It thus plays a significant and independent role in the scheme of Section 305.

As with so many other areas of Section 305, however, Section 305(b)(4) is not without its legislative curiosity. Tacked onto the general rule that any distribution on preferred stock is taxable is the following exception:

> . . . other than an increase in the conversion ratio of convertible preferred stock made solely to take account of a stock dividend or stock split with respect to the stock into which such convertible stock is convertible.

This is curious for two reasons. First, an adjustment to a conversion ratio involves a deemed rather than an actual distribution of stock. Accordingly, it is surprising that this language was not included in Section 305(c) rather than in Section 305(b)(4). Second, it is difficult to understand the reason for this special rule. Where convertible preferred stock is outstanding, a distribution of common stock on common stock will be nontaxable to common shareholders (under Section 305(a) and 305(b)(2)) if either (1) the conversion ratio of the preferred is adjusted, or (2) common stock is distributed to the holders of the convertible preferred. However, with respect to the preferred shareholders, only the first of the two alternatives is a nontaxable transaction. A direct distribution to them of common stock would be taxable under Section 305(b)(4), as a distribution on preferred, but an adjustment to the conversion ratio, even though having identical effect (insofar as proportionate interest is concerned), would not be taxable. This statutory bias in favor of conversion ratio adjustment and against direct distribution of stock probably results from a recognition that, in the real world of finance, stock dividends on common stock are virtually always compensated, vis-à-vis convertible issues, by adjusting to the conversion ratio of the latter.

LIMITATION ON SECTION 305 — ADJUSTMENT OF PURCHASE PRICE

By the terms of Section 305(a), the rules of that section apply only to a distribution of stock of the corporation "with respect to its

61. Senate Report, p. 55.

stock." As interpreted by the Regulations,[62] this language precludes application of Section 305 where stock is transferred (or a conversion ratio or redemption price is changed) and the purpose is to adjust the purchase price being paid by the corporation in the acquisition of property. Thus, for example, if in an acquisition transaction, there is a contingent computation of consideration, with additional stock to be paid upon the occurrence of the contingency, the payment of that additional stock is not a distribution of stock with respect to stock — it is a payment of additional consideration pursuant to the terms of the transaction. . . .

CONCLUSION

The area of stock distributions will doubtless always be mysterious. The mysteries should, however, be restricted to those arising from the subject matter itself and should not be compounded by mysteries arising from the structure of the statute. Unfortunately, the existing statute contributes more than its share of mystery.

NOTES

1. The reach of §306 was diminished by the addition of §§305(b)(2) et seq. in 1969. Now, the issuance of a dividend in preferred stock may be taxable as ordinary income under §305(b); consequently, the shares will not be §306 stock. See §306(c)(1)(A).

In Rev. Rul. 76-258, 1976-2 C.B. 95, the Service ruled that immediately redeemable preferred stock, distributed as a pro rata stock dividend on the common, was taxable on receipt by reason of §305(b)(1) (a provision carried over in substance from the 1939 Code). The preferred would appear to be §306 stock, a point ignored in the ruling. If the redemption feature alone is sufficient to make the distribution taxable under §305(b)(1), the role of §306 is further narrowed. See also Rev. Rul. 83-68, 1983-1 C.B. 75 (dividend of redeemable common-on-common taxable under §305(b)(1)). Is the Service right?

2. Which approach is preferable, "tainting" but deferring tax, as under §306, or taxing up-front, when stock is issued and a disproportionate interest is created, as under §305(b)(2)? Is it sound to have both approaches, as the Code has had since 1969? When should stock appreciation be treated as "realized"? What influence does §1014 have on your thinking? Consider these questions as you work through the materials that follow under §§305(b)(2) et seq. Indeed,

---

62. Reg. §1.305-1(c).

you should consider these questions in connection with virtually every issue you study in this chapter.

3. See B. Bittker and J. Eustice, Federal Income Taxation of Corporations and Shareholders, 7-71 to 7-82 (5th ed. 1987); Metzer, the "New" Section 305, 27 Tax L. Rev. 93 (1971); Pehrson, Jr., Final 305 Regs Generally Restrict Stock Dividend Benefits But Some Openings Remain, 42 J. Taxn. 280 (1975); Stone, Back to Fundamentals: Another Version of the Stock Dividend Saga, 79 Colum. L. Rev. 898 (1979). See also Treas. Reg. §1.305-3(c) with respect to distributions of money in lieu of fractional shares to which shareholders would otherwise be entitled. Cf. Chirelstein, Optional Redemptions and Optional Dividends: Taxing the Repurchase of Common Shares, 78 Yale L.J. 739 (1969).

FRONTIER SAVINGS ASSOCIATION v. COMMISSIONER
87 T.C. 665 (1986), *aff'd sub nom.* Colonial Sav. Assn. v. Commissioner, 854 F.2d 1001 (7th Cir. 1988)

SWIFT, Judge. . . .

Following concessions, the issue remaining for decision is whether stock dividends received by petitioner in 1978 and 1979 from the Federal Home Loan Bank of Chicago are taxable to petitioner under section 305(b)(1). The resolution of this issue will affect the taxability of stock dividends received by the other 496 stockholders of the Federal Home Loan Bank of Chicago which also received stock dividends in 1978 and 1979.

Petitioner, Frontier Savings Association ("Frontier Savings"), is a mutual savings and loan association which was organized on February 19, 1919. It operates as a mutual savings association pursuant to Wisconsin law.

Frontier Savings has been a member and stockholder of the Federal Home Loan Bank of Chicago (the "Chicago Bank") at all times since the organization of the Chicago Bank. The Chicago Bank is one of 11 district banks (12 prior to 1946) established pursuant to the Federal Home Loan Bank Act of 1932, 47 Stat. 725, 12 U.S.C. sec. 1421 et seq. The district banks were capitalized with stock subscriptions from member institutions and the U.S. Treasury. District banks operate under the supervision of the Federal Home Loan Bank Board, an administrative agency in the Executive branch of the Federal government. The Federal Home Loan Bank Board also is the chartering and regulatory authority for Federal savings and loan associations and Federal mutual savings banks.

The Federal Home Loan Bank system was designed primarily

as a reserve credit facility for savings and loan associations and other home mortgage credit institutions. Savings and loan associations (such as Frontier Savings) and mutual savings banks that are members or stockholders in the district banks (hereinafter referred to as "members" or "member banks") are required by Federal law to maintain a certain capital stock ownership in the respective district banks of which they are members. The stock ownership requirements are determined at the end of each calendar year and are calculated with reference to each member bank's net home mortgage loans outstanding and total borrowings of each member from the district bank.

Each member bank generally must maintain a capital stock ownership interest in the district bank in an amount equal to at least one percent of the total outstanding balance of its home mortgage loans[2] and at least equal to one-twelfth[3] of total outstanding borrowings of the member bank from the district bank, as of December 31 of each year. Each share of stock in the district banks is valued by statute at its $100 par value. . . .

Based upon the above year-end calculations, member banks that are required to purchase additional stock of district banks must do so by January 31 of the following year at the par value of $100 per share. Member banks that own stock in district banks in excess of the required number of shares ("excess shares") may request that excess shares be redeemed by the district banks.

The policy of the Chicago Bank with respect to the redemption of excess shares is reflected in the minutes of a June 18, 1979, meeting of the Chicago Bank's board of directors, as follows:

> BE IT RESOLVED, that the President of the Bank or any officer designated by him may from time to time increase or decrease the amount of stock of any member in accordance with Section 6 of the Federal Home Loan Bank Act . . . and the Regulations for the Federal Home Loan Bank System; provided, however, that in exercising the Bank's discretion whether or not to grant an application by a member to decrease its stock, the President or his regulatory be guided by all applicable statutory and regulatory provisions, all policies and standards adopted from time to time by this Board, including, but not limited to, the Bank's credit standards contained in the "Policies Governing Extension of Credit" as adopted by this Board and all relevant facts and circumstances.

[After purchasing a number of shares in January 1978, Frontier Savings owned 9,066 shares of the common stock of the Chicago Bank. As shareholders they received dividends whenever they were

2. Each bank that became a member before September 8, 1961, is required to maintain a stock ownership interest of two percent of its total outstanding balance of home mortgage loans.
3. This requirement was changed to one-twentieth in 1979. . . .

paid. Prior to 1978 these dividends were always paid in cash. On December 29, 1978 the Chicago Bank paid a dividend in stock and on December 31, 1979 paid a dividend that was half stock and half cash. In both cases the Chicago Bank paid cash in lieu of fractional shares. On December 22, 1978 the Chicago Bank sent its member banks a bulletin explaining the decision to pay a stock dividend:]

> (1) Providing a stock rather than a cash dividend may enable your association to defer the payment of income taxes on the value of the stock dividend. You may wish to consult your tax adviser for the proper handling of a stock dividend.
>
> (2) A stock dividend can be applied toward satisfying the stock investment requirement for members that experienced a growth in assets during 1978 or that will be required to purchase additional stock due to increased borrowings from the Bank.

The bulletin also explained that most member banks would be required to increase their stock holdings in the Chicago Bank due to that year's general increase in outstanding home mortgage loans. [Enclosed with the bulletin was a form that a bank could use to purchase additional shares as required by the Home Loan Bank Act. If a bank anticipated that it would have more than enough shares as of the end of the year, it could request a redemption. The Chicago Bank was not obligated to redeem any shares, but had done so as a matter of routine in the past.

[On December 29, 1978, Frontier Savings received its share of the dividend, which came to 588 shares and $51.07 in cash. Frontier Savings did not request a redemption that year. It was required to purchase additional shares, which it did in January 1979. In total, 302 of the 497 member banks had to buy additional shares that year. Sixty-nine member banks requested a redemption, and all of these requests were granted. On December 31, 1979, Frontier Savings received, as a dividend, 514 shares on Chicago Bank common stock and $51,567.87 in cash.]

The December 21, 1979, bulletin mailed to member banks concerning the 1979 dividends explained that "to help preserve the nontaxable characteristics of the stock dividend" a new procedure was being adopted for the purchase and disposition of excess shares of stock in the Chicago Bank. Instead of having member banks purchase additional shares of stock from the Chicago Bank and instead of having the Chicago Bank redeem excess shares from member banks, the new procedure called for member banks who had excess shares they wished to dispose of to sell such excess shares to other member banks who wished to buy additional shares.

Enclosed with the December 21, 1979, bulletin was a form entitled "Calculation of Bank Stock Requirement" as of December 31, 1979, and a separate form that could be used by the member banks to notify the Illinois and Wisconsin League Offices of their desire to sell excess shares of stock in the Chicago Bank to other member banks. Each member bank was required to notify the Chicago Bank of any purchases of shares of stock in the Chicago Bank so the changes in ownership of the stock could be reflected on its records. . . .

[At the end of 1979, Frontier was 520 shares short of the number it needed. It purchased the necessary shares in January 1980. Of the 497 member banks, 215 needed to purchase additional shares. Thirty-one member banks sold stock to other member banks, and 10 purchased stock from other member banks. In all, 85,859 shares were exchanged among member banks. Shares were exchanged among member banks only in January. After that 64 banks requested the Chicago Bank to redeem shares. Of those, 60 banks requested redemptions of at least as many shares as they received in their 1979 dividends. All redemption requests were granted. Frontier Savings did not request any stock redemptions during this time.]

The receipt of common stock dividends generally is not taxable to stockholders. Sec. 305(a). Where, however, dividends from a corporation are payable, at the election of the stockholders, in stock or property (such as cash), the receipt of dividends will be taxable to the stockholders under the provisions of section 301. Sec. 305(b)(1). In that circumstance the receipt of stock dividends will be taxable under sections 305(b)(1) and 301 regardless of whether the stockholders exercise their election to receive the dividends in cash or other property. See Regs. §1.305-2(a). . . .

Respondent argues that by redeeming all of the common stock it was requested to redeem from its member banks in 1979 and 1980 (and apparently doing so in years before 1979), the Chicago Bank established such a policy and practice of redeeming excess stock upon request of the member banks that the member banks should be regarded as having had an "election" to receive the 1978 and 1979 stock dividends in cash. Respondent therefore argues that the stock dividends in question do not qualify for exemption from taxability under section 305(a) and should be taxable to the member banks under sections 305(b)(1) and 301. For the reasons explained below, we disagree.

The Federal statute under which the Federal Home Loan Bank Board and the district banks regulate certain activities of member banks addresses the authority of district banks to redeem common stock from its member banks and explicitly describes that authority as discretionary with each district bank. Section 1426(c) of the Federal Home Loan Bank Act as amended in 1961 provides, in relevant part, as follows:

> If the bank finds that the investment of any member in stock is greater than that required under this subsection it may, unless

prohibited by said Board [i.e., the Federal Home Loan Bank Board] or by the provisions of paragraph (2) of this subsection, in its discretion and upon application of such member retire the stock of such member in excess of the amount so required. . . .

[12 U.S.C. §1426(c) (1961), as amended by Act of Sept. 8, 1961, subsec. (c), Pub. L. No. 87-210, 75 Stat. 482.]

A comparison of the language quoted above (reflecting the 1961 amendment to section 1426(c)) with the language of the predecessor statute to section 1426(c) (as originally enacted in 1932) is particularly significant. As originally enacted, section 1426(c) of the Federal Home Loan Bank Act of 1932, supra, provided as follows:

If the board finds that the investment of any member in stock is greater than that required under this section, upon application of such member, the bank shall pay such member for each share of stock in excess of the amount so required an amount equal to the value of such stock. . . .

[Federal Home Loan Bank Act of 1932, supra, §1426(c).]

The language quoted immediately above suggests that member banks may have had the right to require district banks to redeem excess shares before the 1961 amendment to section 1426(c) (12 U.S.C.). That is suggested by use in the statutory language of the mandatory "shall." Nothing, however, in the Federal Home Loan Bank Act, in its present form, suggests that since 1961 anyone other than the district banks and the Federal Home Loan Bank Board have the authority to determine whether excess shares will be redeemed.

The policy of the Chicago Bank with respect to the redemption of excess shares, as reflected in the minutes of the June 18, 1979, meeting of its board of directors, is entirely consistent with the above statutory provisions. Also, the bulletins mailed in December of 1978 and 1979 by the Chicago Bank to its members do not communicate any contrary policy to member banks. Those bulletins acknowledged that although the issuance of stock dividends was attributable, in part, to a perceived tax planning opportunity, the distributions of stock dividends also were attributable to the recognized need for a number of member banks to acquire additional shares of common stock in the Chicago Bank. With respect to the holding of excess shares, the bulletin dated December 22, 1978, simply suggested that member banks "may want to retire" such stock. The bulletin dated December 21, 1979, stated that it was "hoped that the majority of those holding excess stock will choose to hold the stock to meet future needs and for investment purposes," but that if they chose to sell excess shares to another member bank the league offices will "make every effort to bring you in contact with a member . . . willing to purchase" the excess shares. Neither bulletin suggested that the Chicago Bank necessarily would grant any or all redemption requests.

Congress vested in the district banks and in the Federal Home Loan Bank Board discretionary authority to redeem excess shares of common stock held by member banks. Our careful examination of the record herein satisfies us that the manner in which stock dividends were paid and redeemed in 1978 and 1979 by the Chicago Bank was consistent with that grant of discretionary authority and did not vest in the member banks the unilateral right to elect or to require the Chicago Bank to redeem excess shares upon request.

Respondent concedes that the Chicago Bank did not completely abdicate its discretionary authority to redeem its stock but respondent argues that that authority was exercised so consistently in favor of redemption that member banks, as a practical matter, had the option or election to have excess shares redeemed at any time. Respondent contends that the option arose "from the circumstances of the distribution," citing section 1.305-2(a)(4), Income Tax Regs. As indicated, we have carefully examined the circumstances of the stock dividends in question and conclude that the member banks, including Frontier Savings, did not have the option or election to have the Chicago Bank redeem excess shares of common stock in the Chicago Bank.

In addition to the factors explained above, we think it significant that the stock dividends of the Chicago Bank were declared and distributed in late December of 1978 and 1979. Member banks, however, normally would not be able to determine until early in the following year (after actual distribution of the stock dividends) whether they would be able even to request a redemption of some of their common stock in the Chicago Bank. In other words, on the day of distribution of the stock dividends, member banks could not know (other than through estimates and projections) whether they would be required to retain the stock dividends they received as part of their required investments in the district bank or whether the stock dividends would qualify as excess shares, in which case redemption thereof, if requested, might occur depending on the decision of the Chicago Bank.[5]

The parties have cited only one case that involves facts at all similar to those involved herein. In Rinker v. United States, 297 F. Supp. 370, 371 (S.D. Fla. 1968), the board of directors of a corporation adopted a resolution with respect to stock dividends and the ability to redeem the stock dividends, as follows:

> RESOLVED, that a stock dividend of 5% be paid to holders of record on March 31, 1960, on or before July 15, 1960, and that said dividends may be cashed at the request of the stockholders at a value per share yet to be determined.

5. In one case a member bank, apparently on December 29, 1978, was able to determine that its stock dividend would constitute excess shares and was able to request a redemption on the same day the stock distribution occurred.

Among other factors, the district court emphasized the use of the word "may" in the corporate resolution and held that the stockholders did not have an election to receive cash, in lieu of the stock dividends.

We recognize that the issuance by the Chicago Bank in 1978 and 1979 of stock dividends instead of or in addition to cash dividends was motivated in part by tax considerations. We cannot conclude, however, on the facts before us that the stock dividends were a mere subterfuge for cash distributions (see Rinker v. United States, supra at 372), or that the Chicago Bank had relinquished its discretionary authority to decline to grant stock redemption requests.

Respondent refers to Rev. Rul. 76-258, 1976-2 C.B. 95. Revenue Rulings are, of course, not binding on this Court. . . . Respondent's litigating position herein is reflected in Rev. Rul. 83-68, 1983-1 C.B. 75. For the reasons explained above and under the facts of this case, we reject the conclusion reached therein that a history or practice of redemptions by the Chicago Bank makes the stock dividends received by petitioner herein taxable under sections 305(b)(1) and 301. . . .

Reviewed by the Court.

Simpson, J., dissents.

HAMBLEN, J., concurring. I concur in the conclusion of the majority based upon the limited factual circumstances involved. If a discretionary act of the Board of Directors of a shareholder corporation to redeem stock dividends becomes a routine matter, it might, in my opinion, develop into an "option" that arises after the distribution or a distribution pursuant to a "plan." See secs. 1.305-2(a) and 1.305-3(b), Income Tax Regs. In such a situation, it seems the redemptions might be periodic rather than isolated. The broad rules of section 305 could invoke different considerations under other circumstances.

Sterrett, Cohen, and Jacobs, JJ., agree with this concurring opinion.

REVENUE RULING 78-375
1978-2 C.B. 130

Advice has been requested as to the treatment for federal income tax purposes of a "dividend reinvestment plan" where the shareholder may not only elect to receive stock of greater fair market value than the cash dividend such shareholder might have received instead, but also the shareholder may, through the plan, purchase additional stock from the corporation at a discount price which is less than the fair market value of the stock.

X is a corporation engaged in commercial banking whose shares of common stock are widely held and are regularly traded in the over-the-counter market. In order to raise additional equity capital for corporate expansion and to provide holders of X's common stock with a simple and convenient way of investing their cash dividends and optional payments in additional shares of X common stock without payment of any brokerage commission, X established an automatic dividend reinvestment plan. An independent agent will administer the plan and will receive the stock from X in the manner described below on behalf of a participating shareholder.

The plan provides the following:

(1) Shareholders can elect to have all their cash dividends (less a quarterly service charge of 3x dollars that is paid to an independent agent of the shareholder) otherwise payable on common stock registered in the name of the shareholder automatically reinvested in shares of X common stock. The service charge is paid to the agent for administering the plan and maintaining the stock certificates for the shareholders. The shareholders who elect to participate in the plan acquire X stock at a price equal to 95 percent of the fair market value of such stock on the dividend payment date. The shareholder's option to receive a dividend in additional common stock in lieu of a cash dividend is not transferable apart from a transfer of the common shares themselves.

(2) A shareholder who participates in the dividend reinvestment aspect of the plan as described in paragraph (1) above, in addition, has the option to invest additional amounts to purchase shares of X common stock at a price equal to 95 percent of the fair market value of such stock on the dividend payment date. Optional investments by a shareholder in any quarterly dividend period must be at least 4x dollars and cannot exceed 100x dollars. The shareholder's right to invest additional amounts under the plan is not transferable apart from a transfer of the common shares themselves.

There is no requirement to participate in the plan and shareholders who do not participate receive their cash dividend payments in full. Certain shareholders have chosen not to participate; therefore, they receive their regular quarterly cash dividend. While the plan continues in effect, a participant's dividends will continue to be invested without further notice to X.

Prior to the dividend payment date no cash dividend is available to either X's participating or nonparticipating shareholders. On the dividend payment date the participant receives written notification that X is acting to effectuate the participant's option to receive stock on that date. The crediting on the plan account and notification to the participant of the exact number of shares acquired (including fractional shares) takes place shortly after the dividend payment date.

A participant may withdraw from the plan at any time, upon written request. Upon withdrawal, certificates for whole shares credited to the participant's account under the plan will be issued and a cash payment based upon the market value of the participant's fractional share interest will be paid by X, through the participant's agent, to the participant. As an alternative, the shareholder may request that all or part of the whole shares credited to its account in the plan be sold for the shareholder's account. The sale will be made by an independent agent acting on behalf of such participant and the proceeds of the sale (less any brokerage commission and transfer tax) will be forwarded to the participant. With regard to the whole shares, X will neither purchase any shares of a participant nor pay any expense attributable to the sale of such stock. Upon a request for sale of a participant's shares, a cash payment equal to the market value of the participant's fractional share interest will be paid by X, through the participant's agent, to the participant. The purpose of the payment of cash is to save X the trouble, expense, and inconvenience of issuing and transferring fractional shares and is not designed to give any particular group of shareholders an increased interest in the assets or earnings and profits of X. . . .

Section 1.305-3(b)(2) of the regulations provides that in order for a distribution of stock to be considered as one of a series of distributions, it is not necessary that such distribution be pursuant to a plan to distribute cash or property to some shareholders and to increase the proportionate interests of other shareholders. It is sufficient if there is an actual or deemed distribution of stock and, as a result of such distribution, some shareholders receive cash or property and other shareholders increase their proportionate interests. This is so whether the stock distributions and the cash distributions are steps in an overall plan or are independent and unrelated. In addition, section 1.305-3(b)(3) states that there is no requirement that both elements of section 305(b)(2) . . . (receipt of cash or property by some shareholders and an increase in proportionate interests of other shareholders) occur in the form of a distribution or series of distributions as long as the result of a distribution of stock is that some shareholders' proportionate interests increase and other shareholders in fact receive cash or property.

Rev. Rul. 76-53, 1976-1 C.B. 87, concerns a situation where a widely held corporation that regularly distributes its earnings and profits adopted a plan permitting the shareholders to choose to have all of the cash dividends, otherwise payable on common shares owned by the shareholder, automatically invested to purchase additional shares of the corporation's stock. The shareholders who elect to participate under this plan acquire the company's stock at a price equal to 95 percent of the fair market value of such stock on the dividend payment date. That Revenue Ruling concludes that the distributions made by the corporation while the plan is in effect are properly treated as payable either in stock or in cash at the election of the shareholder within the meaning of section 305(b)(1) . . . and, therefore, such participating shareholders will be treated as having received a distribution to which section 301 applies by reason of section 305(b)(1).

Rev. Rul. 77-149, 1977-1 C.B. 82, concerns a situation where a corporation established a dividend reinvestment plan administered by a local bank, acting as agent for the shareholders. At a shareholder's direction the shareholder's cash dividends would be received by the participating shareholders' agent, the bank, who would then purchase the corporation's stock on the open market at 100 percent of fair market value. That Revenue Ruling held that section 301 applies directly to the cash dividends without reference to section 305(b)(1) because the distribution is payable by the corporation only in cash, and the shareholders of the corporation do not have the election of receiving their dividend distribution from the corporation in either stock or cash.

In the present case, the distributions made by X while the plan is in effect are properly treated as payable either in X's stock or in cash at the election of X's common shareholders within the meaning of section 305(b)(1). . . . The acquisition of stock through the dividend reinvestment aspect of the plan is identical to the situation in Rev. Rul. 76-53. Further, the present case and Rev. Rul. 76-53 are distinguishable from Rev. Rul. 77-149 because the distribution described in Rev. Rul. 77-149 was payable by the corporation only in cash, and the shareholder, through the agent, purchased the corporation's stock on the open market.

The optional investment aspect of the present case results in an increase in the proportionate interests of the shareholders making the purchase at a 5 percent discount, and this event increases their proportionate interests in the assets or earnings and profits of X within the meaning of section 305(b)(2)(B). . . . Furthermore, the fact that X shareholders who do not participate in the plan receive cash dividends constitutes a receipt of property by those shareholders within the meaning of section 305(b)(2)(A).

Accordingly, under the circumstances described above, it is held as follows:

(a) A shareholder of X who participates in the dividend reinvestment aspect of the plan will be treated as having received a distribution to which section 301 . . . applies by reason of the application of section 305(b)(1). Pursuant to section 1.305-1(b) of the regulations, the amount of the distribution to a participating shareholder (including participating corporate shareholders) will be the fair market value of the X stock received on the date of the distribution (sections 1.301-1(b) and (d)), plus, pursuant to section 301, 3x dollars, the service charge subtracted from the amount of the shareholder's distribution.

(b) The basis of the shares credited to the account of a participating shareholder pursuant to the dividend reinvestment aspect of the plan will equal the amount of the dividend distribution, as provided in section 301(c) . . . , measured by the fair market value of the X common stock as of the date of the distribution both as to noncorporate and corporate shareholders, pursuant to section 301(d). Section 1.301-1(h)(1) and (2)(i) of the regulations. The quarterly service charge paid by a participant who is an individual for the production of income or for the management, conservation, or maintenance of property held for the production of income, is deductible in the year paid by such participant under section 212, provided the individual itemizes deductions. See Rev. Rul. 70-627, 1970-2 C.B. 159, and Rev. Rul. 75-548, 1975-2 C.B. 331. The quarterly service charge, which is paid in carrying on a trade or business by a participant who is an individual, is deductible in the year paid by such participant under section 162. A participant who is a corporation may deduct the service charge under section 162.

(c) A shareholder of X who participates in the optional payment aspect of the plan will be treated as having received a distribution to which section 301 . . . applies by reason of the application of section 305(b)(2). Pursuant to section 1.305-3(a) of the regulations, the amount of the distribution to a participating shareholder will be the difference between the fair market value on the dividend payment date of the shares purchased with the optional payment and the amount of the optional payment. Section 1.305-3(b)(2).

(d) The basis to the shareholder who participates in the optional payment aspect of the plan is the excess of fair market value of the shares purchased with the optional payment over the optional payment (provided that this deemed distribution is taxable as a dividend under section 301(c)(1)) . . . pursuant to section 301(d) and sections 1.301-1(h)(1) and (2)(i) of the regulations, plus the amount of the optional payment, pursuant to section 1012.

(e) A participant in the plan will not realize any taxable income upon receipt of certificates for whole shares that were credited to the participant's account pursuant to the plan. Rev. Rul. 76-53. Any cash received by an X shareholder in lieu of a fractional share interest will be treated as a redemption of that fractional share interest, subject to the provisions and limitations of section 302. . . . See Rev. Rul. 66-365, 1966-2 C.B. 116.

(f) A participant will recognize gain or loss pursuant to section 1001 . . . when shares are sold or exchanged on behalf of the participant upon the participant's withdrawal from the plan, or when the participant sells the shares after its withdrawal from the plan. In accordance with section 1001, the amount of such gain or loss will be the difference between the amount that the participant receives for the whole shares and the participant's tax basis. Any cash received by the participants, who withdraw from the plan, in lieu of their fractional share interests will be treated as a redemption of that fractional share interest, subject to the provisions and limitations of section 302. See Rev. Rul. 66-365.

Rev. Rul. 77-149 is distinguished.

NOTE

See also Rev. Rul. 76-53, 1976-1 C.B. 87 (dividend reinvestment plan permitting shareholders to purchase corporation's stock at 5-percent discount from market price held taxable); Rev. Rul. 79-42, 1979-1 C.B. 130.

REVENUE RULING 78-60
1978-1 C.B. 81

Advice has been requested whether under section 302(a) . . . the stock redemptions described below qualified for exchange treatment, and whether under section 305(b)(2) and (c) the shareholders who experienced increases in their proportionate interests in the redeeming corporation as a result of the stock redemptions will be treated as having received distributions of property to which section 301 applies.

Corporation Z has only one class of stock outstanding. The Z common stock is held by 24 shareholders, all of whom are descendants, or spouses of descendants, of the founder of Z.

In 1975, when Z had 6,000 shares of common stock outstanding, the board of directors of Z adopted a plan of annual redemption to provide a means for its shareholders to sell their stock. The plan provides that Z will annually redeem up to 40 shares of its outstanding stock at a price established annually by the Z board of directors. Each shareholder of Z is entitled to cause Z to redeem two-thirds of one percent of the shareholder's stock each year. If some shareholders choose not to participate fully in the plan during any year, the other shareholders can cause Z to redeem more than two-thirds of one percent of their stock, up to the maximum of 40 shares.

Pursuant to the plan of annual redemption, Z redeemed 40 shares of its stock in 1976. Eight shareholders participated in the redemptions. The following table shows the ownership interests of the Z shareholders before and after the 1976 redemptions:

[Table omitted. No shareholder actually owned as much as 13 percent, and none constructively owned as much as 15 percent, of the outstanding stock at any time. The greatest change in actual and constructive ownership as a result of the redemption was incurred by shareholder G, whose actual and constructive ownership declined respectively from 188 to 182 and from 195 to 189 shares.]

ISSUE 1

[The Service concluded that none of the shareholders participating in the redemptions experienced a meaningful reduction in interest. Consequently, the redemptions were taxable under §301.]

ISSUE 2

... Section 1.305-7(a) of the ... regulations provides that a redemption treated as a section 301 distribution will generally be treated as a distribution to which sections 305(b)(2) and 301 ... apply if the proportionate interest of any shareholder in the earnings and profits or assets of the corporation deemed to have made the stock distribution is increased by the redemption, and the distribution has the result described in section 305(b)(2). The distribution is to be deemed made to any shareholder whose interest in the earnings and profits or assets of the distributing corporation is increased by the redemption.

Section 1.305-3(b)(3) of the regulations provides that for a distribution of property to meet the requirements of section 305(b)(2) ..., the distribution must be made to a shareholder in the capacity as a shareholder and must be a distribution to which section 301 [or one of several other specified sections] applies. A distribution of property incident to an isolated redemption will not cause section 305(b)(2) to apply even though the redemption distribution is treated as a section 301 distribution.

Section 305 ... does not make the constructive stock ownership rules of section 318(a) applicable to its provisions.

The 16 shareholders of Z who did not tender any stock for redemption in 1976 experienced increases in their proportionate interests of the earnings and profits and assets of Z (without taking into account constructive stock ownership under section 318 ...) as a result of the redemptions. Shareholders B and X, who surrendered small amounts of their stock for redemption in 1976, also experienced increases in their proportionate interests. The 1976 redemptions were not isolated but were undertaken pursuant to an ongoing plan of annual stock redemptions. Finally, the 1976 redemptions are to be treated as distributions of property to which section 301 . . . applies.

Accordingly, B, X and the 16 shareholders of Z who did not participate in the 1976 redemptions are deemed to have received stock distributions to which sections 305(b)(2) and 301 . . . apply. See examples (8) and (9) of section 1.305-3(e) of the regulations for a method of computing the amounts of the deemed distributions.

REVENUE RULING 78-115
1978-1 C.B. 85

Advice has been requested whether, under the circumstances described below, a series of redemptions of preferred stock by a corporation constitute a periodic redemption plan the effect of which is to increase the proportionate interests of certain shareholders within the meaning of section 305(b)(2) and (c). . . .

Corporation X wanted to acquire all of the stock of corporation Y. X and Y were unrelated, except that shareholders of X owning 10 percent of its stock owned 5 percent of the stock of Y. The shareholders of Y initially offered to sell their stock for a consideration of 8,000x dollars in cash. Because of previously existing debt commitments, however, X could only offer 75 percent of the consideration in cash and the remaining 25 percent portion of the consideration in the form of X preferred stock. The shareholders of Y accepted this offer. The exchange of Y stock for cash and X preferred stock was taxable to the Y shareholders. In accordance with section 1001 . . . , the amount of gain or loss to a shareholder is measured by the difference between the amount of the cash and the fair market value of the X preferred stock received over the shareholder's adjusted basis in the Y stock exchanged therefor.

X amended its articles of incorporation to authorize 2,000x shares of no par value preferred stock which would pay a cumulative annual dividend of nine dollars per share. X issued these shares to the shareholders of Y along with 6,000x dollars in cash in exchange for all of the stock of Y. Each share of preferred stock had a fair market value of $100 and the total value of the preferred stock issued to the Y shareholders was 2,000x dollars.

The preferred stock is nonparticipating and nonconvertible. Upon liquidation, each preferred share is entitled to $100, plus all unpaid accumulated dividends. The preferred stock is nonvoting, except for special voting powers whenever dividend arrearages on the stock exceed a certain amount. The shareholder may not cause the preferred stock to be redeemed.

The articles of incorporation of X provide that X shall redeem that number of whole shares equal to 5 percent of the authorized 2,000x shares of preferred stock commencing on June 30, 1983 and on each June thereafter for a period of 20 years. The redemption price is $100 per share, plus all dividends which shall have accrued to such mandatory redemption date. Such redemption shall be of whole shares pro rata or by lot among all the then outstanding shares of preferred stock. It is possible that certain redemptions of preferred stock will be treated as distributions to which section 301 applies by reason of section 302.

X's articles further provide that no additional shares of the class of preferred stock may be authorized while any shares of preferred stock are outstanding and that any shares of preferred stock which have been redeemed or otherwise acquired by X shall be cancelled and not be reissued. Finally, the articles provide that any class of preferred stock that X might authorize in the future would be fully subordinated to the existing class of preferred stock while any shares of the existing preferred stock remained outstanding.

[Summary of §§305(b)(2) and 305(c), and Treas. Reg. §1.305-7(a) omitted.]

Example (8) under section 1.305-3(e) of the regulations involves a situation in which corporation T has 1,000 shares of stock outstanding. C owns 100 shares. Nine other shareholders each own 100 shares. Pursuant to a plan for periodic redemptions, T redeems up to 5 percent of each shareholder's stock each year. During the year, each of the nine other shareholders has 5 shares of such shareholder's stock redeemed for cash. Thus, C's proportionate interest in the assets and earnings and profits of T is increased. Assuming that the cash received by the nine other shareholders is taxable under section 301 . . . , C is deemed under section 305(c) to have received a distribution under section 305(b)(2) of 5.25 shares of T stock to which section 301 applies.

Sections 305(c) and 305(b)(2) . . . are intended to apply to corporate stock redemptions that are in pursuance of a plan to periodically redeem the interest of some of a corporation's shareholders. See S. Rep. No. 91-522, 91st Cong., 1st Sess. 153 (1969), 1969-3 C.B. 423, 521, which states, in part, as follows:

> A periodic redemption plan may exist, for example, where a corporation agrees to redeem a small percentage of each common shareholder's stock annually at the election of the shareholder. The shareholders whose stock is redeemed receive cash, and the shareholders whose stock is not redeemed receive an automatic increase in their proportionate interests.

Example (14) under section 1.305-3(e) of the regulations involves a situation in which corporation U is a large manufacturing company whose products are sold through independent dealers. In order to assist individuals who lack capital to become dealers, the corporation has an established investment plan under which it provides 75 percent of the capital necessary to form a dealership corporation and the individual dealer provides the remaining 25 percent. Corporation U receives class A stock and a note representing its 75 percent interest. The individual dealer receives class B stock representing the dealer's 25 percent interest. The class B stock is nonvoting until all the class A shares are redeemed. At least 70 percent of the earnings and profits of the dealership corporation must be used each year to retire the note and redeem the class A stock. The class A stock is redeemed at a fixed price. The individual dealer has no control over the redemption of stock and has no right to have that dealer's stock redeemed during the period the plan is in existence. U's investment is thus systematically eliminated and the individual becomes the sole owner of the dealership corporation. Since this type of plan is akin to a security arrangement, the redemptions of the class A stock will not be deemed under section 305(c) . . . as distributions taxable under sections 305(b)(2) and 301 during the years in which the class A stock is redeemed.

Example (8) under section 1.305-3(e) of the regulations and the Senate Report cited above make it clear that a common shareholder, who does not elect to redeem stock when other common shareholders redeem their stock, receives a marked increase in the assets and earnings and profits of the corporation. This increase, when coupled with the redemption distributions that are taxable under section 301 . . . , causes the nonredeeming shareholder to be deemed under section 305(b)(2) to have received a distribution of stock to which section 301 applies. However, the instant redemptions of X's nonconvertible, nonparticipating preferred stock at its $100 call price and liquidation value, does not so clearly increase the interest of the X common shareholders in the assets and earnings and profits of X as the interests in X represented by the preferred stock is limited.

While the redemptions in the instant case do not cause the X common shareholders to receive an increased interest in X's assets, the redemption of a share of preferred stock does remove an annual $9 priority claim on X's earnings and profits, which increases the common shareholders' interest in the earnings and profits of X to this limited extent. However, as illustrated by example (14) under section 1.305-3(e) of the regulations certain periodic redemptions have been exempted from sections 305(b)(2) and (c). . . . Example (14) states that the periodic redemption of a class of stock at a fixed redemption price per share pursuant to a buy out plan designed to eliminate a shareholder was akin to a security arrangement, and consequently the redemptions of one shareholder's stock were not deemed under section 305(c) to constitute distributions taxable to the remaining shareholder under sections 305(b)(2) and 301. The instant case is analogous to example (14) in that the particular class of stock, subject to the periodic redemption plan, was created solely to facilitate the ownership of a business when other forms of financing were not readily available.

Accordingly, it is held that the redemptions of the preferred stock of X will not be deemed under section 305(c) . . . as distributions taxable to the common shareholders under sections 305(b)(2) and 301 during the years in which the X preferred stock is redeemed. See, however, section 302 with respect to individual redeeming shareholders.

NOTES

1. See also Rev. Rul. 77-37, 1977-1 C.B. 85 (adjustment in conversion ratio of preferred stock to reflect nontaxable distributions to common shareholders not a deemed distribution); Rev. Rul. 77-19, 1977-1 C.B. 83 (isolated redemptions do not result in distributions under §305(b)(2) or (c) where there is no plan to periodically redeem some shareholders); Rev. Rul. 76-186, 1976-1 C.B. 86 (effect on basis and earnings and profits where adjustment in conversion ratio of debentures results in deemed distribution); Rev. Rul. 75-468, 1975-2 C.B. 115 (calculation of "reasonable redemption premium" under Treas. Reg. §1.305-5(b)(2)). See Minasian and Walz, Guidelines for Determining When Discount on Preferred Stock Will Create Taxable Income, 53 J. Taxn. 2 (1980).

2. In Rev. Rul. 83-42, 1983-1 C.B. 76, the Service ruled that a distribution of common stock to holders of convertible preferred will constitute a distribution under §301 by reason of §305(b)(4) even though the distribution is made in order to take account of a dilution of the holders' conversion rights. See also Rev. Rul. 84-141, 1984-2 C.B. 80, where the Service ruled that a holder of cumulative preferred stock with the right to receive common stock equal in value to accrued dividends if cash dividends are not paid for two successive quarters, received a distribution of common stock taxable under §305(b)(4) on the passage of two successive quarters without the payment of cash dividends.

3. There is a perplexing policy puzzle that is larger and more engrossing than all of the technical detail in §§305 and 306. In a regime that had taxed ordinary investment income as high as 70 percent or even 50 percent and long-term capital gains at a maximum of only 20 percent, perhaps the complexity of §305(b)(2)-(5) and (c) could be justified. Yet, even then, it is hard to comprehend why the deferral-but-assured-ordinary income approach of §306 was appro-

priate to deal with *some* bailout cases, but yet the immediate ordinary income consequence of §§305(b)(2) et seq. was thought necessary in others. Today, with all income taxed at ordinary rates, it is even harder to rationalize the termination of deferral when §305(b)(2) is applicable since, in cases only marginally different, §306 allows deferral to continue. As long as the taxation of appreciation must generally await "realization," and as long, therefore, as §305(a) remains as a corollary to that principle, it may make sense to repeal §§305(b)(2) et seq. and, at the same time, to expand §306 to include most of the cases that §§305(b)(2)-(5) and (c) now embrace.

4. See Walter, Section 305: Its Implications in Reorganizations and Corporate Capital Structures, 54 Taxes 888 (1976).

C. STOCK DIVIDEND vs. COMPENSATION — §§305, 267, 61, 83

COMMISSIONER v. FENDER SALES, INC.
338 F.2d 924 (9th Cir.), *cert. denied*, 382 U.S. 813 (1965)

Before Pope and Barnes, Circuit Judges, and Thompson, District Judge.

THOMPSON, District Judge. . . . The Tax Court held neither the corporate taxpayer, Fender Sales, Inc., nor the individual stockholder-taxpayers, Donald D. and Jean Randall, and C. Leo and Esther Fender, liable for a deficiency of income taxes. . . .

The taxpayer Fender Sales, Inc. was incorporated in 1953 as a California corporation. It was authorized to issue 2,500 shares of common stock with a par value of $100 per share. At the commencement of the events material to this case, only 100 shares were outstanding, 50 of which were held by the taxpayer Donald D. Randall, and the other 50 by the taxpayer C. Leo Fender. Randall and Fender were also employees of Fender Sales and as such, were entitled to receive, as compensation for their services, $15,000 a year plus amounts equal to four percent and one percent, respectively, of annual sales. . . .

Although Fender Sales has always been financially solvent, from its inception it has been plagued by the shortage of cash. This financial predicament was brought about primarily because it had to pay for its purchases upon receipt of the merchandise while it was often required to finance the dealers who purchased merchandise from it. Accordingly, in 1955, Fender Sales found it necessary to seek bank financing. Originally the bank did not ask for security for its loan, but later it required the subordination of other liabilities and personal guarantees from the corporate officers. In addition it became concerned about accrued (but unpaid) officers' salary liabilities that appeared on Fender Sales' balance sheet; it felt that these liabilities could represent potential priority claims over the bank's claim. To remedy this, the bank suggested that these liabilities be capitalized.

In each case of its fiscal years ending May 31, 1954, 1955 and 1956, Fender Sales, which used the accrual method of accounting for federal income tax purposes, accrued $30,000 on its books of account as representing officers' salaries payable, but unpaid, in the amount of $15,000 a year each to Randall and Fender. In each of those years, Fender Sales deducted the $30,000 on its federal income tax return. Accordingly, as of August 6, 1956, Fender Sales owed Randall and Fender each $45,000 for salaries payable for the fiscal years ended May 31, 1954 through 1956.

On or about August 6, 1956, Randall and Fender, in order to comply with the bank's suggestion, offered to discharge Fender Sales' liability for salaries due and payable to them by accepting from Fender Sales an additional share of $100 par value common stock for each $100 of salary debt. On August 6, 1956, the board of directors of Fender Sales, consisting of Mr. and Mrs. Randall and Mr. and Mrs. Fender, resolved to accept the offers by Randall and Fender. After obtaining a permit from the Commissioner of Corporations of the State of California, Fender Sales, on December 3, 1956, issued to Randall and to Fender 450 shares each of its $100 par value common stock in discharge and cancellation of its indebtedness of $45,000 owing to each of them. As a result of this issuance of stock, Sales' capital stock account was increased from $10,000 to $100,000 and its $90,000 liability for salaries owed to Randall and Fender was discharged and cancelled.

[A similar transaction occurred discharging Sales' liability for salaries for the fiscal year ended May 27, 1957.]

On their federal income tax returns for the years 1956 and 1958, Fender and his wife did not report any amount as taxable income resulting from Fender's receipt of 450 shares of Fender Sales' stock on December 3, 1956, and 150 shares of Fender Sales' stock on May 9, 1958. On their federal income tax returns for the year 1956 and on their joint federal income tax returns for the year 1958, Randall and his wife did not report any amount as taxable income resulting from Randall's receipt of 450 shares of Fender Sales' stock on December 3, 1956, and 150 shares of Fender Sales' stock on May 9, 1958. On its corporate federal income tax returns for the fiscal years ended May 31, 1957 and May 31, 1958, Fender Sales did not report any amount as taxable income resulting from the discharge and cancellation on December 3, 1956 and May 9, 1958 of its indebtednesses for officers' salaries payable to Fender and Randall.

The Commissioner determined that the receipt of the stock constituted taxable salary income to Fender and Randall and, alternatively, that if it did not constitute taxable income to them, Fender Sales realized taxable income upon the cancellation of the salary indebtedness. The Tax Court held, however, that the cancellation of the indebtedness and issuance of the stock did not result in taxable income either to Fender and Randall or to Fender Sales. . . .

It is . . . conceded by respondents that the shares of Fender Sales, Inc. issued to each of the shareholders, Fender and Randall, had a fair market value of $100 per share (par value).

TAX LIABILITY OF FENDER AND RANDALL

Cases numbered 19075 to 19079, inclusive, present petitions by the Commissioner to review decisions by the Tax Court that the individuals, Donald D. Randall and his wife, Jean Randall, and C. Leo Fender and his wife, Esther Fender, incurred no income tax liability arising from the transactions related in the statement of facts. The complete rationale of the Tax Court decision is found in the following quotation:

> Fender and Randall were the sole shareholders of Sales regardless of whether they each owned 50 shares or 1,000 shares. Their wealth was no more increased by the issuance of additional shares than if the corporation had caused its stock to be split 20 for 1. The issuance of such additional shares to Fender and Randall did not constitute income to them within the meaning of the 16th Amendment to the Constitution regardless of whether it represented a stock dividend or represented compensation for services. Eisner v. Macomber [252 U.S. 189 . . .], supra. . . .

We disagree, and reverse the decision of the Tax Court in these cases.

The stockholder-employees received and accepted capital stock in discharge of the delinquent obligations of the corporation to them for salaries. If these were not equal stockholders to whom the corporation owed equal sums for unpaid salaries, there would be no semblance of a basis for dispute. The law and regulations plainly tax "all income from whatever source derived" (. . . §61), and provide: ". . . if a corporation transfers its own stock to an employee . . . as compensation for services, the fair market value of the stock at the time of transfer shall be included in the gross income of the employee." Regulations, §1.61-2(d)(4). Here the parties agree the fair market value of the stock of Fender Sales, Inc. equalled its par value, and the additional stock issued is, in any event, presumptively equal in value to the liquidated obligations discharged. Regulations, §1.61-2(d)[(1)].

Respondents say this case is different because the taxpayers were stockholders as well as employees and the equal (50-50) stock ownership by Fender and Randall remained equal after the additional stock was issued; and that they, therefore, "received nothing which they did not already possess, i.e., the entire capital stock of Fender Sales, Inc."

But the corporation was a substantially different corporation after the transactions than before. After the transactions on August 6, 1956, for example, the net worth of the company (excluding capital stock as a liability) was increased by $90,000, resulting from the cancellation of the accrued salary indebtedness. The fact is clear that the interests of Fender and Randall in Fender Sales, Inc. were substantially enhanced in value and that they did, in effect, receive something of value constituting taxable income under the Sixteenth Amendment to the Constitution. In this context, Eisner v. Macomber (1920), 252 U.S. 189, . . . is not even apposite, let alone controlling. True, a stock dividend is just a piece of paper and, when issued proportionately to all stockholders, represents nothing of value and does not result in the realization of taxable income. But this is only because the basic net worth of the corporation, excluding capital stock as a liability, has not been changed. The stockholders have retained an equal interest in the same investment. In our situation, the stockholders have retained an equal interest in a substantially different investment. The *Eisner* opinion was explicit in pointing out that a stock dividend is "paper certificates that evidence an *antecedent* increase in the value of the stockholder's capital interest" (not, as here, a contemporaneous quid pro quo increase thereof), and "merely bookkeeping that does not affect the aggregate assets of the corporation or its outstanding liabilities" (not, as here, a $90,000 reduction in debts of Fender Sales, Inc. in August, 1956). The obvious differences between the economic interests represented by an unsecured debt as compared with stock ownership need no elaboration.

We interpret Lidgewood Manufacturing Co. v. Commissioner (2 CCA 1956), 229 F.2d 241, as supporting our conclusions. In *Lidgewood*, the debts which were cancelled arose from loans, and if paid would not have represented taxable income to the stockholder. In that case, a sole stockholder cancelled debts, receiving capital stock in exchange, to enable the corporation to obtain bank loans. The debts cancelled were uncollectible and the stockholder-taxpayer claimed bad debt deductions on its income tax returns. The Court rejected the taxpayer's contention that nothing had been received by virtue of the issuance of the additional stock and, denying the bad debt deduction, said:

> The petitioner contends that since the debts were assumed to
> be uncollectible, the cancellation of worthless debts and the issu-
> ance of stock therefor were meaningless formalities. We disagree.

When a creditor cancels a debt in return for stock, he gives up the right to repayment, however prosperous the debtor may become, and he acquires a right to dividends from future prosperity. If he owns less than all of the debtor's stock, the issuance of additional shares increases his share of possible dividends. If, as here, the creditor owns all the debtor's stock, his share is not increased but he has retained his 100 percent right to future dividends, and, if the cancelled debts had any value whatever, to that extent he has increased his capital investment. It is not entirely clear what the Tax Court meant by its assumption that the debts were "uncollectible." Although the petitioner had contended that the subsidiaries were insolvent both before and after the cancellations, no finding of insolvency was made. But even on the assumption that the debtors were insolvent after as well as before the cancellations, wiping out the debts was a valuable contribution to the financial structure of the subsidiaries. It enabled them to obtain bank loans, to continue in business and subsequently to prosper.

Finally, Respondents say, in substance — break the transaction down to its component parts, none of them is a taxable event, therefore in the aggregate, they cannot generate a tax liability. The argument is: First, the receipt by equal stockholders of equal additional shares of capital stock, without more, is nontaxable; second, the forgiveness by a stockholder of the corporation's debt to him is, without more, a contribution to the capital of the corporation which is expressly excluded from the corporation's gross income. Therefore, a combination of the two cannot impose income tax liability on anyone. The answer is that the argument is a complete non-sequitur. The first statement deals with the tax liability of the individual stockholders and the second with the tax liability of the corporation.

To be persuasive with respect to the tax liability of the individual stockholders, Respondents' contentions should be: First, the acquisition of additional stock in equal proportionate shares is not a taxable event; second, the cancellation of a debt which, if collected, would represent taxable income is not a taxable event; therefore, the two in combination cannot generate tax liability. This Court does not accept the second premise. We are not prepared to hold that the voluntary surrender or forgiveness by a taxpayer of a receivable which, if collected, would represent taxable income, is, in all circumstances, a non-taxable event. We believe the authorities are opposed to such a conclusion.

In Helvering v. Horst, 1940, 311 U.S. 112, . . . the Supreme Court held that the income received on payment of coupons clipped from coupon bonds and given by a father to his son was taxable to the father, and said, in part:

Admittedly not all economic gain of the taxpayer is taxable income. From the beginning the revenue laws have been interpreted as defining "realization" of income as the taxable event rather than the acquisition of the right to receive it. And "realization" is not deemed to occur until the income is paid. But the decisions and regulations have consistently recognized that receipt in cash or property is not the only characteristic of realization of income to a taxpayer on the cash receipts basis. Where the taxpayer does not receive payment of income in money or property realization may occur when the last step is taken by which he obtains the fruition of the economic gain which has already accrued to him. Old Colony Trust Co. v. Commissioner, 279 U.S. 716 . . . ; Corliss v. Bowers, 281 U.S. 376, 378. . . . Cf. Burnet v. Wells, 289 U.S. 670. . . .

Underlying the reasoning in these cases is the thought that income is "realized" by the assignor because he, who owns or controls the source of the income, also controls the disposition of that which he could have received himself and diverts the payment from himself to others as the means of procuring the satisfaction of his wants. The taxpayer has equally enjoyed the fruits of his labor or investment and obtained the satisfaction of his desires whether he collects and uses the income to procure those satisfactions, or whether he disposes of his right to collect it as the means of procuring them. Cf. Burnet v. Wells, supra. . . .

The dominant purpose of the revenue laws is the taxation of income to those who earn or otherwise create the right to receive it and enjoy the benefit of it when paid. See Corliss v. Bower, supra. . . . The tax laid by the 1934 Revenue Act upon income "derived from . . . wages, or compensation for personal service, of whatever kind and in whatever form paid . . . ; also from interest . . ." therefore cannot fairly be interpreted as not applying to income derived from interest or compensation when he who is entitled to receive it makes use of his power to dispose of it in procuring satisfactions which he would otherwise procure only by the use of the money when received.

In *Lidgewood* (supra), the case in which the taxpayer sought a bad debt deduction in addition to the capital stock received for the cancelled obligation, the Court succinctly said: "If the debtor has received a contribution to capital, the creditor must have made the contribution. Consistency requires that both parties treat it alike."

In Helvering v. Horst, the coupons were actually paid in the year of the gift, and Respondents point to this as a distinguishing feature, claiming the salaries due from Fender Sales, Inc. were never "paid." But, in *Horst*, the Supreme Court relied on the broader concept of "realization of income" rather than a restricted notion of actual payment for its conclusions, and we think it necessary and logical, in the just administration of the tax laws, that the Courts continue to recognize that a taxpayer may realize the income represented by an account receivable by exercising his rights of control and disposition of it for his economic benefit in ways other than receipt of payment in money. In Commissioner of Internal Revenue v. Lester, 1961, 366 U.S. 299, 304, . . . the Supreme Court approvingly quoted from *Horst*:

"The power to dispose of income is the equivalent of ownership of it." We add, the exercise of the power to dispose of income is the equivalent of the realization of it. Fortunately, under the agreed facts of this case, we have no problem respecting the taxable value of the income thus realized and no problem respecting the tax year in which the income is reportable.

Randall and Fender, when they voluntarily elected to exercise their dominion and control over the choses in action against Fender Sales, Inc. for unpaid salaries by extinguishing them for the benefit of the corporation, of which they were sole owners, thereby augmenting the intrinsic worth of the capital stock they held, more surely "realized" for their own benefit the value of the obligations discharged than did Horst in his gift of interest coupons to his son.

In summary, we hold that the discharge by a corporation of its salary obligations to any employee (stockholder or not) by the issuance of the corporation's capital stock to the employee is a payment and realization of income by the employee in the amount of the fair market value of the stock. The transaction is controlled by Section 61 of the Internal Revenue Code and Section 1.61-2 of the Regulations. We disagree with the conclusions in Josephson v. Commission, 6 T.C.M. 788 and Daggit v. Commissioner, 23 T.C. 31, cited by Respondents.

The decisions of the Tax Court in cases numbered 19075 to 19079, inclusive, are reversed.

Tax Liability of Fender Sales, Inc.

Case No. 19074 presents a petition to review the determination by the Tax Court that the corporation, Fender Sales, Inc., incurred no income tax liability by reason of the related transactions.

Although the Commissioner argued for assessing tax liability against the corporation, this was only as an alternative should the individuals be held not liable. The Commissioner's brief states: "For the reasons already shown, we believe that Fender and Randall are taxable on the amounts of the accrued salaries and that Fender Sales is not. We do not contend that both are taxable on the same amounts." Whether viewed as payments for stock of the corporation or as the forgiveness by the shareholders of debts owed to them by the corporation, the transactions were nontaxable payments or contributions to capital from the point of view of the corporation's tax liability. . . . §118[(a)]; 1032(a); Reg. 1.10321; Reg. 1.61-12(a). . . .

The petition in Case No. 19074 should be dismissed.

BARNES, Circuit Judge (dissenting in part and concurring in part). I respectfully dissent. I would affirm the Tax Court in respect to the nonliability of the individual taxpayers, i.e., cases 19075 to 19079, inclusive.

I deduce the matter that concerns my brothers is the loophole in present laws which allows a corporation whose stock is owned equally by two principals to take deductions in certain years for accrued salaries payable, never incur actual expenses for such deductions, and then have the liabilities written off without any tax recognition because the item is treated as a capital contribution by the shareholders. If on a balancing of all factors, this method of corporate tax liability reduction is a loophole that should be plugged, then it should be done by legislative action, not by judicial fiat. The majority opinion seeks to remedy the supposed leak by attaching liability to the *individuals* involved by extending the dominion and control cases, represented by Helvering v. Horst, 311 U.S. 112 . . . (1940).

This majority opinion is the first I have encountered which recognizes a realization of income by shareholders upon an increase in corporate net worth, *where no dividend has been declared or capital gain yet realized* by the shareholders. Shareholders' interests in corporations change every day. The net worth of corporations is in a constant state of flux. Surely, when it increases, the shareholders are not *yet* deemed to have made a taxable gain. Rather the increase in corporate net worth is merely a paper increase of the shareholders' equity, not taxable until such time as the shareholders realize the increase by virtue of a dividend, or the sale or exchange of the security investment above cost. Then, and only then, have the courts traditionally recognized "a taxable event."

The use of the *Horst* line of cases as authority for recognizing the creation of a taxable event for the individuals in the case at bar is to me misleading. The evasionary device attacked in *Horst* and its progeny was different from the present situation. Those cases involved assignments of income rights to others prior to the point of realization of the income by the taxpayer himself. Such an anticipatory device by a taxpayer with complete control over the income was clearly a loophole in our tax laws that required plugging. Otherwise a taxpayer could assign his earnings directly to his creditors or family and claim there was never any income realization on his part. The case at bar does not involve a flagrant example of this potential loophole. The taxpayers here have no benefits *realized* by the issuance of additional stock for the cancellation of a corporate debt; their income has not been *diverted* to anyone else for their own personal benefit. They did not exert any power to dispose of their alleged "income" in a manner equivalent to ownership, and will not do so until the ordinary taxable event occurs — the sale of their stock.

The *Lidgewood* case, cited, is in my opinion not controlling on the facts of this case. In fact the opinion seems to overlook the corporate nature of the stockholder in that case. The bad debt deduction was disallowed the parent-stockholder, but the cancellation was treated not as income to the parent *or its creditor subsidiaries*; rather it was properly treated as a capital contribution. To the extent the *Lidgewood* case is relevant to the facts before us, it supports the conclusion that the taxpayers have not yet realized income by the receipt of additional shares of stock (while maintaining their identical proportional interests) for a debt cancellation.

> This court and others have held that cancellation of a debt owed by a corporate debtor to a stockholder of the debtor does not constitute taxable income to the debtor but is a capital contribution by the creditor. For many years the Treasury Regulations have so provided. . . . If the debtor has received a contribution to capital, the creditor must have made the contribution. Consistency requires that both parties treat it alike. *Whether the creditor's investment will result in profit or loss to the investor cannot be determined forthwith. Loss, if any is eventually realized, occurs when the investment is closed out; that is, when the shares of stock of the debtor are sold or become worthless.* (Emphasis supplied.) [Lidgewood Mfg. Co. v. Commissioner, 229 F.2d 241, at 242-243 (2d Cir. 1956).]

Another approach to the problem, which to me supports the decision of the Tax Court, is as follows:

The two equal owners of the corporation are cash basis taxpayers. They each work on behalf of the corporation for three years without drawing a salary. Thus each has no current employment income subject to tax. However, the full time services each renders to the corporation are of some value; and are here valued at $15,000 per year. These services have their effect on the corporate performance. Consequently, these gratuitous services result, at the end of three years, in a corporate net worth presumably $90,000 greater than it would have been without their services. If at any time one or both of the individual owners decides to sell his investment, he will be taxed in effect for his gratuitous services because the proceeds from any sale would presumably be $45,000 greater than they would have been had he not contributed his services. He has not taken advantage of any tax loophole that does not already exist. Rather, he has just chosen not to take a current salary which would be taxed at ordinary income rates, and has instead increased the value of his investment to be taxed at a subsequent time at capital gain rates. I contend that, from the individual's standpoint, this is exactly what has occurred in the case at bar.

As to the corporation tax liability (case No. 19074), I would affirm.

Under the Internal Revenue Code and regulations, the corporation did not realize income on account of its issuance of capital stock to Fender and Randall, and did not realize income on account of the cancellation of the salary indebtedness to Fender and Randall. From the point of view of the corporation, any consideration received by it upon an original issue of its corporate stock, whether more or less than the actual or the stated value thereof, is a receipt of capital, not income. Merten's "Law of Federal Income Taxation," Vol. 7, p. 67; I.R.C. 1032(a); Reg. 1.1032-1.

Also, should we treat the capital stock issued as valueless and view the transactions as the gratuitous forgiveness of the salary obligations of the corporation by the respective stockholder-employees, still the corporation would not thereby have realized taxable income. It is established both by regulation and court decision that the gratuitous forgiveness by a shareholder of a debt owed to him by the corporation represents a contribution to the capital of the corporation and is not taxable income. Regulation 1.61-12(a). . . . Under the Internal Revenue Code, a contribution to the capital of a corporate taxpayer is expressly excluded from the definition of reportable gross income. . . . §118. In this case, the corporate obligations which were cancelled were unpaid salary obligations to the shareholders which had been deducted as operating expenses by the corporate taxpayer in its annual accrual-accounting income tax returns and which, if paid, would have represented taxable income to the shareholder-employees. In dealing with a corporation's possible tax liability arising from the gratuitous forgiveness of a debt by a shareholder, the law makes no distinction on the basis of how the obligation arose, that is, whether or not it arose out of a transaction which had permitted the corporation, in an earlier tax year, to deduct the charge from reportable gross income, or whether or not the obligation, if paid, would have constituted reportable income to the shareholder-taxpayer. The forgiveness of the debt by the shareholder is, in either case, from the viewpoint of the corporate taxpayer, a contribution to capital, and not a taxable event. In Helvering v. American Dental Co., 318 U.S. 322 . . . (1943), the Supreme Court held the forgiveness of interest on notes and of rentals due by nonstockholder creditors to be gifts and capital contributions to a corporation, though "the motives leading to the cancellation were those of business or even selfish." Also, in Commissioner v. Auto Strop Safety Razor Co., 74 F.2d 226 (2d Cir. 1934), the court, under regulations like those now prevailing, held the voluntary cancellation by the sole stockholder of a subsidiary corporation of over two million dollars in debts, a portion of which represented expense items previously deducted, such as royalties and interest, to be a nontaxable contribution to the capital of the subsidiary corporation, and said: "When the indebtedness was canceled, whether or not it was a contribution to the capital of the debtor depends upon considerations entirely foreign to the question of the payment of income taxes in some previous year."

I believe a word or two of further explanation is required. The amounts now being treated as contributions to capital have previously been deducted by the corporation on its accrual-method tax returns. Had the individual taxpayers merely loaned money to the corporation and now cancelled the indebtedness, the cancellation would clearly be a contribution to capital, and such contribution should not be treated as taxable income to the corporation. However, the case at bar involves an indebtedness in the nature of accrued salaries which, unlike the hypothetical taxpayer loans, have once been deducted from income in prior years, consequently lessening the corporation's tax liability. Where sums have been deducted as expenses in previous years under an accrual method of accounting, and are now forgiven and are no longer corporate liabilities, the corporation ordinarily must add back the amount of the cancellation to its current income. If it need not, a flagrant loophole is created whereby expense deductions are taken without expenses ever being incurred or paid out. I refer to the language in Helvering v. Jane Holdin Corp., 109 F.2d 933 (8th Cir. 1940).

> The above cases recognize the principle that an obligation, once deducted but not paid, represents income when, because of subsequent circumstances, it is cancelled or it may be determined with reasonable certainty that it will never be enforced. None of the cases attach any importance to the means by which the cancellation is effected. That is immaterial, the controlling factors being the previous deductions offsetting income otherwise taxable and the subsequent release of the indebtedness before payment.
>
> The Trust filed all of its returns for prior years on the cash basis and never reported as taxable income the interest accrued and deducted by the Corporation. The Trust, through the trustees, has, at all times since its creation, been in a position to determine and dictate the policies of the Corporation. It has chosen to earmark the payments which it received from the Corporation as payments on account of principal and at the same time, throughout the entire period, these payments have been in effect deducted as interest accrued in the Corporation's returns. To now permit this accrued liability, after the forgiveness thereof, to be called surplus and addition to capital without taxing the income actually received by the Corporation would result in an unjustifiable avoidance of tax.

While I agree with Judge Thompson's ultimate conclusion that the company has not realized income by the cancellation of the accrued salaries obligation, I do believe to properly justify that conclusion requires same discussion of the conflicting line of cases dealing with shareholder cancellations of indebtedness where the indebtedness has previously been deducted by the corporation as an operating expense.

Regulation §1.61-12(a) addresses itself directly to the problem of the cancellation of an indebtedness by a shareholder of a corporation. *Generally*, it maintains that the gratuitous forgiveness of a debt constitutes a contribution to capital, the corporation thus realizing no income. The leading precedent for this line of reasoning is Helvering v. American Dental Co., supra. In that case, the Commissioner had increased the taxpayer's reported income by the sum of the items of the cancelled indebtedness which had served to offset income in like amounts in prior years. But the Supreme Court held that the gratuitous cancellation of rent and interest due should be deemed a gift and not income.

The leading precedent for the opposing point of view, recognizing income to the taxpayer relieved of an indebtedness, is the later case of Commissioner v. Jacobson, 336 U.S. 28 . . . (1949), which taxed the difference between the face amount of the taxpayer's personal indebtedness as the maker of secured bonds issued at face value, and a lesser amount paid by him for their repurchase. There was no evidence that there had been a transfer of something for nothing: the seller received the maximum price attainable.

Neither of these cases serves as exact precedent for the situation we have here; the cancellation of accrued salaries which have been deducted by the debtor-corporation in prior years. The leading exponents of the conflicting points of view in the accrued salary cases are Helvering v. Jane Holding Corp., supra, in favor of income recognition, and Carroll-McCreary Co. v. Commissioner, 124 F.2d 303 (2d. Cir. 1941), holding no realization of income from the gratuitous cancellation of debts for unpaid salaries owing to officer-shareholders. The *Jane* case preceded the decision in *American Dental Co.*, supra, and the trend of the case law since the latter decision has been to follow *Carroll-McCreary* and hold no income is recognized if there was no consideration given as inducement for the cancellation. The cases have interpreted "gratuitous" forgiveness of a debt as simply meaning that no consideration was paid by the corporation for release of the debt. The prior deduction of the debt as a corporate expense has been held immaterial to the question of whether a nontaxable capital contribution was effected by the debt release. . . .

In the absence of evidence of consideration passing from Fender Sales, Inc., to the individual shareholders for cancellation of the accrued salaries indebtedness, the above case law supports the conclusion that the corporation did not realize income by the release of the accrued salaries liability, though the corporation had already taken the amount as deduction for expense of doing business.

Any potential loophole that is created by attaching no tax liability to the individuals or the corporation is a product of the legislature's failure to compel the corporation to make an income recognition when their accrued deductions are cancelled. This is an error which the legislature should be called upon to reconsider. It should not be corrected by committing a second error in the present case to offset the first.

NOTES

1. Why was §267(a)(2) inapplicable to the deductions claimed by Fender Sales, Inc., for salaries accrued but unpaid? Note that §267(A) now refers to "personal service corporations." Thus, if the principal activity of the corporation "is the performance of personal services and such services are substantially performed by employee-owners," see §269A(b)(1), then the corporation may not deduct compensation payments made to an employee-owner who owns, actually or constructively, more than 10 percent of the corporation's stock, unless the employee-owner takes the compensation in income. See §§267(a) and 269A.

2. Does the *Fender Sales* majority or the dissent present the more persuasive case as to the taxability of the individuals? Is the majority's position consonant with the premise underlying §305? What would be the dissenting judge's position if the shareholders had had unequal share interests but the stock-for-salary distribution had been 50-50? What should it be? See the Commissioner's view in Rev. Rul. 67-402, 1967-2 C.B. 135.

3. If the dissenting judge is right in his position that the individuals had no income on the stock distribution, is he right that the termination of the corporate liability was a tax-free contribution to capital? In a tax sense, did the shareholders have "property" to contribute? How would you have decided the *Fender Sales* issue involving the corporate taxpayer? Why?

In Putoma Corp., 66 T.C. 652 (1976), *aff'd*, 601 F.2d 734 (5th Cir. 1979), a corporation's two equal shareholders, on the cash basis, canceled the corporation's accrued (and previously deducted) interest liability, receiving no stock in exchange. The court refused to find income to either the corporation or its shareholders. It distinguished *Fender Sales* on the ground that no stock had been issued, and in addition found on the facts before it that the shareholders had not exercised sufficient dominion and control over the interest obligation to justify taxing them on its receipt. Accord, as to the corporation's nonrecognition, Hartland Associates, 54 T.C. 1580 (1970), *nonacq.* 1976-2 C.B. 3; contra, Rev. Rul. 76-316, 1976-2 C.B. 22. Cf. Treas. Reg. §1.61-12(a). See also, as to the shareholders, Dwyer v. United States, 622 F.2d 460 (9th Cir. 1980) (taxing shareholder after distinguishing *Putoma*).

The 1980 Bankruptcy Tax Act overruled *Putoma* in §108(e)(6). See S. Rep. No. 1035, 96th Cong., 2d Sess. 1980-2 C.B. 620 (1980). Now, if no stock is issued in such a transaction, the corporation will be treated as having satisfied the indebtedness with an amount of money equal to the shareholder's adjusted basis in the indebtedness. Thus, in *Putoma*, where the cash method shareholders had an adjusted basis of zero in the indebtedness, the corporation would recognize cancellation of indebtedness income in the full amount of the debt (subject to reduction of tax attributes or election to decrease basis under §1017).

Suppose, however, that additional stock is issued for the amount of the cancelled debt, as in *Fender Sales*. When a corporation issues stock in cancellation of its indebtedness, §108(e)(10)(A) now provides that the corporation, if not insolvent and if not in certain bankruptcy proceedings, is treated as if it had satisfied the indebtedness with an amount of money equal to the fair market value of the stock.* Thus, the corporation will have discharge-of-indebtedness income to the extent the debt exceeds the value of the stock. It would seem that if shareholder-creditors in the *Fender Sales* situation forgave the debt and no stock were issued, under §108(e)(6) the corporation would have discharge of debt income. If stock equal in value to the debt were issued, then it would appear that under §108(e)(10)(A), the corporation would have no income, but the shareholders would — all as under the *Fender Sales* decision. Is this a wise outcome?

4. An employee of Corporation A is given an option to purchase 20 percent of the corporation's shares. Thereafter Corporation A and Corporation B agree to a plan of reorganization in which the shares of A will be exchanged for voting stock of B (a "B" reorganization). The employee transfers his option to purchase A stock to B in exchange for voting stock of B. Must the employee recognize income? If so, when? What other facts should you know? Compare LeVant v. Commissioner, 376 F.2d 434 (7th Cir. 1967).

5. Ordinarily, when employees are not the sole and equal shareholders, as they were in *Fender Sales*, it is not questioned that they have ordinary income on receipt of their employer's stock in compensation for their services. See §§61 and 83.

ALVES v. COMMISSIONER
734 F.2d 478 (9th Cir. 1984)

Before Kennedy, Schroeder, and Boochever, Circuit Judges.
SCHROEDER, Circuit Judge. . . .

---

*Prior to the passage of the Tax Reform Act of 1984, the "stock-for-debt" exception allowed a corporation to replace its debt with stock without recognizing any cancellation of indebtedness income.

Section 83 requires that an employee who has purchased restricted stock in connection with his "performance of services" must include as ordinary income the stock's appreciation in value between the time of purchase and the time the restrictions lapse, unless at the time he purchased the stock he elected to include as income the difference between the purchase price and the fair market value at that time. The issue here is whether section 83 applies to an employee's purchase of restricted stock when, according to the stipulation of the parties, the amount paid for the stock equaled its full fair market value, without regard to any restrictions. The Tax Court, with two dissenting opinions, held that section 83 applies to all restricted stock that is transferred "in connection with the performance of services," regardless of the amount paid for it. We affirm. . . .

Alves joined [General Digital Corporation] as vice-president for finance and administration. As part of an employment and stock purchase agreement dated May 22, 1970, the company agreed to sell Alves 40,000 shares of common stock at ten cents per share "in order to raise capital for the Company's initial operations while at the same time providing the Employee with an additional interest in the Company. . . ." 79 T.C. at 867. The six other named individuals signed similar agreements on the same day. The agreement divided Alves's shares into three categories: one-third were subject to repurchase by the company at ten cents per share if Alves left within four years; one-third were subject to repurchase if he left the company within five years; and one- third were unrestricted. In addition, the company retained an option to repurchase up to one-half of the shares for their fair market value at any time between July 1, 1973 and July 1, 1975.

In transactions not at issue here, Alves sold some of his shares to friends and relatives. In 1973 he sold 4,667 four-year shares to Technology Ventures, Inc. (TVI), the assignee of General Digital's repurchase option, for $18 per share, and in 1974 he sold TVI 2,240 five-year shares for $4 per share.[2]

On July 1, 1974, when the restrictions on the four-year shares lapsed, Alves still owned 4,667 four-year shares that had a fair market value at that time of $6 per share. On March 24, 1975, the restrictions on the 7,093 remaining five-year shares lapsed with the fair market value at $3.43 per share.

Although Alves reported the $8,736 of gain on the sale of the 2,240 five-year shares to TVI as ordinary income on his 1974 tax return, he did not report the difference between the fair market value of the four and five-year shares when the restrictions ended, and the purchase price paid for the shares. The Commissioner

2. No claim is made here with regard to any section 83 income Alves may have received during the 1973 tax year.

treated the difference as ordinary income in 1974 and 1975, pursuant to section 83(a).[3]

In proceedings before the Tax Court, the parties stipulated that: (1) General Digital's common stock had a fair market value of 10 cents per share on the date Alves entered into the employment and stock purchase agreement; (2) the stock restrictions were imposed to "provide some assurance that key personnel would remain with the company for a number of years"; (3) Alves did not make an election under section 83(b) when the restricted stock was received; (4) the free shares were not includable in gross income under section 83; and (5) the four and five-year restricted shares were subject to a substantial risk of forfeiture until July 1, 1974, and March 24, 1975, respectively.

The Tax Court sustained the Commissioner's deficiency determination. It found as a matter of fact that the stock was transferred to Alves in connection with the performance of services for the company, and, as a matter of law, that section 83(a) applies even where the transferee paid full fair market value for the stock.

Resolution of the legal issue presented here requires an understanding of section 83's background and operation. Congress enacted section 83 in 1969 in response to the existing disparity between the tax treatment of restricted stock plans and other types of deferred compensation arrangements. . . . Prior to 1969, an individual purchasing restricted stock was taxed either when the restrictions lapsed or when the stock was sold in an arm's length transaction. Tax was imposed upon the difference between the purchase price and the fair market value at the time of transfer or when the restrictions lapsed, whichever was less. See Cohn v. Commissioner, 73 T.C. 443, 446 (1979). This had both tax deferral and tax avoidance advantages over, for example, employer contributions to an employee's pension or profit sharing trust, which were immediately taxable in the year of receipt. . . .

Section 83 resolved this disparity by requiring the taxpayer either to elect to include the "excess" of the fair market value over the purchase price in the year the stock was transferred, or to be taxed upon the full amount of appreciation when the risk of forfeiture was removed. . . . By its terms, the statute applies when property is: (1) transferred in connection with the performance of services; (2) subject to a substantial risk of forfeiture; and (3) not disposed of in an arm's length transaction before the property becomes transferable or the risk of forfeiture is removed. In the present case, it is undisputed that the stock in question was subject to a substantial risk of

3. In his Tax Court petition, Alves claimed error in reporting as ordinary income the $8,736 gain on the 2,240 five-year shares sold to TVI in 1974. Our disposition here necessarily resolves that issue.

forfeiture, that it was not disposed of before the restrictions lapsed, and that Alves made no section 83(b) election. Alves's contention is that because he paid full fair market value for the shares, they were issued as an investment, rather than in connection with the performance of services.

The Tax Court concluded that Alves obtained the stock "in connection with the performance of services" as company vice-president. . . . Although payment of full fair market value may be one indication that stock was not transferred in connection with the performance of services, the record shows that until the company sold stock to TVI, it issued stock only to its officers, directors, and employees, with the exception of the shares sold to the underwriter. Alves purchased the stock when he signed his employment agreement and the stock restrictions were linked explicitly to his tenure with the company. In addition, the parties stipulated that the restricted stock's purpose was to ensure that key personnel would remain with the company. Nothing in the record suggests that Alves could have purchased the stock had he not agreed to join the company.

Alves maintains that, as a matter of law, section 83(a) should not extend to purchases for full fair market value. He argues that "in connection with" means that the employee is receiving compensation for his performance of services. In the unusual situation where the employee pays the same amount for restricted and unrestricted stock, the restriction has no effect on value, and hence, Alves contends, there is no compensation.

The plain language of section 83(a) belies Alves's argument. The statute applies to all property transferred in connection with the performance of services. No reference is made to the term "compensation." Nor is there any statutory requirement that property have a fair market value in excess of the amount paid at the time of transfer. Indeed, if Congress intended section 83(a) to apply solely to restricted stock used to compensate employees, it could have used much narrower language. Instead, Congress made section 83(a) applicable to all restricted "property," not just stock; to property transferred to "any person," not just to employees; and to property transferred "in connection with . . . services" not just compensation for employment. . . . As the Second Circuit has noted, Congress drafted section 83(a) as a "blanket rule" in an effort to create "a workable, practical system of taxing employees' restricted stock options." Sakol v. Commissioner, 574 F.2d 694, 699-700 (2d Cir.) *cert. denied,* 439 U.S. 859 . . . (1978).

Section 83's legislative history also reveals that while Congress was concerned primarily with the favorable tax treatment afforded restricted stock plans, it also was concerned that such plans were a means of allowing key employees to become shareholders in businesses without adhering to requirements in other sections of the Code. The Senate Report stated:

> To the extent that a restricted stock plan can be considered a means of giving employees a stake in the business, the committee believes the present tax treatment of these plans is inconsistent with the specific rules provided by Congress in the case of qualified stock options, which were considered by Congress as the appropriate means by which an employee could be given a shareholder's interest in the business. . . .

The legislative history reveals that Congress perceived restricted stock as more than a problem of deferred compensation. It also demonstrates that Congress intended section 83 to apply to taxpayers like Alves who allege that they purchased restricted stock as an investment.

Alves suggests that the language of section 83(b) indicates that Congress meant for that section to apply only to bargain purchases and that section 83(a) should be interpreted in the same way. Section 83(b) allows taxpayers to elect to include as income in the year of transfer "the excess" of the full fair market value over the purchase price. Alves contends that a taxpayer who pays full fair market value would have "zero excess," and would fall outside the terms of section 83(b).

Section 83(b), however, is not a limitation upon section 83(a). Congress designed section 83(b) merely to add "flexibility," not to condition section 83(a) on the presence or absence of an "excess." . . . Moreover, nothing in section 83(b) precludes a taxpayer who has paid full market value for restricted stock from making an 83(b) election. Treasury Regulations promulgated in 1978 and made retroactive to 1969 specifically provide that section 83(b) is available in situations of zero excess:

> If property is transferred . . . in connection with the performance of services, the person performing such services may elect to include in gross income under section 83(b) the excess (if any) of the fair market value of the property at the time of transfer . . . over the amount (if any) paid for such property. . . . *The fact that the transferee has paid full value for the property transferred, realizing no bargain element in the transaction, does not preclude the use of the election as provided for in this section.* . . .

§1.83.2(a) (1983) (emphasis supplied). These regulations are consistent with the broad language of section 83 and, as the Tax Court stated, simply make "more explicit a fact which is inherent in the statute itself." 79 T.C. at 877-78 n.7. . . .

Alves last contends that since every taxpayer who pays full fair market value for restricted stock would, if well informed, choose the section 83(b) election to hedge against any appreciation, applying section 83(a) to the unfortunate taxpayer who made no election is simply a trap for the unwary. The tax laws often make an affirmative election necessary. Section 83(b) is but one example of a provision requiring taxpayers to act or suffer less attractive tax consequences. A taxpayer wishing to avoid treatment of appreciation as ordinary income must make an affirmative election under 83(b) in the year the stock was acquired. . . .

The decision of the Tax Court is affirmed.

NOTES

1. In *Alves* the Ninth Circuit was no doubt influenced by the Treasury Regulations which, as the court pointed out, had been issued with retroactive effect. The Supreme Court has often called for substantial judicial deference to Treasury Regulations, but how faithful is the Supreme Court itself to its own utterances on that subject? See Wolfman, Foreword, Supreme Court Decisions in Taxation: 1980 Term, 35 Tax Law. 443 (1982).

2. Because Congress was concerned that the decision in *Alves* may have caused investors in start-up companies unfairly to lose capital gains treatment because of their failure to make timely §83(b) elections, the 1984 Act extended the time period in which to make an election for stock transfers occurring before the date of the Tax Court's decision in *Alves*. The legislation relieved the taxpayer in *Alves* itself as well as some others from the result in that case. See §556 of the TRA of 1984, Pub. L. No. 98-369, 98 Stat. 898.

3. See Maurice J. Cohn, 73 T.C. 443 (1979), where the Tax Court held that §83 applies to independent contractors, and not merely to employees, with respect to restricted shares received as compensation for services rendered.

4. In Commissioner v. LoBue, 351 U.S. 243 (1956), the Court held that employees exercising stock options granted by their employers realize ordinary income on the date of exercise as measured by the difference between the option price and the fair market value of the stock on the date of exercise. See Treas. Reg. §1.61-15. Sections 421-425 enacted special rules which mitigated the *LoBue* result, offering opportunities to defer the income until the stock was sold and to convert the income into long-term capital gain. The Tax Reform Act of 1976 repealed the favorable rules for "qualified stock options," delegating their tax consequences to §83. See H. R. Rep. No. 94-1515, 94th Cong., 2d Sess. 438-439 (1976); Treas. Reg. §§1.83-2(a), 1.83-3(a), and 1.83-7. A concomitant of the 1976 change was a business expense deduction for the employer equal to the amount

includible in the employee's income. The Economic Recovery Tax Act of 1981 (ERTA) reversed the direction taken in 1976, enacting §422A which provides for "incentive stock options." The report of the Senate Committee on Finance states:

> The committee believes that reinstitution of a stock option provision will provide an important incentive device for corporations to attract new management and retain the service of executives who might otherwise leave, by providing an opportunity to acquire an interest in the business. Encouraging the management of business to have a proprietary interest in its successful operation will provide an important incentive to expand and improve the profit position of the companies involved. The committee bill is designed to encourage the use of stock options for key employees without reinstituting the alleged abuses which arose with the restricted stock option provisions of prior law. . . .
>
> The bill provides for "incentive stock options," which will be taxed in a manner similar to the tax treatment previously applied to restricted and qualified stock options. That is, there will be no tax consequences when an incentive stock option is granted or when the option is exercised, and the employee will be taxed at capital gains rates when the stock received on exercise of the option is sold. Similarly, no business expense deduction will be allowed to the employer with respect to an incentive stock option.
>
> The term "incentive stock option" means an option granted to an individual, for any reason connected with his or her employment, by the employer corporation or by a parent or subsidiary corporation of the employer corporation, to purchase stock of any of such corporations. . . .
>
> To receive incentive stock option treatment, the bill provides that the employee must not dispose of the stock within two years after the option is granted, and must hold the stock itself for at least one year. If all requirements other than these holding period rules are met, the tax will be imposed on sale of the stock, but gain will be treated as ordinary income rather than capital gain, and the employer will be allowed a deduction at that time [limited to the spread between the sale price and option price]. . . .
>
> The difference between the option price and the fair market value of the stock at the exercise of the option will not be an item of tax preference. . . . [S. Rep. No. 97-144, 97th Cong., 1st Sess. 98-100.]

See Sobeloff, Payment of Compensation in the Form of Restricted Property — Problems of Employer and Employee — The Rules of New Code Section 83, 28 N.Y.U. Inst. Fed. Taxn. 1041 (1970).

Should compensation paid in the form of stock be treated differently from that paid in cash? Why?

738-3032

WOLFMAN

527-534   §368(a)(1)(E)
                    (F)
751-814   §1368-2(g)

5. Prior to the enactment of ERTA in 1981, if stock or other property received was not transferable or was subject to a substantial risk of forfeiture, taxation was generally postponed until the stock or the property was transferable or no longer subject to a substantial risk of forfeiture. In Horwith v. Commissioner, 71 T.C. 932 (1979), the Tax Court held that §16(b) of the Securities Exchange Act of 1934, under which an insider's profit may be recovered by a corporation if the stock is sold within six months of receipt, does not make the stock nontransferable and therefore does not affect the taxation of the stock. Thus, the value of the stock (less any amount paid) was treated as compensation when received. ERTA changed the law by adding §83(c)(3), which provides that stock received by a taxpayer that is subject to the application of §16(b) of the Securities Exchange Act of 1934 is treated as being nontransferable and subject to a substantial risk of forfeiture for the six-month period following receipt of the stock. Thus, at the expiration of the six-month period, the employee must include in income, and the employer may deduct, the difference between the value of the stock at that time and the amount paid (if any). Under §83(b), however, an employee may elect to include in income at the time of the transfer the excess of the value of the property at that time (determined without regard to the §16(b) restriction) over any amount paid.

III. RECAPITALIZATIONS AND CERTAIN INVESTOR EXCHANGES

A. RECAPITALIZATION — §§368(a)(1)(E), 354, 356

BAZLEY v. COMMISSIONER
331 U.S. 737 (1947)

Mr. Justice FRANKFURTER delivered the opinion of the Court. The proper construction of provisions of the Internal Revenue Code relating to corporate reorganizations is involved in [this case]. Their importance to the Treasury as well as to corporate enterprise led us to grant certiorari, . . . 329 U.S. 701. . . .

. . . [T]he Commissioner . . . assessed an income tax deficiency against the taxpayer for the year 1939. Its validity depends on the legal significance of the recapitalization in that year of a family corporation in which the taxpayer and his wife owned all but one of the Company's one thousand shares. These had a par value of $100. Under the plan of reorganization the taxpayer, his wife, and the holder of the additional share were to turn in their old shares and receive in exchange for each old share five new shares of no par value, but of a stated value of $60, and new debenture bonds, having a total face value of $400,000, payable in ten years but callable at any time. Accordingly, the taxpayer received 3,990 shares of the new stock for the 798 shares of his old holding and debentures in the amount of $319,200. At the time of these transactions the earned surplus of the corporation was $855,783.82.

The Commissioner charged to the taxpayer as income the full value of the debentures. The Tax Court affirmed the Commissioner's determination against the taxpayer's contention that as a "recapitalization" the transaction was a tax-free "reorganization" and that the debentures were "securities in a corporation a party to a reorganization," "exchanged solely for stock or securities in such corporation" "in pursuance of the plan of reorganization," and as such no gain is recognized for income tax purposes. . . . [Sections 368(a)(1)(E) and 354(a)(1)].* The Tax Court found that the recapitalization had "no legitimate corporate business purpose" and was therefore not a "reorganization" within the statute. The distribution of debentures, it concluded, was a disguised dividend, taxable as earned income under [§§61(a)(7), 301, and 302]. . . . The Circuit Court of Appeals for the Third Circuit, sitting en banc, affirmed, two judges dissenting. . . .

Unless a transaction is a reorganization contemplated by §[368], any exchange of "stock or securities" in connection with such transaction, cannot be "in pursuance of the plan of reorganization" under §[354(a)(1)]. While §[368(a)(1)] informs us that "reorganization" means, among other things, "a recapitalization," it does not inform us what "recapitalization" means. "Recapitalization" in connection with the income tax has been part of the revenue laws since 1921. . . . Congress has never defined it and the Treasury Regulations shed only limited light. Treas. Reg. [§1.368-2(e)]. One thing is certain. Congress did not incorporate some technical concept, whether that of accountants or of other specialists, into §[368] assuming that there is agreement among specialists as to the meaning of recapitalization. And so, recapitalization as used in §[368(a)(1)(E)] must draw its meaning from its function in that section. It is one of the forms of reorganization which obtains the privileges afforded by §[354(a)(1)]. Therefore, "recapitalization" must be construed with reference to the presuppositions and purpose of [the reorganization provisions]. It

---

*The 1939 Code under which this case was litigated had no counterparts to §§354(a)(2) and 356(d). — Ed.

was not the purpose of the reorganization provision to exempt from payment of a tax what as a practical matter is realized gain. Normally, a distribution by a corporation, whatever form it takes, is a definite and rather unambiguous event. It furnishes the proper occasion for the determination and taxation of gain. But there are circumstances where a formal distribution, directly or through exchange of securities, represents merely a new form of the previous participation in an enterprise, involving no change of substance in the rights and relations of the interested parties one to another or to the corporate assets. As to these, Congress has said that they are not to be deemed significant occasions for determining taxable gain.

These considerations underlie §[368] and they should dominate the scope to be given to the various sections, all of which converge toward a common purpose. Application of the language of such a revenue provision is not an exercise in framing abstract definitions. In a series of cases this Court has withheld the benefits of the reorganization provision in situations which might have satisfied provisions of the section treated as inert language because they were not reorganizations of the kind with which [the reorganization provisions], in [their] purpose and particulars, concern [themselves]. See Pinellas Ice & Cold Storage Co. v. Commissioner, 287 U.S. 462 [page 580 infra]; Gregory v. Helvering, 293 U.S. 465 [page 545 infra]; LeTulle v. Scofield, 308 U.S. 415 [page 589 infra].

Congress has not attempted a definition of what is recapitalization and we shall follow its example. The search for relevant meaning is often satisfied not by a futile attempt at abstract definition but by pricking a line through concrete applications. Meaning frequently is built up by assured recognition of what does not come within a concept the content of which is in controversy. Since a recapitalization within the scope of [the reorganization provisions] is an aspect of reorganization, nothing can be a recapitalization for this purpose unless it partakes of those characteristics of a reorganization which underlie the purpose of Congress in postponing the tax liability.

No doubt there was a recapitalization of the Bazley corporation in the sense that the symbols that represented its capital were changed, so that the fiscal basis of its operations would appear very differently on its books. But the form of a transaction as reflected by the correct corporate accounting opens questions as to the proper application of a taxing statute; it does not close them. Corporate accounting may represent that correspondence between change in the form of capital structure and essential identity in fact which is of the essence of a transaction relieved from taxation as a reorganization. What is controlling is that a new arrangement intrinsically partake of the elements of reorganization which underlie the congressional exemption and not merely give the appearance of it to accomplish a distribution of earnings. In the case of a corporation which has undistributed earnings, the creation of new corporate obligations which are transferred to stockholders in relation to their former holdings, so as to produce, for all practical purposes, the same result as a distribution of cash earnings of equivalent value, cannot obtain tax immunity because cast in the form of a recapitalization-reorganization. The governing legal rule can hardly be stated more narrowly. To attempt to do so would only challenge astuteness in evading it. And so it is hard to escape the conclusion that whether in a particular case a paper recapitalization is no more than an admissible attempt to avoid the consequences of an outright distribution of earnings turns on details of corporate affairs, judgment on which must be left to the Tax Court. See Dobson v. Commissioner, 320 U.S. 489.

What have we here? No doubt, if the Bazley corporation had issued the debentures to Bazley and his wife without any recapitalization, it would have made a taxable distribution. Instead, these debentures were issued as part of a family arrangement, the only additional ingredient being an unrelated modification of the capital account. The debentures were found to be worth at least their principal amount, and they were virtually cash because they were callable at the will of the corporation which in this case was the will of the taxpayer. One does not have to pursue the motives behind actions, even in the more ascertainable forms of purpose, to find, as did the Tax Court, that the whole arrangement took this form instead of an outright distribution of cash or debentures, because the latter would undoubtedly have been taxable income whereas what was done could, with a show of reason, claim the shelter of the immunity of a recapitalization-reorganization.

The Commissioner, the Tax Court and the Circuit Court of Appeals agree that nothing was accomplished that would not have been accomplished by an outright debenture dividend. And since we find no misconception of law on the part of the Tax Court and the Circuit Court of Appeals, whatever may have been their choice of phrasing, their application of the law to the facts of this case must stand. A "reorganization" which is merely a vehicle, however elaborate or elegant, for conveying earnings from accumulations to the stockholders is not a reorganization under [the reorganization provisions]. This disposes of the case as a matter of law, since the facts as found by the Tax Court bring them within it. And even if this transaction were deemed a reorganization, the facts would equally sustain the imposition of the tax on the debentures under §[356(a)(1) and (2)]. Commissioner v. Estate of Bedford, 325 U.S. 283. . . .

. . . [A]ffirmed.

Mr. Justice Douglas and Mr. Justice Burton dissent . . . for the reasons stated in the joint dissent of Judges Maris and Goodrich in the court below. Bazley v. Commissioner, 155 F.2d 237, 244.

NOTES

1. Does *Bazley* hold that a distribution of securities is always to be treated as a distribution of cash? A number of subsequent decisions under the 1939 Code allowed reorganization treatment for some exchanges in which bonds were issued in exchange for some of the issuing corporation's outstanding stock. See B. Bittker and J. Eustice, Federal Income Taxation of Corporations and Shareholders 14-89 to 14-92 (5th ed. 1987). The 1939 Code did not contain provisions corresponding to §§354(a)(2) and 356(d), which were added in 1954. The latter was said to be "a restatement of the principle stated by the Supreme Court in *Bazley*." S. Rep. No. 1622, 83d Cong., 2d Sess., 3 U.S. Code Cong. & Admin. News 4907 (1954). Do you agree with that statement? In any event, the 1954 changes greatly reduced the incentive for taxpayers to characterize stock-for-bond exchanges as reorganizations.

The Commissioner was soon on the other side of the fence, arguing that a distribution of bonds in exchange for stock of lesser value was a reorganization and therefore could not give rise to original issue discount, described in what is now §§1271-1275, which would be deductible over the life of the bond by the corporation under Treas. Reg. §§1.163-3, 1.163-4. In Commissioner v. National Alfalfa Dehydrating & Milling Co., 417 U.S. 134 (1974), the Court held that no discount was created when the taxpayer issued $50 bonds in exchange for shares of $50 preferred stock, in part because it incurred no additional cost of capital. Subsequent cases have allowed the discount where the face value of newly issued bonds exceeded the face value or issue price (as well as the fair market value) of stock surrendered in exchange therefor. See Gulf, Mobile & Ohio R.R. v. United States, 579 F.2d 892 (5th Cir. 1978); Cities Serv. Co. v. United States, 522 F.2d 1281 (2d Cir. 1974), *cert. denied*, 423 U.S. 827 (1975). A 1969 amendment, however, explicitly excluded securities distributed in reorganizations from original issue discount treatment. And in Microdot, Inc. v. United States, 728 F.2d 593 (2d Cir. 1984), the Court held that under the 1969 amendment to the original issue discount rules, a transaction in which a corporation exchanged debentures for approximately 10 percent of its outstanding common stock was a "recapitalization," and thus the debentures did not have deductible original issue discount, even though the shareholders were taxed on the exchange.

The 1984 Act significantly revised and expanded the scope of the original issue discount provisions to cover a wider range of transactions including reorganization exchanges. If either the debt instrument or the stock or securities for which it is exchanged is publicly traded, the amount of original issue discount is generally determined by reference to the market value of the traded position. If neither is traded the issue price of the new bonds is determined by their discounted present value using the "applicable federal rate." See §§1271-1275, esp. §1275(a)(4), replacing §§1232 and 1232A. See also §§1276-1278 as to so-called market discount bonds.

2. The stock received in a recapitalization may be §306 stock or may give rise to §305(b) problems. Consider G.C.M. 39088, in which the Treasury Department concluded that §305(b)(3) did not apply to a transaction in which some common shareholders exchanged their shares for an equal number of new common shares plus nonvoting nonconvertible preferred stock while other shareholders received shares of the same class of new common plus shares of nonvoting common. Such a transaction was found to be an "E" reorganization and not a §305(b)(3) distribution, on the assumption that it had a bona fide business purpose, was an isolated transaction, and was not "part of a plan to increase periodically the proportionate interest of any shareholder in the assets or earnings and profits of the corporation." In the fact pattern described in the memorandum, the transaction was designed as a one-time event to shift permanently the future equity growth of a family-owned corporation from an older generation of shareholders to a younger generation. Cf. Note 4, page 473 supra; Rodewald and Cohen, Preferred Stock Recapitalizations: A Basic Look at Some Tax Problems, 17 Duq. L. Rev. 785 (1979).

B.   EXERCISE OF CONVERSION PRIVILEGES

In Rev. Rul. 57-535, 1957-2 C.B. 513, the Commissioner ruled that there is no realization in a transaction in which a security, convertible by its terms, is converted into another. The transaction is treated as a transformation, not an "exchange" or "disposition." Since no "closed transaction" has occurred, there is no "realization"; and so no nonrecognition provision, such as §354 or §1031 or §1036 (see page 534 infra), is needed to defer taxation. See Treas. Reg. §1.1001-1(a).

Compare Rev. Rul. 72-265, 1972-1 C.B. 222 (conversion of debenture into stock of same corporation is not a taxable event) and

Rev. Rul. 79-155, 1979-1 C.B. 153 (conversion of debenture into stock of a different corporation that was also an obligor on the debenture not a taxable event), *with* Rev. Rul. 72-264, 1972-1 C.B. 131 (result where debenture is an "installment obligation" under §453) and Rev. Rul. 69-135, 1969-1 C.B. 198 (conversion of debenture into stock of a different corporation that is not liable for the debenture is a taxable event).

When is (or is not) a conversion of one security into another a part of a recapitalization? See Rev. Rul. 77-238, 1977-2 C.B. 115 (provisions in articles of incorporation to require or encourage conversions are plans of reorganizations, and conversions are exchanges pursuant to plan).

C. DEBT REFUNDING

The exchange of bonds for other bonds of the same issuer that differ only in immaterial details (e.g., extended maturity) does not produce a "realization." Such "refunding" does not constitute an "exchange" or "other disposition." See West Missouri Power Co., 18 T.C. 105 (1952), *acq.* 1952-2 C.B. 3. But see Rev. Rul. 81-169 1981-1 C.B. 469; Treas. Reg. §1.1001-1(a). Cf. Rev. Rul. 77-437, 1977-2 C.B. 28, holding that a corporation that refunded an outstanding bond issue by replacing the outstanding bonds with new bonds of lesser face amount (but of equal or greater market value) realized income from discharge of indebtedness even though the refunding was a recapitalization. In Rev. Rul. 89-122, 1989-47 I.R.B. 6, the Service ruled that debt restructuring under which, in one case, the interest rate was reduced substantially and in another, the interest rate remained the same, but the principal was reduced, constituted a material modification, triggering realization under §1001 on a deemed exchange of old debt for new. The issue price of the modified instruments were determined under §1274.

In Letter Rul. 8815003 (Dec. 11, 1987), the IRS granted "E" reorganization treatment to a transaction in which, pursuant to an agreement with the reorganizing corporation, an underwriter purchased the corporation's outstanding bonds at a discount and then surrendered them to the corporation in exchange for new bonds yielding a lower rate of interest.

What distinguishes a "refunding" or "conversion" from a "sale," "exchange," or "other disposition"? What should the law be?

See Hariton, Recapitalizations: The Issuer's Treatment, 40 Tax Law. 873 (1987)

D. EXCHANGE OF INVESTOR INTEREST

1. *For Assets — §1031*

Normally, an investor who exchanges his appreciated (or depreciated) corporate stock or debt for assets has recognized gain (or loss), although a few provisions (e.g., §§267, 1091) provide for nonrecognition of loss. Why is §1031, a nonrecognition provision applicable to the exchange of business and investment assets, made expressly inapplicable to an exchange involving stock or securities? See §1031(a)(2)(B).

2. *For Stock or Securities — §§1031, 1036*

Section 1036 provides for nonrecognition (and §1031(d) for carryover of basis) where common stock is exchanged for common stock in the same corporation and where preferred stock is exchanged for preferred stock in the same corporation. Note that a "reorganization" is not a prerequisite for this provision to operate, as it is for §354.

Why is §1036 in the Code? Why is it limited to stock "in the same corporation"? Why does it not cover an exchange of common for preferred (or vice versa) in the same corporation? Does §1036 cover an exchange between investors only? Between an investor and his corporation only? Among investors as well as between the investor and his corporation? See Treas. Reg. §1.1036-1.

Is §1036 applicable to an exchange of Class A (voting) common stock for Class B (nonvoting) common stock in the same corporation? Is it applicable to an exchange of a 6-percent, participating, cumulative, nonvoting preferred stock for an 8-percent, nonparticipating, noncumulative, voting preferred stock in the same corporation?

IV. *THE STATUTE IN PERSPECTIVE*

A. BEFORE SPECIAL TREATMENT

MARR v. UNITED STATES
268 U.S. 536 (1925)

Mr. Justice BRANDEIS delivered the opinion of the Court. Prior to March 1, 1913, Marr and wife purchased 339 shares of the preferred and 425 shares of the common stock of the General Motors Company of New Jersey for $76,400. In 1916, they received in exchange for this stock 451 shares of the preferred and 2,125 shares of the common stock of the General Motors Corporation of Delaware which (including a small cash payment) had the aggregate market value of $400,866.57. The difference between the cost of their stock in the New Jersey corporation and the value of the stock in the Delaware corporation was $324,466.57. The Treasury Department ruled that this difference was gain or income under the Act of September 8, 1916, c. 463, Title I, §§1 and 2 . . . ;* and assessed, on that account, an additional income tax for 1916 which amounted, with interest, to $24,944.12. That sum Marr paid under protest. He then appealed to the Commissioner of Internal Revenue by filing a claim for a refund; and, upon the disallowance of that claim, brought this suit in the Court of Claims to recover the amount. Judgment was entered for the United States. . . .

The exchange of securities was effected in this way. The New Jersey corporation had outstanding $15,000,000 of 7 percent preferred stock and $15,000,000 of the common stock, all shares being of the par value of $100. It had accumulated from profits a large surplus. The actual value of the common stock was then $842.50 a share. Its officers caused to be organized the Delaware corporation, with an authorized capital of $20,000,000 in 6 percent non-voting preferred stock and $82,600,000 in common stock, all shares being of the par value of $100. The Delaware corporation made to stockholders in the New Jersey corporation the following offer for exchange of securities: For every share of common stock of the New Jersey corporation, five shares of common stock of the Delaware corporation. For every share of the preferred stock of the New Jersey corporation, one and one-third shares of preferred stock of the Delaware corporation. In lieu of a certificate for fractional shares of stock in the Delaware corporation payment was to be made in cash at the rate of $100 a share for its preferred and at the rate of $150 a share for its common stock. On this basis all the common stock of the New Jersey corporation was exchanged and all the preferred stock except a few shares. These few were redeemed in cash. For acquiring the stock of the New Jersey corporation only $75,000,000 of the common stock of the Delaware corporation was needed. The remaining $7,600,000 of the authorized common stock was either sold or held for sale as additional capital should be desired. The Delaware corporation, having thus become the owner of all the out-

*Section 61(a) of the 1986 Code. — ED.

standing stock of the New Jersey corporation, took a transfer of its assets and assumed its liabilities. The latter was then dissolved.

It is clear that all new securities issued in excess of an amount equal to the capitalization of the New Jersey corporation represented income earned by it; that the new securities received by the Marrs in excess of the cost of the securities of the New Jersey corporation theretofore held were financially the equivalent of $324,466.57 in cash; and that Congress intended to tax as income of stockholders such gains when so distributed. The serious question for decision is whether it had power to do so. Marr contends that, since the new corporation was organized to take over the assets and continue the business of the old, and his capital remained invested in the same business enterprise, the additional securities distributed were in legal effect a stock dividend; and that under the rule of Eisner v. Macomber [page 431 supra], applied in Weiss v. Stearn, 265 U.S. 242, he was not taxable thereon as income, because he still held the whole investment. The Government insists that identity of the business enterprise is not conclusive; that gain in value resulting from profits is taxable as income, not only when it is represented by an interest in a different business enterprise or property, but also when it is represented by an essentially different interest in the same business enterprise or property; that, in the case at bar, the gain actually made is represented by securities with essentially different characteristics in an essentially different corporation; and that, consequently, the additional value of the new securities, although they are still held by the Marrs, is income under the rule applied in United States v. Phellis, 257 U.S. 156; Rockefeller v. United States, 257 U.S. 176; and Cullinan v. Walker, 262 U.S. 134. In our opinion the Government is right.

In each of the five cases named, as in the case at bar, the business enterprise actually conducted remained exactly the same. In United States v. Phellis, in Rockefeller v. United States and in Cullinan v. Walker, where the additional value in new securities distributed was held to be taxable as income, there had been changes of corporate identity. That is, the corporate property, or a part thereof, was no longer held and operated by the same corporation; and, after the distribution, the stockholders no longer owned merely the same proportional interest of the same character in the same corporation. In Eisner v. Macomber and in Weiss v. Stearn, where the additional value in new securities was held not to be taxable, the identity was deemed to have been preserved. In Eisner v. Macomber the identity was literally maintained. There was no new corporate entity. The same interest in the same corporation was represented after the distribution by more shares of precisely the same character. It was as if the par value of the stock had been reduced, and three shares of reduced par value stock had been issued in place of every two old shares. That is, there was an exchange of certificates but not of interests. In Weiss v. Stearn a new corporation had, in fact, been organized to take over the assets and business of the old. Technically there was a new entity; but the corporate identity was deemed to have been substantially maintained because the new corporation was organized under the laws of the same State, with presumably the same powers as the old. There was also no change in the character of securities issued. By reason of these facts, the proportional interest of the stockholder after the distribution of the new securities was deemed to be exactly the same as if the par value of the stock in the . old corporation had been reduced, and five shares of reduced par value stock had been issued in place of every two shares of the old stock. Thus, in Weiss v. Stearn, as in Eisner v. Macomber, the transaction was considered, in essence, an exchange of certificates representing the same interest, not an exchange of interests.

In the case at bar, the new corporation is essentially different from the old. A corporation organized under the laws of Delaware does not have the same rights and powers as one organized under the laws of New Jersey. Because of these inherent differences in rights and powers, both the preferred and the common stock of the old corporation is an essentially different thing from stock of the same general kind in the new. But there are also adventitious differences, substantial in character. A 6 percent, non-voting preferred stock is an essentially different thing from a 7 percent, voting preferred stock. A common stock subject to the priority of $20,000,000 preferred and a $1,200,000 annual dividend charge is an essentially different thing from a common stock subject only to $15,000,000 preferred and a $1,050,000 annual dividend charge. The case at bar is not one in which after the distribution the stockholders have the same proportional interest of the same kind in essentially the same corporation.

Affirmed.

The separate opinion of Mr. Justice VAN DEVANTER, Mr. Justice McREYNOLDS, Mr. Justice SUTHERLAND and Mr. Justice BUTLER. We think this cause falls within the doctrine of Weiss v. Stearn, 265 U.S. 242, and that the judgment below should be reversed. The practical result of the things done was but the reorganization of a going concern. The business and assets were not materially changed, and the stockholder received nothing actually severed from his original capital interest — nothing differing in substance from what he already had.

Weiss v. Stearn did not turn upon the relatively unimportant circumstance that the new and old corporations were organized under the laws of the same State, but upon the approved definition of income from capital as something severed therefrom and received by the taxpayer for his separate use and benefit. Here stockholders got nothing from the old business or assets except new statements of their undivided interests, and this, as we carefully pointed out, is not enough to create taxable income.

B. SINCE SPECIAL TREATMENT

1. Statutory "Close-Order Drill" — §§368, 354, 355, 356, 357, 358, 361, 362, 332, 334

Before studying the overlay of judicial doctrines that have developed in connection with reorganizations, it will be useful to gain familiarity with the pattern and interrelationship of the relevant sections of the 1986 Code. When you examine the reorganization provisions of the Code, consider which, if any, of the current reorganization definitions might cover the transaction in *Marr*.

a. Start with §368(a). It *defines* the various reorganizations. It is not a section that fixes tax consequences or determines recognition. Subsection (a)(1) lists and defines seven types of "reorganization," from (A) to (G). Tax lawyers, familiar with the definitions, use a shorthand reference system in identifying a particular type of reorganization. They refer to an "A reorganization," or just an "A," if they mean one defined in §368(a)(1)(A), and to a "B," if they mean one defined in §368(a)(1)(B), and so forth. This book will use that shorthand.

(i) An "A" reorganization is a statutory merger or consolidation of two or more corporations. By "statutory" the Code means a merger or consolidation effected pursuant to state or federal statutory law.

(ii) A "B" reorganization contemplates one corporation's acquisition, in exchange solely for a portion of its voting stock, of "control" of another corporation. When the reorganization is completed the acquiring corporation will be the parent and the acquired corporation will be a subsidiary (although not necessarily a 100-percent owned subsidiary). The former shareholders of the subsidiary corporation will now own voting shares in the parent.

(iii) A "C" reorganization is sometimes referred to as a "de facto" merger, in contrast with the "de jure" merger embraced in the "A" reorganization. In general, a "C" reorganization contemplates one corporation's transfer of "substantially all of its properties" to another corporation in exchange solely for voting stock of the latter, although §368(a)(2)(B) does mitigate this requirement somewhat. Under §368(a)(2)(G), added in 1984, the transferor corporation in a "C" reorganization must, as a general matter, completely liquidate, i.e., distribute to its shareholders pursuant to the plan of reorganization the stock, securities, and other property it receives, as well as any other properties not transferred in the reorganization. The latter requirement may be waived by the Service.

(iv) A "D" reorganization requires the transfer of a portion of one corporation's assets to another in circumstances in which the transferor or its shareholders are immediately thereafter "in control" of the transferee corporation. Ordinarily, the transferee issues stock to the transferor, and the transferor then liquidates, distributing to its shareholders the stock received from the transferee corporation. The last clause of §368(a)(1)(D) requires a distribution that meets particular statutory patterns. Essentially, a "D" contemplates the division of one corporation into two or more or the substitution of one for another, in either case with substantial continuity of control.

(v) An "E" reorganization is a "recapitalization," studied earlier in this chapter, page 527 supra.

(vi) An "F" reorganization, at least on its face, involves very little, a "mere change in identity, form or place of organization."

(vii) A "G" reorganization requires the transfer of "all or part" of a corporation's assets to a second corporation in a bankruptcy proceeding, as further defined, followed by a distribution of the transferee's stock in a transaction that conforms to specified statutory provisions. See Asofsky, Reorganizing Insolvent Corporations, 41 N.Y.U. Inst. Fed. Taxn. 5 (1983); Henderson and Goldring, Failing and Failed Businesses (CCH Tax Trans. Lib.).

b. Section 368(a)(2) sets forth modifications and amplifications of the sometimes stark and restrictive definitional rules in §368(a). Read the section carefully. Its full impact will become clearer as you work through the development of the case law. Two provisions of §368(a)(2) are particularly worthy of mention at this point.

(i) An "(a)(2)(D)" or "forward triangular subsidiary merger" under §368(a)(2)(D) involves the statutory merger of a target corporation into a subsidiary of the acquiring corporation, with the target's shareholders receiving stock of the corporation that controls the subsidiary. For the transaction to qualify, the surviving corporation (the controlled subsidiary) must receive "substantially all" the assets of the target, and no stock of the controlled subsidiary may be used in the transaction. Moreover, the transaction must meet all of the requirements (like the continuity of interest requirement, see page 568 infra) that would have been applicable if the merger had been into the corporation controlling the subsidiary.

(ii) An "(a)(2)(E)" or "reverse triangular subsidiary merger" under §368(a)(2)(E) involves the statutory merger of the acquiring corporation's controlled subsidiary into the target corporation, with the target surviving. The shareholders of the target must receive only voting stock of the corporation controlling the subsidiary for an amount of the target's stock that constitutes "control" of the target, as defined in §368(c)(1). After the transaction, the target must hold "substantially all" of its own assets and those of the controlled subsidiary. See Beller, Final Regulations Ease Planning for Tax-Free Reverse Subsidiary Mergers, 64 J. Taxn. 80 (1986).

c. The provisions that determine the tax consequences of "reorganization" refer to those who are "a party to a reorganization." Section 368(b) defines a "party." It will become clearer in significance as you study the case law, but it is important now to keep in mind the necessity of determining who is a "party."

d. "Control" is a frequent requirement for particular tax consequences in reorganizations. For most cases, it is defined in §368(c), as it was for purposes of §351, as 80 percent of the combined voting power of all voting classes of stock and 80 percent of the shares of each remaining class. See Rev. Rul. 59-259, 1959-2 C.B. 115. For "D" reorganizations, however, "control" is defined as it is in §304(c), i.e., the ownership of stock possessing at least 50 percent of the total combined voting power of all classes of stock entitled to vote, or at least 50 percent of the total value of all shares of all classes of stock (see §368(a)(2)(H)). The constructive ownership rules of §318(a), as modified by §304(c)(3)(B), apply for purposes of determining whether this control requirement is met.

e. With the definitions of §368 in mind, move to §354(a)(1), a section that provides tax consequences for corporate investors who exchange "stock or securities in a corporation a party to a reorganization . . . in pursuance of the plan of reorganization. . . ." Note the reference to "reorganization," defined in §368(a)(1), and to "a party," defined in §368(b). Note, too, the requirement for a "plan," a term not defined by statute, and for "stock or securities," similarly undefined. Since the term "securities" presumably means something other than "stock," it is taken to mean corporate debt, but not all corporate debt. Case and administrative law flesh out the meaning, somewhat painstakingly, somewhat irritatingly. Cf. Note 3, page 381 supra.

If §354(a)(1) is applicable, the investor's gain or loss is not recognized. If §354(a)(1) does not apply because the consideration received by the investor is not exclusively stock or securities, or because the securities received are as described in §354(a)(2)(A), §354(a)(3)(A) remits the taxpayer to §356. Section 356(a) describes the tax treatment when "boot" is received, taxing the gain to the extent of the "boot" as capital gain if §356(a)(1) applies, and as a dividend if §356(a)(2) applies. Despite the presence of "boot," loss is not recognized. §356(c). Section 354(a)(2)(B) denies nonrecognition to the receipt of both stock and securities if attributable to accrued interest owed to the investor under certain circumstances.

f. If §354 or §356 applies to the investor transaction, his basis for the consideration received on the exchange is determined under §358, much as it is in the case of an investor in a §351 transaction.

g. Section 355 is applicable to corporate proliferations — spin-offs, split-offs, split-ups, and spin-aways. It is not dependent on a "reorganization," defined in §368(a)(1), but frequently operates on a "D" reorganization. Look at the provisions of §355 now, and the accompanying "boot" provisions in §356(b), but their full impact must await the material that begins on page 680 infra. Mark for inquiry later the fact that the "boot" taxable under §356(a) is limited to "gain." No such limitation encumbers §356(b).

h. Corporations are transferors of assets in "A," "C," "D," "F," and "G" reorganizations. Recognition of their gain or loss is determined by §361. Note the special "boot" provision in §361(b), applicable if property not permitted by §361(a) is received. It works quite differently from §356, the "boot" provision applicable to investors. Section 357 determines the tax effect of a transfer of indebtedness.

The transferor corporation's basis for the consideration (usually stock or securities) it receives for its assets is determined under §358, the section generally applicable to investors receiving stock or securities in a reorganization exchange.

i. The corporate transferee in an "A," "C," "D," "F," or "G" reorganization has no gain or loss on the issuance of its stock. See §1032. Its basis for the assets received is determined under §362(b). Section 362(b) also determines the basis to the acquiring corporation of the stock it acquires in a "B" reorganization in exchange for its own voting stock.

j. An intercorporate liquidation (subsidiary into parent) is not technically a "reorganization" as defined in §368(a)(1). Such a liquidation, if covered by §332, results in the nonrecognition of the parent's gain or loss in its stock investment. Section 332 is studied together with reorganizations because the effect of an intercorporate liquidation is substantially the same as a merger, and sometimes such a liquidation can be effected as an "A" reorganization. If §332 provides nonrecognition for the parent's gain or loss, the assets the parent receives from the subsidiary will take their basis under §334(b)(1). Section 337(a) bars recognition of gain or loss to an 80-percent-or-more-owned subsidiary with respect to assets distributed to its parent in a complete liquidation. Section 337(b) does the same with respect to the appreciation in the subsidiary's assets distributed to its parent in satisfaction of indebtedness.

The foregoing general summary of the Code provisions applicable to corporate reorganization is only that. It is no substitute for detailed analysis, close reading of the relevant Regulations, and an understanding of how the law came to be (and what it may become), which your study of the case law may help to provide. As you deal with specific and seemingly narrow statutory issues, take the time necessary to reflect and to consider the general perspective in which courts view reorganizations.

2. Business Purpose

HELVERING v. GREGORY
69 F.2d 809 (2d Cir. 1934), aff'd, 293 U.S. 465 (1935)*

Before L. Hand, Swan, and Augustus N. Hand, Circuit Judges.

L. HAND, Circuit Judge. This is an appeal (petition to review), by the Commissioner of Internal Revenue from an order of the Board of Tax Appeals expunging a deficiency in income taxes for the year 1928. The facts were as follows: The taxpayer owned all the shares of the United Mortgage Corporation, among whose assets were some of the shares of another company, the Monitor Securities Corporation. In 1928 it became possible to sell the Monitor shares at a large profit, but if this had been done directly, the United Mortgage Corporation would have been obliged to pay a normal tax on the resulting gain, and the taxpayer, if she wished to touch her profit, must do so in the form of a dividend, on which a surtax would have been assessed against her personally. To reduce these taxes as much as possible, the following plan was conceived and put through: The taxpayer incorporated in Delaware a new company, organized ad hoc, and called the Averill Corporation, to which the United Mortgage Corporation transferred all its shares in the Monitor Securities Corporation, under an agreement by which the Averill Corporation issued all its shares to the taxpayer. Being so possessed of all the Averill shares, she wound up the Averill company three days later, receiving as a liquidating dividend the Monitor shares, which she thereupon sold. It is not disputed that all these steps were part of one purpose to reduce taxes, and that the Averill Corporation, which was in existence for only a few days, conducted no business and was intended to conduct none, except to act as conduit for the Monitor

*Page 545 infra. — ED.

shares in the way we have described. The taxpayer's return for the year 1928 was made on the theory that the transfer of the Monitor shares to the Averill Corporation was a "reorganization" under section 112(i)(1)(B) of the Revenue Act of 1928* . . . , being "a transfer by a corporation of . . . a part of its assets to another corporation" in such circumstances that immediately thereafter "the transferor or its stockholders or both are in control of the corporation to which the assets are transferred." Since the transfer was a reorganization, she claimed to come within section 112(g) . . . , ** and that her "gain" should not be "recognized," because the Averill shares were "distributed, in pursuance of a plan of reorganization." The Monitor shares she asserted to have been received as a single liquidating dividend of the Averill Corporation, and that as such she was only taxable for them under section [331] . . . and upon their value less the cost properly allocated to the Averill shares. That cost she determined as that proportion of the original cost of her shares in the United Mortgage Corporation, which the Monitor shares bore to the whole assets of the United Mortgage Corporation. This difference she returned, and paid the tax calculated upon it. The Commissioner assessed a deficiency taxed upon the theory that the transfer of the Monitor shares to the Averill Corporation was not a true "reorganization" within section 112(i)(1)(B), . . . being intended only to avoid taxes. He treated as nullities that transfer, the transfer of the Averill shares to the taxpayer, and the winding up of the Averill Corporation ending in the receipt by her of the Monitor shares; and he ruled that the whole transaction was merely the declaration of a dividend by the United Mortgage Corporation consisting of the Monitor shares in specie, on which the taxpayer must pay a surtax calculated at their full value. The taxpayer appealed and the Board held that the Averill Corporation had been in fact organized and was indubitably a corporation, that the United Mortgage Corporation had with equal certainty transferred to it the Monitor shares, and that the taxpayer had got the Averill shares as part of the transaction. All these transactions being real, their purpose was irrelevant, and section 112(i)(1)(B) was applicable, especially since it was part of a statute of such small mesh as the Revenue Act of 1928; the finer the reticulation, the less room for inference. The Board therefore expunged the deficiency, and the Commissioner appealed.

We agree with the Board and the taxpayer that a transaction, otherwise within an exception of the tax law, does not lose its immunity, because it is actuated by a desire to avoid, or, if one choose,

---

*Cf. §368(a)(1)(D) of the 1986 Code. — Ed.

**Section 112(g) is set forth in the Supreme Court's opinion in this case, page 546 infra. No 1986 Code section is the exact counterpart to §112(g), but today, §355(a) permits some tax free "spin-offs." Spin-offs and similar transactions are studied at page 680 et seq. infra. — Ed.

to evade, taxation. Any one may so arrange his affairs that his taxes shall be as low as possible; he is not bound to choose that pattern which will best pay the Treasury; there is not even a patriotic duty to increase one's taxes. . . . Therefore, if what was done here, was what was intended by section 112(i)(1)(B), it is of no consequence that it was all an elaborate scheme to get rid of income taxes, as it certainly was. Nevertheless, it does not follow that Congress meant to cover such a transaction, not even though the facts answer the dictionary definitions of each term used in the statutory definition. It is quite true, as the Board has very well said, that as the articulation of a statute increases, the room for interpretation must contract; but the meaning of a sentence may be more than that of the separate words, as a melody is more than the notes, and no degree of particularity can ever obviate recourse to the setting in which all appear, and which all collectively create. The purpose of the section is plain enough; men engaged in enterprises — industrial, commercial, financial, or any other — might wish to consolidate, or divide, to add to, or subtract from, their holdings. Such transactions were not to be considered as "realizing" any profit, because the collective interests still remained in solution. But the underlying presupposition is plain that the readjustment shall be undertaken for reasons germane to the conduct of the venture in hand, not as an ephemeral incident, egregious to its prosecution. To dodge the shareholders' taxes is not one of the transactions contemplated as corporate "reorganizations."

This accords both with the history of the section, and with its interpretation by the courts, though the exact point has not hitherto arisen. It first appeared in the Act of 1924, §203(h)(1)(B), . . . and as the committee reports show (Senate Reports 398), was intended as supplementary to section 112(g), . . . then section 203(c) . . . ; both in combination changed the law as laid down in U.S. v. Phellis, 257 U.S. 156, . . . and Rockefeller v. U.S., 257 U.S. 176. . . . [T]he purpose was stated to be to exempt "from tax the gain from exchanges made in connection with a reorganization in order that ordinary business transactions will not be prevented." . . . Moreover, we regard Pinellas Ice & Cold Storage Co. v. Commissioner, 287 U.S. 462 . . . [page 580 infra], and our own decision in Cortland Specialty Co. v. Commissioner, 60 F.2d 937, [page 581 infra] as pertinent, if not authoritative. In each the question was of the applicability of a precursor of section 112(i)(1)(A) of 1928, . . . to the sale of all the assets of one company to another, which gave in exchange, cash and short time notes. The taxpayer's argument was that this was a "merger or consolidation," because the buyer acquired "all the property of another corporation," the seller, that being one statutory definition of "merger or consolidation." That assumed, the exemption was urged to fall within section 112(g) as here. It might have been enough to hold that short time notes were not "securities," within section 112(g); but both courts went further and declared that the transaction was not a "merger or consolidation," but a sale, though literally it fell within the words of section 112(i)(1)(A). This they did, because its plain purpose was to cover only a situation in which after the transaction there continued some community of interest between the companies, other than holding such notes. The violence done the literal interpretation of the words is no less than what we do here. Moreover, the act itself gives evidence that, on occasion anyway, the purpose of a transaction should be the guide; thus in section 115(g),* . . . the cancellation of shares is to be treated as a dividend — though otherwise it would not be such — if it is "essentially equivalent to the distribution of a taxable dividend"; again in section 112(c)(2),** . . . a distribution is in part taxable as a dividend, if it "has the effect of the distribution of a taxable dividend."

We do not indeed agree fully with the way in which the Commissioner treated the transaction; we cannot treat as inoperative the transfer of the Monitor shares by the United Mortgage Corporation, the issue by the Averill Corporation of its own shares to the taxpayer, and her acquisition of the Monitor shares by winding up that company. The Averill Corporation had a juristic personality, whatever the purpose of its organization; the transfer passed title to the Monitor shares and the taxpayer became a shareholder in the transferee. All these steps were real, and their only defect was that they were not what the statute means by a "reorganization," because the transactions were no part of the conduct of the business of either or both companies; so viewed they were a sham, though all the proceedings had their usual effect. But the result is the same whether the tax be calculated as the Commissioner calculated it, or upon the value of the Averill shares as a dividend, and the only question that can arise is whether the deficiency must be expunged, though right in result, if it was computed by a method, partly wrong. Although this is argued with some warmth, it is plain that the taxpayer may not avoid her just taxes because the reasoning of the assessing officials has not been entirely our own.

Order reversed; deficiency assessed.

GREGORY v. HELVERING

293 U.S. 465 (1935)

Mr. Justice SUTHERLAND delivered the opinion of the Court. Petitioner in 1928 was the owner of all the stock of United Mortgage Corporation. That corporation held among its assets 1,000 shares of

*Cf. §§302(a) and 317(b) of the 1986 Code. — ED
**Cf. §356(a)(2) of the 1986 Code. — ED.

the Monitor Securities Corporation. For the sole purpose of procuring a transfer of these shares to herself in order to sell them for her individual profit, and, at the same time, diminish the amount of income tax which would result from a direct transfer by way of dividend, she sought to bring about a "reorganization" under §112(g) of the Revenue Act of 1928, c. 852, . . . set forth later in this opinion. To that end, she caused the Averill Corporation to be organized under the laws of Delaware on September 18, 1928. Three days later, the United Mortgage Corporation transferred to the Averill Corporation the 1,000 shares of Monitor stock, for which all the shares of the Averill Corporation were issued to the petitioner. On September 24, the Averill Corporation was dissolved, and liquidated by distributing all its assets, namely, the Monitor shares, to the petitioner. No other business was ever transacted, or intended to be transacted, by that company. Petitioner immediately sold the Monitor for $133,333.33. She returned for taxation as capital net gain the sum of $76,007.88, based upon an apportioned cost of $57,325.45. Further details are unnecessary. It is not disputed that if the interposition of the so-called reorganization was ineffective, petitioner became liable for a much larger tax as a result of the transaction.

The Commissioner of Internal Revenue, being of opinion that the reorganization attempted was without substance and must be disregarded, held that petitioner was liable for a tax as though the United corporation had paid her a dividend consisting of the amount realized from the sale of the Monitor shares. In a proceeding before the Board of Tax Appeals, that body rejected the commissioner's view and upheld that of petitioner. . . . Upon a review of the latter decision, the circuit court of appeals sustained the commissioner and reversed the board, holding that there had been no "reorganization" within the meaning of the statute. . . . Petitioner applied to this court for a writ of certiorari, which the government, considering the question one of importance, did not oppose. We granted the writ.

Section 112 of the Revenue Act of 1928 deals with the subject of gain or loss resulting from the sale or exchange of property. Such gain or loss is to be recognized in computing the tax, except as provided in that section. The provisions of the section, so far as they are pertinent to the question here presented, follow:

> Sec. 112. (g) *Distribution of stock on reorganization.* — If there is distributed, in pursuance of a plan of reorganization, to a shareholder in a corporation a party to the reorganization, stock or securities in such corporation or in another corporation a party to the reorganization, without the surrender by such shareholder of stock or securities in such a corporation, no gain to the distributee from the receipt of such stock or securities shall be recognized. . . .
>
> (i) *Definition of reorganization.* — As used in this section . . .

(1) The term "reorganization" means . . . (B) a transfer by a corporation of all or a part of its assets to another corporation if immediately after the transfer the transferor or its stockholders or both are in control of the corporation to which the assets are transferred, . . .

It is earnestly contended on behalf of the taxpayer that since every element required by the foregoing subdivision (B) is to be found in what was done, a statutory reorganization was effected; and that the motive of the taxpayer thereby to escape payment of a tax will not alter the result or make unlawful what the statute allows. It is quite true that if a reorganization in reality was effected within the meaning of subdivision (B), the ulterior purpose mentioned will be disregarded. The legal right of a taxpayer to decrease the amount of what otherwise would be his taxes, or altogether avoid them, by means which the law permits, cannot be doubted. . . . But the question for determination is whether what was done, apart from the tax motive, was the thing which the statute intended. The reasoning of the court below in justification of a negative answer leaves little to be said.

When subdivision (B) speaks of a transfer of assets by one corporation to another, it means a transfer made "in pursuance of a plan of reorganization" [§112(g)] of corporate business; and not a transfer of assets by one corporation to another in pursuance of a plan having no relation to the business of either, as plainly is the case here. Putting aside, then, the question of motive in respect of taxation altogether, and fixing the character of the proceeding by what actually occurred, what do we find? Simply an operation having no business or corporate purpose — a mere device which put on the form of a corporate reorganization as a disguise for concealing its real character, and the sole object and accomplishment of which was the consummation of a preconceived plan, not to reorganize a business or any part of a business, but to transfer a parcel of corporate shares to the petitioner. No doubt, a new and valid corporation was created. But that corporation was nothing more than a contrivance to the end last described. It was brought into existence for no other purpose; it performed, as it was intended from the beginning it should perform; no other function. When that limited function had been exercised, it immediately was put to death.

In these circumstances, the facts speak for themselves and are susceptible of but one interpretation. The whole undertaking, though conducted according to the terms of subdivision (B), was in fact an elaborate and devious form of conveyance masquerading as a corporate reorganization, and nothing else. The rule which excludes from consideration the motive of tax avoidance is not pertinent to the situation, but it is plain that the taxpayer may not avoid her just taxes because the reasoning of the assessing officials has not been entirely our own.

Order reversed; deficiency assessed.

NOTES

1. The Court of Appeals said that "the result is the same whether the tax be calculated as the Commissioner calculated it, or upon the value of the Averill shares as a dividend . . ." (page 545 supra). The Commissioner, according to that court, argued that "the whole transaction was merely the declaration of a dividend by the United Mortgage Corporation consisting of the Monitor shares in specie . . ." (page 543 supra). The Supreme Court, however, thought that the Commissioner claimed the transaction should be taxed "as though the United [C]orporation had paid her a dividend consisting of the amount realized from the sale of the Monitor shares." Might there be any difference in result?

2. The Supreme Court said (page 545 supra) that a "plan of reorganization" does not exist where the transfer has "no relation to the business of either" corporation. If the transfer has some relation to the business of the parent, must there be a nontax reason for the particular method of disposition chosen in order to avoid the result in *Gregory*?

Should the result in a reorganization case depend on the purpose or motive of the parties? How might the Supreme Court have reached the result it did without weighing the taxpayer's tax objectives against her nontax objectives?

3. See Bittker, Pervasive Judicial Doctrines in the Construction of the Internal Revenue Code, 21 Howard L.J. 693 (1978); Isenberg, Musings on Form and Substance in Taxation, 49 U. Chi. L. Rev. 859 (1982); Willens, The Significance of Form: Some Subchapter C Manifestations, 12 J. Corp. Taxn. 72 (1985).

GRANITE TRUST CO. v. UNITED STATES
238 F.2d 670 (1st Cir. 1956)

Before Magruder, Chief Judge, and Woodbury and Hartigan, Circuit Judges.

MAGRUDER, Chief Judge. . . . In 1928 the Building Corporation was organized by Granite Trust Company for the purpose of acquiring land and constructing an office building thereon to be occupied by the bank. The land and building cost over $1,000,000

and were financed through the purchase by the taxpayer bank of all
the stock of the Building Corporation. The Building Corporation
rented a portion of the premises to Howard D. Johnson Company
for a rental of approximately $ 13,700 per year. This last-named
corporation was in 1943 wholly owned by Howard D. Johnson, an
individual. Neither Howard D. Johnson Company, nor Johnson,
owned any stock in Granite Trust Company, and no shareholder or
officer of Howard D. Johnson Company was a director in, or otherwise connected with, Granite Trust Company, though both Howard
D. Johnson Company, and Johnson, were depositors in the taxpayer
bank.

Beginning at least as early 1936, the amount at which the stock
of the Building Corporation was carried upon the taxpayer's books
was subjected to continuous criticism by various banking authorities.
As a result, the taxpayer wrote down the value of the stock on its
books, but nevertheless the examining authorities continued to press
for further annual reductions.

At some time prior to October, 1943, the taxpayer's management
commenced the formulation of a plan to bring this issue to a close
by the expedient of having Granite Trust Company purchase the
real estate from the Building Corporation for $550,000, a fair current
appraisal, after which the subsidiary Building Corporation was to be
liquidated. The practical problem in the execution of this plan resulted from the fact that the distribution in the liquidation of the
subsidiary corporation was expected to amount to something between
$65 and $66 per share upon the shares of common stock in the
Building Corporation for which the taxpayer had paid $100 per
share. In thus contributing to the simplification of the corporate
structure of the taxpayer as a holding company, an end deemed
desirable by the Congress, Granite Trust Company naturally wanted
to be assured that its prospective loss to be realized upon the liquidation of its subsidiary would lawfully be "recognized" at once so as
to be available as a tax deduction.

In order that this forthcoming loss upon its investment might
not be denied recognition by §[332] . . . , the taxpayer, on advice of
counsel, proceeded to divest itself of some of its shares of common
stock in the Building Corporation by means of several purported
sales and of a gift, the facts concerning which are as follows:

[As of December 1, 1943, the taxpayer owned all of the outstanding stock of the Building Corporation — 2,250 shares of
preferred and 5,000 shares of common stock. The latter was the sole
voting stock of the corporation. On December 6, 1943, the taxpayer
sold, or went through the form of selling, 1,025 shares — 20.5 percent
— of the outstanding common stock to Howard D. Johnson Company
for $65.50 per share. The buyer paid the purchase price to the tax-

payer and received the Building Corporation certificates which it held until the final liquidation of the Building Corporation.

[On December 10, 1943, the shareholders of the Building Corporation voted to accept the taxpayer's offer to purchase the real estate. At the same meeting, the shareholders also voted to liquidate the corporation and to distribute the proceeds pro rata provided that such liquidation would be completed before December 30, 1943. The taxpayer's shares were the only shares represented and voted at the meeting.

[Subsequently, on December 13, 1943, the taxpayer sold, or went through the form of selling, 10 shares of the Building Corporation stock to each of two individuals, Howard D. Johnson and Ralph E. Richmond, for $65.50 per share. On the same day, the taxpayer gave two shares of the Building Corporation stock to the Greater Boston United War Fund. The purchase prices were paid and all of the stock certificates were delivered.

[The taxpayer acquired no additional shares of the Building Corporation stock at any time after making the above sales or gift.

[On December 15, 1943, the $550,000 purchase price was paid by the taxpayer, and the real estate was conveyed to it by the Building Corporation. The real estate was recorded on the taxpayer's books at fair market value.

[On December 17, 1943, the Building Corporation retired its preferred stock. On the same day, each of the shareholders of common stock — the taxpayer, Howard D. Johnson Company, Howard D. Johnson, Ralph E. Richmond, and the Greater Boston United War Fund — received $65.77 per share as a final liquidating distribution.

[On December 30, 1943, in a meeting at which all of the shareholders of the Building Corporation were represented, the shareholders voted to dissolve the corporation and to give the directors the authority necessary to effect the dissolution.]

The taxpayer concedes that it would not have made the sales described above had it not been for §[332]. . . . While the taxpayer maintains that the gift to the United War Fund was but part of the total gift to that organization for the year 1943, it seems clear, because this was the only case where shares of stock rather than cash were distributed to the charity, that at least the specific object given at this time was dictated by §[332].

The precise issue before us is whether or not to give effect for tax purposes to the aforesaid sales and gift by the taxpayer. If the answer is in the affirmative, there is no doubt that the liquidation distribution of the property of the Building Corporation was not in "complete liquidation" within the very special meaning of that phrase in §[332] . . . and, accordingly, the taxpayer may recognize the loss on its investment.

Although there is no dispute that the transactions in form at least purport to be sales and a gift, the Commissioner nevertheless maintains that we should not accord them that significance. The Commissioner's argument is in two parts: The first proposition derives from the basic finding of the district court that the taxpayer effected the liquidation "in such manner as to achieve a tax reduction" and that this was "without legal or moral justification." The Commissioner attempts to bolster this argument by his traditional corporation reorganization analysis to the effect that, so long as the "end-result" of the transactions involved complies with the "criteria of the statute," intermediary steps (in this case the sales and gift) should be ignored as if they were nonexistent. His reasoning is that, if the final outcome is complete liquidation of a subsidiary corporation which at the outset was wholly owned by the taxpayer, the entire procedure comes within the intendment of the statute and "[c]ircuitous steps to avoid Section [332]" occurring prior to the ultimate liquidation should be disregarded.

The Commissioner's second proposition is that there were *in fact* no valid sales or gift of stock made by the taxpayer. This argument rests on the taxpayer's admission that the transfers were motivated solely by tax considerations and were made in a friendly atmosphere to friendly people who knew of the decision to liquidate the corporation before the end of the year. As the Commissioner points out, the liquidation took place shortly after the transfers, and the transferees then received back the money they had paid in, plus a small profit. Therefore, the Commissioner argues, relying heavily on Gregory v. Helvering, . . . [page 545 supra], that "the stock transfers in question had no independent purpose or meaning — either for the transferor or the transferees — but constituted merely a transitory and circuitous routing of legal title for the purpose of avoiding taxes, within the meaning of Gregory v. Helvering. . . . It was not expected or intended by any of the parties that the transferees should become true stockholders. Legal title passed; but beneficial ownership surely never passed. The transferees who paid money for their stock knew that the subsidiary would be liquidated in a few days and that they would get their money back — as in fact they did, with additional amounts to pay them for their cooperation in serving as conduits of title." The gift of stock to the United War Fund is dismissed as "nothing more than a gift of the cash." . . .

Our conclusion is that the Commissioner's arguments must be rejected, and that the taxpayer should be permitted to "recognize" the loss on its investment, which it undoubtedly realized upon the liquidation of the Building Corporation.

Initially we may note, without ruling upon it, one legal argument made by the Commissioner having to do with the efficacy of the purported sale of 1,025 shares of stock to Howard D. Johnson Company on December 6, 1943. The Commissioner contends that, to satisfy the first condition of nonrecognition prescribed in §[332], it is not necessary to have a formal plan of liquidation, evidenced by a corporate resolution, but it is sufficient if there is a "definitive determination" to achieve dissolution. It is claimed by the Commissioner that such a definitive determination existed here by November 10, 1943, and, therefore, that the sale of stock to Howard D. Johnson Company which took place on December 6, 1943 (before the formal adoption of the plan of liquidation) occurred *after* the "adoption of the plan of liquidation" within the meaning of §[332]. In this view the taxpayer owned 100 percent of the subsidiary's stock on the date the plan of liquidation was adopted, from which it would follow, on the basis of the first condition of §[332], that the loss should not be "recognized."

We need not consider the foregoing legal argument on its merits, because the subsequent actions by the taxpayer — the sales to Johnson individually and to Richmond on December 13, 1943, and the gift of stock on the same day to the United War Fund — of themselves, if valid, successfully accomplished the taxpayer's purpose of avoiding the nonrecognition provisions of §[332] under the second condition contained in that subsection. This second condition prescribes, in a sort of backhanded way, that gain or loss shall be recognized if, at any time on or after the date of adoption of the plan of liquidation and prior to the date of the receipt of the property distributed in final liquidation, the receiving corporation is the owner of a greater percentage of any class of stock of the corporation being liquidated than the percentage of such stock owned by it at the time of the receipt of the property — which means that this condition precedent to the nonrecognition of a realized gain or loss is not satisfied if, in the described period, the receiving corporation has made an effective disposition of any of the shares of stock held in the subsidiary corporation, without making any countervailing acquisitions of such stock.

Turning then to the basic contentions of the Commissioner, not much need be said with reference to the proposition that the tax motive for the sales and gift rendered the transactions "immoral" and thus vitiated them. Again and again the courts have pointed out that a "purpose to minimize or avoid taxation is not an illicit motive." . . . The *Gregory* case itself makes this clear, Gregory v. Helvering. . . .

As for the Commissioner's "end-result" argument, the very terms of §[332] make it evident that it is not an "end-result" provision, but rather one which prescribes specific conditions for the nonrecognition of realized gains or losses, conditions which, if not strictly met, make the section inapplicable. In fact, the Commissioner's own regulations (Reg. [§1.332-2]) emphasize the rigid requirements of the section and make no allowance for the type of "step transaction" theory advanced in this case.

The legislative history of §[332] likewise tends to support the position of the taxpayer. That history indicates that Congress was primarily concerned with providing a means of facilitating the simplification of corporate structures pursuant to the general policy enunciated in the Public Utility Holding Company Act of 1935, 49 Stat. 803, 15 U.S.C.A. §79 et seq. . . . This fact, while perhaps not conclusive as to the proper interpretation of §[332], nevertheless does lend a favorable background to the taxpayer's contention that the subsection, as a relief measure, was "not designed as a straitjacket into which corporations should be forced at the penalty of forfeiture of losses on liquidation of subsidiaries."

The more specific and more important bit of legislative history is found in the Report of the Senate Finance Committee at the time that §112(b)(6) [of the 1939 Code] was reenacted, with amendments, as §332 of the Internal Revenue Code of 1954. At this time, when Congress was engaged in a comprehensive reexamination of the Internal Revenue Code, the well-known case of Commissioner of Internal Revenue v. Day & Zimmermann, Inc., 3 Cir., 1945, 151 F.2d 517, had been decided in favor of the taxpayer, and it reasonably could be supposed that Congress, had it disapproved of the decision in that case, would have overturned its conclusion by making over §[332] into an "end-result" provision. In the *Day & Zimmermann* case, the taxpayer, admittedly in order to avoid the nonrecognition provisions of §[332] had sold at public auction a sufficient number of shares of a wholly owned subsidiary corporation to reduce its holdings below 80 percent. These shares were bought, after general bidding, by the treasurer of the taxpayer, who, after receiving cash dividends in the subsequent liquidation of the companies, reported his gain and paid income tax thereon. The Third Circuit held that §[332] did not apply to the liquidation, emphasizing that the treasurer had paid a fair price for the shares, had used his own money, had not been directed by anyone to bid, and that there had been no showing of any understanding existing between him and the corporation by which the latter was to retain any sort of interest in the securities or in the proceeds therefrom. . . . The significant thing in the case is its ultimate rationale that the purported sales of stock to the treasurer were in fact sales, notwithstanding the tax motive which prompted the corporation to enter into the transaction; from which it would seem to be irrelevant how the transfer was arranged, or whether or not it occurred at a public auction or exchange, so long as the beneficial as well as legal title was intended to pass and did pass. . . .

We come then to the Commissioner's second major contention,

resting on Gregory v. Helvering, . . . that the sales of stock by the corporation should be ignored on the ground that they were not bona fide, and that the taxpayer therefore retained "beneficial ownership." The Commissioner characterizes the transfers as artificial, unessential, transitory phases of a completed tax avoidance scheme which should be disregarded.

In answer to this contention, it is first necessary to determine precisely what the *Gregory* case held. Judge Learned Hand, in Chisholm v. Commissioner, 2 Cir., 1935, 79 F.2d 14, 15, . . . *certiorari denied* 1935, 296 U.S. 641, . . . analyzed the case as follows:

> *The question always is whether the transaction under scrutiny is in fact what it appears to be in form*; a marriage may be a joke; a contract may be intended only to deceive others; an agreement may have a collateral defeasance. In such cases the transaction as a whole is different from its appearance. . . . In Gregory v. Helvering, supra, 293 U.S. 465, . . . the incorporators adopted the usual form for creating business corporations; but their intent, or purpose, was merely to draught the papers, in fact not to create corporations as the court understood that word. That was the purpose which defeated their exemption, not the accompanying purpose to escape taxation; that purpose was legally neutral. Had they really meant to conduct a business by means of the two reorganized companies, they would have escaped whatever other aim they might have had, whether to avoid taxes, or to regenerate the world. [Italics added.]

In the present case the question is whether or not there actually were sales. Why the parties may wish to enter into a sale is one thing, but that is irrelevant under the *Gregory* case so long as the consummated agreement was no different from what it purported to be.

Even the Commissioner concedes that "[l]egal title" passed to the several transferees on December 13, 1943, but he asserts that "beneficial ownership" never passed. We find no basis on which to vitiate the purported sales, for the record is absolutely devoid of any evidence indicating an understanding by the parties to the transfers that any interest in the stock transferred was to be retained by the taxpayer. If Johnson or Richmond had gone bankrupt, or the assets of both had been attached by creditors, on the day after the sales to them, we do not see how the conclusion could be escaped that their Building Corporation stock would have been included in their respective assets. . . .

In addition to what we have said, there are persuasive reasons of a general nature which lend weight to the taxpayer's position. To strike down these sales on the alleged defect that they took place between friends and for tax motives would only tend to promote duplicity and result in extensive litigation as taxpayers led courts into hairsplitting investigations to decide when a sale was not a sale. It is no answer to argue that, under Gregory v. Helvering, there is an inescapable judicial duty to examine into the actuality of purported corporate reorganizations, for that was a special sort of transaction, whose bona fides could readily be ascertained by inquiring whether the ephemeral new corporation was in fact transacting business, or whether there was in fact a continuance of the proprietary interests under an altered corporate form. See Lewis v. Commissioner, 1 Cir., 1949, 176 F.2d 646.

What we have said so far is related chiefly to the validity of the sales. When we turn to the gift on December 13, 1943, to the United War Fund, the taxpayer is on even firmer ground. The Commissioner says that the gift was nothing more than a gift of cash, that the charity "was, at most, a passive transferee, without independent purpose, which held legal title to two shares for four days." This assertion rests, when examined closely, on the simple fact that the purpose for the gift was a tax avoidance one. But this does not disqualify it as an effective gift, transferring title. A gift certainly may have a tax motive. See Commissioner of Internal Revenue v. Newman, 2 Cir., 1947, 159 F.2d 848; Sawtell v. Commissioner, supra, 82 F.2d at page 222. Charitable contributions of low-cost securities are an everyday type of transfer motivated by tax purposes. The gift to the United War Fund, being valid, transferred two shares from the taxpayer after the adoption of the plan of liquidation, and alone sufficed to put the liquidation beyond the reach of the nonrecognition provisions of §[332].

In short, though the facts in this case show a tax avoidance, they also show legal transactions not fictitious or so lacking in substance as to be anything different from what they purported to be, and we believe they must be given effect in the administration of §[332] as well as for all other purposes. . . .

A judgment will be entered vacating the judgment of the District Court and remanding the case to that court with direction to enter judgment for the sum of $57,801.32, with interest.

NOTES

1. See George L. Riggs, Inc., 64 T.C. 474 (1975), *acq.* 1976-2 C.B. 2, in which the court held that the 80-percent stock ownership requirement of §332 was met where a corporation, by redeeming the stock of its minority shareholders prior to the formal adoption of a plan of liquidation, decreased the number of outstanding shares of stock and thereby increased its percentage share of ownership to greater than 80 percent. No informal adoption of a plan of liquidation occurred prior to the acquisition of the 80-percent ownership even

though the shareholders voted to sell the corporation's assets, the corporation called preferred stock for redemption, and the directors voted to liquidate the corporation's subsidiaries and to offer to redeem the stock of its minority shareholders. See also Rev. Rul. 75-521, 1975-2 C.B. 120 (§332 applied to liquidation where 50-percent corporate shareholder purchased the remaining 50 percent prior to formal adoption of plan, thus resulting in the nonrecognition of gain).

In Letter Rul. 8428006 (Mar. 26, 1984), the Service ruled that a corporate parent was entitled to recognize loss under §331(a) on the liquidation of its 66.7 percent owned subsidiary where the parent had sold the remaining 33.3 percent of the subsidiary's stock to an unrelated corporation only 17 days before the adoption of the plan of liquidation in order to avoid nonrecognition of loss under §332(a).

2. See H. K. Porter Co., 87 T.C. 689 (1986), in which the court held that §332 did not bar the recognition of petitioner's loss on the liquidation of its Australian subsidiary. Ten years prior to the liquidation, the wholly owned subsidiary capitalized loans from its parent and issued preferred stock. Upon liquidation the subsidiary's assets were insufficient to satisfy the preferred stock's liquidation preference. No assets were distributed with respect to the subsidiary's common stock. The court followed Commissioner v. Spaulding Bakeries, 252 F.2d 693 (2d Cir. 1958), and held that the liquidating distribution was not in complete cancellation or redemption of all of the subsidiary's stock.

3. Step Transactions

HELVERING v. ELKHORN COAL CO.
95 F.2d 732 (4th Cir. 1937), *cert. denied*, 305 U.S. 605 (1938)

Before Parker and Northcott, Circuit Judges, and Henry H. Watkins, District Judge.

PARKER, Circuit Judge. This is a petition to review a decision of the Board of Tax Appeals holding profit realized by the Elkhorn Coal & Coke Company upon a transfer of certain mining properties to the Mill Creek Coal & Coke Company to be nontaxable. The ground of the decision was that the transfer was made pursuant to a plan of reorganization within the meaning of section [368(a)(1)(C)]. . . . The facts were stipulated and are set forth at length in the findings of the Board which are reported with its opinion in Elkhorn Coal Co. v. Com'r, 34 B.T.A. 845. Those material to the question presented by the petition are in substance as follows:

Prior to December 18, 1925, the Elkhorn Coal & Coke Company, to which we shall hereafter refer as the old company, owned certain coal mining properties in West Virginia and certain stocks in other mining companies engaged in business in that state. It was closely associated with the Mill Creek Coal & Coke Company, which owned neighboring property; and a majority of the directorate of both corporations consisted of the same persons. Early in December, 1925, a plan was formed whereby the old company was to transfer its mine, mining plant, and mining equipment at Maybeury, W. Va., to the Mill Creek Company in exchange for 1,000 shares of the capital stock of that company. This exchange was accomplished on December 31, 1925, at which time, it is stipulated, the stock received by the old company had a fair market value of $550,000 which is in excess of the deficiency asserted by the Commissioner. There is no contention that the transfer by the old company was to a corporation controlled by it or by its stockholders and therefore within the nonrecognition provision of [the progenitor of section 368(a)(1)(D)] of the act; but the argument of the taxpayer is that the transfer was of all the properties of one corporation for the stock of another, and therefore within the nonrecognition provision of section [368(a)(1)(C)].

The contention . . . depends upon the legal conclusion to be drawn from certain evidentiary facts relating to the prior organization of another corporation and the transfer to it of all the property of the old company which was not to be transferred to the Mill Creek Company. These facts, which were found by the Board and are undisputed, are as follows: At the time that the transfer to the Mill Creek Company was decided upon, the officers of the old company caused another corporation to be organized under the name of the Elkhorn Coal Company, which we shall refer to hereafter as the new company, and on December 18, 1925, transferred to it, in exchange for 6,100 shares of its stock, all of the property of the old company which was not to be transferred to the Mill Creek Company except certain accounts, which were transferred to the new company on December 28, 1931, in consideration of its assuming the liabilities of the old company. The 6,100 shares of stock in the new company were promptly distributed by the old company as a dividend to its stockholders. This left the old company owning only the property which was to be transferred to the Mill Creek Company under the plan and which was transferred to that company on December 31st, as mentioned in the preceding paragraph. Following that transfer and the receipt by the old company of the 1,000 shares of the stock of the Mill Creek Company pursuant thereto, the new company proceeded to place itself in the same position relative to the stockholders of the old company that the old company had occupied, and then to wind up its affairs. It accomplished that result in the following manner: On January 22, 1926, it exchanged 1,440 shares of its capital stock for the 7,540 shares of the outstanding capital stock of the old company, making the exchange with the stockholders of that company. This gave those who had been stockholders in the old company the same interest in the new company that they had had in the old, and gave to the new company the ownership of all of the stock in the old. The 1,000 shares of stock received from the Mill Creek Company were then transferred to the new company and the old company was dissolved. No business whatever was done by the old company after the transfer of assets to the Mill Creek Company on December 31st; and no reason appears for the organization of the new company except to provide a transferee to take over and hold the assets which were not to be transferred to the Mill Creek Company so that the transfer to that company when made would be a transfer of all the assets of the old company.

The Board was of opinion that all of these transactions were carried through pursuant to prearranged plan, saying: "We do not doubt that before a single step was taken a plan had been formulated for regrouping the corporate assets"; and "The stipulated facts justify the inference that one of the motives which the stockholders of Elkhorn had in organizing the new corporation and causing the three corporations to adopt the several steps or plans of reorganization which were adopted and carried out, was to make the transfer of the mining properties from Elkhorn to Mill Creek without resulting tax liability to Elkhorn or to themselves." The Board thought, however, with five members dissenting, that because the transfers from the old company to the new were genuine and were separate and distinct from the transfer to the Mill Creek Company, the latter must be treated as a transfer of substantially all of the properties of the corporation within the meaning of the reorganization statute. . . .

While we are bound by the Board's findings of evidentiary facts, we are not bound by the foregoing conclusion set forth in the opinion and embodying a mixed question of law and fact. . . . Helvering v. Tex-Penn Oil Co., 300 U.S. 481. . . .

A careful consideration of the evidentiary facts discloses no purpose which could have been served by the creation of the new company and the transfer of the assets to it, except to strip the old company of all of its properties which were not to be transferred to the Mill Creek Company, in anticipation of that transfer. The creation of the new company and its acquisition of the assets of the old was not a corporate reorganization, therefore, within the meaning of the statute or within any fair meaning of the term "reorganization." It did not involve any real transfer of assets by the business enterprise or any rearranging of corporate structure, but at most a mere shifting of charters, having no apparent purpose except the avoidance of taxes on the transfer to the Mill Creek Company which was in contemplation. To use in part the language of the Supreme Court in Gregory v. Helvering, [page 545 supra], . . . it was "simply an operation having no business or corporate purpose — a mere device which put on the form of a corporate reorganization as a disguise for concealing its real character, and the sole object and accomplishment of which was the consummation of a preconceived plan, not to reorganize a business or any part of a business," but to give to the intended transfer to the Mill Creek Company the appearance of a transfer of all the corporate assets so as to bring it within the nonrecognition provision of section [368(a)(1)(C)].

Under such circumstances we think that the decision in Gregory v. Helvering . . . is controlling. In that case, for the purpose of avoiding taxes on a liquidating dividend of shares of stock held by a corporation, a subsidiary was organized within the terms of the reorganization statute and the shares were transferred to it. The stock of the subsidiary was then delivered to the sole stockholder of the original corporation and shortly thereafter the subsidiary was dissolved and the shares which had been transferred to it were delivered to the stockholder. The court held that although the organization of the subsidiary came within the letter of the reorganization statute, such corporate manipulation would be ignored when it fulfilled no proper corporate function and was not in reality a reorganization within the meaning of the statute. The court said:

> "In these circumstances, the facts speak for themselves and are susceptible of but one interpretation. The whole undertaking, though conducted according to the terms of [§368(a)(1)(D)], was in fact an elaborate and devious form of conveyance masquerading as a corporate reorganization, and nothing else. The rule which excludes from consideration the motive of tax avoidance is not pertinent to the situation, because the transaction upon its face lies outside the plain intent of the statute. To hold otherwise would be to exalt artifice above reality and to deprive the statutory provision in question of all serious purpose."

We do not see how that case can be distinguished from this. If the property which was to be transferred to Mill Creek had been transferred to a new company created for the purpose and had been by that company transferred to Mill Creek, no one would contend that there was a distinction; and certainly there is no difference in principle between creating a subsidiary to take and convey the property to the intended transferee and creating a subsidiary to take over the other assets and having the old company make the transfer. In either case, the apparent reorganization is a mere artifice; and it can make no difference which of the affiliated corporations makes the transfer of assets which it is desired to bring within the nonrecognition provisions of the statute.

It is suggested in the opinion of the Board that the case before us is analogous to that which would have been presented if the old company, prior to the transfer to Mill Creek, had distributed to its stockholders all of the assets except those destined for such transfer; but the distinction is obvious. In the case supposed, the business enterprise would have definitely divested itself of the property distributed. Here it did not divest itself of the property at all, but merely made certain changes in the legal papers under which it enjoyed corporate existence. No rule is better settled than that in tax matters we must look to substance and not to form; and no one who looks to substance can see in the mere change of charters, which is all that we have here, any reason for permitting a transfer of a part of the corporate assets to escape the taxation to which it is subject under the statute.

Congress has seen fit to grant nonrecognition of profit in sale or exchange of assets only under certain conditions, one of which is that one corporation shall transfer "substantially all" of its properties for stock in another. If nonrecognition of profit can be secured by the plan adopted in this case, the exemption is broadened to cover all transfers of assets for stock, whether "substantially all" or not, if only the transferor will go to the slight trouble and expense of getting a new charter for his corporation and making the transfer of assets to the new corporation thus created in such way as to leave in the old only the assets to be transferred at the time the transfer is to be made. We do not think the statutory exemption may be thus broadened by such an artifice.

Having reached this conclusion, it is unnecessary to decide whether the unity of the plan under which the transfer was made brings it, without a unifying contract, within the principles laid down in Starr v. Commissioner (C.C.A. 4th) 82 F.(2d) 964, 968, wherein we said,

> "Where transfers are made pursuant to such a plan of reorganization, they are ordinarily parts of one transaction and should be so treated in application of the well-settled principle that, in applying income tax laws, the substance, and not the form, of the transaction shall control. . . . This is demanded also by the principle, equally well settled, that a single transaction may not be broken up into various elements to avoid a tax. . . .

For the reasons stated, the decision of the Board will be reversed, and the cause will be remanded to it for further proceedings in accordance with this opinion.

Reversed.

Henry H. Watkins, District Judge (dissenting). [Opinion omitted.]

ON REHEARING

PARKER, Circuit Judge. The rehearing granted in this case and careful consideration of the briefs filed and arguments made thereon have served only to strengthen the majority of the court in the opinion heretofore expressed; and we see no basis whatever for the contention that our former opinion was based on a ground not considered by the Board of Tax Appeals. The question before the Board was whether the transfer to Mill Creek was of all the assets of the old company. . . .

It was not intended by what was said in the original opinion, to the effect that the transfer of assets from the old company to the new did not constitute a bona fide reorganization, to suggest that the transfer was a taxable transaction, but to point out that the creation of the new company and the transfer of the assets to it was a mere shifting of charters having no purpose other than to give to the later transfer to Mill Creek the appearance of a transfer of all the corporate assets so as to bring that transfer within the non-recognition provisions of section [368(a)(1)]. . . . The transfer to the new company was non-taxable whether it was a real reorganization or a mere shifting of charters, which would of course come within the terms of the reorganization statute. It is only in relation to the subsequent transfer to Mill Creek that it becomes important to determine whether the organization of the new company and its taking over of the assets was a genuine reorganization. If there was no real reorganization and transfer, but a mere shifting of charters, the subsequent transfer to Mill Creek was not within the terms of the nonrecognition provision of the statute.

We are confirmed in our original opinion by the recent decision of the Supreme Court in Minnesota Tea Co. v. Helvering [302 U.S. 609]. In that case there was a reorganization in which stockholders paid the debts of a corporation from the cash distributed to them in the course of the reorganization. The question was whether the corporation was taxable on the amount of the debts thus paid on the theory that the cash used for that purpose was in reality received by the corporation, or whether it was nontaxable on the theory that the distribution to the stockholders was within the nonrecognition provisions of the statute. In holding the corporation taxable thereon the court said:

> The conclusion is inescapable, as the court below very clearly pointed out, that by this roundabout process petitioner received the same benefit "as though it had retained that amount from distribution and applied it to the payment of such indebtedness." Payment of indebtedness, and not distribution of dividends, was, from the beginning, the aim of the understanding with the stock-

holders and was the end accomplished by carrying that
understanding into effect. *A given result at the end of a straight path
is not made a different result because reached by following a devious path.*
The preliminary distribution to the stockholders was a meaningless
and unnecessary incident in the transmission of the fund to the
creditors, all along intended to come to their hands, so transpar-
ently artificial that further discussion would be a needless waste
of time. (Italics ours.)

In the case at bar, the "aim" of the incorporation of the new
company and the transfer made to it, was that the transfer to Mill
Creek should appear to be a transfer of all of the assets of the company; and this was the end accomplished, and the only end
accomplished so far as the record shows, by the incorporation and
transfer. The incorporation of the new company and the transfer to
it was a "meaningless and unnecessary incident." It is true that the
new company was incorporated under the laws of a different state
from the old; but it does not appear that any corporate purpose was
served by this change of jurisdictions and certainly the integrity of
the existing business was not affected by the change. . . . It is said
that the transfer to Mill Creek had a real corporate purpose. This is
true, but it was taxable unless constituting a transfer of all of the
assets of the corporation. The incorporation of and transfer to the
new company, which had no proper corporate purpose, were resorted to in order to give the transfer to Mill Creek the appearance
of being a transfer of all the assets of the transferor and hence not
taxable. All that was done by the complicated corporate maneuvering
employed was the transfer of a part of the assets of the old company
to Mill Creek in exchange for 1,000 shares of its stock, leaving the
business of the old company in the hands of the old stockholders,
with a new charter, but otherwise unaffected. This result is "not a
different result because reached by following a devious path."

And we think it clear that the incorporation of the new company
and the transfer made to it were but parts of a single plan under
which the transfer was made to Mill Creek and that they should be
treated as parts of one transaction. When this is done, there is no
room for the contention that all of the assets of the corporation were
transferred to Mill Creek. Even though there was no unifying contract, the unity of the plan brings the case within the rule applied in
Starr v. Commissioner, 4 Cir., 82 F.2d 964.

For the reasons stated here and in our former opinion, the decision of the Board of Tax Appeals will be reversed.

Reversed.

Henry H. Watkins, District Judge, dissents.

REVENUE RULING 76-123
1976-1 C.B. 94

Advice has been requested concerning the treatment for Federal income tax purposes of the transaction described below.

Individual A owned all the stock of X corporation, which was incorporated in State O. Individual B, who is unrelated to A, owned all the stock of Y corporation, which was incorporated in State P. A and B determined that the businesses operated by X and Y could be improved if their interests in X and Y were combined while at the same time preserving the separate corporate existence of X and Y. A and B also decided that the laws of State P were more favorable to the operation of the combined enterprise. To carry out their plan, A and B transferred all of their stock in X and Y to a newly organized corporation, Z, incorporated in State P, in exchange for, respectively, 60 percent and 40 percent of all of the outstanding stock of Z. In addition, B received from Z 10x dollars in cash. The consideration received by A and B was in each case equal to the fair market value of the stock exchanged. As part of this plan, X then distributed all of its assets to Z in complete liquidation, and Y remained as a wholly owned subsidiary of Z. . . .

In Rev. Rul. 67-274, 1967-2 C.B. 141, a corporation, pursuant to a plan of reorganization, acquired all the outstanding stock of another corporation from the shareholders in exchange for voting stock of the acquiring corporation and thereafter, as part of the same plan, the acquiring corporation completely liquidated the acquired corporation. Rev. Rul. 67-274 holds that under these circumstances the acquisition of the stock of the acquired corporation and its liquidation by the acquiring corporation are part of the overall plan of reorganization and may not be considered independently of each other for Federal income tax purposes. Rev. Rul. 67-274 concludes that the transaction is not an acquisition of the stock of the acquired corporation qualifying as a reorganization under section 368(a)(1)(B) of the Code but is an acquisition of the assets of the acquired corporation qualifying as a reorganization under section 368(a)(1)(C).

Rev. Rul. 68-357, 1968-2 C.B. 144, holds that section 351 of the Code applies where, as part of an overall plan to consolidate the operations of five businesses, an individual and three corporations transfer property to a corporation that they control immediately after the transfers within the meaning of section 368(c) even though the transfers of property by the corporations are reorganizations within the meaning of section 368(a)(1)(C).

The transfer by A of A's X stock to Z and, as part of the overall transaction, the liquidation of X by Z are interdependent steps in an overall reorganization plan the substance of which is treated for Federal income tax purposes as an acquisition by Z of all of the assets of X solely in exchange for Z voting stock in a transaction qualifying as a reorganization under section 368(a)(1)(C) of the Code, followed by a distribution by X of the Z stock to A in exchange for all of A's X stock. Accordingly, no gain or loss is recognized by X upon the exchange of its property solely for Z stock as provided by section 361(a), and no gain or loss is recognized to A on the exchange of A's X stock solely for voting stock of Z as provided in section 354(a).

Furthermore, the transfer by X of its property to Z in liquidation and the transfer by B of B's Y stock to Z is a transaction within the provisions of section 351(a) of the Code since X and B are in control of Z immediately after the exchanges within the meaning of section 368(c). Pursuant to section 351(c) the distribution by X of the Z stock to A does not violate the control requirement of section 368(c). Accordingly, no loss is recognized to B and no gain is recognized to B in excess of the 10x dollars received by B, as provided in section 351(b), upon the exchange of B's Y stock solely for cash and voting stock of Z. See Rev. Rul. 68-357.

Rev. Rul. 68-349, 1968-2 C.B. 143, holds that the transfer of property by an individual [C] to a newly formed corporation [M] does not qualify under section 351 of the Code where another corporation [N] simultaneously transfers all of its property to the new corporation for the purpose of qualifying the individual's transfer under section 351. Rev. Rul. 68-349 states that the organization of the new corporation is considered under the circumstances to be merely a continuation of the transferor corporation. Rev. Rul. 68-349 is distinguishable from the instant case in that Z was not employed solely for the purpose of enabling B to transfer B's Y stock without the recognition of gain and was not merely a continuation of X. Z was organized to enable X to be reincorporated in State P. Further, the transfer by B of his Y stock to Z effected the combination of A's and B's former business interests in the form of affiliated corporations.

Rev. Rul. 68-349 is distinguished.

WEST COAST MARKETING CORP. v. COMMISSIONER
46 T.C. 32 (1966)

The Commissioner determined a deficiency in petitioner's income tax for the fiscal year ended June 30, 1960, in the amount of $50,911.97.

The sole issue is whether the substance of a certain transaction was a taxable sale or exchange by the taxpayer of its interest in certain land or whether the realized gain in respect thereof is to escape taxation under section 354(a)(1) of the 1954 Code through the use of an intermediate corporation to which such property was first transferred.

FINDINGS OF FACT

[Petitioner owned a 25-percent interest in a certain tract of real estate. Cohen, petitioner's president and sole shareholder, owned a 25-percent interest in two neighboring tracts. The 50-percent owner of all three tracts negotiated a sale to Universal Marion Corporation ("Universal") for $360 an acre, payable in voting convertible preferred stock of Universal. Cohen orally agreed to the terms of the sale, which were embodied in a letter agreement dated April 16, 1959.]

The final sale of all three tracts of land to Universal was consummated in the fall of 1959, in accordance with the terms of the letter of April 16, 1959.

Meanwhile, however, Cohen caused to be organized on April 30, 1959, a Florida corporation named Manatee Land Co. (Manatee), and, on May 1, 1959, he and petitioner transferred to Manatee their remaining respective one-fourth interests in the three tracts — petitioner's in the Middle Tract and Cohen's in the North and South tracts.

Petitioner received 645 shares of the stock of Manatee for its undivided one-quarter interest in the Middle Tract. Cohen received the remaining 769 shares of Manatee stock for his undivided one-quarter interest in the North and South tracts.

Subsequent to the issuance of the 1,414 shares of stock to the petitioner and Cohen, Manatee issued two shares to William B. McKechnie and two additional shares to Donald E. Thurlow. Payment was made for these four shares of stock in cash on the basis of $100 per share. . . .

In carrying out the terms of the agreement for the sale or exchange of the three tracts of land as proposed in the letter of April 16, 1959, the stockholders of Manatee, on October 27, 1959, transferred their stock in the corporation to Universal in exchange for 10,800 shares of Universal's 4½ percent $100 par value voting cumulative preferred stock. . . .

Manatee was not engaged in the conduct of any business. It was used by petitioner and Cohen for no purpose other than to hold title to their respective undivided one-fourth interests in the three tracts of land, and to serve as a conduit for transferring title thereto to Universal.

On December 18, 1959, Manatee was liquidated by Universal.

In its income tax return for the year ended June 30, 1960, petitioner reported the transfer of all of the stock which it owned in Manatee in exchange for 4,913 shares of Universal "having an indeterminate market value" and did not report any taxable income from that transaction. Those shares in fact had a fair market value of $67 per share, as stipulated by the parties herein. The Commissioner determined that petitioner realized a long-term capital gain of $203,647.91 "on the exchange in form of stock of Manatee Land Co. for stock of Universal Marion Corporation" and increased the taxable income reported in its return by that amount.

OPINION

RAUM, Judge. If petitioner had transferred its one-fourth interest in the Middle Tract directly to Universal in exchange for the preferred shares of Universal, there is no dispute that the resulting gain would have been taxable. Counsel for the parties so agreed at the trial. Is a different result required by the use of Manatee, an intermediate agency that was employed to effectuate the transfer? On this record, we think the answer must be no.

Petitioner's position has been that Manatee was organized for a bona fide business purpose and that the transfer of its stock to Universal in exchange for stock of the latter constituted a tax-free "reorganization" under sections 354(a)(1) and 368(a)(1)(B) of the 1954 Code. To be sure, the transaction before us falls literally within those provisions. But if Manatee served no business purpose and the substance of the transaction was simply an exchange of land for stock of Universal, the tax consequences must turn upon the substance of the transaction rather than the form in which it was cast. "A given result at the end of a straight path is not made a different result because reached by following a devious path." Minnesota Tea Co. v. Helvering, 302 U.S. 609, 613. In such circumstances there would not be any bona fide "reorganization" to which the nonrecognition provisions in question could apply.[3] Gregory v. Helvering [page 545 supra]. What was the situation here?

Cohen testified before us in an effort to show that there were bona fide business reasons for incorporating Manatee and transferring to it his and petitioner's respective undivided one-quarter interests in the three tracts. We found his testimony slippery and unconvincing. The burden was upon petitioner and it has not been carried. To the contrary, the record persuasively indicates that Manatee was incorporated for the purpose of being used as a conduit for

3. See Income Tax Regulations, sec. 1.368-1(b): "a sale is nevertheless to be treated as a sale even though the mechanics of a reorganization have been set up."

passing title to petitioner's and Cohen's interests in the three tracts to Universal.[4]

Manatee was brought into existence when the sale of the land was imminent. Petitioner's and Cohen's interests in the land were transferred to it. It engaged in no business and served no purpose other than to hold title pending the contemplated transfer to Universal. We reject as unworthy of belief any testimony that might be construed as suggesting that it had any other purpose.

All of the steps taken by petitioner and Cohen were but component parts of a single transaction the substance of which was a taxable disposition by them of their property interests to Universal. Accordingly, the Commissioner did not err in including in petitioner's taxable income, the long-term capital gain which it realized in that transaction. . . .

NOTES

1. Suppose the Elkhorn shareholders had cast their transaction as a "B" reorganization? *Compare* Rev. Rul. 70-225, 1970-1 C.B. 80, *with* Rev. Rul. 70-434, 1970-2 C.B. 83.

See Rev. Rul. 88-48, 1988-1 C.B. 531, in which the Service found "substantially all the assets" transferred for "C" reorganization purposes despite the considerable tailoring that had occurred prior to the transfer.

2. If the transaction in *West Coast Marketing Corp.* was in substance a sale between the taxpayer and Universal, and the transaction in Rev. Rul. 68-349 was in substance a sale between C and N, why was the transaction in Rev. Rul. 76-123 tax-free to both A and B? Cf. Rev. Rul. 78-250, 1978-1 C.B. 83 (merger of X Corporation into newly organized Y Corporation, with majority shareholder of X receiving Y stock and minority receiving cash, treated as redemption of minority by X).

3. For an example of the nonapplication of the step transaction doctrine to a series of events undertaken pursuant to a single plan, see Rev. Rul. 79-250, 1979-2 C.B. 156 (forward triangular merger followed by a change in the place of organization of the parent treated

---

4. The record shows, in addition, that a small minority interest (less than three-tenths of 1 percent in the aggregate) in Manatee was acquired by two persons named McKechnie and Thurlow, not otherwise identified. However, there is no evidence as to what part, if any, these persons played in the transaction or whether their interests represented anything more than mere window dressing. In the circumstances, since the burden was upon petitioner, we do not give any substantial weight to their participation in the transaction.

as two separate transactions qualify as an "A" and an "F" reorganization, respectively).

4. Compare Maurice M. Weikel, 51 T.C.M. (CCH) 432 (1986), in which the court distinguished *West Coast Marketing Corp.* and found a "B" reorganization and not a sale, although the exchange occurred shortly after the unincorporated property was incorporated. The court emphasized that the incorporation was for a substantial business purpose, that the corporation was not a mere conduit but continued in operation for three years after the exchange, and that no prearranged plan existed at the time of incorporation.

4.   *Continuity of Business Enterprise*

BENTSEN v. PHINNEY
199 F. Supp. 363 (S.D. Tex. 1961)

GARZA, District Judge. This is a suit for refund of federal income taxes paid by plaintiffs to defendant.

All of the facts have been stipulated, and the case has been submitted to the Court on written briefs and on oral argument.

A brief summary of the stipulated facts is as follows:

Plaintiff taxpayers were shareholders of Rio Development Company, a Texas corporation, which in 1955 was engaged in the land development business in the Rio Grande Valley, along with two other corporations, Bentsen Brothers, Inc., and Bentsen Loan & Investment Company.

The shareholders in such three corporations were all members of the families of Lloyd M. Bentsen, Sr., and Elmer C. Bentsen.

On March 7, 1955, the three corporations transferred all of their respective properties, subject to their liabilities, to the newly formed Consolidated American Life Insurance Company. For the sake of brevity and consistency, the former will be referred to as the "Transferor Corporations," and the latter will be referred to as the "Insurance Company."

Immediately thereafter, the stockholders of the three transferor corporations surrendered all of their stock in the three transferor corporations for cancellation. The three transferor corporations were liquidated and dissolved, and the Insurance Company issued all of its voting stock directly to the former stockholders of the three transferor corporations which had been dissolved to Bentsen Development Company, a partnership, and to Lloyd M. Bentsen, Sr., individually. [These latter two recipients] had also transferred their assets to the Insurance Company.

It is stipulated that prior to the transaction, the transferor corporations were going concerns in the land development business in the Rio Grande Valley of Texas. The Insurance Company was a going concern created to carry on the corporate business of selling life insurance.

It has been stipulated that there were business reasons and purposes for the transaction.

It is the exchange by the plaintiff taxpayers of their stock in Rio Development Company for Insurance Company stock that was the specific event out of which this refund suit arose.

It has been stipulated that there was continuity of corporate activity as between the Rio Development Company and the Insurance Company, the only change being that the type of business carried on was changed from the land development business to the insurance business.

The net result of the transactions involved in this case was that all and the same assets which had been owned by the transferor corporations, were, after the transaction, owned by the Insurance Company. The same individuals who had owned stock in the transferor corporations now owned the stock of the Insurance Company.

It has also been stipulated that prior to the consummation of the corporate transaction involved here, the Commissioner of Internal Revenue was requested to rule in advance on the federal income tax consequences of the transaction, and that the said Commissioner on two separate occasions ruled that in his opinion an exchange of stock in the Insurance Company for the land development companies' or transferor corporations' stock, was taxable because the Insurance Company engaged in a different business from the three land development corporations.

Although the plaintiff taxpayers disagreed with the Commissioner's ruling, in their respective 1955 income tax returns they reported the exchange of their Rio Development Company stock for Insurance Company stock as a taxable event and paid a tax thereon.

Thereafter the necessary procedural steps were taken to bring this refund suit before the Court for a decision as to the income tax consequences of such exchange of stock by the taxpayers.

The question for the Court to decide is: Was such corporate transaction a corporate "reorganization," as the term "reorganization" is defined in §368(a)(1), ... even though Rio Development Company engaged in the land development business and thereafter the new Insurance Company engaged in the insurance business?

The plaintiff taxpayers contend there was a corporate reorganization. The Government, defendant in this cause, maintains that there was not a corporate reorganization under §368(a)(1) ..., because there was not a continuity of business enterprise before and after the reorganization; and that this is a prerequisite as set out in the Treasury Regulations.

This case is governed by [§§368(a)(1)(C) and (D) and 354(a)(1)]. . . .

It is conceded that the 1939 Internal Revenue Code was the same in this respect as the 1954 Code, and that the corresponding Treasury Regulations issued under the 1939 Code are similar to the corresponding Treasury Regulations issued under the 1954 Code.

The Treasury Regulation states: "Requisite to a reorganization under the Code, are a continuity of business enterprise under the modified corporate form."[1]

The Government contends that since there was a lack of "continuity of the business enterprise," there was not a reorganization as contemplated under the statutes.

The question for this Court to decide is the meaning of "continuity of business enterprise," and whether or not it exists in this case.

The Government takes the position that "continuity of business enterprise" means that the new corporation must engage in the same identical or similar business. Stated in another manner, the Government maintains it is necessary that there must be an identity of type of business before and after the reorganization.

The plaintiff taxpayers have cited to the Court the case of Becher v. Commissioner, 221 F.2d 252 (2d Cir. 1955) . . . which the Government has tried to distinguish. In this case the taxpayer owned all the stock in a corporation engaged in the sponge rubber and canvas-product manufacturing business. The new corporation engaged in the business of manufacturing upholstered furniture. In that case, the Government took the position that there had been a reorganization and that a cash distribution to the shareholders of the old corporation was taxable as "boot" and was ordinary income to the shareholders. The Government prevailed in that case, and the Court, at 221 F.2d 252, said: ". . . but the Tax Court here correctly held that a business purpose does not require an identity of business before and after the reorganization. . . ."

Other cases cited are Pebble Springs Distilling Co. v. Commissioner, 231 F.2d 288 (7th Cir. 1956), cert. denied 352 U.S. 836. . . . There the old corporation had the power to carry on both a whiskey distilling business and a real estate business, but it engaged solely in the real estate business.

Another case cited to the Court is Morley Cypress Trust v. Commissioner, 3 T.C. 84 (1944). In that case the old corporation owned land held for timber and the land was conveyed to a new corporation engaged in the oil business.

The Government tries to distinguish these last two cases by saying

---

1. Treasury Regulation 118, Section 39.112(g)-1(b) under the 1939 Code; and Section 1.368-1(b) under the 1986 Code.

that in the *Pebble Springs Distilling Co.* case the new corporation could engage in the whiskey distilling business if it had wanted to, and that in the *Morley Cypress Trust* case, after the problem of continuity of business enterprise had been presented, the required continuity could have been found because both the old and the new corporations were actively engaged in exploiting the natural resources of the same land.

The Government also contends that under Texas law an insurance company cannot engage in any business other than that of insurance.

The *Morley Cypress Trust* case cited above, this Court believes, is the case most like the case before the Court. In the *Morley Cypress Trust* case the land was held for timber. In this case it was held for development. In the *Morley* case land was conveyed to a new oil corporation for use in the oil business. In this case, land (plus proceeds from the sale of land) was conveyed to a new corporation to furnish the means to capitalize a new insurance business.

The Government contends that the corresponding Treasury Regulation issued under the 1939 Code was in existence when the 1954 Code was enacted and Congress did not see fit to make any changes; that Treasury Regulations have the force of law when the Code section which they interpret is reenacted after they have once been promulgated, and cites Roberts v. Commissioner, 9 Cir., 176 F.2d 221. . . .

The Government has been unable to present the Court with any decision in which the meaning of "continuity of business enterprise" as used in the Treasury Regulations, has been interpreted. Since no Court had upheld the contention made by the Government as to the interpretation to be given said words in the Regulations, it is unfair to say that Congress had an opportunity to make a change in passing the 1954 Code. Congress was not apprised of the meaning that the Government wishes to give to said language in the Regulations, and therefore the rule expressed in Roberts v. Commissioner, supra, is not controlling here.

This Court finds that no court has passed on the question of whether "continuity of business enterprise," as used in the Regulations, means that the new corporation must engage in the identical type of business or a similar business; and it is, therefore, held that this Court is not bound by any Treasury Regulation since it is the province of the Court to decide whether the Treasury Regulation means what the Government contends it means; and whether or not if it means what the Government contends, said regulation is one that could be promulgated under the appropriate sections of the Internal Revenue Code.

This Court finds that "continuity of business enterprise," as used in the Regulations, does not mean that the new corporation must engage in either the same type of business as the old or a similar business, for if this be the requirement, then said Regulation is without authority.

To qualify as a "reorganization" under the applicable statutes, the new corporation does not have to engage in an identical or similar type of business. All that is required is that there must be continuity of the business activity.

This Court therefore finds that there was a reorganization under the applicable sections of the Internal Revenue Code.

Under the facts stipulated in this case, it is found that there was a continuity of the business activity and all requisites having been complied with, the plaintiff taxpayers have a right to a refund of the income taxes paid on the exchange of stock. The amounts to be refunded by the Government are to be those as stated in the Stipulation. . . .

REVENUE RULING 63-29
1963-1 C.B. 77

Advice has been requested whether the transaction described below qualifies as a reorganization under section 368(a)(1)(C) of the Internal Revenue Code of 1954.

M corporation and N corporation were respectively engaged in the manufacture of children's toys and in the distribution of steel and allied products. At some time in the past, M corporation sold a substantial part of its operating assets for cash and notes to a third party and more recently sold all but a small part of the remaining operating assets for cash, also to a third party. Thereafter, for valid business reasons, it acquired all of the property of N corporation solely in exchange for its voting stock. N corporation distributed the M stock received to its shareholders and then dissolved. M corporation used the assets resulting from the sale of its operating assets to expand the operations of the steel distributing business acquired from N corporation.

Section 368(a)(1)(C) of the Code states that the term "reorganization" means the acquisition by one corporation, in exchange solely for all or part of its voting stock, of substantially all the properties of another corporation.

Section 1.368-1(b) of the Income Tax Regulations specifies that a reorganization, to satisfy the requirements of the Code, must result in a continuity of the business enterprise under modified corporate form. This requirement will not be satisfied unless the surviving corporation is organized to engage in a business enterprise. See, for example, Standard Realization Company v. Commissioner, 10 T.C.

708 (1948), *acquiescence,* C.B. 1948-2, 3. However, the surviving corporation need not continue the activities conducted by its predecessors. See Donald L. Bentsen et al. v. Phinney, 199 Fed. Supp. 363 (1961); and Ernest F. Becher v. Commissioner, 221 Fed. (2d) 252 (1955). See also Pebble Springs Distilling Co. v. Commissioner, 231 Fed. (2d) 288 (1956), *certiorari denied,* 352 U.S. 836 (1956); . . . and Morley Cypress Trust, Schedule "B" et al. v. Commissioner, 3 T.C. 84, (1944), *acquiescence* C.B. 1944, 20.

Since M corporation engaged in the steel distribution business after the merger, the requirement that the reorganization result in a continuity of the business enterprise within the meaning of section 1.3681(b) of the regulations was satisfied in the instant case, even though the toy business formerly conducted by M corporation was discontinued.

Accordingly, it is held that the acquisition by M corporation of all of the properties of N corporation solely in exchange for its voting stock constitutes a reorganization as defined in section 368(a)(1)(C) of the Code.

In view of these conclusions, reconsideration has been given to Revenue Ruling 56-330, C.B. 1956-2, 204, which held, in part, that the required continuity of the business enterprise was lacking where the successor corporation in a transaction otherwise qualifying as a reorganization engaged in a new business enterprise entirely different from that conducted by its predecessors. The conclusions reached in the instant case are equally applicable to the question involved in Revenue Ruling 56-330.

Accordingly, Revenue Ruling 56-330 is revoked.

NOTES

1. Regulations that clarify and reaffirm the continuity of business enterprise requirement became applicable to acquisitions occurring after February 1, 1981. See Treas. Reg. §1.368-1(d). These regulations take the position that continuity of business enterprise exists only when the transferee corporation either continues the historic business of the transferor or uses a significant portion of the transferor's historic business assets. See Rev. Rul. 79-434, 1979-2 C.B. 155, (manufacturing corporation sold its operating assets for cash and, prior to dissolving, transferred its remaining assets — cash and short-term Treasury notes -– to an investment company in exchange for stock; held, the transaction constituted a purchase of the investment company shares and a taxable liquidation rather than a reorganization). There is evidence, however, that at least the Sixth

Circuit will not construe the regulations to impose excessive constraints. See Laure v. Commissioner, 653 F.2d 253 (6th Cir. 1981).

In Rev. Rul. 81-25, 1981-1 C.B. 65, the Service strictly interpreted the regulations when it ruled that the continuity of business enterprise requirement does not relate to the pre-reorganization business or business assets of the transferee corporation. Hence, Rev. Rul. 63-29, the holding of which is reflected in the regulations, remains in force.

2. What purpose do the regulations on continuity of business enterprise serve? Does it make sense to look at the historical business of the transferor corporation but not deal with the situation in which the transferee sells its assets, and the transferor, which retains its historic business, merges into it?

3. In addition to *Laure*, Note 1 supra, see Atlas Tool Co., 614 F.2d 860 (3d Cir.) (reorganization where transferor's assets not used, but held for possible use in transferee's business), *cert. denied sub nom.* Schaffan v. Commissioner, 449 U.S. 836 (1980), and Ernest F. Becher, 22 T.C. 932 (1954), *aff'd*, 221 F.2d 252 (2d Cir. 1955) (reorganization where assets transferred consisted of cash and assets to be liquidated). See Aidinoff and Lopata, The Continuity of Business Enterprise Requirement and Investment Company Reorganizations, 58 Taxes 914 (1980); Faber, Continuity of Interest and Business Enterprise: Is It Time to Bury Some Sacred Cows?, 34 Tax Law. 239 (1981).

4. See Rev. Rul. 70-357, 1970-2 C.B. 79, holding that a parent corporation need not continue the business of a liquidated subsidiary in order to claim the benefit of §332. Cf. Rev. Rul. 75-223, 1975-1 C.B. 109, holding that a parent corporation will be considered to have conducted the business of its liquidated subsidiary so that the distribution to the parent's shareholders of the proceeds of sale of the subsidiary's assets may qualify as a partial liquidation under what is now §302(b)(4) and (e). The size of the subsidiary's discontinued trade or business is immaterial. See Rev. Rul. 77-376, 1977-2 C.B. 107.

5. The Service followed a vacillating policy with respect to investment company reorganizations prior to the Tax Reform Act of 1976. See Rev. Proc. 73-15, 1973-2 C.B. 464; Rev. Proc. 74-10, 1974-1 C.B. 420; Rev. Proc. 76-13, 1976-1 C.B. 553. The 1976 Act resolved this issue with the enactment of §368(a)(2)(F). See Rev. Proc. 77-1, 1977-1 C.B. 534; Rev. Rul. 87-76, 1987-2 C.B. 84.

6. In Rev. Rul. 81-92, 1981-1 C.B. 133, the Service ruled that an attempted "B" reorganization fails as such if the target corporation's assets consist only of the cash that it realized on the sale of the assets it had employed previously in its manufacturing business. For a liberal interpretation of the continuity of business enterprise rules

of Treas. Reg. §1.368-1(d) in a case in which a transferee corporation disposes of a significant portion of the historic assets received from its transferor, see Rev. Rul. 81-247, 1981-2 C.B. 87.

7. In Rev. Rul. 85-198, 1985-2 C.B. 120, the Service concluded that the acquiring corporation's indirect operation of one of the target's indirect businesses was sufficient to satisfy the continuity of business enterprise requirement. The target operated two businesses through its wholly owned subsidiaries, S1 and S2. After the target merged into the acquiring corporation, the acquiring corporation transferred the stock of S2 to one of its wholly owned subsidiaries and sold the stock of S1 to an unrelated purchaser. Because the acquiring corporation, through its subsidiary, continued to operate one of the target's two significant businesses, the continuity of business requirement was met.

8. Another pervasive judicial doctrine, the one requiring "continuity of proprietary interest" for a transaction to be treated as a reorganization, will be studied in Part V of this chapter, page 576 et seq. infra.

V. CORPORATE FUSION — MERGERS AND OTHER AMALGAMATIONS

A. INTRODUCTION AND HISTORY

Well before cases like Marr v. United States, page 535 supra, reached the Supreme Court, Congress had adopted its first nonrecognition provision and had done so in circumstances limited to corporate reorganizations. Primitive in retrospect, §202(b) of the Revenue Act of 1918 provided that "when in connection with the reorganization, merger, or consolidation of a corporation a person receives in place of stock or securities owned by him new stock or securities of no greater aggregate par or face value, no gain or loss shall be deemed to occur from the exchange, and the new stock or securities received shall be treated as taking the place of the stock, securities, or property exchanged." According to the Senate Finance Committee that proposed the section, it was "to negative the assertion of tax in the case of certain purely paper transaction." Seidman's Legislative History 1938 – 1861 899 (1938); R. Blakey and G. Blakey, The Federal Income Tax 175 (1940).

The federal income tax law has contained reorganization and nonrecognition provisions continuously since 1918. They have become more complex and have taken crucial turns at different times.

Study of some of the cases that dealt with the statute as it was during the years prior to those covered by present law is essential to a full understanding of present law and to the continuing administrative and judicial attitudes toward particular types of problems.

B. STATUTORY ISSUES

1. *Continuity of Proprietary Interest*

a. Interest Acquired

PINELLAS ICE & COLD STORAGE CO. v.
COMMISSIONER

57 F.2d 188 (5th Cir. 1932), *aff'd*, 287 U.S. 462 (1933)

[The factual statement set forth below is taken from the opinion of Mr. Justice McREYNOLDS, speaking for the Supreme Court in its affirmance of this case.* . . . Excerpts from Judge FOSTER's opinion, speaking for the Court of Appeals, follow the factual statement.]

"Petitioner, a Florida corporation, made and sold ice at St. Petersburg. Substantially the same stockholders owned the Citizens Ice and Cold Storage Company, engaged in like business at the same place. In February, 1926, Lewis, general manager of both companies, began negotiations for the sale of their properties to the National Public Service Corporation. Their directors and stockholders were anxious to sell, distribute the assets and dissolve the corporations. The prospective vendee desired to acquire the properties of both companies, but not of one without the other.

"In October, 1926, agreement was reached and the vendor's directors again approved the plan for distribution and dissolution. In November, 1926, petitioner and the National Corporation entered into a formal written contract conditioned upon a like one by the Citizens Company. This referred to petitioner as 'vendor' and the National Corporation as 'purchaser.' The former agreed to sell, the latter to purchase the physical property, plants, etc., 'together with the goodwill of the business, free and clear of all defects, liens, encumbrances, taxes and assessments for the sum of $1,400,000, payable as hereinafter provided.' The specified date . . . for consummation [was] eleven A.M., December 15, 1926, . . . when 'the vendor shall deliver to the purchaser instruments of conveyance and transfer

---

*Page 580 infra. — Ed.

by general warranty in form satisfactory to the purchaser of the property set forth. . . . The purchaser shall pay to the vendor the sum of $400,000.00 in cash.' The balance of the purchase price ($1,000,000.00) shall be paid $500,000.00 on or before January 31, 1927; $250,000.00 on or before March 1, 1927; $250,000.00 on or before April 1st, 1927. Also, the deferred installments of the purchase price shall be evidenced by the purchaser's 6% notes, secured either by notes or bonds of the Florida West Coast Ice Company, thereafter to be organized to take title, or other satisfactory collateral; or by 6% notes of such Florida company secured by first lien on the property conveyed, or other satisfactory collateral.

"The vendor agreed to procure undertakings by E. T. Lewis and Leon D. Lewis not to engage in manufacturing or selling ice in Pinellas County, Florida, for ten years.

"The $400,000 cash payment was necessary for discharge of debts, liens, encumbrances, etc. The Florida Company, incorporated December 6, 1926, took title to the property and executed the purchase notes secured as agreed. These were paid at or before maturity except the one for $100,000, held until November, 1927, because of flaw in a title. As the notes were paid petitioner immediately distributed the proceeds to its stockholders according to the plan.

"The property conveyed to the Florida Company included all of petitioner's assets except a few vacant lots worth not more than $10,000, some accounts — $3,000 face value — also a small amount of cash. Assets, not exceeding 1% of the whole, were transferred to the Citizens Holding Corporation as trustee for petitioner's stockholders — 99% of all vendor's property went to the Florida Company. The plan of the whole arrangement as carried out was accepted by petitioner's officers and stockholders prior to November 4, 1926.

"The Commissioner of Internal Revenue determined that the petitioner derived taxable gain exceeding $500,000 and assessed it accordingly under the Act of 1926. The Board of Tax Appeals and the Circuit Court of Appeals approved this action.

"The facts are not in controversy. The gain is admitted; but it is said this was definitely exempted from taxation by §203, Revenue Act of 1926.

"The Act, . . . —

Sec. 202. (a) Except as hereinafter provided in this section, the gain from the sale or other disposition of property shall be the excess of the amount realized therefrom over the basis provided in subdivision (a) or (b) of section 204, and the loss shall be the excess of such basis over the amount realized. . . .

(c) The amount realized from the sale or other disposition of property shall be the sum of any money received plus the fair market value of the property (other than money) received.

(d) In the case of a sale or exchange, the extent to which the gain or loss determined under this section shall be recognized for the purposes of this title, shall be determined under the provisions of section 203. . . .

Sec. 203. (a) Upon the sale or exchange of property the entire amount of the gain or loss, determined under section 202, shall be recognized, except as hereinafter provided in this section. . . .

(b)(3) No gain or loss shall be recognized if a corporation a party to a reorganization exchanges property, in pursuance of the plan of reorganization, solely for stock or securities in another corporation a party to the reorganization. . . .

(e) If an exchange would be within the provisions of paragraph (3) of subdivision (b) if it were not for the fact that the property received in exchange consists not only of stock or securities permitted by such paragraph to be received without the recognition of gain, but also of other property or money, then

(1) If the corporation receiving such other property or money distributes it in pursuance of the plan of reorganization, no gain to the corporation shall be recognized from the exchange, but

(2) If the corporation receiving such other property or money does not distribute it in pursuance of the plan of reorganization, the gain, if any, to the corporation shall be recognized, but in an amount not in excess of the sum of such money and the fair market value of such other property so received, which is not so distributed. . . .

(h) As used in this section and sections 201 and 204 —

(1) The term "reorganization" means (A) a merger or consolidation (including the acquisition by one corporation of at least a majority of the voting stock and at least a majority of the total number of shares of all other classes of stock of another corporation, or substantially all the properties of another corporation), or (B) a transfer by a corporation of all or a part of its assets to another corporation if immediately after the transfer the transferor or its stockholders or both are in control of the corporation to which the assets are transferred, or (C) a recapitalization, or (D) a mere change in identity, form, or place of organization, however effected.

(2) The term "a party to a reorganization" includes a corporation resulting from a reorganization and includes both corporations in the case of an acquisition by one corporation of at least a majority of the voting stock and at least a majority of the total number of shares of all other classes of stock of another corporation. . . ."

Before Bryan, Foster, and Walker, Circuit Judges.

FOSTER, Circuit Judge. . . . Relying on the provisions of section 203, paragraphs (b)(3), (e)(1) and (h)(1)(A) . . . , it is contended by petitioner: That there was a reorganization to which petitioner and the West Coast Company were parties; that the notes were securities of the new company; that there was an exchange of the property of petitioner for cash and securities; that this was distributed in pursuance of a plan of reorganization; and that therefore no gain to the corporation should be recognized.

Apparently there are no decisions in point, and it would be useless to review the cases cited by either side.

Section 203* appeared first in the 1924 Revenue Act. . . . Prior thereto the profit resulting from all exchanges of property was taxable. It is evident that in enacting section 203 Congress intended to exempt from consideration for either profit or loss transfers of property which were really exchanges of capital assets, and, to a certain extent, to brush aside technicalities in so construing them. It is equally clear that there was no intention to exempt profit arising from an outright sale of property, or an exchange of property, between corporations where there was in fact no reorganization.

There is no doubt that the written agreement of November 4, 1926, for the disposition of petitioner's property to a new corporation, contemplated an outright sale and not an exchange or a reorganization. The conveyance of the property on December 17, 1926, was in form a sale and not an exchange. This is not seriously disputed by petitioner, but it is contended that under the definition of paragraph (h)(1)(A)* the mere acquisition by the Florida West Coast Ice Company of substantially all the property of petitioner was a reorganization. . . .

As applied to corporations, the terms "merger" and "consolidation" have well known legal meanings. While the result is practically the same in either event, there is this difference. In a merger one corporation absorbs the other and remains in existence while the other is dissolved. In a consolidation a new corporation is created and the consolidating corporations are extinguished. In either event, the resulting corporation acquires all the property, rights, and franchises of the dissolved corporations, and their stockholders become its stockholders. . . .

It must be assumed that in adopting paragraph (h) Congress intended to use the words "merger" and "consolidation" in their ordinary and accepted meanings. Giving the matter in parenthesis the most liberal construction, it is only when there is an acquisition of substantially all the property of another corporation in connection with a merger or consolidation that a reorganization takes place. Clause (B) of the paragraph removes any doubt as to the intention of Congress on this point.

It follows that there was no reorganization, and consequently no

---

*The precursor, inter alia, to §§354 and 361 of the 1986 Code. — ED.
*Cf. §368(a)(1)(C) of the 1986 Code. — ED.

party to a reorganization, in connection with the disposition of petitioner's property. It is unnecessary to pass upon petitioner's other contentions.

The record presents no reversible error. The petition is denied.

PINELLAS ICE & COLD STORAGE CO. v. COMMISSIONER
287 U.S. 462 (1933)

Mr. Justice McREYNOLDS delivered the opinion of the Court. . . . Counsel for the petitioner maintain —

The record discloses a "reorganization" to which petitioner was party and a preliminary plan strictly pursued. The Florida West Coast Ice Company acquired substantially all of petitioner's property in exchange for cash and securities which were promptly distributed to the latter's stockholders. Consequently, under §203, the admitted gain was not taxable.

The Board of Tax Appeals held that the transaction in question amounted to a sale of petitioner's property for money and not an exchange for securities within the true meaning of the statute. It, accordingly and as we think properly, upheld the Commissioner's action.

The "vendor" agreed "to sell" and "the purchaser" agreed "to purchase" certain described property for a definite sum of money. Part of this sum was paid in cash; for the balance the purchaser executed three promissory notes, secured by the deposit of mortgage bonds, payable, with interest, in about forty-five, seventy-five, and one hundred and five days, respectively. These notes — mere evidence of obligation to pay the purchase price — were not securities within the intendment of the act and were properly regarded as the equivalent of cash. It would require clear language to lead us to conclude that Congress intended to grant exemption to one who sells property and for the purchase price accepts well-secured, short-term notes, (all payable within four months), when another who makes a like sale and receives cash certainly would be taxed. We can discover no good basis in reason for the contrary view and its acceptance would make evasion of taxation very easy. In substance the petitioner sold for the equivalent of cash; the gain must be recognized.

The court below held that the facts disclosed failed to show a "reorganization" within the statutory definition. And, in the circumstances, we approve that conclusion. But the construction which the court seems to have placed upon clause A, paragraph (h)(1), §203, we think is too narrow. It conflicts with established practice of the tax officers and if passed without comment may produce perplexity.

The court said — "It must be assumed that in adopting paragraph (h) Congress intended to use the words 'merger' and 'consolidation' in their ordinary and accepted meanings. Giving the matter in parenthesis the most liberal construction, it is only when there is an acquisition of substantially all the property of another corporation in connection with a merger or consolidation that a reorganization takes place. Clause (B) of the paragraph removes any doubt as to the intention of Congress on this point."

The paragraph in question directs — "The term 'reorganization' means (A) a merger or consolidation (including the acquisition by one corporation of at least a majority of the voting stock and at least a majority of the total number of shares of all other classes of stock of another corporation, or substantially all the properties of another corporation)." The words within the parenthesis may not be disregarded. They expand the meaning of "merger" or "consolidation" so as to include some things which partake of the nature of a merger or consolidation but are beyond the ordinary and commonly accepted meaning of those words — so as to embrace circumstances difficult to delimit but which in strictness cannot be designated as either merger or consolidation. But the mere purchase for money of the assets of one company by another is beyond the evident purpose of the provision, and has no real semblance to a merger or consolidation. Certainly, we think that to be within the exemption the seller must acquire an interest in the affairs of the purchasing company more definite than that incident to ownership of its short-term purchase-money notes. This general view is adopted and well sustained in Cortland Specialty Co. v. Commissioner of Internal Revenue [infra]. It harmonizes with the underlying purpose of the provisions in respect of exemptions and gives some effect to all the words employed.

The judgment of the court below is affirmed.

NOTE

See Griswold, "Securities" and "Continuity of Interest," A Suggestion for the Reexamination of Two Concepts in the Reorganization Provisions of the Tax Laws, 58 Harv. L. Rev. 705 (1945).

CORTLAND SPECIALTY CO. v. COMMISSIONER
60 F.2d 937 (2d Cir. 1932), *cert. denied*, 288 U.S. 599 (1933)

[As in *Pinellas*, the principal issue was seen to be whether a corporation's transfer of substantially all its properties to another corporation for cash and notes payable within 14 months was a "reorganization" within the meaning of §203 of the Revenue Act of 1926. Like the Fifth Circuit in *Pinellas,* the Second Circuit concluded (at 940) that a transfer of assets, to constitute a reorganization, must smack of "merger" or "consolidation," and those concepts imply "a continuance of interest on the part of the transferor in the properties transferred."

[If the Supreme Court had reviewed *Cortland* it probably would have affirmed on grounds like those employed in *Pinellas,* rejecting the notion of required nexus to "merger" or "consolidation." As the concluding paragraph in the Supreme Court's opinion in *Pinellas* indicates, however, a second ground for decision was employed by the Second Circuit in *Cortland,* this one very much to the Supreme Court's liking, as indicated by its statements in *Pinellas* and in later cases. As seen by the Second Circuit, this secondary issue was posed: Even if the transfer of assets for cash and short term notes had been made pursuant to a "plan of reorganization," did the payment that *Cortland* received in exchange have to include some "stock or securities," and if so, had they been included in this case?]

Before L. Hand, Augustus N. Hand, and Chase, Circuit Judges.

AUGUSTUS N. HAND, Circuit Judge. . . . Furthermore the Cortland Company cannot come within the exception to the general rule that gains realized from exchanges of property represent taxable income unless section 203(e) and section 203(e)(1)* apply. Under those clauses, even if the transfer to Deyo was an exchange in pursuance of a "plan of reorganization," the property received by Cortland had to include *some* "stock or securities" (§203(e)), or the exemption could not be had. As no stock was issued against the transfer, the conditions for an exemption were not fulfilled unless the notes, all payable within fourteen months of the date of the transfer, and all unsecured, can be considered "securities" under section 203(e). Inasmuch as a transfer made entirely for cash would not be enough, it cannot be supposed that anything so near to cash as these notes payable in so short a time and doubtless readily marketable would meet the legislative requirements.

The very reason that section 203(e) requires that some of the property received in exchange should be "*stock or securities*" is to deprive a mere sale for cash of the benefits of an exemption and to require an amalgamation of the existing interests. There can be no justice or propriety in taxing one corporation who transfers its properties for cash and in relieving another that takes part of its pay in short time notes. The situation might be different had the "securities," though not in stock, created such obligations as to give creditors or others some assured participation in the properties of the trans-

---

*Cf. §361(b) of the 1986 Code. — ED.

feree corporation. The word "securities" was used so as not to defeat the exemption in cases where the interest of the transferor was carried over to the new corporation in some form. . . .

The orders of the Board of Tax Appeals are affirmed.

NOTES

1. Suppose the "notes" were payable in five years, or ten years. Would it make any difference if they were redeemable at the issuer's option? At any time? If there were a plan for their redemption? If there were or were not a ready market in the "securities" of the issuer?

2. The Supreme Court regarded the Court of Appeals' construction of §203(h)(1)(A) in *Pinellas* as "too narrow." Why? Was it "too narrow" in your judgment? What function would clause (A) serve if the Court of Appeals' construction had been accepted? The effects of the Supreme Court's view that the parenthetical clause had independent significance were far-reaching, as later cases show. As you read the cases consider whether the Supreme Court's construction was helpful or harmful in the evolution of the law of reorganization.

JOHN A. NELSON CO. v. HELVERING
296 U.S. 374 (1935)

Mr. Justice McREYNOLDS delivered the opinion of the Court. The petitioner contests a deficiency income assessment made on account of alleged gains during 1926. It claims that the transaction out of which the assessment arose was reorganization within the statute. Section 203, Revenue Act, 1926, c. 27, . . . is relied upon. The pertinent parts are in the margin of the opinion in Helvering v. Minnesota Tea Co.* . . .

In 1926, under an agreement with petitioner, the Elliott-Fisher Corporation organized a new corporation with 12,500 shares nonvoting preferred stock and 30,000 shares of common stock.** It purchased the latter for $2,000,000 cash. This new corporation then acquired substantially all of petitioner's property, except $100,000, in return for $2,000,000 cash and the entire issue of preferred stock.*** Part of this cash was used to retire petitioner's own pre-

---

*Page 585 infra. — ED.
**The preferred stock was callable in whole or in part on any dividend date at the option of the corporation. No redemption premium was to be paid if the preferred stock was redeemed prior to 1932. — ED.
***Taxpayer actually received 14,060 shares of preferred with a par value of $100 each, the added shares representing profits earned by taxpayer between the date of the agreement and the date of transfer. — ED.

ferred shares, and the remainder and the preferred stock of the new company went to its stockholders. It retained its franchise and $100,000, and continued to be liable for certain obligations. The preferred stock so distributed, except in case of default, had no voice in the control of the issuing corporation.

The Commissioner, Board of Tax Appeals and the court all concluded there was no reorganization. This, we think, was error.

The court below thought the facts showed

> that the transaction essentially constituted a sale of the greater part of petitioner's assets for cash and the preferred stock in the new corporation, leaving the Elliott-Fisher Company in entire control of the new corporation by virtue of its ownership of the common stock. . . .
>
> The controlling facts leading to this conclusion are that petitioner continued its corporate existence and its franchise and retained a portion of its assets; that it acquired no controlling interest in the corporation to which it delivered the greater portion of its assets; that there was no continuity of interest from the old corporation to the new; that the control of the property conveyed passed to a stranger, in the management of which petitioner retained no voice.
>
> It follows that the transaction was not part of a strict merger or consolidation or part of something that partakes of the nature of a merger or consolidation involving a continuance of essentially the same interests through a new modified corporate structure. Mere acquisition by one corporation of a majority of the stock or all the assets of another corporation does not of itself constitute a reorganization, where such acquisition takes the form of a purchase and sale and does not result in or bear some material resemblance to a merger or consolidation.

True, the mere acquisition of the assets of one corporation by another does not amount to reorganization within the statutory definition. Pinellas Ice Co. v. Commissioner, 287 U.S. 462 [page 580 supra], so affirmed. But where, as here, the seller acquires a definite and substantial interest in the affairs of the purchasing corporation, a wholly different situation arises. The owner of preferred stock is not without substantial interest in the affairs of the issuing corporation, although denied voting rights. The statute does not require participation in the management of the purchaser; nor does it demand that the conveying corporation be dissolved. A controlling interest in the transferee corporation is not made a requisite by §203(h)(1)(A). This must not be confused with par. (h)(2).

Finally, as has been pointed out in the *Minnesota Tea* case, [page 585 infra], par. (h)(1)(B) was not intended to modify the provisions of par. (h)(1)(A). It describes a class. Whether some overlapping is possible is not presently important.

The judgment below must be reversed.

HELVERING v. MINNESOTA TEA CO.
296 U.S. 378 (1935)

Mr. Justice McREYNOLDS delivered the opinion of the Court. . . . Respondent, a Minnesota corporation with three stockholders, assailed a deficiency assessment for 1928 income tax, and prevailed below. The Commissioner seeks reversal. He claims the transaction out of which the assessment arose was not a reorganization within §112, par. (i)(1)(A), Revenue Act, 1928, c. 852 . . . : "The term 'reorganization' means (A) a merger or consolidation (including the acquisition by one corporation of at least a majority of the voting stock and at least a majority of the total number of shares of all other classes of stock of another corporation, or substantially all the properties of another corporation)." The Circuit Court of Appeals held otherwise and remanded the cause for determination by the Board whether the whole of the cash received by the Minnesota Tea Company was in fact distributed as required by the act. We granted certiorari because of alleged conflicting opinions.

The petition also stated that, as the taxpayer made an earlier conveyance of certain assets, the later one, here in question, of what remained to the Grand Union Company did not result in acquisition by one corporation of substantially all property of another. This point was not raised prior to the petition for certiorari and, in the circumstances, we do not consider it.

Statutory provisions presently helpful are in the margin.*.

---

*. . . **Sec. 203.** (a) Upon the sale or exchange of property the entire amount of the gain or the loss, determined under section 202, shall be recognized, except as hereinafter provided in this section. . . .

(b)(2) No gain or loss shall be recognized if stock or securities in a corporation a party to a reorganization are, in pursuance of the plan of reorganization, exchanged solely for stock or securities in such corporation or in another corporation a party to the reorganization.

(3) No gain or loss shall be recognized if a corporation a party to a reorganization exchanges property, in pursuance of the plan of reorganization, solely for stock or securities in another corporation a party to the reorganization. . . .

(e) If an exchange would be within the provisions of paragraph (3) of subdivision (b) if it were not for the fact that the property received in exchange consists not only of stock or securities permitted by such paragraph to be received without the recognition of gain, but also of other property or money, then —

(1) If the corporation receiving such other property or money distributes it in pursuance of the plan of reorganization, no gain to the corporation shall be recognized from the exchange, but

(2) If the corporation receiving such other property or money does not distribute it in pursuance of the plan of reorganization, the gain, if any, to the corporation shall be recognized, but in an amount not in excess of the sum of such money and the fair market value of such other property so received, which is not so distributed.

(h) As used in this section and sections 201 and 204 —

(1) The term "reorganization" means (A) a merger or consolidation (including the acquisition by one corporation of at least a majority of the voting stock and at least a majority of the total number of shares of all other classes of stock of another corporation, or substantially all the properties of another corporation), or (B) a transfer by a corporation of all or a part of its assets to another corporation if immediately

July 14, 1928, respondent caused Peterson Investment Company to be organized and transferred to the latter real estate, investments and miscellaneous assets in exchange for the transferee's entire capital stock. The shares thus obtained were immediately distributed among the three stockholders. August 23, 1928, it transferred all remaining assets to Grand Union Company in exchange for voting trust certificates, representing 18,000* shares of the transferee's common stock, and $426,842.52 cash. It retained the certificates; but immediately distributed the money among the stockholders, who agreed to pay $106,471.73 of its outstanding debts. Although of opinion that there had been reorganization, the Commissioner treated as taxable gain the amount of the assumed debts upon the view that this amount of the cash received by the company was really appropriated to the payment of its debts.

The matter went before the Board of Tax Appeals upon the question whether the Commissioner ruled rightly in respect of this taxable gain. Both parties proceeded upon the view that there had been reorganization. Of its own motion, the Board questioned and denied the existence of one. It then ruled that the corporation had realized taxable gain amounting to the difference between cost of the property transferred and the cash received plus the value of the 18,000 shares — $712,195.90.

The Circuit Court of Appeals found there was reorganization within the statute and reversed the Board. It concluded that the words "the acquisition by one corporation of . . . substantially all the property of another corporation" plainly include the transaction under consideration. Also that Clause (B), §112(i)(1), . . . did not narrow the scope of Clause (A). Further, that reorganization was not dependent upon dissolution by the conveying corporation. And finally, that its conclusions find support in Treasury regulations long in force.

These conclusions we think are correct.

The Commissioner maintains that the statute presents two definitions of reorganization by transfer of assets. One, Clause (B),

---

after the transfer the transferor or its stockholders or both are in control of the corporation to which the assets are transferred, or (C) a recapitalization, or (D) a mere change in identity, form, or place of organization, however effected.

(2) The term "a party to a reorganization" includes a corporation resulting from a reorganization and includes both corporations in the case of an acquisition by one corporation of at least a majority of the voting stock and at least a majority of the total number of shares of all other classes of stock of another corporation.

Revenue Act, 1926 c. 27. . . .

Revenue Act, 1928, c. 852. . . .

Section 112(a), (b)(3), (b)(4), . . . (d), (d)(1), (d)(2), (i), (i)(1) and (i)(2) repeat the words of Section 203(a), (b)(2), (b)(3), . . . (e),(e)(1), (e)(2), (h), (h)(1) and (h)(2) of the Act of 1924. [Footnote by the court.]

*The 18,000 shares amounted to 7½ percent of Grand Union's outstanding stock. — ED.

requires that the transferor obtain control of the transferee. The other, Clause (A), is part of the definition of merger or consolidation, and must be narrowly interpreted so as to necessitate something nearly akin to technical merger or consolidation. These clauses have separate legislative histories and were intended to be mutually exclusive. Consequently, he says, Clause (A) must be restricted to prevent overlapping and negation of the condition in Clause (B). Also, the transaction here involved substantially changed the relation of the taxpayer to its assets; a large amount of cash passed between the parties; there are many attributes of a sale; what was done did not sufficiently resemble merger or consolidation as commonly understood.

With painstaking care, the opinion of the court below gives the history of Clauses (A) and (B), §112(i)(1). We need not repeat the story. Clause (A) first appeared in the Act of 1921; (B) was added by the 1924 Act. We find nothing in the history or words employed which indicates an intention to modify the evident meaning of (A) by what appears in (B). Both can have effect, and if one does somewhat overlap the other the taxpayer should not be denied, for that reason, what one paragraph clearly grants him. Treasury regulations long enforced support the taxpayer's position, as the opinion below plainly points out.

Pinellas Ice Co. v. Commissioner, 287 U.S. 462, 470, [page 580 supra] considered the language of §203(h)(1)(A), Act of 1926, which became §112(i)(1)(A), Act of 1928, and held that a sale for money or short-term notes was not within its intendment. We approved the conclusion of the Commissioner, Board of Tax Appeals and Court of Appeals that the transaction there involved was in reality a sale for the equivalent of money — not an exchange for securities. . . . And we said:

> The words within the parenthesis may not be disregarded. They expand the meaning of "merger" or "consolidation" so as to include some things which partake of the nature of a merger or consolidation but are beyond the ordinary and commonly accepted meaning of those words — so as to embrace circumstances difficult to delimit but which in strictness cannot be designated as either merger or consolidation. But the mere purchase for money of the assets of one Company by another is beyond the evident purpose of the provision, and has no real semblance to a merger or consolidation. Certainly, we think that to be within the exemption the seller must acquire an interest in the affairs of the purchasing company more definite than that incident to ownership of its short-term purchase-money notes.

And we now add that this interest must be definite and material; it must represent a substantial part of the value of the thing transferred. This much is necessary in order that the result accomplished may genuinely partake of the nature of merger or consolidation.

Gregory v. Helvering [page 545 supra] revealed a sham — a mere device intended to obscure the character of the transaction. We, of course, disregarded the mask and dealt with realities. The present record discloses no such situation; nothing suggests other than a bona fide business move.

The transaction here was no sale, but partook of the nature of a reorganization in that the seller acquired a definite and substantial interest in the purchaser.

True it is that the relationship of the taxpayer to the assets conveyed was substantially changed, but this is not inhibited by the statute. Also, a large part of the consideration was cash. This, we think, is permissible so long as the taxpayer received an interest in the affairs of the transferee which represented a material part of the value of the transferred assets.

Finally, it is said the transferor was not dissolved and therefore the transaction does not adequately resemble consolidation. But dissolution is not prescribed and we are unable to see that such action is essential to the end in view.

The challenged judgment is affirmed. . . .

NOTES

1. In 1984 Congress overruled the holding in *Minnesota Tea* (along with dicta in earlier cases as well), which had countenanced a "C" reorganization even though the transferor stayed alive, not transferring or distributing all of its assets. See §368(a)(2)(G).

After remand of *Minnesota Tea*, the case again came before the Supreme Court on the issue whether the transferor corporation was taxable on money received in the reorganization and transferred to the shareholders pursuant to an agreement that the shareholders assume and pay off corporate debt. See 302 U.S. 609 (1938). Interpreting a provision similar to §361(b)(1), the Supreme Court held that the receipt of the money was taxable to the corporation because it was not "distributed" to (or for the benefit of) the *shareholders*. According to the Court, the shareholders had received the money not as a distribution for their own benefit, but as a fund that they were bound to pass on to the corporation's creditors. The outcome had been roundly criticized and was finally overruled in the 1986 Act amendments to §361. See §361(b)(3).

2. After *Pinellas, Cortland,* and *Minnesota Tea,* the transferor corporation or its shareholders had to acquire a "definite and substantial interest" in the transferee corporation, representing a "material part

of the value of the transferred assets," in order that the transfer qualify as a reorganization. In terms of tax planning, counseling, or litigating, did these developments contribute much to certainty? Given the ends that the courts indicate the reorganization provisions are designed to serve, how likely were the Supreme Court's formulations to contribute to their attainment?

LETULLE v. SCOFIELD
308 U.S. 415 (1940)

Mr. Justice ROBERTS delivered the opinion of the court. We took this case because the petition for certiorari alleged that the Circuit Court of Appeals had based its decision on a point not presented or argued by the litigants, which the petitioner had never had an opportunity to meet by the production of evidence.

The Gulf Coast Irrigation Company was the owner of irrigation properties. Petitioner was its sole stockholder. He personally owned certain lands and other irrigation properties. November 4, 1931, the Irrigation Company, the Gulf Coast Water Company, and the petitioner, entered into an agreement which recited that the petitioner owned all of the stock of the Irrigation Company; described the company's properties, and stated that, prior to conveyance to be made pursuant to the contract, the Irrigation Company would be the owner of certain other lands and irrigation properties. These other lands and properties were those which the petitioner individually owned. The contract called for a conveyance of all the properties owned, and to be owned, by the Irrigation Company for $50,000 in cash and $750,000 in bonds of the Water Company, payable serially over the period January 1, 1933, to January 1, 1944. The petitioner joined in this agreement as a guarantor of the title of the Irrigation Company and for the purpose of covenanting that he would not personally enter into the irrigation business within a fixed area during a specified period after the execution of the contract. Three days later, at a special meeting of stockholders of the Irrigation Company, the proposed reorganization was approved, the minutes stating that the taxpayer, "desiring also to reorganize his interest in the properties," had consented to be a party to the reorganization. The capital stock of the Irrigation Company was increased and thereupon the taxpayer subscribed for the new stock and paid for it by conveyance of his individual properties.

The contract between the two corporations was carried out November 18, with the result that the Water Company became owner of all the properties then owned by the Irrigation Company including the property theretofore owned by the petitioner individually. Subsequently all of its assets, including the bonds received from the Water Company, were distributed to the petitioner. The company was then dissolved. The petitioner and his wife filed a tax return as members of a community in which they reported no gain as a result of the receipt of the liquidating dividend from the Irrigation Company. The latter reported no gain for the taxable year in virtue of its receipt of bonds and cash from the Water Company. The Commissioner of Internal Revenue assessed additional taxes against the community, as individual taxpayers, by reason of the receipt of the liquidating dividend, and against the petitioner as transferee of the Irrigation Company's assets in virtue of the gain realized by the company on the sale of its property. The tax was paid and claims for refund were filed. Petitioner's wife having died he brought suit individually and as her executor and representative in the community property against the respondent to recover the amount of the additional taxes so assessed. He alleged that the transaction constituted a tax-exempt reorganization as defined by the Revenue Act.[1] The respondent traversed the allegations of the complaints and the causes were consolidated and tried by the District Court without a jury. The respondent's contention that the transaction amounted merely to a sale of assets by the petitioner and the Irrigation Company and did not fall within the statutory definition of a tax-free reorganization was overruled by the District Court and judgment was entered for the petitioner.

The respondent appealed, asserting error on the part of the District Court in matters not now material and also assigning as error the court's holding that the transaction constituted a nontaxable reorganization.

The Circuit Court of Appeals concluded that, as the Water Company acquired substantially all the properties of the Irrigation Company, there was a merger of the latter within the literal language of the statute, but held that, in the light of the construction this Court has put upon the statute, the transaction would not be a reorganization unless the transferor retained a definite and substantial interest in the affairs of the transferee. It thought this requirement was satisfied by the taking of the bonds of the Water Company, and, therefore, agreed with the District Court that a reorganization had been consummated. It added, however, "We find a reason for reversing the judgment which has not been argued." Adverting to the fact that the transfer of the petitioner's individual properties to the Irrigation Company was for the purpose of including them in the latter's assets to be transferred in the proposed reorganization, the court said the statute did not extend to the reorganization of an

---

1. Section 112(i) of the Revenue Act of 1928, c. 852. . . .

individual's business or affairs, and the transaction was a reorganization within the meaning of the Revenue Act as respects the corporation's assets owned on November 4, 1931, but not as respects the petitioner's individual properties included in the sale. It concluded:

> Only so much of the consideration as represents the price of the properties and business of the Irrigation Company is entitled to be protected from taxation as arising from a reorganization. It does not appear what the proper apportionment is. The burden was upon LeTulle to show not only that he had been illegally taxed, but how much of what was collected from him was illegal. The latter he did not do. The evidence does not support the judgment for the full amount paid by him. It is accordingly reversed, that further proceedings may be had consistent herewith.

The petitioner sought certiorari asserting that the Circuit Court of Appeals had departed from the usual and accepted course of judicial proceedings by deciding the cause upon a ground not presented or argued and hence had deprived the petitioner of his day in court. The respondent, though he had contended below that the transaction in question did not amount to a tax-free statutory reorganization, did not file a cross petition asking for a review of that part of the judgment exempting from taxation gain to the Irrigation Company arising from the transfer of its assets owned by it on and prior to November 4, 1931, and the part of the liquidating dividend attributable thereto.

We find it unnecessary to consider petitioner's contention that the Circuit Court of Appeals erred in deciding the case on a ground not raised by the pleadings, not before the trial court, not suggested or argued in the Circuit Court of Appeals, and one as to which the petitioner had never had the opportunity to present his evidence, since we are of opinion that the transaction did not amount to a reorganization and that, therefore, the petitioner cannot complain, as the judgment must be affirmed on the ground that no tax-free reorganization was effected within the meaning of the statute.

Section 112(i) provides, so far as material:

> (1) The term "reorganization" means (A) a merger or consolidation (including the acquisition by one corporation of at least a majority of the voting stock and at least a majority of the total number of shares of all other classes of stock of another corporation, or substantially all the properties of another corporation). . . .

As the court below properly states, the section is not to be read literally as denominating the transfer of all the assets of one company for what amounts to a cash consideration given by the other a reorganization. We have held that where the consideration consists of cash and short term notes the transfer does not amount to a reorganization within the true meaning of the statute, but is a sale upon which gain or loss must be reckoned.[3] We have said that the statute was not satisfied unless the transferor retained a substantial stake in the enterprise and such a stake was thought to be retained where a large proportion of the consideration was in common stock of the transferee,[4] or where the transferor took cash and the entire issue of preferred stock of the transferee corporation.[5] And, where the consideration is represented by a substantial proportion of stock, and the balance in bonds, the total consideration received is exempt from tax under §112(b)(4) and 112(g).[6]

In applying our decision in the *Pinellas* case the courts have generally held that receipt of long term bonds as distinguished from short term notes constitutes the retention of an interest in the purchasing corporation. There has naturally been some difficulty in classifying the securities involved in various cases.

We are of opinion that the term of the obligations is not material. Where the consideration is wholly in the transferee's bonds, or part cash and part such bonds, we think it cannot be said that the transferor retains any proprietary interest in the enterprise. On the contrary, he becomes a creditor of the transferee; and we do not think that the fact referred to by the Circuit Court of Appeals, that the bonds were secured solely by the assets transferred and that, upon default, the bondholder would retake only the property sold, changes his status from that of a creditor to one having a proprietary stake, within the purview of the statute.

We conclude that the Circuit Court of Appeals was in error in holding that, as respects any of the property transferred to the Water Company, the transaction was other than a sale or exchange upon which gain or loss must be reckoned in accordance with the provisions of the revenue act dealing with the recognition of gain or loss upon a sale or exchange.

Had the respondent sought and been granted certiorari the petitioner's tax liability would, in the view we have expressed, be substantially increased over the amount found due by the Circuit Court of Appeals. Since the respondent has not drawn into question so much of the judgment as exempts from taxation gain to the Irrigation Company arising from transfer of its assets owned by it on and prior to November 4, 1931, and the part of the liquidating dividend attributable thereto, we cannot afford him relief from that portion of the judgment which was adverse to him.

3. Pinellas Ice & Cold Storage Co. v. Commissioner, 287 U.S. 462 [page 580 supra].
4. Helvering v. Minnesota Tea Co., 296 U.S. 378 [page 585 supra].
5. Nelson Co. v. Helvering, 296 U.S. 374 [page 583 supra].
6. ... See Helvering v. Watts, 296 U.S. 387.

A respondent or an appellee may urge any matter appearing in the record in support of a judgment, but he may not attack it even on grounds asserted in the court below, in an effort to have this Court reverse it, when he himself has not sought review of the whole judgment, or of that portion which is adverse to him.

The judgment of the Circuit Court of Appeals is affirmed and the cause is remanded to the District Court with directions to proceed in accordance with the opinion and mandate of the Circuit Court of Appeals.

Affirmed.

NOTES

1. In Helvering v. Watts, 296 U.S. 387 (1935), decided the same day as *Nelson* and *Minnesota Tea*, the shareholders of one corporation exchanged all of their shares for common stock of another corporation having an agreed value of $963,090 and mortgage bonds valued at $1,161,184.50. The first bond was to be retired within two months, and the remaining bonds were due at one year intervals over the next seven years. The acquiring corporation also paid $338,815 to the creditors of the acquired corporation, and the payment was treated as a loan from the transferee to the transferor. The Supreme Court held that the bonds were "securities" and could not be regarded as a cash equivalent, unlike the short-term notes in *Pinellas*. The Court ignored the payment to the creditors of the acquired corporation and held that the transaction constituted a valid reorganization.

2. The taxpayers in *LeTulle* received $50,000 cash and $750,000 in bonds redeemable over 11 years; in *Watts* the taxpayers received 32,103 shares of common stock, with a value of $963,090, and mortgage bonds of approximately $1,161,184.50; and in *Nelson* the taxpayer received $2 million cash and 14,060 shares of nonvoting preferred stock, valued at $1,406,000. Is there a sufficient difference, in terms of the concept of "reorganization," to justify the treatment of the taxpayers in *LeTulle*? In any event, who has a more significant interest in the corporate assets: the owner of ten-year, fixed-interest bonds or the owner, e.g., of nonvoting, noncumulative preferred stock?

3. In this connection, consider Roebling v. Commissioner, 143 F.2d 810 (3d Cir.), *cert. denied*, 323 U.S. 773 (1944). In *Roebling*, South Jersey Gas, Electric and Traction Co. (South Jersey) in 1903 leased all its plants and operating equipment to Public Service Gas and Electric Company (Public Service) for 900 years. The net rentals received by South Jersey were distributed yearly to its stockholders at a rate of 8 percent of the par value of the stock. In 1937, South

Jersey merged into Public Service, and South Jersey's shareholders received in exchange for their stock 8-percent 100-year first mortgage bonds of Public Service.

After unsuccessfuly contending that the continuity of interest doctrine was superseded by the reorganization provision of the Revenue Act of 1938, the taxpayer, a former South Jersey shareholder, argued that the continuity of interest requirement was met because "prior to the merger, the stockholders of South Jersey had no *proprietary interest* in its properties in any real sense" and the South Jersey stock "was substantially equivalent to a perpetual 8% bond." Therefore, he argued, the interest received by the former shareholders in the merger was equivalent to the interest they held before the merger. The court, however, rejected this argument, finding that the South Jersey shareholders held a proprietary interest before the merger, but not after the merger.

The court thought that the taxpayer's interest was less remote before the merger than after. Is the right to income from a corporation that owns and operates the assets more remote than the expectancy of income from a corporation which, for 900 years, has only a right to income from the assets? What relevance do questions like these have to the meaning of "reorganization?"

REVENUE PROCEDURE 77-37
1977-2 C.B. 568

[The Internal Revenue Service has announced an "operating rule" to guide it in issuing rulings where the "continuity of interest" requirement of Treas. Reg. §1.368-1(b) is involved.]

... The "continuity of interest" requirement of section 1.368-l(b) of the Income Tax Regulations is satisfied if there is a continuing interest through stock ownership in the acquiring or transferee corporation (or a corporation in "control" thereof within the meaning of §368(c) of the Code) on the part of the former shareholders of the acquired or transferor corporation which is equal in value, as of the effective date of the reorganization, to at least 50 percent of the value of all of the formerly outstanding stock of the acquired or transferor corporation as of the same date. It is not necessary that each shareholder of the acquired or transferor corporation receive in the exchange stock of the acquiring or transferee corporation or a corporation in "control" thereof, which is equal in value to at least 50 percent of the value of his former stock interest in the acquired or transferor corporation, so long as one or more of the shareholders of the acquired or transferor corporation have a continuing interest through stock ownership in the acquiring or transferee corporation (or a corporation in "control" thereof) which is, in the aggregate, equal in value to at least 50 percent of the value of all of the formerly outstanding stock of the acquired or transferor corporation. Sales, redemptions, and other dispositions of stock occurring prior or subsequent to the exchange which are part of the plan of reorganization will be considered in determining whether there is a 50 percent continuing interest through stock ownership as of the effective date of the reorganization. . . .

REVENUE RULING 66-224

1966-2 C.B. 114

Corporation X was merged under state law into corporation Y. Corporation X had four stockholders (A, B, C, D), each of whom owned 25 percent of its stock. Corporation Y paid A and B each $50,000 in cash for their stock of corporation X, and C and D each received corporation Y stock with a value of $50,000 in exchange for their stock of corporation X. There are no other facts present that should be taken into account in determining whether the continuity of interest requirement of §1.368-1(b) of the Income Tax regulations has been satisfied, such as sales, redemptions or other dispositions of stock prior to or subsequent to the exchange which were part of the plan of reorganization.

Held, the continuity of interest requirement of Section 1.368-1(b) of the regulations has been satisfied. It would also be satisfied if the facts were the same except corporation Y paid each stockholder $25,000 in cash and each stockholder received corporation Y stock with a value of $25,000.

MAY B. KASS v. COMMISSIONER

60 T.C. 218 (1973), aff'd without opinion, 491 F.2d 749 (3d Cir. 1974)

DAWSON, Judge. Respondent determined a deficiency in petitioner's Federal income tax for the year 1966 in the amount of $10,134.67.

The only issue for decision is whether petitioner, a minority shareholder of an 84-percent-owned subsidiary, must recognize gain upon the receipt of the parent's stock pursuant to a statutory merger of the subsidiary into the parent. . . .

[May B. Kass (petitioner) owned 2,000 shares of the common stock of Atlantic City Racing Association (ACRA) which had a basis of $1000.

[Track Associates, Inc. (TRACK) was formed on November 19, 1965, by the Levy and Casey families, minority shareholders in ACRA, for the purpose of gaining control over ACRA's racetrack business. These two families owned over 58 percent of TRACK's outstanding stock, part of which was received in exchange for their ACRA stock.

[Control in ACRA was to be acquired by having TRACK purchase 80 percent or more of ACRA's stock and by then merging ACRA into TRACK. Pursuant to this plan, TRACK offered to buy ACRA's stock from its 500 shareholders for $22 per share, conditioned on the tendering of 80 percent or more of the outstanding shares. TRACK acquired more than the requisite number of shares.

[Thereafter, upon shareholder approval, ACRA was merged into TRACK. The shares of ACRA that were neither tendered nor sold by dissenting shareholders were exchanged, one for one, for TRACK stock. The petitioner exchanged her 2,000 shares of ACRA stock, valued at $22 per share, for 2,000 shares of TRACK stock. She reported no capital gain.]

Petitioner contends that the merger of ACRA into TRACK, although treated at least in part as a liquidation at the corporate level, is at her level, the shareholder level, (1) a true statutory merger and (2) a section $368(a)(1)(a)(A)^2$ reorganization, occasioning no recognition of gain on the ensuing exchange. In support of this she cites Madison Square Garden Corp., 58 T.C. 619 (1972). Respondent, on the other hand, argues that the purchase of stock by TRACK and the liquidation of ACRA into TRACK, which took the form of a merger, must be viewed at all levels as an integrated transaction; that the statutory merger does not qualify as a reorganization because it fails the continuity-of-interest test; and that, as a consequence, petitioner falls outside of section 354(a)(1) and must recognize gain pursuant to section 1002.

The problems presented by these facts are somewhat complex, and the solutions, according to the commentators, are less than clear. Stated one way, the question is whether a statutory merger that follows a section 334(b)(3) "purchase" and serves the purpose of a Section 332, 334(b) "complete liquidation" can qualify as an "A" reorganization at the shareholder level and, if so, when. Put another way, does the merger of ACRA into TRACK fall under section 368(a)(1)(A), thus placing the exchange of petitioner's ACRA stock for TRACK stock within the applicable nonrecognition provision?

Respondent does not take the position that a statutory merger, such as the one we have here, can never qualify for reorganization-

---

2. ... Hereafter we will use "statutory merger" to refer to a merger which might or might not qualify as a sec. 368 reorganization and "A" reorganization to refer to a statutory merger that definitely does qualify.

nonrecognition status. He admits that "Theoretically, it is possible for TRACK to get a stepped-up basis in 83.95 percent of the assets of ACRA per section 334(b)(2), . . . upon a section 332, . . . liquidation of ACRA into TRACK and at the same time allow nonrecognition reorganization treatment to minority shareholders." Rather, his position is simply that the merger in question fails to meet the time-honored continuity-of-interest test. We agree with this and so hold.

Section 334(b)(2) and the reorganization provisions might apply to the same transaction only in certain cases where the continuity-of-interest test is met. See sec. 332 (last sentence, last independent clause); sec. 1.332-2(d) and (e). . . . Reorganization treatment is appropriate when the parent's stock ownership in the subsidiary was not acquired as a step in a plan to acquire assets of the subsidiary: the parent's stockholding can be counted as contributing to continuity-of-interest, so that since such holding represented more than 80 percent of the stock of the subsidiary, the continuity-of-interest test would be met. Reorganization treatment is inappropriate when the parent's stock ownership in the subsidiary was purchased as the first step in a plan to acquire the subsidiary's assets in conformance with the provisions of section 334(b)(2).[9] The parent's stockholding could not be counted towards continuity-of-interest so in the last example there would be a continuity-of-interest of less than 20 percent. (Less than 20-percent continuity would be significantly less continuity-of-interest than that allowed in John A. Nelson Co. v. Helvering, 296 U.S. 374 (1935) [page 583 supra].) In short, where the parent's stock interest is "old and cold," it may contribute to continuity-of-interest. Where the parent's interest is not "old and cold," the sale of shares by the majority of shareholders actually detracts from continuity-of-interest.

In petitioner's case, TRACK's stock in ACRA was acquired as part of an integrated plan to obtain control over ACRA's business. The plan called for, first, the purchase of stock and, second, the subsidiary-into-parent merger. Accordingly, continuity-of-interest must be measured by looking to all the pre-tender offer stockholders rather than to the parent (TRACK) and the nontendering stockholders only; and by that measure the merger fails and petitioner must recognize her gain.

The result reached in *Madison Square Garden Corp.*, supra, is, at first blush, inconsistent with the result reached in this case. . . .

In *Madison Square Garden* the principal issue was whether the taxpayer could "back around" the 80-percent ownership test imbed-

9. We express no opinion as to whether such treatment would be appropriate in the case of a plan to acquire the subsidiary's assets, which is then not implemented so as to meet the requirements of sec. 334(b)(2). Cf. American Potash & Chemical Corporation v. United States, 399 F.2d 194 (Ct. Cl. 1968).

ded in section 334(b)(2) by purchasing a controlling interest in the corporation to be acquired, having that corporation redeem some of its stock from other shareholders, and then purchasing a little more stock — just enough to increase its stockholdings over the 80-percent mark. We held that the transaction qualified, section 334(b)(2) being a largely mechanical area. The issue with which we are presently concerned in this case was raised by the taxpayer (Madison Square Garden) in an amendment to its petition. The taxpayer, the acquiring parent corporation, claimed that it was entitled to a step-up in the basis of the assets received with reference to the stock that it had purchased *and* a step-up in the basis of the assets received in the statutory merger, though the stock to which those assets were "attached" belonged to minority shareholders. The latter portion of the claim conflicted with the position taken on its return. It is important to note that in *Madison Square Garden*, as in the instant case, there was a section 334(b)(2) "purchase" followed by a statutory merger and that the two steps were obviously part of an integrated plan. On this secondary issue, the Commissioner argued that section 334(b)(2) gives a stepped-up or cost-of-stock basis only to "property received with reference to stock owned immediately before the liquidation [or statutory merger treated as a liquidation for section 332 purposes]." Since Madison Square Garden owned only 80.22 percent of the stock immediately before the merger, it should be limited in a step-up in basis to only 80.22 percent of the assets received. Thus the Commissioner took a very narrow view of the applicable law, basing his arguments on section 334(b)(2) and the regulations thereunder. Likewise, Madison Square Garden argued solely in terms of section 334(b)(2). Neither party mentioned the possibility that the minority shareholders, who were not parties to the proceeding, might recognize gain (because the two-step transaction was integrated and thus there was no continuity-of-interest) and therefore the corporation should get a step-up in basis to reflect the tax at the shareholder level, on the theory that a nonqualifying reorganization is simply a purchase or sale. Confronted with these arguments and the narrowly framed issue, this Court held that Madison Square Garden, the acquiring parent, was not entitled to a step-up in basis *under section 334(b)(2)* as to part of the property.

In the present case, with essentially the same facts but the minority shareholder as petitioner, respondent argues that the statutory merger is a nonqualifying reorganization, thus a sale, thus taxable at the shareholder level. Although technically he need not mention the corporate basis aspects nor sections 334(b)(2) and 332, respondent frankly admits that at the corporate level he would allow the assets received with reference to the stock belonging to the minority shareholders a stepped-up basis. This admission by the respondent unavoidably conflicts with the result argued for and achieved in *Madison Square Garden*.

Faced with the general rule as the applicability of the continuity-of-interest test, petitioner makes the following arguments, which we will deal with separately.

One, the continuity-of-interest doctrine should not be applied because TRACK was formed by a few stockholders in ACRA in order to purchase the business and, in the process, to acquire a stepped-up basis for as many of the assets as possible via section 334(b)(2). "In effect, the situation was the same as the sale of stock by some shareholders to other shareholders." The petitioner meets herself coming, so to speak, when making this argument. Confronted with the problem of how to characterize the second event in the present two-event transaction, she contends that the transaction was a true statutory merger in both form and substance, at least insofar as she, a minority shareholder, was concerned. Now, confronted with the continuity-of-interest problem, she would have us treat the transaction in a manner inconsistent with the characterization previously given to the transaction, that of a merger. . . .

Two, in applying the continuity-of-interest test, if it is applied, the purchase of stock by TRACK and the subsequent merger should not be viewed as steps in an integrated transaction because the choice of merger over liquidation as a second step had independent significance to the minority shareholders and either choice would have suited TRACK. By so arguing, the petitioner attempts in effect to avoid the step-transaction doctrine and thus to limit the application of the continuity-of-interest test. If the merger can be separated from the stock purchase, the continuity-of-interest test might be applicable only with regard to ACRA's shareholders at the time of the statutory merger, namely, the parent corporation, TRACK, and the minority shareholders, including petitioner. We note at least one flaw: The choice — liquidation or merger — did make a difference to TRACK. If it had liquidated ACRA, TRACK would not have received all of ACRA's assets. Some of the assets would have gone to the minority shareholders, and it would have had to have purchased them from these shareholders at an additional price. By choosing to merge ACRA into itself, it was able to avoid this and other problems. . . .

Four, assuming that the continuity-of-interest test is applied, it is met where all 16 percent of the stockholders of ACRA exchanged their stock for a total of 35 percent of the stock of TRACK. The 16-percent figure (really 16.04 percent) is the sum of the percentage of ACRA stock transferred to TRACK at the time of TRACK's formation (10.22 percent) plus the percentage of ACRA stock exchanged for TRACK stock following the statutory merger (5.82 percent). Fortunately, we need not engage in a game of percentages since the continuity figure argued for by petitioner, 16 percent, is not "tantalizingly" high. The plain fact that more than 80 percent of the shareholders of ACRA sold out for cash is sufficient to prevent this merger from meeting the quantitative test expressed in the Southwest Natural Gas Co. v. Commissioner, 189 F.2d 332, 334 (C.A. 5, 1951). . . . The two Supreme Court cases on point are John A. Nelson Co. v. Helvering, supra, and Helvering v. Minnesota Tea Co., 296 U.S. 378 (1935) [page 585 supra].

Finally, we emphasize that the petitioner is not any worse off than her fellow shareholders who sold their stock. She could have also received money instead of stock had she chosen to sell or to dissent from the merger. The nonrecognition of a realized gain is always an important matter. We hold that petitioner is not entitled to such favorable treatment in this case.

Reviewed by the Court.

NOTES

1. Is the court's last paragraph persuasive? Should Mrs. Kass be treated like those who receive cash? How would she have been treated if TRACK had merged into ACRA? Should her tax treatment depend on which corporation survived?

2. See also Kansas Sand & Concrete, Inc., 56 T.C. 522, *aff'd,* 462 F.2d 805 (10th Cir. 1972) (a corporation was required to compute the basis of assets acquired in liquidation of its subsidiary under old §334(b)(2) rather than §362 when both were literally applicable); American Mfg Co., 55 T.C. 204 (1970) (the complete liquidation of a subsidiary was held to be a step in a "D" reorganization so that the tax treatment of the gain was governed by §356 rather than §332).

McDONALD'S RESTAURANTS OF ILLINOIS, INC. v. COMMISSIONER
688 F.2d 520 (7th Cir. 1982)

Before Cummings, Chief Judge, Bauer, Circuit Judge, and Grant, Senior District Judge.

Cummings, Chief Judge.

This income tax case is an appeal by taxpayers from 27 decisions of the Tax Court determining deficiencies in their federal income tax totaling $566,403. . . .

[T]axpayers [are] 27 wholly owned subsidiaries of McDonald's Corporation (McDonald's), the Delaware corporation that franchises and operates fast-food restaurants. . . .

On the opposite end of the transaction at issue here were Melvin Garb, Harold Stern and Lewis Imerman (known collectively as the Garb-Stern group). The group had begun with a single McDonald's franchise in Saginaw, Michigan, in the late 1950s and expanded its holdings to include McDonald's restaurants elsewhere in Michigan and in Oklahoma, Wisconsin, Nevada and California. After 1968 relations between the Garb-Stern group and McDonald's deteriorated. In 1971 McDonald's considered buying some of the group's restaurants in Oklahoma, but abandoned the idea when it became clear that the acquisition could not be treated as a "pooling of interests" for accounting purposes[2] unless all of the Garb-Stern group's restaurants were acquired simultaneously. In November 1972, however, negotiations resumed, McDonald's having decided that total acquisition was necessary to eliminate the Garb-Stern group's friction.

The sticking point in the negotiations was that the Garb-Stern group wanted cash for its operations, while McDonald's wanted to acquire the Garb-Stern group's holdings for stock, consistent with its earlier expressed preference for treating the transaction as a "pooling of interests" for accounting purposes. McDonald's proposed a plan to satisfy both sides: it would acquire the Garb-Stern companies for McDonald's common stock, but it would include the common stock in a planned June 1973 registration so that the Garb-Stern group could sell it promptly.[3]

[The parties agreed that the] Garb-Stern companies would be merged in stages into McDonald's, which would in turn transfer the restaurant assets to the 27 subsidiaries that are the taxpayers here. In return the Garb-Stern group would receive 361,235 shares of unregistered common stock. The agreement provided that the Garb-Stern group could participate in McDonald's planned June 1973 registration and underwriting or in any other registration and underwriting McDonald's might undertake within six years . . . ; the

2. The Tax Court's opinion describes "pooling of interests" as follows:

"The pooling of interests method accounts for a business combination as the uniting of the ownership interests of two or more companies by exchange of equity securities. No acquisition is recognized because the combination is accomplished without disbursing resources of the constituents. Ownership interests continue and the former bases of accounting are retained. The recorded assets and liabilities of the constituents are carried forward to the combined corporation at their recorded amounts. Income of the combined corporation includes income of the constituents for the entire fiscal period in which the combination occurs. The reported income of the constitutents for prior periods is combined and restated as income of the combined corporation."

3. The stock the Garb-Stern group received was unregistered. It could not be sold until it was registered or until the Garb-Stern group met the conditions of S.E.C. Rule 144 (2-year holding period and limitation on number of shares sold within a 6-month period thereafter). . . . Sale rather than retention was attractive to the Garb-Stern group, because McDonald's stock had paid no cash dividends from 1968 to the time of this transaction. . . .

group also had a one-time right to demand registration in the event that McDonald's did not seek registration within the first year. . . . The Garb-Stern group was not obligated by contract to sell its McDonald's stock but fully intended to do so.

. . . In mid June a widely publicized negative report about McDonald's stock caused the price to drop from $60 to $52 a share in two weeks, and McDonald's therefore decided to postpone the registration and sale of additional stock. The Garb-Stern group acquiesced, although it had made no effort to withdraw from the registration before McDonald's decided to cancel it.

Through the rest of the summer, the price of McDonald's stock staged a recovery. In late August McDonald's decided to proceed with the registration, and the Garb-Stern group asked to have its shares included. The registration was announced on September 17 and completed on October 3, 1973. The Garb-Stern group thereupon sold virtually all of the stock it had acquired in the transaction at a price of more than $71 per share.

In its financial statements McDonald's treated the transaction as a "pooling of interests." In its tax returns for 1973, however, it treated it as a purchase.[6] Consistent with that characterization, McDonald's gave itself a stepped-up basis in the assets acquired from the Garb-Stern group to reflect their cost ($29,029,000, representing the value of the common stock transferred and a $1-2 million "nuisance premium" paid to eliminate Garb-Stern group from the McDonald's organization). It allocated that basis among various Garb-Stern assets, then dropped the restaurant assets to the 27 taxpayer subsidiaries pursuant to Section 351 . . . governing transfers to corporations controlled by the transferor. The subsidiaries used the stepped-up basis allocable to them to compute depreciation and amortization deductions in their own 1973 tax returns.

It is those deductions by the subsidiary taxpayers that the Commissioner reduced. He ruled that the transfer of the Garb-Stern group's assets to McDonald's was not a taxable acquisition but a statutory merger or consolidation under Section 368(a)(1)(A) . . . , and that under Section 362(b) McDonald's was required to assume the Garb-Stern group's basis in the assets acquired. In turn, the subsidiaries were required to compute depreciation and amortization deductions on this lower, carryover basis. With properly computed deductions, the subsidiary taxpayers owed an additional $566,403 in 1973 income taxes. The Tax Court upheld the Commissioner's deficiency assessments, and this appeal is the result.

6. The Commissioner's brief makes much of the differences between the accounting and the tax treatment (Br. 9, 20), characterizing McDonald's strategies as "disingenuous" and "bordering on the duplicitous." The short answer to this argument is found in McDonald's Reply Br. at 9-10: such variations are common and accepted. The service has a special form (Schedule M) for corporations to file in order to reconcile the financial and tax records. McDonald's duly filed such a form. . . .

The Code distinguishes between taxable acquisitions and non-taxable (or more accurately tax-deferrable) acquisitive reorganizations under Sections 368(a)(1)(A)-(C) and 354(a)(1) for the following common-sense reason: If acquired shareholders exchange stock in the acquired company for stock in the acquiring company, they have simply readjusted the form of their equity holdings. . . .

To ensure that the tax treatment of acquisitive reorganizations corresponds to the rationale that justifies it, the courts have engrafted a "continuity of interest" requirement onto the Code's provisions. . . . That test examines the acquired shareholder's proprietary interest before and after the reorganization to see if "the acquired share-holders' investment remains sufficiently 'at risk' after the merger to justify the nonrecognition tax treatment." . . .

The taxpayers, the Commissioner, and the Tax Court all agree that the Garb-Stern group holdings were acquired by statutory merger. They also all agree that the "continuity of interest" test is determinative of the tax treatment of the transaction of which the statutory merger was a part. But the taxpayers on the one hand, and the Commissioner and the Tax Court on the other, part company over how the test is to be applied, and what result it should have produced. In affirming the Commissioner, the Tax Court recognized that the Garb-Stern group had a settled and firm determination to sell their McDonald's shares at the first possible opportunity rather than continue as investors. . . . It nonetheless concluded that because the Garb-Stern group was not contractually bound to sell, the merger and the sale could be treated as entirely separate transactions and the continuity-of-interest test applied in the narrow time-frame of the April transaction only. Thus tested, the transaction was in Judge Hall's view a nontaxable reorganization, and the taxpayer subsidiaries were therefore saddled with the Garb-Stern group's basis in taking depreciation and amortization deductions. The taxpayers by contrast argue that the step-transaction doctrine should have been applied to treat the April merger and stock transfer and the October sale as one taxable transaction. They also argue that the Tax Court's extremely narrow view of both the step-transaction doctrine and the continuity-of-interest test in this case is not consonant with appellate court case law, the Tax Court's own precedents, or the Service's practices hitherto. We agree with the taxpayers.

The step-transaction doctrine is a particular manifestation of the more general tax law principle that purely formal distinctions cannot obscure the substance of a transaction. See, e.g., Redding v. Commissioner [page 728 infra]. As our Court there noted:

The commentators have attempted to synthesize from judicial decisions several tests to determine whether the step transaction doctrine is applicable to a particular set of circumstances. . . . Unfortunately, these tests are notably abstruse — even for such an abstruse field as tax law.

Nonetheless, under any of the tests devised — including the intermediate one nominally adopted by the Tax Court and the most restrictive one actually applied in its decision — the transactions here would be stepped together. For example, under the "end result test," "purportedly separate transactions will be amalgamated with a single transaction when it appears that they were really component parts of a single transaction intended from the outset to be taken for the purpose of reaching the ultimate result." 76 T.C. at 994, citing King Enterprises, Inc. v. United States, 418 F.2d 511, 516 (Ct. Cl. 1969) and referring to *Redding*, supra. . . . Here there can be little doubt that all the steps were taken to cash out the Garb-Stern group, although McDonald's sought to do so in a way that would enable it to use certain accounting procedures. . . .

A second test is the "interdependence" test, which focuses on whether "the steps are so interdependent that the legal relations created by one transaction would have been fruitless without a completion of the series." *Redding*, supra, . . . quoting with approval Paul, Selected Studies in Federal Taxation (2d Series 1938) 200, 254. This is the test the Tax Court purported to apply, . . . although its version of the test is indistinguishable from yet another formulation, the "binding commitment" test. That is, the Tax Court would have found interdependence only if the Garb-Stern group had itself been legally bound to sell its stock. In fact, the "interdependence" test is more practical and less legalistic than that. It concentrates on the relationship between the steps, rather than on the "end result." . . . Here it would ask whether the merger would have taken place without the guarantees of saleability, and the answer is certainly no. The Garb-Stern group's insistence on this point is demonstrated both by its historic stance in these negotiations and by the hammered-out terms of the agreement. Although the Tax Court emphasized the permissive terms about "piggyback" registration, it glossed over the Garb-Stern group's one-time right to force registration — and hence sale — under the agreement. The very detail of the provisions about how McDonald's would ensure free transferability of the Garb-Stern group's McDonald's stock shows that they were the quid pro quo of the merger agreement.

Finally the "binding commitment" test most restricts the application of the step-transaction doctrine, and is the test the Tax Court actually applied, despite its statements otherwise. The "binding commitment" test forbids use of the step-transaction doctrine unless "if one transaction is to be characterized as a 'first step' there [is] a binding commitment to take the later steps." *Redding*, supra, . . . quoting Commissioner v. Gordon [page 722 infra]. The Tax Court found the test unsatisfied because the Garb-Stern group was not legally obliged to sell its McDonald's stock. We think it misconceived the purpose of the test and misapplied it to the facts of this case.

In the first place, the "binding commitment" test is the most rigorous limitation on the step-transaction doctrine because it was formulated to deal with the characterization of a transaction that in fact spanned several tax years and could have remained "not only indeterminable but unfixed for an indefinite and unlimited period in the future, awaiting events that might or might not happen." *Gordon*, supra. . . . By contrast this transaction was complete in six months and fell entirely within a single tax year. The degree of uncertainty that worried the *Gordon* court is absent here, and a strong antidote for uncertainty is accordingly not needed.

In the second place, the Tax Court underestimated the extent to which the parties were bound to take the later steps. The registration and underwriting provisions in the parties' agreement did not just enhance saleability; they were essential to it. Unless and until McDonald's registered the stock, it was essentially untransferrable. . . . Second, although McDonald's had the choice of when during the first year after the merger it would seek registration, if it did nothing the Garb-Stern group could make a legally enforceable demand for registration in either year two or year three. On the other hand, if McDonald's did register stock during the first year but the Garb-Stern group chose not to "piggyback," the group's demand registration rights would be lost. These limitations made it extremely likely that the sale would — as it did — take place promptly. They are enough to satisfy the spirit, if not the letter, of the "binding commitment" test.

Under any of the three applicable criteria, then, the merger and subsequent sale should have been stepped together. Substance over form is the key. . . . Had the Tax Court taken a pragmatic view of the actions of the Garb-Stern group, it would have found that they clearly failed to satisfy the continuity-of-interest requirement that has been engrafted onto the Code provisions governing nonrecognition treatment for acquisitive reorganizations.

Quite apart from the proper application of the step-transaction doctrine, the available precedents dealing with statutory mergers and the effect of postmerger sales by acquired shareholders — though scanty — strongly support the taxpayers. . . .

The taxpayers rely on, and the Tax Court was unsuccessful in distinguishing, Heintz v. Commissioner, 25 T.C. 132 (1955). The *Heintz* case differs from this case only in focusing on the tax liability of the acquired shareholders rather than the acquiring corporation. . . .

Heintz and Jack (taxpayers) formed a company (Jack & Heintz, Inc.) to manufacture arms and ammunition during World War II. At the war's end, they determined to sell it rather than try to reorganize its production for peacetime. The buyer was the Precision Corporation, which had been formed to acquire Jack & Heintz. On March 5, 1946, Precision acquired almost all the outstanding shares of Jack & Heintz from the taxpayers for $5 million cash and 50,000 preferred shares of Precision, with a par value of $50 each. On March 6 Precision merged its newly acquired subsidiary with itself. At the time the deal was being negotiated, two of the parties representing the buyer assured the taxpayers that the Precision shares they had received as part payment would be sold in a public offering planned for thirty days after the merger, . . . but this promise was nowhere reflected in the thirty-five page written agreement covering the whole transaction. . . . Owing to unforeseen delays, the contemplated registration and sale did not take place, but the buyers helped arrange a private sale at $30 per share in August 1946. In their 1946 returns, the taxpayers reported long-term capital gain computed on a figure arrived at by deducting from the sale proceeds ($5 million in cash plus $2,500,000 worth of Precision stock) their $112,000 basis in the Jack & Heintz stock. They also reported short-term capital losses of $1 million on the August private sale of the Precision stock.

The Commissioner assessed deficiencies, using exactly the reasoning the Tax Court has adopted in McDonald's case. He treated the transaction as a statutory reorganization, which had no immediate tax consequences (except that the cash component of the price was ordinary income). He then gave the taxpayers a carryover basis of $112,000, rather than a cost basis, in the Precision stock. Finally he treated the August sale as producing sizable capital gains ($1,500,000 less $112,000) rather than capital losses. Although the Commissioner's position is sketchily presented in the Tax Court's opinion, his treatment must have involved a conviction that neither the promise to sell the Precision stock nor the actual sale changed the character of the reorganization.

The Tax Court rejected the Commissioner's position unequivocally.[13] Although a statutory merger had occurred,

> [e]ssential to this arrangement was the promise made to petitioners
> by members of the purchasing group that the preferred stock . . .
> would shortly thereafter be sold on their behalf. . . .

13. At oral argument counsel for the commissioner argued that both the Tax Court and the author of the Commissioner's brief in the *McDonald* case had misconstrued the *Heintz* case. He advocated treating it as first, last, and always a sale (on March 5, 1946). The March 6, 1946, merger was, he maintained, entirely irrelevant. That was in fact the taxpayer's position in *Heintz*, . . . but the Tax Court gives no hint to having accepted it. We suspect that the Tax Court was rightly unwilling to separate transactions that occurred within 24 hours of each other.

... The term "reorganization as used in [the predecessor of Section 354(a)(1)], contemplates a readjustment of the corporate structure of an enterprise and requires that those individuals who are owners of the enterprise prior to such readjustment continue to maintain a substantial proprietary interest therein. ... The terms of the instant plan did not contemplate the petitioners' maintenance of a proprietary interest in the continuing operation. ... [P]etitioners wished to dispose of their entire interest in Jack & Heintz, Inc. ... [T]hey settled for cash plus preferred stock ... only after obtaining the promise of the promoters of [the] purchasing corporation that their preferred stock in that corporation would be sold together with a public offering of that corporation's stock within 30 days." 25 T.C. 142-143.

As in the present case, the taxpayer's wishes to sell were clear and the transaction was designed to accommodate them. As in the present case, the acquiring corporation's promise was to facilitate the sale, not to guarantee it. As in the present case, the acquiring corporation did not require a reciprocal commitment from the acquired shareholders — for all that appears, Heintz and Jack were free to retain their equity interest in Precision. As in the present case, these understandings of the parties were not reflected in the written agreement. There is no principled way to distinguish the two cases, and the Tax Court's efforts to do so here ... are unsuccessful. ...

Given the dearth of precedent and the aptness of the Tax Court's reasoning in *Heintz*, we think that case dictates a consistent — and favorable — treatment of the taxpayers in this appeal.

Part of the reason that there is so little litigation about statutory mergers and the effect of postmerger events on tax treatment is that people involved in nontaxable reorganizations usually seek advice in the form of private letter rulings, beforehand. ...

The Commissioner's usual position in this context is not the one adopted by the Tax Court, namely, that the intent of the acquired shareholders is irrelevant and no period of postmerger retention is required. 76 T.C. at 990, 992, 997. See, for example, Rev. Proc. 77-37 [page 594 supra]:

The "continuity of interest" requirement of section 1.368-1(b) of the Income Tax Regulations is satisfied if there is a *continuing* interest through stock ownership in the acquiring or transferee corporation (or a corporation in "control" thereof within the meaning of section 368(c) of the Code) on the part of the former shareholders of the acquired or transferor corporation which is equal in value, as of the effective date of the reorganization, to at least 50 percent of the value of all of the formerly outstanding stock of the acquired or transferor corporation as of the same date. ... *Sales, redemptions, and other dispositions of stock occurring prior or subsequent to the exchange which are part of the plan of reorganization*

*will be considered in determining whether there is a 50 percent continuing
interest through stock ownership as of the effective date of the reorganization.* (Emphasis added.)

. . . Moreover, the Commissioner usually does not limit his scrutiny to explicit, contemporaneous commitments to sell out, Rev. Rul.
77-479, 1977-2 C.B. 119; Rev. Rul. 66-23, 1966-1 C.B. 67. In fact,
taxpayers who seek a ruling in advance of a reorganization must
represent that there is "no plan *or intention* on the part of the Acquired
shareholders to [reduce their new holdings] to a number of shares
having, in the aggregate, a value of less than 50 percent of the total
value of the Acquired stock outstanding immediately prior to the
proposed transaction." . . .

Against this background, the Commissioner's treatment of the
McDonald's transaction — as affirmed by the Tax Court — seems
opportunistic. The agency's practice, described above, suggests that
if McDonald's had laid its plan before the Internal Revenue Service
ahead of time, it would not have been deemed a nontaxable reorganization. . . .

If, on the other hand, the treatment here represents a considered
change in the Service's treatment of reorganizations, then the Commissioner's victory in the Tax Court was Pyrrhic and he should
welcome reversal. The Tax Court's decision was barely six months
old before tax planners were publicizing the possibilities for manipulating it. Prusiecki, [Continuity of Interest in Tax-Free Mergers:
New Opportunities after *McDonald's of Zion,* 55 J. Tax. 378,] at 380-
381, notes nine new types of tax avoidance that the case opens up,
all taking advantage of the newfound ability to obtain reorganization
status without constraining postmerger sales. The key to all of them
is the extraordinary rigidity of the "binding commitment" test and
the ephemeral continuity of interest the Tax Court seems to require.

The decisions appealed from are reversed, with instructions to
enter fresh decisions in the taxpayers' favor.

NOTES

1. For another expansive application of the continuity of interest
doctrine, see Superior Coach of Florida, Inc. v. Commissioner, 80
T.C. 895 (1983).

2. In light of *McDonald's,* how long after a merger must parties
wait before they will know whether a tax-free reorganization was
effected? *Compare McDonald's with* Robert A. Penrod, 88 T.C. 1415
(1987), where the Tax Court found a valid reorganization even
though 80 percent of the stock was sold immediately after the transaction.

PAULSEN v. COMMISSIONER
469 U.S. 13 (1985)

REHNQUIST, J., delivered the opinion of the Court. . . .

Commerce Savings and Loan Association of Tacoma, Wash., merged into Citizens Federal Savings and Loan Association of Seattle in July 1976. Petitioners Harold and Marie Paulsen sought to treat their exchange of stock in Commerce for an interest in Citizens as a tax-free reorganization under . . . sections 354(a)(1) and 368(a)(1)(A). The Court of Appeals for the Ninth Circuit, disagreeing with the Court of Claims and other Courts of Appeals, reversed a decision of the Tax Court in favor of petitioners. 716 F.2d 563 (1983). . . .

At the time of the merger, petitioner Harold T. Paulsen was president and a director of Commerce. He and his wife, petitioner Marie B. Paulsen, held as community property 17,459 shares of "guaranty stock" in Commerce. In exchange for this stock petitioners received passbook savings accounts and time certificates of deposit in Citizens. Relying on . . . sections 354(a)(1) and 368(a)(1)(A), they did not report the gain they realized on their 1976 federal income tax return because they considered the merger to be a tax-free reorganization.

Before it ceased to exist, Commerce was a state-chartered savings and loan association incorporated and operated under Washington State law. It was authorized to issue "guaranty stock," to offer various classes of savings accounts, and to make loans. Each stockholder, savings account holder, and borrower was a member of the association. Each share of stock and every $100, or fraction thereof, on deposit in a savings account carried with it one vote. Each borrower also had one vote.

The "guaranty stock" had all of the characteristics normally associated with common stock issued by a corporation. Under the bylaws, a certain amount of guaranty stock was required to be maintained as the fixed and nonwithdrawable capital of Commerce. . . . [H]olders of guaranty stock, but no other members, had a proportionate proprietary interest in its assets and net earnings, subordinate to the claims of creditors. Dividends could not be declared or paid on the guaranty stock unless certain reserves had been accumulated and dividends had been declared and paid on withdrawable savings accounts.

Citizens is a federally chartered mutual savings and loan association under the jurisdiction of the Federal Home Loan Bank Board. . . . It offers savings accounts and makes loans, but has no capital stock. Its members are its depositors and borrowers. Each savings account holder has one vote for each $100, or fraction thereof, of the withdrawal value of his savings account up to a maximum of 400 votes. Each borrower has one vote.

Citizens is owned by its depositors. Twice each year its net earnings and any surplus are to be distributed to its savings account holders pro rata to the amounts on deposit. Its net assets would similarly be distributed if liquidation or dissolution should occur. It is obligated to pay written withdrawal requests within 30 days, and may redeem any of its accounts at any time by paying the holder the withdrawal value.

The merger was effected pursuant to a "Plan of Merger," under which Commerce's stockholders exchanged all their stock for passbook savings accounts and certificates of deposit in Citizens. The plan was designed to conform to the requirements of Wash. Rev. Code section . . . which provides for mergers between business entities, and to qualify as a tax-free reorganization under the terms of sections 354(a)(1) and 368(a)(1)(A). Under the plan, Commerce stockholders received for each share a $12 deposit in a Citizens passbook savings account, subject only to the restriction that such deposits could not be withdrawn for one year. They also had the alternative of receiving time certificates of deposit in Citizens with maturities ranging from one to 10 years at the same $12-per-share exchange rate. The plan further provided that former Commerce stockholders could borrow against their deposits resulting from the exchange at 1.5 percent above the passbook rate as opposed to a two percent differential for other depositors. Following the exchange, the merged entity continued to operate under the Citizens name.

Petitioners had a cost basis in their Commerce stock of $56,802; in the exchange they received passbook accounts and certificates of deposit worth $209,508. . . . [Section 1001(c)] require[s] that ["the entire amount of the gain or loss . . . on the sale or exchange of property shall be recognized."] Accordingly, petitioners were required to declare as income on their 1976 return the $152,706 profit unless one of the exceptions incorporated by reference in section [1001(c)] applied.

Included among the exceptions to section [1001(c)] were the corporate reorganization provisions set out in sections 354 to 368. As already noted, petitioners have attempted to rely on section 354(a)(1). . . . Section 368(a)(1)(A) defines a "reorganization" to include "a statutory merger or consolidation." . . . There is no dispute that at the time of the merger Commerce and Citizens qualified as associations, petitioners qualified as shareholders, Commerce's guaranty stock and Citizens' passbook accounts and certificates of deposit qualified as stock, and the merger qualified as a statutory merger within these provisions of the Code. Accordingly, under the literal terms of the Code the transaction would qualify as a tax-free "reorganization" exchange rather than a sale or exchange on which gain must be recognized and taxes paid.

Satisfying the literal terms of the reorganization provisions, however, is not sufficient to qualify for nonrecognition of gain or loss. The purpose of these provisions is "to free from the imposition of an income tax purely 'paper profits or losses' wherein there is no realization of gain or loss in the business sense but merely the recasting of the same interests in a different form." Southwest Natural Gas Co. v. Commissioner, 189 F.2d 332, 334 (C.A.5), *cert. denied,* 342 U.S. 860 (1951) (quoting Commissioner v. Gilmore's Estate, 130 F.2d 791, 794 (C.A.3 1942)). See Treas. Reg. section 1.368-l(b). . . . In order to exclude sales structured to satisfy the literal terms of the reorganization provisions but not their purpose, this Court has construed the statute to also require that the taxpayer's ownership interest in the prior organization must continue in a meaningful fashion in the reorganized enterprise, Pinellas Ice & Cold Storage Co. v. Commissioner [page 580 supra]. In that case we held that "the seller must acquire an interest in the affairs of the purchasing company more definite than that incident to ownership of its short-term purchase-money notes." . . . We soon added the requirement that "this interest must be definite and material; it must represent a substantial part of the value of the thing transferred." Helvering v. Minnesota Tea Co. [page 585 supra]. *Compare* LeTulle v. Scofield [page 589 supra] (no retained property interest where transferor received transferee's bonds), *with* John A. Nelson Co. v. Helvering [page 583 supra] (continuity of interest satisfied where nonvoting preferred stock received). Known as the "continuity-of-interest" doctrine, this requirement has been codified in Treas. Reg. sections 1.368-1(b), 1.368-2(a).

The present case turns on whether petitioners' exchange of their guaranty stock in Commerce for their passbook savings accounts and certificates of deposit in Citizens satisfies this continuity-of-interest requirement. More generally, we must decide whether a merger of a stock savings and loan association into a mutual savings and loan association qualifies as a tax-free reorganization. Following his ruling in Rev. Rul. 69-6, 1969-1 Cum. Bull. 104, which itself apparently was at odds with his earlier policy expressed in Rev. Rul. 54-624, 1954-2 Cum. Bull. 16, the Commissioner rejected petitioners' treatment of the Commerce-Citizens merger as a tax-free reorganization under sections 354(a)(1) and 368(a)(1)(A) and issued a statutory notice of deficiency finding petitioners liable for tax on their entire $152,706 gain.

Petitioners sought redetermination of the deficiency in the Tax Court, which found that the Commissioner's position had been uniformly rejected by the courts. Following Capital Savings and Loan

Assn. v. United States, 221 Ct. Cl. 557, 607 F.2d 970 (1979); West Side Federal Savings and Loan Assn. v. United States, 494 F.2d 404 (C.A.6 1974); Everett v. United States, 448 F.2d 357 (C.A. 10 1971), the Tax Court reasoned that the savings accounts and certificates of deposit were the only forms of equity in Citizens, and it held that the requisite continuity of interest existed. 78 T.C. 291 (1982).

The Commissioner appealed to the Court of Appeals for the Ninth Circuit, which declined to follow the cases cited by the Tax Court and reversed. 716 F.2d 563 (1983). It reasoned that "despite certain formal equity characteristics" the passbook savings accounts and time certificates of deposit "are in reality indistinguishable from ordinary savings accounts and are essentially the equivalent of cash." Id., at 569. For the reasons that follow we affirm the decision of the Court of Appeals.

Citizens is organized pursuant to [a Federal Home Loan Bank Board regulation] which provides for raising capital "by accepting payments on savings accounts representing share interests in the association." These shares are the association's only means of raising capital. Here they are divided into passbook accounts and certificates of deposit. In reality, these shares are hybrid instruments having both equity and debt characteristics. They combine in one instrument the separate characteristics of the guaranty stock and the savings accounts of stock associations like Commerce.

The Citizens shares have several equity characteristics. The most important is the fact that they are the only ownership instrument of the association. Each share carries in addition to its deposit value a part ownership interest in the bricks and mortar, the goodwill, and all the other assets of Citizens. Another equity characteristic is the right to vote on matters for which the association's management must obtain shareholder approval. The shareholders also receive dividends rather than interest on their accounts; the dividends are paid out of net earnings, and the shareholders have no legal right to have a dividend declared or to have a fixed return on their investment. The shareholders further have a right to a pro rata distribution of any remaining assets after a solvent dissolution.

These equity characteristics, however, are not as substantial as they appear on the surface. Unlike a stock association where the ownership of the assets is concentrated in the stockholders, the ownership interests here are spread over all of the depositors. The equity interest of each shareholder in relation to the total value of the share, therefore, is that much smaller than in a stock association. The right to vote is also not very significant. A shareholder is limited to 400 votes, thus any funds deposited in excess of $40,000 do not confer any additional votes. The vote is also diluted each time a loan is made, as each borrower is entitled to one vote. In addition the Commissioner asserts, and petitioners do not contest, that in practice, when depositors open their accounts, they usually sign proxies giving management their votes.

The fact that dividends rather than interest are paid is by no means controlling. Petitioners have not disputed the Commissioner's assertion that in practice Citizens pays a fixed, preannounced rate on all accounts. As the Court of Appeals observed, Citizens would not be able to compete with stock savings and loan associations and commercial banks if it did not follow this practice. Potential depositors are motivated only by the rate of return on their accounts and the security of their deposits. In this latter respect, the Citizens accounts are insured by the Federal Savings and Loan Insurance Corporation (FSLIC), up to $40,000 in 1976 and now up to $100,000. . . . The Code treats these dividends just like interest on bank accounts rather than like dividends on stock in a corporation. The dividends are deductible to Citizens, . . . and they do not qualify for dividend exclusion by the Citizens shareholders under section 116.

The right to participate in the net proceeds of a solvent liquidation is also not a significant part of the value of the shares. Referring to the possibility of a solvent liquidation of a mutual savings association, this Court observed: "It stretches the imagination very far to attribute any real value to such a remote contingency, and when coupled with the fact that it represents nothing which the depositor can readily transfer, any theoretical value reduces almost to the vanishing point." Society for Savings v. Bowers, 349 U.S. 143, 150 (1955).

In contrast, there are substantial debt characteristics to the Citizens shares that predominate. Petitioners' passbook accounts and certificates of deposit are not subordinated to the claims of creditors, and their deposits are not considered permanent contributions to capital. Shareholders have a right on 30 days' notice to withdraw their deposits, which right Citizens is obligated to respect. While petitioners were unable to withdraw their funds for one year following the merger, this restriction can be viewed as akin to a delayed payment rather than a material alteration in the nature of the instruments received as payment. In this case petitioners were immediately able to borrow against their deposits at a more favorable rate than Citizens' depositors generally. As noted above, petitioners were also in effect guaranteed a fixed, preannounced rate of return on their deposits competitive with stock savings and loan associations and commercial banks.

In our view, the debt characteristics of Citizens' shares greatly outweigh the equity characteristics. The face value of petitioners' passbook accounts and certificates of deposit was $210,000. Petitioners have stipulated that they had a right to withdraw the face amount of the deposits in cash, on demand after one year or at stated intervals thereafter. Their investment was virtually risk free and the dividends received were equivalent to prevailing interest rates for savings accounts in other types of savings institutions. The debt value of the shares was the same as the face value, $210,000; because no one would pay more than this for the shares, the incremental value attributable to the equity features was, practically, zero. Accordingly, we hold that petitioners' passbook accounts and certificates of deposit were cash equivalents.

Petitioners have failed to satisfy the continuity-of-interest requirement to qualify for a tax-free reorganization. In exchange for their guaranty stock in Commerce, they received essentially cash with an insubstantial equity interest. Under *Minnesota Tea Co.*, their equity interest in Citizens would have to be "a substantial part of the value of the thing transferred." . . . Assuming an arms'-length transaction in which what petitioners gave up and what they received were of equivalent worth, their Commerce stock was worth $210,000 in withdrawable deposits and an unquantifiably small incremental equity interest. This retained equity interest in the reorganized enterprise, therefore, is not a "substantial" part of the value of the Commerce stock which was given up. We agree with the Commissioner that the equity interests attached to the Citizens shares are too insubstantial to satisfy *Minnesota Tea Co.* The Citizens shares are not significantly different from the notes that this Court found to be the mere "equivalent of cash" in *Pinellas Ice & Cold Storage Co.* . . . The ownership interest of the Citizens shareholders is closer to that of the secured bondholders in LeTulle v. Scoffield . . . than to that of the preferred stockholders in John A. Nelson Co. v. Helvering. . . . The latter case involved a classic ownership instrument — preferred stock carrying voting rights only in the event of a dividend default — which we held to represent "a definite and substantial interest in the affairs of the purchasing corporation."

Petitioners argue that the decision below erroneously turned on the relative change in the nature and extent of the equity interest, contrary to the holding in *Minnesota Tea Co.*, that "the relationship of the taxpayer to the assets conveyed [could] substantially chang[e]," and only a "material part of the value of the transferred assets" need be retained as an equity interest. . . . In that case, taxpayers received voting trust certificates representing $540,000 of common stock and $425,000 cash; 56 percent of the value of the assets given up was retained as an equity interest in the transferee. In *John A. Nelson Co.*, . . . the taxpayer received consideration consisting of 38 percent preferred stock and 62 percent cash. Here, in contrast, the retained equity interest had almost no value. It did not amount to a "material part" of the value of the Commerce stock formerly held by petitioners. See Southwest Natural Gas Co. v. Commissioner, 189 F.2d, at 335 (insufficient continuity of interest where stock received represented less than one percent of the consideration).

Petitioners' real complaint seems to be our willingness to consider the equity and debt aspects of their shares separately. Clearly, if these interests were represented by separate pieces of paper — savings accounts on the one hand and equity instruments of some kind on the other — the value of the latter would be so small that we would not find a continuity of proprietary interest. In order not "to exalt artifice above reality and to deprive the statutory provision in question of all serious purpose," Gregory v. Helvering [page 545 supra], it is necessary in the present case to consider the debt and equity aspects of a single instrument separately. See Rev. Rul. 69-265, 1969-1 Cum. Bull. 109, 109-110, which treats the conversion rights incorporated in convertible preferred stock as "property other than voting stock" for purposes of section 368(a)(1)(C).

Petitioners also complain that the result reached by the court below is inconsistent with the Commissioner's position that a merger of one mutual savings and loan institution into another mutual association or into a stock association would still qualify as a tax-free reorganization. See Rev. Rul. 69-3, 1969-1 Cum. Bull. 103. If the continuity-of-interest test turns on the nature of the thing received, and not on the relative change in proprietary interest, argue petitioners, the interest received in the merger of two mutual associations is no different from the interest received in the instant case.

As already indicated, shares in a mutual association have a predominant cash-equivalent component and an insubstantial equity component. When two mutual associations merge, the shares received are essentially identical to the shares given up. As long as the cash value of the shares on each side of the exchange is the same, the equity interest represented by the shares received — though small — is equivalent to the equity interest represented by the shares given up. Therefore, to the extent that a mutual association share reflects an equity interest, the continuity-of-interest requirement, as defined in *Minnesota Tea Co.*, is satisfied in an exchange of this kind. The fact that identical cash deposits are also exchanged does not affect the equity aspect of the exchange. In the case of a merger of a mutual association into a stock association, the continuity-of-interest requirement is even more clearly satisfied because the equity position of the exchanging shareholders is not only equivalent before and after the exchange, but it is enhanced. . . .

Justice Powell took no part in the decision of the case. [The dissenting opinion of Justice O'Connor, in which Chief Justice Burger joined, is omitted.]

NOTES

1. What is the focus of continuity of interest when a corporation has no shareholders? In addition to Rev. Rul. 69-3, 1969-1 C.B. 109, noted in *Paulsen*, see Rev. Rul. 78-286, 1978-2 C.B. 145, in which the Service ruled that a merger of two mutual savings banks qualified as an "A" reorganization, even though neither corporation had capital stock outstanding and the banks were controlled by self-perpetuating boards of trustees. When a mutual savings institution "converts" to one in stock form, it does so in an "F" reorganization. See Rev. Rul. 80-105, 1980-1 C.B. 78. See generally Soukup, The Continuity-of-Proprietary Interest Doctrine and Thrift Institution Mergers, 12 J. Corp. Taxn. 141 (1985).

2. See Wolfman, "Continuity of Interest" and the American Law Institute Study, 57 Taxes 840 (1979), explaining and criticizing the development and reach of the continuity doctrine.

REVENUE RULING 84-71
1984-1 C.B. 106

The Internal Revenue Service has reconsidered Rev. Rul. 80-284, 1980-2 C.B. 117, and Rev. Rul. 80-285, 1980-2 C.B. 119, in which transfers that satisfied the technical requirements of section 351(a) of the Internal Revenue Code were nevertheless held to constitute taxable exchanges because they were part of larger acquisitive transactions that did not meet the continuity of interest test generally applicable to acquisitive reorganizations.

In Rev. Rul. 80-284, fourteen percent of T corporation's stock was held by A, president and chairman of the board, and eighty-six percent by the public. P, an unrelated, publicly held corporation, wished to purchase the stock of T. All the T stockholders except A were willing to sell the T stock for cash. A wished to avoid recognition of gain.

In order to accommodate these wishes, the following transactions were carried out as part of an overall plan. First, P and A formed a new corporation, S. P transferred cash and other property to S in exchange solely for all of S's common stock; A transferred T stock to S solely in exchange for all of S's preferred stock. These transfers were intended to be tax-free under section 351 of the Code. Second,

S organized a new corporation, D, and transferred to D the cash it had received from P in exchange for all the D common stock. Third, D was merged into T under state law. As a result of the merger, each share of T stock, except those shares held by S, was surrendered for cash equal to the stock's fair market value and each share of D stock was converted into T stock.

Rev. Rul. 80-284 concluded that if a purported section 351 exchange is an integral part of a larger transaction that fits a pattern common to acquisitive reorganizations, and if the continuity of shareholder interest requirement of section 1.368-1(b) of the Income Tax Regulations is not satisfied with respect to the larger transaction, then the transaction as a whole resembles a sale and the exchange cannot qualify under section 351 because that section is not intended to apply to sales. Rev. Rul. 80-285 reached a similar conclusion with respect to an asset, rather than stock, acquisition in which a purported section 351 exchange was also part of a larger acquisitive transaction.

Upon reconsideration, the Service has concluded that the fact that "larger acquisitive transactions," such as those described in Rev. Rul. 80-284 and Rev. Rul. 80-285, fail to meet the requirements for tax-free treatment under the reorganization provisions of the Code does not preclude the applicability of section 351(a) to transfers that may be described as part of such larger transactions, but also, either alone or in conjunction with other transfers, meet the requirements of section 351(a). . . .

Rev. Rul. 80-284 and Rev. Rul. 80-285 are revoked. . . .

NOTES

1. Compare *May B. Kass*, page 595 supra. In light of Rev. Rul. 84-71, how might Mrs. Kass have achieved a tax-free exchange?

2. Who must satisfy the continuity of interest requirement? See Rev. Rul. 84-30, 1984-1 C.B. 115, in which the Service ruled that the continuity of interest requirement was satisfied where the stock interest in the continuing enterprise was held by the 100-percent corporate parent of the original shareholder.

REVENUE RULING 77-479
1977-2 C.B. 119

Advice has been requested whether the recapitalization described below qualifies as a reorganization under section 368(a)(1)(E) of the Internal Revenue Code of 1954 when part of the stock received in the recapitalization is sold pursuant to a prearranged plan.

Individuals A and B each owned one half of each class of the outstanding stock of Z corporation, which consisted of 50,000 shares of voting common stock and 50,000 shares of non-voting preferred stock. Under a plan to offer some of the Z stock to the public, A and B made arrangements with an investment broker for a secondary offering of 80 percent of their stock. To facilitate the sale by making the stock a more attractive investment, the broker suggested that the existing common and preferred stock be converted into one new class of common stock. Thus, Z effected a recapitalization in which all of its outstanding shares of common and preferred stock were exchanged by A and B for shares of one new class of voting common stock of Z on a share-for-share basis. A and B each then sold 40,000 shares of the new voting common stock to the public through the broker.

Section 368(a)(1)(E) of the Code provides that a "recapitalization" is a "reorganization." For this purpose a recapitalization has been defined as a "reshuffling of a capital structure within the framework of an existing corporation." Helvering v. Southwest Consolidated Corp., 315 U.S. 194 (1942). . . .

The exchange by A and B of their common and preferred stock for new common stock meets the definition of a reorganization under section 368(a)(1)(E) of the Code. However, when a shareholder receives stock in a reorganization described in section 368(a)(1) and any of the stock received is disposed of pursuant to a prearranged plan, a question arises whether the continuity of interest requirement for a reorganization is satisfied. See Rev. Rul. 66-23, 1966-1 C.B. 67.

In Rev. Rul. 77-415, 1977-2 C.B. 311, a shareholder who owned only preferred stock in a corporation exchanged all of this stock for bonds of the corporation pursuant to a plan of recapitalization. Rev. Rul. 77-415 states, consistent with several court decisions, that the continuity of interest requirement need not be applied to a recapitalization under section 368(a)(1)(E) of the Code because the considerations that make the continuity of interest requirement necessary in acquisitive reorganizations are not present in recapitalizations involving a single corporation. Thus, Rev. Rul. 77-415 concludes that the transaction was a recapitalization under section 368(a)(1)(E) even though the shareholder did not retain a proprietary interest in the corporation.

Accordingly, since continuity of interest is not required for the recapitalization of Z to qualify as a reorganization described in section 368(a)(1)(E) of the Code, the subsequent sale by A and B of the stock received by them as a result of the recapitalization does not affect the qualification under section 368(a)(1)(E). Therefore, no gain or loss is recognized to A or B on the exchange of their common and preferred Z stock for new Z common stock pursuant to section 354(a).

The basis to A and B of the new common stock is the same as the basis of the Z common and preferred stock exchanged therefor pursuant to section 358(a). Any gain realized or loss sustained by A or B upon the sale of the new Z stock to the public is recognized to them pursuant to section 1001.

NOTE

In the version of the 1954 Code proposed by the House Ways and Means Committee, recapitalizations theretofore treated as reorganizations would have been dealt with entirely under the sections dealing with corporate distributions. See H. Rep. No. 1337, 83d Cong., 2d Sess., 3 U.S. Code Cong. & Admin. News 4253 (1954).Do you think such an approach would be sensible?

b. Interest Surrendered

HELVERING v. ALABAMA ASPHALTIC LIMESTONE CO.
315 U.S. 179 (1942)

Mr. Justice DOUGLAS delivered the opinion of the Court. Respondent in 1931, acquired all the assets of Alabama Rock Asphalt, Inc., pursuant to a reorganization plan consummated with the aid of the bankruptcy court. In computing its depreciation and depletion allowances for the year 1934, respondent treated its assets as having the same basis which they had in the hands of the old corporation. The Commissioner determined a deficiency, computed on the price paid at the bankruptcy sale.[1] The Board of Tax Appeals rejected the position of the Commissioner. . . . The Circuit Court of Appeals affirmed. . . . We granted the petition for certiorari because of the conflict between that decision[2] and Commissioner v. Palm Springs Holding Corp., 119 F.2d 846, decided by the Circuit Court of Appeals for the Ninth Circuit, and Helvering v. New President Corp., 122 F.2d 92, decided by the Circuit Court of Appeals for the Eighth Circuit.

The answer to the question[3] turns on the meaning of that part

1. Petitioner now takes the position that the new basis should be measured by the market value of the assets rather than the bid price. See Bondholders Committee v. Commissioner, [315 U.S. 189 (1942)].
2. And see Commissioner v. Kitselman, 89 F.2d 458, and Commissioner v. Newberry Lumber & Chemical Co., 94 F.2d 447, which are in accord with the decision below.
3. If there was a "reorganization," the respondent was entitled to use the asset basis of the old corporation as provided in §113(a)(7) [362(b)].

of §112(i)(1) of the Revenue Act of 1928 . . . which provides: "The term 'reorganization' means (A) a merger or consolidation (including the acquisition by one corporation of . . . substantially all the properties of another corporation). . . ."

The essential facts can be stated briefly. The old corporation was a subsidiary of a corporation which was in receivership in 1929. Stockholders of the parent had financed the old corporation taking unsecured notes for their advances. Maturity of the notes was approaching and not all of the noteholders would agree to take stock for their claims. Accordingly, a creditors' committee was formed, late in 1929, and a plan of reorganization was proposed to which all the noteholders, except two, assented. The plan provided that a new corporation would be formed which would acquire all the assets of the old corporation. The stock of the new corporation, preferred and common, would be issued to the creditors in satisfaction of their claims. Pursuant to the plan, involuntary bankruptcy proceedings were instituted in 1930. The appraised value of the bankrupt corporation's assets was about $155,000. Its obligations were about $838,000, the unsecured notes with accrued interest aggregating somewhat over $793,000. The bankruptcy trustee offered the assets for sale at public auction. They were bid in by the creditors' committee for $150,000. The price was paid by $15,000 in cash, by agreements of creditors to accept stock of a new corporation in full discharge of their claims, and by an offer of the committee to meet the various costs of administration, etc. Thereafter, respondent was formed and acquired all the assets of the bankrupt corporation. It does not appear whether the acquisition was directly from the old corporation on assignment of the bid or from the committee. Pursuant to the plan, respondent issued its stock to the creditors of the old corporation — over 95% to the noteholders and the balance to small creditors. Non-assenting creditors were paid in cash. Operations were not interrupted by the reorganization and were carried on subsequently by substantially the same persons as before.

From the *Pinellas* case (287 U.S. 462) [page 580 supra] to the *LeTulle* case (308 U.S. 415) [page 589 supra] it has been recognized that a transaction may not qualify as a "reorganization" under the various revenue acts though the literal language of the statute is satisfied. See Paul, Studies in Federal Taxation (3d Series), pp. 91 et seq. The *Pinellas* case introduced the continuity of interest theory to eliminate those transactions which had "no real semblance to a merger or consolidation" . . . and to avoid a construction which "would make evasion of taxation very easy." . . . In that case, the transferor received in exchange for its property cash and short term notes. This Court said . . . : "Certainly, we think that to be within the exemption the seller must acquire an interest in the affairs of the purchasing company more definite than that incident to ownership of its short-term purchase-money notes." In the *LeTulle* case, we held that the term of the obligation received by the seller was immaterial. "Where the consideration is wholly in the transferee's bonds, or part cash and part such bonds, we think it cannot be said that the transferor retains any proprietary interest in the enterprise." . . . On the basis of the continuity of interest theory as explained in the *LeTulle* case, it is now earnestly contended that a substantial ownership interest in the transferee company must be retained by the holders of the ownership interest in the transferor. That view has been followed by some courts. . . . Under that test, there was "no reorganization" in this case, since the old stockholders were eliminated by the plan, no portion whatever of their proprietary interest being preserved for them in the new corporation. And it is clear that the fact that the creditors were for the most part stockholders of the parent company does not bridge the gap. The equity interest in the parent is one step removed from the equity interest in the subsidiary. In any event, the stockholders of the parent were not granted participation in the plan qua stockholders.

We conclude, however, that it is immaterial that the transfer shifted the ownership of the equity in the property from the stockholders to the creditors of the old corporation. Plainly, the old continuity of interest was broken. Technically that did not occur in this proceeding until the judicial sale took place. For practical purposes, however, it took place not later than the time when the creditors took steps to enforce their demands against their insolvent debtor. In this case, that was the date of the institution of bankruptcy proceedings. From that time on, they had effective command over the disposition of the property. The full priority rule of Northern Pacific Ry. Co. v. Boyd, 228 U.S. 482, applies to proceedings in bankruptcy as well as to equity receiverships. . . . It gives creditors, whether secured or unsecured, the right to exclude stockholders entirely from the reorganization plan when the debtor is insolvent. . . . When the equity owners are excluded and the old creditors become the stockholders of the new corporation, it conforms to realities to date their equity ownership from the time when they invoked the processes of the law to enforce their rights of full-priority. At that time they stepped into the shoes of the old stockholders. The sale "did nothing but recognize officially what had before been true in fact." . . .

That conclusion involves no conflict with the principle of the *LeTulle* case. A bondholder interest in a solvent company plainly is not the equivalent of a proprietary interest, even though upon default the bondholders could retake the property transferred. The mere possibility of a proprietary interest is, of course, not its equivalent. But the determinative and controlling factors of the debtor's insolvency and an effective command by the creditors over the property were absent in the *LeTulle* case.

Nor are there any other considerations which prevent this transaction from qualifying as a "reorganization" within the meaning of the Act. The *Pinellas* case makes plain that "merger" and "consolidation" as used in the Act include transactions which "are beyond the ordinary and commonly accepted meaning of those words." . . . Insolvency reorganizations are within the family of financial readjustments embraced in those terms as used in this particular statute. Some contention, however, is made that this transaction did not meet the statutory standard because the properties acquired by the new corporation belonged at that time to the committee and not to the old corporation. That is true. Yet, the separate steps were integrated parts of a single scheme. Transitory phases of an arrangement frequently are disregarded under these sections of the revenue acts where they add nothing of substance to the completed affair. Gregory v. Helvering [page 545 supra]; Helvering v. Bashford, 302 U.S. 454. Here they were no more than intermediate procedural devices utilized to enable the new corporation to acquire all the assets of the old one pursuant to a single reorganization plan.

Affirmed.

NOTES

1. Before the transaction in *Alabama Asphaltic Limestone Co.*, the "equity" interest in the assets was owned by the parent corporation. The parent, in turn, was owned by the same persons who held the subsidiary's notes. Why is the readjustment that took place not a prototype "reorganization"? Of what relevance is the *LeTulle* line of cases to the basis of assets of a corporation after it has been taken over by creditors in an insolvency proceeding? Should the character of the pre-insolvency interest of the subsequent stockholders have any effect on these questions?

Today, §368(a)(1)(G), enacted as part of the Bankruptcy Tax Act of 1980, is the primary section governing insolvency reorganizations. The Senate Finance Committee Report recommending this provision makes clear that the "continuity of interest" doctrine is not to be strictly applied to such reorganizations. See S. Rep. No. 1035, 96th Cong., 2nd Sess. 36-37 (1980). Rather, all creditors, including all senior and junior classes, and all shareholders who receive stock for their claims in a corporation to which the insolvent company's assets have been transferred, will generally be included in determining whether the continuity of interest requirement has been met. See Asofsky and Tatlock, Reorganizations, Procedures and Corporate

Taxes Greatly Affected by Bankruptcy Tax Act, 54 J. Taxn. 170 (1981); G. Henderson and S. Goldring, Failing and Failed Businesses (CCH Tax Trans. Lib.).

2. In Helvering v. Cement Investors, Inc., 316 U.S. 527 (1942), property of two corporations, a bankrupt parent and its subsidiary, was transferred to a new corporation by the debtor companies, the trustee in bankruptcy, and the trustee under the indenture agreement securing the bonds of the bankrupt subsidiary. The bondholders of the old subsidiary received common stock and income bonds in place of their former securities. The old shareholders received warrants. The issue was whether the bondholders of the new corporation could be treated as transferring property to the new company so that their gain would not be recognized under the predecessor of §351. Although the Commissioner argued that the bondholders themselves had transferred no property to the corporation, and thus they could not receive §351 treatment, the Supreme Court held otherwise. Citing *Alabama Asphaltic Limestone Co.*, the Court noted that it would not be unrealistic to treat the bondholders as having received an equity interest in the old corporation when they sought to enforce their rights. Regardless of how that interest was described, the bondholders had an equitable interest in the property transferred and such an interest was sufficient to treat them as transferring property within the meaning of §351 even if the actual conveyance was made by a trustee. The bondholders therefore received tax-free treatment under §351.

2. "Party to a Reorganization"

REVENUE RULING 63-234
1963-2 C.B. 148

Advice has been requested whether the successive exchanges of corporate stock described below constitute, separately or in concert, a reorganization as defined in section 368(a)(1)(B) of the Internal Revenue Code of 1954.

In 1960, the M corporation directly and through its subsidiaries operated a chain of retail stores. It owned 60 shares (60 percent) of the 100 outstanding shares of N corporation's voting common stock. A group of taxpayers, hereinafter referred to as the X group, owned 18 shares (18 percent) of N's voting stock, and the remaining 22 shares (22 percent) were held by other shareholders.

Among the assets of the N corporation was 50 percent of the voting stock of the O corporation. The remaining 50 percent of O's voting stock was owned by members of the X group.

For the purpose of affecting certain economies in operation and to make the filing of a consolidated income tax return possible, the above-mentioned parties adopted a plan of reorganization pursuant to which the following action was taken:

(1) The charter of the N corporation was amended to enlarge its board of directors from ten to 12 members and to provide that the two new members of the board would be elected by the owners of a newly authorized class of preferred stock.

(2) Newly created preferred stock of the N corporation was issued to the members of the X group in exchange for all their holdings of the O corporation's voting stock.

The N corporation thus acquired 100 percent of the outstanding stock of the O corporation and the holdings of the X group in the N corporation were increased to include all of that corporation's preferred stock.

(3) Immediately thereafter, the X group transferred all of its stock of the N corporation (18 percent of the common stock and 100 percent of the preferred stock) to the M corporation in exchange for the latter's voting common stock. As a result, the M corporation became the owner of 78 percent of N's common stock and 100 percent of the preferred shares.

The voting power of the N corporation preferred stock confers upon the holders of such stock the right to significant participation in the management of the affairs of the corporation. This preferred stock is therefore "voting stock" within the meaning of the reorganization provision. See I.T. 3896, C.B. 1948-1, 72. Under the principles set forth in I.T. 3896, the voting rights of the M corporation respecting the affairs of the N corporation, when properly weighted, totaled 81.67 percent of the "voting power" of all classes of "voting stock" of the N corporation. Thus, the M corporation acquired "control" of the N corporation within the meaning of section 368(c) of the Code.

Section 368(a)(1)(B) of the Code provides that, for purposes of parts I, II, and III of subchapter C of chapter 1 of subtitle A of the Code, the term "reorganization" means —

> the acquisition by one corporation, in exchange solely for all or a part of its voting stock, of stock of another corporation if, immediately after the acquisition, the acquiring corporation has control of such other corporation (whether or not such acquiring corporation had control immediately before the acquisition);

Among the requisites to a reorganization under the Code is that of continuity of interest on the part of those persons who, directly or indirectly, were the owners of the enterprise prior to the reorganization. See section 1.368-1(b) of the Income Tax Regulations.

Taking into account all the facts and circumstances, it is concluded that the two exchanges of corporate stock in the instant case were but successive steps in the execution of the single plan adopted earlier by the parties. See Whitney Corporation v. Commissioner, 105 Fed. (2d) 438 (1939), and United Light and Power Co. v. Commissioner, 105 Fed. (2d) 866 (1939), *certiorari denied,* 308 U.S. 574 (1939). When the component steps in the plans are combined it becomes apparent that the X group exchanged its stock in the O corporation for stock of the M corporation, which did not thereafter directly own either stock of O corporation or its assets. The receipt of N corporation preferred shares by the X group may be disregarded for purposes of the reorganization provisions of the Code since the X group's holding of such shares was "transitory and without real substance." Helvering v. Raymond I. Bashford, 302 U.S. 454 (1938) . . . ; see also the *United Power and Light Co.* case, supra.

Under the principles established by the Supreme Court of the United States in Herman C. Groman v. Commissioner, 302 U.S. 82 (1937), . . . and the *Bashford* case, the stock of M corporation does not provide the X group with the requisite continuity of interest in the O corporation stock transferred to the N corporation because the group had only an indirect interest in the O stock following the transaction. The rule of the *Groman* and *Bashford* cases is still applicable to reorganizations sought to be brought within the provisions of section 368(a)(1)(B). See S. Report No. 1622, Eighty-third Congress, Second Session, 51 and 273.

Accordingly, it is held that the transfer by the X group of its shares in the O corporation to the N corporation in exchange for the latter's newly issued preferred stock and the subsequent transfer of the newly acquired preferred shares of N to the M corporation in exchange for voting stock in M does not qualify, either in whole or in part, as a reorganization within the meaning of section 368(a)(1)(B) of the Code.

However, it is held that the exchange of N corporation stock owned by the X group before any of the exchanges described above for voting common stock of M corporation constitutes a reorganization within the meaning of section 368(a)(1)(B) of the Code, and that M and N corporations are each a party to such reorganization within the meaning of section 368(b)(2) of the Code.

NOTES

1. Is the result in Rev. Rul. 63-234 wise or compelled by the decisions in Groman v. Commissioner, 302 U.S. 82 (1937), and Hel-

vering v. Bashford, 302 U.S. 454 (1938)? Were the results in *Groman* and *Bashford* compelled by the statute or desirable?

2. What impact do the 1964 amendments to §368(a)(1)(B) and §368(a)(2)(C) have on the specific problem posed in Rev. Rul. 63-234?

3. In Rev. Rul. 63-234 the Commissioner declined to recognize the X group's holding of the N Corporation's newly issued voting preferred stock because it was "transitory and without real substance." For what purpose, however, does the ruling implicitly recognize the reality of the N Corporation's newly issued voting preferred stock? In this connection, consider the last paragraph of Rev. Rul. 63-234.

REVENUE RULING 64-73
1964-1 C.B. 142

Advice has been requested whether the transaction described below constitutes a reorganization within the meaning of section 368(a) of the Internal Revenue Code of 1954.

L corporation owns 100 percent of the outstanding stock of corporation M. M owns 100 percent of the outstanding stock of corporation N. L entered into an agreement with X, an unrelated corporation, under which L acquired all of the assets of X, solely in exchange for L voting stock. Some of the X assets were transferred from X to N, and the remaining X assets were transferred to L. Neither the assets which were transferred to N nor the assets transferred to L constituted substantially all of X's assets, but together they constituted all of X's assets.

Section 368(a)(1)(C) of the Code provides, in part, that the term reorganization means —

> (C) the acquisition by one corporation, in exchange solely for all or a part of its voting stock (or in exchange solely for all or a part of the voting stock of a corporation which is in control of the acquiring corporation), of substantially all of the properties of another corporation. . . .

Prior to the enactment of the 1954 Code, the described transaction would not have qualified as a reorganization, as it was believed that the ultimate lodging of some of the assets in any subsidiary of the acquiring corporation failed to satisfy the continuity-of-interest requirements of the reorganization provisions. See Herman C. Groman v. Commissioner, 302 U.S. 82 (1937) . . . ; and Helvering v. Raymond I. Bashford, 302 U.S. 454 (1938). . . .

The Congress, in 1954, modified the *Groman-Bashford* doctrine to provide that the placement of acquired assets in a controlled corporation would no longer destroy the continuity-of-interest requirements of section 368(a)(1)(C) reorganizations. See S. Report No. 1622, Eighty-third Congress, Second Session, at 51-52 and 273, 275.

In applying specific statutory relief to certain factual situations previously governed by the *Groman* and *Bashford* cases and section 112(g) of the Internal Revenue Code of 1939 (the predecessor of section 368(a)(1)(C) of the 1954 Code), Congress indicated its desire to remove the continuity-of-interest problem from the section 368(a)(1)(C) reorganization area. Having modified the continuity-of-interest rule where assets move to a corporation directly controlled by the parent in exchange for the parent's stock, there is no sound reason to assume the Congress intended to have the *Groman-Bashford* rule apply where the assets are caused to be transferred by the parent to a wholly owned subsidiary of a corporation controlled by the parent corporation.

No cases involving the transfer of some of the acquired assets to remote subsidiaries in attempted section 368(a)(1)(C) reorganizations had arisen prior to the enactment of the 1954 Code. The specific statutory exceptions to the *Groman-Bashford* doctrine contained in sections 368(a)(1)(C), 368(a)(2)(C), and 368(b) are not intended to exclude a transfer of assets to a wholly owned subsidiary of a corporation which is controlled by the parent corporation.

However, it should be noted that the Congress in 1954 did not change the definition of a reorganization contained in section 368(a)(1)(B) of the Code so as to modify the continuity-of-interest doctrine in that area. See Revenue Ruling 63-234, C.B. 1963-2, 148.

The described transaction is viewed as an acquisition by L, in exchange solely for part of its voting stock, of substantially all of the properties of X. The fact that in the instant case the plan of reorganization provides that some of the assets are to be transferred directly from X to N, rather than through L and M, does not detract from the conclusion that in substance L is to acquire substantially all the X assets. To hold otherwise would defeat the purpose of the 1954 Code change in the definition of a section 368(a)(1)(C) reorganization. The subsequent transfer of assets acquired in a reorganization under section 368(a)(1)(C) of the 1954 Code to a wholly owned subsidiary of a corporation controlled by the acquiring corporation, even though pursuant to the plan of reorganization, will not affect the reorganization.

Accordingly, it is held that the transaction described in the instant case constitutes a reorganization as defined in section 368(a)(1)(C) of the Code.

NOTES

1. If the facts of Rev. Rul. 64-73 were modified to provide that X is to receive voting stock of L for the assets lodged in L and voting stock of M for the assets lodged in N, would the transaction constitute a reorganization? Why?

2. There is no indication in Rev. Rul. 64-73 that X was liquidated. Section 368(a)(2)(G), which generally requires the liquidation of the transferor corporation in a "C" reorganization, had not yet been enacted. If the plan of reorganization in Rev. Rul. 64-73 had called for liquidation, what provision of the Code would have governed the tax consequences to the shareholders of X?

REVENUE RULING 67-326

1967-2 C.B. 143

Advice has been requested whether the nonrecognition provisions of section 361(a) of the Internal Revenue Code of 1954 apply to a transaction qualifying as a merger under applicable State law where the acquiring corporation exchanged the stock of its parent for all of the assets of an unrelated corporation and whether section 354(a) of the Code will apply to the exchange by the shareholders of the acquired corporation of all of their stock of the acquired corporation for stock of the parent of the acquiring corporation.

Corporation S is a wholly owned subsidiary of P corporation. In a transaction which qualified as a merger under the law of the State in which S and X are incorporated, S acquired from X, an unrelated corporation, all of its assets and assumed all of its liabilities in exchange for stock of P which had previously been contributed to S. Pursuant to the plan of reorganization, the shareholders of X exchanged their stock of X for stock of P.

Section 361(a) of the Code provides in part for the nonrecognition of gain or loss if a corporation a party to a reorganization exchanges property, in pursuance of a plan of reorganization, solely for stock in another corporation a party to the reorganization. In order for this section to be applicable to the exchange of assets by X for stock of P, X and P must be parties to the reorganization.

Section 354(a) of the Code provides in part for the nonrecognition of gain or loss if stock in a corporation a party to a reorganization is, in pursuance of the plan of reorganization, exchanged solely for stock in such corporation or in another corporation a party to the reorganization. In order for this section to be applicable to the exchange of X stock by the shareholders of X for stock of P, X and P must be parties to the reorganization.

Section 368(b) of the Code defines a party to a reorganization as: "(1) a corporation resulting from a reorganization, and (2) both corporations, in the case of a reorganization resulting from the acquisition by one corporation of stock or properties of another."

Section 368(b) of the Code provides that in the case of a reorganization qualifying under paragraph (1)(B) or (1)(C) of section 368(a) of the Code, if the stock exchanged for the stock or properties of another corporation is stock of a corporation which is in control of the acquiring corporation, the term "a party to a reorganization" includes the corporation so controlling the acquiring corporation. Section 368(b) of the Code does not include, however, as a party to a reorganization a corporation which is in control of the acquiring corporation in a reorganization qualifying under section 368(a)(1)(A) of the Code.*

Accordingly, although the transaction described is a statutory merger of S and X under State law, the nontaxable provisions of section 361(a) of the Code will not apply to the exchange of the assets of X for stock of P and section 354(a) will not apply to the exchange by the shareholders of X of their stock of X for stock of P.

A reorganization under section 368(a)(1)(C) of the Code is the acquisition by one corporation, in exchange solely for all or a part of its voting stock (or in exchange solely for all or a part of the voting stock of a corporation which is in control of the acquiring corporation), of substantially all of the properties of another corporation. As indicated, section 368(b) of the Code includes as a party to a reorganization described in section 368(a)(1)(C) of the Code a corporation which is in control of the acquiring corporation. Therefore, if the transaction otherwise qualifies as a reorganization as defined in section 368(a)(1)(C) of the Code, the nonrecognition provisions of sections 361(a) and 354(a) of the Code will apply to the exchanges described.

NOTES

1. Was the ruling correct in holding that the transaction could not qualify as an "A," but could qualify as a "C," reorganization? Can it matter to either the taxpayer or the government that the transaction is a "C," but not an "A," reorganization? Why?

2. The doctrine arising from the cases of Groman v. Commissioner, 302 U.S. 82 (1937), and Helvering v. Bashford, 302 U.S. 454 (1937), precluded the use of the reorganization provisions of the

---

*Section 368(b), as now constituted, includes the corporation controlling the acquiring corporation as a "party to [the] reorganization" in a merger qualifying under §368 (a)(1)(A). — Ed.

1939 Code in transactions in which the acquiring corporation transferred the stock or assets of the acquired corporation to a subsidiary or in transactions in which the subsidiary directly acquired the transferor's stock or assets in exchange for its parent's stock. In the 1954 Code Congress attempted to overrule this doctrine. It started by adding the parenthetical in the definition of a "C" reorganization. It later added the parenthetical in the "B" reorganization, §368(a)(2)(C) which allows tax-free status to a reorganization even if the assets of the acquired company are dropped down into a subsidiary, and §368(a)(2)(D) which allows "forward" subsidiary mergers. It also made the necessary changes to the definition of a "party to the reorganization" in §368(b). Then, in 1970, Congress added subparagraph (E) to §368(a)(2) and the last sentence in §368(b). The effect of these changes was to afford tax-free status to "reverse" statutory mergers in which a corporation's subsidiary is merged into an unrelated corporation that survives, and the voting stock of the subsidiary parent is exchanged for control of the corporation surviving the merger.

Today, these triangular mergers have taken on a life of their own. Many if not most corporate acquisitions are effected through the use of subsidiaries. One reason for this prevalent practice is that state corporation statutes do not require that the shareholders of the parent corporation approve the merger. Rather, only the shareholder of the subsidiary, i.e., the directors of the parent corporation, must approve. The use of subsidiary mergers, therefore, eliminates a proxy statement and shareholder vote.

3. In Rev. Rul. 84-104, 1984-2 C.B. 94, the Service ruled that although §368(a)(2)(E) applies by its terms only to "mergers," under the National Banking Act a "consolidation" of a wholly owned bank subsidiary of a bank holding company into an existing bank is considered a "merger" qualifying under §368(a)(2)(E). The Service said that the "consolidation" in question was correctly classified as a merger, since under the National Banking Act a "consolidation" results in the survival of one of the existing corporations (there the target), and no new corporation is formed. This seems to confirm that a "true consolidation" will *not* qualify under section 368(a)(2)(E).

4. See Posin, A Case Study in Income Tax Complexity: The Type A Reorganization, 47 Ohio St. L.J. 627 (1986).

REVENUE RULING 74-565
1974-2 C.B. 125

Advice has been requested whether the transaction described below qualifies as a reorganization within the meaning of section

368(a)(1)(B) of the Internal Revenue Code of 1954, even though it does not qualify as a reorganization under section 368(a)(1)(A) and (a)(2)(E) of the Code.

The stock of corporations P and Y is publicly held. Corporation S1 is a wholly owned subsidiary of P. S1 desired to acquire all the stock of Y and in order to eliminate the possibility of having minority shareholders in Y, the following steps were taken pursuant to a plan:

(a) P transferred shares of its voting stock to S1 in exchange for shares of S1 stock.

(b) S1 transferred the shares of P voting stock to its newly formed subsidiary S2, in exchange for shares of S2 stock.

(c) S2 (whose only asset consisted of a block of the voting stock of P) merged into Y in a transaction which qualified as a statutory merger under the applicable state law.

(d) Y stock held by Y shareholders (except for dissenters) was exchanged for the P stock received by Y on the merger of S2 into Y. At the same time the S2 stock owned by S1 was exchanged for Y stock. The end result of these transactions was that S1 acquired from the shareholders of Y, in exchange for voting stock of P, more than 95 percent of the stock of Y.

(e) Y shareholders owning less than 5 percent of the stock of Y dissented to the merger and had the right to receive the appraised value of their shares paid solely from assets of Y. No funds, or other property, have been or will be provided by P or S1 for this purpose.

After the consummation of the plan of reorganization described above, Y continued its business as a wholly owned subsidiary of Sl.

Section 368(a)(2)(E) of the Code, which is applicable to statutory mergers occurring after December 31, 1970, was enacted to permit, under certain circumstances, a tax-free statutory merger when stock of a parent corporation is used in a merger between a controlled subsidiary of the parent and another corporation, and the other corporation survives. See S. Rep. No. 91-1533, 91st Cong., 2d Sess. 1 (1970), 1971-1 C.B. 622. . . .

In the instant case, the transaction does not qualify as a reorganization under section 368(a)(1)(A) and (a)(2)(E) of the Code, because stock of P, rather than stock of the controlling corporation S1, was transferred to the Y shareholders in the transaction. . . .

In Rev. Rul. 67-448, 1967-2 C.B. 144, pursuant to a plan of reorganization, a parent corporation, P, issued some of its voting stock to its new subsidiary S and S, pursuant to the plan, merged into unrelated corporation, Y, with the Y shareholders exchanging their Y stock (amounting to 95 percent of the outstanding stock of Y) for the P stock received by Y in the merger of S into Y. Rev. Rul. 67-448 states that the net effect of this series of steps for Federal income tax purposes is a direct acquisition by P of 95 percent of the stock of Y from the Y shareholders in exchange solely for P voting stock and that the transitory existence of S is disregarded. Thus, Rev. Rul. 67-448 holds that the transaction will be treated as an acquisition by P, in exchange solely for a part of its voting stock, of stock of Y in an amount constituting control (as defined in section 368(c) of the Code) of Y, which qualifies as a reorganization within the meaning of section 368(a)(1)(B) of the Code.

In the instant case, the net effect of the steps taken was that S1 acquired, solely for voting stock of P (which was in control of S1), stock of Y in an amount constituting control of Y.

Accordingly, the transaction in the instant case will be treated as an acquisition by S1, in exchange solely for a part of P voting stock (P being in control of S1), of stock of Y (S1 being in control of Y after the transaction), which qualifies as a reorganization within the meaning of section 368(a)(1)(B) of the Code.

Pursuant to section 354(a) of the Code the former shareholders of Y will recognize no gain or loss on the exchange of their Y stock for P stock.

See Rev. Rul. 74-564, . . . which holds that a similar transaction that does not qualify as a reorganization under section 368(a)(1)(A) and (a)(2)(E) of the Code is treated as a reorganization qualifying under section 368(a)(1)(B).

NOTES

1. Compare Rev. Rul. 78-250, 1978-1 C.B. 83, in which A, the majority shareholder in Corporation X, created Corporation Y in exchange for his X stock and, thereafter, Y merged into X. The minority shareholders of X received cash for their shares, and A received X stock for his Y shares. Held, the net result is that the minority shareholders received cash for their X shares, and, therefore, the creation of Y and merger of Y into X will be disregarded and the transaction will be treated as a redemption of X stock.

2. In Letter Rul. 7921075 (May 31, 1979), the Service ruled that when P creates S to merge into target company T, and when upon the merger the shareholders of T have the right to receive either cash or convertible notes of P, and P acquires the stock of T, the transitory existence of S will be ignored and the transaction will be treated as a sale of T stock by the shareholders of T for cash or notes of P. Thus, if all of the other requirements of the pre-1980 provisions of §453 were met, since P is considered the purchaser of the T stock, the T shareholders could report their gain on the installment sale method. See Emory, Penick, and Swensen, Reverse Triangular Merger Eligible for Section 453, 51 J. Taxn. 372 (1979). Would the result be different if T had merged into S?

3. "Solely for ... Voting Stock" — "B" and "C" Reorganizations

In both "B" and "C" reorganizations, the acquisition must be made solely in exchange for all or part of the acquiring corporation's voting stock. The statute, however, relaxes the "solely for voting stock" requirement for the "C" reorganization in two ways. First, in determining whether the exchange is solely for voting stock, liabilities of the transferor that are assumed by the acquiring corporation are disregarded. See §368(a)(1)(C). Second, §368(a)(2)(B) permits a limited amount of money or other property to be exchanged by the acquiring corporation. In this case, however, liabilities assumed by the acquiring corporation are treated as money or other property.

The "solely for voting stock" requirement of the "B" reorganization is much more restrictive. For example, in an early decision, Helvering v. Southwest Consolidated Corp., 315 U.S. 194 (1942), the taxpayer contended that the requirement was met when the target shareholders received voting stock of the acquiring corporation and warrants to purchase additional stock. The Supreme Court rejected this argument, finding that the warrants were impermissible consideration. In so doing, the Court stated that the "solely for voting stock" requirement of §368(a)(1)(B) "leaves no leeway. Voting stock plus some other consideration does not meet the statutory requirement."

The Supreme Court again considered the "solely for voting stock" requirement of the "B" reorganization in Turnbow v. Commissioner, 368 U.S. 337 (1961). The taxpayer in *Turnbow* transferred all the shares of his wholly owned corporation to the acquiring corporation in exchange for $1.2 million of the acquiror's voting stock and $3 million in cash. The taxpayer conceded that the transaction failed as a "B" reorganization to the extent he received cash, but he argued that the exchange was nontaxable to the extent he received voting stock. The Supreme Court disagreed, holding that "an exchange of stock *and* cash — approximately 30 per centum in stock and 70 per centum in cash for 'at least 80 per centum of the ... stock of another corporation' cannot be a 'reorganization' as defined in [§368(a)(1)(B)]."

Turnbow left unresolved the issue whether the requirements of a "B" reorganization are met when some of the target's stock is acquired for cash but at least 80 percent of the target's stock is acquired in exchange for the acquiring corporation's voting stock. This issue was squarely presented in a group of cases involving the target shareholders in an acquisition of Hartford Fire Insurance Company (Hartford) by ITT. Between November 1968 and March 1969, ITT purchased for cash approximately 8 percent of Hartford's outstanding shares. Over a year later, in a transaction approved by Hartford's

Board of Directors, ITT received from Hartford's shareholders more than 90 percent of Hartford's stock in exchange for voting stock of ITT. Conceding *arguendo* that the cash purchases were part of the same transaction, the former Hartford shareholders argued that the transaction nevertheless was a nontaxable "B" reorganization since more than 80 percent of Hartford's stock (an amount constituting control under §368(a)(1)(B) and 368(c)) was acquired in exchange for ITT voting stock.

The Tax Court agreed with the taxpayers. C. E. Graham Reeves, 71 T.C. 927 (1979). On appeal, after extensively examining the legislative history, the regulations, and the decisions construing §368(a)(1)(B), the First Circuit reversed. Chapman v. Commissioner, 618 F.2d 856 (1st Cir. 1980). The court said that the taxpayers' argument incorrectly emphasized the 80-percent control test as the primary requirement of a "B" reorganization. Instead, the court held that the transaction must meet both the "solely for voting stock" and "control immediately after" requirements. It concluded that "the presence of non-stock consideration in such an acquisition, regardless of whether it is necessary to the gaining of control, is inconsistent with treatment of the acquisition as a nontaxable ['B'] reorganization."

The Third Circuit, also reviewing the Tax Court's decision in *Reeves*, reached the same result as the First. See Heverly v. Commissioner, 621 F.2d 1227 (3d Cir. 1980). Appeals from the Tax Court's decision were pending in the Fourth and Ninth Circuits, and petitions for certiorari were pending in *Chapman* and *Heverly*, when, in early 1981, the litigation was settled by an agreement on the part of ITT to pay the government $18.5 million, with the shareholders effectively bound to carry over their Hartford stock basis into their ITT stock.

Is the result in *Chapman* a sound construction of §368(a)(1)(B)? Contrast the language in §368(a)(2)(E). Are the differing continuity of interest requirements for the "A," "B," and "C" reorganizations sensible legislative policy?

REVENUE RULING 79-4
1979-1 C.B. 150

ISSUE

Is the "solely for . . . voting stock" requirement of section 368(a)(1)(B) of the Internal Revenue Code of 1954 violated in the situation described below where an acquired corporation's debt that is treated for federal income tax purposes as a debt of its guarantor-shareholder is repaid by the acquired corporation with funds furnished to it by the acquiring corporation?

FACTS

A, an individual, was the sole shareholder of corporation Y, and was the guarantor on an unsecured note of Y in the principal amount of 200x dollars issued to Z, an unrelated party, in exchange for a loan. Because of Y's inadequate capitalization, Z required that A guarantee the note as to principal and interest. The facts and circumstances, including but not limited to Y's thin capitalization, resulted in Z being treated for federal income tax purposes as having made the loan to A rather than Y and A being treated as having made a capital contribution of the 200x dollar loan proceeds to Y. A's initial basis in A's Y stock (100x dollars) was therefore increased to 300x dollars pursuant to section 1.118-1 of the Income Tax Regulations. Payments of principal and interest by Y to Z with respect to the loan were treated as discharging A's obligation to Z, and such amounts were taxable to A as constructive distributions under section 301 of the Code. In addition, Y's interest payments on the loan were considered as having been made by A. See Plantation Patterns, Inc. v. Commissioner, 462 F.2d 712 (1972). . . . For financial accounting purposes, however, the loan was considered as made to Y and listed among its liabilities. At the time of the situation described below, Y had made all previous principal and interest payments on the loan as they became due.

In accordance with an agreement and plan of reorganization, X acquired all of the outstanding stock of Y from A in exchange for voting stock of X. The fair market value of the Y stock was calculated at 400x dollars with the 180x dollar remaining indebtedness on the Z loan being included in such calculation as an indebtedness of Y. A received 390x dollars of X stock, an amount equal to the 400x dollar fair market value of the Y stock at the date of the exchange less 10x dollars consideration for X's agreement to contribute 180x dollars to Y to satisfy the indebtedness to Z. The satisfaction of such indebtedness would eliminate A's potential liability as guarantor and would improve A's borrowing ability. X was willing to satisfy the indebtedness immediately to strengthen Y's financial position and to prevent a suit for reimbursement that would have arisen if A, as guarantor, had been required to pay the indebtedness on Y's default.

LAW AND ANALYSIS

Because the contribution of cash by X to Y and the repayment by Y of the indebtedness plus accrued interest was a condition for the exchange of the Y stock for the X stock, such contribution and repayment constitute additional consideration for the Y stock within the meaning of section 1.368-2(c) of the regulations and the "solely for . . . voting stock" requirement contained in section 368(a)(1)(B) of the Code is not satisfied. Consequently, the nonrecognition provisions of section 354(a)(1) are inapplicable and gain or loss realized on the exchange is recognized under section 1001.

In addition, because under *Plantation Patterns*, the indebtedness of Y to Z is considered as indebtedness of A to Z despite Y's timely payment of principal and interest to Z, and because the repayment of the outstanding indebtedness by Y was a condition for exchange of stock, A has received income in the amount of such repayment. Section 61 . . . , and Douglas v. Willcuts, 296 U.S. 1 (1935). . . . Therefore, pursuant to section 1001, A will realize and recognize a gain on the exchange to the extent such income and the fair market value of the X stock received exceeds A's basis in the Y stock:

income from Y's repayment of indebtedness	180x
fair market value of X stock received	390x
Total	570x
Less A's basis in Y stock	300x
gain realized by and recognized to A	270x

A will therefore realize and recognize a gain of 270x dollars on the exchange, and A's basis in the X stock received will be 400x dollars, its cost in Y stock exchanged. Section 1012 of the Code.

HOLDING

The "solely for . . . voting stock" requirement of section 368(a)(1)(B) of the Code is violated when the debt of Y (which is treated for federal income tax purposes as the debt of A) is repaid by Y with funds furnished by X, if such repayment is a condition for the exchange of the X and Y stock.

NOTE

Compare Rev. Rul. 79-89, 1979-1 C.B. 152, where, in a "B" reorganization, the acquiring corporation contributed cash to the acquired corporation, which the latter used to discharge its debt. The debt had been guaranteed by one of the two shareholders of the acquired corporation, but the ruling held that the cash did not constitute boot because (1) the contribution was not a condition of the exchange; (2) the fair market value of the acquiring corporation's stock received by each shareholder was equal in value to the stock exchanged; and (3) the acquired corporation was not "thinly capitalized" as was the acquired corporation in Rev. Rul. 79-4.

REVENUE RULING 66-365
1966-2 C.B. 116

Advice has been requested whether the payment of cash by an acquiring corporation to the shareholders of the acquired corporation in lieu of issuing fractional shares to the shareholders who are entitled to receive fractional share interests violates the "solely for voting stock" requirement of section 368(a)(1)(B) and (C) of the Internal Revenue Code of 1954. Advice has also been requested concerning the tax treatment of cash received by shareholders in lieu of fractional shares in certain reorganizations defined in section 368(a)(1) of the Code.

In Mills, et al. v. Commissioner, 331 F.2d 321 (1964), . . . the United States Court of Appeals for the Fifth Circuit held that the "solely for voting stock" requirement of section 368(a)(1)(B) of the Code was satisfied where the acquiring corporation received all of the stock of several corporations and distributed in return for such stock, shares of its voting common stock and a small amount of cash in lieu of fractional shares. After finding that the cash given in lieu of fractional shares was simply a mathematical rounding-off for the purpose of simplifying the corporate and accounting problems which would have been caused by the actual issuance of fractional shares, the Court concluded that the receipt of the stock of the acquired corporations was for all practical purposes "solely in exchange for voting stock."

The Internal Revenue Service will follow the decision of the Court of Appeals in Mills, et al. v. Commissioner in similar factual situations. Accordingly, the "solely for voting stock" requirement of section 368(a)(1)(B) and (C) of the Code will not be violated where the cash paid by the acquiring corporation is in lieu of fractional share interests to which the shareholders are entitled, representing merely a mechanical rounding-off of the fractions in the exchange, and is not a separately bargained-for consideration. Where, however, the cash paid by the acquiring corporation is not in lieu of fractional share interests to which the shareholders are entitled or is a separately bargained-for consideration, the "solely for voting stock" requirement of section 368(a)(1)(B) and (C) of the Code will not be satisfied.

In a transaction qualifying as a reorganization under section 368(a)(1)(A) or (D) (or (C) by reason of section 368(a)(2)(B)) of the Code where the cash paid by the acquiring corporation represents a separately bargained-for consideration it will be treated as the receipt of "boot" under sections 361(b) and 356(a) of the Code. See Tenney Ross v. United States, 173 F. Supp. 793 (1959), in which the cash distributed to the shareholders of the acquired corporation pursuant to a reorganization under section 368(a)(1)(A) of the Code was held to be dividend boot under section 356(a)(2) of the Code where the cash paid did not result in a mere mechanical rounding-off of fractions but was a separately bargained-for consideration. See also Revenue Ruling 56-220, C.B. 1956-1, 191, which holds, in effect, that all of the cash paid to the shareholders of the acquired corporation was separately bargained-for consideration in the exchange. The Revenue Ruling states that the acquiring corporation did not desire to give the stockholders of the acquired corporation a large common stock ownership in itself.

In all reorganizations described in the preceding paragraphs where the cash payment made by the acquiring corporation is not bargained for, but is in lieu of fractional share interests to which the shareholders are entitled, such cash payment will be treated under section 302 of the Code as in redemption of the fractional share interests. Therefore, each shareholder's redemption will be treated as a distribution in full payment in exchange for his fractional share interest under section 302(a) of the Code provided the redemption is not essentially equivalent to a dividend. The *Mills* case is an example of the type of case in which capital gain or loss treatment will be accorded a redemption where cash is paid in lieu of fractional share interests. If the redemption is essentially equivalent to a dividend, it will be treated as a distribution under section 301 of the Code as provided in section 302(d) of the Code. All the facts and circumstances of each case will be considered in determining whether the cash distribution in lieu of the fractional shares is essentially equivalent to a dividend.

The foregoing principles are illustrated by the following example. If, in a reorganization described in section 368(a)(1)(A) of the Code, a shareholder receives stock worth $100 and cash boot of $20, the gain, if any, realized on the exchange, will be recognized under section 356(a) of the Code but not in excess of $20. If the shareholder also receives $4 and it is not bargained for but is in lieu of a fractional share interest, the $4 will be considered as the proceeds from a redemption of the fractional share interest under section 302 of the Code.

If the cash payment made by the acquiring corporation is in lieu of fractional share interests of stock which is section 306 stock, such cash payment will be treated as a distribution in redemption to which section 301 applies unless it is established to the satisfaction of the Commissioner that the distribution of cash was not in pursuance of a plan having as one of its principal purposes the avoidance of Federal income tax. See section 306(b)(4) of the Code.

Revenue Ruling 56-220, C.B. 1956-1, 191, is clarified to remove any implication that the cash paid by the acquiring corporation to the shareholders of the acquired corporation was in lieu of fractional shares, rather than bargained-for additional consideration.

NOTES

1. According to Rev. Rul. 66-365, cash paid in lieu of fractional shares in a reorganization of the "A," "C," or "D" variety will be regarded as "boot" if separately bargained for. If it has the effect of a dividend, taxation under §356(a)(2) may result. If the cash is not separately bargained for, however, the conception is that of a redemption of the fractional shares. If the redemption distribution has dividend equivalence, then taxation under §301 may result. What may be the practical tax difference to the shareholder? In a would-be "B" reorganization, the separate bargain for the cash will destroy the reorganization because of the "solely for voting stock" requirement. When might it have that effect in a would-be "C" reorganization?

2. Rev. Rul. 66-365 refers to cash that is not separately bargained for *and* not in excess of the amount representing the value of the fractional share interest. Can you conceive of a case in which cash representing only and precisely the value of the fractional shares is paid, but where it is held nevertheless that there had been a "separate bargain" that destroys an otherwise qualifying "B" reorganization?

3. The tax treatment prescribed by Rev. Rul. 66-365 for cash paid in lieu of fractional shares was extended to "E" and "F" reorganizations in Rev. Rul. 69-34, 1969-1 C.B. 105, and Rev. Rul. 74-36, 1974-1 C.B. 85. In Rev. Rul. 81-81, 1981-1 C.B. 122, the Service amplified Rev. Rul. 66-365 to cover fractional shares of §306 stock received by minority shareholders in a recapitalization. See also Rev. Proc. 77-41, 1977-2 C.B. 574, stating the conditions under which a ruling will be issued that cash paid for fractional shares will be treated as payment in exchange for stock.

REVENUE RULING 85-138
1985-2 C.B. 122

ISSUE

Whether the acquisition of substantially all the properties of X by S1 under the facts described below meets the requirements of a reorganization pursuant to section 368(a)(1)(C) of the Internal Revenue Code.

FACTS

Corporation P owned all the stock of corporation S1 and corporation S2. It was P's desire that S1 acquire substantially all the properties of X, a corporation unrelated by stock ownership to P, S1 or S2. In order to eliminate any possible adverse minority interest in X, and pursuant to a plan adopted by P, P caused S2 to purchase with S2's own cash some of the shares of outstanding voting stock of X. S2, along with the other shareholders of X, then approved an agreement between P and X under which X transferred substantially all its properties to S1 in exchange for voting stock of P and the assumption by S1 of all of X's liabilities. The liabilities assumed by S1 were in excess of twenty percent of the fair market value of X's assets. Subsequent to this exchange, X was dissolved and the P stock was distributed to the shareholders of X (including S2) in exchange for the surrender and cancellation of all the S stock.

Law and Analysis

Section 368(a)(1)(C) of the Code provides that the term "reorganization" means the acquisition by one corporation, in exchange solely for all or a part of its voting stock (or in exchange solely for all or part of the voting stock of a corporation which is in control of the acquiring corporation), of substantially all the properties of another corporation, but in determining whether the exchange is solely for stock, the assumption by the acquiring corporation of a liability of the other, or the fact that property acquired is subject to a liability, shall be disregarded.

Section 368(a)(2)(B) of the Code provides that if (i) one corporation acquires substantially all of the properties of another corporation, (ii) the acquisition would qualify under section 368(a)(1)(C) but for the fact that the acquiring corporation exchanges money or other property in addition to voting stock, and (iii) the acquiring corporation acquires, solely for voting stock described in section 368(a)(1)(C), property of the other corporation having a fair market value which is at least 80 percent of the fair market value of all of the property of the other corporation, then such acquisition will (subject to section 368(a)(1)(A)) be treated as qualifying under section 368(a)(1)(C). Solely for the purpose of determining whether clause (iii) of the preceding sentence applies, the amount of any liability assumed by the acquiring corporation, and the amount of any liability to which any property is subject, will be treated as money paid for the property. Thus, if nonqualifying consideration such as cash is furnished by the acquiring corporation, liabilities of the acquired corporation assumed by the acquiring corporation are added to cash paid in order to determine whether 80 percent of the fair market value of the assets of the acquired corporation are exchanged solely for voting stock. In the instant case, S1's assumption of X liabilities in excess of 20 percent of the fair market value of X assets effectively precludes the application of the boot relaxation rule of section 368(a)(2)(B) of the Code. As a result, if S1 is deemed to have exchanged partly P voting stock and partly cash for substantially all the assets of X, the transaction will not qualify as a reorganization under section 368(a)(1)(C) of the Code.

In Rev. Rul. 69-48, 1969-1 C.B. 106, corporation P purchased for cash nineteen percent of the stock of corporation X and acquired an option to purchase an additional thirty percent as part of a plan for P's wholly owned subsidiary, S, to acquire the assets of X.

Under the option agreement, P was able to vote the optioned stock as well as the stock it had purchased outright. Twenty-two months later, P voted for the transfer of X's assets to S in exchange for P voting stock and the assumption by S of X's liabilities. After the transfer of its assets, X was liquidated. Rev. Rul. 69-48 concludes that P's cash purchase of X stock violated the "solely for voting stock" requirement of section 368(a)(1)(C) because it was an integral step in the plan to require substantially all of X's assets.

In the present case, S2's prearranged cash purchase of X shares was an integral step in the plan for S1 to acquire substantially all the assets of X. Therefore, as in Rev. Rul. 69-48, the consideration for the acquisition of X's properties by S1 is deemed to consist of cash in addition to the voting stock of P and the assumption of liabilities by S1 permitted under section 368(a)(1)(C) of the Code.

Holding

The transaction does not qualify as a reorganization defined in section 368(a)(1)(C) of the Code. Compare Rev. Rul. 85-139 wherein the same conclusion is reached in a purported reorganization under section 368(a)(1)(B).

REVENUE RULING 85-139
1985-2 C.B. 123

Issue

Whether the transaction described below qualifies as a reorganization under section 368(a)(1)(B) of the Internal Revenue Code.

Facts

P corporation owned all the stock of S corporation. P desired to obtain control of X corporation by acquiring all the shares of the one outstanding class of stock of X solely in exchange for P voting stock. Certain shareholders of X, owning ten percent of its stock, insisted, however, on receiving cash for their stock. Since P wanted to eliminate any possible adverse minority interest in X, and pursuant to one overall plan to acquire the stock of X, P acquired ninety percent of the stock of X solely in exchange for P voting stock, and P caused S to purchase for cash the remaining ten percent of the X stock. The cash paid by S for X's stock was not obtained directly or indirectly from P. S retained ownership of the X stock it had purchased.

LAW AND ANALYSIS

Section 368(a)(1)(B) of the Code provides that the term "reorganization" means the acquisition by one corporation, in exchange solely for all or a part of its voting stock (or in exchange solely for all or a part of the voting stock of a corporation which is in control of the acquiring corporation), of stock of another corporation, if, immediately after the acquisition, the acquiring corporation has control of such other corporation (whether or not such acquiring corporation had control immediately before the acquisition).

Section 1.368-2(c) of the Income Tax Regulations illustrates the application of the "solely for voting stock" requirement under section 368(a)(1)(B) as follows:

If, for example, corporation X in one transaction exchanges nonvoting preferred stock or bonds in addition to all or a part of its voting stock in the acquisition of stock of corporation Y, the transaction is not a reorganization under section 368(a)(1)(B).

The "solely for voting stock" requirement applies to the entire transaction in which stock of a corporation is acquired, not just to the acquisition of a block of stock constituting control. Therefore, the acquisition by a corporation of eighty percent of the stock of a corporation in exchange for its voting stock and the remaining twenty percent in exchange for cash violates "solely for voting stock." Rev. Rul. 75-123, 1975-1 C.B. 115; Chapman v. Commissioner, 618 F.2d 856 (1st Cir. 1980); *cert. dism.* 451 U.S. 1012 (1981). . . .

Accordingly, if P had acquired all the stock of X in exchange for its voting stock and cash, the acquisition would not have qualified as a reorganization under section 368(a)(1)(B). P's structuring of the transaction to have its wholly owned subsidiary acquire some of the X stock for cash does not produce a different result. Compare Rev. Rul. 69-48, 1969-1 C.B. 106, which holds that the purchase for cash by P of stock of corporation X as part of a plan for P's wholly-owned subsidiary, S, to acquire substantially all the assets of X for P voting stock, violates the "solely for voting stock" requirement of section 368(a)(1)(C).

HOLDING

The purchase by S of ten percent of X's stock for cash violates the "solely for voting stock" requirement of section 368(a)(1)(B) of the Code. Compare Rev. Rul. 85-138, wherein it was held that a similar transaction does not qualify as a reorganization under section 368(a)(1)(C).

REVENUE PROCEDURE 77-37
1977-2 C.B. 568

In reorganizations under sections 368(a)(1)(A), 368(a)(1)(B) and 368(a)(1)(C) . . . where the requisite stock or property has been acquired, it is not necessary that all of the stock of the acquiring corporation or a corporation in "control" thereof, which is to be issued in exchange therefor, be issued immediately provided (1) that all of the stock will be issued within five years from the date of the transfer of assets 368(a)(1)(C), . . . or within five years from the date of the initial distribution in the case of reorganization under section 368(a)(1)(B) . . . [;] (2) there is a valid business reason for not issuing all of the stock immediately, such as the difficulty in determining the value of one or both of the corporations involved in the reorganization; (3) the maximum number of shares which may be issued in the exchange is stated; (4) at least 50 percent of the maximum number of shares of each class of stock which may be issued is issued in the initial distribution; (5) the agreement evidencing the right to receive stock in the future prohibits assignment (except by operation of law) or, in the alternative, if the agreement does not prohibit assignments, the right must not be evidenced by negotiable certificates of any kind and must not be readily marketable; and (6) such right can give rise to the receipt of only additional stock of the acquiring corporation or a corporation in "control" thereof, as the case may be. Stock issued as compensation royalties or any other consideration other than in exchange for stock or assets will not be considered to have been received in exchange. Until the final distribution of the total number of shares of stock to be issued in the exchange is made, the interim basis of the stock of the acquiring corporation received in the exchange by the shareholders of the acquired corporation (not including that portion of each share representing interest) will be determined, pursuant to section 358(a), as though the maximum number of shares to be issued (not including that portion of each share representing interest) had been received by the shareholders.

NOTE

In Rev. Proc. 84-42, 1984-1 C.B. 521, the IRS indicated that the guidelines set forth in Rev. Proc. 77-37 with respect to the issuance of rulings in contingent stock transactions (relating to A, B, and C reorganizations) would be extended to D and E reorganizations and to §351 transactions. It also added the following additional conditions to those set forth in Rev. Proc. 77-37:

> (7) such stock issuance will not be triggered by an event the occurrence or nonoccurrence of which is within the control of shareholders; (8) such stock issuance will not be triggered by the payment of additional tax or reduction in tax paid as a result of a Service audit of the shareholders of the corporation either (a) with respect to the reorganization or section 351 transaction in which the contingent stock will be issued, or (b) when the reorganization or section 351 transaction in which the contingent stock will be issued involves persons related within the meaning of section 267(c)(4) . . . ; and (9) the mechanism for the calculation of the additional stock to be issued is objective and readily ascertainable.

REVENUE RULING 67-90
1967-1 C.B. 79

Advice has been requested whether the transaction described below satisfies the "solely for voting stock" requirement of section 368(a)(1)(B) of the Internal Revenue Code of 1954.

Corporation X and corporation Y are both publicly held corporations. The stock of each corporation is listed and actively traded on a national stock exchange. Pursuant to a plan of reorganization X will acquire all of the Y stock from the Y shareholders. On the date the plan of reorganization was adopted by X and the Y shareholders the X stock closed at $45 per share and the Y stock closed at $52 per share. After substantial arms-length negotiations the agreed plan of reorganization provides that all of the Y shareholders will exchange all of their 50,000 shares of Y voting stock for 50,000 shares of X voting stock and a contingent contractual right to receive additional X voting stock.

The contingent right to receive additional X voting stock is evidenced only by the plan of reorganization agreed to by the parties, is not evidenced by a negotiable certificate of any kind, is not readily marketable, and can give rise to the receipt of only additional X stock. All additional X stock will be issued 4 years from the date of the initial distribution. All of the stock cannot be issued immediately because the parties are unable to agree on the value of the X stock for purposes of the exchange, notwithstanding that it is listed and traded on a national stock exchange. The maximum number of additional X shares that may be issued to the Y shareholders is 50,000.

The plan of reorganization provides that the Y shareholders will receive the additional X shares only if on the fourth anniversary of the initial distribution the closing market price of the X stock is less than $50 per share. If the market price is below $50 per share, X will issue sufficient additional shares (but in no event more than 50,000) so that the total market value of the shares of both the initial and fourth anniversary distributions computed on the basis of the fourth anniversary closing price will equal $2,500,000. Subject to the 50,000 additional share limitation, this formula guarantees the exchanging Y shareholders a $50 per share value for the X stock they receive pursuant to the plan of reorganization.

Section 368(a)(1)(B) of the Code provides that the term "reorganization" includes the acquisition by one corporation, exchange solely for all or a part of its voting stock, of stock of another corporation, if, immediately after the acquisition, the acquiring corporation has control of such other corporation (whether or not such acquiring corporation has control immediately before the acquisition).

Revenue Ruling 66-112, C.B. 1966-1, 68, holds that the "solely for voting stock" requirement of section 368(a)(1)(B) of the Code is satisfied where the number of additional shares to be issued under the provisions of a nonassignable contractual right is determined by a formula contingent upon the future earnings of the acquired corporation. In this case the number of additional shares is contingent upon the future market price of the acquiring corporation's stock. Where the parties are unable to agree on the value of the stock of the acquiring corporation for purposes of the exchange, notwithstanding that the stock is traded on a national stock exchange, a valid business reason exists for issuing less than all of the stock immediately.

Accordingly, in the present case where the parties cannot agree on the value of the X stock, the proposed plan of reorganization satisfies the "solely for voting stock" requirement of section 368(a)(1)(B) of the Code.

The facts of every delayed stock issuance case arising under section 368 of the Code will be carefully examined to insure that bona fide business reasons justify issuing less than all of the stock immediately, and will also be examined to insure that the stock issued is issued solely in exchange for stock or assets, as the case may be, and is in fact not being issued in lieu of other consideration, such as compensation or royalties.

For the effect section 483 of the Code, dealing with interest on certain deferred payments, has on delayed issuance of stock exchanges see sections 1.483-1(b)(6), Example 7; 1.483-1(e)(3), Example 2; and 1.483-2(a)(2) of the Income Tax Regulations. . . .

NOTES

1. In William H. Bateman, 40 T.C. 408 (1963), Corporation A and Corporation B merged. Corporation A survived and changed its name to C. Each shareholder of B was entitled to two and one-fourth shares of C common and one stock purchase warrant for each share of B surrendered. Each warrant entitled the holder to purchase one share of C within 10 years for a stated price. Are the warrants "stock"? Are they "securities"? Does it matter whether they are securities? Cf. §354(a)(2)(B).

Does the exchange have the effect of a distribution of a dividend? What adjustment would be made to earnings and profits? To the shareholders' basis in their stock? If the exchange does not have the effect of a distribution of a dividend at the time, what result when exercised? If the warrants are sold in the meantime to a third party? How should the distribution of warrants be treated?

2. What is the relevance of each of the criteria set forth in Rev. Proc. 77-37 to the statutory "voting stock" requirement? Is the Commissioner's position in Rev. Rul. 67-90 correct? See Murphy, Contingent Share Reorganizations, 1969 S. Calif. Tax Inst. 255; Tillinghast, Contingent Stock Pay-Outs in Tax-Free Reorganizations, 22 Tax Law. 467 (1969).

What is the point of the "voting stock" requirement of the "B" and "C" reorganizations? Should "voting stock" be required in an "A" reorganization as well?

3. If a reorganization involving contingent or escrowed stock satisfies whatever conditions are imposed for meeting the "solely for voting stock" requirement on the date of the exchange, should the qualification be vulnerable to attack on the basis of future events? See Rev. Rul. 76-334, 1976-2 C.B. 108 (following "C" reorganization, cash payment by acquiring corporation to shareholders of acquired corporation in settlement of dispute over entitlement to escrowed shares, was "a transaction separate from the reorganization" and treated as a redemption); Rev. Rul. 75-456, 1975-2 C.B. 128 (following "B" reorganization, acquiring corporation underwent "F" reorganization and successor assumed contingent obligation to issue stock; successor's voting stock would be effectively the same as voting stock of the acquiring corporation); Rev. Rul. 78-376, 1978-2 C.B. 149 (return of escrowed shares to satisfy contingent liability with number of shares returned computed on the basis of current fair market value, was a taxable disposition); but cf. Rev. Rul. 76-42, 1976-1 C.B. 102 (return of escrowed stock under agreement is part of the reorganization transaction and does not give rise to gain or loss); Rev. Rul. 75-94, 1975-1 C.B. 111 (similarly, as to additional voting stock issued after discovery that acquiring corporation's stock was over-valued in reorganization agreement).

4. The regulations requiring §483 "unstated interest" to be imputed on the delayed issuance of stock have been upheld. See, e.g., Vorbleski v. Commissioner, 589 F.2d 123 (3d Cir. 1978); Katkin v. Commissioner, 570 F.2d 139 (6th Cir. 1978); Solomon v. Commissioner, 570 F.2d 28 (2d Cir. 1977).

The original issue discount provisions added in 1984 (§§1271-1275) cover a number of transactions that previously were within the purview of §483. How should they apply to delayed stock issuances?

5. In Rev. Rul. 67-275, 1967-2 C.B. 142, the Commissioner ruled that the costs paid by an acquiring corporation in an "A" reorganization to register with the SEC the stock it was to issue to the acquired corporation's shareholders do not constitute "boot" to the shareholders, since "the costs of registering its own stock are properly attributable to the acquiring corporation. . . ." What arguments might be made for and against that result? What would the result be if the acquiring corporation had paid the legal fees of the lawyers who advised the acquired corporation and its shareholders? Would it matter whether the lawyers' advice related to the reorganization or to legal affairs of the acquired corporation and its shareholders antedating the plan of reorganization?

In Rev. Rul. 73-54, 1973-1 C.B. 187, the Commissioner ruled that payment by the acquiring corporation of all expenses incurred by the acquired corporation or its shareholders "solely and directly related to the reorganization" did not violate the solely for voting stock requirement of a "B" or "C" reorganization. However, a transfer of property other than voting stock directly to the acquired corporation or its shareholders for the payment of such expenses would violate that requirement.

In a "C" reorganization, the "solely for voting stock" requirement is not violated if the acquiring corporation merely assumes the acquired corporation's liability to pay reorganization expenses. See Rev. Rul. 76-365, 1976-2 C.B. 110. What would be the tax consequences if the acquired corporation agreed to pay the reorganization expenses of its shareholder, and the acquiring corporation assumed that liability? Cf. Rev. Rul. 75-421, 1975-2 C.B. 108.

BAUSCH & LOMB OPTICAL CO. v.
COMMISSIONER
267 F.2d 75 (2d Cir. 1959), *cert. denied,* 361 U.S. 835 (1959)

Before Medina and Hincks, Circuit Judges, and Mathes, District Judge.

MEDINA, Circuit Judge. Petitioner Bausch & Lomb Optical Company, a New York corporation engaged in the manufacture and sale of ophthalmic products, on March 1, 1950 owned 9923¼ shares of the stock of its subsidiary Riggs Optical Company, or 79.9488% of the 12,412 outstanding shares of Riggs. In order to effectuate certain operating economies, Bausch & Lomb decided to amalgamate Riggs with itself. To this end on April 22, 1950 Bausch & Lomb exchanged 105,508 shares of its unissued voting stock for all of the Riggs assets. An additional 433 shares of Bausch & Lomb stock went to 12 Riggs' employees.

On May 2, 1950, according to a prearranged plan, Riggs dissolved itself, distributing its only asset, Bausch & Lomb stock, pro rata to its shareholders. Bausch & Lomb thus received back 84,347 of its own shares which became treasury stock, while 21,161 shares went to the Riggs minority shareholders.

The Commissioner determined that the substance of these transactions was that Baush & Lomb received the Riggs assets partly in exchange for its Riggs stock and partly for its own stock, and that the gain which Bausch & Lomb realized upon the Riggs "liquidation" was subject to tax. In other words, that Bausch & Lomb parted with 21,161 shares of its own voting stock, plus 9923¼ shares of its Riggs stock, for the transfer to it of all of the Riggs assets. Bausch & Lomb contends, however, that a "reorganization" was effected under Section 112(g)(1)(C) of the 1939 Internal Revenue Code,[1] and that it is therefore entitled to tax-free treatment.[2] The Tax Court sustained the Commissioner's position and held that the acquisition of the Riggs assets and the dissolution of Riggs must be viewed together, and that the surrender by Bausch & Lomb of its Riggs stock was additional consideration. The Tax Court accordingly held that the Riggs assets were not obtained "solely for all or a part of its voting stock." We agree.

Bausch & Lomb concedes that to qualify as a "C" reorganization, it could not furnish any additional consideration over and above its own stock. Helvering v. Southwest Consolidated Corp., 1942, 315 U.S. 194. . . . Moreover, Bausch & Lomb admits, as the correspondence and minutes of pertinent meetings plainly show, that the acquisition of the Riggs assets and the dissolution of Riggs were both part of the same plan. Nevertheless, Bausch & Lomb asserts that the

---

1. Section 112(g)(1)(C) provides: "(1) The term 'reorganization' means . . .

"(C) the acquisition by one corporation, in exchange solely for all or a part of its voting stock, of substantially all the properties of another corporation, but in determining whether the exchange is solely for voting stock the assumption by the acquiring corporation of a liability of the other, or the fact that property acquired is subject to a liability, shall be disregarded, . . ."

2. Section 112(b)(3) provides: "(b) *Exchanges solely in kind.* . . .

(3) *Stock for stock on reorganization.* No gain or loss shall be recognized if stock or securities in a corporation a party to a reorganization are, in pursuance of the plan of reorganization, exchanged solely for stock or securities in such corporation or in another corporation a party to the reorganization."

exchange of the Riggs assets for its stock should be treated as separate and distinct from the dissolution. The argument runs to the effect that, if the two steps are viewed apart from one another, a "C" reorganization is effected.

Petitioner contends that, even if a qualification according to the literal terms of Section 112(g)(1)(C) is not found, the amalgamation was in substance a "reorganization" because it has the attributes of one, including "continuity of interest" and business purpose. This is factually not quite true for, while the amalgamation may have been for genuine business reasons, the division into two steps served only to facilitate the liquidation of Riggs. It was considered easier to distribute Bausch & Lomb stock than distribute the Riggs assets. Hence the "business purpose" of dividing the liquidation into two steps lends no support to Bausch & Lomb's contention that in substance and actuality a reorganization was achieved. Moreover, the Congress has defined in Section 112(g)(1)(C) how a reorganization thereunder may be effected, and the only question for us to decide, on this phase of the case, is whether the necessary requirements have been truly fulfilled. It is for the Congress and not for us to say whether some other alleged equivalent set of facts should receive the same tax free status.

Nor does the fact that Bausch & Lomb may well have desired to hold the 84,347 shares of its own voting shares as treasury stock change our opinion of the transaction as a whole.

Bausch & Lomb suggests that under our present holding even if it had but a 1% interest in Riggs, the requirement that the acquisition be "solely for . . . its voting stock" could defeat Section 112(g)(1)(C) reorganization treatment. This hypothesis is a far cry from the facts disclosed in this record, and the lack of controlling interest surrounds it with a mist of unreality. In any event, it will be time to consider such a situation in all its aspects when, as and if it comes before us. We merely hold that the attempt to thwart taxation in this case by carrying out the liquidation process in two steps instead of one fell short of meeting the requirements of a "C" reorganization. See Gregory v. Helvering, 1935 . . . [page 545 supra]; Helvering v. Alabama Asphaltic Limestone Co., 1942, 315 U.S. 179 . . . ; Helvering v. Bashford, 1938, 302 U.S. 454 . . . ; Minnesota Tea Co. v. Helvering, 1938, 302 U.S. 609. . . .

Of course, the fact that Bausch & Lomb "could have" merged with Riggs and hence qualified the transaction as a reorganization under [section 112(g)(1)(A)] is beside the point. For reasons of its own it chose not to do so. This is clearly not an "A" reorganization.

Bausch & Lomb also claims that a tax-free liquidation was effected under Section [332] although it plainly lacked the necessary 80% of the voting stock. This belabored effort to claim ownership of the 51 shares of Riggs voting stock for which 12 of Riggs' employees had received credit on Riggs' books, so as to raise Bausch & Lomb's interest slightly above the 80% required by Section [332] has nothing whatever to commend it. As found by the Tax Court, Bausch & Lomb never was the legal or equitable owner of these shares, there was never any agreement on the part of the employees to assign them to Bausch & Lomb, and the original stock-for-stock purchase agreements of the Riggs employees provided that if Riggs should be reorganized and its business acquired by another corporation, a successor corporation would have the right to assume the contract and substitute its stock in the place of the Riggs stock originally reserved under the stock purchase agreements. New arrangements were made later, in line with the provision of the original stock purchase agreements just referred to, and the employees received certain cash payments and the 433 shares of Bausch & Lomb stock mentioned in the opening part of this opinion. We find in the facts of this case no foundation whatever for the claim that a liquidation was effected under Section [332].

Affirmed.

NOTES

1. Was there a way by which Bausch & Lomb might have proceeded (without recognition) to get a substituted basis? If so, what was it and why was it not used? See generally Trimble, Creeping Control: An Analysis of Tax Problems of the Multi-stage Acquisition, 28 J. Taxn. 135 (1968). Compare Rev. Rul. 68-526, 1968-2 C.B. 156, and Rev. Rul. 69-585, 1969-2 C.B. 56.

2. In Rev. Rul. 85-107, 1985-2 C.B. 121, the Service ruled that the *Bausch & Lomb* doctrine notwithstanding, an acquiring corporation's preexisting stock ownership in an acquired corporation would not prevent the transaction from qualifying as a "D" reorganization if it otherwise met the requirements of §368(a)(1)(D).

3. In American Potash & Chemical Corp. v. United States, 399 F.2d 194 (Ct. Cl. 1968), P Corporation had acquired all of the outstanding stock of W Corporation in exchange solely for its voting stock. As part of the same plan, W Corporation was completely liquidated and its assets distributed to P. The Court of Claims held that the stock for stock exchange did not qualify as a "B" reorganization solely because P obtained voting control of Y in two separate transactions over a period of 14 months, two months longer than the 12-month period suggested in Reg. §1.368-2(c). The court further held that a nonqualifying "B" reorganization followed by a liquidation of the acquired corporation could not be integrated under the step transaction doctrine and treated as an exchange of stock for assets

pursuant to a valid "C" reorganization. In so holding, the court distinguished Rev. Rul. 67-274, 1967-2 C.B. 141, which states that a valid "B" reorganization followed promptly by liquidation of the acquired company will be treated as a "C" rather than a "B" reorganization. On the defendant's motion for reconsideration, the court ordered the case to trial on the question of whether there had been a valid "B" reorganization, as well as on issues involving the *Kimbell-Diamond* doctrine and §334(b)(2). See Note 2, page 51 supra. See Rev. Rul. 76-123, page 563 supra. But cf. Rev. Rul. 75-521, 1975-2 C.B. 120 (§332 governed transaction in which corporate 50 percent shareholder bought out other shareholders for cash, then liquidated subsidiary); Rev. Rul. 74-35, 1974-1 C.B. 85 (declining to extend the *Kimbell-Diamond* principle to a series of transactions in which an exchange of stock intended to qualify as a "B" reorganization was followed by the distribution of only a portion of the acquired corporation's assets).

4. Control

a. Acquiring Control

The Service construes the §368(c) control requirement as ownership of at least 80 percent of the voting power of a corporation and at least 80 percent of the stock of *each* nonvoting class. See Rev. Rul. 59-259, 1959-2 C.B. 115, page 359 supra.

b. Yielding Control

Reread Granite Trust Co. v. United States, page 548 supra.

Can the shareholders of Corporation X ensure recognition of some of their stock investment loss by transferring in the aggregate only 79.9 percent of the outstanding stock in X (which has only common outstanding) to Corporation Y in exchange for 50 percent of Corporation Y's voting stock? Will this not constitute a "B" reorganization, and will §354(a)(1) not apply? Is the result a wise one? If not, what would you propose?

5. "Substantially All of the Properties" — §368(a)(1)(C)

In Rev. Proc. 77-37, 1977-2 C.B. 568, the Internal Revenue Service restated the "operating rule" that will guide it in issuing rulings where the "substantially all" requirement of §§354(b)(1)(A),

368(a)(1)(C), and 368(a)(2)(B) is involved. Acknowledging that its operating rule does not, as a matter of law, define the lower limits, the Service held the requirement "is satisfied if there is a transfer of assets representing at least 90 percent of the fair market value of the net assets and 70 percent of the fair market value of the gross assets held by the [transferor] corporation immediately prior to the transfer."

In some cases a transfer of a corporation's *operating* assets may be treated as substantially all the properties of the transferor for the purpose of §354(b)(1)(A) even though the transferred assets constitute only a small part of the corporation's total assets. See American Mfg Co., 55 T.C. 204 (1970) (a transfer of 20 percent of the total assets, constituting all of the operating assets, was held to be substantially all of the assets); Smothers v. United States, page 751 infra (15 percent of the total assets, constituting all of the operating assets, were held to be substantially all of the assets).

In Rev. Rul. 88-48, 1988-1 C.B. 531, a corporation sold one of its two historic lines of business to an unrelated party immediately before a "C" reorganization. Although that line of business had accounted for 50 percent of the transferor corporation's historic assets, the pre-reorganization tailoring did not lead the Service to rule that the "substantially all" requirement of §368(a)(1)(C) was not satisfied.

6. *Assumption of Liabilities — §357*

UNITED STATES v. HENDLER
303 U.S. 564 (1938)

Mr. Justice BLACK delivered the opinion of the Court. The Revenue Act of 1928 [§13] imposed a tax upon the annual "net income" of corporations. It defined "net income" as "gross income . . . less the deductions allowed . . . ," and "gross income" as including "gains, profits and income derived from . . . trades . . . or sales, or dealings in property, . . . or gains or profits and income . . . from any source whatever." [§§21-22.]

Section 112 of the Act exempts certain gains which are realized from a "reorganization" similar to, or in the nature of, a corporate merger or consolidation. Under this section, such gains are not taxed if one corporation, pursuant to a "plan of reorganization" exchanges its property "solely for *stock* or *securities*, in another corporation a party to the reorganization." But, when a corporation not only receives "stock or securities" in exchange for its property, but also receives "other property or money" in carrying out a "plan of reorganization,"

(1) If the corporation receiving such other property or money distributes it in pursuance of the plan of reorganization, no gain to the corporation shall be recognized from the exchange, but

(2) If the corporation receiving such other property or money does not distribute it in pursuance of the plan of reorganization, the gain, if any, to the corporation shall be recognized [taxed] . . .

In this case, there was a merger or "reorganization" of the Borden Company and the Hendler Creamery Company, Inc., resulting in gains of more than six million dollars to the Hendler Company, Inc., a corporation of which respondent is transferee. The Court of Appeals, believing there was an exemption under §112, affirmed the judgment of the District Court holding all Hendler gains non-taxable.

This controversy between the government and respondent involves the assumption and payment—pursuant to the plan of reorganization—by the Borden Company of $534,297.40 bonded indebtedness of the Hendler Creamery Co., Inc. We are unable to agree with the conclusion reached by the courts below that the gain to the Hendler Company, realized by the Borden Company's payment, was exempt from taxation under §112.

It was contended below and it is urged here that since the Hendler Company did not actually receive the money with which the Borden Company discharged the former's indebtedness, the Hendler Company's gain of $534,297.40 is not taxable. The transaction, however, under which the Borden Company assumed and paid the debt and obligation of the Hendler Company is to be regarded in substance as though the $534,297.40 had been paid directly to the Hendler Company. The Hendler Company was the beneficiary of the discharge of its indebtedness. Its gain was as real and substantial as if the money had been paid it and then paid over by it to its creditors. The discharge of liability by the payment of the Hendler Company's indebtedness constituted income to the Hendler Company and is to be treated as such.

Section 112 provides no exemption for gains—resulting from corporate "reorganization"—neither received as "stock or securities," nor received as "money or other property" and distributed to stockholders under the plan of reorganization. In Minnesota Tea Co. v. Helvering, 302 U.S. 609, it was said that this exemption "contemplates a distribution to stockholders, and not payment to creditors."* The very statute upon which the taxpayer relies provides that "If the corporation receiving such other property or money does not distribute in pursuance of the plan of reorganization, the gain, if any, to the corporation shall be recognized [taxed]. . . ."

---

*This is not the opinion in *Minnesota Tea*, page 585 supra, but it grows out of the same transaction.

Since this gain or income of $534,297.40 of the Hendler Company was neither received as "stock or securities" nor distributed to its stockholders "in pursuance of the plan of reorganization" it was not exempt and is taxable gain as defined in the 1928 Act. This $534,297.40 gain to the taxpayer does not fall within the exemptions of §112, and the judgment of the court below is reversed. . . .

NOTES

1. How would you have argued for a contrary result in *Hendler*? If Congress had permitted the *Hendler* decision to stand, what impact would the decision have had on corporate reorganizations? To what extent does §357 overrule *Hendler*? What is the reason for §357(c)?

2. Section 357(c)(1), taxing transferors on their gains to the extent that the liabilities transferred exceed the basis of the accompanying assets, does not apply to corporate transferors of assets in reorganization except in the case of a §368(a)(1)(D) reorganization (§357(c)(1)(B)). The Service has ruled that if a transaction is both a "D" reorganization and an "A" reorganization (Rev. Rul. 75-161, 1975-1 C.B. 114) or a "C" reorganization (and also a §351 exchange) (Rev. Rul. 76-188, 1976-1 C.B. 99), it is to be treated as a "D" and gain recognized. But if the transaction is both a "D" and an "F" reorganization, the latter dominates and no gain is recognized (Rev. Rul. 79-289, 1979-2 C.B. 145). Why does §357(c)(1)(B) mark the "D" reorganization for special treatment? Should it? Are the Commissioner's positions right when the "D" overlaps with the "A," "C," and "F"?

See New York State Bar Association Tax Section, Committee on Reorganizations, Report on the Ancillary Tax Effects of Different Forms of Reorganizations, 34 Tax L. Rev. 475 (1979); Steiner, Liabilities in Excess of Basis in Corporate Reorganizations — When Should Gain Be Recognized?, 6 J. Corp. Taxn. 39 (1979).

See Rev. Rul. 68-637, 1968-2 C.B. 158, in which the assumption of stock options and warrants was held to be "liabilities" and not "boot" under §368(a)(1)(C).

3.(a) Corporation X is in control of Corporation Y. Y acquires all of the assets of Corporation Z in exchange for voting stock of X and the assumption by X of some of the liabilities of Z. What are the tax consequences of the transaction to Y? To Z? *Compare* Rev. Rul. 70-107, 1970-1 C.B. 78, *with* Rev. Rul. 70-224, 1970-1 C.B. 79.

(b) See Rev. Rul. 78-330, 1978-2 C.B. 147, in which the parent corporation's forgiveness of debt due from subsidiary, to avoid application of §357(c) to subsequent "D" reorganization, was given effect as a contribution to capital.

(c) Section 357(c)(3), discussed at page 399 et seq. supra, applies only to §351 exchanges. What implications does this raise in the reorganization area? Cf. Rev. Rul. 78-442, 1978-2 C.B. 143.

(d) What is the effect if, in a "C" reorganization, the transferor corporation is liquidated and its liabilities are assumed by its shareholders? Cf. Rev. Rul. 75-450, 1975-2 C.B. 166.

(e) For the impact of §357(c) in a "D" reorganization and the active trade or business requirement of §355(b)(2)(C), see Rev. Rul. 78-442, 1978-2 C.B. 143, page 705 infra.

7. Effect of "Boot"

a. On Corporations

1. If a transferor corporation in an "A," "C," or "D" reorganization receives "boot" (anything in addition to stock or securities in another corporation that is a party to the reorganization), §361(b)(1)(A) provides that no gain will be recognized to the transferor if it distributes the "boot" "in pursuance of the plan of reorganization." Why does it so provide? If the transferor retains the "boot," gain to the extent of the retained "boot" will be recognized. Section 361(b)(1)(B). In what types of reorganizations might such "boot" retention occur? Despite retention of "boot," no loss is recognized. Section 361(b)(2).

Section 354(a)(2) and (3) treats "securities" as "boot" in designated circumstances. Section 361 does not so provide. Should it? What about §351?

2. Section 361 does not prevent taxation of the transferor corporation's gain if instead of distributing all transferee's stock to its shareholders or creditors, it sells some of it and distributes the sale proceeds along with the balance of transferee's stock. It is a very unfortunate if not mindless result, exalting the form, and paying no attention to the fact that transferee corporation does not get a step-up in asset basis despite the gain recognition. Thus §361, esp. §361 (c)(3), codifies General Housewares Corp. v. United States, 615 F.2d 1056 (5th Cir. 1980), in providing nonrecognition in the case of an in-kind distribution, but also leaves intact the decision in FEC Liquidating Corp. v. United States, 548 F.2d 924 (Ct. Cl. 1977), which taxed the transferor on its sale for cash of some of transferee's stock.

3. If a corporation receives a "boot" distribution that is taxable to it as a dividend under §356(a)(2), is it entitled to the dividends-received deduction under §243? See Tribune Publishing Co. v. United States, 836 F.2d 1176 (9th Cir. 1988).

4. See Rev. Rul. 72-327, 1972-2 C.B. 197, in which the corporate

shareholder of an acquired corporation in a statutory merger received a distribution consisting of stock of the acquiring corporation and appreciated property. Its realized gain was recognized to the extent of the fair market value of the appreciated property; it received a dividend to the extent of its ratable share of the acquired corporation's earnings and profits; and it was allowed a dividends received deduction. See also Carlson, Boot at the Corporate Level in Tax-Free Reorganizations, 27 Tax L. Rev. 499 (1972).

b. On Shareholders

COMMISSIONER v. ESTATE OF BEDFORD
325 U.S. 283 (1945)

Mr. Justice FRANKFURTER delivered the opinion of the Court. . . . The estate of Edward T. Bedford, who died May 21, 1931, included 3,000 shares of cumulative preferred stock (par value $100) of Abercrombie & Fitch Company. Pursuant to a plan of recapitalization respondent, as executor of the estate, in 1937 exchanged those shares for 3,500 shares of cumulative preferred stock (par value $75), 1,500 shares of common stock (par value $1), and $45,240 in cash (on the basis of $15.08 for each of the old preferred shares). The recapitalization had been proposed because the company, after charging against its surplus account stock dividends totaling $844,100, distributed in 1920, 1928, and 1930, had incurred a book deficit in that account of $399,771.87. Because of this deficit, the company, under applicable State law, was unable to pay dividends although for the fiscal year ending January 31, 1937 it had net earnings of $309,073.70.

By comparing the fair market value of the old preferred shares at the date of Bedford's death with the market value of the new stock and cash received the gain to his estate was $139,740. Admittedly the recapitalization was a reorganization, §[368(a)(1)(E)], so that only the cash received, but none of the stock is taxable. Sections [354(a)(1), 356(a)]. The sole issue is whether the cash, $45,240, is taxable as a dividend, or merely as a capital gain. . . . The Tax Court sustained the determination of the Commissioner that the cash was taxable as a dividend, . . . but was reversed by the Circuit Court of Appeals. . . . On a showing of importance to the administration of the Revenue Acts, we granted certiorari. . . .

The precise question is whether the distribution of cash in this recapitalization "has the effect of the distribution of a taxable dividend" under §[356(a)(2)] and as such is fully taxable, or is taxable only . . . as a capital gain under §[356(a)(1)].

The history of this legislation is not illuminating. Section [356(a)(2)] originated in §203(d)(2) of the Revenue Act of 1924. . . . But the reports of the Congressional Committees merely use the language of the section to explain it. H. Rep. No. 179, 68th Cong., 1st Sess., pp. 14-15; S. Rep. No. 398, 68th Cong., 1st Sess., pp. 15-16. Nor does the applicable Treasury Regulation add anything; it repeats substantially the Committee Reports. Treas. Reg. 94, Art. 112(g)-4. We are thrown back upon the legislative language for ascertaining the meaning which will best accord with the aims of the language, the practical administration of the law and relevant judicial construction.

Although Abercrombie & Fitch showed a book deficit in the surplus account because the earlier stock dividends had been charged against it, the parties agree that for corporate tax purposes at least earnings and profits exceeding the distributed cash had been earned at the time of the recapitalization. That cash therefore came out of earnings and profits and such a distribution would normally be considered a taxable dividend, see §[316(a)], and has so been treated by the courts in seemingly similar situations. It has been ruled in a series of cases that where the stock of one corporation was exchanged for the stock of another and cash and then distributed, such distributions out of earnings and profits had the effect of a distribution of a taxable dividend under §[356(a)(2)]. . . . The Tax Court has reached the same result, that is, has treated the distribution as a taxable dividend, in the case of the recapitalization of a single corporation. . . . We cannot distinguish the two situations and find no implication in the statute restricting §[356(a)(2)] to taxation as a dividend only in the case of an exchange of stock and assets of two corporations.

Respondent, however, claims that this distribution more nearly has the effect of a "partial liquidation" as defined in §115(i).[5] But the classifications of §115, which governs "Distribution of Corporations" apart from reorganizations, were adopted for another purpose. They do not apply to a situation arising within §112 [the reorganization and nonrecognition provisions]. The definition of a "partial liquidation" in §115(i) is specifically limited to use in §115. To attempt to carry it over to §112 would distort its purpose. That limitation is not true of §[316(a)] which defines "dividends" for the purpose of the whole title. Accordingly, this definition is infused into §112(c)(2) [356(a)(2)]. Under §[316(a)] a distribution out of accumulated earnings and profits is a "dividend," thus confirming the conclusion that

5. "(i). *Definition of Partial Liquidation.* — As used in this section the term 'amounts distributed in partial liquidation' means a distribution by a corporation in complete cancellation or redemption of a part of its stock, or one of a series of distributions in complete cancellation or redemption of all or a portion of its stock."

a distribution of earnings and profits has the "effect of the distribution of a taxable dividend" under §[356(a)(2)].

Recapitalization does not alter the "effect." Although the capital of a company is reduced the cash received is a distribution of earnings and profits and as such falls within the federal tax. That the company's treatment of its stock dividends may bring consequences under State law requiring a capital reduction does not alter the character of the transactions which bring them within the federal income tax. Recapitalization is one of the forms of reorganization under §112. . . . It cannot therefore be urged as a reason for taking the transaction out of the requirements of §112 and forcing it into the mold of §115. The reduction of capital brings §112 into operation and does not give immunity from the requirements of §[356(a)(2)].

Treating the matter as a problem of statutory construction for our independent judgment, we hold that a distribution, pursuant to a reorganization, of earnings and profits, "has the effect of a distribution of a taxable dividend" within §[356(a)(2)]. As is true of other teasing questions of construction raised by technical provisions of Revenue Acts the matter is not wholly free from doubt. But these doubts would have to be stronger than they are to displace the informed views of the Tax Court. And if the case can be reduced to its own particular circumstances rather than turn on a generalizing principle we should feel bound to apply Dobson v. Commissioner, 320 U.S. 489, and sustain the Tax Court.

Reversed.

COMMISSIONER v. CLARK
109 S. Ct. 1455 (1989)

Justice STEVENS delivered the opinion of the Court.

This is the third case in which the Government has asked us to decide that a shareholder's receipt of a cash payment in exchange for a portion of his stock was taxable as a dividend. In the two earlier cases, Commissioner v. Estate of Bedford, 325 U.S. 283 (1945), and United States v. Davis, 397 U.S. 301 (1970), we agreed with the Government largely because the transactions involved redemptions of stock by single corporations that did not "result in a meaningful reduction of the shareholder's proportionate interest in the corporation." Id., at 313. In the case we decide today, however, the taxpayer in an arm's length transaction exchanged his interest in the acquired corporation for less than one percent of the stock of the acquiring corporation and a substantial cash payment. The taxpayer held no interest in the acquiring corporation prior to the reorganization. Viewing the exchange as a whole, we conclude that the cash payment is not appropriately characterized as a dividend. We accordingly agree with the Tax Court and with the Court of Appeals that the taxpayer is entitled to capital gains treatment of the cash payment.

I

In determining tax liability under the Internal Revenue Code, gain resulting from the sale or exchange of property is generally treated as capital gain, whereas the receipt of cash dividends is treated as ordinary income.[2] The Code, however, imposes no current tax on certain stock-for-stock exchanges. In particular, §354(a)(1) provides, subject to various limitations, for nonrecognition of gain resulting from the exchange of stock or securities solely for other stock or securities, provided that the exchange is pursuant to a plan of corporate reorganization and that the stock or securities are those of a party to the reorganization. 26 U.S.C. §354(a)(1).

Under §356(a)(1) of the Code, if such a stock-for-stock exchange is accompanied by additional consideration in the form of a cash payment or other property — something that tax practitioners refer to as "boot" — "then the gain, if any, to the recipient shall be recognized, but in an amount not in excess of the sum of such money and the fair market value of such other property." 26 U.S.C. §356(a)(1). That is, if the shareholder receives boot, he or she must recognize the gain on the exchange up to the value of the boot. Boot is accordingly generally treated as a gain from the sale or exchange of property and is recognized in the current tax-year.

Section 356(a)(2), which controls the decision in this case, creates an exception to that general rule. It provides:

> If an exchange is described in paragraph (1) but has the effect of the distribution of a dividend (determined with the application of section 318(a)), then there shall be treated as a dividend to each distributee such an amount of the gain recognized under paragraph (1) as is not in excess of his ratable share of the undistributed earnings and profits of the corporation accumulated after February 28, 1913. The remainder, if any, of the gain recognized under paragraph (1) shall be treated as gain from the exchange of property.

2. In 1979, the tax year in question, the distinction between long-term capital gain and ordinary income was of considerable importance. Most significantly, §1202(a) of the Code allowed individual taxpayers to deduct 60% of their net capital gain from gross income. Although the importance of the distinction declined dramatically in 1986 with the repeal of §1202(a), see Tax Reform Act of 1986, Pub. L. 99-514, §301(a), 100 Stat. 2216, the distinction is still significant in a number of respects. For example, §1211(b) allows individual taxpayers to deduct capital losses to the full extent of their capital gains, but only allows them to offset up to $3000 of ordinary income insofar as their capital losses exceed their capital gains.

Thus, if the "exchange . . . has the effect of the distribution of a dividend," the boot must be treated as a dividend and is therefore appropriately taxed as ordinary income to the extent that gain is realized. In contrast, if the exchange does not have "the effect of the distribution of a dividend," the boot must be treated as a payment in exchange for property and, insofar as gain is realized, accorded capital gains treatment. The question in this case is thus whether the exchange between the taxpayer and the acquiring corporation had "the effect of the distribution of a dividend" within the meaning of §356(a)(2).

The relevant facts are easily summarized. For approximately 15 years prior to April 1979, the taxpayer was the sole shareholder and president of Basin Surveys, Inc. (Basin), a company in which he had invested approximately $85,000. The corporation operated a successful business providing various technical services to the petroleum industry. In 1978, N. L. Industries, Inc. (NL), a publicly owned corporation engaged in the manufacture and supply of petroleum equipment and services, initiated negotiations with the taxpayer regarding the possible acquisition of Basin. On April 3, 1979, after months of negotiations, the taxpayer and NL entered into a contract.

The agreement provided for a "triangular merger," whereby Basin was merged into a wholly owned subsidiary of NL. In exchange for transferring all of the outstanding shares in Basin to NL's subsidiary, the taxpayer elected to receive 300,000 shares of NL common stock and cash boot of $3,250,000, passing up an alternative offer of 425,000 shares of NL common stock. The 300,000 shares of NL issued to the taxpayer amounted to approximately 0.92% of the outstanding common shares of NL. If the taxpayer had instead accepted the pure stock-for-stock offer, he would have held approximately 1.3% of the outstanding common shares. The Commissioner and the taxpayer agree that the merger at issue qualifies as a reorganization under §368(a)(1)(A) and (a)(2)(D).

Respondents filed a joint federal income tax return for 1979. As required by §356(a)(1), they reported the cash boot as taxable gain. In calculating the tax owed, respondents characterized the payment as long-term capital gain. The Commissioner on audit disagreed with this characterization. In his view, the payment had "the effect of the distribution of a dividend" and was thus taxable as ordinary income up to $2,319,611, the amount of Basin's accumulated earnings and profits at the time of the merger. The Commissioner assessed a deficiency of $972,504.74.

Respondents petitioned for review in the Tax Court, which, in a reviewed decision, held in their favor. 86 T.C. 138 (1986). The court started from the premise that the question whether the boot payment had "the effect of the distribution of a dividend" turns on the choice between "two judicially articulated tests." Id., at 140. Under the test advocated by the Commissioner and given voice in Shimberg v. United States, 577 F.2d 283 (CA5 1978), *cert. denied,* 439 U.S. 1115 (1979), the boot payment is treated as though it were made in a hypothetical redemption by the acquired corporation (Basin) immediately prior to the reorganization. Under this test, the cash payment received by the taxpayer indisputably would have been treated as a dividend. The second test, urged by the taxpayer and finding support in Wright v. United States, 482 F.2d 600 (CA8 1973), proposes an alternative hypothetical redemption. Rather than concentrating on the taxpayer's pre-reorganization interest in the acquired corporation, this test requires that one imagine a pure stock-for-stock exchange, followed immediately by a post-reorganization redemption of a portion of the taxpayer's shares in the acquiring corporation (NL) in return for a payment in an amount equal to the boot. Under §302 of the Code, which defines when a redemption of stock should be treated as a distribution of dividend, NL's redemption of 125,000 shares of its stock from the taxpayer in exchange for the $3,250,000 boot payment would have been treated as capital gain.

The Tax Court rejected the pre-reorganization test favored by the Commissioner because it considered it improper "to view the cash payment as an isolated event totally separate from the reorganization." 86 T.C., at 151. Indeed, it suggested that this test requires that courts make the "determination of dividend equivalency fantasizing that the reorganization does not exist." Id., at 150 (footnote omitted). The court then acknowledged that a similar criticism could be made of the taxpayer's contention that the cash payment should be viewed as a post-reorganization redemption. It concluded, however, that since it was perfectly clear that the cash payment would not have taken place without the reorganization, it was better to treat the boot "as the equivalent of a redemption in the course of implementing the reorganization," than "as having occurred prior to and separate from the reorganization." Id., at 152.[8]

---

8. The Tax Court stressed that to adopt the pre-reorganization view "would in effect resurrect the now discredited 'automatic dividend rule' . . . , at least with respect to pro rata distributions made to an acquired corporation's shareholders pursuant to a plan of reorganization." 86 T.C., at 152. On appeal, the Court of Appeals agreed. 828 F.2d 221, 226-227 (CA4 1987).

The "automatic dividend rule" developed as a result of some imprecise language in our decision in Commissioner v. Estate of Bedford, 325 U.S. 283 (1945). Although Estate of Bedford involved the recapitalization of a single corporation, the opinion employed broad language, asserting that "a distribution, pursuant to a reorganization, of earnings and profits 'has the effect of a distribution of taxable dividend' within [§356(a)(2)]." Id., at 292. The Commissioner read this language as establishing as a matter of law that all payments of boot are to be treated as dividends to the extent of undistributed earnings and profits. See Rev. Rul. 56-220, 1956-1 Cum. Bull. 191. Commentators, see, e.g., Darrel, The Scope of Commissioner v. Bedford Estate, 24 Taxes 266 (1946); Shoulson, Boot Taxation: The Blunt Toe of the Automatic Div-

The Court of Appeals for the Fourth Circuit affirmed. 828 F.2d 221 (1987). Like the Tax Court, it concluded that although "[s]ection 302 does not explicitly apply in the reorganization context," id., at 223, and although §302 differs from §356 in important respects, id., at 224, it nonetheless provides "the appropriate test for determining whether boot is ordinary income or a capital gain," id., at 223. Thus, as explicated in §302(b)(2), if the taxpayer relinquished more than 20% of his corporate control and retained less than 50% of the voting shares after the distribution, the boot would be treated as capital gain. However, as the Court of Appeals recognized, "[b]ecause §302 was designed to deal with a stock redemption by a single corporation, rather than a reorganization involving two companies, the section does not indicate which corporation [the taxpayer] lost interest in." Id., at 224. Thus, like the Tax Court, the Court of Appeals was left to consider whether the hypothetical redemption should be treated as a pre-reorganization distribution coming from the acquired corporation or as a post-reorganization distribution coming from the acquiring corporation. It concluded:

> Based on the language and legislative history of §356, the change-in-ownership principle of §302, and the need to review the reorganization as an integrated transaction, we conclude that the boot should be characterized as a post-reorganization stock redemption by N. L. that affected [the taxpayer's] interest in the new corporation. Because this redemption reduced [the taxpayer's] N. L. holdings by more than 20%, the boot should be taxed as a capital gain. Id., at 224-225.

This decision by the Court of Appeals for the Fourth Circuit is in conflict with the decision of the Fifth Circuit in *Shimberg*. [There] the court concluded that it was inappropriate to apply stock redemption principles in reorganization cases "on a wholesale basis." Id., at 287; see also ibid, n.13. . . . In addition, the court adopted the pre- reorganization test, holding that "§356(a)(2) requires a determination of whether the distribution would have been taxed as a dividend if made prior to the reorganization or if no reorganization had occurred." Id., at 288.

To resolve this conflict on a question of importance to the administration of the federal tax laws, we granted certiorari. 485 U.S. — (1988).

---

idend Rule, 20 Tax L. Rev. 573 (1965), and courts, see, e.g., Hawkinson v. Commissioner, 235 F.2d 747 (CA2 1956), however, soon came to criticize this rule. The courts have long since retreated from the "automatic dividend rule," see, e.g., Idaho Power Co. v. United States, 161 F. Supp. 807 (Ct. Cl.), *cert. denied*, 358 U.S. 832 (1958), and the Commissioner has followed suit, see Rev. Rul. 74-515, 1974-2 Cum. Bull. 118. As our decision in this case makes plain, we agree that Estate of Bedford should not be read to require that all payments of boot be treated as dividends.

II

We agree with the Tax Court and the Court of Appeals for the Fourth Circuit that the question under §356(a)(2) of whether an "exchange . . . has the effect of the distribution of a dividend" should be answered by examining the effect of the exchange as a whole. We think the language and history of the statute, as well as a common-sense understanding of the economic substance of the transaction at issue, support this approach.

The language of §356(a) strongly supports our understanding that the transaction should be treated as an integrated whole. Section 356(a)(2) asks whether "an exchange is described in paragraph (1)" that "has the effect of the distribution of a dividend." The statute does not provide that boot shall be treated as a dividend if its payment has the effect of the distribution of a dividend. Rather, the inquiry turns on whether the "exchange" has that effect. Moreover, paragraph (1), in turn, looks to whether "the property received in the exchange consists not only of property permitted by section 354 or 355 to be received without the recognition of gain but also of other property or money." Again, the statute plainly refers to one integrated transaction and, again, makes clear that we are to look to the character of the exchange as a whole and not simply its component parts. Finally, it is significant that §356 expressly limits the extent to which boot may be taxed to the amount of gain realized in the reorganization. This limitation suggests that Congress intended that boot not be treated in isolation from the overall reorganization. See Levin, Adess, & McGaffey, Boot Distributions in Corporate Reorganizations — Determination of Dividend Equivalency, 30 Tax Lawyer 287, 303 (1977).

Our reading of the statute as requiring that the transaction be treated as a unified whole is reinforced by the well-established "step-transaction" doctrine, a doctrine that the Government has applied in related contexts, see, e.g., Rev. Rul. 75-447, 1975-2 Cum. Bull. 113, and that we have expressly sanctioned, see Minnesota Tea Co. v. Helvering, 302 U.S. 609, 613 (1938); Commissioner v. Court Holding Co., 324 U.S. 331, 334 (1945). Under this doctrine, interrelated yet formally distinct steps in an integrated transaction may not be considered independently of the overall transaction. By thus "linking together all interdependent steps with legal or business significance, rather than taking them in isolation," federal tax liability may be based "on a realistic view of the entire transaction." 1 B. Bittker, Federal Taxation of Income, Estates and Gifts, para. 4.3.5, p. 4-52 (1981).

Viewing the exchange in this case as an integrated whole, we are unable to accept the Commissioner's pre-reorganization analogy. The analogy severs the payment of boot from the context of the reorganization. Indeed, only by straining to abstract the payment of boot from the context of the overall exchange, and thus imagining that Basin made a distribution to the taxpayer independently of NL's planned acquisition, can we reach the rather counterintuitive conclusion urged by the Commissioner — that the taxpayer suffered no meaningful reduction in his ownership interest as a result of the cash payment. We conclude that such a limited view of the transaction is plainly inconsistent with the statute's direction that we look to the effect of the entire exchange.

The pre-reorganization analogy is further flawed in that it adopts an overly expansive reading of §356(a)(2). As the Court of Appeals recognized, adoption of the pre-reorganization approach would "result in ordinary income treatment in most reorganizations because corporate boot is usually distributed pro rata to the shareholders of the target corporation." 828 F.2d, at 227; see also Golub, "Boot" in Reorganizations — The Dividend Equivalency Test of Section 356(a)(2), 58 Taxes 904, 911 (1980); Note, 20 Boston College L. Rev. 601, 612 (1979). Such a reading of the statute would not simply constitute a return to the widely criticized "automatic dividend rule" (at least as to cases involving a pro rata payment to the shareholders of the acquired corporation), see n. 8, supra, but also would be contrary to our standard approach to construing such provisions. The requirement of §356(a)(2) that boot be treated as dividend in some circumstances is an exception from the general rule authorizing capital gains treatment for boot. In construing provisions such as §356, in which a general statement of policy is qualified by an exception, we usually read the exception narrowly in order to preserve the primary operation of the provision. See Phillips, Inc. v. Walling, 324 U.S. 490, 493 (1945) ("To extend an exemption to other than those plainly and unmistakably within its terms and spirit is to abuse the interpretative process and to frustrate the announced will of the people"). Given that Congress has enacted a general rule that treats boot as capital gain, we should not eviscerate that legislative judgment through an expansive reading of a somewhat ambiguous exception.

The post-reorganization approach adopted by the Tax Court and the Court of Appeals is, in our view, preferable to the Commissioner's approach. Most significantly, this approach does a far better job of treating the payment of boot as a component of the overall exchange. Unlike the pre-reorganization view, this approach acknowledges that there would have been no cash payment absent the exchange and also that, by accepting the cash payment, the taxpayer experienced a meaningful reduction in his potential ownership interest.

Once the post-reorganization approach is adopted, the result in this case is pellucidly clear. Section 302(a) of the Code provides that if a redemption fits within any one of the four categories set out in §302(b), the redemption "shall be treated as a distribution in part or full payment in exchange for the stock," and thus not regarded as a dividend. As the Tax Court and the Court of Appeals correctly determined, the hypothetical post-reorganization redemption by NL of a portion of the taxpayer's shares satisfies at least one of the subsections of §302(b). In particular, the safe harbor provisions of subsection (b)(2) provide that redemptions in which the taxpayer relinquishes more than 20% of his or her share of the corporation's voting stock and retains less than 50% of the voting of stock after the redemption, shall not be treated as distributions of a dividend. . . . Here, we treat the transaction as though NL redeemed 125,000 shares of its common stock (i.e., the number of shares of NL common stock foregone in favor of the boot) in return for a cash payment to the taxpayer of $3,250,000 (i.e., the amount of the boot). As a result of this redemption, the taxpayer's interest in NL was reduced from 1.3% of the outstanding common stock to 0.9%. See 86 T.C., at 153. Thus, the taxpayer relinquished approximately 29% of his interest in NL and retained less than a 1% voting interest in the corporation after the transaction, easily satisfying the "substantially disproportionate" standards of §302(b)(2). We accordingly conclude that the boot payment did not have the effect of a dividend and that the payment was properly treated as capital gain.

III

The Commissioner objects to this "recasting [of] the merger transaction into a form different from that entered into by the parties," Brief for the United States 11, and argues that the Court of Appeals' formal adherence to the principles embodied in §302 forced the court to stretch to "find a redemption to which to apply them, since the merger transaction entered into by the parties did not involve a redemption," id., at 28. There are a number of sufficient responses to this argument. We think it first worth emphasizing that the Commissioner overstates the extent to which the redemption is imagined. As the Court of Appeals for the Fifth Circuit noted in Shimberg, "[t]he theory behind tax-free corporate reorganizations is that the transaction is merely a 'continuance of the proprietary interests in the continuing enterprise under modified corporate form.' Lewis v. Commissioner of Internal Revenue, 176 F.2d 646, 648 (1 Cir. 1949); Treas. Reg. §1.368-1(b). See generally Cohen, Conglomerate Mergers and Taxation, 55 A.B.A.J. 40 (1969)." 577 F. 2d at 288. As a result, the boot-for-stock transaction can be viewed as a partial repurchase of stock by the continuing corporate enterprise — i. e., as a redemption. It is of course true that both the pre-

and post-reorganization analogies are somewhat artificial in that they imagine that the redemption occurred outside the confines of the actual reorganization. However, if forced to choose between the two analogies, the post-reorganization view is the less artificial. Although both analogies "recast the merger transaction," the post-reorganization view recognizes that a reorganization has taken place, while the pre-reorganization approach recasts the transaction to the exclusion of the overall exchange.

Moreover, we doubt that abandoning the pre- and post-reorganization analogies and the principles of §302 in favor of a less artificial understanding of the transaction would lead to a result different from that reached by the Court of Appeals. Although the statute is admittedly ambiguous and the legislative history sparse, we are persuaded — even without relying on §302 — that Congress did not intend to except reorganizations such as that at issue here from the general rule allowing capital gains treatment for cash boot. 26 U.S.C. §356(a)(1). The legislative history of §356(a)(2), although perhaps generally "not illuminating," Estate of Bedford, 325 U.S., at 290, suggests that Congress was primarily concerned with preventing corporations from "siphon[ing] off" accumulated earnings and profits at a capital gains rate through the ruse of a reorganization. See Golub, 58 Taxes, at 905. This purpose is not served by denying capital gains treatment in a case such as this in which the taxpayer entered into an arm's length transaction with a corporation in which he had no prior interest, exchanging his stock in the acquired corporation for less than a one percent interest in the acquiring corporation and a substantial cash boot.

Section 356(a)(2) finds its genesis in §203(d)(2) of the Revenue Act of 1924. See 43 Stat. 257. Although modified slightly over the years, the provisions are in relevant substance identical. The accompanying House Report asserts that §203(d)(2) was designed to "preven[t] evasion." H.R. Rep. No. 179, 68th Cong., 1st Sess. 15 (1924). Without further explication, both the House and Senate Reports simply rely on an example to explain, in the words of both Reports, "[t]he necessity for this provision." Ibid.; S. Rep. No. 398, 68th Cong., 1st Sess., 16 (1924). Significantly, the example describes a situation in which there was no change in the stockholders' relative ownership interests, but merely the creation of a wholly owned subsidiary as a mechanism for making a cash distribution to the shareholders:

> Corporation A has capital stock of $100,000, and earnings and profits accumulated since March 1, 1913, of $50,000. If it distributes the $50,000 as a dividend to its stockholders, the amount distributed will be taxed at the full surtax rates.
>
>   On the other hand, Corporation A may organize Corporation B, to which it transfers all its assets, the consideration for the

transfer being the issuance by B of all its stock and $50,000 in cash
to the stockholders of Corporation A in exchange for their stock
in Corporation A. Under the existing law, the $50,000 distributed
with the stock of Corporation B would be taxed, not as a dividend,
but as a capital gain, subject only to the 12½ per cent rate. The
effect of such a distribution is obviously the same as if the corporation had declared out as a dividend its $50,000 earnings and
profits. If dividends are to be subject to the full surtax rates, then
such an amount so distributed should also be subject to the surtax
rates and not to the 12½ per cent rate on capital gain.

Id., at 16; H. R. Rep. No. 179, at 15.

The "effect" of the transaction in this example is to transfer
accumulated earnings and profits to the shareholders without altering
their respective ownership interests in the continuing enterprise.

Of course, this example should not be understood as exhaustive
of the proper applications of §356(a)(2). It is nonetheless noteworthy
that neither the example, nor any other legislative source, evinces a
congressional intent to tax boot accompanying a transaction that involves a bona fide exchange between unrelated parties in the context
of a reorganization as though the payment was in fact a dividend.
To the contrary, the purpose of avoiding tax evasion suggests that
Congress did not intend to impose an ordinary income tax in such
cases. Moreover, the legislative history of §302 supports this reading
of §356(a)(2) as well. In explaining the "essentially equivalent to a
dividend" language of §302(b)(1) — language that is certainly similar
to the "has the effect . . . of a dividend" language of §356(a)(2) —
the Senate Finance Committee made clear that the relevant inquiry
is "whether or not the transaction by its nature may properly be
characterized as a sale of stock. . . ." S. Rep. No. 1622, 83d Cong.,
2d Sess., 234 (1954); cf. United States v. Davis, 397 U. S., at 311.

Examining the instant transaction in light of the purpose of
§356(a)(2), the boot-for-stock exchange in this case "may properly be
characterized as a sale of stock." Significantly, unlike traditional single
corporation redemptions and unlike reorganizations involving commonly owned corporations, there is little risk that the reorganization
at issue was used as a ruse to distribute dividend. Rather, the transaction appears in all respects relevant to the narrow issue before us
to have been comparable to an arm's length sale by the taxpayer to
NL. This conclusion, moreover, is supported by the findings of the
Tax Court. The court found that "[t]here is not the slightest evidence
that the cash payment was a concealed distribution from BASIN."
86 T. C., at 155. As the Tax Court further noted, Basin lacked the
funds to make such a distribution:

Indeed, it is hard to conceive that such a possibility could even
have been considered, for a distribution of that amount was not
only far in excess of the accumulated earnings and profits

($2,319,611), but also of the total assets of BASIN ($2,758,069). In fact, only if one takes into account unrealized appreciation in the value of BASIN's assets, including good will and/or going-concern value, can one possibly arrive at $3,250,000. Such a distribution could only be considered as the equivalent of a complete liquidation of BASIN. . . .

Ibid.

In this context, even without relying on §302 and the post-reorganization analogy, we conclude that the boot is better characterized as a part of the proceeds of a sale of stock than as a proxy for a dividend. As such, the payment qualifies for capital gains treatment.

The judgment of the Court of Appeals is accordingly Affirmed.

Justice WHITE, dissenting.

The question in this case is whether the cash payment of $3,250,000 by N. L. Industries, Inc. (NL) to Donald Clark, which he received in the April 18, 1979, merger of Basin Surveys, Inc. (Basin), into N. L. Acquisition Corporation (NLAC), had the effect of a distribution of a dividend under the Internal Revenue Code, 26 U.S.C. §356(a)(2), to the extent of Basin's accumulated undistributed earnings and profits. Petitioner, the Commissioner of Internal Revenue (Commissioner) made this determination, taxing the sum as ordinary income, to find a 1979 tax deficiency of $972,504.74. The Court of Appeals disagreed, stating that because the cash payment resembles a hypothetical stock redemption from NL to Clark, the amount is taxable as capital gain. 828 F.2d 221 (CA4 1987). Because the majority today agrees with that characterization, in spite of Clark's explicit refusal of the stock-for-stock exchange imagined by the Court of Appeals and the majority today, and because the record demonstrates, instead, that the transaction before us involved a boot distribution that had "the effect of the distribution of a dividend" under §356(a)(2) — hence properly alerted the Commissioner to Clark's tax deficiency — I dissent.

The facts are stipulated. Basin, Clark, NL, and NLAC executed an Agreement and Plan of Merger dated April 3, 1979, which provided that on April 18, 1979, Basin would merge with NLAC. The statutory merger, which occurred pursuant to §§368(a)(1)(A) and (a)(2)(D) of the Code, and therefore qualified for tax-free reorganization status under §354(a)(1), involved the following terms: Each outstanding share of Basin common stock was exchanged for $56,034.482 cash and 5,172.4137 shares of NL common stock; and each share of Basin common stock held by Basin was canceled. NLAC's name was amended to Basin Surveys, Inc. The Secretary of State of West Virginia certified that the merger complied with West

Virginia law. Clark, the owner of all 58 outstanding shares of Basin, received $3,250,000 in cash and 300,000 shares of NL stock. He expressly refused NL's alternative of 425,000 shares of NL common stock without cash. See App. 56-59.

Congress enacted §354(a)(1) to grant favorable tax treatment to specific corporate transactions (reorganization) that involve the exchange of stock or securities solely for other stock or securities. See Paulsen v. Commissioner, 469 U.S. 131, 136 (1985) (citing Treas. Reg. §1.368-1(b), 26 CFR §1.368-1(b) (1984), and noting the distinctive feature of such reorganizations, namely continuity-of-interests). Clark's "triangular merger" of Basin into NL's subsidiary NLAC qualified as one such tax-free reorganization, pursuant to §368(a)(2)(D). Because the stock-for-stock exchange was supplemented with a cash payment, however, §356(a)(1) requires that "the gain, if any, to the recipient shall be recognized, but in an amount not in excess of the sum of such money and the fair market value of such other property." Because this provision permitted taxpayers to withdraw profits during corporate reorganizations without declaring a dividend, Congress enacted the present §356(a)(2), which states that when an exchange has "the effect of the distribution of a dividend," boot must be treated as a dividend, and taxed as ordinary income, to the extent of the distributee's "ratable share of the undistributed earnings and profits of the corporation. . . ." Ibid.; see also H.R. Rep. No. 179, 68th Cong., 1st Sess., 15 (1924) (illustration of §356(a)(2)'s purpose to frustrate evasion of dividend taxation through corporate reorganization distributions); S. Rep. No. 398, 68th Cong., 1st Sess., 16 (1924) (same).

Thus the question today is whether the cash payment to Clark had the effect of a distribution of a dividend. We supplied the straightforward answer in United States v. Davis, 397 U.S. 301, 306, 312 (1970), when we explained that a pro rata redemption of stock by a corporation is "essentially equivalent" to a dividend. A pro rata distribution of stock, with no alteration of basic shareholder relationships, is the hallmark of a dividend. This was precisely Clark's gain. As sole shareholder of Basin, Clark necessarily received a pro rata distribution of monies that exceeded Basin's undistributed earnings and profits of $2,319,611. Because the merger and cash obligation occurred simultaneously on April 18, 1979, and because the statutory merger approved here assumes that Clark's proprietary interests continue in the restructured NLAC, the exact source of the pro rata boot payment is immaterial, which truth Congress acknowledged by requiring only that an exchange have the effect of a dividend distribution.

To avoid this conclusion, the Court of Appeals — approved by the majority today — recast the transaction as though the relevant distribution involved a single corporation's (NL's) stock redemption, which dividend equivalency is determined according to §302 of the Code. Section 302 shields distributions from dividend taxation if the cash redemption is accompanied by sufficient loss of a shareholder's percentage interest in the corporation. The Court of Appeals hypothesized that Clark completed a pure stock-for-stock reorganization, receiving 425,000 NL shares, and thereafter redeemed 125,000 of these shares for his cash earnings of $3,250,000. The sum escapes dividend taxation because Clark's interest in NL theoretically declined from 1.3% to 0.92%, adequate to trigger §302(b)(2) protection. Transporting §302 from its purpose to frustrate shareholder sales of equity back to their own corporation, to §356(a)(2)'s reorganization context, however, is problematic. Neither the majority nor the Court of Appeals explains why §302 should obscure the core attribute of a dividend as a pro rata distribution to a corporation's shareholders;[1] nor offers insight into the mechanics of valuing hypothetical stock transfers and equity reductions; nor answers the Commissioner's observations that the sole shareholder of an acquired corporation will always have a smaller interest in the continuing enterprise when cash payments combine with a stock exchange. Last, the majority and the Court of Appeals' recharacterization of market happenings describes the exact stock-for-stock exchange, without a cash supplement, that Clark refused when he agreed to the merger.

Because the parties chose to structure the exchange as a tax-free reorganization under §354(a)(1), and because the pro rata distribution to Clark of $3,250,000 during this reorganization had the effect of a dividend under §356(a)(2), I dissent.[2]

---

1. The Court of Appeals' zeal to excoriate the "automatic dividend rule" leads to an opposite rigidity — an automatic nondividend rule, even for pro rata boot payments. Any significant cash payment in a stock-for-stock exchange distributed to a sole shareholder of an acquired corporation will automatically receive capital gains treatment. Section 356(a)(2)'s exception for such payments that have attributes of a dividend disappears. Congress did not intend to handicap the Commissioner and courts with either absolute; instead, §356(a)(1) instructs courts to make fact-specific inquiries into whether boot distributions accompanying corporate reorganizations occur on a pro rata basis to shareholders of the acquired corporation, and thus threaten a bailout of the transferor corporation's earnings and profits escaping a proper dividend tax treatment.

2. The majority's alternative holding that no statutory merger occurred at all — rather a taxable sale — is difficult to understand: All parties stipulate to the merger, which, in turn was approved under West Virginia law; and Congress endorsed exactly such tax-free corporate transactions pursuant to its §368(a)(1) reorganization regime. However apt the speculated sale analogy may be, if the April 3 Merger Agreement amounts to a sale of Clark's stock to NL, and not the intended merger, Clark would be subject to taxation on his full gain of over $10 million. The fracas over tax treatment of the cash boot would be irrelevant.

NOTE

The issue decided by *Clark* involved higher stakes under the 1954 Code than it does today, this because the 1968 Act eliminated the capital gains preference. As a matter of sound statutory construction and sensible Subchapter C policy, which of the opinions in *Clark* is the more persuasive?

REVENUE RULING 84-114
1984-2 C.B. 90

ISSUE

When nonvoting preferred stock and cash are received in an integrated transaction by a shareholder in exchange for voting common stock in a recapitalization described in section 368(a)(1)(E) . . . , does the receipt of cash have the effect of the distribution of a dividend within the meaning of section 356(a)(2)?

FACTS

Corporation X had outstanding 420 shares of voting common stock of which A owned 120 shares and B, C and D each owned 100 shares. A, B, C and D were not related within the meaning of section 318(a). . . . X adopted a plan of recapitalization that permitted a shareholder to exchange each of 30 shares of voting common stock for either one share of nonvoting preferred stock or cash. Pursuant to the plan, A first exchanged 15 shares of voting common stock for cash and then exchanged 15 shares of voting common stock for 15 shares of nonvoting preferred stock. The facts and circumstances surrounding these exchanges were such that the exchanges constituted two steps in a single integrated transaction for purposes of sections 368(a)(1)(E) and 356(a)(2). The nonvoting preferred stock had no conversion features. In addition, the dividend and liquidation rights payable to A on 15 shares of nonvoting preferred stock were substantially less than the dividend and liquidation rights payable to A on 30 shares of voting common stock. B, C, and D did not participate in the exchange and will retain all their voting common stock in X. X had a substantial amount of post-1913 earnings and profits.

The exchange by A of voting common stock for nonvoting preferred stock and cash qualified as a recapitalization within the meaning of section 368(a)(1)(E) of the Code.

LAW AND ANALYSIS

Rev. Rul. 74-515, 1974-2 C.B. 118, and Rev. Rul. 74-516, 1974-2 C.B. 121, state that whether a reorganization distribution to which section 356 of the Code applies has the effect of a dividend must be determined by examining the facts and circumstances surrounding the distribution and looking to the principles for determining dividend equivalency developed under section 356(a)(2) and other provisions of the Code. . . . Rev. Rul. 74-516 indicates that in making a dividend equivalency determination under section 356(a)(2), it is proper to analogize to section 302 in appropriate cases. In Shimberg v. United States [577 F.2d 283 (5th Cir. 1978)], the courts indicated that in making a dividend equivalency determination under section 356(a)(2), an analogy to section 302 may be appropriate in cases involving single entity reorganizations.

In United States v. Davis [page 195 supra], the Supreme Court of the United States held that a redemption must result in a meaningful reduction of the shareholder's proportionate interest in the corporation in order not to be essentially equivalent to a dividend under section 302(b)(1) of the Code.

Rev. Rul. 75-502, 1975-2 C.B. 111, sets forth factors to be considered in determining whether a reduction in a shareholder's proportionate interest in a corporation is meaningful within the meaning of *Davis*. The factors considered are a shareholder's right to vote and exercise control, to participate in current earnings and accumulated surplus, and to share in net assets on liquidation. The reduction in the right to vote is of particular significance when a redemption causes a redeemed shareholder to lose the potential for controlling the redeeming corporation by acting in concert with only one other shareholder. See Rev. Rul. 76-364, 1976-2 C.B. 91.

The specific issue is whether, in determining dividend equivalency under section 356(a)(2) . . . , it is proper to look solely at the change in A's proportionate interest in X that resulted from A's exchange of voting common stock for cash, or instead, whether consideration should be given to the total change in A's proportionate interest in X that resulted from the exchange of voting common stock for both cash and nonvoting preferred stock.

In Rev. Rul. 55-745, 1955-2 C.B. 223, the Internal Revenue Service announced that for purposes of section 302(b)(3) . . . , it would follow the decision in Zenz v. Quinlivan [page 259 supra], that a complete termination of shareholder interest may be achieved when a shareholder's entire stock interest in a corporation is disposed of partly through redemption and partly through sale. See also Rev. Rul. 75-447, 1975-2 C.B. 113, in which the *Zenz* rationale was applied to section 302(b)(2).

Since the exchange of voting common stock for cash and the exchange of voting common stock for nonvoting preferred stock constitute an integrated transaction, in this situation involving a single corporation it is proper to apply the *Zenz* rationale so that both exchanges are taken into consideration in determining whether there has been a meaningful reduction of A's proportionate interest in X within the meaning of *Davis*. Compare Rev. Rul. 75-83, 1975-1 C.B. 112, which holds that a distribution in connection with a transaction qualifying under section 368(a)(1)(A) . . . will be viewed as having been made by the acquired or transferor corporation and not by the acquiring or transferee corporation for purposes of making a dividend equivalency determination under section 356(a)(2).

If the exchange of voting common stock for preferred stock and cash in this situation had been tested under section 302 . . . as a redemption, it would not have qualified under section 302(b)(2) or (3) because there was neither an adequate reduction in A's voting stock interest nor a complete termination of that interest. In determining whether this situation is analogous to a redemption meeting the requirements of section 302(b)(1), it is significant that A's interest in the voting common stock of X was reduced from 28.57 percent (120/420) to 23.08 percent (90/390) so that A went from a position of holding a number of shares of voting common stock that afforded A control of X if A acted in concert with only one other shareholder, to a position where such action was not possible. Moreover, it is significant that A no longer holds the largest voting stock interest in X. In addition, although A received dividend and liquidation rights from the 15 shares of nonvoting preferred stock, these were substantially less than the dividend and liquidation rights of the 30 shares of voting common stock A surrendered. Accordingly, the requirements of section 302(b)(1) would have been met if the transaction had been tested under section 302, and, therefore, the cash received by A did not have the effect of the distribution of a dividend within the meaning of section 356(a)(2).

HOLDING

When A received cash and nonvoting preferred stock of X in an integrated transaction in exchange for voting common stock of X in a recapitalization described in section 368(a)(1)(E) . . . , the receipt of cash did not have the effect of the distribution of a dividend within the meaning of section 356(a)(2).

8. Subsidiary's Dealings with Stock in Parent

AMERICAN LAW INSTITUTE, FEDERAL INCOME TAX PROJECT — SUBCHAPTER C*
145-150 (Tent. Draft No. 5, 1980)

PARENT STOCK OWNED BY A SUBSIDIARY

Under present law a corporation does not recognize gain or loss from buying and selling its own shares. Prior to 1954, if a corporation dealt in its own shares as it might in the shares of another corporation, then it would have a cost basis for its own purchased shares and taxable gain if it resold them for more than basis. But the determination whether a corporation was dealing as it might in shares of another corporation was difficult to make, and in any event the tax was not an effective one since a corporation holding low-basis treasury stock could avoid it by issuing new shares instead of selling the treasury shares. The Congress therefore eliminated taxable gain or loss in all cases, after 1954, by enacting section 1032.

Suppose, however, that a corporation organizes a subsidiary, which then buys and sells stock of the parent corporation. The Revenue Service has ruled that gain or loss is to be computed and recognized by the subsidiary in such a case as if the parent stock were stock of an unrelated entity. Rev. Rul. 70-305, 1970-1 C.B. 169. Thus the pre-'54 possibility of an enterprise conducting taxable investment transactions in its own stock is still open after all, though not on the same condition. Investing through a subsidiary is a more formal condition than dealing as one might in shares of another corporation, and will not raise difficult factual issues of classification, but it is even more subject to manipulation. It is difficult to imagine how the tax on a subsidiary's gains in its parent's stock can function either as an effective tax or as a deterrent to avoidance or escape from any other tax on anything else.

A special problem has arisen if a subsidiary acquires parent stock directly from the parent, either in exchange for its own stock or as a contribution to capital. The Revenue Service has ruled that the transfer of parent stock in such a case is covered by section 351, with the consequence that the subsidiary's basis for the parent stock is to be determined under section 362. The Service reads section 1032 as implying that the parent has no basis for its own stock, even treasury stock it may have purchased from investors, and therefore concludes that the basis of the parent stock in the hands of the subsidiary is zero. Rev. Rul. 74503, 1974-2 C.B. 117.

---

*Copyright © 1980 by the American Law Institute. Reprinted by permission. — ED.

This interpretation creates the possibility of subsequent gain far beyond anything the parent might ever have had from dealing in its own stock. Section 1032 may be taken to imply the absence of any basis for a corporation's stock in its own hands, but that is quite different from a zero basis, since a zero basis operates to make sales proceeds taxable in full while section 1032 eliminates any tax at all.

The general effect of section 362 is to cause a corporate transferee to step into the shoes of a transferor of property so that the transferee will pick up whatever potential tax liabilities a transferor may be relieved of under section 351 or 361. Assigning a zero basis to parent stock in the hands of a subsidiary has a drastically different effect, creating the possibility of artificial and arbitrary tax liabilities on a subsequent disposition, which would not have accrued on a disposition by the parent corporation itself.

Some relief has been granted from the implications of this reasoning in the case of acquisitions covered by the reorganization definitions and in the case in which the subsidiary holding parent stock has only a transitory existence in an acquisition transaction. See, e.g., Rev. Rul. 67-326, 1967-2 C.B. 143; Rev. Rul. 73-427, 1973-2 C.B. 301. But this relief is only partial and incomplete and leaves practitioners with the necessity of complying with the applicable conditions. While the resulting distortions have primarily to do with the form in which transactions are carried out, there is no policy justifying even a minor distortion, and the existing law creates booby traps with no substantial justification.

In general, section 1032 appears to have operated sensibly and satisfactorily and not to have engendered notable abuses. Moreover, the use of a subsidiary to carry out a transaction should not substantially alter its tax effect. That is, indeed, the main import of section 362 in its normal application. The problems concerning parent stock held by a subsidiary can best be resolved by extending section 1032 to embrace transactions in parent stock carried out through a subsidiary, and that is what is here proposed.

A parent may dispose of its own stock held in a subsidiary in either of two ways: (1) by the subsidiary selling the parent stock, or (2) by the parent selling the subsidiary. The proposal has two paragraphs, one dealing with each mode of disposition, and both providing for nonrecognition of gain or loss with respect to the parent stock being disposed of.

PROPOSAL VIID — PARENT STOCK OWNED BY A SUBSIDIARY

1. *DISPOSITION BY SUBSIDIARY.* — NO GAIN OR LOSS SHOULD BE RECOGNIZED TO A SUBSIDIARY CORPORATION ON THE RECEIPT OF MONEY OR OTHER PROPERTY

IN EXCHANGE FOR STOCK OF ANY CORPORATION WHICH
IS IN CONTROL OF SUCH SUBSIDIARY CORPORATION.

2. *DISPOSITION BY CONTROLLING CORPORATION.* — NO
GAIN OR LOSS SHOULD BE RECOGNIZED TO A CONTROL-
LING CORPORATION ON THE RECEIPT OF MONEY OR
PROPERTY IN EXCHANGE FOR STOCK OF A SUBSIDIARY,
TO THE EXTENT ALLOCABLE TO STOCK OF THE CON-
TROLLING CORPORATION OWNED BY THE SUBSIDIARY.

3. *DEFINITIONS.* —

A) ["CONTROL" MEANS OWNERSHIP OF STOCK POS-
SESSING AT LEAST 80 PERCENT OF THE TOTAL COMBINED
VOTING POWER OF ALL CLASSES OF STOCK ENTITLED TO
VOTE AND AT LEAST 80 PERCENT OF THE TOTAL NUMBER
OF SHARES OF ALL OTHER CLASSES OF STOCK OF THE
CORPORATION.]

B) "SUBSIDIARY" MEANS A CORPORATION CON-
TROLLED BY A CONTROLLING CORPORATION.

GENERAL OPERATION . . .

Example (1): P organizes S, a wholly owned subsidiary. S then
purchases stock of P from outsiders for $100x and subsequently
sells that stock for $150x.

No gain would be recognized to S, under paragraph 1 of the
proposal.

Example (2): The facts are the same as in Example (1), except
that S transfers the P stock in exchange for a parcel of real estate
with a fair market value of $150x.

Again no gain would be recognized to S, under paragraph 1 of
the proposal. In this case, there would be an additional issue concerning the basis of the real estate to S. Assuming the transfer of the
real estate is not part of some transaction in which the transferor
does not recognize gain or loss and basis carries over, the basis to S
should be cost, which would mean the fair market value of the P
stock. The guiding principle is that the tax consequences of the transaction should be the same as if it had been carried out by the parent
directly without the intervention of any subsidiary.

Example (3): P organizes S, contributing $250x for all its stock.
S then purchases, from outsiders, stock of P for $100x and real
estate for $150x. Later when the P stock is worth $170x and the
real estate is worth $180x, P sells the S stock for $350x.

Under paragraph 2 of the proposal, P would not recognize $70x
of gain attributable to the P stock held by S. P would recognize the

remaining gain of $30x, however, attributable to S's investment in the real estate.

> *Example (4)*: P organizes S, contributing P stock in exchange for all S's stock. Subsequently, S exchanges the P stock partly for cash and partly for real estate.

Again, S would have no gain or loss, under paragraph 1 of the proposal, and the basis for the real estate would be the fair market value of the P stock exchanged to acquire it.

BASIS

Under existing law, one is accustomed to ask what is the basis of stock of one corporation held by another, even if the two corporations are part of a single affiliated group. One may, accordingly, ask what is the basis of P stock held by S, and of S stock held by P, in various situations, including perhaps the examples in comment 1.

In one sense, this proposal by-passes that question, or makes it irrelevant, just as section 1032 makes it irrelevant to inquire about the basis of treasury stock held directly by its own issuer. Since gain or loss is not to be recognized by S in any event, S could be considered to have no basis for P stock it may own. . . .

NOTES

1. Rev. Rul. 70-305, 1970-1 C.B. 169, held that stock purchased and resold on the open market by a subsidiary of the issuing corporation was not treasury stock, and that gain or loss would be recognized to the subsidiary on the transaction. Compare Litton Business Systems, Inc., 61 T.C. 367 (1973), in which a subsidiary acquired a cost basis in its parent's stock through a bona fide purchase on "advance account," then used that stock to acquire the assets of an unrelated company in a qualifying "C" reorganization.

In Rev. Rul. 74-503, 1974-2 C.B. 117, X Corporation transferred its own treasury shares to Y Corporation in exchange for newly issued Y shares of equal aggregate value, constituting 80 percent of the latter's outstanding stock. Sections 351 and 1032 prevented recognition of gain to X or Y, and each was said to take a zero basis in the other's stock.

2. See Committee on Corporate Taxation, Tax Section of The New York State Bar Association, Sale or Exchange by a Subsidiary Corporation of its Parent Corporation's Stock, 47 Taxes 146 (1969); Manning, The Issuer's Paper: Property of What? Zero Basis and Other Income Tax Mysteries, 39 Tax L. Rev. 159 (1984). For the Treasury's current solution, see Prop. Treas. Reg. §§1.1032-2 and 1.358-6.

9. Proposals for Reform

A number of bad puns press hard for recognition as one reflects on the morass into which the rules relating to corporate fusion have devolved. It seems preferable, however, to forego the puns and to raise a few questions of policy which may evoke others:

The American Law Institute's study (American Law Institute, Federal Income Tax Project — Subchapter C — Proposals on Corporate Acquisitions and Dispositions and Reporter's Study on Corporate Distributions (1982)) proposes a radical, elegant, and simplifying revision of the tax law affecting corporate amalgamation. Many results that are only "effectively elective" under present law would become explicitly elective, free of unnecessary and insubstantial formal trappings.* The ABA's Section of Taxation, however, has conducted a "Narrow Project," with a resulting proposal that is less radical. It departs less than the ALI's from the structure and terminology of current law, but offers a substantial degree of internal harmony and simplification, while cutting the "continuity of proprietary interest" doctrine down to size. What is your reaction to the following proposal of the Section of Taxation?

> The Internal Revenue Code of . . . should be amended to provide that:
>
> (1) An acquisitive transaction will constitute a corporate "reorganization" described in Internal Revenue Code section 368 only if at least 50 percent of the consideration issued in the transaction by the acquiring corporation or a corporation controlling the acquiring corporation is "qualifying consideration," that is, either
>
> (i) stock of the acquiring corporation; or
> (ii) stock of a corporation that directly or indirectly controls the acquiring corporation immediately after the transaction.
>
> (2) A corporation is deemed to control all corporations in an unbroken chain of corporations controlled by it or by any other corporation it controls.
>
> (3) In determining the amount of qualifying consideration,
>
> (i) stock of the acquiring corporation, or stock of a corporation controlling the acquiring corporation, but not both, is qualifying consideration;
> (ii) except as provided in sections 357(b) and (c) the assumption of a liability of the acquired corporation or the acquisition of property subject to a liability shall not be considered consideration given by the acquiring or controlling corporation;
> (iii) the value of all consideration issued or transferred for assets or stock of the acquired corporation in transactions that

*See also American Law Institute, Federal Income Tax Project — Subchapter C (Supplemental Study) — Reporter's Study Draft 103 – 137 (June 1, 1989).

are a part of the plan of reorganization will be taken into account;

(iv) if the acquired corporation is liquidated or merged into the acquiring corporation "old and cold" stock of the acquired corporation previously owned by the acquiring corporation will be disregarded.

(4) In transactions described in section 368(a)(1)(C)

(i) the transferor corporation must transfer substantially all of its assets, measured immediately before the transfer, to the acquiring corporation;

(ii) the transferor corporation must liquidate, distributing all its assets to its creditors and shareholders pursuant to the plan of reorganization; and

(iii) the transferor corporation may not have been a transferor corporation in another reorganization described in section 368(a)(1)(C) within the twelve months preceding the transfer.

(5) In transactions qualifying under section 368(a)(1)(A), (1)(B) or (1)(C), all or part of the acquired assets or stock may be transferred (i) to one or more corporations directly or indirectly controlled by the acquiring corporation; or (ii) to one or more corporations that directly or indirectly control the acquiring corporation; or (iii) to one or more corporations directly or indirectly controlled by a corporation directly or indirectly controlling the acquiring corporation.

(6) "Triangular mergers" will be tested for reorganization status under the traditional forms of acquisitive reorganizations which they most resemble. A "forward" subsidiary merger will be tested as a merger described in paragraph (1)(A) while a "reverse" subsidiary merger will be tested as a stock exchange described in paragraph (1)(B).

(7) The term "properties," wherever it appears in section 368, is changed to "assets."

(8) The definition of a "party to a reorganization" is clarified to include specifically (i) a corporation that effects a recapitalization, and (ii) the corporation to which assets are "dropped down" following an acquisitive reorganization.

The report accompanying the foregoing proposal notes the following with respect to one aspect of the recommendation's impact on continuity of interest:

Notwithstanding the admonition in the private rulings guidelines, the Internal Revenue Service has largely ignored changes in the composition of T's* historical shareholder ownership brought

*Throughout the report the following definitions are used:

P	The corporation whose stock is issued in an exchange. Normally P or its subsidiary S will be the acquiring or transferee corporation.
S	P's controlled subsidiary (100% owned by P unless otherwise stated).
T	The target or acquired or transferor corporation.
A	T's shareholder or shareholders. — ED.

about by transactions not directly related to the reorganization. [We] . . . discern no valid reason for making reorganization status depend upon static shareholder ownership.

Similarly, under the recommendation (as we believe is the case under existing law) none of the forms of acquisitive reorganization require that T's former or historical shareholders control P immediately after the reorganization. Consequently, it should not matter whether 100%, 66⅔%, 50% or 10% of T's historical shareholders (whether measured by number of shareholders or number of shares) actually participate in the reorganization exchange:

[T]he transmutation of the concern about proprietary interest into one about the identity of the proprietors is a distortion of enormous magnitude. Perhaps it was only innocently careless, perhaps more than that. But, in any event, it was costly and mischievous beyond measure. . . . [T]he mandate to look to shareholder identity had no legislative or judicial imprimatur. [Wolfman, "Continuity of Interest" and The American Law Institute Study, 57 Taxes 840, 841-842 (Dec. 1979.]

Under the recommendation sales of T stock to third parties in the open market or in privately negotiated transactions (other than to P or an affiliated corporation) immediately prior or subsequent to the reorganization will not affect the measurement of continuity of interest. . . . [Recommendation No. 1981-5, 34 Tax Law. 1386 (1981)].

VI. CORPORATE FISSION—SPIN-OFFS AND OTHER CORPORATE PROLIFERATIONS

A. INTRODUCTION AND HISTORY

Lawyers have coined brief phrases to describe four of the most common types of corporate divisions—transactions in which some or all of the assets held by one corporation are transferred to one or more corporations, and some or all of the shareholders of the transferor become shareholders in the transferee:

Spin-off: Corporation A transfers some of its assets to Corporation B in exchange for all of the latter's authorized stock. Corporation A thereupon distributes a pro rata dividend to its shareholders consisting of the stock it receives in B. A's shareholders now own stock in both A and B. (In some cases a spin-off involves the pro rata distribution of the stock of an old subsidiary, one not formed or one whose stock was not purchased as part of a plan that included distribution of the stock.)

Split-off: The transaction is very much the same as a spin-off, except that Corporation A distributes the B stock to its shareholders in redemption of a proportionate share of their stock in A. As with a spin-off, the shareholders of A now own stock in both A and B, but in the aggregate they own fewer shares (not a lower percentage) of the A stock.

Split-up: Corporation A transfers part of its assets to Corporation B in exchange for all of B's stock and transfers the remainder of its assets to Corporation C for all of its stock. A then liquidates, distributing the stock of B and C in retirement of its own outstanding stock. The shareholders now own stock in B and C in place of their stock in the defunct Corporation A.

Spin-away: B, a corporation with two separate businesses, desires to merge one of its businesses with A, an unrelated corporation. Prior to the merger, B transfers one of its businesses to a separate corporation in either a spin-off or split-off. As a result of the "spin-away," the stock in one of B's businesses is owned exclusively by shareholders of B, while the shares in the corporation resulting from the merger are owned by both A's and B's shareholders.

The cases posed are prototypes, not exclusive. The principal tax issues are usually these: (1) recognition of income or loss to the shareholders on receipt of stock in the transferee corporations; (2) basis to the shareholders of the stock they receive; (3) recognition of gain or loss to the transferor corporation; and (4) basis of assets in the hands of the transferee corporations. Sections 355, 356(b), and 368(a)(1)(D) are the provisions primarily involved. Sections 351, 361, and 358 also play roles.

Gregory v. Helvering, page 545 supra, concerned a spin-off in which the taxpayer unsuccessfully claimed that the distribution of the transferee corporation's stock was tax-free under §112(g) of the Revenue Act of 1928 (the earliest version of the current §355(a)(1)) as part of a reorganization plan under §112(i)(1)(B) of that Act (an early version of the "D" reorganization). Why did Mrs. Gregory fail under the 1928 Act? Would she fail under current law?

In 1934 Congress repealed §112(g) of the 1928 Act as part of a legislative program to eliminate what it then thought were unwarranted tax avoidance devices. Tax-free spin-offs returned to the statute in 1951 as §112(b)(11) of the 1939 Code. With modification, the provision was continued in the 1954 Code as §355. Although earlier statutory versions required a "plan of reorganization," §355 does not. Frequently, however, a corporate division may be part of a "D" reorganization. When it is not (and even when it is), §351 may operate to avoid recognition to the transferor corporation. If there is a "D" reorganization, §361 will be operative, often along with §351.

See generally Kaden and Wolfe, Spin-offs, Split-offs and Split-ups: A Detailed Analysis of Section 355, Tax Notes, July 31, 1989,

p. 565; Silverman, Keyes, and Berry, Satisfying the Continuity of Interest Requirement of the Section 355 Regulations, 71 J. Taxn. 118 (1989); and Wells, Continuity of Interest Under the New Section 355 Regulations, 16 J. Corp. Taxn. 203 (1989).

B. STATUTORY ISSUES

1. *Purpose*

RAFFERTY v. COMMISSIONER
452 F.2d 767 (1st Cir. 1971), *cert. denied,* 408 U.S. 922 (1972)

Before Aldrich, Chief Judge, McEntee and Coffin, Circuit Judges.

McEntee, Circuit Judge. Taxpayers, Joseph V. Rafferty and wife, appeal from a decision of the Tax Court which held that a distribution to them of all the outstanding stock of a real estate holding corporation did not meet the requirements of §355 of the Internal Revenue Code of 1954 and therefore was taxable as a dividend. Our opinion requires a construction of §355 and the regulations thereunder.

The facts, some of which have been stipulated, are relatively simple. The taxpayers own all the outstanding shares of Rafferty Brown Steel Co., Inc. (hereinafter RBS), a Massachusetts corporation engaged in the processing and distribution of cold rolled sheet and strip steel in Longmeadow, Massachusetts. In May 1960, at the suggestion of his accountant, Rafferty organized Teragram Realty Co., Inc., also a Massachusetts corporation. In June of that year RBS transferred its Longmeadow real estate to Teragram in exchange for all of the latter's outstanding stock. Thereupon Teragram leased back this real estate to RBS for ten years at an annual rent of $42,000. In 1962 the taxpayers also organized Rafferty Brown Steel Co., Inc., of Connecticut (RBS Conn.), which corporation acquired the assets of Hawkridge Brothers, a general steel products warehouse in Waterbury, Connecticut. Since its inception the taxpayers have owned all of the outstanding stock in RBS Conn. From 1962 to 1965 Hawkridge leased its real estate in Waterbury to RBS Conn. In 1965 Teragram purchased some unimproved real estate in Waterbury and built a plant there. In the same year it leased this plant to RBS Conn. for a term of fourteen years. Teragram has continued to own and lease the Waterbury real estate to RBS Conn. and the Longmeadow realty to RBS, which companies have continued up to the present time to operate their businesses at these locations.

During the period from 1960 through 1965 Teragram derived all of its income from rent paid by RBS and RBS Conn. Its earned surplus increased from $4,119.05 as of March 31, 1961, to $46,743.35 as of March 31, 1965. The earned surplus of RBS increased from $331,117.97 as of June 30, 1959, to $535,395.77 as of June 30, 1965. In August 1965, RBS distributed its Teragram stock to the taxpayers. Other than this distribution, neither RBS nor Teragram has paid any dividends.

Joseph V. Rafferty has been the guiding force behind all three corporations, RBS, RBS Conn., and Teragram. He is the president and treasurer of Teragram which, while it has no office or employees, keeps separate books and records and filed separate tax returns for the years in question.

On various occasions Rafferty consulted his accountant about estate planning, particularly about the orderly disposition of RBS. While he anticipated that his sons would join him at RBS, he wanted to exclude his daughters (and/or his future sons-in-law) from the active management of the steel business. He wished, however, to provide them with property which would produce a steady income. The accountant recommended the formation of Teragram, the distribution of its stock, and the eventual use of this stock as future gifts to the Rafferty daughters. The taxpayers acted on this advice and also on the accountant's opinion that the distribution of Teragram stock would meet the requirements of §355.

In their 1965 return the taxpayers treated the distribution of Teragram stock as a nontaxable transaction under §355. The Commissioner viewed it, however, as a taxable dividend and assessed a deficiency. He claimed (a) that the distribution was used primarily as a device for the distribution of the earnings and profits of RBS or Teragram or both, and (b) that Teragram did not meet the active business requirements of §355.

We turn first, to the Tax Court's finding that there was no device because there was an adequate business purpose for the separation and distribution of Teragram stock. In examining this finding we are guided by the rule that the taxpayer has the burden of proving that the transaction was not used principally as a device. . . . Initially, we are disturbed by the somewhat uncritical nature of the Tax Court's finding of a business purpose. Viewing the transaction from the standpoint of RBS, RBS Conn., or Teragram, no immediate business reason existed for the distribution of Teragram's stock to the taxpayers. Over the years the businesses had been profitable, as witnessed by the substantial increase of the earned surplus of every component, yet none had paid dividends. The primary purpose for the distribution found by the Tax Court was to facilitate Rafferty's desire to make bequests to his children in accordance with an estate plan. This was a personal motive. Taxpayers seek to put it in terms relevant to the corporation by speaking of avoidance of possible interference with the operation of the steel business by future sons-in-law, pointing to Coady v. Commissioner, 33 T.C. 771 (1960), *aff'd per curiam*, 289 F.2d 490 (6th Cir. 1961) [page 694 infra.].

In *Coady*, however, the separation was in response to a seemingly irreconcilable falling-out between the owners of a business. This falling-out had already occurred and, manifestly, the separation was designed to save the business from a substantial, present problem. . . . In the case at bar there was, at best, only an envisaged possibility of future debilitating nepotism. If avoidance of this danger could be thought a viable business purpose at all, it was so remote and so completely under the taxpayers' control that if, in other respects the transaction was a "device," that purpose could not satisfy the taxpayers' burden of proving that it was not being used "principally as a device" within the meaning of the statute.

Our question, therefore, must be whether taxpayers' desire to put their stockholdings into such form as would facilitate their estate planning, viewed in the circumstances of the case, was a sufficient personal business purpose to prevent the transaction at bar from being a device for the distribution of earnings and profits. While we remain of the view, which we first expressed in Lewis v. Commissioner, 176 F.2d 646 (1st Cir. 1949), that a purpose of a shareholder, qua shareholder, may in some cases save a transaction from condemnation as a device, we do not agree with the putative suggestion in Estate of Parshelsky v. Commissioner, 303 F.2d 14, 19 (2d Cir. 1962), that any investment purpose of the shareholders is sufficient. Indeed, in *Lewis*, although we depreciated the distinction between shareholder and corporate purpose, we were careful to limit that observation to the facts of that case, and to caution that the business purpose formula "must not become a substitute for independent analysis." . . . For that reason we based our decision on the Tax Court's finding that the transaction was "undertaken for reasons germane to the continuance of the corporate business." Id. at 647.

This is not to say that a taxpayer's personal motives cannot be considered, but only that a distribution which has considerable potential for use as a device for distributing earnings and profits should not qualify for tax-free treatment on the basis of personal motives unless those motives are germane to the continuance of the corporate business. . . . We prefer this approach over reliance upon formulations such as "business purpose," and "active business." . . . The facts of the instant case illustrate the reason for considering substance. Dividends are normally taxable to shareholders upon receipt. Had the taxpayers received cash dividends and made investments to provide for their female descendants, an income tax would, of course, have resulted. Accordingly, once the stock was distributed, if it could potentially be converted into cash without thereby impairing tax-payers' equity interest in RBS, the transaction could easily be used to avoid taxes. The business purpose here alleged, which could be fully satisfied by a bail-out of dividends, is not sufficient to prove that the transaction was not being principally so used.

Given such a purpose, the only question remaining is whether the substance of the transaction is such as to leave the taxpayer in a position to distribute the earnings and profits of the corporation away from, or out of the business. The first factor to be considered is how easily the taxpayer would be able, were he so to choose, to liquidate or sell the spun-off corporation. Even if both corporations are actively engaged in their respective trades, if one of them is a business based principally on highly liquid investment-type, passive assets, the potential for a bail-out is real. The question here is whether the property transferred to the newly organized corporation had a readily realizable value, so that the distributee-shareholders could, if they ever wished, "obtain such cash or property or the cash equivalent thereof, either by selling the distributed stock or liquidating the corporation, thereby converting what would otherwise be dividends taxable as ordinary income into capital gain. . . ." . . . In this connection we note that the Tax Court found that a sale of Teragram's real estate properties could be "easily arranged." . . . Indeed, taxpayers themselves stressed the fact that the buildings were capable of multiple use.

There must, however, be a further question. If the taxpayers could not effect a bail-out without thereby impairing their control over the ongoing business, the fact that a bail-out is theoretically possible should not be enough to demonstrate a device because the likelihood of it ever being so used is slight. "[A] bail-out ordinarily means that earnings and profits have been drawn off without impairing the shareholder's residual equity interest in the corporation's earning power, growth potential, or voting control." . . . If sale would adversely affect the shareholders of the on-going company, the assets cannot be said to be sufficiently separated from the corporate solution and the gain sufficiently crystallized as to be taxable. . . . In this case, there was no evidence that the land and buildings at which RBS carried on its steel operations were so distinctive that the sale of Teragram stock would impair the continued operation of RBS, or that the sale of those buildings would in any other way impair Rafferty's control and other equity interests in RBS.[7]

In the absence of any direct benefit to the business of the original company, and on a showing that the spin-off put saleable assets in the hands of the taxpayers, the continued retention of which was not

---

7. Our conclusion is reinforced by the fact that RBS and RBS Conn. were guaranteed occupancy of Teragram property under long-term leases at fixed rents.

needed to continue the business enterprise, or to accomplish tax-payers' purposes, we find no sufficient factor to overcome the Commissioner's determination that the distribution was principally a device to distribute earnings and profits.

[The court's discussion of whether Teragram failed to meet the "active business" requirement of §355 is omitted.*]

NOTES

1. In view of the outer parenthetical in §355(a)(1)(B), what circumstances might demonstrate that the transaction was used as a device for the siphoning of earnings and profits? What do you think led to the outer and inner parentheticals? See Treas. Reg. §1.355-2(c).

2. In Estate of Parshelsky v. Commissioner, 303 F.2d 14, 19, (2d Cir. 1962) the court held that the reason for the reorganization may properly be related to the personal or noncorporate business interests of the shareholders. The *Rafferty* court criticizes this, see page 684 supra. Regarding the "business purpose" requirement, Treas. Reg. §1.355-2(b) states:

> Depending upon the facts of a particular case, a shareholder purpose for a transaction may be so nearly coextensive with a corporate business purpose as to preclude any distinction between them. In such a case, the transaction is carried out for purposes germane to the business of the corporations. On the other hand, if a transaction is undertaken solely for the purpose of fulfilling the personal planning purposes of a shareholder, the distribution will not qualify under section 355. . . .

Cf. Rev. Rul. 76-527, 1976-2 C.B. 103 (spin-off to make subsidiary more attractive to prospective merger partner had a valid business purpose); Rev. Rul. 75-337, 1975-2 C.B. 124 (distribution of a subsidiary's stock in complete redemption of inactive shareholders, and in reduction of interest of aging majority shareholder, served to protect corporation's automobile dealership franchise).

3. The question whether a distribution under §355 has a business purpose must be distinguished from the question whether expenses incident to the distribution are deductible "business expenses." See Bilar Tool & Die Corp. v. Commissioner, 530 F.2d 708 (6th Cir. 1976) (split-up to resolve shareholder dispute had a lasting benefit to both resulting corporations, so the expenses incident to the split-up were paid "to enhance capital" and nondeductible).

*The "active business" requirements will be treated at page 687 et seq. infra. — ED.

2.   *"Active Conduct of a Trade or Business"*

ELLIOTT v. COMMISSIONER
32 T.C. 283 (1959)

DRENNEN, Judge. . . . The only issue for determination is whether the distribution of all the stock of Centrifix Management Corporation, a wholly owned subsidiary, hereinafter referred to as Management, by Centrifix Corporation, hereinafter referred to as Centrifix, to Randall T. Elliott, the principal stockholder of Centrifix, on December 15, 1954, was taxable as a long-term capital gain to Elliott or qualified as a nontaxable "split-off" under section 355. . . .

FINDINGS OF FACT

. . . At all times material hereto, Centrifix was an Ohio corporation formed in 1926. . . . Centrifix was organized to engineer and develop apparatus for the purification and separation of liquids and gases, and at all times material hereto was engaged in said business.

Management was incorporated under the laws of Ohio on April 22, 1950, as a wholly owned subsidiary corporation of Centrifix. At all times material hereto it had authorized capital of 150 shares of no-par common stock having a stated value of $100 per share.

In 1946, Centrifix acquired property at 3029 Prospect Avenue, Cleveland, Ohio, consisting of an old 2-story house with caretakers quarters and a carriage house in the rear. Centrifix occupied approximately one-half of the available space in the house and carriage house as an office and shop for its engineering business and made available for rent to various tenants the balance of the property. Centrifix continued to use part of this property in its business and rented the balance of the property until it was sold in 1950.

In 1950, Centrifix sold the property at 3029 Prospect Avenue and acquired property at 3608 Payne Avenue, Cleveland, Ohio. When the new property on Payne Avenue was acquired, it was transferred to Management in exchange for all of the stock of Management in a transaction that was tax free under section [351]. . . .

During the period from April 27, 1950, to December 15, 1954, Management owned and operated the Payne Avenue property. The property consisted of land and a 3-story brick loft building having a total area of 28,144 square feet, of which Centrifix leased 14,468 square feet, Tetrad Company, unrelated, leased approximately 5,200 square feet, and the balance was unoccupied but was available for rental to third parties.

On December 15, 1954, Randall T. Elliott surrendered to Centrifix the 1,852¾ shares of cumulative preferred stock of Centrifix which he owned, in exchange for which Centrifix transferred to Elliott 150 shares being all of the authorized common stock of Management, and canceled an indebtedness of $5,241.48 which had been owing from Elliott to Centrifix. No other consideration was involved in this transaction. . . . At the same time Elliott agreed to the cancellation of cumulative past-due dividends on the preferred stock in the amount of $242,894.75.

On December 15, 1954, the 150 shares of no-par-value common stock of Management distributed in the above transaction to Elliott had a fair market value of $78,837.34, and the adjusted basis of 1,852¾ shares of Centrifix cumulative preferred stock in the hands of Elliott was $750. . . . As of December 15, 1954, and December 31, 1954, Centrifix had no accumulated earnings and profits.

In their 1954 return, petitioners reported no gain or loss on the above transaction.

During that part of the year 1946 after Centrifix acquired the Prospect Avenue property, and through that part of the year 1950, prior to the time said property was sold, Centrifix realized gross rental income from the Prospect Avenue property, gross income from all sources, net income from all sources, and reported net taxable income for each of the years 1946 through 1950 as follows:

Period covered	Gross rental income	Gross income[1]	Net income[1]	Net taxable income
1946	$380.90	$150,120.18	$ 2,461.26	($ 707.39)
1947	591.00	253,193.64	20,927.09	24,609.37
1948	780.00	238,280.53	13,516.60	17,424.16
1949	780.00	243,344.39	16,765.13	20,152.71
1950[2]	325.00	324,253.26	19,932.20	26,176.20

[1]All sources.
[2]5 months

The gross rental value of the entire Prospect Avenue property would have been between $1,700 and $1,800 per year during the period it was owned by Centrifix, if rented on a commercial basis. Centrifix made no allocation of expenses in connection with the Prospect Avenue property and it could not be determined from its books whether the rental portion of the property produced a net income or a net loss.

During the period April 22, 1950, to December 31, 1954, Management realized gross rental income and net income as follows:

Period covered	Gross rental income	Net income
1950	$ 7,257.17	$ 484.37
1951	14,682.44	1,884.79
1952	17,080.00	1,840.43
1953	19,292.00	3,034.64
1954	19,179.00	3,757.60

OPINION

. . . The only issue is whether the distribution by Centrifix of all the stock of its wholly owned subsidiary, Management, to its principal stockholder, Elliott, qualifies as a nontaxable distribution under section 355. . . .

. . . Respondent agreed in the opening statement of his counsel that the transaction was not used principally as a distribution of earnings and profits of either corporation. Both parties are in agreement that all requirements of section 355(a) are satisfied, except the requirement of subsection (b) relating to the active conduct of businesses.

Respondent does not question the fact that Management had been engaged in the real estate rental business from the date the Payne Avenue property was conveyed to it in April of 1950 to the date of distribution of its stock to Elliott on December 15, 1954, a period of less than 5 years, but does contend that such business had not been actively conducted by either Centrifix or Management prior to April of 1950, so that the 5-year active conduct of business requirement of subsection (b) was not satisfied. Respondent, therefore, determined that the distribution, to the extent that it exceeded basis, was taxable to Elliott as a capital gain, Centrifix having had no earnings or profits at the time of the distribution.

Petitioners contend that all the requirements of subsection (b), including the 5-year active conduct of the real estate rental business, were satisfied. So we are concerned only with whether the requirements of subsection (b) relating to active conduct of businesses are satisfied.

Subsection (b) of section 355 subjects the nonrecognition of gain or loss to a shareholder provided in subsection (a) to certain conditions. One of those conditions is that the distributing corporation and the controlled corporation are engaged immediately after the distribution in the active conduct of a trade or business. A corporation may be regarded as engaged in the active conduct of a trade or business only if, inter alia, "such trade or business has been actively conducted throughout the 5-year period ending on the date of the distribution." See sec. 355(b)(2)(B). Respondent concedes that Management was engaged in the real estate rental business immediately after the distribution, but argues that it was not actively engaged in that business for a total of 5 years prior to the distribution.

Management was not incorporated until April 22, 1950. The Payne Avenue property was acquired by Centrifix at some time during 1950 and was transferred to Management in exchange for its stock. This stock was distributed to Elliott on December 15, 1954. Obviously, Management did not actively conduct and could not have actively conducted any business for 5 years prior to the distribution since it had been in existence for less than 5 years prior to December 15, 1954. Thus, the 5-year requirement of section 355(b)(2)(B) is not satisfied by the activities of Management alone, and cannot be satisfied under any circumstances in this case unless Centrifix actively conducted the same business for a period of at least 4½ months prior to the transfer of the Payne Avenue property to Management, and unless such a period of operation by Centrifix can be added to the period that Management conducted the business in order to satisfy the above requirement. We will assume for the purpose of further discussion that two such periods may be added together.

The issue then becomes whether Centrifix actively conducted a real estate rental business within the meaning of section 355(b) for a period of time prior to the formation of Management in 1950.

. . . Centrifix purchased an old house with a carriage house in the rear located on Prospect Avenue in Cleveland, Ohio, in 1946. Centrifix occupied about half the space in this property as its office and shop and rented the balance of the property to various tenants from the time it was acquired until it was sold in 1950. The gross rentals received did not exceed $780 per year in any of these years, which sum represented about 40 percent of the rental value of the entire property, based on an 8 percent gross return on the cost of the property. No allocation was made on the books of the company of that portion of the expenses attributable to the rented portion of the property, and there is no evidence with respect to the net income or loss attributable to that portion of the property.

. . . The gross rental income represented a very small part of the total gross income of Centrifix. There is no evidence of any specific activity on the part of the management of Centrifix in renting this property and no evidence that Centrifix ever engaged in any other real estate rental activities.

When the Prospect Avenue property was sold in 1950 and the new Payne Avenue property acquired, the new property was put in the name of the newly formed subsidiary corporation, Management, which thereafter leased about one-half of the new property to Centrifix, and the balance to other tenants. Management did not engage in any other business activities and Centrifix continued in the engineering business.

On this evidence we are not convinced that prior to 1950 Centrifix could be considered to have been actively conducting the same business subsequently conducted by Management within the meaning of section 355(b). What constitutes a trade or business is not defined in section 355 or anywhere else in the Internal Revenue Code. This Court held in John D. Fackler, 45 B.T.A. 708 (1941), *aff'd*, 133 F.2d 509 (C.A. 6), that where the owner of depreciable property devotes it to rental purposes and exclusively to the production of taxable income, the property is used by him in a trade or business and depreciation is allowable thereon. Since the *Fackler* case, we have also held that a single piece of rental property constitutes property used in a trade or business so as to be excluded from the definition of "capital assets" regardless of whether taxpayer was engaged in any other trade or business, Leland Hazard, 7 T.C. 372 (1946), and in Anders I. Lagreide, 23 T.C. 508 (1954), that real estate devoted to rental purposes constitutes use of the property in trade or business for purposes of determining operating loss carrybacks regardless of whether it is the only property so used, without too much inquiry into the activity of the taxpayer in renting and managing the property. . . . However, the *Fackler, Hazard*, and *Lagreide* cases are not authority for holding that the incidental rental of that portion of real estate used in a trade or business which is not needed for the principal business constitutes the active conduct of a rental business within the meaning of section 355(b). . . . By this we do not mean to imply that rental of a substantial part of property occupied in part by the owner for the conduct of its principal business cannot qualify as the active conduct of a trade or business within the meaning of section 355(b). But in section 355, we are concerned with the *active conduct of a trade or business*, and we must examine that phraseology in the light of the purpose for which it is used in this particular section of the Code. . . .

This provision was a part of section 353 of the Revenue Act of 1954 as originally introduced in the House of Representatives (H.R. 8300, 83d Cong., 2d Sess.). That section had no requirement relative to the active conduct of a trade or business either before or after the distribution. The Senate Finance Committee rewrote this provision as section 355 of its version of the bill, to introduce the requirement of active conduct of a trade or business both before and after the distribution, the stated purpose for the 5-year predistribution active conduct of a trade or business requirement being to provide a safeguard against avoidance not contained in the present law. See S. Rept. No. 1622, 83d Cong., 2d Sess., p. 50. The Senate thereby chose the

5-year active conduct of a trade or business limitation as one method of safeguarding against tax avoidance rather than a 10-year post-distribution penalty provision contained in the House version of the bill. The House accepted the Senate version but with the understanding that a trade or business which had been actively conducted throughout the 5-year period described would meet the requirements even though such trade or business underwent change during the 5-year period, such as an addition of new or the dropping of old products, changes in production capacity, and the like, provided the changes were not of such a character as to constitute the acquisition of a new or different business. See H. Rept. No. 2543, 83d Cong., 2d Sess., pp. 37-38.

This requirement in section 355(b) therefore necessitates an examination of the activities of the parent and subsidiary corporations in each of the two or more businesses conducted to determine whether this requirement is satisfied in each individual case. We do not think a mere passive receipt of income from the use of property which is used in the principal trade or business and which is only incidental to, or an incidental use of a part of property used primarily in, the principal business would constitute the active conduct of a trade or business within the meaning of section 355(b) of the Code, whether or not such use of property might constitute a trade or business within the meaning of other sections of the Code.

The Commissioner of Internal Revenue has defined a trade or business for purposes of section 355, in section 1.355-1(c), Income Tax Regs., as consisting of a "specific existing group of activities being carried on for the purpose of earning income or profit from only such group of activities, and the activities included in such group must include every operation which forms a part of, or a step in, the process of earning income or profit from such group. Such group of activities ordinarily must include the collection of income and payment of expenses." . . .

In this case the evidence does not support a conclusion that Centrifix was ever actively conducting a real estate rental business within the meaning of section 355. . . .

Why Centrifix did not hold the stock of Management for 4 or 5 additional months to complete the 5-year period prior to distributing Management's stock is not our concern. The fact is that Management had not been actively conducting its trade or business for a period of 5 years at the time of distribution, and we cannot find that Centrifix was actively conducting the same business within the meaning of section 355 prior to the formation of Management. The transaction therefore failed to qualify as a tax-free distribution under section 355, and the distribution was taxable as determined by respondent. . . .

Decision will be entered for the respondent.

NOTES

1. Would the House proposal in 1954 (page 691 supra) have been a better approach to permitting business readjustments on a tax-free basis while taxing bail-outs? Why? Note the attempt in Treas. Reg. §1.355-4 to give content and some measure of certainty to the phrase "active conduct of a trade or business." Would the House's idea of a bail-out period have been preferable?

2. In 1990 X incorporates Y Corporation to conduct the wholesale and retail plumbing fixture businesses that he has conducted as an individual since 1982. He soon finds it impracticable to run both businesses under one corporate roof. Must he wait five years from incorporation to spin off one of the businesses on a tax-free basis? See §355(b)(2)(C).

In W. E. Gabriel Fabrication Co., 42 T.C. 545 (1964), the taxpayer and his brother, owners of 70 percent of A Corporation, had a falling out and wanted to separate business interests without waiting the 14 months necessary for the expiration of five years. Corporation A therefore "loaned" taxpayer the assets which, 14 months later, were transferred to a new subsidiary and split off to taxpayer. The Tax Court held the distribution tax-free under §355, and the Commissioner has acquiesced (see 1965-2 C.B. 5).

3. In King v. Commissioner, 458 F.2d 245 (6th Cir. 1972), spun-off subsidiaries were originally formed for the purpose of constructing truck terminal facilities and leasing them to their parent corporation on a net lease. The leasing activity was held to constitute the active conduct of a trade or business. But see Rafferty v. Commissioner, 452 F.2d 767, 772 (1st Cir. 1971), stating the active business test as follows: "It is our view that in order to be an active trade or business under §355 a corporation must engage in entrepreneurial endeavors of such a nature and to such an extent as to qualitatively distinguish its operations from mere investments. Moreover, there should be objective indicia of such corporate operations." A subsidiary whose sole activity was holding real estate leased to its parent was ruled not to satisfy these requirements. See Rev. Rul. 73-236, 1973-1 C.B. 183; Rev. Rul. 73-237, 1973-1 C.B. 185.

Rev. Rul. 79-394, 1979-2 C.B. 141, holds that in order to qualify as an active trade or business under §355, a corporation engaged in leasing real estate must demonstrate considerable day-to-day management and operational activity sufficient to distinguish such conduct from passive investment in real estate. A corporation's lack of salaried employees (the corporation reimbursed a sister corporation for the use of its employees) does not result in its failure to meet the "active trade or business" requirement. Rev. Rul. 80-181, 1980-2 C.B. 121 ruled that the active trade or business requirement is satisfied even though a corporation does not reimburse another corporation for the use of its employees and officers in the conduct of the former's real estate activities. The non-reimbursement, the Service says, should be dealt with under §482 and not by disqualification under §355. See Rev. Rul. 73-236, 1973-1 C.B. 183; Rev. Rul. 73-237, 1973-1 C.B. 185.

See Rev. Rul. 86-125, 1986-2 C.B. 57, in which the Service ruled that the active business requirement under §355(b) is not met with regard to a rental office building if the building is managed by an unrelated real estate management company acting as an independent contractor. See also Rev. Rul. 86-126, 1986-2 C.B. 58, in which the Service likewise found that the active business requirement was not met where a corporation leased farmland to tenant farmers who planted, raised, harvested, and sold their crops with limited involvement with the corporation.

4. How are earnings and profits to be allocated between the distributing and controlled corporations after a tax-free corporate division under §355? See §312(h) and Treas. Reg. §1.312-10. See also Bennett v. United States, 427 F.2d 1202 (Ct. Cl. 1970).

Does Treas. Reg. §1.312-10 provide for a sensible allocation? In 1984, Congress instructed the Treasury to promulgate regulations for the allocation of earnings and profits in "C" and nondivisive "D" reorganizations. The legislative commentary states that under the regulations the consequences of a "C" or nondivisive "D" reorganization followed by a distribution should generally be the same as the consequences of an "A" merger preceded by a distribution. "In this regard, the Treasury might reconsider its regulations relating to allocations of earnings and profits in transactions under section 355." H.R. Rep. No. 861, 98th Cong., 2d Sess. 846 (1984).

COADY v. COMMISSIONER

33 T.C. 771 (1960), *aff'd per curiam*, 289 F.2d 490 (6th Cir. 1961)

OPINION

TIETJENS, Judge. . . . The issue for decision is whether the transfer by the Christopher Construction Company of a portion of its assets to E.P. Coady and Co. in exchange for all of the Coady Company's stock, and the subsequent distribution by the Christopher Company of such Coady stock to petitioner in exchange for his Christopher stock, constituted a distribution of stock qualifying for tax-free treatment on the shareholder level under the provisions of section 355. . . .

Christopher Construction Co., an Ohio corporation, is now engaged, and for more than 5 years prior to November 15, 1954, was engaged, in the active conduct of a construction business primarily in and around Columbus, Ohio. In an average year the Christopher Company undertook approximately 6 construction contracts, no one of which lasted for more than 2 years. Its gross receipts varied between $1,500,000 and $2,000,000 per year.

At its central office . . . , the Christopher Company kept its books of account, paid its employees, prepared bids for its jobs, and, excepting minor amounts of tools and supplies, made its purchases. In addition, it maintained temporary field offices at each jobsite. It also maintained a central repair and storage depot for its equipment. Equipment in use on particular jobs was kept at the jobsite until work was terminated.

Then, it would either be returned to the central depot or moved to another jobsite.

At all times material hereto, the stock of the Christopher Company was owned by M. Christopher and the petitioner. For a number of years, petitioner owned 35 per cent of that stock and Christopher owned 65 per cent. However, on April 19, 1954, petitioner purchased 15 per cent of the total stock from Christopher. From that date until November 15, 1954, each owned 50 per cent of the company's stock.

Sometime prior to November 15, 1954, differences arose between the petitioner and Christopher. As a result, they entered into an agreement for the division of the Christopher Company into two separate enterprises. Pursuant to that agreement, the Christopher Company, on November 15, 1954, organized E.P. Coady and Co., to which it transferred the following assets, approximating one half the Christopher Company's total assets:

A contract for the construction of a sewage disposal plant at Columbus, Ohio, dated June 1, 1954.

A part of its equipment.

A part of its cash, and certain other items.

In consideration for the receipt of these assets, E.P. Coady and Co. transferred all of its stock to the Christopher Company. The Christopher Company retained the following assets, which were of the same type as those transferred to E.P. Coady and Co.:

A contract for a sewage treatment plant in Charleston, West Virginia.

A part of its equipment.

A part of its cash.

Immediately thereafter, the Christopher Company distributed to the petitioner all of the stock of E.P. Coady and Co. held by it in exchange for all of the stock of the Christopher Company held by petitioner. The fair market value of the stock of E.P. Coady and Co. received by petitioner was $140,000. His basis in the Christopher Company stock surrendered was $72,500.

Since the distribution, both E.P. Coady and Co. and the Christopher Company have been actively engaged in the construction business.

On their 1954 Federal income tax return, petitioner and his wife reported no gain or loss on the exchange of the Christopher Company stock for the stock of E.P. Coady and Co.

Respondent determined that petitioner realized a capital gain on that exchange in the amount of $67,500. . . .

Petitioner contends that the distribution to him of the E.P. Coady and Co. stock qualified for tax-free treatment under the provisions of section 355 . . . arguing that it was received pursuant to a distribution of a controlled corporation's stock within the meaning of that section.

Respondent on the other hand maintains petitioner's receipt of the Coady stock did not fall within those distributions favored by section 355, inasmuch as the 5-year active business requirements of 355(b) were not met. More particularly he argues that section 355 does not apply to the separation of a "single business"; and, inasmuch as the Christopher Company was engaged in only one trade or business (construction contracting) the gain realized by petitioner upon receipt of the Coady stock was taxable. As authority for his position respondent points to [Treas. Reg. §1.355-1(a)] . . . which expressly provides that section 355 does not apply to the division of a single business.

Conceding that the Christopher Company was engaged in a "single business" immediately prior to the instant transaction, petitioner contends that the regulations, insofar as they limit the applicability of section 355 to divisions of only those corporations which have conducted two or more separate and distinct businesses for a 5-year period, are without support in the law, are without justification, are unreasonable and arbitrary, and therefore are invalid.

Thus, the issue is narrowed to the question of whether the challenged portion of the regulations constitutes a valid construction of the statute, or whether it is unreasonable and plainly inconsistent therewith. . . . [T]his appears to be a case of first impression. . . .

Section 355 . . . represents the latest of a series of legislative enactments designed to deal with the tax effect upon shareholders of various corporate separations. Where the 1939 Code contained three sections, 112(b)(3), 112(b)(11), and 112(g)(1)(D), which controlled the tax impact of these exchanges, present law groups the statutory requirements into two sections, 355 and 368(c). A careful reading of section 355, as well as the Finance Committee report which accompanied its enactment, reveals no language, express or implied, denying tax-free treatment at the shareholder level to a transaction, otherwise qualifying under section 355, on the grounds that it represents the division or separation of a "single" trade or business.

In general, section 355(a) prescribes the form in which a qualifying transaction must be cast, providing that a divisive distribution will not give rise to taxable gain or loss if: (1) The distributing corporation distributes stock or securities of a corporation of which it has, immediately prior to the distribution, 80 per cent control as defined in section 368(c); (2) the distribution is not principally a device for distributing earnings and profits of either the distributing or controlled corporations; (3) the 5-year active business requirements of 355(b) are satisfied; and (4) the distributing corporation distributes either all its stock and securities in the controlled corporation, or so much thereof as constitutes control, as defined in 368(c), and retention of the balance is shown not to be in pursuance of a plan having as one of its principal purposes tax avoidance. The distribution itself must be either to a shareholder with respect to its stock, or a security holder with respect to its securities. With respect to a distribution of stock, the distribution need not be on a pro rata basis; the shareholder need not surrender stock in the distributing corporation; and the distribution need not have been made in pursuance of a plan of reorganization. However, subsection (a) contains no language which would require that the distributing corporation be engaged in more than one trade or business prior to the distribution.

The active business requirements of 355(b)(1) prohibit the tax-free separation of a corporation into active and inactive entities. Section 355(b)(1)(A) extends the provisions of 355(a) only to those divisive distributions where the distributing corporation and the controlled corporation are engaged immediately after the distribution in the active conduct of a trade or business. In the case of those distributions which involve liquidation of the transferor, 355(b)(1)(B) requires that immediately before the distribution the transferor have no assets other than stock or securities in the controlled corporations, and that immediately thereafter each of the controlled corporations is engaged in the active conduct of a trade or business. Neither 355(b)(1)(A) nor (B) concerns itself with the existence of a plurality of businesses per se; rather both speak in terms of a plurality of corporate entities engaged in the active conduct of *a* trade or business, a distinction we believe to be vital in light of provisions of 355(b)(2).

Section 355(b)(2) details the rules for determining whether a corporation is engaged in the active conduct of a trade or business, and provides that a corporation shall be treated as so engaged, if, and only if: (1) It is engaged in the active conduct of a trade or business, or substantially all its assets consist of stock and securities of a corporation controlled by it immediately after the distribution which is so engaged; (2) such trade or business has been actively conducted throughout the 5- year period ending on the date of the distribution; (3) such trade or business was not acquired within that 5-year period in a transaction in which gain or loss was recognized; and (4) control of a corporation, which at the time of acquisition of control was conducting such trade or business, was not acquired within that 5-year period, or, if acquired within that period, was acquired by reason of a transaction in which no gain or loss was recognized or by reason of such transactions combined with acquisitions made before the beginning of the 5-year period. Again we note the statute avoids the use of the plural when referring to "trade or business," but rather provides that: "[A] corporation shall be treated as engaged in the active conduct of *a* trade or business if and only if . . . it is engaged in the active conduct of *a* trade or business . . . [and] such trade or business has been actively conducted through the 5-year period ending on the date of the distribution." (Emphasis supplied.)

Respondent maintains that a reading of 355(b)(2)(B) in conjunction with the requirement of 355(b)(1) that both "the distributing corporation, *and* the controlled corporation . . . , [be] engaged immediately after the distribution in the active conduct of a trade or business" (emphasis supplied) indicates Congress intended the provisions of the statute to apply only where, immediately after the distribution, there exist two separate and distinct businesses, one operated by the distributing corporation and one operated by the controlled corporation, both of which were actively conducted for the 5-year period immediately preceding the distribution. In our judgment the statute does not support this construction.

As noted, the only reference to plurality appears in section 355(b)(1), and deals with corporate entities, not businesses. Recognizing the divisive nature of the transaction, subsection (b)(1) contemplates that where there was only one corporate entity prior to the various transfers, immediately subsequent thereto, there will be two or more *corporations*. In order to insure that a tax-free separation will involve the separation only of those assets attributable to the carrying on of an active trade or business, and further to prevent the tax-free division of an active corporation into active and inactive entities, (b)(1) further provides that each of the surviving corporations must be engaged in the active conduct of *a* trade or business.

A careful reading of the definition of the active conduct of a trade or business contained in subsection (b)(2) indicates that its function is also to prevent the tax-free separation of *active* and *inactive* assets into *active* and *inactive* corporate entities. This is apparent from the use of the adjective "such," meaning before-mentioned, to modify "trade or business" in subsection (b)(2)(B), thus providing that the trade or business, required by (b)(2)(B) to have had a 5-year active history prior to the distribution, is the same trade or business which (b)(2)(A) requires to be actively conducted immediately after the distribution. Nowhere in (b)(2) do we find, as respondent suggests we should, language denying the benefits of section 355 to the division of a single trade or business.

Nor can respondent derive support for his position by reading subsections (b)(1) and (b)(2) together, inasmuch as the plurality resulting therefrom is occasioned, not by any requirement that there be a multiplicity of businesses, but rather by the divisive nature of the transaction itself: i.e., one corporation becoming two or more corporations. Moreover, from the fact that the statute requires, immediately after the distribution, that the surviving corporations each be engaged in the conduct of a trade or business with an active 5-year history, we do not think it inevitably follows that each such trade or business necessarily must have been conducted on an individual basis throughout the 5-year period. As long as the trade or business which has been divided has been actively conducted for 5 years preceding the distribution, and the resulting businesses (each of which in this case, happens to be half of the original whole) are actively conducted after the division, we are of the opinion that the active business requirements of the statute have been complied with.

Respondent argues his construction of section 355 is confirmed by the report of the Senate Committee on Finance which accompanied the 1954 Internal Revenue Code. He refers us to that portion of the report which provides:

> Present law contemplates that a tax-free separation shall involve only the separation of assets attributable to the carrying on of an active business. Under the House bill, it is immaterial whether the assets are those used in an active business but if investment assets, for example, are separated into a new corporation, any amount received in respect of such an inactive corporation, whether by a distribution from it or by a sale of its stock, would be treated as ordinary income for a period of 10 years from the date of its creation. Your committee returns to existing law in not permitting the tax free separation of an existing corporation into active and inactive entities. It is not believed that the business need for this kind of transaction is sufficiently great to permit a person in a position to afford a 10-year delay in receiving income to do so at capital gain rather than dividend rates. Your committee requires that *both* the business retained by the distributing company and the business of the corporation the stock of which is distributed must have been actively conducted for the 5 years preceding the

distribution, a safeguard against avoidance not contained in existing law. [Emphasis supplied.]

He argues that use of the term "both," with reference to the business retained by the distributing corporation and that operated by the controlled corporation, indicates that Congress intended there be in operation and existence during the 5 years preceding the distribution two or more separate and distinct businesses. We do not agree.

A reading of the quoted section of the report in its entirety reveals that the committee was addressing itself to the nature and the use of the particular assets which were transferred (active v. inactive), rather than to any distinction between one or more businesses. This is obvious when the entire paragraph is considered in the light of its topic sentence. The committee notes that under present law only assets attributable to the carrying on of an active trade or business may be separated tax free. After acknowledging a departure from this requirement in the House bill, the committee disapproves of the position taken by the House, and indicates it is returning to existing law by not permitting the tax-free separation of a corporation into active and inactive entities, and strengthens this provision by requiring that *both* the business retained by the distributing corporation and that of the controlled corporation must have been actively conducted for 5 years preceding the distribution. The excerpt makes no mention of trades or businesses per se. . . .

There being no language, either in the statute or committee report, which denies tax-free treatment under section 355 to a transaction solely on the grounds that it represents an attempt to divide a single trade or business, the Commissioner's regulations which impose such a restriction are invalid, and cannot be sustained. Commissioner v. Acker, 361 U.S. 87 (1959). . . .

Inasmuch as the parties treat the distribution as otherwise qualifying under section 355 for tax-free treatment, and inasmuch as we have found that portion of the regulations denying application of section 355 to the division of a single business to be invalid, we conclude that petitioner properly treated the distribution to him of the stock of E.P. Coady and Co. as a nontaxable transaction.

No evidence having been introduced with respect to the addition to tax under section 294(d)(2) of the 1939 Code, it is sustained subject to our holding on the above issue.

Reviewed by the Court. . . .

Pierce, J., dissents.

Harron, J., dissenting. The petitioner claims that no gain is to be recognized from the distribution of all of the Coady corporation stock in exchange for all of his Christopher corporation stock. In order to obtain such tax-free treatment of the exchange, he relies upon the provisions of section 355. . . . The provisions of section 355 provide exceptions to the rule recognizing gain or loss. In considering whether the transaction in dispute is entitled to the nonrecognition provisions of section 355, we must inquire whether the transaction before us is the kind of transaction that Congress intended to relieve of tax. Cf. Commissioner v. Gregory, 69 F.2d 809, *aff'd*, 293 U.S. 465; and Bazley v. Commissioner, 331 U.S. 737. . . .

Section 355 requires that two tests shall be met to obtain tax-free treatment: (1) The transaction must not be "principally . . . a device for the distribution of the earnings and profits of the distributing corporation." (2) The transaction must satisfy "the requirements of subsection (b) (relating to *active businesses*)." (Emphasis added.) Subsection (b) states the requirements as to "active businesses." It is required by (b)(1)(A) that subsection (a) shall apply only if the distributing corporation, and the controlled corporation, are engaged immediately after the distribution "in the active conduct of a trade or business." That is to say, immediately after the distribution, *both* the distributing corporation and the controlled corporation must be engaged in the active conduct of a trade or business. The punctuation of (b)(1)(A) has meaning. The words, "and the controlled corporation" are set off by commas; the verb, "is engaged," has two singular subjects, "the distributing corporation," and "the controlled corporation." The statute then defines the phrase "active conduct of a trade or business" (subsec. (b)(2)). The definition specifies that the trade or business which is actively conducted immediately after the distribution (referred to in subsection (a) and subsection (b)(1)) must be a trade or business which has been actively conducted throughout a 5-year period ending on the date of distribution. I believe there can be no doubt that since it is required by subsection (b)(1)(A) that *both* the distributing corporation and the controlled corporation must be engaged immediately after the distribution in the active conduct of a trade or business, the meaning of subsection (b)(2)(B) is that *both* the distributing corporation and the controlled corporation must actively conduct a business, respectively, which had been conducted for 5 years prior to the date of the distribution; each corporation must carry on a business after the distribution which had been carried on for 5 years before the distribution. I disagree with the conclusion that the statute does not so require. . . .

. . . Furthermore, I strongly disagree with the view that the purpose of the active business requirements of section 355(b)(1) is limited to the prohibition of a tax-free separation of a corporation into active and inactive entities, and to the prevention of "the tax-free separation of *active* and *inactive* assets into *active* and *inactive* corporate entities." Of course, such results are not allowed by section 355, but that kind of separation is not involved here and the point is not relevant to the issue in this case.

The error which I believe is made here in the construction of subsection (b) of section 355 is found in the failure to agree that the definition of the phrase "active conduct of a trade or business" contained in (b)(2) has reference to "a corporation"; that by reference to (b)(1), "a corporation" must refer to both the distributing corporation and the controlled corporation; and that the first sentence of (b)(2) deals with "a corporation" as a matter of convenience in drafting the definition so as not to engage in repetitions of the words "the distributing corporation" and "the controlled corporation." In this context, I think it is entirely clear that the word "such" in (b)(2)(B) refers back to the active conduct of a trade or business by "a corporation," be the corporation either the distributing corporation or the controlled corporation. . . .

. . . I respectfully dissent.

ATKINS, J., dissenting. I think the majority opinion errs in holding that section 1.355-1 of the Income Tax Regulations . . . is invalid in providing that section 355 does not apply to the division of a single business.

The Supreme Court has many times held that Treasury regulations must be sustained unless unreasonable and plainly inconsistent with the revenue statutes, and that they constitute contemporaneous constructions by those charged with administration of these statutes which should not be overruled except for weighty reasons. Commissioner v. South Texas Lumber Co., 333 U.S. 496. It has also been stated by the Supreme Court that the practical interpretation of an ambiguous or doubtful statute that has been acted upon by officials charged with its administration will not be disturbed except for weighty reasons. Brewster v. Gage, 280 U.S. 327, and cases therein cited.

Section 355 is not clear. It might be susceptible to different interpretations. However, it seems that the interpretation adopted in the regulations is not unreasonable and plainly inconsistent with the statute, specifically section 355(b)(2)(B). This is particularly true if the legislative history of the statutory provision is taken into consideration. See section 353 of the House bill (H.R. 8300), which required that a corporation would be treated as an "inactive corporation" unless separate books and records had been maintained for the business transferred to it. This clearly contemplated the separation of distinct businesses. See H. Rept. No. 1337, 83d Cong., 2d Sess., p. A124. The law as finally adopted did not incorporate this particular requirement that separate books should be kept, but in S. Rept. No. 1622, 83d Cong., 2d Sess., p. 50, it is stated that the changes made by the Senate in existing law correspond substantially to those made in the House bill and, as shown in the quotation from the Senate report, contained in the majority opinion, it was the intention that "both the business retained by the distributing company and the business of the corporation the stock of which is distributed must have been actively conducted for the 5 years preceding the distribution, a safeguard against avoidance not contained in existing law." . . .

Turner, Harron, Opper, and Train, JJ., agree with this dissent.

NOTES

1. Did the Commissioner's solicitude for the revenue lead him to adopt a wholly unreasonable regulation? What potential for tax avoidance did the Commissioner perceive in the *Coady* situation? In Rev. Rul. 75-160, 1975-1 C.B. 112, the Commissioner announced that, pending issuance of revised regulations, the Service would follow *Coady* and *Marett* on the issue of active trade or business. New Treas. Reg. §§1.355-1 to 1.355-4 were made effective on January 5, 1989. The Treasury's current position on the issue in *Coady* is reflected in §1.355-1(a).

2. In Estate of Lockwood v. Commissioner, 350 F.2d 712 (8th Cir. 1965), the issue was whether the five-year rule was satisfied when a "D" reorganization separated the Maine sales organization from the midwestern-based parent only three years after the Maine business was actively conducted. The court held that, under *Coady*, the question is whether the two corporations existing after the distribution are doing the same type of work and using the same type of assets as before in the original business, without reference to geographic area. Section 355(b)(2) was held satisfied.

3. Suppose a restaurant chain opens a new restaurant location, deducts the initial operating losses incurred in establishing the new location, reduces its earnings and profits by its losses, and then separately incorporates the new restaurant and distributes the stock to its shareholders. Is the distribution tax-free? Why?

REVENUE RULING 59-400
1959-2 C.B. 114

Advice has been requested whether a distribution of stock by a corporation engaged in the hotel and real estate business qualifies under the nontaxable provisions of section 355 of the Internal Revenue Code of 1954.

M corporation was engaged in two businesses, operating a hotel and renting improved real estate (both commercial and residential). The hotel business was started upon organization in 1920 and has been actively conducted up to the present time. In 1934, M corporation also entered into the rental real estate business when it purchased property, constructed a garage and automobile agency facilities thereon and rented it to a dealer. In the intervening years, it acquired other rental properties which it has continued to operate. In 1954, the hotel had a fair market value of 550x dollars and a net book value of 350x dollars. The rental properties had a fair market value of 350x dollars and a net book value of 167x dollars.

During the five-year period commencing with 1954, the operation of the hotel business resulted in earnings, after taxes, of 240x dollars, and the operation of the real estate business resulted in earnings of approximately 75x dollars. In 1958, a new rental office building was built for 400x dollars, some 175x dollars thereof being provided by loans from banks. At the beginning of 1959, the hotel business was placed in a new corporation N, and the stock thereof distributed to the shareholders of M on a pro rata basis. N corporation received the hotel, plus certain receivables and other hotel business assets. M corporation retained the real estate liabilities and assets, which at that time had a net book value of 372x dollars and a fair market value of 705x dollars.

Section 355 of the Code states, in part, that in order for a distribution of stock to qualify under the nontaxable provisions of such section, each of the corporations involved must be engaged in a trade or business which has been actively conducted throughout the five-year period ending on the date of distribution, and that the transaction must not be used principally as a device to distribute the earnings and profits of either corporation.

The purpose behind the five-year limitation of section 355 is to prevent the corporate earnings of one business from being drawn off for such a period and put into a new business and thereby, through the creation of a marketable enterprise, convert what would normally have been dividends into capital assets that are readily saleable by the shareholders.

It is the position of the Internal Revenue Service that where a corporation which is devoted to one type of business also engages in the rental business, and substantial acquisitions of new rental property are made within the five-year period preceding the separation of these businesses, a "spin-off" transaction will not qualify under section 355 unless it can be shown that the property acquisitions were substantially financed out of the earnings of the rental business and not out of the earnings of the other business.

From the facts presented herein, it is readily apparent that there has been a very substantial increase in the rental properties subsequent to 1954, primarily as a result of the addition of the large office building in 1958. Further, it is also apparent that, viewing the transaction most favorably to the taxpayer, earnings properly attributable to the hotel business, in the amount of approximately 150x dollars, have been employed in increasing the real estate business. In view of this substantial financing out of the earnings of the hotel business, it is held that the distribution of the stock of N corporation to the shareholders of M corporation will not qualify as a nontaxable distribution under section 355 of the Code.

NOTE

How were corporate earnings "drawn-off . . . and put into a new business"? Note the form in which the reorganization was structured; what purpose was to be achieved by this structure? Is this properly a §355 problem, or should this transaction be approached under §312(h)? See Treas. Reg. §1.312-10(a). Is this a "proper case" for "such other method as may be appropriate under the facts and circumstances . . ."? Even if all the earnings and profits produced by the hotel properties are allocated to N Corporation, will that ensure proper tax treatment when the M stock is sold or M is liquidated? Since it is held that the distribution of N stock does not qualify as a nontaxable distribution under §355, what are the consequences to M, N, and their shareholders?

REVENUE RULING 78-442
1978-2 C.B. 143

Advice has been requested whether the "active trade or business" requirements of section 355(b)(2)(C) of the Internal Revenue Code of 1954 have been satisfied and if so, whether section 355(a)(3) is applicable to the distribution of stock, under the circumstances described below.

X corporation has conducted two active businesses, within the meaning of section 355(b) of the Code, for more than 5 years. X transferred the property of one of the businesses to Y, a newly formed corporation, in exchange for all the stock of Y and the assumption by Y of certain liabilities of X attributable to the business transferred. Thereafter, X distributed all the stock of Y to the shareholders of X in a transaction intended to meet the requirements of sections 368(a)(1)(D) and 355. The transaction was undertaken for valid business purposes and was not used principally as a device to distribute earnings and profits of either X or Y. Immediately after the transaction, the shareholders of X were in control of both X and Y within the meaning of section 368(c). On the date of the transfer, the amount of the liabilities assumed by Y exceeded the total adjusted basis of the property transferred by X but the amount of the liabilities was less than the total fair market value of the transferred property. . . .

In the instant case, section 351 of the Code applies to the transfer, and if the transaction is a reorganization within the meaning of section 368(a)(1)(D), section 361 applies. Therefore, gain will be recognized to X under section 357(c) on the transfer of property to Y and the assumption by Y of the liabilities of X.

The specific question is whether the gain required to be recognized under section 357(c) of the Code prevents Y from satisfying the trade or business test of sections 355(b)(1)(A) and (b)(2)(C).

The rules of section 355(b)(2)(C) of the Code are intended to prevent the acquisition of a trade or business by the distributing or the controlled corporation from an outside party in a taxable transaction within 5 years of a distribution by the distributing corporation of the stock of a controlled corporation in a transaction to which section 355 would otherwise apply. It was not intended to apply to an acquisition of a trade or business by the controlled corporation from the distributing corporation. Therefore, the acquisition by Y of an active business from X in exchange for Y stock does not violate the provisions of section 355(b)(2)(C), even though gain is recognized to X on the transaction by reason of section 357(c).

Likewise, for the same reasons, section 355(a)(3) of the Code is not applicable to the distribution of the Y stock by X. Section 355(a)(4) provides that for purposes of section 355 (other than section 355(a)(1)(D)) and so much of section 356 as relates to this section, stock of a controlled corporation acquired by the distributing corporation by reason of any transaction which occurs within 5 years of the distribution of such stock and in which gain or loss was recognized in whole or in part, shall not be treated as stock of such controlled corporation, but as other property.

Accordingly, since the active business acquired by Y had been actively conducted by X for more than 5 years prior to the distribution of the Y stock to the shareholders of X, the requirements of section 355(b)(2)(C) of the Code are satisfied. Since all the other requirements of section 355 are met, the transaction qualifies as a reorganization within the meaning of section 368(a)(1)(D), and no gain or loss will be recognized to (and no amount will be includible in the income of) the X shareholders under section 355(a)(1) on the distribution of the Y stock to them.

REVENUE RULING 89-37
1989-11 I.R.B. 4

... A corporation purchased all of the stock of another corporation in a transaction in which gain or loss was recognized. Two years later, the acquired corporation distributed the stock of its wholly owned subsidiary, whose stock it had acquired more than five years before that time, to the acquiring corporation. The distribution fails to meet the active trade or business requirement of section 355(b)(2)(D) of the Code, as amended by the Revenue Act of 1987 and the Technical and Miscellaneous Revenue Act of 1988. ...

PURPOSE

This revenue ruling obsoletes Rev. Rul. 74-5, 1974-1 C.B. 82, in light of the amendment of section 355(b)(2)(D) of the Internal Revenue Code by section 10223(b) of the Revenue Act of 1987 ... and section 2004(k)(1) of the Technical and Miscellaneous Revenue Act of 1988 (TMRA). ...

LAW AND ANALYSIS

Rev. Rul. 74-5 involved a distribution of the stock of a controlled corporation, Y, by a distributing corporation, X, to X's parent corporation, P, 2 years after P acquired the stock of X for cash in a transaction in which gain or loss was recognized ("first distribution"). At the time of the first distribution, X had owned the stock of Y for more than 5 years. P subsequently distributed the stock of Y to its shareholders at a time when it had not owned the stock of Y directly or indirectly through X for a 5-year period prior to the distribution ("second distribution"). Rev. Rul. 74-5 considered whether the requirements of section 355(b)(2)(D) of the Code were met with regard to each of the distributions, since P acquired control of X directly and Y indirectly in a transaction in which gain or loss was recognized within the 5-year period prior to each of the distributions.

Section 355(b)(2)(D) of the Code, prior to its amendment by the Act and TMRA, provided that control of a corporation that, at the time of acquisition of control, was conducting an active trade or business, must not have been acquired directly (or through one or more corporations) by "another corporation" within the 5-year period described in section 355(b)(2)(B), or if so acquired by "another corporation" within such period, such control must not have been acquired by reason of transactions in which gain or loss was recognized in whole or in part, or acquired by reason of such transactions combined with acquisitions before the beginning of such period. Rev. Rul. 74-5 reasoned that the purpose of section 355(b)(2)(D) was to prevent a distributing corporation from accumulating excess funds to purchase the stock of a corporation having an active business and then immediately distributing such stock to its shareholders. Rev. Rul. 74-5 concluded that the first distribution was not the type of transaction to which section 355(b)(2)(D) of the Code was directed because P was merely the shareholder receiving the distribution and not the distributing corporation or the controlled corporation and, therefore, the ruling held that section 355(b)(2)(D) was inapplicable to the first distribution. Rev. Rul. 74-5 further held that the second distribution did not meet the requirements of section 355(b)(2)(D) because the distributing corporation, P, indirectly acquired control of the controlled corporation, Y, through another corporation, X, in a transaction in which gain or loss was recognized within the 5-year period prior to the distribution.

Section 10223(b) of the Act and section 2004(k)(1) of TMRA amended section 355(b)(2)(D) of the Code to provide that a corporation is engaged in the active conduct of a trade or business only if control of a corporation which (at the time of acquisition of control) was conducting such trade or business (i) was not acquired by any distributee corporation directly (or through one or more corporations, whether through the distributing corporation or otherwise) within the 5-year period ending on the date of the distribution, and was not acquired by the distributing corporation directly (or through one or more corporations) within such period, or (ii) was so acquired by any such corporation within such period, but, in each case in which such control was so acquired, it was so acquired only by reason of transactions in which gain or loss was not recognized in whole or in part, or only by reason of such transactions combined with acquisitions before the beginning of such period.

Under section 355(b)(2)(D) of the Code, as amended by section 10223(b) of the Act and section 2004(k)(1) of TMRA, the first distribution described in Rev. Rul. 74-5 is now a transaction described in section 355(b)(2)(D). Therefore, because Y was acquired by a distributee corporation within the meaning of section 355(b)(2)(D) in a transaction in which gain or loss was recognized within the 5-year period prior to the distribution, the first distribution fails to meet the active trade or business requirement of section 355(b)(2)(D).

The holding as to the second distribution in Rev. Rul. 74-5 has not been affected by the Act or by TMRA.

3. *"Device" for Siphoning Earnings and Profits*

COMMISSIONER v. MORRIS TRUST
367 F.2d 794 (4th Cir. 1966)

Before Haynsworth, Chief Judge, J. Spencer Bell, Circuit Judge, and Stanley, District Judge.

HAYNSWORTH, Chief Judge. Its nubility impaired by the existence of an insurance department it had operated for many years, a state bank divested itself of that business before merging with a national bank. The divestiture was in the form of a traditional "spin-off," but, because it was a preliminary step to the merger of the banks, the Commissioner treated their receipt of stock of the insurance company as ordinary income to the stockholders of the state bank. We agree with the Tax Court, that gain to the stockholders of the state bank was not recognizable under §355 of the 1954 Code.

In 1960, a merger agreement was negotiated by the directors of American Commercial Bank, a North Carolina corporation with its principal office in Charlotte, and Security National Bank of Greensboro, a national bank. American was the product of an earlier merger of American Trust Company and a national bank, the Commercial National Bank of Charlotte. This time, however, though American was slightly larger than Security, it was found desirable to operate the merged institutions under Security's national charter, after changing the name to North Carolina National Bank. It was contemplated that the merged institution would open branches in other cities.

For many years, American had operated an insurance department. This was a substantial impediment to the accomplishment of the merger, for a national bank is prohibited from operating an insurance department except in towns having a population of not more than 5000 inhabitants. To avoid a violation of the national banking laws, therefore, and to accomplish the merger under Security's national charter, it was prerequisite that American rid itself of its insurance business.

The required step to make it nubile was accomplished by American's organization of a new corporation, American Commercial Agency, Inc., to which American transferred its insurance business assets in exchange for Agency's stock which was immediately distributed to American's stockholders. At the same time, American paid a cash dividend fully taxable to its stockholders. The merger of the two banks was then accomplished.

Though American's spin-off of its insurance business was a "D" reorganization, as defined in §368(a)(1), provided the distribution of Agency's stock qualified for non-recognition of gain under §355, the

Commissioner contended that the active business requirements of §355(b)(1)(A) were not met, since American's banking business was not continued in unaltered corporate form. He also finds an inherent incompatibility in substantially simultaneous divisive and amalgamating reorganizations.

Section 355(b)(1)(A) requires that both the distributing corporation and the controlled corporation be "engaged immediately after the distribution in the active conduct of a trade or business." There was literal compliance with that requirement, for the spin-off, including the distribution of Agency's stock to American's stockholders, preceded the merger. The Commissioner asks that we look at both steps together, contending that North Carolina National Bank was not the distributing corporation and that its subsequent conduct of American's banking business does not satisfy the requirement.

A brief look at an earlier history may clarify the problem.

Initially, the active business requirement was one of several judicial innovations designed to limit nonrecognition of gain to the implicit, but unelucidated, intention of earlier Congresses.

Nonrecognition of gain in "spin-offs" was introduced by the Revenue Act of 1924. Its §203(b)(3), as earlier Revenue Acts, provided for nonrecognition of gain at the corporate level when one corporate party to a reorganization exchanged property solely for stock or securities of another, but it added a provision in subsection (c) extending the nonrecognition of gain to a stockholder of a corporate party to a reorganization who received stock of another party without surrendering any of his old stock. Thus, with respect to the nonrecognition of gain, treatment previously extended to "split-offs" was extended to the economically indistinguishable "spin-off."

The only limitation upon those provisions extending nonrecognition to spin-offs was contained in §203(h) and (i) defining reorganizations. The definition required that immediately after the transfer, the transferor or its stockholders or both be in control of the corporation to which the assets had been transferred, and "control" was defined as being the ownership of not less than eighty per cent of the voting stock and eighty per cent of the total number of shares of all other classes of stock.

With no restriction other than the requirement of control of the transferee, these provisions were a fertile source of tax avoidance schemes. By spinning-off liquid assets or all productive assets, they provided the means by which ordinary distributions of earnings could be cast in the form of a reorganization within their literal language.

The renowned case of Gregory v. Helvering, 293 U.S. 465, 55 S. Ct. 266, 79 L. Ed. 596, brought the problem to the Supreme Court. [The recitation of the *Gregory* facts is omitted.]*

*See page 545 supra. — ED.

The Supreme Court found the transaction quite foreign to the congressional purpose. It limited the statute's definition of a reorganization to a reorganization of a corporate business or businesses motivated by a business purpose. It was never intended that Averill engage in any business, and it had not. Its creation, the distribution of its stock and its liquidation, the court concluded, was only a masquerade for the distribution of an ordinary dividend, as, of course, it was.

In similar vein, it was held that the interposition of new corporations of fleeting duration, though the transactions were literally within the congressional definition of a reorganization and the language of a nonrecognition section, would not avail in the achievement of the tax avoidance purpose when it was only a mask for a transaction which was essentially and substantively the payment of a liquidating dividend, a sale for cash, or a taxable exchange.

Such cases exposed a number of fundamental principles which limited the application of the nonrecognition of gain sections of the reorganization provisions of the Code. Mertens defines them in terms of permanence, which encompasses the concepts of business purpose and a purpose to continue an active business in altered corporate form. As concomitants to the primary principle and supplements of it, there were other requirements that the transferor, or its stockholders, retain a common stock interest and that a substantial part of the value of the properties transferred be represented by equity securities.

Underlying such judicially developed rules limiting the scope of the nonrecognition provisions of the Code, was an acceptance of a general congressional purpose to facilitate the reorganization of businesses, not to exalt economically meaningless formalisms and diversions through corporate structures hastily created and as hastily demolished. Continuation of a business in altered corporate form was to be encouraged, but immunization of taxable transactions through the interposition of short-lived, empty, corporate entities was never intended and ought not to be allowed.

While these judicial principles were evolving and before the Supreme Court declared itself in Gregory v. Helvering, an alarmed Congress withdrew nonrecognition of gain to a stockholder receiving securities in a spin-off. It did so by omitting from the Revenue Act of 1934, a provision comparable to §203(c) of the Revenue Act of 1924.

Nonrecognition of gain to the stockholder in spin-off situations, however, was again extended by §317(a) of the Revenue Act of 1951, amending the 1939 Code by adding §112(b)(11). This time, the judicially developed restrictions upon the application of the earlier statutes were partially codified. Nonrecognition of gain was extended "unless it appears that (A) any corporation which is a party to such reorganization was not intended to continue the active conduct of a trade or business after such reorganization, or (B) the corporation whose stock is distributed was used principally as a device for the distribution of earnings and profits to the shareholders of any corporation a party to the reorganization."

If this transaction were governed by the 1939 Code, as amended in 1951, the Commissioner would have had the support of a literal reading of the A limitation, for it was not intended that American, in its then corporate form, should continue the active conduct of the banking business. From the prior history, however, it would appear that the intention of the A limitation was to withhold the statute's benefits from schemes of the Gregory v. Helvering type. It effectively reached those situations in which one of the parties to the reorganization was left only with liquid assets not intended for use in the acquisition of an active business or in which the early demise of one of the parties was contemplated, particularly, if its only office was a conduit for the transmission of title. The B limitation was an additional precaution intended to encompass any other possible use of the device for the masquerading of a dividend distribution.

The 1954 Code was the product of a careful attempt to codify the judicial limiting principles in a more particularized form. The congressional particularization extended the principles in some areas, as in the requirement that a business, to be considered an active one, must have been conducted for a period of at least five years ending on the distribution date and must not have been acquired in a taxable transaction during the five- year period.[10] In other areas, it relaxed and ameliorated them, as in its express sanction of non-prorata distributions.[11] While there are such particularized variations, the 1954 Code is a legislative re-expression of generally established principles developed in response to definite classes of abuses which had manifested themselves many years earlier. The perversions of the general congressional purpose and the principles the courts had developed to thwart them, as revealed in the earlier cases, are still an enlightening history with which an interpretation of the reorganization sections of the 1954 Code should be approached.

Section 355(b) requires that the distributing corporation be engaged in the active conduct of a trade or business "immediately after the distribution." This is in contrast to the provisions of the 1951 Act, which, as we have noted, required an intention that the parent, as well as the other corporate parties to the reorganization, continue the conduct of an active business.[12] It is in marked contrast to §355(b)'s

10. Section 355(b)(2).
11. Section 355(a)(2). . . .
12. See, also, the Senate Finance Committee Report explaining §317 of the

highly particularized requirements respecting the duration of the active business prior to the reorganization and the methods by which it was acquired. These contrasts suggest a literal reading of the post-reorganization requirement and a holding that the Congress intended to restrict it to the situation existing "immediately after the distribution."

Such a reading is quite consistent with the prior history. It quite adequately meets the problem posed by the Gregory v. Helvering situation in which, immediately after the distribution, one of the corporations held only liquid or investment assets. It sufficiently serves the requirements of permanence and of continuity, for as long as an active business is being conducted immediately after the distribution, there is no substantial opportunity for the stockholders to sever their interest in the business except through a separable, taxable transaction. If the corporation proceeds to withdraw assets from the conduct of the active business and to abandon it, the Commissioner has recourse to the backup provisions of §355(a)(1)(B) and to the limitations of the underlying principles. At the same time, the limitation, so construed, will not inhibit continued stockholder conduct of the active business through altered corporate form and with further changes in corporate structure, the very thing the reorganization sections were intended to facilitate.

Applied to this case, there is no violation of any of the underlying limiting principles. There was no empty formalism, no utilization of empty corporate structures, no attempt to recast a taxable transaction in nontaxable form and no withdrawal of liquid assets. There is no question but that American's insurance and banking businesses met all of the active business requirements of §355(b)(2). It was intended that both businesses be continued indefinitely, and each has been. American's merger with Security, in no sense, was a discontinuance of American's banking business, which opened the day after the merger with the same employees, the same depositors and customers. There was clearly the requisite continuity of stockholder interest, for American's former stockholders remained in 100% control of the insurance company, while, in the merger, they received 54.385% of the common stock of North Carolina National Bank, the remainder going to Security's former stockholders. There was a strong business purpose for both the spin-off and the merger, and tax avoidance by American's stockholders was neither a predominant nor a subordinate purpose. In short, though both of the transactions be viewed together, there were none of the evils or misuses which the limiting principles and the statutory limitations were designed to exclude.

Revenue Act of 1951. Sen. Rep. No. 781, 82 Cong. 1st Sess., (1951) U.S. Code Congressional and Administrative News, p. 1969.

We are thus led to the conclusion that this carefully drawn statute should not be read more broadly than it was written to deny non-recognition of gain to reorganizations of real businesses of the type which Congress clearly intended to facilitate by according to them nonrecognition of present gain.

The Commissioner, indeed, concedes that American's stockholders would have realized no gain had American not been merged into Security after, but substantially contemporaneously with, Agency's spin-off. Insofar as it is contended that §355(b)(1)(A) requires the distributing corporation to continue the conduct of an active business, recognition of gain to American's stockholders on their receipt of Agency's stock would depend upon the economically irrelevant technicality of the identity of the surviving corporation in the merger. Had American been the survivor, it would in every literal and substantive sense have continued the conduct of its banking business.

Surely, the Congress which drafted these comprehensive provisions did not intend the incidence of taxation to turn upon so insubstantial a technicality. Its differentiation on the basis of the economic substance of transactions is too evident to permit such a conclusion.

This, too, the Commissioner seems to recognize, at least conditionally, for he says that gain to the stockholders would have been recognized even if American had been the surviving corporation. This would necessitate our reading into §355(b)(1)(A) an implicit requirement that the distributing corporation, without undergoing any reorganization whatever, whether or not it resulted in a change in its corporate identity, continue the conduct of its active business.

We cannot read this broader limitation into the statute for the same reasons we cannot read into it the narrower one of maintenance of the same corporate identity. The congressional limitation of the post-distribution active business requirement to the situation existing "immediately after the distribution" was deliberate. Consistent with the general statutory scheme, it is quite inconsistent with the Commissioner's contention.

The requirement of §368(a)(1)(D) that the transferor or its stockholders be in control of the spun-off corporation immediately after the transfer is of no assistance to the Commissioner. It is directed solely to control of the transferee, and was fully met here. It contains no requirement of continuing control of the transferor. Though a subsequent sale of the transferor's stock, under some circumstances, might form the basis of a contention that the transaction was the equivalent of a dividend within the meaning of §355(a)(1)(B) and the underlying principles, the control requirements imply no limitation upon subsequent reorganizations of the transferor.

There is no distinction in the statute between subsequent amalgamating reorganizations in which the stockholders of the spin-off transferor would own 80% or more of the relevant classes of stock of the reorganized transferor, and those in which they would not. The statute draws no line between major and minor amalgamations in prospect at the time of the spin-off. Nothing of the sort is suggested by the detailed control-active business requirements in the five-year predistribution period, for there the distinction is between taxable and nontaxable acquisitions, and a tax free exchange within the five-year period does not violate the active business-control requirement whether it was a major or a minor acquisition. Reorganizations in which no gain or loss is recognized, sanctioned by the statute's control provision when occurring in the five years preceding the spin-off, are not prohibited in the post-distribution period. . . .

Nor can we find elsewhere in the Code any support for the Commissioner's suggestion of incompatibility between substantially contemporaneous divisive and amalgamating reorganizations. The 1954 Code contains no inkling of it; nor does its immediate legislative history. The difficulties encountered under the 1924 Code and its successors, in dealing with formalistic distortions of taxable transactions into the spin-off shape, contain no implication of any such incompatibility. Section 317 of the Revenue Act of 1951 and the Senate Committee Report, to which we have referred, did require an intention that the distributing corporation continue the conduct of its active business, but that transitory requirement is of slight relevance to an interpretation of the very different provisions of the 1954 Code and is devoid of any implication of incompatibility. If that provision, during the years it was in effect, would have resulted in recognition of gain in a spin-off if the distributing corporation later, but substantially simultaneously, was a party to a merger in which it lost its identity, a question we do not decide, it would not inhibit successive reorganizations if the merger preceded the spin-off.

The Congress intended to encourage six types of reorganizations. They are defined in §368 and designated by the letters "A" through "F." The "A" merger, the "B" exchange of stock and the "C" exchange of stock for substantially all of the properties of another are all amalgamating reorganizations. The "D" reorganization is the divisive spin-off, while the "E" and "F" reorganizations, recapitalizations and reincorporations, are neither amalgamating nor divisive. All are sanctioned equally, however. Recognition of gain is withheld from each and successively so. Merger may follow merger, and an "A" reorganization by which Y is merged into X corporation may proceed substantially simultaneously with a "C" reorganization by which X acquires substantially all of the properties of Z and with an "F" reorganization by which X is reincorporated in another state.

The "D" reorganization has no lesser standing. It is on the same plane as the others and, provided all of the "D" requirements are met, is as available as the others in successive reorganizations. . . .

. . . After the merger, North Carolina National Bank was as much American as Security. It was not one or the other, except in the sense of the most technical of legalisms; it was both, and with respect to the Charlotte operation, old American's business, it was almost entirely American. North Carolina National Bank's business in the Charlotte area after the merger was American's business conducted by American's employees in American's banking houses for the service of American's customers. Probably the only change immediately noticeable was the new name.

. . . [I]t is important to the result that, as in every merger, there was substantive continuity of each constituent and its business. In framing the 1954 Code, the Congress was concerned with substance, not formalisms. Its approach was that of the courts in the Gregory v. Helvering series of cases. Ours must be the same. The technicalities of corporate structure cannot obscure the continuity of American's business, its employees, its customers, its locations or the substantive fact that North Carolina National Bank was both American and Security.

A decision of the Sixth Circuit[16] appears to be at odds with our conclusion. In *Curtis*, it appears that one corporation was merged into another after spinning-off a warehouse building which was an unwanted asset because the negotiators could not agree upon its value. The Court of Appeals for the Sixth Circuit affirmed a District Court judgment holding that the value of the warehouse company shares was taxable as ordinary income to the stockholders of the first corporation.

A possible distinction may lie between the spin-off of an asset unwanted by the acquiring corporation in an "A" reorganization solely because of disagreement as to its value and the preliminary spin-off of an active business which the acquiring corporation is prohibited by law from operating. We cannot stand upon so nebulous a distinction, however. We simply take a different view. The reliance in *Curtis* upon the Report of the Senate Committee explaining §317 of the Revenue Act of 1951, quite dissimilar to the 1954 Code, reinforces our appraisal of the relevant materials. . . .

For the reasons which we have canvassed, we think the Tax Court, which had before it the opinion of the District Court in *Curtis*, though not that of the affirming Court of Appeals, correctly decided that American's stockholders realized no recognizable taxable gain upon their receipt in the "D" reorganization of the stock of Agency.

Affirmed.

16. Curtis v. United States, 6 Cir., 336 F.2d 714.

NOTES

1. What is it about the transactions in *Morris Trust* and *Curtis* (cited in the *Morris Trust* opinion at page 716 supra) that gave the Commissioner concern? What are the significance of the inner and outer parenthetical clauses in §355(a)(1)(B)? If you were Government counsel in *Morris Trust*, what argument might you have advanced, based on the inner parenthetical clause? As the taxpayer's counsel, how might you have responded? What decision should a court reach with respect to the applicability of the inner parenthetical clause in cases like *Morris Trust* and *Curtis*? Why? In Rev. Rul. 68-303, 1968-2 C.B. 148, the Commissioner indicated that he would no longer attack the "spin-away" transaction sustained under §355 in *Morris Trust*.

Treas. Reg. §1.355-2(c)(2) now reflects the conclusion that the spin-away is not a "device." See also Rev. Rul. 76-527, noted at page 686 supra; Rev. Rul. 75-406, 1975-2 C.B. 125 (spin-off, followed by statutory merger of former subsidiary into unrelated corporation, was not a "device" since shareholders had a continuing interest in the businesses of the former parent and the former subsidiary).

See Handler, Variations on a Theme: The Disposition of Un-wanted Assets, 35 Tax. L. Rev. 389 (1980); New York State Bar Association, Tax Section, Committee on Reorganizations, Report on the Ancillary Tax Effects of Different Forms of Reorganizations, 34 Tax. L. Rev. 475 (1979).

But cf. Rev. Rul. 70-225, 1970-1 C.B. 80, involving a series of prearranged steps whereby Corporation R transferred assets in exchange for stock in a newly created subsidiary, S; R distributed the S stock to its sole shareholder, A, who exchanged it for some of the stock of an unrelated corporation, T. The Service ruled that the transaction was:

> a series of integrated steps which . . . may not be considered independently of each other. Accordingly, neither R nor . . . A is in control of S after the transfer and the transaction does not constitute a [D reorganization nor a §351 transfer]. Section 368(a)(1)(B) . . . is not applicable to the transaction, since in effect R transferred part of its assets to T in exchange for a part of the T stock, rather than T having acquired all of the stock of a previously existing corporation solely in exchange for its own voting stock.
>
> Accordingly, the receipt by A of the stock of T is not a distribution to which section 355 . . . applies. The fair market value of the stock of T is taxable to A as a distribution by R under section 301. . . . In addition, gain or loss is recognized to R on the transaction.

Compare also Letter Rul. 8821001 (May 27, 1988), in which T, a subsidiary of D, was merged into S1, a subsidiary of F, in exchange for which F stock was given to D. D shareholders who tendered their D stock received F stock. The Service did not consider this a valid reorganization and required the tendering D shareholders to recognize gain. Rev. Rul. 75-406, supra, was distinguished on the ground that in that situation the subsidiary was spun-off and only subsequently did the shareholders vote to merge the former subsidiary into another corporation.

2. Redemption of some shares in one or both surviving corporations will not automatically result in a §355 distribution's being treated as a "device." See Rev. Rul. 78-251, 1978-1 C.B. 89 (cash redemption of target corporation's dissenting shareholders, following spin-away of unwanted subsidiary); Rev. Rul. 77-377, 1977-2 C.B. 111 (redemption of shares in both surviving corporations following split-up, where redemption prior to split-up would have qualified for exchange treatment under §303).

3. Do you agree with the way that §355 is drafted? In this connection consider the history of the spin-off provisions as summarized in *Morris Trust*. What is the relevance of the "active conduct of a trade or business"? Does it reflect the best way to deal with the underlying congressional concern? Cf. Brown, An Approach to Subchapter C, 3 Tax Revision Compendium 1619, 1621-1627 (1959).

4. In Rev. Rul. 64-102, 1964-1 C.B. 136, the issue was whether a nonpro-rata distribution of stock in a subsidiary in exchange for all of certain minority shareholders' stock in the parent was a "device," when shortly before the distribution the parent transferred a sizable amount of cash to the subsidiary in order to equalize the value of the subsidiary's and parent's stock. What result would you expect? Cf. H. Grady Lester, 40 T.C. 947 (1963), where the distributing corporation transferred $200,000 to the controlled corporation. Of that sum $140,000 was used to purchase starting inventory, and the remaining $60,000 was needed to begin business immediately. The court held this was not "principally" a "device," and the Commissioner has acquiesced. 1964-2 C.B. 6.

See also Rev. Rul. 83-114, 1983-2 C.B. 66, in which the parent corporation, P, was required to divest itself of the subsidiary corporation, S, as the result of an antitrust decree. In order to permit S to expand its operations and attract additional investment capital, P canceled a large debt owed to it by S. Although the cancellation resulted in a 100-percent increase in S's net worth, the Service ruled that because the cancellation was for legitimate business reasons the spin-off of S was not a "device." The Service also held that the device restriction was not violated per se merely because an unrelated corporation merged into S after the spin-off.

5. What is the relationship between §355(a)(1)(B) and §356(a)(2)? Should a transaction which is not principally a "device for the dis-

tribution of . . . earnings and profits" be considered "substantially equivalent to a dividend"? See Rev. Rul. 74-516, 1974-2 C.B. 121. That ruling holds that dividend equivalence of a redemption that is a split-off with "boot" must be determined as if the exchanging shareholder had redeemed only the shares attributable to the "boot." Do you agree?

6. See Rev. Rul. 77-335, 1977-2 C.B. 95, holding that the preferred stock of a subsidiary distributed (along with the subsidiary's common stock) in a transaction qualifying under §355 became §306 stock.

7. When Corporation A effects a split-off by distributing all the stock of Corporation B in redemption of a proportionate share of the A shareholders' stock in A, does A recognize gain under §311(b)(1)? Consider the limiting effect to be given the statutory language: "to which subpart A applies." See §§355(c) and 361(c)(4); see also §336(c). Cf. G.C.M. 38882, Tax Notes, Aug. 9, 1982, p. 507.

In Rev. Rul. 86-4, 1986-1 C.B. 174, the Service ruled that the transfer of even a small percentage of investment assets (relative to the other assets transferred to a controlled corporation) prior to the distribution of stock is a factor to be considered in determining whether the transaction is a "device" under §355.

8. See Rev. Proc. 86-41, 1986-2 C.B. 716, amplified by Rev. Proc. 89-28, 1989-15 I.R.B.20. They detail a checklist questionnaire that must be answered in connection with all ruling requests under §355. As revised, the checklist requires taxpayers to submit greater information than before in regard to the active business requirement and business purpose.

4. Distribution of "Control" Stock

REVENUE RULING 63-260
1963-2 C.B. 147

A owned all of the stock of X which owned 70 shares of the stock of Y. A also owned the remaining 30 shares of Y stock directly. A contributed 10 shares of his Y stock to X. Immediately thereafter, X distributed all 80 shares of Y stock now held by it to A.

Held, the distribution by X does not qualify as a nontaxable distribution under the provisions of section 355 of the Internal Revenue Code of 1954, because X did not have "control" of Y within the meaning of section 368(c) of the Code immediately before the distribution except in a transitory and illusory sense.

Section 355 of the Code cannot be made to apply to a transaction in which an immediately preceding contribution to capital by the distributor corporation's shareholder is made solely to attempt to qualify the transaction as a nontaxable distribution under that section.

NOTE

Should §355(b)(2)(D) have wrought a different result? Why? Is Rev. Rul. 63-260 consonant with the statute? What relevance does §318(a)(3)(C) have to this problem?

REVENUE RULING 71-593

1971-2 C.B. 181

Advice has been requested whether section 355 of the Internal Revenue Code of 1954 applies to a distribution of stock under the circumstances described below.

X and Y were corporations engaged in manufacturing. A and B each owned 50 percent of the X stock. A owned 25 percent of the Y stock (its only class of outstanding stock) and X owned 75 percent of the Y stock, which it had owned for more than five years. X and Y have each been engaged in the active conduct of a trade or business for more than five years.

For valid corporate business purposes, within the meaning of section 1.355-2(c) of the Income Tax Regulations, it was decided to separate the ownership of the X and Y stock, with A to own all of the stock of Y, and B to own all of the stock of X. A and B plan to continue the operations of Y and X, respectively.

Pursuant to a plan and in order to make the value of the Y stock to be distributed to A equal in value to the X stock surrendered by A in exchange therefor, X transferred some of its assets to Y in exchange for newly issued stock of Y. The stock of Y received by X was equal in value to the assets transferred by X to Y. As a result of this exchange, X owned 90 percent of the Y stock. As part of the same plan, X then transferred all of its Y stock to A in exchange for all of A's stock of X. After the exchanges, A owned all of the Y stock and B owned all of the X stock.

In view of all the facts and circumstances of the transactions, particularly the fact that the distribution of the Y stock to A in exchange for his stock of X completely terminated his interest in X, it was determined that the transactions were not a device for the distribution of the earnings and profits of X or Y or both. . . .

Revenue Ruling 63-260, C.B. 1963-2, 147, holds, in effect, that the requirement in section 355(a)(1)(A) of the Code that the distributing corporation be in control of the distributed corporation immediately before the distribution is not met where the transaction in which control was obtained was entered into immediately prior to the distribution for the sole purpose of qualifying the distribution under section 355 of the Code.

Two questions are raised by the facts of this case. First, did X have control of Y (immediately before it distributed the Y stock to A) within the meaning of section 355(a)(1)(A) of Code? Secondly, if X did have such control of Y, was that control acquired in a transaction in which no gain or loss was recognized in whole or in part as required by section 355(b)(2)(D) of the Code?

The value of the assets transferred by X to Y was equal to the value of the stock of Y received by X in exchange therefor. Moreover, the transfer by X of a portion of its assets to Y in exchange for additional Y stock was necessary to equalize the values of stocks to be received and surrendered by A. Since this exchange was value-for-value, and since it was necessary to equalize the values of the stocks to be received and surrendered by A, it must be viewed as a meaningful exchange and not as an exchange made solely to attempt to qualify the distribution of Y stock to A as a non-taxable distribution under section 355 of the Code. Consequently, X had control of Y immediately before the distribution of Y stock to A within the meaning of section 355(a)(1)(A) of the Code.

Since X did have control of Y immediately before the distribution of the Y stock to A in exchange for his X stock, and since that control was acquired within the five-year period immediately preceding the distribution, it must be determined whether gain or loss was recognized in whole or in part on the transaction in which X acquired control of Y. If no gain or loss was recognized on that transaction, then the requirements of section 355(b)(2)(D) of the Code were met and section 355 of the Code applies to the distribution of the Y stock by X to A in exchange for his X stock.

Under the facts of this case, the transfer by X of a portion of its assets to Y in exchange for additional stock of Y met all of the requirements of section 368(a)(1)(D) of the Code. As a result, no gain or loss was recognized to X on the exchange by reason of section 361(a) of the Code. Under section 1032 of the Code, no gain or loss was recognized to Y on the receipt of X's assets for its stock. Consequently, no gain or loss was recognized in whole or in part on the transaction and the requirements of section 355(b)(2)(D) of the Code were met.

Accordingly, since all of the requirements of section 355(a) of the Code were met, no gain or loss will be recognized to A (and no amount will be includible in the income of A) upon the receipt of Y stock in exchange for his X stock.

NOTE

Is there an inconsistency between the approach in Rev. Rul. 63-260 and that in Rev. Rul. 71-593 and *Granite Trust* (page 548 supra)? What might the result have been in *Granite Trust* if the sales had been to a majority shareholder?

COMMISSIONER v. GORDON
391 U.S. 83 (1968)

Mr. Justice HARLAN delivered the opinion of the Court.

These cases, involving the interpretation of §355 of the Internal Revenue Code of 1954, have an appropriately complex history.

American Telephone and Telegraph Company (hereafter A.T. & T.) conducts its local communications business through corporate subsidiaries. Prior to July 1, 1961, communications services in California, Oregon, Washington, and Idaho were provided by Pacific Telephone and Telegraph Company (hereafter Pacific). A.T. & T. held about 90% of the common stock of Pacific at all relevant times. The remainder was widely distributed.

Early in 1961, it was decided to divide Pacific into two separate corporate subsidiaries of A.T. & T. The plan was to create a new corporation, Pacific Northwest Bell Telephone Company (hereafter Northwest) to conduct telephone business in Oregon, Washington, and Idaho, leaving the conduct of the California business in the hands of Pacific. To this end, Pacific would transfer all its assets and liabilities in the first three States to Northwest, in return for Northwest common stock and debt paper. Then, Pacific would transfer sufficient Northwest stock to Pacific shareholders to pass control of Northwest to the parent company, A.T. & T.

Pacific had, however, objectives other than fission. It wanted to generate cash to pay off existing liabilities and meet needs for capital, but not to have excess cash left over. It also feared that a simple distribution of the Northwest stock would encounter obstacles under California corporation law. Consequently, the "Plan for Reorganization" submitted to Pacific's shareholders on February 27, 1961, had two special features. It provided that only about 56% of the Northwest common stock would be offered to Pacific shareholders immediately after the creation of Northwest. It also provided that, instead of simply distributing Northwest stock pro rata to shareholders, Pacific would distribute to its shareholders transferable rights entitling their holders to purchase Northwest common from Pacific at an amount to be specified by Pacific's Board of Directors, but expected to be below the fair market value of the Northwest common. . . .

The plan was approved by Pacific's shareholders on March 24, 1961. Pacific transferred its assets and liabilities in Oregon, Washington, and Idaho to Northwest, and ceased business in those States on June 30, 1961. On September 29, 1961, Pacific issued to its common stockholders one right for each outstanding share of Pacific stock. These rights were exercisable until October 20, 1961. Six rights plus a payment of $16 were required to purchase one share of Northwest common. The rights issued in 1961 were sufficient to transfer some 57.3% of the Northwest stock.

By September 29, 1961, the Internal Revenue Service had ruled that shareholders who sold rights would realize ordinary income in the amount of the sales price, and that shareholders who exercised rights would realize ordinary income in the amount of the difference between $16 paid in and the fair market value, measured as of the date of exercise, of the Northwest common received. . . .

On June 12, 1963, the remaining 43% of the Northwest stock was offered to Pacific shareholders. This second offering was structured much as the first had been, except that eight rights plus $16 were required to purchase one share of Northwest.

The Gordons . . . and the Baans, . . . were minority shareholders of Pacific as of September 29, 1961. In the rights distribution that occurred that day the Gordons received 1,540 rights under the plan. They exercised 1,536 of the rights on October 5, 1961, paying $4,096 to obtain 256 shares of Northwest, at a price of $16 plus six rights per share. The average price of Northwest stock on the American Stock Exchange was $26 per share on October 5. On the same day, the Gordons sold the four odd rights for $6.36. The Baans received 600 rights on September 29, 1961. They exercised them all on October 11, 1961, receiving 100 shares of Northwest in return for their 600 rights and $1,600. On October 11, the agreed fair market value of one Northwest share was $26.94.

In their federal income tax returns for 1961, neither the Gordons nor the Baans reported any income upon the receipt of the rights or upon exercising them to obtain Northwest stock at less than its fair market value. The Gordons also did not report any income on the sale of the four rights. The Commissioner asserted deficiencies against both sets of taxpayers. He contended, in a joint proceeding in the Tax Court, that taxpayers received ordinary income in the amount of the difference between the sum they paid in exercising their rights and the fair market value of the Northwest stock received. He contended further that the Gordons realized ordinary income in the amount of $6.36, the sales price, upon the sale of their four odd rights.

The Tax Court upheld taxpayers' contention that the 1961 distribution of Northwest stock met the requirements of §355 of the

Code, with the result that no gain or loss should be recognized on the receipt by them or their exercise of the rights. The Tax Court held, however, that the Gordons' sale of the four odd rights resulted in ordinary income to them. The Commissioner appealed the *Baan* case to the Court of Appeals for the Ninth Circuit, and the *Gordon* case to the Court of Appeals for the Second Circuit; in the latter, the Gordons cross-appealed. The Ninth Circuit reversed the Tax Court, holding that the spread between $16 and fair market value was taxable as ordinary income to the Baans. The Second Circuit disagreed, sustaining the Tax Court on this point in the *Gordon* case. The Second Circuit went on to hold that the amount received by the Gordons for the four odd rights was taxable as a capital gain rather than as ordinary income, reversing the Tax Court on this point.

Because of the conflict, we granted certiorari. . . . We affirm the decision of the Court of Appeals for the Ninth Circuit, and reverse the decision of the Court of Appeals for the Second Circuit on both points.

Under §§301 and 316 of the code, subject to specific exceptions and qualifications provided in the code, any distribution of property by a corporation to its shareholders out of accumulated earnings and profits is a dividend taxable to the shareholders as ordinary income. . . . It is here agreed that on September 28, 1961, Pacific's accumulated earnings and profits were larger in extent than the total amount the Commissioner here contends was a dividend — the difference between the fair market value of all Northwest stock sold in 1961 and the total amount, at $16 per share, paid in by purchasers.

Whether the actual dividend occurs at the moment when valuable rights are distributed or at the moment when their value is realized through sale or exercise, it is clear that when a corporation sells corporate property to stockholders or their assignees at less than its fair market value, thus diminishing the net worth of the corporation, it is engaging in a "distribution of property" as that term is used in §316.[4] Such a sale thus results in a dividend to shareholders unless

4. See, e.g., Choate v. Commissioner, 129 F.2d 684 (C.A. 2d Cir.). In Palmer v. Commissioner, 302 U.S. 63, 69, this Court said, "While a sale of corporate assets to stockholders is, in a literal sense, a distribution of its property, such a transaction does not necessarily fall within the statutory definition of a dividend. For a sale to stockholders may not result in any diminution of its net worth and in that case cannot result in any distribution of its profits.

"On the other hand such a sale, if for substantially less than the value of the property sold, may be as effective a means of distributing profits among stockholders as the formal declaration of a dividend."

In *Palmer*, rights were distributed entitling shareholders to purchase from the corporation shares of stock in another corporation. Finding that the sales price represented the reasonable value of the shares at the time the corporation committed itself to sell them, this Court found no dividend. It held that the mere issue of rights

some specific exception or qualification applies. In particular, it is here agreed that the spread was taxable to the present taxpayers unless the distribution of Northwest stock by Pacific met the requirements for nonrecognition stated in §355, or §354, or §346(b) of the code.[5] Since the Tax Court concluded that the requirements of §355 had been met, it did not reach taxpayers' alternative contentions. . . .

Section 355 provides that certain distributions of securities of corporations controlled by the distributing corporation do not result in recognized gain or loss to the distributee shareholders. The requirements of the section are detailed and specific, and must be applied with precision. It is no doubt true, as the Second Circuit emphasized, that the general purpose of the section was to distinguish corporate fission from the distribution of earnings and profits. However, although a court may have reference to this purpose when there is a genuine question as to the meaning of one of the requirements Congress has imposed, a court is not free to disregard requirements simply because it considers them redundant or unsuited to achieving the general purpose in a particular case. Congress has abundant power to provide that a corporation wishing to spin off a subsidiary must, however bona fide its intentions, conform the details of a distribution to a particular set of rules.

The Commissioner contends that the 1961 distribution of North-

---

was not a dividend. It has not, however, been authoritatively settled whether an issue of rights to purchase at less than fair market value itself constitutes a dividend, or the dividend occurs only on the actual purchase. In the present case this need not be decided.

5. It is important to begin from this premise. In our view, the Court of Appeals for the Second Circuit erred in its approach to the §355 problem because it assumed, at the outset, that the Commissioner essentially sought to tax a transaction that brought no "income" to Pacific shareholders. Whether the shareholders received income, however, cannot in practice be determined in the abstract, before looking at §355.

Any common shareholder in some sense "owns" a fraction of the assets of the corporation in which he holds stock, including those assets that reflect accumulated corporate earnings. Earnings are not taxed to the shareholder when they accrue to the corporation, but instead when they are passed to shareholders individually through dividends. Consequently it does not help to note, as the Second Circuit here did, that the distribution of Northwest stock merely changed the form of ownership that Pacific's shareholders enjoyed and did not increase their wealth. This is only very roughly true at best, but in the rough sense in which it is here true, it is true of any dividend. The question is not whether a shareholder ends up with "more" but whether the change in the form of his ownership represents a transfer to him, by the corporation, of assets reflecting its accumulated earnings and profits.

There may be a genuine theoretical difference between a change in form representing a mere corporate fission, separating what the shareholder owns into two smaller but essentially similar parts, and a change in form representing a dividend, separating what a shareholder owns qua shareholder from what he owns as an individual. This difference, however, must be defined by objectively workable tests, such as Congress supplied in §355. Neither the Second Circuit nor the taxpayers have suggested any other way of identifying a true fission.

west stock failed to qualify under §355 in several respects.[7] We need, however, reach only [§]355(a)(1)(D). . . .

On September 28, 1961, the day before the first rights distribution, Pacific owned all of the common stock of Northwest, the only class of securities that company had issued. The 1961 rights offering contemplated transferring, and succeeded in transferring, about 57% of the Northwest common to Pacific shareholders. It therefore could not be clearer that this 1961 distribution did not transfer "all" of the stock of Northwest held by Pacific prior to it, and did not transfer "control" as that term is defined in §368(c).

Nevertheless, taxpayers contend, and the Second Circuit agreed, that the requirements of subsection (a)(1)(D) were here met because Pacific distributed the remaining 43% of the Northwest stock in 1963. The court said that the purpose of the subsection "in no way requires a single distribution." The court apparently concluded that so long as it appears, at the time the issue arises, that the parent corporation has in fact distributed all of the stock of the subsidiary, the requirements of §(a)(1)(D)(i) have been satisfied.

We are forced to disagree. The code requires that "the distribution" divest the controlling corporation of all of, or 80% control of, the controlled corporation. Clearly, if an initial transfer of less than a controlling interest in the controlled corporation is to be treated for tax purposes as a mere first step in the divestiture of control, it must at least be identifiable as such at the time it is made. Absent other specific directions from Congress, code provisions must be interpreted so as to conform to the basic premise of annual tax accounting. It would be wholly inconsistent with this premise to hold that the essential character of a transaction, and its tax impact, should remain not only undeterminable but unfixed for an indefinite and unlimited period in the future, awaiting events that might or might not happen. This requirement that the character of a transaction be determinable does not mean that the entire divestiture must necessarily occur within a single tax year. It does, however, mean that if one transaction is to be characterized as a "first step" there must be a binding commitment to take the later steps.[11]

---

7. The Commissioner contends, first, that Pacific did not distribute "solely stock or securities" as required by §355(a)(1)(A), because it distributed rights rather than stock. He contends, second, that Pacific did not distribute the Northwest stock "to a shareholder, with respect to its stock" as required by §355(a)(1)(A)(i), because it did not distribute the stock to shareholders but sold it to holders of transferable rights, for cash consideration. He contends, third, that Northwest did not meet the quantity requirements of §355(a)(1)(D) because it parted with only 57% of the stock in 1961.

Any one of these arguments, if established, would support the result the Commissioner seeks. The Court of Appeals for the Second Circuit perforce rejected all three. The Court of Appeals for the Ninth Circuit accepted all three. We reach only the last.

11. The Commissioner contends that a multistep divestiture presents special problems in preventing bailouts of earnings and profits. The Second Circuit, recog-

Here, it was little more than a fortuity that, by the time suit was brought alleging a deficiency in taxpayers' 1961 returns, Pacific had distributed the remainder of the stock. The plan for reorganization submitted to shareholders in 1961 promised that 56% of that stock would be distributed immediately. The plan went on,

> It is expected that within about three years after acquiring the stock of the New Company, the Company by one or more offerings will offer for sale the balance of such stock, following the procedures described in the preceding paragraph. The proceeds from such sales will be used by the Company to repay advances then outstanding and for general corporate purposes including expenditures for extensions, additions and improvements to its telephone plant.
>
> The prices at which the shares of the New Company will be offered pursuant to the offerings referred to . . . will be determined by the Board of Directors of the Company at the time of each offering.

It was further stated that such subsequent distributions would occur "[a]t a time or times related to its [Pacific's] need for new capital." Although there is other language in the plan that might be interpreted to prevent Pacific management from dealing with the Northwest stock in any way inconsistent with eventual sale to Pacific shareholders, there is obviously no promise to sell any particular amount of stock, at any particular time, at any particular price. If the 1961 distribution played a part in what later proved to be a total divestiture of the Northwest stock, it was not, in 1961, either a total divestiture or a step in a plan of total divestiture.

Accordingly, we hold that the taxpayers, having exercised rights to purchase shares of Northwest from Pacific in 1961, must recognize ordinary income in that year in the amount of the difference between $16 per share and the fair market value of a share of Northwest common at the moment the rights were exercised.

The second question presented . . . , whether the $6.36 received by taxpayers Gordon upon the sale of four rights was taxable as ordinary income, as a capital gain, or not at all, does not require extended discussion in light of our view upon the first question. Since receipt and exercise of the rights would have produced ordinary income, receipt and sale of the rights, constituting merely an alter-

---

nizing such potential problems, held that they can be dealt with under §(a)(1)(B), which provides that nonrecognition shall result only when it appears that "the transaction was not used principally as a device for the distribution of the earnings and profits of the distributing corporation or the controlled corporation or both. . . ."

Congress may, of course, have chosen not to leave problems created by multistep divestitures to specific adjudication under this "device" subsection, but to require *both* a unitary divestiture *and* satisfaction of the "device" requirement. Whether §(a)(1)(D) would prohibit or limit a divestiture of control committed from the outset but spread over a series of steps is a problem we need not reach.

native route to realization, also produced income taxable at ordinary rates. Helvering v. Horst, 311 U.S. 112; Gibson v. Commissioner, 133 F.2d 308.

The judgment of the Court of Appeals for the Second Circuit is reversed. The judgment of the Court of Appeals for the Ninth Circuit is affirmed. . . .

NOTES

1. On remand, see Gordon v. Commissioner, 424 F.2d 378 (2d Cir. 1970), *aff'g* 51 T.C. 1032 (1969), *cert. denied,* 400 U.S. 848 (1970). The two arguments made by the Commissioner but not reached by the *Gordon* court (see footnote 7) were dealt with by the Seventh Circuit in Redding v. Commissioner, infra.

2. Cf. Rev. Rul. 77-11, 1977-1 C.B. 93, in which two commonly controlled corporations transferred part of their assets in exchange for stock of a newly formed corporation, then distributed the new corporation's stock in complete redemption of one shareholder's stock in both transferors. Since one transferor had acquired control of the new corporation prior to the redemption, its distribution was nontaxable. The distribution by the other transferor corporation was a §302(b)(3) redemption.

REDDING v. COMMISSIONER
630 F.2d 1169 (7th Cir. 1980), *cert. denied,* 101 S. Ct. 1353 (1981)

Before Bauer, Wood and Cudahy, Circuit Judges.

CUDAHY, Circuit Judge. This is an appeal by the Commissioner of Internal Revenue from determinations of the United States Tax Court that Gerald R. and Dorothy M. Redding and Thomas W. and Anne M. Moses ("taxpayers") do not owe any income tax on account of the receipt or exercise of stock warrants.[1] These warrants were distributed as part of a series of transactions involving distribution by the Indianapolis Water Company (the "Water Company") to its stockholders of all the stock of its wholly owned subsidiary, Shorewood Corporation ("Shorewood"). The distribution of warrants was made preliminarily to the distribution of stock, which was distributed upon the exercise of the warrants. The Tax Court treated the two

---

1. The terms "stock rights" (or "rights") will be used in this opinion interchangeably with the term "warrants" since both terms have been used interchangeably in this litigation. In financial circles, "warrants" usually refer to *longer term* options to purchase stock at a stated price (a "subscription price" or "exercise price" or "option price") than do stock rights. . . .

distributions as being part of a single transaction, sheltered from taxation under section 355 . . . , granting nonrecognition to a corporation's distribution to its stockholders of stock or securities in a controlled corporation. We hold that the distribution of stock warrants to the taxpayers constituted a dividend to them and that section 355 is not available to render the transaction nontaxable. We, therefore, reverse.

The Water Company, which is a public utility, owned all of the stock of Shorewood, which in turn owned most of the waterfront property surrounding the reservoirs used by the Water Company. Shorewood wished to develop its waterfront realty, but the Indiana Public Service Commission determined that real estate development was not an appropriate activity for a public utility and suggested that Shorewood be separated from the Water Company.

To achieve this end, Shorewood's capital structure was altered. In 1970, Shorewood's authorized common stock was increased from 1,000 to 2,500,000 shares. On the same day, Shorewood issued to the Water Company 481,291 shares of common stock in exchange for Shorewood's 1,000 shares then outstanding and held by the Water Company. On January 6, 1971, the Water Company agreed to purchase an additional 855,630 shares of common stock from Shorewood for a total ownership of 1,336,921 shares. The board of directors of the Water Company decided to distribute to its shareholders of record on January 6, 1971, stock rights or warrants to purchase Shorewood stock on the basis of one warrant for each share of the Water Company common stock outstanding. The warrants gave the holder the right to receive one share of Shorewood stock upon surrender of two warrants and the payment of $5.00 to the Water Company and further right to subscribe to any remaining Shorewood shares by allotment. The warrants were transferable.

The total offering of Shorewood shares by the Water Company thus amounted to 1,069,537 shares, which comprised slightly more than 80% of the total outstanding amount of Shorewood stock. Of these shares to be offered, 50,000 shares were reserved for the underwriters, and 1,019,537 shares were available for distribution to warrant holders. Any shares not sold to warrant holders were to be bought by the underwriters, on a "firm commitment" basis, at a slightly discounted price. The Water Company thus retained slightly less than 20% of the outstanding Shorewood stock. Immediately after the distribution, the shareholders of the Water Company held substantially more than 50% of the outstanding shares of Shorewood.

The warrants were issued on January 7, 1971, and expired and became valueless if not exercised by 3:30 p.m. on January 22, 1971. During this subscription period, shareholders or their transferees or assignees subscribed to all 1,069,537 Shorewood shares offered, except for 50,000 shares acquired by the underwriters. Hence, 1,019,537 shares of Shorewood stock were actually distributed to the warrant holders and 50,000 shares conveyed to the underwriters on February 2, 1971. As contemplated by the Water Company, an over-the-counter market in warrants developed during the subscription period, with the price ranging from $0.39 to $1.05 per warrant. There is no dispute that both at the time of issuance and at the time of exercise of the warrants the subscription price of $5.00 was less than the fair market value of Shorewood stock. . . .

Taxpayers were stockholders of the Water Company. Gerald and Dorothy Redding owned 7,000 Water Company shares, and Thomas and Anne Moses owned 35,543 shares. They received a corresponding number of warrants and exercised all of them. The Moseses also exercised an additional subscription privilege to obtain an additional 6,228 shares of Shorewood stock.

Taxpayers contended that both the receipt and the exercise of the warrants were tax free to them under the provisions of section 355. It was stipulated that the transaction was not a "device" for the distribution of earnings and profits pursuant to section 355(a)(1)(B); that the separately conducted "active business" requirements of section 355(a)(1)(C) were met; that the 1,069,537 shares of Shorewood distributed in the offering amounted to 80% control; and that the shares retained by the Water Company were not held for tax avoidance purposes within the meaning of section 355(a)(1)(D)(ii).

The Tax Court agreed with taxpayers that the transactions involved in these cases met the requirements for a corporate division, in this case a "spin-off," contained in section 355 and were, accordingly, taxfree. . . .

In reversing the Tax Court, we find taxpayers have failed to meet their burden of showing that the several transactions here meet the tests of section 355 so as to qualify for nonrecognition of the gain otherwise subject to tax. As the parties and the Tax Court acknowledged to be the case were we to find section 355 inapplicable, we conclude the distribution of the warrants by the Water Company is taxable as a dividend. It is not controlling that taxpayers sold none of their rights, exercised all of them, and received stock for them (for which taxpayers also paid the additional consideration of $5.00 per Shorewood share). The tax treatment of taxpayers must depend upon an analysis of the transaction as a whole rather than only of the specific facts applicable to these taxpayers. This is true because the nonrecognition of gain afforded by section 355 requires adherence to requirements governing the transaction as a whole.

The Tax Court, in determining whether the issuance of the warrants and their exercise by warrant holders should be immunized from tax by section 355, purported to rely heavily on its prior ruling granting tax-free status to warrants used in somewhat similar trans-action in Baan v. Commissioner, 45 T.C. 71 (1965), *rev'd,* 382 F.2d 485 (9th Cir. 1967), *aff'd sub nom.* Commissioner v. Gordon, 382 F.2d 499 (2d Cir. 1967), 9th Cir. *aff'd sub nom.* Commissioner v. Gordon, 2d Cir. *rev'd,* 391 U.S. 83 [page 722 supra] . . . (1968). In *Baan,* the Tax Court apparently felt that it could ignore the issuance of warrants as a taxable event under the dictum of Palmer v. Commissioner, 302 U.S. 63 . . . (1937), that an issuance of stock rights is not a dividend,[10] and that it could proceed to consideration of the warrant *exercise* and stock issuance only. In the instant case, on the other hand, the Tax Court expressly declined to state a view on the current vitality of the *Palmer* dictum. Instead, it applied the "step transaction doctrine" to reach its conclusion that the two transactions which took place should be viewed as "steps" in a single transaction meeting the requirements of section 355 and that, hence, neither the receipt nor the exercise of the warrants results in tax. We shall, therefore, address first the applicability of the step transaction doctrine, which we think is sig-nificantly related to the current status of the *Palmer* dictum, to be discussed later. As to the application of the step transaction doctrine, we believe the Tax Court erred.

The attempted application of the step transaction doctrine in this case to shift the focus from the issuance of the stock rights or warrants to the subsequent distribution of stock is important, because, to qualify under section 355, a distribution must consist solely of stock or securities, which do not include stock rights such as these. See Treas. Reg. §1.3551(a) (1979). . . . As the Court of Appeals for the Ninth Circuit said in Commissioner v. Baan,

> . . . Stock rights are not stocks or securities and, most assuredly, are not stock or securities carrying voting rights. They are only options to purchase stock. . . .

See Gordon v. Commissioner, 424 F.2d 378, 381-83 (2d Cir. 1970) construing the similar language of section 354(a)(1).

The Tax Court does not disagree with this conclusion but seeks to keep the related transactions within the ambit of section 355 by integrating through the step transaction doctrine the distribution of stock warrants and the subsequent exercise of these warrants. By that technique the overall transaction can be viewed as a distribution solely of stock, which is allegedly immunized from tax by section 355.

The commentators have attempted to synthesize from judicial decisions several tests to determine whether the step transaction doc-trine is applicable to a particular set of circumstances in order to combine a series of steps into one transaction for tax purposes. Un-

---

10. "The mere issue of rights to subscribe and their receipt by stockholder, is not a dividend." Palmer v. Commissioner, 302 U.S. at 71. . . . See, infra, at 1181.

fortunately, these tests are notably abstruse — even for such an abstruse field as tax law. . . . [O]ne of the tests which the parties ask us to consider is the "end result" test, whereby purportedly separate transactions will be amalgamated into a single transaction when it appears that "the successive steps were made 'in furtherance of, and for the purpose of executing and putting into effect, the plan of reorganization.'" . . . Here, the distribution of stock warrants was not made for the purpose of reaching the end result of distributing stock to the Water Company shareholders. Indeed, the workings of the stock warrant mechanism indicate that it was a matter of relative indifference to the Water Company, from the standpoint of raising capital for Shorewood or for itself, whether the Shorewood stock went to Water Company shareholders, or to their assignees of warrants (or to the underwriters). Had the paramount purpose of the Water Company been to distribute its portfolio Shorewood stock in a way that Water Company shareholders would in the end become Shorewood shareholders, the obvious way to proceed would have been simply to omit the first "step" and to distribute Shorewood stock directly to Water Company shareholders. But such an approach would have made it difficult to raise new capital, which was a paramount and somewhat inconsistent goal. . . .

. . . Here where the Water Company's purpose went far beyond a simple corporate division, the use of transferable warrants made it possible to bring in *new* distributees for the Shorewood stock (together with new capital for Shorewood and for Water Company). Therefore, the reason for using transferable warrants was to arrange in advance for Water Company shareholders to be excluded as recipients of Shorewood stock in favor of new investors prepared to make a capital contribution. Hence, to the extent that the rights distribution was a step, it was not a necessary step in the sort of corporate division contemplated by section 355.[14] Our conclusion is directly buttressed by the stipulation of the parties that "[t]he use of rights that required payment of a subscription price as a method of distribution of the Shorewood common stock was dictated by the need of Shorewood for capital to develop its assets and business" . . .

The reference of the Tax Court to the warrant issue as a "merely procedural device" is misleading. Insofar as the warrants had a readily

---

14. "[T]he purpose [of section 355] and the purpose of its predecessors is to give to stockholders in a corporation controlled by them the privilege of separating or 'spinning off' from their corporation a part of its assets and activities and lodging the separated part in another corporation which is controlled by the same stockholders. Since, after the spin off, the real owners of the assets are the same persons who owned them before, Congress has been willing that these owners should be allowed, without penalty, to have their real ownership divided into smaller . . . entries than the single original corporation, if the real owners decide that such a division would be desirable." Commissioner v. Wilson, 353 F.2d at 186.

ascertainable market value, they had independent economic significance, and, as indicated, their function in the series of transactions was to make it possible for Water Company shareholders to defer profitably to others who were prepared to make an investment in Shorewood. Further, since the warrant distribution had independent economic significance, that distribution was a matter of substance rising above mere form or procedure.

Taxpayers also contend that it was not essential to use warrants as evidence of "legal rights" to receive stock and that this fact is significant. They describe several alternative procedures not involving the issuance of warrants which would have provided the same "legal benefits or opportunities" as those provided by warrants. . . . But simply because some other means (which arguably comply with section 355) might have been used to reach ultimate results similar to those sought in this case does not suggest that the procedures followed here are entitled to section 355 treatment.

First, " '[t]he Commissioner is justified in determining the tax effects of transactions on the basis in which taxpayers have molded them.' "

. . . Second, taxpayers do not explain precisely how the suggested alternative means would raise capital (a paramount objective). Third, Congress narrowly constrained the means for gaining the tax benefit; the issue here is whether the means of using transferable warrants comply with the "detailed and specific requirements of section 355." Commissioner v. Gordon. . . . Fourth, the fact that the rights were "evidenced by a piece of paper" gave them a marketable identity and helped endow them and their receipt with independent economic significance.

The second "test" for determining whether the step transaction doctrine applies is the so-called "interdependence test," which requires an evaluation "whether on a reasonable interpretation of objective facts the steps are so interdependent that the legal relations created by one transaction would have been fruitless without a completion of the series." . . . Although there is some question whether the "interdependence test" is even relevant to the corporate division situation, were we to apply the test to the facts before us we would not find use of the warrants sufficiently indispensable to achieving a spin-off to compel us to view this as a unitary transaction. . . . While the exercise of the warrants here was obviously dependent upon warrants having been issued, the issuance of warrants did not require their exercise by shareholders in the purchase of stock from the Water Company. . . . Insofar as the issuance of warrants contemplated the raising of capital through the disposition of stock, the result would have been essentially the same whether the warrants were exercised by Water Company shareholders or by non-shareholder assignees.

Even if the warrants were not exercised at all, the underwriters had agreed to purchase the stock (albeit at a slightly reduced price). Although the use of warrants made it more likely than a public offering that Water Company shareholders would end up as Shorewood shareholders, the money would have come in and the stock gone out with or without the exercise of the warrants. On the other hand, the transferable warrants led away from, rather than toward, a goal of spinning off to *shareholders*, which could have occurred by direct stock distribution without warrants. . . .

Finally, the Commissioner argues that the transactions before us also fail to satisfy a third test permitting invocation of the step transaction doctrine, the "binding commitment" test. As explained by the Supreme Court in Commissioner v. Gordon, . . . the step transaction doctrine should not apply unless "if one transaction is to be characterized as a 'first step' there must be a binding commitment to take the later steps." The Commissioner, noting that the Tax Court in the instant case found that there was no binding commitment for a stock distribution to follow the rights issuance, stresses that the absence of such commitment renders the step transaction doctrine inapplicable. Although this is a valid contribution to the analysis, we do not find the point determinative.

The Supreme Court articulated the binding commitment test in the factual context of a multi-step distribution similar to that before us. Given this similarity, we would embrace and apply the "binding commitment" test were it not for one important difference between the *Gordon* case and that before us. The multi-step distribution in *Gordon* took place in successive tax years, a time-span obviously exceeding the several weeks involved in the instant case. This lengthy time period raised the possibility that the transactions' tax impact would remain indefinite and indeterminable for an unlimited period, an eventuality inconsistent with the premise of annual tax accounting and one the Court may have thought necessitated the "binding commitment" test. We cannot say that the Court intended that the failure to satisfy the test in the circumstance of a much shorter period would automatically preclude application of the step transaction doctrine. Hence, the lack of "binding commitment" is simply one factor to which we give appropriate consideration here. Certainly, it is not necessary for us to rely on this factor to reach our result.

Our examination of the facts in light of the various tests convinces us that the issuance of transferable warrants not only had independent economic significance but added nothing to the essential process of effecting a spin-off, "to permit the real owners of enterprises to arrange their units and evidences of ownership to suit their own ideas of how best to carry on their business." . . . It may be, as the Tax Court emphasizes, that the warrants were in existence for only a short period of time but their economic value is clear, and they were actively traded during the period of their existence. Fundamentally, we think it inappropriate to substitute the step transaction doctrine as a tax shield for the warrant issuance if the dictum of Palmer v. Commissioner is no longer available to immunize the warrant transaction. . . .

Even were we to agree that the step transaction doctrine permits these transactions to be viewed as simply a distribution of Shorewood stock, the requirement of section 355(a)(1)(A) that this stock be distributed *with respect to* the stock of the Water Company has not been met. What has instead happened has been that the stock warrants have been distributed with respect to the stock of the Water Company, and the Shorewood stock has then been distributed with respect to the warrants (as well as to the underwriters). It was the warrant distribution rather than the stock distribution which conformed to this statutory test.

After the distribution of warrants to Water Company stockholders had taken place, the subsequent distribution of shares of Shorewood stock was made "with respect to" the holders of warrants — some Water Company shareholders and some not — and to the underwriters. This was not, in the words of the Supreme Court, "conform[ing] the details of a distribution to a particular set of rules." Commissioner v. Gordon. . . .

It has been argued that the status of the Water Company shareholders was important because their existence created any purchaser's right to receive the stock "through" the stockholders of the Water Company, as the Tax Court suggested in the comparable situation of Baan v. Commissioner. . . . But, in comparison with the more straightforward view that section 355 contemplates simply distributions to shareholders, this analysis is painfully strained. The Tax Court was apparently not unduly troubled by the problem of distributions to non-stockholders or the fact that the use of transferable warrants structured the transaction in the direction of transfers to third parties. The Tax Court was apparently satisfied by the fact that the shareholders of the Water Company actually received more than 50% of the Shorewood stock, a sufficient percentage to satisfy the so-called continuity-of-shareholder-interest test.

The continuity-of-shareholder-interest test is "a doctrine of judicial origin based on what is conceived to be the unstated but fundamental statutory purpose of providing for nonrecognition of gain or loss only if the reorganization exchange is distinguishable from a sale. . . ." Generally, if one-half or more of the stock remains in the hands of the original shareholders, such continuity of interest is adequate proof that a sale was not effected. Here, the Tax Court found it harmless from the standpoint of fulfilling the "with respect to its stock" requirement of section 355(a)(1)(A) that Shorewood stock was sold to third parties so long as 50% or more of it ended up with Water Company shareholders. The Tax Court apparently reasoned (although this is not explicit in its opinion) that, when section 355 applied to a rights offering, it was enough, for purposes of section 355(a)(1)(A) that at least 50% of the stock or securities of the subsidiary come to rest in the hands of shareholders of the parent.

This way of thinking conflicts with that of the Court of Appeals for the Ninth Circuit which stated in Commissioner v. Baan, "Congress could well conclude that the prospect that the same people (shareholders of the distributing company) will continue to own the same business would be undermined if a distribution was effectuated by means of transferable stock rights, the exercise of which required substantial cash payments." . . . We cannot agree with the Tax Court, if we understand its reasoning, that the failure of the distribution of Shorewood stock to be "with respect to" Water Company stock was harmless merely because 50% or more of Shorewood stock came to rest with Water Company shareholders. We know of no authority that mere satisfaction of the 50% standard is enough to meet the section 355(a)(1)(A) problem.[22]

We reach only in passing the further issue upon which Judge Sterrett relied in his dissenting opinion below that the Water Company did not distribute 80% of the Shorewood stock within the meaning of section 355(a)(1)(D), and therefore that the transaction was not tax-free under section 355. The Tax Court found that this issue was foreclosed by the stipulations entered into by the parties for purposes of this litigation.

Section 355(a)(1)(D) requires that stock constituting "control" of the controlled corporation, defined under section 368(c) as at least 80%, must be distributed. We think the "distribution" referred to in section 355(a)(1)(D) is the same "distribution" as that referred to in section 355(a)(1)(A) requiring a "distribution" to shareholders of the issuing corporation with respect to its stock. In other words the statute "requires distribution of control to *shareholders of the distributing corporation.*" Redding v. Commissioner, 71 T.C. at 617 (Sterrett, J., dissenting).

---

22. In addition, because of the requirements of section 355(a)(1)(B), . . . the 50% standard is presumably applicable where there has been no prearrangement of stock transfers to third parties after the distribution. In the instant circumstances, a distribution of stock *based on a prior distribution of rights*, where some of the rights are sold before the stock is distributed, is a situation where "stock . . . [is] sold . . . pursuant to an arrangement . . . agreed upon prior to . . . [the] distribution [of the stock]." I.R.C. §355(a)(1)(B). Any such transfer by prearrangement to non-stockholders might render the transaction at least presumptively nonconforming under section 355. . . . We are, of course, aware of the stipulation here with respect to section 355(a)(1)(B), but, in divining the intent of Congress, we think all the subsections of section 355 must be read together to arrive at the meaning, for example, of section 355(a)(1)(A).

Here, after the transaction at issue, the Water Company retained 267,384 shares or exactly 20%, less one share, of the total 1,336,921 shares of Shorewood stock issued and outstanding. The Water Company thus must have distributed slightly more than 80%. But of the shares constituting this 80%, 50,000 were acquired by the underwriters. As Judge Sterrett found, the transfer of the 50,000 shares to the underwriters reduced the percentage of the stock "distributed" to Water Company shareholders to, at most, 76.26% of all Shorewood shares issued.[23] Were it not for the stipulation, we would probably be persuaded by the Commissioner on this point, and the issue would necessarily be significant in our decision.

Given our conclusion that the step transaction doctrine does not require this transaction to be seen simply as a distribution of Shorewood stock and our further finding that even if it could be so viewed, there has been a failure to comply with the requirements of section 355, we must turn finally to a determination of what constitutes the taxable event.

The Commissioner contends that the taxable event is the receipt of the warrants; taxpayers contend that, if the transaction is taxable at all, the taxable event would be the exercise of the warrants. There is also a difference of view as to how to measure the income received with respect to the warrants. In our view these matters are rather simply dealt with under the Internal Revenue Code of 1954.

The method of taxing corporate distributions was extensively revised in the 1954 Code. A distribution to shareholders, as such, of rights to acquire stock of the distributing corporation is, with exceptions not germane here, excluded from gross income under section 305. Rights distributed to shareholders to acquire the stock of another corporation, however, are *not* specifically excluded from gross income by the 1954 Code.

Section 301(a) of the Code states that, except as otherwise provided in chapter 1 of the Code, a distribution of property, as defined in §317(a), made by a corporation to a shareholder with respect to

23. We do not know to what level this figure was further reduced by the exercise of warrants by individuals who received or purchased them from Water Company shareholders.

We find somewhat persuasive the reasoning applied by Judge Sterrett in concluding his analysis of the section 355(a)(1)(D) issue: "In order to sustain the Court's decision herein one would have not only to ignore the substance and importance of the rights issuance, but also assume that all [the recipients of] the rights traded over the counter and all the underwriters were also Water Co. shareholders. I cannot join in this assumption and it seems, in any event, to be contrary to the . . . [statutory] language. The petitioner has not shown to whom Water Co. transferred 'control' inasmuch as no one related group of distributees had 80 percent of Shorewood's stock immediately after the transfer. It is not this Court's function to assume petitioners' prima facie case. Rather, such case must be proven." 71 T.C. at 617 (Sterrett, J., dissenting).

its stock, will be treated as provided in section 301(c). Section 301(c) provides that where section 301(a) applies to a distribution, that amount of the distribution that is a dividend, as defined in section 316, will be included in gross income.

Under section 316(a), any distribution of "property" by a corporation to its shareholders out of its earnings and profits accumulated after February 28, 1913 is a "dividend." "Property" as defined in section 317(a) "means money, securities, and any other property; except that such term does not include stock in the corporation making the distribution (or right to acquire such stock)." The specific *exclusion* of rights to acquire stock of the distributing company implies that rights to acquire stock of another corporation are *included* in the term "property." Indeed, the legislative history of the 1954 Code leaves no doubt that this broad definition of property includes stock warrants:

> As a result of [the exclusion in] this definition, the receipt of stock, of a corporation which is not stock of the distributing corporation (or is not treated as such stock under . . . section 353 [later renumbered as section 355]) would be treated as property for the purpose of section 301 (and other relevant provisions of this subsection). H. Rep. No. 1337, 83d Cong., 2d Sess., reprinted in [1954] U.S. Code Cong. & Admin. News pp. 4017, 4238.

See also Baumer v. United States, 580 F.2d 863, 881 (5th Cir. 1978); Rev. Rul. 70-521, 1970-2 C.B. 72; . . .

Thus, since the distribution of warrants here was not sheltered from taxation by section 355, taxpayers received a dividend upon receipt of the warrants and the amount of the dividends was the fair market value of the warrants received. See Rev. Rul. 70-521, 1970-2 C.B. 72.

It is argued, of course, that such a result contradicts the dictum of Palmer v. Commissioner. In that opinion Mr. Justice Stone said:

> The mere issue of rights to subscribe and their receipt by stockholders, is not a dividend. No distribution of corporate assets or diminution of the net worth of the corporation results in any practical sense. Even though the rights have a market or exchange value, they are not dividends within the statutory definition. . . . [Citations omitted.] They are at most options or continuing offers, potential sources of income to the stockholders through sale or the exercise of their rights. Taxable income might result from their sale, but distribution of the corporate property could take place only on their exercise. 302 U.S. at 71. . . .

But this analysis in the *Palmer* dictum was made under the Revenue Act of 1928, which did not contain the broad definition of "property" added in 1954 as section 317(a) of the Code.[24] Obviously, the Internal Revenue Code of 1954 must govern our decision. Although the superseding legislation and the congressional commentary it generated did not specifically discuss the *Palmer* dictum, several provisions of the 1954 Code governing corporate distributions seem incompatible with the principle that income never results from the mere issuance of stock rights. Whether, in enacting these provisions, Congress intended to "overrule" *Palmer* with respect to its famous dictum is left for us to intuit. We believe, though, that a "reasonable interpretation" of the corporate distribution provisions as a whole yields the conclusion that, even if the dictum was authoritative prior to 1954, it must now make way for a result consonant with the 1954 Code (and, incidentally, more reflective of economic reality).

In addition to the definition of "property" in section 317(a), which we find includes stock rights in the shares of a non-issuing corporation, the 1954 Code added a provision in section 305 which indicates another change in the law of tax-free receipt of stock rights. The general rule of section 305(a) excludes from taxability stock rights to acquire stock in the issuing corporation. However, one exception to this rule in section 305(b) is designed to tax distributions when they are effectively granted "in lieu of money." If the exception applies, the distribution of stock or of stock rights "shall be treated as a distribution of property to which section 301 applies." This exception precludes any inference that Congress intended to perpetuate the *Palmer* dictum. Thus, both sections 305(b) and 317(a) vitiate the "no property" rationale of the *Palmer* dictum. . . .

Indeed, the Supreme Court itself has apparently done the next thing to explicitly rejecting the *Palmer* dictum in light of the 1954 Code. In Commissioner v. Gordon, the Court discussed the relevant provisions of the Code and said that when a corporation sells its property to its stockholders or their assignees at less than fair market value, the transaction diminishes the net worth of the corporation and is a "distribution of property" within section 316. In attempting to relate this statement to discussion of the same subject in *Palmer*, the Court made broader observations:

> In *Palmer*, rights were distributed entitling sharesholders to pur-
> chase from the corporation shares of stock in another corporation.
> Finding that the sales price represented the reasonable value of

24. As has been noted, "[T]he 1928 revenue statue, . . . defined a dividend as 'any distribution made by a corporation to its shareholders, whether in money or in other property, out of its earnings and profits.' The *Palmer* Court concluded that the issuance of an option did not constitute a distribution out of corporate profits, and so was not a dividend." Gann, . . . [Taxation of Stock Rights and Other Options: Another Look at the Persistence of Palmer v. Commissioner, 1979 Duke L.J. 911, 940 (1979).]

the shares at the time the corporation committed itself to sell them, the Court found no dividend. It held that the mere issue of rights was not a dividend. *It has not, however, been authoritatively settled whether an issue of rights to purchase at less than fair market value itself constitutes a dividend, or the dividend occurs on the actual purchase.* . . .

This statement in *Gordon,* which as we have noted was quite similar on its facts to the instant case, withdraws any compulsion which may previously have arisen from the dictum in *Palmer* to prohibit treating the receipt of stock rights as the receipt of a dividend. In the instant case, the Tax Court pointedly refused to assess the *Palmer* doctrine's current vitality. . . . Further, in Baumer v. United States, the Court of Appeals for the Fifth Circuit, confronted with a problem similar to ours, carefully limited the *holding* in *Palmer* to its precise facts. . . .[26] We think the better interpretation under the provisions of the 1954 Code and the regulations construing them is that, in the case of stock rights, where the subscription price is lower than fair market value, there is a dividend at the time of issuance (and receipt) of the rights measured by the fair market value of the rights at the time of issuance.

We believe that we are required under the provisions of the 1954 Code to move beyond the dictum of *Palmer* and its pre-1954 progeny such as Choate v. Commissioner, 129 F.2d 684 (2d Cir. 1942). A fair reading of the decision of the Supreme Court in Commissioner v. Gordon requires that *Palmer* be limited to its facts, namely, a situation where there was no spread between option (subscription) price and market value on the date the corporation adopted its plan of distribution. When a substantial spread between market and option price prevails at all relevant times, we perceive no requirement to follow rigidly the *Palmer* dictum. Since options (warrants) are "property" as defined in the 1954 code, they fall easily within the scope of the statutory scheme for the taxation of dividends. Such an approach better reflects economic reality since an option incorporating a spread is a thing of value capable of being actively traded in public markets. Further, from an administrative point of view the valuation approach

26. "[T]he Fifth Circuit in *Baumer* limited the application of *Palmer* to a situation in which no spread exists on the date of issuance and the option period is so short that it is contemplated that the property subject to the option will be immediately sold to the shareholder before any substantial appreciation in the value of the underlying property can occur. Under the *Baumer* opinion, the issuance of the option is the distribution of a valuable asset to be taxed as a dividend if a spread exists on the date the option is issued, or if no spread exists on the date of issuance, but the option period is long enough so that the corporation contemplates appreciation. This analysis looks at the economic effect of the transaction to determine the existence of a dividend, and it correctly encompasses the two factors that attribute value to options — that is, both the existence of a spread on the date of issuance, and the length of the option period and potential appreciation during that period." *Gonn,* supra note [24], at 956-57.

dictated by the Code and regulations seems simpler than that developed in valuation cases purportedly based on *Palmer*. . . . Hence, based on careful analysis of relevant authority and a perception of the economic realities, we believe that the step we take here is fully justified. The time has come to put *Palmer* in perspective, and we do so with full confidence that our conclusion meets the most exacting standards of deference to the precedents of the Supreme Court, which in all respects control the decisions of the inferior federal courts. . . .

Reversed and remanded. . . .

NOTE

The parties in *Redding* stipulated that the shares of Shorewood retained by the Water Company were not held for tax avoidance purposes. In Rev. Rul. 75-469, 1975-2 C.B. 469, a parent corporation retained securities (long-term debentures) in its subsidiaries after distributing its subsidiaries' stock in a transaction that otherwise complied with the requirements of §355(a). The Service ruled that the distribution was nontaxable to the shareholders of the parent who received the subsidiaries' stock because the retention of the debentures would not permit the parent to maintain any practical control over its former subsidiary and because a sufficient business purpose for the retention of the debentures existed (the subsidiary's stock had been held by a bank as collateral for a loan; the bank agreed to release the stock for distribution to the shareholders if the debentures were substituted as collateral). See also Rev. Rul. 75-321, 1975-2 C.B. 123, where a corporation distributed 95 percent of the stock of a controlled corporation to its shareholders and retained the remaining 5 percent of the stock to serve as collateral for loans. The Service ruled that the retention of 5 percent of the stock was not in pursuance of a plan having as one of its principal purposes the avoidance of Federal income tax. For the Service's guidelines under §355(a)(1)(D)(ii), see Rev. Proc. 89-28, 1989-15 I.R.B. 200.

EDNA LOUISE DUNN TRUST v. COMMISSIONER
86 T.C. 745 (1986)

TANNENWALD, Judge. Respondent determined a deficiency of $29.64 in petitioner's Federal income taxes for the taxable year ended May 31, 1984. The issue for decision is whether a portion of the stock distributed to petitioner pursuant to a reorganization and divestiture plan constituted "other property" under section 355(a)(3)(B). . . .

Throughout its fiscal year ended May 31, 1984, petitioner owned 400 shares of common stock of American Telephone and Telegraph Company ("AT&T") a corporation organized and existing under the laws of the State of New York. Petitioner received, as of January 1, 1984, a distribution with respect to its AT&T stock of 40 shares of stock of each of American Information Technologies Corporation, Bell Atlantic Corporation, BellSouth Corporation, NYNEX Corporation, Pacific Telesis Group ("PacTel Group"), Southwestern Bell Corporation and U S West, Inc. (AT&T's seven regional holding Companies ("RHCs")). Petitioner did not include in its gross income on its Federal income tax return for the year in question any amount on account of the receipt of these shares of the RHCs.

Until January 1, 1984, AT&T was the common parent corporation of a group of corporations known as the Bell System, whose principal business was the furnishing of communications services and equipment. The group included 22 Bell operating companies ("BOCs") which were direct or indirect subsidiaries of AT&T, Western Electric Company, Incorporated, Bell Telephone Laboratories, Incorporated, and other companies. . . .

On August 24, 1982, a longstanding antitrust suit between AT&T and the United States Government was disposed of by a judicially approved agreement between the parties. United States v. American Telephone and Telegraph Company, et al., 552 F. Supp. 131 (D.D.C. 1982), *affd. sub nom.* Maryland v. United States, 460 U.S. 1001 (1983). Under the terms of that decision and its subsequent judicially approved implementation . . . , certain "local exchange" functions of the BOCs were to be placed in the aforementioned seven RHCs and AT&T was to divest itself of its holdings therein.

In an action unrelated to the antitrust suit, the Federal Communications Commission ("FCC"), on April 2, 1980, ordered that, on or before March 1, 1982, certain acts be taken to separate the functions of the BOCs. . . .

In 1980, AT&T owned all of the outstanding stock of the BOCs, with the exception of some minority shares held by unrelated third parties in the New England Telephone and Telegraph Company, the Mountain States Telephone and Telegraph Company, Pacific Northwest Bell Telephone Company and the Pacific Telephone and Telegraph Company ("Pacific").

Various steps were taken to implement the FCC mandate and at the same time serve the business interests of the Bell system, of which only those steps relating to Pacific need to be described herein.

Under an agreement of merger, dated November 5, 1981, between AT&T, Pacific and Pacific Transition Corporation ("Transition"), a newly formed, wholly owned subsidiary of AT&T, Transition would merge into Pacific and Pacific voting stockholders (other than AT&T and dissenting shareholders) would receive .35 shares of AT&T common stock (and cash in lieu of fractional shares) in exchange for each share of Pacific common stock and $60 in cash for each share of Pacific 6 percent voting preferred stock. The outstanding Pacific common and percent voting preferred stock would be cancelled and the outstanding share of Pacific Transition Corporation (held by AT&T) would be converted into one share of Pacific common stock.

The merger was consummated on May 12, 1982. At that time, Pacific had 224,504,982 shares of voting common stock, 205,345,275 (91.5 percent) of which were owned by AT&T, 820,000 shares of 6 percent voting preferred stock, 640,957 (78.2 percent) of which were owned by AT&T, and 21,120,000 shares of nonvoting preferred stock, none of which were owned by AT&T. The balance of the voting stock was publicly held, and the nonvoting preferred stock was held by institutional investors. Because the nonvoting preferred stock remained outstanding after the merger, AT&T did not acquire control of Pacific within the meaning of section 368(c) and the merger therefore resulted in recognition of gain or loss to Pacific's common and voting preferred shareholders.

On February 19, 1982, AT&T announced that, to accomplish the divestiture, the 22 BOCs would be grouped into seven regions. A separate, independent holding company structure was established for each region. This structure was subsequently incorporated in the Plan of Reorganization filed by AT&T on December 16, 1982, and approved by the court in United States v. Western Electric Company, Inc., 569 F. Supp. 1057 (D.D.C.), *affd. sub nom.* California v. United States, 464 U.S. 1013 (1983).

The Plan of Reorganization provided that the Articles of Incorporation of Pacific would be amended to convert the one outstanding share of Pacific voting common stock into 224,504,982 shares of voting common stock (the number of common shares outstanding prior to the merger), and to modify the rights of the nonvoting preferred stock to entitle each share to one vote per share with cumulative voting for directors as authorized by California law. By this change, AT&T would acquire control of Pacific by means of a tax-free reorganization, and then PacTel Group would be in control of Pacific within the meaning of section 368(c) at divestiture.

On January 21, 1983, AT&T applied to the Internal Revenue Service ("IRS") for rulings (the "Application") that, inter alia, the amendment to Pacific's Articles of Incorporation would be a reorganization within the meaning of section 368(a)(1)(E), and no gain or loss would be recognized by AT&T or by the preferred shareholders on the constructive exchange of their preferred stock. Under date of October 6, 1983, the IRS ruled that the amendment qualified as a reorganization within the meaning of section 368(a)(1)(E), and that no gain or loss would be recognized by Pacific, AT&T or the preferred shareholders.

In accordance with the Plan of Reorganization, AT&T and its affiliates would transfer to each regional holding company, in exchange for the latter's voting stock, the stock of the appropriate BOCs and other assets. Among the assets to be transferred to the PacTel Group were 224,504,982 shares of Pacific voting common stock. Thereafter, AT&T would then distribute to its stockholders one share of stock in each of the seven regional holding companies for every ten shares of AT&T stock owned by AT&T shareholders of record at the close of business on December 30, 1983. Fractional shares would not be issued but would be aggregated and sold and the cash proceeds distributed to the stockholders.

The January 21, 1983, Application also asked for rulings that, inter alia, no gain or loss would be recognized on the transfers of the stock of the BOCs and other assets to the regional holding companies in exchange for stock and that no income, gain or loss would be recognized by AT&T shareholders upon the receipt by them of the stock in the holding companies.

The IRS ruled that no gain or loss would be recognized on the transfer of stock of the BOCs and other property to the seven regional holding companies in exchange for their stock and that no income, gain or loss would be recognized by AT&T shareholders upon the receipt of the stock of the six regional holding companies other than PacTel Group. With respect to the latter, the IRS ruled that a portion of the PacTel Group stock was taxable to the AT&T shareholders. The IRS thereafter advised that this portion of the PacTel Group stock had a value at the time of distribution equal to $.39 per share of AT&T stock and the parties have accepted that value for the purposes of this case.

Section 355(a)(1) allows a corporation to make a tax-free distribution of the stock of a controlled corporation (control being defined in section 355(a)(1)(D)(ii) by reference to section 368(c)) to its shareholders in a tax-free distribution, provided the active business requirement of section 355(b) is met and the transaction is deemed not to be merely a "device" to distribute tax free, earnings and profits which otherwise would be taxable as a dividend. There is no dispute between the parties that these conditions have been satisfied. The issue upon which they have parted company is whether the limitations of section 355(a)(3)(B) apply. That section provides for the taxation of part of the distribution as follows —

> (B) Stock Acquired in Taxable Transactions Within 5 Years Treated As Boot. — For purposes of this section (other than paragraph (1)(D) of this subsection) and so much of section 356 as

relates to this section, stock of a controlled corporation acquired by the distributing corporation by reason of any transaction —

> (i) which occurs within 5 years of the distribution of such stock, and
>
> (ii) in which gain or loss was recognized in whole or in part,
>
> shall not be treated as stock of such controlled corporation, but as other property.

Section 356(b), in turn, provides that "the fair market value of such other property shall be treated as a distribution of property to which section 301 applies."

Petitioner concedes that, if AT&T had distributed the Pacific stock directly to its shareholders, the Pacific stock acquired in the merger would have been treated as "other property" under section 355(a)(3)(B), because the merger was a taxable transaction that took place within five years of the divestiture. Petitioner argues, however, that it was PacTel Group stock, not Pacific stock, which AT&T distributed to its shareholders. Since this stock was acquired in what respondent concedes was a tax-free exchange, petitioner argues that none of such stock can be categorized as "other property."

Respondent contends that petitioner's position is overly simplistic and that the language of section 355(a)(3)(B) is sufficiently broad to permit an interpretation which will be more accommodating to what he views as the legislative purpose behind the section's enactment, namely to preclude not only direct distributions of purchased interests in an active business but also indirect distributions of such interests emanating from a holding company structure. By way of amplification of his position, respondent argues that (1) we should treat a portion of the PacTel Group common stock as having been acquired via the prior taxable acquisition of Pacific stock with the result that the "by reason of any transaction" provision of section 355(a)(3)(B) is satisfied, or (2) in view of the overall statutory framework of section 355, Pacific, as part of the PacTel Group, falls within the ambit of the statutory phrase "controlled corporation" as that term is used in section 355(a)(3)(B). As a consequence, respondent concludes that such portion of PacTel stock as represents the fair market value of the Pacific stock (stipulated to be $.39 per share of AT&T stock) constitutes "other property" and is taxable as a dividend.

A literal reading of section 355(a)(3)(B) appears to support petitioner's position. On its face, the statutory language is directed to the distribution "*of stock of a controlled corporation*, acquired by the distributing corporation by reason of any [taxable] transaction [occurring] within 5 years of the *distribution of such stock*." (Emphasis added.) As used in section 355(a)(1)(A) the term "controlled corporation" means a corporation which the distributing corporation "controls immediately before the distribution" within the meaning of section 368(c). Since AT&T did not own directly any stock of Pacific immediately before the distribution, and because the stock attribution rules of section 318 are not applicable to section 368(c), it follows that, from a literal standpoint, Pacific was not a "controlled corporation" of AT&T for purposes of section 355(a)(3)(B). On this basis, petitioner would prevail.

We think it appropriate, however, not simply to adhere to the literal meaning of section 355(a)(3)(B). It can be argued — as indeed respondent does herein — that the words of that section are sufficiently ambiguous to permit a resort to legislative history, an aspect of this case to which we now turn our attention.

The stock boot rule of section 355(a)(3)(B) made its first appearance in the Senate version of the Internal Revenue Code of 1954, H.R. 8300, 83d Cong., 2d Sess. (1954). Section 355(a)(3) in the amendments to the Bill as reported by the Senate Finance Committee on page 122 (June 18, 1954) provided that —

> stock of a controlled corporation acquired by the distributing corporation within 5 years of its distribution, in a transaction in which gain or loss was recognized in whole or in part, shall not be treated as stock of such controlled corporation, but as other property.

In commenting on the addition of this section, the Senate Finance Committee stated that —

> For purposes of determining the taxable nature of part of the exchange or distribution, stock in a controlled corporation acquired by purchase within 5 years of its distribution is treated as "other property." Thus, for example, if a corporation has held a minority stock interest in a corporation for 5 years or more prior to the distribution and within such 5-year period purchases control of such corporation only the stock so purchased will be considered "other property." . . . [S. Rept. No. 1622, 83d Cong., 2d Sess. 267-68 (1954).]

The Conference Committee modified this proposal, however, and explained the modification as follows —

> In section 355(a)(3), the phrase "by reason of any transaction which occurs within 5 years of the distribution of such stock" has been inserted in lieu of the phrase "within 5 years of its distribution, in a transaction." The effect of this change is to make certain that, in addition to treating stock of a controlled corporation purchased directly by the distributing corporation as "other property," similar treatment will be given such stock if it is purchased within 5 years through the use of a controlled corporation or of a corporation which, prior to a "downstairs merger," was in control of the distributing corporation. For example, if the parent corporation has

> held 80 percent of the stock of an active subsidiary corporation for more than 5 years but purchases the remaining 20 percent of such stock within the 5-year period, and distributes all of the stock, gain or loss will not be recognized nor will dividend treatment be accorded the stock distributed to the extent of 80 percent. The 20 percent of the stock will be treated as "other property" for purposes of section 356. Similarly, under the amendment made, where such parent causes another subsidiary to acquire the 20 percent of the stock and then itself acquires such stock in a liquidation in which no gain or loss is recognized to such parent under section 332, or where the subsidiary having held 80 percent of the stock of its subsidiary for more than 5 years, acquires the 20 percent of the stock which has been purchased by the parent within the 5-year period through a nontaxable "downstairs" merger of the parent into the subsidiary, and all of the stock is distributed, such 20 percent of the stock will in either case be treated as "other property." [H. Rept. No. 2543, 83d Cong., 2d Sess. 38 (1954).]

Thus, the "by reason of any transaction" language was added to prevent a distributing corporation from avoiding taxation by acquiring additional controlled corporation stock via a purchase by a related entity coupled with some type of tax-free combination. The focus of section 355(c)(3)(B) both before and after the change remained the same; on the acquisition and distribution of stock of the controlled corporation, not on the acquisition of stock of the underlying, active subsidiary which was not actually distributed.

This brings us to respondent's second argument, namely that the overall statutory framework of section 355 requires section 355(a)(3)(B) to be interpreted as focusing not merely on the stock of the controlled corporation being distributed, but on the actual operating subsidiary included in the spin-off. Respondent correctly points out that the statutory framework of section 355(b)(2)(A) "itself envisions situations where a holding company will be used as the distributing mechanism for an active subsidiary." It provides that a corporation will qualify as an "active business" if for the 5 year period ending on the date of distribution it has been—

> engaged in the active conduct of a trade or business, or substantially all of its assets consist of stock and securities of a corporation controlled by it (immediately after the distribution) which is so engaged. . . .

Thus, section 355(b)(2)(A) allows the distributing corporation to "look through" the controlled corporation to its underlying active subsidiary in order to satisfy the active business requirement. Similarly, to qualify as an active trade or business under section 355(b)(2)(D) during the 5 years prior to the distribution of stock, it must be established that—

control of a corporation which (at the time of acquisition of control) was conducting such trade or business —

    (i) was not acquired directly (or through one or more corporations) by another corporation. . . .

Therefore, much like section 355(b)(2)(A), this section cuts through the form of the spin-off and focuses directly on the underlying active subsidiary when considering whether or not a corporation qualifies as an active trade or business.

From this legislative framework, respondent concludes that, since it is the activity of the underlying subsidiary that qualifies the spin-off as a tax-free section 355 distribution to begin with, it is only logical and consistent that for section 355(a)(3)(B) purposes, we must also focus on the underlying active subsidiary. Unfortunately for respondent, as we have already observed, neither the words of section 355(a)(3)(B), nor its legislative history, support his conclusion. Furthermore, although respondent discusses at great length the congressional purpose behind the passage of the "active business" provisions of section 355(b), his attempts to explain why we should interpret section 355(a)(3)(B) in a similar light, so that these two sections are read in "symmetry," with a focus on the active subsidiary, are far from convincing. Absent a clearer statement of legislative intent that we should look through the stock of the controlled corporation, we find it difficult to make the analytical jump respondent asks of us. . . . In fact, in light of the clear and detailed statutory scheme of section 355(b), the conspicuous absence of similar language in section 355(a)(3)(B) suggests that Congress was not only aware of the claimed "inconsistency," but intended just such a result.[1] Moreover, we have not overlooked the interpretative implications of the fact that, both in operative text and examples, respondent's regulations under section 355 have been for some thirty years, and are anticipated to continue to be, conspicuously silent in respect of transactions of the type involved herein.

However, our inquiry is not over. While it appears that both the plain meaning of section 355(a)(3)(B), as well as its legislative history, support petitioner's position, we also recognize that —

> the courts have some leeway in interpreting a statute if the adoption of a literal or usual meaning of its words "would lead to absurd results . . . or would thwart the obvious purpose of the statute." . . .

---

1. Moreover, Congress has proven itself quite capable of enacting stock-taint rules when it has desired to do so. See, e.g., section 306(c)(1)(B)(ii) in which the same Congress that enacted section 355(a)(3)(B) provided for an "inherited taint" rule with respect to preferred stock received in exchange for section 306 stock pursuant to a plan of reorganization.

Or, to put it another way, we should not adopt a construction which would reflect a conclusion that Congress had "legislate[d] eccentrically." . . . We are satisfied that our reliance on the wording of the statute involved herein would not have any such deleterious consequences either in terms of sections 355(a)(3)(B) specifically or section 355 generally. To begin with, pursuant to the merger, AT&T issued 6,705,897 shares of its common stock, with a fair market value of $370,500,834, in exchange for the 19,159,707 publicly held shares of Pacific common stock, and paid $10,742,580 for the 179,043 publicly held shares of Pacific 6 percent voting preferred stock. Thus, over 97% of the consideration furnished by AT&T to acquire the Pacific stock consisted of newly issued shares of its own stock. Since the underlying purpose of section 355(a)(3)(B) is to prevent the conversion of excess, liquid funds, such as cash and marketable securities, into additional controlled corporation stock that can then be distributed tax-free in a spin-off, we fail to see how respondent can argue that the spin-off of PacTel Group stock in any way frustrated the "obvious purpose of the statute."

Furthermore, by spinning off PacTel Group stock, AT&T did not bail out earnings and profits and thus undermine the general statutory purpose of section 355, because the Pacific stock acquired from the minority shareholders pursuant to the merger has remained in corporate solution and has never passed into the hands of AT&T's shareholders. Although respondent argues that this is merely a form over substance argument because the benefit of the purchased interest in the Pacific stock was transferred to PacTel Group, and thus was indirectly distributed to AT&T's shareholders, we note that—

> A dividend does not confer an economic benefit on its recipient. The distribution leaves the shareholder no richer, since his directly owned assets increase only by the same amount that the beneficial ownership of those assets represented by his stock interest diminishes. A dividend therefore is included in gross income not because it affects the shareholder's net worth (which is increased even by undistributed corporate profits), but because the distributed property no longer is in corporate solution. [Kingston, The Deep Structure of Taxation: Dividend Distributions, 85 Yale L.J. 861, 863-864 (1976).]

Thus, even assuming, arguendo, that the net worth of each shareholder increased as a result of the AT&T stock purchase,[2] the

2. We note that AT&T's shareholders did not in fact benefit from the Pacific merger. While we recognize that the acquisition, on AT&T's books, resulted in an increase in total net assets and corporate net worth (because AT&T acquired the majority of the Pacific stock for newly issued shares instead of for cash or debt securities), this increase did not filter down to the existing AT&T shareholders. When a corporation issues new stock in exchange for adequate consideration, existing share-

simple fact remains that this did not give rise to a taxable event because AT&T did not distribute the Pacific stock. A bailout, like a dividend, by definition requires a distribution out of corporate solution. This has not occurred.

That the Pacific stock which was acquired in a taxable transaction remained in corporate solution is most significant. It has caused us to focus on some of the problems which would arise if respondent's approach were adopted herein. For example, how would a future distribution of Pacific stock be treated? Another problem which would arise, if respondent's approach were adopted, involves the necessity of determining the value of the "tainted" stock transferred in the later nontaxable exchange and allocating that value to the shares of stock acquired in that exchange which then become the subject of a section 355 distribution—a problem which we are not required to face herein because of the parties' agreement as to the value attributable to the purchased Pacific stock and allocable to the distributed PacTel stock. The problem is even more difficult when more than one class of stock of the controlled corporation is received by the distributing corporation in the nontaxable exchange. Beyond this is a still further complication if respondent should carry his approach to its logical conclusion and, in a later case, should ask us to extend the view which he asks us to adopt herein to a purchase of stock of a subsidiary of the controlled corporation within 5 years of a section 355 distribution. Granted that the courts often deal with problems of allocation without specific legislative mandate, it does not necessarily follow that they should extend the interpretation of a statute to create such a problem.

The long and the short of the matter is that we see no thwarting of legislative purpose by confining section 355(a)(3)(B) to the situations which Congress obviously had in mind at the time of its enactment. In so concluding, we are constrained to observe that, if respondent feels that a transaction of the type involved herein represents an obvious attempt to bail out earnings and profits in violation of the purpose behind section 355, he is not without his remedy. He can challenge such a transaction as a "device" under section 355(a)(1)(B). He has chosen not to do so in this case, because of the conceded business purposes involved in implementing the antitrust decree and FCC order, and we are satisfied that he should not be permitted to avoid this channel of attack by means of an overly broad construction of section 355(a)(3)(B). Thus, while we agree with respondent that business purpose is irrelevant to the proper construction of section 355(a)(3)(B), we do not agree with his con-

---

holders realize no increase in the value of their individual holdings, because although the overall net worth of the company rises, so does the number of shares outstanding.

tentions, that "Congress, in enacting section 355, intended to put direct distributions of stock of existing corporations on a par with indirect distributions of such stock through the use of holding companies [and that the 'by reason of any transaction' language was specifically added to section 355(a)(3)(B) to make it clear that the section was to be applied not only to direct purchase of stock by distributing corporations, but also to any conceivable indirect purchase of stock within five years of the distribution." (Respondent's brief, p. 40.)

The absolutism of respondent's contentions is unacceptable. Essentially respondent seeks to have us do what Congress might have done if the type of transaction involved herein had been brought to its attention. But it is not within the province of this Court thus to expand upon the handiwork of the legislature. . . .

In view of the foregoing, decision will be entered for petitioner.

Reviewed by the Court.

NOTE

Does *Dunn* provide a roadmap for a taxpayer seeking to avoid the constraints of §355(a)(3)(B)? How would you have decided *Dunn*, and how would you have written your opinion?

What is the purpose of §355(a)(3)(B) and how does it (should it) fit into the legislative scheme? What is the role of §355(b)(2)(d), enacted more recently?

VII.   *CORPORATE SUBSTITUTION — REINCORPORATIONS, "F" REORGANIZATIONS, AND RELATED PROBLEMS*

SMOTHERS v. UNITED STATES
642 F.2d 894 (5th Cir. 1981)

Before Wisdom, Garza and Reavley, Circuit Judges.

WISDOM, Circuit Judge. . . . This dispute arises from the dissolution of one of . . . [the Smothers'] wholly owned business corporations. The taxpayers contend that the assets distributed to them by that corporation should be taxed at the capital gain rate applicable to liquidating distributions. The Internal Revenue Service . . . counters by characterizing the dissolution as part of a reorganization, thereby rendering the taxpayers' receipt of the distributed assets taxable at ordinary income rates. The district court viewed the transaction as a reorganization and ruled for the IRS. We affirm.

In 1956, . . . [the taxpayers] and an unrelated third party organized Texas Industrial Laundries of San Antonio, Inc. (TIL). The taxpayers owned all of its outstanding stock from 1956 through the tax year in issue, 1969. TIL engaged in the business of renting industrial uniforms and other industrial cleaning equipment, such as wiping cloths, dust control devices, and continuous toweling. It owned its own laundry equipment as well.

Shortly after the incorporation of TIL, the taxpayers organized another corporation, Industrial Uniform Services, Inc. (IUS), specifically to oppose a particular competitor in the San Antonio industrial laundry market. The taxpayers owned all of the stock of IUS from the time of its organization until its dissolution. Unlike TIL, IUS did not own laundry equipment; it had to contract with an unrelated company to launder the uniforms it rented to customers. J. E. Smothers personally managed IUS, as well as TIL, but chose not to pay himself a salary from IUS in any of the years of its existence.

IUS evidently succeeded in drawing business away from competing firms, for TIL purchased its main competitor in 1965. IUS continued in business, however, until 1969. On the advice of their accountant, the taxpayers then decided to dissolve IUS and sell all of its non-liquid assets to TIL. On November 1, 1969, IUS adopted a plan of liquidation in compliance with §337, and on November 30, it sold the following assets to TIL for cash at their fair market value (stipulated to be the same as their book value):

Assets	Amount
Noncompetitive covenant	$ 3,894.60
Fixed assets	491.25
Rental property	18,000.00
Prepaid insurance	240.21
Water deposit	7.50
Total	$22,637.56

The noncompetitive covenant constituted part of the consideration received by IUS from its purchase of a small competitor. The fixed assets consisted of incidental equipment (baskets, shelves, and a sewing machine), two depreciated delivery vehicles, and IUS's part interest in an airplane. The rental property was an old apartment building in Corpus Christi on land with business potential. These assets collectively represented about 15% of IUS's net value. The parties stipulated that none of these assets were necessary to carry out IUS's business.

After this sale, IUS promptly distributed its remaining assets to its shareholders, the taxpayers, then dissolved under Texas law:

Assets	Amount
Cash (received from TIL)	$ 22,637.56
Cash (of IUS)	2,003.05
Notes receivable	138,000.00
Accrued interest receivable	35.42
Claim against the State of Texas	889.67
Liabilities assumed	(14,403.35)
Total	$149,162.35

TIL hired all three of IUS's employees immediately after the dissolution, and TIL continued to serve most of IUS's customers.

In computing their federal income tax liability for 1969, the taxpayers treated this distribution by IUS as a distribution in complete liquidation within §331(a)(1). Accordingly, they reported the difference between the value of the assets they received in that distribution, $149,162.35, and the basis of their IUS stock, $1,000, as long-term capital gain. Upon audit, the IRS recharacterized the transaction between TIL and IUS as a reorganization within §368(a)(1)(D), and therefore treated the distribution to the taxpayers as equivalent to a dividend under §356(a)(2). Because IUS had sufficient earnings and profits to cover that distribution, the entire distribution was therefore taxable to the Smothers' at ordinary income rates. The IRS timely assessed a $71,840.84 deficiency against the Smothers.' They paid that amount and filed this suit for a refund.

The district court held that the transaction constituted a reorganization and rendered judgment for the IRS. . . .

Subchapter C of the Internal Revenue Code broadly contemplates that the retained earnings of a continuing business carried on in corporate form can be placed in the hands of its shareholders only after they pay a tax on those earnings at ordinary income rates. That general rule is, of course, primarily a consequence of §301, which taxes dividend distributions as ordinary income. The Code provides for capital gain treatment of corporate distributions in a few limited circumstances, but only when there is either a significant change in relative ownership of the corporation, as in certain redemption transactions, or when the shareholders no longer conduct the business themselves in corporate form, as in true liquidation transactions. The history of Subchapter C in large part has been the story of how Congress, the courts, and the IRS have been called upon to foil attempts by taxpayers to abuse these exceptional provisions. Ingenious taxpayers have repeatedly devised transactions which formally come within these provisions, yet which have the effect of permitting shareholders to withdraw profits at capital gain rates while carrying on a continuing business enterprise in corporate form without substantial change in ownership. This is just such a case.

The transaction in issue here is of the genus known as liquidation-reincorporation, or reincorporation. The common denominator of such transactions is their use of the liquidation provisions of the Code, which permit liquidating distributions to be received at capital gain rates, as a device through which the dividend provisions may be circumvented.[7] Reincorporations come in two basic patterns. In one, the corporation is dissolved and its assets are distributed to its shareholders in liquidation. The shareholders then promptly reincorporate all the assets necessary to the operation of the business, while retaining accumulated cash or other surplus assets. The transaction in this case is of the alternate form. In it, the corporation transfers the assets necessary to its business to another corporation owned by the same shareholders in exchange for securities or, as here, for cash, and then liquidates. If the minimal technical requirements of §337 are met, as they indisputably were here, the exchange at the corporate level will not result in the recognition of gain by the transferor corporation. If formal compliance with the liquidation provisions were the only necessity, both patterns would enable shareholders to withdraw profits from a continuing corporate business enterprise at capital gain rates by paper-shuffling. Unchecked, these reincorporation techniques would eviscerate the dividend provisions of the Code.

That result can be avoided by recharacterizing such transactions, in accordance with their true nature, as reorganizations. A reorganization is, in essence, a transaction between corporations that results merely in "a continuance of the proprietary interests in the continuing enterprise under modified corporate form" — a phrase that precisely describes the effect of a reincorporation. Lewis v. Commissioner, 1 Cir. 1949, 176 F.2d 646, 648. Congress specifically recognized that the throw-off of surplus assets to shareholders in the course of a reorganization can be equivalent to a dividend, and if so, should be taxed as such. §§356(a)(1)-(2). The reincorporation transactions described above result in a dividend payment to the shareholders in every meaningful financial sense. The assets retained by the shareholders therefore should be taxed as dividends as long

---

7. Other tax benefits may be reaped from reincorporation transactions in appropriate circumstances: e.g., elimination of the earnings and profits account of the old corporation in order to avoid the §531 tax on unreasonable accumulations; and a step-up in the tax basis of depreciable corporate assets at capital gain rates to the extent permitted by §1245 and §1250. In light of IUS's relatively large earnings and profits account, the former benefit is not a trivial one here.

as the transaction can be fitted within the technical requirements of one of the six classes of reorganization recognized by §368(a)(1).

In general, reincorporation transactions are most easily assimilated into §368(a)(1)(D) ("D reorganization"), as the IRS attempted to do in this case.[9] A transaction qualifies as a D reorganization only if it meets six statutory requirements.

(1) There must be a transfer by a corporation (§368(a)(1)(D));

(2) of substantially all of its assets (§354(b)(1)(A));

(3) to a corporation controlled by the shareholders of the transferor corporation, or by the transferor corporation itself (§368(a)(1)(D));

(4) in exchange for stock or securities of the transferee corporation (§354(a)(1));

(5) followed by a distribution of stock or securities of the transferee corporation to the transferor's shareholders (§354(b)(1)(B));

(6) pursuant to a plan of reorganization (§354(b)(1)).

On this appeal, the taxpayers concede that the transaction in issue meets every technical prerequisite for characterization as D reorganization, except for one. They argue that since the assets sold by IUS to TIL amounted to only 15% of IUS's net worth, TIL did not acquire "substantially all of the assets" of IUS within the meaning of §354(b)(1)(A).

We hold to the contrary. The words "substantially all assets" are not self-defining. What proportion of a corporation's assets is "substantially all" in this context, and less obviously, what "assets" are to be counted in making this determination, cannot be answered without reference to the structure of Subchapter C. To maintain the integrity of the dividend provisions of the Code, "substantially all assets" in this context must be interpreted as an inartistic way of expressing the concept of "transfer of a continuing business." As this Court implied in Reef Corp. v. Commissioner, 5 Cir. 1966, 368 F.2d 125, 132, *cert. denied,* 1967, 386 U.S. 1018, . . . it is in a sense simply a limited codification of the general nonstatutory "continuity of business enterprise" requirement applicable to all reorganizations.

9. Reincorporations may also fit within §368(a)(a)(F) ("[a] mere change in identity form or place of organization, however effected"). See Davant v. Commissioner, . . . [page 779 infra]; Reef Corp. v. Commissioner, 5 Cir. 1966, 368 F.2d 125, 133-37, *cert. denied,* 1967, 386 U.S. 1018. . . . The government did not press that theory on appeal. Doubtless that owes to its general reluctance to extend the scope of §368(a)(1)(F) to acquisitive reorganizations, which derives from the fact that net operating losses may be carried back after an F reorganization. §381(b)(3). . . . The IRS has in the past occasionally advanced more exotic arguments against reincorporations — e.g., the theory that no real "liquidation" occurs in such transactions, and the theory that even if a liquidation does occur, the distribution of surplus assets is a dividend functionally unrelated to the liquidation — but it did not so argue here. Cf. Rev. Rul. 61-156, 1961-2 C.B. 62; Telephone Answering Service Co., Inc. v. Commissioner, . . . [page 773 infra]; Breech v. United States, 9 Cir. 1971, 439 F.2d 409; Joseph C. Gallagher, 1962, [page 761 infra].

This interpretation finds support in the history of §368(a)(1)(D) and §354(b)(1)(A). The Internal Revenue Code of 1939 had no provision equivalent to the "substantially all assets" requirements, and courts almost uniformly approved attempts by the IRS to treat reincorporation transactions as reorganizations within the predecessor of §368(a)(1)(D) in the 1939 Code. The "substantially all assets" requirement of §354(b)(1)(A) and the amendment of §368(a)(1)(D) incorporating that requirement were added during the 1954 recodification as part of a package of amendments aimed at plugging a different loophole — the bail-out of corporate earnings and profits at capital gains rates through divisive reorganizations. There is no indication that Congress wished to relax the application of the reorganization provisions to reincorporation transactions. Indeed, the committee reports indicate the contrary. The Senate report accompanying the bill that contained the "substantially all assets" requirement of §354(b)(1)(A) and the parallel amendment to §368(a)(1)(D) stated that the purpose of those changes was only "to insure that the tax consequences of the distribution of stocks or securities to shareholders or security holders in connection with divisive reorganizations will be governed by the requirements of section 355." The report expressly noted that except with respect to divisive reorganizations, the reorganization provisions "are the same as under existing law and are stated in substantially the same form." Even more significantly, the original House version of the 1954 Code contained a provision specifically dealing with reincorporation transactions. That provision was dropped in conference because the conferees felt that such transactions "can appropriately be disposed of by judicial decision or by regulation within the framework of the other provisions of the bill." As the court said in Pridemark, Inc. v. Commissioner, 4 Cir. 1965, 345 F.2d 35, 40, this response shows that "the committee was aware of the problem and thought the present statutory scheme adequate to deal with it." By implication, this passage approved the IRS's use of the predecessor of §368(a)(1)(D) to meet the problem, and shows that the "substantially all assets" amendment was not thought to restrict its use.

Courts have almost unanimously so interpreted the "substantially all assets" language. Moreover, they have also interpreted the other technical conditions for a D reorganization in ways which accomplish the congressional intent to reach reincorporation transactions. For example, the literal language of §368(a)(1)(D) and §§354(a), 354(b)(1)(B), requires that the transferee corporation "exchange" some of its "stock or securities" for the assets of the transferor, and that those items be "distributed" to the shareholders of the transferor, before a D reorganization can be found. Yet both of those requirements have uniformly been ignored as "meaningless gestures" in the reincorporation context, in which the same shareholders own all the stock of both corporations.[14] Smothers does not even challenge the applicability of that principle here.

Properly interpreted, therefore, the assets looked to when making the "substantially all assets" determination should be all the assets, and only the assets, necessary to operate the corporate business — whether or not those assets would appear on a corporate balance sheet constructed according to generally accepted accounting principles. Two errors in particular should be avoided. Inclusion of assets unnecessary to the operation of the business in the "substantially all assets" assessment would open the way for the shareholders of any enterprise to turn dividends into capital gain at will. For example, if we assume that "substantially all" means greater than 90%, then a corporation need only cease declaring dividends and accumulate surplus liquid assets until their value exceeds 10% of the total value of all corporate assets. The shareholders could then transfer the assets actively used in the business to a second corporation owned by them and liquidate the old corporation. Such a liquidating distribution would be a dividend in any meaningful sense, but an interpretation of "substantially all assets" that took surplus assets into account would permit the shareholders to treat it as capital gain. Indeed, such an interpretation would perversely treat a merely nominal distribution of retained earnings as a dividend, but would permit substantial distributions to be made at capital gain rates. Courts therefore have invariably ignored all surplus assets and have focused on the operating assets of the business — the tangible assets actively used in the business — when making the "substantially all assets" assessment.

Second, exclusion of assets not shown on a balance sheet constructed according to generally accepted accounting principles from the "substantially all assets" assessment would offer an unjustified windfall to the owners of service businesses conducted in corporate form. The most important asset of such a business may be its reputation and the availability of skilled management and trained employees, none of which show up on a standard balance sheet. Other courts have correctly recognized that in appropriate cases those in-

14. The "meaningless gesture," language is from James Armour, Inc., 1964, 43 T.C. 295, 307. See also, e.g., Atlas Tool Co. v. Commissioner, 3 Cir. 1980, 614 F.2d 860, 865, *cert. denied*, 1980, _____ U.S. _____, . . . Davant v. Commissioner, . . . [page 779 infra]. Other technical requirements have been liberally construed in appropriate situations to foil reincorporations. For instance, §354(b)(1)(B) technically requires that all properties received from the transferor corporation be distributed before a D reorganization can be found, but a "constructive distribution" was found in David T. Grubbs, 1962, 39 T.C. 42. Similarly, §368(a)(1)(D) requires a "plan of reorganization," but a formal written plan is not necessary and the taxpayer's phraseology is not controlling if the transaction is in substance a reorganization. Atlas Tool Co. v. Commissioner, 614 F.2d at 866. . . .

tangible assets alone may constitute substantially all of the corporate assets. Otherwise for example, a sole legal practitioner who owns nothing but a desk and chair could incorporate himself, accumulate earnings, and then set up a new corporation and liquidate the old at capital gain rates — as long as he is careful to buy a new desk and chair for the new corporation, rather than transferring the old.

When these principles are applied to this case, it is plain that "substantially all of the assets" of IUS were transferred to TIL, and that the transaction as a whole constituted a reorganization. TIL and IUS were both managed and wholly owned by Smothers. By the nature of its business, IUS was wholly a service enterprise; indeed, the parties stipulated that none of the tangible assets of IUS were necessary to the operation of its business. The extent to which those tangible assets were transferred to TIL is therefore entirely irrelevant. IUS's most important assets — its reputation, sales staff, and the managerial services of Smothers — were all transferred to TIL. TIL rehired all three of IUS's employees immediately after IUS's liquidation, and continued to serve IUS's old customers. The same business enterprise was conducted by the same people under the same ownership, and the only assets removed from corporate solution were accumulated liquid assets unnecessary to the operation of the business. To treat this transaction as other than a reorganization would deny economic reality; to permit Smothers to extract the retained earnings of IUS at capital gain rates would make a mockery of the dividend provisions of the Internal Revenue Code.

We do not perceive ordinary income treatment here to be particularly harsh or a "tax trap for the unwary." It places the Smothers only in the position they would have been in if they had extracted the retained earnings of IUS as the Code contemplates they should have — by periodically declaring dividends.[18]

Affirmed.

GARZA, Circuit Judge, dissenting. After carefully reading the majority's opinion, I find that I must respectfully dissent. Unlike my Brothers, who apparently feel that it is their duty to "plug loopholes," I would remain content in applying the tax law as it reads leaving the United States Congress to deal with the consequences of the tax

---

18. Of course, the progressive structure of the income tax in a sense penalizes the plaintiff, since dividend income that could have been spread over many years is concentrated in one year, but that result was avoidable at the taxpayer's discretion. Similarly, he could have taken out some of the earnings in the form of a salary. Note that in all probability, Smothers did not actually defer enjoyment of the retained earnings of IUS until the reincorporation transaction. IUS's major asset by far was $138,000 in "notes receivable." Although the record does not reveal who issued those notes, the inference could be drawn that Smothers took the earnings out of IUS as they were earned, tax-free, by simply borrowing them from the corporation.

law as it has been drafted. The only issue before this Court on appeal is whether or not IUS transferred "substantially all of its assets" to TIL. Instead of dealing with this straightforward question, the majority has made a case of evil against liquidation-reincorporation abuses and, in an attempt to remedy every such perceived abuse, they have relieved the Congress of its burden to change the law heretofore requiring that "substantially all" of a corporation's assets be transferred to now read that "only those assets necessary to operate the corporate business" be transferred in order to meet the "D reorganization" requirements. Essentially, the majority has changed the definition of "substantially all assets" to mean only "necessary operating assets." I believe if Congress had meant "necessary operating assets" it would have said so instead of specifically requiring that "substantially all" of the assets be transferred. In my mind "substantially all" plainly means *all* of the assets except for an *insubstantial* amount. Under such a definition, the sale of 15% IUS's assets to TIL could hardly be defined as "substantially all" of IUS's assets.

However, even after having redefined "substantially all" to mean "necessary operating assets," the IUS liquidation still falls short of the "D reorganization" requirements because the stipulated facts are that absolutely none of the assets sold from IUS to TIL were necessary operating assets for either corporation. Faced with an absence of a proper factual setting, the majority goes on to define necessary operating assets as including a corporation's intangible assets. Now while a sale of intangible assets might be an appropriate consideration in determining whether or not "substantially all" assets of a corporation have been transferred, such a consideration simply has no bearing in this case. All of the assets transferred to TIL were depreciated tangible objects sold at book value after which IUS completely ceased all business operations. There simply was no other transfer of IUS's intangible assets as a continuing business.

The majority has placed great emphasis on the fact that three of IUS's route salesmen were subsequently employed by TIL and that Mr. Smothers' managerial services were available to TIL. Regardless of whether or not these facts enhanced TIL's business, the fact remains that neither the route salesmen nor Mr. Smothers' services were *transferred* as assets from one corporation to another. After IUS ceased business its route salesmen were free to seek any employment they desired. Likewise, Mr. Smothers was never obligated to perform services for TIL. From these facts I cannot agree that there was a transfer of a continuing business. The majority imputes adverse tax consequences to IUS's stockholders simply because TIL offered new employment to the route salesmen who were unemployed upon cessation of IUS's business operations. The majority places future stockholders, in Mr. Smothers' position, of choosing between unfavorable tax consequences and helping secure future employment to loyal and deserving employees who otherwise would be unemployed.

Although the Internal Revenue Service has never questioned the bona fides of IUS's liquidation, the majority has gone beyond the stipulated facts by characterizing the liquidation as a tax avoidance scam. I simply cannot agree. After starting from scratch, Mr. Smothers worked for over a dozen years refraining from drawing salary in order that IUS could pay its taxes, employees and other operating expenses and in order for IUS to become a successful self-sustaining business enterprise. Mr. Smothers was successful but, now that he no longer could devote his service to IUS, his years of labor are now labeled by the majority as a mere "paper shuffle." I do not share the majority's attitude.

The reasons for my position can be more easily understood by a simple review of the bottom-line facts. After IUS began showing a profit and started accumulating a cash surplus, instead of immediately investing in a building or in other equipment for its operations, it continued its operations as before. Now, if IUS had purchased real property or depreciable personal property for its operations (instead of leasing as it had been) and had sold these properties pursuant to its plan of liquidation, certainly no argument would be made that the money initially invested in those properties should have been declared by IUS as dividends. However, instead of investing its accumulations, IUS simply put them in its bank account as the tax laws allow and presumably faced any tax consequences posed by such an accumulation.

After IUS ceased operations, was liquidated, and its assets distributed to its stockholders in exchange for their stock, the I.R.S. issued a deficiency, not because IUS was reorganized within the meaning of . . . §368(a)(1)(D), but rather because the I.R.S. felt the accumulated earnings of IUS coupled with long-term capital gains rates applicable to the stock exchange provided an undesirable windfall to IUS's stockholders. In essence, the I.R.S. sought to expand the "D reorganization" provisions, lessen the availability of long-term capital gains treatment to corporate stockholders, and totally ignore the purpose of the tax upon improperly accumulated surplus as provided in . . . §531. The majority seeks to do equity for the I.R.S. position by "treating" the IUS liquidation as a "D reorganization." I do not believe the taxpayers or the tax laws are served by upholding an I.R.S. deficiency for the sole purpose of "plugging loopholes." The lesson to be learned from the majority's opinion is clear — future corporations faced with similar circumstances need only invest their otherwise accumulated surplus in some method other than savings. In the process of liquidation they need sell whatever assets exist to third parties unrelated to their stockholders and their stockholders should make no effort to find future employment for the corporation's employees.

It seems to me that in its attempt to "plug" a perceived "loophole," the majority is giving this Court's imprimatur to a variation of the same so-called "mockery" of the tax laws sought to be prevented by its opinion.

For these reasons, I respectfully dissent.

NOTE

In Walter S. Heller, 2 T.C. 371 (1943), aff'd, 147 F.2d 376 (9th Cir.), cert. denied, 325 U.S. 868 (1945), one of the very early liquidation-reincorporation cases, the shareholders were denied a loss on liquidation under the predecessor of §331 since, upon a finding that "reorganization" had occurred, the predecessor of §354(a)(1) barred its recognition. Compare Capital Sales, Inc., 71 T.C. 416 (1978) (P Corporation's principal asset, a franchise from an unrelated manufacturer, was cancelled and granted to commonly controlled S Corporation; P sold its remaining assets to S and liquidated; held, no "D" reorganization because franchise was not "transferred"), with Commissioner v. Morgan, 288 F.2d 676 (3rd Cir. 1961), cert. denied, 368 U.S. 836 (1962), (lack of "transfer" of investment advisory contract not sufficient basis for denying a "D" reorganization). Not surprisingly, in Rev. Rul. 70-240, 1970-1 C.B. 81, the Commissioner ruled that a corporation's sale of its operating assets to another corporation under common control with the transferor, followed by liquidation of the transferor and distribution of nonoperating assets to the sole shareholder, resulted in a "D" reorganization and a dividend. To the same effect as Smothers, see Commissioner v. Simon, 644 F.2d 339 (5th Cir. 1981).

GALLAGHER v. COMMISSIONER
39 T.C. 144 (1962), acq. and nonacq., 1964-2 C.B. 5, 9

Respondent has determined deficiencies in income tax in these consolidated cases. . . .

. . . The issues remaining for determination are (1) whether a series of distributions received in liquidation of a corporation should be treated as taxable dividends or distributions of earnings and profits incidental to a reorganization within the meaning of sections 354, 356, and 368 of the Internal Revenue Code of 1954 and, if either, (2) whether the amount taxed as ordinary income should be reduced by the capital contribution to the original corporation or the capital contributed to a new corporation formed to conduct the business of the original corporation.

FINDINGS OF FACT

. . . West Coast Terminals, Inc., a Delaware corporation with its principal business office in San Francisco, California (hereinafter called Delaware), was organized on May 13, 1946. Delaware was at all material times until its dissolution, hereinafter described, engaged in the general stevedoring and terminal business, which consisted of providing under contract the services (including labor and equipment) required to load, unload, and handle cargo carried on vessels, including both loading and unloading of vessels and both loading and unloading of freight cars, trucks, and other vehicles for the purpose of transferring cargo to or from vessels. The business was conducted principally at various points on San Francisco Bay, at the port of Stockton, at the port of Los Angeles, at Long Beach harbor, all in California, and at Portland, Oregon. . . .

William J. Bush (hereinafter called Bush) . . . , was president and a director and stockholder of Delaware, holding 391 shares of its stock at all material times until its dissolution. Bush was the chief executive officer of Delaware and devoted full time to its management, including the supervision of its stevedoring and terminal operations, the supervision of its financial affairs, and the supervision of relations with the ship operators who were its customers or potential customers.

Joseph C. Gallagher (hereinafter called Gallagher) . . . , was vice president and general manager and a director and stockholder of Delaware, holding 58 shares of its stock, at all material times until its dissolution. Gallagher was the second highest executive officer of Delaware and devoted full time to participation in its management, including participation in the supervision of its stevedoring and terminal operations, the supervision of its financial affairs, and the supervision of relations with the ship operators who were its customers or potential customers.

George H. Grant (hereinafter called Grant) . . . , was a director and stockholder of Delaware, holding 57 shares of its stock at all material times until its dissolution. Grant was a member of the board of directors having general control of the management of Delaware and, in addition, assisted in its relations with the ship operators who were its customers or potential customers.

Thomas E. Cuffe (hereinafter called Cuffe) . . . , was a director and stockholder of Delaware, holding 267 shares of its stock, at all material times until its dissolution. Cuffe was a member of the board of directors having general control of the management of Delaware and, in addition, assisted in its relations with the ship operators who were its customers or potential customers and was himself president of one of the ship operators who were customers of Delaware, namely, Pacific Far East Lines, Inc. . . .

The nine shareholders of Delaware consisted of two groups, as shown by the following schedule:

Stockholders	Percentage of stock	Shares of stock
Bush	30.24	391
Cuffe	20.65	267
Gallagher	4.49	58
Grant	4.41	57
Burkman	2.16	28
Total	61.95	801
Sexton (an estate)	20.65	267
Seid (an estate)	5.80	75
Lyon (a widow)	5.80	75
Seidenspinner (a widow)	5.80	75
Total	38.05	492
Grand total	100.00	1,293

The first group consisted of active executives and directors, as follows: Bush, Cuffe, Gallagher, and Grant, who were all directors of Delaware and two of whom were officers, and D. R. Burkman (hereinafter called Burkman), who was district manager in direct charge of all operations of Delaware in southern California, including Los Angeles and Long Beach harbor. The second group consisted of the remaining shareholders of record . . . (hereinafter referred to as the estates and widows), all of whom were . . . shareholders who had acquired their stock through the death of persons formerly active in Delaware. . . . The estates and widows were inactive and of no assistance to Delaware, and several members of this group wished to liquidate their interest because of the low yield and speculative nature of the business. . . .

The minutes of a meeting of the board of directors of Delaware on May 31, 1955, state in part as follows:

> The President stated that he and certain other of the share-holders of [Delaware], together with other persons, were planning to organize a California corporation for the purpose of offering to purchase the operating assets and goodwill of [Delaware]. The President then presented to the meeting a Plan of Complete Liquidation of [Delaware] involving the sale of the operating assets of [Delaware] as aforesaid, to be followed by the dissolution and liquidation of [Delaware]. . . .

A special meeting of the stockholders of Delaware was held on June 14, 1955. The minutes of this meeting state in part as follows:

... *Resolved*, that the Plan of Complete Liquidation of ... [Delaware] submitted to this meeting and hereby ordered to be made a part of the records of this meeting, be and same is hereby adopted;

Resolved, that, when and if ... [Delaware] shall receive an offer to purchase the operating assets of ... [Delaware], including its goodwill and the assignment of its operating contracts, then the President or Vice-President and Secretary are authorized and empowered to sell such assets at any price which in their judgment is deemed advisable; provided, however, that such price shall not be less than the book value thereof as of May 31, 1955, or as of the time of sale, whichever is less;

... The Chairman stated that the assets to be sold comprised equipment and prepaid insurance having April 30, 1955 book values of $86,760.26 and $10,754.71 respectively.

The plan of liquidation of Delaware provided in part as follows:

2. Immediately upon adoption of the Plan, the shareholders voting for its adoption shall adopt appropriate resolutions authorizing the appropriate officers of ... [Delaware] to take all necessary steps to sell and transfer the operating assets of ... [Delaware], including its goodwill, and to assign its operating contracts. The sales price of such assets shall be not less than the book value thereof as of May 31, 1955, or as of the time of sale, whichever is less. It is understood and contemplated that such assets may be sold to a corporation some of the shareholders of which are also shareholders and/or officers of ... [Delaware]. ...

5. If and when the operating assets of ... [Delaware] have been sold as contemplated by Section 1 hereof, the officers and directors in so far as possible shall reduce all other assets of ... [Delaware] to cash and upon compliance with the applicable laws of the State of Delaware may from time to time make one or more pro rata distributions in cash to the shareholders of ... [Delaware]. ...

6. On or before, but not later than, May 1, 1956, all known assets of ... [Delaware], except such assets as may be retained to meet claims against ... [Delaware] which it shall not have been possible to discharge prior to that date, shall be distributed pro rata to the shareholders of ... [Delaware] in complete liquidation of ... [Delaware]. If any of ... [Delaware's] assets shall not have been reduced to cash prior to the date of such distribution, which shall take place on May 1, 1956, if not earlier, undivided interests in such assets shall be distributed to the shareholders or such assets shall be otherwise divided ratably among the shareholders of ... [Delaware]. Such distribution of all of the assets of ... [Delaware] shall be in complete cancellation of all outstanding shares of ... [Delaware].

... On June 17, 1955, there was incorporated West Coast Terminals Co. of California, a California corporation (hereinafter referred to as California). California had only one class of stock. It issued this capital stock on July 15, 1955, and received full payment therefor in cash in the aggregate amount of $300,000.

Certain employees, important in the operation of the business and who had not owned any stock in Delaware, became stockholders in California. . . .

The capital stock of California at all material times has been owned, by petitioners and others, as shown by the following schedule:

Stockholders	Percentage of stock	Shares of stock
Bush, W. J.	30	900
Gallagher, J. C.	21	630
Cuffe, T. E.	10	300
Grant, G. H.	62⅔	200
Burkman, D. R.	5	150
Total	72⅔	2,180
Kurtz, M. O.	5	150
Johnson, A. E.	4⅔	140
Johnson, O.	4⅔	140
Kavanaugh, L. B.	4⅔	140
Linden, N. R.	4⅔	140
Cervelli, G. F.	1⅚	55
O'Leary, J.	1⅚	55
Total	27⅓	820
Grand total	100.00	3,000

On July 18, 1955, Delaware effected a sale of all of its operating assets and prepaid expenses and an assignment of its current trade contracts to California. The consideration for the above purchase was a check dated July 18, 1955, for the book value of the property in the amount of $100,264.56, said to be the fair market value of the properties. Nothing was paid for the partially performed contracts with customers beyond the purchaser's assumption of the obligations of these contracts. The opening balance sheet of California on July 18, 1955, was set up on the books as follows:

Assets:	
Tangible Property	$100,264.56
Cash	199,735.44
Total	$300,000.00

Liabilities	0
Capital Contributed	$300,000.00
Retained Earnings	0
Total	$300,000.00

In all cases the assignment of the contracts was agreed to by the third party involved, except in the case of the United States Government, which required that a new contract in the form of a novation be entered into. In securing these assignments, the customers were informed that the same key personnel would be with California and that Bush and Gallagher would control the company. . . .

After July 18, 1955, Delaware completely terminated its business, retaining only the personnel and office facilities necessary to effect an orderly liquidation. After July 18, 1955, the principal assets remaining to be converted to cash by Delaware were its accounts receivable. On July 21, 1955, Delaware was issued a document entitled "Certificate of Dissolution" by the State of Delaware.

By May 3, 1956, Delaware had made a series of distributions of all remaining assets to its shareholders pro rata. . . . After these distributions, Delaware had no remaining assets and all of its outstanding shares of stock were surrendered and canceled.

Delaware's total accumulated earnings and profits since its organization did not exceed $949,221, and petitioner's respective shares thereof did not exceed the following:

Bush	$287,044.30
Cuffe	196,014.14
Gallagher	42,620.02
Grant	41,860.65

Petitioners' respective shares of Delaware capital and the individual adjusted basis for Federal income tax purposes were as follows:

	Capital	Basis
Bush	$39,100	$59,209.36
Cuffe	26,700	26,700.00
Gallagher	5,800	15,206.00
Grant	5,700	14,943.82

As of May 31, 1955, Delaware had retained earnings of $838,329.80 and capital contributed in the amount of $156,000. . . .

The business of the two corporations required only a small amount of operating assets. . . .

The principal business of California was substantially the same as that of Delaware. When California commenced operations in 1955, the use of a name similar to that of Delaware was convenient for the purpose of indicating the same personnel of directors and executives, but was not necessary.

. . . About eight customers accounted for 75 percent of Delaware's business. One of these customers was the United States Army, which accounted for more than 40 percent of Delaware's business. . . . At the beginning of 1956, California lost the Army contract. . . .

Throughout the 4 fiscal years immediately preceding May 31, 1955, the earned surplus was invested in assets required by business needs. The cash in the business was enough to meet approximately 1 week's operating expenses. Bush had sought counsel as to Delaware's dividend policy with respect to the accumulated earnings tax for each of the fiscal years during 1953 through 1955 and was advised that it was not necessary to have a dividend in either 1953, 1954, or 1955 as long as the first distribution in dissolution was made before August 15, 1955. Adams opposed any dividends and wanted Delaware to build its net worth to reduce the risk of borrowing.

The following were some of the corporate business reasons for liquidating Delaware: To eliminate the inactive estates and widows, representing 38 percent of the outstanding stock, from the business; to permit Gallagher to acquire more stock so that Bush and Gallagher could control the business; to bring into stock ownership seven or eight executives who had helped in making a success of Delaware; to limit Cuffe's ownership of the business. Cuffe had previously withdrawn his account in San Francisco and stated his intention of going into the stevedoring business. The liquidation was intended to limit the possibility of Cuffe's 20.65 percent being combined with the estates and widows to control the business.

The dissolution of Delaware, incorporation of California, and transfer of the assets were all part of a single plan formulated by petitioners upon the advice of their attorney and tax counsel to effect the stated ends and achieve favorable tax results. . . .

None of the shareholders of Delaware and none of the shareholders of California occupied a relationship to any other shareholder of either Delaware or California, either by reason of being a member of a family or of owning any interest in any partnership, estate, trust, or corporation or for any other reason which would make applicable the constructive ownership rules of section 318 of the Internal Revenue Code of 1954. . . . All of the stock of each petitioner here involved had been held for more than six months before January 1, 1955.

Petitioners, in their individual returns, treated the liquidating distributions of Delaware as part or full payment in exchange for their stock and reported the amounts received in excess of the adjusted basis as long-term capital gains. Respondent, in his deficiency notices, "determined that the amount[s] . . . received . . . from [Delaware] . . . [are] taxable in full as dividend income."

OPINION

OPPER, Judge. Respondent's position consists of two alternative contentions which are so mutually exclusive as to make it desirable to consider them separately. His first argument, as stated in his brief, is "predicated basically on the thesis that the facts show that a complete [or partial] liquidation did not in substance occur." He therefore insists that the amount received by the individuals consisted of a dividend within the purview of section 301 of the 1954 Code. Although he does not specifically refer to section 302, the implication appears to be that the redemption, which he does not dispute, was essentially equivalent to a dividend under section 302(b)(1), see Neff v. United States, 305 F.2d 455 (Ct. Cl. 1962), *vacating and withdrawing* 301 F.2d 330 (Ct. Cl. 1962), and hence is not to be treated as a capital transaction under section 302(a), but as a dividend under section 301(c)(1), with ordinary income consequences. His alternative argument is that this was a reorganization within the meaning of section 368, that presumably the proceeds of the redemptions constituted "boot," and, accordingly, under section 356, are, at least to some extent, to be treated as ordinary income.

There can be no doubt that the stock of Delaware was redeemed and, if that were all there was to it, we might look to section 302, and then to section 301, for guidance in settling the ordinary-income problem. But the redemption was only one step in what was undoubtedly a liquidation-reincorporation operation, see David T. Grubbs, 39 T.C. 42 (1962), as respondent himself suggests in his second alternative.

As to the first proposition, we are accordingly able to resort to the step-transaction theory and to view the entire series of transactions as interrelated and inextricable. . . . Respondent does not, in fact, suggest anything to the contrary, but merely contends that some of the steps actually taken can be disregarded.[12] But, at least in such a situation as this, we cannot justify the inclusion of some and the exclusion of other essential steps. . . .

The concept of a continuation of the existing business through a section 331 liquidation, coupled with an intercorporate transfer,

---

12. "Furthermore, the 27⅓ [%] stock interest purchased in the new corporation by third parties should be disregarded and reorganization treatment applied to the step transaction. This step can be disregarded since without it the dominant purpose — to withdraw corporate earnings while continuing the equity interest in substantial part — was fully achieved."

falls into the general area of corporate reorganizations, so that it is in the so-called reorganization sections, if anywhere, that we should expect it to be dealt with.

The fact that the assets of a business are transferred to a new corporation does not by itself change the effect of the liquidation of the original corporation. If, for example, the assets had been transferred to another corporation in which the old shareholders had no interest, even though the business continued, Fowler Hosiery Co., 36 T.C. 201 (1961), *aff'd*, 301 F.2d 394 (C.A. 7, 1962); or if they had been transferred to another corporation, but the old corporation's business had not been continued, it seems clear respondent would have had no possible ground for contending that the liquidating distribution, even though partly composed of accumulated earnings, could be taxed as an ordinary dividend. Hellmich v. Hellman, 276 U.S. 233 (1928). So that it is only the continuance of the business in a new corporation, preponderantly owned by the shareholders of the old, upon which respondent can rely for his first contention.

But, generally speaking, it is exactly where the same enterprise is in essence wholly or partly continued even after some more or less radical change in its organization or conduct that it is the purpose of the so-called "reorganization" section of the law to operate. The basic approach of the complicated series of enactments incorporated in the 1954 Code appears to be that all such situations are to be tested by the "reorganization" portion of the statute, and that it was intended that if a transaction of a similar kind does not fall within them, but lies in the general area of arrangements which may, in effect, constitute the continuation of an existing business, it shall be treated as a transaction giving rise to gain or loss and not as a distribution.

Respondent's first contention includes the insistence that we should ignore the liquidation of Delaware and test these transactions solely as a redemption. Yet he makes no reference in his brief to section 302 which is the primary redemption section. It is not clear whether for this proposition he relies on the rationale of such cases as Bazley v. Commissioner, 331 U.S. 737 (1947), *rehearing denied and prior opinion amended* 332 U.S. 752 (1947); see also Gregory v. Helvering, 293 U.S. 465 (1935), although there it was a "recapitalization," not a liquidation, that was held not to fall within the statute. In *Bazley*, the Supreme Court found that a transaction which literally complied with the reorganization provisions was not to be accorded reorganization treatment because it was primarily a vehicle for the distribution of undistributed earnings. *Gregory* similarly denied the benefits of the reorganization provisions to a plan which met the literal definition of the Code because the plan had no relation to the business of either corporation.

Respondent would have us hold here that the liquidation of

Delaware was not a liquidation, although it literally complied with all the terms, because the transaction is alleged to have been primarily a vehicle for the distribution of undistributed earnings. But, unlike the reorganization sections which were involved in *Bazley* and similar cases, liquidation is usually accompanied by some kind of distribution which may well include accumulated earnings of the liquidating corporation. Hellmich v. Hellman, supra. That this is recognized by the statutory provisions themselves seems to us to permit of no uncertainty. Even though respondent from time to time refers to the section relating to complete liquidation,[19] no definition of this term appears in the statute nor in the regulations. A complete liquidation of a corporation can apparently exist only where the definition of partial liquidation does not apply, since otherwise there would be no purpose in distinguishing between complete and partial liquidation as defined in section 346(a)(1); although, of course, there may be situations in which, since the result would be the same, it is unnecessary to determine whether the liquidation is complete or partial.

Instead, it appears that what actually occurred here must be treated as a partial liquidation since it falls squarely within the definition of such a transaction which does appear in the statute.[20] It is difficult to find any ground for holding that this was not in every respect a partial liquidation to which section 331(a)(2) would expressly apply. . . .

We think it follows that the distributions made by Delaware are governed by the rules established by section 346. There was unquestionably a series of distributions in complete redemption of all of Delaware's stock pursuant to a plan. Although these distributions completely liquidated Delaware, the transaction literally falls within section 346(a)(1).

The conclusion that the redemption of Delaware's stock in the course of its liquidation is not to be considered as an ordinary dividend is fortified by an examination of the provisions of section 346. From the language of section 346(a), it would appear that a distribution in redemption of all of the stock of the corporation pursuant to a plan can never be essentially equivalent to a dividend as referred to in section 302(b)(1). This is because Congress found it necessary to include that condition in section 346(a)(2), which refers to the redemption of a part of the stock of the corporation, but omitted it in section 346(a)(1). We cannot assume that this was without significance.

Furthermore, "Section 302 does not apply to that portion of any distribution which qualifies as a distribution in partial liquidation under section 346." Sec. 1.302-1(a), Income Tax Regs. Not only this,

19. Sec. 331. . . .
20. Sec. 346 [now §302(b)(4) and (e) — Ed.]. . . .

but we have been referred to no authority, either under the 1954 Code or under the less restrictive language of the preceding revenue acts, in which a liquidation-reincorporation has been held to give rise to ordinary income, except where that result could be accomplished by applying the provisions relating to reorganizations. . . .

Of course, this does not eliminate respondent's second argument contending for the existence of a reorganization and accompanying "boot." With the limited exception of special situations specifically provided for by statute, see, e.g., sections 333, 341, this would be the only time a series of redemptions of all the stock of a corporation pursuant to a plan, or distributions in complete liquidation of a corporation, would receive treatment as a distribution to which section 301 applies. When the redemption, whether in complete or partial liquidation, is in pursuance of a plan of reorganization, as defined by section 368, and section 356 regarding "boot" comes into play, it is apparent that the dividend provisions of section 301 must apply.

The difficulty is that this series of steps does not amount to a statutory reorganization. Although several cases have found reorganization upon similar facts under subsection (D) relating to intercorporate transfers of assets with retention of "control," . . . those cases differ from the instant case in one important respect. Respondent specifically renounces subsection (D). This may be because only 72⅔ percent of California's stock was owned by former shareholders of Delaware. In this respect, if no other, the present case is unlike David T. Grubbs, supra. "Since the [shareholders of the transferor] owned less than 80 percent of the stock of the new corporations, the acquisition of the assets of the [transferor] is precluded from being a tax-free reorganization within the meaning of section [368(a)(1)(D)]." Austin Transit, Inc., 20 T.C. 849, 856 (1953).

The step-transaction approach makes it possible to view this arrangement as an acquisition of Delaware's assets by California in exchange for California's voting stock to petitioners. But then we must consider that there was also a payment of cash to the retiring 38 percent owned by the estates and widows. Possibly, this is the reason respondent has not attempted to apply subsection (C), relating to the acquisition of assets, "in exchange *solely* for . . . voting stock." (Emphasis added.) . . .

The remaining arguments for reorganization treatment are even less persuasive. Respondent's own regulation under section 368, section 1.368-1,2, Income Tax Regs., disposes of respondent's contention on brief that "[r]eorganization treatment can be ascribed . . . without literal satisfaction of the requirements of Sec. 368." Furthermore, "there was not that reshuffling of a capital structure, *within the framework of an existing corporation,* contemplated by the term 'recapitalization,'" as now described in subsection (E). . . . (Emphasis added.) And the shift that occurred in the proprietary interest of the two corporations was hardly the *"mere* change in identity, form, or place of organization" (emphasis added) required by subsection (F). . . .

We rest the conclusion that there was no reorganization here on the form and content of the reorganization sections, not on the ground that there was no business purpose. . . .

Section 1.331-l(c), Income Tax Regs., does not interfere with our ultimate conclusion. This regulation adopts the holding of Richard H. Survaunt, supra. In *Survaunt,* a transaction in which the original corporation was liquidated and the shareholders and directors transferred the assets to a new corporation in exchange for stock was found to be a reorganization under the intercorporate transfer of assets provision of subsection (D) when petitioners failed to prove the absence of a business purpose. The regulation describes similar facts and the . . . language invokes section 356 to cover the distribution of "boot" in pursuance of a plan of reorganization. Since we cannot conclude that the facts in the instant case constitute a reorganization, the reference to section 356 will not support respondent's position.

Section 1.331-1(c), Income Tax Regs., also cites section 301 as authority. This may be explained as further description of section 356. See section 356(a)(2). Respondent, however, takes the position that the regulation may require dividend treatment in any case of liquidation-reincorporation. It is argued that Congress did not intend a liquidation followed by a reincorporation of the business into a corporation with similar equity interests to be a liquidation within the meaning of section 331, with the result that section 331(b) should not apply. As we have already concluded, however, Congress accorded ordinary income treatment to liquidations only, if at all, in reorganization situations. . . .

We accordingly think petitioners correctly treated the cash and property received from Delaware as a payment in exchange for the Delaware stock redeemed by them. . . .

Reviewed by the Court.

[Dissenting opinion omitted.]

NOTES

1. In 1984 Congress effectively overruled *Gallagher* by relaxing the control requirement for acquisitive "D" reorganizations. See §368(a)(2)(H). Congress indicated that this amendment was not intended to "supersede or otherwise replace the various doctrines that have been developed by the Service and the courts to deal with"

transactions such as those in *Telephone Answering Service Co.* (infra) and *J. E. Smothers* (page 751 supra).

2. What was the basis of the Commissioner's first argument in *Gallagher?* See Treas. Reg. §1.301-1(1). Would this approach lead to dividend treatment of *all* the shareholders of Delaware? Of *all* who continued in California? By what factors did the Commissioner determine that there was "in substance a separate transaction"? What is the Commissioner's authority for disregarding the "net effect" here, while disregarding the separate steps in *Morgan?* What is the basis for the court's distinguishing *Grubbs,* discussed in *Gallagher* at page 768 supra?

TELEPHONE ANSWERING SERVICE CO. v. COMMISSIONER
63 T.C. 423 (1974), *aff'd by order,* 546 F.2d 423 (4th Cir. 1976), *cert. denied,* 431 U.S. 914 (1977)

TANNENWALD, Judge. . . . [T]he sole issue for determination is whether the gain realized by petitioner on the sale of all the stock of one of its subsidiaries to a third party is to be recognized. The resolution of this issue depends upon whether the factual pattern involved herein meets the requirements of section 337. . . . [TASCO, the petitioner, operated telephone answering services and provided managerial services to its two subsidiaries, Houston and North American, both of which also operated telephone answering services. The stock of Houston had been acquired in 1961 in exchange for stock of TASCO. North American was organized in 1962 to acquire services in other parts of the country. TASCO's income was derived from its separate answering services and from its management contracts; neither Houston nor North American ever paid a dividend.

[In April 1966, a general agreement was reached between TASCO and an unrelated party for the sale of the Houston stock. In May 1966, the board of directors adopted a "Plan of Complete Liquidation and Dissolution," and approved a contract for the sale of Houston. The sale was consummated for cash in October 1966, resulting in a realized gain to TASCO of approximately $270,000.

[In March 1967, TASCO transferred all of the assets necessary to its answering service and management operations to a newly organized, wholly owned subsidiary, New TASCO, in exchange for the latter's stock. The only assets retained by TASCO were the North American stock, the New TASCO stock, and the cash received on the sale of Houston. New TASCO entered into a management contract with North American.

[In April 1967, TASCO distributed all of its remaining assets to its shareholders and filed articles of dissolution under state law. New TASCO changed its name to TASCO and continued in business with the same customers, employees and offices as its predecessor.

[Also in April 1967, Houser, a 15.7-percent shareholder of New TASCO following the above distribution, surrendered all of his stock in exchange for the assets of a telephone answering service owned by North American. This stock was later transferred by North American to New TASCO.]

Petitioner claims that following these steps it was completely liquidated, and therefore section 337 requires nonrecognition of the gain realized on its sale of Houston. We disagree, and hold that the requirements of that section have not been satisfied.[9] Our decision is founded on both the history and the purpose of the statute.

Section 337 was first enacted as part of the 1954 Code. It was intended by Congress to avoid the "shadowy and artificial" distinction between a closely held corporation and its shareholders required by Commissioner v. Court Holding Co., . . . and United States v. Cumberland Public Service Co., . . . when corporate assets are sold during liquidation. . . . That section permits the avoidance of a double tax by allowing nonrecognition of gain at the corporate level, without the *Court Holding-Cumberland* requirement of proving that the shareholders, not the corporation, made the sale. Congress placed a price on nonrecognition, however, which is that the sale shall be followed by complete liquidation.

The Internal Revenue Code does not define a complete liquidation. Clearly, the term conveys more than the formal dissolution of a corporation under state law. Pridemark, Inc. v. Commissioner, 345 F.2d 35, 41 (C.A. 4, 1965). In contrast with some other parts of the Code (compare, e.g., sections 331 and 336), section 337 is hedged with specific provisions designed to describe, at least in outline, the complete liquidations entitled to its benefits. The sale and distribution must be preceded by the adoption of a "plan of complete liquidation." More importantly, "*all of the assets* of the corporation" (less assets retained to meet claims) must be "*distributed* in complete liquidation."

---

9. Although the notice of deficiency merely denied the applicability of section 337, respondent in this Court concentrates principally on the argument that the instant transaction was a reorganization meeting the requirements of sections 354 and 368(a)(1)(D). We find it unnecessary to reach this issue particularly with regard to the question whether New TASCO acquired "substantially all" of TASCO's assets, and we express no opinion as to its proper resolution. Similarly, we do not consider the proposition, disavowed by respondent, that the exchange should be treated in whole or in part as a divisive reorganization qualifying under section 355. In this context, we emphasize that we are dealing herein with the question of nonrecognition of gain *at the corporate level* and not with the tax consequences of the transactions *at the shareholder level*; in view of the complexities involved in determining those consequences, under a variety of permutations and combinations, it is conceivable that they might be subjected to a different analysis. . . .

(Emphasis added.) This language evidences an intent to require a bona fide elimination of the corporate entity and does not include a transaction in which substantially the same shareholders continue to utilize a substantial part of the directly owned assets of the same enterprise in uninterrupted corporate form.[10] . . .

The record herein demonstrates that TASCO sought to avoid the recognition of gain on the sale of Houston. But, the presence or absence of a tax avoidance objective is irrelevant in determining what is a "complete liquidation" for tax purposes. United States v. Cumberland Public Service Co., supra. . . . While a complete liquidation is a prerequisite to the application of section 337, the mere adoption of a plan denominated as one of "complete liquidation" and purported compliance therewith does not preclude further inquiry on our part. It is the reality and substance of the liquidation that counts. . . .

In Pridemark, Inc. v. Commissioner, supra, the Fourth Circuit stated . . . :

> The corporation must have ceased to be a going corporate concern, or if the enterprise is continued in corporate form, the shareholder must have disassociated himself from it. See Regs. 1.332-2(c) (1955). If the liquidated business is not resumed by the new corporation as a continuation of a going concern, there is a "complete liquidation."

Similarly, in Davant v. Commissioner, 366 F.2d 874, 882 (C.A. 5, 1966), . . . the Fifth Circuit stated:

> Those provisions [dealing with complete liquidation] contemplate that the operating assets will no longer be used by the stockholders to carry on the business as a corporation.

. . . Both *Court Holding Co.* and *Cumberland Public Service Co.*, supra, which prompted the adoption of section 337, involved the sale of a corporate enterprise and the termination of the shareholders' interest in the business. It is not without significance that the Supreme Court, in the latter case, specifically distinguished gains in the course of a "genuine liquidation" from those of a "going concern." . . . Moreover, during its consideration of the Internal Revenue Code of 1954, the House Ways and Means Committee stated:

> [A] corporation will be deemed to have completely liquidated

---

10. This interpretation is supported by Congress' failure to make section 337 applicable to sales of property in connection with partial liquidations and nonliquidating distributions in which the corporate form is retained, despite the possibility of the same "double tax" dilemma arising as with complete liquidations. . . . Section 333 of the House bill would have extended nonrecognition treatment to partial liquidations; the limitation to complete liquidations originated in the Senate Finance Committee. . . .

even though the business previously carried on by it is continued in partnership or sole proprietorship *or other noncorporate form.* [Emphasis added. . . .][12]

Clearly, the transactions under consideration herein did not meet the foregoing standards. The businesses which petitioner directly operated were continued without interruption by New TASCO, with substantial continuity of shareholder interest. The only result of the transaction was to place the North American stock and a sizable amount of cash in the shareholders' hands. New TASCO was merely the alter ego of petitioner with respect to all of its directly owned business assets; its formation and utilization served no purpose other than masking a distribution as one in complete liquidation. It is possible that the transactions can be treated as accomplishing a partial liquidation of petitioner within the meaning of section 346. We express no opinion on this score because, even if the requirements of a partial liquidation were found to have been met, section 337 would not apply. That section requires a "complete liquidation." . . . The transitory co-existence of TASCO and New TASCO does not support the conclusion that the subsequent but prearranged liquidation of the former effected a sufficient transmutation of the assets of petitioner out of corporate solution to satisfy the requirement of section 337 that "all of the assets of the corporation" be distributed. To hold for the petitioner in the instant case would frustrate the congressional purpose to deny section 337 treatment in connection with distributions of ongoing corporations. We cannot give tax effect to the "mere shifting of charters," Helvering v. Elkhorn Coal Co., . . . masquerading as a complete liquidation.

The facts before us are unlike those in Breech v. United States, 439 F.2d 409 (C.A. 9, 1971), and Hyman H. Berghash, 43 T.C. 743 (1965), *aff'd,* 361 F.2d 257 (C.A. 2, 1966). Those cases applied section 337 to liquidation-reincorporation transactions in which the continuity of shareholder interest between the old and new corporations was insufficient to satisfy the definition of a statutory reorganization. It was felt inappropriate to deny the existence of a complete liquidation where Congress had found the shift in ownership adequate to justify considering the transferee as a new, rather than a continuing, enterprise. . . . Where such divergence in shareholder interest does not exist and the transferee corporation continues the business of the transferor, the courts have consistently held that no complete liquidation occurs. . . .

Here, immediately after the dissolution of TASCO both of its

---

12. . . . The House bill contained, in section 336, definitions of complete and partial liquidations, which required inter alia a plan "under which the *termination of the business* or businesses and the *transfer of assets in redemption* of all or part of the stock is authorized. . . ." [Emphasis added.]

directly owned businesses were continued by New TASCO, and, even if the contemporaneous, but apparently unrelated, redemption of the Houser shares . . . is taken into account, there remains a degree of shareholder continuity in excess of 84 percent. In short, petitioner has not satisfied the requirements of section 337.[14] . . .

STERRETT, J., dissenting: As argued by the parties the issue presented to the Court is whether the sale in question was made pursuant to a plan of complete liquidation as contended by petitioner or was merely part of an integrated transaction constituting a reorganization as maintained by respondent.

Specifically respondent asserts that the entire transaction qualifies as a reorganization within the meaning of sections 368(a)(1)(D) and 354. I would hold otherwise on the grounds that the legislative history makes it quite clear that section 354(b) was not designed to cover divisive reorganizations (a split-up in this case).

This Court has faced before, on several occasions, the issue of how to categorize a transaction that does not meet the requirements of the reorganization provisions. In Joseph C. Gallagher, 39 T.C. 144 (1962), we said:

> . . . The liquidation of Delaware, although the business was continued by California with considerable change in the corporate structure, falls squarely within the first definition of a partial liquidation. Congress intended that in this situation, any redemption could not be treated as essentially equivalent to a dividend, and that *this problem of the continuation of a business must be dealt with, if at all, under the reorganization sections. Since these facts do not fall within the careful language of those sections, the distributions should be treated as payment in exchange for the stock.* To find differently would be to enact that provision which has failed on two separate occasions to be enacted by Congress. See H. Conf. Rept. No. 2543, to accompany H.R. 8300 (Pub. L. 591), 83rd Cong., 2d Sess., page 41 (1954), and H.R. 4459, 86th Cong., 1st Sess., sec. 26 (1959). [Footnotes omitted; Emphasis added.] . . .

Since the transaction then does not fall within the reorganization provisions, which are designed to cover the instances of the continuation of an existing business through a liquidation coupled with an intercorporate transfer, it follows under the teachings of prior case law that the transaction must, perhaps by definition of terms, be treated as a liquidation.

14. Nothing we have said should be construed as holding that section 337 does not apply where one corporate tier is eliminated through the complete liquidation of a parent corporation and no directly held assets of the parent corporation remain in corporate solution. Nor do we necessarily preclude the applicability of section 337 where the amount of such assets remaining in corporate solution can be said to be de minimis. . . .

For years respondent, when faced with a liquidation-reincorporation transaction, had sought to extract an ordinary income tax on the distribution either by calling the transaction a reorganization with boot or a naked distribution taxable under sections 301 or 302. Insofar as I am aware respondent has only prevailed when this or any court has found a reorganization accompanied by a nonqualifying distribution taxable as boot. When a court has not found a reorganization, respondent has inevitably lost with the distribution deemed to be made in exchange for stock. Never has the respondent prevailed on the section 301-302 argument.

Now for the first time, if the logic of the majority's holding is extended, the respondent will win his point. "How sweet it will be" and who could have expected it when the respondent was simply trying to forestall the applicability of section 337 by invoking the reorganization provisions. The majority's holding is rather gratuitous, to say the least.

The majority seeks to make its decision at the corporate level more palatable by suggesting that consistency is not required between the transaction's treatment at the corporate level and at the shareholder level, implying that a section 337 liquidation must be more "complete" than a section 331 liquidation. This novel suggestion finds no support in any decisional law. . . . In my judgment the majority is simply playing with words in order to reach what is, I suspect, a preconceived desired result. An unfortunate by-product of this form of rationalization is the creation of uncertainty where none had existed and, if there is one thing our income tax laws do *not* need, it is more uncertainty.

The majority seems preoccupied with a continuity of shareholder interest approach. The minimal (less than 15 percent) continuity of assets is ignored. Even the House version of section 357 of the 1954 Code required, among other things, a 50 percent continuity of assets before ignoring a purported liquidation. The opinion leaves up in the air what magic percentage combination of shareholder and asset transfer will, in the future, invalidate an asserted liquidation.

In this fully stipulated case I note that there is no evidence that there was, or was not, a business purpose to the transaction in issue. Of course, it is well established that the existence of a business purpose is irrelevant to the determination of whether a complete liquidation took place. . . .

Finally, the majority relies heavily on certain dicta in Pridemark, Inc. v. Commissioner. . . . This reliance is rather odd since the fact of the matter is that the final holding of that court was that a liquidation had in fact taken place. I must also note that in *Pridemark*, as in the instant case, the controlling shareholders remained the same and that, also in both cases, minimal assets were "reincorporated." It may well be argued that the majority has misconstrued its authority.

For the foregoing reasons I would stick with existing law and find for petitioner.

Dawson and Drennen, JJ., agree with this dissent.

NOTES

1. What are the implications of footnote 14 in the court's opinion? Was it right of the court not to carry through the analysis?

2. See Lester J. Workman, 36 T.C.M. (CCH) 1534 (1977) (corporation sold its operating assets and distributed proceeds in liquidation to shareholder, who transferred them to new corporation; no reorganization); Rev. Rul. 77-191, 1977-1 C.B. 94 (distribution of assets of one of two corporate businesses to shareholders, who transferred them to a new corporation, was a §355-§368(a)(1)(D) reorganization, not a partial liquidation); Rev. Rul. 76-429, 1976-2 C.B. 97 (a subsidiary sold one of two businesses, then liquidated; the parent reincorporated the remaining business in a new subsidiary; held, not a §332 liquidation).

DAVANT v. COMMISSIONER
366 F.2d 874 (5th Cir. 1966), *cert. denied,* 386 U.S. 1022 (1967)

Before Rives and Bell, Circuit Judges, and Fulton, District Judge.

Rives, Circuit Judge. The petitioners are persons who claim that the income from the sale of their stock in the South Texas Rice Warehouse Company should be taxed solely as a capital gain. The Tax Court found that a corporate reorganization had taken place and held that at least part of petitioners' income should be taxed as a dividend constituting ordinary income. The government took a cross appeal contending that the Tax Court should have held that a greater portion of petitioners' income was ordinary income. Since we agree with the government, we affirm in part and reverse in part.

South Texas Rice Warehouse Co. [Warehouse] was incorporated under the laws of the State of Texas in 1936. The principal business of Warehouse consisted of drying, cleaning, and storing rice. Warehouse's principal source of rice was land owned by a brother corporation, South Texas Water Co. [Water].

Water was incorporated under the laws of the State of Texas in 1934. Water had two principal businesses. It owned land which it rented to a partnership, South Texas Rice Farms [Farms], and it owned and operated an irrigation canal system used to irrigate the ricelands that it leased to Farms.

The principal business of Farms was releasing the land rented from Water to tenant farmers on a sharecrop arrangement. Generally, the tenant retained 50% of the rice produced and Farms received the other 50% as payment for the land provided.

The riceland which was leased by Farms from Water was irrigated by Water and the rice which Farms received from its tenants was put through Warehouse's dryer and stored by Warehouse. Water's lessees generally put their rice through Warehouse's dryer, and then stored their rice in Warehouse's facilities.

Warehouse and Water were each owned in equal proportions by four families. The partners in Farms were the same persons who were the stockholders of Warehouse and Water and their respective interests were in substantially the same proportions as their stock ownership in the two corporations. The books and records of these three enterprises, while separately prepared, were all kept in the same office.

In 1960 a number of the stockholders consulted an attorney, Homer L. Bruce, Esq., about the possibility of transferring Warehouse's operating assets to Water for $700,000 and then liquidating Warehouse. This attorney had represented Warehouse, Water, and their stockholders for many years.

In the attorney's opinion, section 337 would allow the individuals to obtain capital gains treatment for any income they might receive in the transaction they contemplated.[8] However, Mr. Bruce advised against such a course of conduct. He told them that in a situation where a sale and distribution was made when the stockholders of the two corporations were identical it was probable that the Internal Revenue Service would take the position that the stockholders had received a dividend taxable at ordinary rates and not a capital gain.

Mr. Bruce then suggested an alternate course of conduct which he believed would have the desired effect of having any gains taxed at the capital rather than the ordinary rate. The suggestion was that if the stockholders made a sale of their stock to a person not connected with them or their corporations at a fair price which would allow that person to make a reasonable profit, then that person could sell Warehouse's operating assets to Water and liquidate Warehouse without endangering the original stockholders' capital gains treatment.

Homer L. Bruce, Jr., a practicing attorney and the son of petitioners' attorney, was suggested by one of the stockholders as an appropriate person to buy their stock. Both Water and Warehouse had a corporate account with the Bank of the Southwest[9] and the Bank had for many years been represented by Mr. Bruce's law firm.

Mr. Bruce contacted A. M. Ball, a vice-president of the Bank. He told Mr. Ball that his son wished to buy Warehouse for $914,200

8. While the attorney spoke in terms of section 337, he, of course, meant sections 337 and 331.
9. Hereafter, Bank.

and wished to borrow the necessary funds from the Bank. The stock of Warehouse was to be the collateral for the $914,200 note of Bruce, Jr. It was understood that Water would then buy the assets of Warehouse for $700,000, and that this money plus part of the approximately $230,000 which Warehouse had in its bank account would be used, after Warehouse was liquidated, to repay the loan. This procedure allowed Bruce, Jr. to receive $15,583.30 for his part in the transaction, and allowed the Bank to receive what the parties designated as one day's interest on its $914,200 loan or $152.37.

Homer L. Bruce, Jr. was not present during his father's discussions with Mr. Ball nor did Bruce, Jr. participate in the discussions which determined that $914,200 should be the purchase price for the Warehouse stock and $700,000 the purchase price of Warehouse's operating assets to be paid by Water. No appraisals were made of the properties of Warehouse during 1960, although the Tax Court later found their fair market value to be at least the $700,000 paid for them by Water. The Bank loaned Bruce, Jr. $914,200, yet was never furnished a statement of his finances nor an appraisal or statement on Warehouse.

Mr. Ball, who approved the $914,200 loan, had no authority to approve loans in excess of $25,000 without prior approval of the Bank's discount committee. This particular transaction was not approved by the discount committee until after it was entirely a fait accompli.

On August 26, 1960 the stockholders of Warehouse, Mr. Ball, Mr. Bruce and his son met at the Bank. In accordance with a detailed instruction sheet, the respective parties went through the motions of making a loan, selling stock, electing new corporate officials, selling Warehouse's assets, liquidating Warehouse, and repaying the loan. Thanks to the careful prearrangement of all the details, the parties were able to act out their respective roles in approximately one hour.[11]

In terms of the actual physical carrying on of Warehouse's business, absolutely no disruption was occasioned by the paper transfer to Water. Every part of the business was carried on as before with the sole change being that it was necessary to keep one less set of books at the office. August 26 came during the busy rice drying season, but for those physically involved in carrying on Warehouse's business affairs, August 26, 1960 came and went like any other day — the dryers kept right on drying.

Petitioners take the position that the sale of their stock in Warehouse to Bruce, Jr. was a bona fide sale and that they properly reported their profits as the gain from the sale of a capital asset held

11. In addition to the instruction sheet, all of the necessary documents had been prepared in advance. These documents included the necessary papers for Warehouse's "sale" of its operating assets to Water.

over six months. The Commissioner argues that the transaction involved in this case is a corporate reorganization and that to the extent of the earnings and profits of both Warehouse and Water the gain reported here must be considered as a dividend taxable as ordinary income. The Tax Court held that the instant transaction constituted a corporate reorganization coming under section 368(a)(1)(D) of the Internal Revenue Code of 1954. However, the Tax Court also held that the gain was taxable as a dividend only to the extent of Warehouse's earnings and profits. . . .

In order to effectuate the intent of Congress the dividend, liquidation, redemption and reorganization sections of the Code must be examined and viewed as a functional whole. The basic framework by which Congress sought to tax corporate distributions is contained in sections 301(a), 301(c) and 316. Distributions of corporate funds to stockholders made with respect to their stockholdings must be included in their gross income to the extent that those distributions are made out of the corporation's earnings and profits. Such distributions are termed by the Code as dividends and are taxed as ordinary income.

All of the steps taken by taxpayer in this case with regard to the $200,000 worth of earnings and profits generated by Warehouse and the $700,000 worth of earnings and profits generated by Water were for the sole purpose of turning what otherwise would be a dividend taxed at the ordinary income rate into a gain made on the sale or exchange of a capital asset taxed at the much lower capital gains rate.

First, petitioners tell us that all they have done is sell their entire stock interest in Warehouse in a bona fide sale to an outside party. The sale of all of one's stock in a corporation, thus terminating a taxpayer's proprietary interest in a corporation and its assets, is probably one of the most common forms of capital sales. But the Tax Court held, "The facts in this case show that Homer L. Bruce, Jr., was not a purchaser of the stock in any real sense but merely a conduit through which funds passed from Water Co. to Warehouse and from Warehouse to petitioners." In this Court petitioners stress the fact that there was never a binding, written obligation on Water to buy Warehouse's assets or on Bruce, Jr. to sell them. Like the Tax Court, in view of all the circumstances, we can attach very little importance to the absence of any written obligations.

For the purposes of the personal income tax provisions, courts have never been shackled to mere paper subterfuges. It is hard to imagine a transaction more devoid of substance than the purported "sale" to Bruce, Jr. . . . Congress has provided in great detail what the tax consequences of a reorganization or partial or complete liquidation of a corporation should be. The tax consequences of this transaction must be judged by those standards because to allow the "sale" to Bruce, Jr. to divert our attention from the tax policies enacted by Congress would be to exalt form above all other criteria. He served no function other than to divert our attention and avoid tax. Stated another way, his presence served no legitimate nontax-avoidance business purpose. . . .

The petitioners insist that, even if we recognize that Bruce, Jr. was merely their agent and impute his acts to them, they are entitled to capital gains treatment. They stress that they did no more than completely liquidate Warehouse corporation, which entitled them to a capital gain under section 331. The sale to Water of Warehouse's operating assets should not be treated as a taxable event, the petitioners argue, because of section 337. The "general rule" pronounced by section 337 is that if a corporation adopts a plan of complete liquidation and distributes all of its assets in complete liquidation within 12 months after the date the plan was adopted, no recognition of gain or loss shall be recognized on the sale of its property made during those 12 months.

Section 331 provides that when a corporation is completely liquidated section 301 is inapplicable and the gain shall be treated as if derived from a sale or exchange of the stock. In short, the gain is to be treated as a capital gain. It would appear at first blush that petitioners have carefully fitted themselves directly within the statutory wording. But in the landmark case of Gregory v. Helvering, 293 U.S. 465 (1935) the Supreme Court refused to give effect to a corporate transaction which complied precisely with the formal requirements for a nontaxable corporate reorganization, on the ground that the transaction had served no function other than that of a contrivance to bail out corporate earnings at capital gains tax rates. That is precisely the charge made here. Let us examine what legitimate purposes might be served by the transactions here under consideration. Three distinct and separate things occurred.

First, $700,000 in earnings and profits possessed by Water were passed through Warehouse to petitioners. Second, $200,000 in earnings and profits from Warehouse were distributed to petitioners. Third, the operating assets of Warehouse were combined with Water and were from that point on owned and controlled through Water. Only one business nontax-avoidance purpose can be found to support any of these events: petitioners wished to eliminate one of the corporate shells and thereafter control all of the properties under one roof. This motive legitimately explains why petitioners transferred the operating assets of Warehouse to Water. But it does not explain either of the first two steps. Under the reorganization provisions of the Code petitioners could have transferred all of Warehouse's assets, including its earnings and profits, to Water without paying any tax. Thus the payment of $200,000 from Warehouse to petitioners cannot be explained as necessary in order to place both businesses under the same roof. Likewise, there was no need for petitioners to cast the transfer of Warehouse's operating assets in the form of a sale. The businesses could be combined under one roof without the $700,000 from Water ever coming over to Warehouse. It is apparent that no functional relationship exists between either the $200,000 coming to petitioners from Warehouse or the $700,000 coming to petitioners from Water and the transfer of Warehouse's assets to Water. Petitioners make no attempt to provide a nontax-avoidance purpose for their actions, but instead argue that these events cannot be a reorganization because they do not come under the literal language of the reorganization provisions. They then reason they must be a complete liquidation since they do come under the literal language of the complete liquidation provisions. As Justice Frankfurter once put it, "The syllogism is perfect. But this is a bit of verbal logic from which the meaning of things has evaporated."[20]

Clearly, this liquidation cannot come within the intention of Congress in enacting the complete liquidation provisions. Those provisions contemplate that operating assets will no longer be used by the stockholders to carry on the business as a corporation. It has long been recognized that taxpayers cannot liquidate a corporation with the intention of immediately reincorporating it in order to hold back liquid assets and cash for the purpose of getting capital gains treatment or to obtain a stepped-up basis for the operating assets or to wipe out old earnings and profits or other tax attributes. Such a liquidation reincorporation transaction does not qualify for section 331 treatment. . . . Applying the concept that we must look at petitioners' plan as a whole to the extent that the parts are functionally related, and not at its constituent parts individually, for the purpose of determining whether section 331 applies, we conclude that section 331 does not apply in this case.

Petitioners never intended to give up the corporate form of doing business. At all times relevant their intention was to transfer Warehouse's operating assets to Water. Water and Warehouse were owned by identical shareholders with identical distribution of shares. At no time did the petitioners' interest in the operating assets change. Most of the reported cases involve situations where the stockholders create a new corporate shell to receive the assets, but we see no difference between a liquidation followed by a transfer to a new corporate shell and a liquidation followed by a transfer to an already existing corporate shell.

Since this interchange of events cannot be viewed as a complete liquidation, we must now decide, for the purposes of the federal tax

20. Phelps Dodge Corp. v. NLRB, 313 U.S. 177, 191 (1941).

code, what it is. In the Tax Court the Government contended that this was a 368(a)(1)(D) or (F) reorganization.

A section 368(a)(1)(F) reorganization is defined as "a mere change in identity, form, or place of organization, however effected." Since the Tax Court held that this transaction was a (D) reorganization, it apparently believed that it was unnecessary to decide the (F) question. In the past, type (F) reorganizations have overlapped with type (A), (C) and (D) reorganizations. For this reason this provision has received almost no administrative or judicial attention. It is true that a substantial shift in the proprietary interest in a corporation accompanying a reorganization can hardly be characterized as a mere change in identity or form. Helvering v. Southwest Consolidated Corp., 315 U.S. 194 (1942).

The term "mere change in identity [or] form" obviously refers to a situation which represents a mere change in *form* as opposed to a change in substance. Whatever the outer limits of section 368(a)(1)(F), it can clearly be applied where the corporate enterprise continues uninterrupted, except for a distribution of some liquid assets or cash. Under such circumstances, there is a change of corporate vehicles but not a change in substance. If Water had no assets of its own prior to the transfer of Warehouse's operating assets to it, could we say that Water was any more than the alter ego of Warehouse? The answer is no. The fact that Water already had other assets that were vertically integrated with Warehouse's assets does not change the fact that Water was Warehouse's alter ego. Viewed in this way, it can make no practical difference whether the operating assets were held by Water or Warehouse, and a shift between them is a mere change in identity or form. At least where there is a complete identity of shareholders and their proprietary interests, as here, we hold that the type of transaction involved is a type (F) reorganization.

In the alternative, we also hold that the Tax Court correctly held that these events constituted a 368(a)(1)(D) reorganization. The (D) question is more complex than the (F) question. . . . In this case, it is clear that the petitioners have satisfied part one of the type (D) definition. Warehouse is a "corporation" and it transferred "a part of its assets to another corporation," Water. Since both corporations were owned identically by petitioners the "control" requisite was fulfilled.

Petitioners argue that the provision cannot apply to them because in part two Congress specifically required that "stock or securities" of the transferee corporation be passed to petitioners. They, of course, point out that they received no new stock in Water as a part of their transaction. We cannot agree that this statutory requirement must be taken literally, especially where it would prevent the effectuation of the tax policies of Congress.

The (D) reorganization provisions have never been confined to a strictly literal application. It will be noted that section 368(a)(1)(D) requires that the transferor be "a corporation." But it has been consistently held that a proper interpretation and application does not prevent from coming under the aegis of 368(a)(1)(D) a transfer made by "persons" who have received assets from a corporation with the intention of transferring them to another corporation. . . .

Nor in ascertaining the intention of Congress should we ignore the function intended for part two of the type (D) definition. Section 368 is not an operative provision but merely defines what Congress meant by the term reorganization. The operative provisions for a 368(a)(1)(D) reorganization are those which Congress has cited, sections 354, 355 and 356. These latter three sections determine what will be the tax consequences of a type (D) reorganization. . . .

In sections 354, 355 and 356 Congress has provided for the tax consequences of holding out cash or liquid assets in a 368(a)(1)(D) reorganization. Congress has drawn these provisions to cover the normal procedure for a taxpayer legitimately wishing to take advantage of the tax-free reorganization provisions. It is only natural then that Congress would speak in terms of stock transferred in the course of a reorganization. The exchange of stock in the course of a legitimate reorganization was the specific case most likely to occur to the mind and the most logical way to draw the statute. The fact that Congress drew the statute to fit the most common form of the problem does not mean that it had any intention of allowing the two evils most inherent in a reorganization scheme to persist. . . .

Moreover, since the operative sections were cast in terms of stock transfers, it was only normal that in referring to those sections in 368(a)(1)(D) . . . Congress referred to "stock or securities" "distributed in a transaction which qualifies under section 354, 355, or 356." Congress thus did not intend to place any special emphasis on the idea that stock *must* be transferred, rather Congress only intended to use this convenient terminology in referring to the operating provisions of the Code.

Petitioners' major argument against the application of 368(a)(1)(D) and 354, 356 thus rests on the weak foundation that Congress required stock to pass before a reorganization under section 368(a)(1)(D) could be found. Section 354 when coupled with section 356 requires that cash or liquid assets received by stockholders as part of a reorganization be taxed as a dividend. In Commissioner of Internal Revenue v. Morgan, 288 F.2d 676 (3 Cir. 1966), the taxpayer also claimed that Congress' clear intent could be avoided by a transaction where no new stock passed.

. . . Applying the rationale of *Morgan* to the instant case requires the same result. The same stockholders owned all of the stock of both Water and Warehouse. Before the transaction the operating assets' value of Warehouse was reflected in the value of its stock. Similarly, the operating assets' value of Water was reflected in the value of its stock. The stockholders had both stocks and their combined certificates reflected the value of their combined operating assets. After the transaction petitioners only had the stock of Water, but it then reflected the value of the combined operating assets of Water and Warehouse. Therefore, the appreciation of the value of Water's stock certificates caused by the transfer of Warehouse's operating assets to Water was the equivalent of issuing $700,000 worth of new or additional stock to Water's stockholders.[26] *Here the issuance of new stock would have been a meaningless gesture. . . ."* Commissioner of Internal Revenue v. Morgan, supra; accord, Liddon v. Commissioner, 230 F.2d 304 (6 Cir. 1956), *cert. den.,* 352 U.S. 824, 77 S. Ct. 34 (1956). To require the actual transfer of stock certificates where such a transfer would be a meaningless gesture would be to make the reorganization provisions optional with the taxpayer, a result which Congress clearly did not intend. . . .

We come now to the last leg of our journey; the question of whether the earnings and profits of Warehouse and Water should be combined in determining whether the full $900,000 cash received by petitioners should be treated as a dividend. We hold that the $700,000 coming indirectly from Water and the $200,000 coming from Warehouse must be tested against their combined earnings and profits. Whether we reach this result by means of calling this transaction a type (D) or type (F) reorganization, or a dividend declared simultaneously with a reorganization, makes no difference. But, in order to avoid future confusion, we think it appropriate to explain our three separate rationales.

Taking in inverse order the separate methods of reaching our conclusion, we hold that the $700,000 petitioners received from Water and the $200,000 petitioners received from Warehouse were dividends under section 301, declared incident to a reorganization. See Bazley v. Commissioner, 331 U.S. 737, 67 S. Ct. 1489 (1947). In *Bazley,* a corporation attempted to transfer liquid assets to a taxpayer, claiming they were a part of a reorganization under what is now section 368(a)(1)(E) which provides for recapitalizations. The Supreme Court characterized the modification of the capital account

26. It follows logically from what we have said that the basis formerly belonging to petitioners' Warehouse stock must now be added to the basis of their Water stock. Had the assets of Warehouse been transferred to Water for Water's stock, as they would have been if this transaction had actually been cast as a reorganization, the Water stock would have received the basis of petitioners' Warehouse stock when Warehouse was liquidated. See Treasury Reg. 1.358-1. A different result should not be obtained just because petitioners received no new stock but merely allowed their existing stock to appreciate in value. Cf. Treasury Reg. 1.302-2(c).

which constituted the reorganization-recapitalization as "unrelated" to the transfer of the liquid assets which the Court held to be a dividend under what is now section 301.

The same characterization is apt in the instant case. Three separate events took place. The distribution of $700,000 which had been generated incident to the earnings and profits of Water has no rational connection with the reorganization involving Warehouse. It was not necessary to pass this money through Warehouse and Bruce, Jr. in order to accomplish the reorganization. Everything that we said about Bruce, Jr. may be said about Warehouse in regard to the $700,000. Warehouse, under the circumstances of this case, was in no real sense a seller of assets to Water but merely a conduit through which funds passed from Water to Water's stockholders. Since both Warehouse and Water were owned in exactly the same way by the same stockholders, after the funds ended their circuitous route through Warehouse and Bruce, Jr., we see that they were a distribution "with respect to its stock" as required by section 301. The effect was precisely the same as if Water had passed them up directly to its stockholders.

The fact that we held that the transfer of Warehouse's assets and the "sale"-liquidation of Warehouse's stock should be viewed as an integrated transaction does not mean that we are being inconsistent when we separate the distribution of Water's cash to its stockholders. We are merely recognizing that two distinct and functionally unrelated types of transactions were carried on simultaneously — one was a dividend and the other a reorganization. The Code does the same thing in section 356. It recognizes that a series of complicated events may occur which are legitimately a reorganization. These are not taxed. Simultaneously, a taxpayer may receive boot having the effect of a dividend. The dividend's only relation to the reorganization is that it occurred at the same time. The boot where appropriate is taxed as a dividend.

Water, if it chose, could have declared the $700,000 as a dividend before the reorganization with Warehouse ever took place. Or Water could have waited and a week, a month or a year later distributed this dividend. Had it chosen any of these courses, the reorganization involving Warehouse would not have been affected in the slightest. We, therefore, hold that the $700,000 received by petitioners from Water is a distribution governed by sections 301(a), 301(c) and 316. The same reasoning demonstrates that $200,000 coming from Warehouse was a dividend since it was functionally unrelated to the reorganization. We, therefore, hold that the $200,000 received by petitioner from Warehouse is a distribution governed by sections 301(a), 301(c) and 316.

Even if the $700,000 received from Water were not a dividend under sections 301(c) and 316, it would be boot under section 356. Section 356 tells us that, when a taxpayer as part of a reorganization receives not only stock but liquid assets or cash to boot, that boot shall be taxed as a dividend to the extent of the earnings and profits of the distributing corporation. The Tax Court believed the words "of the corporation" referred only to Warehouse and, therefore, held that the $900,000 received should be taxed only to the extent of Warehouse's earnings and profits since it was the only distributing corporation.

We cannot agree with this narrow construction in a case where there is complete identity of ownership of both corporations. Water and Warehouse were but different pockets in the same pair of trousers worn by petitioners. It would be illogical to say that $700,000 would be used to measure how much of the $900,000 distribution had the effect of a dividend if Water were merged into Warehouse and only $200,000 should be used to measure how much of the $900,000 distribution had the effect of a dividend just because Warehouse was merged into Water.

Where there is complete identity of stockholders, the use of the earnings and profits of both corporations is the only logical way to test which distributions have the effect of a dividend. Before the reorganization the petitioners had two pockets with $900,000 in cash divided between them. After the reorganization the petitioners had removed all that cash from both pockets, and it should not matter that before removing it completely they took it out of the right pocket and put it in the left.

The statute in speaking of "the corporation" means the corporation controlled by the stockholders receiving the distribution. Where there is complete identity, as here, the stockholders control both corporations and it is virtually impossible to tell which corporation is in reality "the corporation" distributing the cash. We have two corporations each one of which is distributing cash; therefore, we must look at the earnings and profits of both corporations to see if the distribution is essentially equivalent to a dividend or has the effect of a dividend.

The Tax Court was correct that section 356(a)(2) in using the term "the corporation" meant the distributing corporation. However, the Tax Court erred when it failed to see that in this case there were two distributing corporations, each of which was a party to this reorganization. As we said in connection with our holding for purposes of applying section 301, Warehouse was a conduit for Water's distribution of $700,000 and thus, in determining which corporation was the distributing corporation for purposes of 356(a)(2), we must look through Warehouse and reach Water. . . .

It would not benefit petitioners even if they prevailed on their argument that "the corporation" means only the last distributing corporation. Section 482 permits the Commissioner to "allocate" such tax attributes as are here involved between two corporations "owned" "by the same interests" if "such" "allocation is necessary in order to prevent evasion of taxes." No clearer evasion of taxes can be imagined than converting what would be a dividend taxable at ordinary rates into a capital gain by merely passing it through another corporate shell. We hold that under section 356 and/or section 482 the effect of distributing the $700,000 and the $200,000 must be tested by the combined earnings and profits of both Warehouse and Water.

We need pause for only a moment at the door of 368(a)(1)(F). The effect of a type (F) reorganization is largely uncharted ground; we hold that the funds passed to stockholders in a type (F) reorganization must be tested by the standards laid down under sections 301 and 316. As we showed earlier, that would result in the $900,000 being tested by the earnings and profits of both Warehouse and Water.

Since the Tax Court did not find that Water's earnings and profits were at the time relevant for determining the effect of its distribution of $700,000, we must remand this case. The opinion of the Tax Court is affirmed in part and reversed in part, and the case is remanded for further proceedings not inconsistent with this opinion.

Affirmed in part and reversed in part.

NOTES

1. Rev. Rul. 70-240, 1970-1 C.B. 81, following *Davant*, holds that where there is complete identity of stock interest in the distributing and acquiring corporations, for purposes of §356(a)(2) earnings and profits are to be determined with reference to the combined earnings and profits of the two corporations. The Tax Court and the Third Circuit have rejected this view and have held that only the transferor corporation's earnings and profits are to be considered in determining the amount of the distribution that is to be treated as a dividend under §356(a)(2). See American Manufacturing Co., 55 T.C. 204 (1970), and Atlas Tool Co. v. Commissioner, 614 F.2d 860 (3rd Cir.), *cert. denied sub nom.* Schaffan v. Commissioner, 449 U.S. 836 (1980).

2. In Warsaw Photographic Associates v. Commissioner, 84 T.C. 21 (1985), the court reached a doubtful result denying the taxpayer the benefit of a "D" reorganization primarily because stock of the acquiring corporation (the taxpayer) was not formally issued to the transferor corporation and distributed to the transferor's shareholders as part of the transaction. In doing so, it distinguished *Davant*, and stated that "[w]e have not found, and petitioner has not cited us

to, any case . . . in which the court has acceded to a taxpayer's urging that the taxpayer be permitted to obtain a "D" reorganization tax benefit even though the form of the transaction . . . did not meet the literal requirement of the statute."

3. Suppose the ownership of Water and Warehouse had not been exactly the same. Might this still have been an "F" reorganization? A "D"? Would it have been proper to combine the earnings and profits of Water and Warehouse? Suppose there were a 5-percent stockholder in Warehouse who had no interest in Water. What accounting would be made for his basis in his Warehouse stock? What effect would his situation have on the other stockholders?

Suppose Warehouse had an accumulated deficit. Would this have been set off against the earnings and profits of Water?

4. On the assumption that the court properly measured earnings and profits in *Davant*, does it follow that there is a dividend to the extent of all ratable earnings and profits? What is the significance of the formula in §356(a)(2) which limit taxation to *gain*? Is Treas. Reg. §1.301-1(1) valid in light of the provisions of §356(a), which limit taxation of the "boot" to the "gain" realized? Why is the limitation to "gain" found in §356(a) but not in §356(b) or §356(e)? Should §356(a) be limited to "gain" or, to the extent of ratable earnings and profits, should the full dividend-equivalent distribution be taxable? Cf. §302(d).

REEF CORP. v. COMMISSIONER
368 F.2d 125 (5th Cir. 1966), *cert. denied*, 386 U.S. 1018 (1967)

Before Rives and Bell, Circuit Judges and Fulton, District Judge.

BELL, Circuit Judge. [The court, dealing with a complex set of facts, decided unanimously that, in effect, (1) Reef Fields Gasoline Corporation (Reef Fields) first redeemed all the stock of a shareholder group owning 48 percent of its outstanding shares; (2) Reef Fields transferred about 80 percent of its assets to a new corporation (new Reef) wholly owned by the controlling (52 percent) shareholder group of Reef Fields; (3) the transfer of assets was pursuant to a plan of reorganization under §368(a)(1)(D); (4) the assets transferred met the "substantially all" requirement of §354(b)(1)(A); and (5) there was a "distribution" sufficient to meet the requirements of §354(b)(1)(B). The court then considered whether the "D" reorganization might also constitute an "F" reorganization. If an "F" reorganization had occurred, Reef Fields would not have been entitled to file a return for the "short period" from the beginning of its taxable year on July 1, 1958, to April 27, 1959, the date of its dissolution, and the Commissioner's deficiency notice, sent to new Reef as successor in name only, would be valid to cover the entire period, July 1, 1958, to June 30, 1959.]

... The Commissioner, by way of a cross-appeal, contends that the Tax Court erred in not holding that the transaction . . . constituted a corporate reorganization under §368(a)(1)(F) of the Internal Revenue Code of 1954, as amended. Additional taxes would be due under such a holding. We . . . reverse on the cross-appeal. . . .

Reef Fields, which filed its income tax returns on an accrual basis and whose fiscal year ran from July 1 to June 30, filed an income tax return for the short taxable period July 1, 1958 to the date of dissolution, April 27, 1959. . . . The Commissioner disallowed the return on the basis that new Reef was the successor in name to Reef Fields and thus the return should have been for the full fiscal year. This position, rejected by the Tax Court, was based on the premise that the transaction resulted in a reorganization under §368(a)(1)(F).

Reef Corporation (new Reef), the petitioner, which had adopted the accrual method and the July 1 to June 30 fiscal year, filed an income tax return covering the short period December 15, 1958, the date of its incorporation, to June 30, 1959. . . .

. . . The Commissioner contends on his appeal that the Tax Court erred in holding that the transaction did not constitute a reorganization under §368(a)(1)(F), and in thus holding that the notice of deficiency to petitioner as the successor in name to Reef Fields Gasoline Corporation for a full fiscal year was invalid. . . .

. . . It is his contention that the Tax Court erred in failing to hold that the transaction resulted in a corporate reorganization within the scope of §368(a)(1)(F). His position is that no more took place than a mere change in identity, form, or place of organization of Reef Fields. Judges Rives and Fulton are of the view that this contention should be sustained. This means that the notice of deficiency sent to petitioner as the successor in name to Reef Fields will be validated and a remand will be necessary so that the Tax Court may consider the Commissioner's position under that deficiency notice.

The Commissioner sent two statutory notes of deficiency as a protective measure. One notice, addressed to "Reef Corporation (successor in name to Reef Fields Corporation)," was based on the position that new Reef, although a new corporate entity, was the same taxable entity as Reef Fields. The deficiency under this notice was claimed to be $111,894.40. The other notice, addressed to "Reef Corporation," treated new Reef as a new taxable entity to file a return covering the short taxable period but the depreciation and interest deductions were disallowed, as stated, and the additional tax due was claimed to be $70,695.18.*

---

*The depreciation and interest deductions were claimed in the theory that there had not been a reorganization but a sale of assets by Reef Fields to new Reef, with a step-up in basis and part of the purchase price represented by interest-bearing debt. — ED.

The Tax Court rejected the Commissioner's position with respect to §368(a)(1)(F), and thus the deficiency notice to petitioner as successor in name to Reef Fields was invalid. As noted, the Tax Court did adopt the Commissioner's alternative position that the transaction resulted in a corporate reorganization under §368(a)(1)(D), and concluded that the assets transferred by Reef Fields to new Reef had a substituted basis for depreciation and not a stepped-up basis.

The reasoning which supports the conclusion of Judges Rives and Fulton that this is a §368(a)(1)(F) reorganization follows.

In concluding that the instant case was not a type (F) reorganization, the Tax Court interpreted the Supreme Court's last sentence in Helvering v. Southwest Consolidated Corporation, 1942, 315 U.S. 194, . . . as holding §368(a)(1)(F) is "inapplicable when there is a shift in proprietary interest." *Southwest Consolidated* was decided under the 1939 Internal Revenue Code, and we think that the complete revision of the Code in 1954 compels a different result under the instant circumstances from that reached in *Southwest Consolidated*. Further, this case is distinguishable on its facts from *Southwest Consolidated*.

A

The intricate and confusing facts of this case have been carefully explained. Distilled to their pure substance, two distinct and unrelated events transpired. First, the holders of 48% of the stock in Reef Fields had their stockholdings completely redeemed. Second, new Reef was formed and the assets of Reef Fields were transferred to new Reef. The business enterprise continued without interruption during both the redemption and the change in corporate vehicles.

Much confusion flows from the fact that the corporate reorganization took place simultaneously with the stock redemption. But taking the Code as a standard, these two elements were functionally unrelated. Reef Fields could have completely redeemed the stock of 48% of its shareholders without changing the state of its incorporation. A complete redemption is not a characteristic of a reorganization. Congress clearly indicated this when it defined reorganization in section 368. Section 368(a)(1)(A) speaks of a "merger or consolidation" which looks to the joining of two or more corporations. Section 368(a)(1)(B) and (C) look to one corporation acquiring the assets of another or control of another corporation solely for its voting stock. Section 368(a)(1)(D) looks to the consolidation of two or more corporations or the division of two or more going businesses into separate corporations. Only sections 368(a)(1)(E) and (F) look to adjustments within a corporation. But none of these provisions focuses on a complete redemption as a characteristic of a reorganization. Congress did not have redemption of stock as a primary purpose of any of the forms of a reorganization.

That subject came under consideration when it undertook to enact specific legislation on complete and partial redemptions, section 302.

The boot provision, section 356, is adequate to cover a complete redemption when it occurs incident to a reorganization whose primary purpose conforms to the intent of section 354 or 355. But section 356 was principally designed to cover dividends incident to a reorganization. When the primary characteristics of the reorganization conform to those described by 368(a)(1)(F), we should parse the occurrences into their functional elements. The reorganizational characteristics present in the instant case do not conform to those generally intended to be covered by section 354 and therefore we should not be blinded by the 356 boot provision. To effectuate the intention of Congress manifested in the Code, we must separate this transaction into its two distinctly separate functional parts. The test of whether events should be viewed separately or together as part of a single plan is not temporal but is functional. See Davant v. Commissioner of Internal Revenue, 5 Cir. 1966, 366 F.2d 874. Applying this test to the instant case, it is clear that the redemption and the change of corporate vehicles must be viewed as separate and distinct occurrences. Cf. Bazley v. Commissioner of Internal Revenue, 1947, 331 U.S. 737. . . .

B

In 1954 Congress completely overhauled the sections of the Code detailing the tax consequences of many types of corporate transactions. Grouped together by Congress were the sections dealing with corporate distributions and adjustments, including the sections dealing with partial liquidations, stock redemptions (complete or partial), and corporate reorganizations. As we said in Davant v. Commissioner of Internal Revenue, 5 Cir. 1966, 366 F.2d 874 at 879: "In order to effectuate the intent of Congress the dividend, liquidation, redemption and reorganization sections of the Code must be examined and viewed as a functional whole."

Prior to 1954 Congress had not specifically provided for the tax treatment of partial liquidations or redemptions. This problem had been handled by judicial decisions which caused "considerable confusion" and in some cases resulted in "unwarranted" taxes and in others allowed taxpayers to "avoid" proper taxation. To correct this situation, Congress enacted a comprehensive set of rules governing the complete and partial redemptions of a stockholder's interest in a corporation. Section 302.

In the instant case the only way to protect the statutory intent of Congress is to test the redemption of stock by the provisions of section 302. A similar result as to the stockholders comes from applying sections 368, 354 and 356. But this method may not always reach the same result and in the instant case would cause an improper result with regard to the corporation. Since the reorganization and the redemption are functionally unrelated in this case, the redemption should be tested by the standard Congress has laid down in section 302.

Prior to 1954 Congress had not specifically provided which tax attributes should be carried over to the surviving or new corporation remaining after a reorganization. . . .

These adjustments had been left to judicial interpretation. . . . Thus, in 1954, in order to correct the existing problems created by unrealistic and conflicting judicial decisions, Congress enacted a comprehensive set of rules governing the carry-over of tax attributes from one corporation to another as a result of a reorganization. Section 381.

In section 381 Congress made a rational distinction between reorganizations that constitute a mere change in form and those that integrate two previously separate and independent enterprises. Where two or more separate businesses are unified into a single enterprise under a 368(a)(1)(D), 354 reorganization, Congress recognized that the resulting new enterprise should be allowed to change certain of its accounting procedures. See for example section 381(b). But Congress also realized that when the business enterprise is carried on as before, with no change in its substance, this is not a proper time to allow the business to change its accounting procedures. See for example 381(b).[12] Thus for the first time, in 1954 it became important to determine whether a reorganization was considered a (D) type or an (F) type reorganization.

Virtually all (F) reorganizations also qualify as (D) reorganizations. When a transaction qualifies as both an (F) and a (D) reorganization, if the new entity were governed by the less stringent continuity rules of (D) reorganizations, provided by section 381, the (F) rules would become a dead letter. The (F) rules are stricter than the (D) rules because a mere change of corporate charter or state of incorporation is not the proper occasion for wholesale accounting method changes that would not have been permitted if no reorganization had taken place.

Only those reorganizations which reflect a substantial change in the corporate operation should be viewed as *solely* (D) reorganizations qualifying for the more liberal rules. Where there is no substantial change in the corporate operation, (F) should be applied since it invokes the stricter rules.

12. Section 381(b) excludes type (F) reorganizations from the liberal treatment accorded type (D) reorganizations.

In the instant case there has been no substantial change in the operation of the corporate business. It is carried on just as before but in a new corporate vehicle. This is not a 354 "integration of two or more separate businesses into a unified business enterprise," which Congress considered when it adopted the more liberal rules applicable to a (D) reorganization.

What characteristics of reorganization are present in this case? The only characteristics of a corporate reorganization are the changes in name and state of incorporation. Those are primarily the characteristics of an (F), not a (D), reorganization. The redemption is not a characteristic of a reorganization, as is demonstrated by the fact that a redemption standing alone would not allow a corporation to make wholesale changes in its method of accounting.

If a corporation did no more than completely redeem the stock interest belonging to 48% of its shareholders, it could not under the Code make wholesale accounting method changes. Likewise, if a corporation did no more than change its name and state of incorporation, it could not under the Code make wholesale accounting method changes. Combining these two events, neither of which would be sufficient alone, will not permit a corporation to make wholesale accounting method changes. Nothing in the Internal Revenue Code of 1954 contemplates such a result.

. . . The Tax Court's position might have more force if the change in proprietary interests were to new persons and less than 50% of the former stockholders' interest in the old corporation remained in the new corporation. Then the change begins to look like a sale of the assets to a new and legally separate entity followed by a bona fide liquidation. . . . But just how much of a complete redemption would be required to avoid the impact of section 381? Would 1% be enough? Sufficient continuity of interest has been found where 67% or 69% of the old corporation's stockholders control the new corporation. Reilly Oil Co. v. Commissioner of Internal Revenue, 5 Cir. 1951, 189 F.2d 382; Western Mass. Theaters v. Commissioner of Internal Revenue, 1 Cir. 1956, 236 F.2d 186. Changes of less than 50%, as we have here, or for that matter any change not sufficient to prevent the finding of a reorganization should not be sufficient to prevent the operation of section 381. The corporate enterprise went on as before, no new blood was injected and all that took place was a redemption followed by a change in name.

We hold, therefore, that the changes made in the Code in 1954 make the *Southwest Consolidated* decision inapplicable here. We hold also that under the 1954 Code this transaction constituted both a 368(a)(1)(D) and a 368(a)(1)(F) reorganization. . . .

BELL, Circuit Judge, dissenting in part. I respectfully dissent from [the latter part] of the majority opinion. I do not think that the transaction in question constituted a corporate reorganization within the meaning of §368(a)(1)(F). That section has been construed by the Supreme Court as being inapplicable where there is a shift in proprietary interest. Helvering v. Southwest Consolidated Corporation, 1942, 315 U.S. 194. . . . Mertens, Law of Federal Income Taxation, §20.94. Here there was a clear and substantial change in proprietary interest. [One] group was eliminated.

This is to be distinguished from the situation where only minor and technical differences between the original and surviving corporation will justify classification as a reorganization under §368(a)(1)(F). See, for example, Davant v. Commissioner of Internal Revenue, 5 Cir., 1966, 366 F.2d 874, involving two corporations having precisely the same stockholders and proprietary interests. The assets of one corporation were conveyed to the other. And the court held the result to be a §368(a)(1)(F) corporate reorganization. The court concluded that whether the assets were held by one or the other corporations made no practical difference and that the shift of the assets between them in view of the complete identity of stockholders and their proprietary interest, resulted in a mere change in identity or form. There was a change in corporate vehicles but not in substance. . . .

There is nothing in §381 of the Code . . . , or elsewhere, to overrule the specific holding of Helvering v. Southwest Consolidated Corporation, supra, and it is our duty, as was the case with the Tax Court, to follow that decision in the absence of more specific congressional direction. My view is that this was not an appropriate case for the application of §368(a)(1)(F).

NOTES

1. Is it likely that Congress would have wanted to equate the absence of "substantial change in the corporate operation" with "a mere change in identity, form, or place of organization"? Is it likely that Congress contemplated an "F" reorganization where 48 percent of the equity interest is redeemed? In Russell v. Commissioner, 832 F.2d 349 (6th Cir. 1987), a 98-percent shift in ownership prevented a transaction from qualifying as an "F" reorganization.

2. In 1982, Congress changed the language of §368(a)(1)(F) to read as it now does. Would the transactions in either *Davant* or *Reef Corp.* be "F" reorganizations today? If not, would the results in either case differ today from what they were?

REVENUE RULING 66-284
1966-2 C.B. 115

In determining the applicability of Revenue Ruling 57-276, C.B. 1957-1, 126, relating to the requirements for filing Federal income tax returns in cases involving certain reorganizations described in section 368(a)(1) of the Internal Revenue Code of 1954, advice has been requested whether the statutory merger described below qualifies as a reorganization within the meaning of section 368(a)(1)(F) of the Code.

For a valid business purpose, X corporation, a publicly held State A Corporation, desired to reincorporate in State B. Accordingly, X organized a new X Corporation in State B and then merged itself into new X pursuant to the laws of States A and B.

Shareholders owning less than one percent of the outstanding shares of old X voted against the plan of merger. These dissenting shareholders elected to have their shares appraised under State law and they received payment representing the fair value of their shares. All other shareholders participated in the merger and received one share of new X stock for each share of old X stock surrendered.

Pursuant to the plan of merger, new X received the assets and assumed the liabilities of old X and continued the same business without interruption.

Section 368(a)(1)(F) of the Code provides, in part, that a mere change in place of organization is a reorganization. Revenue Ruling 58422, C.B. 1958-2, 145, states, in part, that section 368(a)(1)(F) of the Code is applicable to all reorganizations where there is no change in existing shareholders or in the assets of the corporation involved. A question has been raised whether the instant transaction, which qualifies as a reorganization described in section 368(a)(1)(A) of the Code, also qualifies as a reorganization described in section 368(a)(1)(F) of the Code in view of the action taken by the dissenting shareholders.

Where, as in the instant case, a plan of merger is designed only to effect a change in the corporation's place of organization, the Internal Revenue Service considers the failure of dissenting shareholders owning a total of less than 1 percent of the outstanding shares to participate in the plan of merger to be such a de minimis change in the corporation's shareholders and its assets as not to disqualify the merger as a reorganization under section 368(a)(1)(F) of the Code. Accordingly, pursuant to the provisions of section 381(b) of the Code, old X Corporation is not required to file a Federal income tax return for that portion of the taxable year prior to the effective date of the reorganization, but that portion of the taxable year prior to the effective date of the reorganization and that portion of the taxable year after such effective date constitute a single taxable year for new X Corporation. See Revenue Ruling 57-276, supra.

Revenue Ruling 58-422, C.B. 1958-2, 145, amplified.

NOTES

1. How do you explain the Commissioner's litigating position in *Reef* (page 791 supra) in light of his position in Rev. Rul. 66-284? Should a court be less willing to find an "F" reorganization when pressed by the taxpayer (who has structured the transaction) than when pressed by the Commissioner? Why?

2. The "de minimis" rule of Rev. Rul. 66-284 was applied to the merger of sister corporations (which was an "F" reorganization under Rev. Rul. 75-561, 1975-2 C.B. 129) in Rev. Rul. 78-441, 1978-2 C.B. 152.

Rev. Rul. 78-441 indicates that a change in proprietary interest will not be disregarded if it exceeds 1 percent, without application of any constructive ownership rules.

CASCO PRODUCTS CORP. v. COMMISSIONER
49 T.C. 32 (1967)

TANNENWALD, Judge. Respondent determined deficiencies in petitioner's income tax for the taxable years ended February 28, 1959 and February 29, 1960 and the taxable period March 1, 1960 to December 31, 1960 in the amounts of $247,870.91, $399,861.84, and $245,540.69, respectively. The essential issue involved is the extent to which petitioner should be permitted to carry back its 1961 net operating loss as an offset against prior earnings of its predecessor.

FINDINGS OF FACT

All of the facts have been stipulated and are incorporated herein by this reference.

The Casco Products Corporation (hereinafter referred to as "Old Casco") was organized in 1928 as a Connecticut corporation. It filed its returns for the fiscal years ended February 28, 1959 and February 29, 1960 and, having validly elected to change its fiscal year, for the period March 1, 1960 to December 31, 1960 with the district director of internal revenue, Hartford, Connecticut.

On June 9, 1960, Standard Kollsman Industries Inc., by a public tender, offered to purchase all of the issued and outstanding shares of Old Casco. On July 12, 1960, it acquired by a single purchase 310,483 shares out of a total of 511,356 shares issued and outstanding at that time. On the same date, Standard Kollsman extended its previous offer to purchase the remaining shares. By February 28, 1961, it had acquired a total of 464,515 shares. Difficulties had been and continued to be encountered in acquiring the remaining shares, which were owned by dissident shareholders.

The parties have stipulated that "for the sole purpose of providing a legal technique by which Standard Kollsman could become owner of 100% of the outstanding stock" of Old Casco, Standard Kollsman on February 28, 1961 formed SKO, Inc. as a Connecticut corporation. SKO, Inc. issued 25 shares of no-par stock to Standard Kollsman for $1,000 and thus became the wholly owned subsidiary of Standard Kollsman.

On March 2, 1961, Old Casco and SKO, Inc. entered into an agreement to merge Old Casco into SKO, Inc. under the laws of Connecticut.

The merger agreement provided, inter alia:

> At the time the merger becomes effective, (a) all shares of common stock, without par value, of Casco which are owned by SKO shall be cancelled and shall not receive any distribution with respect to such shares, and all rights attaching to such shares shall terminate; (b) all shares of common stock, without par value, of Casco which are owned by [Standard Kollsman] shall be cancelled and shall not receive any distribution with respect to such shares, and all rights attaching to such shares shall terminate; (c) there shall be distributed the sum of $10.15 in cash on each of the issued and outstanding shares of common stock, without par value, of Casco owned by persons other than SKO and [Standard Kollsman], and all shares of common stock, without par value, of Casco owned by persons other than SKO and [Standard Kollsman] shall be cancelled and shall not be converted into any securities of SKO, and all rights attaching to such shares shall terminate.

The merger agreement was approved at duly constituted meetings of the directors and shareholders of both corporations. At the meeting of the shareholders of Old Casco on March 16, 1961, several of the minority shareholders filed formal objections to the merger. These shareholders were informed that their sole right was to be paid in cash for their shares. Despite these objections, Standard Kollsman voted its shares in Old Casco for the merger. Because only a two-thirds majority was necessary, the approximately 91 percent interest held by Standard Kollsman provided sufficient votes to pass the merger resolution. Accordingly, on March 16, 1961, Old Casco was merged into SKO, Inc., which then changed its name to The Casco Products Corporation (hereinafter "New Casco").

SKO, Inc. conducted no business before the merger, except to incorporate and to agree to the merger. New Casco continued business in exactly the same manner as had Old Casco. It had the same programs and activities, the same customers (except for normal variations), the same employees, the same bank accounts, etc. Except for the $1,000 capital invested by Standard Kollsman in SKO, Inc., the assets of Old Casco immediately before the merger were the same as the assets of New Casco immediately after the merger. At all times relevant, including the time of filing of the petition herein, New Casco continued to have its principal place of business in Bridgeport, Connecticut, at the same location used by Old Casco prior to the merger.

New Casco filed its income tax return for the calendar year 1961 with the district director of internal revenue, Hartford, Connecticut, disclosing a net operating loss of approximately $1,500,000. New Casco then filed applications for tentative allowance of a loss carryback against the income shown on the returns filed by Old Casco for the fiscal years ended February 28, 1959 and February 29, 1960 and the fiscal period March 1, 1960 to December 31, 1960. The applications were tentatively allowed.

The December 31, 1960 return was the last return filed by Old Casco. No return was filed by Old Casco for the period January 1, 1961 to March 16, 1961, the date of the merger.

Respondent subsequently issued a deficiency notice disallowing the loss carryback in its entirety. Respondent did not allocate any portion of the 1961 loss to the period prior to the merger on the ground that petitioner had not shown that a portion of the loss was so allocable.

OPINION

The factual situation against which the decision herein must be made is extremely narrow. Standard Kollsman set out in 1960 to become the sole shareholder of Old Casco. Pursuant to a public tender, it succeeded in acquiring approximately 91 percent thereof through voluntary sales by existing shareholders. Having found that its public tender could not entirely accomplish its purpose, Standard Kollsman resorted to the legal technique of a merger, permitted under Connecticut law, to force out the remaining shareholders of Old Casco. As its instrument, it formed New Casco and acquired 100 percent of its issued and outstanding stock. By virtue of that ownership and its ownership of 91 percent of the shares of Old Casco, it accomplished a merger of Old Casco into New Casco, pursuant to which its shares in Old Casco were cancelled without payment and the shares of the remaining shareholders were to be paid for in cash.

Simultaneously with the merger becoming effective, the obligation to make such cash payment devolved upon New Casco.[1]

Against this factual background, petitioner makes these arguments: First, it asserts that the loss carryback is allowable under section 172 on the ground that no reorganization took place and that realistically there was a legal identity between Old Casco and New Casco. Alternatively, petitioner argues that, if a reorganization did in fact occur, it was an "F" reorganization under section 368(a)(1) and that therefore the loss carryback is allowable under section 381(b).

Respondent counters with the arguments that, given the presence of business purpose, continuity of business enterprise and continuity of proprietary interest, petitioner's use of the reorganization form requires that the transaction be treated as a reorganization; that it cannot be an "F" reorganization because of the 9 percent shift in proprietary interest between Old Casco and New Casco; and that consequently the loss carryback was properly disallowed under section 381(b).

Thus, both parties invite us to engage in an interpretative exercise as to the scope of section 368(a)(1)(F) and the relationship between sections 381(b) and 172. We decline the invitation to attempt to navigate these treacherous shoals. See Reef Corporation v. Commissioner, 368 F.2d 125 (C.A. 5, 1966), *certiorari denied* 386 U.S. 1018, affirming in part and reversing as to the "F" reorganization issue a Memorandum Opinion of this Court; Estate of Bernard H. Stauffer, 48 T.C. 277 (1967), *on appeal* (C.A. 9, Sept. 5, 1967); Associated Machine, 48 T.C. 318 (1967), *on appeal* (C.A. 9, Sept. 15, 1967); Dunlap & Associates, 47 T.C. 542 (1967). Instead, we take a different tack.

There is no question, and indeed, respondent so concedes, that if Old Casco had redeemed the shares of the minority shareholders and had continued in business the loss carryback would have clearly been available. As we see it, the circumstances herein should not produce a different result. To hold otherwise would be to exalt form over substance and to accord an unjustifiable vitality to the merger format which was admittedly adopted only as a "legal technique."

In this case, Standard Kollsman sought to become the sole shareholder of Old Casco. Its voluntary efforts having failed as to 9 percent of the shares, it resorted to a "squeeze-out" technique via the merger route, as permitted by Connecticut law. It formed a new corporation

---

1. It is not clear under Connecticut law whether this obligation first became that of Old Casco and was then assumed by New Casco or whether it originally arose as an obligation of New Casco, but resolution of this esoteric question of local law is unnecessary to our decision.

(New Casco) under the same state law[3] to conduct the same business at the same location with the same employees. In fact, upon the accomplishment of the merger, the New Casco was identical in all respects to the Old Casco with a single exception. That exception was that, although there were no new shareholders, 9 percent of the holders of Old Casco shares did not hold any shares in New Casco.

Taxwise, New Casco was merely a meaningless detour along the highway of redemption of the minority interests in Old Casco. The merger itself, although in form a reorganization, had as its sole purpose the accomplishment of the redemption — an objective which Standard Kollsman had not been able to achieve through its original program of voluntary acquisition of all of the Old Casco shares. On this basis, we think that the instant case falls squarely within the ambit of the principles which we laid down in Utilities & Industries Corporation, 41 T.C. 888 (1964), *reversed on this issue sub nom.* The South Bay Corporation v. Commissioner, 345 F.2d 698 (C.A. 2, 1965). That case involved a question of the basis of certain assets acquired by the taxpayer through the purchase-of-stock-merger route rather than by direct purchase of the assets themselves. Since the taxpayer had not shown its inability to accomplish its objective by such direct purchase, we held that the mergers had to be treated as reorganizations because they were not so integrated or interdependent as to have been *solely for the purpose* of acquiring assets. The Second Circuit Court of Appeals reversed us on the ground that we imposed too strict a test. We need not now decide the extent to which we will adopt the broader approach of the Court of Appeals, for it is clear that the instant situation falls within our stricter test. Cf. Long Island Water Corporation, 36 T.C. 377 (1961); Kimbell-Diamond Milling Co., 14 T.C. 74 (1950), *affirmed per curiam* 187 F.2d 718 (C.A. 5, 1951). Here, New Casco was formed and the merger route utilized for the sole purpose of redeeming the minority shares. This course was followed because Standard Kollsman had no alternative way of accomplishing its objective of sole ownership of Old Casco; its efforts to do so via the stock acquisition route had been tried and had failed. Under these circumstances, the merger was a reorganization in form only and should consequently be ignored as such. What took place was a redemption of 9 percent of the Old Casco shares and no more.[4] Under

3.   Where incorporation takes place in another state, different corporation laws imposing different rights and obligations apply. Often such incorporation is accomplished in a state such as Delaware in order to obtain the greater flexibility provided by its laws. Under these circumstances, an independent significance may attach to the merger so as to require it to be treated as a true reorganization. Cf. Reef Corporation v. Commissioner, 368 F.2d 125 (C.A. 5, 1966) (Texas to Delaware): Dunlap & Associates, Inc., 47 T.C. 542 (1967) (New York to Delaware).

4.   The fact that Standard Kollsman did not seek to acquire 100-percent own-

the limited circumstances of this case, we hold that New Casco was simply a continuation of Old Casco and the loss carryback should have been allowed.

In view of our holding, we do not reach the question whether, if there had been a reorganization which did not qualify under section 368(a)(1)(F), petitioner would nevertheless have been entitled to carry back that portion of the 1961 loss allocated to the period to the effective date of the merger.

Reviewed by the Court.

Decision will be entered for the petitioner.

BAUM, Judge, dissenting. I cannot agree that the merger of Old Casco into New Casco was only "in form a reorganization" and that New Casco was "merely a meaningless detour." New Casco was not a corporation with transitory life; it was not a mere stopping place en route to an ultimate destination; it was itself the end product of the transactions before us, and indeed is the petitioner herein. Old Casco was a corporation existing for a number of years and the deficiencies in controversy were determined with respect to *its* tax years, not those of New Casco. Both Old Casco and New Casco were separate, distinct viable corporations. One was merged into the other in order to squeeze out a 9 percent minority stockholder interest. Such merger was a corporate reorganization, and section 381(b)(3) forbids the carryback of a post reorganization net loss to a taxable year of the predecessor corporation unless the transaction is a reorganization "described in subparagraph (F) of section 368(a)(1)." I can see no escape from the necessity of determining whether this reorganization fell within (F).

The question whether the elimination of a 9 percent adverse minority interest may be ignored or regarded as de minimis in order to satisfy the requirement of (F) that there is a "mere change in identity, form, or place of organization" is a teasing and difficult one. And I can understand why one might wish to avoid it. But it cannot be sidestepped here and must be faced. In failing to address itself to the issue thus presented and argued by the parties, I think the majority erred. I express no opinion on the question itself at this time until it is considered by the Court.

Withey, Atkins, Scott and Featherston, JJ., agree with this dissenting opinion.

SCOTT, Judge, dissenting. I respectfully disagree with the holding of the majority that the merger of Old Casco into New Casco was a

---

ership of Old Casco by causing that corporation to attempt voluntary redemption of the minority shares is not significant. To have endeavored so to do would have constituted a meaningless ritual in view of the unsuccessful efforts to acquire such shares directly.

reorganization in form only and should be ignored. The reorganization was in accordance with provisions of the laws of Connecticut whereby the holders of 91 percent of the stock of Old Casco were able to accomplish their objective of becoming 100 percent stockholders of a new corporation which owned the operating assets and conducted the business previously conducted by Old Casco. Corporate reorganizations provided for by State laws often effect little substantive change in the equitable ownership of a corporation or the nature of the corporate business. However, the Federal tax consequences of any reorganization are controlled by the specific provisions of the Internal Revenue Code.

In my opinion the case should have been decided by a determination of whether the reorganization here involved was "a mere change in identity, form, or place of organization," so as to constitute a reorganization within the meaning of section 368(a)(1)(F).

Baum, Withey and Atkins, JJ., agree with this dissenting opinion.

NOTES

1. Was the court majority in *Casco* justified in failing to decide whether the transaction was an "F" reorganization? Why do you think it did not wish to decide? Was the transaction an "F" reorganization? Apart from what they said, what do the *votes* of the dissenting judges signify?

2. Would the statutory changes made in 1982 in defining an "F" reorganization (see Note 2, page 797 supra) affect either the majority or dissent in *Casco*?

AETNA CASUALTY & SURETY CO. v. UNITED STATES
568 F.2d 811 (2d Cir. 1976)

Before Timbers, Circuit Judge, and MacMahon and Newman, District Judges.

Timbers, Circuit Judge. The questions here presented under the corporate reorganization provisions of the Internal Revenue Code appear to be of first impression, at least in this Circuit. . . .

The central question is whether the corporate taxpayer, which was a subsidiary organized by its parent solely for the purpose of acquiring the assets and business of one of the parent's other subsidiaries, should be allowed as a deduction its post-reorganization net operating losses as carrybacks against the pre-reorganization income of its predecessor under §§172 and 381(b)(3) of the Internal Revenue

Code. The answer to this question turns on whether the reorganization qualifies as "a mere change in identity [or] form" within the meaning of §368(a)(1)(F). . . .

I. FACTS AND PRIOR PROCEEDINGS

(A) PRIOR PROCEEDINGS

Aetna Life Insurance Company (Aetna Life) is a Connecticut corporation which writes and sells life, accident and health insurance. Prior to December 29, 1964 Aetna Life held 61.61% of the outstanding voting common stock of The Aetna Casualty and Surety Company (Old Aetna), a Connecticut corporation which wrote and sold liability, fire, theft, property damage and surety insurance. In November or December 1964 Aetna Life organized Farmington Valley Insurance Company (Farmington Valley), a Connecticut corporation which was a wholly owned shell subsidiary with no business or assets of its own, for the sole purpose of acquiring the business and assets of Old Aetna. On December 29, 1964 Old Aetna was merged into Farmington Valley in a complex, three-party reorganization described more fully below. As a result of this merger and the related stock transfers, minority shareholders of Old Aetna received shares of Aetna Life in return for their Old Aetna shares and the shares of Farmington Valley were placed in trust for the shareholders of Aetna Life. The name of Farmington Valley later was changed to The Aetna Casualty Surety Company (New Aetna), plaintiff herein.

Pursuant to the loss carryback provisions of the Code, New Aetna sought to carry back its net operating losses for the taxable period December 30 through 31, 1964 and the calendar year 1965 against the net income of Old Aetna for the calendar year 1963 and the period January I through December 29, 1964.

The IRS allowed New Aetna to carry back the $7,213,547 net operating loss allocated to the period prior to the December 29, 1964 reorganization, . . . to offset a part of Old Aetna's 1963 taxable income; but no part of New Aetna's net operating losses for the periods subsequent to December 29, 1964 was allowed as a carryback to offset Old Aetna's other 1963 taxable income. . . .

(B) DECEMBER 29, 1964 MERGER . . .

As a result of the Life Insurance Company Income Tax Act of 1959, . . . the federal income tax liability of insurance companies such as Aetna Life depended in part on the value of the assets held by the company. The greater the value of the company's assets, the greater the portion of its income which was subject to tax. . . . Understandably, Aetna Life wished to remove its 61.61% ownership of Old Aetna from its tax base.

Aetna Life also wished to achieve an identity of ownership between the shareholders of Aetna Life and those of Old Aetna. Although the officers and directors of the two companies had been identical for several years prior to the reorganization, they had fiduciary duties to different groups of shareholders because of Aetna Life's 61.61% stock interest in Old Aetna. This prevented the two companies from further integrating their operations, from selling insurance together, and from taking other business steps which might have achieved operational economies. The diverse stock ownership of the two companies also required elaborate cost allocation accounting procedures.

The obvious way for Aetna Life to remove Old Aetna from its tax base would have been for Aetna Life to distribute its Old Aetna stock to the Aetna Life shareholders. This would have resulted in taxable income to Aetna Life under §802(b)(3) which makes certain portions of distributions to shareholders taxable to the life insurance company. . . .

Aetna Life therefore sought to persuade Congress to amend these provisions of the Code. In 1964 Congress enacted the Act of September 2, 1964, Pub. L. No. 88-571, §4(a)(2), 78 Stat. 859, which added, inter alia, what is now §815(f)(3)(B) of the Code. . . . §815(f)(3)(B)(ii) excluded from the definition of taxable distributions certain distributions of the stock of a 100% controlled insurance corporation provided (i) that control was obtained in exchange for the distributing corporation's own stock; (ii) that the controlled corporation immediately exchanged the distributing corporation's stock to a third corporation in a §368(a)(1)(A) reorganization (statutory merger or consolidation) or a §368(a)(1)(C) reorganization (exchange of stock for assets); and (iii) that the distributing corporation had owned at least 50% of the third corporation's voting stock.

In order to bring itself within the provisions of the new law and thus avoid incurring tax liability to itself as a result of distributing its Old Aetna stock to its shareholders, Aetna Life devised a plan substantially as follows.

Aetna Life would organize Farmington Valley as a wholly owned shell subsidiary with no business of its own. Aetna Life would issue 13,300,000 shares of its voting common stock and exchange them for all 1,000 shares of Farmington Valley. Then, . . . Farmington Valley would exchange its Aetna Life stock for the voting common stock held by Old Aetna shareholders. . . . Aetna Life would retire the Aetna Life stock which it received in return for its 61.61% stock interest in Old Aetna. Farmington Valley would cancel its newly acquired Old Aetna stock. Then by operation of Connecticut's merger law Farmington Valley would succeed to all of the assets and liabilities of Old Aetna. Farmington Valley would change its name to The Aetna Casualty and Surety Company (New Aetna). Under that name

New Aetna would carry on the business of Old Aetna. Aetna Life would distribute the 1,000 shares of Farmington Valley (now New Aetna) by putting them into a trust for the benefit of the Aetna Life shareholders. . . .

On October 23, 1964 the IRS issued a number of rulings which had been requested by Aetna Life with respect to the plan, including the following: that the merger of Old Aetna into Farmington Valley and the transfer of Aetna Life stock held by Farmington Valley to Old Aetna's shareholders would constitute a §368(a)(1)(C) reorganization; and that the transfer by Aetna Life of its New Aetna stock to a trustee for the benefit of Aetna Life shareholders would be nontaxable to Aetna Life and its shareholders under §§355 and 311.

On November 24, 1964 the shareholders of Aetna Life and Old Aetna approved the plan. The reorganization was carried out on December 29, 1964.

(C) CLAIMS IN DISTRICT COURT AND RULINGS THEREON . . .

New Aetna made three basic arguments in the district court. First, it argued that the transactions pursuant to which it merged with Old Aetna did not constitute a "reorganization" within the meaning of §§368 and 381, but merely a "redemption" of the minority shareholders' interest in Old Aetna. *Casco Products Corp.* . . . Second, it argued that, even if there was a "reorganization," the merger of Old Aetna into New Aetna constituted a §368(a)(1)(B) reorganization even if it also constituted a reorganization under §368(a)(13)(C) and that §381(b)(3) does not prohibit carrybacks in the case of a §368(a)(1)(B) reorganization. Third, it argued that the merger of Old Aetna into the shell which later became New Aetna was a "mere change in identity [or] form" within the meaning of §368(a)(1)(F). . . .

Judge Blumenfeld held that the merger of Old Aetna into New Aetna was a "reorganization"; that the transactions did constitute a §368(a)(1)(C) reorganization; and that the merger of Old Aetna into the new shell which became New Aetna was not a "mere change in identity [or] form." . . . In support of this holding the judge emphasized the fact that the 38.39% minority shareholders were forced to exchange their Old Aetna stock for Aetna Life stock, together with the interest in New Aetna which they received as a result of Aetna Life's placing the New Aetna stock in a trust for the benefit of Aetna Life shareholders.

II. INTERNAL REVENUE CODE PROVISIONS AND THEIR
     APPLICATION TO THIS REORGANIZATION

. . . Section 381(b)(3) does not prevent the acquiring corporation from carrying back its losses against its *own* pre-reorganization income, even if those losses resulted from the operations of the non-surviving corporation. The purpose of §381(b)(3) was to provide a hard and fast rule that the acquiring corporation may not carry back losses to the pre-reorganization tax years of the transferor corporation — unless the acquisition qualifies as a §368(a)(1)(F) reorganization. Section 381(b)(3) avoids the need for divisional accounting and prevents the manipulation that would result if the acquiring corporation were allowed to apportion current losses between the operations acquired from each of the predecessor corporations. . . .

Prior to the 1954 revision of the Code, the lines of demarcation between what are now §368(a)(1)(F) reorganizations and other types of reorganization under §368(a)(1) were not nearly as significant as the boundaries between reorganizations in general and transactions which did not qualify as reorganizations. Under §§354 and 361 certain transactions were tax free if carried out pursuant to a plan of reorganization. Distributions to shareholders might be taxed at capital gains rates if made as part of a corporate "liquidation," while certain distributions of corporate profits to shareholders pursuant to "reorganizations" could be taxed as regular income.

In 1954 Congress completely revised the Code. With the addition of §381 and the significance of §368(a)(1)(F) to the operation of the carryback and accounting provisions of §381, it became more important to delineate the boundaries between a §368(a)(1)(F) reorganization and other types of reorganizations than previously had been the case. . . .

Unlike the other subsections of §368(a)(1) which contain definitions of various types of reorganizations, §368(a)(1)(F) on its face says very little. What may be "a mere change in identity [or] form" for one purpose may not be for another purpose. At least one other Circuit which has dealt with this provision of the Code, in the context of interpreting the provisions relating to tax-exempt transactions, or determining whether certain corporate transactions constitute liquidations or reorganizations, has assumed that a transaction deemed an (F) reorganization for those purposes must also be an (F) reorganization for those purposes of §381. . . . That is a matter we need not decide in the instant case.

(B) CLAIMS IN COURT OF APPEALS AND OUR RULINGS
    THEREON

Stripped to its essentials, the critical elements of the reorganization here involved were the following: Aetna Life owned 61.61% of Old Aetna. Aetna Life organized New Aetna (the Farmington Valley) as a 100% owned subsidiary solely to acquire Old Aetna. New Aetna had no business or assets of its own. New Aetna acquired Old

Aetna's assets on December 29, 1964. As an incident of the reorganization, the 38.39% minority shareholders of Old Aetna exchanged their Old Aetna stock for Aetna Life stock. These minority shareholders retained a reduced proprietary interest in the business of the subsidiary upon the distribution by Aetna Life of the New Aetna stock which was placed in a trust for the benefit of Aetna Life shareholders. . . .

We need not resolve Aetna's claim that its merger with Old Aetna was a reorganization under §368(a)(1)(B) even if it also was covered by §368(a)(1)(C), since under the circumstances of this case §368(a)(1)(B) does not bar the loss carryback. While the transactions did involve the type of stock-for-stock exchange contemplated by §368(a)(1)(B), they also involved acquisition of Old Aetna's assets by New Aetna.

As the district court recognized, however, reorganizations under §368(a)(1)(A)-(E) may qualify also under §368(a)(1)(F); and it is well settled that many (F) reorganizations do fit within the types of reorganizations defined by the other subsections of §368(a)(1). . . .

Absent the shift in the proprietary interests of the minority shareholders of Old Aetna, there would be no basis for contending that the merger of Old Aetna into a shell corporation, which had no business or assets of its own, did not qualify as a §368(a)(1)(F) reorganization. . . .

The government argues, however, that we should reach a different result here merely because the 38.39% minority shareholders of Old Aetna were forced to exchange their Old Aetna stock for Aetna Life stock.[11] We disagree. . . .

The Code deals extensively with the tax consequences of redemptions. See §§302 et seq. Those provisions represent a comprehensive set of rules relating to the problems of partial and complete redemptions. Clearly a corporation which merely redeems its minority shareholders' stock has not undergone a reorganization at all under §368(a)(1) and is entitled to carry back its losses under §172. We see no reason why the result should be different simply because the redemption occurs in the course of merging one corporation into a different shell. . . . If the redemption, reorganization and carryback provisions were not intended to preclude carrybacks where there has been a simple redemption, we do not believe those

11. Actually the minority shareholders of Old Aetna who exchanged their Old Aetna stock for Aetna Life stock retained a significant interest in New Aetna, since Aetna Life placed all of its New Aetna shares in a trust for the benefit of Aetna Life shareholders. It is not necessary to determine to what extent the Old Aetna minority shareholders' proprietary interest in the subsidiary was reduced as a result of the entire reorganization, for we do not believe that this reorganization would lose its character as a §368(a)(1)(F) reorganization even if there had been a complete redemption of the minority shareholders' stock.

provisions should be construed to preclude the carryback here involved.

Accepting arguendo the government's contention that Aetna Life had independent business reasons for freezing out the minority shareholders during the course of the merger of Old Aetna into New Aetna, we do not believe that a redemption which occurs in the course of what otherwise would be a §368(a)(1)(F) reorganization should strip the reorganization of its subsection (F) character. Even assuming that the merger could not be separated from the redemption, as apparently it was possible for the court to do in Reef Corp. v. Commissioner, we agree with the reasoning of the Fifth Circuit that a "redemption is not a characteristic of a reorganization. . . ." . . . This view also is implicit in the Tax Court's reasoning in Casco Products Corp. v. Commissioner. . . .[13]

We believe that where the issue is whether a corporation is entitled to a carryback after a corporate reorganization §368(a)(1)(F) should be construed with particular sensitivity to the purposes of §381(b). The interplay between subsections (F) and (A)-(E) gains its principal significance under the Code through the application of §381(b). Since New Aetna was merely a corporate shell with no business of its own, none of the accounting problems which motivated §381(b)(3) is present here.[14] Indeed, since New Aetna had no pre-reorganization tax history of its own, application here of the carryback prohibition contained in §381(b)(3) would prevent New Aetna from obtaining *any* carryback of its current losses, even though §381(b)(3) does not prevent acquiring corporations in other types of reorganizations from carrying back losses to their *own* pre-reorganization tax years. We do not believe that the mere fact that a redemption has occurred should lead to so Draconian a result, particularly since §172 manifests a legislative policy in favor of carrybacks which ordinarily would not be affected by a simple redemption.

Moreover, even assuming that §368(a)(1)(F) should be given a fixed meaning in its application to the different provisions of the Code — a question which we need not decide here — our view of

13. We do not agree with the Tax Court's conclusion in *Casco Products* that there was no "reorganization." We believe that the language of §368(a)(1), and that of §368(a)(1)(F), in particular, is adequate to cover such transactions as the merger of a corporation into another shell. But the Tax Court's holding in *Casco Products* does accord with our view that a redemption which occurs in the course of what otherwise would have been a §368(a)(1)(F) reorganization does not change its subsection (F) character.

14. Other Circuits have found §368(a)(1)(F) reorganizations, for purposes of the carryback provisions, where two or more corporations merged — each with a business of its own and each owned in identical proportions by the same persons. . . . This result may be consistent with the purposes of §381(a)(1)(F) where the respective business operations of the predecessor corporations continue to function separately and do not raise problems of accounting apportionment. . . .

§368(a)(1)(F) is not inconsistent with the implementation of those other provisions.

In holding that the merger of Old Aetna into New Aetna did not qualify as a §368(a)(1)(F) reorganization, the district court relied on Helvering v. Southwest Consolidated Corp. 315 U.S. 194, 202-203 (1942), where the Supreme Court stated that "a transaction which shifts the ownership of the proprietary interest in a corporation is hardly 'a mere change in identity, form, or place of organization.' . . ." There the assets of an insolvent corporation were transferred to a new corporation which was owned and controlled by the old corporation's creditors. The shareholders of the old corporation received only a small minority interest in the new corporation. In determining whether there had been a "sale" of the old corporation's assets to the new corporation, or merely a reorganization, the Court dealt in one sentence with what is now §368(a)(1)(F).

Here, unlike *Southwest Consolidated,* there was merely a shift in the proprietary interest of the *minority* shareholders of Old Aetna. The transaction here involved cannot be described accurately as a "sale" of one corporation's assets to another corporation. We agree with the Fifth Circuit that the instant reorganization might begin to look more like a "sale" — or at least might look less like a §368(a)(1)(F) reorganization and a redemption — "if the change in proprietary interests were to new persons and less than 50% of the former stockholders' interest in the old corporation remained in the new corporation." Reef Corp. v. Commissioner. . . . But that is not the situation here.

We conclude that the reorganization of Old Aetna into New Aetna was a §368(a)(1)(F) reorganization and that New Aetna is entitled to carry back its post-reorganization losses against the pre-reorganization income of Old Aetna pursuant to §§172 and 381(b)(3).

On Petition for Rehearing

Per Curiam. The government has petitioned for rehearing, contending that our decision of December 15, 1976 in this case is in conflict with decisions of this and other courts as to the scope of §368(a)(1)(F) of the Internal Revenue Code of 1954.

We think the government misapprehends the point of our decision. We are concerned in this case only with whether §381(b)(3) of the Code bars the loss carryback that New Aetna claimed it was entitled to offset against pre-reorganization income of Old Aetna. In ruling that §381(b)(3) did not bar the loss carryback, we concluded that the reorganization was exempted from the prohibition of §381(b)(3) because it fell within the definition of §368(a)(1)(F) and (F) reorganizations are specifically exempted from the bar of

§381(b)(3). We ruled that the reorganization was an (F) reorganization only for purposes of determining the reach of §381(b)(3). We specifically declined to decide whether classifying a reorganization as an (F) reorganization for purposes of §381(b)(3) would necessarily mean it is an (F) reorganization for purposes of other provisions of the Code.

None of the decisions of the Supreme Court or of the Courts of Appeals cited to us by the government as allegedly in conflict with ours involves the issue of whether a reorganization is an (F) reorganization for purposes of §381(b)(3). Hence we consider our decision to be far narrower than the government apprehends and not in conflict with any appellate case that has been called to our attention.

We are concerned here with a reorganization in which a corporation is merged into a corporate shell with no prior business or tax history of its own. Since this reorganization presents none of the accounting or allocation problems that might arise in reorganizations involving two corporations each with a prior business and tax history, we concluded that Congress did not intend the loss carryback to be unavailable. In our view, it makes no difference whether effectuating congressional intent in the circumstances of this reorganization is achieved by construing §368(a)(1)(F) somewhat broadly to include the reorganization of Old and New Aetna, or by construing §381(b)(3) somewhat narrowly so as to be inapplicable to this particular reorganization. Either way, a loss carryback favored by the policies of the Code, see §§172 and 832(c)(10), and not presenting the problems with which the prohibition of §381(b)(3) was concerned, is allowed. Having decided only that narrow point, we hold that the petition for rehearing should be denied.

Petition denied.

NOTES

1. In National Tea Co. & Consolidated Subsidiaries, 83 T.C. 8 (1984), aff'd, 793 F.2d 864 (7th Cir. 1986), a subsidiary corporation was merged into its parent corporation in 1974 in an "F" reorganization. The subsidiary had been organized in 1902 and acquired by its parent in 1954; the parent had been formed in 1929. Both corporations operated retail food stores. Noting that no portion of the postmerger loss was attributable to the business formerly operated by the subsidiary, the Tax Court denied the carryback of the postmerger net operating loss to a premerger year of the subsidiary.

2. As discussed in Note 2, page 797 supra, in 1982 Congress narrowed the definition of an "F," intending to restrict the kinds of

transactions after which net operating loss carrybacks would be allowed. The legislative history indicates that Congress intended to limit "F" reorganizations to transactions involving one *operating* corporation, although that word does not appear in the law. See Staff of the Joint Committee on Taxation, General Explanation of the Revenue Provisions of the Tax Equity and Fiscal Responsibility Act of 1982, at 141 (Dec. 31, 1982). If the word "operating" is properly inferred from the history, then a change of place of incorporation is properly classified as an "F" reorganization even if its form is a statutory merger of the operating coporation into a newly formed corporation that has not yet operated.

3. Why do you think Congress limited net operating loss carrybacks to "F" reorganizations? Does the decision in *Aetna* meet or frustrate that purpose? Would the *Aetna* court decide that case today (after the 1982 legislation) the same way as it did?

See Note, Corporate Reorganizations and Loss Carrybacks — Aetna Casualty & Surety Co. v. United States, 46 Geo. Wash. L. Rev. 299 (1978).

VIII.   CARRYOVERS — §§381, 382, 172, 269

A.   EARNINGS AND PROFITS

COMMISSIONER v. SANSOME
60 F.2d 931 (2d Cir. 1932), *cert. denied,* 287 U.S. 667 (1932)

Before L. Hand, Augustus N. Hand, and Chase, Circuit Judges.

L. HAND, Circuit Judge. Sansome, the taxpayer, on January 1, 1921, bought some shares of stock, having $100 par value, in a New Jersey company, which on April 1, 1921, sold out all its assets to another company of the same state. The new company assumed all existing liabilities, and issued its shares to the shareholders of the old, without change in the proportion of their holdings, though the number of new shares was increased five times, and they were without par value. The new charter differed only in that the company could manufacture other products besides silk, to which the charter of the old company had been confined. There was no other change in the "financial structure," as the phrase is.

The old company had carried upon its books a large surplus and undivided profits, which we may assume to have been altogether earned before January 1, 1921, and which the new company carried over at the same figure upon its books for the year, 1921, but somewhat reduced because of losses in 1922. The business made no profit, and the company was dissolved in 1923. During this year Sansome received payments upon his shares in liquidation which the Commissioner included in his returns as dividends for the year 1923, for the distribution of that year did not exhaust the surplus and undivided profits which still remained. Sansome protested; he wished to use these dividends to compute the "gain" upon his investment; that is, to take all liquidating dividends first to amortize his cost, or "base," and return any overplus as profit in the year, 1924, when the last payment was made. The question is whether section 201 of the Revenue Act of 1921 (42 Stat. 228) justified the Commissioner's position. The Board held that as the companies were separate juristic persons, the later one had distributed nothing "out of *its* earnings or profits."

Section 201 of 1921 differed from the same section in the Act of 1918 (40 Stat. 1059), which expressly provided that all liquidation dividends should be taken as in exchange for shares, and that the gain should be computed by the formula which Sansome wished to use; and the Act of 1924, §201(c), 26 USCA §932(c), restored the law to its original form. The change of 1921 must have been deliberate and we cannot disregard it; it is also unequivocal, only distributions not allocated to profits by subdivision b may be used to reduce the subtrahend for computing the gain derived, or the loss sustained. This means that the shareholder is to be taxed upon the dividends as such so far as they represent profits, calculated under the preceding subdivision and that what is left shall be treated as amortizing his cost. The rule would work in some cases to the taxpayer's advantage and in others not; he escapes normal taxes pro tanto, provided he has enough income in later years to use as a deduction the loss calculated upon the reduced payments. . . .

Nor is there doubt as to the constitutionality of the section. When Sansome bought the old shares, the profits had indeed been already earned; yet he might be taxed upon ordinary dividends paid out of them. . . . He could not successfully assert that such dividends must be computed as part of his gain on the transaction, but must be content with a corresponding allowance when he sold. If so, Congress might insist that a dividend in liquidation should be treated like any other, for while this may violate ordinary usage, once we conceive of income as the change from undivided profits to an immediately available dividend, the rest follows. The taxpayer gets his quid pro quo in the closing transaction. Though it is a chance whether the final resultant will be favorable or not, the dice are not loaded against him. Thus, there was income to tax as much as though the company continued its life; and it was not an unfair method.

All this the Board accepted, but held with Sansome, because it treated the company as new and independent, and the liquidating dividends as distributed out of capital, not "out of its earnings or profits," of which there were none. Under the Act of 1916, which had not yet developed the elaborate definition of the later statutes, greater corporate differences have been considered not to break the identity of the older company. . . . In Marr v. U.S., 268 U.S. 536, . . . still greater differences did indeed change the result, but for our purposes the decision is irrelevant, for the facts were wide of those at bar. . . .

However, we prefer to dispose of the case as a matter of statutory construction, quite independently of decisions made in analogous, though not parallel, situations. It seems to us that section 202(c)(2) (42 Stat. 230) should be read as a gloss upon section 201. That section provides for cases of corporate "reorganization" which shall not result in any "gain or loss" to the shareholder participating in them, and it defines them with some particularity. He must wait until he has disposed of the new shares, and use his original cost as the "base" to subtract from what he gets upon the sale. Such a change in the form of the shares is "an exchange of property," not "a sale or other disposition" of them. Section 201 was passed, in some measure at least, to fix what should come into the computation of "gain or loss"; it allowed all payments except those cut out by subdivision c. It appears to us extremely unlikely that what was not "recognized" as a sale or disposition for the purpose of fixing gain or loss, should be "recognized" as changing accumulated profits into capital in a section which so far overlapped the latter. That in substance declared that some corporate transactions should not break the continuity of the corporate life, a troublesome question that the courts had beclouded by recourse to such vague alternatives as "form" and "substance," anodynes for the pains of reasoning. The effort was at least to narrow the limits of judicial inspiration, and we cannot think that the same issue was left at large in the earlier section. Hence we hold that a corporate reorganization which results in no "gain or loss" under section 202(c)(2) (42 Stat. 230) does not toll the company's life as continued venture under section 201, and that what were "earnings or profits" of the original, or subsidiary, company remain, for purposes of distribution, "earnings or profits" of the successor, or parent, in liquidation. As the transaction — "reorganization" — between the companies at bar fell plainly within section 202(c)(2), it seems to us that the Board was wrong.

Order reversed; cause remanded for further proceedings in accord with the foregoing.

NOTE

What kind of reorganization was involved in *Sansome*? Would Judge Hand's reasoning apply equally to an amalgamating merger of two ongoing businesses? With differing shareholder interests? Compare *Davant*, page 779 supra.

UNITED STATES v. SNIDER

224 F.2d 165 (1st Cir. 1955)

Before Magruder, Chief Judge, and Woodbury and Hartigan, Circuit Judges.

HARTIGAN, Circuit Judge. . . . The plaintiffs sued to recover an alleged over payment of taxes for the calendar year 1950, stating in their complaint that $3,909.01 of a $9,000 dividend paid to the plaintiff, Abraham Snider, by the Hotel Kenmore Corp. in 1950 had been erroneously reported by them as taxable income whereas in fact it was not taxable income being a distribution of the capital of the Hotel Kenmore Corp. rather than a distribution of earnings and profits.

The stipulated facts deal mainly with the tax-free reorganization of a Massachusetts real estate trust, which owned and operated two Boston hotels, the Hotel Braemore and Hotel Kenmore, into two corporations, the Hotel Braemore Corp. and the Hotel Kenmore Corp. The dividend, the nature of which is the principal issue in this case, was declared by the Hotel Kenmore Corp.

The plaintiff, Abraham Snider, owned 25 shares of the 100 shares outstanding of the Massachusetts real estate trust which had been organized in 1922. In 1947 the stockholders of the trust agreed that it would be preferable that the hotel properties be owned and operated by two corporations rather than a real estate trust. At this time the trust had a deficit of about $327,000. The Hotel Braemore Corp. was organized on May 29, 1947. The real estate trust transferred the Hotel Braemore property to this Hotel Braemore Corp. in exchange for all the outstanding stock of the latter corporation except for four shares which had previously been issued to the trust for a nominal sum. Also on May 29, 1947 the Hotel Kenmore Corp. was organized and this corporation issued all its outstanding stock to the four stockholders of the real estate trust in exchange for their trust stock except for four shares which had been issued to these four stockholders for a nominal sum. The Hotel Kenmore Corp. then liquidated the real estate trust and transferred all its assets to itself. Thus the Hotel Kenmore Corp. acquired ownership of the Hotel Kenmore and through its ownership of the stock of the Hotel Braemore Corp., the Hotel Braemore. The new corporations were apparently more successful than the real estate trust, although there was no change in any material manner in the operation of the business, and profits were earned by the Hotel Kenmore Corp. in the fiscal years ending March 31, 1948, 1949, 1950 and 1951 of about $140,000. On December 8, 1950 a cash dividend of $36,000 was paid to the stockholders of the Hotel Kenmore Corp., the plaintiff Abraham Snider, receiving $9,000. The Hotel Kenmore Corp. had available for distribution in 1950 as current earnings and profits a little over $20,000 and there is no question that approximately $5,100 of the $9,000 received by the plaintiff was clearly dividend income attributable to current earnings and profits and taxable to the plaintiffs.

The issue in this case is whether any portion of this $36,000 distribution to stockholders of the Hotel Kenmore Corp. may be offset by the 1947 deficit of the Massachusetts real estate trust (which deficit is greater than the earnings and profits accumulated by the Hotel Kenmore Corp. since 1947) despite the fact that the real estate trust was terminated in 1947 following the tax-free reorganization of the ownership of the hotel properties. The sections of the Internal Revenue Code of 1939 involved are Sec. 115(a), (b) and (d) . . . , the pertinent parts of which provide as follows:

§115. **Distributions by corporations** — *(a) Definition of dividend.*

The term "dividend" when used in this chapter . . . means any distribution made by a corporation to its shareholders, whether in money or in other property, (1) out of its earnings or profits accumulated after February 28, 1913, or (2) out of the earnings or profits of the taxable year (computed as of the close of the taxable year without diminution by reason of any distributions made during the taxable year), without regard to the amount of the earnings and profits at the time the distribution was made. . . .

(b) Source of distributions.

For the purposes of this chapter every distribution is made out of earnings or profits to the extent thereof, and from the most recently accumulated earnings or profits. . . .

(d) Other distributions from capital.

If any distribution made by a corporation to its shareholders is not out of increase in value of property accrued before March 1, 1913, and is not a dividend, then the amount of such distribution shall be applied against and reduce the adjusted basis of the stock provided in section 113, and if in excess of such basis, such excess shall be taxable in the same manner as a gain from the sale or exchange of property. . . .*

*Cf. §§316 and 301 of the 1986 Code. — Ed.

In applying this statute to the facts in the instant case it is apparent that whether or not the $3,909.01 in question is a "dividend" and taxable depends on whether at the date of distribution there existed any assets which could be attributed to "earnings and profits accumulated after February 28, 1913," as the other source of dividends — "the earnings and profits of the taxable year" — had been already exhausted. It would be logical to assume that the earnings and profits of the Hotel Kenmore Corp. would have no relation to the earnings and profits of the trust, they being two separate entities. However, it was decided in Commissioner of Internal Revenue v. Sansome [page 814 supra] . . . that a corporate reorganization which did not result in the gain or loss in the value of the corporate stock being recognized for tax purposes "does not toll the company's life as continued venture . . . and that what were 'earnings or profits' of the original, or subsidiary, company remain, for purposes of distribution, 'earnings or profits' of the successor, or parent, in liquidation." In that case the original enterprise was a corporation which had large accumulated earnings and profits. Its assets were conveyed to a new corporation, the stock of the new corporation being issued to the shareholders of the old corporation. The new corporation made no profits, and payments in distribution of its assets were made to the taxpayer who treated such payments as return of capital and not as income, maintaining that the distributions could not have been dividends as the corporation had never had any earnings and profits. The court, however, held that the first corporation's earnings and profits were attributable to the second corporation and consequently the second corporation's cash distribution was a taxable dividend to the extent of such earnings and profits.

It would appear to follow from the reasoning used in the *Sansome* case that the plaintiffs are entitled to recover, for logic would seem to require that if the prior business organization's profits and losses must be attributed to the successor corporation following a tax-free reorganization, similarly the prior enterprise's deficits should be attributed to the successor corporation. However, the Supreme Court in Commissioner of Internal Revenue v. Phipps, 1949, 336 U.S. 410, . . . dealt with this problem as it affected parent and subsidiary corporations and it is clear from its opinion that subtracting the deficit of a subsidiary business from the accumulated earnings and profits of the parent corporation is not a corollary to the carrying over of the subsidiary's earnings and profits to the parent. The Court stated in 336 U.S. at page 417, . . . "that the *Sansome* rule is grounded not on a theory of continuity of the corporate enterprise but on the necessity to prevent escape of earnings and profits from taxation." See Commissioner of Internal Revenue v. Munter, 1947, 331 U.S. 210, 215. . . .

In the *Phipps* case, a parent corporation had large accumulated earnings and profits but it owned several subsidiary corporations possessing deficits. By means of a tax-free reorganization the parent acquired the assets of its subsidiaries and later made pro rata cash distributions to its preferred stockholders. The Court held that the deficits of the subsidiaries could not be used to reduce the accumulated earnings and profits of the parent and consequently the cash distribution was in the nature of a taxable dividend.

In the instant case the district court said that the *Phipps* opinion did not repudiate the entire doctrine of continuity of venture that had been advanced in the *Sansome* case but that it superimposed on the *Sansome* rule the further principle that it is inconsistent with the idea of a tax-free reorganization that the Government should lose by the process. The district court further said that the *Phipps* opinion did not hold that the Government should gain through this process and consequently in the instant case the taxpayer would be allowed to utilize the deficit of the defunct real estate trust in determining the taxability of cash distributions made by its corporate successor.

The plaintiff contends in support of the district court's decision that there is a crucial distinction between the situation presented in the instant case and that which was presented in the *Phipps* case. In the instant case the transferee, Hotel Kenmore Corp., had no accumulated earnings and profits at the time of the reorganization while in the *Phipps* case the parent corporation did possess accumulated earnings and profits at the date of the tax-free reorganization. Any distributions made by the parent corporation in the *Phipps* case would have undoubtedly been dividends and therefore taxable to the recipient if the reorganization had not taken place. The result in the *Phipps* case was necessary in order to prevent corporations which had earnings and profits from distributing these earnings and profits so as to avoid taxation merely by acquiring the assets of a business possessing a deficit. In the instant case, however, where there were no accumulated earnings and profits at the date of the reorganization of the ownership of the Hotel Braemore and Hotel Kenmore, the taxpayer could not have obtained a tax advantage through a reorganization. In other words, if the taxpayer's business had continued in its trust form and there had been no reorganization, the $3,909.01 distribution clearly would not have qualified as a dividend under the 1939 Internal Revenue Code and therefore would not have been taxable to the plaintiffs.

There is language in the *Phipps* opinion which tends to support the plaintiff's contention. At page 420 of 336 U.S. . . . it is said ". . . the effect of the *Sansome* rule is simply this; a distribution of assets that would have been taxable as dividends absent the reorganization or liquidation does not lose that character by virtue of a tax-free transaction." At page 421 of 336 U.S. . . . . : "There has been judicially superimposed by the *Sansome* rule, with the subsequent explicit ratification of Congress, the doctrine that tax-free reorganizations shall not disturb the status of earnings and profits otherwise available for distribution."

Thus, the Supreme Court seems to emphasize the possession by one of the business entities involved in the tax-free reorganization of accumulated earnings and profits at the time of the reorganization. The nonexistence of such earnings and profits in the instant case clearly distinguishes it from the *Phipps* case. We consequently hold that a logical application of the *Sansome* rule, even as that rule has been defined by the Supreme Court in the *Phipps* case, compels us to conclude that in determining whether distributions made to its stockholders by the Hotel Kenmore Corp. are dividends, the deficit of its real estate trust predecessor must be taken into account.

The judgment of the district court is affirmed.

NOTES

1. Do §381(a) and (c)(2) modify or codify the law as you glean it from *Sansome, Phipps*, and *Snider*? How would the following distributions be treated under current law?

(a) B merges into C on the last day of their taxable years in an "A" reorganization. B has an accumulated deficit of $50,000; C has accumulated earnings and profits of $10,000. In the year following the consummation of the merger C breaks even. During that year C distributes the $10,000.

(b) B merges into C as above. B had accumulated earnings and profits of $50,000. C had neither a deficit nor accumulated earnings and profits. In the year following the merger C broke even and on the last day of the year distributed $10,000.

(c) B merges into C as above. B had a deficit of $50,000. C had neither a deficit nor accumulated earnings and profits. In the year following merger C earned over $10,000 after all corporate taxes. In the second year following merger C broke even and distributed $10,000.

2. In Dunning v. United States, 353 F.2d 940 (8th Cir. 1965), *cert. denied*, 384 U.S. 986 (1966), a bankrupt corporation was reorganized in 1935 under what became Chapter 11 of the Bankruptcy Code. The common stock was wiped out, and the preferred stock and the indebtedness were adjusted downward. There was a pre-reorganization deficit of almost $1,500,000. The court held that the pre-reorganization deficit could not be offset against subsequent earnings of the successor corporation, although the court stated there

might be a different result in a less drastic reorganization. What should the result be? Why?

3. In Rev. Rul. 73-552, 1973-2 C.B. 116, the Commissioner ruled that the acquiring corporation in a "C" reorganization would succeed to the transferor corporation's tax attributes, including earnings and profits, despite the fact that the transferor corporation retained liquid assets and continued in existence. Today, of course, there would not be a "C" if the transferor corporation continued (§368(a)(2)(G)). Cf. Rev. Rul. 71-364, 1971-2 C.B. 182 (excess cash retained by transferor corporation in "C" reorganization and distributed to shareholders one year later, treated as a dividend to the extent of the transferor corporation's earnings and profits at the time of the reorganization).

4. See Nesson, Earnings and Profits Discontinuities Under the 1954 Code, 77 Harv. L. Rev. 450 (1964); Phelan, Carryover of Tax Attributes, 51 Taxes 273 (1973).

B.   NET OPERATING LOSSES

1.   The Libson Shops Doctrine and Section 381

LIBSON SHOPS, INC. v. KOEHLER
353 U.S. 382 (1957)

Mr. Justice BURTON delivered the opinion of the Court. The issue before us is whether, under §§23(s) and 122 of the Internal Revenue Code of 1939, as amended, a corporation resulting from a merger of 17 separate incorporated businesses, which had filed separate income tax returns, may carry over and deduct the pre-merger net operating losses of three of its constituent corporations from the post-merger income attributable to the other businesses. We hold that such a carryover and deduction is not permissible.

Petitioner, Libson Shops, Inc., was incorporated on January 2, 1946, under the laws of Missouri, as Libson Shops Management Corporation, to provide management services for corporations selling women's apparel at retail. Its articles of incorporation also permitted it to sell apparel. At about the same time, the same interests incorporated 16 separate corporations to sell women's apparel at retail at separate locations. Twelve were incorporated and went into business in Missouri; four in Illinois. Each of these 16 sales corporations was operated separately and filed separate income tax returns. Petitioner's sole activity was to provide management services for them. The outstanding stock of all 17 corporations was owned, directly or indirectly, by the same individuals in the same proportions.

On August 1, 1949, the 16 sales corporations were merged into petitioner under the laws of Missouri and Illinois. New shares of petitioner's stock were issued, pro rata, in exchange for the stock of the sales corporations. By virtue of the merger agreement, petitioner's name was changed, the amount and par value of its stock revised, and its corporate purposes expanded. Following the merger, petitioner conducted the entire business as a single enterprise. Thus, the effect of the merger was to convert 16 retail businesses and one managing agency, reporting their incomes separately, into a single enterprise filing one income tax return.

Prior to the merger, three of the sales corporations showed net operating losses. . . . In the year following the merger, each of the retail units formerly operated by these three corporations continued to sustain a net operating loss. . . .

Section 23(s) authorizes a "net operating loss deduction computed under section 122."[1] Section 122 prescribes three basic rules for this calculation. Its pertinent parts provide generally (1) that a "net operating loss" is the excess of the taxpayer's deductions over its gross income (§122(a)); (2) that, if the taxpayer has a net operating loss, the loss may be used as a "net operating loss carry-back" to the two prior years (§122(b)(1)(A)) and, if not exhausted by that carry-back, the remainder may be used as a "net operating loss carry-over" to the three succeeding years (§122(b)(2)(C)); and (3) that the aggregate of the net operating loss carry-backs and carry-overs applicable to a given taxable year is the "net operating loss deduction" for the purposes of §23(s) (§122(c)).

We are concerned here with a claim to carry over an operating loss to the immediately succeeding taxable year. The particular provision on which petitioner's case rests is as follows: "If for any taxable year beginning after December 31, 1947, and before January 1, 1950, *the taxpayer* has a net operating loss, such net operating loss shall be a net operating loss carry-over for each of the three succeeding taxable years. . . ." (Emphasis supplied.) §122(b)(2)(C). . . . The controversy centers on the meaning of "the taxpayer."[2] The conten-

---

1. As originally added to the 1939 Code by the Revenue Act of 1939 . . . §122 relating for the computation and carry-over of net operating losses without expressly relating them to a given taxpayer. Section 153(a) of the Revenue Act of 1942 . . . amended §122(b) not only to allow carry-backs for the first time, but also to provide, as to both carry-backs and carry-overs, that it was only the net operating losses of "the taxpayer" which could be so utilized.

2. These words have been omitted from the new provisions of the Internal Revenue Code of 1954 relating to carry-backs and carry-overs after corporate acquisitions of assets of another corporation. See §§381, 382. [See also §172, the successor to §§23(s) and 122. — Ed.]

tions of the parties require us to decide whether it can be said that petitioner, a combination of 16 sales businesses, is "the taxpayer" having the pre-merger losses of three of those businesses.

In support of its denial of the carry-over, the Government argues that this statutory privilege is not available unless the corporation claiming it is the same taxable entity as that which sustained the loss. In reliance on New Colonial Co. v. Helvering, 292 U.S. 435, . . . the Government argues that separately chartered corporations are not the same taxable entity. Petitioner, on the other hand, relying on Helvering v. Metropolitan Edison Co., 306 U.S. 522, . . . argues that a corporation resulting from a statutory merger is treated as the same taxable entity as its constituents to whose legal attributes it has succeeded by operation of state law. However, we find it unnecessary to discuss this issue since an alternative argument made by the Government is dispositive of this case. The Government contends that the carry-over privilege is not available unless there is a continuity of business enterprise. It argues that the prior year's loss can be offset against the current year's income only to the extent that this income is derived from the operation of substantially the same business which produced the loss. Only to that extent is the same "taxpayer" involved.

The requirement of a continuity of business enterprise as applied to this case is in accord with the legislative history of the carry-over and carry-back provisions. Those provisions were enacted to ameliorate the unduly drastic consequences of taxing income strictly on an annual basis. They were designed to permit a taxpayer to set off its lean years against its lush years, and to strike something like an average taxable income computed over a period longer than one year. There is, however, no indication in their legislative history that these provisions were designed to permit the averaging of the pre-merger losses of one business with the post-merger income of some other business which had been operated and taxed separately before the merger. What history there is suggests that Congress primarily was concerned with the fluctuating income of a single business.[6]

---

6. The House Committee on Ways and Means, reporting on §122 as it was originally added to the 1939 Code by the Revenue Act of 1939, c. 247, 53 Stat. 862, 867-868, stated that — "The bill together with the committee amendments, permits taxpayers to carry over net operating business losses for a period of 2 years. Prior to the Revenue Act of 1932 such 2-year carry-over was allowed. No net loss has ever been allowed for a greater period than 2 years. In the Revenue Act of 1932, the 2-year net loss carry-over was reduced to 1 year and in the National Industrial Recovery Act the net loss carry-over was entirely eliminated. As a result of the elimination of this carry-over, *a business* with alternating profit and loss is required to pay higher taxes over a period of years than *a business* with stable profits, although the average income of the two firms is equal. New enterprises and the capital-goods industries are especially subject to wide fluctuations in earnings. It is, therefore, believed that the allowance of a net operating business loss carry-over will greatly aid business and stimulate new enterprises." (Emphasis supplied.) H.R. Rep. No. 855, 76th Cong., 1st Sess. 9.

This distinction is recognized by the very cases on which petitioner relies. In Stanton Brewery, Inc. v. Commissioner, 176 F.2d 573, 577, the Court of Appeals stressed the fact that the merging corporations there involved carried on "essentially a *continuing enterprise*, entitled to all ... benefits [of the carryover provisions] in ameliorating otherwise harsh tax consequences of fluctuating profits or expanding business." (Emphasis supplied.) And in Newmarket Manufacturing Co. v. United States, 233 F.2d 493, 497, the court expressly distinguished the case before it from the instant case on the ground that there "one single business" was involved in the merger, while in this case there were "several businesses."[7]

This difference is not merely a matter of form. In the *Newmarket* case, supra, a corporation desiring to change the state of its domicile caused the organization of a new corporation and merged into it. The new corporation sought to carry back its post-merger losses to the premerger income of the old corporation. But for the merger, the old corporation itself would have been entitled to a carry-back. In the present case, the 16 sales corporations, prior to the merger, chose to file separate income tax returns rather than to pool their income and losses by filing a consolidated return. Petitioner is attempting to carry over the pre-merger losses of three business units which continued to have losses after the merger. Had there been no merger, these businesses would have had no opportunity to carry over their losses. If petitioner is permitted to take a carry-over, the 16 sales businesses have acquired by merger an opportunity that they elected to forego when they chose not to file a consolidated return.

We do not imply that a question of tax evasion or avoidance is involved. Section [269(a)] ... does contain provisions which may vitiate a tax deduction that was made possible by the acquisition of corporate property for the "principal purpose" of tax evasion or avoidance. And that section is inapplicable here since there was no finding that tax evasion or avoidance was the "principal purpose" of the merger. The fact that §[269(a)] is inapplicable does not mean that petitioner is automatically entitled to a carry-over. The availability of this privilege depends on the proper interpretation to be given to the carry-over provisions. We find nothing in those provi-

---

7. Koppers Co. v. United States, 133 Ct. Cl. 22, 134 F. Supp. 290, also involves a situation in which the corporation resulting from the merger carried on essentially the same taxable enterprise as before, since the merged corporations had been filing consolidated tax returns. E. & J. Gallo Winery v. Commissioner, 227 F.2d 699, is inconclusive on this point since the opinion does not disclose whether or not a continuing enterprise was involved. Cf. §382(a) of the Internal Revenue Code of 1954 relating to the purchase of a corporation and change in its trade or business. Under circumstances there defined, that section precludes a carry-over by the *same* corporation, unless it continues to engage in "substantially the same" trade or business as before the change in ownership. §382(a)(1)(C).

sions which suggests that they should be construed to give a "windfall" to a taxpayer who happens to have merged with other corporations. The purpose of these provisions is not to give a merged taxpayer a tax advantage over others who have not merged. We conclude that petitioner is not entitled to a carry-over since the income against which the offset is claimed was not produced by substantially the same businesses which incurred the losses.[9]

The Judgment of the Court of Appeals is affirmed.

Mr. Justice Douglas dissents.

Mr. Justice Whittaker took no part in the consideration or decision of this case.

FRANK IX & SONS v. COMMISSIONER
375 F.2d 867 (3d Cir. 1967), *cert. denied*, 389 U.S. 900 (1967)

FREEDMAN, Circuit Judge. Petitioner attacks the Tax Court's disallowance of net operating loss carryover deductions on losses which it incurred prior to a reorganization.

The Ix family, through a number of corporations, was engaged in the manufacture and sale of woven synthetic fibers. Separate corporations operated separate mills which manufactured the same types and styles of cloth within the multi-corporation structure. A central office was maintained for accounting, bookkeeping, inventory control and yarn purchasing. There was also provided a central sales force as well as complete technical and production and control staffs. Orders were solicited and returned to a central office in New York where the production and control department determined on the basis of work load and availability of skilled operators which corporation would manufacture the cloth.

In 1952 Frank Ix & Sons, Inc., borrowed $3,000,000 from a bank to make loans to a number of Ix family corporations. To secure the bank indebtedness it pledged as collateral all the capital stock which it owned in the other Ix family corporations and the promissory notes which it received from them for their participation in the loan. One of the conditions of the bank's loan was the maintenance in specified amounts of the working capital of the family corporations.

One of the Ix family corporations operated a mill in Cornelius, North Carolina. Because of the similarity in names of the various Ix corporations and the change in the corporate name of the petitioner,

---

9. We do not pass on situations like those presented in Northway Securities Co. v. Commissioner, 23 B.T.A. 532; Alprosa Watch Corp. v. Commissioner, 11 T.C. 240; A.B. & Container Corp. v. Commissioner, 14 T.C. 842; WAGE, Inc. v. Commissioner, 19 T.C. 249. In these cases a *single* corporate taxpayer changed the character of its business and the taxable income of one of its enterprises was reduced by the deductions or credits of another.

we shall refer to this entity as "Cornelius Ix." Cornelius Ix received $2,550,000 from Frank Ix & Sons, Inc., the major share of the bank loan. In accordance with the bank's requirement, Cornelius Ix agreed that it would maintain its working capital in the amount of $2,800,000. More than a year and a half later, when Cornelius Ix's working capital had fallen nearly a million dollars below the stipulated requirement, a plan of reorganization was adopted with the bank's approval by which there were transferred to Cornelius Ix all of the assets of another Ix family corporation which operated a mill in Charlottesville, Virginia, and which we shall for convenience refer to as "Charlottesville Ix." Both corporations were engaged in the manufacture and sale of woven synthetic fibers, and their common stock was owned in the same proportions by Ix family members. Pursuant to the plan of reorganization Charlottesville Ix transferred all its assets to Cornelius Ix, in return for which Charlottesville Ix received new common stock of Cornelius Ix on the basis of thirteen shares of Cornelius Ix for each outstanding share of Charlottesville Ix. Charlottesville Ix then distributed these shares to its stockholders in complete liquidation and was dissolved. The plan of reorganization was fully consummated on September 30, 1953, and Cornelius Ix changed its name to Frank Ix & Sons Virginia Corporation, the petitioner. It is conceded that the transaction constituted a valid, tax-free "D reorganization." . . . After the reorganization the same persons held the common stock in the new corporation in the same proportions as their pre-reorganization holdings in Cornelius Ix and Charlottesville Ix.

   Cornelius Ix had operated its mill at a loss before the reorganization for the years ending March 31, 1952 and March 31, 1953. After the reorganization, petitioner operated both the mill in Cornelius, North Carolina and the mill in Charlottesville, Virginia, maintaining separate records for each of them, until July 22, 1954, when it shut down the North Carolina mill, which had continued to operate at a loss. The Charlottesville, Virginia mill had realized taxable net income in the years prior to the reorganization and continued to operate at a profit thereafter. For the year ending March 31, 1954, the first fiscal year after the reorganization, petitioner showed a net loss from the operation of the Cornelius mill for the period from September 30, 1953 to the end of the fiscal year, and sustained a net operating loss for the full fiscal year.

   What is before us now is the determination by the Commissioner of deficiencies resulting from petitioner's deduction on its 1957, 1958 and 1959 income tax returns of net operating losses sustained by Cornelius Ix for the fiscal year ending March 31, 1953,[1] and by

   1. The net operating loss for the fiscal year ending March 31, 1953 was carried over only in part to the years here involved. Petitioner utilized a portion of it in earlier returns which the Commissioner did not challenge.

Cornelius Ix and petitioner for the fiscal year ending March 31, 1954. The action of the Commissioner was upheld by the Tax Court on the ground that the deductibility of the net operating loss carryovers was determined by the 1939 Code, under which the deduction was barred by the doctrine of Libson Shops, Inc. v. Koehler, 353 U.S. 382 (1957). Frank Ix & Sons Virginia Corporation (N.J.) v. C.I.R., 45 T.C. 533 (1966).

In the Tax Court petitioner's argument for the deductions rested on two grounds. One was that the *Libson Shops* doctrine was inapplicable to the transaction because Cornelius Ix, which acquired the assets of Charlottesville Ix, was a loss corporation, which made the situation radically different from that with which the *Libson Shops* doctrine dealt. The second contention was that in any event the "continuity of business enterprise" requirement of the *Libson Shops* doctrine had been met.

These two contentions lead us back to the *Libson Shops* case, which the Supreme Court decided in 1957 under the 1939 Code. There a number of individuals directly or indirectly owned in the same proportions the stock of seventeen corporations. One of the corporations provided management services for the remaining sixteen corporations, each one of which, separately operated, as engaged in the retail sale of women's apparel. Each corporation filed a separate income tax return. In a tax-free reorganization the sixteen operating corporations, three of which had been sustaining losses and thirteen of which had been profitable, were merged into the management corporation. The Commissioner disallowed the deduction by the surviving corporation from its net income derived from the thirteen profitable units of the losses carried over from former years of the three unprofitable corporations. The Supreme Court found it unnecessary to decide the Commissioner's primary contention that the surviving corporation was not the same "taxpayer" as that which had sustained the losses in the prior years.[2] Instead the Court disallowed the deduction on the ground that the losses, and the profits from which they were sought to be deducted, were not produced by "substantially the same businesses." The Court thus chose to decide the case on the basis of economic substance rather than on the more technical question whether the surviving corporation was the same "taxpayer" as the constituent units which had sustained the losses.

The *Libson Shops* case has given rise to a flood of discussion and much dispute regarding its application in particular circumstances. The facts in the present case however, fall so remarkably close to the circumstances which existed in *Libson Shops* and we therefore stand

2. Sections 23(s) and 122(b)(C) of the 1938 Code authorized a net operating loss carryover for three years "if for any taxable year beginning after December 31, 1947, and before January 1, 1950, *the taxpayer* has a net operating loss. . . . (Emphasis added.)

so close to the center of the doctrine that there is no need to consider its application in the more remote areas in which its repercussions may be felt. The decisive fact in *Libson Shops* was that a number of individuals had chosen to cast their investment into seventeen separate corporations and thus to spread the risk of their undertaking among separate business units and to enjoy the benefits of separate incorporation and separate tax returns for each of them. Thus, by their own choice they made each corporation a separate business unit as well as a separate taxpayer. The Court therefore determined that they could not disregard this choice in order to enjoy the deduction of a net operating loss carryover of one taxpayer-business unit from the profits of another, separate taxpayer-business unit by a formal act of corporate merger. The court believed that such a deduction was forbidden by the policy underlying the allowance of net operating loss carryovers, which was to protect a single business from the hazards of fluctuating income. The establishment of the seventeen separate business units was a choice in the opposite direction; within each individual unit the loss carryover provision applied, but the investors could not enjoy that benefit and also reap the contradictory advantage, by merger, of enjoying the loss carryover advantage beyond the boundaries of the individual unit.

In the present case, as in *Libson Shops*, individuals chose to cast their investment into separate corporate units, each of which was a separate economic entity as well as a separate legal entity, and the assets which produced the income against which earlier losses were sought to be applied were different from the assets which produced the losses. If the separate businesses had not been combined there would have been no right to utilize the net operating loss carryover from the unprofitable corporation to reduce the taxable income of the profitable corporation. Whatever differences exist between the factual circumstances in the present case and in *Libson Shops* are not of decisive significance. The fact that what occurred here was not an "A reorganization," a statutory merger, but instead a "D reorganization," a transfer of assets for stock, is a factual difference without any legal distinction. The policy of *Libson Shops*, where indeed there was a retention of one hundred per cent control, cannot be diminished because the "D reorganization" involved here was subject to a statutory requirement of eighty per cent retention of control of the transferee corporation by the owners of the transferor corporation.

Petitioner earnestly contends that the fact that here the loss corporation acquired in reorganization the assets of the profitable corporation significantly distinguishes this case from *Libson Shops*, where the central service corporation absorbed by merger the remaining sixteen corporations including the three loss corporations.

Shortly after the Supreme Court decided *Libson Shops* the view was advanced that the decision might have been different had the loss corporations survived. For there would then not be present the implication that the transaction was without a business purpose, which is so clearly evident when a loss corporation is acquired by a profitable corporation, a transaction which ordinarily has no economic advantage except for the net operating loss carryover which the absorbing corporation, as a result of taking over the shell, can apply against its net taxable income. On the other hand, if the loss corporation is the survivor in the reorganization, it is to be looked upon as the business enterprise which continues, and this prevents regarding it as an empty shell acquired by another merely for the purpose of enjoying its accumulated net losses. In addition, where the loss corporation is the survivor, the identity of the corporation which had sustained the original losses and the corporation which is carrying them forward to the tax year for deduction is the same, and this satisfies the requirement, which *Libson Shops* had emphasized, that the deduction must be taken by the same taxpayer which had suffered the original loss.

These distinctions, however, are too artificial for application in dealing with economic realities. It is easy enough for those planning a reorganization to turn the shell on end and make it the surviving corporation if this difference will have substantial tax advantages. The courts to which the question has been presented therefore have rejected the distinction. Allied Central Stores, Inc. v. C.I.R., 339 F.2d 503 (2 Cir. 1964), *cert. denied*, 381 U.S. 903 (1965); see Julius Garfinckel & Co., Inc. v. C.I.R., 335 F.2d 744 (2 Cir. 1964), *cert. denied*, 379 U.S. 962 (1965). We agree with this view, especially where, as in this case, the corporations involved were originally owned by the same individuals, whose proportionate interest in each corporation was the same. The conclusion is compelled by the underlying policy of *Libson Shops* that losses incurred by a business unit should not be applied against profits which come from other assets which the shareholders had originally decided to operate separately, even though each unit is owned by the same group of shareholders. . . .

Petitioner invokes Revenue Ruling 63-40,[7] which permits the carryover of a net operating loss where a corporation which is sustaining losses in its business acquires from unrelated sellers the assets of another business which it then carries on. This change in activity by the same corporation presents a situation which the Supreme Court in *Libson Shops* expressly noted was not reached by its opinion.[8] The Revenue Ruling is inapplicable where a group of shareholders

---

7. 1963-1 Cum. Bull. 46. [See Note 2, page 833 infra. — ED.]
8. See 353 U.S. at 390, n.9; C.I.R. v. Virginia Metal Products, Inc., 290 F.2d 675, 677 (3 Cir. 1961), *cert. denied*, 368 U.S. 889 (1961); Julius Garfinckel & Co., Inc. v. C.I.R., supra.

choose originally the benefits of separate incorporation. It merely recognizes the general principle acknowledged by the Second Circuit in Norden-Ketay Corp. v. C.I.R., 319 F.2d 902, 906 (2 Cir. 1963): "It may well be that shareholders who sustain a loss and then are wise enough to liquidate an uneconomic enterprise and embark on a different and profitable field of endeavor through the same corporation are equally entitled to offset the earlier losses as those who see an unprofitable corporation through the lean years into the good ones in the same activity." . . .

Section 172(a) of the 1974 Code is a general provision authorizing the deduction of net operating losses which are carried over from former years; it is similar to the provision of §23(s) of the 1939 Code. The 1954 Code, however, contains new provisions in §381 and §382 which deal with carryovers in certain corporate acquisitions and special limitations on net operating loss carryovers. Section 381, to the extent it is relevant here, provides that a corporation which acquires the assets of another corporation in certain tax-free transactions, such as a "D reorganization," shall succeed to the net operating loss carryover of the acquired corporation. Section 381(a)(2), (c)(1). Section 382 establishes two limitations on the carryover of a net operating loss: (1) it completely disallows any loss carryover where there has been a change of fifty percentage points or more in the ownership of the total fair market value of the outstanding stock of the corporation among any one or more of the ten persons who own the greatest percentage of the stock, and where the corporation has not continued to carry on substantially the same trade or business as that conducted before the change in ownership (§382(a)); and (2) it imposes a proportionate reduction in the amount of the net-operating loss carryover permitted where in a reorganization such as a "D reorganization" the shareholders of the loss corporation immediately after the reorganization own less than twenty per cent of the fair market value of the outstanding stock of the acquiring corporation (§382(b)), a proportionate limitation which does not apply, however, if the transferor corporation and the acquiring corporation are owned substantially by the same persons in the same proportions. (§382(b)(3)).

Petitioner argues that the maze of provisions in §381 and §382 which provide for the survival of a loss carryover in the hands of a transferee corporation and place limitations upon it, are inapplicable under their terms where it is the loss corporation which survives. From this it claims that it enjoys the right to the deduction of the net operating loss carryover under the simple authority of §172(a), which, with §§381 and 382 inapplicable, is accordingly without limitation.[10]

10. Section 269, which deals with attempts to avoid tax, concededly is not here involved.

The result of their contention would be that a loss corporation absorbing by reorganization a profitable corporation would enjoy without any limitation the right under §172(a) to deduct net operating loss carryovers. Although the language of §382 does not indubitably lead to petitioner's construction of its meaning,[11] we are not required to decide the question. For by the express terms of the Code,[12] neither §381 nor §382 is applicable to the present case because they are effective only where the plan of reorganization is adopted on or after June 22, 1954. Petitioner argues, however, that since under its view §§381 and 382 would by their terms be inapplicable where the loss corporation survives and thus §172(a) would be operative without limitation, it is true a fortiori where §§381 and 382 are inapplicable because of their effective dates. In effect, this argument if accepted would mean that petitioner would obtain the benefit of whatever plan the 1954 Code envisages even though essential portions of the plan had not yet come into effect.

The law which existed on September 30, 1953 when the plan of reorganization was consummated was the 1939 Code. Its §23(s) was substantially reincorporated in the 1954 Code as §172(a). In these circumstances we see no reason why the taxpayer should be freed from the judicially created *Libson Shops* doctrine before the restrictions of §381 and §382 went into effect even if they should be considered to be congressional substitutes for the *Libson Shops* doctrine. If they were such substitutes, the fact that Congress held them in abeyance until June 22, 1954 in order to permit taxpayers to complete pending transactions in reliance on the former law,[13] can result in no less than the continued validity of the *Libson Shops* doctrine until they went into effect. In saying this we do not mean to indicate what our view would be in the case of a plan of reorganization adopted after June 22, 1954 which would bring into the problem the extent to which §§381 and 382 are substitutes for the *Libson Shops* doctrine and their applicability where an acquisition is made by loss corporation by way of merger or other reorganization. . . .

The decision of the Tax Court will be affirmed.

NOTES

1. In Rev. Rul. 58-603, 1958-2 C.B. 147, and Rev. Rul. 59-395, 1959-2 C.B. 475, the Service ruled that the *Libson Shops* doctrine

---

11. Thus §382(b)(1) applies "If . . . the transferor corporation or the acquiring corporation" has the net operating loss.

12. Sections 393(b)(1) and 394.

13. Senate Committee Report accompanying H.R. 8300, 1954-3 U.S. Code Cong. & Admin. News, p. 4925.

would not be relied upon under the 1954 Code in cases to which
§381(a) applied. In Rev. Rul. 66-214, 1966-2 C.B. 98, it construed
its prior rulings to bar the application of the *Libson Shops* doctrine to
the carryover of a net operating loss in the case of an "A" reorganization (statutory merger) in which the surviving corporation, no
longer engaged in its premerger business, sought to set off its earlier
loss against the profits of the business previously conducted by the
constituent corporation whose identity had not survived reorganization. This was a liberalization of the Service's prior rulings, since
§381(a) does not speak to the surviving corporation's own loss carryover. What does? Compare §382 in this respect.

2. Although the facts in *Libson Shops* involved a reorganization,
in Rev. Rul. 63-40, 1963-1 C.B. 46, the Service indicated clearly that
in some non-reorganization cases under the 1954 Code it would apply
the doctrine of that case to deny a corporation the use of its own loss
carryover. This application would be made, presumably, where the
facts of a given case did not invoke the bar of old §382(a). Excerpts
from Rev. Rul. 63-40 are set forth below. What is the principle the
Service follows in distinguishing those non-reorganization cases in
which it will apply a *Libson Shops* approach from those in which it will
not?

> Advice has been requested whether either the rationale or the
> decision in Libson Shops, Inc. v. Koehler, 335 U.S. 382 (1957),
> Ct. D. 1809, C.B. 1957-2, 891, . . . prevent[s] the use of a net
> operating loss carryover under the circumstances described below.
> 1. The M Corporation was organized in 1947 by three indi-
> viduals who owned an equal number of shares of its authorized
> and outstanding stock. From the date of its incorporation until the
> early part of 1958 it was engaged in the fabrication and sale,
> through distributors, of household light steel products. The busi-
> ness was successful during its early years of operation. However,
> commencing in 1953 it sustained losses in each of its taxable years
> and over the period ending December 31, 1957, had accumulated
> substantial net operating losses.
> In 1958 M Corporation purchased for cash, at fair market
> value, all of the assets of N corporation, which had a history of
> successful operation of drive-in restaurants. M and N were un-
> related corporations and none of the shareholders of M
> corporation owned, directly or indirectly, any stock of N corpo-
> ration. The funds for the cash purchase were derived in part from
> M corporation's own business assets and in part from an equal
> contribution to its capital of cash by its three stockholders. Shortly
> thereafter, M corporation discontinued its former business activity,
> sold the assets connected therewith, and engaged exclusively in
> the business of operating the chain of drive-in restaurants formerly
> operated by the N corporation.

Under the facts presented, . . . the sole question raised is whether the rationale of the *Libson Shops* decision bars the allowance of the net operating loss deduction attributable to losses incurred prior to the acquisition of the new business activity for M corporation's taxable year ended December 31, 1958.

In cases, like the one discussed above, arising under §122 of the Internal Revenue Code of 1939 or §172 of the 1954 Code in which losses have been incurred by a single corporation and there has been little or no change in the stock ownership of the corporation during or after the period in which the losses were incurred, the Internal Revenue Service will not rely on the rationale of the *Libson Shops* decision to bar the corporation from using losses previously incurred by it solely because such losses are attributable to a discontinued corporate activity. Accordingly since there was no change in stock ownership in M corporation either before the discontinuance of its former business activity or after the commencement of its new business activity, a net operating loss deduction is allowable for its taxable year ended December 31, 1958.

However, if there is more than a minor change in stock ownership of a loss corporation which acquires a new business enterprise, the Service may continue to contest the deductibility of the carryover of the corporation's prior losses against income of the new business enterprise. See, for example, as involving substantial changes in stock ownership, Mill Ridge Coal Co. v. Patterson, 264 Fed. (2d) 713 (1959), *certiorari denied,* 361 (U.S. 816 (1959); A.C. Willingham v. United States, 289 Fed. (2d) 283 (1961), *certiorari denied,* 368 U.S. 828 (1961); Commissioner v. Virginia Metal Products, Inc., 290 Fed. (2d) 675 (1961), *certiorari denied,* 368 U.S. 889 (1961); J.G. Dudley Co., Inc. v. Commissioner, 298 Fed. (2d) 750 (1962); and Huyler's v. Commissioner, 38 T.C. 773 (1962). Compare Kolker Bros., Inc. v. Commissioner, 35 T.C. 299 (1960), *nonacquiescence* at page five of this Bulletin, where part of the funds used by the corporation to purchase assets of a new business activity were borrowed from some nonstockholders who several months after the purchase acquired about 46 percent of the corporation's stock in exchange for the indebtedness owed them.

For a discussion of the Service position with respect to the application of *Libson Shops* to a merger or other transaction described in §381(a) of the Code, see Revenue Ruling 58-603, C.B. 1958-2, 147. Further Service views concerning the application of *Libson Shops* are set out in Revenue Ruling 59-395, C.B. 1959-2, 475.

2. Advice has also been requested whether the Service would apply different treatment to a case involving the same facts as are set out in the foregoing except for a difference in the method of acquisition by M corporation of the assets of N corporation. In this second case M corporation first attempted in extended

negotiations to purchase the assets of N corporation, but the shareholders of N corporation were unwilling to consummate the transaction except by way of the sale of their stock to M corporation. M corporation purchased the stock of N corporation for cash, at fair market value, solely for the purpose of acquiring its assets to earn a profit with those assets and *immediately* liquidated that corporation under such circumstances that the basis of the assets to M corporation will be determined by the amount it paid for the stock of N corporation.

Under the facts of this second case, . . . the conclusion reached with respect to the first case is equally applicable here.

No opinion is expressed as to other cases where the facts show that the purchase price is payable over a substantial period of time (whether or not specifically payable only out of earnings of the business) or exceeds fair market value or where other circumstances may justify the application of §269 of the Code. . . .*

3. The House Conference Report discussing the 1986 amendments to §382 indicates that "the *Libson Shops* doctrine will have no application to transactions subject to the provisions of [§382]." H.R. Conf. Rep. No. 841, 99th Cong., 2d Sess. II-194 (1986). See Peaslee and Cohen, Section 382 As Amended by the Tax Reform Act of 1986, page 837 infra.

REVENUE RULING 77-133
1977-1 C.B. 96

Advice has been requested concerning the Federal income tax treatment of a net operating loss (NOL) incurred prior to a corporate reorganization under the circumstances described below.

A and B, both individuals, owned all of the stock of M, a domestic corporation engaged in farming. Serious disputes arose between A and B regarding the operation of the farming business that endangered the continued operation of the business. As a result, M formed S, also a domestic corporation, by transferring 50 percent of its assets and liabilities to S in exchange for all of the S stock. M, immediately thereafter, distributed all of the S stock to B in exchange for all of B's stock in M. The non pro rata distribution was undertaken for reasons germane to corporate business problems and was necessary for the future conduct of the farming business. This split-off transaction, the formation of S followed by the distribution and exchange

*Rev. Rul. 63-40 was modified in part by T.I.R. 773 (1965). — ED.

between M and B, qualified as a reorganization under section 368(a)(1)(D) . . . and satisfied the requirements of section 355. Prior to the split-off, M had incurred a NOL that was available to be carried forward to years subsequent to the split-off.

The specific questions presented are whether the entire NOL is available to M after the split-off and, if not, whether any portion of the NOL carries over to S under section 381. . . .

Section 381(c) . . . states, in part, that in the case of the acquisition of assets of a corporation by another corporation in a transfer to which section 361 (relating to nonrecognition of gain or loss to corporations) applies, but only if the transfer is in connection with a reorganization described in section 368(a)(1)(D) that satisfies the requirements of section 354(b)(1)(A) and (B), the acquiring corporation shall succeed to and take into account as of the close of the day of distribution, the items described in section 381(c).

Section 381(c) . . . states, in part; that one of the items to be taken into account under section 381(a) is a NOL of the transferor corporation.

Section 354(b)(1)(A) . . . provides, in part, that no gain or loss will be recognized in connection with certain exchanges of stock or securities pursuant to a reorganization within the meaning of section 368(a)(1)(D) if the corporation to which the assets are transferred in the reorganization acquires substantially all of the assets of the transferor of such assets.

Rev. Rul. 56-373, 1956-2 C.B. 217, holds that under section 381(a)(2) . . . where a corporate reorganization, to which sections 361 and 368(a)(1)(D) apply, is a "split-up" within the purview of section 355, an unused NOL carryover of the transferor corporation may not be taken into account by any of the successor corporations.

The split-off in the present transaction is similar in many respects to the split-up described in Rev. Rul. 56-373. Both a split-up and a split-off are divisive reorganizations but a split-off does not involve the liquidation of the transferor corporation, as does a split-up.

In the present situation, substantially all of the assets of M, the transferor corporation, have not been transferred to S, so that the requirements of section 354(b)(1)(A) of the Code and section 381(a)(2) have not been met. Furthermore, the congressional committee reports underlying section 381 of the Code, S. Rep. No. 1622, 83rd Cong., 2nd Sess. 52 (1954), state that section 381 does not apply in the case of split-ups, spin-offs or other divisive reorganizations.

In addition, section 382(a) . . . does not preclude M from deducting the NOL, without regard to whether M's business is changed within the meaning of section 382(a), because the split-off transaction was a tax-free reorganization. . . .

Accordingly, the entire NOL is available to M following the split-off. . . .

NOTES

1. Why in the case of a "D" reorganization did Congress limit the applicability of §381(a)(2) to situations in which the requirements of §354(b)(1)(A) and (B) are met? How else might Congress have achieved its basic objective in the case of a "D" reorganization that is within the ambit of §355 but not within §354(b)(1)?

2. Section 381 deals with much more than just earnings and profits and net operating losses. For example, if an acquiring corporation settles and pays a liability of the corporation it acquired in an "A" reorganization, it may deduct its payment under §162 by application of §381(c)(4). Reimbursement by the (former) shareholders of the acquired corporation is not includible in the acquiring corporation's gross income. It is a capital contribution, increasing the shareholders' basis in the stock they receive in the acquiring corporation. See Rev. Rul. 83-73, 1983-1 C.B. 84.

3. The 1989 Act substantially curtailed the right of a corporation to carry back its net operating losses if they are incurred after a CERT, a "corporate equity reducing transaction," occurs. See §172(b)(1)(M) and §172(m).

2. Section 382

The 1986 Act repealed old §382. The new §382, which offers a very different approach to the problem of trafficking in corporations with net operating losses, is well summarized in the following excerpt:

PEASLEE AND COHEN, SECTION 382 AS AMENDED BY THE TAX REFORM ACT OF 1986*
Tax Notes, Dec. 1, 1986, p. 849

I.   BACKGROUND

A. PURPOSE OF SECTION 382

Section 382[1] is intended to avoid "trafficking" in loss carryovers by restricting the availability of net operating loss ("NOL") carryovers of a corporation following changes in the ownership of the stock of that corporation. (By operation of section 383, these rules also apply to carryovers of other losses, such as capital losses, and of certain credits, such as investment tax credits, research credits, minimum tax credits, and foreign tax credits.)

*Excerpted and reprinted with permission.

1. References herein to "section 382" are to that section as amended by the Tax Reform Act of 1986 ("TRA 1986"). References to "old section 382" are to that section as in effect before the effective date of section 382.

B. OLD SECTION 382

Old section 382 provided two separate rules governing the carryover of NOLs:

1. *Taxable Purchases.* In the case of taxable purchases of stock, NOL carryovers were unaffected unless:

(i) the 10 largest shareholders of the corporation had increased their stock ownership by 50 percentage points (not by 50 percent) over a two-year period and

(ii) the corporation discontinued a trade or business that it had conducted prior to the change in ownership (or was not engaged in any active trade or business).

If both of these tests were met, then the corporation's NOL carryovers were eliminated.

2. *Tax-free Reorganizations.* Following a tax-free reorganization, a corporation's NOL carryovers were unaffected unless the former loss corporation's shareholders had less than a 20 percent continuing stock interest in the surviving corporation. If the continuing stock interest was less than 20 percent, the NOL carryovers were reduced by five percent for each percentage point that the continuing stock interest was less than 20 percent.

3. *Practical Effect.* Old section 382 rarely applied in practice to taxable acquisitions because of the change of business requirement. It also rarely applied to reorganizations for the reason that, when the loss corporation was acquired through a subsidiary, in applying the 20 percent continuity test, the value of the former loss corporation's shareholders' stock was compared with the value of the equity of the subsidiary, not the value of the equity of the parent. Also, old section 382 did not apply to "B" reorganizations. Finally, old section 382 did not affect built-in losses (potential tax losses that were unrealized at the time of an acquisition).

C. PRIOR ATTEMPTS TO AMEND OLD SECTION 382

The provisions of old section 382 were substantially amended by the Tax Reform Act of 1976. The amended version of section 382 potentially disallowed NOL carryovers completely if there was a change in ownership regardless of whether a business was continued. This was thought to be too harsh and the effective date of amended section 382 was repeatedly postponed. As a practical matter, it never came into effect. (Technically, amended section 382 was in effect during three separate periods, the latest of which began on January 1, 1986; in each case, however, it was later repealed on a retroactive basis.)

D. SECTION 382 UNDER TRA 1986

1. *General Rule.* As amended by TRA 1986, section 382 provides, in general, that following a change in the ownership of a corporation's stock aggregating more than 50 percentage points over a three-year period (regardless of whether the change occurs as a result of taxable purchases, reorganizations, or a combination of both), NOL carryovers (including built-in losses) are generally not reduced, but the maximum amount of taxable income that can be offset with those carryovers or losses in years ending after the change in ownership is limited. The annual limit equals the product of (x) the value of the corporation at the time of the change in ownership and (y) a prescribed rate fixed at that time equal to the long-term Federal rate, adjusted for the difference between interest rates on taxable and tax-exempt bonds. In addition, the annual limitation is scaled back if the loss corporation has more than a de minimis amount of investment assets, and NOL carryovers are completely disallowed if the corporation does not meet a generous business continuity test for two years following the change in ownership.

2. *Rationale.* This rule (except for the business assets and business continuity requirements) reflects the so-called "neutrality principle" under which an acquiror of a loss corporation is permitted to utilize that corporation's NOL carryovers to the same extent that the loss corporation itself would have been able to realize benefits from those carryovers. The annual limitation is intended to approximate the income that the corporation would have produced as a return on its equity and thus the income that could have been sheltered by the NOL carryovers absent the acquisition. The limitation incorporates its own economic tax avoidance test in that the limitation will be more significant the greater the amount of NOL carryovers is by comparison with the value of the loss corporation.

3. *Continuity of Business Irrelevant.* It is important to bear in mind that, unlike old section 382, which required that, in the case of a taxable stock purchase, both a change of ownership and a change of business test be met before a corporation's NOL carryovers would be affected, the application of section 382 under TRA 1986 is triggered solely by an ownership change. Thus, the limitations imposed by section 382 become effective following the requisite ownership change even though the corporation maintains exactly the same businesses (or, indeed, expands those businesses) that it had operated prior to the change in ownership. Also, in the reorganization context, the limitations cannot be avoided through a subsidiary acquisition. . . .

III. DETAILED DESCRIPTION OF SECTION 382

A. OWNERSHIP CHANGE

Section 382 is triggered by an "ownership change." An ownership change occurs if after either an owner shift involving a 5-percent shareholder or an equity structure shift, the percentage of loss corporation stock owned by one or more 5-percent shareholders exceeds by more than 50 percentage points the lowest total percentage holdings of those shareholders during the testing period. All transactions during the testing period are counted even if they are isolated events and not part of a plan to acquire the loss corporation.

Example: On January 2, 1987, Corp L is owned equally by four shareholders: A, B, C, and D. On that date, A buys B's 25 percent interest. On June 30, 1989, in a transaction unrelated to A's purchase of B's stock, E buys the stock held by C and D. There is an ownership change on June 30, 1989 because on that date A's percentage interest (50 percent) exceeds by 25 percentage points his lowest interest in Corp L during the preceding three years and E's interest exceeds by 50 percentage points his lowest interest (zero) during that period, resulting in a total increase of 75 percentage points.

1. *Owner Shift Involving a 5-Percent Shareholder.* An owner shift involving a 5-percent shareholder includes any change in the percentage stock ownership of 5-percent shareholders, regardless of how that change is effected, including a change that results from a reorganization or other corporate transaction, or from redemptions or issuances of stock. For these purposes, a 5-percent shareholder includes any shareholder who holds five percent of the corporation's stock either before or after the change in stock ownership. In general, any transaction affecting the ownership of stock of a corporation, other than a pro rata redemption, exchange, or distribution of stock, would be an owner shift involving a 5-percent shareholder. . . .

2. *Equity Structure Shift.* Includes a reorganization within the meaning of section 368(a)(1) except for (i) a divisive "D" or "G" reorganization, or (ii) an "F" reorganization.

See, however, . . . below for illustrations of transactions that may be treated as equity structure shifts under regulatory authority. Because an equity structure shift would almost invariably also constitute an owner shift involving a 5-percent shareholder, the only significance of qualifying as an equity structure shift is that a special rule may apply to segregate groups of public shareholders . . . and a different effective date may apply. . . .

3. *Definitions and Computational Rules.* Again, it is necessary to be familiar with a number of definitions.

a. Stock. For purposes of determining whether there has been an ownership change, all stock is included, whether common or preferred, except stock that would not be treated as such for purposes of the consolidated return rules (i.e., nonvoting, nonconvertible non-participating preferred stock that is not issued at a significant discount).

Under regulatory authority granted in TRA 1986, however, se-curities that would otherwise be treated as stock may be treated as non-stock and vice versa.

b. 5-Percent Shareholder. Changes in stock ownership are mea-sured by aggregating increases in the ownership of stock by "5-percent shareholders" (owners of 5 percent or more of a corporation's stock). However, all owners of *less than* 5 percent are aggregated and treated as a single 5-percent shareholder (a "section 382 public share-holder"). Thus, any sale of stock by a 5-percent shareholder to other shareholders will be counted as an increase in stock ownership by a 5-percent shareholder regardless of the size of the holdings of the other shareholders. The only sales that will not be counted are sales by one less than 5-percent shareholder to another.

Example: Corp L is held by a single shareholder. In a public offering, stock of Corp L that represents 60 percent of the stock of Corp L outstanding after the offering is sold to public investors, with no investor acquiring as much as five percent of the Corp L stock. This would constitute an ownership change because the section 382 public shareholder has increased its ownership of Corp L stock from zero to 60 percent. . . .

4. *Segregating Public Shareholders.* Public shareholders are treated differently and must be segregated in several cases.

a. Acquisitive Reorganizations. A reorganization in which a loss corporation is combined with another corporation can result in an ownership change because of the increase in the ownership of stock of the loss corporation by the shareholders of the other party to the reorganization. In a case where both the loss corporation and that other party have less than 5-percent shareholders, the true increase in ownership of the loss corporation would be understated if the two groups were treated as a single section 382 public shareholder. Ac-cordingly, in the case of an equity structure shift that is a reorganization with more than one party, section 382 treats the less than 5-percent shareholders of each party as a separate section 382 public shareholder that is considered to be a 5-percent share-holder. . . .

b. Stock Offerings. Under regulatory authority to be applied prospectively only, in the case of a public offering of shares of a corporation that has public shareholders before the offering, the pre-offering group of public shareholders may generally be segregated from the new group of public shareholders, with each group being treated as a different section 382 public shareholder. As a result, the increase in ownership by the new public shareholders would be counted in full in determining whether an ownership change has occurred.

Example: Corp L is widely held with no individual 5-percent shareholders. The value of the Corp L stock is $500 million. On January 2, 1987, Corp L issues stock with a value of $750 million. Assuming that regulations relating to public offerings have been issued with an effective date of January 1, 1987, an ownership change has occurred because the new group of Corp L public shareholders have increased their ownership interest from zero to 60 percent ($750 million/$1,250 million) except to the extent that it can be demonstrated that the new Corp L stock has been purchased by old shareholders. . . .

c. Recapitalizations. Regulations also will be issued that will segregate different groups of public shareholders following a recapitalization.

Example: Corp L is widely held with no person owning 5 percent of its stock. After the issuance of regulations relating to recapitalizations, 60 percent of the Corp L stock is redeemed for preferred stock that is not treated as "stock" for purposes of the definition of ownership change. An ownership change occurs because the remaining common shareholders are treated as a separate section 382 public shareholder that has increased its percentage ownership interest in Corp L stock by 60 points (from 40 percent to 100 percent). . . .

d. Multiple Transactions. In determining whether an ownership change has occurred, owner shifts involving 5-percent shareholders and equity structure shifts that occur within the testing period are combined. The total increase in percentage ownership of 5-percent shareholders is calculated simply by comparing the current ownership of such shareholders with their ownership throughout the testing period. In the case of acquisitions following an equity structure shift that results in the creation of two section 382 public shareholders, however, section 382 provides that subsequent acquisitions of stock from the public are deemed to have been made on a proportionate basis from each section 382 public shareholder unless the actual source can be shown. . . .

5. *Attribution Rules.* Generally, section 382 follows the section 318 attribution rules, with the following exceptions:

a. Family Members. Owner of stock and spouse, children, parents, and grandparents are treated as a single individual. It is not clear, however, how this mechanism avoids double-counting of stock. Thus, for example, a single share of stock owned by a parent would, on the face of the statute, be attributed separately to each of that person's children. Presumably, this result was not intended.

b. Attribution to Entities. No attribution to entities (i.e., partnerships, corporations, estates, and trusts), except to extent provided in regulations. Thus, if Corp P owns stock of Corp L and Corp P forms a subsidiary (Corp S), Corp S is not treated as a new owner of Corp L stock.

c. Options. The term option includes warrants, convertible debt, contingent purchase arrangements, puts, stock subject to a risk of forfeiture, and contracts to acquire stock. Except as provided in regulations, any such option is treated as exercised if that treatment would result in an ownership change. Inconsistent assumptions may apply to different options if that would result in an ownership change. If an option is considered to be exercised, then the actual exercise is disregarded. . . .

d. Attribution from Entities. An entity (corporation, partnership, trust, or estate) is "looked through" so that all stock owned by it is treated as owned by the holders of interests in the entity in proportion to their interests, without regard to the minimum 50 percent stock ownership generally required for corporation-to-shareholder attribution under section 318.

Example: Corp P owns all of the stock of Corp L, and distributes the Corp L stock pro rata to its shareholders. No ownership change occurs because, for purposes of section 382, shareholders of Corp P are deemed to have held the Corp L stock even before the distribution.

e. Coordination of Attribution Rule With 5-Percent Shareholder Rule. In general, less than 5-percent shareholders of a corporation that is a stockholder in a loss corporation are aggregated and treated as a separate shareholder from other less than 5-percent shareholders of the loss corporation.

Example: Corp P and Corp L are widely held. Each has no shareholder owning 5 percent or more. Corp P purchases all of the stock of Corp L. An ownership change occurs with respect to Corp L because all of its stock is now owned, under the attribution rule, by the public shareholders of Corp P whereas, before the purchase, all of that stock had been owned by the public shareholders of Corp L.

B. TESTING PERIOD

The testing period generally is a rolling three calendar year period preceding any owner shift involving a 5-percent shareholder or any equity structure shift.

There are two exceptions to this general rule:

1. Following any ownership change, the testing period for determining whether a second ownership change has occurred does

not start before the day following the day on which the preceding ownership change occurred.

2. Generally, the testing period does not start before the first day of the first taxable year in which the NOL carryovers arose. Except as provided in regulations, this rule will not apply to corporations with unrealized built-in losses (that are subject to the section 382 limitation as discussed in Part IV.D.2.c. below). Regulations, however, will provide that the testing period will not start before the year in which any such built-in loss arose.

C. OTHER RULES RELATING TO TRIGGERING OF SECTION 382

1. *Nonconsideration Transfers.* Stock acquired by gift, upon death, incident to a divorce, or from a spouse, is treated as if the acquiror had owned the stock during the period that it was owned by the transferor, so that such transfer would not contribute to an ownership change. Otherwise, there is no general exception for carryover basis transactions and any relief in the case of transfers between related parties must come from the ownership attribution rules.

2. *ESOPs.* Special rules apply so that certain acquisitions by an ESOP of 50 percent or more of the stock of a corporation, or acquisitions by participants from an ESOP, are not counted in determining whether an ownership change has occurred.

3. *Value Fluctuations.* Changes in relative stock ownership attributable solely to fluctuations in the fair market value of different classes of stock are not counted in determining whether an ownership change has occurred. . . .

IV.   EFFECT OF OWNERSHIP CHANGE

A. IN GENERAL

If the application of section 382 is triggered by an ownership change, then "pre-change losses" may reduce taxable income in a "post-change year" only up to the "section 382 limitation" for that year.

B. PRE-CHANGE LOSSES

A pre-change loss includes (i) NOL carryovers to the taxable year in which the ownership change occurs and (ii) NOLs generated in that year, to the extent allocable to the period preceding the date of the ownership change ("change date"). The allocation generally will be made ratably, i.e., by reference to the number of days in the taxable year preceding and following the change date. Unrealized but economically accrued losses of the corporation also may be treated as pre-change losses. See paragraph D.2.c. below.

C. POST-CHANGE YEAR

A post-change year is any taxable year ending after the change date. This would include the taxable year in which the ownership change occurs. Under a special rule, however, the section 382 limitation for that year applies only to taxable income generated after the change date, calculated, generally, on a ratable basis. . . .

D. SECTION 382 LIMITATION

1. *General Rule.* The "section 382 limitation" for any taxable year equals the product of (x) the value of the loss corporation and (y) the "long-term tax-exempt" bond rate.

a. "Value" of the Loss Corporation. Value is determined based on the value of the corporation's stock immediately prior to the ownership change. Thus, in the case of an ownership change triggered by, for example, a merger of Corp L into Corp P, the value of the loss corporation would refer only to the value of Corp L. Similarly, in a consolidation of three corporations, two of which undergo ownership changes in the consolidation, separate section 382 limitations would apply to each of those two corporations based on their respective pre-consolidation values. . . .

For purposes of determining "stock" value, *all* stock is counted, *including* preferred stock that would not be treated as stock for purposes of determining whether an ownership change has occurred. Regulations may provide rules treating other equity-flavored interests (such as options, warrants, convertible debt) as stock for these purposes.

Generally, the latest price paid for stock of the loss corporation would be the best evidence of value. However, where the ownership change is effected through a purchase of stock at a price that reflects a "control premium," the value of the loss corporation cannot be determined simply by "grossing-up" the cost of that stock. Instead, regulations may allow the value to be determined by "grossing up" the cost of all the acquired loss corporation stock if a control block is acquired within a 12-month period.

b. Long-Term Tax-Exempt Bond Rate. Generally equal to the highest long-term applicable Federal rate ("AFR"), as determined under section 1274(d), for the month in which the ownership change occurs or the preceding two months, adjusted for the difference between taxable and tax-exempt rates. In making this adjustment, the AFR will not be simply tax-effected to reflect the 34-percent corporate tax rate but will, instead, be adjusted to reflect the actual spread between the AFR and market rates on a diversified pool of long-term, prime quality, general obligation tax-exempt bonds. The rate will be based on the date of the ownership change and not on an earlier contract date. However, stock that is subject to a purchase contract may be considered to have been purchased under the attribution rules so that an ownership change may occur on the contract date.

2. *Special Rules Relating to Section 382 Limitation.* The section 382 limitation is burdened with special rules.

a. Short Taxable Years. Regulations will provide for a prorated section 382 limitation based on the number of days in the taxable year compared with 365.

b. Carryovers. The section 382 limitation for any taxable year will be increased by any excess section 382 limitation from previous years, i.e., the amount, if any, by which the section 382 limitation in a previous taxable year exceeded the amount of taxable income in that year that was offset by pre-change losses.

c. Built-in Gains and Losses. Built-in gains and losses present a number of problems that are specially treated:

(i) In general. The section 382 limitation for any taxable year that falls in whole or in part within the "recognition period" is increased by the amount of "recognized built-in gains" for that year, while any recognized built-in losses for any such taxable year are subject to the section 382 limitation in the same manner as pre-change NOL carryovers. The "recognition period" is the five calendar year period beginning on the change date.

(ii) Built-in gain rules.*

Net unrealized built-in gain. A corporation can have recognized built-in gains only if it has a "net unrealized built-in gain." A corporation's net unrealized built-in gain is the excess, if any, of the fair market value of all of its assets over their basis at the time of an ownership change. This calculation reflects a netting of unrealized gains and losses.

De minimis rule. If net unrealized built-in gain does not exceed 25 percent of the fair market value of the corporation's assets at the time of the ownership change, the net unrealized built-in gain of the corporation is considered to be zero. For purposes of applying the de minimis rule, cash, cash items, and any marketable security if the value of such security does not differ substantially from its adjusted basis, are disregarded.

Recognized built-in gain. Gain recognized upon disposition of an asset is recognized built-in gain to the extent the taxpayer can demonstrate that such gain existed economically on the change date.

---

*The 1989 Act amended the built-in gain and loss rules in §382(h)(3)(B)(i). — Ed.

However, the aggregate amount of recognized built-in gains for any taxable year cannot exceed the net unrealized built-in gain, as defined above, less the amount of recognized built-in gains for prior taxable years. (Because net unrealized built-in gain takes into account assets with respect to which there is a built-in loss, this cap is necessary in order to avoid recognition of individual built-in gains that exceed, in the aggregate, the net unrealized built-in gain.)

Note: A special rule increases the section 382 limitation by the amount of gain recognized as a result of a section 338 election (to the extent not already taken into account in computing recognized built-in gains for the taxable year). Accordingly, while the repeal of General Utilities under TRA 1986 generally will make the exercise of a section 338 election uneconomic, it may be advantageous to make the election for an acquired corporation with NOL carryovers in order to obtain a stepped-up basis while sheltering any gain to the extent of pre-acquisition losses (without limitation under section 382).

(iii) Built-in loss rules.

Definitions. A corporation can have recognized built-in losses only if it has a net unrealized built-in loss. The definition of "net unrealized built-in loss" is parallel to the definition of "net unrealized built-in gain," including a similar 25-percent de minimis rule. The definition of "recognized built-in loss" for a taxable year is parallel to the definition of "recognized built-in gain," except that the burden is on the taxpayer to show that a recognized loss is not a recognized built-in loss. Under regulations to be issued, amounts that accrue before the change date but are not deductible until a later date, such as amounts deferred under the rules of section 267 or section 465, will be treated as built-in losses. In a legislative compromise, depreciation deductions cannot be treated as built-in losses under the regulations, but the Treasury is directed to issue a report with respect to this issue not later than January 1, 1989.

Operating rules. Recognized built-in losses are subject to the same limitations are pre-change NOL carryovers. Amounts disallowed because of the operation of the section 382 limitation may be carried over to succeeding taxable years under rules similar to the rules for the carrying forward of NOLs (presumably for a maximum of 15 years following the year in which the loss was recognized). Section 382 does not contain ordering rules that would determine whether recognized built-in losses are utilized prior to pre-change losses. Apparently, it is intended that built-in losses would be utilized first under general tax principles that provide for first utilizing a current year loss before the offsetting of taxable income by NOL carryforwards from prior taxable years. . . .

d. Anti-Stuffing Rules

(i) General. In determining the value of a loss corporation for purposes of calculating the section 382 limitation, capital contributions that are made principally for the purpose of increasing the value of the corporation (and, thereby, the section 382 limitation) are not taken into account. For these purposes, except as provided in regulations, any capital contribution within the two-year period preceding the ownership change will be irrebutably presumed to have been made for the purpose of increasing the value.

(ii) Exceptions. The Conference Report indicates that it is anticipated that the regulations, when issued, will exclude from the two-year presumption:

(1) Capital contributions made in connection with the formation of a corporation, unless the incorporation involved assets with built-in losses;

(2) Capital contributions received before the first year in which any NOLs or built-in losses arose; and

(3) Capital contributions made in order to meet working capital requirements.

In addition, the regulations also may consider the extent to which capital contributions should not reduce the corporation's value because of subsequent distributions or because the capital contribution is allocable to investments in nonbusiness assets that would, in any event, reduce the section 382 limitation.

(iii) Note on liquidations of loss subsidiaries. In the case of an affiliated group of corporations that includes some loss corporations, the section 382 limitation ordinarily would apply to each loss corporation separately because an ownership change with respect to the common parent would typically result in an ownership change with respect to each group member under the ownership attribution rules. While the anti-stuffing rules would significantly inhibit pre-change capital contributions to loss corporations, they would not affect the pre-change liquidation of loss corporations into profitable parent corporations. Assuming that the liquidated corporations were solvent, NOL carryovers and other tax attributes would be continued in the parent. It would seem that the parent's assets could then be taken into account in determining the value of the loss corporation for purposes of subjecting those attributes to limitation under section 382.

e. Nonbusiness Assets

(i) General. The value of the loss corporation for purposes of calculating the section 382 limitation is also reduced by the excess of the value of any nonbusiness assets of the corporation at the time of the ownership change over indebtedness of the corporation attributable to such assets.

(1) De minimis rule. The nonbusiness assets rule does not apply unless one-third of the corporation's gross assets consist of nonbusiness assets.

(2) Nonbusiness assets. Defined as assets held for investment. Generally would include cash and marketable stock or securities except to the extent necessary as an integral part of the corporation's business (such as insurance company reserves or inventory of a securities dealer). . . .

E. SUCCESSIVE OWNERSHIP CHANGES

Section 382 contains no special rule governing the section 382 limitation in the case of a second ownership change. Instead, this issue is to be dealt with under regulations. One possible regulatory scheme would be to provide that if a second ownership change occurs at a time when the value of the loss corporation and/or the long-term tax-exempt bond rate are lower than at the time of the earlier ownership change, the section 382 limitation that applies to NOL carryovers from periods before the first ownership change in succeeding taxable years would be correspondingly decreased, but that the limitation applied to such carryovers would not be increased as a result of increases in value and/or the long-term tax-exempt bond rate. . . .

F. APPLICATION TO OTHER LOSSES AND CREDITS

By application of section 383, old section 382 applied to carryovers of other losses and credits, including capital loss carryovers and foreign tax credits, investment tax credits, and research credits. The Conference Report indicates that section 382 under TRA 1986 is similarly intended to apply to those carryovers and to carryovers of passive activity losses and credits and minimum tax credits. As drafted, however, the statute appears to make no reference to carryovers of passive activity losses and credits.

V.   OTHER LIMITATIONS ON NOL CARRYOVERS

A. CONTINUITY OF BUSINESS ENTERPRISE

While the application of section 382 generally results only in limitations on the utilization of NOL carryforwards, if the loss corporation fails to maintain continuity of its business enterprise for a two-calendar-year period after the ownership change, its section 382 limitation for any taxable year ending after the change date will be reduced to zero (except for amounts attributable to recognized built-in gains or gain attributable to a section 338 election). Thus, a corporation that fails the continuity of business enterprise test in the second year following an ownership change would be required to amend its return for the previous year to the extent that any pre-change NOL carryovers had been utilized to offset taxable income.

The continuity of business test is the same test that applies in tax-free reorganizations (and less stringent than the change of business test under old section 382(a)). . . .

B. SECTION 269; *LIBSON SHOPS*

Section 269, relating to acquisitions for the principal purpose of making use of favorable tax attributes, continues to be applicable. The practical significance of section 269 is likely to be significantly diminished, however, because it will be a rare case when the opportunity to use tax attributes, as limited by section 382, is the principal purpose for an acquisition. The Conference Report also indicates that the *Libson Shops* doctrine will not be applicable to transactions that are subject to section 382. . . .

D. ANTI-AVOIDANCE REGULATIONS

Broad regulatory authority is granted to issue regulations to prevent the avoidance of the purposes of section 382 through the use of related persons, pass-through entities, or other intermediaries. . . .

NOTES

1. Is the approach taken by the new §382 preferable to that of the old?

2. The Peaslee and Cohen article was written before the regulations under §382 were promulgated. For a full discussion of these regulations, see Silverman and Keyes, An Analysis of the New Ownership Regs. Under Section 382 (pt. 1), 68 J. Taxn. 68 (1988); (pt. 2), 68 J. Taxn. 142 (1988); (pt. 3), 68 J. Taxn. 300 (1988); (pt. 4), 69 J. Taxn. 42 (1988).

3. See B. Bittker and J. Eustice, Federal Income Taxation of Corporations and Shareholders, 16-66 to 16-95 (5th ed. 1987); Rizzi, Section 382 and the Trigger Rules: Is Congress Beating a Dead Horse?, 14 J. Corp. Taxn. 99 (1987); Wooton, Section 382 After the Tax Reform Act of 1986, 64 Taxes 874 (1986).

3.   Acquisitions Made to Avoid Tax—§269

COMMISSIONER v. BRITISH MOTOR CAR
DISTRIBUTORS, LTD.
278 F.2d 392 (9th Cir. 1960)

Before Pope, Hamlin and Merrill, Circuit Judges.

MERRILL, Circuit Judge. The taxpayer corporation incurred losses while engaged in the business of selling home appliances. It disposed of all its assets and the corporate shares were then sold to new owners, who used the corporation to operate a previously going automobile business. The question here presented is whether the taxpayer is entitled to carry over the losses incurred in the old business, where it is clear that the principal purpose of the acquisition of the taxpayer by the new owners was to avoid taxes. The Tax Court, five judges dissenting, ruled in the affirmative, 31 T.C. 437 (November 26, 1958), and the Commissioner has appealed. We here hold that carryover of the loss is forbidden under §[269(a)]. . . . The judgment of the Tax Court accordingly must be reversed.

Empire Home Equipment Company, Inc., was incorporated under the laws of California on November 13, 1948. Empire engaged in the business of selling home appliances at wholesale and retail. During its fiscal years ending in 1949, 1950 and 1951, Empire incurred net operating losses in the sum of $374,406.57. In December, 1949, Empire's lease of its premises at 40 Drumm Street in San Francisco was cancelled. Unamortized leasehold improvements were written off by January, 1950. In February, 1950, its merchandise inventory was liquidated in bulk at a considerable loss. All of its furniture and fixtures were sold by February 20, 1950. On April 1, 1950, its accounts receivable were sold. On its tax return for the fiscal year ending October 31, 1951, Empire reported its assets as "Nil."

British Motor Car Company was a partnership consisting of Kjell H. Qvale, who had an 85 per cent interest, and his wife, who had a 15 per cent interest. The partnership had existed from about May 1, 1948, and engaged, in San Francisco, in the business of importing, distributing and selling foreign automobiles and parts. On September 11, 1951, the partnership submitted an offer to counsel for the Empire Home Equipment Company, in which the former offered to buy the outstanding stock of the corporation from its then owners for $21,250.00, upon the conditions, inter alia, that the corporation would increase its authorized capital and change its name. The offer was accepted. On November 2, 1951, Empire changed its name to British Motor Car Distributors, Ltd. On November 30, 1951, the partnership acquired all the outstanding shares of stock and immediately thereafter transferred its net assets (exclusive of the acquired

shares) to the corporation in exchange for an additional 15,923 shares
of stock. It is not claimed that there was any business purpose in the
acquisition.

In the tax years ending October 31, 1952, and October 31, 1953,
the corporation operated profitably in the automobile business. In
its income and excess profits tax returns for those years, it carried
forward the net operating losses that it had sustained in the appliance
business in its fiscal years ending in 1949, 1950 and 1951.

The Commissioner disallowed the claimed deductions and gave
notice of deficiency. The corporation then petitioned the Tax Court
for a redetermination.

The Tax Court, in its construction of §[269(a)], adhered to its
view as expressed in T.V.D. Company, 27 T.C. 879, 886,[2] following
the dictum in Alprosa Watch Company, 11 T.C. 240, to the effect
that "it is manifest from the unambiguous terms of §129* that it
applies only to an acquiring corporation." The court points out that
here the corporation is seeking to make use of its own previous loss;
that it is the corporation, and not its new stockholders, which is
securing the benefit of the deduction. *Alprosa Watch* is quoted to the
effect that §129(a) "would seem to prohibit the use of a deduction,
credit or allowance only by the acquiring person or corporation and
not their use by the corporation whose control was acquired."

We do not read the language of the section, "securing the benefit
of a deduction," as applying only to the actual taking of such deduction by the taxpayer. We should be closing our eyes to the realities
of the situation were we to refuse to recognize that the persons who
have acquired the corporation did so to secure *for themselves* a very
real tax benefit to be realized by them *through* the acquired corporation and which they could not otherwise have realized.

This is not, as the corporation protests, a disregard of its corporate entity. Since §[269(a)] is expressly concerned with the persons
acquiring control of a corporation, we must recognize such persons
as, *themselves*, having a significant existence or entity apart from the
corporation they have acquired. To ignore such independent entity
simply because such persons are also the stockholders of their acquisition is to ignore the clear demands of §[269(a)]. It is not the fact
that they are stockholders which subjects them to scrutiny. Rather,
it is the fact that they are the persons specified by the section: those
who have acquired control of the corporation. They may not escape

2. This case involved an attempt to *tax income* to an acquired corporation which
had been merged into the acquirer. No question of disallowance of losses was before
the Court. In W.A.G.E., Inc., 1952, 19 T.C. 249, and in A.B. & Container Corporation, 1950, 14 T.C. 842, also referred to by the Tax Court, business purpose was
expressly found.

*Section 129 is the 1939 Code predecessor to §269. — ED.

the scrutiny which the section demands by attempting to merge their identity with that of their acquisition.

Section [269(a)] contemplates that it shall not be limited to corporate acquirers. While Clause (2) is specifically limited to corporate acquirers, Clause (1) deals with "persons" as acquirers. That Clause (1) is to include noncorporate acquirers could not be more clearly implied. Nor do we find any sound reason, if this device for tax avoidance is to be struck down, for doing the job only when the tax avoider is a corporation. Legislative history indicates that a much broader construction was intended.[3]

To limit the effect of §[269(a)] to cases in which the taxpayer is seeking to deduct as its own a loss incurred by another would seem to limit Clause (1) to corporate acquirers. Who but a corporation could claim as its *own* a loss which had been incurred by an acquired corporation? Certainly an individual could not do so. The construction here contended for by the taxpayer corporation would then clearly frustrate legislative purpose.

Such construction is not the necessary result of the language used. To construe "benefit" as limited to the taking of the deduction, or "deduction" as limited to one claimed by the acquirer is to read something into the section which is not expressly there and which serves to prevent its application in an area clearly intended to have been included.

---

3. H.R. No. 871, 78th Congress, First Session (1944 Cum. Bull. 901, 938):

"This section is designed to put an end promptly to any market for, or dealings in, interests in corporations or property which have as their objective the reduction through artifice of the income or excess profits tax liability.

"The crux of the devices which have come to the attention of your committee has been some form of acquisition on or after the effective date of the Second Revenue Act of 1940, but the devices take many forms. Thus, the acquisition may be an acquisition of the shares of a corporation, or it may be an acquisition which follows by operation of law in the case of a corporation resulting from a statutory merger or consolidation. The person, or persons, making the acquisition likewise vary, as do the forms or methods of utilization under which tax avoidance is sought. Likewise, the tax benefits sought may be one or more of several deductions or credits, including the utilization of excess profits credits, carry-overs and carry-backs of losses or unused excess profits credits, and anticipated expense of other deductions. In the light of these considerations, the section has not confined itself to a description of any particular methods for carrying out such tax avoidance schemes but has included within its scope these devices in whatever form they may appear. For similar reasons, the scope of the terms used in the section is to be found in the objective of the section, namely, to prevent the tax liability from being reduced through the distortion or perversion effected through tax avoidance devices."

The taxpayer corporation contends that the Conference Report, H. Rep. 1079, 78th Congress, Second Session (1944 Cum. Bull. 1069) shows a narrowing of the intendment of the section. However, reference to Sen. Rep. 627, 78th Congress, First Session (1944 Cum. Bull. 973, 1016-1018) clearly shows that restriction on the sweep of the house bill was confined to the elimination of overlaps with existing sections and the formulation of a standard for "control" and that the spirit of the measure was left unaffected.

The corporation contends, as stated by the Tax Court, that the benefit to the stockholders (as distinguished from that to the corporate taxpayer) is too tenuous to bring the section into play. Tenuous or not, it is the benefit which actuated these persons in acquiring this corporation and is thus the very benefit with which this section is concerned. It is not for the courts to judge whether the benefit to the acquiring persons is sufficiently direct or substantial to be worth acquiring. That judgment was made by the acquirers. The judicial problem is whether the securing of the benefit was the principal purpose of the acquisition. If it was, the allowance of the deduction is forbidden. . . .

Judgment reversed. The deductions claimed by the taxpayer are disallowed and judgment is entered for the Commissioner.

ZANESVILLE INVESTMENT CO. v. COMMISSIONER
335 F.2d 507 (6th Cir. 1964)

Before Phillips, Circuit Judge, McAllister, Senior Circuit Judge, and Levin, District Judge.

Levin, District Judge. The question presented for decision is whether Section 269 of the Internal Revenue Code of 1954 or some judicially enunciated principle of law prevents the offsetting in a consolidated return of cash operating losses and losses realized on the sale of physical assets sustained after affiliation by one corporate member of an affiliated group with the post-affiliation profits of another corporate member thereof, where it could be anticipated that such operating losses would be incurred.

The cases principally relied on by the Government are not apposite, as they all concern situations where a taxpayer was attempting to utilize built-in tax losses (i.e., losses which had economically accrued prior to the affiliation but which had not as yet been realized in a tax sense), whereas the taxpayer in this case is attempting to offset actual cash losses incurred both economically and taxwise after the affiliation.

Since the Government cites no authority in point and independent research discloses none, it will be necessary to review the history of Section 269 and the consolidated returns provisions to determine whether the interpretation sought by the Commissioner is correct. The facts of this case are as follows:

During the period 1951 through August 31, 1955, a coal mine corporation (Muskingum Coal Company), which in prior years had been highly profitable (almost four million dollars of net income in the period 1945 to 1950), sustained operating losses of about

$730,000 in an attempt to develop a new mine opening to replace the prior mine opening which had been exhausted. These losses had been financed in part by loans from the taxpayer and its wholly owned subsidiary, Earl J. Jones Enterprises, Inc., totaling $320,268.68, during the period from September 1953 to August 1955, of which $42,930.79 was repaid. Enterprises was profitably engaged in operating a newspaper.

In September 1955, Muskingum was in the process of attempting to solve its problems through a new type of mechanization, but encountered continuing difficulty. Muskingum did not have adequate funds either to finance the purchase of such equipment or absorb the operating losses that almost certainly would continue to be sustained before profitable operations might be expected.

At this juncture, on September 1, 1955, Earl J. Jones, the sole stockholder[3] of Muskingum since 1945, transferred all the stock thereof to the taxpayer (of which, since 1948, he was also the sole stockholder).

The Tax Court found (38 T.C. at p. 414) that the principal purpose of the transfer to the taxpayer of the stock of Muskingum (the losing coal mine business) was to utilize Muskingum's "anticipated" losses on a consolidated return to be filed with the other members of the affiliated group, including the profitable newspaper publisher (Enterprises) and that this was interdicted under the provisions of Section 269 of the Internal Revenue Code of 1954 and the principle enunciated in J.D. & A.B. Spreckels Co., 41 B.T.A. 370 (1940).

The taxpayer, Enterprises, and Muskingum filed consolidated returns for 1955 and 1956. Muskingum sustained an operating loss of $176,806 during the period September 1 to December 31, 1955, and an operating loss of $369,950 during the period January 1 to July 10, 1956. In July 1956 Muskingum sold its mine properties at a net loss of about $480,000 and later filed a petition in bankruptcy. Enterprises' taxable income in 1955 was $175,283.61 and during the first seven months of 1956 was $102,496.46. Enterprises operated profitably also in subsequent periods.

Both prior and subsequent to affiliation, Muskingum's operations were extensive, its sales were at an annual rate in excess of two million dollars, and it employed several hundred persons throughout the period in question. Muskingum attempted to sell its properties between October 1955 and June 1956, and various transactions were discussed, negotiated, and, in two cases, documented; but none was consummated. Had any been consummated, Muskingum's properties would have been disposed of at a tax gain rather than a loss.

3. Less than one percent of the stock was held by others.

It is not disputed that Muskingum and the other members of the affiliated group that were financing it were engaged in a good faith but unsuccessful attempt to overcome the engineering problems and thereby render operations at the second mine opening economically profitable. In this connection, the taxpayer and Enterprises made further advances of $161,359.28 to Muskingum in the post-affiliation period, of which $44,966.59 was repaid. The total investment in physical assets, in an attempt to bring in the second mine opening, was $1,026,610.30, of which $247,309.01 was spent in the post-affiliation period. It would thus appear that approximately $247,000 of the $480,000 net loss realized on the sale of Muskingum's properties was paid for in cash after affiliation. The Government has not contended that such loss was incurred in an economic sense prior to affiliation.

. . . Most of the cases that have arisen under Section 269 and its predecessor, Section 129, have dealt with the sale by one control group to another of a corporation with, typically, a net-operating loss carryover, and the efforts of the new control group to utilize this carryover by funneling otherwise taxable income to a point of alleged confluence with the carryover.[4]

Until this case, the Commissioner made no attempt in the approximately twenty years since enactment of Section 129 (now Section 269), so far as the reported cases indicate, to deny a taxpayer the right to offset an out-of-pocket dollar loss incurred after affiliation with post-affiliation income. We do not believe that §269 requires such a result.

An examination of the Senate Finance Committee report accompanying the Revenue Act of 1943, which enacted Section 129 of the I.R.C. of 1939, reveals that the statutory language cannot be mechanically interpreted and that all acquisitions that result in tax saving are not prohibited. The test, according to the Senate Finance Committee, is: ". . . whether the transaction or a particular factor thereof 'distorts the liability of the particular taxpayer' when the 'essential nature' of the transaction or factor is examined in the light of the 'legislative plan' which the deduction or credit is intended to effectuate." 1944 Cum. Bull., p. 1017. (Emphasis added.)

This legislative explanation found its way into [Treas. Reg. §1.269-2(b)]. . . .

In deciding whether the essential nature of the transaction before this court violates the "legislative plan," the fact that the Tax Court's decision is the first[5] in the heavily litigated tax field where a court

4. In each of the following cases cited by the Government, there was a change in the stockholding group after the occurrence of the operating losses and before the income sought to be offset against the same was earned. . . .
5. In R.P. Collins & Co., Inc. [303 F.2d 142], discussed later in this opinion, the

was asked to deny a taxpayer the right to use real post-affiliation losses, incurred and paid in cash after affiliation, against post-affiliation income suggests that the legislative plan may not be violated by allowing the deduction. . . .

But here, the loss was incurred by one entity, and the profit was realized by another. What is the legislative plan in this regard?

Congress first required[7] and now permits[8] certain affiliated corporations to file consolidated returns and to offset the losses of one against the profits of another. The consolidated return regulations forbid the use of pre-affiliation losses of one entity against pre- or post-affiliation consolidated income (Reg. 1.1502-31(b)(3)) but have never suggested that post-affiliation losses may not be utilized against post-affiliation consolidated income. In fact, these regulations specifically permit the use of post-affiliation losses against post-affiliation consolidated income (Reg. 1.1502-31(b)).

All the cases cited by the Government where consolidation was denied involved situations where the taxpayer sought to take advantage of the realization after affiliation of losses which in an economic sense had occurred prior to the affiliation. . . .

. . . *Collins* [see footnote 5] is not authority for the proposition here advanced by the Government because even the majority would not have disallowed the post-affiliation operating loss if it stood by itself, as it does in this case, and only denied the post-affiliation operating loss because it was thought to be tainted as in respect to the built-in loss the use of which, as we have seen, Section 269 was designed to prevent. The fact that the dissenting judge in *Collins* would have allowed the post-affiliation operating loss and the two majority judges denied it only because it was tainted ("They are tarred by the same brush," 303 F.2d at p. 146), as incidental to the built-in loss, tends to support the taxpayer's view that post-affiliation operating losses standing by themselves are not within the coverage of Section 269. . . .

. . . [H]ad Earl Jones dissolved all three corporations he could have utilized the Muskingum losses against the publishing company's profits; or if he had dissolved Muskingum and contributed its property to the taxpayer or to Enterprises he could have accomplished a similar result.

In Revenue Ruling 63-40, 1963-1 Cum. Bull. 46, the Internal

---

out-of-pocket dollar loss incurred after affiliation was not allowed because a majority of the court felt that it was tainted — being in respect to the built-in loss, the obtaining of which was the primary purpose of the acquisition, and hence within the proscription of Section 269. . . .

7. Internal Revenue Regulations 41, Article 77; Sec. 1331 of the Internal Revenue Act of 1921; Sec. 240 of the Internal Revenue Act of 1918.

8. Section 240 of the Internal Revenue Act of 1921; Sec. 1501 et seq. of the 1954 I.R.C.

Revenue Service stated its view that where there is no change in the control group, Section 269 was not applicable to the addition of a new profitable business to a loss corporation, which had discontinued the money losing business, even if the means by which this was accomplished was the purchase by the loss corporation of the stock of the money-making business and the transfer of its assets in liquidation to its new stockholder. Compare Kolker Brothers, Inc., 35 T.C. 299 (1960).

Section 382 of the Internal Revenue Code of 1954 expressly permits the use of historical losses against the income of other businesses where either there has not been a change in the control group (as defined therein) or there has not been a substantial change in the trade or business conducted before the change in control.[12] One would think that if the same control group could, after the loss, add new income (Revenue Ruling 63-40, supra), there would be no objection to the offsetting of a future loss against future income. The latter case, which is the case before this court, would appear to be a stronger one for the taxpayer. . . .

. . . [O]ne is left with the definite impression that there is no legislative plan to deny the utilization of post-affiliation losses against post-affiliation income and one suspects that one of the basic reasons why taxpayers consolidated corporations and paid the two per cent penalty that prior to the enactment of the Revenue Act of 1964 was payable on consolidated taxable income, was to be able to offset the losses of one corporation against the profits of another. Inherent in the concept of consolidation is the offsetting of loss against income. . . .

We have seen that the principal purpose of Section 269 was to deny those losses, credits, deductions, etc., which could only be obtained by acquiring (generally, by buying) a corporation which, because of its own history, had obtained such benefits and which benefits the acquiring person could not otherwise obtain.

The regulations and the courts included within the scope of Section 269 the organization of a corporation as an "acquisition," on the ground that the stockholders are the underlying persons obtaining the benefit. Regulation 1.269-3(b)(2). James Realty Company v. United States, 280 F.2d 394 (8th Cir. 1960); Coastal Oil Storage Co. v. Commissioner of Internal Revenue, 242 F.2d 396 (4th Cir. 1957). . . .

In this case, it may well be, as the Tax Court found, that the

---

12. Compare Commissioner of Internal Revenue v. Goodwyn Crockery Company, 315 F.2d 110 (6th Cir. 1963), where this court held that the net operating losses could be utilized against future income even though there was a change in the control group because it was found that there was no substantial change in the trade or business conducted.

taxpayer desired to offset anticipated losses against income; but there is no evidence that such objective is violative of the legislative plan which permits just that in an effort to counter-balance profits with losses. The over-all purpose of Section 269 was to prevent distortion of a taxpayer's income resulting from the utilization of *someone else's loss* or a *built-in but unrealized loss* or, as found by the court in Coastal Oil Storage Co. v. Commissioner of Internal Revenue, supra, through the utilization of the corporate veil to acquire a benefit (the multiplying of surtax exemptions through the organization of so-called "multiple corporations") which otherwise was unobtainable; but there is no indication that Section 269 was designed to prohibit the utilization of future losses against future income merely because a corporate rather than a partnership or individual proprietorship form of business enterprise was involved. . . .

In view of this court's decision, it is unnecessary to consider taxpayer's alternative arguments that there was no acquisition because Earl J. Jones (the underlying controlling person) owned the stock of Muskingum many years before the prohibited purpose could come to mind,[14] or that a loss deduction should be allowed alternatively at least to the extent of the loss realized on the sale of the physical assets in July 1956; the Government does not contend that this is a built-in loss (Regulation 1.1502-31(b)(9)). Likewise, taxpayer's alternative theory seeking the allowance of bad debt deductions under Section 166(a)(1) need not be reached.

This case is remanded to the Tax Court for the entry of a judgment not inconsistent with this opinion.

Reversed.

NOTES

1. *Compare Zanesville Investment* and Herculite Protective Fabrics Corp. v. Commissioner, 387 F.2d 475 (3d Cir. 1968), *with* R.P. Collins & Co., Inc. v. United States, 303 F.2d 142 (1st Cir. 1962); Luke v. Commissioner, 351 F.2d 568 (7th Cir. 1965); Borge v. Commissioner, 405 F.2d 673 (2d Cir. 1968), *cert. denied sub nom.* Danica Enterprises, Inc. v. Commissioner, 395 U.S. 933 (1969); *and* Hall Paving Co. v. United States, 471 F.2d 261 (5th Cir. 1973).

2. The 1984 Act added the new §269(b) to provide that in the case of a "qualified stock purchase" (within the meaning of §338) of

14. The taxpayer relies on the dictum in Thomas E. Snyder Sons v. Commissioner of Internal Revenue, 288 F.2d 36 (7th Cir. 1961), that if the individual there concerned had (as did Earl J. Jones) acquired the stock in the loss corporation prior to the earliest date that he could have had any purpose to evade or avoid taxes, the Tax Court's decision in *Snyder* "could not stand." . . .

the stock of a target corporation as to which the acquiring corporation does *not* make a §338 election, but *does* liquidate the target pursuant to a plan adopted within two years after acquisition, the Service may deny the acquiring corporation the use of the target's net operating loss carryover (otherwise available under §381(a)(1)) if tax avoidance motivated the transaction.

3. The enactment of new §382 in 1986 greatly reduces the number of situations in which §269 will apply. Some of the cases in which §269 may still be applicable are those where the taxpayer seeks such benefits as earnings deficits, rapid amortization write-offs, and favorable tax elections to which §382 does not apply.

REVENUE RULING 67-202
1967-1 C.B. 73

Advice has been requested whether under Section 269 of the Internal Revenue Code of 1954 the carryover of net operating losses will be disallowed under the circumstances presented below.

A, an individual, in January 1961, purchased all of the stock of unrelated corporations X and Y, each of which was actively engaged in a business. In the 5-year period preceding the acquisition, both corporations operated at a profit. During 1961 and 1962 the corporations were operated separately and both corporations showed a small profit. During 1963, 1964, and 1965, both corporations incurred substantial losses. In 1964, the Federal Government initiated procedures to condemn a portion of Y's land. In February 1966, in anticipation of the large gain to be realized from the condemnation, A contributed his X stock to Y. Five days later X was liquidated into Y so that the losses of both businesses could be used to partially offset Y's gain. . . .

While Y, as a matter of form, acquired control of X, the transitory control lacked substance since it was merely the initial step of a prearranged plan to liquidate X into Y. Thus, the "essential nature of the transaction" involved in the present case was the indirect acquisition by Y of the X property. See section 1.269(b) of the Income Tax Regulations. Accordingly, since section 269(a)(1) of the Code pertains only to the acquisition of control of a corporation and not to the acquisition of its assets, the section is not applicable to the described transaction. Moreover, section 269(a)(2) of the Code is not applicable since A owned all of the stock of each corporation prior to the acquisition of X's property by Y.

The net operating losses in this type of case will carry over under section 381 of the Code provided the transaction qualifies as a reorganization under section 368(a)(1) of the Code. Thus, the taxpayer here would have to demonstrate that corporations X and Y were combined for a valid business purpose and not merely in order to secure the benefits of the net operating loss carryovers. See section 1.368-1 of the Income Tax Regulations.

NOTES

1. In Briarcliff Candy Corp. v. Commissioner, 54 T.C.M. (CCH) 667 (1987), the Tax Court held that §269(a)(1) applied to a loss corporation's acquisition of a profitable corporation even though there was no shift in the ownership of the loss corporation. How does the statute support that result?

2. See Capri, Inc., 65 T.C. 162 (1975) (§269 did not preclude use of acquired corporation's net operating loss carryover on a consolidated return, where 56 percent of the loss corporation's stock was acquired for a valid business purpose before tax avoidance purpose was formed and 80-percent control acquired); O'Mealia Research & Development, Inc., 64 T.C. 491 (1975) (§269(a)(2) was inapplicable to transaction in which parent corporation purchased income-producing assets and transferred them to a subsidiary which had net operating losses; subsidiary had a cost basis in the assets); Rocco, Inc., 72 T.C. 140 (1979) (§269 not applicable to deny choice of cash basis method of accounting).

3. In Rev. Rul. 80-46, 1980-1 C.B. 62, the taxpayer, M Corporation, owned 45 percent of X Corporation's stock. A, an individual, owned 10 percent of X's stock and 100 percent of M's stock. The balance of X's stock was owned by unrelated third parties. X's assets consisted solely of 100 percent of the stock of Corporations Y and Z. By statutory merger under §368(a)(1)(A), X was merged into M. The Service ruled that the stock of X Corporation owned by A before merger was not attributable to M for the purpose of determining "control" under §269(a), since neither §318 nor any other attribution provision is applicable to it. Therefore, the merger constituted an acquisition of control of Y and Z Corporations under §269(a)(1), and it matters not that control was acquired by acquisition of X's assets and not its stock. Cf. Brick Milling Company, 22 T.C.M. (CCH) 1603 (1963).

4. Net operating loss carryovers have been the subject of a substantial number of law review articles. In addition to those previously cited, see, e.g., Campisano and Romano, Recouping Losses: The Case for Full Loss Offsets, 76 Nw. U.L. Rev. 709 (1981); Eustice and Portney, The Destiny of Net Operating Losses, 22 San Diego L. Rev. 115 (1985).

IX. *THE FUTURE OF SUBCHAPTER C*

In 1980 The American Law Institute concluded a study of Subchapter C and recommended a fundamental revision and simplification. See ALI Federal Income Tax Project—Subchapter C—Proposals on Corporate Acquisitions and Dispositions and Reporter's Study on Corporate Distributions (1982). Following the theme of the ALI proposals, the Staff of the Senate Committee on Finance recommended significant changes in the taxation of corporate acquisitions, both taxable and tax-free: The Subchapter C Revision Act of 1985, A Final Report Prepared by the Staff, S. Prt. 99-47, 99th Cong., 1st Sess. (Comm. Print, May 1985). See, in particular, pages 5 and 38-58 with respect to acquisition transactions and pages 8, 47-49, 55-57, and 68-72 with respect to net operating losses. And see ALI Federal Income Tax Project — Subchapter C (Supplemental Study) — Reporter's Study Draft (June 1, 1989).

Consider the following excerpts in which the casebook author discusses important issues facing Congress with respect to Subchapter C.

WOLFMAN, SUBCHAPTER C AND THE 100TH CONGRESS*
Tax Notes, Nov. 17, 1986, p. 669

II. ITEMS FOR THE LEGISLATIVE AGENDA

In the Tax Reform Act of 1986 Congress instructed the Treasury to make a comprehensive study of Subchapter C and to report to Congress by the end of 1987. . . . The '86 changes lay the way for a comprehensive revision of Subchapter C with the potential for elimination of many of the unnecessary remaining complexities and for a system of corporate and shareholder taxation with systemic soundness and integrity. Fortunately, there have been a number of earlier studies on which to build in 1987. Indeed, several of the legislative changes made in 1986 and earlier as well found their underpinning and direction in the American Law Institute's recent eight year examination of Subchapter C.[8] The Senate Finance Committee Staff had proposed a rather thoroughgoing revision of Subchapter C in 1985,[9] relying heavily on the American Law Institute's recommendations. In the 1986 Act, following the House's lead, Congress

---

*Excerpted and reprinted with permission.

8. ALI Federal Income Tax Project — Subchapter C — Proposals on Corporate Acquisitions and Dispositions and Reporter's Study on Corporate Distributions (1982).

9. The Subchapter C Revision Act of 1985, A Final Report Prepared by the Staff, S. Prt. 99-47, 99th Cong., 1st Sess. (Comm. Print, May 1985).

enacted two major Code revisions which are traceable to those recommendations—the repeal of the *General Utilities* doctrine and the substitution of a new approach to the management of net operating loss carryovers following a corporate acquisition.

With repeal of *General Utilities* accomplished, with the rate distinction between capital gain and other income eliminated, and with the top corporate tax rate higher than the individual, it seems to make sense to reexamine the prior studies and undertake new studies to see what this new tax environment can use to make it as healthy and fruitful as possible. What follows are only preliminary suggestions of candidates for inclusion on the study agenda.

A. CORPORATE DISTRIBUTIONS AND COLLAPSIBLE
    CORPORATIONS

1. *The Demise of Capital Gains.* Elimination of the capital gains preference substantially reduces the stakes involved in the question whether a distribution should be treated as a dividend or a payment "in exchange" for the stock. In both cases the taxable amount of the distribution will be taxed at the same rate. If there is an exchange, however, the shareholder's stock basis will be recoverable tax free. If there are adequate earnings and profits and the distribution is a dividend or dividend equivalent, there will be no basis recovery, but if the earnings are inadequate, even a pro-rata distribution, one with all of the earmarks of a garden variety dividend, will permit tax-free basis recovery. Some of the questions worth considering in light of the limited stakes and the remaining complexity are these:

(a). *Timing.* How and when should stock basis be recovered? Why, in an exchange transaction, should basis be treated as *first out* when, in a dividend transaction, it is ignored and in an installment sale transaction basis and profit are recoverable ratably?

(b). *Dividend Equivalence and Attribution.* It may be sensible for us to gain the simplification that would come from Congress's limiting the concept of *dividend* to distributions that are substantially pro-rata, with attribution-of-ownership limited essentially to family. If the timing of basis recovery in an exchange transaction were made somewhat less generous than it is, a proposal to narrow or eliminate dividend equivalency would no doubt gain adherents.

(c). *Earnings and Profits.* Powerful arguments have been levied against the earnings and profits concept, at least with respect to the domestic tax issues to which it relates.[10] The real cost of preserving the concept is high, high in dollars for both the private sector and the Commissioner, and high in complexity. With only

---

10. Andrews, "Out of Its Earnings and Profits": Some Reflections on the Taxation of Dividends, 69 Harv. L. Rev. 1403 (1956); Blum, The Earnings and Profits Limitation on Dividend Income: A Reappraisal, 53 Taxes 68 (1975).

the limited issue of basis recovery in a dividend-like situation hinged to it, the proposal to eliminate the earnings and profits test should make it to the Subchapter C study agenda. When it does, of course, it will be intertwined with questions involving the new *book income* preference under the alternative minimum tax and the prospect that, in three years, earnings and profits may become the standard. Analysts should keep in mind that even if something like earnings and profits is to be an alternative minimum tax reference point, there may be a net gain for simplification and equity in removing it as the touchstone of *dividend*.

(d). *Boot in Reorganization.* Sections 356(a)(1) and (a)(2) are essentially redundant. With either applicable, the shareholder receiving boot in a reorganization is taxable at the same rate on his *gain*, whether or not the distribution has the effect of a dividend. But in the case of a dividend equivalent boot distribution it has long been thought by many practitioners, the organized tax bar, and government and academic analysts that taxing *only* the gain is irrational, completely inconsistent with the taxation of dividends and dividend equivalents outside the reorganization area, e.g., under §302, §304, and §306. The study agenda should include the question of eliminating the "boot within gain" limitation of §356(a)(2), particularly but not only if the timing of basis recoveries in corporate distributions is examined. If the limitation is removed, and if the concept of dividend equivalence is narrowed, for §356 purposes and §302 as well, the Treasury should be asked (or told) to reconsider the dis-integration approach of Reg. §1.301-1(*l*).

2. *Collapsibles.* The collapsible corporation provisions came into the law in 1950 because corporations were being liquidated or sold without realization of any substantial corporate income. The confluence of the *General Utilities* and *Kimbell-Diamond* doctrines permitted a step-up in basis notwithstanding the avoidance of corporate tax. Section 341 was created to deal with "abuses" of those doctrines. When it codified those doctrines in 1954, Congress also strengthened §341 and made it more complicated. Later, in 1958, thinking it now too tough, Congress enacted relief[11] in statutory language fathomable by only a select if admirable few. In 1964 Congress granted additional relief[12], this time intelligible and with obvious recognition of the continuing problem rooted in *General Utilities* and the Code provisions which codified it. In 1986 Congress provided for the complete repeal of the *General Utilities* doctrine and its statutory superstructure.

With the elimination of the capital gains preference, the only significance of §341(a) is that a gain which it taxes at 28% is "ordinary income." In the absence of §341(a) the gain, though taxed at 28%, would be capital gain and available, as ordinary income is not, for full offset against capital losses. Even if the offset limitation is desir-

---

11. Section 341(e).
12. Section 341(f).

able in general, it is hard to justify our preservation of the §341 maze just for that purpose. Moreover, even if the offset limitation is to be retained generally, nothing leaps to mind to suggest why gain realized on the disposition of collapsible corporation stock should not be available for the offset. And astute tax lawyers have already come to understand that a §341(f) election in the new world does no more or less at the corporate level than the repeal of *General Utilities* has accomplished, and yet making the election will have the same positive effect for capital loss offset purposes as the repeal of §341 would have. All of this leads me to believe that repeal should be high on the study agenda.

B. CORPORATE ACQUISITIONS AFTER THE REPEAL OF GENERAL UTILITIES

Once we are past the transition periods, acquisition transactions in the new world will be simpler than they have been, not simple but simpler, and many tax outcomes will be less arbitrary than in the past. But the law remains more complex than may be necessary or wise. The ALI study and the Senate Finance Committee Staff Report both concluded that, with the repeal of *General Utilities*, other changes could and should follow.

1. The Corporate Tax — When and How Often?

The repeal of *General Utilities* assures the imposition of a corporate tax on asset appreciation as the price of a step-up in asset basis. With that assurance, and as long as the realization doctrine generally prohibits taxation of unrealized appreciation, should the parties to an acquisition transaction be able to continue the deferral which that doctrine ordinarily affords unless and until there is a step-up in basis? As indicated earlier, in the name of *General Utilities* repeal the '86 Act imposes corporate taxation in cases where no concurrent step-up in asset basis will occur, and it poses the real possibility of multiple rounds of corporate tax on essentially the same gain. . . . It would seem highly desirable for the study groups to consider whether subsidiary stock should be saleable without tax on the stock appreciation as long as the sale proceeds are distributed to shareholders, none of whom is a controlling corporation. A corporate tax will be payable when and if the assets are transferred in a taxable transaction or a §338 election is made. The shareholders receiving the proceeds will be taxed, and a further question for study groups will be whether and to what extent they should recover basis tax-free.

2. Freeing Shareholder Tax Consequences from the Corporate

The Senate Finance Committee Staff Report, like the ALI, recommends that tax consequences for the shareholder be liberated from their current law dependence on whether the corporate parties to an acquisition have decided on a "cost basis" (taxable, basis step-up) transaction or a "carryover basis" (tax-free reorganization) transaction. The recommendations would allow the corporate parties to determine freely whether or not basis is to step up (with imposition of the corporate tax when it does), and without regard to whether the consideration is stock or boot. If boot, whether or not basis steps up, the corporate transferor would be taxed unless the boot is distributed. The recommendations would eliminate the hoary term "reorganization," and with its passing the irrational, hypertechnical distinctions such as those which differentiate an "A" from a "B" from a "C," and an "(a)(1)(D)" from an "(a)(1)(E)," would disappear.

The shareholders would be taxed on their receipt of boot, and they would not be taxed on their receipt of stock. These results would be independent of the *corporate decision* as to carryover or cost basis. Moreover, the recommendations also call for the repeal of the *continuity of proprietary interest* doctrine, with its many perverse effects.[13] Each shareholder's tax consequences would be determined by what he or she received, and not by reference to the quantum of stock interest secured by others.

The earlier studies have provided most of the analysis necessary to reach informed judgments on these important questions. The study groups of 1987 should help Congress come to closure.

3. Incorporation

Although less pressing than the need for revision of the reorganization area, any comprehensive review of Subchapter C should include the principles governing incorporation of assets. Does the "control" requirement of §351 make sense? What does it accomplish, what does it permit which it should not, and what does it burden which it should not?

Instead of a "control" requirement, or in addition to a more relaxed "control" requirement than we have now, should the Code restrict tax-free incorporation of assets to situations in which the contributor's interest is not substantially diluted? And would it not make sense to treat "securities" as boot, just as §354 does?*

Should cash constitute "property" under §351, even when contributed by persons who had no prior affiliation with those who contribute appreciated property? If so, why should the contribution of services by a party who does not contribute appreciated assets adversely affect one who does?

Should unrealized receivables and inventory contributed by a cash basis taxpayer constitute "property," as the *government* suc-

---

13. See Wolfman, "Continuity of Interest" and the American Law Institute Study, 57 Taxes 840 (1979).

*In 1989 Congress amended §351 to treat securities as boot even more comprehensively than §354 does.

cessfully contended in Hempt Brothers, Inc. v. United States?[14] The outcome, a boon to most taxpayers when the top individual rate exceeded the corporate, has a different complexion after '86. All of these §351 questions present intertwined issues which are ripe for the Subchapter C agenda of 1987.

C. THE REALIZATION DOCTRINE

Much of our prior thinking has been premised on the realization doctrine which prohibits the taxation of "unrealized" appreciation. We have taken it as both given and fundamental. Now may be the time to reconsider that notion, at least in part.[15] We have learned how to "mark to the market" in the case of straddles. Perhaps we can use that learning to deal with appreciation generally, taxing it periodically without regard to "realization." But should we?[16]

If Congress limits the deductibility of capital losses because we do not tax capital gains until the shareholder chooses to realize them, we might end that deferral privilege (one that turns into exemption at death) by periodic tax accrual of unrealized gain. If that goes too far, however, we might consider accruing unrealized capital gains to the extent of the excess of realized capital losses over realized capital gains. This would permit Congress to allow a full deduction for realized capital losses in excess of realized and unrealized capital gains, and to provide a basis step-up for the unrealized capital gains that are accrued and offset by realized capital losses. With changes like these, the "capital asset" concept might well be limited to marketable securities and certain real estate.

Sections 305 and 306 deal with overlapping aspects of the same basic problem and by no means consistently. With the realization requirement a given, §305(a) makes a great deal of sense. Unless there is to be periodic accrual of gain, taxing appreciation upon the mere issuance of a stock dividend makes little sense. But the bailout potential of some stock dividends moved Congress in 1954 to enact §306 to prevent the use of preferred stock dividends as redemption vehicles for converting ordinary income to capital gain. It did not insist on terminating the deferral of taxation afforded by the realization doctrine just because a preferred stock dividend was issued. In 1969, however, Congress went the other way. It limited the de-

14. 490 F.2d 1172 (3rd Cir. 1974), *cert. denied,* 419 U.S. 826 (1974).
15. See Shakow, Taxation without Realization: A Proposal for Accrual Taxation, 134 U. Pa. L. Rev. 1111 (1986).
16. The realization doctrine carries to its extreme in treating a nonrecourse borrowing in excess of the basis of the property securing it as a nontaxable event. The problem it creates permeates all of the income tax, with special difficulties for Subchapter C. See Woodsam Associates, Inc. v. Commissioner, 198 F.2d 357 (2d Cir. 1952).

ferral, expanding and complicating §305 by taxing unrealized appreciation when certain stock dividends and rearrangements changed the proportionate interests of shareholders. If the realization doctrine is not relaxed more generally, and in light of the elimination of the preferential capital gains rate, the study groups should consider a proposal to harmonize §305(b) and §306, tainting most of the stock issuances which §305(b)(2) would now tax, but deferring the tax until there is a disposition, as §306 does.

D. CORPORATE CLASSIFICATION AND INTEGRATION

With a top corporate rate 21% higher than the top individual rate and without a capital gains preference on the sale of stock, partnerships, big and little, public and private, will grow in number and, if they are not classified as C corporations, will be free of the corporate tax. S corporations will also grow in popularity and with the same goal. Is it not time to rationalize all of this? Do we want a corporate tax? If not, let us do what is needed to create and implement a system of integration. If we want a corporate tax, when? On what kinds of enterprises and in what form? What are the criteria for choice? The rules that now tell us when an unincorporated enterprise should be treated as a corporation are learnable and workable, but there is little else to be said in their defense.

The various groups which will study the new corporate tax world should provide an economically and conceptually sound basis for determining when and which business enterprises should be subject to an unintegrated corporate tax. In examining the questions, they should consider the recommendation made by the ALI reporter for permitting C corporations to deduct dividends paid on new corporate equity. If that recommendation were accepted, perhaps some of the other questions would disappear or be less intractable.

E. THE CORPORATE PENALTY TAXES AND THE DIVIDEND RECEIVED DEDUCTION

The study groups ought to give serious consideration to the desirability of repealing the accumulated earnings and personal holding company taxes. They are complicated. They produce little revenue. They apply unevenly, perhaps capriciously. Moreover, with the top corporate rate at 34% and the individual at 28%, the reason for the taxes under §§531 and 541 tends to disappear. At least in the case of the accumulated earnings tax the case for repeal is strong. In the personal holding company situation the case is almost but not quite as compelling because of the dividends received deduction. A corporation whose income is mainly dividends from portfolio investment can continue to accumulate at very low corporate tax rates. Is that low corporate tax a sufficient price to pay for deferral of the 28% tax on the shareholder? It hardly seems so, particularly with the knowledge that in many cases death will turn shareholder deferral into exemption.

The ALI has proposed the repeal of the dividends received deduction for portfolio stock, and the study groups should weigh this.[17] But even if the deduction is to remain in general, its elimination is attractive and worth considering as the sole "penalty" for personal holding companies and other "mere holding or investment compan[ies] as well."[18]

III.   Conclusion

Since 1981 we have had lots of tax reform, real and imagined. The 1986 Act, having provided us with the potential for real reform, requires time to be understood, time for its effects to occur and be studied. There is a need and a widespread desire for respite from legislative tax tinkering. But Congress has recognized that the 1986 Act began without finishing a large design for comprehensive reform and simplification of Subchapter C. For that reason it has ordered the Treasury to study and report on the rest of the project. The private sector should help the Treasury where appropriate and make its own, independent contributions as well. Prompt completion of the unfinished Subchapter C task can go a long way to assure that the reforms in place will stick and that the future will be filled with fewer calls for the complicated quick if ephemeral fix.

WOLFMAN, WHITHER "C"?*
Tax Notes, Mar. 14, 1988, p. 1269

With its place in the scheme of things never fully rationalized, our corporate income tax has always lacked coherence. In light of the substantial disagreement among economists as to the incidence of the tax, many have argued that real coherence is impossible and that "reform" worthy of the term requires complete integration with the individual income tax. Others, mainly lawyers (practitioners and professors alike), have felt that as long as there is to be a corporate income tax, it would be good to perfect its structure and systemic logic and to harmonize it with the individual tax on shareholder

---

17. See Francis, The Taxation of Intercorporate Dividends: Current Problems and Proposed Reforms, 64 Taxes 427 (1986).

18. Cf. Code §533(b).

*Reprinted with permission.

income, thereby to reduce much of the arbitrariness and transactional complexity to which we all bear witness.

The General Utilities (GU) doctrine and its codification had been a daunting barrier to significant structural revision because it countenanced a corporate step-up in the basis of appreciated assets without a corresponding tax on the appreciation. Although "tax-free" transactions produced mere deferral of the corporate tax, the so-called "taxable" transactions provided for corporate tax exemption.[1]

Over the years a number of tax policy analysts proposed the repeal of General Utilities whether or not it was accompanied by other structural changes, perhaps as a predicate for broader reforms as well, but good in its own right even without more.[2] Others had more general revision of subchapter C as their primary objective, and they saw GU repeal as the essential precondition, rationally required in the minds of a substantial number of them and required at least as a political matter in the view of the rest. Among those in the latter group were a number who actually disfavored GU repeal, but since they wanted an explicitly elective carryover basis regime, they supported GU repeal as the only way to achieve it. Most of those in the former group believed that the political hurdles standing in the way of GU repeal would be formidable if not insurmountable, and so they supported what they thought was the widely appealing proposal for elective carryover basis only if hinged to GU repeal. The decision of the 99th Congress to repeal General Utilities and to do essentially nothing with the reorganization area of the Code surprised both groups and left one of them quite unhappy.

Although charged by Congress to report on more general subchapter C reform by December 31, 1987, the Treasury has yet to do so. The most comprehensive issue to tackle, although by no means the only one, is whether and under what conditions to allow the corporate parties to an asset sale to elect to have the purchaser carry over the target's asset basis even when the purchase price is cash and to free the target from any tax on its gain. Proponents of such an election would give as one of their clearest cases a statutory merger of T into P, with T's shareholders receiving cash for their stock. They would tax T's former shareholders on their stock gain, as under current law, but T itself would be tax free. P, however, would continue T's low asset basis after the merger, and the operating income from those assets would continue to be measured in P's hands just as it had been in T's hands prior to the merger. Under current law, of course, T would have to recognize all its asset appreciation, and the asset basis in P's hands would step up to the purchase price. With a few exceptions, taxpayers would elect a carryover regime because in

---

1. There were, of course, the familiar exceptions to the exemption for recapturable and similar income items.
2. To expose a possible bias I want to note that I was in this group.

present value terms the burden of an immediate tax to T would exceed the tax benefit to P of a stepped-up asset basis.[4]

The first question is why any objective person should seriously consider an elective carryover basis regime. At first blush it seems to flout the widely held notion that tax on gain, deferred as it accrues prior to realization, is due when the taxpayer cashes out. But when the tax lawyer looks for analogies, as he usually does in his search for the paradigm, he sees that when A, the sole shareholder of T, sells his T stock to P, A pays tax on his stock gain (as he would in a cash merger), but that there is no tax on the appreciation in T's assets since there has been no realization at the corporate level. Furthermore, if P subsequently liquidates T, P will take T's assets with a carryover basis, and T will recognize none of its gain.[*]

The objective person might then conclude that these two cases, one of the statutory merger for cash and the other the sale of stock, producing diametrically opposed corporate tax results under current law must be harmonized. He sees that today the law provides an election, not an explicit one but an effective one, that depends entirely on choice of corporate forms and procedures, and he fails to see the sense in that. He concludes that either the election should be made explicit and available without the financial and procedural complexity that may be required when, to buy T's stock without dealing through T's management, P has to deal with thousands of shareholders (not just A in our hypothetical), or the corporate tax should be exacted when A sells his T stock to P. Either approach would require a major change in the taxing scheme of subchapter C. To do neither leaves a significant degree of structural incoherence, complexity, and uncertainty, with rewards (after high transaction costs) to those who know how and are able to elect effectively and with substantial uncompensated burdens to the others.

As a result of its eight-year study concluded in 1982, the American Law Institute (the ALI) proposed the repeal of General Utilities and a detailed scheme for a carryover basis regime.[5] The staff of the Senate Finance Committee, although differing in some detail, concurred.[6] Congress repealed General Utilities in terms more sweeping than the ALI proposed,[7] but it has not moved towards the adoption

---

4. An exceptional case would arise if T had current losses or net operating loss carryovers to offset its gain and no equally good alternative vehicle for gain offset.

*Of course, P's tendering directly to T's shareholders is not the only way to effect a stock sale. If T's management is friendly to P, a sale of T's stock can be effected for tax purposes by using the mechanism of a reverse subsidiary merger.

5. ALI Federal Income Tax Project — Subchapter C — Proposals on Corporate Acquisitions and Dispositions and Reporter's Study on Corporate Distributions (1982) (the ALI Study). . . .

6. The Subchapter C Revision Act of 1985, A Final Report Prepared by the Staff, S. Prt. 99-47, 99th Cong., 1st Sess. (Comm. Print, May 1985).

7. For example, the ALI would not have taxed the transfer of corporate goodwill. See the ALI Study, supra note 5 at 120-133.

of a carryover basis regime. For a long time it seemed that the practical options were only two: the proposal for carryover basis as one and the status quo, the other. Recently, however, James B. Lewis has taken up the cudgel, opposing both the status quo and the ALI. He would harmonize the two cases I have posed by imposing a corporate tax on T's asset appreciation when A sells his T stock to P. Indeed, he would impose such a corporate tax even if A were to exchange his T stock for P stock and receive no cash. And Lewis has composed a proposal, the Uniform Corporate-Level Recognition (UCLR) tax, one which deals with my simple hypotheticals as well as with the many more intricate transactions that involve dispositions of less than all of the stock of T.[8] Under Lewis' UCLR it would take a sale of 50 percent or more of the stock of T to trigger the corporate tax. UCLR would not require the monitoring of market transactions in the stock of publicly held corporations, but the merger of public or private T into P would call for a corporate tax on T's asset appreciation, just as a tender offer would if it succeeded in having P acquire 50 percent or more of T's outstanding stock.[9]

Lewis restricts the tax to the asset appreciation of the target, making it a very important planning matter for the parties to determine which corporation is to live and which to die in the merger. Under UCLR the formal identity of the survivor could become as significant a factor as it was before the adoption of section 381 in 1954.

It is not the purpose of this essay to deal with the detail of the UCLR proposal but to address its theme. In the jargon of current law one could say that it calls for a mandatory section 338 election. I leave for another day whether, if we are to have a UCLR, the corporate tax trigger should click only as to bulk stock dispositions (or dispositions within a contained period of time) aggregating 50 percent or more of the stock, whether the gain taxable should be proportionate to the quantum of stock sold, whether the basis step-up should also be only proportionate, whether bootless stock swaps should press the trigger, and whether, in a transaction that is tax free to shareholders but taxable at the corporate level, it is only the des-

8. See Lewis, A Proposal for a Corporate Level Tax on Major Stock Sales, Tax Notes, December 7, 1987, p. 1041. Lewis would continue current law as to the shareholder, indeed liberalize it, as the ALI would, by repealing the continuity-of-interest rule, free A from current tax to the extent that he received stock, and tax him on his gain to the extent of any boot he received. See also, Wolfman, "Continuity of Interest" and the American Law Institute Study, 57 Taxes 840 (1979).

9. The logic of UCLR might have called for a tax on the asset appreciation of both T and P when T merges into P, but Lewis restricts the tax to the asset appreciation of the target, making it a very important planning matter for the parties to determine which corporation is to live and which to die in the merger. Under UCLR the formal identity of the survivor could become as significant a factor as it was before the adoption of section 381 in 1954.

ignated target's appreciation that should be taxed or whether the gain in the assets of both corporations should be taxed and stepped up. And I will certainly leave for that other day the mechanisms to be used after answering the questions "whether." For now the questions I would like to raise are why we should depart from the status quo, why, if we do, we should move to an explicitly elective, carryover basis regime and with what general conditions for nonrecognition of a target's gain, or why, instead, we should require recognition of a target's asset appreciation upon the transfer of, say, 50 percent or more of the target's stock in a cash sale. This paper will not answer the questions. At most it will suggest some points of departure. My hope is that it will serve as a stimulus to thought and discussion.

THE STATUS QUO

Ordinarily the realization doctrine operates to defer the corporate tax on the appreciation in value of corporate assets. Codification of GU in the 1954 congressional embroidery of sections 311, 334(b)(2), 336, and 337 converted the deferral into exemption for many corporations in many circumstances. GU repeal in 1986 has eliminated that distortion. A goal of GU repeal was to assure that corporate asset appreciation would be subjected to corporate tax no later than the time the assets leave corporate solution or the corporate asset basis steps up to market value. I know of no position put forth during the many years of debate on the subject that suggested that it would be desirable to subject corporate asset appreciation to corporate tax more than once. The single-corporate-tax model is exemplified when A, the sole shareholder of T, sells all of his T stock to P for cash. There is no corporate tax on the corporate assets however much they have appreciated. After P owns T, the portion of the operating income of T that is derived from its old assets will continue to be measured from the low basis those T assets had when A was the owner. Operating income will not be affected by the sale of stock. A will pay his individual income tax on his share gain. P will be free to continue T as a subsidiary or to absorb T's assets into its own corporate structure. The gain on T's assets will be taxed when and if P distributes them to its shareholders or it sells the assets to another corporation whose basis will then be stepped up to cost.

But suppose T was not a stand-alone (nonsubsidiary) corporation owned by Mr. A. Suppose it was a subsidiary of X corporation, and that the stock of T had appreciated in X's hands as much as the T assets had appreciated in T's hands. A sale of the T stock would generate a corporate tax even if the purchaser had no desire to make the section 338 election required to alter the measuring rod of T's operating income by stepping up its asset basis. Indeed, under current law the only sure way to avoid the prospect of two corporate taxes on essentially the same gain is to have the sale of stock treated as an asset sale, thereby terminating the deferral on the asset gain and stepping up the asset basis. Had T's stock been owned by X's shareholders, however, they, like Mr. A, could have sold the stock without incurring a current corporate tax, with basis undisturbed and operating income measured as before.

To be sure, if Mr. A had sold the T stock, he would have been taxed. If corporation X sells its T stock, would one propose the elimination of the tax on the stock gain without a current tax on X's shareholders? Not very persuasively, I think, and so the question is whether it makes sense to keep the status quo, with its potential for more than one corporate tax on the same gain unless the parties accept a current tax on the asset appreciation, or whether it is preferable to devise a method that treats the sale of subsidiary stock as much as possible like the sale of nonsubsidiary stock.

ELECTIVE CARRYOVER BASIS

If X corporation were free to sell its T stock without a current tax, and the basis of T's assets remained as it was, the treatment would be analogous to A's sale of T's stock, provided that X's shareholders were taxed on their share gain. At a minimum, therefore, one would condition nonrecognition to X on its distribution of the sale proceeds to its shareholders who would then be taxed.[10] But if the analogy is to A's sale of T stock, perhaps distribution of only the proceeds of X's sale of T is not enough. The arguments are strong that X's sale should be taxed unless X completely liquidates. And there are arguments the other way. I do not want to probe that issue now, but to ask whether we want to get to the point where it must be resolved.[11]

Under a carryover basis regime that sought coherence and similar results without regard to the corporate form of a transaction, if T merged into P, with P paying cash to T's shareholders, the parties could elect to treat the transaction as A's sale of the T stock to P. A would be taxed on his stock gain; T would not be taxed; T's asset basis would carry over to P. Whether T should be able to sell part of its assets implicates the same kind of question raised in X corporation's sale of its subsidiary. Should a distribution of the sale

---

10. There would, of course, be the issue of whether the shareholders should be treated as dividend recipients or distributees in a partial liquidation, today implicating mainly the question of basis recovery.

11. The ALI Subchapter C Reporter, William D. Andrews, is working on a new set of tentative draft proposals which, inter alia, will restate with modifications the ALI's 1982 recommendations for elective carryover basis. For a critical analysis, supporting but proposing limitations on some of the outstanding carryover basis proposals, see Yin, A Carryover Basis Asset Acquisition Regime?: A Few Words of Caution, Tax Notes, October 26, 1987, p. 415.

proceeds do the trick, or should a complete liquidation be required, or might some in-between solution be appropriate?

Current law, particularly as embellished by the 1987 Act, views spin-offs and similar divisions with suspicion. After all, they may be devices to put subsidiary stock into the hands of a parent's shareholders without incurring a corporate tax on the appreciation of the subsidiary stock, and those shareholders — like Mr. A — might then be in a position to sell the distributed stock without a corporate tax. But the basis of the corporate assets would remain low, and operating income would continue relatively high. Why, particularly in a world without a capital gains preference, should spin-offs be made more difficult? Maybe the answer lies in the notion that freedom from corporate tax should be conditioned on complete liquidation of the parent corporation, a question raised above. Maybe the answer is that the analogue to A's sale of T's stock is not only not compelling, but wrong-headed; that a wise tax policy would treat A's sale of all of T's stock as an appropriate time not only to tax him but to tax T as well, just as though T had sold its assets and distributed the proceeds, with P taking a cost basis in the assets it has purchased. Enter James B. Lewis.

UCLR

Lewis agrees that in non-tax financial terms a sale of T's corporate assets, followed by its complete liquidation, would not be different from A's selling his stock. But he asserts that the complete disposition of a corporate enterprise, whether by stock sale or asset sale, presents the appropriate time to terminate the corporate tax deferral that the realization doctrine had required as well as to tax the shareholders on their stock gain. He recognizes the difficulty if not impossibility of tracking market transactions in publicly traded stock, and so would pass them by. He would also continue corporate tax deferral on a sale of closely held stock unless it carried control (50 percent or more). Mergers, tender offers, and presumably redemptions would trigger a corporate tax whether the corporations were private or public, but only on the target's gain, and not on the acquiror's. In all cases he would tax corporate gain only on a basis proportionate to the percentage of the outstanding stock transferred, and the corporate step-up in asset basis would also be proportionate.

Some questions: What role does the UCLR see for the corporate tax? Is it to be more than a proxy for the shareholders' deferral of tax on the corporation's accumulated earnings? Certainly before the top individual rate was pushed below the top corporate rate, that proxy notion made a lot of sense and had its adherents.

If competitive corporations are operating at roughly the same rate and under the same external conditions, is it wise to impose a corporate tax and a change in tax basis for one, and not the other, just because in the former case, but not in the latter, the UCLR trigger was pressed by the requisite sale of shareholders' stock?

Why is it right not to tax the acquiring corporation's gain if we are to tax the target's gain in a stock-for-stock corporate acquisition? And why should the shareholders not be taxed in a stock-for-stock swap if the corporation is to be taxed?

Lewis, like the ALI, wants generally to unhinge stockholder tax consequences from those that occur at the corporate level. Neither he nor the ALI would tax a small shareholder who receives only stock in a corporate acquisition transaction even if all of the other shareholders took cash, the selling corporation paid tax, and the purchasing corporation took a cost basis in the assets. Why, then, particularly in light of that attitude that favors the separation of the corporation from its shareholders for tax purposes, should a shareholder's stock swap or shareholder sale be an event that justifies termination of deferral (some would say acceleration of tax) at the corporate level? Perhaps the answer lies in a perception of fault in our realization system. But if that is so, might it not be better to tax appreciation more generally, more uniformly, and more regularly than we do now rather than to impose a tax on corporate asset acquisition on the occasion when shareholders dispose of their stock? Or moving in the other direction, still seeking a solution of general application, should we consider adopting a system that never taxes gain upon reinvestment (providing for more universal tax-free rollover), but that always taxes disinvestment and consumption?

Just some questions.

GENERAL REFERENCES

See generally B. Bittker and J. Eustice, Federal Income Taxation of Corporations and Shareholders 13-1 to 14-239, 16-1 to 16-101 (5th ed. 1987); M. Ginsberg and J. Levin, Mergers, Acquisitions, and Leveraged Buyouts (CCH Tax Trans. Lib.)

See also Coven, Taxing Corporate Acquisitions: A Proposal for Uniform Mandatory Rules, 44 Tax L. Rev. 145 (1989); Bloom, Corporate Tax Changes in the Revenue Act of 1987, 15 J. Corp. Taxn. 138 (1988); Nicholls, 1987 Tax Provisions Affecting Corporate Acquisitions and Dispositions, Tax Notes, May 2, 1988, p. 637; Pollack and Goldring, Filing for Bankruptcy Can Alter Tax Consequences of Numerous Transactions, 66 J. Taxn. 330 (1987); Posin, Treatment of the Participants in a Reorganization: Policy After the 1986 Act, 40 Sw. L.J. 1169 (1987). For the views of two economists, see Auerbach and Reishus, The Effects of Taxation on the Merger Decision, NBER Working Paper No. 2192 (1987).

5

The Corporate Identity—Special Problems

I. CORPORATION VEL NON—§7701(a)(3); TREAS. REG. §§301.7701-1 TO 301.7701-4

A corporation is a corporation is a corporation, but for federal income tax purposes the reach of the term "corporation" is not precise. Although the Code does not define "corporation," §7701(a)(3) tells us that it "includes associations, joint stock companies, and insurance companies." In their effort to explain what "partnership" includes, §§7701(a)(2) and 761(a) provide that "partnership" does not include a trust, estate, or corporation. "Trust" and "estate" are undefined. The fact that "corporation" includes "associations" evidences a congressional design to have the term "corporation" embrace organizations that may not bear the label of, or be recognized for nontax purposes as, corporations.

Ordinarily, there is no difficulty in determining whether an organization is a trust, estate, partnership, or corporation. In most cases the characterization applicable under state law, as selected by the parties, will be apt for tax purposes. That is not always the case, however, and where it is not, the stakes may be high. More often than not, where the issue is raised the question is whether a trust under state law is to be treated as a corporation under the Code, or whether a partnership is to be so treated. In addition, the question has also been raised whether corporations organized under state laws applicable only to professionals (e.g., lawyers and doctors) might be treated as taxpayers other than corporations, i.e., as partnerships or individual proprietors.

When the Commissioner seeks to treat a trust or partnership as a corporation, his purpose is usually to impose the corporate tax under §11(a), sometimes after the entity has distributed its earnings and the individual income tax on the "dividend" has accrued, or perhaps to prevent the pass-through of losses. When taxpayers urge corporate status and the Commissioner resists, the taxpayers are usually seeking special tax benefits that are available to "employees" of corporations (even when they are also the shareholders) but that are not available to "partners" (even partners who work for the partnership).

The problem of corporate identity is more important under the 1986 Code than it was before. Three elements of the 1986 Act increased the stakes involved in the question of whether the organization or enterprise should be treated as a corporation: (1) the Act set the maximum individual rate well below the maximum corporate rate; (2) it repealed the *General Utilities* doctrine together with its statutory appendages; and (3) it eliminated the preferential rate for long-term capital gains. Thus, noncorporate or partnership-like tax status now results in a single 28-percent maximum tax, whereas C corporation status results in a higher maximum corporate rate of 34 percent and, of course, a second level of tax on corporate earnings when they are distributed. As a result, taxpayers in many instances will seek to avoid C corporation status in favor of partnership or S corporation status, and the Commissioner may well give the issue of corporate identity much closer attention than he has in the recent past.

MORRISSEY v. COMMISSIONER
296 U.S. 344 (1935), *aff'g* 74 F.2d 803 (9th Cir. 1935)

Mr. Chief Justice HUGHES delivered the opinion of the Court. Petitioners, the trustees of an express trust, contest income taxes for the years 1924 to 1926, inclusive, upon the ground that the trust has been illegally treated as an "association." . . . We granted certiorari because of a conflict of decisions as to the distinction between an "association" and a "pure trust," the decisions being described in one of the cases as "seemingly in a hopeless state of confusion." Coleman-Gilbert Associates v. Commissioner, 76 F.(2d) 191, 193.

The facts were stipulated. In the year 1921 petitioners made a declaration of trust of real estate in Los Angeles. They were to be designated in "their collective capacity" as "Western Avenue Golf Club." The trustees were authorized to add to their number and to choose their successors; to purchase, encumber, sell, lease and operate the "described or other lands"; to construct and operate golf courses, club houses, etc.; to receive the rents, profits and income; to make loans and investments; to make regulations; and generally to manage the trust estate as if the trustees were its absolute owners. The trustees were declared to be without powers to bind the beneficiaries personally by "any act, neglect or default," and the beneficiaries and all persons dealing with the trustees were required to look for payment or indemnity to the trust property. The beneficial interests were to be evidenced solely by transferable certificates for shares which were divided into 2,000 preferred shares of the par value of $100 each, and 2,000 common shares of no par value, and the rights of the respective shareholders in the surplus, profits, and capital assets were defined. "Share ledgers" showing the names and addresses of shareholders were to be kept.

The trustees might convene the shareholders in meeting for the purpose of making reports or considering recommendations, but the votes of the shareholders were to be advisory only. The death of a trustee or of a beneficiary was not to end the trust, which was to continue for twenty-five years unless sooner terminated by the trustees.

During the years 1921 and 1922, the trustees sold beneficial interests and paid commissions on the sales. About 42 acres (of the 155 acres described by the declaration of trust) were plotted into lots which were sold during the years 1921 to 1923, most of the sales being on the installment basis. On the remaining property a golf course and club house were constructed, and in 1923 this property with the improvements was conveyed to Western Avenue Golf Club, Inc., a California corporation, in exchange for its stock. Under a lease from the corporation, petitioners continued the operation of the golf course until January 12, 1924. After that date petitioners' activities were confined to collections of installments of principal and interest on contracts of purchase, the receipt of interest on bank balances and of fees on assignments by holders of purchase contracts, the execution of conveyances to purchasers, the receipt of dividends from the incorporated club, and the distribution of moneys to the holders of beneficial interests. On December 31, 1923, the total number of outstanding beneficial interests was 3,016, held by 920 persons; by December 31, 1926, the number of interests had been gradually decreased to 2,172, held by 275 persons. The holdings by the trustees ranged approximately from 16 to 29 per cent.

Petitioners contend that they are trustees "of property held in trust," within [§641(a)], and are taxable accordingly and not as an "association." They urge that, to constitute an association, the applicable test requires "a quasi-corporate organization in which the beneficiaries, whether or not certificate holders, have some voice in the management and some control over the trustees and have an opportunity to exercise such control through the right to vote at meetings"; and that, in any event, the activities in which petitioners were engaged, during the tax years under consideration, did not constitute "a carrying on of business" within the rule applied by this Court.

The Government insists that the distinction between associations and the trusts taxed under [§641(a)] is between "business trusts on the one side" and other trusts "which are engaged merely in collecting the income and conserving the property against the day when it is to be distributed to the beneficiaries"; that Congress intended that all "business trusts" should be taxed as associations.

[Section 770 1(a)(3) provides:]

> The term "corporation" includes associations, joint-stock companies, and insurance companies. . . .

"Association" implies associates. It implies the entering into a joint enterprise, and, as the applicable regulation imports, an enterprise for the transaction of business. This is not the characteristic of an ordinary trust — whether created by will, deed, or declaration — by which particular property is conveyed to a trustee or is to be held by the settlor, on specified trusts, for the benefit of named or described persons. Such beneficiaries do not ordinarily, and, as mere cestuis que trustent, plan a common effort or enter into a combination for the conduct of a business enterprise. Undoubtedly the terms of an association may make the taking or acquiring of shares of interests sufficient to constitute participation, and may leave the management, or even control of the enterprise, to designated persons. But the nature and purpose of the cooperative undertaking will differentiate it from an ordinary trust. In what are called "business trusts" the object is not to hold and conserve particular property, with incidental powers, as in the traditional type of trusts, but to provide a medium for the conduct of a business and sharing its gains. Thus a trust may be created as a convenient method by which persons become associated for dealings in real estate, the development of tracts of land, the construction of improvements, and the purchase, management and sale of properties; or for dealings in securities or other personal property; or for the production, or manufacture, and sale of commodities; or for commerce, or other sorts of business; where those who become beneficially interested, either by joining in the plan at the outset, or by later participation according to the terms of the arrangement, seek to share the advantages of a union of their interests in the common enterprise.

The Government contends that such an organized community of effort for the doing of business presents the essential features of an association. Petitioners stress the significance of, and the limitations said to be implied in, the provisions classifying associations with corporations.

The inclusion of associations with corporations implies resemblance; but it is resemblance and not identity. The resemblance points to features distinguishing associations from partnerships as well as from ordinary trusts. As we have seen, the classification cannot be said to require organization under a statute, or with statutory priv-

ileges. The term embraces associations as they may exist at common
law. Hecht v. Malley, 265 U.S. 144 (1924). We have already referred
to the definitions, quoted in that case, showing the ordinary meaning
of the term as applicable to a body of persons united without a charter
"but upon the methods and forms used by incorporated bodies for
the prosecution of some common enterprise." These definitions,
while helpful, are not to be pressed so far as to make mere formal
procedure a controlling test. The provision itself negatives such a
construction. Thus unincorporated joint-stock companies have
generally been regarded as bearing the closest resemblance to corporations. But, in the revenue acts, associations are mentioned
separately and are not to be treated as limited to "joint-stock companies," although belonging to the same group. While the use of
corporate forms may furnish persuasive evidence of the existence of
an association, the absence of particular forms, or of the usual terminology of corporations, cannot be regarded as decisive. Thus an
association may not have "directors" or "officers," but the "trustees"
may function "in much the same manner as the directors in a corporation" for the purpose of carrying on the enterprise. The
regulatory provisions of the trust instrument may take the place of
"by-laws." And as there may be, under the reasoning in the *Hecht*
case, an absence of control by beneficiaries such as is commonly exercised by stockholders in a business corporation, it cannot be
considered to be essential to the existence of an association that those
beneficially interested should hold meetings or elect their representatives. Again, while the faculty of transferring the interests of
members without affecting the continuity of the enterprise may be
deemed to be characteristic, the test of an association is not to be
found in the mere formal evidence of interests or in a particular
method of transfer.

What, then, are the salient features of a trust — when created
and maintained as a medium for the carrying on of a business enterprise and sharing its gains — which may be regarded as making it
analogous to a corporate organization? A corporation, as an entity,
holds the title to the property embarked in the corporate undertaking. Trustees, as a continuing body with provision for succession,
may afford a corresponding advantage during the existence of the
trust. Corporate organization furnishes the opportunity for a centralized management through representatives of the members of the
corporation. The designation of trustees, who are charged with the
conduct of an enterprise — who act "in much the same manner as
directors" — may provide a similar scheme, with corresponding effectiveness. Whether the trustees are named in the trust instrument
with power to select successors, so as to constitute a self-perpetuating
body, or are selected by, or with the advice of, those beneficially

interested in the undertaking, centralization of management analogous to that of corporate activities may be achieved. An enterprise carried on by means of a trust may be secure from termination or interruption by the death of owners of beneficial interests and in this respect their interests are distinguished from those of partners and are akin to the interests of members of a corporation. And the trust type of organization facilitates, as does corporate organization, the transfer of beneficial interests without affecting the continuity of the enterprise, and also the introduction of large numbers of participants. The trust method also permits the limitation of the personal liability of participants to the property embarked in the undertaking.

It is no answer to say that these advantages flow from the very nature of trusts. For the question has arisen because of the use and adaptation of the trust mechanism. The suggestion ignores the postulate that we are considering those trusts which have the distinctive feature of being created to enable the participants to carry on a business and divide the gains which accrue from their common undertaking, — trusts that thus satisfy the primary conception of association and have the attributes to which we have referred, distinguishing them from partnerships. In such a case, we think that these attributes make the trust sufficiently analogous to corporate organization to justify the conclusion that Congress intended that the income of the enterprise should be taxed in the same manner as that of corporations.

Applying these principles to the instant case, we are of the opinion that the trust constituted an association. The trust was created for the development of a tract of land through the construction and operation of golf courses, club houses, etc. and the conduct of incidental businesses, with broad powers for the purchase, operation and sale of properties. Provision was made for the issue of shares of beneficial interests, with described rights and priorities. There were to be preferred shares of the value of $100 each and common shares of no par value. Thus those who took beneficial interests became shareholders in the common undertaking to be conducted for their profit according to the terms of the arrangement. They were not the less associated in that undertaking because the arrangement vested the management and control in the trustees. And the contemplated development of the tract of land held at the outset, even if other properties were not acquired, involved what was essentially a business enterprise. The arrangement provided for centralized control, continuity, and limited liability, and the analogy to corporate organization was carried still further by the provision for the issue of transferable certificates. . . .

The judgment is affirmed.

LARSON v. COMMISSIONER
66 T.C. 159 (1976)

TANNENWALD, Judge. . . .

FINDINGS OF FACT

. . . [P]etitioner was a limited partner in Mai-Kai Apartments (hereinafter Mai-Kai), a limited partnership formed under the laws of the State of California. . . . [P]etitioner was also a limited partner in Somis Orchards (hereinafter Somis), a limited partnership formed under the laws of the State of California.

Grubin, Horth & Lawless, inc. (hereinafter GHL), a California corporation, the sole general partner of both Mai-Kai and Somis, was formed . . . primarily to organize so-called "real estate syndications" as limited partnerships. . . . GHL had a paid-in capital of $21,300. . . . [I]ts capital and surplus ranged between a maximum of $49,593 at the close of the fiscal year 1970 to a minimum of $18,764 as of the close of the fiscal year 1974. Cash on hand was generally negligible. GHL organized both Mai-Kai and Somis and managed and administered the partnership properties. . . .

Mai-Kai was formed . . . for the purpose of owning and operating a student apartment complex. . . . Upon the formation of Mai-Kai, GHL transferred to Mai-Kai, as a contribution to its capital, the right to acquire the Mai-Kai Apartments under a contract negotiated by . . . GHL's predecessor in interest. . . .

GHL was not required to make any further capital contributions to Mai-Kai. The limited partnership interests in Mai-Kai were divided into 10 "units" of $9,500 per "unit." All of the "units" were sold to a total of eight limited partners. The total capital contribution to Mai-Kai by the limited partners was $95,000 in cash. GHL's total capital contribution to Mai-Kai was reflected and carried at zero ($0) on Mai-Kai's books and records.

GHL and the limited partners in the Mai-Kai venture subscribed to an agreement of limited partnership which defined their respective rights and obligations. Concurrently with the execution of the agreement of limited partnership, the Mai-Kai partners also executed a certificate of limited partnership which was filed and recorded in accordance with California law.

After its formation, Mai-Kai purchased the Mai-Kai Apartments from Century Land Co., . . . for a purchase price of $450,000. The purchase price was paid by the execution of a promissory note . . . in the amount of $450,000. . . . The promissory note was secured by a deed of trust upon the Mai-Kai Apartments . . . in the event of default by Mai-Kai under the promissory note no money judgment would lie against Mai-Kai, and Century Land Co.'s remedy would be limited to requiring the sale of the Mai-Kai Apartments pursuant to the deed of trust. . . .

The Mai-Kai partnership agreement . . . provided, in pertinent part:

AGREEMENT Of LIMITED PARTNERSHIP

3. *Term.*

The partnership shall commence as of December 1, 1968 and shall continue for a period of thirty-three (33) years . . . unless sooner terminated as hereinafter provided for, or unless extended for such longer term as may be determined by the election of the Limited Partners entitled to sixty per cent (60%) or more of the profits of the partnership allocable to the Limited Partners. . . .

7. *Withdrawal of Capital.*

No Limited Partner may withdraw his capital contribution to the partnership without the consent of the General Partner. . . .

8. *Rights, Duties, Obligations of the Limited Partners.*

(a) Except as otherwise expressly provided herein, no Limited Partner shall participate in the management of the partnership business.

(b) A Limited Partner shall have the right to withdraw his capital account upon the termination of the partnership. . . .

10. *Profits, Losses and Distributions.*

(a) *Profits.* The net profits of the partnership shall be equal to the taxable income of the partnership. . . .

Except as provided in Paragraph 11 below, profits shall be divided as follows:

(1) Twenty Per Cent (20%) to the account of the General Partner.

(2) Eighty Per Cent (80%) to the accounts of the Limited Partners. . . .

(b) *Losses.* All losses of the partnership shall be allocated entirely to the Limited Partners in proportion to their capital contributions, subject however to the limitation of liability of each Limited Partner to the amount of his individual investment in the partnership. . . .

(c) *Distributions.* Subject to the provisions of Paragraph 11 below, in the event of the sale of the real property, or the liquidation of the partnership, the net proceeds realized from such sale . . . or the proceeds of any liquidation, as the case may be, and the cash flow of the partnership shall be distributed as follows:

(1) Twenty Per Cent (20%) to the General Partner.

(2) Eighty Per Cent (80%) to the Limited Partners. . . .

(e) The General Partner shall distribute the cash flow of the partnership . . . not less frequently than quarterly.

11. *Limitation on Allocations and Distributions to General Partner.*

Notwithstanding Paragraph 10 above, it is agreed that the General Partner shall not participate in the cash flow or profits of the project until such time as a Limited Partner (assuming 50% tax bracket) has been returned his initial investment through a combination of cash flow and operating losses. . . .

15. *Assignment of Partners' Interests.*

(a) *General Partner.* The General Partner shall not assign, mortgage, encumber or sell its interest as General Partner in the partnership or enter into any agreement as a result of which any firm, person or corporation shall become interested with it in the partnership. . . .

(b) *Limited Partners' Right to Receive Income.* The right of a Limited Partner to receive any income from the partnership shall not be transferred, sold or assigned without the prior written consent of the General Partner. The General Partner shall not unreasonably withhold such consent.

(c) *Transfer of Capital Interest — Limited Partner.* The capital interest of a Limited Partner may not be transferred, sold or assigned by such Limited Partner except in accordance with the following provisions:

. . . If the General Partner, . . . in good faith determines that the purchase price offered by the proposed transferee is less than the then fair market value of the interest to be transferred, the General Partner shall have the option to notify the proposed transferor within said ten day period, that the transferor cannot effect a transfer of the interest unless he first offers the interest to the remaining Limited Partners. . . .

17. *Termination.*

Notwithstanding anything to the contrary contained herein, the partnership shall terminate upon any of the following events:

(a) A disposition of [sic] the partnership of its entire interest in the real property.

(b) The adjudication of bankruptcy of the General Partner or otherwise as provided by the Uniform Limited Partnership Act, unless the business is continued by a General Partner elected in place thereof.

(c) A determination by the election of Limited Partners entitled to sixty per cent (60%) or more of the profits of the partnership allocable to the Limited Partners that the partnership shall terminate.

(d) The removal of the General Partner by the vote of Limited Partners entitled to sixty per cent (60%) or more of the profits of the partnership allocable to the Limited Partners. In such event, there shall be a distribution of assets . . . unless the Limited Partners, by an affirmative vote of Limited Partners owning 100% of the profits in the partnership allocable to the Limited Partners, elect to form a new partnership to continue the partnership business. . . .

18. Limited Partners entitled to 60% or more of the profits of the limited partnership allocable to the Limited Partners may by a vote remove the General Partner. In the event of such removal the partnership shall terminate except that by the vote of 100% of the Limited Partners a new partnership may be formed to continue the partnership business.

In the case of Mai-Kai, GHL thus had a 20-percent "subordinated" participation interest in operating profits, cash flow, and net proceeds upon the sale of partnership assets. GHL's participation interest in Mai-Kai became unsubordinated after December 31, 1972. The amount by which GHL's participation interest was subordinated prior to December 31, 1972 — i.e., the amount remaining in the partners' investment accounts (which amount was to be recovered by the limited partners before GHL was entitled to participate) — was as follows:

End of year	Subordinated amount
1968	$46,707
1969	27,692
1970	14,947
1971	1,431

During 1973 Mai-Kai did not generate a profit or cash flow to be distributed to either the limited partners or to the general partner.

For each of the taxable years 1968 to 1973, inclusive, Mai-Kai reported losses on its U.S. Partnership Income Tax Returns. . . .

Somis Orchards was formed . . . for the purpose of acquiring, holding, operating, improving, leasing, selling, and otherwise managing approximately 265 acres of citrus groves and related assets. . . . The purchase price was paid by $102,750 in cash and the execution of three installment notes . . . totaling $3,709,630. . . . The first and second installment notes totaling $3,434,500 were nonrecourse liabilities. . . . The third installment note was paid in full by Somis in March 1970.

GHL's capital contributions to Somis consisted of the transfer to the partnership of GHL's rights to acquire the citrus groves. . . . In addition, GHL assigned to Somis the management contract negotiated by GHL for management of the citrus groves by Kaiser Aetna.

A total of 44 limited partners contributed $420,000 in cash to Somis. Each limited partner also executed a series of promissory notes reflecting annual contributions to be made by the limited partners. . . .

The partnership agreement and certificate signed by GHL and the Somis limited partners were generally similar to those of Mai-Kai, with the following material differences:

(1) The initial 15-year term could be extended by a 51-percent vote of limited partners. . . .

(4) Profits, proceeds from sales of assets, and liquidation proceeds were allocated, 15 percent to the general partner and 85 percent to the limited partners. The general partner had no interest in cash flow.

(5) Fifty-one percent of the limited partnership interests could elect to terminate the partnership. The same percentage could vote to remove the general partner, in which event the partnership would terminate unless 51 percent of the limited partnership interests elected to form a new partnership to continue the business. On removal, the general partner would be paid the value of its interests, as determined by arbitration. . . .

(7) The rights of the parties were contingent on approval by the State department of corporations of the sale of the limited partnership interests.

(8) The agreement could be amended by a 51-percent vote of limited partners.

On two separate occasions individual limited partnership interests in Somis were transferred from the individual limited partner to a joint tenancy between the limited partner and his wife. . . .

In the case of Somis, GHL had a 15-percent "subordinated" participation interest in operating profits and net proceeds upon the sale of partnership assets. . . . The amount by which GHL's participation interest in the net profit was subordinated . . . was as follows:

End of year	Subordinated amount (including 6-percent interest)
1969	$271,992
1970	252,714
1971	277,074
1972	281,232
1973	300,342

During the taxable years 1969 to 1973 inclusive, Somis operated at a loss. . . .

No limited partner in Somis or Mai-Kai was a stockholder of GHL, with the exception of Harris E. Lawless, who at all pertinent times held a 1.905-percent limited partnership interest in Somis and owned 23.125 percent of the stock of GHL. Neither Somis nor Mai-Kai issued certificates to the limited partners representing shares in the partnerships. During the period 1968 to 1973, no meetings of the limited partners in Mai-Kai were held, nor were any decisions with respect to either Mai-Kai or Somis referred to the limited partners for their vote or approval. Meetings of the Somis partners were held in December of 1972 and 1973 to allow Kaiser Aetna to inform them of progress in obtaining master plan approval for the planned city development covering the land owned by Somis.

Pursuant to the provisions of the California Corporate Securities Law . . . GHL applied for and secured from the California Corporations Commissioner a permit authorizing it to offer for sale, negotiate for the sale of, and sell security interests (or subscriptions therefor) in Somis.

Offering circulars, prepared by GHL, were distributed by GHL to prospective limited partners in Somis and Mai-Kai. The circulars advertised the limited partnership interests as "tax-sheltered real estate investments," and contained extensive descriptions of the underlying real property, the investment terms, and the anticipated return on the proposed investments. . . .

Opinion

Petitioners owned limited partnership interests in Mai-Kai and Somis, two real estate ventures organized under the California Uniform Limited Partnership Act . . . (hereinafter referred to as CULPA). Petitioners allege that the partnerships fail all of the tests of corporate resemblance established by respondent's regulations (sec. 301.7701-2, Proced. & Admin. Regs.); respondent contends that all those tests are satisfied. Both sides agree that the regulations apply and are controlling, and our opinion and decision are consequently framed in that context; the validity of respondent's regulations is not before us. In our previous (now withdrawn) opinion dated October 21, 1975, we concluded that respondent should prevail. Upon reconsideration, we have come to the opposite conclusion and hold for petitioners.

The starting point of the regulations' definition of an "association" is the principle applied in Morrissey v. Commissioner, 296 U.S. 344 (1935), that the term includes entities which resemble corporations although they are not formally organized as such. *Morrissey* identified several characteristics of the corporate form which the regulations adopt as a test of corporate resemblance. For the purpose of comparing corporations with partnerships, the significant characteristics are: continuity of life; centralization of management; limited liability; and free transferability of interests. Other corporate or noncorporate characteristics may also be considered if appropriate in a particular case. An organization will be taxed as a corporation if, taking all relevant characteristics into account, it more nearly resembles a corporation than some other entity. . . .

The regulations discuss each major corporate characteristic separately, and each apparently bears equal weight in the final balancing. . . . This apparently mechanical approach may perhaps be explained as an attempt to impart a degree of certainty to a subject otherwise fraught with imponderables. In most instances, the regulations also make separate provision for the classification of limited partnerships. Petitioners rely heavily on those provisions, while respondent seeks to distinguish them or to minimize their importance.

1. CONTINUITY OF LIFE

. . . A corporation possesses a greater degree of continuity of life than a partnership, since its existence is not dependent upon events personally affecting its separate members. Because of their more intimate legal and financial ties, partners are given a continuing right to choose their associates which is denied to corporate shareholders. A material alteration in the makeup of the partnership, as through the death or incapacity of a partner, either dissolves the partnership relation by operation of law or permits dissolution by order of court. Uniform Partnership Act, . . . (hereinafter referred to as UPA). Partners are then free to withdraw their shares from the business, though they may agree to form a new partnership to continue it. A partner is also given the right to dissolve the partnership and withdraw his capital . . . at will at any time . . . although he may be unable to cause the winding up of the business and may be answerable in damages to other partners if his act breaches an agreement among them. . . . The significant difference between a corporation and a partnership as regards continuity of life, then, is that a partner can always opt out of continued participation in and exposure to the risks of the enterprise. A corporate shareholder's investment is locked in unless liquidation is voted or he can find a purchaser to buy him out.

In a partnership subject to the Uniform Limited Partnership Act (hereinafter referred to as ULPA), this right of withdrawal is modified. A limited partner can withdraw his interest on dissolution . . . but he can neither dissolve the partnership at will . . . nor force dissolution at the retirement, death, or insanity of a general partner if the remaining general partners agree to continue the business in accordance with a right granted in the partnership certificate. . . . CULPA section 15520 further provides that a new general partner can be elected to continue the business without causing dissolution, if the certificate permits.

The sole general partner in the limited partnerships involved herein was a corporation, whose business was the promotion and management of real estate ventures. As a practical matter, it is unlikely that either Mai-Kai or Somis would have been dissolved midstream and the partners afforded an opportunity to withdraw their investments. Petitioners argue that the partnerships neverthe-less lacked continuity of life because they could be dissolved either at will by, or on the bankruptcy of, the general partner. We turn first to the effect of bankruptcy of GHL.

California Uniform Partnership Act . . . (hereinafter referred to as CUPA) provides that a partnership is dissolved on the bankruptcy of a partner. CUPA . . . makes that act applicable to limited part-nerships unless inconsistent with statutes relating to them. CULPA nowhere provides for dissolution or nondissolution in the event of bankruptcy. . . . CUPA . . . therefore applies. Since the bankruptcy of GHL would bring about dissolution by operation of law, each limited partner would be entitled to demand the return of his con-tribution. . . . Somis and Mai-Kai simply do not satisfy the regulations' test of continuity, which requires that the "bankruptcy . . . of *any member* will *not* cause a dissolution of the organization." (Emphasis supplied.)[11]

The fact that under the agreements involved herein a new gen-eral partner might be chosen to continue the business does not affect this conclusion. . . . [I]f GHL became bankrupt while it was the gen-eral partner of Somis and Mai-Kai, there would at best be a hiatus between the event of bankruptcy and the entry of a new general partner so that, from a legal point of view, the old partnerships would have been dissolved. Moreover, at least in the case of Mai-Kai, a vote of 100 percent of the limited partners was required to elect a new general partner. Glensder Textile Co., 46 B.T.A. 176 (1942), held that such contingent continuity of life did not resemble that of a corporation. Respondent's regulations incorporate this conclusion.

. . . We recognize that our application of respondent's existing regulations to the event of bankruptcy results in a situation where it is unlikely that a limited partnership will ever satisfy the "continuity of life" requirement of those regulations. But the fact that the reg-ulations are so clearly keyed to "dissolution" (a term encompassing the legal relationships between the partners) rather than "termination of the business" (a phrase capable of more pragmatic interpretation encompassing the life of the business enterprise) leaves us with no viable alternative. In this connection, we note that respondent is not without power to alter the impact of our application of his existing regulations. . . .

---

11. In light of our conclusion, infra . . . that GHL has not been shown to have had a substantial interest in the partnerships, it may be argued that it was not a "member" for the purpose of the regulations. Such an argument, however, we find to be structurally incompatible with the regulations, which consider the substantiality of a partner's interest in the partnership only in connection with centralization of management and transferability of interests. Cf. sec. 301.7701-2(d)(2), Proced. & Admin. Regs., . . . (fourth sentence).

2. CENTRALIZED MANAGEMENT

In the corporate form, management is centralized in the officers and directors; the involvement of shareholders as such in ordinary operations is limited to choosing these representatives. In a general partnership, authority is decentralized and any partner has the power to make binding decisions in the ordinary course. . . . In a limited partnership, however, this authority exists only in the general partners . . . and a limited partner who takes part in the control of the business loses his limited liability status. . . . From a practical standpoint, it is clear that the management of both Mai-Kai and Somis was centralized in GHL. The sole general partner was empowered by law as well as by the partnership agreements to administer the partnership affairs. However, respondent's regulations specify that —

> In addition, limited partnerships subject to a statute corresponding to the Uniform Limited Partnership Act, generally do not have centralized management, but centralized management ordinarily does exist in such a limited partnership if substantially all the interests in the partnership are owned by the limited partners. . . .

. . . In specifying this additional condition, respondent has adopted the theory of Glensder Textile Co., supra, that managing partners with . . . interests in the business are not "analogous to directors of a corporation" because they act in their own interests "and not *merely* in a representative capacity for a body of persons having a limited investment and a limited liability." . . .

. . . [P]etitioners herein have failed to show that the limited partners did not own all or substantially all the interests in the partnerships involved herein within the meaning of the regulations. GHL's interests in Mai-Kai and Somis were subordinated to those of the limited partners. Petitioners have not attempted to demonstrate that GHL's capital interests had any present value during the years in issue, and it is clear that, because of the subordination provisions, it had no present right to income during those years. Petitioners would have us look to the anticipated return on the partnership properties in future years to determine that GHL had a substantial proprietary stake in the business independent of its management role. They have not, however, proved by competent evidence that such a return could in fact be expected, relying instead on unsupported projections; nor have they shown that any such future profit would be reflected in the present value of GHL's interest. Although there was testimony that GHL expected profits from the subordinated interests when the limited partnerships were liquidated, we are not convinced that the possibility of such income at an indefinite future date had value during the years at issue. GHL reported gross income of $906,930.89 from fiscal 1969 to fiscal 1974, out of which only $118 represented a partnership distribution (from a partnership not involved herein).

Furthermore, the limited partners in Somis and Mai-Kai possessed the right to remove GHL as the general partner. Thus, GHL's right to participate in future growth and profits was wholly contingent on satisfactory performance of its management role, and not at all analogous to the independent proprietary interest of a typical general partner. In Glensder Textile Co., supra, our conclusion that centralization of management was lacking rested not only on the fact that management retained a proprietary interest but also on the fact that the limited partners could not "remove the general partners and control them as agents, as stockholders may control directors." . . .

Petitioners argue that such power of removal and control could be given to limited partners under ULPA. . . . In our opinion, the regulation was not intended to provide a blanket exemption from association status for ULPA limited partnerships, regardless of the extent to which the partners by agreement deviate from the statutory scheme. . . . We have repeatedly held that an organization is to be classified by reference to the rights and duties created by agreement as well as those existing under State law. . . . The effect of such organic laws as ULPA (and CULPA) is to provide a rule which governs in the absence of contrary agreement. Where the theme is obscured by the variations, it is the latter which set the tone of the composition. Neither ULPA nor CULPA requires that the limited partners be given the right to remove the general partner; in fact, ULPA does not even mention such a possibility. By reserving that right, the limited partners in Mai-Kai and Somis took themselves out of the basic framework of ULPA and hence out of the shelter of the regulation, which is based on Glensder. . . .

3. LIMITED LIABILITY

Unless some member is personally liable for debts of, and claims against, an entity, . . . the entity possesses the corporate characteristic of limited liability. The regulation provides that "in the case of a limited partnership subject to a statute corresponding to the Uniform Limited Partnership Act, personal liability exists with respect to each general partner, except as provided in subparagraph (2) of this paragraph." The first sentence of subparagraph (2) establishes a conjunctive test. . . . [P]ersonal liability exists if the general partner either has substantial assets or is not a dummy for the limited partners. . . . Although the purpose of subparagraph (2) was ostensibly to delineate the conditions under which personal liability of a general partner *does not exist*, practically all the remaining material in the subparagraph outlines the conditions under which such personal liability does exist. In several examples, personal liability is said to exist, either because the general partner has substantial assets or because he is not a dummy for the limited partners. See Zuckman v. United States, supra. In no instance is there a suggestion that both conditions established by the first sentence of subparagraph (2) need not be satisfied.

In so concluding, we are mindful that in Glensder Textile Co., supra, the apparent source of the language in the regulations, the term "dummy" was arguably considered applicable to any general partner without substantial assets risked in the business. The opinion in *Glensder* states . . . :

> If, for instance, the general partners were not men with substantial assets risked in the business *but* were mere dummies without real means acting as the agents of the limited partners, whose investments made possible the business, there would be something approaching the corporate form of stockholders and directors. . . . [Emphasis added.]

Thus, lack of substantial assets seems to be considered the equivalent of being a dummy — an equivalence which respondent apparently sought to avoid by using the word "and" in his existing regulations.

While it may be doubtful that GHL could be considered to have had substantial assets during the years in issue, we find it unnecessary to resolve this question since it is clear that GHL was not a dummy for the limited partners of Somis and Mai-Kai. Respondent contends that GHL fell within the "dummy" concept because it was subject to removal by the limited partners, and thus was subject to their ultimate control. While it is true that a mere "dummy" would be totally under the control of the limited partners, it does not follow that the presence of some control by virtue of the power to remove necessarily makes the general partner a "dummy." It seems clear that the limited partners' rights to remove the general partner were designed to give the limited partners a measure of control over their investment without involving them in the "control of the business"; the rights were not designed to render GHL a mere dummy or to empower the limited partners "to direct the business actively through the general partners." Glensder Textile Co. . . . Moreover, the record indicates that the limited partners did not use GHL as a screen to conceal their own active involvement in the conduct of the business; far from being a rubber stamp, GHL was the moving force in these enterprises. With a minor exception, the persons controlling GHL were independent of and unrelated to the limited partners. . . .

4. TRANSFERABILITY OF INTERESTS

A stockholder's rights and interest in a corporate venture are, absent consensual restrictions, freely transferable by the owner without reference to the wishes of other members. A partner, on the other hand, can unilaterally transfer only his interest in partnership "profits and surplus," and cannot confer on the assignee the other attributes of membership without the consent of all partners. . . . Respondent's regulations recognize and rely upon this distinction.

The regulations state that if substantially all interests are freely transferable, the corporate characteristic of free transferability of interests is present. Since we have concluded, for the purposes of this case, that the limited partners should be considered as owning substantially all the interests in Mai-Kai and Somis . . . we turn our attention to the question whether their interests were so transferable. . . .

Both partnership agreements permit the assignment of a limited partner's income interest with the consent of the general partner, which may not unreasonably be withheld. Petitioners have not suggested any ground on which consent could be withheld. The requirement of consent, circumscribed by a standard of reasonableness, is not such a restriction on transfer as is typical of partnership agreements; nor is it the sort referred to by the regulations. . . .

Petitioners also argue that transferability is limited by the requirement that, in the event of a proposed assignment, a limited partner's capital interest first be offered to other members under certain circumstances. While an assignment for less than fair market value could be prevented in this manner, there was no requirement that such an offer be made if an interest was to be sold to a third party at fair market value. Thus, there was no "effort on the part of the parties to select their business associates," as is characteristic of the usual partnership arrangement. . . . We think that these interests possessed considerably more than the "modified" form of free transferability referred to in subparagraph (2) of the regulation. . . .

5. OTHER CHARACTERISTICS

Both parties have identified other characteristics of Mai-Kai and Somis which they allege are relevant to the determination whether those entities more closely resemble partnerships or corporations. . . . Petitioners point to the fact that, unlike a corporate board of directors, GHL as manager lacked the discretionary right to retain or distribute profits according to the needs of the business. This argument is in reality directed to the issue of centralized management. The same is true of respondent's analogy between the limited partners' voting rights and those of corporate shareholders. To be sure the partnership interests were not represented by certificates but this factor conceivably is more properly subsumed in the transferability issue. . . . Moreover, those interests were divided into units or shares and were promoted and marketed in a manner similar to corporate securities — an additional "characteristic" which we have not ignored, . . . but which we do not deem of critical significance under the circumstances herein. Similarly, we do not assign any particular additional importance to the facts that the partnerships have not observed corporate formalities and procedures . . . or that, unlike general partners, limited partners were not required personally to sign the partnership certificates. Finally, respondent argues that the limited partnerships resemble corporations because they provide a means of pooling investments while limiting the liability of the participants. . . . As it relates to the facts of this case, this point is subsumed in our earlier discussion. To the extent that it presages an attempt to classify *all* limited partnerships as corporations, it is in irreconcilable conflict with respondent's own regulations.

6. CONCLUSION

The regulations provide that an entity will be taxed as a corporation if it more closely resembles a corporation than any other form of organization. They further state that such a resemblance does not exist unless the entity possesses *more* corporate than noncorporate characteristics. If every characteristic bears equal weight, then Mai-Kai and Somis are partnerships for tax purposes. . . . On the other hand, if the overall corporate resemblance test, espoused by *Morrissey* and adhered to by the regulations, permits us to weigh each factor according to the degree of corporate similarity it provides, we would be inclined to find that these entities were taxable as corporations. Each possessed a degree of centralized management indistinguishable from that of a pure corporation; the other major factors lie somewhere on the continuum between corporate and partnership resemblance. Were not the regulations' thumb upon the scales, it appears to us that the practical continuity and limited liability of both entities would decisively tip the balance in respondent's favor. However, we can find no warrant for such refined balancing in the regulations or in cases which have considered them. . . . Only in connection with free transferability of interests do the regulations recognize a modified and less significant form of a particular characteristic.

Our task herein is to apply the provisions of respondent's regulations as we find them and not as we think they might or ought to have been written. . . . On this basis, petitioners must prevail. . . .

Reviewed by the Court.

Fay and Hall, JJ., did not participate. . . .

[Concurring opinions of Dawson, C.J., and Goffe, J., and dissenting opinions of Baum, Drennen, Scott, and Quealy, JJ., omitted.]

SIMPSON, J., dissenting. The majority has presented a careful analysis of the complex matters involved in this case. However, I respectfully suggest that, while becoming involved with the intricacies of the regulations, they have lost sight of the ultimate objective of the regulations, which is to decide whether Mai-Kai and Somis more nearly resemble corporations or partnerships.

. . . Both parties have asked that we make such decision based on the present regulations so that our task is merely to interpret those regulations, and we are not asked to pass upon their validity.

1. OTHER SIGNIFICANT CHARACTERISTICS

. . . The regulations enumerate the major characteristics of a corporation . . . and set forth many rules to assist in applying those criteria. The regulations also recognize that there may be other characteristics which should be taken into consideration. . . .

. . . Since under both the cases and the regulations, the ultimate test is to decide whether an organization more nearly resembles a corporation or a partnership, we must consider all characteristics which have any relevancy in making that judgment. The even-split rule of the regulations applies only when there are no other significant characteristics. Here, we do have other significant characteristics.

. . . The interests in the limited partnerships are securities under California and Federal law, just as is corporate stock. . . . Further, such interests were sold through licensed brokers just as corporate stock. GHL prepared and distributed offering circulars which advertised the interests as "tax-sheltered real estate investments." Thus, the method of raising capital and marketing the interests in the organizations was very similar, if not identical, to the methods customarily used by corporations. . . .

Moreover, Mai-Kai and Somis possess another significant characteristic which also increases their resemblance to corporations. . . . CULPA provides that the limited partners may possess and exercise voting rights with respect to any matter "affecting the basic structure" of the limited partnership. Such rights include the right of the limited partners to remove the general partner at any time and to select a replacement and the right to vote on the sale of all, or substantially all, of the assets of the partnership. The certificates of Mai-Kai and Somis provided that the limited partners in each organization had the rights to remove the general partner and to select a replacement. Such rights could not be conferred upon limited partners under ULPA. . . .

By conferring such rights on limited partners, California has created greater democracy in limited partnerships. It has thus enabled the limited partners to exercise control over the affairs of the enterprise in much the same manner as shareholders can control the affairs of a corporation. . . .

. . . Even if we assume, as does the majority, that there is an even split among the major characteristics, the method of marketing the interests in the organizations and the control conferred upon the limited partners are surely significant characteristics. . . .

2. LIMITED LIABILITY

I am in complete agreement with the majority that limited liability exists only when the general partner lacks substantial assets and also is "merely a 'dummy' acting as the agent of the limited partners." . . . The majority finds that GHL was not a "dummy" since "the limited partners did not use GHL as a screen to conceal their own active involvement in the conduct of the business; far from being a rubber stamp, GHL was the moving force in these enterprises." I disagree with that construction of the term "dummy" and conclude that GHL was a "dummy" within the meaning of the regulations.

I have two reasons for my disagreement: In the first place, the majority's construction of the regulations will render the provision meaningless. . . . The regulations surely contemplate that under some situations, an organization formed as a limited partnership may have limited liability, but the construction of the regulations adopted . . . by a majority of this Court, will result in limited partnerships never possessing such characteristic. . . .

Unfortunately, the term "dummy" has no precise meaning, but as the majority recognizes, the regulations adopted the language from Glensder Textile Co. . . .

. . . [W]hen the Board spoke of "mere dummies . . . acting as the agents of the limited partners," they did not have in mind a private understanding in which the general partners were merely straw men for the limited partners. The Board had in mind the relationship between a board of directors and the shareholders of a corporation and was looking to State law to ascertain what powers were conferred upon the limited partners. . . .

It is true that GHL was not a mere straw man for the limited partners in Mai-Kai and Somis, but it is also true that the limited partners in those organizations possessed rights very similar to those of shareholders in a corporation. As in the case of a board of directors of a corporation and the corporate officers chosen by it, GHL was expected to exercise its discretion in the management of the day-to-day affairs of the enterprises, but the limited partners, through their power to remove GHL, could exercise general control over the policies of the enterprises. In other respects, the limited partners possess the powers with which the Board was concerned in *Glensder. . . .*

3. CONTINUITY OF LIFE

Although I agree with the majority's conclusion that Mai-Kai and Somis lacked continuity of life within the meaning of the regulations,[2] I do not agree with their reasons for that conclusion. Their conclusion is based on the finding that bankruptcy of the general partner would cause a dissolution of each of the organizations. . . .

Under *Glensder,* there is no continuity of life whenever an organization's continuity is contingent, and if its continuity depends upon the agreement of remaining partners, it is contingent, irrespective of whether all, or merely a majority, of the remaining partners must agree. . . . In the case of Mai-Kai, dissolution could be avoided by an agreement of 100 percent of the limited partners, and in the case of Somis, a majority of the limited partners could prevent dissolution. In either event, the continuation of the organization depended upon the agreement of some or all of the limited partners, and consequently, continuity was contingent. For this reason, both organizations lack continuity of life within the meaning of the regulations and *Glensder.*

Drennen and Sterrett, JJ., agree with this dissent.

NOTES

1. See Zuckman v. United States, 524 F.2d 729 (Ct. Cl. 1975), a case reaching the same result as *Larson,* but with a somewhat different analysis. The terms of the Service's acceptance of *Larson* are set forth in Rev. Rul. 79-106, 1979-1 C.B. 448, and it reaffirmed its position in Rev. Proc. 88-44, 1988-38 I.R.B. 1, and in Rev. Rul. 88-76, 1988-38 I.R.B. 1. Should the Service have accepted *Larson*?

2. The conditions for obtaining an IRS ruling that an organization will be accorded partnership treatment for tax purposes are found in Rev. Proc. 89-12, 1989-7 I.R.B. 22. Cf. Peel, Definition of

---

2. However, it may be persuasively argued that, on the record in this case, there was, realistically, continuity of life within the meaning of *Morrissey*. . . . On this record, the possibility that the bankruptcy of the general partner would affect the continuity of the organizations is minimal and hardly distinguishable from the situation that would exist when a corporation becomes bankrupt.

a Partnership: New Suggestions on an Old Issue, 1979 Wis. L. Rev. 989. For a case in which the government sought unsuccessfully to treat a real estate trust as an association taxable as a corporation, see Elm Street Realty Trust, 76 T.C. 803 (1981).

3. In recent years, the use of so-called master limited partnerships proliferated. These partnerships typically have hundreds or even thousands of limited partners, and their interests are traded on public markets, including the New York Stock Exchange. Master limited partnerships were initially designed to pool existing passive investments in income-producing assets (such as interests in oil and gas tax shelters) in order to make the investments more marketable. However, their use soon spread from these passive enterprises to actively managed businesses.

The potential for abuse of the master limited partnership vehicle in connection with actively managed businesses is evident. The vehicle could be used to to gain most of the benefits of corporate form (e.g., ready transferability of interest) without incurring a corporate level tax. As a result, the corporate tax base could be substantially eroded. See Freeman, Some Early Strategies for the Methodical Disincorporation of America After the Tax Reform Act of 1986, 64 Taxes 962 (1986); Friedrich, The Unincorporation of America?, 14 J. Corp. Taxn. 3 (1987). In 1987, Congress acted to limit the possibilities for abuse by enacting §7704. Under this section, a publicly traded partnership is treated as a corporation for tax purposes unless 90 percent or more of its gross income is passive income. The following report discusses §7704.

H.R. REP. NO. 391
100th Cong., 1st Sess., pt. 1, at 1063-1071 (1987)

. . .

PRESENT LAW

Under present law, a partnership is not subject to tax at the partnership level, but rather, income and loss of the partnership is subject to tax at the partner's level. A partner's share of partnership income is generally determined without regard to whether he receives any corresponding cash distributions. Similarly, partnership deductions, losses and credits are taken into account at the partner level for tax purposes. A corporation, by contrast, generally is subject to tax at the entity level, and distributions with respect to corporate stock generally are subject to tax at the shareholder level.

The Supreme Court articulated standards applicable in determining whether an entity should be taxed as a corporation in the case of Morrissey v. Commissioner, 296 U.S. 344 (1935). The Court reasoned that the entity in that case resembled a corporation. Thus, the *Morrissey* case is said to have set forth the "resemblance" test referred to in the current Treasury regulations regarding entity classification. These regulations govern classification under present law. . . .

The Treasury regulations distinguishing partnerships from corporations currently provide that whether a business entity is taxed as a corporation depends on which form of enterprise the entity "more nearly" resembles (Treas. Reg. sec. 301.7701-2(a)). The regulations list six corporate characteristics, two of which are common to corporations and partnerships, and the other four of which are: (1) continuity of life, (2) centralization of management, (3) liability for corporate debts limited to corporate property, and (4) free transferability of interests. The regulations provide that an association is treated as a corporation (rather than a partnership) for Federal income tax purposes if it has more corporate than non-corporate characteristics. The effect of the regulations generally is to classify an entity as a partnership if it lacks any two of these four corporate characteristics, without further inquiry as to how strong or weak a particular characteristic is or how the evaluation of the factors might affect overall resemblance. . . .

REASONS FOR CHANGE

The recent proliferation of publicly traded partnerships has come to the committee's attention. The growth in such partnerships has caused concern about long-term erosion of the corporate tax base. To the extent that activities would otherwise be conducted in corporate form, and earnings would be subject to two levels of tax (at the corporate and shareholder levels), the growth of publicly traded partnerships engaged in such activities tends to jeopardize the corporate tax base.

The problem is exacerbated by changes in the Tax Reform Act of 1986 that make conduit entities more attractive as vehicles for business activity than corporations. For example, under the 1986 Act, the maximum regular corporate tax rate is higher than the maximum individual tax rate. Thus, in addition to the fact that corporate earnings bear a second level of tax when distributed, retained earnings are generally taxed at a higher rate than amounts directly earned by an individual. In addition, by increasing the tax rate on capital gains and making that rate generally equivalent to the rate on ordinary income, the Act reduced an investor's incentive to realize income through sales of appreciated stock rather than in the form of current income.

Further, the 1986 Act generally imposed a corporate level tax on certain liquidating sales and distributions that were not taxed under prior law. Appreciation in corporate assets is thus now subject to a corporate level tax on the ultimate disposition of the business. The 1986 Act also included a new corporate minimum tax regime that includes as a preference item a portion of the excess of the income that is reported for financial purposes over the amount of corporate alternative minimum taxable income.

These changes reflect an intent to preserve the corporate level tax.[7] The committee is concerned that the intent of these changes is being circumvented by the growth of publicly traded partnerships that are taking advantage of an unintended opportunity for disincorporation and elective integration of the corporate and shareholder levels of tax.

The committee believes that, in important respects, publicly traded partnerships resemble corporations. Publicly traded partnerships resemble publicly traded corporations in their business functions and in the way their interests are marketed, and limited partners as a practical matter resemble corporate shareholders in that they have limited liability, may freely transfer their interests, generally do not participate in management, and expect continuity of life of the entity for the duration of the conduct of its business enterprise. Consequently, the committee believes that these types of entities and their holders generally should be treated similarly for tax purposes.

The committee is also concerned that the availability of publicly traded partnerships as an alternative to corporations creates an unintended unfair competitive advantage for certain types of businesses. Mature businesses with a steady cash flow, that can be marketed effectively as public partnerships because of the tax-advantaged yield, are unfairly favored over start-up companies or those with high capital expenditures, which cannot take advantage of the publicly traded partnership structure. Favoring one type of business investment over another creates new economic inefficiencies of the type that the 1986 Act was designed to reduce.

In certain circumstances, however, the committee believes that the tax-created competitive advantage of publicly traded partnerships may be less significant. If the publicly traded partnership's income

7. For example, in repealing the *General Utilities* rule (which had permitted liquidating distributions free of tax to the distributing corporation), it was Congress' express intent to prevent the corporate tax from being undermined. See H.R. 3838, as reported by the House Committee on Ways and Means on December 7, 1985, sec. 331, and H. Rep. 99-426, p. 282.

is from sources that are commonly considered to be passive investments, then there is less reason to treat the publicly traded partnership as a corporation, either because investors could earn such income directly (e.g., interest income), or because it is already subject to corporate-level tax (in the case of dividends). Therefore, under the bill, an exception is provided to the treatment of publicly traded partnerships as corporations in the case of partnerships whose income is principally from passive-type investments.

Further, certain types of natural resources and rental real estate activities have commonly or typically been conducted in partnership form, and the committee considers that disruption of present practices in such activities is currently inadvisable due to general economic conditions in these industries. . . .

The provision affects partnerships whose interests are publicly traded, or in which a market is effectively made. The committee believes it is appropriate to classify partnerships as corporations if interests in the partnership are publicly traded or a market is effectively made in them for several reasons.

Historically, free transferability of interests has been one of several factors that have been considered important in entity classification. As a practical matter, publicly traded partnerships have many or most of the attributes of corporations, and are accessing capital markets in a manner similar to that traditionally performed by corporations. Further, because of the trading in interests, these partnerships present unique administrative difficulties and enforcement concerns if the tax law relating to partnerships is applied to them. The partnership tax rules under present law contemplate an entity in which the identity of the investors is known and transfers of interests are easily identifiable, and public trading in partnership interests does not conform to this model.

Thus, the committee concluded that public trading involves a degree of lack of identity of the investor with the entity that particularly justifies separate taxation of the entity, rather than partnership conduit treatment. . . .

The provision in the bill addresses the concerns of the committee by treating certain publicly traded partnerships as corporations.

EXPLANATION OF PROVISION

Under the provision, publicly traded partnerships are treated as corporations for Federal income tax purposes. An exception is provided for certain partnerships, 90 percent or more of whose gross income is passive-type income (as defined for purposes of the provision).

PASSIVE-TYPE INCOME

Passive-type income, for purposes of the provision, is defined as certain interest, dividends, real property rents, gains from the sale or other disposition of real property, and income and gains from certain natural resources activities. Also treated as passive-type income is any gain from the sale or disposition of a capital asset or property described in sec. 1231(b) that is held for the production of income that is treated as passive-type income (e.g., typical commodity pools). . . .

The definition of passive-type income for purposes of this provision is not coextensive with existing statutory categories of passive income (e.g., the passive loss rule or the S corporation rules), but rather, is specific to the purposes of this provision.

In general, the purpose of distinguishing between passive-type income and other income is to distinguish those partnerships that are engaged in activities commonly considered as essentially no more than investments, and those activities more typically conducted in corporate form that are in the nature of active business activities. In the former case, the rationale for imposing an additional corporate-level tax on investments in publicly traded partnership form is less compelling, because purchasers of such partnership interests could in most cases independently acquire such investments (or the income has already been subject to corporate-level tax, in the case of dividends). Where the activity of the partnership does not fall into the category of generating passive-type income, however, it is less likely that direct interests in the activity would be available to investors; rather, it is more likely that such activities would be conducted in corporate form and would therefore be subject to corporate level tax before profits reached the hands of investors. In the case of other types of activities treated under the provision as giving rise to passive-type income (i.e., those where the provision more broadly defines passive-type income), the rationale relates to the traditional conduct of such activities in partnership form, and the consequent reluctance to impose entity-level tax in such circumstances. . . .

INADVERTENT TERMINATIONS

The bill provides relief from classification as a corporation for tax purposes, where a partnership inadvertently fails to meet the requirement that 90 percent of its gross income be passive-type income. Under this relief provision, if (1) the Secretary determines that the failure was inadvertent, (2) the partnership takes steps within a reasonable time to meet the 90 percent requirement, and (3) the partnership and each holder of an interest in the partnership during the failure period agree to make adjustments determined by the Secretary, then the partnership will be treated as continuing to meet the 90 percent requirement during the failure period. A reasonable time, for this purpose, would be one year, unless otherwise determined in regulations.

PUBLICLY TRADED PARTNERSHIPS

Publicly traded partnerships are defined for purposes of the provision as partnerships whose interests are (1) traded on an established securities market, or (2) offered with the expectation that there will be a secondary market for such interests, or (3) readily tradeable in a secondary market (or the substantial equivalent thereof).*

For this purpose, an established securities market includes any national securities exchange registered under the Securities Exchange Act of 1934 or exempted from registration because of the limited volume of transactions, and any local exchange. It also includes any over the counter market. An over the counter market is characterized by an interdealer quotation system which regularly disseminates quotations of obligations by identified brokers or dealers, by electronic means or otherwise. . . .

An interest is treated as readily tradeable on a secondary market (or the substantial equivalent thereof) if the interest is regularly quoted by brokers or dealers making a market in the interest. (See Treas. Reg. section 1.453-3(d)(3).) Thus, for example, an interest is readily tradeable in a secondary market where the interest is traded on a market essentially equivalent to an over the counter market, or where the holder has a readily available, regular and ongoing opportunity to sell or exchange his interest.

A partner's ability to trade the interest, without more, will not cause the interest to be treated as readily tradeable, nor will occasional sales of interests in the partnership, the terms of which are not widely publicized, indicate the existence of a secondary market.

The existence of a buy-sell agreement among the partners, without more, will not cause a partnership to be treated as publicly traded. Nor will the occasional and irregular repurchase or redemption by the partnership, or acquisition by the general partner, of interests in the partnership, cause the partnership to be considered as publicly traded under the provision. A regular plan of redemptions or repurchases, or similar acquisitions of interests in the partnership such that holders of interests have readily available opportunities to dispose of their interests, that is essentially equivalent to a secondary

---

*As enacted, §7704 treats partnerships as "publicly traded" only if their interests are (1) traded on an established securities market or (2) readily tradeable in a secondary market. See §7704(b). — Ed.

market, indicates that the interests are readily tradeable on what is the substantial equivalent of a secondary market. . . .

TREATMENT AS A CORPORATION

The bill provides that, in the case of a partnership that is treated as a corporation under this provision, the partnership is treated as contributing all of its assets (subject to all of its liabilities) to a newly formed corporation in exchange for all of the corporation's stock. The stock of the corporation is treated as distributed to the corporation in complete liquidation of the partnership. In general, the tax consequences to the partnership, the corporation, and the distributee holders of interests in the partnership who become shareholders in the new corporation are governed by secs. 351 (permitting tax-free contributions to corporations that are controlled immediately after the contribution transaction), 731 and 732 (governing the treatment of liquidating distributions from partnerships). Rules applicable to recognition of income upon recapture of tax benefits also apply.

Income from publicly traded partnerships that are classified as corporations under the bill generally is treated as dividend income. Regardless of whether such income is characterized as income or gain (e.g., depending on whether it represents a distribution of earnings and profits under section 301), income from such entities is properly treated as portfolio income for purposes of the passive loss rule. . . .

NOTES

1. See Banoff, Avoiding Publicly Traded Partnership Status: Living and Dying with Notice 88-75, 66 Taxes 561 (1988); Haney and Holmes, Publicly Traded Partnerships After the Revenue Act of 1987, 66 Taxes 331 (1988); Loffman, Presant, and Lipton, The Impact of Notice 88-75 Concerning Publicly Traded Partnerships, Tax Notes, August 15, 1988, p. 747.

2. The 1987 Act also specified the treatment of publicly traded partnerships under the passive activity loss rules of §469. It provides that net income from publicly traded partnerships is not treated as passive income under the passive loss rules, but instead is treated as portfolio income. Losses from one publicly traded partnership may not be used to offset income from another publicly traded partnership. See §469(k).

REVENUE RULING 70-101
1970-1 C.B. 278

The Internal Revenue Service has been requested to state its position with respect to the classification of professional service organizations formed under state professional association or corporation statutes.

In the light of recent decisions of the Federal courts, the Service generally will treat organizations of doctors, lawyers, and other professional people organized under state professional association acts as corporations for tax purposes.

The Government has not applied for certiorari in the cases of United States v. O'Neill, 410 F.2d 888 (6th Cir. 1969); Kurzner v. United States, 413 F.2d 97 (5th Cir. 1969); Empey v. United States, 406 F.2d 157 (10th Cir. 1969); and Holder v. United States, 289 F. Supp. 160 (1968), *affirmed, per curiam,* 412 F.2d 1189 (5th Cir. 1969). Also the Government will not further press its appeals in Wallace v. United States, 294 F. Supp. 1225 (1968). Furthermore, no appeal will be prosecuted in any other pending cases decided adversely to the Government on the same issue involving similar facts and all similar cases now in litigation or under audit are being reviewed to see if they should be conceded. However, the Government reserves the right to conclude differently in any cases reflecting special circumstances. . . . [Citations omitted.]

It is held that a professional service organization will be treated as a corporation in any case arising in the same state as, and having facts similar to, the cases cited above.

A professional service organization that is organized and operated under the statutes listed below for each state will also be treated as a corporation except in those instances in which it is illegal, as a matter of state law, for the professional service organization claiming corporate status to engage in the practice of the particular profession that it is organized to engage in. [Listing of state statutes omitted.]

Furthermore, if a corporation is organized and operated as a professional service business under the general business corporation statute of its state, it will generally be recognized as a corporation.

In addition, a professional service organization that meets the requirements for corporate classification under section 301.7701-2 of the Procedure and Administration Regulations, exclusive of the 1965 amendments (section 301.7701-2(h) of the regulations) made thereto, in its organization and operation will be classified as a corporation. . . .

A professional service organization must be both organized and operated as a corporation to be classified as such. See Jerome J. Roubik and Joan M. Roubik, et al., v. Commissioner, 53 T.C. 365, No. 36 (1969).*

Notwithstanding that a professional service organization is, in accordance with this Revenue Ruling, classified as a corporation, if it reported income as a partnership in accordance with then existing regulations for taxable years ending prior to the issuance of this Revenue Ruling, March 2, 1970, it will not be required to report income as a corporation for such prior years. Also, a professional service organization that qualifies as a corporation under this Revenue Ruling and is presently reporting income as a partnership will be permitted to continue reporting such income as a partnership for any taxable year ending on or before December 31, 1970.

The foregoing position relates solely to the issue of the tax classification of professional service organizations. Professional service organizations classifiable as corporations are subject to audit to the same extent as other corporations, and nothing contained herein is to be construed as waiving the assertion of any issues against such organizations other than that of classification.

NOTES

1. The enactment in 1962 of the Self-Employed Individuals Retirement Act reduced — but did not eliminate — the attractiveness of tax benefits that are available only to "employees." See, for example, §§101(b), 105. Physicians and lawyers, who sometimes cannot do business in corporate form, have sought to become eligible for such benefits by forming and becoming the employees of professional service "associations." In 1965 The Service promulgated regulations that were designed to prevent organizations of this type from qualifying as corporations for federal tax purposes. These regulations spawned litigation summarized in Rev. Rul. 70-101, supra, with the government's losing consistently on the ground that the regulations were arbitrary and without statutory support.

The regulations were eventually revoked. T.D. 7515, 1977-2 C.B. 482. Rev. Rul. 77-31, 1977-1 C.B. 409, held that a professional service organization legally organized and operated in a state listed in Rev. Rul. 70-101 (as amplified and modified on several occasions) need not be tested by the criteria prescribed in the §7701 regulations. Cf. Rev. Rul. 75-19, 1975-1 C.B. 382 (Uniform Partnership Act partnership organized among four subsidiaries of a single parent corporation treated as a partnership where the subsidiaries existed for other business purposes and there was no tax avoidance purpose).

---

*In *Roubik* the Commissioner successfully contended that the income of a professional service corporation was taxable directly to the shareholders as those who had earned it, applying the assignment of income doctrine. — ED.

2. In 1982, as part of TEFRA, Congress eliminated the requirement that lawyers, doctors, and other professionals use a corporate vehicle to obtain the substantial "qualified plan" retirement and other tax benefits that had been unavailable to the unincorporated under prior law. See Joint Committee of Taxation Staff Summary, Aug. 24, 1982, p. 66.

3. Before the 1986 Act, "personal service corporations" selected a taxable year just as other corporations did, that is, by adopting a year on the corporation's first federal income tax return. The 1986 Act restricted this deferral opportunity by adding §441(i) to require all personal service corporations to be on the calendar year, "unless the corporation establishes, to the satisfaction of the Secretary, a business purpose for having a different period . . . [and] deferral of income to shareholders shall not be treated as a business purpose."

4. Congress enacted §269A in 1982, overruling Keller v. Commissioner, 77 T.C. 1104 (1981), *aff'd*, 723 F.2d 58 (10th Cir. 1983). According to the August 24, 1982, Joint Committee of Taxation Staff Summary, at p. 69,

> Under the Act, if a corporation, the principal activity of which is the performance of personal services substantially all of which are performed by employee-owners for or on behalf of another corporation, partnership, or entity (including related parties), is availed of for the principal purpose of evasion or avoidance of Federal income tax by securing for any employee-owner significant tax benefits which would not otherwise be available, then the Secretary may allocate all income, as well as such deductions, credits, exclusions, etc., as may be allowable, between or among the corporation and employee-owners involved. For this purpose, an employee-owner is defined as any employee who owns (after application of the attribution rules under section 318) more than 10 percent of the outstanding stock of the corporation. . . .

5. See Sargent v. Commissioner, 93 T.C. No. 48 (1989); and Sheppard, Sargent v. Commissioner: A Renewed Attack on Personal Service Corporations, Tax Notes, December 4, 1989, p. 1161.

In issuing its proposed regulations under §269A, the Treasury published the following:

DEPARTMENT OF THE TREASURY, INTRODUCTION: PROPOSED REGULATIONS UNDER §269A
48 Fed. Reg. 13,438 (March 31, 1983), 1983-1 C.B. 1052

BACKGROUND

Section 269A was added to the Internal Revenue Code by the Tax Equity and Fiscal Responsibility Act of 1982. Section 269A permits the Secretary to allocate all income, deductions, credits, exclusions, and other tax benefits between a personal service corporation and its employee-owners in order to prevent the avoidance or evasion of Federal income taxes or to reflect clearly the income of the personal service corporation or any of its employee-owners if substantially all of the services are performed for one other entity and if the principal purpose for forming, or availing of, the corporation is the avoidance or evasion of Federal income taxes. Avoidance or evasion of Federal income taxes may be either the reduction of income of an employee-owner through the use of the corporation or the securing of one or more tax benefits that would not otherwise be available. These regulations define benefits that would not otherwise be available as benefits that would not be available to a taxpayer providing services as an unincorporated individual.

These regulations also provide a safe-harbor, excluding from the application of section 269A those situations in which the Federal income tax liability of each employee-owner is reduced by not more than 10 percent or $2,500, whichever is less.

Prior to "parity" between qualified retirement plans of corporations and those of noncorporate employers (effective generally for taxable years beginning after December 31, 1983), an employee-owner can make larger contributions to a corporate qualified retirement plan than could have been made to a Keough or H.R. 10 plan had the corporation not been in existence. For corporations in existence before the date of enactment of TEFRA (September 3, 1982), qualified retirement plans available to corporations generally will not be taken into account for purposes of determining the corporation's principal purpose. Thus, a corporation created principally to take advantage of the higher contributions to corporate plans may still have an impermissible purpose if its principal purpose (other than qualified retirement plan benefit) was to reduce income or secure one or more tax benefits. If a corporation is found to have an impermissible principal purpose, the contributions to the qualified retirement plan will neither be reallocated to the employee-owner nor reduced as a result of reallocation of other income to the employee-owner. For corporations formed after the date of enactment of TEFRA, this protection is not available for contributions or benefits that would not have been available to the employee-owner absent the corporation. In that case, contributions to a qualified retirement plan will be considered in determining the corporation's principal purpose and may be reallocated or reduced through application of section 269A.

Section 269A does not override other sections of the Code or existing tax law principles. Nothing in these regulations, including the safe-harbor provision, precludes application of any other Code section (e.g., sections 61 or 482) or principle of tax law (e.g., assignment of income doctrine) to reallocate or reapportion income, deductions, credits or any other tax benefits if such reallocation is necessary to reflect the true earner of the income.

The regulations provide guidance regarding certain specific section 269A issues determined to be of major interest. No inference should be drawn regarding issues not included in the regulations, or as to why some issues, and not others, are addressed. . . .

II.　IGNORING THE CORPORATION

A.　IN GENERAL

JACKSON v. COMMISSIONER
293 F.2d 289 (2d Cir. 1956)

Before Frank, Medina and Waterman, Circuit Judges.

FRANK, Circuit Judge. The basic question here is whether certain corporations should be disregarded with the result that transactions carried out by them should be treated as if the corporations did not exist and as if the transactions had been those of the taxpayers themselves. . . .

Taxpayers and two others, Cohn and Harris, each owned one-third of the stock of Empire Industries, Inc. (hereafter Empire). Empire owned numerous other corporations whose acquisition had been financed by loans personally guaranteed by Mr. Jackson. Attempts by Jackson to reduce this large contingent liability engendered such friction between Jackson and Cohn that it was decided to form a new corporation, Lewis of Delaware (hereafter Lewis), to which would be transferred one-third of the assets of Empire in exchange for all the capital stock of Lewis. Lewis was to be either a wholly owned subsidiary controlled and managed by Jackson or a separate corporation owned, as well as controlled, by Jackson. The latter alternative was eventually chosen, and the taxpayers proceeded to exchange their one-third interest for all of the Lewis stock by a series of transactions involving two corporations, Dumelle Corporation (Dumelle) and Belgrade Properties, Inc. (Belgrade), wholly owned and controlled by taxpayers. Taxpayers first created Dumelle and then transferred their one-third interest in Empire to Dumelle in exchange for all of Dumelle's capital stock. Then a pre-existing corporation, Belgrade, which was wholly owned by Mrs. Jackson and had never conducted any business, purchased the Empire stock from Dumelle in exchange for $1,000 in cash and $469,000 in interest-bearing notes payable over 2 years. The final step in the overall transaction was an exchange between Belgrade and Empire — Belgrade receiving the entire capital stock of Lewis in exchange for the one-third interest in Empire which Belgrade then held. The activity of the two corporations in question was of a very limited nature. Dumelle's only activity was the receipt of Empire stock from the taxpayers and the sale of the same stock to Belgrade. Belgrade's only activity was to purchase the Empire stock from Dumelle, exchange it for Lewis stock with Empire, and to hold the Lewis stock.

The taxpayers had this purpose in creating the Dumelle Company and using the Belgrade Company: to insure that Mrs. Jackson, as owner of all the stock of Belgrade, should have, as her sole property, free of any claim of Jackson's creditors, any future increment in the value of the stock of the Lewis Company over and above its fair market value in April 1949 (that value as of that date being $1,000 more than the face amount of the note for $469,000 given by Belgrade to Dumelle). Although Belgrade was to and did become the owner of the Lewis stock, it was intended not to and did not exercise any functions with respect to the management of Lewis.

Unquestionably, the taxpayers had a personal business purpose other than (or in addition to) that of avoiding taxation. Consequently, if a taxpayer's personal purpose, in creating a corporation, controls, the Tax Court erred. But we read the pertinent Supreme Court decisions, and our own decisions interpreting the Supreme Court's views, as follows: A corporation may not be disregarded in respect of taxation if, inter alia, a bona fide intention in creating it was that the corporation itself should have some real substantial business function,[1] or if it actually engages in business; on the other hand, the corporation may be disregarded, in the absence of such an intention or activity. The intended or actual business functioning of the corporation itself, not the taxpayer's aim to be accomplished via the corporation, is the test.[2]

Reviewing previous decisions, including Higgins v. Smith, 308 U.S. 473, 477-478, the Supreme Court in Moline Properties v. Commissioner, 319 U.S. 436, 439, said: "The doctrine of corporate entity fills a useful purpose in business life. Whether the purpose be to gain an advantage under the law of the state of incorporation or to avoid

1. When there is such an intention, but the intended business functioning does not become effective the corporation is not to be disregarded in the interval before it becomes evident that the corporation will not so function. See National Investors Corp. v. Hoey, 2 Cir., 144 F.2d 466.

2. A natural person may be used to receive income which in fact is another's. So, too, a corporation, although for other purposes a jural entity distinct from its stockholders, may be used as a mere dummy to receive income which in fact is the income of the stockholders or of someone else; in such circumstances, the company will be disregarded.

or to comply with the demands of creditors or to serve the creator's personal or undisclosed convenience, so long as that purpose is the equivalent of business activity or is followed by the carrying on of business by the corporation, the corporation remains a separate taxable entity." In National Investors Corp. v. Hoey, 2 Cir., 144 F.2d 466, 468, a parent company wished to combine itself and several subsidiaries into a single corporation; as a preliminary step, it transferred the stock of the subsidiaries to another corporation which had no other assets or liabilities; during the time when the plan of consolidation was being formulated and submitted to the stockholders of the parent, the new company engaged in no activity except to receive and hold the stock of the subsidiary companies; the plan of consolidation was rejected by the stockholders of the parent company, and the new company was subsequently liquidated. We ruled that the corporate entity of the new company could not be disregarded up to the time when the stockholders rejected the plan of consolidation, because its use, meanwhile, as a means of achieving the consolidation and holding the transferred securities, "was a 'business' activity." We said that *Moline Properties* "merely declares that to be a separate jural person for purposes of taxation, a corporation must engage in some industrial, commercial, or other activity besides avoiding taxation: in other words, that the term 'corporation' will be interpreted to mean a corporation which does some 'business' in the ordinary meaning. . . ." In Paymer v. Commissioner, 2 Cir., 150 F.2d 334, 337, a corporation was formed with the sole intention of serving "as a blind to deter the creditors of one of the partners" who had organized it. We said that it "was at all times but a passive dummy which did nothing but take and hold the title to the real estate conveyed to it. . . . It was but a sham, to be disregarded for tax purposes." We think the instant case comes within this *Paymer* ruling.[3]

Affirmed.

NOTE

For a review of case law on recognition of the corporate entity, see Britt v. United States, 431 F.2d 227 (5th Cir. 1970) (Wisdom, J.). Was Averill's corporate existence "disregarded" in Gregory v. Helvering, page 545 supra?

---

3. This conclusion is fortified by the fact that taxpayers' purpose would have been as well served if the Lewis shares had been transferred to Mrs. Jackson as her property in consideration of her giving the $470,000 note, or if they had been transferred to a trustee for Mrs. Jackson and the trustee had given the note.

We disagree with the Tax Court as to the following: We think it immaterial (1) that the transactions between the Jacksons, the Dumelle Company and the Belgrade Company were not "at arm's length," and (2) that there was no disclosure of those transactions to Harris and Cohn.

B. STRAW CORPORATIONS

KURTZ AND KOPP, TAXABILITY OF STRAW CORPORATIONS IN REAL ESTATE TRANSACTIONS*
22 Tax Law. 647 (1969)

One who holds record title as a nominee or agent for a beneficial owner of property is commonly referred to as a "straw." The tax consequences surrounding the use of corporate straws are in a sufficiently confused state to deter many from using them. In this article we will try to point out how this uncertainty developed, why it is unnecessary and how we believe straw corporations can be organized and handled to avoid any substantial doubt about their tax status.

REASONS FOR USING STRAWS IN REAL ESTATE

There are a number of non-tax reasons why it is frequently desirable to have title to property held by one other than the beneficial owner of the property. This practice is particularly useful where the property is real estate, primarily because of the title recording systems and financing practices unique to real estate. Some of the reasons for using a straw for real estate are:

1. To avoid mortgage liabilities. In some jurisdictions a straw is used in a mortgage transaction to limit the liability of the beneficial owner to the property.

2. To secure anonymity of ownership.

3. To simplify conveyancing. This is particularly advantageous where the property is beneficially owned by a relatively large group of individuals. In these circumstances, straw ownership permits leases or deeds to be executed by the straw rather than by each member of the large owning group and perhaps also by their spouses.

4. To avoid title complications occasioned by the death of an owner. Where beneficial owners are individuals, a death of one will cloud title until the administration of his estate.

While an individual may serve as a straw, an individual straw presents these problems:

1. He is not immortal and, therefore, while he avoids title delays on the death of a beneficial owner, his own death may cause problems.

2. Although he may protect the beneficial owner from contract liability, he may incur it himself. Therefore, an individual can only be a straw for a single piece of property, since any property of which he is record holder will be subject to claims. Moreover, he must be

*Copyright © 1969 by the American Bar Association. Reprinted by permission. — ED.

and remain impecunious. Bachelorhood is also desirable, otherwise marital difficulties can cause considerable title problems.

These problems are eliminated if the straw is a corporation. A corporation is immortal. Separate straws can be used for each piece of property, thereby insulating each property from the liabilities of others. A corporation can be kept impecunious. Its officers can execute all documents, and officers can easily be changed if necessary.

Tax Problems — Introduction

The use of corporate straws raises troublesome and confusing tax problems.[1] The confusion and doubts seem unwarranted as a policy matter and result more from historical development than careful analysis.

The courts appear to have approached the problem of taxing straw corporations in terms of whether the corporation should be disregarded or ignored for tax purposes on the one hand, or whether it has sufficient activities to constitute a taxable entity on the other, and if it has such activities to tax it on the income from the property to which it holds title. The question properly, it seems, is not whether there is or is not a corporation for tax purposes, but rather whether an admittedly existing corporation is taxable on the income from the property in question and this, in turn, involves a factual determination as to whether the corporation is the beneficial owner of the property or only serving as a nominal titleholder.

In deciding whether a straw is a taxable entity, the courts have sometimes discussed the problem in terms of whether the real owners of the property derive any advantage from using a corporation and, if they do, the conclusion that the corporation is an entity which is taxable on the income from the property is presumed to follow. This analysis may well lead to erroneous conclusions for again the real question is not whether the use of a corporation to hold title is advantageous to the owners — presumably it always is, otherwise they would not use this form — but rather whether the corporation beneficially owns the property.

In short, the approach in the straw corporation cases should not be directed toward a determination of whether or not a particular corporation should be disregarded for tax purposes but, rather, toward a factual determination of who owns the property in question, and then taxing the income from the property to the beneficial owner.

To put the question in perspective, the straw corporation may be compared with an individual straw. If title to real estate is put in

1. See generally, Watts, Tax Problem of Regard for the Corporate Entity, 20 N.Y.U. Inst. on Fed. Taxn. 867 (1962).

the name of an individual straw, there is no doubt that the real owner alone is taxable on the income from the property and not the straw. This result has nothing to do with the question whether the straw exists — he obviously does — or whether he might be paying taxes on some other income which he has, or whether he might, in fact, have income from fees which he charges for acting as a straw in this particular transaction, or whether the beneficial owner gains some non-tax advantage by using the straw. The only question is whether the straw is taxable on the income from the real estate, and this depends on whether the income is his.

Some courts have recognized the foregoing distinction. In United States v. Brager Building and Land Corp.,[2] the court held income from property taxable to a partnership where a corporation served as nominal titleholder. The court said:

> But it is going too far to say that if a taxpayer forms a corporation for his convenience, he is thereafter estopped from disclosing the true nature of the arrangement, whenever it is of advantage to the government to recognize only the corporate form. . . . In a number of these cases . . . under circumstances quite similar to those found in the case at bar, it has been held that when a corporation has been formed merely as an agency to hold title to real estate for the convenience of the owner, and has served this purpose with little or no independent activity on its part, the property and the income therefrom should be regarded as belonging to the stockholder.[3]

Unfortunately, not all courts have adopted this analysis. The reason they have not is perhaps best explained by a look at history.

HISTORICAL DEVELOPMENT

Although many cases dealing with straw corporations were decided prior to 1943, the logical starting point for any discussion of the subject is the Supreme Court's 1943 opinion in Moline Properties, Inc. v. Commissioner.[4] In that case, Moline Properties, Inc. sought to have its corporate existence ignored as merely fictitious for tax purposes and to have the gain on sales of real property titled in its name treated as the gain of its sole shareholder.

The facts in *Moline* were as follows: Moline Properties, Inc. was organized in 1928 at the suggestion of the second mortgagee of certain Florida realty owned by one Thompson, who was at all times Moline's sole stockholder and president. Under the mortgagee's plan, Thompson conveyed the property to the corporation, which assumed

2. 124 F.2d 349 (4th Cir. 1941).
3. Id. at p. 351.
4. 319 U.S. 436 (1943).

the outstanding mortgages on the property, in exchange for all but the qualifying shares of stock. Thompson then transferred the stock to a voting trustee appointed by the second mortgagee as security for an additional loan to himself.

From 1928 to 1933, the activities of the corporation consisted of the assumption of a certain obligation of Thompson to the original creditor, the defense of certain condemnation proceedings, and the institution of a suit to remove restrictions imposed on the property by a prior deed. The expenses of the suit were paid by Thompson. In 1933, the loan which occasioned the creation of the corporation was repaid through a refinancing, and control of the corporation was returned to Thompson. In 1934, the corporation leased a portion of the property for a rental of $1,000.

The refinanced mortgage debt was paid in 1936 by means of a sale of a portion of the property titled in the corporation. The remaining property titled in the corporation's name had been sold in three parcels, one each in 1934, 1935 and 1936, the proceeds being received by Thompson and deposited in his bank account.

The corporation had no activity after the sale of the last property in 1936 but was not dissolved. It kept no books and maintained no bank account during its existence, and owned no assets other than those referred to above. The sales made in 1934 and 1935 were reported on the corporation's income tax returns, a small loss being reported in 1934 and a gain of over $5,000 being reported for 1935. Subsequently, Thompson filed a claim for refund on the corporation's behalf for 1935, and sought to report the 1935 gain on his individual return. He reported the gain on the 1936 sale.

The Supreme Court held that the corporation could not be disregarded for tax purposes in this case, and set forth the following principle which has been stated over and over again in later cases:

> The doctrine of corporate entity fills a useful purpose in business life. Whether the purpose be to gain an advantage under the law of the state of incorporation or to avoid or to comply with the demands of creditors or to serve the creator's personal or undisclosed convenience, so long as that purpose is the equivalent of business activity or is followed by the carrying on of business by the corporation, the corporation remains a separate taxable entity.[5]

Applying the foregoing principle to the facts in the case, the Supreme Court said:

> The petitioner corporation was created by Thompson for his advantage and had a special function from its inception. At that time it was clearly not Thompson's alter ego and his exercise of control over it was negligible. It was then as much a separate entity as if

5. Id. at pp. 438-439.

its stock had been transferred outright to third persons. The argument is made by petitioner that the force of the rule requiring its separate treatment is avoided by the fact that Thompson was coerced into creating petitioner and was completely subservient to the creditors. But this merely serves to emphasize petitioner's separate existence. . . . Business necessity, i.e., pressure from creditors, made petitioner's creation advantageous to Thompson.[6]

Although the decision in this case may have been correct — after all Thompson had, for tax purposes, treated the corporation as the taxpayer by filing corporate returns showing all the income and expenses of the property and paying tax — the language of the opinion is at the root of the trouble in this area.

PROBLEMS WITH *MOLINE* APPROACH

Evidence of the difficulties stemming from *Moline* can be seen in cases such as Paymer v. Commissioner.[7] In that case, two parcels of income-producing real estate owned by two partners were transferred respectively to two newly organized corporations in order to prevent possible attachment of the real estate by creditors of one of the partners. The partners each received half of the stock of the grantee corporations. The corporate minutes expressly stated that the corporations received the property as mere titleholders and that the full beneficial ownership and control and rights to profits remained in the two partners. The corporation had no further meetings and no office or bank accounts.

Six years after incorporation, one of the corporations (Raymep) obtained a loan from an insurance company and, as part security for the loan, executed an assignment of all of the lessor's rights in two leases on the property and expressly covenanted that it was the sole lessor.

The second corporation (Westrich) never had any activity after it took title to the real estate.

The Court of Appeals for the Second Circuit held that the second corporation was a passive dummy that could be disregarded for tax purposes but that Raymep, which engaged in the financing transaction, was not a mere dummy and should not be disregarded for tax purposes.

The court said:

We think that Raymep was active enough to justify holding that it did engage in business in 1938. The absence of books, records and offices and the failure to hold corporate meetings are not

6. Id. at pp. 439-440.
7. 150 F.2d 334 (2d Cir. 1945).

decisive on that question. Though Raymep was organized solely to deter creditors of one of the partners, it apparently was impossible or impracticable to use it solely for that purpose when it became necessary or desirable to secure the above mentioned loan in a substantial amount. . . .

Westrich, however, was at all times but a passive dummy which did nothing but take and hold the title to the real estate conveyed to it. It served no business purpose in connection with the property and was intended to serve only as a blind to deter the creditors of one of the partners.[8]

The *Paymer* court did not face the question of the relevance of the corporate resolutions indicating that the corporations were acting as nominal title holders. The activity of Raymep does not seem inconsistent with its role as a straw. Being the record title holder, it might well be required to execute financing documents in that capacity. The business activity test set forth in *Paymer* which is derived from *Moline* seems entirely inappropriate where the corporate records clearly indicate from the outset that the corporation is a straw and its subsequent activities are consistent with its role as a straw. To repeat an earlier example, we would not tax an individual straw on the income from property to which he held record title if he happened to execute a mortgage agreement on the property. The question properly is not whether the corporation has activity or is carrying on a business, but whether its activities or its business are those of a beneficial owner or the activities or business of a straw or agent.

The Agency Approach

Even though a number of cases have adopted an interpretation of *Moline* similar to that of the *Paymer* court,[9] another group of cases has developed the test suggested, that is, whether the corporation, admittedly in existence and having activity is acting on its own behalf or as an agent for the beneficial owners.

The foundation for the agency approach to the problem actually goes all the way back to *Moline*. In that case the Supreme Court, while setting forth the test discussed above, pointed out that there was no contract of agency nor the usual incidents of an agency relationship in the case before it. This language naturally suggested that the Court might not have taxed the income to the corporation had it been shown that the corporation was acting pursuant to an agency contract with its shareholder.

A few years after *Moline*, in National Carbide Corporation v.

---

8. Id. at pp. 336-337.
9. See, e.g., Commissioner v. State-Adams Corporation, 283 F.2d 395 (2d Cir. 1960); Tomlinson v. Miles, 316 F.2d 710 (5th Cir. 1963).

Commissioner of Internal Revenue,[10] the Supreme Court had the
opportunity to consider a case firmly grounded on the agency theory.
In that case, a parent corporation had entered into a contract with
three of its subsidiaries under which the parent agreed to make available to the subsidiaries certain assets, executive management and
working capital in return for which the subsidiaries agreed to turn
over to the parent all of their profits from operations except a nominal amount. The Supreme Court held that ownership and control
of a subsidiary does not constitute an agency relationship for tax
purposes, that the contractual arrangements were entirely consistent
with a corporation – sole stockholder relationship whether or not any
agency relationship existed (and with other relationships as well), and
that the subsidiaries were all taxable on their entire net income.

The Court went on to state, however:

> What we have said does not foreclose a true corporate agent or
> trustee from handling the property and income of its owner-prin-
> cipal without being taxable therefor. . . . If the corporation is a
> true agent, its relations with its principal must not be dependent
> upon the fact that it is owned by the principal, if such is the case.
> Its business purpose must be the carrying on of the normal duties
> of an agent.[11]

The dicta in *Moline* and *National Carbide* have been followed in
several instances by the Tax Court. In two cases decided after *Moline*,
but before *National Carbide*, the Tax Court held against the Commissioner on the theory that the title holding corporation was an
"agent" of the beneficial owner and was, therefore, not taxable on
the income received from the property held in its name. First, in
Worth Steamship Corporation,[12] the Tax Court held that a corporation with record title to a steamship and an agreement to operate
the ship for a joint venture owning the vessel was not taxable on the
net income earned from operating the ship. The fees paid to the
"agent" corporation for managing the ship's operations were reported by the corporation as its income and a tax paid thereon. In
addition to a complete set of documents clearly stating that the corporation was merely holding title for the beneficial owners rather
than for itself, the record in this case indicated that the beneficial
owners of the vessel were not all shareholders of the title-holding
corporation. One of the three joint venturers held no stock in the
corporation.[13] And, in the other case — Industrial Union Oil

10. 336 U.S. 422 (1949).
11. Id. at p. 437.
12. 7 T.C. 654 (1946).
13. The separation of ownership of the real estate and the stock of the nominal
titleholder was also considered an important factor in K-C Land Company, Inc., 19
T.C.M. 183 (1960), where the Tax Court held that a titleholding corporation was
not taxable on income with respect to property titled in its name.

Company[14] — the Tax Court held that a corporation which held oil leases in its name was not taxable on the income from such leases because it was specifically provided by appropriate corporate resolution that all property standing in the name of the corporation would not belong to the corporation but would be held by it as agent or trustee for the beneficial owner. In holding for the taxpayer in *Industial Union Oil*, the court stated:

> The respondent relies on Moline Properties, Inc. v. Commissioner, which lays down the rule, bottomed on corporate entity, that where a corporation is engaged in business it has a "tax identity" distinct from its stockholder and gain to the corporation cannot be treated as gain to the stockholder. In the *Moline* case "there was no actual contract of agency nor the usual incidents of agency relationship" and the Court said that "the mere fact of the existence of a corporation with one or several stockholders, regardless of the corporation's business activities, does not make the corporation the agent of its stockholders."
>
> Undoubtedly, the rule laid down in the *Moline* case is thoroughly sound, but in our judgment it has no application under the facts of the case before us. . . .
>
> The Petitioner does not contend that it was not a distinct corporate entity nor does it seek to have its corporate entity disregarded. It stands on the perfectly simple proposition that the property involved was in fact the property of Miller and the income therefrom taxable to him.[15]

The "agency" approach to the straw corporation problem is to be found continuing in the Tax Court in Caswal Corporation.[16] In that case the Tax Court held that a corporation was not taxable on the rental income from real property titled in its name because it was acting only in a fiduciary capacity (in this case called a "trustee" rather than an "agent" because the documents in the case described the corporation as "trustee" rather than "agent" for the beneficial owners) in collecting and remitting net rentals to its shareholders, the beneficial owners of the property.

The court's approach to the problem was as follows:

> We need not say here . . . that the separate entity of petitioner is to be disregarded. . . . We shall assume that it was an existing and functioning corporation which was operated for the purpose of acting as fiduciary. As such, its existence separate from that of stockholders or trust beneficiaries is to be respected. But neither do we feel free to disregard the trust instrument or its effect upon the relationship of the parties. . . .

14. T.C.M. 879 (1946).
15. Id. at pp. 881-882.
16. 19 T.C.M. 757 (1960).

That petitioner did not actually engage in any business in its own right also seems clear. The mere collection and transmittal of the rents, with such incidental activities as negotiating with tenants and keeping the property in repair, do not on this record justify dignifying petitioner's operations as engaging in business, any more than would have been the case if an unrelated corporate fiduciary had done the same. . . . Petitioner's business, if any, was acting as fiduciary, not owning and operating an enterprise.[17]

PROBLEMS OF PROOF

There are, of course, considerable difficulties facing courts in applying the agency approach in certain situations. These difficulties involve making factual determinations as to whether activities performed by a corporation are performed in the capacity of beneficial owner or in the capacity of agent for the beneficial owner. Closely held corporations are controlled directly by their shareholders, just as agents are controlled by their principals. Therefore, where the shareholders of a closely held corporation argue that the corporation is in reality their agent, it is difficult to establish an agency relationship since there are few meaningful criteria available for determining the capacity in which the corporation really is acting. Many facts relied upon in support of an agency relationship are also consistent with a shareholder-corporation relationship.

The proof questions, however, only seem difficult where the stock of the corporation purporting to act as an agent as to property is owned by the beneficial owners of the property. There is little difficulty in making this determination where the beneficial owners have no interest in the stock of the corporation. That obviously is the reason that we have no problem in deciding that stock owned in street name is not owned by the brokerage firm; the beneficial owners typically have no interest in the brokerage firm and therefore the relationships are clear. This is true notwithstanding the fact that the brokerage firm may perform substantial acts in its name in connection with the stock, such as collecting dividends, voting, or selling all of part of the stock.

The ambiguous nature of the shareholder-owner-corporation-agent relationships, it is submitted, is at the heart of the problem and is the underlying reason for the courts' decisions in the cases like *Moline* and *Paymer*. A careful reading of the *Moline* case indicates that the court was not denying that a corporation could be a straw. It was more likely concerned, however, with the substantial problems of proof that would ensue if it adopted fairly liberal views as to when

17. Id. at p. 763.

a corporation could be considered the agent for its shareholders. It seems to have adopted what amounts to a presumption that a corporation is the beneficial owner of property titled in its name, as against the claimed beneficial ownership of its shareholders. Some other courts, unfortunately, have misinterpreted *Moline* and seem to have made the presumption conclusive except where the corporation did absolutely nothing.

It should be pointed out, in all fairness, that most of the cases were apparently decided properly on their facts.[18] It seems appropriate that the taxpayer be faced with a substantial burden of proof where he claims that a corporation is not the beneficial owner of property titled in its name. But the burden of proof should not be insurmountable — the presumption should not be conclusive against him. Where the corporate documents are clear from the beginning that the corporation is an agent and where its activities are consistent with its agent's role, the agency should be recognized. Moreover, an agent may well have activities in connection with the property, such as signing documents incident to its role as title holder.

The burden of proof problem could be more easily met by individuals wishing to use corporate straws if they used corporate straws in which they had no interest as shareholders. If the agency cases are correct, and it is believed they are, and if *Moline* and the cases following it are essentially failure of proof cases, as it is believed they are, then there is nothing in any of the cases which would imply that a corporation would be taxed with the income of property titled in its name where it is clearly acting as a straw.

Such a corporation would not be claiming that it did not exist for tax purposes or that it was a dummy, but rather that it was an existing corporation in the business of acting as a straw or agent, and, in fact, it would probably have income from fees charged for this service.

SUMMARY AND RECOMMENDATIONS

To summarize, the basic problem of straw corporations should not be a theoretical one of whether a corporation should be ignored for tax purposes or whether it should be viewed as a taxable entity where the shareholder-owners chose to use the corporate form to hold legal title for non-tax reasons, but rather should be one of proof of who owns the property. However, the courts — witness the recent

18. In Commissioner v. State-Adams Corporation, 283 F.2d 395 (2nd Cir. 1960), for example, there were no specific corporate documents to indicate that the corporation was to act in the capacity of agent rather than beneficial owner. On the other hand, in Tomlinson v. Miles, 316 F.2d 710 (5th Cir. 1963), there were appropriate corporate documents but the corporation's activities were more consistent with the role of beneficial owner than of agent.

Miles case[19] — still speak in terms of the shareholder's personal reasons for forming the corporation, the business activities of the corporation and whether the corporation should be disregarded or not for tax purposes. Therefore, it remains difficult for a taxpayer to feel at all secure in using a straw corporation to hold title to real estate where, as in the normal case, the corporation is admittedly formed for the personal convenience of the shareholder, and will in fact engage in business activities involving the execution of various documents for acquisitions, mortgages, leases, sales, etc.

The situation is, of course, particularly risky where the taxpayer is striving to bring his case under the *Moline* rule of having the straw corporation disregarded for tax purposes. Any corporate activity such as obtaining a loan — as in *Paymer* — can cause a court to hold that the corporation cannot be ignored for tax purposes. Moreover, any one or a combination of maintaining a corporate bank account, using corporate funds to acquire and maintain the property, executing a substantial number of leases, mortgages, sales, etc., in its name, or failing to have documentary evidence that the corporation is acting only as a nominal titleholder for the real owners, may well cause a court to treat a corporation as a separate entity for tax purposes. It is believed, however, that a taxpayer should be relatively safe in having the income or loss from real estate taxed directly to him where he transfers record title to a corporation formed to act as an *agent* for himself, the beneficial owner.

In the "agency" approach, the importance of carefully drawn documents clearly describing the limited purposes, duties and powers of the corporate agent or nominee and the control and beneficial ownership in the principal cannot be overstated. A straw corporation should be recognized as such if (1) it sets forth in its articles of incorporation that its corporate powers are limited to holding title to property on behalf of others and not itself, (2) it executes appropriate agreements and corporate resolutions spelling out clearly that the corporation's sole business is acting as agent and nominal titleholder for the beneficial owners, (3) under the terms of its agreements with the beneficial owners, the corporation has no discretionary authority to act with respect to the property titled in its name but may act only upon written direction from the beneficial owners, (4) the corporation agrees by contract to terminate the agency relationship upon notice from the beneficial owners and to retransfer legal title to such owners at their direction, (5) all income and expenses with respect to the property are paid to and out of the beneficial owners' bank account, the only funds passing through the straw corporation's bank account being the fees it receives for acting as nominal title-

19. Supra note 18.

holder and executing specific documents on behalf of the beneficial owners, and amounts which it pays out for professional fees, etc., incurred as a result of conducting its business as an agent, and (6) all other corporate documents are consistent with the proposition that the straw corporation has no interest in, or duties or responsibilities toward, the property except to perform purely ministerial tasks at the direction of the real owners. And, as a final and important step in avoiding difficult proof problems concerning the tax status of the straw corporation as an agent, the shareholders of the straw corporation should be different from and independent of the beneficial owners of the property.

In these circumstances, the taxpayer would not argue that the corporation should be disregarded for tax purposes. He would concede that the corporation exists and, in fact, the corporation would file tax returns showing the income from nominee fees received and expenses incurred by the corporation from its business of acting as a nominal titleholder. If the factual situation conforms with the above patterns, it is believed that the profit or loss from the property should properly be taxed to the beneficial owners and not to the agent or nominee corporation.

COMMISSIONER v. BOLLINGER
485 U.S. 340 (1988)

Justice SCALIA delivered the opinion of the Court.

Petitioner, the Commissioner of Internal Revenue, challenges a decision by the United States Court of Appeals for the Sixth Circuit holding that a corporation which held record title to real property as agent for the corporation's shareholders was not the owner of the property for purposes of federal income taxation. . . .

I

Respondent Jesse C. Bollinger, Jr., developed, either individually or in partnership with some or all of the other respondents, eight apartment complexes in Lexington, Kentucky. (For convenience we will refer to all the ventures as "partnerships.") Bollinger initiated development of the first apartment complex, Creekside North Apartments, in 1968. The Massachusetts Mutual Life Insurance Company agreed to provide permanent financing by lending $1,075,000 to "the corporate nominee of Jesse C. Bollinger, Jr." at an annual interest rate of eight percent, secured by a mortgage on the property and a personal guaranty from Bollinger. The loan commitment was structured in this fashion because Kentucky's usury law at the time limited the annual interest rate for noncorporate borrowers to seven percent. . . . Lenders willing to provide money only at higher rates required the nominal debtor and record title holder of mortgaged property to be a corporate nominee of the true owner and borrower. On October 14, 1968, Bollinger incorporated Creekside, Inc., under the laws of Kentucky; he was the only stockholder. The next day, Bollinger and Creekside, Inc., entered into a written agreement which provided that the corporation would hold title to the apartment complex as Bollinger's agent for the sole purpose of securing financing, and would convey, assign, or encumber the property and disburse the proceeds thereof only as directed by Bollinger; that Creekside, Inc., had no obligation to maintain the property or assume any liability by reason of the execution of promissory notes or otherwise; and that Bollinger would indemnify and hold the corporation harmless from any liability it might sustain as his agent and nominee.

Having secured the commitment for permanent financing, Bollinger, acting through Creekside, Inc., borrowed the construction funds for the apartment complex from Citizens Fidelity Bank and Trust Company. Creekside, Inc., executed all necessary loan documents including the promissory note and mortgage, and transferred all loan proceeds to Bollinger's individual construction account. Bollinger acted as general contractor for the construction, hired the necessary employees, and paid the expenses out of the construction account. When construction was completed, Bollinger obtained, again through Creekside, Inc., permanent financing from Massachusetts Mutual Life in accordance with the earlier loan commitment. These loan proceeds were used to pay off the Citizens Fidelity construction loan.

Bollinger hired a resident manager to rent the apartments, execute leases with tenants, collect and deposit the rents, and maintain operating records. The manager deposited all rental receipts into, and paid all operating expenses from, an operating account, which was first opened in the name of Creekside, Inc., but was later changed to "Creekside Apartments, a partnership." The operation of Creekside North Apartments generated losses for the taxable years 1969, 1971, 1972, 1973, and 1974, and ordinary income for the years 1970, 1975, 1976, and 1977. Throughout, the income and losses were reported by Bollinger on his individual income tax returns.

Following a substantially identical pattern, seven other apartment complexes were developed by respondents through seven separate partnerships. For each venture, a partnership executed a nominee agreement with Creekside, Inc., to obtain financing. (For one of the ventures, a different Kentucky corporation, Cloisters, Inc., in which Bollinger had a 50 percent interest, acted as the borrower and titleholder. For convenience, we will refer to both Creekside and

Cloisters as "the corporation.") The corporation transferred the construction loan proceeds to the partnership's construction account, and the partnership hired a construction supervisor who oversaw construction. Upon completion of construction, each partnership actively managed its apartment complex, depositing all rental receipts into, and paying all expenses from, a separate partnership account for each apartment complex. The corporation had no assets, liabilities, employees, or bank accounts. In every case, the lenders regarded the partnership as the owner of the apartments and were aware that the corporation was acting as agent of the partnership in holding record title. The partnerships reported the income and losses generated by the apartment complexes on their partnership tax returns, and respondents reported their distributive share of the partnership income and losses on their individual tax returns.

The Commissioner of Internal Revenue disallowed the losses reported by respondents, on the ground that the standards set out in National Carbide Corp. v. Commissioner, 336 U.S. 422 (1949), were not met. The Commissioner contended that National Carbide required a corporation to have an arm's-length relationship with its shareholders before it could be recognized as their agent. Although not all respondents were shareholders of the corporation, the Commissioner took the position that the funds the partnerships disbursed to pay expenses should be deemed contributions to the corporation's capital, thereby making all respondents constructive stockholders. Since, in the Commissioner's view, the corporation rather than its shareholders owned the real estate, any losses sustained by the ventures were attributable to the corporation and not respondents. Respondents sought a redetermination in the United States Tax Court. The Tax Court held that the corporations were the agents of the partnerships and should be disregarded for tax purposes. . . . On appeal, the United States Court of Appeals for the Sixth Circuit affirmed. . . . We granted the Commissioner's petition for certiorari.

II

For federal income tax purposes, gain or loss from the sale or use of property is attributable to the owner of the property. See Helvering v. Horst, 311 U.S. 112, 116-117 (1940); Blair v. Commissioner, 300 U.S. 5, 12 (1937). . . . The problem we face here is that two different taxpayers can plausibly be regarded as the owner. Neither the Internal Revenue Code nor the regulations promulgated by the Secretary of the Treasury provide significant guidance as to which should be selected. It is common ground between the parties, however, that if a corporation holds title to property as agent for a partnership, then for tax purposes the partnership and not the corporation is the owner. Given agreement on that premise, one would suppose that there would be agreement upon the conclusion as well. For each of respondents' apartment complexes, an agency agreement expressly provided that the corporation would "hold such property as nominee and agent for" the partnership, . . . and that the partnership would have sole control of and responsibility for the apartment complex. The partnership in each instance was identified as the principal and owner of the property during financing, construction, and operation. The lenders, contractors, managers, employees, and tenants — all who had contact with the development — knew that the corporation was merely the agent of the partnership, if they knew of the existence of the corporation at all. In each instance the relationship between the corporation and the partnership was, in both form and substance, an agency with the partnership as principal.

The Commissioner contends, however, that the normal indicia of agency cannot suffice for tax purposes when, as here, the alleged principals are the controlling shareholders of the alleged agent corporation. That, it asserts, would undermine the principle of Moline Properties v. Commissioner, 319 U.S. 436 (1943), which held that a corporation is a separate taxable entity even if it has only one shareholder who exercises total control over its affairs. Obviously, *Moline*'s separate-entity principle would be significantly compromised if shareholders of closely held corporations could, by clothing the corporation with some attributes of agency with respect to particular assets, leave themselves free at the end of the tax year to make a claim — perhaps even a good-faith claim — of either agent or owner status, depending upon which choice turns out to minimize their tax liability. The Commissioner does not have the resources to audit and litigate the many cases in which agency status could be thought debatable. Hence, the Commissioner argues, in this shareholder context he can reasonably demand that the taxpayer meet a prophylactically clear test of agency.

We agree with that principle, but the question remains whether the test the Commissioner proposes is appropriate. The parties have debated at length the significance of our opinion in National Carbide Corp. v. Commissioner, supra. In that case, three corporations that were wholly owned subsidiaries of another corporation agreed to operate their production plants as "agents" for the parent, transferring to it all profits except for a nominal sum. The subsidiaries reported as gross income only this sum, but the Commissioner concluded that they should be taxed on the entirety of the profits because they were not really agents. We agreed, reasoning first, that the mere fact of the parent's control over the subsidiaries did not establish the existence of an agency, since such control is typical of all shareholder-corporation relationships, . . . ; and second, that the agreements to pay the parent all profits above a nominal amount were not determinative since income must be taxed to those who actually earn it without regard to anticipatory assignment, . . . We acknowledged, however, that there was such a thing as "a true corporate agent . . . of [an] owner-principal," id., at 437, and proceeded to set forth four indicia and two requirements of such status, the sum of which has become known in the lore of federal income tax law as the "six National Carbide factors": "[1] Whether the corporation operates in the name and for the account of the principal, [2] binds the principal by its actions, [3] transmits money received to the principal, and [4] whether receipt of income is attributable to the services of employees of the principal and to assets belonging to the principal are some of the relevant considerations in determining whether a true agency exists. [5] If the corporation is a true agent, its relations with its principal must not be dependent upon the fact that it is owned by the principal, if such is the case. [6] Its business purpose must be the carrying on of the normal duties of an agent." Id., at 437 (footnotes omitted).

We readily discerned that these factors led to a conclusion of nonagency in *National Carbide* itself. There each subsidiary had represented to its customers that it (not the parent) was the company manufacturing and selling its products; each had sought to shield the parent from service of legal process; and the operations had used thousands of the subsidiaries' employees and nearly $20 million worth of property and equipment listed as assets on the subsidiaries' books. . . .

The Commissioner contends that the last two *National Carbide* factors are not satisfied in the present case. To take the last first: The Commissioner argues that here the corporation's business purpose with respect to the property at issue was not "the carrying on of the normal duties of an agent," since it was acting not as the agent but rather as the owner of the property for purposes of Kentucky's usury laws. We do not agree. It assuredly was not acting as the owner in fact, since respondents represented themselves as the principals to all parties concerned with the loans. Indeed, it was the lenders themselves who required the use of a corporate nominee. Nor does it make any sense to adopt a contrary-to-fact legal presumption that the corporation was the principal, imposing a federal tax sanction for the apparent evasion of Kentucky's usury law. To begin with, the Commissioner has not established that these transactions were an evasion. Respondents assert without contradiction that use of agency arrangements in order to permit higher interest was common practice, and it is by no means clear that the practice violated the spirit of the Kentucky law, much less its letter. It might well be thought that the borrower does not generally require usury protection in a transaction sophisticated enough to employ a corporate agent — assuredly not the normal modus operandi of the loan shark. That the statute positively envisioned corporate nominees is suggested by a provision which forbids charging the higher corporate interest rates "to a corporation, the principal asset of which shall be the ownership of a one (1) or two (2) family dwelling," Ky. Rev. Stat. section 360.025(2) (1987) — which would seem to prevent use of the nominee device for ordinary home-mortgage loans. In any event, even if the transaction did run afoul of the usury law, Kentucky, like most States, regards only the lender as the usurer, and the borrower as the victim. See Ky. Rev. Stat. section 360.020 (1987) (lender liable to borrower for civil penalty), section 360.990 (lender guilty of misdemeanor). Since the Kentucky statute imposed no penalties upon the borrower for allowing himself to be victimized, nor treated him as in pari delictu, but to the contrary enabled him to pay back the principal without any interest, and to sue for double the amount of interest already paid (plus attorney's fees), see Ky. Rev. Stat. section 360.020 (1972), the United States would hardly be vindicating Kentucky law by depriving the usury victim of tax advantages he would otherwise enjoy. In sum, we see no basis in either fact or policy for holding that the corporation was the principal because of the nature of its participation in the loans.

Of more general importance is the Commissioner's contention that the arrangements here violate the fifth *National Carbide* factor — that the corporate agent's "relations with its principal must not be dependent upon the fact that it is owned by the principal." The Commissioner asserts that this cannot be satisfied unless the corporate agent and its shareholder principal have an "arm's-length relationship" that includes the payment of a fee for agency services. The meaning of *National Carbide*'s fifth factor is, at the risk of understatement, not entirely clear. Ultimately, the relations between a corporate agent and its owner-principal are *always* dependent upon the fact of ownership, in that the owner can cause the relations to be altered or terminated at any time. Plainly that is not what was meant, since on that interpretation all subsidiary-parent agencies would be invalid for tax purposes, a position which the *National Carbide* opinion specifically disavowed. We think the fifth *National Carbide* factor — so much more abstract than the others — was no more and no less than a generalized statement of the concern, expressed earlier in our own discussion, that the separate-entity doctrine of *Moline* not be subverted.

In any case, we decline to parse the text of *National Carbide* as though that were itself the governing statute. As noted earlier, it is uncontested that the law attributes tax consequences of property held by a genuine agent to the principal; and we agree that it is reasonable for the Commissioner to demand unequivocal evidence of genuineness in the corporation-shareholder context, in order to prevent evasion of *Moline*. We see no basis, however, for holding that unequivocal evidence can only consist of the rigid requirements (arm's-length dealing plus agency fee) that the Commissioner suggests. Neither of those is demanded by the law of agency, which permits agents to be unpaid family members, friends, or associates. See Restatement (Second) of Agency sections 16, 21, 22 (1958). It seems to us that the genuineness of the agency relationship is adequately assured, and tax-avoiding manipulation adequately avoided, when the fact that the corporation is acting as agent for its shareholders with respect to a particular asset is set forth in a written agreement at the time the asset is acquired, the corporation functions as agent and not principal with respect to the asset for all purposes, and the corporation is held out as the agent and not principal in all dealings with third parties relating to the asset. Since these requirements were met here, the judgment of the Court of Appeals is

Affirmed.

Justice Kennedy took no part in the consideration or decision of this case.

NOTES

1. In Betson v. Commissioner, 802 F.2d 365 (9th Cir. 1986), a taxpayer, who was a physician, unsuccessfully sought to deduct expenditures he made in connection with four liquor stores operated by a corporation owned by him and his wife. Taxpayer argued that he, not the corporation, could deduct the expenditures because the payments were necessary to protect the businesses and licenses, that petitioner believed himself liable for the stores' debts as record-licensee, and that the corporation operated the stores as his agent. Citing *Moline Properties*, however, the court accepted the Commissioner's position that no deduction was available to the taxpayer. The court saw the business as that of the corporation only, not the taxpayer's. Would *Bollinger* call for a different outcome?

2. The taxpayer succeeded in having a straw corporation disregarded in Louis Steinmetz, 32 T.C.M. (CCH) 669 (1973), where the corporation had no business activities and was used only to unite title to two parcels of land in anticipation of a condemnation award. Cf. Taylor v. Commissioner, 445 F.2d 455, 457 (1st Cir. 1971): "If [the corporation] were to serve only as a straw, it should have only performed those transactions essential to the holding and transferring of title."

III. MULTIPLE CORPORATIONS — §§1561, 1563, 1551, 269

Corporations are taxed at graduated rates set by §11, as follows:*

	Taxable Income	Tax Rate
(1)	Not over $50,000	15%
(2)	Over $50,000 but not over $75,000	25%
(3)	Over $75,000	34%

The benefit of the graduation in rates is phased out for corporations with taxable income in excess of $100,000 so that when it reaches $335,000 they are effectively taxed at a flat rate of 34 percent.

Corporations, like individuals, have been quick to recognize the tax saving potential of assigning income among multiple, low tax bracket recipients. Section 1551 is nominally intended to prevent this type of abuse, but in fact §§1561 and 1563 have evolved to the point where they almost entirely preempt §1551. See generally B. Bittker and J. Eustice, Federal Income Taxation of Corporations and Shareholders 15-1 to 15-14 (5th ed. 1987).

UNITED STATES v. VOGEL FERTILIZER CO.
455 U.S. 16 (1982)

Justice BRENNAN delivered the opinion of the Court.

Section 1561(a) limits a "controlled group of corporations" to a single corporate surtax exemption.[1] Section 1563(a)(2) provides that a "controlled group of corporations" includes a "brother-sister controlled group," defined as "[t]wo or more corporations if 5 or fewer persons . . . own . . . stock possessing (A) at least 80 percent of the total combined voting power . . . or at least 80 percent of the total value . . . of each corporation, and (B) more than 50 percent of the total combined voting power . . . or more than 50 percent of the total

---

*The 1986 Act replaced a five-step rate structure (with a top rate of 46%) that was enacted in 1978. Before 1978, there was in effect a two-step rate structure created by a "surtax" applied to corporate income in excess of $25,000.

1. For two of the tax years in question in this case — the years ending November 30, 1973 and 1974 — the Code exempted the first $25,000 of corporate earnings from the federal surtax on corporate income . . . and for the third year — ending November 30, 1975 — the Code exempted the first $50,000. . . . For each of these tax years, however, §1561 of the Code limited the members of a "controlled group" of corporations to a single shared surtax exemption. Amendments to the Code in 1978 replaced the surtax exemption with a graduated five-step tax rate structure on taxable corporate income. 26 U.S. §11 (1976 ed., Supp. III). Now members of a controlled group must share a single rate schedule. [§1561(a)].

value . . . of each corporation, taking into account the stock ownership of each such person only to the extent such stock ownership is identical with respect to each such corporation." The interpretation of the statutory provision by Treas. Reg. §1.1563-1(a)(3) is that the "term 'brother-sister controlled group' means two or more corporations if the same five or fewer persons . . . own . . . singly or in combination" the two prescribed percentages of voting power or total value. The question presented is whether the regulatory interpretation — that the statutory definition is met by the ownership of the prescribed stock by five or fewer persons "singly or in combination" — is a reasonable implementation of the statute or whether Congress intended the statute to apply only where each person whose stock is taken into account owns stock in each corporation of the group.

I

Respondent, Vogel Fertilizer Co. (Vogel Fertilizer), an Iowa corporation, sells farm fertilizer products. During the tax years in question — 1973, 1974, and 1975 — Vogel Fertilizer had only common stock issued and outstanding and Arthur Vogel (Vogel) owned 77.49 percent of that stock. Richard Crain (Crain), who is unrelated to Arthur Vogel, owned the remaining 22.51 percent. Vogel Popcorn Co. (Vogel Popcorn), another Iowa corporation, sells popcorn in both the wholesale and retail markets. For the tax years in question Crain owned no stock in Vogel Popcorn. Vogel, however, held 87.5 percent of the voting power, and between 90.66 percent and 93.42 percent of the value of Vogel Popcorn's stock.

Vogel Fertilizer did not claim a full surtax exemption on its tax returns for the years in question, believing that Treas. Reg. §1.1563-1(a)(3) barred such a claim. But when the United States Tax Court, in 1976, held that Treas. Reg. §1.1563-1(a)(3) was invalid because the statute did not permit the Commissioner to take a person's stock ownership into account for purposes of the 80-percent requirement unless that person owned stock in each corporation within the brother-sister controlled group, Fairfax Auto Parts of Northern Virginia, Inc. v. Commissioner, 65 T.C. 798 (1976), *rev'd*, 548 F.2d 501 (CA4 1977), Vogel Fertilizer filed timely claims for refunds, asserting that Vogel Fertilizer and Vogel Popcorn were not members of a controlled group and that Vogel Fertilizer was therefore entitled to a full surtax exemption for each taxable year. The Internal Revenue Service disallowed the claims and respondent brought this suit for a refund in the United States Court of Claims. The Court of Claims held that Vogel Fertilizer and Vogel Popcorn did not constitute a brother-sister controlled group within the meaning of §1563(a)(2)(A); that Treas. Reg. §1.1563-1(a)(3) is invalid to the extent that it takes into account, with respect to the 80-percent requirement, stock held by a shareholder who owns stock in only one corporation of the controlled group; and that respondent was, accordingly, entitled to a refund. 225 Ct. Cl. 15, 634 F.2d 497 (1980). We granted certiorari to resolve a conflict among the Circuits on this issue, 450 U.S. 994 (1981),[6] and now affirm.

II

Vogel's ownership of more than 50 percent of both Vogel Fertilizer and Vogel Popcorn satisfies Part (B) of the statutory test—the 50-percent identical-ownership requirement. The controversy centers on Part (A) of the test—the 80-percent requirement.

Respondent argues that the statute must be construed as including a common-ownership requirement—Congress was attempting to identify interrelated corporations that are in reality subdivided portions of a larger entity. In the taxpayer's view, Congress thus did not intend that a person's stock ownership be taken into account for purposes of the 80-percent requirement unless that shareholder owned stock in all of the corporations within the controlled group. The same "5 or fewer" individuals cannot be said to control 80 percent of both Vogel Fertilizer and Vogel Popcorn because Crain owns no stock in Vogel Popcorn and therefore his 22.51 percent of Vogel Fertilizer cannot be added to Vogel's 77.49 percent of that corporation to satisfy §1563(a)(2)(A). The Commissioner takes the position, however, reflected in his addition of the words "singly or in combination" in Treas. Reg. §1.1563-1(a)(3) to the statutory language, that there is no common-ownership requirement—various subgroups of "5 or fewer persons" can own the requisite 80 percent of the different corporations within the controlled group. The Commissioner acknowledges that under this interpretation, Part (A)'s 80-percent requirement in no respect measures the interrelationship between two corporations. The Commissioner's view is that only the 50-percent requirement measures this interrelationship. He contends the 80-percent requirement "continues to have independent significance" in that it "insures that all the members of the corporate group will be closely held," so that "the more-than-50-percent shareholder control group can obtain additional control in those instances where a greater interest is needed without the necessity of dealing with a large number of other shareholders." Brief for United States 35.

6. The Court of Appeals for the Fifth Circuit is in agreement with the Court of Claims and the Tax Court that Treas. Reg. §1.1563-1(a)(3) . . . is invalid insofar as it permits the 80-percent requirement to be satisfied without common ownership. . . . The Tax Court has adhered to its view that the Regulation is invalid . . . in the face of reversals by the Courts of Appeals for the Second, Fourth, and Eighth Circuits. . . .

A

Our role is limited to determining the validity of Treas. Reg. §1.1563-1(a)(3). Deference is ordinarily owed to the agency construction if we can conclude that the regulation "implement[s] the congressional mandate in some reasonable manner." United States v. Correll, 389 U.S. 299, 307 (1967). But this general principle of deference, while fundamental, only sets "the framework for judicial analysis; it does not displace it." United States v. Cartwright, 411 U.S. 546, 550 (1973).

The framework for analysis is refined by consideration of the source of the authority to promulgate the regulation at issue. The Commissioner has promulgated Treas. Reg. §1.1563-1(a)(3) interpreting this statute only under his general authority to "prescribe all needful rules and regulations." 26 U.S.C. §7805(a). Accordingly, "we owe the interpretation less deference than a regulation issued under a specific grant of authority to define a statutory term or prescribe a method of executing a statutory provision." Rowan Cos. v. United States, 452 U.S. 247, 253 (1981). . . .

B

We consider first whether the Regulation harmonizes with the statutory language. . . . That language . . . while not completely unambiguous, is in closer harmony with the taxpayer's interpretation than with the Commissioner's Regulation. The term that the statute defines — "brother-sister controlled group" — connotes a close horizontal relationship between two or more corporations, suggesting that the same indivisible group of five or fewer persons must represent 80 percent of the ownership of each corporation.

This interpretation is strengthened by the structure of the statute. Section 1563(a)(2) defines the controlling group of shareholders ("5 or fewer"), and then sets forth the two ownership requirements (80-percent and 50-percent). This structure suggests that precisely the same shareholders must satisfy both the 80-percent and 50-percent requirements. As the Tax Court stated it, "5 or fewer persons" is the "conjunctive subject" of both requirements. Fairfax Auto Parts of Northern Virginia, Inc. v. Commissioner, 65 T.C., at 803. Since under Part (B)'s 50-percent requirement, stock ownership is taken into account only to the extent it is "identical," that part of the statutory test clearly includes a common-ownership requirement. If, as the statutory structure suggests, the shareholders whose holdings are considered for purposes of Part (A) must be precisely the same shareholders as those whose holdings are considered for purposes of Part (B), the former also requires common ownership. . . .

C

The legislative history of §1563(a)(2) resolves any ambiguity in the statutory language and makes it plain that Treas. Reg. §1.1563-1(a)(3) is not a reasonable statutory interpretation. Through the controlled-group test, Congress intended to curb the abuse of multiple incorporation — large organizations subdividing into smaller corporations and receiving unintended tax benefits from the multiple use of surtax exemptions, accumulated earnings credits, and various other tax provisions designed to aid small businesses. S. Rep. No. 91-552, p. 134 (1969). . . . The intended targets of §1563(a)(2) were groups of *interrelated* corporations — corporations characterized by *common* control and ownership. Although the 50-percent requirement measures, to a lesser degree, the overlap between two corporations, the history of the enactment of §1563(a)(2) illustrates that Congress intended that the *80-percent* requirement be the primary requirement for defining the interrelationship between two or more corporations.

Until 1964, the method prescribed by the Code to curb the abuse of multiple incorporation was subjective: Multiple exemptions or benefits were allowed or disallowed depending on the reasons for the taxpayer's actions.[9] The Revenue Act of 1964 changed this approach, adding §§1561-1563 to the Code. Pub. L. 88-272, §235(a), 78 Stat. 116-125. These sections prescribed the application of mechanical, objective tests for determining whether two corporations were a "controlled group" and thereby restricted to one surtax exemption. . . .

In 1969 Congress adopted the present two-part percentage test codified in §1563(a)(2). Pub. L. 91-172, §401(c), 83 Stat. 602. This change was proposed by the Treasury Department as part of an extensive package of tax reform proposals. . . . The Treasury Department proposed, inter alia, that the definition of a brother-sister controlled group "be broadened to include groups of corporations owned and controlled by five or fewer persons, rather than only those owned and controlled by one person," as was the case under then existing law. . . . In setting forth the "Technical Explanation" for this new definition of brother-sister controlled groups, the Treasury Department was most explicit that the 80-percent requirement, like the 50-percent requirement, included common ownership: "[T]he *same five* or fewer persons [must] own at least 80 percent of the voting stock or value of shares of *each* corporation and . . . *these* five or fewer

---

9. Before 1964, the Code provisions designed to prevent taxpayers from using the multiple form of corporate organization in order to avoid taxes were §§269, 482 and 1551. . . . All of these sections are still in effect, but they are no longer the primary weapons employed against the abuse of multiple incorporation. Rather, the purely objective tests of §§1561-1563 have proved to be more effective. See Thomas, Brother-Sister Multiple Corporations — The Tax Reform Act of 1969 Reformed by Regulation, 28 Tax L. Rev. 65, 66-67 (1972).

individuals" must satisfy the 50-percent requirement in Part (B) . . .
(emphasis added except for "*five*"). . . .

The [Treasury Department's "General Explanation"] made it
clear that, under the 1969 amendment to §1563(a)(2), the 80-percent
requirement would remain the primary basis for determining
whether two or more corporations represent the *same* financial interests. Part (A) of the 1969 test was simply an expansion of the 1964
test, which considered the two or more corporations to be a brother-
sister controlled group only when one person owned 80 percent of
all of the corporations. This "expansion" was necessary to "close the
present opportunity for easy avoidance" of the 80-percent test. . . .
Because five persons now played the role previously played by one,
this expanded version of the test required a new safeguard — the
50-percent requirement — to "insure that the new expanded definition is limited to cases where the brother-sister corporations are,
in fact, *controlled* by the group of stockholders as one economic enterprise." . . .

The "singly or in combination" provision of Treas. Reg. §1.1563-
1(a)(3) is clearly incompatible with the explanation offered by the
Treasury Department when it proposed the statute. In addition to
the explicit statement that the members of the controlling group must
own stock in "each" corporation, the Treasury Department presented
a test in which the 80-percent requirement remained the primary
indicia of interrelationship. But under the challenged Regulation,
the 80-percent requirement measures *only* whether or not the
brother-sister corporations are closely held. The fact that a corporation is closely held, absent common ownership, is irrelevant to the
congressional purpose of identifying interrelationship: "It is not the
smallness of the number of persons in each company that triggers
§1563; it is the *sameness* of that small number." T. L. Hunt, Inc. v.
Commissioner, 562 F.2d 532, 537 (CA8 1977) (Webster, J. dissenting).

. . . The subsequent legislative history of §1563(a)(2) confirms
that Congress adopted not only the proposal of the Treasury Department, but also the Department's explanation and interpretation
which are wholly incompatible with the "singly or in combination"
interpretation of the Regulation. The Ways and Means Committee
Report stated:

> This bill expands the definition [of a brother-sister controlled
> group] to include two or more corporations which are owned 80
> percent or more (by voting power or value) by five or fewer persons
> (individuals, estates, or trusts) provided that these five or fewer
> persons own more than 50 percent of each corporation when the
> stock of each person is considered only to the extent it is owned
> identically with respect to each corporation. H.R. Rep. No. 91-
> 413, pt. 1, p. 99 (1969).

The House Committee Report thus reflects the Treasury Department's explanations — the 80-percent requirement is an expanded version of the 1964 statute and measures overlapping interests, while the 50-percent requirement is an additional proviso necessary in light of the expanded number of shareholders whose overlapping interests were to be considered.

D

The Commissioner's further reasons for sustaining his interpretation are unpersuasive.

The Commissioner relies on the fact that, in expanding the coverage of §1563(a)(2), Congress expressly adopted part of the language used in §1551(b)(2) of the Code to describe a transfer from one corporation to another "controlled" by the same "five or fewer" individuals. The Commissioner contends that Congress thereby approved the interpretation the Commissioner had placed on §1551(b)(2). Even if we could assume that Congress was aware of Treasury Regulations interpreting §1551, promulgated only two years before §1563 was enacted, see 32 Fed. Reg. 3214-3216 (1967), the promulgated regulations do not support the Commissioner's present interpretation of the statutory language in §1563(a)(2). The Regulations defining control under §1551 contain no language similar to the words "singly or in combination" found in Treas. Reg. §1.1563-1(a)(3) and they contain no suggestion that the Treasury Department had interpreted §1551(b)(2) as not having a common-ownership requirement. See Treas. Reg. §1.1551-1(e). . . .

Finally, the Commissioner seeks to uphold the Regulation on the ground that a common-ownership requirement leads to the assertedly nonsensical result that ownership of only one share could be determinative. For example, if Richard Crain owned but one share of Vogel Popcorn, then the 80-percent requirement would be met and the taxpayer corporation would be part of a controlled group even under the taxpayer's interpretation of the statute. This argument is without merit, for several reasons. First, Congress purposefully substituted the mechanical formula of §1563(a)(2) for the subjective, case-by-case analysis that had previously prevailed. Inherent in such an objective test is a sharp dividing line that is crossed by incremental changes in ownership. Moreover, it is obvious that a shareholder would not buy a small amount of stock in order to create a controlled group, since it is to the taxpayer's advantage not to be part of such a group. Finally, a person's "mere" ownership of one share of stock plays an important role in the operation of the test. It insures that each of the "5 or fewer" shareholders representing the bulk of the financial interest of the corporations actually knows of the other corporations within the putative brother-sister controlled group.

Under this construction of the statute, controlled-group membership cannot catch such a shareholder by surprise, as it could under the Commissioner's construction.

Affirmed.

Justice BLACKMUN, with whom Justice White joins, dissenting.

I cannot deny that the Court's opinion persuasively defends a possible interpretation of §1563(a)(2). In my view, however, the Court has totally failed to establish that the Commissioner's interpretation is incorrect. Because I believe that the only certainty about the language and history of §1563(a)(2) is that both are ambiguous, I would defer to the Commissioner's judgment.

The Court begins by declaring that the statutory language, "while not completely unambiguous, is in closer harmony with the taxpayer's interpretation than with the Commissioner's Regulation" because the term " 'brother-sister controlled group' — connotes a close horizontal relationship between two or more corporations." . . . In taking this approach, however, the Court simply assumes its conclusion. The 50-percent test of Part (B) already ensures a horizontal relationship between the corporations that constitute the controlled group; nothing in the language of the statute suggests that Part (A) was designed directly to serve the same purpose. At most, §1563(a)(2) can be read to require that the same set of five or fewer persons must satisfy the 50- and 80-percent tests; the statute is entirely silent as to whether each member of the set must own stock in each corporation. . . .

Similar problems attend the Court's analysis of the statute's structure. In the Court's view, the fact that the controlling group of shareholders is defined as "5 or fewer" for both the 50- and 80-percent tests "suggests that precisely the same shareholders must satisfy both the 80-percent and 50-percent requirements." . . . Even if this were true, however, it would not mean that each member of the set of five or fewer shareholders must own stock in each corporation; it suggests only that the total number of shareholders considered in relation to both tests may not exceed five. In any event, the common-ownership requirement — which takes "into account the stock ownership of each such person only to the extent such stock ownership is identical with respect to each such corporation," §1563(a)(2)(B) — is embedded in Part (B), and the simpler and normal reading of the statute therefore would apply the common-ownership restriction only to Part (B)'s 50-percent test. It is the Court's reading, then, that seemingly runs counter to the structure of the statute, for under its approach the 80-percent test would "tend to overlap or swallow the 50% identical ownership requirement." Allen Oil Co. v. Commissioner, 614 F.2d 336, 339 (CA2 1980).

The confusing nature of the statutory text leads the Court to rely principally on §1563(a)(2)'s legislative history, which it cheerfully reads as "resolv[ing] any ambiguity in the statutory language." . . . It seems to me that this conclusion is substantially overstated. It is undoubtedly true, as the Court observes, that §1563(a)(2) was aimed at curbing the abuses of multiple incorporation. But this is beside the point, for — as the Court notes — the 50-percent test of Part (B) itself serves to "measur[e] . . . the overlap between two corporations." . . . The Court's further conclusion "that Congress intended that the *80-percent* requirement be the primary requirement for defining the interrelationship between two or more corporations," . . . (emphasis in original), is entirely without support in the legislative history. Certainly, such a view appears nowhere in the congressional Reports. These simply echo the statutory definition, declaring that a controlled group includes "two or more corporations which are owned 80 percent or more . . . by five or fewer persons . . . provided that these five or fewer persons own more than 50 percent of each corporation when the stock of each person is considered only to the extent it is owned identically with respect to each corporation." H.R. Rep. No. 91-413, pt. 1, p. 99 (1969). . . .

Ironically, then, the Court at bottom is forced to rely on the rationale advanced by the Treasury Department when it proposed the legislation eventually adopted as §1563(a)(2). The Court's analysis of this proposal, which it explores in some detail . . . is certainly credible. But even this legislative material contains an essential ambiguity. Neither the "General Explanation" nor the "Technical" one addresses whether the 80-percent test requires common ownership, or whether a person excluded from the 50-percent calculation because he owns no stock in one of the controlled corporations may nevertheless be included in the 80-percent test, so long as the total number of relevant shareholders does not exceed five. For example, while the Treasury Department suggested that "the same *five* or fewer persons [must] own at least 80 percent of the voting stock or value of shares of each corporation" to satisfy Part (A), and that "these five or fewer individuals" must satisfy the 50-percent test of Part (B), Hearings Before the House Committee on Ways and Means on the Subject of Tax Reform, 91st Cong., 1st Sess., pt. 14, p. 5168 (1969) (emphasis in original), the Department's explanation — despite the Court's suggestion to the contrary — need not be read as requiring that *each* of the five own stock in every controlled corporation. To the contrary, the Technical Explanation declares that the 80-percent test "is satisfied if the *group* of five or fewer persons as a whole owns at least 80 percent of the voting stock or value of shares of each corporation, *regardless of the size of the individual holdings of each person.*" Id., at 5169 (emphasis added). This obviously suggests that the crucial inquiry is whether a given set of five satisfies both tests, not whether each individual owns stock in each corporation.

Certainly, I do not suggest that the Commissioner's interpretation is compelled by the legislative materials. But the Court, by putting so much effort into reading between the lines, has lost sight of the fact that certain statutory ambiguities cannot be neatly and finally resolved. Here, the Commissioner's interpretation is not "unreasonable or meaningless," for "it insures that the stock is closely held." Allen Oil Co. v. Commissioner, 614 F.2d, at 340. In such a situation, "[t]he choice among reasonable interpretations is for the Commissioner, not the courts." National Muffler Dealers Assn., Inc. v. United States, 440 U.S. 472, 488 (1979). . . . For that reason, I respectfully dissent.

NOTES

1. After the Supreme Court's decision in *Vogel*, the Tax Court held that *constructive* stock ownership under §1563(e) is sufficient to satisfy the ownership requirement of §1563(a)(2). See Complete Finance Corp. v. Commissioner, 80 T.C. 11062 (1983), *aff'd*, 766 F.2d 436 (10th Cir. 1985).

2. *Vogel* was invoked in a different context in Tribune Publishing Co. v. Commissioner, 731 F.2d 1401 (9th Cir. 1984), *aff'g* 79 T.C. 1029 (1982). One corporation held 175 out of 250 shares of stock in another company; the remaining 75 shares were held by two individuals. The individual shareholders could dispose of their stock only after giving the majority holding corporation a "right of first refusal." The question was whether that restriction rendered the stock "excluded" under §1563(c), so that the corporate shareholder would, in effect, hold 100 percent of the stock and become part of an affiliated group limited to a single surtax exemption. A panel of the Ninth Circuit held that the stock was so excluded, over a variety of taxpayer objections related to the informality of the restrictions. In reaching its decision, the court cited *Vogel* as evidence of a statutory preference for "mechanical, objective tests" in the affiliated group area. But cf. Superior Beverage Co. v. Commissioner, 525 F.2d 186 (9th Cir. 1975) (employee's stock subject to corporation's right of first refusal not excluded where controlling shareholder's stock was similarly restricted).

3. In addition to requiring members of a controlled group to share a single rate structure, §1561 restricts other tax benefits. The section requires members of a controlled group to share (1) the $250,000 allowance in computing the accumulated earnings credit; (2) the $40,000 alternative minimum tax exemption; and (3) the $2 million exemption in calculating the environmental superfund tax under §59A.

COASTAL OIL STORAGE CO. v. COMMISSIONER
242 F.2d 396 (4th Cir. 1957)

Before Parker, Chief Judge, Sobeloff, Circuit Judge, and Gilliam, District Judge.

PARKER, Chief Judge. These are cross appeals from the decision of the Tax Court of the United States reported in 25 T.C. 1304. The questions involved relate to the right of a corporate taxpayer to the $25,000 corporate surtax exemption and minimum excess profits credit. . . . The corporation was organized February 1, 1951. The surtax exemption and minimum excess profits credit were claimed for the months of February to June 1951. They were denied by the Tax Court for the months of April, May and June 1951 under the restrictions imposed by section 15(c) of the Tax Code but allowed for the months of February and March for the reason that the restrictions imposed by that section were not applicable in the latter months. The taxpayer appeals from the denial for the months of April, May and June, the Commissioner from the allowance for February and March, the Commissioner contending that they should be denied for those months under the provisions of section [269(a)]. . . .

TAXPAYER'S APPEAL

Coastal Terminals, Inc. was organized in 1944 for the purpose of supplying and storing petroleum products. It constructed a terminal at North Charleston, S.C. and leased some of the storage facilities there to the office of the Quartermaster General under renegotiable contracts. On February 1, 1951 Coastal Terminals, Inc., caused the taxpayer, the Coastal Oil Storage Company, to be organized and transferred to it seven oil storage tanks, with a capacity of 150,000 barrels, for $100,000 of the capital stock of taxpayer, which was all of the capital stock that taxpayer issued, and a note for $38,706.79, which taxpayer paid off at the rate of $5,062.50 per month until it was extinguished. The reason given in the testimony before the Tax Court for the creation of taxpayer was to separate storage operations under storage contracts with the government from operations under contracts with others; but it was admitted that tax aspects of the transaction were taken into consideration and no satisfactory reason was given why the same advantages could not have been obtained by separate bookkeeping that were obtained by separate incorporation, which necessarily resolved itself into little more than separate bookkeeping. As a result of the incorporation of taxpayer, the operations at North Charleston received two $25,000 surtax exemptions and minimum excess profits credits instead of one; and the Tax Court found that taxpayer had failed to establish by a clear preponderance of the evidence that the securing of the extra exemption or credit, or both, was not a major purpose of the transfer of the property to the taxpayer. It, therefore, denied the exemption for the months of April, May, and June 1951, under section 15(c) of the Tax Code,[1] the pertinent portion of which is as follows:

> If any corporation transfers, on or after January 1, 1951, all or part of its property (other than money) to another corporation which was created for the purpose of acquiring such property or which was not actively engaged in business at the time of such acquisition, and if after such transfer the transferor corporation or its stockholders, or both, are in control of such transferee corporation during any part of the taxable year of such transferee corporation, then such transferee corporation shall not for such taxable year (except as may be otherwise determined under section [269]) be allowed either the $25,000 exemption from surtax . . . or the $25,000 minimum excess profits credit . . . unless such transferee corporation shall establish by the clear preponderance of the evidence that the securing of such exemption or credit was not a major purpose of such transfer.

We agree with the Tax Court that the taxpayer failed to sustain the burden of proof imposed by the statute to "establish by the clear preponderance of the evidence that the securing of such exemption or credit was not a major purpose of such transfer." Since the keeping of separate records as to government business would have accomplished the separation of government business from other business just as well as the incorporation of a subsidiary corporation, it is difficult to see how the incorporation and transfer could have had any real purpose other than tax avoidance. At all events, we would not be justified in setting aside the finding of the Tax Court as clearly erroneous.

THE COMMISSIONER'S APPEAL

While admitting that the section of the Revenue Code above quoted has no application to income for the months of February and March 1951, the Commissioner contends that the taxpayer should be denied the surtax exemption and minimum excess profits credit for those months under the provisions of section [269]. . . .

The Tax Court considered this contention of the Commissioner but held the section inapplicable, without passing on the question as to whether or not tax evasion or avoidance was the principal purpose of the transfer in question. In this we think there was error. It is

---

1. This section was added by section 121(f) of the Revenue Act of 1951 and is applicable only after March 31, 1951. . . .
[The 1986 Code successor is §1551.]

clear that the parent corporation acquired complete control of taxpayer through stock ownership and the parent corporation was certainly a person within the meaning of subsection (1) of the statute. As a result of the transfer of its property in exchange for the stock, it was able to obtain through this splitting up of its corporate business the benefit of an exemption and credit which it would not otherwise have enjoyed. While the exemption is claimed by taxpayer, the sole benefit thereof would accrue to the parent corporation, the sole owner of its stock. Cf. Higgins v. Smith, 308 U.S. 473, 476. . . . We see no reason, therefore, why subsection (1) of the section is not applicable. Subsection (2) is applicable also, since taxpayer, as a result of the transfer from the parent corporation, received property having a basis for tax purposes which would be determined by reference to its basis in the hands of the parent corporation,[2] and the transfer resulted in the securing of a surtax exemption and minimum profits credit, to which neither the taxpayer nor the parent corporation would have been entitled otherwise; for the taxpayer could not have enjoyed the benefit of the surtax exemption and excess profits tax credit but for the acquisition of the property producing the income from or against which the exemption and credit are claimed. That the section was intended to reach just such schemes for tax evasion or avoidance by the splitting up of a business enterprise clearly appears from the H. Rep. No. 871, 78th Cong. 1st Sess., p. 49 where it is said:

> This section . . . provid[es] that in the case of acquisitions on or after October 8, 1940, of an interest in or control of corporations or property which the Commissioner finds to be principally motivated by or availed of for the avoidance of income or excess profits tax by securing the benefit of a deduction, credit, or other allowance, then the tax benefits are to be disallowed or allowed only in part in a manner consistent with the prevention of tax avoidance. This section is designed to put an end promptly to any market for, or dealings in, interests in corporations or property which have as their objective the reduction through artifice of the income or excess profits tax liability.
>
> The crux of the devices which have come to the attention of your committee has been some form of acquisition on or after the effective date of the Second Revenue Act of 1940, but the devices take many forms. Thus, the acquisition may be an acquisition of the shares of a corporation, or it may be an acquisition which follows by operation of law in the case of a corporation resulting from a statutory merger or consolidation. The person, or persons, making the acquisition likewise vary, as do the forms or methods

2. It is not disputed that the basis of the seven storage tanks in the hands of the taxpayer should be determined by reference to the basis in the hands of the parent corporation [under §362]. . . .

of utilization under which tax avoidance is sought. Likewise, the tax benefits sought may be one or more of several deductions or credits, including the utilization of excess profits credits, carry-overs, and carry-backs of losses or unused excess profits credits, and anticipated expense of other deductions. In the light of these considerations, the section has not confined itself to a description of any particular methods for carrying out such tax avoidance schemes but has included within its scope these devices in whatever form they may appear. *For similar reasons, the scope of the terms used in the section is to be found in the objective of the section, namely, to prevent the tax liability from being reduced through the distortion or perversion effected through tax avoidance devices. . . .* (Italics supplied.)

This accords with the interpretation placed upon the section by a later Congress, where in the Senate report on proposed amendments to the corporate surtax exemption provisions, it was said (S. Rep. No. 2375, 81st Cong. 2d Sess. p. 70, 2 Cum. Bull. 483, 533):

It is not intended, however, that the exemption of the first $25,000 of a corporation's surtax net income from the surtax shall be abused by the splitting up, directly or indirectly, of a business enterprise into two or more corporations or the forming of two or more corporations to carry on an integrated business enterprise. It is believed that sections [482 and 269] will prevent this form of tax avoidance.

The Tax Court refers to its decision in Commodores Point Terminal Corp. v. Com'r, 11 T.C. 411; but that was an entirely different case from this and is no precedent for its decision here. There a corporation had acquired a controlling interest in another corporation and the question was whether it was entitled to a dividends received credit on the stock purchased in the transaction. The Tax Court in allowing the credit pointed out that the dividends, and consequent credit, were not dependent on the taxpayer's having acquired control of the other corporation. In this case, as pointed out above, the taxpayer could not have enjoyed the exemption and credit claimed but for the acquisition of the property producing the income, which was transferred to it by the parent corporation. There not only was there a holding that there was no purpose of tax avoidance, but the transaction was not one which involved tax avoidance. Here there can be no question but that tax avoidance necessarily resulted from the corporate splitting which was involved. . . .

Affirmed on Taxpayer's Appeal.

Reversed and Remanded for further proceedings on Commissioner's Appeal.

JAMES REALTY CO. v. UNITED STATES
280 F.2d 394 (8th Cir. 1960)

Before Gardner, Woodrough, and Blackmun, Circuit Judges.

WOODROUGH, Circuit Judge. The taxpayer James Realty Company, a corporation, . . . received and made return of income of $24,699.05 for the period and claimed deduction under the $25,000 corporate surtax exemption and $25,000 minimum excess profits tax credit. . . .

The Commissioner disallowed the deduction and credit on the ground that the corporation was created solely for the purpose of tax avoidance and was deprived of the right to the exemption and credit by Sections [269(a) and 1551]. . . .

It appeared on the trial that Adolph Fine organized Adolph Fine, Inc., in 1944 to engage in the construction business and later in 1949 he incorporated Fine Realty, Inc., whose principal activity was to sell homes built by Adolph Fine, Inc. Both of these corporations were controlled and managed by Adolph Fine and his wife, Mildred, who owned the stock of such corporations individually or in trust for their children. Also, at all times pertinent hereto, Adolph Fine was president and treasurer, Mildred Fine was vice president and secretary, and June Myslajek was assistant secretary to Adolph Fine, Inc.; Mildred Fine was president and treasurer, M. L. Grossman was vice president, and June Myslajek was secretary of Fine Realty, Inc.

In 1952, Adolph Fine, as an individual, owned certain undeveloped land located in the village of St. Louis Park, Minnesota, which he caused to be subdivided and platted for the purpose of home development, and named it the Jeffrey, James Fine Addition to St. Louis Park.

On November 20, 1952, Adolph Fine caused the taxpayer, James Realty Company, to be organized with an initial authorized capital of $25,000, consisting of ten shares of Class A common stock at a par value of $100 (voting) and two hundred and forty shares of Class B common stock at a par value of $100 (non-voting). According to the articles of incorporation, the purpose of the corporation was, among other things: "To acquire, improve, and develop real property; to erect dwellings of all kinds and to sell, or rent the same; also to acquire, by purchase, lease, or otherwise, and to take, own, hold, sell, exchange, transfer, lease, repair, maintain, improve, mortgage, or in any other manner deal in and with real property. . . ."

On November 24, 1952, Adolph Fine conveyed eighteen of the lots in the Jeffrey, James Fine Addition to the taxpayer corporation in exchange for two shares of its Class A common stock and thirty-four shares of its Class B common stock. The value of the lots in terms of the thirty-six shares was $200 per lot or $3,600. On the same day, Adolph Fine transferred seventeen shares of the Class B stock to his wife Mildred in trust for their sons Jeffrey and James.

Also on November 24, 1952, the taxpayer corporation, acting through its president, Adolph Fine, entered into two written contracts. The first was an agreement with Adolph Fine, Inc., by which that corporation would construct houses on the lots owned by the taxpayer James Realty Co., at cost plus 12½%. By the terms of a second contract, with Fine Realty, Inc., that corporation was made the exclusive selling agent of the homes to be constructed for taxpayer by Adolph Fine, Inc. Sales commissions were to be from 5% to 7½% depending upon financing arrangements and costs.

In August, 1953, taxpayer purchased thirty-six lots located in the neighboring West Tonka Hills Addition from Fine Realty, Inc. at a price of $650 per lot, or a total price of $23,000.

During its fiscal year ended November 30, 1953, when taxpayer reported taxable income in the amount of $24,699.05, only $355.56 of this amount was attributable to the sale of lots purchased from Fine Realty, Inc., while the remaining income was derived from sales of houses built on lots acquired from Adolph Fine.

Taxpayer was one of nine development companies formed by Adolph Fine between 1950 and 1954. All of them occupied offices owned by Adolph Fine, Inc., and were supplied with bookkeeping services by the same personnel who kept the books of Adolph Fine, Inc. . . .

The Court considered the testimony tendered by the taxpayer to show that its existence was justified by bona fide business purposes although as Mr. Fine testified, "he was aware" of the tax results of the multiple corporations he caused to be organized.

The District Court found as ultimate facts: (a) that there was no real business purpose for the creation of the taxpayer corporation and that it derived no income from independent activities of a nature different from those of Adolph Fine, Inc., and Fine Realty, Inc.; (b) that the principal purpose for the acquisition of the taxpayer corporation by Adolph Fine was tax avoidance by securing the benefit of another corporate surtax exemption and excess profits credit which he would not otherwise enjoy; (c) that taxpayer was created for the purpose of acquiring property from other corporations controlled by the same stockholders and was not actively engaged in business in August, 1953, when it acquired the thirty-six lots from Fine Realty, Inc.; (d) that at the time of the formation of the taxpayer-corporation Adolph Fine, Inc., and Fine Realty, Inc., were conducting trades or businesses substantially similar to that of the taxpayer corporation during its taxable year ended November 30, 1953; (e) and that during its taxable year ended November 30, 1953, the taxpayer did not permit earnings or profits to accumulate beyond the reasonable needs of its business.

Accordingly, the court concluded that the Commissioner properly disallowed the surtax exemption and minimum excess profits tax credit under Sections [1551 and 269(a)].

The question presented here is whether control of the taxpayer was acquired by Adolph Fine for the principal purpose of avoiding federal income and excess profits taxes by securing the benefit of another surtax exemption and excess profits tax credit which he would not otherwise enjoy so that the disallowance of the exemption and credit was proper. . . .

The determination by the District Court that Mr. Fine organized and acquired control of the taxpayer corporation for the principal purpose of tax avoidance was a finding of fact which is conclusive on this appeal if supported by substantial evidence and not clearly erroneous. Although Mr. Fine testified that in forming the taxpayer and eight other corporations he had in mind the two purposes of implementing his estate plan and of spreading and minimizing risks of loss from business reversal or tort liability and that tax saving was not the principal purpose, he admitted that he was aware of the tax consequences of the multiple corporate set up and testimony of his secretary and bookkeeper was to the effect that "she made adjusting entries" in the books of Adolph Fine, Inc., Fine Realty, Inc., and the development companies including taxpayer; that "a great deal of consideration was given to taxes" by Mr. Fine and his accountants and that "we were very careful to keep the figures under $25,000.00, the profit figures." An office memorandum from Mr. Fine made in 1957 concerning "the land status" of "the following companies" "to determine what company should own and develop" certain lands included the statement: "This will depend upon the possible profit status for the year 1957 in each of the companies." The tax returns of the various corporations formed by Mr. Fine as shown in the Exhibit B which the District Court included in its opinion shows that in 1950 the income from development and sale of homes reported by Adolph Fine, Inc. and Fine Realty, Inc. was $202,268.00 and $34,212.00. For the ensuing years 1951-1956 following the creation of the various development companies the taxable income of the two named companies dropped with but few exceptions to less than $25,000.00 and each of those companies reported less than $25,000.00. Notwithstanding Mr. Fine's testimony that avoidance of tax was not a prime consideration in splitting his home building business, there was substantial evidence to support the finding of the Court that the principal purpose was to avoid federal income or excess profit tax by securing the benefit of deductions and credits which he would not otherwise enjoy.

Appellant contends here as it did below that creation of a new corporation and obtaining its stock is not an acquisition of the control of a corporation within the meaning of Section [269(a)]. The court in rejecting the contention said [176 F. Supp. 310]:

> Although the legislative history and the case law under Section 129 [now 269] indicate that it was aimed at the abuses of one corporation acquiring going concerns which had accrued certain tax exemptions, see J. E. Dilworth Co. v. Henslee, D.C. Tenn. 1951, 98 F. Supp. 957, 960 (dictum); Rudick, Acquisitions to Avoid Income or Excess Profits Tax: Section 129 [now 269] of the Internal Revenue Code, 58 Harv. L. Rev. 196 (1944), there is no settled view that "acquisition of control" cannot and should not include the organization of a new corporation such as was done here. See Alcorn Wholesale Co., 1951, 16 T.C. 75, 88; 7 Mertens, Federal Taxation, §38.66, n.75 (1956). The regulations promulgated under the 1939 Code provide that acquisition of control of a corporation may be accomplished by acquiring the stock of a newly organized corporation. . . .

We find no error in the Trial Court's ruling on this contention. . . .

In view of our conclusion in this case that the deduction claimed by the taxpayer was forbidden by Section [269(a)] it is not necessary for us to pass upon the application and effect of Section [1551] and we expressly refrain from doing so.

The judgment appealed from is affirmed.

IV. REALLOCATION OF CORPORATE INCOME — §482

A. ALLOCATION AND "CREATION" OF INCOME

E.I. DUPONT DE NEMOURS AND CO. v. UNITED STATES
608 F.2d 445 (Ct. Cl. 1979), *cert. denied*, 445 U.S. 962 (1980)

Before Friedman, Chief Judge, Davis, Nichols, Kashiwa, Kunzig, Bennett and Smith, Judges en banc.

Davis, Judge. . . . Taxpayer Du Pont de Nemours, the American chemical concern, created early in 1959 a wholly owned Swiss marketing and sales subsidiary for foreign sales — Du Pont International S.A. (known to the record and the parties as DISA). Most of the Du

Pont chemical products marketed abroad were first sold by taxpayer to DISA, which then arranged for resale to the ultimate consumer through independent distributors. The profits on these Du Pont sales were divided for income tax purposes between plaintiff and DISA via the mechanism of the prices plaintiff charged DISA. For 1959 and 1960 the Commissioner of Internal Revenue, acting under section 482 of the Internal Revenue Code which gives him authority to reallocate profits among commonly controlled enterprises, found these divisions of profits economically unrealistic as giving DISA too great a share. Accordingly, he reallocated a substantial part of DISA's income to taxpayer, thus increasing the latter's taxes for 1959 and 1960 by considerable sums. The additional taxes were paid and this refund suit was brought in due course. Du Pont assails the Service's reallocation, urging that the prices plaintiff charged DISA were valid under the Treasury regulations implementing section 482. We hold that taxpayer has failed to demonstrate that, under the regulation it invokes and must invoke, it is entitled to any refund of taxes.

1. DESIGN, OBJECTIVES AND FUNCTIONING OF DISA[1]

A. Du Pont first considered formation of an international sales subsidiary in 1957. A decreasing volume of domestic sales, increasing profits on exports, and the recent formation of the Common Market in Europe convinced taxpayer's president of the need for such a subsidiary. He envisioned an international sales branch capable of marketing Du Pont's most profitable type of products — Du Pont proprietary products, particularly textile fibers and elastomers[2] specially designed for use as raw materials by other manufacturers. Du Pont had utilized two major marketing techniques to sell such customized products.[3] One mechanism consisted of technical sales services: an elaborate set of laboratory services making technical improvements, developing new applications, and solving customer

1. We adopt (with minor modifications) Trial Judge Will's findings of fact (see our order of this date). Because of their length the findings are not reproduced with this opinion. Plaintiff has requested numerous changes in the findings, almost all designed to down-grade the trial judge's findings with respect to (a) taxpayer's purpose to allocate as much income as possible to DISA, (b) taxpayer's establishment of a pricing system for sales to DISA designed to further that objective, and (c) the aspects and functioning of DISA which differentiate it from other selling and merchandising agencies. We are satisfied, however, that the trial judge's findings properly reflect the evidence on these points.

2. An elastomer is "an elastic rubberlike substance (as a synthetic rubber or a plastic) having some of the physical properties of natural rubber." Webster's Third International Dictionary 730 (unabridged ed. 1968).

3. Du Pont also had several other types of products which did not require the specialized sales effort contemplated for DISA. These products included direct "commodity-type" goods (such as household paints) or standard chemical products (e.g., sulphuric acid).

problems for Du Pont products. The other was "indirect selling," a method of promoting demand for Du Pont products at every point in the distribution chain. These two techniques were to be developed by DISA, Du Pont's international branch in Europe. DISA was not to displace plaintiff's set of independent European distributors, but rather to augment the distributors' efforts by the two marketing methods and to police the independents adequately.

B. Neither in the planning stage nor in actual operation was DISA a sham entity; nor can it be denied that it was intended to, and did, perform substantial commercial functions which taxpayer legitimately saw as needed in its foreign (primarily European) market. Nevertheless, we think it also undeniable that the tax advantages of such a foreign entity were also an important, though not the primary, consideration in DISA's creation and operation. During the planning stages, plaintiff's internal memoranda were replete with references to tax advantages, particularly in planning prices on Du Pont goods to be sold to the new entity. The tax strategy was simple. If Du Pont sold its goods to the new international subsidiary at prices below fair market value, that company, upon resale of the goods, would recognize the greater part of the total profit (i.e., manufacturing and selling profits). Since this foreign subsidiary could be located in a country where its profits would be taxed at a much lower level than the parent Du Pont would be taxed here, the enterprise as a whole would minimize its taxes. Cf. Baldwin-Lima-Hamilton Corp. v. United States, 435 F.2d 182, 184 (7th Cir. 1970). The new company's accumulated profits would be used to finance further foreign investments. The details of this planning are set forth in the findings, and they leave us without doubt that a significant objective of plaintiff was to create a foreign subsidiary which would be able to accumulate large profits with which to finance Du Pont capital improvements in Europe.[4]

---

4. Du Pont is divided into a series of semi-autonomus departments which report to the Executive Committee. An early draft of a memorandum on this subject to the Executive Committee from the International Department (then known as the Foreign Relations Department) stated that the Treasury Department (responsible for Du Pont's tax planning) was considering the possibility of a "transfer of goods to a tax haven subsidiary at prices less than such transfers would be made to other subsidiaries or industrial Departments. . . ." A memorandum from the Treasury Department reviewed the possibility of an IRS attack on such pricing and concluded:

"It would seem to be desirable to bill the tax haven subsidiary at less than an 'arm's length' price because: (1) the pricing might not be challenged, by the revenue agent; (2) if the pricing is challenged, we might sustain such transfer; (3) if we cannot sustain the prices used, a transfer price will be negotiated which should not be more than an 'arm's length' price and might well be less; thus we would be no worse off than we would have been had we billed at the higher price."

A subsequent Treasury Department report on "Use of a Profit Sanctuary Company by the Du Pont Company" advised pricing goods to the "profit sanctuary" at considerably lower levels than other intercorporate sales, suggesting that such prices

C. Consistently with that aim, plaintiff's prices on its intercorporate sales to DISA were deliberately calculated to give the subsidiary the lion's share of the profits. Instead of allowing each individual producing department to value its goods economically and to set a realistic price,[5] Du Pont left pricing on the sales to DISA with the Treasury and Legal Departments. Neither department was competent to set an economic value on goods sold to DISA, and no economic correlation of costs to prices was attempted.[6] Rather, an official of the Treasury Department established a pricing system designed to leave DISA with 75 percent of the total profits. If the goods' cost was greater than DISA's selling price, the department would price the item at its cost *less* DISA's selling expense. This latter provision was designed to insulate DISA from any loss. On the whole, the pricing system was based solely on Treasury and Legal Department estimates of the greatest amount of profits that could be shifted to DISA without evoking IRS intervention.[7]

As it turned out, for the taxable years involved here, 1959 and 1960, the actual division of total profits between plaintiff and DISA was closer to a 50-50 split. In 1959 DISA realized 48.3 percent of the total profits, while in 1960 its share climbed to 57.1 percent. This departure from the original plan was the result of the omission of

---

could probably be sustained against an IRS challenge. In the spring of 1958, an International Department memorandum stated that the principal advantages of a "profit sanctuary trading company" (dubbed by its initials as a "PST company") depended "largely upon the amount of profits which might be shifted (through selling price) from Du Pont to the 'PST company'." The report concluded that Du Pont could find "a selling price sufficiently low as to result in the transfer of a substantial part of the profits on export sales to the 'PST company.'" A corporate task force selected Switzerland as the best location for the foreign trading subsidiary, principally because of Swiss tax incentives.

The two industrial departments expected to provide the main source of DISA's sales were not overly enthusiastic about a new layer of company organization. However, both departments agreed to formation of DISA for tax reasons. The Elastomer Department concluded: "The decisive factor in our support of the organization is the potential tax saving." The Textile Fibers Department recognized that tax considerations "will command the establishment of lowest practical transfer prices from the manufacturing subsidiaries to Du Pont Swiss [DISA]. . . ." A memorandum to the Executive Committee in late 1958 (shortly before the Committee approved DISA) spoke of *the modest mark-up* (emphasis in original) of goods sold to the foreign trading subsidiary. A prior draft of the memorandum used the phrase "the 'artificially' low price."

5. The individual industrial departments which manufactured goods sold to DISA had little reason to care about the pricing of such goods. Under a special accounting system DISA was ignored in computing departmental earnings, bonuses, etc. All profits from DISA were attributed to the department manufacturing the respective goods. This internal treatment of DISA's profits conflicted with Du Pont's standard practice of treating each subsidiary as a distinct profit center.

6. The responsible official did not solicit the views of the manufacturing departments as to an appropriate pricing system.

7. Finding 71 summarizes the testimony of the key Treasury Department official, who conceded he would have set prices so as to shift 99 percent of total profits to DISA if he had thought such an allocation would have survived IRS scrutiny.

certain intercorporate transfers — a result not contemplated in the initial pricing scheme.

D. In operation, DISA enjoyed certain market advantages which helped it to accumulate large, tax-free profits. For its technical service function, the subsidiary did not develop its own extensive laboratories (with resulting costs and risks), but could rely on its parent's laboratory network in the United States and England. DISA was not required to hunt intensively (or pay as highly) for qualified personnel, since in both 1959 and 1960 it drew extensively on its parent's reservoir of talent. The international company's credit risks were very low, in part because of a favorable trade credit timetable by Du Pont. DISA also selected its customers to avoid credit losses, having a bad debt provision of less than one-tenth of one percent of sales. Unlike other distributor or advertising service agencies, DISA, because of its special relationship to the Du Pont manufacturing departments, had relatively little risk of termination.[8] And as explained *supra*, Du Pont's pricing formula was intended to insulate DISA from losses on sales.[9]

In operating DISA, Du Pont also maximized its subsidiary's income by funneling a large volume of sales through DISA which did not call for large expenditures by the latter. Many of the products Du Pont sold through DISA required no special services, or already had ample technical services provided. Du Pont routed sales to Australia and South Africa through DISA although the latter provided no additional services to sales in these non-European countries. DISA made sales of commodity-type products and opportunistic spot sales to competitors temporarily short in a raw material, although neither type of sale required DISA's specialized marketing expertise. Du Pont also routed all European sales of elastomers through DISA, even though the parent had a well-established English subsidiary which had all the necessary technical services and marketing ability.

E. We have itemized the special status of DISA — as a subsidiary intended and operated to accumulate profits without much regard to the functions it performed or their real worth — not as direct proof, in itself, supporting the Commissioner's reallocation of profits under Section 482, but instead as suggesting the basic reason why

8. Du Pont's individual Industrial Departments could terminate sales with DISA, and two smaller departments did terminate. However, there is no evidence that Du Pont as an entity, particularly the important Elastomer and Textile Fiber Departments, would have seriously considered terminating DISA, a child of their own creation. Further, any such termination would have imposed less financial risk to DISA than for an independent distributor.

9. In actual fact, the pricing system malfunctioned to some extent and DISA incurred some minor losses. As in the case of profit allocation (see supra), this discrepancy was the product of a miscalculation in selling costs for a few low-volume goods. The design of Du Pont's pricing policy was to prevent any loss.

plaintiff's sales to DISA were unique and without any direct comparable in the real world. As we shall see in Part II, infra, taxpayer has staked its entire case on proving that the profits made by DISA in 1959 and 1960 were comparable to those made on similar resales by uncontrolled merchandizing agencies. DISA's special status and mode of functioning help to explain why that effort has failed. It is not that there was anything "illegal" or immoral in Du Pont's plan; it is simply that that plan made it very difficult, perhaps impossible, to satisfy the controlling Treasury regulations under Section 482.[10]

II. SECTION 482 AND THE RESALE PRICE METHOD OF ALLOCATING PROFITS

A. Section 482 gives the Secretary of the Treasury (or his delegate) discretion to allocate income between related corporations when necessary to "prevent evasion of taxes or clearly to reflect the income" of any of such corporations. The legislative history parallels the general purpose of the statutory text to prevent evasion by "improper manipulation of financial accounts," "arbitrary shifting of profits," and to accurately reflect "true tax liability." See H.R. Rep. No. 350, 67th Cong., 1st Sess. 14 (1921) (section 240(d) of 1921 Act); S. Rep. No. 275, 67th Cong., 1st Sess. 20 (1921) (same section); H.R. Rep. No. 2, 70th Cong., 1st Sess. 16 (1928) (predecessor section to §482). . . . Morton-Norwich Products, Inc. v. United States, Ct. Cl. No. 83-77, (July 18, 1979).[12]

B. We do not, however, have the initial problem of considering this case on the words of Section 482 alone, or on comparable broad criteria. In 1968 the Secretary of the Treasury issued revised regulations governing action under the statute, and setting forth rules for certain specific situations. Treas. Reg. §1.482-1, et seq. These regulations, which were issued before the trial here, were made retroactive to cover the taxable years before us (1959-1960), and both sides agree that the regulations must control. In some quarters these regulations have been faulted as not giving enough meaningful guidance in specific situations, or as being too narrow in the specific situations they do cover, but there is here no challenge to the validity of the regulations and we have to apply them as they are, with fidelity to both their words and their spirit.

---

10. The regulations make it clear (§1.482-1(c)) that they apply, not only to fraudulent, or shady cases, but "to any case in which either by inadvertence or design the taxable income, in whole or in part, of a controlled taxpayer, is other than it would have been had the taxpayer in the conduct of his affairs been an uncontrolled taxpayer dealing at arm's length with another uncontrolled taxpayer."

12. In this case there is, of course, no question that the two organizations involved were controlled by the same interests.

For sales of tangible goods, the directive mandates determination of an arm's length price for the sale by one controlled entity to the other, and then sets out (in order of preference) four methods for calculating such an arm's length price: the comparable uncontrolled price method, the resale price method, the cost plus method, and any other appropriate method. The parties correctly agree upon the inapplicability of the comparable uncontrolled price method (which calls for comparison with an uncontrolled sale of an almost identical product). Plaintiff makes no argument as to the possible application of the cost plus method. Instead it posits its whole case on the resale price method (Treas. Reg. §1.4822(e)(3)) — which we now consider.

C. Essentially, the resale price method reconstructs a fair arm's length market price by discounting the controlled reseller's selling price by the gross profit margin (or markup percentage) rates of comparable uncontrolled dealers.[14] Thus, if DISA's gross profit margin for resale was 35% and the prevailing margin for comparable uncontrolled resellers was 25%, the Commissioner could reallocate 10% of DISA's gross income. But the vital prerequisite for applying the resale price method is the existence of substantially comparable uncontrolled resellers. Subpart (vi) of Section 1.482-2(e)(3) requires determination of the "most similar" resale or resales, considering the type of property, reseller's functions, use of any intangibles, and similarity of geographic markets.[15] Cases which have considered the regulation uniformly require substantial comparability. See, e.g., Woodward Governor Co. v. Commissioner, 55 T.C. 56, 65 (1970) (resale price method applicable only when evidence shows uncontrolled purchases and resales by same or similar reseller); American Terrazzo Strip Co. v. Commissioner, 56 T.C. 961, 972-73 (1971) (uncontrolled sales must be comparable in terms of similar goods and circumstances of sale); Edwards v. Commissioner, 67 T.C. 224, 236 (1976) (rejecting use of industry gross profit statistic when no evidence that such sales were comparable to taxpayer). Commentators agree on the need for close similarity of uncontrolled sales, and some criticize the regulation when no uncontrolled sales by the *same* party

14. Subpart (vi) of Section 1.482-2(e)(2) declares that the proper markup, described as "the appropriate markup percentage," is "equal to the percentage of gross profit (expressed as a percentage of sales) earned by the buyer (reseller) or another party on the resale of property which is both purchased and resold in an uncontrolled transaction, which resale is most similar to the applicable resale of the property involved in the controlled sale."

15. Subpart (vii) directs that, "[w]henever possible markup percentages should be derived from uncontrolled purchases and resale of the buyer (reseller) involved in the controlled sale [here, DISA]. . . . In the absence of [such] resales by the same buyer (reseller) . . . evidence of an appropriate markup percentage may be derived from resales by other resellers selling *in the same or a similar market* in which the controlled buyer (reseller) is selling, *providing such resellers perform comparable function.*" [Emphasis added.]

exist. See Fuller, Section 482 Revisited, 31 Tax L. Rev. 475, 505-07, 510-11 (1976); Jenks, Treasury Regulations under Section 482, 23 Tax Lawyer 279, 310 (1970) [hereinafter cited as Jenks]; Note, Multinational Corporations Income Allocation under Section 482 of the Internal Revenue Code, 89 Harv. L. Rev. 1202, 1220 (1976). It is quite plain from the text of the regulation itself that the evident purpose for the use of the particular resale price method, as set forth in the regulation, is to proffer a relatively precise mechanism for determining a realistically comparable, uncontrolled, arm's length resale price — not to leave the taxpayer, the Service, or the courts to grope at large for some figure drawn out of overly general indices or statistics.

The common starting point for our search in this case for a comparable meeting the requirements of the regulation is our finding 101 which states: "The parties agree, and their agreement is supported by the record, that there is not known to exist, presently or heretofore, an independent organization circumstanced as DISA was during the period in suit and performing the marketing functions that were assigned to it by plaintiff." That being so, the regulation requires us (§1.4822(e)(3)(vi)(a), (b), and (d)) to look for the "most similar" resales and "in determining the similarity of resales" to consider as the "most important characteristics" the type of property sold, the functions performed by the seller with respect to the property, and the geographic market in which the functions are performed by the reseller. There is also special stress on the performance of "comparable functions" by the seller making the "most similar" resales. See subpart (vii).

Taxpayer tells us that a group of 21 distributors, whose general functions were similar to DISA's, provides the proper base of comparison.[16] Beyond the most general showing that this group, like DISA, distributed manufactured goods, there is nothing in the record showing the degree of similarity called for by the regulation. No data exist to establish similarity of products (with associated marketing

---

16. The 21 companies were selected by defendant from a group of 32 businesses. Defendant chose the 32 from a much larger random sample of the three types of organizations functionally comparable (in general) to DISA — management consultant firms, advertising agencies, and distributors. Defendant introduced this group of 32 solely to demonstrate its general economic thesis that companies with higher profits also incurred higher selling costs. Taxpayer asserts that at trial defendant conceded that these companies were in fact sufficiently comparable to DISA for use in applying the resale price method. A review of the trial transcript reveals no such concession. Similarly, taxpayer's reliance on the finding that, of the three types of organizations, the distributors "are most functionally comparable to DISA. . . ." is misplaced. That statement means merely that, as between management consultant firms, advertising agencies, and distributors, the latter are closest to DISA. Moreover, a mere finding of general functional similarity does not provide precise enough data to allow use of the resale price method.

costs), comparability of functions, or parallel geographic (and economic) market conditions. Rather, the record suggests significant differences. Defendant has introduced evidence that the six companies plaintiff identifies most closely with DISA all had average selling costs much higher than DISA.[17] Because we agree with the trial judge and defendant's expert that, in general, what a business spends to provide services is a reasonable indication of the magnitude of those services, and because plaintiff has not rebutted that normal presumption in this case, we cannot view these six companies as having made resales similar to DISA's. They may have made gross profits comparable to DISA's but their selling costs, reflecting the greater scale of their services or efforts, were much higher in each instance.[18] Moreover, the record shows that these companies dealt with quite different products (electronic and photographic equipment) and functioned in different markets (primarily the United States).

Other industrial group or individual resales relied on by taxpayer also fall short of comparability to DISA. We are cited to the gross profit margin of certain drug and chemical wholesalers contained in the Internal Revenue Service's Source Book of Statistics of Income

---

17. Defendant's comparison is derived from data in various exhibits and is summarized in the following table:

Reseller	Average Annual Markup Percentages	Average Annual Operating Expenses (percentage of net sales)
AIC Photo	38%	27.5%
Superscope	33%	20.5%
Lloyd Electronics	26%	20.5%
DISA	26%	6.7% or 7.1%*
Soundesign	23%	20.0%
Interphoto	20.5%	16.0%
Telecor	19.5%	11.5%

*The trial judge used a 6.7% figure while our own computation shows 7.1% (both figures have been adjusted to exclude certain one-time starting costs in 1959; including such costs our result would be the slightly higher average figure of 7.8%.

Finding 123 summarizes the evidence on DISA's unusually low selling costs: "The evidence shows that DISA so dramatically exceeded the profitability of the independent distributor community [the sample of 21 firms taxpayer relies on] ... because to earn the dollars represented by that [gross profit] margin it did not have to spend nearly so many dollars to provide service and otherwise operate its business as did the distributors who bought and sold their products and services at prices determined by free market forces."

18. Taxpayer itself compensated its independent distributors by a system of price discounts ranging from 4% for textile fibers and 5% for elastomers (the two product lines accounting for more than 90% of DISA's sales and earnings) to 35% for photo products and agricultural chemicals, depending on the amount of effort and expense taxpayer thought necessary for the proper merchandising by the independent of the product involved (finding 81).

for 1960. Because the gross profit for this group of undisclosed companies[19] in 1960 averaged 21 percent, taxpayer infers that DISA's gross profit of 26 percent was reasonable. Again, the lack of any data establishing comparability between DISA and the category of Source Book companies precludes any such conclusion. The fact that, within the wholesaler category, gross profits varied from 9 to 33 percent indicates that to take a mere arithmetic average, without considering underlying factual details, would risk a total distortion. See Simon, Section 482 Allocations, 46 Taxes 254 (1968) (criticizing lack of relevance, unavailability of third party data in gauging arm's length prices); Edwards v. Commissioner, 67 T.C. 224, 236-37 (1976) (industry average of uncertain reliability in determining arm's length sale price); cf. Major Coat Co. v. United States, 211 Ct. Cl. 1, 34, 543 F.2d 97, 116 (1976) (Source Book statistics on profitability of firms in same manufacturing category rejected in renegotiation case; no showing of relative character, efficiencies or risks of other companies). Plaintiff tells us that the IRS itself used these Source Book figures for 1960 and later years (not now before us). But the Service utilized net profit figures, not those for gross profit or gross markup. Whether or not this use of net profit computations contravened the regulations (which call for comparisons of gross profits in using the resale price method) or means that the IRS was following the "fourth method" (see Part III infra), we cannot say, as plaintiff wants us to, that the Service must have considered these drug and chemical wholesalers as comparable companies making similar resales, but that the IRS simply made a mistake in using net profits. The little we have on the IRS practice does not permit us to conclude anything as to the Service's position on comparability of these companies for the purposes of the resale price method.[20]

---

19. Defendant is precluded by statute from disclosing the names of companies contained in the Source Book.

20. Subpart (vii) of the regulation says that "[i]n the absence of data on markup percentages of particular sales or groups of sales, the *prevailing* markup percentage in the *particular industry* involved *may* be appropriate" (emphasis added), but we do not consider that this record (with its wide range of markups and variation in products) shows, with respect to these Source Book companies, the "prevailing" markup in DISA's own "particular industry."

Taxpayer also invites comparison of DISA's gross profits with several other uncontrolled transactions, none of which is apposite. The contract for marketing of film between Du Pont and Bell & Howell involved minimal volume requirements, the expectation of initial marketing losses, and a gross profit contingent on meeting maximum selling cost levels. Such risks are so different from DISA's as to make Bell & Howell's proposed compensation rate "irrelevant for comparative purposes." Finding 105. The rate of return by a Du Pont subsidiary marketing urea herbicides involved special technology loans and missing details which preclude "a meaningful analogy," Finding 109. The sale of a "commodity-type" NA-22 elastomer (not requiring DISA's special selling skills) at a very low volume also precludes the use of such sales as a meaningful comparison. Finding 108. See also Findings 106, 107, 110 (discussing in detail other purported comparable profits introduced by taxpayer at trial).

The lack of any significantly comparable resale (or group of resales) in this record is underscored by taxpayer's failure to suggest any means for adjusting for differences between DISA and the uncontrolled resellers. Subpart (ix) of section 1.482-2(e)(3) requires "appropriate adjustment" for "any material differences between the uncontrolled purchases and resales used as the basis for the calculation of the appropriate markup percentage and the resales of property involved in the controlled sale." Such material differences must be "differences in functions or circumstances" and must have a "definite and reasonably ascertainable effect on price." The trial judge premised his rejection of plaintiff's case on the failure to suggest appropriate adjustments under this subpart, particularly for DISA's lack of "entrepreneurial risk." Taxpayer mounts a vigorous assault on this position, arguing that DISA was exposed to all normal risks, including shipping and warehouse risks, sudden European market declines, or termination by manufacturing departments of Du Pont. Even if we assume *arguendo* that DISA did assume full market risks,[21] we think taxpayer cannot escape the ultimate point of subpart (ix) — assuming a roughly comparable uncontrolled reseller (or resellers), taxpayer still bears the burden of showing adjustments to arrive at an arm's length price.[22] However, plaintiff proposes no adjustments for differences in marketing locations, selling functions, or production differences between DISA and the "comparable" 21 distributors. Taxpayer's brief selects one of the distributors, Superscope, as the company "most similar in function" to DISA, but fails to suggest the appropriate adjustments for such aspects as Superscope's different product line (tape recorders), different geographic market (the United States), or contractual obligation to make minimum purchases from the manufacturer.

The failure to proffer adjustments reflects the stark fact that, on this record, there is no company or group of companies so near and so comparable to DISA that the few material differences can be properly adjusted for under the regulatory pattern. Subpart (ix) and the example given under it (the same reseller selling two very similar products with only a difference in warranty coverage between the controlled and uncontrolled transactions) reinforce the view that

21. This is not an easy assumption to accept, since Du Pont's pricing system for DISA was designed to protect the latter from losses, and DISA's operations seemed geared to help it make profits with little risk. See Part I, *supra.* Furthermore, the risk of complete termination by the parent which established and operated DISA for a number of particular purposes (including profit accumulation), seems substantially less than that of a wholly independent distributor.

22. Plaintiff should have been aware at trial that this was considered its burden. Before the trial, the trial judge ruled that taxpayer could not rest on a showing that the IRS determination was erroneously computed, but had to prove that it owed either nothing at all or a lesser amount than the Service had determined. Plaintiff did not seek court review of this ruling.

under the resale price method the resales of uncontrolled companies must be substantially similar to those of the controlled reseller before that method can be used. And even if there is greater initial latitude in finding a comparable reseller than seems to us appropriate, subpart (ix) demands "appropriate adjustment . . . to reflect any material differences" which "have a definite and reasonably ascertainable effect on price." Plaintiff, which urges that the resale price method be used, bears the burden of fulfilling all the requirements of the regulation, but has failed to do so.

Plaintiff contends, finally, that requiring it to prove the proper amount of adjustment is an unfair burden. The suggestion is that once Du Pont shows that its prices were arm's length prices (by demonstrating that DISA's gross profit margin was equivalent to that of uncontrolled alleged comparables can be accepted as such under the resale price method portion of the regulation. And if we surmount that hurdle, we see no good reason why a taxpayer should be free from suggesting the appropriate adjustments under subpart (ix). As the opening words of the paragraph show, the adjustments called for by the subpart are integral to the determination of an "arm's length price," and the determination of an "arm's length price" is the essence of the resale price method which plaintiff invokes.[23]

D. The upshot is that plaintiff has failed to bring itself within the resale price method. The record before us does not support use of that formula for this case.[24] Indeed, it may very well be that, because of DISA's unique position, the showing required by the regulation could simply not be made. At any rate, we have to conclude that, on this record, it is not possible to apply the resale price method.

As we have intimated in Part I, D, supra, this total failure of proof is no surprise. Taxpayer's prices to DISA were set wholly without regard to the factors which normally enter into an arm's length price (see Part I, C, supra), and it would have been pure happenstance if those prices had turned out to be equivalent to arm's length prices. This is not a case in which a taxpayer does attempt, the best it can, to establish intercorporate prices on an arm's length basis, and then runs up against an IRS which disagrees with this or that detail in the

23. Insofar as the trial judge may have indicated in his opinion that, apart from adjustment for entrepreneurial risk under subpart (ix), Du Pont's prices to DISA were fully comparable to arm's length prices, we disagree — as seen from the foregoing portions of this opinion.

24. Defendant says, somewhat weakly, that, although plaintiff made insufficient proof, the Government itself presented adequate evidence to comply with the resale price method by using as comparables Du Pont's independent distributors in Europe (to whom DISA resold) — and whose markup margins were normally much less than DISA's. But these "comparables" were not shown to be similar to DISA, which performed many other functions, and no effort was made by defendant to adjust upward for the differences. Therefore, we do not believe that the evidence as to the margin of these independent resellers enables us to apply the resale price method here.

calculation. Plaintiff never made that effort, and it would have been undiluted luck—which under the regulation it probably could enjoy—if it had managed to discover comparable resales falling within the resale price method as set forth in the regulation (including adjustments to be made under subpart (ix)).

III. VALIDITY OF THE COMMISSIONER'S ALLOCATION UNDER THE REGULATION

In reviewing the Commissioner's allocation of income under Section 482, we focus on the reasonableness of the result, not the details of the examining agent's methodology. See Eli Lilly & Co. v. United States, 178 Ct. Cl. 666, 676, 372 F.2d 990, 997 (1967); Young & Rubicam, Inc. v. United States, 187 Ct. Cl. 635, 654-55, 410 F.2d 1233, 1245 (1969).[25] Plaintiff contends that the Commissioner's result does not conform to any of the specific methods under the regulations and is therefore unreasonable per se. But the regulations (§1.482-2(e)(1)(iii)) specifically allow for another appropriate method — "some appropriate method of pricing other than those described . . . or variations on such methods"—when, as here, none of the three specific methods can properly be used. That alternative "fourth method" now comes into play, and we consider the reasonableness of the Commissioner's result under its very broad delegation. This other "appropriate method of pricing" must, of course, conform to the general directives (stated at the outset of the regulation): "to place a controlled taxpayer on a tax parity with an uncontrolled taxpayer" and "in every case" to apply the standard "of an uncontrolled taxpayer dealing at arm's length with another uncontrolled taxpayer." See §1.482-1(b)(1) and (c).[26]

That some reallocation was reasonable is demonstrated by recalling the facts of DISA's operation. See Part I, supra. Several of the products sold through DISA received none of its special marketing or technical services. Nonetheless, DISA obtained its usual profit from Du Pont for minimal work on these goods—a result contrary to selling practices in the real world. Examples include: (1) opportunistic sales and sales of commodity-type products; (2) sales to South Africa and Australia routed through DISA; (3) sales of elastomers produced and serviced by Du Pont's British subsidiary. DISA's selling "expertise" was not employed on any of these goods, and the sole reason to sell them through DISA seems to have been

25. On July 7, 1969, before the trial, the court denied taxpayer's motion for summary judgment which was based on the ground that, once it is shown that the IRS computation is erroneous in method, the taxpayer must necessarily prevail. Our order cited *Eli Lilly* and *Young & Rubicam*.

Defendant does not now contend that the Service's method of calculating the reallocations was correct, but does support the result.

26. Again, plaintiff has the burden of showing that the IRS result is unacceptable under the "fourth method."

to increase the volume of profits for that special subsidiary.[27] Above all of these specific indications that DISA did not earn its profits is the overriding fact (discussed in Parts I and II, supra) that Du Pont's prices to DISA were deliberately set high and with little or no regard to economic realities.

The amount of reallocation would not be easy for us to calculate if we were called upon to do it ourselves, but Section 482 gives that power to the Commissioner and we are content that his amount (totalling some $18 million) was within the zone of reasonableness. The language of the statute and the holdings of the courts recognize that the Service has broad discretion in reallocating income. . . . Once past the three specific methods for computing intercompany prices of tangible property, the determiner of realistic intercompany prices is hardly exercising an economic art susceptible of precision. A "broad brush" approach to this inexact field seems necessary and conforms with this court's experience up to now under the Renegotiation Act, requiring post hoc and de novo determination of excessive profits on war and defense Government business. See, e.g., A.C. Ball Co. v. United States, 209 Ct. Cl. 223, 229, 531 F.2d 993, 996 (1976); Bata Shoe Co. v. United States, . . . 595 F.2d 9, 25 (Ct. Cl. 1979) (and cases cited). Du Pont has not convinced us, on this record, that the Commissioner abused the broad discretion he possessed (the specific methods being inapplicable), or that he acted unreasonably.

On the contrary, two economic indices presented by defendant support the result of the Commissioner's reallocation: One index compares DISA's ratio of gross income to total operating costs with the ratios for the 32 advertising, management-consultant, and distributor firms functionally similar, in general, to DISA. These are the results:

Organization	Average gross income/ total cost percentage
6 management-consultant firms	108.3%
5 advertising firms	123.9%
21 distributors	129.3%
DISA (before reallocation)*	281.5% (1959)
	397.1% (1960)**
DISA (after reallocation)*	108.6% (1959)
	179.3% (1960)

*DISA's percentages are not averages, but its actual returns for 1959-1960.

**The 285.1% figure for 1959, if readjusted to exclude one-time start-up costs, would be over 336%.

27. An early memorandum to the Executive Committee during the formative stages of DISA stated that the amount of export profits to be realized by the tax haven subsidiary would depend (in part) "upon the extent to which export sales can be funnelled through the trading company. . . ." In operation, taxpayer set out to maximize sales "funnelled through" DISA, even though DISA's skills contributed minimally to such sales.

Only twice in over a hundred years of these companies' experience did any of the distributing firms attain income/cost ratios of over 200%, and no distributor ever achieved the 280-400% range experienced by DISA.

The second index does not rely at all on general functional similarities, but rests solely on a very comprehensive study of the rates of return (along with margin and turnover ratios) of over 1,100 companies. The following table illustrates the results:

Index	10-year average of 1,133 companies	DISA before allocation 1959	1960	DISA after allocation 1959	1960
Return on capital	9.47%	450 %	147.2 %	20%	38%
Margin	7.12%	13.1%	17.3 %		
Turnover	1.33	34.0	8.516		

Whether measured by income/cost ratios of functionally similar firms or by capital return rates for industry as a whole, DISA's profits, before reallocation, vastly exceeded the uppermost limits. After reallocation, DISA's return on capital would still be better than over 96% of the 1133 companies surveyed. Using the two indices as a general measure of economic profits, DISA stands supreme before reallocation.

Plaintiff attacks the validity of the two studies, arguing that return on capital is an inaccurate measuring rod, and that the income/cost ratio is inappropriate because profits vary with the skills of the individual companies. Whatever the general limits of any particular gauge of industry profitability, plaintiff cannot escape the basic thrust of defendant's proof. Defendant has shown that DISA made extraordinarily high profits which the Commissioner reallocated to an economically reasonable level. Plaintiff has not shown any specific comparable transactions refuting the general trend, and the record reveals none. See Part II, supra. Given the Commissioner's general discretion and the necessary inexactitude of such economic allocations, we conclude that the Commissioner's allocation was reasonable and should be accepted.

CONCLUSION OF LAW

Upon the findings of fact, which are made a part of the judgment herein, and the foregoing opinion, the court concludes as a matter of law that plaintiff is not entitled to recover, provided that plaintiff is accorded the opportunity to demonstrate in further proceedings in the Trial Division that it is entitled to relief under the provisions of Rev. Proc. 64-54, 1964-2 Cum. Bull. 1008. The cases are returned to the Trial Division for such further proceedings. . . .

[Concurring opinion omitted.]

NOTES

1. See Eli Lilly & Co., 84 T.C. 996 (1985), *aff'd in part and rev'd in part,* 856 F.2d 855 (7th Cir. 1988) (employing a profit-split method, analyzing the relative value of each member's contribution to the income production process).

2. The Government recently issued an important study dealing with the intercompany pricing rules. See Treasury Department Study of Intercompany Pricing (Oct. 19, 1988), known as "The Section 482 White Paper." One of the most important aspects of the study is its discussion of the valuation of intangibles such as patents and trademarks. It suggests that the use of "exact comparables," prices between unrelated parties in which the same property is transferred under very similar market conditions, be required when available. If exact comparables are unavailable, the report recommends the use of either (1) "inexact comparables," (2) an arm's length return method, or (3) a profit-split method.

The study also suggests that companies be required to document their intercompany pricing methods before filing their tax returns. The documentation would include such pertinent information as financial analyses of the rates of returns on assets and markups on costs incurred.

For a discussion of the Treasury study, see Carlson, Fogarasi and Gordon, The Section 482 White Paper: Highlights and Implications, Tax Notes, Oct. 31, 1988, p. 547; Langbein, Transaction Cost, Production Cost, and Tax Transfer, Tax Notes, Sept. 18, 1989, p. 1391. See also Bausch & Lomb Inc., et al., 92 T.C. No. 33 (1989); Frisch and Horst, Bausch & Lomb and the White Paper, Tax Notes, May 8, 1989, p. 725.

3. In Rev. Rul. 82-135, 1982-2 C.B. 104, the Service made an interest allocation where a corporation was required by its parent to make a prepayment for merchandise purchased from the parent. No allocation was made where the prepayment arose in the ordinary course of business and was not required by the parent.

4. See Central Bank of the South v. United States, 834 F.2d 990 (11th Cir. 1987), in which the court sustained the Commissioner's allocation to a taxpayer of rental income never paid him by a lessee corporation owned by his wife and children.

In Dolese v. Commissioner, 811 F.2d 543 (10th Cir. 1987), the court upheld the Commissioner's decision to reallocate a charitable contribution deduction and capital gains between an individual and a wholly owned corporation on the basis of their respective interests in a partnership. The court rejected the taxpayer's position that the reallocation should be made on the basis of the partnership's distribution of land (later sold to a city for tax purposes) to the individual and the corporation in percentages disproportionate to their respective partnership interests.

5. See generally Higinbotham, Asper, Stoffregen, and Wexler, Effective Application of the Section 482 Transfer Pricing Regulations, 42 Tax L. Rev. 293 (1987); Rafferty, The Profit-Split Method of Income Allocation in Intercompany Pricing Disputes: The *Eli Lilly* Case, 64 Taxes 662 (1986).

REVENUE RULING 78-83
1978-1 C.B. 79

Advice has been requested whether income of X corporation diverted to Y corporation will be treated as a distribution taxable as a dividend to P corporation to the extent of the earnings and profits of X and a capital contribution by P to Y, under the circumstances described below.

The taxpayer, P, a domestic corporation, owned all of the stock of X, a foreign corporation incorporated in country M. X produces and exports fiber for sale on the world market, but due to monetary restrictions, X has had difficulty in securing dollars needed to pay refunds to foreign customers and to pay travel expenses of its employees outside country M. P, therefore, formed Y, a wholly owned foreign corporation incorporated in country T to act on behalf of X to receive part of the sales price charged by X. Thereafter, some of these dollars accumulated by Y were used to pay the above-mentioned refunds and expenses, as well as certain promotion expenses in connection with the fiber sales. P provided incidental services for X in connection with these disbursements, but performed no services in connection with the fiber sales. The funds diverted from X to Y were in excess of the amounts necessary to provide Y with reasonable compensation for its services to X and to reimburse Y for the expenses it incurred on behalf of X. . . .

Section 482 of the Code applies to transactions between brother-sister corporations involving the performance of services by one for the benefit of the other that result in significant shifting of income.

Where an allocation is made under section 482 as a result of an excessive charge for services rendered between brother-sister corporations, the amount of the allocation will be treated as a distribution to the controlling shareholder with respect to the stock of the entity whose income is increased and as a capital contribution by the controlling shareholder to the other entity involved in the transaction. See Rev. Rul. 69-630, 1969-2 C.B. 112, relating to a bargain sale between brother-sister controlled corporations.

A constructive dividend is paid when a corporation diverts property, directly or indirectly, to the use of a shareholder without expectation of repayment, even though no formal dividend has been declared.

Generally, in those cases involving corporations controlled by the same persons, the courts have found a constructive dividend to have been distributed to the common shareholders where one of the corporations was used as a device for siphoning off the earnings and profits. See Helvering v. Gordon, 87 F.2d 663 (8th Cir. 1937); Commissioner v. Greenspun, 156 F.2d 917 (5th Cir. 1946); Biltmore Homes, Inc. v. Commissioner, 288 F.2d 336 (4th Cir. 1961).

However, a constructive dividend is a diversion of the property, not of the income. Income is a characterization which tax law attributes to certain receipts of property, whereas a constructive distribution is that of property itself. Thus, where property is transferred from one affiliate to a sister corporation without adequate consideration therefor, there is a constructive distribution to the common parent whether or not the motive for the transfer was an attempt improperly to allocate income or deductions between the corporations.

However, any amount diverted to Y for disbursements on behalf of X, or as reasonable compensation for services rendered to X, would not be considered as constructive dividend income to P.

Accordingly, the income of X diverted to Y in excess of the disbursements on behalf of X and reasonable compensation for services of Y will be treated as a distribution taxable as a dividend to P to the extent of the earnings and profits of X, and a capital contribution by P to Y.

NOTE

The facts of Rev. Rul. 78-83 are derived from Columbian Rope Co., 42 T.C. 800 (1964). The government did not appear to rely on §482 in *Columbian Rope*, but the court referred to that section in the course of its discussion (42 T.C. at 811-813):

> The first issue is whether respondent was correct in including the undistributed income of Empresa (Y) (a wholly owned foreign subsidiary of petitioner) in the taxable income of petitioner in 1959, 1960, and 1961. Respondent contends that Empresa's principal function in Panama was to serve as a "conduit of dollars"

from the Philippine subsidiary (X) to the petitioner. Respondent states on brief that Empresa was no more than the petitioner's "bank account in Panama" and that petitioner withdrew money as it was needed for petitioner's own purposes, such as the payment of dividends or financing other ventures. Respondent states that the routing of dollars to Empresa was accomplished by an "arbitrary overcharge" for the fiber sale by the Philippine subsidiary to its customers (other than petitioner) and that this overcharge was credited to Empresa.

It is difficult to discern the basis for respondent's contentions. The Philippine subsidiary was a wholly owned foreign subsidiary of the petitioner. It was generally true prior to 1962 that the earnings of foreign subsidiaries were taxable to the domestic parent only when such earnings were actually distributed to the parent. The Philippine subsidiary conducted its own business as a leading exporter of abaca fiber to markets in all parts of the world. Although petitioner obtained much of its abaca fiber from the Philippine subsidiary, the record shows that sales by the subsidiary to other customers in the United States exceeded the sales to petitioner in each of the years 1959, 1960, and 1961. Income derived from the sale of fiber clearly belonged to the Philippine subsidiary, not to petitioner. Petitioner was not in the business of selling fiber. It would seem that no justification existed to attribute the income of the Philippine subsidiary to the petitioner.

When Empresa was formed by petitioner in 1957 as a wholly owned foreign subsidiary in Panama, it was presumably for the purpose of alleviating some of the dollar-shortage difficulties faced by the Philippine subsidiary as a result of Philippine exchange restrictions. Among Empresa's functions were (1) to settle claims (in dollars) made by customers of the Philippine subsidiary as to quality, quantity, color, or other defects in the fiber sold by the subsidiary and (2) to provide travel expenses in dollars for the business trips made outside the Philippines by executives and employees of the Philippine subsidiary.

The funds obtained by Empresa for these and other purposes came out of the proceeds of fiber sales made by the Philippine subsidiary to its customers (other than petitioner). The portion of the sales price so diverted by the Philippines subsidiary to Empresa amounted to about $1 per bale of fiber, plus 1 percent of the amount of "cost plus insurance" per bale. Petitioner performed no services for the Philippine subsidiary in connection with these fiber sales, so that it cannot be said that a part of *petitioner's* income was being diverted to Empresa. There is no problem here as to a reallocation of income between related taxpayers to properly reflect their respective income, which might arise where a taxpayer sells to a foreign subsidiary at an unrealistic discount, or buys from a foreign subsidiary at an artificially high price. See sec. 482, I.R.C. 1954.

If Empresa had not been formed and, instead, all of the proceeds from the world sales of fiber were remitted directly to the Philippine subsidiary, it is clear (as we have indicated earlier) that its profits would not be includable in petitioner's taxable income until they were actually distributed to the petitioner. We do not see how the presence of Empresa calls for any different result. Nothing is changed: the income is still generated by the same fiber sales by the Philippine subsidiary on the world market, except that now some of the income, instead of returning to the Philippines, comes to rest in Panama.

Respondent urges on brief that we should disregard the entity of Empresa and "attribute the earnings which were temporarily passing through Empresa as actually having been received by the ultimate beneficiary," i.e., the petitioner. Empresa was a separate corporate entity duly organized under the laws of Panama, where it actually performed certain business functions. Under these circumstances, its separate corporate identity cannot be ignored. Moline Properties, Inc. v. Commissioner, 319 U.S. 436.

COMMISSIONER v. FIRST SECURITY BANK
405 U.S. 394 (1972)

Mr. Justice POWELL delivered the opinion of the Court. This case presents for review a determination by the Commissioner of Internal Revenue (Commissioner), pursuant to §482 . . . that the income of taxpayers within a controlled group should be reallocated to reflect the true taxable income of each. . . .

Respondents, First Security Bank of Utah, N.A., and First Security Bank of Idaho, N.A. (the Banks), are national banks that, during the tax years, were wholly owned subsidiaries of First Security Corp. (Holding Company). Other, non-bank, subsidiaries of the Holding Company, relevant to this case, were First Security Co. (Management Company), Ed. D. Smith & Sons, an insurance agency (Smith), and —from June 1954—First Security Life Insurance Company of Texas (Security Life). Beginning in 1948, the Banks offered to arrange for borrowers credit life, health, and accident insurance (credit life insurance). The Tax Court found that they did this "for several reasons," including (1) offering a service increasingly supplied by competing financial institutions, (2) obtaining the benefit of the additional collateral that credit insurance provides by repaying loans upon the death, injury, or illness of the borrower, and (3) providing an "additional source of income—part of the premiums from the insurance—to Holding Company or its subsidiaries."

Until 1954, any borrower who elected to purchase this insurance was referred by the Banks to two independent insurance companies. The premium rate charged was $1 per $100 of coverage per year, the rate commonly charged in the industry. The Insurance Commissioners of the States involved — Utah, Idaho, and Texas — accepted this rate. The Banks followed a routine procedure in making this insurance available to customers. The lending officer would explain the function and availability of credit insurance. If the customer desired the coverage, the necessary form was completed, a certificate of insurance was delivered, and the premium was collected or added to the customer's loan. The Banks then forwarded the completed forms and premiums to Management Company, which maintained records of the insurance purchased and forwarded the premiums to the insurance carrier. Management Company also processed claims filed under the policies. The cost to each of the Banks for the actual time devoted to explaining and processing the insurance was less than $2,000 per year, characterized by the courts below as "negligible." The cost to Management Company of the services rendered by it was also negligible, slightly in excess of $2,000 per year.

It was the custom in the insurance business (although not invariably followed), regardless of the cost of incidental paperwork, to pay a "sales commission" — ranging from 40% to 55% of net premiums collected — to a party who originated or generated the business. But the Banks had been advised by counsel that they could not lawfully conduct the business of an insurance agency or receive income resulting from their customers' purchase of credit life insurance. Neither the Banks nor any of their officers were licensed to sell insurance, and there is no question here of unlawfully acting as unlicensed agents. The Banks received no commissions or other income on or with respect to the credit insurance generated by them. During the period from 1948 to 1954 commissions were paid by the independent companies writing the insurance directly, to Smith, one of the wholly owned subsidiaries of Holding Company. These commissions were reported as taxable income, not by Smith, but by Management Company which had rendered the services above described. During this period (1948-1954), the Commissioner did not attempt to allocate the commission to the Banks.

In 1954, Holding Company organized Security Life, a new wholly owned subsidiary licensed to engage in the insurance business. A new procedure was then adopted with respect to placing credit life insurance. It was referred by the Banks to, and written by an independent company, American National Insurance Company of Galveston, Texas (American National), at the same rate to the customer. American National then reinsured the policies with Security Life pursuant to a "treaty of reinsurance." For assuming the risk under the policies sold to the Banks' customers, Security Life retained 85% of the premiums. American National, which furnished actuarial and accounting services, received the remaining 15%. No sales commissions were paid. Under this new plan, the Banks continued to offer credit life insurance to their borrowers in the same manner as before.

Security Life was not a paper corporation. It commenced business in 1954 with an initial capital of $25,000, which was increased in 1956 to $100,000. Although it did not become a full-line insurance company (contemplated as a possibility when organized), its reinsurance business was substantial. The risks assumed by it had grown to $41,350,000 by the end of 1959, and it had paid substantial claims.

Security Life reported the entire amount of reinsurance premiums, 85% of the premiums charged, in its income for the years 1955-1959. Because the income of life insurance companies then was subject to a lower effective tax rate than that of ordinary corporations, the total tax liability for Holding Company and its subsidiaries was less than it would have been had Security Life paid a part of the premium to the Banks or Management Company as sales commissions. Pursuant to his §482 power to allocate gross income among controlled corporations in order to reflect the actual incomes of the corporations, the Commissioner determined that 40% of Security Life's premium income was allocable to the Banks as compensation for originating and processing the credit life insurance. It is the Commissioner's view that the 40% of the premium income so allocated is the equivalent of commissions that the Banks earned and must be included in their "true taxable income."

The parties agree that §482 is designed to prevent "artificial shifting, milking, or distorting of the true net incomes of commonly controlled enterprises." . . .

The question we must answer is whether there was a shifting or distorting of the Banks' true net income resulting from the receipt and retention by Security Life of the premiums above described.

We note at the outset that the Banks could never have received a share of these premiums. National banks are authorized to act as insurance agents when located in places having a population not exceeding 5,000 inhabitants, 12 U.S.C.A. §92. Although §92 does not explicitly prohibit banks in places with a population of over 5,000 from acting as insurance agents, courts have held that it does so by implication. The Comptroller of the Currency has acquiesced in this holding, and the Court of Appeals for the Tenth Circuit expressed its agreement in the opinion below.

The penalties for violation of the banking laws include possible forfeiture of a bank's franchise and personal liability of directors. The Tax Court found that the Banks, upon advice of counsel, "held the belief that it would be contrary to Federal banking law . . . to receive income resulting from their customers' purchase of credit insurance" and, pursuant to this belief, "the two Banks have never received or attempted to receive commissions or reinsurance premiums resulting from their customers' purchase of credit insurance."

. . . [W]e assume for purposes of this decision that the Banks were prohibited from receiving insurance-related income, although this prohibition did not apply to non-bank subsidiaries of Holding Company.

We know of no decision of this Court wherein a person has been found to have taxable income that he did not receive and that he was prohibited from receiving. In cases dealing with the concept of income, it has been assumed that the person to whom the income was attributed could have received it. The underlying assumption always has been that in order to be taxed for income, a taxpayer must have complete domination over it. . . .

It is, of course, well established that income assigned before it is received is nonetheless taxable to the assignor. But the assignment-of-income doctrine assumes that the income would have been received by the taxpayer had he not arranged for it to be paid to another. . . .

One of the Commissioner's regulations for the implementation of §482 expressly recognizes the concept that income implies a dominion or control of the taxpayer. It provides as follows:

> The interests controlling a group of controlled taxpayers are assumed to have complete power to cause each controlled taxpayer so to conduct its affairs that its transactions and accounting records truly reflect the taxable income from the property and business of each of the controlled taxpayers.

This regulation is consistent with the control concept heretofore approved by this Court, although in a different context. The regulation, as applied to the facts in this case, contemplates that Holding Company — the controlling interest — must have "complete power" to shift income among its subsidiaries. It is only where this power exists, and has been exercised in such a way that the "true taxable income" of a subsidiary has been understated, that the Commissioner is authorized to reallocate under §482. But Holding Company had no such power unless it acted in violation of federal banking laws. The "complete power" referred to in the regulations hardly includes the power to force a subsidiary to violate the law.

Apart from the inequity of attributing to the Banks taxable income that they have not received and may not lawfully receive, neither the statute nor our prior decisions require such a result. We are not faced with a situation such as existed in those cases, urged by the Commissioner, in which we held the proceeds of criminal activities to be taxable. Those cases concerned situations in which the taxpayer had actually received funds. Moreover, the illegality involved was the act that gave rise to the income. Here the originating and referring of the insurance, a practice widely followed, is acknowledged to be legal. Only the receipt of insurance commissions or premiums thereon by national banks is not. Had the Banks ignored the banking laws, thereby risking the loss of their charters and subjecting their officers to personal liability, the illegal-income cases would be relevant. But the Banks from the inception of their use of credit life insurance in 1948 were careful never to place themselves in that position. We think that fairness requires the tax to fall on the party that actually receives the premiums rather than on the party that cannot.

In L.E. Shunk Latex Products, Inc. v. Commissioner, 18 T.C. 940 (1952), the Tax Court considered a closely analogous situation. The same interest controlled a manufacturer and a distributor of rubber prophylactics. The OPA Price Regulations of World War II became effective on December 1, 1941. Prior thereto the distributor had raised its prices to retailers, but the manufacturer had not increased the prices charged to its affiliated distributor. The Commissioner, acting under §482, attempted to allocate some of the distributor's income to the manufacturer on the ground that a portion of the distributor's profits was in fact earned by the manufacturer, even though the manufacturer was prohibited by the OPA regulations from increasing its prices. In holding that the Commissioner had acted improperly, the Tax Court said that he had "no authority to attribute to petitioners income which they could not have received.[22] . . .

It is argued, finally, that the "services" rendered by the Banks in making credit insurance available to customers "would have been compensated had the corporations been dealing with each other at arm's length." The short answer is that the proscription against acting as insurance agent and receiving compensation therefore applies to *all* national banks located in places with population in excess of 5,000 inhabitants. It applies equally to such banks whether or not they are controlled by a holding company. If these Banks had been independent of any such control — as most banks are — no commissions or premiums could have been received lawfully and there would have been no taxable income.[24] As stated in the Treasury Regulations, the

22. . . . See Teschner v. Commissioner, 38 T.C. 1003, 1009 (1962): "In the case before us the taxpayer while he had no power to *dispose* of income, had a power to appoint or designate its recipient. Does the existence or exercise of such a power alone give rise to taxable income in his hands? We think clearly not. In Nicholas A. Stavroudis, 27 T.C. 583, 590 (1956), we found it to be settled doctrine that a power to direct the distribution of trust income to others is not alone sufficient to justify the taxation of that income to the possessor of such a power."

24. If an unaffiliated bank were able to provide the insurance at a cheaper rate because no commissions were paid, this would benefit the customers but would result in no taxable income.

"purpose of section 482 is to place a controlled taxpayer on a tax parity with an uncontrolled taxpayer. . . ." We think our holding comports with such parity treatment.

We conclude that the premium income received by Security Life could not be attributable to the Banks. Holding Company did not utilize its control over the Banks and Security Life to distort their true net incomes. The Commissioner's exercise of his §482 authority was therefore unwarranted in this case. The judgment below is affirmed.

Mr. Justice MARSHALL, dissenting.

The facts of this case illustrate the national affinity that lending institutions and insurance companies have for each other. Congress depends on the ability of the Commissioner of Internal Revenue to utilize §482 . . . to insure that this affinity does not provide a basis for tax avoidance. . . . In my opinion, today's decision renders §482 a less efficacious weapon against tax avoidance schemes than Congress intended and provides the respondents with an unwarranted tax advantage. I dissent. . . .

First enacted as §45 of the Revenue Act of 1928, . . . the statute was intended to prevent the avoidance of tax liability through fictions and "to deny the power to shift income . . . arbitrarily among controlled corporations, and to place such corporations rather on a parity with uncontrolled concerns." Central Cuba Sugar Co. v. Commissioner, 198 F.2d 214, 216 (C.A.2 1952). . . . It is intended to serve the same purpose in the present Code.

It is well-established law that in analyzing a transaction under §482, the test is whether the arrangement as structured for income tax purposes by interlocking corporate interests would have been similarly structured by taxpayers dealing at arm's length. See, e.g., Borge v. Commissioner, 405 F.2d 673 (C.A.2 1968), *cert. denied sub nom.* Danica Enterprises v. Commissioner, 395 U.S. 933 (1969); Eli Lilly & Co. v. United States, 178 Ct. Cl. 666, 372 F.2d 990 (1967).

Applying that test to this case, the following facts are relevant. Before 1954, an independent insurance company paid respondents commissions ranging from 40% to 45% for their services in offering insurance to borrowers designed to discharge their debts in the event that they died or became disabled during the term of their loans. After 1954, respondents offered borrowers policies issued by a different insurance company. At this time the holding company that controlled respondents created a new subsidiary to reinsure the borrowers who purchased policies. By paying off the independent insurance company with 15% of the proceeds of the policies, the subsidiary assumed the insurance risks and garnered the remaining 85% of the proceeds. No commission was paid to respondents by either the independent company or the insurance subsidiary.

The tax advantage of the post-1954 structure derived from the fact that the Life Insurance Company Tax Act for 1955 . . . , as amended, 26 U.S.C. §801 et seq., gives preferential tax treatment to life insurance companies. By funneling all proceeds from the sales of the insurance policies to a subsidiary that qualified for tax treatment as a life insurance company, the holding company avoided the heavier tax that would have been imposed on respondents had they been paid commissions.

The Commissioner's analysis of this case is not overly complex: He saw that respondents performed essentially the same services and generated the same income after 1954 that they did before, and he concluded that §482 required that they should be taxed on the premiums that they were actually earning.

Based on respondents' earlier experience dealing *at arm's length* with an independent insurance company and on the well-known fact that insurers pay solicitors a portion of the premium as a commission for generating income, see Local Finance Corp. v. Commissioner, 48 T.C. 733, 786 (1967), *aff'd,* 407 F.2d 629, 631-632 (C.A.7 1969), the Commissioner determined that 40% of the premium income was properly allocated to respondents.

The respondents make, in essence, two arguments in their attempt to rebut the Commissioner's position. First, they urge that they never received any funds as a result of offering the policies to borrowers, and that it is therefore unfair to tax them on any portion of said proceeds. If §482 is to have any meaning, that argument must be rejected. It makes absolutely no sense to examine this case with a technical eye as to whether respondents actually received or had a "right" to receive any commissions. This is not a case involving independent companies or private individuals where we must scrupulously avoid taxing someone on money he will never receive regardless of his will in the matter. See, e.g., Blair v. Commissioner, 300 U.S. 5 (1937); cf. Teschner v. Commissioner, 38 T.C. 1003 (1962). This is a case involving related corporations, and §482 recognizes that such corporations may be treated differently from natural persons or unrelated corporations for certain tax purposes.

We need not look far to find that this entire complicated economic structure — established, designed, administered, and amendable by the holding company — had the right to the proceeds. Pursuant to §482, the Commissioner properly attempted to insure that the proceeds would be equitably allocated.

The Court apparently concedes that if respondents' only argument against taxation were that they have received no money, that argument would fail. This concession is, in fact, mandated by various decisions of this Court, including Harrison v. Schaffner, 312 U.S. 579 (1941); Helvering v. Horst, 311 U.S. 112 (1940), and Lucas v. Earl, 281 U.S. 111 (1930).

Having implicitly rejected the argument that mere nonreceipt of money is sufficient to avoid taxation, the Court proceeds to accept respondents' second argument that in this case the taxpayer is legally barred from ever receiving money, and in this circumstance he cannot be taxed on it. Respondents find a legal bar to receipt of the proceeds at issue here in 12 U.S.C.A. §92. . . .

This statute by inference and the regulations of the Comptroller of the Currency, 12 CFR §§2.1-2.5, by explicit language bar national banks in communities with more than 5,000 inhabitants from selling, soliciting, or receiving the proceeds from selling insurance. Respondents are within the legal prohibition and the penalties provided for a violation are indeed severe. Assuming that the respondents will not attempt to violate the law and not wishing to appear to encourage a violation, the Court concludes that respondents will receive none of the proceeds and that they cannot be taxed on money they will never receive.

But the crucial fact in this case is that under their own theory respondents have already violated the federal statute and regulations by soliciting insurance premiums. Title 12 U.S.C.A. §92 was added to the federal banking laws in 1916 at the suggestion of John Skelton Williams, who was then Comptroller of the Currency. He wrote to Congress to recommend that national banks in small communities be permitted to associate with insurance companies, but that banks in larger communities be prohibited from doing the same. . . .

There is nothing in the history of the provision to indicate that Congress was more concerned with banks' actually receiving money than with their performing the activities that generated the money. In fact, the history that is available indicates that it is the activities themselves that Congress wished to stop. Banks in large communities were simply not permitted to do anything that insurance agents might do, i.e., they were not permitted to solicit insurance.

Under respondents' theory of the case, the legal violation is thus a fait accompli and the respondents are taxable as if there had been no illegality. See, e.g., United States v. Sullivan, 274 U.S. 259 (1927); Rutkin v. United States 343 U.S. 130 (1952); James v. United States, 366 U.S. 213 (1961). . . .

The Court seeks, however, to distinguish all of the prior cases holding that a taxpayer may be taxed on income illegally earned on the ground that the issue was never raised as to whether the taxpayers in those cases had actually received the income. The distinction is valid but it does not warrant a different result in this case.

The reasoning of the majority runs along these lines: If A violates the law — by attempted embezzlement or by illegally soliciting insurance sales, for example — but he receives no money and has no "legal right" to receive any money then he cannot be taxed as if the money had been received; but, if A actually embezzles money or receives insurance premiums in violation of the law, A can be taxed even though he may have transferred the money without any personal gain to a third party from whom he has no right of recovery.

I would agree with this analysis in most cases. Where I differ from the Court is in which category to place this transaction. To pretend that respondents have not received any money and have no right to any money is to ignore the thrust of §482. That section requires that we treat this case as if the commissions had been paid to respondents and had been transferred to the insurance subsidiary by them. Of course, that did not occur. But, we know that the whole notion of the section is to look behind the form in which a transaction is structured to its substance. The substance is either that the respondents violated federal law, earned illegal income, attempted to avoid taxation on the income by channeling it elsewhere, and were caught by the Commissioner; or, that they did not violate federal law by soliciting sales of insurance and that there is no legal bar to their receiving the proceeds from their sales. In either case, the result is the same, and respondents cannot prevail.

If respondents had actually received the proceeds and transferred them to the insurance subsidiary, they would still be free to make essentially the same argument that they make in this case, i.e., they could argue that federal law prohibited them from receiving the money; that they violated federal law, but had no right to keep the money; and that they should not be taxed on receipt of funds which they could not legally keep.

To be consistent with the assignment-of-income cases, Helvering v. Horst, supra, and Lucas v. Earl, supra, and the line of cases that includes Rutkin v. United States, supra, and James v. United States, supra, the Court would have to reject this argument. Yet, I maintain that this is just what the taxpayer is arguing here. The Commissioner has determined that in reality the respondents have earned income, and he has taxed it under §482. To reject his position is to give undue weight to the absence of technical temporary possession of money and some abstract concept of a "right" to receive it. I had thought that this kind of technical reasoning was rejected in James v. United States, supra, when the Court overruled Commissioner v. Wilcox, 327 U.S. 404 (1946).

Finally, even if there is some mysterious reason why the banking laws should be read in the manner suggested by respondents, there is still another reason why they should not prevail. The fact would remain that they consciously chose to perform services in order that their parent holding company would reap financial rewards. Certainly, there is nothing in the federal banking laws that required the performance of these services. In the context of a complex corporate structure ministered by one large holding company, the purposes of §482 are best served by permitting the Commissioner to allocate income to the company that earns it, rather than to the company that receives it. Again, we must remember that this is not a case of unrelated private individuals or independent corporations where there might be some danger that in allocating income to the person who generated but did not receive it, the Commissioner would render that person financially unable to pay his taxes. This case involves one large interrelated system. It would be total fiction to assume that the holding company would leave its subsidiaries in a financial bind. Hence, there is no good reason to bar the Commissioner from taxing respondents on the money that they earn.

In my view, the Commissioner has done exactly what §482 requires him to do in this case. . . .

[Dissenting opinion of Blackmun, J., with whom White, J. joined, is omitted.]

NOTES

1. See Comment, Commissioner v. First Security Bank: Allocability Under Section 482 of Legally Nonreceivable Income, 122 U. Pa. L. Rev. 184 (1973).

2. Rev. Rul. 76-243, 1976-1 C.B. 134, refused to extend *First Security Bank* to preclude allocation of interest on an interest-free loan made to a foreign subsidiary, pursuant to a binding contract made with a foreign government. Despite the possibility of sanctions for nonperformance, the transaction was initially consensual. See also Rev. Rul. 82-43, 1982-1 C.B. 89 (holding of *First Security Bank* does not apply to foreign law restrictions).

HUBER HOMES, INC. v. COMMISSIONER
55 T.C. 598 (1971)

FINDINGS OF FACT

The facts stipulated by the parties are incorporated herein by this reference.

Huber Homes, Inc. (sometimes referred to as "Huber Homes" or "petitioner") is an Ohio corporation, formed on April 28, 1958. . . .

The Commissioner determined deficiencies in the income tax of petitioner for the taxable year ended March 31, 1963 and the taxable period beginning March 29, 1965 and ending August 31, 1965, in the respective amounts of $25,973.15 and $79,311.41.

After concessions by both parties, the issue presented is whether the Commissioner properly "allocated" income to the petitioner, under the terms of section 482, I.R.C. 1954, in respect of its transfer of 52 houses to its wholly owned subsidiary at cost.

From its incorporation through August 31, 1965, Charles H. Huber ("Huber") owned all of the outstanding stock of petitioner. He was also chairman of its board of directors and its chief executive officer at all times involved herein. It was the successor to a Huber family enterprise that was concerned with the construction and sale of houses.

During the period from April 28, 1958 through August 31, 1965, petitioner was engaged principally in the construction and sale of single-family houses in developments. These developments were located in the metropolitan areas of Dayton, Ohio, Cincinnati, Ohio, Columbus, Ohio, and Fort Lauderdale, Florida.

Huber Heights, located a few miles outside of Dayton, Ohio, is one of the developments. At the time of the formation of Huber Homes, approximately 700 houses had already been completed in Huber Heights. Huber Homes built approximately 3,700 more houses in that area during the period from April 28, 1958 through August 31, 1965, of which approximately 3,300 were sold to the general public. The remaining houses built during that period, about 400 in number, were acquired by Huber Investment Corporation, hereinafter described.

Huber Investment Corporation ("Huber Investment") is an Ohio corporation, organized on April 10, 1959. From the date of incorporation through August 31, 1965, all of its outstanding stock was owned by petitioner. At all times involved herein Huber was the chairman of its board of directors and its chief executive officer.

Huber Investment was formed for the purpose of acquiring and holding property not directly connected with petitioner's business of building and selling single-family houses. From its incorporation until August 31, 1965, Huber Investment was engaged principally in the real estate rental business. It owned approximately 400 rental houses in Huber Heights, approximately 100 houses in Indianapolis, Indiana, and an unspecified number of houses in Columbus, Ohio, Cincinnati, Ohio, and Fort Lauderdale, Florida. The majority of the houses owned by Huber Investment on August 31, 1965, were acquired from petitioner. Huber Investment itself never built any houses.

After forming Huber Investment, with only comparatively minor exceptions, petitioner did not own, manage, or maintain any rental houses in Huber Heights. From its incorporation through the year in issue, Huber Investment sold only one of its Huber Heights homes, a single-family residence which was first rented to petitioner for use as an office and later sold to a realtor.

Petitioner and Huber Investment were operated as two separate and autonomous companies, and the books, records, and bank accounts of each were separately maintained. Each company had its own payroll and its own employees. Huber Investment's employees performed all the activities of a landlord with respect to the houses which it owned. Petitioner's employees never performed any of such activities with respect to Huber Investment's properties.

Petitioner developed the land in Huber Heights in sections, ranging in size from approximately 50 to 200 houses. As soon as a new section was opened for development, petitioner's sales department was permitted to sell the houses which were to be built there through the use of furnished and landscaped model homes. On the average, approximately 70 percent of the houses in a section were sold by the time all the houses in that section had been completed. In the late summer and fall of each year, however, petitioner would begin construction of houses beyond its immediate needs and in anticipation of sales during the following winter and spring, since it found it impractical to start construction between the beginning of November and the middle of the following April.

Based upon previous sales and upon the then current market conditions, Charles Huber, plus the sales manager, production manager, and other officers of petitioner determined, at a meeting held sometime in August, 1964, that 148 houses could be built and sold in Huber Heights from the fall of 1964 through the spring of 1965 when construction could start again. Thus, petitioner started construction on 148 houses in the late summer and early fall of 1964.

The prices at which the foregoing 148 houses and lots were offered to the public were set by petitioner on the basis of direct labor and material costs, land and land development costs, overhead, and profit. The base prices at which the houses were offered to the public varied according to the model of the particular house, ranging from $12,995 to $19,995. After the prices were established, they were made known to the public by advertising, through brochures, and in the sales office. It was petitioner's established policy never to offer any house to the public at a price below its published price.

During the period from the commencement of construction of the 148 aforementioned houses through the period in question, ending August 31, 1965, petitioner employed four full-time salesmen, working seven days a week, to solicit the sales of these houses. The salesmen were instructed to sell every house they could, and they were compensated on a salary plus commission basis.

Of the 148 houses started in the late summer and early fall of 1964, petitioner succeeded in selling only 95 to the public. Four more houses were acquired by Huber Investment during its taxable year ended March 28, 1965. Despite petitioner's sales effort from the fall of 1964 until the early summer of 1965, the 49 houses which remained out of the original 148 could not be sold at the prices asked due to the then existing market conditions. Three other houses, constructed by petitioner at other times, were also unsold as of the early summer of 1965; one was a new style, model "Q," which had been built as a model home, and two were houses started prior to the construction of the aforementioned 148 houses. Thus, a total of 52 houses were unsold as of this time.

Petitioner transferred 38 of the 52 unsold houses and lots to Huber Investment by journal entry on July 1, 1965, approximately 8½ to 9½ months after construction on the 38 houses had begun, and approximately 2½ to 6 months after the 38 houses had been finished. It transferred another 13 of the 52 houses and lots to Huber Investment by journal entry on August 1, 1965, approximately 9½ to 10½ months after construction on the 13 houses had begun, and approximately 3 to 7 months after the 13 houses had been finished. Finally, it transferred the model "Q" house and lot to Huber Investment by journal entry on August 31, 1965.

Title to the 52 houses and lots was formally transferred by petitioner to Huber Investment by deeds during August 1965.

Huber Investment acquired the aforementioned 52 houses at petitioner's actual cost of $723,003.25. On petitioner's books and records there was an "Account Receivable" from its subsidiary, Huber Investment, and the debt on that inter-company open account was increased in the aggregate amount of $723,003.25 to reflect the transfer of the 52 houses at cost. During the taxable period ending August 31, 1965, the monthly balance of petitioner's "Account Receivable" from Huber Investment, as reflected on petitioner's books and records, was as follows:

March 31, 1965	$ 546,301.42
April 20, 1965	546,301.42
May 31, 1965	544,248.13
June 30, 1965	544,248.13
July 31, 1965	1,067,411.96
August 31, 1965	465,342.84

The aggregate sales price to the general public of the 52 houses was $907,807.28.

The 52 houses were transferred to Huber Investment in order that they be converted to rental properties. The decision to do so was based on the belief that the houses could not be sold to the public at the published selling prices, and that by continuing to hold the unsold houses, petitioner not only would incur interest charges and other expenses but would also sustain losses arising from vandalism and deterioration.

After their transfer, Huber Investment, with a view towards renting the houses, obtained insurance on all the 52 houses in issue, and, in addition, installed venetian blinds and curtain and drapery rods in all 52 houses except the model "Q" house, and installed stair carpeting in the eight 2-story houses that were included within the 52 houses.

The 52 houses have been rental units ever since their acquisition by Huber Investment. The rentals which it charged were usually set by model, depending upon the size of the model, with certain adjustments for "extras" such as a 2-car garage, fireplace, custom kitchen, etc. The rental price of the houses ranged from $105 to $180 per month.

In July and September 1965, the vice president in charge of the Appraisal Department of Citizens Federal Savings and Loan Association, Dayton, Ohio, Thomas J. Gilfoil, appraised each of the 52 houses and lots in issue in connection with applications for mortgage loans made by Huber Investment. He appraised the aggregate fair market value of the individual houses and lots in issue to be $852,045 as of that time. Because 38 houses and lots were transferred to Huber Investment on July 1, 1965 in a bulk transaction, and on August 1, 1965, 13 more houses and lots were also transferred in a bulk transaction, the fair market value of these houses and lots as a group was five percent less than the total of the fair market value of each individual house and lot.

During the summer of 1965, there was a resale market for houses in Huber Heights built by Huber Homes. The prices for such houses were generally lower than the prices of comparable new houses offered for sale by Huber Homes. During its taxable year ended August 31, 1966, Huber Homes sold 132 houses in Huber Heights to the general public. The model types of these houses were generally the same as those sold in previous years.

In its return for the taxable period ended August 31, 1965, Huber Homes reported a net loss of $61,882. 13. This amount was carried back to its fiscal year ended March 31, 1963.

On its return for the taxable period ended August 31, 1965, Huber Investment reported gross rental income of $470,181.09 and a net loss in the amount of $56,517.99.

From the date of its incorporation through the taxable period ended August 31, 1965, Huber Investment has computed its depreciation deduction on buildings on the double-declining-balance method using a 30-year life for all single family residences.

The Commissioner determined deficiencies in the income tax of Huber Homes for its taxable year ending March 31, 1963 and the taxable period ending August 31, 1965. In his notice of deficiency he stated:

> (a) It is determined that during the taxable year ended August 31, 1965 you had a profit of $205,113.85 upon transfer of houses to your wholly owned subsidiary, Huber Investment Corp. The profit is allocated to you under the provisions of section 482 of the Internal Revenue Code since it is determined that this allocation is necessary in order to prevent evasion of taxes and a clearly reflect income. Therefore, taxable income is increased $205,113.85 as shown below.

Cost of houses transferred	$723,003.25
Estimated sales prices	928,117.10
Profit	$205,113.85

This determination resulted not only in a deficiency for the taxable period ending August 31, 1965, but also a deficiency for the taxable year ending March 31, 1963, by reason of the elimination of the reported net loss for the period ending August 31, 1965, which in turn eliminated the net operating loss carryback to the year ending March 31, 1963.

The report of the Internal Revenue Service agent in respect of an audit of Huber Investment's books and records and its tax return for the taxable period beginning March 29, 1965 and ending August 31, 1965 stated, in part:

> The income of one member of a controlled group was increased by $205,113.85. . . . The correlative adjustment to this member of the controlled group resulted in the basis of real estate being increased by $205,113.85. . . .
>
> The $205,113.85 was allocated between land and buildings as follows:

land	$39,931.00
buildings	$165,182.85

OPINION

RAUM, Judge. During 1965 petitioner transferred, at its actual cost, 52 newly constructed houses to its wholly owned subsidiary, Huber Investment, which then rented the houses to the public. It is conceded by petitioner that at the time of the transfer the houses had a fair market value in excess of cost — though the exact amount thereof is in dispute herein. The Commissioner has determined that, pursuant to section 482, . . . income should be "allocated" to petitioner to the extent of the difference between the cost of the houses and their fair market value at the time of transfer. The petitioner argues that this determination is unreasonable and arbitrary because no income was realized in respect of the transfer. . . .

The purposes of section 482, and the Commissioner's authority thereunder, were set out in Pauline W. Ach, 42 T.C. 114, 125-126, *affirmed* 358 F.2d 342 (C.A. 6), *certiorari denied* 385 U.S. 899:

> Respondent may allocate income under section 482 in order to prevent "evasion of taxes or clearly to reflect the income." The legislative history of section 482 indicates that it was designed to prevent evasion of taxes by the arbitrary shifting of profits, the making of fictitious sales, and other such methods used to "milk" a taxable entity. Ballentine Motor Co., Inc., 39 T.C. 348, *affirmed* 321 F.2d 796 (C.A. 4); Seminole Flavor Co., 4 T.C. 1215, 1228. The Commissioner has considerable discretion in applying this section and his determinations must be sustained unless he has abused his discretion. We may reverse his determinations only where the taxpayer proves them to be unreasonable, arbitrary, or capricious. . . .

In order to prevent the artificial shifting of income from one related business to another, section 482 places a controlled taxpayer on a parity with an uncontrolled taxpayer, by determining according to the standard of an uncontrolled taxpayer, the true net income of a controlled taxpayer. See, e.g., Asiatic Petroleum Co. v. Commissioner, 79 F.2d 234, 236 (CA. 2), *affirming* 31 B.T.A. 1152, *certiorari denied* 296 U.S. 645, *rehearing denied* 296 U.S. 664; . . . Regs. section 1.482-1(b) and 1.482-1(c). Thus, income which has been artificially diverted to one member of a controlled group but which in fact was earned by another member of the group may be "allocated" by the Commissioner under section 482 to the entity which really earned it. However, in the present case Huber Investment has not received any income — indeed, it has sustained losses — which was earned by petitioner and should be "allocated" to it. Nevertheless, the Commissioner seeks to apply section 482, relying upon Regs. section 1.482-1(a)(6), which states:

> Sec. 1.482-1. Allocation of income and deductions among taxpayers. — (a) *Definitions.* . . .
> (6) The term "true taxable income" means, in the case of a controlled taxpayer, the taxable income (or as the case may be, any item or element affecting taxable income) which would have resulted to the controlled taxpayer, had it in the conduct of its affairs (or, as the case may be in the particular contract, transaction, arrangement, or other act) dealt with the other member or members of the group at arm's length. It does not mean the income, the deductions, the credits, the allowances, or the item or element of income, deductions, credits, or allowances, resulting to the controlled taxpayer by reason of the particular contract, transaction, or arrangement, the controlled taxpayer, or the interests control-

ling it, chose to make (even though such contract, transaction, or arrangement be legally binding upon the parties thereto).

The Commissioner argues that had the transaction between petitioner and its subsidiary been at arm's length, additional income would have inured to petitioner in the amount of the excess of the fair market value of the houses transferred over petitioner's cost. And, if Huber Investment had dealt with its parent at arm's length it would have paid the fair market value of the houses. Hence, contends the Commissioner, in order "clearly to reflect the income" of both corporations, petitioner's income should be increased by what it would have earned in an arm's length sale and Huber Investment's basis in the houses should be increased accordingly. This approach finds at least some support in the Regulations, sections 1.482-1(a)(6), 1.482-1(d)(1), and 1(d)(4), particularly the latter.

The arm's-length standard relied upon by the Commissioner has traditionally been upheld where it has served as the basis for a reallocation of income derived from dealings with third parties — i.e., parties other than the controlled corporations which have engaged in transactions at less than arm's length. For example, in Oil Base, Inc. v. Commissioner . . . , 362 F.2d 212 (C.A. 9), the parent corporation granted its wholly owned subsidiary commissions and discounts twice as large as those allowed uncontrolled sales representatives. The Commissioner allocated portions of the subsidiary's sales income to the parent on the basis of what would have been the parent's arm's length arrangements with uncontrolled parties. The Commissioner's determination was approved. Likewise, in Eli Lilly & Co. v. United States, 372 F.2d 990 (Ct. Cl.), the Commissioner successfully charged the parent manufacturing company with portions of the profits received on sales to outsiders by its wholly owned subsidiary where the parent's sales to the subsidiary were at less than arm's length prices. In these cases, as in the other cases relied upon by the Commissioner, e.g., Dillard-Waltermire, Inc. v. Campbell, 255 F.2d 433 (C.A. 5); Grenada Industries, Inc., 17 T.C. 231, *affirmed* 202 F.2d 873 (C.A. 5), *certiorari denied* 346 U.S. 819, the determinations in issue were based on the *reallocation* of income derived from dealings with third parties. And the arm's length formula simply played a part in determining what portion of the income received by a member of the controlled group was really earned by and therefore properly allocable to another member of the group. However, we are not faced with that situation here. Huber Investment did not resell the houses transferred to it, and thereby receive a profit that was in fact attributable to petitioner but which was artificially channeled to Huber Investment by means of an intercompany sale at cost. Moreover, in contrast to his position in the foregoing cases, the Commissioner does not here contend that any of Huber Investment's gross rental income was not earned by it or that any portion of *its* income should be allocated to Huber Homes. Rather, the Commissioner is purporting to exercise his authority under section 482 to create income, i.e., to charge petitioner with the income it would have realized had its sale to Huber Investment been at arm's length. We hold that this determination is not authorized by section 482.

Essential to the application of section 482 is the distribution, apportionment, or allocation of income realized at some time by the controlled group. This was made clear in Tennessee-Arkansas Gravel Co. v. Commissioner, 112 F.2d 508 (C.A. 6), reversing a Memorandum Opinion of this Court. In that case, the taxpayer made available certain movable equipment to an affiliate, "Mississippi." During the year in issue no rental charge was made for the use of the equipment and, pursuant to section 45 of the Revenue Act of 1934 (predecessor of section 482), the Commissioner determined that the taxpayer had rental income of $12,000, the value of the use of the equipment based on arrangements made the previous year. The Court of Appeals rejected the Commissioner's position, stating (112 F.2d at 510):

> Regardless of what he [the Commissioner] may have contemplated the undisputed fact is, that he made no distribution, apportionment or allocation of gross income between petitioner and Mississippi. He made no attempt to allocate any portion of the $51,427.70, representing the gross income of Mississippi in 1934, to petitioner. The record clearly discloses what he did. He simply concluded that petitioner should have charged Mississippi rent upon the equipment for the year 1934, notwithstanding the fact that petitioner neither charged, collected nor could have collected rent under its agreement with Mississippi. Having so determined, the Commissioner fixed the rental to be charged at $1,000 per month based upon the rate charged by petitioner for a portion of 1933. Having so fixed the rental, he charged it to petitioner as income in the following language: "Add: . . . 2. Rent of equipment $12,000."
>
> Section 45, supra, *did not authorize the Commissioner to set up income where none existed.* The principal purpose of the section was to clearly reflect income that did exist.
>
> It is suggested that the law will imply that the Commissioner apportioned the $12,000 to petitioner from the gross income of Mississippi, but the law permits no inferences contrary to fact. (Emphasis supplied.)

The present case closely parallels *Tennessee-Arkansas* in that the Commissioner here, as there, did not *allocate* to the taxpayer any of the gross income of the related party to which there was a transfer at less than arm's length. Instead, here, as there, the Commissioner *created* income out of a transaction which, in the Commissioner's opinion, only *would have* produced income had the petitioner dealt with the controlled party at arm's length. Thus, it is apparent that the Commissioner here did not "distribute, apportion, or allocate gross income" within the meaning of section 482.

The Commissioner seeks to distinguish the *Tennessee-Arkansas* case on the ground that the decision was based on the Commissioner's failure to make a correlative adjustment to the income or deductions of the related entity. We think, however, that the Sixth Circuit's decision rests on a broader ground: that the allocation under section 482 must be of income actually realized by a member of the controlled group.

Nor do we think that the Commissioner's proposed adjustment to Huber Investment's basis in the houses transferred to it sufficiently effects an allocation of Huber Investment's income to petitioner. The fact remains that even in light of this adjustment income is being attributed to petitioner that was not in fact realized by the controlled group. Compare V & M Homes, Inc., 28 T.C. 1121, *affirmed* 263 F.2d 837 (C.A. 6). Had petitioner retained the 148 houses and rented them itself to tenants, it could not conceivably have been charged with income to the extent that the fair market value of the houses exceeded cost, and certainly its basis for depreciation would have been only cost. Plainly, section 482 was not intended to produce a different result; it was designed merely to "unscramble" (Grenada Industries, Inc., supra, 17 T.C. at 253) a situation where income realized by the controlled group and earned by one member of the group is diverted to another group member by means of transactions not carried out at arm's length.

In E.C. Laster, 43 B.T.A. 159, *acq.* 1941-1 C.B. 7, *modified on other grounds,* 128 F.2d 4 (C.A. 5), the Board rejected the Commissioner's attempt to attribute income to a transferor of valuable oil payment rights, without charge, to its wholly owned subsidiary, the owner of the working interest. There, as in the present case, income was not realized by the transferee of the rights during the taxable year. After citing the *Tennessee-Arkansas* case, supra, the Board stated, at p. 177:

> The acquisition by the Retsal Drilling Co. of the oil payments without cost did not result in income to it or the transferor. It follows therefrom that there was no income to distribute or allocate under section 45.

In Smith-Bridgman & Co., 16 T.C. 287, *acq.* 1951-1 C.B. 3,[4] the petitioner, a wholly owned subsidiary of Continental, made interest-free loans to its parent. The Commissioner included in the taxpayer's gross income an amount representing a four percent interest charge

4. The Commissioner's acquiescence is explained in Rev. Rul. 67-79, 1967-1 C.B. 117.

in respect of its loan to its parent. The Court disapproved the Commissioner's determination (16 T.C. at 293):

> In support of his action the respondent argues that Continental, in securing these non-interest-bearing loans from petitioner, was enabled to relieve itself from paying interest on its outstanding debentures; and, furthermore, he argues, petitioner could have loaned the funds which Continental borrowed without interest to third parties at 4 per cent interest. Therefore, in order to prevent evasion of taxes and to clearly reflect the income of such related businesses, he has "allocated" to petitioner part of the income of its parent, in the exercise of the discretion conferred by section 45 of the code. The decisions involving section 45 make it clear that its principal purpose is to prevent the manipulation of or improper shifting of gross income and deductions between two or more organizations, trades, or businesses. Its application is predicated on the existence of income. The courts have consistently refused to interpret section 45 as authorizing the creation of income out of a transaction where no income was realized by any of the commonly controlled businesses. Tennessee-Arkansas Gravel Co. v. Commissioner, 112 Fed. (2d) 508; E.C. Laster, 43 B.T.A. 159, *modified on other issues,* 128 Fed. (2d) 4; Epsen-Lithographers, Inc. v. O'Malley, 67 Fed. Supp. 181, cf. Hugh Smith, Inc., 8 T.C. 660, *aff'd,* 173 Fed. (2d) 224, *certiorari denied,* 337 U.S. 918.

The Court in *Smith-Bridgman* further noted that no correlative adjustment was made in the income of or deductions of Continental to account for the increase in the taxpayer's income. The Commissioner contends that this factor explains the decision and thereby distinguishes it from the present case. We disagree. We view this factor as no more than a possible supporting ground for the decision and not the controlling reason. It is no different in this respect from the similar situation in *Tennessee-Arkansas.*

Finally, in Texsun Supply Corp., 17 T.C. 433, *acq.* 1952-1 C.B. 4, Texsun's subsidiary sold boxes to it at its manufacturing cost, which Texsun, a cooperative supply corporation, then resold to its members. Texsun was required by its by-laws to sell to its members at cost, and it accomplished this by first selling to them at prevailing market prices and then rebating its "profits" to them at year-end. It thus realized no profit on such sales. The Commissioner attempted to "allocate" a profit to Texsun's subsidiary on the sales based on prevailing arm's length prices. The Court, citing *Smith-Bridgman & Co.,* again refused to approve the allocation.

Against the foregoing background of decided cases favorable to the petitioner, the Commissioner argues that he would be foreclosed from correcting distortions in income where goods or services are transferred to a related party at less than arm's-length prices and the goods or services are consumed rather than sold by the transferee. But if, as a consequence of such use or consumption by the transferee, income is realized within the controlled group, an entirely different question would be presented as to whether such income or a portion thereof might be allocated to the transferor under section 482. That situation, however, is not before us.

In deciding that section 482 is inapplicable here we do not reach the question whether the regulations . . . relied upon by the Commissioner are valid. They plainly contemplate a situation where one member of a controlled group sells to another at less than fair market value and where it is expected that the controlled vendee would in turn resell the product to a third party. In order properly to reflect income the profit on such resale would have to be fairly allocated between the two controlled corporations; the regulations provide that in such circumstances the allocation of its share of the profit to the original vendor need not await the year of ultimate sale but may be made immediately. We think that the regulations do not cover the present case where there was no intention to resell the 52 houses in issue, where they were converted to rental use, where they are still held for rental purposes, and where they do not appear to be productive of any net income whatever. In the circumstances we do not pass upon the validity of the regulations in situations where resale of the transferred property was contemplated regardless of when or even whether such resale in fact occurred.

The taxpayer has argued that the excess of the fair market value of the houses transferred to Huber Investment over their cost should be treated as a tax-free contribution of capital under section 118. Since we have held that section 482 is not applicable herein we need not pass upon this issue. Further, in light of the inapplicability of section 482 we need not determine the fair market value of the houses transferred to Huber Investment. . . .

NOTES

1. The Tax Court has now held that the current Regulations under §482 acceptably authorize the "creation" of income, if necessary to produce an arm's length result. See Latham Park Manor, Inc., 69 T.C. 199 (1977), *aff'd,* (unpublished opinion) (4th Cir. Jan. 28, 1980). Earlier decisions to the contrary had been reversed. *Compare* Kerry Investment Co., 58 T.C. 479 (1972), *aff'd in part and rev'd in part,* 500 F.2d 108 (9th Cir. 1974), *with* Kahler Corp., 58 T.C. 496, *rev'd,* 486 F.2d 1 (8th Cir. 1973). In addition, the Fifth Circuit had rejected the Tax Court's tracing requirement and followed B. For-

man Co., infra, and Fitzgerald Motor Co. v. Commissioner, 508 F.2d 1096 (5th Cir. 1975).

2. What sort of obligation does Treas. Reg. §1.482-1(d)(2) impose on the IRS? See Continental Equities, Inc. v. Commissioner, 551 F.2d 74 (1977) (§482 allocation permitted although statute of limitations has expired for period with respect to which related taxpayer would be entitled to correlative adjustment); cf. OTM Corp. v. United States, 572 F.2d 1046 (5th Cir.) (per curiam), *cert. denied,* 439 U.S. 1002 (1978) (no correlative adjustment required where IRS relied on §162, not §482, to disallow excessive portion of rent paid related taxpayer.)

3. See Crane & Tractor Parts, 48 T.C.M. (CCH) 1207 (1984), for an interesting example of a §482 allocation of income from a C corporation to an S.

B. CONTROL

B. FORMAN CO. v. COMMISSIONER
453 F.2d 1144 (2d Cir.), *cert. denied,* 407 U.S. 934 (1972)

ZAVATT, District Judge. These are cross-appeals from a decision of the Tax Court, 54 T.C. 913 (1970), holding (1) that . . . §482 . . . did not authorize the Commissioner to allocate to B. Forman Co., Inc. (Forman) and McCurdy & Co., Inc. (McCurdy) (both referred to herein as taxpayers) interest income attributable to interest free loans made by the taxpayers to Midtown Holdings Corp. (Midtown), because of the absence of the requisite §482 control of Midtown by the taxpayers. . . . We reverse the decision of the Tax Court. . . .

For several years prior to and as of the date of incorporation of Midtown, McCurdy . . . operated a retail general department store . . . and Forman . . . operated a retail department store, specializing in men's and women's apparel. . . . All of the stock of McCurdy was owned by or in behalf of members of the McCurdy family. All of the stock of Forman was owned by or in behalf of members of the Forman family. McCurdy and Forman had no common shareholders, directors or officers. Both corporations were competitors.

In an effort to stem declining incomes, McCurdy and Forman caused Midtown to be formed in 1958. On March 23, 1959 they entered into an agreement with reference to their participation in the building and development of a midtown shopping center in Rochester which would adjoin the rear entrances to their respective stores.

By that time the Board of Directors and officers of Midtown consisted of the following:

	Relationship to McCurdy and Forman
Gilbert J.C. McCurdy (President and Chairman of Board of Directors of Midtown)	Chairman of the Board of Directors and President of McCurdy
Gordon W. McCurdy (Secretary and a Director of Midtown)	Vice-Chairman of the Board of Directors and Senior Vice-President of McCurdy
Maurice R. Forman (Vice-President and a Director of Midtown)	Chairman of the Board of Directors and President of Forman
Fred Forman (Treasurer and a Director of Midtown)	Member of the Board of Directors and Senior Vice-President of Forman
Lynn Johnston (Vice-President and General Manager of Midtown)	

. . . McCurdy and Forman had already acquired 50% each of the issued and outstanding shares of Midtown. In exchange for the real estate interests they were to assign and convey to Midtown, each of them was to receive an additional 810 common, no par value shares of Midtown, thus continuing their equal stock ownership in Midtown. If, prior to January 1, 1965, the Board of Directors of Midtown should determine, by resolution, that additional funds were necessary or advisable, McCurdy and Forman agreed to purchase additional shares of Midtown "so that their aggregate holding shall be One Million Dollars ($1,000,000) each, at any time, and from time to time. . . ." In addition, each party to this agreement agreed to loan to Midtown additional amounts "so that their aggregate loans to Midtown shall be One Million Dollars ($1,000,000) each, at any time and from time to time, if, prior to January 1, 1965, the Board of Directors of Midtown, by resolution, shall determine that such additional funds in the form of borrowing are necessary or advisable. Loans shall be made equally by the parties. Such loans shall be represented by notes, or other evidence of indebtedness, of Midtown. . . ."

This agreement also provided for the control of Midtown by McCurdy and Forman by requiring each party thereto to vote its respective Midtown stock so as to provide for a Board of Directors consisting of three Directors designated by the Board of Directors of McCurdy and three Directors designated by the Board of Directors of Forman. At the request of either McCurdy or Forman, each party to the agreement undertook to vote its Midtown stock for a seventh Director. In the event they were unable to agree upon the seventh Director, McCurdy and Forman were to designate their respective representatives who would designate the seventh Director to be elected "by the parties hereto. . . ." In the event that these representatives were unable to agree upon a seventh Director, a Justice of the Appellate Division of the Supreme Court, Fourth Judicial Department, was to act with the two representatives and the seventh Director of Midtown was then to be designated by majority vote of the Justice and the two representatives of the parties.

The agreement also limited the right of the parties to dispose of their Midtown stock to detailed conditions set forth therein.

Although the agreement provided for the designation of three Midtown Directors each by the parties, there were only four. During all of the relevant times the officers and directors of Midtown were:

President and Director	Gilbert J.C. McCurdy
Vice President and Director	Maurice R. Forman
Secretary and Director	Gordon W. McCurdy
Treasurer and Director	Fred Forman (until his death)
	Robert Aex (after Fred Formans death; Aex represented Forman's interests)
Vice President and General Manager	Lynn Johnston (to April 1, 1963)
	Angelo Chiarella (from May 27, 1963 on)

Construction commenced in 1959. The record does not reveal all of the financing for this project. It does show that Midtown entered into a building loan agreement with Lincoln Rochester Trust Company (Lincoln), dated April 18, 1961, providing for advances not to exceed $11,000,000.00 to be evidenced by notes bearing interest at the rate of six percent per year, secured by the "personal guarantees of certain officers of the Company and others" and "a conditional assignment of rents of the premises." During 1958 and 1959, McCurdy and Forman made several loans to Midtown, the amounts of which are not revealed by the record or stated in the stipulation of facts in the proceeding before the Tax Court. It was so stipulated, however, that, on May 1, 1959, the several loans were consolidated into single obligations of Midtown of $662,500.00 each to McCurdy and Forman, represented by thirty-year notes of Midtown, each bearing interest at the rate of five percent per annum. (These notes were satisfied in July of 1959, without interest, from the proceeds of a $2,700,000.00 line of credit established by Midtown with Lincoln.

The fact that McCurdy and Forman each waived interest on these notes is not involved in the instant case.)

ALLOCATION OF INTEREST INCOME UNDER 26 U.S.C. §482

The issue as to allocation of income to McCurdy and Forman for the fiscal years 1965, 1966 and 1967 stems from loans of $1,000,000.00 each by the taxpayers to Midtown on September 9, 1960, each represented by a three-year note of Midtown to each taxpayer, bearing interest at the rate of three and one-half percent per annum. These notes were cancelled in April 1961, without payment of any principal or interest. In lieu thereof, they were replaced by notes of $1,000,000.00 each, predated September 9, 1960 and bearing no interest. On their due date, September 9, 1963, they were replaced by three-year notes in the same principal amounts, bearing no interest — without any payment of principal or interest having been made thereon. These notes, dated September 9, 1963, were replaced on September 9, 1966 by three-year notes in the same amounts, bearing no interest, without any payment of principal or interest having been paid thereon. No payments of principal or interest have ever been made on the notes dated, respectively, September 9, 1960, September 9, 1963 and September 9, 1966. The issue as to the Commissioner's allocation of income to McCurdy and Forman relates to the notes dated September 9, 1963 and September 9, 1966.

The Commissioner imputed interest income at the rate of five percent per annum on those $1,000,000.00 loans by McCurdy and Forman to Midtown ($50,000.00 of income to each taxpayer during their fiscal years 1965, 1966 and 1967), pursuant to . . . §482. . . .

The Tax Court reversed the Commissioner's determination, holding in effect that Midtown was not "controlled directly or indirectly" by either McCurdy or by Forman and that McCurdy and Forman may not be regarded as a single entity controlling Midtown.

> The clear language of section 482 requires that there be *two* business entities with respect to which direct or indirect control by the same interests can be found. If we look at Midtown and Forman's or Midtown and McCurdy's, no such control existed. To import a *common objective test* into section 482, and thereby create a theoretical partnership between Forman's and McCurdy's, would require an unwarranted elasticized reading of the statutory language. [54 T.C. at 923.]

LEGISLATIVE HISTORY

. . . [Section] 482 derives from section 45 of the Internal Revenue Code of 1928. The House report with reference to section 45 of the

1928 Code explained that its purpose was to allow the Commissioner to "distribute the income or deductions between or among [commonly controlled taxpayers] . . . , as may be necessary in order to prevent evasion (by the shifting of profits, the making of fictitious sales, and other methods frequently adopted for the purpose of 'milking'), and in order clearly to reflect their true tax liability." . . .

Provisions somewhat similar to those in section 45 were contained in prior Revenue Acts. Section 240(d) of the Revenue Act of 1924, . . . authorized the Commissioner to consolidate the accounts of two or more related trades or businesses owned or controlled by the same interests. It did not authorize him to distribute, apportion, or allocate, as in section 482. . . . Section 45 of the Revenue Act of 1928, . . . effected a change. The sections of the prior acts were under the caption "Consolidated Returns of Corporations." The caption of section 45 of the Revenue Act of 1928 was "Allocation of Income and Deductions." Its language is substantially identical to that in present section 482. . . . The Revenue Act of 1928 eliminated the right of affiliated corporations to file consolidated returns and the right of the Commissioner to consolidate the accounts of two or more related trades or businesses controlled by the same interests. In lieu thereof section 45 was inserted which "broadened considerably" former section 240(f) of the 1926 Act "in order to afford adequate protection to the Government made necessary by the elimination of the consolidated return provisions of the 1926 Act." National Securities Corp. v. Commissioner of Internal Revenue, 137 F.2d 600, 602 (3d Cir.), *cert. denied,* 320 U.S. 794 . . . (1943). . . .

LAKE ERIE

The decision of the Tax Court in Lake Erie & Pittsburg Railway Co. v. Commissioner, 5 T.C. 558 (1945), is the only judicial determination based on facts substantially similar to those in the instant case. . . . In *Lake Erie,* the New York Central Railroad and the Pennsylvania Railroad (two independent competing corporations, having no common stockholders, officers or directors), formed a third corporation, the Lake Erie & Pittsburg Railway Co. (Lake Erie), for the purpose of acquiring, building, maintaining, leasing and operating a railroad. . . . New York Central and Pennsylvania railroads were the sole, equal stockholders of Lake Erie. They used the facilities of Lake Erie for which use they originally paid rent pursuant to a 1908 agreement and Lake Erie paid dividends to these two stockholders. This agreement was modified in 1939 so as to release the two railroads from their obligation to pay rent to Lake Erie and release Lake Erie of its obligation to pay them (as stockholders) dividends. The Commissioner allocated to Lake Erie as income to it . . . and amount equal to the rent which the railroads were originally obligated to pay to Lake Erie. . . . The Tax Court reversed the determination of the Commissioner on the ground that he was without authority to make the questioned allocation. . . .

> The stockholders of the New York Central are not the "same interests" as the stockholders of Pennsylvania and neither the New York Central nor the Pennsylvania has control of the petitioner. Together they do have. But that amounts to saying nothing more than that the stockholders of a corporation control it. We do not think it can be said that where two or more corporations owned by different sets of stockholders control another corporation such other corporation is controlled by the same interests. . . .

The Commissioner acquiesced in the decision of the Tax Court in *Lake Erie*. . . . In 1965, however, the Commissioner withdrew the prior acquiescence and substituted nonacquiescence. . . .

The courts recognize the congressional purpose of section 482 to prevent evasion or avoidance of otherwise payable taxes by means of shifting profits or by other financial devices and have given broad scope to the Commissioner's discretion in making reallocations of income, where the exercise of this power is not unreasonable or arbitrary. . . . The courts have also construed this statute liberally in order to achieve the declared purpose of Congress. . . .

ORGANIZATION

The terms "organization," "trade," "business" are broadly defined in Treas. Reg. §1.482-1(a)(1) and (2). . . . Certainly, Midtown, McCurdy and Forman satisfy this prerequisite.

CONTROL

No definition of "control" is contained in section 482. It has been opined that this omission was intentional in order to allow for flexibility of administration. . . .

As to "same interests," there is no statutory definition and no Treasury regulations guidelines.

In order to find control, no percentage requirements are specified nor are any precise requirements necessary. The trend in the recent case law is to apply the realistic approach. . . .

If Midtown was the creature of only one of the taxpayers, and all of its stock were owned by that single parent, i.e., if Midtown were a strange creature having a father but no mother, the most rigid, literal wooden interpretation of section 482 would bring Midtown within the ambit of that section. It is the contention of the taxpayers, however, that section 482 is not applicable because Midtown is the normal child of a father and a mother, the product of an earthy relationship between McCurdy and Forman, twentieth century parents exercising no control over their progeny.

Midtown is the creation of a union of McCurdy and Forman — not in holy matrimony but in a legitimate business enterprise. Their interests in the existence and career of Midtown and the interests of Midtown are identical.

To contend that these parents do not control their child is to fly in the face of reality. They have had complete control of Midtown from the day of conception (its incorporation) throughout the years relevant to this case. Every act of Midtown has been dictated by papa and mamma who, directly or indirectly, have financed its career and controlled its every move.

In apparent disregard of the reality of the circumstances, the Tax Court below looked only to the record ownership of Midtown. Ignored was reality of the control of Midtown. In withdrawing his acquiescence in *Lake Erie*, the Commissioner concluded that *Lake Erie* was inconsistent with the broad language of §482 and the trend of cases discussed supra, and noted that *Lake Erie* ignored the reality of the control in that case.

The Commission[er] is supported by the views of commentators.

The loans by taxpayers to Midtown, without interest, affected the incomes of taxpayers and of Midtown. By not reporting interest on these loans, taxpayers reported lower earnings and, in turn, lower taxes. Midtown, in not paying interest, eliminated a business expense which would have further increased its yearly losses. Because of Midtown's unfavorable financial condition, it was encountering difficulty in the rental of stores, a matter of concern to McCurdy and Forman, the actual owners of Midtown. Midtown, McCurdy and Forman were loath to show as further losses annual interest payments on $2,000,000.00 of loans at 5%, i.e. $100,000.00 per year, and the elimination of annual payments of $150,000.00 by McCurdy and Forman. . . . Mr. Chiarella, general manager of Midtown, testifying before the Tax Court to these annual payments of $150,000.00, said that they definitely helped to narrow Midtown's deficit; that without these payments Midtown would have had to get that money from some place. . . . This explanation is equally applicable to the waiver of interest on the loans aggregating $2,000,000.00.

Whether McCurdy and Forman are regarded as a partnership or joint venture, de facto, in forming Midtown, the conclusion is inescapable that they acted in concert in making loans without interest to a corporation, all of whose stock they owned and all of whose directors and officers were their alter egos. They were not competitors in their dealings with one another or with Midtown as to Midtown. Their interests in Midtown were identical. When the Commissioner withdrew his acquiescence in *Lake Erie*, he gave reality of control as one of the reasons for doing so. . . . We agree. . . .

Having found two businesses under common control, we reach the question as to whether the Commissioner properly allocated interest on the two loans of $1,000,000.00 each as income to the taxpayers.

. . . To justify the allocation as income to McCurdy and Forman of interest on their loans, it must be found that their waiver of interest "is other than it would have been had the taxpayer in the conduct of his affairs been an uncontrolled taxpayer dealing at arm's length with another controlled taxpayer." Treas. Reg. 1.4821(c). . . . "In determining the true taxable income of a controlled taxpayer, the district director is not restricted to the case of improper accounting, to the case of a fraudulent, colorable, or sham transaction, or to the case of a device designed to reduce or avoid tax by shifting or distorting income, deductions, credits, or allowances." Treas. Reg. 1.482-1(c).

Reallocation is necessary here in order to properly reflect the income of taxpayers and Midtown. Taxpayers have advanced an argument, supported by case law, that the Commissioner may not create income where none actually existed. . . .

Several cases have held that one related party is not required to charge another related party interest on a loan; that the lender is not to be taxed on interest, with respect to a loan, where it was not intended that interest be collected. In Combs Lumber Co. v. Commissioner, 41 B.T.A. 339 (1940), it was the practice of the corporation to lend money to its stockholders without interest. The Board of Tax Appeals ruled that, under the circumstances, no liability for interest was created and, thus, the Commissioner could not impute interest to the lender. In Society Brand Clothes, Inc. v. Commissioner, 18 T.C. 304 (1952), a corporation held a ten year note of its wholly owned subsidiary. The note provided for the payment of interest, but it was executed with the understanding that no interest would be charged until some date in the future. The Tax Court held that the corporation was not required to report any interest not received by it. . . .

To the extent that the above cases cited by taxpayers may be read as holding that no interest can be allocated under §482 under the facts of this case, they are not in accord with either economic reality, or with the declared purpose of section 482. They seriously impair the usefulness of §482. Those cases may be correct from a pure accounting standpoint. Nevertheless, interest income may be added to taxpayers' incomes, as long as a correlative adjustment is made to Midtown, for then the true taxable income of all involved will be properly reflected. Treas. Reg. §1.482-1(a)(6) provides:

> The term "true taxable income" means . . . the taxable income . . .
> which would have resulted to the controlled taxpayer, had it in the
> conduct of its affairs . . . dealt with the other member . . . at arm's
> length. It does not mean the income . . . or allowances, resulting
> to the controlled taxpayer by reason of the particular . . . trans-
> action . . . the controlled taxpayer . . . chose to make (even though
> such . . . transaction . . . may be legally binding upon the parties
> thereto).

Treas. Reg. §1.482-2(a) provides:

> Where one member of a group of controlled entities makes
> a loan or advance directly or indirectly to, or otherwise becomes
> a creditor of, another member of such group, and charges no
> interest . . . the district director may make appropriate allocations
> to reflect an arm's length interest rate for the use of such loan. . . .

These regulations must prevail, for they are entirely consistent
with the scope and purpose of §482. The instant loans without interest
are obviously not at arm's length, since no unrelated parties would
loan such large sums without interest. The allocation of the interest
income to taxpayers was necessary in order to properly reflect their
taxable incomes. . . .

Our remaining concern is with whether the allocation of interest
at 5% was proper. The Tax Court in its decision did not reach this
issue. A remand is not necessary because, under both the regulations
and the circumstances of this case, the 5% interest charge was emi-
nently reasonable. Treas. Reg. 1.482-2(a)(2) provides the standard
for determining the appropriate interest to be charged. . . .

Midtown's balance sheets reveal that it paid interest on various
loans, ranging from 4½% to 6% per annum. . . . Midtown had outstanding loans from Lincoln Rochester Trust Co. payable at 5½%
interest; from Central Trust Co. payable at 5½% per annum and
from D. Raffelson payable at 5% per annum. Considering the rate
of interest Midtown paid on its arm's length loans and the Treasury
Regulations, 5% is an appropriate rate of interest. . . .

NOTE

See Nauheim, B. Forman & Co., Inc. — A Crucial Test of the
Future of Section 482, 26 Tax Law. 107 (1972). See also Robert M.
Brittingham, 66 T.C. 373 (1976), aff'd per curiam, 598 F.2d 1375 (5th
Cir. 1979), holding that the family relationship between the shareholders of two corporations did not permit a finding that the two
were "owned or controlled directly or indirectly by the same interests," where the financial interests of the two groups of shareholders
were adverse to any misallocation of income between them.

C. "TRADE OR BUSINESS"

RUBIN v. COMMISSIONER

56 T.C. 1155 (1971), *aff'd per curiam*, 460 F.2d 1216 (2d Cir. 1972)

FAY, Judge. . . . In the prior opinion of this Court we held that fees paid to a corporation for management services rendered by a controlling shareholder to a second corporation, controlled by the same shareholder, were taxable to the shareholder rather than to the corporation under section 61 and principles enunciated in Lucas v. Earl, 281 U.S. 111 (1930), despite the existence of a contract purporting to attribute the earnings to the corporation. In light of this conclusion, we did not reach respondent's attempted allocation of a portion of the income received by the corporation to petitioner under the authority of section 482.

The Court of Appeals held our reliance on section 61 to have been erroneous and remanded the case for consideration under section 482. . . .

. . . [P]etitioner contends that section 482 is inapposite in the present situation on the theory that what is involved here is not an allocation among two or more organizations, trades, or businesses, as the terms of that section require, but rather an attempted allocation of income between a corporation and its employee. For the proposition that employment is not deemed a trade or business, petitioner places primary reliance on the Supreme Court case of Whipple v. Commissioner, 373 U.S. 193 (1963), which in another context held that devoting one's time to a corporation is not of itself and without more a trade or business. While there may well be truth in the latter assertion of petitioner, the weakness of his argument, in our view, rests not in any proposition of law relied upon but in his conception and characterization of the facts presented. The evidence in this case does not, in our judgment, support the factual conclusion which lies at the heart of petitioner's opposition to the proposed application of section 482, to wit, that petitioner engaged in no trade or business other than that of being a corporate employee. In reaching this result, we rely heavily upon the decisions of this court in Pauline W. Ach, 42 T.C. 114 1964), *aff'd*, 358 F.2d 342 (C.A. 6, 1966), *certiorari denied* 385 U.S. 899 (1966), and of the Second Circuit in Borge v. Commissioner, 405 F.2d 673 (C.A. 2, 1968), affirming a Memorandum Opinion of this Court, *certiorari denied* 395 U.S. 933 (1969). . . .

In *Ach* the taxpayer's son had for some time owned a controlling interest in a corporation which consistently incurred losses in its operations. During the same period the taxpayer conducted a highly successful dress business in the form of a proprietorship. In 1953, in a transaction apparently designed to secure for the dress business the benefits of net operating losses which had in prior years accrued to the corporation, the corporation discontinued its unprofitable operations and simultaneously acquired from taxpayer her interest in the dress business. Taxpayer thereafter, presumably as an employee of the corporation, continued to operate the dress business but received no compensation for her efforts. She was neither bound by contract to continue rendering her crucial services for the benefit of the corporation nor inhibited by covenant or otherwise from competing with it. . . . [T]he court over an objection of the taxpayer predicated upon arguments similar to those put forth by petitioners in the present case, sustained the right of the Commissioner to allocate a portion of the income received by the corporation to the taxpayer. Commenting on the scope of section 482 the court stated:

> Section 482 is remedial in character. It is couched in broad, comprehensive terms, and we should be slow to give it a narrow, inhospitable reading that fails to achieve the end that the legislature plainly had in view. We think that the statute is not made inapplicable by its reference to "two or more organizations, trades, or businesses."

The court apparently found it unnecessary to decide whether section 482 warranted an allocation between a corporation and an employee, concluding, on the facts, that taxpayer was not a mere employee but rather continued after the purported transfer of the proprietorship assets to conduct a dress business jointly with the corporation.

The facts of *Borge* . . . bear even closer resemblance to those of the case at bar. The taxpayer in that case, a well-known entertainer, owned a poultry farm which produced losses in 5 consecutive years. Prompted by a desire to avoid the consequences of a Code section then in effect limiting the amount of deductions allowable in the case of individuals, Borge formed a corporation and transferred to it, in exchange for all its stock, the assets of the poultry business. To offset expected losses from farm operations, Borge then entered into a contract with the corporation under which he agreed to perform entertainment services for it in return for a fixed salary of $50,000 per year. His annual net entertainment income for the years in dispute far exceeded the $50,000 stipulated in the contract. On these facts the Second Circuit affirmed the conclusion of the Tax Court that section 482 was applicable to authorize the Commissioner's allocation of a portion of the income received by the corporation to Borge. Again, proceeding on the premise that he was a mere employee of the corporation, Borge contended, as did petitioner in *Ach* and as does petitioner in the case at bar, that section 482 does not apply. The court held otherwise, stating:

> We accept, as supported by the record, the Tax Court's findings: that Borge operated an entertainment business and *merely assigned to Danica* [the corporation] *a portion of his income from that business,* that Danica did nothing to earn or to assist in the earning of the entertainment income; that Borge would not have contracted for $50,000 per year with an unrelated party to perform the services referred to in his contract with Danica. Thus Borge was correctly held to be in the entertainment business. [Emphasis added. . . .]

Directing itself to Borge's reliance upon *Whipple,* the court pointed out:

> Here, however, Borge was in the business of entertaining. He was not devoting his time and energies to a corporation; he was *carrying on his career as an entertainer, and merely channeling a part of his entertainment income through the corporation.* [Emphasis added. . . .]

As in *Ach,* the court in *Borge* did not consider whether employment status, standing alone, constituted a trade or business for purposes of section 482. . . .

It is true, as petitioner is quick to point out, that the individuals in both of the cited cases had engaged in business as a proprietorship prior to the formation of corporations to take over their business operations. However, we regard this factor as only one of many to be weighed in determining whether activities of a shareholder constituted a trade or business. . . . Moreover, in the present case, as in *Borge,* the services for which the corporation became entitled to compensation were rendered to parties other than the employing corporation. . . .

Nor do we believe that the purpose for which the corporation was formed serves to distinguish these cases from the case at hand. Admittedly, the use of the corporate device in *Borge* and *Ach* was seized upon to permit the taxpayer to offset the losses of one business against those of another whereas in the immediate case it merely resulted in a deflection of income from one taxpayer to another. But to the extent that the transactions gave rise to a distortion of income, each of the cases presents an equally cogent case for an application of section 482. In some respects, it should be noted, the facts of the instant case make out an even stronger plea for the application of section 482 than those of *Borge.* For example, petitioner in this case, unlike Borge, neither entered into contract with his putative employer nor relinquished to the slightest degree his control over production of the income. In view of the control he possessed over both payor and payee corporations, petitioner could have terminated his employment status virtually at will, thereby divesting Park of any further claim to the proceeds of his labor. We recognize, of course, that there are also factors in this case which tend to militate in the opposite direction, such as the existence of other shareholders and their contribution of substantial sums of capital to the corporation. These factors, along with others mentioned in our present and prior opinions, are to be thrown into the hopper in performing an allocation under section 482; they do not, however, warrant a conclusion that section 482 is wholly inapplicable.

Petitioner has also invoked the personal holding company provisions and accompanying legislative history as evidencing the congressional belief that section 482 was not intended to be applied to personal service corporations in the manner presently sought by the Commissioner. At best, as petitioner himself recognizes, these provisions show only that Congress, in assessing the merits of the personal holding company proposals then under consideration, acted under a belief that existing provisions of the Code were inadequate to deal with the varied problems surrounding personal holding companies. . . . As the court in *Borge*, rejecting a similar contention advanced by the taxpayer in that case, said:

> We do not read those provisions, however, as the only available methods for dealing with situations there involved. As the Third Circuit said in National Sec. Corp. v. Commissioner, 137 F.2d 600, 602 (3d Cir.), *cert. denied*, 320 U.S. 794 . . . (1943).
>
> In every case in which [Section 482] is applied its application will necessarily result in an apparent conflict with the literal requirements of some other provision of the [Internal Revenue Code]. If this were not so Section [482] would be wholly superfluous. . . .

Petitioner has characterized the present efforts of the Commissioner in seeking to tax petitioner on some or all of the income received by the corporation as an attempt to increase the salary of a corporate employee, an attempt which, petitioner asserts, is entirely novel and one which has not to date received the approval of any court. He expresses "horror" at the prospect should the respondent prevail in this case that the effect of such a decision would be to confer upon the Commissioner the authority to freely increase the salary of corporate employees upon a finding at his discretion that the compensation paid to the employee was inadequate. We emphasize, however, that having found it unnecessary to consider this question, we do not today hold that employment status constitutes, in and of itself, a trade or business within the meaning of section 482. Nor have we ruled that section 482 empowers the Commissioner at will to readjust the salaries of corporate employees. We merely hold, as is the clear import of both the *Ach* and *Borge* decisions, that where the particular facts of a case are such as to justify a finding that a shareholder operated an independent business and merely assigned to the corporation a portion of the income therefrom, the business activity of the taxpayer may constitute a trade or business to which allocation of all or part of the income attributable to his efforts is authorized under section 482. . . .

NOTES

1. See also Stanley W. Haag, 88 T.C. 604 (1987). But see Foglesong v. Commissioner, 621 F.2d 865 (7th Cir. 1980), where the court held that §482 does not permit the Commissioner to allocate personal service income from a corporation to its controlling shareholder-employee when the controlling shareholder's only trade or business is the performance of services for the corporation. The Service has announced that it will not follow *Foglesong*. See Rev. Rul. 88-38, 1988-21 I.R.B. 17. In 1982, Congress passed §269A, which overrules *Foglesong* with respect to "personal service corporations" that perform services primarily for one other entity.

See Wood, The *Keller, Foglesong*, and *Pacella* Cases: Section 482 Allocations, Assignments of Income and New §269A, 10 J. Corp. Taxn. 65 (1983).

2. See General Electric Co. v. United States, 83-2 U.S.T.C. ¶9532(Cl. Ct. 1983), in which the court held that §482 could trump the carryover basis provision normally applicable to assets received in a §332 liquidation, thereby denying the parent corporation the loss it claimed on selling high basis, low value property received from its subsidiary. The loss in value had accrued during the subsidiary's ownership of the property, but the subsidiary, to which the government had allocated the loss under §482, could get no benefit from the deduction. Cf. *National Securities Corp.,* page 1002 infra.

3. In G. D. Searle & Co., 88 T.C. 252 (1987), the Service had sought to reallocate to the taxpayer, a U.S. pharmaceutical company, the income earned by a wholly owned subsidiary operating in Puerto Rico. Refusing to disregard the taxpayer's transfers of intangibles to the subsidiary, which it concluded had been made for business reasons, the Tax Court reduced the reallocation to the amount attributable to the fact that the taxpayer had not received arm's-length consideration for the transferred intangibles.

4. In situations where the individual taxpayer is clearly not an "organization, trade or business," the Commissioner may rely on the "substance-over-form" doctrine to achieve the same result as a §482 reallocation. For an interesting example of such a case, see the opinion of Justice Stewart, sitting by designation, in Stewart v. Commissioner, 742 F.2d 977 (9th Cir. 1983) ("substance-over-form" doctrine used to impute gain on the sale of appreciated securities to controlling taxpayer, who had transferred them to the corporation

in a §351 exchange, where funds were subsequently distributed to pay off corporate debt to shareholders).

D. EFFECT ON DEDUCTIONS AND LOSSES

NATIONAL SECURITIES CORP. v. COMMISSIONER
137 F.2d 600 (3d Cir. 1943), *cert. denied*, 320 U.S. 794 (1943)

Before Biggs, Maris, and Goodrich, Circuit Judges.

MARIS, Circuit Judge. The petitioner, National Securities Corporation, is the successor of the taxpayer, American Gas & Electric Securities Corporation, and is liable by reason of its merger with the taxpayer for all obligations of the latter, including federal income taxes. During its entire existence the taxpayer was a wholly owned subsidiary of American Equitable Assurance Company of New York. The taxpayer's income and expenses were recorded in separate books of account kept by it and its accounts were not commingled with those of the parent. In August and September, 1929 the parent purchased as an investment 1,000 shares of the common stock of Standard Gas and Electric Company at a cost of $140,378.06. By 1933 the parent's purchases of Standard stock had increased to a total of 3,500 shares, at a cost of $418,780.19. During 1935 reorganization of Standard was commenced under §77B of the Bankruptcy Act. . . . At the close of that year the Standard stock, for which the parent had paid an average of approximately $120 per share, had decreased in value to $6.25 per share. In January, 1936 the parent sold 2,500 shares of Standard stock in the open market at prices ranging from $7.75 to $9.125 per share. On February 13, 1936 the parent delivered its remaining 1,000 shares of Standard to the taxpayer in exchange for the latter's capital stock having a stated value of $10 per share and a market value of more than $92 per share. These shares on the date when delivered to the taxpayer had a market value of $8,562.50. On December 11, 1936 the taxpayer sold the Standard stock for $7,175.00. The proceeds of the sale were received and kept by the taxpayer. In its income tax return for 1936 the taxpayer claimed as a deductible loss $133,203.06 representing the difference between the cost of the 1,000 shares to the parent ($140,378.06) and the amount for which the taxpayer sold them ($7,175.00).

The Commissioner disallowed in its entirety the deduction claimed by the taxpayer and assessed a deficiency. At the hearing before the Board of Tax Appeals, however, he conceded that the taxpayer was entitled to that part of the claimed deduction which represented the difference between $8,562.50, the fair market value of the Standard shares when acquired by the taxpayer, and $7,175.00, the amount for which the taxpayer sold them, or $1,387.50. The Board of Tax Appeals sustained the Commissioner's action as thus modified. 1942, 46 B.T.A. 562.

The Commissioner disallowed the loss upon authority of Section [482]. . . .

The taxpayer's first contention is that since Section [482] is a general statute dealing with the allocation of gross income and deductions it cannot be controlling here because Congress has specifically provided by Sections [351 and 362(a)] that a corporation, which has acquired property from its controlling stockholder and which sells that property for an amount less than the original cost of the property to its stockholder, may deduct the difference as a loss in computing its own net income for the year of the sale.

We think, however, that the petitioner misconceives the distinct functions of these provisions of the statute. Sections [351 and 362(a)(1)] were intended to regulate the time when certain gains or losses are to be recognized for tax purposes and the cost bases to be used in determining the amounts of such gains or losses. It is true that they likewise lay down a general rule to determine which taxpayer shall take such gains or losses into account. These sections were followed in the present case by the Commissioner when he determined that no loss should be recognized upon the transfer of the Standard shares by the parent to the taxpayer and that the loss sustained by the taxpayer upon the later sale of these shares should be measured by their original cost to the parent.

Section [482] on the other hand is addressed to the wholly different problem of providing a more appropriate manner of allocating income and deductions when the application of the general rules of the statute will not clearly reflect the true income. . . . Section [482] is directed to the correction of particular situations in which the strict application of the other provisions of the act will result in a distortion of the income of affiliated organizations. In every case in which the section is applied its application will necessarily result in an apparent conflict with the literal requirements of some other provision of the act. If this were not so Section [482] would be wholly superfluous. We accordingly conclude that the application of Section [482] may not be denied because it appears to run afoul of the literal provisions of Sections [351 and 362(a)(1)] if the Commissioner's action in allocating under the provisions of Section [482] the loss involved in this case was a proper exercise of the discretion conferred upon him by the section.

By Section [482] Congress has conferred authority upon Commissioner to allocate deductions "if he determines" that such allocation "is necessary." This is a broad discretion, limited only in that the necessity must arise "in order to prevent evasion of taxes or clearly to reflect the income." G.U.R. Co. v. Commissioner, 7 Cir., 1941, 117 F.2d 187.

The Commissioner takes the position that allocation was necessary in order clearly to reflect the income. In this determination he was sustained by the Board. Our examination of the facts convinces us that this determination was neither arbitrary nor capricious. The parent made the investment in Standard stock in 1929, held on to the stock as an investment until 1936, concluded to rid its own portfolio at a time when the stock had become well nigh valueless and then, instead of selling on the market, taking its loss and marking "finis" to a most unprofitable venture, transferred the stock to its wholly owned subsidiary. It seems most reasonable to treat the loss as one which had in fact been sustained by the parent rather than by its subsidiary. The shifting of the loss to the subsidiary gives an artificial picture of its true income and one which it was unnecessary for the Commissioner to accept. The shares for which the taxpayer claims a loss of $133,203.06 had been acquired by it for its own stock having a declared value on its books of only $8,000 and a market value of only about $75,000. The Commissioner was not bound to accept the petitioner's explanation that the parent transferred the stock solely for the purpose of ridding itself of an investment which it was unwise for an insurance company to retain and not for the purpose of tax avoidance. The Commissioner was justified in finding that the taxpayer's income was not clearly reflected by its return for 1936 since the return included a loss which was in fact incurred by the parent. We conclude that the Commissioner's action was neither arbitrary nor capricious.

Finally the taxpayer contends that in fact the Commissioner did not allocate the loss as Section [482] requires but merely disallowed it to the taxpayer. As we have seen, counsel for the Commissioner at the hearing before the Board conceded that $1,387.50 of the $133,203.06 loss should be allowed to the taxpayer and the Board's decision approved this allowance. For all practical purposes this was an allocation of the remainder of the loss to the parent. For in his deficiency notice the Commissioner stated that he was disallowing the deduction to the taxpayer "by application of the provisions of Section [482]. . . ." There is clearly implicit in this disallowance of the loss to the subsidiary on the authority of Section [482] a finding that the loss has been allocated to the parent. This is true even though under the circumstances of this case such an allocation would have had no practical effect upon the parent's income tax for 1936.[3]

---

3. Though the parent's liability for tax is not here involved it appears from the stipulation that in its income tax return for that year the parent reported $1,706,683.76 profits from the sales of stock and $1,723,376.88 losses. This resulted in a net capital loss of $16,693.12. Since Sections 23(j) and 117(d) of the Revenue

The decision of the Board of Tax Appeals is affirmed.

NOTES

1. Does the basis provision of §362(a) apply only when §351 bars recognition of a gain, or does it also apply when §351 bars recognition of a loss? If so, when? Cf. *General Electric Co.*, Note 2, page 1001 supra.

2. See Northwestern National Bank v. United States, 556 F.2d 889 (8th Cir. 1977) (charitable deduction allocated from parent to subsidiary where donated property had been distributed by subsidiary as a dividend; subsidiary would not have engaged in such a transaction with a noncontrolling corporate shareholder); Southern Bancorporation, 67 T.C. 1022 (1977) (gain on sale of appreciated property distributed as dividend allocated to subsidiary; purpose of distribution was to avoid application of §482 to sale by subsidiary); Rev. Rul. 77-83, 1977-1 C.B. 139 (§482 may apply to bargain sale of stock of second-tier foreign subsidiaries to foreign parent corporation by domestic first-tier subsidiary, where one purpose was avoidance of tax on income derived from ownership of distributed stock).

W. BRAUN CO. v. COMMISSIONER
396 F.2d 264 (2d Cir. 1968)

Before Moore, Woodbury* and Smith, Circuit Judges.

MOORE, Circuit Judge. This case was brought to contest an asserted deficiency of $8,665.98 in the income tax return of W. Braun Co., Inc., petitioner-appellant, for the fiscal year ended February 29, 1960. The deficiency arose because the Commissioner, acting pursuant to . . . §482, attributed to the petitioner all the taxable income of Braunware Products Co., Inc., a corporation wholly owned by petitioner.

Three corporations are involved. Both the ownership interest therein and the chronology of the events are important in deciding the proper tax consequences of the facts hereinafter set forth.

1. W. Braun Co., an Illinois corporation ("Braun Chicago"), was owned in equal shares by Mary Braun and her three children, Morris, Julius, and Mrs. E. C. Erenberg. "Braun Chicago was engaged in the

---

Act of 1936 permit deductions arising from losses from sales or exchanges of capital assets to be taken only to the extent of $2,000 the parent could not have derived any actual tax benefit from an allocation of the losses from the sale of the Standard stock.

*Of the First Circuit, sitting by designation.

sale at wholesale of bottles and glass products to manufacturers of pharmaceuticals and cosmetics and to others" (Op. T.C.).

2. W. Braun Co. Inc., petitioner was incorporated in New York in 1946. Two-thirds of its stock were owned by the Brauns in equal shares. The other one-third was owned equally by two persons, A. A. Friedberg and M. J. Tauger, who were unrelated to the Brauns. Petitioner had been "organized to conduct the same type of business in the northeastern part of the United States as was conducted in the midwest by Braun Chicago" (Op. T.C.) under a territorial agreement that was in effect between them. Friedberg had been hired by the Brauns to run the petitioner. Both Friedberg and Tauger were employed full time by petitioner, were vice-presidents and received the major portion of the salaries paid, Friedberg receiving various amounts ranging between $14,638 and $20,250 and Tauger between $12,615 and $20,250 for the taxable years ending, respectively, in February 1956 to 1960.

3. Braunware Products Co., Inc. ("Braunware"), was incorporated in New York in 1956. Petitioner was the sole owner of its stock and its officers and directors occupied the same positions in Braunware. Braunware's business was to sell "at wholesale cosmetic travel packages and glass containers of the same type sold by the petitioner. It conducted its business on the petitioner's premises and used the petitioner's office, telephone and correspondence facilities" (Op. T.C.). Braunware during its first taxable year ending July 31, 1957, sustained a net operating loss of $4,772.68. It remained inactive thereafter until November 1959. As of August 1, 1959, its net assets were $5,172.32.

The business arrangements between Braun Chicago and petitioner (primarily a selling organization) called for the purchase by Braun Chicago from manufacturers of the merchandise sold by petitioner. The manufacturers shipped directly to petitioner's customers and looked to Braun Chicago for payment. Braun Chicago in turn billed petitioner at cost and petitioner billed its customers, paying Braun Chicago 2% of its net sales for its services.

In June 1959 a substantial customer of Braun Chicago, Lanolin Plus, Inc., a cosmetic manufacturer, moved its plant from Chicago to Newark, New Jersey, to wit, out of Braun Chicago's territory into petitioner's. Thus, for all practical purposes the responsibility for this account fell on petitioner's operating officers Friedberg and Tauger. As owners of a one-third interest in petitioner, they had a real financial stake in the account. Their concern with respect to the Lanolin Plus account (evidenced as early as June 11, 1959 — letter from Friedberg to Julius Braun (Exh. 17)), has been well summarized by the Tax Court as follows:

> Plus account was a profitable account for the petitioner to have, were concerned about the risk entailed in dealing with Lan-

olin Plus because of the size of the account and some of the ventures that Lanolin Plus was engaged in. They thought that the business of the petitioner, and consequently their individual interests in the petitioner, might very well be destroyed if Lanolin Plus should become insolvent, and therefore wanted to eliminate the risk of such account. Both Friedberg and Tauger expressed their concern to Morris and Julius Braun. Friedberg recommended to them that the petitioner cease making shipments to Lanolin Plus and that the sales of Lanolin Plus be handled by the petitioner's inactive subsidiary, Braunware. The other officers of the petitioner agreed to Friedberg's suggestion.

There was a factual basis for the worries of Friedberg and Tauger. While Lanolin Plus returned a modest profit in 1959, it sustained a substantial loss in 1958. A large part of its assets were intangibles (patents, etc.) and a very high proportion of its costs were advertising and other selling expenses. When petitioner acquired the account, Lanolin Plus' debt to Braun Chicago stood at $250,000, one-fifth of which was past due. It took Friedberg six months to succeed in collecting the full amount for Braun Chicago. Finally, several Dun & Bradstreet reports showed that while Lanolin Plus paid most of its bills on time, it was "slow" or in arrears with several of its creditors.

Subsequent to September 1959, the Lanolin Plus account was transferred to the 1956-incorporated Braunware. Under an agreement with Braunware, Braun Chicago received as its fee for services rendered 50% of Braunware's gross profits or approximately 10% of its net sales [petitioner's gross profit was some 20% of its net sales]. In September 1959 petitioner ceased making shipments to Lanolin Plus and in November 1959 Braunware commenced handling the account. Braunware did not have separate offices but it kept its own bank account, books, and records. Friedberg was still in charge of the account and it was agreed that petitioner would receive 2% of Braunware's net sales for the use of its facilities and Friedberg's talents. For the fiscal year ended February 29, 1960, Braunware reported net profit of $17,208.00 from which it deducted its net operating loss of $4,827.00. Petitioner's net income for the same period totalled $23,461.25. The deficiency arose because the Commissioner, acting under powers bestowed upon him by Section 482 of the Internal Revenue Code of 1954, allocated all the taxable income of Braunware to petitioner.

The congressional purpose of Section 482 was to prevent the use of controlled corporations to evade or avoid otherwise payable taxes by means of shifting profits or by other financial devices. The courts have given broad scope to the Commissioner's discretion in making such allocations. On the other hand, the exercise of this power cannot be unreasonable or arbitrary. The Tax Court and other reviewing courts have endeavored to examine carefully the relationship between the controlled corporations to ascertain whether there was a "sound business purpose" served by the use of the other corporation or whether the transaction was a mere sham to effect tax evasion. Before analyzing the facts, the precepts must be noted that a taxpayer "is not required to adopt or continue with that form of organization which results in the maximum tax upon business income" and that when a taxpayer chooses to conduct his business in a certain form, "the tax collector may not deprive him of the incidental tax benefits flowing therefrom, unless it first be found to be but a fiction or a sham." Polak's Frutal Works, Inc. v. Comm'r, 21 T.C. 953, 973-74 (1954). In final analysis, "[e]ach case must be decided on its own facts." (Id. 974.)

The facts as found by the Tax Court so far as applicable are accepted as basic. The Commissioner contends "that the purpose of the petitioner's transfer of the Lanolin Plus account to Braunware was to take advantage of the net operating loss deduction which Braunware had available and Braunware's surtax exemption" (Op. T.C.). The Tax Court held that "[w]hile there is no evidence which specifically indicates that such was the purpose, the evidence does not affirmatively establish that such was not the purpose." True, "the petitioner did not, in connection with the transfer, have the advice of an attorney or an accountant" and one of petitioner's officers and stockholders knew of the unused tax loss and surtax exemption but business transactions conducted without the advice of attorney or accountant are not per se illegal and knowledge of the law permitting corporate surtax exemptions creates no presumption that the purpose of the transaction was the evasion of income taxes. The Tax Court also held that "petitioner has failed to show that the allocation was not necessary in order clearly to reflect the income of the petitioner, within the meaning of Section 482" (Op. T.C.).

Although the facts justified both Commissioner and Tax Court in critically analyzing the Braunware transaction in the light of the family control of these corporations, we believe that the petitioner has shown sufficiently "sound business reasons" for the Braunware transaction and that to hold otherwise would be to substitute the Commissioner's business judgment for that of petitioner's officers and directors without a factual showing of unlawful purpose.

The financial welfare of Friedberg and Tauger was dependent upon petitioner's welfare and stability. Since 1956 at least they had received moderately substantial salaries from petitioner. The Brauns were in a way absentee owners but Friedberg and Tauger were the actual owner-executives on location managing the business.

The 1959 acquisition of the Lanolin Plus account was therefore not an unmixed blessing to Friedberg and Tauger. It was not unreasonable for them to assume that Lanolin Plus would continue to run a receivable balance on petitioner's books about two-and-one-half times greater than petitioner's net worth of $102,000. Since most of this money was invested in special order merchandise, if Lanolin Plus went bankrupt because of the failure of a promotional campaign, petitioner could not hope to resell its inventory. While petitioner did have credit insurance in the amount of $75,000 (this amount was later doubled when Braunware took over the account), in the event of Lanolin Plus' insolvency, petitioner's continued existence and Friedberg's and Tauger's investment therein would be in dire jeopardy. Nor was the subsequent collection of the $250,000 Lanolin Plus indebtedness proof of its stability. The transfer to Braunware must be viewed prospectively from the date June 1959.

While the transfer of the account was mainly desired by petitioner's New York management, it also appealed to the Brauns. Braun Chicago would still supply most of the merchandise requirements of petitioner as well as Braunware. From the Brauns' point of view, one effect of the transfer of Lanolin Plus from the petitioner to Braunware was the loss of security afforded by petitioner's net worth ($102,000) compared to that of Braunware (only $5,000 as of August 1, 1959). However, they felt adequately compensated because under the agreement with Braunware, Braun Chicago received as its fee 50% of Braunware's gross profits or approximately 10% of its net sales [petitioner's gross profit was approximately 20% of net sales]. Under its agreement with petitioner Braun Chicago received only 2% of net sales as its fee, or one-fifth as much for the same service.

The Tax Court took the position that there was no reasonable business purpose behind the transfer of the Lanolin Plus account to Braunware and that the primary reason for the transaction was the evasion of income taxes (via utilization of the net operating loss carryover and the additional surtax exemption). We find this holding to be based on an overly optimistic view of the risks involved in handling the Lanolin Plus account. The court's own findings as to the motivation of the parties in transferring the account and the record evidence compel the conclusion that the transfer was for a good business reason.[2] While the Tax Court might disagree with the soundness of, or the necessity for, the decision reached by petitioner's management, their decision was nevertheless a reasonable business judgment which must be respected as such.

The Commissioner was therefore not justified in arbitrarily allocating all of Braunware's taxable income to petitioner. Such an

---

2. See Johnson Bronze Co. v. Comm'r, 24 T.C.M. 1542, 1552 (1965). Counsel for the Commissioner suggested on oral argument that the Lanolin Plus account was not any riskier than petitioner's other accounts. It was conceded, however, that there was nothing in the record to support this contention, and the size of the account alone would appear to place it in a different category from petitioner's other accounts.

allocation is authorized only when there is no business purpose to the challenged transactions or corporate structure. Section 482 does not give the Commissioner the power to disregard separate corporate entities if they are being used for a bona fide business purpose. The mere fact that the Lanolin Plus account could have been handled by petitioner is irrelevant.[5]

In Simon J. Murphy Co. v. Commissioner, 231 F.2d 639, 644 (6th Cir. 1956), the court stated that Section 45, the predecessor of Section 482, was aimed at:

> circumstances involving an improper manipulation of financial accounts, an improper juggling of the accounts between the related organizations, an improper "milking" of one business for the benefit of the other, or some similar abuse of proper financial accounting, all made possible by the control of the two businesses by the same interests. When the Commissioner determined that a transaction between the controlled parties was not "at arm's length," an allocation would be justified in order to reflect the true net income which would have resulted if one uncontrolled taxpayer had dealt at arm's length with another uncontrolled taxpayer. Substance has been substituted for form.

. . . In summary, in opposition to the Commissioner's unsupported finding of unlawful purpose, there are definite facts which point to an opposite conclusion, i.e., (1) Braunware was not organized for tax evasion purposes but prior to the occasion of the Lanolin Plus account transfer; (2) the financial positions of Friedberg and Tauger in petitioner were quite distinct from those of the Braun family; (3) the relocation of the Lanolin Plus plant was not part of some scheme on petitioner's part; (4) the territorial division agreement pursuant to which the Lanolin Plus account was transferred from Braun Chicago to petitioner; and (5) the admitted concern of Friedberg and Tauger with respect to the Lanolin Plus account.

To give recognition to salesmen's interests, the Tax Court in Bush Hog Manufacturing Co., 42 T.C. 713 (1964), found that the formation of six additional separate sales corporations was for "sound business reasons" and "to permit the salesmen to acquire proprietary interests in the company they worked for. . . ." Id. 727. There would seem to be as sound business reasons here for protecting the salesmen responsible for petitioner's business activities and welfare.

The Tax Court, as an alternative ground of decision, held that "petitioner has failed to show that the allocation was not necessary in order clearly to reflect the income of the petitioner. . . ." The Commissioner therefore argues that even if his allocation of income was not necessary to prevent the evasion of tax, it was necessary to

---

5. . . . Regulation §1.482-1(b)(3). . . .

reflect the "true taxable income" of petitioner. See Regulation §1.482-1(a)(6). The Tax Court, which was in agreement with this view, supported its conclusion by pointing to the fact that "the record fails to show that Braunware paid petitioner any consideration whatever for the account" and by questioning whether 2% of Braunware's net sales was adequate to reimburse petitioner for the use of its personnel and facilities when petitioner's ratio of expense to sales was much higher. Petitioner argues that as to the latter item, the Tax Court, in comparing expense ratios, failed to make any allowance for the fact that Braunware was a cash basis taxpayer while petitioner was on the accrual system — hence, Braunware's obligation to pay one-half of its gross profit to Braun Chicago and other expenses were not accrued on its books. Furthermore, payment by Braunware to petitioner for the Lanolin Plus account was not the only way by which consideration could be shown. The mutual corporate undertakings of the respective owners under some circumstances might well be adequate consideration. Be that as it may, even if both points were decided favorably to the Commissioner, petitioner has still shown that an allocation of all of Braunware's net income to it is unreasonable and arbitrary, Oil Base, Inc. v. Comm'r, 362 F.2d 212, 214 (9th Cir. 1966); Comm'r v. Chelsea Products, 197 F.2d 620, 624 (3rd Cir. 1952), because it is clear that an uncontrolled taxpayer would insist on receiving some net income after expenses before agreeing to take over the Lanolin Plus account. The Commissioner has considerable discretion as to the amount which he may allocate from one controlled taxpayer to another (see Eli Lilly & Co. v. United States, 372 F.2d 990 (Ct. Cl. 1967)), but he cannot make entirely arbitrary apportionments.

We therefore remand to the Tax Court for a determination of the proper amount of income, if any, that should be allocated to petitioner from Braunware. . . .

REVENUE RULING 76-88
1976-1 C.B. 52

. . . S, a life insurance company . . . is a wholly owned subsidiary of P and is subject to tax under section 802; P, a finance company, . . . also owns all of the outstanding stock of S-1 and S-2, both of which are casualty insurance companies subject to Federal income tax under section 831. . . . P, S-1, and S-2 file consolidated returns. However, in the instant case, by reason of section 1504(b)(2), which defines an "includible corporation" for affiliated group purposes, S is precluded from joining in the filing of a consolidated return. Therefore, S files separate Federal income tax returns.

The life insurance business of S and the casualty insurance business of S-1 and S-2 are conducted separately by different operating personnel and each company is an active business corporation. However, the investment portfolios, as well as the accounting, legal, and other non-insurance functions of S, S-1, and S-2, are supervised and managed by the same personnel.

For many years the casualty companies sustained substantial operating losses so that they generally derived a lesser economic yield from tax-exempt bonds than from taxable bonds. In order to preserve the greatest economic yield, the casualty companies' portfolios during these years consisted primarily of taxable bonds. However, by 1974, the casualty companies were in a profit situation and wanted to acquire tax-exempt bonds for their portfolios. The taxable bonds that the casualty companies . . . wanted to eliminate from their portfolios were the type of securities that S desired in order to increase the investment yield of its investment portfolio, while the tax-exempt bonds that S possessed and wanted to eliminate were those desired by the casualty companies. Because the disposition through bond dealers would result in large commissions to be paid by the companies involved, the investment managers decided to accomplish the portfolio improvements, to the extent possible, by inter-company exchanges. Pursuant to this decision, S transferred tax-exempt bonds to S-1 and S-2 in exchange for taxable bonds in 1974. All of the bonds were capital assets in the hands of S, S-1, and S-2.

All values used in the exchanges were obtained from independent market sources and reflected the fair market value of the bonds. As a result of increasing interest rates and deteriorating market values for debt obligations, losses were sustained by all parties to the exchanges. As a result of these exchanges, S's replacement of tax-exempt bonds with taxable bonds increased its pre-tax investment yield.

The specific question presented is whether, under the above circumstances, the losses incurred by S, S-1, and S-2 are allowable even though all the stock of each is held by P.

In the instant case section 267 of the Code cannot apply to disallow the loss because the relationship described in section 267(b) does not exist. Further, section 482 is not applicable because no avoidance of tax or distortion of income resulted from the transactions between the commonly controlled entities. In the instant case gains or losses from the exchanges between the controlled parties are the same as would have resulted from an arm's length transaction between uncontrolled parties.

Accordingly, the losses sustained by S, S-1, and S-2 on the exchanges described above meet the requirements of section 1.165-1(b) of the regulations and such losses are allowable as capital losses under the provisions of section 165(f) of the Code.

NOTE

See also Pitchford's, Inc., 34 T.C.M. (CCH) 384 (1975) (uncertainty that interest, if charged, would have been paid by financially weak related corporation prevented allocation of interest on interest-free loan).

E. SECTION 482 vs. FORCED CONSOLIDATIONS

FULLER, SECTION 482 REVISITED*
31 Tax L. Rev. 475, 516 (1976)

NET INCOME ALLOCATIONS

Section 482 authorizes the Service to allocate gross income, deductions, credits or allowances. Some older cases interpreted this language to mean the Service could not allocate an entity's entire net income to a related entity. More recent cases have permitted net income allocations, however, and it is now quite clear that the Service may make net income allocations in proper circumstances. The Service, however, has attempted to make many more such allocations than the courts have approved.

There are two categories of net income allocations. The first category, the true earner, is represented by the *Philipp Brothers Chemicals, Inc.* decision,[178] and is the broader, more significant category. The second, forced consolidations, is represented by the *Marc's Big Boy-Prospect*[179] decision and is of less importance.

TRUE EARNER

Philipp Brothers Chemicals, Inc. (Chemicals) was a New York corporation. The Service allocated gross income and deductions of ten related corporations to Chemicals. Five of these corporations, the foreign sales corporations, were engaged in the group's export sales activities and five, the domestic sales corporations, were engaged in the group's domestic sales activities. The Tax Court permitted a net income allocation of the foreign sales corporations' income because

---

*Copyright © 1976 by the Tax Law Review. Excerpts reprinted by permission. — ED.

178. Philipp Bros. Chem., Inc. (Md.), 52 T.C. 240 (1969), *acq.*, *aff'd in part sub nom.* Philipp Bros. Chems., Inc. (N.Y.) v. Comm'r, 435 F.2d 53 (2d Cir. 1970).

179. Marc's Big Boy-Prospect, Inc., 52 T.C. 1073 (1969), *acq.*, *aff'd sub nom.* Wisconsin Big Boy Corp. v. Comm'r, 452 F.2d 137 (7th Cir. 1971).

there was no evidence to show that the foreign sales corporations earned their income. None reported deductions for salaries and wages and there was no indication they had employees. Chemicals handled all of the foreign sales corporations' bookkeeping and shipping arrangements. In short, there was no showing that the foreign sales corporations carried on any business activity.

However, the Service's allocation of the domestic sales corporations' net income was not sustained. The five domestic sales corporations maintained their own offices and carried on substantial activities, which produced the income reported on the returns. They had employees and they maintained substantial inventories. Although Chemicals performed their bookkeeping and traffic functions the court felt these services were purely routine. In any event, the corporations paid Chemicals for such services.

The taxpayers appealed with regard to the allocation of the net income from foreign sales corporations. The Second Circuit, however, affirmed the Tax Court and on the same grounds. . . . The court also stated that business purpose becomes relevant only where the corporation performed some business function.

The *Philipp Brothers Chemicals* case provides an excellent example of the true earner category because it involved both corporations that earned income and corporations that did not. . . . Channeling income to a shell corporation, whether for business reasons or otherwise, will not withstand a section 482 true earner attack by the Service. However, if the income is in fact earned by the corporation's employees or its property, a true earner attack should prove to be unsuccessful.

A portion of the Internal Revenue Manual is relevant here. The Manual provides that all section 482 cases can be reduced to a functional analysis:

> (1) What was done?
> (2) What economically significant functions were involved in doing it?
> (3) Who performed each function?
> (4) What is the measure of the economic value of each function performed by each party?

The Manual provides that frequently a function consists of services that must be performed by individuals. Accordingly, agents are directed to obtain information regarding how many employees were employed by each organization, the compensation paid to individual employees and the functions performed by those employees in connection with the questioned transactions. Agents are directed to provide the basis for their conclusions that the individuals involved were employees of one organization rather than another. For example, this might be a reference to employment or withholding records.

In situations where a domestic corporation sells goods to a foreign subsidiary, agents are directed to determine, in addition to the intercompany price and terms of sale, what the subsidiary did with the goods and, if the subsidiary resold the goods, who purchased them, at what prices or profit margins, and what functions the subsidiary performed in reselling. A number of inquiries are suggested:

(1) Did the subsidiary have a staff of salesmen?

(2) Was it necessary to provide technical assistance to the foreign purchasers?

(3) Did the parent or another affiliate sell in the territory before the subsidiary was created?

(4) Were distributors selling in the territory before the subsidiary was created and, if so, at what commission rate?

(5) Is the subsidiary actively selling or only using the prior established distributor network?

(6) Did the subsidiary develop new distributors and accounts in the territory and, if so, did sales increase because of these new distributors or sales?

Although the Manual's provisions presumably were not designed for use in considering net income allocations . . . the functional analysis approach offers some guidelines in this area. Often true earner cases can be reduced to a functional analysis. If a corporation reports income that it has not really earned (perhaps because it is a "shell") it is ripe for challenge under section 482 and it may suffer a net income allocation. However, if a corporation has earned the income that it reports by performing the functions that gave rise to that income, it should be able to avoid a net income allocation.

Forced Consolidations

Net income allocations as discussed above are understandable. Planning is possible. The outcome of litigation can be predicted with reasonable accuracy. But now we will consider *Marc's Big Boy-Prospect, Inc.* and its brethren. Understanding vanishes, planning possibilities decrease and anything becomes possible. Uncertainty rules.

Section 1.482-1(b)(3) of the regulations provides that: "It is not intended . . . to effect in any case such a distribution, apportionment or allocation of gross income . . . as would produce a result equivalent to a computation of consolidated taxable income."

Nevertheless, there have been at least three cases which seem directly to contravene section 1.482-1(b)(3) of the regulations: *Hamburgers York Road, Inc.,*[187] *Marc's Big Boy-Prospect, Inc.,* and, at least in part, *Your Host, Inc.*[189]

187. 41 T.C. 821 (1964).
189. 58 T.C. 10 (1972), *aff'd* 489 F.2d 957 (2d Cir. 1973), *cert. denied,* 419 U.S. 829 (1974).

Hamburgers York Road, Inc., involved two corporations: Isaac Hamburger & Sons Co. (H&S), which operated the oldest and largest retail men's wear business in Baltimore, and Hamburgers York Road, Inc. (York), which operated a newly opened store in the suburbs of Baltimore. The two were brother-sister corporations. The Service allocated all of York's income to H&S on the grounds that the operation of both stores was substantially the function of H&S. Alternatively, the Service sought to disallow York's surtax exemption under sections 269 and 1551.[190]

The Tax Court upheld the Service's net income allocation. It held there was a single integrated business enterprise and that its taxable income was produced by and due to the long established business reputation and goodwill of H&S, H&S's business organization and procedures, the brands of merchandise which H&S handled and H&S's advertising program. H&S handled all of the essential functions for both corporations, namely, advertising, selection of merchandise and supervision of sales personnel and, in addition, York apparently was able to obtain the lease on its business premises only on the strength of H&S's guarantee.

The court felt that H&S, had it dealt with York at arm's length, "would have claimed for itself the profits in their entirety of the York Road segment of the integrated business."[192] Moreover, the Tax Court saw no pressing business need that required a separate corporation to operate the York suburban store.

The court also brushed away the no consolidated return provision of section 1.482-1(b)(3) of the regulations above, by quoting from the Second Circuit's opinion in Advance Machinery Exchange v. Commissioner: "Whatever valid interpretation may be given this regulation, the unsoundness of that of the petitioner is illustrated by the fact that it would exclude from the 'policing' provisions of [section 482] the most flagrant evasion by arbitrary shifting of income."[193] The court stated that consolidated returns could not have been filed anyway because the two corporations lacked a common parent. The court did not seem concerned with true earner concepts, as little or no consideration was given to the sales activities performed by York.

Marc's Big Boy involved a restaurant franchising operation, a

---

190. It is submitted that all three forced consolidation cases were really surtax disallowance cases. The Tax Court did not permit the Service to disallow surtax exemptions under section 482. . . . However, a net income allocation accomplishes the same thing. Unfortunately, the success achieved by the Service in combating surtax exemptions has left in its wake substantial confusion as to when net income allocations will be made.

192. What third party would enter into an agreement to perform services and turn over all of the net profits? It is submitted that the court did not apply an arm's length standard.

193. 196 F.2d 1006 (2d Cir.), *cert. denied*, 344 U.S. 835 (1952).

principal product of which was a nationally known hamburger sandwich called the Big Boy. Wisconsin Big Boy Corporation (WBB) obtained a license from unrelated third parties exclusively to use the Big Boy trademark and designs incidental thereto in Wisconsin, Iowa and Minnesota. WBB granted sublicenses to ten of its wholly owned subsidiary corporations. The Service allocated all of the income of the ten restaurant subsidiaries to WBB under section 482 or, alternatively, on the grounds that their separate corporate entities should be disregarded for tax purposes. The Service also sought to disallow the corporations' surtax exemptions under sections 269 and 1551. The Tax Court and the Seventh Circuit upheld the Service under section 482.

The subfranchise agreements between WBB and its subsidiaries contained certain management and administration provisions pursuant to which WBB had the power and authority to determine all policies, including matters with respect to the financial affairs and operations of the restaurants, leasehold matters, personnel practices and procedures, advertising and purchases and sales of goods. In fact, WBB did determine corporate policies, which it implemented by overseeing and supervising all aspects of its subsidiaries' restaurants' businesses, including their day to day routine of obtaining and merchandising foods. In addition, advertisements, telephone listings, menus and employees and management recruitment practices suggested that the Wisconsin Big Boy restaurants were operated by a single integrated enterprise.

The Tax Court followed its *Hamburgers York Road, Inc.*, approach, to wit "if WBB and its subsidiaries had dealt at arm's length as uncontrolled corporations WBB would have required all profits of the subsidiaries to be turned over to it." The court found that there was a single, integrated restaurant operation that was completely dominated by WBB and which was dependent for success upon WBB's reputation, goodwill, resources, skills and experience. Consequently, it held that WBB generated the income for the years in issue.

On appeal, the Seventh Circuit affirmed the Tax Court's decision. However, its opinion was much less broad in scope than the Tax Court's. It stated the particular problem in the case was posed by the fact that the taxpayers made no claim that license and management fees met the arm's length test.[198] The Seventh Circuit seemed to feel that each restaurant operation must have contributed to some degree to the overall net income. Nevertheless, it felt the issue on appeal boiled down to the burden of proof and that the taxpayers

198. Marc's Big Boy charged its subsidiaries management and sublicense fees. . . . The management fees were designed to earn Wisconsin Big Boy a small profit and the sublicense fees were billed at the same rate which Wisconsin Big Boy paid. . . .

had not shown the Service's section 482 allocation was unreasonable, arbitrary or capricious.

Against this background, the decision in *Your Host* has much significance. Your Host and a number of related corporations operated some 40 restaurants. Your Host, the largest corporation and the center of the group's activities, operated 15 restaurants and each of ten related corporations operated between one and four restaurants. Other related corporations included Sher-Del Foods (Sher-Del), a food wholesaler, Your Host Bakery, Inc. (Bakery), a bakery, and Chef Foods, Inc. (Chef), which operated cigarette vending machines and leased certain facilities to Sher-Del. The Service allocated under section 482 all of the net income of the ten restaurant corporations and Chef to Your Host and all of Bakery's net income to Sher-Del. Alternatively, the Service sought to disallow most of the corporations' surtax exemptions under section 269.

. . . The Your Host restaurants were very simple establishments. Their advertising and telephone listings gave the impression that each Your Host restaurant was a member of a chain with a single management. Menus were standardized and all corporations were required to purchase their food supplies from Sher-Del. The corporations shared the same top management and all personnel were nominally the employees of Your Host. Moreover, none of the corporations paid Your Host for the use of its trademark.

However, the outcome in *Your Host* was substantially different from that in *Marc's Big Boy*. . . .

The court indicated that the Your Host restaurant corporations were more viable economically than were Marc's Big Boy's subsidiaries. The Your Host corporations paid most of their own costs of doing business and Your Host was not required to guarantee rental payments for any locations except its own (unlike WBB). Landlords apparently relied upon the financial responsibility and resources of each respective Your Host corporation.

The Service argued that Your Host and most of its related corporations shared the same administrative staff and maintenance crew. However, during the years before the court, the cost of providing such services was apportioned among the corporations according to gross sales and the Service had not contended that the apportionment method was unreasonable. Moreover, Your Host operated 15 of its own restaurants (unlike WBB which had no restaurants of its own). Consequently, Your Host's activities were not limited to running its related corporations' restaurants. In addition, each Your Host restaurant had its own manager, who generally was responsible for the operation of his restaurant, and whose compensation depended upon the success of his location.

The court also felt that the trademark and goodwill possessed by Your Host differed considerably from those of WBB in *Marc's Big Boy* and of H&S in *Hamburgers York Road*. As to goodwill, the restaurants operated by Your Host were on the average no older nor more well established than those operated by the ten other restaurant corporations. . . . Thus, the court stated the situation in *Your Host* was obviously different from that which obtained in *Hamburgers York Road*. . . .

As to the trademarks, the court felt that the Your Host trademark could not be compared with the Big Boy trademark which was used nationally and which enabled the Milwaukee area restaurants to benefit from the goodwill generated by others across the country. The restaurant corporations in *Your Host* were dependent upon local advertising and local management. Consequently, the court felt the Your Host trademark had little value in addition to the goodwill generated from the operation of the restaurants themselves.

Thus, decentralized operating management and economically viable corporations that generated their own goodwill were sufficient to preclude a forced consolidation.

However, the outcome was different in the case of Chef and Bakery, and allocations of their net income were approved by the court. Chef had third-party cigarette sales (through vending machines in Your Host restaurants) averaging $130,000 per year and intercompany rental income averaging about $30,000 per year. It had a salaried employee (a vending machine repairman) for whom it paid workman's compensation and made social security contributions; it owned its own vending machines; it maintained a substantial inventory; and it paid its own utilities, taxes, automobile expenses and, as did the ten restaurant corporations, a proportionate share of group insurance and general and administrative costs. Chef conducted its business no differently than did its competitors. It serviced its own machines, collected receipts and paid commissions based upon the amount of merchandise sold. Moreover, Chef was a wholly owned subsidiary of Sher-Del (its income was allocated to Your Host . . .), an admittedly viable entity . . . , and Chef received no services from Your Host for which it did not adequately compensate Your Host.

Bakery was responsible for the baking of pies, cakes, doughnuts and other sweet goods, the sale of which accounted for a significant portion of the business of Your Host restaurants. It apparently owned its own bakery and ran a successful operation. Sher-Del took orders for baked goods from the Your Host restaurants and made purchases from Bakery. Bakery sold only to Sher-Del and at the same prices for which Sher-Del resold the baked products to the restaurant corporations. These prices were based upon the wholesale price list of a commercial baking corporation. Bakery had sales in excess of $175,000; it had a sizeable work force with a payroll of approximately

$50,000; it purchased more than $80,000 worth of raw materials; it paid for its own insurance, linen, laundry and operating supplies; and there were clear indicia of operational autonomy.

Nevertheless, the Tax Court and, on appeal, the Second Circuit, sustained the Service's allocations of Chef's net income to Your Host and Bakery's net income to Sher-Del. The Tax Court felt that neither Chef nor Bakery could be considered to have conducted any business. On appeal, the Second Circuit stated that it viewed Chef and Bakery as kinds of sham enterprises.

There was a strong dissent from the Second Circuit's decision by Judge Timbers. He felt that section 482 does not permit the Service to disregard a separate corporate entity if it exists for a bona fide business purpose, conducts substantial business activities and earns its own income. He also felt the statute does not permit the Service to substitute its business judgment for that of management and, if operational autonomy was a bar to income allocation with respect to the ten restaurant corporations, he failed to understand the majority's conclusion with respect to Chef and Bakery. He saw no basis for the Tax Court's conclusion that Bakery (and Chef) "could hardly be considered to have conducted any business." Rather, he suggested a pricing adjustment was in order with regard to Bakery.

At first glance, the Tax Court's holding in *Your Host* appears to be somewhat of a retreat from its holding in *Marc's Big Boy*. Indeed it seems to define some principles that should be helpful in future planning. Related corporations that may be vulnerable to a *Marc's Big Boy* attack should be careful to deal at arm's length. . . . If possible, responsible, decentralized operating management and viable subsidiaries which contribute to the group's goodwill should be established. Care also should be taken to avoid having an overseeing, supervising parent corporation that becomes involved in the subsidiaries' day to day activities. It apparently is permissible to have a centralized top management that sets general policy, centralized accounting, some centralization of advertising (although local advertising was important in *Your Host*) and standardized procedures even though they may go to the heart of the operation.

On the other hand, *Your Host* may prove to be troublesome, perhaps more troublesome than the now somewhat watered down, or at least better defined, *Hamburgers York Road-Marc's Big Boy* problems. It is difficult to understand why Chef and, especially, Bakery were found not to have conducted any business. The courts did not seem to focus on the true earner concept and offered no guidelines that might assist in future planning. . . .

NOTES

1. After holding that a subsidiary created to run a hospital in Saudi Arabia was not a "sham," to be disregarded, the Tax Court sustained a §482 allocation to the American parent. In a lengthy discussion citing, inter alia, *Wisconsin Big Boy Corp.* and *Hamburgers York Road,* the court, however, refused to allocate *all* of the income, as the Service had urged, concerned that such an allocation "would in fact disregard the separate corporate existence of the subsidiary." It found 75 percent a reasonable figure to allocate to the parent. See Hospital Corp. of America v. Commissioner, 81 T.C. 520 (1983).

2. In an opinion of excessive length, the Tax Court dealt with intangibles that had been created and then transferred by an American parent to its Puerto Rican subsidiary. Although the court recognized ownership in the subsidiary, it held, inter alia, that the prices that the subsidiary charged the parent caused an income distortion that justified reallocation and arm's-length pricing under §482. See Ely Lilly & Co. v. Commissioner, 84 T.C. 996 (1985).

V. CONSOLIDATED RETURNS — §§1501-1504

The rules governing consolidated returns are of major importance in the corporate tax world. Under §1501, a group of affiliated corporations, instead of filing separate returns, may file a consolidated return that encompasses all of the group's dealings with the outside world. There are several advantages to filing a consolidated return. First, the operating losses of an affiliate corporation can be used to offset the profits of other affiliates. Second, many intercorporate distributions between affiliates can be received tax-free. Finally, gain or loss on certain transaction between affiliates is deferred until it is realized outside the group or until a specified "triggering" event takes place.

There are, however, some disadvantages. To the extent losses of one affiliate corporation are used to offset gains of the other affiliates, the basis of the stock of the loss corporation must be reduced. In addition, members of the affiliated group must make consistent elections and maintain consistent accounting periods. Moreover, certain intercompany transactions must be reflected immediately. And once the election is made, it is very difficult to revoke it in the absence of Service consent.

Congress has delegated to the Treasury broad authority to promulgate regulations with respect to consolidated returns, and therefore much of the law in this area is contained in the Treasury regulations. Nevertheless, the courts have been unwilling to give the Treasury completely free reign.

See generally B. Bittker and J. Eustice, Federal Income Taxation of Corporations and Shareholders 15-42 to 15-84 (5th ed. 1987); F. Peel, Consolidated Tax Returns (1984); J. Crestol, K. Hennessey and A. Rua, The Consolidated Tax Return (4th ed. 1988); Eisenberg, Consolidated Returns: Family Ties for Financial Gain, 64 Taxes 907 (1986).

A. ELIGIBILITY

LETTER RULING 8022017
CCH IRS Letter Rulings (Feb. 22, 1980)

ISSUE

Whether Corp. X has properly filed returns including therein losses resulting from certain subsidiaries formed by Corp. X in which it held more than 80% of the voting power of all classes of stock entitled to vote?

FACTS

During the years 1971 through 1973, Corp. A through Corp. M were formed with similar capital structures and stock ownership arrangements. . . . Losses incurred by the various corporations were included in the consolidated returns of Corp. X for the years 1971 through 1973.

Common or similar factors of importance with respect to Corp. A through Corp. M include the following:

1. Corp. X owns only voting preferred stock which is limited and preferred as to dividends.

2. The common voting stock is owned primarily by foreign trusts.

3. The voting rights attached to the common and preferred stock allow for one vote per share. Preferred shares were issued to Corp. X sufficient to give it 80% of the voting power in each case.

4. The capital contributions by Corp. X and the other shareholders were about equal with the exception of two companies where the related shareholders contributed greater amounts of capital.

5. The preferred stock held by Corp. X in the various corporations in most cases is subject to redemption and liquidation provisions which provide for little more than a return of contributed capital.

6. The preferred stock provides for fixed cumulative dividends that range between 7 percent and 10 percent as a rate of return on contributed capital.

In 1975, Corp. X sold its preferred stock interest in Corp. L to the foreign trust holding the common stock interest in Corp. L. In prior years, Corp. X had included losses from Corp. L. No excess loss account was established by Corp. X for the Corp. L stock and none was taken into consideration when this transaction occurred. In 1976, Corp. X lost the requisite 80 percent control of voting power for Corp. L. Losses had been claimed in prior years that exceeded Corp. X's basis in Corp. L. No excess loss account was ever established or taken into consideration when this transaction occurred. During the years 1971 through 1973, Corp. X included in its consolidated returns losses from Corp. A through Corp. M of $____ compared with a capital investment of approximately $____.

The examining agent believes that Corp. A through Corp. M should not be included in the consolidated Federal income tax return of Corp. X because these corporations are not part of the affiliated group. He states that Corp. X does not really own Corp. A through Corp. M, but merely controls them. Further, the examining agent believes that Congress did not intend that limited preferred stock should be used as the sole basis for affiliation.

The taxpayer argues that the inclusion of Corp. A through Corp. M in the consolidated Federal income tax return of Corp. X is proper, established by section 1504 of the Internal Revenue Code of 1954. The taxpayer further argues that the examining agent has misconstrued Congressional intent underlying the enactment of the affiliation requirement for consolidated filing.

APPLICABLE LAW

Section 1501 of the Code provides that an affiliated group of corporations shall, subject to the provisions of this chapter, have the privilege of making a consolidated return with respect to the income tax imposed by Chapter 1 for the taxable year in lieu of separate returns. The making of a consolidated return shall be upon the condition that all corporations which at any time during the taxable year have been members of the affiliated group consent to all the consolidated return regulations prescribed under section 1502 prior to the last day prescribed by law for the filing of such return. The making of a consolidated return shall be considered as such consent.

Section 1502 of the Code provides that the Secretary shall prescribe such regulations as he may deem necessary in order that the tax liability of any affiliated group of corporations making a consolidated return and of each corporation in the group, both during and after the period of affiliation, may be returned, determined, computed, assessed, collected and adjusted, in such a manner as clearly to reflect the income tax liability and the various factors necessary for the determination of such liability, and in order to prevent avoidance of such tax liability.

Section 1504(a) of the Code defines the term "affiliated group" to mean one or more chains of includible corporations connected through stock ownership with a common parent corporation which is an includible corporation if —

(1) Stock possessing at least 80 percent of the voting power of all classes of stock and at least 80 percent of each class of the nonvoting stock of each of the includible corporations (except the common parent corporation) is owned directly by one or more of the other includible corporations; and

(2) The common parent corporation owns directly stock possessing at least 80 percent of the voting power of all classes of stock and at least 80 percent of each class of the nonvoting stock of at least one of the other includible corporations.

As used in this subsection, the term "stock" does not include nonvoting stock which is limited and preferred as to dividends.

Section 1.1502-19(a)(1) of the regulations provides that immediately before the disposition of stock of a subsidiary, there shall be included in the income of each member disposing of the stock that member's excess loss account, determined under sections 1.1502-14 and -32, with respect to the disposed stock. Under section 1.1502-19(b)(2)(ii) a member shall be considered as having disposed of all of its shares of stock in a subsidiary on the day the subsidiary ceases to be a member or on the day such member ceases to be a member.

Section 1.1502-32(a) of the regulations provides, generally, investment adjustment rules, as of the end of each consolidated return year, for members owning stock in a subsidiary. Subsection (a) further states that if a subsidiary owns stock in any other subsidiary the adjustment with respect to the stock of the higher tier subsidiary shall not be made until after the adjustment is made with respect to the stock of the lower tier subsidiary. In the case of a disposition (as defined in section 1.150219(b)) of the stock of a subsidiary before the end of the taxable year, the adjustment with respect to such stock shall be made as of the date of disposition. The amount of such adjustment shall be the difference between the positive adjustment described in section 1.1502-32(b)(1) or (c)(1), whichever is applicable, and the negative adjustment described in section 1.1502-32(b)(2) or (c)(2), whichever is applicable. Such difference is referred to in this section as the "net positive adjustment" or the "net negative adjustment," as the case may be.

Section 1.1502-32(b)(1) and (2) provides positive and negative adjustments, respectively, for stock which is not limited and preferred as to dividends. In general, the positive adjustment is the sum of (i) an allocable part of the undistributed earnings and profits of the subsidiary for the taxable year; (ii) an allocable part of any consolidated net operating loss or consolidated net capital loss for the year that is not carried back and used in an earlier year; and (iii) if such subsidiary owns stock in another subsidiary and section 1.1502-33(c)(4)(i) applies to the taxable year, an allocable part of the net positive adjustment made by the higher tier subsidiary for the taxable year with respect to its stock in such other subsidiary.

Section 1.1502-80 of the regulations provides that other provisions of the law shall be applicable to the group to the extent that the regulations do not exclude its application.

Section 1016 of the Code provides, in part, that a proper adjustment in respect of the property shall in all cases be made for expenditures, receipts, losses, or other items, properly chargeable to the capital account.

Section 1.1016-6(a) of the regulations provides that adjustments must always be made to eliminate double deductions or their equivalent. Thus, in the case of stock of a subsidiary company, the basis thereof must be properly adjusted for the amount of the subsidiary company's losses for the years in which consolidated returns were made.

RATIONALE

Section 1504(a) of the Code defines the term "affiliated group" as basically a group of includible corporations in which at least 80% of the voting power of all classes of stock entitled to vote and at least 80% of each class of non-voting stock is owned directly by one or more includible corporations and the common parent corporation must satisfy the same two 80% tests for one of the includible corporations. Because the provisions of section 1504(a) relate to voting power, this term ("voting power") includes any kind of voting stock (i.e., common or preferred) and the ability to elect directors is the essential element in determining if the test has been met.

Rev. Rul. 69-126, 1969-1 C.B. 218, provides an example of the use of preferred stock to meet the voting power test. The Rev. Rul. presents two questions — (1) whether the preferred is considered voting stock and (2) if it is voting stock has the 80% voting power test been satisfied. The facts of the Rev. Rul. are that the common parent of an affiliated group of corporations owns 100 percent of the common stock and 50 percent of the preferred stock of a subsidiary. No other members of the group own any of the preferred stock of the subsidiary. Pursuant to the certificate of incorporation and by-laws of the subsidiary, the holders of its preferred stock have the right to elect three directors. The holders of the common stock of the subsidiary have the right to elect five of its eight directors and have all other voting powers. The preferred stock is limited and preferred as to dividends. The subsidiary has no other class of stock outstanding. In resolving the first issue presented, the Rev. Rul. relies on Rudolph Wurlitzer Co. et al. v. Commissioner, 29 B.T.A. 443 (1933), *aff'd* 81 F.2d 971 (1936), *cert. denied,* 298 U.S. 676 (1936), and holds that the preferred stock, since it participates in the election of directors, qualifies as voting stock within the meaning of section 1504(a) of the Code. Turning to the second question, the Rev. Rul. goes on to hold that since the common parent owns 81.25% of the voting power to elect directors, it satisfies the 80% voting power test in section 1504(a)(1) and (2).

In the present situation, Corp. X also appears to satisfy the literal requirements for meeting the voting power tests in section 1504. That is, by holding 100% of the voting preferred stock but none of the common stock, it satisfies the voting power requirements of section 1504. However, literal compliance with a particular requirement of the affiliation/consolidation provisions does not automatically mean that a taxpayer may file a consolidated return. For example, in Spreckels Co. v. Commissioner, 41 B.T.A. 370 (1940), the parent corporation acquired all of the stock of a subsidiary during the taxable year but the acquisition was without a business purpose. The court held that the subsidiary was not a member of the affiliated group notwithstanding the fact that the parent corporation satisfied the literal requirement of consolidation. In reaching its conclusion the court stated at 375 that "The framers of the statute evidently believed and intended 'that no ultimate advantage under the tax laws results' from the granting of the privilege to make consolidated returns and that 'No improper benefits are obtained from the privilege.' " In addition at 378 the court stated "If Congress did not intend that the privilege of making a consolidated return should be enjoyed by a corporation which acquired ownership of another corporation in order to take advantage of a loss already sustained by that corporation, it seems to follow that Congress did not intend that the privilege should be enjoyed by a corporation which acquired the ownership of another corporation in order to take advantage of a loss certain to be sustained by that corporation in the immediate future, particularly where the acquisition of the ownership of the other corporation served no business purpose." See also Elko Realty Co. v. Commissioner, 29 T.C. 1013 (1957), *aff'd,* 260 F.2d 949 (3rd Cir. 1958) and United States v. Skelly Oil Co., 394 U.S. 678 (1969).

Based on the above, it can readily be argued that literal compliance is not the sole test for purposes of affiliation. One of the underpinnings of the consolidation provisions is that as losses of a subsidiary are utilized appropriate adjustments to the basis of the subsidiary's stock must be made. Section 1.1502-32. The basis of the stock is reduced and an excess loss account is established for losses availed of below a zero basis. This excess loss account is then recaptured or reduced depending upon events that occur in subsequent taxable years. This excess loss account concept is indicative of the fact that there are certain burdens for filing consolidated returns in addition to the benefits that can be gained. In the present situation, the taxpayer desires that its voting preferred stock be treated as the element that entitled it to the benefits of consolidation on the one hand (i.e., voting power) while on the other hand denies that it is the type of stock that requires basis adjustments. In other words, Corp. X seeks the benefits of consolidation without the corresponding burdens. We cannot attribute such an intent to the consolidated return provisions.

The consolidated return regulations are legislative in character and have been recognized to have the force and effect of law. The legislative character of the consolidated return regulations and the broad power given the Secretary or his delegate have been frequently recognized by the courts. . . .

Case law construing consolidated return regulations has developed a number of principles based primarily on the decision of the Supreme Court in Charles Ilfeld Co. v. Hernandez, 292 U.S. 62 (1934), *aff'g* 66 F.2d 236 and 67 F.2d 236 (9th Cir. 1933). In that case, the taxpayer claimed a deduction for an investment loss on the liquidation of two subsidiaries whose operating losses for prior years had been deducted by the taxpayer on its consolidated returns. The Court denied the deduction by interpreting it as an intercompany transaction eliminated by the consolidated return regulations, and went on to say:

> The allowance claimed would permit petitioner twice to use the subsidiaries' losses for the reduction of its taxable income. By means of the consolidated returns in earlier years it was enabled to deduct them. And now it claims for 1929 deductions for diminution of assets resulting from the same losses. If allowed, this would be the practical equivalent of double deduction. In the absence of a provision of the Act definitely requiring it, a purpose so opposed to precedent and equality of treatment of taxpayers will not be attributed to lawmakers. There is nothing in the Act that purports to authorize double deduction of losses or in the regulations to suggest that the Commissioner construed any of its provisions to empower him to prescribe a regulation that would permit consolidated returns to be made on the basis now claimed by petitioner. [292 U.S. at 68.]

Based on *Ilfeld*, we believe the following conclusions can be drawn. First, the consolidated return regulations in the loss in excess of basis area are not read literally. Second, courts will not sanction a double deduction, especially when it is possible to conclude that the consolidated return regulations are inapplicable or do not expressly cover the problem presented. Third, the regulations are interpreted in a manner to achieve a result which is consistent with equality of treatment between taxpayers who file consolidated returns and other taxpayers. And finally, courts apply the law in the loss availed of area in a manner calculated to preclude "a manifest impossibility" so as not "to say what cannot be," a proposition advanced by the Tenth Circuit in *Ilfeld* to characterize the taxpayer's attempt there to claim a loss which was nearly twice its entire investment in its subsidiaries.

Corp. X, in the present situation, desires the practical equivalent of a double deduction — that is, it desires to utilize the subsidiary losses in the consolidated return and then by not reducing the basis of the subsidiary's stock, it will realize less gain on the transfer of the stock outside the affiliated group. Based on the above discussion, particularly the *Ilfeld* case, we do not believe that such a result is justifiable. In particular, we view this question as being directly controlled by one of the *Ilfeld* line of cases, Associated Tel. & Tel. Co. v. United States, 306 F.2d 824 (2nd Cir. 1962), *aff'g on this issue* 199 F. Supp. 452 (S.D.N.Y. 1961). In that case, the predecessor of section 1.1502-34A of the Income Tax Regulations clearly did not provide for a basis reduction for a subsidiary's capital loss availed of it by the parent on a consolidated return. Nevertheless, the court did not regard the absence of such a provision as precluding the adjustment in question, and, following the direction of section 1.1502-3A to refer to other applicable law in such circumstances, applied the principles of *Ilfeld* to require the adjustment, finding additional support for this holding in the provisions of section 1.1016-6(a) necessitating basis adjustments to eliminate double deductions.

There is no indication whatsoever that Congress ever intended the double deduction the taxpayer effectively claims it is entitled to in the instant case. On the contrary, Congress has in effect provided in section 1502 that consolidated returns are to be made on a basis which clearly reflects the income tax liability of the affiliated group and prevents the avoidance of such liability. It is difficult to conceive how the taxpayer's claim may be harmonized with this intention. The taxpayer seems to suggest that the only way of rectifying the claimed double deduction situation is by amending the consolidated return provisions for basis adjustments. However, we believe that the clear weight of authority leads to the conclusion that the proper approach to apply in the instant case is exemplified by the Associated Tel. & Tel. case, supra, in which the Supreme Court indicated that the Code and regulations should not be mechanically applied or construed to permit the practical equivalent of a double deduction in the absence of a clear declaration of intent by Congress to allow such.

Thus, we do not believe that a taxpayer may properly include a subsidiary in its consolidated return when the only stock that is owned is voting preferred stock unless it can be shown that appropriate basis adjustments have been made so that the possibility of a double deduction is avoided. This conclusion is wholly consistent with Rev. Rul. 69-126 because under the facts of that ruling there would not have been any possibility of a double deduction. Similarly Rev. Rul. 79-21, 1979-1 C.B. Wurlitzer, supra, and Atlantic City Electric Company v. Commissioner, 288 U.S. 152 (1933).

CONCLUSION

Corp. X has not properly filed returns including therein losses resulting from certain subsidiaries formed by Corp. X in which it held more than 80% of the voting power of all classes of stock entitled to vote.

ELKO REALTY CO. v. COMMISSIONER
29 T.C. 1012 (1958), aff'd per curiam, 260 F.2d 949 (3d Cir. 1958)

TRAIN, Judge. [Taxpayer, a corporation, acquired 100 percent of the stock of two corporations, Earl Apartments, Inc. and Spiegel Apartments, Inc., which had been operating at losses and which continued to operate at losses after the taxpayer acquired their stock. In each of the years 1951, 1952, and 1953 the taxpayer had a net profit. It filed consolidated returns in those years, however, and on those returns offset the losses of its subsidiaries against its profit. The Commissioner disallowed the deductions attributable to the subsidiaries' losses under the 1939 Code predecessor of §269, and the Tax Court sustained him, finding that the taxpayer failed to prove that the principal purpose of its acquisition of the stock of its subsidiaries was not tax avoidance. The Commissioner's alternative ground was that Earl Apartments, Inc., and Spiegel Apartments, Inc., "were not affiliates of the petitioner within the meaning of §[1504(a)] so as to permit the filing of consolidated returns in the years at issue . . . [under §1501]." (29 T.C. at 1012.) Although the court need not have dealt with the Commissioner's alternative grounds in light of its decision under §269, it did so.]

In J.D. & A.B. Spreckels Co., 41 B.T.A. 370 (1940), we laid down the rule that where the ownership of the subsidiary's stock by a parent corporation served no business purpose, as distinguished from a tax reducing purpose, the subsidiary is not an affiliate within the intent of [the consolidated return sections].

We agree with petitioner that the facts of the instant case differ in a number of respects from the facts in J.D. & A.B. Spreckels Co., supra. However, the rule of that case is applicable, regardless of distinctions of fact, where the petitioner is unable to show that a business purpose, as distinguished from a tax-reducing purpose, was served by the acquisition in question. We have already discussed at considerable length the evidence presented in this proceeding, and it is unnecessary to repeat that discussion here. After a careful examination of all the evidence, we conclude that the petitioner here has failed to show that a business purpose, as distinguished from a tax-reducing purpose, was served by its acquisition of Earl Apartments, Inc., and Spiegel Apartments, Inc.

It follows that the respondent's determination of deficiencies is, in all respects, sustained. . . .

NOTES

1. The Tax Reform Act of 1984 amended §1504(a), redefining "affiliated group" in several significant ways. First, it added an 80% in *value* of the subsidiary's stock test to §1504(a)(2). Second, it provided that, subject to IRS waiver, a corporation ceasing to be a member of an affiliated group must wait five years before reentering the group or any other group "with the same common parent or a successor of such common parent." Section 1504(a)(3). Finally, the Act gave the Service broad authority to promulgate regulations classifying certain interest as "stock" and certain stock as "not stock." See New York State Bar Association Tax Section Committee on Corporations, Report on Tax Reform Act of 1984 Amendments to Section 1504(a), the Definition of "Affiliated Group," Tax Notes, Aug. 19, 1985, p. 895.

2. In Rev. Rul. 84-79, 1984-1 C.B. 190, the Service ruled that a corporation that was the grantor and sole beneficiary of a revocable voting trust "directly owned" the deposited shares for purposes of §1504(a).

3. See U.S. Padding Corp. v. Commissioner, 865 F.2d 750 (6th Cir. 1989), where the court considered whether incorporation in a foreign country must be required by foreign law before a foreign subsidiary may file a consolidated return with an American parent. The court held that a foreign subsidiary is considered as part of an affiliated group under §1504(d) if, as a result of administrative practice, it would be unlikely that the subsidiary would be allowed to operate in a foreign country without incorporation there.

B. COMPUTATION OF CONSOLIDATED TAX LIABILITY

1. Intercompany Transactions

VELVET O'DONNELL CORP. v. UNITED STATES
1 Cl. Ct. 683 (1983)

COLAIANNI, Judge.

This case of first impression is before the court on defendant's motion for partial summary judgment. Generally, the question presented is the effect of Reg. §1.1502-14(d)(1) . . . on a taxpayer's entitlement to a bad debt deduction. Particularly at issue is whether a loss due to the partial worthlessness of the debt of another corporation is, under consolidated return regulations, an allowable deduction on the consolidated return in the year of affiliation where the companies became affiliated after the bad debt was determined partially worthless and its charge-off authorized by resolution of plaintiff's board of directors, but before the charge-off was reflected on the company's books at year's end.

. . . The facts pertinent to this issue are not in dispute, and are summarized below.

Plaintiff in this case is Velvet O'Donnell Corporation (Velvet). . . . Plaintiff filed a consolidated tax return on October 28, 1972, the end of its fiscal year, on behalf of itself and two subsidiaries, O'Donnell Importing Company and Haberstroh Farm Products, Inc. (Haberstroh). This return included a deduction for partially worthless bad debts in the amount of $675,000 from loans made by Velvet to Haberstroh before the date of their affiliation. The company also took a deduction for $50,000, which reflected the purchase price of a loan obligation from Haberstroh to E. E. Dale Shaffer, Chairman of the Board of Haberstroh, and owner of 89.25 percent of its stock. Velvet's loans to Haberstroh began in November 1971, and by July 1, 1972, it had advanced the company a total of $936,000. During this period, Velvet did not own any of the stock of Haberstroh.

As of July 8, 1972, for reasons which do not appear in the record, the Board of Directors of Velvet O'Donnell Corporation decided that approximately $675,000 of the debt owed to the company by Haberstroh was worthless. Minutes of a special meeting of Velvet's board, dated Saturday, July 8, 1972, reflect that a resolution of the board was passed that date authorizing a charge-off of $675,000 on the books and records of Velvet, to reflect the company's loss from its loans to Haberstroh. The resolution further authorized the charge-off of $50,000, an amount representing the cost of a "purchase note" of Haberstroh in the principal amount of $1,998,937.09.

The note evidenced part of Haberstroh's indebtedness to Shaffer, its principal shareholder. The board resolution concluded by directing the appropriate officers of Velvet to take whatever action was necessary to carry out the board's directive.

The only manifestation of the board action on Velvet's books and records, however, was a journal entry, made by plaintiff's accountants on October 28, 1972, the last day of Velvet's fiscal year, crediting its loans receivable account in the amount of the charge-offs. The loans made by Velvet to Haberstroh, as well as the charge-off, were corporate acts which took place within Velvet's 1972 fiscal year but prior to the acquisition of Haberstroh by Velvet.

The government, for the purposes of its summary judgment motion, does not contest the validity of either the advances made to Haberstroh, or the determination of partial worthlessness of these debts within the year. They also allow that the partially worthless portion of the loans were properly charged off as of October 28, 1972, the date the journal entries were made.

On July 22, 1972, two weeks after the charge-offs, Velvet purchased 89 percent of the stock of Haberstroh. It subsequently filed a consolidated corporate tax return for its fiscal year ending October 28, 1972, for itself and O'Donnell Importing Company, a wholly owned subsidiary of Velvet, and for Haberstroh. The consolidated return included Haberstroh's post-affiliation income. In addition, Haberstroh filed a separate return, covering the period from January 1, 1972, the beginning of its fiscal year, to July 21, 1972, the day prior to its affiliation with Velvet, for its pre-affiliation activity.

Plaintiff seeks a refund of $281,110 in taxes for the year ending October 28, 1972, and for $56,016 in taxes for the tax year ending November 1, 1969, based on a net operating loss carryback from 1972 due to the bad debt deduction.

Section 1501 provides for the filing of consolidated income tax returns by affiliated groups of corporations, subject to certain provisions, if the members of the affiliated group so elect. The filing of a consolidated return is considered a privilege, and is conditioned upon the consent by the members of the group to be bound by the regulations governing consolidated returns provided for under §1502 of the Code.

Reg. §1.1502-14(d) is the regulation in controversy in the instant case. It provides, in pertinent part:

> (1) *Deferral of gain or loss.* To the extent gain or loss is recognized under the disposition . . . *of an obligation of another member* (referred to in this paragraph as the "debtor member"), whether or not such obligation is evidenced by a security, such gain or loss shall be deferred. For purposes of this paragraph, a deduction because of the worthlessness of . . . an obligation described in this subpara-

graph shall be considered a loss from the disposition of such obligation. [Emphasis added.]

The provision requires the deferral in a consolidated return year of gains and losses resulting from the disposition "of an obligation of another member" of the affiliated group. Subsumed in the main question to be decided in the instant case is whether plaintiff must defer the loss in its 1972 consolidated return resulting from its declaration of partial worthlessness of the debt owed it by Haberstroh until one of the events described in the regulations triggers the restoration of the deduction.

Plaintiff argues that since Velvet's board charged-off the bad debt by corporate resolution on July 8, 1972, which is before its July 22, 1972, acquisition of Haberstroh, the letter and spirit of §1.1502-14(d)(1) has not been violated because Haberstroh had no obligation at the time it became a member of the Velvet group. Velvet points out that, while the deduction was taken in a year which included Haberstroh in the consolidated return, it did not include that part of Haberstroh's fiscal year during which the events at issue took place. Rather, those events took place during a time prior to the acquisition for which Haberstroh filed a separate return.

Defendant maintains that the bad debt charge-off did not occur until it was mechanically recorded on the books and records of the company at year's end, and that Haberstroh was a member of the affiliated group at this time. Defendant further argues that it does not matter when the charge-off was made because the regulations require deferral of the deduction if the debtor corporation is a member of the consolidated group in the consolidated year in which the deduction is claimed.

The question then comes down to, whether the regulation includes only those debtor companies whose obligations resulted in a loss to another member during a time that the companies are affiliated or whether it means to encompass companies which, regardless of the timing of the loss, became affiliated at any point during the lender company's fiscal year.

Before passing the regulation, it is necessary to answer a threshold question to determine when the loss to the member corporation holding the obligation during the consolidated return year can be considered to have been "recognized," within the meaning of the regulation. A decision that the date of recognition was the date of the journal entry would dispose of the question of deferral in favor of the Government since there is no argument that Haberstroh was a member of the affiliated group as of the end of the fiscal year. However, the question of recognition is not clear cut.

A deduction due to the worthlessness of an obligation of another member is considered as a loss from the disposition of that obligation for the purposes of the regulation, and this loss is to be deferred under Reg. §1.1502-14(d). If recognition is triggered by the deduction because of worthlessness, it is imperative to determine precisely when that disposition occurred. Plaintiff's argument that the proper date of recognition is the date the debt was charged off by the board and its worthlessness evidenced by corporate resolution is, I find, the more persuasive under these circumstances.

In examining this issue, two observations are made at the outset. First, defendant has not questioned the validity of the board's conclusion of worthlessness, so it may be accepted that part of the assets held by Velvet in fact had no value prior to the date of affiliation of the companies. Second, in passing the resolution and directing that its action be reflected on the company's books and records, Velvet's board formally represented that the company no longer possessed assets in the amount of the charge-off. Had Velvet represented its assets to the outside world as of the date of affiliation, it could not have included the value of the notes receivable from Haberstroh. . . .

Despite defendant's reliance on the wording of the resolution to support its contention that the board "merely directed that the charge-off be made on taxpayer's books and records," it concedes the worthlessness of the debt. If the board's determination was valid, it must have been valid as of the time it was made. The debt either was or was not worthless as of July 8, 1972, and since defendant has conceded that the debt was in fact worthless, it may not "postdate" that determination.

Defendant would have the court treat the bad debt deduction as a determination which should be made after considering all the facts and circumstances as of the end of the year. The government argues that to evaluate the bad debt before the end of the year is contrary to accepted practice which requires that an entire year's activity be taken into account. Delaying a determination of worthlessness, the defendant argues, avoids premature resolutions that do not take into account subsequent events which may make the debt valuable again. However, in this situation it is impossible to treat the debt as if nothing out of the ordinary transpired between the time the debt was declared worthless in July and the end of the fiscal year when the deduction was taken. In fact, during this time Haberstroh was not only sold, but it was sold to plaintiff. Velvet purchased the remaining assets of Haberstroh for whatever value they possessed at the time. The relationship between Velvet and Haberstroh became one of parent and subsidiary and these two entities elected to file a consolidated return. Based on these facts, it must be concluded that the change in the relationship between Haberstroh and plaintiff was significant enough to require that the status of the debt be considered and evaluated as of the time of the affiliation. The question at issue of necessity focuses on the treatment which ought to be given the bad debt deduction in the context of the consolidated return of Velvet and Haberstroh, and this simply cannot be done without looking at the relationship of the companies as well as the economic substance of the board's action at the time that the events of affiliation occurred. . . .

While defendant disagrees with plaintiff regarding the date of the recognition of the loss, it contends that the date does not really matter since under the regulations and the facts of this case, plaintiff is not entitled to a deduction under any circumstances. The Government maintains that §1.1502-14(d) prevents the charge-off even if it is made in the period prior to affiliation as long as the debtor is a member of the group during the consolidated return year in which the deduction is claimed. On this point, I also disagree with defendant.

The lack of prior interpretation of the regulation, as well as the unusual fact situation in this case, makes the application of the regulation a tangled thicket.

Defendant's argument in favor of deferral is based on the fact that the taxpaying entity as of the end of the consolidated tax year is a group which includes not only Velvet and its subsidiary, O'Donnell International, Inc., but also Haberstroh, whose debt is reflected as a deduction on the consolidated return. Defendant points out that, even though the loan and the charge-off would have taken place before the acquisition, the deduction would be an element of the return which represented not only Velvet's transactions during the period which included the loan and the charge-off, but also Haberstroh's after July 22, 1972. Since Haberstroh was a member of the consolidated group filing the return, the deduction, defendant argues, represented the disposition of an obligation of a then-member, which §1.1502-14(d)(1) requires to be deferred.

Plaintiff argues that all transactions of the affiliated parent prior to acquisition of the subsidiary should be considered segregated just as the acquired company's preaffiliation income and expenses are segregated from the group with the filing of a separated return for its taxable year ending on the day prior to affiliation. Further, Velvet states that the words of the regulation speak only to members of the group affiliated at the time of the transactions involved, and that Velvet and Haberstroh thus did not come under the regulations. Finally, plaintiff asserts that its reading of the regulation is consistent with the purpose of the regulations governing consolidated returns and their deferral requirements.

In construing Reg. §1.1501-14(d), it is useful to keep in mind the purpose behind the consolidated return, and the goal to be achieved in deferring gains and losses of other members of the affiliated group. "The basic principle of the consolidated return is that the group is taxed upon its consolidated taxable income, representing principally the results of dealings with the outside world after the elimination of inter-company profit and loss." B. Bittker and J. Eustice, Federal Income Taxation of Corporations and Shareholders, ¶15.20 (4th ed. 1979). Additionally, under the broad authority delegated pursuant to §1502 of the Code, the Secretary is directed to —

> [P]rescribe such regulations as he may deem necessary in order that the tax liability of any affiliated group of corporations making a consolidated return and of each corporation in the group, both during and after the period of affiliation, may be returned, determined, computed, assessed, collected, and adjusted, in such manner as clearly to reflect the income-tax liability and the various factors necessary for the determination of such liability, and in order to prevent avoidance of such tax liability.

§1502.

It is with the above principles in mind that the regulations, including the restoration provisions, should be examined. I have concluded that the regulation could not have meant to include pre-affiliation loss within its scope. Several reasons support this conclusion. I begin with the regulation itself.

In looking at the wording of the regulation, two points immediately come to mind. First, the regulation speaks of recognition during a consolidated return year. As shown above, in this instance, the recognition of worthlessness was made by plaintiff before the time of consolidation. Thus, Velvet did not recognize the loss during the consolidated return year. Second, the regulation speaks of a "debtor member." While Haberstroh was a debtor at one point and a member at another, at no point in time was it both a debtor and a member. These facts alone may be dispositive of defendant's argument.

Although the wording of the regulation is hardly a model of clarity, it is only necessary to look to the remainder of the regulations pertaining to the restoration events for support of the above interpretation §1.1502.14(d)(1). It appears that in each case the restoration events contemplate a situation where the subsidiary was part of the affiliated group from the beginning of the fiscal year. This, of course, is not the situation in this instance, since Haberstroh was not a member of the group at the time that the debt was charged-off.

Defendant contended, at the oral argument, that the possibility of double deductions exists if Velvet is allowed to prevail and that this is the evil at which the regulation is directed. Defendant apparently feels that the future depreciation by the group of assets originally purchased by the funds which have now been declared a bad debt will result in a double deduction in favor of plaintiff. I disagree with defendant's conclusion. In the first place, the problem of double deductions is not cured by deferral of deduction. If the bad debt deduction is deferred and taken at a later time, there is still a double deduction. The question in such a case would be, rather, how to effect an elimination of the double deduction. . . .

However, I disagree with defendant that there is a double deduction potential in such circumstances as we have presented here for the more fundamental reason that defendant has not shown that the value of the debt which became worthless is in any way represented in any depreciable assets.[10] At oral argument defendant stated that plaintiff purchased Haberstroh for one dollar. Defendant suggested from this that the debt owed to Velvet entered into the sale of the company. However, the defendant has not challenged the validity of the bad debt. Defendant's double deduction argument is thus not understood since it has not shown that the depreciation of any of Haberstroh's assets entered into the consolidated return.

One further point deserves underscoring. Defendant argues that although a debtor may find a debt to be worthless and writes it off on its books, that debt does not automatically disappear as a legal obligation of the debtor and may be sued on. This may be generally true when the lender is dealing with an unrelated debtor corporation. However, a different result occurs in a situation such as the one at the bar where the lender (plaintiff) acquired 89 percent of the debtor's assets. In this latter situation a suit by the lender would be tantamount to suing itself. Under these circumstances, it would appear that the debt was cancelled by the acquisition. In addition, the possibility of the debt becoming valuable again becomes a moot issue where all subsequent income of the subsidiary is consolidated with lender's pursuant to the regulations governing post-affiliation consolidated income.

Finally, to require, under the facts of this case, that Velvet defer the taking of its partial bad debt does not serve to accomplish the intended goals of the regulation. As set out in §1502, the regulation was intended to foster a clear reflection of the income tax liability of the affiliated corporation and each member and, as well, to prevent the avoidance of the tax liability.

Velvet did not acquire Haberstroh for its tax attributes. The right to a bad debt deduction had vested with Velvet before acquisition of Haberstroh. Instead, plaintiff runs the risk to the extent defendant prevails, of being forced to defer the taking of a deduction by its acquisition of Haberstroh. While it is clear that the taxpayer takes

---

10. Defendant has not fully explained how it can accept the validity of the bad debt on the one hand, and yet allege that assets attributed to the bad debt remain to be depreciated.

the consequences of electing a particular form of filing, the fact that deferral of its bad debt might result shows that the acquisition was not done for the purpose of avoiding liability subsequent to the charge-off. It is true, as defendant freely admitted at oral argument, that Velvet could have avoided this pitfall by simply delaying the purchase of Haberstroh until after plaintiff's new fiscal year, i.e., after October 28, 1982. However, to require this would be in essence to say that Velvet needed to contrive, not to avoid a tax obligation, but rather to preserve a legitimate current deduction which had already vested with it. Under the facts of this case, an interpretation of the regulation requiring such a course of action appears undesirable.

Inasmuch as the "outside world" was concerned, the transactions which included the loans, the charge-off, and the subsequent purchase of Haberstroh by Velvet were those of unrelated entities dealing at arm's length. The fact that these later became affiliated, in the absence of any suggestion of a tax avoidance scheme, does not recast those transactions into dealings between affiliated companies. I do not find that there is a furthering of the purpose of the regulations by deferring the deduction under these circumstances, but to the contrary, feel that a deferral might lead to distorted results upon the restoration of the deduction. Defendant has shown nothing to support a conclusion that such a deduction would open a floodgate of "trafficking" in such losses or any other type of abuse. I therefore conclude that the regulation does not require the deferral of debts of members who were not affiliated during the existence of the obligation. . . .

NOTES

1. Could the Service have presented a stronger argument in *Velvet O'Donnell*? In particular, is there any significance to the fact — which the opinion notes only in passing — that 89 percent of Haberstroh's stock was acquired for $1, two weeks after the bad debt write-off? Is there more merit to the "double deduction" argument than the court seems to think there is?

2. The requirements of Reg. §1.1502-14(d) that bad debt write-offs for liabilities among affiliated group members be deferred are discussed and upheld in First National Bank in Little Rock v. Commissioner, 83 T.C. 202 (1984), and Sooner Federal Savings & Loan Assn. v. United States, 4 Cl. Ct. 746 (1984).

2. Net Operating Losses

REVENUE RULING 74-610
1974-2 C.B. 288

... P is a domestic corporation engaged in the manufacturing business. S_1 was organized on January 1, 1967, as a wholly owned subsidiary of P. S_2 was organized on January 1, 1972, as a wholly owned subsidiary of S_1 by a transfer of assets from S_1 to S_2. Prior to 1973 each of the corporations filed separate Federal income tax returns. For 1973, the affiliated group . . . filed a consolidated Federal income tax return.

For . . . 1973 the affiliated group had a consolidated net operating loss, all of which was attributable to S_2. The assets and operations that generated S_2 . . . loss were formerly owned by S_1. . . .

The specific question is whether the consolidated net operating loss . . . may be carried back to either P or S_1's separate income tax return for 1970.

. . . Carryovers and carrybacks of consolidated net operating losses to separate return years are governed by section 1.1502-79. Subparagraph (a)(2) of that regulation provides that a consolidated net operating loss attributable to a group member not in existence in a carryback year shall be included in the consolidated net operating loss carrybacks to the equivalent consolidated return year of the group, provided that such member was a member of the group immediately after its organization. If such equivalent year is a separate return year, then the carryback shall be made to the separate return year. . . .

Example (1) of section 1.1502-79(a)(4) . . . illustrate[s] that the portion of a consolidated net operating loss attributable to a subsidiary formed by its parent, which owns all the subsidiary's stock, may be carried back to the parent's separate return year, when the subsidiary was not in existence in the prior year. However, . . . there [was not] another group member having direct or indirect ownership of the loss member's stock.

. . . [T]he assets and operations that generated S_2's . . . loss were formerly owned by S_1. But for the formation of S_2, the loss sustained by S_1 would have been sustained by S_1 and could have been carried back . . . to its separate return years.

Accordingly, the 1973 consolidated net operating loss . . . may be carried back to S_1's separate income tax return for 1970. It may not however be carried back to P's separate income tax return for 1970.

NOTE

1. See Electronic Sensing Products, Inc., 69 T.C. 276 (1977) (under Treas. Reg. §1.1502-79(a)(2), portion of consolidated loss attributable to member that was organized 26 days before start of group's first consolidated return year, and that filed a separate return for that 26-day period, could not be carried back to common parent's separate returns); Wolter Construction Co., 68 T.C. 39 (1977), *aff'd,* 634 F.2d 1029 (6th Cir. 1980) (Treas. Reg. §1.1502-21(c) held valid; member's pre-affiliation losses not deductible on consolidated return because no consolidated taxable income was attributable to that member). See Comment, Consolidated Returns: Post-acquisition Losses, 27 Emory L.J. 79 (1978); Ruben, Consolidated Returns: Basis Adjustments for Distributions Out of Pre-acquisition Earnings and Profits, 34 Tax L. Rev. 649 (1979).

2. The 1989 Act added §1503(f), the effect of which is to deny to a subsidiary that pays preferred dividends to a nonmember of the affiliated group the opportunity to shelter the income it paid out with the losses and credits of other corporations in the group.

3. Special Taxes

GOTTESMAN & CO. v. COMMISSIONER
77 T.C. 1149 (1981)

The issues presented are: (1) whether during the years in dispute the regulations promulgated by the Secretary under section 1502 for affiliated groups of corporations filing consolidated returns required a consolidated calculation (as respondent contends) or a separate calculation (as petitioner contends) of accumulated taxable income for purposes of computing the accumulated earnings tax under section 531, and (2) whether, even if a consolidated calculation is required, these regulations adequately provide a method for determining accumulated taxable income on a consolidated basis. . . .

Petitioner is the common parent of an affiliated group of corporations. . . . The affiliated group duly filed consolidated returns for the taxable years 1973, 1974 and 1975.

Under section 1502, Congress granted authority to the Secretary to prescribe regulations for the filing of consolidated returns by affiliated groups of corporations. The filing of a consolidated return is a "privilege," but "[t]he making of a consolidated return shall be upon the condition that all corporations which at any time during the taxable year have been members of the affiliated group consent to all the consolidated return regulations prescribed under section 1502 prior to the last day prescribed by law for the filing of such return." Sec. 1501.

Petitioner contends that to avoid the accumulated earnings tax of section 531 it made distributions to its shareholders prior to the end of each of the taxable years in issue in amounts sufficient to eliminate completely any accumulated taxable income. Petitioner alleges it was advised by counsel that pursuant to the consolidated return regulations (§§1.1502-0 et seq.) for purposes of the accumulated earnings tax its accumulated taxable income was to be determined by reference to its separate taxable income and other relevant items and not on a consolidated basis with the other members of its affiliated group.

Respondent maintains this interpretation by petitioner's counsel was erroneous. Respondent argues that the plain meaning of the language of the regulations is that accumulated taxable income must be computed on a consolidated basis for purposes of the calculation of the accumulated earnings tax.

Petitioner disputes respondent's interpretation. Further, petitioner argues, if the respondent's interpretation is upheld, then the consolidated return regulations dealing with the accumulated earnings tax violate the notice requirement of the Administrative Procedure Act, 5 U.S.C. §553 (1976). In addition, petitioner argues that since the accumulated earnings tax is a penalty tax, Ivan Allen Company v. United States, 422 U.S. 617, 627 (1975), [page 1080 infra], any ambiguity in the regulations should be strictly construed against the respondent and petitioner's attempt to comply with the regulations should relieve it of any liability under section 531.

The first issue for our determination is: How, for the years 1973, 1974 and 1975, did the consolidated return regulations require accumulated taxable income to be computed for purposes of the accumulated earnings tax? To answer this question we must examine the administrative history of various regulations and proposed regulations under the consolidated return provisions of the Code.

Prior to 1966, affiliated corporations making consolidated returns were required to compute their accumulated taxable income on a consolidated basis for purposes of applying section 531. This consolidated calculation was clearly mandated by the regulations then in effect. At that time, section 1.531-1 provided, in part:

> §1.531-1 IMPOSITION OF TAX. Section 531 imposes . . . a graduated tax on the accumulated taxable income of every corporation described in section 532 and §1.532-1. In the case of an affiliated group which makes, or is required to make, a consolidated return, see paragraph (a) of §1.1502-30.

Paragraph (a) of section 1.1502-30, redesignated sec. 1.1502-30A(a) by T.D. 6894, 1966-2 C.B. 362, provided a general list of the various taxes imposed on consolidated filers and how the taxes were to be added to come to a single figure for group tax liability. As to the accumulated earnings tax, the paragraph provided as follows:

§1.1502-30 COMPUTATION OF TAX. (a) *General rule.* In the case of an affiliated group which makes, or is required to make, a consolidated return for any taxable year, the tax liability of each corporation . . . shall be computed . . . in the case of the taxes imposed by section 531 . . . upon the consolidated accumulated taxable income . . . determined . . . in accordance with the regulations under section 1502.

A detailed definition of "consolidated accumulated taxable income" was given in section 1.1502-31, Income Tax Regs., also adopted by T.D. 6140, 1955-2 C.B. 317 (August 29, 1955) (redesignated sec. 1.1502-31A by T.D. 6894, 1966-2 C.B. 362). That definition is reproduced in the margin.[3]

On October 1, 1965, the Internal Revenue Service proposed new consolidated return regulations to replace the 1955 regulations promulgated under section 1502 by T.D. 6140, 1955-2 C.B. 317. 30 Fed. Reg. 12564 (October 1, 1965). In the new proposed regulations, section 1.1502-2, entitled "Computation of tax liability," assumed essentially the function of section 1.1502-30 of the 1955 regulations, namely stating in one place the various taxes that were to be added

---

3. Sec. 1.1502-31(a)(18), Income Tax Regs. (1955) stated:

"(18) *Consolidated accumulated taxable income.* The consolidated accumulated taxable income shall be the consolidated taxable income computed without regard to any capital loss carryover, without regard to any charitable contribution deduction under section 170, without regard to any net operating loss deduction, and without regard to any deduction under part VIII (except section 248) of subchapter B of chapter 1, minus the sum of —

"(i) The combined Federal income and excess profits taxes (other than the excess profits tax imposed by subchapter E of chapter 2 of the Internal Revenue Code of 1939, for taxable years beginning after December 31, 1940) and income, war-profits and excess-profits taxes of foreign countries and possessions of the United States (to the extent not allowable as a deduction under section 164(b)(6)), accrued during the taxable year by the several affiliated corporations, but not including the accumulated earnings tax imposed by section 531, the personal holding company tax imposed by section 541, or the taxes imposed by corresponding sections of a prior income tax law,

"(ii) The consolidated charitable contribution deduction computed without regard to the limitation in section 170(b)(2) except that there shall not be included in the consolidated charitable contribution carryover any amount which has previously been used in the determination of consolidated accumulated taxable income or separate accumulated taxable income,

"(iii) The excess of the sum of the capital losses of the several affiliated corporations (computed without regard to any capital loss carryover) over the sum of the capital gains of such corporations,

"(iv) The excess of the consolidated net long-term capital gain over the consolidated net short-term capital loss (computed without regard to any capital loss carryover) minus the taxes imposed by subtitle A attributable to such excess,

"(v) In the case of an affiliated group including one or more holding company affiliates of a bank, as defined in section 2 of the Banking Act of 1933, the consolidated section 601 deduction, relating to earnings or profits devoted to the acquisition of readily marketable assets, other than bank stock,

"(vi) The consolidated accumulated earnings credit, and

"(vii) The consolidated section 561 dividends paid deduction."

together to determine the total tax liability of the affiliated corporations.

Section 1.1502-2 of the proposed 1965 regulations stated in part:

§1.1502-2 COMPUTATION OF TAX LIABILITY.

The tax liability of a group for a consolidated return year shall be determined by adding together —

(a) The tax imposed by section 11 on the consolidated taxable income for such year (see §1.1502-11 for the computation of consolidated taxable income);

(b) The tax imposed by section 541 on the consolidated undistributed personal holding company income (see §1.1502-42 for the computation of undistributed personal holding company income);

(c) If paragraph (b) of this section does not apply, the aggregate of the taxes imposed by section 541 on the separate undistributed personal holding company income of the members of the group which are personal holding companies (see §1.1502-45 for the computation of separate undistributed personal holding company income);

(d) If paragraph (b) of this section does not apply, the tax imposed by section 531 on the consolidated accumulated taxable income (see §1.1502-51 for the computation of consolidated accumulated taxable income). . . .

30 Fed. Reg. 12565 (October 1, 1965). Section 1.1502-51 was "reserved" and was not included in the 1965 proposals. 30 Fed. Reg. 12564 (October 1, 1965). A Technical Information Release issued the same day as the proposed regulations indicated that further regulations dealing with "special taxes and taxpayers" were to be proposed "in the near future." Technical Information Release 769 (October 1, 1965). It is clear that the Internal Revenue Service intended the reference to "special taxes and taxpayers" to include the accumulated earnings tax; in the 1965 proposals an index reference to "1.1502-37 to 1.1502-74 [Reserved]," was listed under the heading "Special Taxes and Taxpayers." 30 Fed. Reg. 12564 (October 1, 1965). However, when the proposed regulations were adopted in final form in 1966, no regulation defining "consolidated accumulated taxable income" was included. Rather, Proposed Reg. section 1.1502-2(d) was adopted as reproduced above, but with the parenthetical reference to the reserved section 1.1502-51 removed. T.D. 6894, 1966-2 C.B. 362, 367.

The consolidated return regulations promulgated under section 1502 in 1966 (hereinafter "new regulations") by T.D. 6894, 1966-2 C.B. 362, were envisioned as a complete replacement of the existing regulations (hereinafter "old regulations") promulgated by T.D. 6140, 1955-2 C.B. 317 in 1955. The old regulations were each renumbered by inserting a capital "A" after their old numbers and made applicable to tax years beginning before January 1, 1966. Sec. 1.1502-0(b), Income Tax Regs. The new regulations were to be applied to taxable years beginning after December 31, 1965. Sec. 1.1502-0(a), Income Tax Regs. The new regulations are the regulations applicable to the taxable years involved in this case.

During 1966 and 1967, the new regulations contained no provision defining "consolidated accumulated taxable income" as used in section 1.1502-2(d) of the new regulations. In 1968, however, the Commissioner proposed regulations that would provide such a definition. Proposed Income Tax Regs. secs. 1.531-1, 1.533-1(a)(3), 1.1502-2(d), 1.1502-33 and 1.1502-43 to 1.1502-47, inclusive, 33 Fed. Reg. 9830 (July 9, 1968). These complex provisions gave a highly detailed method for applying the accumulated earnings tax to affiliated corporations making consolidated returns. As a general rule, these proposed regulations required a consolidated calculation of accumulated taxable income — one similar, but not identical, to the consolidated calculation under the old regulations. However, in the case of affiliated corporations which did not elect to adjust their earnings and profits under section 1.1502-33(c)(4)(iii), Income Tax Regs. (an adjustment that became mandatory in 1976), proposed regulation section 1.1502-47 provided that "the tax imposed by section 531 shall apply to the separate accumulated taxable income of each member. . . ."

The regulations proposed in 1968 were withdrawn without explanation in 1971. 36 Fed. Reg. 16661 (August 25, 1971). This action again left the new regulations devoid of any definition of "consolidated accumulated taxable income" as used in section 1.1502-2(d) of the new regulations.

In 1979 the Commissioner again attempted to propose a definition of "consolidated accumulated taxable income." Proposed Income Tax Reg. sec. 1.1502-43(b)(1), 44 Fed. Regs. 28001 (May 14, 1979). The 1979 proposed regulations (which had not been adopted as of the date this matter was presented to the Court for decision) provide for a complex calculation of consolidated accumulated taxable income substantially along the lines of the 1968 proposed calculation. This time, though, a consolidated calculation would be uniformly required of all corporations.

As stated, the years before this Court are the taxable years 1973, 1974 and 1975. Petitioner argues that in those years it was reasonable for it to conclude that a separate computation of accumulated taxable income was required of consolidated filers.

Regs. §1.1502-80 provides the general rule that to the extent the consolidated return regulations do not mandate different treatment, corporations filing consolidated returns are to be treated as separate entities when applying other provisions of the Code. Thus, if the new regulations do not mandate a different (i.e., consolidated) treatment, Regs. §1.1502-80 requires that section 531 apply to petitioner only on its separate accumulated taxable income.

The threshold question is thus whether §1.1502-2(d) of the new regulations, standing alone, is sufficient authority for a requirement by the Commissioner in this case of consolidated computations of accumulated taxable income. We again state for emphasis that the accumulated earnings tax is a penalty tax, and as such is to be strictly construed. If the law is vague or ambiguous in this area, we may not impose the tax. Ivan Allen Company v. United States, supra at 627.

Respondent contends that at all times section 1.1502-2(d), Income Tax Regs., has contained the phrase "consolidated accumulated taxable income," and that a reasonable person would have concluded that the plain meaning of these terms mandated a consolidated, not separate, calculation in the years at issue. Even if this inference furnished an adequate substitute for definitive regulations, a postulation we reject, such an approach nevertheless leaves unsupplied a method of calculating the consolidated figure so that a corporate taxpayer could comply with the mandate of the accumulated earnings tax that excess accumulated income be distributed. Respondent maintains that a reasonable method of making the calculation could be found at section 1.1502-31A(a)(18) of the old regulations (quoted above at footnote 3).

A major problem with respondent's argument is that Regs. §1.1502-31A(a)(18) is only by its terms applicable to taxable years beginning before January 1, 1966. Regs. §1.1502-0(b). Were we to adopt respondent's view, we would effectively be inserting a cross-reference in Regs. §1.1502-2(d) to Regs. §1.1502-31A(a)(18), a step which the respondent himself has not seen fit to do.

If respondent had wanted to provide that §1.1502-31A(a)(18) of the old regulations was to govern under §1.1502-2(d) of the new regulations, he had ample opportunity to amend 1.1502-2(d) of the new regulations to so provide. We believe his action in 1966 in deleting a cross-reference to reserved §1.1502-51 and not at the same time inserting a cross-reference to §1.1502-31A(a)(18) can only be explained by a desire on his part to keep his options open as to how accumulated taxable income was eventually to be measured under the new regulations.

In 1968, perhaps concerned with some unspecified abuse if the accumulated earnings tax were applied to affiliated corporations on a consolidated basis when they did not elect to adjust their earnings and profits, respondent proposed that affiliated corporations not electing such an adjustment be subject to separate calculations of accumulated taxable income for purposes of §531. Proposed Income Tax Regs. §1.1502-47, 33 Fed. Reg. 9833 (July 9, 1968). Petitioner here was a member of just such an affiliated group which did not elect to adjust its earnings and profits. Though the 1968 proposed regulations were withdrawn in 1971, before the years involved in this case, we can readily understand petitioner's confusion as to respondent's true position as to whether affiliated corporations in petitioner's position should calculate their accumulated taxable income in a consolidated or separate fashion. Lacking guidance in the regulations as to how a consolidated calculation was to be made in the first place, we do not think petitioner's action unreasonable in concluding that a separate calculation was mandated, or at least permitted, by the consolidated return regulations.

We cannot fault petitioner for not knowing what the law was in this area when the Commissioner, charged by Congress to announce the law (§1502), never decided what it was himself. Petitioner had no reason to assume that the definition provided in the old regulations applied under the new regulations. In fact, for reasons already stated, petitioner had every reason to assume the opposite.

Thus, we find that the Commissioner's regulations regarding the manner in which the accumulated earnings tax was to be imposed on corporations making consolidated returns were ambiguous during the years at issue. This ambiguity was of the Commissioner's making, and as such must be held against him. *Ivan Allen Company*, supra. Petitioner's interpretation of these regulations was reasonable under the circumstances. We think that under these circumstances the failure of petitioner to comply with respondent's post hoc view of the regulations is an insufficient ground on which to impose the accumulated earnings tax and we hold for petitioner on the issues herein presented.

A final word. Respondent vigorously asserts in his memorandum of law that the regulations promulgated in accordance with the statutory mandate of §1502 are legislative in character and must therefore be given special weight by the courts. . . . We would respond by pointing out that 15 years have now elapsed, during which time the statutory mandate remains unfulfilled. By no stretch of the imagination should our decision here be construed as calling into question the validity of the existing regulations. We are merely declining to fill in the gaps.

NOTES

1. Under regulations issued in 1984 an affiliated group filing consolidated returns is generally treated as a single corporation in determining tax liability under §531. Treas. Reg. §1.1502-43.

2. See Rev. Rul. 87-75, 1987-2 C.B. 152, which deals with the

effect of the dividend exclusion provisions of §542(b)(4) in determining whether an affiliated group of corporations may determine
its status as a personal holding company on a consolidated basis under
§542(b)(1).

C. BASIS ADJUSTMENTS AND THE EXCESS LOSS ACCOUNT

COVIL INSULATION CO. v. COMMISSIONER
65 T.C. 364 (1975)

FEATHERSTON, Judge.... Section 1501 permits an affiliated
group of corporations to file a consolidated income tax return, in
lieu of separate returns, for each taxable year. In granting this privilege, Congress did not attempt to prescribe detailed rules governing
the determination of the income tax liability of members of the affiliated group. Rather, section 1502 authorizes the Secretary or his
delegate to prescribe such regulations as he may deem necessary in
order to clearly reflect the affiliated group's income tax liability.

Under the prescribed regulations, the current earnings or losses
of each member of the consolidated group enter into the computation
of consolidated income. . . . Losses of a subsidiary may be utilized in
this matter without limitation, even if the amount of utilized losses
exceeds the group's basis in the affiliate's stock. As a result, the group's
tax liability may be distorted since the tax losses may exceed the
economic losses. This distortion is eliminated, however, through the
vehicle of compensating adjustments to the group's basis in the affiliate's stock.

. . . Under section 1.1502-32, Income Tax Regs., the impact of
the subsidiary's losses (and gains) is reflected in annual adjustments
to the group's basis in the subsidiary's stock. . . . Generally, the subsidiary's undistributed earnings and profits, which contribute to
consolidated income, necessitate a positive adjustment. . . . Losses of
the subsidiary used to reduce the group's consolidated income require
negative adjustments. . . . If the net negative adjustments exceed the
group's basis in the stock, an "excess loss account" — a negative basis
for the stock results. Sec. 1.1502-32(e)(1), Income Tax Regs.

When all of the subsidiary's stock is disposed of, the members
of the affiliated group owning the stock are required to include the
balance of the "excess loss account" in income. . . . The income, in
most cases, is taxable as gain from the sale or exchange of stock.
However, where, as in the instant case, the subsidiary is insolvent,
the income is treated as ordinary income. . . .

. . . With exceptions not here relevant, a member is considered to have disposed of all its shares in the subsidiary on the last day of its taxable year in which, among other situations, the subsidiary's stock is wholly worthless or in which 10 percent or less of the face amount of any obligation for which the subsidiary is liable is recoverable at maturity by its creditors. . . .

Petitioner concedes that its Imesco stock was worthless in 1968, that Imesco could not pay its debts at the end of that year, that Imesco was insolvent within the meaning of applicable regulations, and that these regulations, if valid, would require the excess loss account of $118,661.01 to be included in the consolidated income for 1968. But petitioner contends that section 1.1502-32(e), Income Tax Regs., requiring a parent corporation filing a consolidated return to reduce its basis in its subsidiary's stock to a figure below zero is invalid. Petitioner also challenges the validity of section 1.1502-19(a). . . .

In weighing petitioner's attack on these consolidated return regulations, we begin with the principle that the Income Tax Regulations "should not be overruled except for weighty reasons." . . . Moreover, section 1502 expressly authorizes the issuance of regulations in this area to deal with the complex problems created by the filing of consolidated returns, thus providing an added reason for upholding such a regulation unless it is clearly contrary to the will of Congress. . . .

Further, exercise of the privilege of filing consolidated returns required petitioner to "consent to all the consolidated return regulations prescribed under section 1502 prior to the last day prescribed by law for the filing of such return." . . . As emphasized by petitioner, this consent does not preclude a challenge to arbitrary regulations. . . . The burden of the excess loss account provisions must be accepted with the benefit of unlimited access to the subsidiary's losses. . . .

We think the challenged regulations reflect a permissible exercise of the rulemaking power granted by section 1502. Indeed, the facts of this case amply demonstrate their reasonableness. Petitioner's investment in Imesco was only $45,005, comprised of the $5 paid to acquire Imesco's stock and the $45,000 indebtedness which petitioner capitalized. Yet Imesco's losses, allowed as deductions in computing the tax results of the consolidated group, far exceeded that investment. . . . [T]he regulations merely bring the tax results in line with the economic results of petitioner's ownership of Imesco's stock. The regulation might have been drafted to limit the deductible losses to petitioner's basis in Imesco's stock, but such a regulation would be unnecessarily cumbersome where the loss situation is expected to be temporary. . . . We cannot say that the excess loss account provisions of the regulations are not a permissible alternative technique for limiting the tax deduction to the amount of the group's economic loss. . . .

Petitioner attacks the regulation on the ground that its negative basis adjustment provisions are inconsistent with other Code provisions and the "common law" of taxation which denies that property can have a negative basis. . . . It is true that sections 705(a) and 733 provide that the basis of a partner's interest may not be reduced below zero. . . . It is also true that, under section 1376(b)(1) and (2), . . . a shareholder's adjusted basis in his stock may not be reduced below zero. Also, the basis adjustment provisions of sections 1011 through 1022 do not contemplate bases below zero.

However, the law relating to consolidated returns is unique. It is designed to coordinate the details of treating several corporations as a tax unit. Among the unique features of consolidated returns is the allowance of deductions for a member's losses in amounts in excess of the group's basis in that member for computing consolidated income. Passthrough of losses in the case of a partnership or a small business corporation, in contrast, is specifically limited to the partners' or shareholders' basis in the business enterprise. Since such losses are so limited, reduction of the partners' or the shareholders' basis below zero is unnecessary to prevent tax deductions in excess of economic losses. . . .

Finally, petitioner challenges section 1.1502-19(a)(2)(ii), Income Tax Regs., which provides that, when the subsidiary is insolvent, the amount of the excess loss account is to be taxed as ordinary income rather than capital gain. However, when insolvency occurs, the corporation no longer has assets susceptible to application to its shareholders' claims. The economic loss generated by the insolvent subsidiary is borne by someone other than the shareholder, e.g., a creditor. When the group utilizes those losses, it receives a deduction against ordinary income, unrelated to its then extinct capital investment. Therefore, the excess loss account is justifiably converted to ordinary income, and the regulation is reasonable. . . .

GARVEY, INC. v. UNITED STATES
1 Cl. Ct. 108 (1983), *aff'd*, 726 F.2d 1569 (Fed. Cir.), *cert. denied*,
469 U.S. 823 (1984)

MILLER, Judge. The corporate and individual plaintiffs in these consolidated cases filed to recover an aggregate of $3,447,102 in federal income taxes paid for 1969 through 1977. The cases present issues relating to consolidated return regulations and private annuities. . . .

THE ADJUSTMENT TO BASIS OF THE SUBSIDIARY
CORPORATION'S STOCK

On January 4, 1966, an affiliated group of corporations was formed with Garvey, Inc. (Garvey) as the common parent.[1] Outside this group was another parent-subsidiary chain: Petroleum, Inc. (Petroleum) and its wholly owned subsidiary, Lincoln Grain, Inc. (Lincoln). On January 5, 1966, Garvey acquired from Petroleum all of the outstanding Lincoln stock in exchange for 14 percent of Garvey's own stock, thereby bringing Lincoln into the affiliated group. Immediately before this exchange, the basis of the Lincoln stock in the hands of Petroleum was $2,436,073.

Two years later, on March 28, 1968, Garvey issued 10,404,000 shares of its common stock to the Petroleum shareholders in exchange for 100 percent of the Petroleum stock. This transaction brought Petroleum into the affiliated group and produced reciprocal stock ownership: Garvey owned 100 percent of Petroleum, which in turn owned 14 percent of Garvey. As of the date of the exchange, Petroleum had accumulated earnings and profits of $4,700,000, but the Petroleum shareholders had a collective basis in their Petroleum stock of only $249,602. Because the Petroleum stock was acquired by Garvey in an exchange of stock constituting a reorganization under §368(a)(1)(B), pursuant to §362(b) Garvey took a carryover basis of $249,602 as its basis for its Petroleum stock.

The affiliated group filed consolidated tax returns beginning with the 1966 tax year. Subsequently, the members of the group engaged in several transactions which give rise to the issues in dispute. Specifically, on November 19, 1968, Petroleum distributed its Garvey stock (14 percent) as a dividend to Garvey. The amount of this distribution was $2,426,073, and the distribution was made from Petroleum's preaffiliation earnings and profits, i.e., the earnings and profits accumulated by Petroleum before it became a member of the Garvey group. On August 1, 1970, Garvey contributed all of its Petroleum stock to three of its other wholly owned subsidiaries. On September 22, 1971, Petroleum redeemed this stock from two of the subsidiaries for $2,551,000 ($1,445,961 in cash and the remainder in property). It is stipulated that these redemptions constituted dividend distributions and that these distributions also were made from Petroleum's preaffiliation earnings and profits.

I.R.C. §1502 provides:

REGULATIONS
    The Secretary or his delegate shall prescribe such regulations as he may deem necessary in order that the tax liability of any

---

1. This company is not one of the corporate plaintiffs herein. Rather, plaintiff Garvey, Inc. was formed in 1972 as a result of a reorganization involving the affiliated group. As used herein, the term "Garvey" applies to the 1966 parent corporation.

affiliated group of corporations making a consolidated return and of each corporation in the group, both during and after the period of affiliation, may be returned, determined, computed, assessed, collected, and adjusted, in such manner as clearly to reflect the income-tax liability and the various factors necessary for the determination of such liability, and in order to prevent avoidance of such tax liability.

The consolidated return Treasury Regulations promulgated by the Secretary pursuant to I.R.C. §1502 provide the tax consequences of the above-described distributions by Petroleum. Regulations which deal with investment adjustments, and particularly Treas. Reg. §1.1502-32, T.D. 6909, 1967-1 C.B. 240, provide in pertinent part as follows:

> INVESTMENT ADJUSTMENT
>
> (a) *In general.* As of the end of each consolidated return year, each member owning stock in a subsidiary shall adjust the basis of such stock in the manner prescribed in this section. . . . The amount of such adjustment shall be the difference between the positive adjustment described in paragraph (b)(1) or (c)(1) of this section, whichever is applicable, and the negative adjustment described in paragraph (b)(2) or (c)(2) of this section, whichever is applicable. Such difference is referred to in this section as the "net positive adjustment" or the "net negative adjustment," as the case may be.
>
> (b) *Stock which is not limited and preferred as to dividends.* . . .
>
> (2) *Negative adjustment.* The negative adjustment with respect to a share of stock which is not limited and preferred as to dividends shall be the sum of — . . .
>
> (iii) Distributions made by the subsidiary during the taxable year with respect to such share out of earnings and profits of the subsidiary — . . .
>
> (b) Accumulated in preaffiliation years of the subsidiary. . . .
>
> (e) *Application of adjustment.*
>
> (1) *Net negative adjustment.* A member owning stock in a subsidiary shall apply its net negative adjustment to reduce its basis for such stock. Any excess of such adjustment over basis is herein referred to as such member's "excess loss account."

Because the distributions from Petroleum were made out of its preaffiliation earnings and profits, the investment adjustment rules required a reduction to the basis of the Petroleum stock by the amount of the distributions. Since that amount exceeded Garvey's basis in the stock, an excess loss was created. The creation of the excess loss amount in itself did not generate any tax liability, for, pursuant to Reg. §1.1502-19(a)[5] the member's excess loss account is

---

5. Treas. Reg. §1.1502-19 provides in pertinent part as follows:
"EXCESS LOSSES
"(a) *Recognition of income.* (1) *In general.* Immediately before the disposition (as

included in income, generally as gain from the sale of stock, only upon the "disposition" of the stock as defined in Reg. §1.1502-19(b). In 1972 the group terminated its affiliated status, a transaction considered a "disposition" under Reg. §1.1502-19(b)(2)(vi). Accordingly, the members were required to include in their gross income for their taxable year ending March 31, 1972, the excess loss account previously discussed. They failed to do so, however, and the Commissioner on audit included the excess loss account in the group's income. The validity of the regulation which requires these adjustments is at issue herein.

The purpose of the investment adjustment regulation is self-evident. Corporations in an affiliated group filing consolidated returns are treated as departments of a single entity. . . . Generally transactions between such corporations in a consolidated return year are given no tax effect, and, in particular, a dividend from one member to the other is not taxable to the recipient. Reg. §1.1502-14(a)[6]. However, it is a basic tenet of the tax law that earnings and profits accumulated when there has been no such affiliation are taxable whenever distributed . . . and nothing in the statute allowing affiliated groups to file consolidated returns would suggest that Congress intended such returns to be used as a device to insulate from income taxation the distribution of earnings and profits accumulated in pre-affiliation years. Accordingly, giving due regard to both principles, the regulations reiterate the scheme of §1016 of the Code, which provides:

> ADJUSTMENTS TO BASIS
>   (a) *General rule.* Proper adjustment in respect of the property shall in all cases be made — . . .
>   (4) [I]n the case of stock . . . for the amount of distributions previously made which, under the law applicable to the year in which the distribution was made, either were tax-free or were applicable in reduction of basis. . . .

In other words, the regulation states that even if the distribution of preaffiliation earnings and profits from an affiliate corporation to a parent corporation in a consolidated return year was not taxable when received, upon the disposition of the affiliate's stock the parent's

---

defined in paragraph (b) of this section) of stock of a subsidiary, there shall be included in the income of each member disposing of such stock that member's excess loss account (determined under §§1.1502-14 and 1.1502-32) with respect to the stock disposed of."
   6. Treas. Reg. §1.1502-14 provides in pertinent part as follows:
"STOCK, BONDS, AND OTHER OBLIGATIONS OF MEMBERS
   "(a) *Intercompany distributions with respect to stock.* (1) *Dividends.* A dividend distributed by one member to another member during a consolidated return year shall be eliminated. This provision dates back to the consolidated return regulations under the Revenue Act of 1936. Treas. Reg. 97 Art. 31(b)."

basis for the stock is reduced by the amount it has already received free of tax.

The basis adjustment rules seek to achieve the broad objective of preventing tax avoidance that otherwise might occur through the use of the consolidated return. Authority to so regulate was first delegated to the Secretary by §141(b) of the Revenue Act of 1918, . . . predecessor to I.R.C. §1502. The Conference Report that accompanied §141(b) made clear that Congress expected the Secretary to prescribe regulations dealing with —

> [t]he extent to which gain or loss shall be recognized upon the sale by a member of the affiliated group of stock issued by any other member of the affiliated group or upon the dissolution (whether partial or complete) of a member of the group; . . . [and] the extent to which and the manner in which gain or loss is to be recognized, upon the withdrawal of one or more corporations from the group, by reason of transactions occurring during the period of affiliation. . . .

H.R. Rep. No. 1882, 70th Cong., 1st Sess. 16-17, 1939-1 C.B. (part 2) 444, 449. Nothing in subsequent revisions to the 1928 Act indicates any intent to limit the scope of this authority. . . .

Reg. §1.1502-32(b)(2)(iii)(b) fits squarely within the type contemplated by Congress, for it prevents tax avoidance by fixing the extent to which and the manner in which plaintiff[7] upon disaffiliation, is to recognize gain or loss by reason of transactions that took place during the period of affiliation. Such transactions include the dividend distributions that, pursuant to Reg. §1.1502-14(a), went untaxed due to the filing of the consolidated tax return. The regulation therefore insures that a distribution that would have been taxable absent the consolidated return does not completely escape taxation through the use of the consolidated return.[8]

Since §1502 specifically directs the Secretary to prescribe regulations as he may deem necessary in order clearly to reflect the income tax liability of any affiliated group of corporations making a consolidated return both during and after the period of affiliation and to prevent avoidance of such tax liability, such regulations are legislative in character with the force and effect of law, and the Secretary is allowed wider discretion in their promulgation than in the case of merely interpretative regulations. . . . However, of course even that discretion is not unlimited.

Plaintiff concedes that "the regulations in this complex area should be sustained unless clearly unreasonable" and that the neg-

---

7. In this portion of the opinion, the term "plaintiff" refers only to plaintiff Garvey, Inc.

8. The consolidated return regulations also convert the income from ordinary income to capital gain. See Treas. Reg. §1.1502-19(a)(1).

ative adjustment rules requiring that basis be decreased for distributions out of earnings and profits accumulated by the subsidiary in preaffiliation years of the subsidiary are "logical" and "necessary to prevent double losses and dividend stripping"[9] — except when the parent's basis for the subsidiary's stock is carried over from the prior stockholders and is less than the fair value of the subsidiary's stock at the time acquired.

Plaintiff says that when a corporation buys all of the stock of another corporation for cash, its cost is generally the value of all of the acquired corporation's property, which consists of the original assets plus the cash and other assets acquired by the subsidiary corporation with its accumulated earnings and profits. If the assets derived from the earnings are then paid out to the parent by way of untaxed dividends, the parent receives back part of its cost, and its remaining cost is attributable only to the subsidiary's remaining assets. Therefore, plaintiff concedes that it is logical to reduce the parent's basis for the subsidiary's stock by the amount of the untaxed distribution of preaffiliation earnings. However, plaintiff argues, when the parent issues its own stock having equivalent value for all of the stock of the subsidiary, its basis should not be reduced by the distribution of preaffiliation earnings because the parent's basis for its purchase is reduced (by §362(b)) to the subsidiary's former stockholders' basis for their stock and already excludes the value of the subsidiary's accumulated earnings. Therefore, plaintiff contends, if it disposes of the subsidiary's stock for what it paid less the value of the property received as a dividend, the second reduction in basis causes it to be taxed on "phantom gain."

Although the argument is not without superficial appeal, it is meretricious. First, the assertion that the former stockholders' basis

---

9. A double loss deduction occurs if the loss incurred in a consolidated return year by a subsidiary is used first to offset the taxable income of the group pursuant to Treas. Reg. §1.1502-12, T.D. 6894, 1966-2 C.B. 362, and again to produce a loss if the subsidiary is sold by the parent corporation for an amount that reflects the loss and is less than the parent's original investment in the subsidiary. For example, Corporation P acquires Corporation S for $500. In a consolidated return year, P has taxable income of $300 and S incurs a $200 loss. Under the consolidated return regulations, the taxable income of the group is $100. ($300 − $200). If P then sells S, presumably P could only get $300 (its original $500 value minus the $200 loss). P would then be able to claim a $200 loss on the sale, thereby utilizing the loss twice. This abuse was prohibited by Charles Ilfeld Co. v. Hernandez, 292 U.S. 62 (1934), and now is codified in the consolidated return regulations. Treas. Reg. §§1.1502-19, 1.1502-32.

Dividend stripping is the practice by which a corporation purchases a subsidiary for a price that reflects the subsidiary's accumulated earnings and profits, receives a distribution of those earnings and profits tax-free under Treas. Reg. §1.1502-14(a) (which eliminates dividend distributions between members of the group), sells the subsidiary for its remaining value and claims a loss. See Waterman Steamship Co. v. United States, 430 F.2d 1185 (5th Cir. 1970), cert. denied, 401 U.S. 939 (1971). This abuse also is prohibited by Treas. Reg. §§1.1502-19, 1.1502-32.

for their stock necessarily excludes the value of the subsidiary's accumulated earnings and profits is true only if they were the original stockholders of the subsidiary. It is not accurate if the former stockholders bought their stock from others and some or all of the earnings were accumulated before such purchase.

More important, the reduction in basis for the stock which creates the "phantom gain" is not the reduction required by the regulation but the reduction required by the statute, i.e., §362(b). This does not depend on there being an affiliated group, consolidated returns and preaffiliation earnings. The following examples serve to illustrate this:

(1) Assume that sole stockholder SH acquired the stock of Corporation S for $10,000 and that subsequently S accumulated $10,000 in earnings. If Corporation P then issues to SH P stock having a $20,000 value in exchange for all of SH's shares, pursuant to I.R.C. §362(b) P's basis for the S shares remains the same as that of SH, $10,000. If P then resells the S stock to Y for $20,000, P has a taxable gain of $10,000, even though it has received no more than what it paid.

(2) Assume the same initial facts but that after P acquired the S shares S distributes to P the $10,000 in earnings as a dividend. Since the S assets are thereby depleted, P receives no more than $10,000 when it resells the S shares to Y. Thus, in such a situation P still has $10,000 of taxable income, i.e., the dividend from S, even though the sum of the dividend distribution and resale price of the S stock equals no more than what P paid for the stock in the first place.

(3) Assume again the same initial facts but that after P acquired the S shares P and S become an affiliated group, that they file a consolidated income tax return, and that during the consolidated return year S distributes to P as a dividend the $10,000 in preaffiliation earnings. When thereafter P sells the S shares, because the S assets have been depleted by the dividend P receives no more than $10,000 for the shares. Under Reg. §1.1502-32, P's basis for the S stock is reduced to 0. Therefore, its taxable income is $10,000, the same as in the previous examples, and the operation of the regulation has not affected that amount.

Prior to the enactment of the predecessors to §362(b), P's basis for the S stock in Examples (1) and (2) was $20,000. But Congress became concerned that the reorganization section was being used as a device to deprive the government of its proper taxes by permitting an increased basis for assets and for stock of one corporation acquired by another in exchange for stock in a tax-free reorganization. Therefore, in §204(a)(7) of the Revenue Act of 1924, ch. 234, 43 Stat. 253, 259, Congress provided that if property is acquired by a corporation in connection with a reorganization by the issuance of its stock and immediately thereafter the transferor or transferors are in control of the corporation, then the corporation's basis for the property shall remain the same as it would be in the hands of the transferor. The House Ways and Means Committee explained the purpose of the measure:

> (2) The provisions of the reorganization section have been rewritten to prevent the use of the section to escape proper taxation by increasing the basis for depreciation or depletion or by increasing the basis for determining gain or loss from the sale of assets transferred in connection with a reorganization or by distributing as capital gains what are in effect dividends out of earnings.[11]

H.R. Rep. No. 179, 68th Cong., 1st Sess. 7, 1939-1 C.B. (part 2) 241, 246. The Committee also noted as follows:

> Under the existing law, if the A Corporation owns assets which cost it $10,000 but which are now worth $20,000, it can reorganize into the B Corporation, exchanging shares of stock of the B Corporation for the shares of stock of the A Corporation. Neither Corporation A nor its stockholders realize any taxable gain from the reorganization. The B Corporation, however, can set up the assets received in the reorganization on its books at their market value — that is, $20,000 — and use that amount as the basis for determining the gain or loss from the subsequent sale of the assets and for determining depreciation and depletion. Under paragraph (8) of the draft, however, Corporation B must set up the assets on its books at $10,000, their basis in the hands of Corporation A, and must use that amount as the basis for determining the gain or loss from the subsequent sale of the assets and for determining depreciation and depletion.

Id. at 17, 1939-1 C.B. (part 2) at 253. . . .

Although the 1924 Committee reports indicate that "property" was intended to include stock, in §113(a)(7) of the Revenue Act of 1928, ch. 852, 45 Stat. 791, 819-20, Congress clarified the 1924 measure to remove any doubt that the carryover of basis requirement applies to a stock for stock reorganization. . . . And in 1938 Congress removed the requirement that the transferor of the property or stock retain control over it, in order for the basis to carry over in the reorganization, bringing the statute to the format in which it now reads in §362(b). . . .

Plaintiff's argument comes down to this: Plaintiff has already suffered a statutory reduction in basis because it acquired the stock of its affiliate in a stock-for-stock nontaxable reorganization. There-

---

11. The Senate Finance Committee report contains substantially the same language. S. Rep. No. 398, 68th Cong., 1st Sess. at 7, 18, 1939-1 C.B. (part 2) 266, 278-79.

fore, although generally it is logical for the regulations to require reduction of the basis of an affiliate's stock for the parent's tax-free receipt of a distribution of its affiliate's earnings in a consolidated return year, plaintiff should be entitled to credit for the prior reduction. But as shown, the purposes of the two reductions in basis are unrelated and may exist independently or concurrently. It seems clear that, although couched in terms of an attack on Reg. §1.1502-32, plaintiff's argument really is an effort to nullify the effects of §362(b), a statute dating back to 1924. The validity of that statute, however, has never seriously been questioned and even plaintiff does not challenge it directly here.

Although, as previously mentioned, plaintiff in its main brief conceded that the provisions of Treas. Reg. §1.1502-32(b)(2)(iii)(b) requiring a reduction in the basis because of the receipt of an untaxed distribution of preaffiliation earnings are logical except where the member has a carryover basis in the affiliate's stock, in its reply brief plaintiff urges for the first time that the regulation is at odds with §243 of the Code. That section allows to a corporation receiving a taxable dividend from another corporation a deduction of 85 percent of the amount of the dividend. Plaintiff asserts that applying the 48 percent corporate maximum tax rate in effect during 1968-71 to the 15 percent remainder results in a 7.2 percent tax on the dividends, whereas the effect of the regulation's reduction in the basis of the affiliate's stock because of the untaxed dividend was to subject the increased gain on the disposition in 1972 to a 30 percent capital gains tax. Plaintiff contends that this increased tax violates the principle, enunciated by the Tax Court in Joseph Weidenhoff, Inc. v. Commissioner, 32 T.C. 1222, 1242 (1959), that the Secretary has no authority —

> to prescribe a regulation which will . . . impose a tax on income that would not otherwise be taxed (by limiting the excess profits credit) simply because the taxpayers exercise the privilege of filing consolidated returns, unless it is to prevent tax avoidance.

But the quotation lays down no principle applicable to consolidated return regulations generally. It was merely an expression of the court's frustration over its inability to understand the purpose of a regulation limiting the excess profits credit of corporations becoming members of an affiliated group after a particular date and the failure of both the regulations and the Commissioner to explain such purpose. Therefore, it said, "in the absence of possible tax avoidance or some necessity for its use to properly determine the tax liability, we do not think [the regulation] can be applied, without explanation, in the absolute discretion of the Commissioner." Id.

The obvious purpose of the regulation here at issue, which reduces the plaintiff's basis of its stock in its subsidiary for untaxed dividends from preaffiliation earnings of the subsidiary, is to prevent tax avoidance.

The election to file a consolidated return for an affiliated group inherently carries with it both advantages and disadvantages as compared to filing separate returns. . . . In promulgating consolidated return regulations, the Secretary is not obligated to offer a taxpayer all the benefits of consolidation while simultaneously preserving for it all deductions and benefits of separate returns. As the court stated in Georgia-Pacific Corp. v. Commissioner, 63 T.C. 790, 802 (1975), the affiliated group that voluntarily elects to file a consolidated return "must now take the bitter with the sweet. . . ."

Plaintiff also claims that Petroleum made the distributions in reliance on 1968 and 1971 published proposals by the Treasury to amend Treas. Reg. §1.1502-32, which would have excepted a carryover basis for the stock of an affiliate from reduction of basis for a dividend from preaffiliation earnings and profits, and, although the proposed amendments were not adopted, the Secretary is now estopped from applying the existing regulations to plaintiff without the aborted amendments, even if they are otherwise valid. . . .

It is stipulated that in structuring its transactions plaintiff was advised by experienced tax counsel familiar with the applicable tax statutes and regulations. In multimillion dollar intercorporate transactions, where there is even the slightest doubt as to the tax consequences, it is customary for experienced tax counsel to request an advance private ruling from the I.R.S., which, if favorable, may ordinarily be relied upon by a taxpayer. . . . In the absence of other evidence, it may be fairly inferred that plaintiff's decision not to make such a request and to rely on the proposed regulation instead was prompted by the desire not to "rock the boat." In short, plaintiff's conduct in relying on proposed amendments in structuring its transactions falls far short of conduct that merits an estoppel against the government. . . .

Gottesman & Co. v. Commissioner, 77 T.C. 1149 (1981) [page 1040 supra], another case relied upon by plaintiff, also is inapposite. In that case, the issue was whether the consolidated group was subject to the accumulated earnings tax, and resolution of the issue depended on the manner of computing the group's accumulated taxable income. The regulations on the subject were ambiguous. On one occasion the Secretary proposed new regulations requiring consolidated calculations. He then withdrew this, and proposed different new regulations requiring separate calculations. In turn he withdrew these and never adopted any regulation on the subject. At trial the Commissioner contended that the taxpayer was required by the preexisting regulations to use consolidated calculations. The court first ruled that the preexisting regulations did not resolve the problem at all. It then ruled that in view of the Secretary's inability to make up his mind, there was an unfilled gap in the regulations. Therefore, the Commissioner's ad hoc interpretation of the old regulation was no more reasonable than the taxpayer's and an insufficient basis for the imposition of an accumulated earnings tax (a penalty tax on excessive accumulations). Here, however, there is no gap to be filled: Reg. §1.1502-32(b)(2)(iii)(b) was valid and in effect at the time each distribution was made and plaintiff knew precisely what adjustments to basis it required. . . .

Based on the foregoing, judgment on the consolidated return issue must be entered in favor of defendant. . . .

NOTES

1. See Axelrod, Section 304, Excess Loss Accounts and Other Consolidated Return Gallimaufry, Tax Notes, Aug. 17, 1987, p. 729; Dahlberg, Aggregate vs. Entity: Adjusting the Basis of Stock in a Subsidiary Filing a Consolidated Return, 42 Tax L. Rev. 547 (1987).

2. Craigie, Inc. v. Commissioner, 84 T.C. 466 (1985), presents a good illustration of the "taking the bitter with the sweet" theme of the law affecting affiliated groups. In 1973, the taxpayer corporation was a member of a group which, as a result of a swindle, claimed a sizable theft loss. In 1975, the taxpayer was sold, became independent, and continued to claim its share of net operating losses from the group. Meanwhile, the former parent was audited and signed a statutory waiver giving up its claim to the theft loss. Relying on Treas. Reg. §1.1502-77, the Tax Court held that the parent was the sole agent for the consolidated group, with authority to bind all members as to transactions arising out of the years of affiliation. Hence, the taxpayer's losses were disallowed.

3. In Woods Investment Co., 85 T.C. 274 (1985), a parent (the taxpayer) sold the stock of four wholly owned subsidiaries with which it filed consolidated income tax returns. Taxpayer calculated its gain from the sale by determining its basis in the subsidiaries' stock with reference to the subsidiaries' earnings and profits. Although the subsidiaries used accelerated depreciation in computing their taxable income, the court upheld petitioner's use of straight-line depreciation for earnings and profits purposes under §312(k). The court concluded that if the Commissioner thought the consolidated return regulations in conjunction with §312(k) provide a "double deduction," he should amend the regulations. In 1987, Congress enacted §1503(e) which effectively overrules the *Woods Investment* decision.

4. In 1988 the Service issued regulations under §1502 providing

rules for the adjustment of earnings and profits of group members following certain changes in the affiliated group's structure. Under the regulations, if the group's common parent changes, but the group continues to exist and the shareholders of the old common parent own 80 percent or more of the new common parent, then the earnings and profits of the new parent will be adjusted to reflect the earnings and profits of the old parent. See Temp. Treas. Reg. §1.1502-33.

D. STOCK OWNERSHIP BY AFFILIATES

REVENUE RULING 89-46
1989-14 I.R.B. 16

ISSUE

If a member of an affiliated group that files a consolidated income tax return owns stock of another corporation, do the aggregate stock ownership rules of section 1.1502-34 of the Income Tax Regulations attribute that stock to other members that do not actually own any stock in the corporation?

FACTS

P is the common parent of an affiliated group of corporations that files a consolidated federal income tax return. P has two wholly owned subsidiaries, X and Y, that are members of the P group. On June 1, 1988, X transferred certain property to Y in exchange for a security of Y. The face amount and fair market value of the security equaled the fair market value of the property transferred, but the basis of the property in the hands of X did not equal its fair market value.

LAW AND ANALYSIS

Section 1.1502-34 of the regulations provides that, for purposes of sections 1.1502-1 through 1.1502-80, in determining the stock ownership of a member of the group in another corporation (the "issuing corporation") for purposes of determining the application of section 332(b)(1) or 351(a) (among other sections) in a consolidated return year, there shall be included stock owned by all other members of the group in the issuing corporation. Paragraphs (2) and (3) of section 332(b) are not among the sections whose application is determined according to this special attribution rule.

Section 332(a) of the Internal Revenue Code provides that no gain or loss shall be recognized on the receipt by a corporation of property distributed in complete liquidation of another corporation. Section 332(b)(1) provides that section 332(a) applies only if the corporate distributee satisfies an 80-percent ownership requirement with respect to the liquidating corporation. Further, under section 332(b)(2) and (3), section 332(a) applies only if the liquidating distribution is in complete cancellation or redemption of all the liquidating corporation's stock.

Section 351(a) of the Code provides that no gain or loss shall be recognized if property is transferred to a corporation by one or more persons solely in exchange for stock or securities in the corporation and immediately after the exchange the person or persons are in control (as defined in section 368(c)) of the corporation.

Section 368(c) of the Code generally provides that the term "control" means the ownership of stock possessing at least 80 percent of the total combined voting power of all classes of stock entitled to vote and at least 80 percent of the total number of shares of all other classes of stock of the corporation.

Rev. Rul. 74-598, 1974-2 C.B. 287, amplified by Rev. Rul. 75-383, 1975-2 C.B. 127, concerns an affiliated group filing a consolidated income tax return in which a wholly owned foreign subsidiary (S-1) of one member of the group (P) was to transfer all of its assets to another member of the group (S-2) that did not own any stock of the foreign corporation. The ruling holds that section 1.1502-34 of the regulations applies to attribute stock owned by members of an affiliated group to other members of the group only if the other members actually own some of the stock. The ruling concludes that because S-2 did not actually own any stock of S-1, section 1.1502-34 does not attribute stock ownership to S-2, and thus section 332 of the Code does not prevent recognition of gain on the transfer. This holding is incorrect. Such an interpretation is not required by the plain language of section 1.1502-34 and would not further the purpose of that section.

Rev. Rul. 74-598 is correct, however, in its ultimate conclusion that section 332 of the Code does not apply to S-2's receipt of property from S-1 as described in that ruling. Although section 1.1502-34 of the regulations applies to satisfy the 80-percent ownership requirement of section 332(b)(1), it does not apply to satisfy the requirement of section 332(b)(2) or (3) that the distribution be in complete cancellation or redemption of the liquidating corporation's stock. Since S-2 actually owned no stock in S-1, none of the property received by S-2 from S-1 was received in such a distribution. However, the transaction described in Rev. Rul. 74-598 still may qualify as a reorganization under section 368(a)(1)(D). See Rev. Rul. 75-383.

In the present situation, X, a member of the P group, transferred property to Y, the "issuing corporation," solely in exchange for a security of Y. Thus, the requirements of section 351(a) of the Code, other than the control requirement, are satisfied by the exchange. Under section 1.1502-34 of the regulations, even though X has no actual stock ownership in Y, X is considered, for purposes of section 351(a), the owner of the Y shares owned by P. Because P owns 100 percent of the stock of Y, X is in control of Y immediately after the exchange. Therefore, section 351(a) applies to the exchange, and X recognizes no gain or loss on the exchange. See Rev. Rul. 73-473, 1973-2 C.B. 115. Cf. Rev. Rul. 73-472, 1973-2 C.B. 114. If X were not a member of an affiliated group filing a consolidated income tax return, section 351(a) would not prevent recognition of gain or loss on the transfer of property from X to Y because X did not own at least 80 percent of the Y stock and thus would not be in control of Y immediately after the transaction.

HOLDING

If a member of an affiliated group that files a consolidated income tax return owns stock of another corporation, the aggregate stock ownership rules of section 1.1502-34 of the regulations attribute that stock to other members of the group, regardless of whether the other members actually own any stock in the corporation.

EFFECT ON OTHER REVENUE RULINGS

Rev. Rul. 74-598 is modified to hold that the attribution rules of section 1.1502-34 of the regulations apply for the purpose of determining whether a member satisfies the 80-percent ownership requirement of section 332(b)(1) of the Code, regardless of whether the member actually owns stock in the "issuing corporation." Section 1.1502-34 does not apply, however, for purposes of determining whether the other requirements of section 332 are met. . . .

6

The Accumulated Earnings Tax— §§531-537

I. INTRODUCTION

Over the years, individuals with incomes taxable at very high marginal rates have been willing, sometimes eager, to leave their corporate earnings in corporate solution knowing they could enjoy deferral until they chose to make distribution and could avoid tax at high marginal rates when they did. This was especially true if after death their estates might withdraw the corporate earnings free of the income tax, as a result of a combination of §§1014 and 302(a), 303, or 331. To discourage corporate accumulations designed to avoid the individual income tax, Congress since 1913 has employed special techniques.

From 1913 to 1916, shareholders were taxed individually on their ratable share of undistributed corporate income if the corporation was "formed or fraudulently availed of" to help the shareholders avoid individual taxation. From 1916 to 1921, the individual tax could be imposed even without the showing of a fraudulent purpose. The Supreme Court sustained this tax on the shareholders against charges of unconstitutionality in Helvering v. National Grocery Co., 304 U.S. 282 (1938).

In 1921 Congress changed its approach essentially to that found in the present Code, §§531-537, imposing an added corporate level tax on the undistributed earnings of the corporation if it is formed or availed of for the purpose of avoiding the income tax on its shareholders. A number of statutory amendments were made in 1954, but the basic pattern adopted in 1921 remains. See United States v. Donruss Co., page 1064 infra.

Section 531 imposes its current 28 percent tax on the corporation's "accumulated taxable income," as defined in §535, minus the dividends paid deduction (§561) and the accumulated earnings credit provided by §535(c). Although §531 discourages some corporate accumulations, its effect on the conduct of corporations and shareholders has not been overwhelming. Is it necessary to retain the accumulated earnings tax after the 1986 Act has imposed a maximum tax rate of 34 percent on a corporation's taxable income, one that is 21 percent higher than the 28 percent maximum rate on shareholders? Consider whether it might be sufficient and right just to eliminate the dividends received deduction for "mere investment companies"? See Wolfman, Subchapter C and the 100th Congress, page 862 supra.

See generally B. Bittker and J. Eustice, Federal Income Taxation of Corporations and Shareholders, 8-2 to 8-34 (5th ed. 1987); Apelbaum, The Accumulated Earnings Tax and the Personal Holding Company Tax: Problems and Proposals, 3 Boston U.J. Tax L. 53 (1985); Kwall, Subchapter G of the Internal Revenue Code: Crusade Without a Cause?, 5 Va. Tax Rev. 223 (1985).

II. FORBIDDEN PURPOSE

UNITED STATES v. DONRUSS CO.
393 U.S. 297 (1969), *rev'g* 384 F.2d 292 (6th Cir. 1967)

Mr. Justice MARSHALL delivered the opinion of the Court. This case involves the application of §§531-537 of the Internal Revenue Code of 1954, which impose a surtax on corporations "formed or availed of for the purpose of avoiding the income tax with respect to . . . [their] shareholders . . . by permitting earnings and profits to accumulate instead of being divided or distributed."

Respondent is a corporation engaged in the manufacture and sale of bubble gum and candy and in the operation of a farm. Since 1954, all of respondent's outstanding stock has been owned by Don B. Wiener. In each of the tax years from 1955 to 1961, respondent operated profitably, increasing its undistributed earnings from $1,021,288.58 to $1,679,315.37. The company did not make loans to Wiener or provide him with benefits other than a salary, nor did it make investments unrelated to its business, but no dividends were declared during the entire period.

Wiener gave several reasons for respondent's accumulation policy; among them were capital and inventory requirements, increasing costs, and the risks inherent in the particular business and in the general economy. Wiener also expressed a general desire to expand and a more specific desire to invest in respondent's major distributor, the Tom Huston Peanut Company. There were no definite plans during the tax years in question, but in 1964 respondent purchased 10,000 shares in Tom Huston at a cost of $380,000.

The Commissioner of Internal Revenue assessed accumulated earnings taxes against respondent for the years 1960 and 1961. Respondent paid the tax and brought this refund suit. At the conclusion of the trial, the Government specifically requested that the jury be instructed that:

> [I]t is not necessary that avoidance of shareholder's tax be the sole purpose for the unreasonable accumulation of earnings; it is sufficient if it is one of the purposes for the company's accumulation policy.

The instruction was refused and the court instructed the jury in the terms of the statute that tax avoidance had to be "the purpose" of the accumulations. The jury, in response to interrogatories, found that respondent had accumulated earnings beyond the reasonable needs of its business, but that it had not retained its earnings for the purpose of avoiding income tax on Wiener. Judgment was entered for respondent and the Government appealed.

The Court of Appeals reversed and remanded for a new trial, holding that "the jury might well have been led to believe that tax avoidance must be the sole purpose behind an accumulation in order to impose the accumulated earnings tax." Donruss Co. v. United States, 384 F.2d 292, 298 (C.A. 6th Cir. 1967). The Court of Appeals rejected the Government's proposed instruction and held that the tax applied only if tax avoidance was the "dominant, controlling, or impelling motive" for the accumulation. Ibid. We granted the Government's petition for certiorari to resolve a conflict among the circuits over the degree of "purpose" necessary for the application of the accumulated earnings tax, and because of the importance of that question in the administration of the tax. 390 U.S. 1023 (1968).

I

The accumulated earnings tax is established by §§531-537 of the Internal Revenue Code of 1954. Section 531 imposes the tax. Section 532 defines the corporations to which the tax shall apply. That section provides:

> The accumulated earnings tax imposed by section 531 shall apply to every corporation . . . formed or availed of for the purpose of avoiding the income tax with respect to its shareholders or the shareholders of any other corporation, by permitting earnings and profits to accumulate instead of being divided or distributed.

Section 533(a) provides that:

> For purposes of section 532, the fact that the earnings and profits of a corporation are permitted to accumulate beyond the reasonable needs of the business shall be determinative of the purpose to avoid the income tax with respect to shareholders, unless the corporation by the preponderance of the evidence shall prove to the contrary.

In cases before the Tax Court, §534 allows the taxpayer in certain instances to shift to the Commissioner the burden of proving accumulation beyond the reasonable needs of the business. Section 535 defines "accumulated taxable income." It also provides for a credit for that portion of the earnings and profits retained for the reasonable needs of the business, with a minimum lifetime credit of $100,000. Finally, §537 provides that "reasonable needs of the business" include "reasonably anticipated" needs.

The dispute before us is a narrow one. The Government contends that in order to rebut the presumption contained in §533(a), the taxpayer must establish by the preponderance of the evidence that tax avoidance with respect to shareholders was not "one of the purposes" for the accumulation of earnings beyond the reasonable needs of the business. Respondent argues that it may rebut that presumption by demonstrating that tax avoidance was not the "dominant, controlling, or impelling" reason for the accumulation. Neither party questions the trial court's instructions on the issue of whether the accumulation was beyond the reasonable needs of the business, and respondent does not challenge the jury's finding that its accumulation was indeed unreasonable. We intimate no opinion about the standards governing reasonableness of corporate accumulations.

We conclude from an examination of the language, the purpose, and the legislative history of the statute that the Government's construction is the correct one. Accordingly, we reverse the judgment of the court below and remand the case for a new trial on the issue of whether avoidance of shareholder tax was one of the purposes of respondent's accumulations.

II

Both parties argue that the language of the statute supports their conclusion. Respondent argues that Congress could have used the article "a" in §§532 and 533 if it had intended to adopt the Government's test. Instead, argues respondent, Congress used the article "the" in the operative part of the statute, thus indicating that tax avoidance must at least be the dominant motive for the accumulation. The Government argues that respondent's construction gives an unduly narrow effect to the word "the." Instead, contends the Government, this Court should focus on the entire phrase "availed of for the purpose." Any language of limitation should logically modify "availed of" rather than "purpose" and no such language is present. The Government further argues that Congress has dealt with similar problems in other sections of the Code and has used terms such as "principal purpose," §§269(a), 357(b)(1), and "used principally," §355(a)(1)(B). Similar terms could have been used in

§§532(a) and 533(a), but were not. Finally, the Government points to the fact that prior to adoption of §102 of the Revenue Act of 1938 (52 Stat. 483) the forerunner of §532(a) used the words "the purpose," while the evidentiary section used the words "a purpose," thus indicating that tax avoidance need only be one purpose. Respondent replies that the change from "a" to "the" in the evidentiary section supports its conclusion. Respondent also contends that the statute before the change was consistent with its construction.

We find both parties' arguments inconclusive. The phrase "availed of for the purpose" is inherently vague, and there is no indication in the legislative history that Congress intended to attach any particular significance to the use of the article "the." Nor do we find the change in the evidentiary section from "a" to "the" at all helpful. That change came as part of a significant revision in the operation of the section, and there is no indication that it was other than a mere change in phraseology. Indeed, the Report of the Senate Finance Committee accompanying the bill that was to become the Revenue Act of 1938, insofar as it sheds any light on the question, supports the view of the Government. "The proposal is to strengthen [the evidentiary] section by requiring the taxpayer by a clear preponderance of the evidence to prove the absence of *any* purpose to avoid surtaxes upon shareholders. . . ." S. Rep. No. 1567, 75th Cong., 3d Sess., 5 (1938) (emphasis added). Since the language of the statute does not provide an answer to the question before us,[6] we have examined in detail the relevant legislative history. That history leads us to conclude that the test proposed by the Government is consistent with the intent of Congress and is necessary to effectuate the purpose of the accumulated earnings tax.

III

The accumulated earnings tax is one congressional attempt to deter use of a corporate entity to avoid personal income taxes. The purpose of the tax "is to compel the company to distribute any profits not needed for the conduct of its business so that, when so distributed, individual stockholders will become liable" for taxes on the dividends received, Helvering v. Chicago Stock Yards Co., 318 U.S. 693, 699 (1943). The tax originated in the Tariff Act of 1913, 38 Stat. 114, the first personal income tax statute following ratification of the Sixteenth Amendment. That Act imposed a tax on the shareholders of any corporation "formed or fraudulently availed of for the purpose of preventing the imposition of such tax through the medium of

6. The Regulations shed no light on the problem. See Treas. Reg. §§1.531-1.537. . . .

permitting such gains and profits to accumulate instead of being divided or distributed. . . ." §11(A)(2), 38 Stat. 166. The same section provided that accumulation beyond the reasonable needs of the business "shall be prima facie evidence of a fraudulent purpose to escape such tax. . . ." 38 Stat. 167.

In its first years of operation, difficulties in proving a fraudulent purpose made the tax largely ineffective. To meet this problem, Congress deleted the word "fraudulently." Revenue Act of 1918, §220, 40 Stat. 1072; see S. Rep. No. 617, 65th Cong., 3d Sess., 5 (1918).

During the next few years, numerous complaints were made about the ineffectiveness of the accumulated earnings tax. Various attempts were made to strengthen the tax during the 1920s and 1930s, but the statute remained essentially the same until 1934. See Joint Committee on the Economic Report, The Taxation of Corporate Surplus Accumulations, 82d Cong., 2d Sess., 200-205 (Comm. Print 1952). In 1934, Congress dealt with one of the more flagrant examples of that ineffectiveness, the personal holding company. Personal holding companies were exempted from the general accumulated earnings tax and were subjected to a tax on undistributed income, regardless of the purpose of that accumulation. Revenue Act of 1934, §§102, 351, 48 Stat. 702, 751. The reason for the change was that, "[b]y making partial distribution of profits and by showing some need for the accumulation of the remaining profits, the taxpayer makes it difficult to prove a purpose to avoid taxes." H.R. Rep. No. 704, 73d Cong., 2d Sess., 11 (1934).

Again in 1936, Congress attempted to solve the continuing problem of undistributed corporate earnings. "The difficulty of proving such [tax avoidance] purpose . . . has rendered . . . [the accumulated earnings tax] more or less ineffective." H.R. Rep. No. 2475, 74th Cong., 2d Sess., 5 (1936). However, Congress did not change the requirement that "purpose" must be proved. Rather, it attempted the alternative method of imposing an undistributed profits surtax on most corporations. Revenue Act of 1936, §14, 49 Stat. 1655. The tax on personal holding companies and the general accumulated earnings tax were retained.

The problem continued to be acute and several proposals were made by and to Congress in 1938. The House Ways and Means Committee proposed a surtax on all closely held operating companies. Only minor changes were proposed by the Committee in the accumulated earnings tax. See H.R. Rep. No. 1860, 75th Cong., 3d Sess. (1938). The House rejected all but the changes in the accumulated earnings tax. The Senate approached the problem of retained corporate earnings in a different way. Labeling the House Committee's recommendation a "drastic" remedy, the Senate Finance Committee recommended "dealing with this problem where it should be dealt with — namely, in section 102, relating to corporations improperly accumulating surplus. The proposal is to strengthen this section by requiring the taxpayer by a clear preponderance of the evidence to prove the absence of any purpose to avoid surtaxes upon shareholders after it has been determined that the earnings and profits have been unreasonably accumulated." S. Rep. No. 1567, 75th Cong., 3d Sess., 5 (1938). The change was thought to make it clear that the burden of proving intent, rather than the lesser burden of producing evidence on the question, was to be on the taxpayer. Id., at 16. The Senate proposal was enacted. Revenue Act of 1938, §102, 52 Stat. 483. The Committee felt that a "reasonable enforcement of this revised section will reduce tax avoidance. . . ." S. Rep. No. 1567, supra, at 5.

Only insignificant changes were made in the accumulated earnings tax from 1938 to 1954. Discussion of the problem continued, however, and numerous proposals were made to alter the tax. See, e.g., Joint Committee on the Economic Report, The Taxation of Corporate Surplus Accumulations, 82d Cong., 2d Sess. (Comm. Print 1952). Congress took cognizance of these complaints and incorporated many of them in the Internal Revenue Code of 1954, but no change was made in the required degree of tax avoidance purpose.[9] Rather, the changes, which were generally favorable to the taxpayer, demonstrated congressional disaffection with the effect of the tax and its emphasis on intent. Congress' reaction to the complaints was to emphasize the reasonable needs of the business as a proper purpose for corporate accumulations[11] and to make it easier for the taxpayer to prove those needs.[12] As the House Ways and Means Committee said, "Your committee believes it is necessary to retain the penalty tax on unreasonable accumulations as a safeguard against tax avoidance. However, several amendments have been adopted to minimize the threat to corporations accumulating funds for legitimate business purposes. . . ." H.R. Rep. No. 1337, 83d Cong., 2d Sess., 52 (1954).

As this brief summary indicates, the legislative history of the accumulated earnings tax demonstrates a continuing concern with the use of the corporate form to avoid income tax on a corporation's

9. Congress was urged to adopt a test of purpose similar to that proposed by respondent in the present case. See, e.g., Hearings Before the House Committee on Ways and Means Pertaining to the General Revision of the Internal Revenue Code, 83d Cong., 1st Sess., pt. 3, p. 2142 (1953).

11. Section 535(c) provided a credit for such accumulations.

12. Section 534 allowed the taxpayer to shift to the Commissioner in certain instances the burden of proving unreasonable accumulation. Section 537 included anticipated needs as reasonable needs of the business. In addition to those changes, §533(a) omitted the requirement that the taxpayer negate the existence of tax avoidance purpose by a "clear preponderance of the evidence," and substituted a "preponderance" test.

shareholders. Numerous methods were employed to prevent this practice, all of which proved unsatisfactory in one way or another. Two conclusions can be drawn from Congress' efforts. First, Congress recognized the tremendous difficulty of ascertaining the purpose of corporate accumulations. Second, it saw that accumulation was often necessary for legitimate and reasonable business purposes. It appears clear to us that the congressional response to these facts has been to emphasize unreasonable accumulation as the most significant factor in the incidence of the tax. The reasonableness of an accumulation, while subject to honest difference of opinion, is a much more objective inquiry, and is susceptible of more effective scrutiny, than are the vagaries of corporate motive.

Respondent would have us adopt a test that requires that tax avoidance purpose need be dominant, impelling, or controlling. It seems to us that such a test would exacerbate the problems that Congress was trying to avoid. Rarely is there one motive, or even one dominant motive, for corporate decisions. Numerous factors contribute to the action ultimately decided upon. Respondent's test would allow taxpayers to escape the tax when it is proved that at least one other motive was equal to tax avoidance. We doubt that such a determination can be made with any accuracy, and it is certainly one which will depend almost exclusively on the interested testimony of corporate management. Respondent's test would thus go a long way toward destroying the presumption that Congress created to meet this very problem. As Judge Learned Hand said of the much weaker presumption contained in the Revenue Act of 1921, §220, 42 Stat. 247, "[a] statute which stands on the footing of the participants' state of mind may need the support of presumption, indeed be practically unenforceable without it. . . ." United Business Corp. v. Commissioner, 62 F.2d 754, 755 (C.A. 2d Cir. 1933). And, "[t]he utility of . . . [that] presumption . . . is well nigh destroyed if . . . [it] is saddled with requirement of proof of 'the primary or dominant purpose' of the accumulation." Barrow Mfg. Co. v. Commissioner, 294 F.2d 79, 82 (C.A. 5th Cir. 1961), *cert. denied*, 369 U.S. 817 (1962).

The cases cited by respondent do not convince us to the contrary. For the most part, they lack detailed analysis of the precise problem. Perhaps the leading case for respondent's position is Young Motor Co. v. Commissioner, 281 F.2d 488 (1st Cir. 1960). That case relied in part upon the use of the article "the" instead of "a." We have previously rejected that argument. . . .

Finally, we cannot subscribe to respondent's suggestion that our holding would make purpose totally irrelevant. It still serves to isolate those cases in which tax avoidance motives did not contribute to the decision to accumulate. Obviously in such a case imposition of the tax would be futile. In addition, "purpose" means more than mere knowledge, undoubtedly present in nearly every case. It is still open to the taxpayer to show that even though knowledge of the tax consequences was present, that knowledge did not contribute to the decision to accumulate earnings.

Reversed and remanded.

[Dissenting opinion of Harlan, J., joined by Douglas and Stewart, JJ., is omitted.]

NOTES

1. The wording of §532(a) appears to assume an identity of purpose between a corporation and its shareholders. It might be expected, therefore, that the accumulated earnings tax would be imposed only on the closely held enterprise. However, in Golconda Mining Corp., 58 T.C. 139 (1972), the Commissioner imposed tax on a corporation having from 1,500 to 2,900 shareholders. A controlling group owned 12 to 17 percent of the corporation's stock. The Tax Court said the tax could be imposed on a publicly held company "where the fact of public ownership is neutralized by the manner in which the company has been managed. If the management group is dominated by a single large shareholder or a small group of large shareholders who exercise effective control over the dividend policy of the company or the company represents itself to prospective or existing shareholders as an investment company with the avowed purpose of accumulating its investment income, public ownership of the company becomes a less important factor in determining whether earnings and profits have been accumulated for the proscribed purpose." 58 T.C. at 158 (footnotes omitted). The Court of Appeals reversed, apparently disagreeing with the trial court's finding that the management group had "effective control" of the corporation, but holding that in any event the accumulated earnings tax can never be imposed on a publicly held company. 507 F.2d 594 (9th Cir. 1974).

The Tax Reform Act of 1984 added §532(c), which makes clear that the accumulated earnings tax *can* apply to publicly held corporations. In practice, of course, it may remain difficult to impute to a large, widely held enterprise the forbidden purpose required by §532(a).

2. When stockholders disagree over dividend policy, whose "view" counts? In Atlantic Properties, Inc. 62 T.C. 644 (1974), *aff'd*, 519 F.2d 1233 (1st Cir. 1975), a corporation's articles and bylaws required an 80-percent vote of the shareholders to permit virtually any corporate action. Seventy-five percent of the shareholders wanted to declare dividends, but the remaining 25 percent disagreed, advocating adoption of a plan of expansion. As a result, the corporation

could neither distribute, nor justify accumulation of, its earnings. The accumulated earnings tax was imposed.

3. What should be the result if a corporation accumulates income for *no* purpose? Cf. Starman Investment, Inc. v. United States, 534 F.2d 834 (9th Cir. 1976) (absence of corporate business purpose not dispositive; accumulated earnings tax not imposed where the trial court found no tax avoidance motive).

4. Suppose a corporation with accumulated earnings has no liquid assets or cash but is a creditor of its principal shareholders. The corporation could distribute a dividend by reducing the shareholders' indebtedness but does not do so because the shareholders would have insufficient cash to pay the tax on the dividend. Is the corporation's purpose within the proscription of §532? See Nemours Corp. v. Commissioner, 38 T.C. 585 (1962), *aff'd per curiam*, 325 F.2d 559 (3rd Cir. 1964), page 1097 infra.

5. In Hughes v. Commissioner, 90 T.C. 1 (1988), the taxpayer retained earnings to purchase the stock of a sister corporation for the purpose of preventing a takeover that taxpayer believed would have harmed both it and its sister corporation. The taxpayer convinced the Tax Court that it was not feasible to distribute earnings to shareholders and have them buy the stock. The Tax Court therefore held that the sister corporation's stock was a business-related asset and that petitioner's accumulation was reasonable.

ESTATE OF FRED F. LUCAS v. COMMISSIONER
71 T.C. 838 (1979)

. . . Shawnee, a corporation organized under the laws of the State of Tennessee, was in the coal brokerage business and had one major customer, Louisville Gas & Electric Co., Inc. (Louisville Gas).

At all times material to this case, 75 percent of Shawnee's outstanding stock was owned by [Fred] Lucas, and 25 percent was owned by [his wife] Dorothy; Lucas was president of Shawnee and Dorothy was vice president.

Shawnee employs the accrual method of accounting and has adopted a fiscal year ending April 30. . . .

Shawnee's contract with Louisville Gas was due to expire in 1973. At a special meeting of the board of directors held on February 11, 1971, Lucas, as chairman of Shawnee, suggested that, due to the "unsettled condition of the coal market" it would be advisable for Shawnee to diversify its business by investing in, developing, and selling real estate. During the years prior to this meeting, Lucas individually had owned and leased commercial real estate. He held some valuable, undeveloped land at an interstate interchange which he had inherited from his father and which he wanted Shawnee to develop.

After studying the possibility of investing in real estate, the board met again on April 15, 1971, and gave Lucas authority to seek appropriate commercial, industrial, or residential properties for purchase by Shawnee. As evidenced by the minutes of that meeting, Lucas was instructed "to inform the management to maintain sufficient capital in liquid form to enable the Company to take advantage of real estate investment opportunities as they become available."

On September 15, 1971, pursuant to unanimous consent of Shawnee's shareholders (Lucas and Dorothy), Shawnee's articles of incorporation were amended to permit the corporation to purchase, sell, or lease real estate. Shawnee then began to accumulate capital, but no actual investments were made prior to Lucas' death in 1973.

Shawnee's earnings and profits at the beginning of its fiscal years ended April 30, 1970, 1971, and 1972 were $156,785.29, $173,302.91, and $305,381.63, respectively. Earnings and profits for its fiscal year ended April 30, 1972, were $400,994.45. These earnings and profits were sufficient for the payment of dividends to Lucas in the amounts alleged by respondent. . . . Disregarding the constructive dividends in issue, Shawnee has never paid a dividend. . . .

For the calendar year 1972, any ordinary income of Lucas and Dorothy in addition to the income shown on their joint Federal income tax return would be subject to tax rates of no less than 58 percent. For its fiscal year ended April 30, 1972, Shawnee's income was subject to the maximum corporate tax rate of 48 percent.

In accordance with the provisions of section 534(b), on September 29, 1975, respondent sent Shawnee certified notification that a proposed notice of deficiency included the imposition of an accumulated earnings tax for the taxable year ended April 30, 1972. Pursuant to section 534(c), Shawnee submitted a statement to respondent setting forth the grounds on which it relied to establish that it had not permitted its earnings and profits to accumulate beyond the reasonable needs of the business.

. . . After determining that $18,112.48 of the earnings and profits for Shawnee's fiscal year ended April 30, 1972, was properly retained for reasonable business needs, respondent determined that Shawnee was liable for an accumulated earnings tax of $42,849.77 with respect to the remaining $139,869.52 which respondent determined to have been accumulated unnecessarily. No adjustment to taxable income was made pursuant to section 535(a) for the dividends paid deduction.

On September 13, 1977, a hearing was held pursuant to section 534 at which time it was determined that the burden of proof remained with petitioners on the issue of whether Shawnee is subject to the accumulated earnings tax for the taxable year ended April 30, 1972. . . .

The accumulated earnings tax is imposed upon a corporation which is formed or availed of for the purpose of avoiding income tax with respect to its shareholders by permitting earnings and profits to accumulate instead of being distributed. Secs. 531 and 532. The accumulation of earnings and profits beyond the reasonable needs of the business is determinative of the purpose to avoid income tax unless the corporation proves to the contrary by a preponderance of evidence. Sec. 533(a). A credit is provided, however, against "accumulated taxable income" in the amount of "such part-of the earnings and profits for the taxable year as are retained for the reasonable needs of the business," less the long-term capital gain deduction. Sec. 535(c). Shawnee's defenses against the penalty tax include its assertion that it planned to enter the real estate business and needed the funds to do so and its assertion that Shawnee's accumulations were justified (at least in part) by Federal "dividend guidelines" applicable in 1972.

In 1971, aware that Shawnee's brokerage contract with Louisville Gas (Shawnee's primary customer) was due to end in 1973, Shawnee's board of directors gave Lucas authority to seek commercial, industrial, or residential properties for purchase. The board further directed that Shawnee maintain sufficient liquid capital to enable it to take advantage of real estate opportunities.

By the end of fiscal year 1972, Shawnee's retained earnings and profits reached $400,994.45; however, no real estate investments had been made.

Respondent contends that Shawnee's reasonable business needs for the fiscal year ended April 30, 1972, required the retention of earnings and profits of only $18,112.48 and imposed the accumulated earnings tax upon what he found to be Shawnee's accumulated taxable income (as defined in section 535), in the amount of $139,869.52. Shawnee may avoid the imposed accumulated earnings tax to the extent it can prove that the $139,869.52 it retained in excess of the $18,112.48 respondent allowed was retained for its reasonable business needs.[10] Sec. 535(c).

Section 1.537-2(c), Income Tax Regs., lists indicia of unreasonable accumulations of earnings and profits. Included in that list is:

---

10. Respondent determined in the statutory notice that $18,112.48 was Shawnee's allowable limit of accumulations by using the *Bardahl* formula. See Bardahl Manufacturing Corp. v. Commissioner, 24 T.C.M. 1030 (1965). Shawnee argues that "accrued federal income tax" used in the formula must be adjusted upward to reflect additional tax if we hold against taxpayer on the constructive dividend issue, as we have. However, such adjustment was not a realistically foreseeable contingency and therefore should not be made. See Alma Piston Co. v. Commissioner, 35 T.C.M. 464, 483-485, *aff'd* 579 F.2d 1000 (6th Cir. 1978).

(4) Investments in properties, or securities which are unrelated to the activities of the business of the taxpayer corporation. . . .

Section 1.537-3(a) defines business of a corporation as including "any line of business which it may undertake." Thus it would be permissible under the regulations for a company in the coal brokerage business to enter an active business in the real estate field. See Atlantic Commerce & Shipping Co. v. Commissioner, 500 F.2d 937 (2d Cir. 1974), *aff'g* a Memorandum Opinion of this Court.

Section 537(a)(1) specifically provides that reasonable needs of the business include "reasonably anticipated needs of the business." Section 1.537-1(b)(1), Income Tax Regs., in pertinent part states:

> In order for a corporation to justify an accumulation of earnings and profits for reasonably anticipated future needs, there must be an indication that the future needs of the business require such accumulation, and the corporation must have specific, definite, and feasible plans for the use of such accumulation. . . . Where the future needs of the business are uncertain or vague, where the plans for the future use of an accumulation are not specific, definite, and feasible, or where the execution of such a plan is postponed indefinitely, an accumulation cannot be justified on the grounds of reasonably anticipated needs of the business.

In other words, a specially, definite, and feasible plan for the use of an accumulation of earnings and profits is required.

Plans to enter business have been considered to remain indefinite and vague even where a corporation examines various opportunities, consults attorneys and banks, retains investment brokers, and examines numerous investment proposals. Atlantic Commerce & Shipping Co. v. Commissioner, 500 F.2d at 940. It is not sufficient for the corporation to recognize a future problem and discuss possible and alternative resolutions; what is essential is a definite plan coupled with action taken toward its consummation. Dixie, Inc. v. Commissioner, 277 F.2d 526, 528 (2d Cir. 1960), *aff'g* 31 T.C. 415 (1958), *cert. denied*, 364 U.S. 827 (1960).

Likewise, formal resolutions of a corporation, standing alone, do not substantiate a corporation's objective to expand its business. American Metal Products Corp. v. Commissioner, 287 F.2d 860, 864 (8th Cir. 1961), *aff'g* 34 T.C. 89 (1960). Instead, "the intention claimed must be manifested by some contemporaneous course of conduct directed toward the claimed purpose." Smoot Sand & Gravel Corp. v. Commissioner, 241 F.2d 197, 202 (4th Cir. 1957), *aff'g in part* a Memorandum Opinion of this Court, *cert. denied*, 354 U.S. 922 (1957). . . .

We conclude that petitioners have not shown that any portion of Shawnee's accumulation in excess of the amount determined by respondent was for Shawnee's reasonable business needs insofar as those needs involve planned entry into a real estate business. The record herein as to the reasonable needs of Shawnee's business on this point is barren; it consists almost entirely of corporate minutes, change of the corporate charter, and testimony by Shawnee's secretary of the board of directors, Mr. F. Clay Bailey, Jr., with regard to Lucas' intent. Bailey testified that Lucas intended to have Shawnee develop a certain 4-acre parcel of land owned personally by Lucas. There is no evidence in the record, however, indicating a "contemporaneous course of conduct" by the corporation which verifies Lucas' alleged intent. Merely amending the corporate charter to allow Shawnee to buy, sell, and lease property cannot be construed as a "substantial active move toward implementation." Barrow Manufacturing Co. v. Commissioner, 294 F.2d 79, 81 (5th Cir. 1961).

In reaching our conclusion, we rely on Atlantic Commerce & Shipping Co. v. Commissioner, supra. In that case, the taxpayer consulted its attorneys and took active steps such as examining real estate proposals. Nevertheless, we held (and the Second Circuit affirmed) that the taxpayer's plans for diversification were indefinite and vague. In the instant case, petitioner's position is even weaker, since we have no evidence that Shawnee even explored various investment possibilities. Accordingly, Shawnee has not, by pointing to its real estate aspirations, met the requirements of section 537 or the regulations thereunder with regard to showing that an amount in excess of $18,112.48 of its earnings and profits for fiscal year 1972 was retained for reasonable business needs.

Furthermore, petitioners have not presented us with any evidence showing tax avoidance was not one of the motives for accumulation. United States v. Donruss Co., [page 1064 supra]; GPD, Inc. v. Commissioner, [page 1089 infra]. Shawnee never paid a dividend to its shareholders other than the constructive dividend at issue in this case. The evidence shows that if Shawnee had distributed its current earnings and profits its sole shareholders would have paid income tax at the rate of at least 58 percent on the amount distributed. See Atlantic Commerce & Shipping Co. v. Commissioner, 500 F.2d at 941. In light of the above, we conclude that, but for the impact of the dividend guidelines, discussed below, petitioner Shawnee Coal Co. has not met its burden of showing by a preponderance of evidence, that an amount in excess of $18,112.48 of its earnings and profits was retained for reasonable business needs. . . .

[In 1971 President Nixon imposed a wage and price freeze that led to federal guidelines limiting dividends. The court discusses these guidelines and concludes that they were applicable to Shawnee. — ED.]

We must, accordingly, determine the maximum amount Shawnee could have paid out of its income for the year ended April 30, 1972, without violating the "spirit" of the guidelines. We find that payment of aggregate dividends in excess of 25 percent of 1971 after-tax reported taxable income would have violated the spirit of the guidelines. We construe the guideline "net income" to mean reported after-tax income, i.e., taxable income reported on the return ($254,965.56) less tax paid with the return (including estimated tax payments) ($116,852.26), in this case $138,113.30. Twenty-five percent of $138,113.30 is $34,528.33, and we hold that this constitutes accumulated taxable income, subject to the penalty tax under section 531.

[Concurring and dissenting opinions omitted.]

NOTES

1. In Snow Mfg. Co., 86 T.C. 260 (1986), the court held that a general plan to expand the corporation's business was not enough to justify an accumulation. An expansion plan needs to be "specific, definite, and feasible."

2. Regulations §§1.533-1(a)(2) and 1.537-2(c) detail some factors that are considered by the Service to have evidentiary value in establishing the forbidden purpose:

(a) *Dealings between the corporation and its shareholders, or their relatives or friends, or other businesses owned by the shareholders.* Especially suspect are transactions that appear to be substitutes for dividends — corporate loans to shareholders or expenditures for the personal benefit of shareholders. But not all loans from a corporation to its shareholders are ultimately held to show a tax avoidance purpose. See, e.g., Bardahl Manufacturing Corp., 24 T.C.M. (CCH) 1030 (1965); Sterling Distributors, Inc. v. United States, 313 F.2d 803 (5th Cir. 1963).

(b) *Corporate investments in assets "unrelated" to the firm's business activities. Compare* Sandy Estate Co., 43 T.C. 361 (1964), *with* Cataphote Corp. of Mississippi v. United States, 535 F.2d 1225 (Ct. Cl. 1976), *and* Smith, Inc. v. Commissioner, 292 F.2d 470 (9th Cir., 1961), *cert. denied,* 368 U.S. 948.

(c) *Persistent failure by the corporation to distribute dividends in profitable years.* (Unreasonably small salaries paid to corporate employees who are also principal shareholders are closely analogous evidence.)

3. Section 533(a) makes "unreasonable accumulation" the touchstone in determining tax avoidance purpose. One widely cited approach for drawing the line between reasonable and unreasonable accumulations is the formula adopted in Bardahl Manufacturing Corp., 24 T.C.M. (CCH) 1030 (1965) (cited, for example, in *Lucas,*

at page 1074 supra, in footnote 10). Briefly, a *"Bardahl"* analysis proceeds as follows: "Reasonably anticipated needs" of the business are taken to be normal operating costs for a period determined by the length of a "single operating cycle" — the time the business takes to complete the cash–raw materials–inventory–accounts receivable–cash cycle. "Extraordinary cash reserves" for plant expansion, stockpiling scarce raw materials, expansion with new markets or products, or other extraordinary expenditures may also be deemed reasonable. (Compare Regulation §§1.537-2(b), 1.537-2(c)(5).) The corporation's net cash needs calculated in this way are compared with its net liquid assets at the close of the year in question. Liquid assets include cash and cash-equivalent items such as government securities. Investments that are deemed to be "unrelated" to the corporation's main line of business are also evaluated. The excess (if any) of liquid assets and unrelated investment over reasonable needs is an unreasonable accumulation. For a recent case in which the court applied the "Bardahl" formula, see Snow Mfg. Co., supra Note 1. See also W. L. Mead, Inc., 34 T.C.M. (CCH) 924 (1975), *aff'd by order,* 551 F.2d 121 (6th Cir. 1977).

Taxpayers have been imaginative in their attempts to justify accumulations. The *Bardahl* formula is at best an approximate guide, and its very terms (and similar terms appearing in the Regulations) beg the important questions: What types of investment are "unrelated" to a firm's main business activity? When do reserves for infrequent or uncertain contingencies become unreasonable? How are the reasonable needs of a corporation related to those of its shareholders? The cases and rulings in the following section illustrate how the courts and the Service have reacted to these and other problems.

III. UNREASONABLE ACCUMULATIONS

A. MERE HOLDING COMPANIES

REVENUE RULING 77-399
1977-2 C.B. 200

Advice has been requested whether, under the circumstances described below, the taxpayer, a so-called "tax-sheltered trust," is subject to the accumulated earnings tax provisions of section 531 of the Internal Revenue Code of 1954.

The taxpayer was organized under State law as a corporation. It is registered with the Securities and Exchange Commission as a management open-end investment company but does not qualify as a regulated investment company under section 851 of the Code. The taxpayer is not licensed to operate as a small business investment company under the Small Business Investment Act of 1958, 15 U.S.C. §§661-96 (1971). The taxpayer's investment objective is the accumulation of income from investing in securities that produce dividend income in order to avoid the imposition of any tax on the shareholders for as long as they own their shares. The taxpayer manages its assets so as to avoid the necessity of making annual taxable distributions. As a result, dividends and capital gains are accumulated and are added to the value of each shareholder account. An investment advisor has been retained by the taxpayer to conduct investment research and render service and management services.

During the taxable year 1975, the taxpayer had "accumulated taxable income" as defined in section 535 of the Code, and was not a corporation described in section 532(b). . . .

Section 533(a) of the Code states that for purposes of section 532, the fact that the earnings and profits of a corporation are permitted to accumulate beyond the reasonable needs of the business shall be determinative of the purpose to avoid the income tax with respect to shareholders, unless the corporation by the preponderance of the evidence shall prove to the contrary.

Section 533(b) of the Code states that the fact that any corporation is a mere holding or investment company shall be prima facie evidence of the purpose to avoid the income tax with respect to shareholders.

Section 1.533-1(c) of the Income Tax Regulations provides that a corporation having practically no activities except investing in property shall be considered a holding company under section 533(b) of the Code. Further, if the activities consist substantially of buying and selling stock, real estate, or other investment property so that the income is derived not only from the investment yield but also from profits on market fluctuations, the corporation shall be considered an investment company under section 533(b).

Rev. Rul. 75-305, 1975-2 C.B. 228, sets forth the position of the Service that there is no legal impediment in applying, in an appropriate case, the accumulated earnings tax to a publicly held corporation. Therein, it is stated that the Service will not follow the decision of the United States Court of Appeals, holding to the contrary, in the case of Golconda Mining Corp., 507 F.2d 594 (9th Cir. 1974), *reversing* 58 T.C. 139 and 58 T.C. 736 (1972).

In the instant situation, the taxpayer's activities consist primarily of buying and selling common and preferred stocks and it derived income from both investment yield and market fluctuations. It was organized for the purpose of accumulating investment proceeds without distributing such proceeds to its shareholders so that the shareholders would not incur any immediate tax liability. Instead of distributing the dividends and capital gains each year, the taxpayer accumulates such amounts and adds them to the value of each shareholder account.

Accordingly, the taxpayer is a mere holding or investment company as defined in section 533(b) of the Code. The taxpayer is formed and availed of for the purpose described in section 532(a) and thus is subject to the accumulated earnings tax provisions of section 531.

B. UNRELATED INVESTMENTS

IVAN ALLEN CO. v. UNITED STATES
422 U.S. 617 (1975)

Mr. Justice BLACKMUN delivered the opinion of the Court. . . . The issue here is whether, in determining the application of §533(a), listed and readily marketable securities owned by the corporation and purchased out of its earnings and profits, are to be taken into account at their cost to the corporation or at their net liquidation value, that is, fair market value less the expenses of, and taxes resulting from, their conversion into cash.

I

The pertinent facts are admitted by the pleadings or are stipulated: The petitioner, Ivan Allen Company (the taxpayer), is a Georgia corporation incorporated in 1902 and actively engaged in the business of selling office furniture, equipment, and supplies in the metropolitan Atlanta area. It files its federal income tax returns on the accrual basis and for the fiscal year ended June 30.

For its fiscal years 1965 and 1966, the taxpayer paid in due course the federal corporation income taxes shown on its returns as filed. Taxable income so reported was $341,045.82 for 1965 and $629,512.19 for 1966. During fiscal 1965 the taxpayer paid dividends consisting of cash in the amount of $48,945.30 and 870 shares of Xerox Corporation common that had been carried on its books at a cost of $6,564.34. During fiscal 1966 the taxpayer paid cash dividends of $50,267.49; it also declared a 10% stock dividend. . . . The dividends paid were substantially less than taxable income less federal income taxes for those years.

Throughout fiscal 1965 and 1966, the taxpayer owned various listed and unlisted marketable securities. Prominent among these were listed shares of common stock and listed convertible debentures of Xerox Corporation that, in prior years, had been purchased out of earnings and profits. Specifically, on June 30, 1965, the corporation owned 11,140 shares of Xerox common, with a cost of $116,701 and a then fair market value of $1,573,525, and $30,600 Xerox convertible debentures, with a cost to it of $30,625 and a then fair market value of $48,424. On June 30, 1966, the corporation owned 10,090 shares of Xerox common, with a cost of $102,479 and a then fair market value of $2,479,617, and the same $30,600 convertible debentures, with their cost of $30,625 and a then fair market value of $69,768. . . .

According to its returns as filed, the taxpayer's undistributed earnings as of June 30, 1965, and June 30, 1966, were $2,200,184.77 and $2,360,146.52, respectively. . . . The taxpayer points out that the marketable portfolio assets represented an investment, as measured by cost, of less than 7% of its undistributed earnings and of less than 5% of its total assets. . . .

It is also apparent, however, that the Xerox debentures and common shares had proved to be an extraordinarily profitable investment, although, of course, because these securities continued to be retained, the gains thereon were unrealized for federal income tax purposes. . . .

Throughout fiscal 1965 and 1966 the taxpayer's two major shareholders, Ivan Allen, Sr., and Ivan Allen, Jr., respectively owned 31.20% and 45.46% of the taxpayer's outstanding voting stock. . . .

Following an examination of the taxpayer's federal income tax returns for fiscal 1965 and 1966, the Commissioner of Internal Revenue determined that the taxpayer had permitted its earnings and profits for each of those years to accumulate beyond the reasonable and reasonably anticipated needs of its business, and that one of the purposes of the accumulation for each year was to avoid income tax with respect to its shareholders. . . .

It is agreed that the taxpayer had reasonable business needs for operating capital amounting to $1,198,309 and $1,455,222 at the close of fiscal 1965 and fiscal 1966, respectively. . . . It is stipulated, in particular, that if the taxpayer's marketable securities are to be taken into account at *cost*, its net liquid assets (current assets less current liabilities), at the end of each of those taxable years, and fully available for use in its business, were then exactly equal to its reasonable business needs for operating capital. . . . It is still further stipulated, however, that if the taxpayer's marketable securities are to be taken into account at *fair market value* (less the cost of converting them into cash), as of the ends of those fiscal years,[5] the taxpayer's

---

5. It is stipulated that the cost of converting the taxpayer's marketable securities into cash would have been the sum of a maximum of 6% of the fair market value of the securities (payable as a brokerage commission) and a maximum of 25% of such amount of the fair market value as exceeds the sum of the brokerage commission and the cost of the securities (payable as capital gains taxes). . . .

net liquid assets would then be $2,235,029 and $3,152,009, respectively. . . . From this it would follow that the earnings and profits of the two taxable years *had* been permitted to accumulate beyond the taxpayer's reasonable and reasonably anticipated business needs. Then, if those accumulations had been for "the purpose of avoiding the income tax with respect to its shareholders," under §532(a), accumulated earnings taxes would be incurred. . . .

The District Court held that the taxpayer's readily marketable securities were to be taken into account at cost. . . . The court observed:

> Corporate taxpayers should not be penalized for wise investments; they should be allowed to maximize their capital gains tax advantages in accordance with internal business policies and stock market conditions rather than being forced to sell securities which may have a high value on an arbitrarily selected date merely because the unrealized fair market value of the securities on that date would trigger the accumulated earnings tax. . . . (Footnote omitted.)

The United States Court of Appeals for the Fifth Circuit reversed. . . . It observed:

> [T]he securities involved in the case at bar are of such a highly liquid character as to be readily available for business needs that might arise. Thus the appreciated value of these securities should be taken into account when determining whether the corporation has accumulated profits in excess of reasonable business needs. . . .
>
> This decision does not force the corporation to liquidate these securities at any time when a sale would be financially unwise, but only compels the corporation to comply with the proscriptions of the Code and refrain from accumulating excessive earnings and profits. . . .

The case was remanded, as the parties had agreed, . . . "for the additional factual determination [under §532(a)] of whether one purpose for the accumulation was to avoid income tax on behalf of the shareholders." . . .

Because this conclusion was claimed by the taxpayer to conflict in principle with American Trading & Production Corp. v. United States, 362 F. Supp. 801 (Md. 1972), *aff'd without published opinion,* 474 F.2d 1341 (C.A. 4 1973), and because of the importance of the issue in the administration of the accumulated earnings tax, we granted certiorari. . . .

II

Under our system of income taxation, corporate earnings are subject to tax at two levels. First, there is the tax imposed upon the income of the corporation. Second, when the corporation by way of a dividend, distributes its earnings to its shareholders, the distribution is subject to the tax imposed upon the income of the shareholders. Because of the disparity between the corporate tax rates and the higher gradations of the rates on individuals, a corporation may be utilized to reduce significantly its shareholders' overall tax liability by accumulating earnings beyond the reasonable needs of the business. Without some method to force the distribution of unneeded corporate earnings, a controlling shareholder would be able to postpone the full impact of income taxes on his share of the corporation's earnings in excess of its needs. See B. Bittker & J. Eustice, Federal Income Taxation of Corporations and Shareholders ¶8.01 (3d ed. 1971); B. Wolfman, Federal Income Taxation of Business Enterprise 864 (1971).

In order to foreclose this possibility of using the corporation as a means of avoiding the income tax on dividends to the shareholders, every Revenue Act since the adoption of the Sixteenth Amendment in 1913 has imposed a tax upon unnecessary accumulations of corporate earnings effected for the purpose of insulating shareholders. . . .

It is to be noted that the focus and impositions of the accumulated earnings tax are upon "accumulated taxable income," §531. This is defined in §535(b) to mean the corporation's "taxable income," as adjusted. The adjustments consist of the various items described in §535(b), including federal income tax, the deduction for dividends paid, defined in §561, and the accumulated earnings credit defined in §535(c). The adjustments prescribed by §§535(a) and (b) are designed generally to assure that a corporation's "accumulated taxable income" reflects more accurately than "taxable income" the amount actually available to the corporation for business purposes. This explains the deductions for dividends paid and for federal income taxes; neither of these enters into the computation of taxable income. Obviously, dividends paid and federal income taxes deplete corporate resources and must be recognized if the corporation's economic condition is to be properly perceived. Conversely, §535(b)(3) disallows, for example, the deduction, available to a corporation for income tax purposes under §243, on account of dividends received; dividends received are freely available for use in the corporation's business.

The purport of the accumulated earnings tax structure established by §§531-537, therefore, is to determine the corporation's true economic condition before its liability for tax upon "accumulated taxable income" is determined. The tax, although a penalty and therefore to be strictly construed, . . . is directed at economic reality.

It is important to emphasize that we are concerned here with a tax on "accumulated taxable income," §531, and that the tax attaches only when a corporation has permitted "earnings and profits to accumulate instead of being divided or distributed," §532(a). What is essential is that there be "income" and "earnings and profits." This at once eliminates, from the measure of the tax itself, any unrealized appreciation in the value of the taxpayer's portfolio securities over cost, for any such unrealized appreciation does not enter into the computation of the corporation's "income" and "earnings and profits."

The corporation's readily marketable portfolio securities and their unrealized appreciation, nonetheless, are of profound importance in making the entirely discrete determination whether the corporation has permitted what, concededly, are earnings and profits to accumulate beyond its reasonable business needs. If the securities, as here, are readily available as liquid assets, then the recognized earnings and profits that have been accumulated may well have been unnecessarily accumulated, so far as the reasonable needs of the business are concerned. On the other hand, if those portfolio securities are not liquid and are not readily available for the needs of the business, the accumulation of earnings and profits may be viewed in a different light. Upon this analysis, not only is such accumulation as has taken place important, but the liquidity otherwise available to the corporation is highly significant. In any event — and we repeat — the tax is directed at the accumulated taxable income and at earnings and profits. The tax itself is not directed at the unrealized appreciation of the liquid assets in the securities portfolio. The latter becomes important only in measuring reasonableness of accumulation of the earnings and profits that otherwise independently exist. What we look at, then, in order to determine its reasonableness or unreasonableness, in the light of the needs of the business, is any failure on the part of the corporation to distribute the earnings and profits it has.

Accumulation beyond the reasonable needs of the business, by the language of §533(a), is "determinative of the purpose" to avoid tax with respect to shareholders unless the corporation proves the contrary by a preponderance of the evidence. The burden of proof, thus, is on the taxpayer. A rebuttable presumption is statutorily imposed. To be sure, we deal here, in a sense, with a state of mind. But it has been said that the statute, without the support of the presumption, would "be practically unenforceable. . . ." United Business Corp. v. Commissioner, 62 F.2d 754, 755 (C.A. 2), *cert. denied,* 290 U.S. 635 . . . (1933). What is required, then, is a comparison of accumulated earnings and profits with "the reasonable needs of the business." Business *needs* are critical. And need, plainly, to use mathematical terminology, is a function of a corporation's liquidity, that is, the amount of idle current assets at its disposal. The question, therefore, is not how much capital of all sorts, but how much in the way of quick or liquid assets, it is reasonable to keep on hand for the business. . . .

The taxpayer itself recognizes, and accepts, the liquidity concept as a basic factor, for it "has agreed that the full amount of its realized earnings invested in its liquid assets — their cost — should be taken into account in determining the applicability of section 533(a)." . . . It concedes that if this were not so, "the tax could be avoided by any form of investment of earnings and profits." . . . But the taxpayer would stop at the point of cost and, when it does so, is compelled to compare earnings and profits — not the amount of readily available liquid assets, net — with reasonable business needs.

We disagree with the taxpayer and conclude that cost is not the stopping point; that the application of the accumulated earnings tax, in a given case, may well depend on whether the corporation has available readily marketable portfolio securities; and that the proper measure of those securities, for purposes of the tax, is their net realizable value. Cost of the marketable securities on the assets side of the corporation's balance sheet would appear to be largely an irrelevant gauge of the taxpayer's true financial condition. Certainly, a lender would not evaluate a potential borrower's marketable securities at cost. Realistic financial condition is the focus of the lender's inquiry. It also must be the focus of the Commissioner's inquiry in determining the applicability of the accumulated earnings tax.[11]

This taxpayer's securities, being liquid and readily marketable, clearly were available for the business needs of the corporation, and their fair market value, net, was such that, according to the stipulation, the taxpayer's undistributed earnings and profits for the two fiscal years in question were permitted to accumulate beyond the reasonable and reasonably anticipated needs of the business.

III

Bearing directly upon the issue before us is Helvering v. National Grocery Co., 304 U.S. 282 . . . (1938). There the fact situation was the reverse of the present case inasmuch as that taxpayer corporation had unrealized *losses* in the value of marketable securities it was continuing to hold. After the Court upheld the accumulated earnings tax against constitutional attack, . . . it observed: "Depreciation in any of the assets is evidence to be considered by the Commissioner and the Board [of Tax Appeals] in determining the issue of fact whether the accumulation of profits was in excess of the reasonable needs of

11. We see little force in any observation that our emphasis on liquid assets means that a corporate taxpayer may avoid the accumulated earnings tax by merely investing in nonliquid assets. If such a step, in a given case, amounted to willful evasion of the accumulated earnings tax, it would be subject to criminal penalties. . . .

the business." . . . It went on to hold, however, that such depreciation "does not, as matter of law, preclude a finding that the accumulation of the year's profits was in excess of the reasonable needs of the business." . . . It focused on bonds and stocks held by the corporation, described them as in no way related to the business, and concluded that "there was no need of accumulating any part of the year's earnings for the purpose of financing the business." . . . That language forecloses the present taxpayer's case.

The precedent of *National Grocery* has been applied in accumulated earnings tax cases, with courts taking into account the fair market value of liquid, appreciated securities. . . .

American Trading & Production Corp. v. United States, . . . which the taxpayer continues to assert is in conflict with the present case, deserves mention. The taxpayer there had accumulated earnings and profits of something less than $10 million. Its anticipated business needs were about $12 million. But it owned stocks, primarily oil shares, having a total cost of $5,593,319 and an aggregate current market value in excess of $100 million. The District Court excluded these stocks in making its determination whether earnings had accumulated in excess of reasonable business needs. It did so on several grounds: that the shares constituted "original capital," a term the court used in the sense that the stocks "were properly held and retained as an integral part of its business and were utilized . . . as a base for borrowings for the needs of other parts of its business"; that the statute was not intended to require the conversion of assets of that kind into cash in order to meet business needs, even though that capital "has explosively increased in value," id., at 808; and that "there was substantial evidence" that the stocks "were not readily saleable." . . .

Whatever may be the merit or demerit of the other grounds asserted by the District Court in *American Trading* — and we express no view thereon — we are satisfied that the court's determination as to the absence of ready salability under all the circumstances, provides a sufficient point of distinction of that case from this one, so that it provides meager, if any, contrary precedent of substance to our conclusion here.

IV

The arguments advanced by the taxpayer do not persuade us:

1. The taxpayer, of course, quite correctly insists that unrealized appreciation of portfolio securities does not enter into the determination of "earnings and profits," within the meaning of §533(a). . . . It does not follow, however, that unrealized appreciation is never to be taken into account for purposes of the accumulated earnings tax. . . .

2. We see nothing in the "realization of income" concept of Eisner v. Macomber, . . . that has significance for the issue presently under consideration. . . . We note again, however, that the accumulated earnings tax is not on unrealized appreciation of the portfolio securities. It rests upon, and only upon, the corporation's current taxable income adjusted to constitute "accumulated taxable income."

3. The taxpayer also argues that the effect of the Court of Appeals decision is to force the taxpayer to convert its appreciated assets in order to meet its business needs. It suggests that management should be entitled to finance business needs without resorting to unrealized appreciation. The argument, plainly, goes too far. On the taxpayer's own theory that marketable securities may be taken into account at their cost, a situation easily may be imagined where some conversion into cash becomes necessary, if the corporation is to avoid the accumulated earnings tax.

That our decision does not interfere with corporate management's exercise of sound business judgment, and that it does not amount to a dictation to management as to when appreciated assets are to be liquidated, was aptly answered by the Court of Appeals:

> This decision does not force the corporation to liquidate these securities at any time when a sale would be financially unwise, but only compels the corporation to comply with the proscriptions of the Code and refrain from accumulating excessive earnings and profits. That taxpayer, as a consequence of its own sound judgment in making profitable investments, must sell, exchange or distribute to the shareholders assets in order to avoid an excessive accumulation of earnings and thus comply with the Code's requirements is no justification for precluding its application. . . .

We might add that the existence of the Code's provisions for the accumulated earnings tax, of course, will affect management's decision. So, too, does the very existence of the corporate income tax itself. In this respect, the one is no more offensive than the other. Astute management in these tax-conscious days is not that helpless, and shrinkage, upon liquidation, of one-fourth of the appreciation hardly equates with loss. Such business decision as is necessitated was expressly intended by the Congress. All that is required is the disgorging, at the most, of the taxable year's "accumulated taxable income."

4. It is no answer to suggest that our decision here may conflict with standard accounting practice. The Court has not hesitated to apply congressional policy underlying a revenue statute even when it does conflict with an established accounting practice. . . . It is of some interest that the taxpayer itself, for the tax years under consideration, reflected the market value as well as the cost of its marketable securities on its balance sheets. . . . This appears to be in line with presently accepted practice. . . .

The judgment of the Court of Appeals is affirmed.
[Dissenting opinion omitted.]

NOTE

For a rejection of the "original capital" theory of the *American Trading* case, see D.G. Matthews & Son, Inc. v. United States, 448 F. Supp. 948 (E.D.N.C. 1977).

C. DEPRECIATION RESERVES

REVENUE RULING 67-64
1967-1 C.B. 150

Advice has been requested whether, in justifying the reasonable needs of its business pursuant to section 537 of the Internal Revenue Code of 1954, a corporation may include a fund equal to its depreciation reserves escalated for the economic factor of increased replacement costs.

A corporation is engaged in the manufacturing business and has operated successfully since its inception. Over the years, the corporation has expanded its plant facilities and has made replacements of machinery and equipment. The expenditures with respect to such expansion and replacements were normal for a successful business. The corporation contends that, in justifying the reasonable needs of its business, it should be permitted to include a fund equal to its depreciation reserves escalated for the economic factor of increased costs of replacement regardless of whether it has any specific or definite plans to use the funds in its business.

Section 537 of the Code provides that the term "reasonable needs of the business" includes the reasonably anticipated needs of the business. Section 1.537-1(b) of the Income Tax Regulations provides that in order for a corporation to justify an accumulation of earnings and profits for reasonably anticipated future needs, there must be an indication that the future needs of the business require such accumulation, *and the corporation must have specific, definite, and feasible plans for the use of such accumulation.* Where the future needs of the business are uncertain or vague, where the plans for the future use of an accumulation are not specific, definite, and feasible, or where execution of such a plan is postponed indefinitely, an accumulation cannot be justified on the grounds of reasonably anticipated needs of the business. These regulations express the legislative intent as stated in Senate Report 1622, 83d Congress, 2d Session, 69, and House Report 1337, 83d Congress, 2d Session, A172-A173.

Although the reserve for depreciation itself may be considered and given appropriate weight as a part of the facts and circumstances in considering the reasonable needs of the business, the concept that a non-cash deduction for depreciation based on historic costs requires the setting aside for an indefinite period a cash fund adjusted for economic fluctuations in order to provide for total replacement of plant assets is not within the meaning of the term "reasonable needs of the business."

Accordingly, a corporation may not include a fund equal to its depreciation reserves escalated for the economic factor of increased replacement costs in justifying the reasonable needs of its business pursuant to section 537 of the Code. However, the reserve for depreciation itself may be considered and given appropriate weight as a part of the facts and circumstances in each case.

D. STOCK REDEMPTIONS

GPD, INC. v. COMMISSIONER
508 F.2d 1076 (6th Cir. 1974)

. . . GPD, Inc. (taxpayer) was incorporated in February 1954 under the law of Michigan and has its principal place of business in that State. Continuously since its organization it has been engaged in the sale and distribution of automobile parts in Michigan and Ohio. Taxpayer holds a franchise as exclusive distributor of all Ford "Genuine Parts," except engines, in the Michigan-Ohio area. The parts which taxpayer distributed to its customers, most of whom are Ford automobile dealers, come from the Ford Motor Co. and the Alma Piston Co.

Since taxpayer's incorporation its president and sole or principal shareholder has been Emmet E. Tracy (Tracy), who has never received compensation for services as an officer of the taxpayer corporation. . . .

Taxpayer's net income before taxes for the years 1959 through 1968 ranged from a low of $159,879 for 1959 to highs of $496,636 for 1967 and $596,609 for 1968. Its after-tax net income for the same years ranged from a low of $82,343 for 1959 to highs of $248,946 for 1967 and $278,783 for 1968. It paid no dividends until 1967, when it declared cash dividends of $46,300. In 1968, it declared a cash dividend of $67,440. On December 23, 1968, its Board of Directors voted Tracy, then sole shareholder, a stock dividend of

5,000 shares of one-dollar par seven-dollar cumulative preferred stock.

[In 1959] Tracy, then taxpayer's sole shareholder, . . . made the first of a series of gifts of some of the shares he owned to exempt charities and made one or more further gifts in each of the years 1960 to 1967. These gifts were mostly of taxpayer's common stock, then the only class of stock outstanding, and Tracy took deductions based upon the book value of the shares donated. The gifts, made principally to Catholic Foreign Mission, St. Mary's Church, Jesuit Seminary Guild and Guest House, Inc., aggregated 7,190 shares during the years 1959 through 1967. Tracy took deductions for the gifts in the aggregate amount of $728,325.

In 1961, 1964, 1966 and 1968, taxpayer redeemed the shares that in prior years had been donated to the exempt charities, paying out during these years a total amount of $900,237 in redemption of the 7,190 shares. Of this amount, $434,460 was paid out in 1968 in redemption of the 1,820 shares then outstanding in the hands of the charitable donees. We re-emphasize that at the end of 1968, all the shares which Tracy had given to the charities had been redeemed, and he again was taxpayer's sole shareholder.

Taxpayer's accumulated earnings and profits (without giving effect to the 1968 redemption) as found by the Tax Court was as follows:

December 31, 1966	$1,379,749.18
December 31, 1967	1,582,396.05
December 31, 1968	1,793,739.08

. . . When the 1968 redemption is taken into account, the taxpayer's earnings and profits as of December 31, 1968, reflect a net decrease as compared to 1967.

The joint federal income tax returns filed by Tracy and his wife for 1967 and 1968 reported taxable income of $290,326.46 and $283,954.85, respectively, and tax liability of $174,208 and $182,478, respectively. If taxpayer's after tax income for 1967 and 1968 had been distributed in its entirety the income tax liability of Tracy and his wife would have increased to $248,098.82 for 1967 and to $317,688.52 for 1968.

Pursuant to §534(b) . . . notification was given taxpayer on November 10, 1970, that the Commissioner proposed a notice of deficiency for 1967 and 1968, including an amount with respect to the tax on accumulated earnings imposed by §531. Taxpayer did not file a responding statement to challenge the proposed deficiency, as permitted by §534(c). . . .

The Tax Court rejected taxpayer's contentions that it had accumulated earnings for the reasonable needs of its business and, accordingly, upheld the Commissioner's assessed deficiency for 1967. . . . With respect to 1968, however, the Tax Court accepted taxpayer's argument that it had no increase in its total earnings and profits for that year because of its stock redemption, and that the Commissioner erred in assessing an accumulated earnings tax against it for that year. . . .

II. . . . The Tax Court interpreted §532 as requiring an accumulation of earnings and profits in the taxable year as a condition precedent to the imposition of the accumulated earnings tax. Since there was no accumulation during 1968, the court held the accumulated earnings tax to be improper for that year. . . .

The Commissioner contends now, as he did in the Tax Court, that the statute does not require an accumulation of earnings and profits for the year in which the tax is imposed. He asserts that the phrase "permitting earnings and profits to accumulate instead of being divided or distributed" refers "not only to current profits and earnings . . . but, rather, to the entire amount of the corporation's undistributed profits and earnings." The Commissioner argues that this interpretation is consistent with the purpose behind the statute, the statutory scheme and the legislative history of the accumulated-earnings tax provisions.

III. In analyzing the accumulated earnings tax provisions, it is important to note that "taxable income" and "earnings and profits" are separate and distinct statutory terms. Taxable income serves as a measure of the income tax and related taxes assessed against a particular taxpayer, while earnings and profits reflect a corporation's capacity to pass along tax consequences to its shareholders through distributions to them. . . .

This distinction has been recognized by the Commissioner. In Revenue Ruling 70-497, 1970-2 C.B. 128, the Commissioner stated that the tax exempt interest income was not includible in accumulated taxable income as defined in §535, but was to be included in earnings and profits for the purpose of determining whether they have been accumulated beyond the reasonable needs of the taxpayer's business. . . .

[The Court's discussion of the legislative history of the accumulated earnings tax is omitted.]

We are of the view that the legislative history and the statutory schemes of the Revenue Acts from 1913 to the present show that Congress did not intend to require an accumulation of "earnings and profits" in the taxable year as a condition precedent to imposition of the accumulated earnings tax. This is evidenced by repeated efforts on the part of the Congress in amending the accumulated earnings tax provisions so as to make it more difficult to avoid the tax and by the strong congressional policy of encouraging pro rata distributions as a means of avoiding or lessening the tax.

IV. The Internal Revenue Code is explicit in providing that a non-pro rata redemption does not reduce the "accumulated taxable income," and taxpayer has not disputed this point. There is no question that taxpayer had substantial amounts of income taxable under §531 for 1968. Through the adjustments to taxable income in §535 of the 1954 Code, Congress has effectuated its opposition of excess accumulations of earnings and profits by corporations to save their shareholders from the income tax and has made the resulting amount, i.e., accumulated taxable income, determinative of the issue whether or not there are current earnings and profits that are being used to avoid the tax. To hold as the Tax Court did, that an accumulation of earnings and profits during the tax year is required, would mean that Congress has frustrated the purpose behind the surtax by allowing non-pro rata redemptions to reduce current earnings and profits to such an extent that the corporation would not be subject to the surtax, while at the same time providing that the same redemptions have no effect on the amount of the surtax. We are unwilling to construe the statute as intending such an inconsistency. . . .

Section 532(a) does not of its own terms require an accumulation of current earnings and profits, nor does it require any particular amount of accumulation. The section refers to the proscribed activity of permitting earnings and profits to accumulate, and is unlike §531 which speaks to the accumulated taxable income for the taxable year. Indeed, if the corporation were *formed* for the proscribed purpose of avoiding the income tax on its shareholders, there would be no need for an annual redetermination such as would be required if the corporation were being *availed of* for the proscribed purpose. Had Congress intended a limitation in the scope of the term "permitting earnings and profits to accumulate instead of being divided or distributed," it could have so specified as it did in §535(c)(1)(A), which allows an accumulated earnings credit against taxable income for "an amount equal to such part of the *earnings and profits for the taxable year* as are retained for the reasonable needs of the business."

Also, with respect to the accumulated earnings credit, the Senate Report specifically states that the amount of earnings and profits for a taxable year that may be retained for the reasonable needs of the business is determined by taking into account the amount of earnings and profits that have been accumulated in prior years. . . . If past accumulations are relevant to the propriety of current accumulations, we do not understand how they could be irrelevant in determining that the corporation was availed of for the proscribed purpose. We hold that past accumulations are highly relevant in effecting the congressional intent. . . .

VI. In the case at bar, the repetitive cycles of gifts of stock to exempt charities, followed in a subsequent year by redemptions of the donated stock, demonstrate a purpose of avoiding income taxes owed by Tracy. The charitable deductions enhanced by the retention of earnings in the corporation, provided shelters against other taxable income, and the periodic redemptions of the donated stock permitted Tracy, the controlling shareholder, to retain control over the taxpayer corporation. . . .

Since the Tax Court determined that taxpayer was availed of for the proscribed purpose of avoiding the income tax on its shareholders in 1967 and because the redemption of the donated stock in 1968 was a necessary feature of the method of avoiding the tax, it would appear that taxpayer was availed of for the proscribed purpose during 1968, the year of the redemption. The issues of whether accumulations are beyond the reasonable needs of the business and whether a corporation has been availed of for the proscribed purpose are, however, questions of fact. . . . Because the Tax Court's decision with respect to the 1968 accumulated earnings tax was based on an erroneous interpretation of §532(a), the case is reversed and remanded for further proceedings with respect to the 1968 assessment not inconsistent with this opinion. . . .

NOTES

In Lamark Shipping Agency, Inc., 42 T.C.M. (CCH) 38 (1981), the Tax Court did not decide the issue anew but did comment tersely that it was "not constrained" to follow *GPD* in cases appealable to other circuits. See GPD, Inc. v. Commissioner: Closing a Loophole in the Accumulated Earnings Tax, 70 Nw. U.L. Rev. 651 (1975); cf. Doernberg, The Accumulated Earnings Tax: The Relationship Between Earnings and Profits and Accumulated Taxable Income in a Redemption Transaction, 34 U. Fla. L. Rev. 715 (1982) (criticizing *GPD*).

PELTON STEEL CASTING CO. v. COMMISSIONER
251 F.2d 278 (7th Cir. 1958), *cert. denied,* 356 U.S. 958 (1958)

Before Finnegan, Schnackenberg and Parkinson, Circuit Judges.

FINNEGAN, Circuit Judge. Section [531] . . . imposed a surtax on corporations improperly accumulating surplus. The respondent Commissioner decided that Pelton Steel Casting Co., petitioner, was availed of in 1946 for the purpose of preventing the imposition of such surtax upon its shareholders by accumulating the corporate earnings and profits instead of dividing or distributing them. That determination of the Commissioner covered fiscal years ending November 30, 1945 and November 30, 1946; penalty tax for 1945 was $12,214.22 and for 1946, $69,746.66. The Commissioner conceded there was no deficiency for the year 1945. We have before us for review the Tax Court's lengthy opinion, reported as Pelton Steel Casting Co. v. Commissioner of Internal Revenue, 1957, 28 T.C. 153, approving the 1946 penalty tax, and resting in considerable part on stipulated facts. Detailing of the operative facts is obviated by their presentation in the opinion issued by the Tax Court, and for that reason we merely describe the factual situation.

During its fiscal year 1946 Pelton had earnings and profits of $209,731.58 and its common stock was held, in these proportions, by: Ehne — 60%, Fawick — 20%, and Slichter — 20%. When Ehne and Fawick informed Slichter of their mutual desire to sell Pelton, Slichter decided to avert an outside sale. After Slichter consulted a banker and lawyer the three stockholders agreed on November 11, 1946, that the corporation would buy up and redeem 80% of the common stock held by Ehne and Fawick at their price of $1,200,000 (this being 80% of $1,500,000, the selling price of the Pelton assets when offered to outsiders). Under the plan Ehne and Fawick were to receive $800,000 in cash and $400,000 in Pelton preferred stock. That cash flowed from two sources: (1) $300,000 was Pelton's own money and, (2) $500,000 was borrowed by Pelton on a 10-year agreement, dated April 17, 1947, under which an insurance company covered $300,000 to mature in the last six years, and Pelton's bank covered $200,000 to mature during the first four years. This loan, secured by a mortgage on Pelton's plant, was made May 31, 1947, the date when Slichter became the sole common stockholder as the result of the sale-redemption arrangement of 80% of the outstanding common stock held by Ehne and Fawick. Ehne's preferred stock, newly issued to him under the above plan, was immediately purchased by Slichter who gave Ehne a 20-year installment note.

Financiers planning Pelton's purchase of the common stock advised against declaration and payment of dividends during 1946. Again, to repeat for emphasis, it is the Tax Court's opinion which contains recitals of pertinent facts and reproduces the relevant financial statements. On the other hand, this record clearly establishes Pelton as a closely held corporation whose three director-stockholders did not receive 1946 dividends.

An interesting sidelight here comes from the Tax Court opinion:

> The respective amounts of the personal income tax actually paid by A. J. Ehne for 1946 and the estimated amount of tax for which he would have been liable had all of the 1946 earnings and profits ($209,731.58) been distributed in the form of a dividend

in that year and had his 60 per cent thereof (some $126,000) in addition to his other income for that year ($47,063.93, per his tax return) been taxed to him at ordinary income rates, are as follows:

Actual	Estimated	Estimated difference
$22,786.73	$124,955.96	$102,169.23

The tax paid by A. J. Ehne in 1947 on the $603,571 gain realized under the plan on the retirement of his interest in petitioner under the elective alternative tax rates in effect was approximately $150,000. . . .

The inference, of course, is that instead of dividing all or a portion of the 1946 earnings and profits, totaling $209,731.58, Ehne, Fawick and Slichter countenanced that accumulation and then plowed these earnings into redemption of the common stock. Such an inference is within respectable bounds of reasoning on the evidence before us. On the other hand, Pelton strives to cancel out that inference, and indeed any violation of §[531] by pressing on us, as it did the Tax Court, Slichter's undiminished efforts to preserve Pelton's independent existence. In short, the evidence shows that Slichter envisaged Ehne and Fawick selling Pelton to a corporate cannibal; consequently, complete control through the reorganization plan, already described, of Pelton by Slichter loomed up as the only salvation. That reorganization was rejected by the Tax Court on the grounds that it was not promoted for a valid business purpose.

Clearly the batch of ideas sponsored on Pelton's behalf fails in hurdling this passage in §[531] as amended: "There shall be levied, collected and paid for each taxable year . . . upon the net income of every corporation . . . if such corporation . . . is . . . *availed* of for the *purpose of preventing* the imposition of the surtax upon its shareholders . . . *through the medium of permitting earnings or profits to accumulate* instead of being divided or distributed. . . ." Obviously, the fact an accumulation existed, in Pelton's case, is uncontroverted, and its appeal simply urges that the accumulation was not the type or class penalized by §[531 et seq.].

Regardless of how Pelton's propositions raised in this appeal are analyzed they recur to the basic theme of "reasonable business needs." . . .

Dill Manufacturing Co. v. Commissioner, 1939, 39 BTA 1023 and Gazette Publishing Co. v. Self, D.C. Ark. 1952, 103 F. Supp. 779 are the two main props erected by Pelton's counsel when contending that the reorganization plan was a valid business purpose outside the ambit of §[531]. But reliance on those two cases is misplaced by overlooking the fact that the Pelton plan required, and had, unanimous stockholder approval. The actuality of the consummated plan could only be reached, and was achieved, by the favorable vote of Ehne, alone, or in combination with Fawick. Both *Dill* and *Gazette* are instances where the majority of stockholders bought out a minority, and to that extent *Pelton, Dill* and *Gazette* are all cases where the majority (at bar Ehne, Fawick and Slichter) of stockholders acted, but only in *Pelton* did a minority stockholder remain in the corporation, after the majority sold out and all three men enjoy the tax benefit of the planned action. . . .

Slichter's testimony in the Tax Court demonstrates that Ehne, especially, and Fawick wanted to sell Pelton. Representing 80% of the outstanding capital, as these two men did, they could have ended the independent existence of Pelton. All Slichter's action and motivation indicates is a vague sort of moral obligation toward faithful employees and some understandable pride in perpetuating Pelton as a separate entity. Ransoming Pelton was apparently far from the evidenced state of mind attributable to Ehne or Fawick.

Section [531], containing as it did penalty provisions, was intended as a deterrent. Its aim was to prevent the corporation from being used as a device for avoiding surtax on individual incomes. The singular feature, frequently and conveniently overlooked, is that the penalty tax may be avoided by distributing earnings. See e.g. Carey, Accumulations Beyond The Reasonable Needs Of The Business: The Dilemma Of Section 102(c), 60 Harv. L. Rev. 1282 (1947). The record is utterly devoid of countervailing evidence either palliating or eradicating the situation interdicted . . . , indeed we are satisfied Pelton was "availed of" during the taxable year.

The judgment of the Tax Court is affirmed.

NOTES

1. See Herwitz, Stock Redemptions and the Accumulated Earnings Tax, 74 Harv. L. Rev. 866 (1961); O'Neill, The Accumulated Earnings Tax — Effects of Stock Redemptions, 46 Taxes 172 (1968).
2. The Tax Reform Act of 1969 provided special "relief" in two redemption situations. See §537(b). Is this "relief" wise tax policy?

E. FINANCING OPERATIONS AND EXPANSION

NEMOURS CORP. v. COMMISSIONER
38 T.C. 585 (1962), *aff'd per curiam*, 325 F.2d 559 (3rd Cir. 1964)

The Commissioner originally determined a deficiency in petitioner's income tax for the taxable year 1956 in the amount of $745,302.63 on the theory that petitioner was subject to the personal holding company tax. The Commissioner withdrew this issue at the trial and, by amendment to his answer, determined a deficiency in the amount of $286,281.17 on the theory that petitioner was subject to the accumulated earnings tax in 1956. The correctness of the latter determination is the only issue presented. If the court should hold for petitioner on this issue, petitioner claims an overpayment of tax in the amount of $73,826.91.

FINDINGS OF FACT . . .

During the taxable year 1956, petitioner kept its books and accounting records on a cash receipts and disbursements method of accounting, and its taxable period was the calendar year. . . . [At the time of incorporation in 1924, Paulina duPont Dean and J. Simpson Dean transferred to petitioner securities, real estate, and cash in exchange for petitioner's no-par stock.]

. . . [By] December 31, 1956, petitioner's outstanding no-par common stock in the total amount of 36,172 shares was owned as follows: Paulina duPont Dean, 26,923 shares; J. Simpson Dean, 5,249 shares; trusts for the benefit of the three Dean children, 4,000 shares.

At all times here material J. Simpson Dean was president, treasurer, and a director of petitioner, and Paulina duPont Dean was vice president and a director.

During the taxable years 1934 to 1955, inclusive, petitioner was a personal holding company within the pertinent provisions of the applicable revenue acts, Internal Revenue Codes, and regulations thereunder, and petitioner filed its returns and paid its taxes as such.

Among the assets transferred by and on behalf of Paulina duPont Dean to petitioner on its organization in 1924 were 333 shares of Delaware Realty and Investment Company no-par common stock. As a result of stock splits and stock dividends, petitioner owned 33,300 shares of Delaware Realty and Investment Company no-par common stock as of December 31, 1956, and such stock produced dividend income to petitioner in 1956 in the total amount of $1,273,725. The total cost basis of such stock on petitioner's books was $33,333.33. . . .

[This stock was valued at $1,200.00 per share for loan purposes. See footnote 5 infra.]

On or about April 4, 1956, J. Simpson Dean, hereinafter for convenience sometimes referred to as Dean, was presented with a plan by tax counsel to remove petitioner from its status as a personal holding company under the revenue laws. The plan contemplated the acquisition by petitioner of income from oil and gas production to the end that such gross income from oil and gas sources would exceed 20 percent of its gross income from all sources [and would thus relieve petitioner from personal holding company liability]. The plan appealed to Dean, not only because of the substantial tax saving which it envisioned for petitioner, but also because it offered petitioner an opportunity to earn and retain a sufficient amount to be able to discharge its existing indebtedness (then amounting to $1,260,000) at the Wilmington Trust Company. Dean also considered the purchase of oil and gas properties by petitioner a form of insurance for his and his wife's estate taxes because such assets could be readily sold by petitioner and converted into cash with which the corporation could redeem all or part of their stock in the event of death. . . .

When Dean introduced oil and gas operations into petitioner's corporate activities in 1956, he considered the possibility of having petitioner acquire other gas and oil interests in the future. However, no specific plans were formulated along these lines, nor was anything relating to such possible future acquisitions recorded in a formal corporate resolution in 1956. . . .

[From 1959 to 1961, petitioner acquired a number of additional oil and gas production interests and leases. In some instances the acquisitions were financed with borrowed funds. In one instance petitioner issued shares of its no-par common stock for stock of a corporation that owned leases and whose stock had been held by the Dean children.]

Prior to 1956 (while petitioner was a personal holding company under the applicable revenue laws), petitioner's dividend policy was correlated with the income tax rate of petitioner's principal stockholders, J. Simpson Dean and Paulina duPont Dean. The Deans caused petitioner to declare only sufficient dividends in each year as would produce the smallest overall tax payment for them and for petitioner. Under the statute as a personal holding company petitioner's tax ceiling was set at 85 percent. Since each year the Deans had income from sources other than petitioner which fluctuated in amount, they had petitioner declare a balancing dividend with the result that their own top bracket would not exceed 85 percent. Thus, dividends declared by petitioner fluctuated from year to year according to the outside income of the Deans. An exception to this policy occurred in 1954 when the Deans made a gift of 4,000 shares of petitioner's stock to two trusts created by them in 1937 for the benefit of their three children. To put the trusts in cash the Deans caused petitioner to pay a larger dividend in 1954 and thereby brought their individual tax rate up to 89 percent. Part of the dividend went to the trusts and because the trusts were in a lower tax bracket they retained sufficient funds to pay certain insurance premiums, thereby sparing the Deans the need of giving cash to the trusts and paying gift taxes on such cash transfers.

In 1956, when the Deans no longer considered petitioner a personal holding company, petitioner's dividend policy changed. At first Dean was of the opinion that petitioner should declare no dividend in 1956. However, it was ultimately decided that petitioner declare and pay a dividend of $2 per share or a total of $72,344 on its 36,172 outstanding shares for the year 1956. . . .

As of December 31, 1956, the Deans were indebted to petitioner in the total amount of $2,563,098.07 on non-interest-bearing demand notes. Since 1929 they had been borrowing from petitioner from time to time on such notes and, in addition thereto, since 1938 they had been borrowing from petitioner on open account. On December 31, 1952, the advances to the Deans on open account were transferred to non-interest-bearing demand notes in the amounts of their open account balances. Advances were made in 1953 to Paulina duPont Dean only, which after repayments showed a net amount owing by her on December 31, 1953, of $42,275 for which she gave a non-interest-bearing demand note. Further advances and repayments on open account were made during the year 1954 to both of the Deans, with full repayment of the net amounts then owing by December 31, 1954. During the year 1955 additional advances and repayments were made to the Deans, the principal advances being $250,000 to each on March 15, 1955, with which to pay gift taxes on the gifts of petitioner's stock made by them in 1954 to trusts for the benefit of their children. On December 31, 1955, Dean gave a non-interest-bearing demand note to petitioner in the amount of $133,431.85 covering the balance owed by him on open account, and his wife gave a similar note in the amount of $373,039.95 covering her balance. During 1956 advances were made to Paulina duPont Dean only in the total amount of $462,137.24. Partial repayment was made from time to time throughout the year, and on December 31, 1956, the outstanding balance in the amount of $399,403.01 was fully repaid. The Deans did not borrow additional funds from petitioner on non-interest-bearing demand notes during 1956. . . .

At times (while petitioner was a personal holding company) when the Deans wanted to borrow funds from petitioner and petitioner lacked the necessary cash, Dean caused petitioner to borrow money at prevailing interest rates from the Wilmington Trust Company (in which he was a director), with the prearranged purpose of then borrowing the same funds from petitioner on non-interest-bearing notes. Thus, for example, on March 15, 1955, petitioner borrowed $500,000 from the bank at an interest rate of 3 percent per annum and on the same day advanced such funds to the Deans on open account so that the Deans had cash with which to pay gift taxes owed by them. The Deans did not pay interest to petitioner on their borrowings from petitioner when the corporation was a personal holding company because in their view such interest payments would have involved only cross balancing tax deductions for them and additional income for petitioner, as well as potentially increased taxable dividends from petitioner to them.

Petitioner's accumulated earnings and profits as of December 31, 1955 and 1956, as adjusted by stipulation of the parties, were $1,088,950.15 and $1,626,868.87, respectively. If petitioner's increase of accumulated earnings and profits during the taxable year 1956 had been distributed as dividends, there would have resulted a substantial increase in the Federal income taxes due and payable by J. Simpson Dean and Paulina duPont Dean.

Petitioner was not a mere holding or investment company as of December 31, 1956. . . .

The reasonable needs of petitioner's business (including the reasonably anticipated needs of such business) did not require the accumulation of any of the corporation's earnings and profits for the taxable year 1956.

Opinion

Raum, Judge. The nature of the controversy herein has undergone a complete change since the Commissioner initially sent a deficiency notice to petitioner. The major portion of the $745,302.63 deficiency originally determined by the Commissioner was based on the factual determination that petitioner, which filed its returns and paid its taxes as a personal holding company under the applicable revenue laws each year from 1934 through 1955, remained a personal holding company during the taxable year 1956 and was subject to the personal holding company tax. In its petition filed with this court, petitioner alleged that the Commissioner erred in this determination. Shortly before the trial of this case the Commissioner amended his answer to the petition to allege for the first time that, in the alternative, if petitioner was not a personal holding company in 1956, then it was subject to the accumulated earnings tax for such year, and an alternative, reduced deficiency in the amount of $286,281.17 was claimed. The Commissioner's new theory was necessarily stated as an alternative contention because section 532(b)(1) of the 1954 Code (as did predecessor revenue acts throughout the time petitioner was a personal holding company) provides that the accumulated earnings tax is not applicable to a personal holding company. Hence, it had to be assumed (contrary to the deficiency notice) for purposes of the accumulated earnings tax allegation that petitioner no longer remained a personal holding company in 1956. At the trial the Commissioner entirely abandoned the personal holding company issue, leaving the applicability of the accumulated earnings tax to petitioner in 1956 the only question for decision.

As an accumulated earnings tax dispute, this case has several unusual features. First of all because this issue was raised by the Commissioner for the first time in an amended answer to the petition, under the rules of practice of this court it is the Commissioner and not the petitioner who has the burden of proof regarding the applicability of this special tax, that is, whether petitioner in 1956 was "availed of for the purpose of avoiding the income tax with respect to its shareholders . . . by permitting earnings and profits to accumulate instead of being divided or distributed." Sec. 532(a), I.R.C. 1954. In particular, the Commissioner has the burden in respect of the question whether petitioner permitted earnings and profits to accumulate in 1956 beyond the reasonable needs of its business, a matter upon which he presumably would have the burden in these circumstances in any event since he had not sent the notification provided for in section 534. But it must be noted from the outset that section 533 permits the Commissioner (even in the unusual circumstances of this case) to shift the burden of proof to petitioner on the ultimate question of the purpose of the accumulation by proving that the earnings and profits of petitioner were in fact permitted to accumulate beyond the reasonable needs of the business in 1956 or that petitioner was in fact a mere holding or investment company during the taxable year.

Aside from burden-of-proof responsibilities, there is a second unusual factor which sets this case apart from prior cases considered by this court involving the accumulated earnings tax. This factor is the continuous history of the petitioner as a personal holding company under the revenue laws for over 20 years immediately preceding the taxable year in issue. During this period petitioner was subject to the added personal holding company tax but as already noted was not also subject to the accumulated earnings tax. Thus, the petitioner's business history during the years prior to the taxable year in controversy, a matter generally of considerable importance in an accumulated earnings tax case, is of limited relevance in the instant case. As a personal holding company from 1934 through 1955, for example, petitioner's dividend policy of gearing its distributions to the tax bracket of its shareholders and its loan policy of advancing in excess of $2,500,000 to its principal shareholders on personal loans without interest cannot be viewed in the same light for purposes of decision of the present issue as if petitioner had been other than a personal holding company during this period and had experienced a similar history. While at the Commissioner's request we have made extended findings of fact concerning the petitioner's business and financial history while it remained a personal holding company, we think such findings are of limited usefulness except as a general background to petitioner's changed status during the taxable year in issue.

We do not mean to imply that petitioner's former status as a personal holding company in any sense exempts petitioner from the application of the accumulated earnings tax after it no longer comes within the statutory definition of a personal holding company. On the contrary, in the framework of the 1954 Code both the accumulated earnings and personal holding company taxes are contained within subchapter G which is entitled "Corporations Used to Avoid Income Tax on Shareholders," and thus petitioner's extended history as a personal holding company, if anything, made it suspect in terms of other means, such as accumulating surplus, for avoiding shareholder taxes. We do think, however, in fairness to petitioner that while the corporation was paying its taxes as a personal holding company, petitioner and especially petitioner's principal shareholders, the Deans, had the right to treat and use the corporation as a personal holding company for all purposes and that petitioner's conduct during this period (when the accumulated earnings tax did not apply) should not necessarily prejudice its position once it becomes an ordinary operating corporation under the revenue laws.

We turn then to the issue of the applicability of the accumulated earnings tax to petitioner in 1956. After carefully studying all of the evidence of record and the arguments of counsel, we have concluded that petitioner in 1956 was availed of for the purpose of avoiding the income tax with respect to its shareholders by permitting its earnings and profits to accumulate instead of being distributed and that, therefore, it is subject to the accumulated earnings tax imposed by section 531.

Although the question is not free from doubt, we have made a finding that petitioner was not a "mere holding or investment company" (as the phrase is used in section 533(b), supra) as of December 31, 1956. We think that petitioner's purchase of working interests in 18 gas condensate wells in 1956 constitutes sufficient nonholding or noninvestment company activity to take petitioner out of the "mere holding or investment company" category as used in the statute and the applicable regulations. Sec. 1.533-1(c), Income Tax Regs. In this regard, we reject the Commissioner's argument on brief that petitioner's purchase of oil and gas interests in 1956, because "for the admitted specific purpose of removing petitioner from a personal holding company classification, is incompatible with business status and is legally inadequate to remove petitioner from a holding and investment company status." By conceding that petitioner was no longer a personal holding company in 1956, the Commissioner has recognized the validity of the oil and gas interest purchases. We therefore find it difficult to follow the Commissioner's reasoning that such investments (for whatever purpose) were something less than they purported to be. To be sure, petitioner's working interests in gas condensate wells in 1956 were managed and operated by its agent, Hudson Gas and Oil Company. However, we think this agency arrangement and the gradual takeover of operations by petitioner were consistent with prudent business practice and in no way detract from petitioner's actual entry into the gas condensate business in the taxable year. We think that the scope of this business[3] was of such magnitude that petitioner cannot properly be described as a mere holding or investment company as of the close of the taxable year.[4]

As noted above in our discussion of the burden of proof, section 533(a) provides that the fact that the earnings and profits of a corporation are permitted to accumulate beyond the reasonable needs of the business shall be considered determinative of the purpose to avoid the income tax with respect to shareholders, unless the corporation by the preponderance of the evidence shall prove to the contrary. We think on the record before us that the Commissioner has successfully proved that petitioner's earnings and profits were permitted to accumulate beyond the reasonable needs of the business (including the reasonably anticipated needs of the business as provided in section 537) and that the petitioner has failed to offer a preponderance of evidence to show that such accumulation was not for the interdicted purpose of avoiding shareholder taxes.

As of the start of the taxable year 1956, the parties have stipulated that petitioner's adjusted accumulated earnings and profits amounted

3. The Commissioner relies on language in John Provence #1 Well, 37 T.C. 376, [affirmed sub nom. John Provence #1 Well v. Commissioner, 321 F.2d 840 (3d Cir. 1963)], to argue that petitioner's working interests in the wells represented mere investments and not business activities. However, the working interests sold in that case, unlike those purchased by petitioner, did not include any managerial rights. Since the absence of a transfer of managerial functions was an important factor in reaching the conclusion that the working interests in Provence were akin to corporate stock, we think that case is distinguishable.

4. Petitioner does not argue that its purchase of an oil production payment in 1956 constituted sufficient business activity to remove it from the "mere holding or investment company" category, and therefore we express no opinion on the question whether this phase of petitioner's total activities constituted anything more than an investment or holding of property for the production of income.

to $1,088,950.15. The Commissioner has argued that no further accumulations were necessary for petitioner's business needs in 1956. The petitioner has tried to show that such needs justified the retention of the additional $537,918.72 earnings and profits which it is agreed were accumulated during the taxable year. We think that the Commissioner has proved his case.

In 1956 petitioner's chief income-producing asset continued to be its 33,300 shares of Delaware Realty and Investment Company stock.[5] While its dividend income from such stock in 1956 was slightly less than it had been in 1955, still such income alone, amounting to $1,273,725, was nearly sufficient to pay all of petitioner's operating expenses during the taxable year.[6] In addition, petitioner received over $1 million in gross income from the oil and gas interests it acquired in 1956. By removing itself from the personal holding company classification, petitioner eliminated a Federal income tax expense of in excess of $800,000 in 1956. Thus, although petitioner's net income before taxes in 1956 was almost $150,000 under what it had been in 1955, its net income after taxes was $1,021,492.36 in 1956 as compared to $761,405.70 in 1955. As a result, petitioner's earnings per share after taxes increased from $21.04 in 1955 to $28.24 in 1956.

From these facts it is difficult to understand why, when petitioner was able to pay a dividend of $19.35 per share in 1955, it paid only $2 per share with increased net earnings in 1956. The answer of petitioner's president, J. Simpson Dean, in testimony at the trial was that petitioner's indebtedness incurred in connection with the purchase of its working interests in gas wells, together with its indebtedness on demand notes to the Wilmington Trust Company, was of such magnitude in relation to its cash position at the end of 1956 that a $2 dividend was determined to be all that was "reasonably safe" in the circumstances. If petitioner in fact had no choice but to pay any dividend declared in 1956 in cash, such reasoning might perhaps[7] be persuasive. However, this was not the case. Petitioner

---

5. The Delaware Realty and Investment Company stock was carried on petitioner's books at a cost value of $33,333.33, or approximately $1 a share. . . . [W]e are by no means convinced that if any such stock were offered for sale there would be any real difficulty in disposing of it at a fair price. . . . In regard to the actual value of this stock, it is noteworthy that shares of Delaware Realty were given a value ranging from $884.81 to $1,330 per share for collateral purposes in 1956 by institutions which held such stock as security for loans made to petitioner.

6. Petitioner's total operating expenses in 1956, including a depletion allowance for its newly acquired gas and oil interests in the amount of $882,398.05, amounted to $1,293,787.68.

7. We use the qualifying word "perhaps," because the record strongly indicates that, at least as to petitioner's indebtedness in respect of its oil and gas interests, it was anticipated that such indebtedness would be paid off out of the oil and gas revenues and that no cash accumulation of current earnings was necessary for that purpose.

held non-interest-bearing notes in the total amount of $2,563,098.07 from its principal stockholders, the Deans, and in these circumstances a sizable dividend might have been declared by discharging a substantial portion of these notes without reducing the corporation's cash or general quick assets position.

At the trial when petitioner's counsel asked J. Simpson Dean whether such a method of paying a noncash dividend had been considered in 1956, his answer was as follows: "You could not give much consideration to that because if Mrs. Dean and I had gotten let's say a dividend not in cash from Nemours, we could not get the money to pay the tax on what we got. So it, it could be thought of, but not actually considered. It was not practical or feasible." Such an answer, obviously given in complete candor, furnishes no basis to the corporation for retaining earnings. The inconvenience of a noncash dividend to shareholders, while admittedly a matter of practical concern to the shareholders, can hardly justify a corporation which has more than sufficient accumulated earnings and profits but relatively little cash (in relation to its business needs) from declaring an appropriate dividend in terms of its current earnings. Certainly the cash requirements of the shareholders do not constitute a "business need" of the corporation insofar as the retention of earnings under the statute is concerned. Dean's answer to petitioner's counsel's question can only be viewed as a frank admission that no corporate business reason existed for not paying a dividend in 1956 in the notes of the principal shareholders and that the true reason for not following such a course was to avoid the resulting tax on the shareholders.

In Whitney Chain & Mfg. Co., 3 T.C. 1109, *affirmed per curiam*, 149 F.2d 936 (C.A. 2), a similar situation existed. In that case, a major portion of the corporation's assets was tied up in corporate stock for which there was no ready market and in the form of non-interest-bearing loans to shareholders.[8] The corporation in that case was considering expanding, and it argued that its lack of quick assets fully justified the accumulations involved. This Court's answer to such argument is particularly relevant here (3 T.C. at 1119):

> We think these contentions would acquire force if, in fact there
> was no way to liquidate the assets. However, there is a ready answer

8. While on brief petitioner argues that similarly there was no market in 1956 for its Delaware Realty and Investment Company stock, we do not accept petitioner's contention in this regard nor the corollary contention that such stock did not have a fair market value. See footnote 5, supra. In addition, in *Whitney Chain* the major portion of the non-interest-bearing notes had benefited a predecessor in interest of the then present shareholders who had assumed the debts involved. In the instant case all of such loans were made directly to the present principal shareholders, the Deans. As a result, the facts in these key respects in the present case are not as strong for petitioner as they were in *Whitney Chain*.

to both of these propositions, which might be expected to have occurred to a directorate of the caliber of petitioner's. If the $70,000 retained by the petitioner was, in fact, needed in the business, a complete distribution could have been made on the condition that the stockholders apply the amount of the distribution to the reduction of their indebtedness; or a dividend in kind, payable by the cancellation of the debts of the stockholders to the extent of the $70,000 retained; or a dividend payable in the stock of Hanson-Whitney might have been made, to the extent of the earnings retained. Had any one of these courses been pursued, the petitioner would have been in no worse position, as regards the financing of the proposed expansion, and yet would have avoided any further accumulation of earnings.

Moreover, in *Whitney Chain*, this court concluded that a predominantly independent board of directors could not have been ignorant of the ready means available by which a dividend might have been paid and that the board's failure to follow such a course was indicative of a purpose to reduce the surtax burden of the shareholders. In the present case, where petitioner's board of directors was made up of and controlled by the very shareholders (the Deans) who received the tax benefits of a minimum dividend, the same conclusion follows with even greater force. Cf. Kerr-Cochran, Inc. v. Commissioner, 253 F.2d 121, 128 (C.A. 8), *affirming* a Memorandum Opinion of this Court.

Apart from petitioner's cash position at the end of 1956, the only other reason suggested for petitioner's failure to distribute its current earnings was that petitioner intended to expand its oil and gas activities and in fact did expand such interests in subsequent years and that such expansion plans constituted a reasonable need of the business in 1956 (or, at least, a reasonably anticipated need of the business in such year) for which an accumulation of earnings was required. While there is some indication in the record that Dean, as petitioner's president, did consider the possibility of causing petitioner to acquire other oil and gas properties subsequent to 1956, it appears that no plans were made along such lines during the taxable year. The testimony that we heard showed that petitioner's officers in 1956 were concerned mainly with obtaining sufficient gross income from oil and gas sources to remove petitioner from the personal holding company classification in that year and in subsequent years, and that expansion beyond this goal — while it may possibly have been in Dean's mind — was vague and indefinite. Such nebulous expansion "plans" do not justify the retention of earnings by petitioner over and above the earnings already accumulated prior to the taxable year. . . . Moreover, it must be recalled that the oil and gas interests acquired in 1956 were obtained with borrowed funds rather than out of petitioner's own assets, and it seems plain that any possible future acquisitions could similarly be financed by borrowing. Indeed, the record affirmatively shows that such future purchases were in fact made primarily with borrowed funds. In our judgment, the explanation that petitioner's earnings were retained for this purpose is spurious.

We conclude, on the record as a whole, that the Commissioner has proved that the earnings and profits of petitioner in 1956 were allowed to accumulate beyond the reasonable needs of the business. Under the statute the accumulated earnings tax is thereby applicable, the petitioner having failed to prove by a preponderance of the evidence that the earnings and profits in fact accumulated in 1956 were not for the purpose of avoiding the income tax with respect to its shareholders. . . .

NOTES

1. Treas. Reg. §1.537-2(b)(2) indicates that accumulation for expansion or to acquire a business constitutes an accumulation "for the reasonable needs of the business." Under the 1939 Code it was thought that "a radical change of business" would not be a justifiable basis for accumulation for *the* business. See Treas. Reg. 118, §39.102-3(b). The Commissioner's position under the 1954 Code appears to be more lenient, with Treas. Reg. §1.537-3(a) providing that the corporation's business "is not merely that which it has previously carried on but includes, in general, any line of business which it may undertake."

2. The provision in §537(a)(1) to the effect that the term "reasonable needs of the business" includes its "reasonably anticipated needs" was not in the 1939 Code, but was added in 1954 as a liberalization. See S. Rep. No. 1622, 83d Cong., 2d Sess. 318.

In Rev. Rul. 70-301, 1970-1 C.B. 139, the Service ruled that an accumulation to meet an asserted tax deficiency for prior years under §531 was an accumulation "for the reasonable needs of the business." For another example of a case justifying an accumulation to deal with a *contingent* liability, see William C. Atwater & Co., 10 T.C. 218 (1948), a case relied upon in Rev. Rul. 70-301.

3. Can one corporation's business needs justify another's accumulation of earnings and profits? For a qualified affirmative, see Treas. Reg. §1.537-3(b) (1960) (parent accumulating for subsidiary); Inland Terminals, Inc. v. United States, 477 F.2d 836 (4th Cir. 1973) (subsidiary accumulating for parent); see also Hughes, Inc., 90 T.C. 1 (1988), discussed at Note 5, page 1072 supra. Cf. Myron's Enterprises v. United States, 548 F.2d 331 (9th Cir. 1977) (error to consider shareholder's ability to lend funds to corporation in determining

reasonable needs); Rev. Rul. 78-435, 1978-2 C.B. 181 (where corporation P, subject to accumulated earnings tax, provided services to a subsidiary corporation for less than an arm's length charge, and the purpose of this arrangement was to avoid federal income tax on P's shareholder, allocation of additional income to P under §482 increased P's accumulated taxable income).

In Chaney v. Hope, Inc., 80 T.C. 263 (1983), the Tax Court held that a taxpayer's accumulation for the reasonable business needs of a sister corporation was not an accumulation for the reasonable business needs of *its* business. However, the court held that the taxpayer's accumulation for the period *after* it was to merge with the sister corporation was an accumulation for *its* business, since that business would continue after the merger.

In Letter Rul. 8707019 (Nov. 13, 1986), the Service read Treas. Reg. §1.537-3(b) liberally to permit sibling corporations, wholly owned equally by members of the same family and constituting a "controlled group" within the meaning of §1563(a)(2), to accumulate for the purpose of expanding their respective businesses into a subsidiary corporation in which each sibling would be a 50-percent shareholder.

4. See Treas. Reg. §1.1502-43, as to the accumulated earnings tax liability of an affiliated group of corporations filing a consolidated return.

5. Section 537(b)(4) allows a corporation to accumulate earnings as a fund against "reasonably anticipated product liability losses." For an interesting example of a calculation of such reasonable "self-insurance," see Grob, Inc. v. United States, 565 F. Supp. 391 (E.D. Wis. 1983) (5 percent of annual gross sales times a multiplier of 10; $1.6 million on current facts).

6. In calculating the "accumulated taxable income" subject to tax under §531, the corporation is allowed a "dividends paid deduction," which is the sum of dividends actually paid during the taxable year and so-called consent dividends. See §535(a). "Consent dividends" are treated as deductible "dividends paid" under §565 even though there is no actual distribution if the shareholders consent to the recognition of dividend income.

IV. BURDEN OF PROOF

RHOMBAR CO. v. COMMISSIONER
386 F.2d 510 (2d Cir. 1967)

Before Friendly, Kaufman, and Anderson, Circuit Judges.

KAUFMAN, Circuit Judge. This petition to review a decision of the Tax Court, Atkins, J., reported at 47 T.C. 75 (1967), holding

Rhombar Co., Inc. liable for the accumulated earnings tax imposed
by Section 531 of the Internal Revenue Code of 1954 for the taxable
years ending January 31, 1960, 1961, and 1962, presents what may
be the first instance in which a taxpayer's counsel has had the "ab-
normally strong nervous system"[2] necessary to risk his entire
accumulated earnings tax case on the burden of proof issue under
§534. The Tax Court held that Rhombar had the burden of proving
it was not a "mere holding or investment company" within the meaning of §533(b), and that it had failed to introduce any evidence to
support its position; accordingly, it held against taxpayer. We affirm
the decision of the Tax Court.

The facts are fully set out in the Tax Court's opinion, and we
need recite them here only briefly. Rhombar Co. is a closely held
corporation owned almost entirely by the family of Herbert M. Roths-
child. Before 1952 it engaged in the furniture distribution business
under the name of John Stuart Inc. In that year it sold all its business
assets, including the right to use the John Stuart corporate name, to
John Widdicomb Co., Inc. (New York) [Widdicomb], another closely
held corporation in which the Rothschilds had, after the sale, a controlling interest.[3] Since that time Widdicomb has operated Rhombar's
former business and has adopted Rhombar's old name, John Stuart
Inc. Rhombar, on the other hand, has not re-entered the furniture
business; instead it has steadily accumulated its income, which is derived entirely from dividends, interest, and capital gains from the
sales of securities and from installment payments it receives from
Widdicomb. As a result its surplus had more than doubled, rising to
over $2,000,000, but only de minimis dividends of $700 annually
were paid.[4]

I

The accumulated earnings tax is imposed on corporations
"formed or availed of for the purpose of avoiding the income tax
with respect to its shareholders . . . by permitting earnings and profits
to accumulate instead of being divided or distributed." Code, §532(a).
In this connection, two statutory presumptions have long been spelled
out in the Code. The first of these, found in §533(a), provides that
"the fact that the earnings and profits of a corporation are permitted

2. Bittker & Eustice, Federal Income Taxation of Corporations and Shareholders (2d ed.) 234.
3. Before the agreement of sale was entered into, the Rothschilds owned 50
percent of the outstanding stock of Widdicomb. Afterwards they possessed 66 percent
of the voting power.
4. For the fiscal years ending January 31, 1954 through 1963, Rhombar's net
income before taxes ranged from a high of $468,549.53 in 1961-62, to a low of
$49,827.58 in 1962-63. Surplus increased from $1,167,648.74 to $2,382,494.55, and
the fair market value of its investments was considerably higher.

to accumulate beyond the reasonable needs of the business shall be determinative of the purpose to avoid the income tax with respect to shareholders, unless the corporation by the preponderance of the evidence shall prove to the contrary." The second, contained in §533(b) states: "The fact that any corporation is a mere holding or investment company shall be prima facie evidence of the purpose to avoid the income tax with respect to shareholders." Accordingly, the forbidden purpose of avoiding income tax may be established by either of these statutory presumptions.

Ordinarily, the burden of proving that the Commissioner's determination is wrong rests on the taxpayer, because the Commissioner's deficiency assessment is considered presumptively correct.[5] But Congress recognized this rule might have "several undesirable consequences"[6] when the Commissioner sought to assess an accumulated earnings tax. As a result, in 1954 it enacted §534.[7] This section sets forth the procedures, followed by the Commissioner and the taxpayer in this case, for switching the burden of proof. The Commissioner notified Rhombar on July 23, 1964 that he proposed to issue a statutory notice of deficiency based on the accumulated earnings tax. In response, on September 3, 1964, Rhombar submitted to the Commissioner a 13-page statement setting forth in detail a recitation of its efforts since it sold its business to Widdicomb to acquire another furniture company. The statement claimed that "the reasonable needs of the business of Rhombar required it to set aside and maintain a reserve at least equal to its entire net worth and to build up such reserve out of its earnings and profits, as soon as

5. Tax Court Rule 32: Helvering v. Taylor, 293 U.S. 507 (1935).

6. The Senate Finance Committee Report on the Internal Revenue Code of 1954, S. Rep. No. 1622, 83d Cong., 2d Sess. (1954), reprinted in 3 U.S. Code Cong. & Admin. News 4621, 4702 (1954), states:

"Your committee agrees with the House that this imposition of the burden of proof on the taxpayer has had several undesirable consequences. The poor record of the Government in the litigated cases in this area indicates that deficiencies have been asserted in many cases which were not adequately screened or analyzed. At the same time taxpayers were put to substantial expense and effort in proving that the accumulation was for the reasonable needs of the business. Moreover, the complaints of taxpayers that the tax is used as a threat by revenue agents to induce settlement on other issues appear to have a connection with the burden of proof which the taxpayer is required to assume. It also appears probable that many small taxpayers may have yielded to a proposed deficiency because of the expense and difficulty of litigating their case under the present rules."

7. . . . If Congress hoped that these provisions would make a material difference in tax litigation it has been frustrated, for the Tax Court will not rule in advance on the adequacy of taypayers' statements. See, e.g., Shaw-Walker Co., 39 T.C. 293 (1962). As a result, taxpayers are rarely certain that the burden of proof has been shifted to the Commissioner. Thus, rather than risking all on the burden of proof issue, they continue to introduce evidence just as they did before §534 was enacted. . . . For a criticism of the Tax Court's policy, see Holzman, Burden of Proof in Accumulated Earnings Tax Cases and Its Development in the Second Circuit Court of Appeals, 11 Buff. L. Rev. 328, 36263 (1962).

feasible, to a minimum of at least $3,500,000 in order to finance an acquisition program (adopted in 1952 under circumstances more fully described below) of purchasing interests in businesses engaged in the manufacture of furniture and/or furniture manufacturing facilities. At no time during the years at issue had Rhombar accumulated sufficient amounts for this purpose." Accordingly, Rhombar claimed it had not accumulated its earnings beyond its reasonable business needs.

It appears, therefore, that under §534, the burden of proof under §533(a) (accumulation beyond reasonable needs of business) was shifted to the Commissioner if Rhombar's statement contained "sufficient facts."[8] Rhombar makes the novel claim — rejected by the Tax Court — that the statement submitted to the Commissioner under §534 also shifted the burden of proof to the Commissioner with respect to §533(b) (mere holding or investment company).

Reference to the language of §534 should be sufficient to refute Rhombar's argument. It provides that when a notice of deficiency is based on the allegation that "the earnings and profits have been permitted to accumulate beyond the reasonable needs of the business," the burden of proof "with respect to such allegation" shall be shifted if the taxpayer submits an appropriate statement showing the facts and grounds on which he relies to establish that earnings and profits "have not been permitted to accumulate beyond the reasonable needs of the business." Thus, §534 echoes the exact language of §533(a), but does not give the slightest indication that it is applicable to §533(b). The maxim *expressio unius est exclusio alterius* is not without relevancy under these circumstances.

Moreover, this is not a situation in which a straight-forward reading of the Code does violence to the congressional purpose. Sections 533(a) and 533(b) are alternative presumptions which can be used to prove the ultimate objective of tax avoidance. In fact, when first enacted in the Income Tax Act of 1913, they were explicitly treated in the disjunctive. And, the Revenue Act of 1938 increased the strength of the presumption to be given an accumulation beyond the reasonable needs of the business, but left unchanged the force of the presumption that a holding or investment company was a tax avoidance device.[10] Thus, when §534 was enacted in 1954, Congress was well aware of the distinction between §533(a) and §533(b). That §534 affects only §533(a) is not surprising nor inconsistent, for the Committee Reports indicate that Congress was concerned in the main with the difficulty taxpayers faced in proving that their accumulations were not in excess of the reasonable needs of their businesses. The

8. The Tax Court expressly did not decide whether the statement was sufficient to shift the burden of proof.

10. 52 Stat. 447, 483.

Reports are barren of any indication that Congress had any concern with the distinctly different problems taxpayers faced when proving that they engaged in activities beyond "holding property and collecting the income therefrom or investing therein,"[11] i.e., that they were not mere holding or investment companies.

Rhombar contends, however, that the credit provisions of §535 support its argument that the burden of proving it was a mere holding or investment company rested on the Commissioner. Section 535, like §534, was added to the Internal Revenue Code in 1954. It provides, inter alia, a credit for that portion of a corporation's earnings and profits which were accumulated for the reasonable needs of the business. The tax is thus imposed only on that portion of the accumulation which exceeds the reasonable needs of the business. Specifically, the statute provides, "in the case of a corporation *other than a mere holding or investment company* the accumulated earnings credit is (A) an amount equal to such part of the earnings and profits for the taxable year as are retained for the reasonable needs of the business. . . ." Code, §535(c)(1) (emphasis added). For most corporations this credit is potentially unlimited in amount, but in the case of mere holding or investment companies, credit is limited by §535(c)(3) to a maximum of $100,000.

It is conceded that if a proper §534 statement had been submitted, the Commissioner had the burden of proving the amount of the credit to which the taxpayer was entitled, i.e., the amount of the accumulation retained for reasonable business needs. Rhombar argues from this that if the credit is to be limited because a taxpayer is a mere holding or investment company, the burden of proving this must be on the Commissioner "since it is a necessary part of the [Commissioner's] admitted burden of proving the amount of the credit to which a taxpayer is entitled under §535(c)(1)."

The difficulty with this contention is that a basic maxim of tax law interpretation is that rarely are there occasions when each provision of the Code can be interpreted as if existing in a vacuum. In any event, it is hardly likely that Congress intended that §534 and §535, enacted at the same time, would work at cross purposes. Indeed, to permit the credit section to overpower or submerge and dilute the burden of proof section would be to permit the tail to wag the dog.

The question of the reasonable needs of the business about which §534 speaks is not relevant to §533(b) for, as Congress was informed by a former Secretary of the Treasury, "it is questionable whether any investment company could have a surplus beyond the reasonable needs of its business, since its sole business was to invest."[12] Thus,

11. Treas. Regs. 1.533-1(c).
12. Secretary of the Treasury Mellon, 65 Cong. Record, Part 7, p. 7355 (1924).

the most intelligible reading of the italicized words in §535(c)(1) on
which taxpayer relies is that they constitute a recognition of the truth
of the Secretary's remark.

Accordingly, we believe the Tax Court was correct in holding
that §534 statements do not shift the burden of proof with respect
to §533(b).

NOTES

1. Rule 142(e), Tax Court Rules of Practice and Procedure, provides that the court will ordinarily rule in advance of trial on the
burden of proof under §534.

In Motor Fuel Carriers, Inc. v. Commissioner, 559 F.2d 1348
(5th Cir. 1977), the Fifth Circuit reversed the Tax Court's determination that the §534 statement submitted by the taxpayer was
inadequate to shift the burden of proof. The Court of Appeals held
that the statement need only show the grounds relied on by the
taxpayer to establish the reasonable needs of the business, without
regard to whether those grounds are meritorious as a matter of law.
It observed that "the statement is not supposed to be legally sufficient
on the question of definiteness." See Davidson and Thomson, The
Fifth Circuit Breathes Life into Section 534, 56 Taxes 395 (1978).

2. How strict are the notification requirements of §534(b)? In
Michael DiPeppino, 83 T.C. 979 (1984), the Tax Court held that the
burden of proof remained on the Commissioner because the notification had been sent by ordinary mail. Note, incidentally, that
§534(a) limits the shifting-of-the-burden-of-proof procedure to cases
in the Tax Court. Should the procedure be applicable in other courts?

3. For an interesting dialogue, although it antedates *Donruss* and
Rhombar, see Levy et al., Corporate Accumulations: How to Meet the
Problems of Section 531: A Panel Discussion of Techniques and Is-
sues, 23 N.Y.U. Inst. Fed. Taxn. 745 (1965).

7

Personal Holding Companies— §§541-547

I. INTRODUCTION

In 1934 Congress confronted the fact that, despite the accumulated earnings tax, many wealthy individuals were able to utilize corporations to house their investments and maintain a combined corporate and individual income tax rate far below the effective rate that would have been applicable to their income if "incorporated pocket books" had not been employed. To deal with the problem Congress imposed a high rate of corporate tax on the undistributed income of "personal holding companies." Contrary to the approach taken in §531, the special corporate tax on the undistributed income of personal holding companies was not made dependent upon a subjective test that looked to the purpose of the accumulation. Standards intended to be entirely objective were established. Defects found in the 1934 legislation were addressed in 1937, when the personal holding company tax was strengthened by amendment. In 1964 Congress made a major overhaul, designed to bring the law into phase with the reality of some modern business and investment practices and to streamline procedures, but without changing the basic purpose of the law. As to the 1934 legislation, see H.R. Rep. No. 704, 73d Cong., 2d Sess., 1939-1 C.B. (pt. 2) 554, 562; as to the 1937 legislation, see H.R. Rep. No. 1546, 75th Cong., 1st Sess., 1939-1 C.B. (pt. 2) 704, 705.

Although the legislation that emerged in 1964 is not precisely as recommended by the Senate Finance Committee, and there have been minor changes in the substance of the law since then, and major changes in the tax rate, the following excerpt from the report of the Senate Finance Committee explains the basic thrust of the personal holding company tax provisions as they appear today. When reading the excerpt, however, keep in mind that *today* the personal holding company tax rate is 28 percent. For an excellent, more detailed overview of the 1964 congressional effort, see Lubick, Personal Holding Companies — Yesterday, Today and Tomorrow, 42 Taxes 855 (1964).

REPORT OF THE SENATE COMMITTEE ON FINANCE

S. Rep. No. 830, 88th Cong., 2d Sess., 1964-1 C.B. 505, 608

General explanation of provisions. — The bill makes a series of modifications in the application of the personal holding company tax in the case of domestic corporations. . . . Most of the modifications described below are designed to eliminate various means by which holding companies have been avoiding classification as personal holding companies, although other problems are also dealt with.

(i) Tax rate of 70 percent. — In view of the fact that this bill decreases the maximum tax rate applicable to individuals from 91 to 70 percent, your committee agrees with the House that the rates applicable to personal holding companies also should be lowered from the present rate of 75 percent on the first $2,000, and 85 percent on the excess, to what will be the new top individual income tax rate. Moreover, there appears to be no particular purpose for continuing the graduation in the personal holding company tax rate from 75 percent on the first $2,000 to 85 percent on the balance. In view of this, the bill provides that the personal holding company tax is to be 70 percent of the undistributed personal holding company income.

(ii) Decrease in 80-percent test. — As previously indicated, one of the tests under present law provides that a company, to be a personal holding company, must derive 80 percent or more of its gross income from certain specified types of passive income, called personal holding company income. The bill decreases this 80-percent test to 60 percent. The decrease in this percentage is made because too many holding companies which are essentially holding companies of passive income have avoided the classification as such by holding their "personal holding company income" just slightly below the 80-percent limit. The more realistic 60 percent limit together with other modifications described below will make the avoidance of this classification much more difficult for holding companies generally.

(iii) Adjusted ordinary gross income requirement. — Under present law the 80-percent requirement referred to above is applied to the gross income of the corporation; i.e., if the gross income derived from certain specified passive sources equals 80 percent of the total gross income of the corporation, the corporation is classed as a personal holding company. This has made it possible for corporations to avoid personal holding company classification by seeking out types of income not characterized as passive, or of a personal holding company type, which give rise to a proportionately large amount of gross income even though leaving little, if any, income after the deductions attributable to this income. In this manner, various types of income have been used to shelter investment income and remove the com-

pany from the classification of a personal holding company. Rents, where they constitute more than 50 percent of the gross income of the corporation, are an example of a type of income used to shelter passive income, such as dividends. Mineral, oil, and gas income are the other principal examples of income which have been so used.

To overcome this problem, the bill adjusts downward the income from certain sources to the extent of certain specified deductions attributable to these types of income. Thus, the corporation will be a personal holding company if 60 percent of "adjusted" gross income consists of certain passive income. The adjustments are as follows:

1. In the case of gross income from rents, the deductions for depreciation and amortization, property taxes, interest, and rents paid to the extent attributable to the rental income received, are to be deducted from gross income.

2. In the case of mineral, oil, and gas royalties and also in the case of working interests in oil or gas wells, the deductions attributable to these royalties or working interests for depreciation, amortization and depletion, property and severance taxes, interests and rents paid are to be deducted in computing this adjusted gross income. It should be clearly understood that although income from working interests in an oil and gas well for purposes of the 60-percent limitation are reduced by the deductions referred to above such income is itself never classified as personal holding company income.

3. Interest from U.S. Government bonds held for sale by a dealer who is making a primary market for these obligations and interest on condemnation awards, judgments and tax refunds also are to be excluded in arriving at adjusted gross income for this purpose. This adjustment serves a different purpose from the first two deductions in that it merely excludes from the base on which personal holding company income is computed this particular type of interest income which in reality is not passive in nature.

In applying the 60-percent test, not only is the total gross income adjusted downward by the amount of the deductions (or interest) referred to in the cases specified above, but also in determining the rental income and mineral, oil and gas income for purposes of this test, this income also is reduced by the specified reductions.

(iv) Capital gains. — Under present law capital gains (other than capital gains attributable to stock, securities, or commodities) are not treated as personal holding company income. All capital gains, however, are included in the gross income of the company for purposes of the 80-percent test. As in the case of the deductions referred to above, some companies have timed the realization of their capital gains income in such a manner as to keep their personal holding company income below the 80 percent. The bill avoids this problem by excluding all capital gains from the gross income in determining

whether the 60-percent test is met. Thus, the test under the bill is based on adjusted ordinary gross income.

(v) Rental income. — Under present law rental income is classified as personal holding company income only if it represents less than 50 percent of total gross income. This is based on the concept that where rental income represents the major activity, the activity involved is more likely to be of an active rather than passive character. The House bill retains this 50-percent test (applying it, however, to adjusted income from rents and to adjusted ordinary gross income) but adds a second test providing that rental income may be characterized as passive, or personal holding company income even where it represents 50 percent or more of the adjusted ordinary gross income if, apart from the rental income, more than 10 percent of the ordinary gross income (gross income excluding capital gains) of the company is personal holding company income. For this purpose, income derived from the use of corporate property by shareholders is not viewed as personal holding company income, but income from copyright royalties and the adjusted income from mineral, oil, and gas royalties is included for this purpose as personal holding company income.

Your committee has accepted the House changes in the 50-percent test with one modification. Your committee has made an amendment to this test with regard to rentals of tangible personal property retained by the lessee for three years or less. Under the amendment, in the case of such property, the income is not to be reduced by depreciation attributable to it for purposes of the 50-percent test and also for purposes of computing ordinary gross income. However, in the case of the provision in the House bill that the personal holding company income (apart from rent) may not exceed 10 percent of the ordinary gross income, your committee's amendments provide that the personal holding company income for this purpose may be reduced by dividends paid during the year, by dividends paid in the next year which are treated as if paid in the year in question, and by consent dividends. Your committee believes that this prevents the 10-percent rule from working harshly where the personal holding company income other than rents may exceed 10 percent of ordinary gross income, perhaps by only a small amount but under the House bill, nevertheless, results in the entire amount of rental income being classified as personal holding company income. Your committee's amendment in effect permits taxpayers to meet the 10-percent test after dividend payments (or amounts treated as paid in dividends). At the same time it gives assurance that the personal holding company income (apart from rent) sheltered in the company may not exceed 10 percent of its ordinary gross income.

The fact that rental income, both in applying the 60-percent test and also in applying the 50-percent provision to the rental income itself, is determined on the basis of reducing rental income by depreciation, amortization, property taxes, interest, and rents paid has already been noted above. However, as previously indicated, tangible personal property rented for three years or less is not reduced by depreciation attributable to it for purposes of these tests, under your committee's amendments.

(vi) Mineral, oil, and gas royalties. — Under present law mineral, oil, and gas royalties are considered to be personal holding company income unless they represent 50 percent or more of the gross income of the company and unless the trade or business expense deductions (other than compensation for personal services rendered by shareholders) represent 15 percent or more of the gross income of the company. Thus, under present law, as in the case of rental income, mineral, oil, or gas royalties are treated as personal holding company income unless they represent the bulk of the company's income. However, in this case there also must be business expenses — indicating the active character of the business — constituting 15 percent or more of the gross income.

The bill retains these two tests but applies them on the basis of the adjusted ordinary gross income, thereby reducing, for this purpose, the income considered to be in these categories by depreciation, depletion, property and severance taxes, interest, and rent paid.

In addition, the bill adds another test which must be met in such cases for the mineral, oil, or gas royalty income to escape characterization as personal holding company income. The personal holding company income of the company, apart from this category of income (but including as such income that from copyright royalties and from rents), must not represent more than 10 percent of the ordinary gross income of the company. Thus, the personal holding company type income which mineral, oil, or gas royalty income may shelter even where this income represents the bulk of the income of the company must be relatively small; namely, less than 10 percent of ordinary gross income. Your committee has also added an amendment making it clear that income from mineral, oil, and gas royalties includes production payments and overriding royalties.

(vii) Copyright royalties. — Under present law, copyright royalties also are considered to be personal holding company income unless they represent 50 percent or more of the total gross income. An additional test which must be met in order to escape such classification is that the personal holding company income, apart from the copyright royalty income, must not exceed 10 percent of the company's gross income and the trade or business expense deductions (other than those for compensation for personal services rendered by shareholders or for royalties paid to shareholders) must represent 50

percent or more of the company's gross income. This provision is modified by the bill in that the requirement that deductions equal at least 50 percent of gross income is changed to provide that they must equal 25 percent of ordinary gross income reduced by royalties paid and by depreciation deductions with respect to the copyrights.

(viii) Produced film rents. — Under present law payments received from the distribution and exhibition of motion picture films are treated as rentals. As a result, under present law, a corporation may be formed by an individual who owns a motion picture negative and have its earnings treated as rents for purposes of the personal holding company tax. Since in such a case more than 50 percent of its gross income would be considered to be from rents, there would be no personal holding company tax payable in this case.

To meet this problem, the bill provides that payments received from the use of, or the right to use, films generally will be characterized as copyright royalty income. Thus, such income will be classified as personal holding company income unless 50 percent or more of the company's ordinary income is from this source, not more than 10 percent of the company's ordinary gross income is personal holding company income, and the deductions properly allocable to this film income represent 25 percent or more of the gross income from this source reduced by royalties paid and depreciation taken.

The bill, however, retains what is essentially the treatment of present law for "produced film rents." Produced film rents are rents arising from an interest in a film acquired before the production of the film was substantially complete. It was thought that less severe tests should be applied in such cases because the participation in the production of the film in itself indicates an active business enterprise in this case. For produced film rent to escape characterization as personal holding company income, as under present law, these rents need constitute only 50 percent or more of the ordinary gross income of the company.

(ix) Other types of income characterized as personal holding company income. — Compensation for the use of property by a shareholder, amounts received under a personal service contract, and income from estates and trusts continue to be classified as personal holding company income essentially to the same extent as under present law, except for the fact that capital gain income is not classified as part of gross income in applying the 10-percent test in the case of the use of corporate property by shareholders.

(x) Personal finance companies. — Present law provides that certain types of companies are not to be classified as personal holding companies. These include, for example, banks, life insurance companies, and surety companies. Also excluded from such classification are certain types of personal finance companies. Under present law, there

are four different types of personal finance companies which are excluded from the personal holding company category. These categories in general terms are as follows:

1. Licensed personal finance companies, 80 percent of whose gross income is interest from loans if at least 60 percent of their gross income is received from loans classified as "small loans" by State law (or $500 if there is no State law limit) and if the interest is not payable in advance and computed only on unpaid balances. In addition, loans to a person who is a 10-percent shareholder must not exceed $5,000 in principal amount. These frequently are known as "Russell Sage" type personal finance companies.

2. Other lending companies engaged in the small loan or consumer finance business, 80 percent of whose gross income consists of interest or similar charges on loans to individuals and income from 80-percent-owned subsidiaries which in turn themselves meet this test. In addition, at least 60 percent of the company's income must be from interest or similar charges made in accordance with small loan or consumer finance laws to individuals where the loans do not exceed the State specification for small loans (or if there is no such limit, $1,500) and if the trade or business expenses of the company represent 15 percent or more of the company's gross income. These companies also must not have loans outstanding to shareholders, with a 10-percent interest or more, which exceed $5,000.

3. A loan or investment company (such as a Morris Plan bank), a substantial part of whose business consists of receiving funds not subject to check and evidenced by certificates of indebtedness or investment, and making loans and discounts. Here also loans to a person who is a 10-percent shareholder may not exceed $5,000 in principal amount.

4. A finance company actively engaged in purchasing or discounting accounts or notes receivable, or installment obligations, or in making loans secured by any of these or by tangible personal property, if at least 80 percent of its gross income is derived from such business. In addition, at least 60 percent of such a company's gross income must be derived from certain categories of income. These categories, in general, relate to business or factoring-type loans: such as purchasing or discounting accounts or notes receivable, or installment obligations arising out of the sale of goods or services by the borrower in his business; making loans for not more than 36 months to businesses where the amounts are secured by accounts or notes receivable or installment obligations of the type described above, or secured by warehouse receipts, bills of lading, inventories, chattel mortgages on property used in the borrower's trade or business, etc. In the case of these companies, the trade or business expense deductions must represent at least 15 percent of the gross income of

the company, and loans to those who are 10-percent shareholders in such company must not exceed $5,000 in principal amount.

In the interest of simplification, the House substituted one exclusion for the four now provided these categories of lending or finance companies. At the same time, it saw no need for purposes of the personal holding company provision to restrict the type of loans which these companies could make. It was suggested that this was properly a matter of regulation by State law governing these lending or finance businesses and that in any event the personal holding provisions do not apply to widely held corporations. In these latter cases only State law governs the type of loans which can be made.

In view of these considerations the House bill substituted for all four of the categories described above, one definition of a lending or finance company which is to be excluded from personal holding company tax treatment. This definition provided is designed first to assure that 60 percent of the company's income is from the active, regular conduct of a lending or finance business, and second that its personal holding company income[1] plus interest from U.S. obligations as a dealer in these obligations is not more than 20 percent of the company's ordinary income. These two limitations, and the restriction described below relating to business expense deductions, are designed to give assurance that the company is actively engaged in the lending or finance business and that not more than 20 percent of its remaining income is personal holding company income.

Your committee has modified the requirement that not more than 20 percent of the company's ordinary income may constitute personal holding company income. The House bill permits a company engaged in the small loan business to satisfy the 20-percent test by excluding income which it receives from subsidiaries in the lending or finance business. Your committee's bill would extend this treatment to finance companies. Finally, a technical amendment makes it clear that income received for furnishing services and facilities to a lending or finance company is not to be treated as personal holding company income to members of the same affiliated group which meet the requirement of the exemption for the lending and finance companies, whether they are exempt from the personal holding company tax under the same or another provision.

In addition to 60- and 20-percent tests, the company must have certain business deductions described below, which are directly attributable to its lending or finance business equal to 15 percent of the ordinary gross income up to $500,000 plus 5 percent of the

---

1. For this purpose personal holding company income is computed without regard to income from subsidiaries qualifying under this exemption as lending businesses, but including gross income from rents, royalties, produced film rents, and compensation for use of corporate property by shareholders.

ordinary gross income between $500,000 and $1 million. This provision gives further assurance, as evidenced by the deductions of the company, that it is actively engaged in the lending or finance business. A fourth limitation applicable under present law in the case of all of the categories of lending companies denies the right to make loans to persons who are 10-percent shareholders to the extent of more than $5,000 a year in principal amounts.

The lending or finance business for purposes of this provision is defined as including the business of making loans and purchasing or discounting accounts receivable, notes, or installment obligations receivable, notes or installment obligations. It does not include, however, the making of loans or purchasing or discounting accounts receivable, notes or installment obligations if the remaining period to maturity on the loan or paper exceeds 60 months.* It also does not include the making of loans evidenced by indebtedness issued in a series under a trust indenture and in registered form or with interest coupons attached. Your committee has amended the definition of a lending or finance business to make it clear that this includes the income from rendering services or making facilities available to another member of the same affiliated group which is also in the lending or finance business. This is provided because as a matter of economical operations, one company frequently hires the necessary personnel, acquires the appropriate facilities, and in accordance with the requirements of banks, borrows all of the money for the group. Then all of the corporations in the group pay a service charge for these services to the company performing them.

Business deductions for purposes of the 15-percent or 5-percent test include only those trade or business expense deductions which are deductible only by reason of section 162 or section 404 (other than compensation for personal services rendered by shareholders or members of their family), and depreciation deductions and deductions for real property taxes to the extent that the property to which they relate is used in the regular conduct of the lending or finance business. Trade or business expense deductions which are allowable specifically under other sections, such as the deduction for interest expense which is also allowable under section 163, are not included for purposes of the 15-percent or 5-percent test.

(xi) Liquidating dividends. — Under present law, the 75- or 85-percent tax (70 percent under the bill) on personal holding companies applies only to the undistributed personal holding company income. Thus, this tax is applied after dividend distributions are taken into

---

*TEFRA increased this to 144 months. In addition, loans of indefinite duration come within the exception if they are made under an agreement providing for periodic advances up to a maximum amount and if the debtor may pay in advance. See §542(d)(1)(B) and 542(d)(1)(C).

account. Included among the amounts treated as dividends eligible for the dividends paid deduction are distributions in liquidation to the extent of the accumulated earnings and profits. As a result, in the year of the liquidation of a personal holding company there is no income subject to personal holding company tax for that year. Despite the fact that the distributions are treated as dividends to the personal holding company, its stockholders in that year receive this income and report it at capital gains rates.

Thus, under present law, a company which is a personal holding company may nevertheless avoid both the personal holding company tax and the ordinary income treatment to its shareholders with respect to the personal holding company income the year in which it liquidates.

A problem is also presented in the case of corporations where a subsidiary is liquidated and both the parent and the subsidiary corporation are personal holding companies. In such a case, if the earnings and profits of the subsidiary exceed its undistributable personal holding company income in the year of the liquidating distribution, the parent corporation may use the excess dividend paid deduction in computing its own dividend paid deduction, thereby reducing its own undistributed personal holding company income in the taxable year and also in the 2 succeeding taxable years.

The bill meets these problems by limiting the application of section 562(b) to companies other than personal holding companies or foreign personal holding companies. However, it is provided in section 316(b) that in the case of a complete liquidation of a personal holding company within a 24-month period after the adoption of the plan of liquidation, that the term "dividend" is to include any amounts distributed in this liquidation to other than corporate shareholders to the extent of its undistributed income (before any deductions for this amount) only if the corporation involved designates amounts as dividends (and so notifies the distributee). If the corporation does so designate the distributions as dividends the individuals receiving a liquidating distribution from the personal holding company must report the amount so distributed as a dividend in the year of receipt. The bill also provides that in the case of a foreign personal holding company, the amount included in a United States shareholder's income is not to be diminished by any liquidating distributions made during the year.

An amendment is also made to the code which provides in the case of corporate distributees that where a complete liquidation of a personal holding company occurs within 24 months after the adoption of the plan of liquidation, the distribution is to be treated as a dividend for purposes of the personal holding company tax only to the extent of the corporate distributee's share of the undistributed personal holding company income for the taxable year of the distribution. Thus, the dividends paid deduction is allowed to a personal holding company only to the extent of the undistributed income for the taxable year and with respect to noncorporate distributees, only if such distributees treat such distribution as a dividend. . . .

NOTE

If tax rates established in 1964 had been set as low as they are today, with a maximum corporate rate of 34 percent, a maximum individual rate of 28 percent, and a personal holding company tax rate of 28 percent, do you think any of the substantive provisions then adopted would have differed?

II. DEFINITION

O'SULLIVAN RUBBER CO. v. COMMISSIONER
120 F.2d 845 (2d Cir. 1941)

Before L. Hand, Chase and Frank, Circuit Judges.
FRANK, Circuit Judge. This is a petition for review of a decision of the Board of Tax Appeals, reported at 42 B.T.A. 721, which found a deficiency for 1935 in personal holding company tax of $4,198.37 and a penalty of $1,049.59.

In the disputed year petitioner was a dissolved corporation in process of liquidation. It sold its business of selling rubber heels and dissolved in 1932; since then it has not engaged in business, but has endeavored to liquidate as rapidly as possible. The original sales price, after defaults in payments, was reduced in 1935, and notes, bearing interest payable semi-annually and with serial maturities beginning in 1936, were taken for the unpaid balance of $340,000 due on the adjusted price. Prior to 1935 it had distributed in liquidation about $7 per share, but in that year, the amount available being small, it made no distribution. At least 80 percent of its income in 1935 was derived from interest, and at least 50 percent of its outstanding stock was owned by not more than five individuals. It came, therefore, directly within the definition of "personal holding company" in [§542(a)(1) and §542(a)(2)], unless it was not then a "corporation."

[The court held that although the taxpayer was a "dissolved corporation in process of liquidation, having sold its business and liquidating 'as rapidly as possible,' " it remained a "corporation."]

But, urges the petitioner, the personal holding surtax was enacted to remedy the evil of the "incorporated pocket book," deliberately created to reduce the personal taxes of those who created them, and, therefore, to impose the tax upon a corporation in petitioner's position is a perversion of the Congressional purpose. We may assume that the taxpayer here was not deliberately aiming to relieve its stockholders from personal taxation. It is, however, abundantly clear that Congress, in correcting an evil, is not narrowly confined to the specific instances which suggested the remedy. "Of course, all personal holding companies were not conceived in sin — many were organized for legitimate personal or business reasons; but Congress has made little distinction between the goats and the sheep."[1] In enacting the very section being applied here, Congress was attempting to foreclose the defense, available under [§531], that the accumulation of profits was responsive to a legitimate business need. See Committee on Ways and Means, 73d Cong., 2d Sess., House Report No. 704, p. 12; "The effect of this system . . . is to provide for a tax which will be automatically levied upon the holding company without any necessity for proving a purpose of avoiding surtaxes."

Cf. Committee on Finance, 73d Cong., 2d Sess., Senate Report No. 558, p. 15. It is suggestive that an earlier revenue bill, that of 1928, proposed by the House Committee on Ways and Means, contained in section 104 a definition substantially identical with [§531], but that it was stricken by the Senate because: "As in the case of all arbitrary definitions, the effect was to penalize corporations which were properly building up a surplus and to fail to recognize business necessities and sound practices." Committee on Finance, 70th Cong., 1st Sess., Senate Report No. 960, p. 12; cf. Committee on Ways and Means, 70th Cong., 1st Sess., House Report No. 2, p. 17. Having before us indisputable proof from the exactitude of [§542(a)] itself, reinforced by the Committee reports, that Congress wished to establish objective criteria for imposition of the tax, we cannot, by probing into corporate motives, undertake to relieve from the alleged harshness of a particular application of the statute. The Board of Tax Appeals, therefore, was correct in sustaining the deficiency asserted in personal holding company surtax. . . .

NOTES

1. *Adjusted gross income.* Does §542(a)(1) achieve the goals outlined in the Report of the Senate Committee on Finance, page 1116

---

1. Rudick, Section 102 and Personal Holding Company Provisions of the Internal Revenue Code, 49 Yale L.J. 171, 203 (1939).

supra? Consider the following excerpts from an article by Donald C. Lubick, cited at page 1115 supra.

The 1964 change in the percentage test is significant in two respects: the reduction of the percentage of personal holding company income from 80 per cent to 60 per cent and the use of "adjusted ordinary gross income" as the base rather than "gross income." Personal holding company income still includes dividends, interest, royalties and annuities; the principal changes are to eliminate capital gains altogether and to make adjustments in gross rents and gross mineral, oil and gas royalties to eliminate deductions for depreciation, depletion, property taxes, interest and rent paid. . . .

The old percentage test was liberal and easy to avoid. A corporation had to have nonpersonal holding company income only slightly more than 20 per cent of its gross income to shelter the balance of its portfolio income. Thus numerous cases were discovered of dividends being sheltered by fairly inactive businesses which produced little or no profit but enough gross income to shelter up to four times as much personal holding company income. One of the more startling cases was the telephone answering service which predictably produced gross income of about $100,000 a year but had equally predictable expenses somewhat in excess of that. It was acquired for a nominal investment because it was not capable of producing any real profit; yet it was able to shelter gross income of up to $400,000 from dividends taxable at intercorporate dividend rates and from a portfolio at a 4 per cent yield of $10,000,000.

Even at the new 60 per cent test a nominal investment in a telephone answering service with $100,000 of gross income can shelter up to $150,000 of dividend income from $3,750,000 of portfolio.

Quite obviously in situations like the telephone answering service, even the 60 per cent test is unduly liberal. What about the 60 per cent test in other situations? Suppose a genuine manufacturing operation which has a bad year. Its gross receipts are not its gross income;[10] if its cost of goods sold approaches its gross receipts, and if it has other income from interest and dividends, it may be caught as a personal holding company. This, of course, was possible under the 80 per cent test; under the 60 per cent test the area of danger is increased. If the other income is rents or royalties, the proportion of adjusted ordinary gross income might change to qualify the rents or royalties as nonpersonal holding company income (more than 50 per cent of adjusted ordinary gross income) and this would automatically satisfy the requirement of

10. Treas. Reg. Sec. 1.542-2 points out that gross income is not necessarily synonymous with gross receipts. It refers to Section 61 and the regulations thereunder for a definition of gross income.

more than 40 per cent nonpersonal holding company income. Where the other income is all interest or dividends, or interest or dividends mixed with rentals, or rentals and royalties mixed, the decline in nonpersonal holding company income could conceivably change the normal percentage ratios so that the corporation becomes a personal holding company. . . .

2. Why did Congress choose to define a new taxable entity in §542 instead of adjusting the accumulated earnings tax rates in §531? Do you find this excerpt from the Lubick article persuasive?

There are a number of reasons why Section 531 is not adequate to do the job required of the personal holding company provisions.

First there is the arithmetic of Section 531 rates. The accumulated earnings tax is 27½ per cent of the accumulated taxable income up to $100,000 plus 38½ per cent of the excess.

Using the 27½ per cent rate, applicable to accumulations based on several million dollars of investment, and assuming the rate is not revised upward which, as indicated below, is probably not justifiable, a top bracket shareholder could be ahead by keeping his investment in corporate solution even with the payment of an accumulated earnings tax. For example, $100 subject to corporate tax of 48 per cent leaves $52 subject to 27½ per cent accumulated earnings tax, or $14.30. The total tax is $62.30 which is almost $8 below the top marginal rate. If the balance of $37.70 were subjected to a capital gains tax, the total taxes would rise to $71.725, but the probability of escape of capital gains tax at death or at least the advantage of deferral until liquidation would make the individual better off.

The foregoing example is based on a 48 per cent corporate rate and a 27½ per cent accumulated earnings tax. If the income were subject to only a 22 per cent or 28 per cent corporate tax (because corporate income does not exceed $25,000), or a 7.2 per cent corporate tax on dividend income (or even 3.3 per cent if less than $25,000), obviously the accumulated earnings tax at any feasible rate becomes an insufficient deterrent to corporate shelter. Add to that the factor that the 27½ per cent accumulated earnings tax will not apply to the first $100,000 of accumulations (and that multiple $100,000 accumulation credits may be available) or that it may not apply at all if some business purpose can be established for nondistribution and it is clear why Section 531 is an ineffectual deterrent regardless of rate.

Second, the personal holding company provisions had their origin in the shortcomings of the accumulated earnings tax. The House Committee Report under the 1934 Act (H. Rept. No. 704, 73d Cong., 2d Sess., 1939-1 CB (Part 2) 554, 562) stated that:

"It is true that section 104 of the existing income-tax laws puts a 50 per cent penalty on this accumulation of profits to avoid surtaxes, but, nevertheless, there seems no doubt that this form of avoidance is still practiced to a large extent. By making partial distribution of profits and by showing some need for the accumulation of the remaining profits, the taxpayer makes it difficult to prove a purpose to avoid taxes."[4]

The Congress found that to deal with the extreme cases of avoidance an automatic mechanical penalty tax was needed. The accumulated earnings tax was continued for those cases where avoidance could not be automatically inferred from the high percentage of income of the kind not normally required to be received in corporate form (dividends and interest) or where the income accumulated was from the conduct of an active business, but its retention not needed by the business.

Thus Congress decided that to raise the accumulated earnings tax rate would not be an appropriate solution since that tax was needed for many situations other than incorporated pocketbooks and the like. For instance in the operating corporation which accumulates its earnings and profits from its operating business, Section 531 was still needed to apply to the income from active operations properly derived in corporate form without any tax avoidance motive, but thereafter retained in corporate solution to avoid individual taxes. In the personal holding company situation the very use of the corporate form in deriving the income is the avoidance device. Thus a raise in rate would be unduly severe in many cases where the income itself is legitimately derived in corporate form, though it ought to be distributed,[5] especially since this requires subjective judgment.

---

4. For example, the retention of corporate earnings to amortize corporate indebtedness has always been recognized as a ground to avoid the accumulated earnings tax. See Treas. Reg. Sec. 1.537-2. Thus the Treasury presented cases to Congress in 1963 whereby rental real estate was purchased subject to large indebtedness (as is customary in conducting a real estate business). The gross rentals were sufficiently large under the pre-1964 law to preclude personal holding company liability and the indebtedness was amortized by the net income from the rentals and the dividends from sheltered securities which had been taxed only at intercorporate dividend rates. The net income being required to amortize the indebtedness, Section 531 did not apply and hence the purchase of the real estate could be financed out of retained earnings at practically no tax cost. The 1964 Act by limiting the dividends which can be sheltered by rentals will curtail this practice. Those corporations which had relied on prior law and had counted on earnings to amortize their real estate indebtedness will be permitted to do so without penalty taxes through a special deduction in arriving at undistributed personal holding company income for amounts used to amortize pre-1964 indebtedness. Sec. 545(c).

5. See Rudick, "Effect of the Corporate Income Tax on Management Policies," 2 Howard Law Journal 232, 238-253 (1956).

III.   *PERSONAL HOLDING COMPANY INCOME*

A.   **INTEREST AND ROYALTIES**

LAKE GERAR DEVELOPMENT CO. v. COMMISSIONER
71 T.C. 887 (1979)

IRWIN, Judge. . . . [T]he only issue remaining for our consideration is whether . . . Lake Gerar Development Co. is subject to personal holding company tax pursuant to section 541. Resolution of this issue depends solely on whether certain interest received on a purchase-money mortgage constitutes "interest" for purposes of determining personal holding company income pursuant to section 543(a)(1) and section 1.543-1(b)(2), Income Tax Regs. . . .

Prior to January 1970, Henlopen Hotel Corp. (hereafter Henlopen) and Lake Gerar Hotel Corp., a wholly owned subsidiary of Henlopen, owned certain property (hereafter referred to as the Henlopen Hotel) in Rehoboth Beach, Del. The property was used in the corporation's trade or business and thereby qualified as section 1231(b) property. Michael Fabrizio (hereafter Michael) and Francis Fabrizio (hereafter Francis) jointly owned a parcel of adjacent property. On January 1, 1970, Michael, Francis, Henlopen, and Lake Gerar Hotel Corp. agreed to sell the Henlopen Hotel and adjacent property to Donald Miller and on April 29, 1970, the transaction was closed. The actual purchaser, however, was Miller Properties, a limited partnership, which issued promissory notes secured by a purchase-money second mortgage to Henlopen and Lake Gerar Hotel Corp. for the purchase price.

Both corporations elected the installment method of reporting gain under section 453. Lake Gerar Hotel Corp. received $13,824.67 of interest on the note in its fiscal year ending April 26, 1972[5] and Henlopen received $59,394.39 interest on its note in its fiscal year ending April 30 1972.[6]

OPINION

The precise issue before us is whether the interest income due on the promissory notes issued by Miller Properties on the sale of

---

5. Lake Gerar Hotel Corp.'s only other income during the year was net capital gains of $3,913 from the sale of Henlopen Hotel and a $15.29 refund of its Federal income tax payment for a prior year.

6. Henlopen received additional interest of $1,056.70 on a certificate of deposit savings account and $28,010 net capital gain from the sale of Henlopen Hotel in that year.

Henlopen Hotel and received by Lake Gerar Hotel Corp. and Henlopen is personal holding company income. Both parties agree that if this interest income is personal holding company income, both corporations qualify as personal holding companies, and that if the interest income is not personal holding income, neither corporation falls within the statutory definition of a personal holding company.

Section 543(a)(1) defines personal holding company income, in part, as that portion of the adjusted ordinary gross income which consists of "Dividends, interest, royalties . . . and annuities" with certain exceptions not here relevant. Section 1.543-1(b)(2), Income Tax Regs., further defines interest for purposes of section 543(a) as "any amounts, includible in gross income, received for the use of money loaned." Petitioners maintain that because they did not loan any amount to the purchaser, they have not received interest for purposes of this regulation. Respondent contends that the interest received from the purchase-money mortgage constitutes personal holding company income. . . .

The personal holding company provisions were first enacted as part of the 1934 Act. . . . [S]ection 351(b)(4) of that Act stated that "the terms used in [the personal holding company] section shall have the same meaning as when used in Title I [relating to income taxes]." This provision remained in effect until the 1954 Code, although the section number was changed in the Revenue Act of 1937 to section 357, and in the 1939 Code, to section 507(a)(1). When the 1954 Code was enacted, section 543(a)(1), quoted earlier, continued to define personal holding company income as generally including interest.

The legislative history of the 1954 Code is silent on the reasons for the deletion. Petitioner contends that this silence implies a congressional intent to narrow the meaning of the definition because Congress had previously gone to the trouble of referring the definition of interest to other sections in previous Revenue Acts and the 1939 Code. Respondent maintains that this silence supports his position that the definition was not changed. The Senate Finance Committee stated that the 1954 Code changed the 1939 Code definition of personal holding company in only two aspects, not relevant here. . . . The House Ways and Means Committee stated that section 543(a)(1) "corresponds to section 502 of existing law." House Ways and Means Committee, H. Rept. 1337, 83d Cong., 2d Sess. A 176 (1954). . . . From this history, we can discern no legislative intent to narrow the scope of the definition of "interest" for personal holding company income purposes and we can only surmise that the reason for the removal of section 507(a), 1939 Code, was to remove excess language.

Moreover, no change was made in the regulations defining interest adopted under the 1954 Code. Section 1.543-1(b)(2), Income

Tax Regs. (quoted earlier) which defines interest for purposes of section 543(a)(1) of the 1954 Code defines interest as it was defined in the regulations issued under the 1939 Code, when sec. 19.502-1(2), Income Tax Regs., removed the reference of gross income to the general income tax Provisions which had appeared in the Treasury regulations under the 1934 Act. . . .

It also seems clear that the term "ordinary gross income" as defined in section 543(b)(1) is based upon the concept of "gross income" as defined in section 61. Thus, we believe that for purposes of "ordinary gross income," "interest" must have the same meaning as "interest" for purposes of section 61. In turn, section 543(b)(2) defines "adjusted ordinary gross income" to mean "ordinary gross income" as adjusted in a specific manner and it therefore follows that "interest" as defined for purposes of "adjusted ordinary gross income" also has the same definition as interest for purposes of section 61, except for that interest (not relevant here) which is specifically removed from the definition of "adjusted ordinary gross income." See Bell Realty Trust v. Commissioner, 65 T.C. 766 (1976), *aff'd without published opinion* 546 F.2d 413 (1st Cir. 1976). From this it follows that section 543(a)(1) which defines "personal holding company income" as "the portion of the adjusted ordinary gross income which consists of . . . interest" also includes interest as defined in section 61, except for certain adjustments.

We note, moreover, that the term "rents" as used in section 543(a)(2) includes in its definition interest on the sales price of real property sold to customers in the ordinary course of business (sec. 543(b)(3)). This inclusion was enacted in order to permit real estate dealers receiving interest on purchase money mortgages to avoid personal holding company status. Since this provision would be redundant if a purchase-money mortgage was not included as "interest" for purposes of section 543(a)(1), this further supports our holding that interest includes the interest in issue here. . . .

Petitioner next argues that inclusion of interest received on purchase-money mortgages as personal holding company income would penalize corporations by broadening the congressional intent of taxing the "incorporated pocketbook of the passive investor where the company is merely holding assets which produce the income." However, we fail to perceive a viable policy basis for according more favorable treatment to interest received on a purchase-money mortgage than to interest earned on any other type of debt held. In the case of a purchase-money mortgage, the seller agrees to forego the use of a portion of the proceeds from the selling price. This is no different in substance than if a loan had been made by the seller to the purchaser and then secured by the assets sold.[11] But even assum-

---

11. In this regard, petitioner makes the following argument: lending is the business of A corporation, and it entered upon it voluntarily. It was organized or

ing arguendo that petitioners fall outside the asserted congressional intent, the personal holding company provisions provide for a mechanical test in which the absence of an "incorporated pocketbook" motivation is irrelevant. Bell Realty Trust v. Commissioner, supra. See also Ways and Means Committee, H. Rept. 704, 73d Cong., 2d Sess. 12 (1933): "The effect of this system . . . is to provide for a tax which will be automatically levied upon the holding company without any necessity for proving a purpose of avoiding surtaxes."

We hold, therefore, that interest received on purchase-money mortgages is personal holding company income under section 543(a)(1). . . .

NOTES

1. In Kena Inc., 44 B.T.A. 217 (1941), a subsidiary corporation lent cash to the principal shareholder of its parent corporation. The loan contract called for repayment of principal plus 80 percent of all net profits realized by investment of the principal during the period of the loan "in lieu of interest." Kena's share of the profits was held to be "interest."

2. In Joseph Lupowitz Sons, Inc. v. Commissioner, 497 F.2d 862 (3d Cir. 1974), the taxpayer advanced large sums to a related corporation. Following an IRS audit of its returns for a prior year, taxpayer had agreed to accrue interest on this "indebtedness," and continued to do so during the years in issue. The Service then contended that this accrued interest was personal holding company income. The Third Circuit disagreed, concluding that the advances were capital contributions rather than genuine loans.

3. See Krueger Co., 79 T.C. 65 (1985), where the court sustained the Commissioner's §482 allocation of interest income to the taxpayer on interest-free loans it had made to commonly controlled corporations. The court held further that such imputed interest constituted "interest" for personal holding company purposes under §543,

---

continued in operation for the purpose of collecting interest, which is the only profit from its loan transactions. B corporation is not in the business of lending money; circumstances put it in the position of receiving interest. The interest received was an incidental aspect of the transaction out of which it arose. Considering these substantial distinctions, can it be said that Congress could not have intended to treat the two types of corporations and the two types of interest differently? We agree with petitioner that the two types of interest are taxed differently. Sec. 542(c)(6) excludes from the definition of a personal holding company certain lending or finance companies which derive 60 percent or more of their ordinary gross income directly from the active and regular conduct of a lending or finance business. Although there has been some argument as to whether interest may be "active" or "passive" (see for example the concurring and dissenting opinions in Davenport v. Commissioner, 70 T.C. 922 (1978), dealing with sec. 1244(c)(1)(E)), it does not appear to be a problem in the personal holding company tax area. Moreover, it seems clear that in the example above the interest received by B corporation is "passive" interest.

thereby subjecting the taxpayer to personal holding company tax liability. As to allocations under §482, see Chapter 5, page 948 et seq.

See also Mariani Frozen Foods, 81 T.C. 448 (1983), where the Tax Court held, inter alia, that constructive dividends under §551(b) (attributable to a shareholder's pro rata share of undistributed foreign personal holding company income) were within the scope of §543(a)(1). The court also rejected the taxpayer's argument that the character of the undistributed income should pass through. That argument, if successful, would have resulted in an exclusion, since the corporate gain was derived from the sale of capital assets. See §543(b)(1)(A).

4. In Cloward Instrument Corp., 52 T.C.M. (CCH) 34 (1986), aff'd without opinion, 842 F.2d 1294 (9th Cir. 1988), the Tax Court held that a cash basis corporation could not avoid having interest income by distributing the right to receive the interest to its shareholders at a time when the interest had already accrued. As a result, the corporation was a personal holding company.

AFFILIATED ENTERPRISES, INC. v. COMMISSIONER
140 F.2d 647 (10th Cir. 1944)

Before Phillips and Murrah, Circuit Judges, and Vaught, District Judge.

MURRAH, Circuit Judge. The question presented by this appeal is whether 80 per cent of the taxpayer's income for the taxable year 1937 was derived from "royalties" or "other like property," and consequently taxable as personal holding company income. . . . The answer depends on whether the principles announced by this court in a former case involving the taxpayer's income for the taxable years 1934, 1935 and 1936 is applicable to and controlling of the instant facts. Commissioner v. Affiliated Enterprises, Inc., 10 Cir., 123 F.2d 665, *certiorari denied* 315 U.S. 812. . . . The Tax Court held the facts here insufficiently different on principle to warrant a contrary result, and that accordingly the taxpayer fell within the statutory definition of a personal holding company for the taxable year 1937. By this appeal, the taxpayer does not attack the former holding as applied to those facts, but does contend that these facts, when applied to the principles announced there, require a different result.

Affiliated Enterprises, Inc. (taxpayer and herein called Affiliated), was organized in 1933 to promote the sale of a plan or scheme called "Bank Night" to theater owners throughout the country. The plan was designed to stimulate theater business by encouraging attendance in the following manner: Any person over sixteen years of age who registered in the lobby of a theater using the plan was given a number. These numbers were placed in a box, and on an appointed night a number was drawn from the box on the stage of the theater, and the holder of the number drawn, if present, received a sum of money which had been placed in a special account in a local bank. "Bank Night" was advertised by means of cards, posters, and film trailers which Affiliated sold to the theater owners. The plan was immediately successful, and was used extensively throughout the country. Between 1933 and 1938, Affiliated made repeated attempts to obtain a patent on the "means for conducting prize drawings," but it was denied on the grounds that the art was not patentable. It did succeed however in securing copyrights on certain film trailers and instruction sheets which described the system, and the name "Bank Night" was registered as a trade-mark name in most of the states.

The plan was originally sold to theater owners throughout the country under a written agreement labelled "Bank Night License Agreement," which recited that Affiliated was the owner of the copyrighted and trade-marked name "Bank Night," and of certain copyrights and patents pending, together with other accessories such as cards, posters, registers, film trailers, record books, and instruction sheets used in the operation of "Bank Night." The theater operator was called a licensee, and the agreement recited that the licensee desired to acquire a limited license to use the "Bank Night" system in his theater. The licensee acknowledged Affiliated's ownership of the trade-marks, copyrights, patents pending, and further acknowledged that it was purchasing only the right to use that which Affiliated owned, and agreed to pay damages of $100 per day if it used the system or any modification thereof after the termination of the license agreement. Affiliated reserved the right to defend in the name of the licensee any attack upon the right to exercise the license or any phase thereof, and it paid legal retainers throughout the country to thirty or more attorneys for the purpose of defending various attacks upon the system. By the terms of the license agreement, the theater owners agreed to pay a stipulated fee of from $5 to $10 per week for the right to use the system. Affiliated also sold the theater owners all of the accessories and equipment used in the operation of the plan, but more than 80 per cent of its income for the taxable years 1934, 1935 and 1936 was derived directly from the sale of "Bank Night License Agreements."

On December 3, 1936, this court in Affiliated Enterprises, Inc. v. Gantz, 86 F.2d 597, 599, held that the trade-mark registration of the term "Bank Night" afforded Affiliated no protection of the plan or system employed. It further held that Affiliated had no property right in the plan or system called "Bank Night"; that it was "too closely akin [to a lottery]" to "have the protection . . . of a court of equity."

On December 18, 1936, the First Circuit in Affiliated Enterprises, Inc. v. Gruber, 86 F.2d 958, likewise held that Affiliated had no property right in the plan or system capable of protection in a court of equity.[2] Thereafter, the Commissioner determined that Affiliated fell within the statutory definition of a personal holding company with respect to its tax liability for the taxable years 1934, 1935 and 1936, and assessed a deficiency accordingly. On redetermination, the Board of Tax Appeals (now the Tax Court) held that since Affiliated had no property right in its idea or system which it could protect, or "on which it could give licenses to others," the income from the sale of the license agreements was not royalty or "other like property," and consequently Affiliated was not a personal holding company within the meaning of the Act. Affiliated Enterprises v. Commissioner, 42 B.T.A. 390. The Board thought that the income was in reality derived from a sales promotion scheme, which those purchasing same believed worth the payment of the fee charged under the written agreement.

On appeal (123 F.2d 665, 667), this court held that the test was not whether the system was patentable or capable of protection in a court of equity, but rather "whether the idea is new or novel and has value." The court stated, "it is apparent from the record that respondent [Affiliated] in its dealings with theater operators treated the transaction as one involving the payment of royalty for the use of a creative, novel idea possessing utility"; that since the parties at the time of the transaction "certainly thought they were dealing with reference to an idea subject to protection by patent or copyright, and that the transaction involved royalty payments," the income derived from the sale of the contracts constituted royalty or other likely property for income tax purposes.

Whether Affiliated falls within the arbitrary statutory definition of a personal holding company for the taxable year 1937 depends upon the peculiar facts applicable for that year, and not upon its taxable status in any other year. . . . With the beginning of the year 1937, the *Gantz* and *Gruber* cases had been given wide publicity by means of trade journals and general newspaper comments. Theater owners and managers were given to understand that Affiliated could no longer claim any exclusive right to the use of the "Bank Night" system, and Affiliated also realized that it had nothing to sell capable of protection as a patentable or copyrightable idea. It was faced with the necessity of changing its "mode of operation" if it were to stay in business. Consequently, to meet this exigency, it devised what it

2. Affiliated discontinued operations in 1938 when a fraud order was issued against it by the Post Office Department on the grounds that its system constituted a lottery.

called a "Bank Night Theater Service," which, by means of a manual published early in 1937, it advertised a comprehensive and complete theater service designed to give the independent theater owner specialized advice for the operation of a theater in the most efficient and economical manner. The "Bank Night Theater Service" was advertised through the manual to the theater owners as a "Department of Affiliated Enterprises, Inc., owner of the trade-name, trade-mark, copyrights and/or patents pertaining to Bank Night." Twenty-two items[3] were listed as subjects for specialized advice and counsel. Included in the service offered was the "Bank Night" plan as a "business stimulator," but no exclusive right in the "Bank Night" idea was claimed, and the accessories and supplies used in connection with the system were furnished without extra cost to the purchasers of the service.

Of the total gross income of the taxpayer for the year 1937, 58.32 per cent was realized from the sale of written "License Agreements identical to those used in prior years, some of which were sold in 1936 prior to the *Gantz* and *Gruber* decisions, and others in 1937. With respect to this income, Affiliated concedes that it is controlled by the earlier decision of this court, and that it is to be classified as royalty or other like property for the purposes of this case. But 41.30 per cent of the total gross income of Affiliated for the year 1937 was realized from the sale of the "Bank Night Theater Service" to theater operators who did not sign any contract or agreement, but orally agreed to pay a stipulated amount for the service, with the privilege of termination at will. In other words, 41.30 per cent of the taxpayer's income was derived from sources which cannot be said to be attributable to any written agreements wherein the parties by contract "treated the transaction as one involving the payment of royalty for the use of a creative, novel idea possessing utility." The parties did not treat the idea as one subject to protection by patent, copyright, or otherwise. The Commissioner concedes of course that if the 41.30 per cent of the taxpayer's income was realized for services rendered, having no relation to royalties or other like property, it does not come within the statutory definition of a personal holding company for the taxable year 1937.

To hold that the income derived from the oral contracts constituted royalties or other like property is pushing the rule announced in the earlier case beyond the practical and common sense interpretation accorded that term. It follows that Affiliated does not fall within

---

3. Electrical survey, power costs, heating analysis, accounting, advertising and exploitation, architecture, business stimulators, discounts, decorating, electricity, equipment, financing insurance, laboratories, library, heating and cooling, modernization, physical operation, projection and sound, purchasing advice, valuation, and summary.

the statutory definition of a personal holding company for the taxable year 1937, and the order of the Tax Court is accordingly reversed.

Vaught, District Judge (dissenting). [Opinion omitted.]

DOTHAN COCA-COLA BOTTLING CO. v. UNITED STATES
745 F.2d 1400 (11th Cir. 1984)

Before Roney and Johnson, Circuit Judges, and Morgan, Senior Circuit Judge.

Roney, Circuit Judge.

Plaintiff-taxpayers Dothan Coca-Cola Bottling Company, Inc. and Montgomery Coca-Cola Bottling Company, Inc. sued to recover income taxes and interest paid for the fiscal years ending 1965 through 1969 on the ground that the Internal Revenue Service Commissioner's classification of taxpayers as personal holding companies during these years was erroneous. The district court, 561 F. Supp. 1261, held that payment of certain sums to taxpayers, in connection with the lease of tangible assets and the right to bottle Coca-Cola, were rent for tangible assets and not royalties, therefore, not personal holding company income and taxpayers were not personal holding companies. Judgment was entered for the plaintiff taxpayers for the 70 percent penalty tax imposed on personal holding companies under 26 U.S.C.A. §541 of the Internal Revenue Code, which had been assessed against and paid by them for the period at issue. The Government appeals. We affirm.

Two statutorily defined criteria determine whether a company is subject to the §541 penalty tax: (1) more than 50 percent of the company's stock must be owned by fewer than six individuals, see 26 U.S.C.A. §542(a)(2); and (2) at least 60 percent of the company's adjusted ordinary gross income, as defined in §543(b)(2), for the taxable year must be personal holding company income as defined in §543(a). Since it was stipulated that taxpayers met the first criterion, the controversy in this case revolves around the second.

The issue turns on whether payments made to the taxpayers were rent for tangible assets or royalties for the Coca-Cola franchise. Essentially, this is a question of fact. Since the 1930s, when plaintiff-taxpayers were incorporated, the taxpayers have leased their tangible assets and sublicensed their right to bottle and sell Coca-Cola to the affiliated partnerships which first transferred these assets to the taxpayers in exchange for shares of common stock as an incident of taxpayers' incorporation. Thus, taxpayers have never actively operated as bottling companies.

In late 1955, taxpayers began charging the partnerships ten cents for each gallon of Coke syrup purchased in addition to the fixed rental which taxpayers had collected annually from the date of their incorporation. In 1958, the partnerships sold coolers, mechanical equipment, and delivery equipment to taxpayers, and a revised lease agreement and sub-bottlers contract was executed. This agreement provided, among other things, for gallonage payments of twenty cents to be paid by the partnerships.

The question before the court was whether these payments constituted royalties for a franchise, or compensation for the use of property, or consideration for both. If, as the Government contends, the payments represented a royalty, then taxpayers are holding companies subject to the tax on the undistributed passive income of personal holding companies, see 26 U.S.C.A. §541. If the payments constituted compensation for the use of tangible property, as the district court decided, taxpayers are not personal holding companies for purposes of the tax. If the payments covered both the franchise and the lease of property, plaintiffs are subject to the tax only if more than six cents of each twenty-cent payment were attributable to franchise royalties.

The district court's decision in favor of the taxpayers was based upon a record comprised of documents and transcripts of evidence presented to the Court of Claims trial court in an action involving another taxpayer, but with identical factual and legal issues. That trial lasted over a week and produced a record in excess of 1,300 pages. The Court of Claims trial court, on that record, recommended a decision in favor of the taxpayer. This recommendation, however, was rejected 2-1 by a three judge panel of the Court of Claims which decided the case for the Government. See Coca-Cola Bottling Co., Inc. v. United States, 615 F.2d 1318, 222 Ct. Cl. 356 (1980).

The parties in this action stipulated to use of the record from that proceeding in lieu of relitigating the identical issues before the district court. Specifically, the stipulation provided that "all operating facts concerning entities involved in the Court of Claims proceedings are identical to those concerning the operations of the entities involved in the proceedings before [the District] Court." The court could "consider the transcript [from that proceeding] as applicable in all relevant respects to the entities involved in [this] litigation." . . .

The parties differ in their views of the degree of deference which this Court should afford the district court's decision. The key to this appeal is the standard of review that should be given to the district court's determination. The Government contends we should defer to the Court of Claims decision and overturn the district court's findings. The Government first argued we should make a de novo review since the district court neither conducted a trial nor observed witnesses but decided the cases on the stipulated record from the

Court of Claims. In its reply brief, the Government noted conflicting and unclear intercircuit and intracircuit decisions on the point and argued we should review the decision "free of the constraints of the clearly erroneous rule." It then asserts the decision cannot stand even if the court should apply an "ameliorated clearly erroneous" standard of review. The taxpayer simply argues that the findings and conclusions of the district court are due to be affirmed "under the standard of review of Fed. R. Civ. P. 52(a) which requires affirmance unless these findings are clearly erroneous."

Our review of relevant precedent indicates that the circuits are split on the question of whether a district court's decision on an exclusively documentary record should be reviewed under the same "clearly erroneous" standard which applies to trials where live testimony is presented and witness credibility is a factor. . . . In the interests of finality and for the reasons set forth in the proposed Advisory Committee Note we proceed under the "clearly erroneous" standard and affirm the holding of the district court. Even if we accepted the principle that there may be some amelioration of this standard when applied to documentary evidence, there is no reasoned basis for not applying the clearly erroneous rule to the review of testimony, even though that testimony came before the trier of fact in the form of transcripts. . . .

With the proper standard of review in hand, the controlling facts found by the district court cannot be overturned on appeal. In a thorough and carefully reasoned opinion, the district court held that plaintiff should prevail because the 20-cents-per-gallon payment "was intended to, and actually did, apply to rental of tangible assets and was not a payment of a royalty by the partnerships for the use of Taxpayer's franchise." The court stressed that its review of the evidence indicated that, contrary to the analysis made by the Court of Claims, plaintiffs' position was supported by the preponderance of the objective documentary evidence as well as by the testimony of the plaintiffs' accountant. Specifically, the trial court examined the 1956 and 1958 lease agreements, the testimony of taxpayers' expert witness who agreed that the franchise had no value, and the Government's expert testimony on this point, which the district court found to be in large part "conflicting, ambiguous, and confusing." The court noted that the total rent called for in the leases and sub-bottlers contract was not sufficient to cover the fair rental value of both the tangible and intangible assets leased, a fact which provides further support for plaintiffs' position that the per-gallon payments were for the lease of tangible assets rather than for the Coca-Cola franchises, and that the rentals were not merely a facade.

We therefore affirm the holding of the district court based on the extensive memorandum opinion which carefully evaluated all the evidence in the record. We need not reach plaintiffs' alternative contention that the amounts paid by the partnerships were for shares of a joint venture and are therefore exempt from the tax on personal holding company income.

Affirmed.

JOHNSON, Circuit Judge, dissenting.

The majority holds that the key to this appeal is the standard of review applied to the district court's factual findings. I disagree. Though the proper standard of review is undoubtedly in dispute, even under the clearly erroneous standard the finding that a Coca-Cola bottling franchise has little or no value is in error.

A factual finding is clearly erroneous if "the reviewing court on the entire evidence is left with the definite and firm conviction that a mistake has been committed," . . . and when a trial court's decision is based solely on documentary evidence, "the burden of establishing clear error is not so heavy as in the normal case." . . . Moreover, the taxpaying corporations and the partnerships involved here were under the control of a few related individuals having no adverse economic interests. Under these circumstances the transactions are subject to special scrutiny. . . . After giving this case such scrutiny, I am firmly convinced that the Government has met its burden of establishing a very critical erroneous factual finding by the district court.

The district court held that the gallonage payments consisted entirely of rents for tangible assets and not royalties for franchises. The court endorsed the testimony by expert witnesses that a Coca-Cola franchise has little or no value. With due respect to the district court and the majority, common sense and economic reality dictate a different conclusion. The value of a Coca-Cola franchise is substantial.

Each taxpayer's franchise granted it the exclusive and perpetual right to bottle and sell Coca-Cola within a prescribed geographic territory. The franchises were transferable, and the partnerships' ability to bottle and sell Coca-Cola hinged upon their obtaining the franchise rights from the taxpayers. Of course, obtaining the franchise rights did not guarantee a profitable bottling enterprise. A bottler's profits are a function of its efficiency in managing and operating a bottling plant. To say that "the mere holding of a franchise to bottle and sell Coca-Cola does not assure profit" misses the point. Whether the mere holder of a Coca-Cola franchise realizes a profit depends on the market demand for the franchise. There are no doubt a number of investors willing to purchase the franchise rights from the taxpayers in order that they might set up bottling operations. What these investors are willing to pay is the true value of the taxpayers' franchises.

In this case, however, the sales of franchise rights were made privately and between entities owned by the same individuals. The failure of these individuals to assign the franchises definite values does not alter the economic reality of the transactions. The economic reality is that the franchises have substantial value. . . . Contemporaneous documentation by the taxpayers supports this conclusion. . . .

Taxpayers' expert witnesses testified to the contrary, stating that in evaluating a Coca-Cola bottling company for purposes of merger or acquisition no value is assigned to the company's franchise. According to these witnesses, the value of the franchise is entirely dependent on the company's managerial skills and established good will. Though it is true that managerial ability greatly determines the value of a particular bottling operation, even a well-managed operation can sell no Coca-Cola unless the bottler first purchases the franchise rights.

As for a specific bottling company's good will, it operates only to the extent customers purchase one bottler's Coca-Cola instead of another bottler's Coca-Cola. Yet few consumers know or care which bottler produced the Coca-Cola they consume. The vast national demand among consumers for Coca-Cola products cannot be attributed to an individual bottler's localized efforts toward creating good will. This demand is primarily the result of extensive national advertising directed and financed by the Coca-Cola Company of Atlanta, Georgia. More importantly, this demand is for a product that can be purchased only from a franchised Coca-Cola bottler. While it is true that a Coca-Cola franchise may not give its holder a competitive edge over makers of other soft drinks, such as Pepsi or Seven Up, it does give its holder an extremely valuable monopoly. Only the franchise holder can tap the established demand for Coca-Cola. The competitive edge over other investors interested in bottling and selling Coca-Cola is absolute.

The district court and the majority note that the payments made to the taxpayers were not sufficient to cover the fair rental value of all tangible and intangible assets, including the franchises, that were leased to the partnerships. I am not convinced that the value of "all" the assets has been established, unless the value assigned to the franchises is zero, in which case an error has clearly been made.[2]

2. Moreover, even assuming the payments fell short of the fair rental value of all the assets leased this would not dispose of the Government's contention that the taxpayers created a facade for tax sheltering purposes. The taxpayers argue that, if their intent had been to shelter income they would have sheltered more by making payments in excess of the assets' fair rental value. It is equally plausible, however, that the underpayment evidences an attitude of caution in structuring financial arrangements having the potential for significant tax exposure. The 70-percent penalty tax imposed by Section 541 of the Internal Revenue Code operates specifically to discourage taxpayers from putting large amounts of their income into tax-sheltering corporations. The underpayment in this case may actually be reasonable compensation in light of the risks of audit and penalty assessment.

Because the district court erroneously concluded that the Coca-Cola franchises had little or no value, it did not characterize any portion of the 20-cents per gallon payments as royalties. I would reverse this holding and remand for a specific valuation.

NOTES

1. Who appears to have the firmer grip on reality, the majority or the dissent?

2. When might a corporation's transfer of a trademark constitute a "sale" (yielding capital gain) rather than a "license" (producing a "royalty")? See Tomerlin Trust, 87 T.C. 876 (1986).

3. Section 543(a)(1)(C) now excludes "active business computer software royalties" (as defined in §543(d)) from the "royalties" that might otherwise constitute "personal holding company income." And see §543(b)(3)(E) as well. Although written before the law provided these exclusions, see Morgan, The Domestic Technology Base Company: The Dilemma of an Operating Company Which Might Be a Personal Holding Company, 33 Tax L. Rev. 233 (1978).

B. RENT PAYMENTS TO A CORPORATION BY ITS SHAREHOLDERS

SILVERMAN & SONS REALTY TRUST v. COMMISSIONER
620 F.2d 314 (1st Cir. 1980)

Before Campbell and Bownes, Circuit Judges, and Loughlin, District Judge.

CAMPBELL, Circuit Judge. The Commissioner of Internal Revenue appeals from a decision of the United States Tax Court holding that taxpayer — Silverman & Sons Realty Trust ("the Trust") — was not liable for a tax on personal holding company income under Section 541. . . . The issue presented is whether rental income received by the Trust from a corporation whose principal shareholders were also the sole shareholders of the Trust constituted personal holding company income within the terms of §543(a)(6). The resolution of this issue, in turn, depends upon whether the joint shareholders were, by virtue of their status as stockholders, "individual[s] entitled to the use of the [leased] property" either "directly . . .

or by means of a sublease or other arrangement." Id. As we agree with the Tax Court that they were not, we affirm.

Taxpayer is a Massachusetts business trust with transferable shares, treated for federal tax purposes as a corporation. §7701(a)(3). The principal assets of the Trust during the tax year ending March 31, 1975, were a building acquired in 1957 and a sum of cash, including an interest-bearing certificate of deposit. During the taxable year, the Trust received rental income on its building amounting to $38,900 from Joseph Silverman & Co., Inc., ("the lessee"), a Massachusetts corporation dealing in wholesale floor coverings. The Trust's other income for the year consisted of $13,169 in interest earned on the certificate of deposit.

The Trust was owned in equal shares by two brothers, Donald and Alan Silverman. The Silvermans also owned 73.2 percent of the stock of the lessee, Joseph Silverman & Co., Inc., in equal shares. The remaining 26.8 percent of the lessee's stock was held by six persons who were closely related to Donald and Alan Silverman. See 26 U.S.C. §544(a)(2).

The Commissioner determined that the $38,900 rental income of the Trust constituted personal holding company income within the meaning of Section 543(a)(6), and accordingly determined a deficiency of $6,944 in the Trust's income tax for the taxable year ending March 31, 1975. On September 25, 1979, the Tax Court ruled that no deficiency was due because the rental income did not fall under Section 543(a)(6). This appeal followed.

. . . Personal holding company income, as defined in Section 543, includes dividends, interest, certain types of royalties and other forms of passive investment income. Of particular relevance here, it also includes income received for the use of, or right to use, tangible property of the corporation by a principal stockholder of the corporation where the stockholder as an individual is entitled to the use of the property, "whether such right is obtained directly from the corporation or by means of a sublease or other arrangement." Section 543(a)(6).[4]

---

4. An exception to this rule is made where 10 percent or less of the corporation's other income is personal holding company income. The exception clearly does not apply here, as about 25 percent of the Trust's gross income was interest on a certificate of deposit.

Section 543(a)(6), as it existed when this case arose, provided:

"Personal holding company income

"(a) General rule. — For purposes of this subtitle, the term 'personal holding company income' means the portion of the adjusted ordinary gross income which consists of: . . .

(6) Use of corporation property by shareholder. — Amounts received as compensation (however designated and from whosoever received) for the use of, or right to use, property of the corporation in any case where, at any time during the taxable year, 25 percent or more in value of the outstanding stock of the corporation is

Here, it is conceded that the Trust was a closely held corporate entity within the meaning of Section 542(a)(2). The Trust was thus liable for the personal holding company tax if more than 60 percent of its gross income for the taxable year consisted of personal holding company income. §542(a)(1). The interest income of $13,169, comprising about 25 percent of the Trust's gross income, was admittedly personal holding company income. At issue is the status of the remaining $38,900 in rental income.

Donald and Alan Silverman each owned more than 25 percent of the Trust's shares, making them principal shareholders of the taxpayer. It is also conceded that the lessee corporation — in which the Silvermans were major stockholders — had the right to use the Trust's real property by way of a lease which provided rental income to the Trust. The question remaining is whether the Silvermans' status as stockholders — even assuming they had effective control of the lessee corporation — was sufficient in itself to impute to them as individuals the "right to use" the subject property.

II. The predecessor of current Section 543(a)(6) was added to the Internal Revenue Code in 1937 to close a tax loophole that had developed in the personal holding company provisions of the Revenue Act of 1934. Under Section 351(b) of that Act, the personal holding company tax was imposed only where at least 80 percent of the corporation's gross income was personal holding company income. Since rent was not considered personal holding company income, it was possible for a corporation to avoid the tax if it derived more than 20 percent of its income from rent. This anomaly led some taxpayers to transfer title to yachts, hunting lodges and other items of personal property to their controlled investment corporations, so that by leasing back the items, they could generate rental income sufficient to avoid the personal holding company tax. See H.R. Rep. No. 1546, 75th Cong., 1st Sess. 6 (1937) (1939-1 Cum. Bull. (Part 2) 704, 707-08). The legislative history makes clear that Section 351(b) was enacted specifically to close this loophole by including in personal holding company income amounts received for the use of tangible property by any individual who was a principal shareholder in the would-be personal holding company. Id.

The question posed in the present case first arose before the

---

owned, directly or indirectly, by or for an individual entitled to the use of the property; whether such right is obtained directly from the corporation or by means of a sublease or other arrangement. This paragraph shall apply only to a corporation which has personal holding company income for the taxable year (computed without regard to this paragraph and paragraph (2), and computed by including as personal holding company income copyright royalties and the adjusted income from mineral, oil, and gas royalties) in excess of 10 percent of its ordinary gross income." Section 543(a)(6) was amended by the Tax Reform Act of 1976, Pub. L. No. 94-455, §2106, 90 Stat. 1902, but its material terms remained unchanged.

Tax Court in Minnesota Mortuaries, Inc. v. Commissioner, 4 T.C. 280 (1944). Two prospective partners in the funeral direction business formed separate corporations to hold title to the funeral homes' real property and to manage and operate the business. Each partner owned half of the realty corporation's stock; the realty corporation in turn owned 85 percent of the operating corporation's stock with the remainder in trust for the employees. The operating corporation paid rent to the realty corporation for use of the buildings in which the business was operated, and the issue was whether this rent was personal holding company income under Section 351(b). The Tax Court held it was not, since the stockholders did not, as individuals, have the right to use the property. "The general principal is . . . well established that an individual, as a stockholder of a corporation, has no right, title, or interest in or right to use the corporate property." 4 T.C. at 285. . . .

The Tax Court applied the same reasoning in 320 East 47th Street Corp. v. Commissioner, 26 T.C. 545, 549 (1956), but was reversed by the Second Circuit, which held that rental income from a lessee corporation whose shareholders were identical with those of the lessor did fall within the definition of personal holding company income because the individual shareholder had the right to use the property by way of an "other arrangement." 243 F.2d 894 (2d Cir. 1957). The Second Circuit emphasized that the congressional purpose to close the tax loophole might be frustrated if the statute could be circumvented "by the mere creation of a second corporation which would pay the rent instead of the individual shareholder." Id. at 898.[5] This holding was reaffirmed without further discussion in Hilldun Corp. v. Commissioner, 408 F.2d 1117, 1121 (2d Cir. 1969).

In Allied Industrial Cartage Co. v. Commissioner, 72 T.C. 515 (1979), the Tax Court confronted the question whether, in light of 320 East 47th Street it should abandon the rule of Minnesota Mortuaries and impute to individual shareholders the lessee corporation's right to use the leased property. After carefully reconsidering its position, the Tax Court declined to follow 320 East 47th Street, arguing that, at least where a business purpose exists for the lease arrangement,

---

5. Ironically, the Second Circuit's interpretation of the statute in 320 East 47th Street, now urged by the Treasury, resulted in a benefit to the taxpayer in that case. The Tax Court had held that the rent was not covered by the analogous provision to Section 543(a)(6), but that, considered simply as rent, without regard to its source, it was nonetheless personal holding company income because it constituted less than 50 percent of the corporation's gross income. Cf. 26 U.S.C. §543(a)(2). See 26 T.C. at 548-49. By construing the predecessor of Section 543(a)(6) to cover the rental income, the Second Circuit made the income eligible for a then-available statutory exemption for rent received for property used in the operation of a bona fide business. 243 F.2d at 899. In the present case, the tables are turned, with the Treasury contending Section 543(a)(6) should cover the income, and the taxpayer seeking to avoid its application.

it is consistent with congressional intent to recognize the lessee's separate corporate identity rather than to impute to the shareholders the corporation's legal rights. "We are not dealing here with rental of yachts or hunting lodges to shareholders," the court said, "but rather with rental of trucks and real estate used by the lessee in its corporate business." 72 T.C. at 520.[6]

The Tax Court treated the present case as raising the identical issue posed in *Allied Industrial* and entered a decision for taxpayer on that basis. The Commissioner argues, in effect, that the legal issue in *Allied Industrial* was wrongly decided, and that the Tax Court should have followed the lead of the Second Circuit. The thrust of the Commissioner's argument is that Congress, by providing that the "right to use" property could be obtained directly "or by means of a sublease or other arrangement," implicitly meant to cover the situation where the shareholder has access to property through his control of a lessee corporation. The opposite result, it is argued, would facilitate tax avoidance through interposition of sham corporations as lessees.

Like the Tax Court, we are unpersuaded. Where the lessee corporation is established for tax avoidance purposes — as where the leased property consists of personal or recreational property or where otherwise it is being placed at the disposal of the shareholders — this fact should be readily ascertainable, and appropriate measures may be taken, including piercing the corporate veil to see that the congressional scheme of taxation is not frustrated. Cf. New Colonial Ice Co. v. Helvering, 292 U.S. 435, 442 (1934). Such is manifestly not the case here. The lessee corporation, Joseph Silverman & Co., Inc., is engaged in the wholesale floor covering business; there is not the slightest evidence the subject property is being held for the individual use of Donald and Alan Silverman, or that the corporate lessee is a subterfuge to facilitate personal use of the property by them. As majority shareholders, Donald and Alan Silverman have no legal entitlement to use the corporate property in their individual capacities. 1 Fletcher's Cyclopedia of Corporations §31 at 132-33 (1974). Each of them owes to the other, and to the minority stockholders, certain fiduciary duties which limit their capacity lawfully to convert corporate property to their own individual pursuits. A bona fide corporation is not the equivalent of a "sublease or other arrangement" for the simple reason that whereas the latter would legally authorize personal use, the former does not. Nor is there any showing that these shareholders have, in fact, authorized corporate property to be used other than for a proper corporate and business

---

6. We are informed that *Allied Industrial* is presently being appealed in the Sixth Circuit.

purpose. We therefore do not find the Silvermans to be "individual[s] entitled to the use of the property," and thus do not find the rental income to be personal holding company income.

The Commissioner argues that the Tax Court, in reaching its decision, mistakenly relied on a distinction between those rental arrangements having a business purpose and those having only a tax-related purpose. This distinction, it is argued, is a false one, because the statute has long been interpreted as reaching both types of arrangements where the lease is to an individual or partnership. See, e.g., Hatfried, Inc. v. Commissioner, 162 F.2d 628, 630-31 (3d Cir. 1947). Whatever the force of this argument in other contexts, we do not think it answers the question before us. The issue is whether the statute is to be construed so as to impute to individuals the property rights of a corporation in which they own stock. Absent explicit congressional guidance, this is a step any court should be reluctant to take. See New Colonial Ice Co. v. Helvering, 292 U.S. 435, 442 (1934). We agree with the Tax Court that a relevant consideration is whether the step is necessary to prevent a scheme of tax avoidance. Where, as here, there is no showing the arrangement is other than a bona fide business transaction, we see no necessary implication that Congress intended to impose a personal holding company tax on the lessor corporation.

We are also concerned by the open-ended nature and somewhat sketchy outlines of the Commissioner's position. Eight years after the Second Circuit's decision in *320 East 47th Street*, the Commissioner promulgated a Revenue Ruling adopting the position that use of leased property would be imputed to *any* stockholder of the lessee corporation who was also a principal stockholder of the lessor. Rev. Rul. 65-259, 1965-2 Cum. Bull. 174. At oral argument, counsel for the Commissioner indicated that this extreme version of the rule has been abandoned, but was understandably unable to specify what degree of "control" over the lessee corporation was required in order to impute the corporation's right to the shareholder. Without congressional guidance, we are left in the dark as to whether the proper test is ownership of all the lessee's stock, a majority of the stock, or only enough to give the shareholder effective control of the corporation's actions. Prudence dictates that we not adopt a rule of such uncertain scope and unforeseeable consequences. The Tax Court's interpretation of the statute conforms most nearly with the statutory language and is perfectly reasonable. There is no indication it will signally promote or facilitate tax avoidance.

The decision of the Tax Court is affirmed.

NOTES

1. The Sixth Circuit followed the lead of the First in *Silverman* by affirming the Tax Court in Commissioner v. Allied Industrial Cartage Co., 647 F.2d 713 (6th Cir. 1981). Thereafter, the Commissioner changed his position. In Rev. Rul. 84-137, 1984-1 C.B. 116, the Service made clear that it would no longer challenge "rental income received by a corporate lessor from a corporate lessee, when both corporations are wholly owned by the same individual shareholder and the rented property is used solely in the trade or business of the lessee corporation and not for the individual or personal benefit of the shareholder." Rev. Rul. 84-137 revoked Rev. Rul. 65-259, 1965-2 C.B. 174. In keeping with its new position, the Service revoked its nonacquiescence and substituted an acquiescence in Minnesota Mortuaries, 4 T.C. 280 (1944), *acq.* 1984-2 C.B. 2.

2. In 1968 the Committee on Corporate Stockholder Relationships of the Section of Taxation of the American Bar Association gave consideration to proposing the following "Legislative Recommendation" for treating compensation for the use of corporation property by the shareholders just as all other rental income is treated for personal holding company tax purposes. Should Congress adopt the proposal?

LEGISLATIVE RECOMMENDATION REPEALING
SECTION 543(a)(6)

Resolved, that the American Bar Association recommends to the Congress that the Internal Revenue Code of 1954 be amended so as to treat for personal holding company purposes compensation for the use of corporation property by shareholders in the same manner as all rental income; and

Further resolved, that the Association proposes that this result be achieved by repealing section 543(a)(6) of the Internal Revenue Code of 1954; and

Further resolved, that the Section of Taxation is directed to urge the repeal of section 543(a)(6), effective for taxable years beginning after the effective date of the enactment of the repeal, upon the proper committees of Congress.

Explanation

Summary. The proposed repeal of section 543(a)(6) will treat for purposes of personal holding company classification, compensation for the use of corporation property by shareholders in the same manner as all rental income. Prior to the Revenue Act of 1964, rental income could, if it constituted 50 percent or more of gross income, shelter the other income of the corporation from the personal holding company tax, and a special provision was thus necessary to prevent a corporation from building up its rental income by leasing property to shareholders. The 1964 amendments to section 543(a)(2) prevent rental income from being used to shelter any appreciable amount of other passive income from the personal holding company tax. Accordingly, there is no further need for a special provision relating to rental income from property used by shareholders.

Moreover, the proposed repeal of section 543(a)(6) and the resulting treatment of all rental income under section 543(a)(2) would eliminate an unnecessary distinction under present law whereby a corporation with rental income under section 543(a)(2) may, under certain circumstances, avoid personal holding company classification by distributing most of its other passive income, whereas a corporation whose rental income falls into section 543(a)(6) as income from the use of corporation property by a shareholder may not take advantage of a distribution of its other passive income to avoid personal holding company classification.

C. PERSONAL SERVICE INCOME

GENERAL MANAGEMENT CORP. v. COMMISSIONER
135 F.2d 882 (7th Cir. 1943), *cert. denied*, 320 U.S. 757 (1943)

Before Kerner, Minton, Circuit Judges, and Lindley, District Judge.

LINDLEY, District Judge. Petitioner questions a decision of the Tax Court declaring it a personal holding company in the taxable year 1938, for the reason that more than 80 per cent of its gross income for that year constituted "personal service corporate income" within the meaning of Section [543(a)(7)]. . . . The propriety of the decision depends wholly upon whether a contract with United Printers and Publishers, Inc., hereafter referred to as United, from which it derived $24,000, was a "personal service contract" which "designated" the person who was to perform the services. . . .

Petitioner is a corporation which has, for a number of years, been engaged actively in rehabilitating financially embarrassed business concerns. Grant Gillam owned 100 of its total capital issue of 200 shares; his sister, S. Margaret Gillam, 80 and Marguerite Miller, 20. From 1932 to 1938 petitioner served United, first, at the request of a creditor bankers' committee and, finally, under a contract made in February, 1937, after the bank loans had been retired, wherein it was provided, amongst other matters, that petitioner should render certain services, including specifically those of Gillam, for $2,000 per month. The agreement designated Gillam as comptroller, provided that he should "continue to supervise the physical operations of United, its divisions and subsidiaries" and gave to him full authority over the expenditure and borrowing of money. It provided further that, if he should die or become incapacitated and no one could be obtained to take his place satisfactory to United, the latter might terminate the contract. In addition to the services to be performed by Gillam, petitioner agreed also to furnish budgets, audits, cost accounts and various reports. In pursuance of this employment, petitioner received in 1938, $24,000 as compensation.

Under Section [543(a)(7)] personal service income includes amounts received under contracts under which the corporation is to furnish personal service, provided 25 per cent or more in value of the outstanding stock of the corporation is owned by an individual designated as the one to perform such service. Inasmuch as Gillam owned 50 per cent of the corporate stock, the question narrows to whether he is "designated by the contract as the one to perform such service."

Gillam, as the principal stockholder of petitioner, had for some years been a doctor of financially embarrassed corporations and other business set-ups. He had had wide experience in solutions of problems of management, production, finance and rejuvenation of sick industrial enterprises. Beginning with 1932, as the active agent of petitioner, he had rendered curative administrative service to United, visiting and surveying its plants, its operating divisions and its production, directing its activities, its fiscal and financial policies, acting not only as "comptroller" but also as supervisory administrative head and exercising and making available his discretionary executive talents. Successful results ensuing from his service culminated in 1937 in retirement of United's bank loans, ridding it of supervision by the representatives of bank creditors, whose pressure had brought petitioner into the picture as financial director.

The bank loans having been satisfied, United voluntarily contracted with petitioner to continue to render similar service. This agreement specifically provided for discharge of supervisory functions by Gillam, saying that he should "continue" as comptroller and supervise the physical and financial operations of United, its various divisions and subsidiaries. No money was to be borrowed or paid except as approved by him. Thus he continued as the administrative, financial, fiscal and supervisory head of United. His was the voice of discretionary control. In case of his death, United was to have the option of rescission of the contract. Obviously, the evidence supported the finding that United's desire to avail itself of his constructive discretionary and advisory capacities was the inspiring motive leading to execution of the contract.

In addition to Gillam's designated services under the contract, petitioner, through employees other than Gillam, made projected budgets of United's cash needs, audited its accounts, prepared its income tax returns and made up statements of costs, balance sheets and similar reports. In actual preparation of none of these did Gillam participate. In consequence, petitioner insists, as he was not designated to perform all services rendered United, the income received from United is not within the statute. But the labor supplied by persons other than Gillam consisted, obviously, of preparation of the mechanical tools necessary to efficient discharge of his functions as administrative and controlling head. Such budgets, statements, and reports are some of the implements by which an executive or administrative agent works his way to a definite determination of corporate policy. In their preparation, discretion is not involved but, rather, physical compilation and few if any directors of policies are capable of exercising a wise discretion without their employment. They are the trowel of the mason, the plane of the carpenter, the nurse assisting the physician. The contract designated Gillam as the only agency endowed with discretion, and was made optionally contingent upon his continued ability to act. Under it, anyone included in the personnel of petitioner or found outside might supply the working tools. Their source was a factor of no importance. Clearly the court was justified in finding from this evidence that discretionary service designated to be performed by Gillam was the inspiring motive for his designation and that the makers of the tools utilized supplied only incidental aid necessary to achievement of the desired purpose, — administrative supervision by Gillam.

The value of labor supplied in preparing reports, audits and accounts may be an element proper to be considered in determining the question but where, as here, the evidence amply justifies the ultimate conclusion of fact that such additional service amounted to mere supply of the implements needed in performance of the administrative duties of Gillam, we think that the tax court properly refused to give determinative weight to that factor.

Petitioner insists that the contract was not the type of agreement intended by Section [543(a)(7)]. But we think the statute speaks clearly and covers the kind of service contract here involved.

Inasmuch as it results from inclusion of $24,000 as a part of the personal service income that more than 80 per cent of the gross income of petitioner is personal service income, the decision is affirmed.

Minton, Circuit Judge (dissenting). [Opinion omitted.]

REVENUE RULING 75-67
1975-1 C.B. 169

... B, a doctor specializing in a certain area of medical services, owns 80 percent of the outstanding stock of L, a domestic professional service corporation. B is the only officer of L who is active in the production of income for L, and he is the only medical doctor presently employed by L. B performs medical services under an employment contract with L. L furnishes office quarters and equipment, and employs a receptionist to assist B. P, a patient, solicited the services of and was treated by B.

Section 543(a)(7) of the Code provides, in part, that the term personal holding company income includes amounts received under a contract whereby a corporation is to furnish personal services if some person other than the corporation has the right to designate, by name or description, the individual who is to perform the services, or if the individual who is to perform the services is designated, by name or description, in the contract.

In dealing with a professional service corporation providing medical services, an individual will customarily solicit and expect to receive the services of a particular physician, and he will usually be treated by the physician sought.

A physician-patient relationship arises from such a general agreement of treatment. Either party may terminate the relationship at will, although the physician must give the patient reasonable notice of his withdrawal and may not abandon the patient until a replacement, if necessary, can be obtained. . . . Moreover, if a physician who has entered into a general agreement of treatment is unable to treat the patient when his services are needed, he may provide a qualified and competent substitute physician. . . .

Thus, when an individual solicits, and expects, the services of a particular physician and that physician accepts the individual as a patient and treats him, the relationship of physician-patient established in this manner does not constitute a designation of the individual who is to perform the services under a contract for personal services within the meaning of section 543(a)(7). . . .

If, however, the physician or the professional service corporation contracts with the patient that the physician personally will perform particular services for the patient, and he has no right to substitute another physician to perform such services, there is a designation of that physician as the individual to perform services. . . .

Moreover, if L agreed to perform the type of services that are so unique as to preclude substitution of another physician . . . , there is also a designation. . . .

NOTE

In Kenyatta Corp., 86 T.C. 171 (1986), *aff'd,* 812 F.2d 577 (9th Cir. 1987), a sportscaster organized his business in a manner similar to that of the doctor in Rev. Rul. 75-67, and his corporation was held to be a personal holding company.

IV. EXCEPTIONS

PACIFIC SECURITY COMPANIES v. COMMISSIONER
59 T.C. 744 (1973)

QUEALY, Judge. . . . The only question remaining for decision is whether petitioner was a personal holding company as defined in section 542(a) for the fiscal years ended November 30, 1965 to 1968, inclusive.

FINDINGS OF FACT

. . . Pacific Security Companies (hereinafter referred to as the petitioner) is a corporation organized on May 29, 1963, under the laws of the State of Washington. On November 30, 1971, the name of the corporation was changed to Pacific Security Companies. At all times material herein, Wayne E. Guthrie has owned 100 percent of the outstanding capital stock of the petitioner. . . .

During the fiscal years involved in this proceeding, petitioner was engaged in the general financing business. It made loans, factored accounts receivable, discounted real estate contracts, discounted conditional sales contracts, and entered into chattel lease agreements. . . .

Petitioner did business in the States of Washington, Oregon, Idaho, and Montana, maintaining, in addition to its principal office in Spokane, Wash., offices in the cities of Seattle, Wash., Tacoma, Wash., Portland, Oreg., and Missoula, Mont. The petitioner derived its financing business principally from equipment dealers throughout the four States in which it did business. Representatives of the petitioner called on equipment dealers and maintained constant contact with them for the purpose of selling its financial services to them.

In its financing services to equipment dealers, the petitioner offered to provide financing on either a conditional sales program or a chattel leasing program. Dealers were advised that if their customers wished to purchase equipment on a conditional sales contract, petitioner would purchase the equipment from the dealer and lease it to the customer.

The petitioner provided the dealers with which it did business with a "financing kit." The kit consisted of a plastic binder containing information about petitioner's financial services and a supply of the various forms necessary to put together a financing transaction. Included in the kit were conditional sales contract forms, chattel lease agreement forms, Uniform Commercial Code Financing Statement Forms, various credit application forms, informational brochures about petitioner's financial services, and a financing charge rate card.

The rate card was designed to enable equipment dealers to quote to their customers the monthly cost of leasing a given item of equipment or of purchasing it on a conditional sales contract. The card consisted of various rate factors to be multiplied times the equipment cost. The specific rate factor to be used depended upon the term of the lease or conditional sales contract, and upon the size of the transaction. The rate factors were designed to enable petitioner to recover over the term of the lease or conditional sales contract, its cost of the equipment or contract, plus a satisfactory financing charge.

The rate factors to be used for chattel leasing and for conditional sales contracts were the same. On a given piece of equipment the same rate factors would be used, whether the equipment was to be leased for a given number of months or purchased on a conditional sales contract requiring the same number of payments. The decision, whether a given item of equipment would be acquired through leasing or conditional sale financing, was made by the customer of the dealer with whom the petitioner did business.

A dealer's customer who decided to finance equipment, whether by leasing or conditional sale, would make out a credit application, consisting of bank references, trade references, credit references, and financial statements. After evaluating the credit application, petitioner would either approve or reject the customer's credit. If the customer's credit was approved, petitioner would proceed to close the transaction, purchasing the conditional sales contract from the dealer in the event of a conditional sale, or purchasing the equipment from the dealer and signing a chattel lease agreement with the customer in the case of a lease.

The petitioner used preprinted chattel lease agreement forms. On each lease agreement was set out a description of the equipment, the name of the supplier of the equipment, the cost of the equipment, the amount of each payment, and the number of payments to be made. Included in the terms and conditions of the chattel lease agreement were the following:

(1) Petitioner retained title to the leased property.

(2) Petitioner reserved the right to inspect and label the leased property.

(3) Additions or improvements to the property became property of petitioner.

(4) The lessee was required to pay all taxes with respect to the leased property.

(5) The lessee assumed all risk of loss to the property and was required to maintain casualty and liability insurance with respect to it.

(6) The lessee granted a security interest in the leased property and all of the rights and remedies of a secured creditor under the Uniform Commercial Code to the petitioner.

(7) In the event of default by the lessee, petitioner reserved the right to: (a) Terminate the lease and repossess the property, or (b) declare all of the rent due and sue for it, realizing on the leased equipment for payment, with the lessee liable for any deficiency and the petitioner obligated to return any excess to the lessee.

(8) The lessee was obligated to return the leased equipment to petitioner at the end of the term.

(9) The petitioner disclaimed any liability for injury arising out of the use or condition of leased equipment.

Under the terms of the chattel lease agreement forms used by petitioner, the lessee had no right, obligation, or option to purchase the leased equipment at the end of the term. However, in addition to the durations of the chattel lease agreements as set out above, each lease agreement contained an option, giving the lessee a right to renew the lease agreement for various periods.

All of the chattel lease agreements entered into by petitioner covered equipment sold by equipment dealers in the ordinary course of their business. Petitioner had no inventory of equipment held for lease and no wholesale connections for the purpose of equipment.

In its income tax returns for each of the fiscal years 1965 to 1968, inclusive, petitioner reported payments received from chattel lease agreements as gross rent, and claimed depreciation with respect to the leased property, based upon the terms of the respective leases. During the same period, the petitioner in most cases claimed the investment tax credit with respect to items of equipment covered by chattel lease agreements. In each year in issue, the petitioner in some cases exercised the option granted by section 48(d) of the Internal Revenue Code and passed the investment credit through to the lessee of the equipment.

In the event that petitioner's adjusted gross income from the chattel lease agreements is deemed to constitute "rents" within the meaning of section 543(a)(2), at least 60 percent of its adjusted ordinary gross income would constitute personal holding company income as defined in section 543(a). Unless otherwise excluded under section 542(c)(6), petitioner would meet the definition of a personal holding company as set forth in section 542(a).

In the event that petitioner's ordinary gross income from the chattel lease agreements is deemed to have been derived from the active and regular conduct of a lending or financing business within the meaning of section 542(c)(6)(A), more than 60 percent of petitioner's ordinary gross income as thus defined would be derived from the active and regular conduct of such business in each of the fiscal years involved in this proceeding. The petitioner would thereupon qualify for exclusion from the definition of a personal holding company as a "lending or finance company" within the meaning of section 542(c)(6).

OPINION

... In characterizing the leasing income as personal holding company income, the respondent relies on section 543(a)(2) which defines personal holding income to include "rents," except under certain conditions not present here. Section 543(b)(3) defines "rents" so as to include "compensation, however designated, for the use of, or right to use, property."

In contending that it is not taxable as a personal holding company, the petitioner relies on the exclusion provided in section 542(c)(6). If the income from leasing constitutes a part of the income derived directly from the active and regular conduct of a lending or finance business, admittedly the petitioner would meet the requisite conditions of the exclusion.

In substance, the petitioner concedes that the term "rents" in section 543(a)(2) may be interpreted so as to include income which is received in the form of rent on the chattel leases before the Court. However, petitioner contends that such "rents" may nevertheless also be includable as income derived from the active and regular conduct of a lending or finance business under section 542(c)(6)(A).

In the petitioner's business, the prospective user of the equipment is given an option. The user may purchase the equipment under a conditional sales contract wherein the petitioner provides the funds in the form of a "loan" and is repaid in installments. In the alternative, after selecting the equipment to be purchased, the prospective user may enter into a contract to lease the equipment from the petitioner for a term of years. Petitioner thereupon issues its purchase order to the supplier of the equipment, and the lessee takes possession under the lease. In the chattel lease transaction, the "installments" are in the form of rent.

Petitioner argues that, as a practical matter, the net result is the same. Both transactions are regularly entered into as a part of the finance business. The income should, therefore, be treated the same.

From an economic standpoint, there may be no real distinction between the chattel mortgage form of financing and the chattel lease. In either case, the customer pays pro rata for the use of the equipment, generally over the term of its anticipated service life. Irrespective of the form of financing, the customer is liable to pay the installments prescribed in the contract regardless whether the equipment functions properly, may be damaged through some casualty, or proves to be inoperable. In a majority of the leases, the customer may end up buying the equipment for its residual value.

We are not here concerned, however, with the economic similarities or dissimilarities of the "market place." In the provisions dealing with personal holding companies, the Congress has provided precise definitions and formulae. The "lending or finance business" is what Congress says it is. . . .

It should thus be noted that in section 542(d)(1)(A) the statute refers to "making loans" and to "purchasing or discounting accounts receivable, notes, or installment obligations." Section 542(d)(1)(B) then excludes obligations where the remaining maturity exceeds 60 months, "unless the loans, notes, or installment obligations are evidenced or secured by contracts of conditional sale, chattel mortgages, or chattel lease agreements arising out of the sale of goods or services in the course of the borrower's or transferor's trade or business."

The term "chattel lease agreements" in the statute is not within the enumerated categories of direct transactions constituting permissible activities of the finance business, but is referred to only as the security for such transactions where the property subject to the lease was sold in the ordinary course of the borrower's or transferor's trade or business. The statute thus clearly contemplates a transaction whereby a third party lessor obtains the funds to finance the transaction from the petitioner with the lease as security. If such financing is without recourse against the lessor, the net result insofar as the parties are concerned may be the same as if the lender had acted as lessor. However, the statute does not look to the net result. The statute carefully and specifically defines what is the lending or finance business. While there may be no difference in end result between a direct chattel lease and a non-recourse loan secured by a chattel lease in the "market place," the statute clearly makes the distinction in delineating the activities which constitute the lending or finance business as defined in section 542(d)(1).

Other tax incidents are dependent upon the same distinction. In considering whether taxpayers are entitled to the investment credit under section 38, this Court has upheld the distinction between chattel leasing and chattel financing. . . . [T]his petitioner regarded itself as the owner and lessor of the equipment for purposes of the investment credit. In our opinion, no basis exists for applying a different rule merely because we are dealing with a different section of the Internal Revenue Code. Accordingly, petitioner fails to qualify as a lending or finance company excludable from the term "personal holding company" under section 542(c)(6).

V. DISTRIBUTIONS AND DEDUCTIONS

CALLAN v. COMMISSIONER
54 T.C. 1514 (1970), *aff'd per curiam*, 476 F.2d 509 (9th Cir. 1973)

RAUM, Judge. . . . The only question for decision is whether payments of $19,918.98 and $959.82 made on March 27, 1968, by Callan Investment Co. qualify for the deficiency dividends deduction, authorized by section 547. . . .

[The taxpayers, Michael and Thomas Callan, were stockholders of Callan Investment Co., which was dissolved under state law in 1965. In 1968 the Callans conceded to the Commissioner that the corporation had been a personal holding company, with undistributed personal holding company income totaling nearly $21,000 in its last two taxable years. Michael and Thomas were potentially liable for personal holding company taxes as transferees of the corporation's assets. In order to avert this possibility, a special meeting of the board of directors was called on March 22, 1968. The directors formally called for the shareholders to contribute $21,000 to the corporation.]

On March 27, 1968, the following events occurred (although not necessarily in the order in which they are mentioned): (1) An account in the name of the corporation was opened at an office of the First Western Bank in San Francisco. (2) The Callans delivered checks payable to the corporation in the aggregate amount of $21,000. (3) The checks were deposited in the corporation's account. (4) The corporation's board of directors held a special meeting wherein they purported to declare two "deficiency dividends" pursuant to section 547, . . . 1 cent greater than the corporation's total undistributed personal holding company income for the two periods involved herein of $20,878.79. (5) Four checks, in the aggregate amount of $20,878.80, were drawn on the corporation's newly opened account; two of the checks . . . were payable to Michael . . . the two remaining checks were in the same amounts and were payable to . . . Thomas. . . .

On May 13, 1968, the corporation filed a completed Form 976, "Claim for Deficiency Dividends Deduction, or Credit or Refund Under Section 547 of the Internal Revenue Code." The Commissioner disallowed the claim. . . .

[Michael filed a federal income tax return for the calendar year 1968. Thomas also filed a return for that year.] Neither return disclosed the receipt of any dividend income from the corporation. However, on January 23, 1970, after the hearing in this court, each couple filed an amended joint income tax return for the calendar year 1968 . . . and each of those returns reported an increase in income of $10,439.40 to reflect receipt of the purported "deficiency dividends" from the corporation.

In his statutory notices of deficiency to Michael and Thomas, the Commissioner determined that as a result of his disallowance of the corporation's claim for a deficiency dividends deduction, the petitioners, as transferees of the corporation's assets, were jointly and severally liable for the corporation's deficiencies in income and personal holding company tax, plus interest. . . .

Section 547 grants statutory authority for the deficiency dividends deduction. It provides that once a corporation has been determined to be liable for personal holding company tax, the corporation may reduce its liability for the tax by making a taxable distribution to its shareholders within 90 days of the determination and deducting the amount of that distribution from its personal holding company income as a deficiency dividends deduction.

The general rule for allowance of the deficiency dividends deduction is set forth in section 547(a), which refers to section 547(d) for the definition of "deficiency dividends." By its terms, the definition depends upon the amount of the dividends otherwise includable in the "deduction for dividends paid" authorized by section 561. . . . Section 562(a), in turn, provides that for the purpose of the personal holding company tax, the term "dividend," except as otherwise provided, includes only dividends described in section 316. . . .

Section 316(b)(2) relates to distributions by personal holding companies, and the controversy between the parties herein concerns its interpretation. . . . These provisions expand the definition of "dividend" to include certain "distributions of property" made by personal holding companies. Distributions qualifying as dividends under section 316(b)(2) are, by virtue of section 562, includable in the deduction for dividends paid defined by section 561, and are therefore also taken into account in computing the amount of the deficiency dividends deduction under section 547.

The only question presented for decision is whether the corporation's "distributions" to the Callans on March 27, 1968, may be deducted by it as deficiency dividends under section 547. . . . The controversy turns ultimately on whether the corporation's 1968 "distributions" are treated as dividends by section 316(b)(2). Petitioners concede that the "distributions" do not qualify as "distributions of property" under subparagraph (B) of section 316(b)(2) and hence do not qualify as dividends under subparagraph (A) of that section by virtue of subparagraph (B). However, they urge that the "distributions" do qualify as dividends directly under the more general provisions of subparagraph (A) and that therefore they may be taken into account in computing the deficiency dividends deduction under section 547.

The Commissioner, on the other hand, contends that subparagraph (B) of section 316(b)(2) is the only provision in that section applicable to the so-called distributions in question and that the failure of such distributions to qualify under it precludes allowance of the claimed deduction. In the alternative, even if subparagraph (A) is applicable, the Commissioner urges that as of March 27, 1968, the corporation no longer served a nontax business purpose, that as of March 27, the corporation in fact had no undistributed personal holding company income to distribute, and that the payments in question were simply a return of the Callans' own funds and not a "dividend" within the meaning of section 316(b)(2)(A). We consider these points in inverse order.

1. We think it evident that the so-called "distributions" made on March 27, 1968, were not genuine distributions at all. As of March 27, 1968, the corporation had not held assets or engaged in any business activity whatever for over 3 years. It thus had no assets of any kind, and certainly no earnings and profits, to distribute. The establishment of a bank account in the corporation's name, the deposit of the Callans' checks in that account, and the redistribution of nearly all of the very same funds to the Callans on the same day, was simply an attempt by the Callans to undo what they had done in 1965 and to recast the liquidating distributions made then as deficiency dividends in 1968. The Callans' funds were merely sent on a "planned excursion," . . . or a "round-trip," . . . to the corporation and back for the purpose of qualifying the distributions for the desired deduction. . . . The dormant status of the corporation remained substantially unchanged. We conclude that the "distributions" of March 27, 1968, were not distributions at all for purposes of section 316(b)(2) and that the claimed deficiency dividends deduction may not be allowed.

2. In any event, even if the so-called "distributions" are deemed genuine for purposes of section 316(b)(2), we think that they nevertheless fail to qualify for the deficiency dividends deduction. The 1968 distributions, like the 1965 distributions, were liquidating in

nature. After the 1965 distributions were made, the corporation held no assets and engaged in no business of any kind. The 1968 distributions thus did not alter the corporation's dormant status.

Petitioners urge that section 5400 of the California Corporations Code[9] authorized both the continued existence of the corporation in 1968 and the actions taken in executing the determination of personal holding company tax liability and in engaging in the transactions of March 27, 1968. We do not suggest otherwise. However, we do note that section 5400 expressly withholds authority for the continued existence of a corporation "for the purpose of continuing business except so far as necessary for the winding up thereof." This provision thus lends further support to our conclusion that the 1968 distributions were liquidating in nature.

Once the 1968 distributions are characterized as liquidating distributions, the question before us becomes whether a liquidating distribution may qualify as a "dividend" directly under subparagraph (A) of section 316(b)(2). The legislative history of sections 316(b)(2) and 562(b) makes it clear that it may not, and that a liquidating distribution must qualify under subparagraph (B) in order to be considered a dividend for purposes of the deficiency dividends deduction.

Prior to 1964, section 562(b) treated a liquidating distribution (to the extent of accumulated earnings and profits) made by a personal holding company as a dividend for purposes of computing the dividends paid deduction under section 561:

> *Sec. 562. Rules Applicable in Determining Dividends Eligible for Dividends Paid Deduction*
> (b) Distributions in Liquidation. — In the case of amounts distributed in liquidation, the part of such distribution which is properly chargeable to earnings and profits accumulated after February 28, 1913, shall be treated as a dividend for purposes of computing the dividends paid deduction. In the case of a complete liquidation occurring within 24 months after the adoption of a plan of liquidation any distribution within such period pursuant to such plan shall, to the extent of the earnings and profits (computed without regard to capital losses) of the corporation for the taxable year in which such distribution is made, be treated as a dividend for purposes of computing the dividends paid deduction.

---

9. Cal. Corp. Code sec. 5400: "A corporation which is dissolved by the expiration of its term of existence, by forfeiture of existence by order of court, or otherwise, nevertheless continues to exist for the purpose of winding up its affairs, prosecuting and defending actions by or against it, and enabling it to collect and discharge obligations, dispose of and convey its property, and collect and divide its assets, but not for the purpose of continuing business except so far as necessary for the winding up thereof."

A liquidating distribution was thus deducted (to the extent of accumulated earnings and profits) when computing the liquidating corporation's undistributed personal holding income and consequently reduced its personal holding company tax liability.

Moreover, prior to 1964, section 316(b)(2) provided as follows:

Sec. 316. Dividend Defined
(b) Special Rules. — . . .
(2) Distributions By Personal Holding Companies. — In the case of a corporation which
(A) under the law applicable to the taxable year in which the distribution is made, is a personal holding company (as defined in section 542), or
(B) for the taxable year in respect of which the distribution is made under section 563(b) (relating to dividends paid after the close of the taxable year), or section 547 (relating to deficiency dividends), or the corresponding provisions of prior law, is a personal holding company under the law applicable to such taxable year, *the term "dividend" also means any distribution of property* (whether or not a dividend as defined in subsection (a)) made by the corporation to its shareholders' to the extent of its undistributed personal holding company income (determined under section 545 without regard to distributions under this paragraph) for such year. [Emphasis supplied.]

When that provision was originally enacted in 1942, as an amendment to section 115(a), I.R.C. 1939, both the House and Senate reports declared . . .

The amendments made by this section provide that any distribution to shareholders *(not in complete or partial liquidation)* made on or after the date of enactment of this act by a corporation which, for the taxable year in which such a distribution is made or for the taxable year in respect of which it is made . . . , was under the applicable law a personal holding company, will now constitute a taxable dividend even if not paid out of accumulated or current earnings or profits. [Emphasis supplied.]

That the amended section 115(a) did not govern liquidating distributions was also emphasized in 1956 by the Third Circuit in St. Louis Co. v. United States, 237 F.2d 151, 154-155 (C.A.3), *certiorari denied* 352 U.S. 1001. . . .

Thus, since, prior to 1964, section 316(b)(2) did not govern liquidating distributions, stockholders receiving such a distribution from a personal holding company were taxed on it at favorable capital gain rates. Consequently, in the year of liquidation, a personal holding company could escape liability for the personal holding company tax by virtue of a liquidating distribution, while its stockholders avoided taxation on the distribution at ordinary-income rates.

Such result was at odds with the original purpose of the personal holding company provisions, which was to encourage distribution of accumulated income to the hands of individual stockholders where it would be subjected to individual income tax rates, and the 1964 legislation was designed to remedy the problem. . . . In its report on the 1964 Code amendments, the House Ways and Means Committee again specifically noted . . . : "This special definition of a dividend in section 316(b)(2) does not apply to distributions in partial or complete liquidation of a personal holding company."

Under the 1964 legislation, the introductory clause of current Code section 562(b)(1) was added . . . in order to exclude personal holding treated a liquidating distribution by a personal holding company as a dividend for purposes of the dividends paid deduction.

However, at the same time, section 316(b)(2)(B) was also added to the Code in order to permit certain liquidating distributions made by personal holding companies to noncorporate stockholders to qualify for the dividends paid deduction, but only under conditions designed to ensure that the recipient stockholders would be taxed on such distributions at ordinary-income rates. . . . The House and Senate reports summarized the effect of these provisions as follows . . . :

> it is provided in section 316(b) that in the case of a complete liquidation of a personal holding company within a 24-month period after the adoption of the plan of liquidation, that the term "dividend" is to include any amounts distributed in this liquidation to other than corporate shareholders to the extent of its undistributed income (before any deduction for this amount) only if the corporation involved designates amounts as dividends (and so notifies the distributee). If the corporation does so designate the distributions as dividends the individuals receiving a liquidating distribution from the personal holding company must report the amount so distributed as a dividend in the year of receipt. . . .

The pre-1964 version of section 316(b)(2), however, was preserved unchanged in section 316(b)(2)(A).

Thus, the purpose of the 1964 amendments to sections 316(b)(2) and 562(b)(1) was to prevent a result caused by the fact that a liquidating distribution by a personal holding company was not covered by pre-1964 section 316(b)(2) and consequently was not taxed in the hands of recipient stockholders at ordinary-income rates. Subparagraph (B) of section 316(b)(2) was therefore added in order to ensure that when such a distribution was treated as a dividend for purposes of the dividends paid deduction, the distribution would be taxed to the stockholders at ordinary rates. Section 316(b)(2)(A) preserved the language of the pre-1964 section, and, like its pre-1964 forerunner, it remained completely inapplicable to liquidating distributions by personal holding companies. Regulations section 1.316-l(b)(l), amended in 1968 to reflect the 1964 Code amendments, makes this absolutely clear. . . .

We conclude that the distributions in issue are not governed directly by section 316(b)(2)(A).

While the Code does permit a personal holding company to designate a liquidating distribution as a "dividend" for the purposes of section 316, the procedure outlined in subparagraph (B) of section 316 is the only authorized method for such designation. Subparagraph (B) was added to the Code precisely because liquidating distributions by personal holding companies had not been governed by the forerunner of subparagraph (A) and because compliance with the requirements of subparagraph (B) would ensure that, when properly designated as a dividend, such a distribution would be taxed to the recipients at ordinary rates. Allowing a liquidating distribution to qualify as a dividend directly under subparagraph (A) would thus defeat the purpose of subparagraph (B).[11] Compare sec. 1.316-l(b)(5), Income Tax Regs.

Petitioners urge that if a liquidating distribution must qualify under subparagraph (B), or not at all, an unfair distinction is made between a distribution by a liquidating personal holding company, which must qualify under subparagraph (B), and a distribution by a personal holding company continuing in business, which may qualify directly under subparagraph (A) and thereby avoid the requirements of subparagraph (B). As explained above, however, subparagraph (B) was designed to make just such a distinction, in order to ensure that a liquidating distribution which was treated as a dividend for purposes of the dividends paid deduction would be taxed to the recipients at ordinary rates.

We recognize that our reading of the statute may work a harsh result upon the petitioners. The corporation was not determined to be liable for the personal holding company tax until nearly 4 years after the plan of liquidation was adopted, and by that time it was precluded from making a distribution which qualified under subparagraph (B), since such distribution must be made within 24 months after the adoption of a plan of liquidation. However, we think that the statute leaves us with no other choice, and the claimed deduction must be disallowed. As was stated in St. Louis Co. v. United States, 237 F.2d 151, 157 (C.A.3), *certiorari denied* 352 U.S. 1001:

11. We note that petitioners' original income tax returns for the calendar year 1968 did not disclose receipt of dividend income as a result of the distributions here in issue. Subpar. (B) is designed to ensure that distributions satisfying its requirements are reported by the recipients as ordinary income, and petitioners' initial failure to report the distributions here suggests the opportunity for abuse if the requirements set forth in subpar. (B) need not be followed.

It is recognized that Congress imposed the prohibitive surtax on personal holding companies to destroy the tax advantages accruing to such companies, and to drive them out of business. Since complete liquidation accomplished the desired result in this case, taxpayer urges that imposition of the tax would be contrary to the intent of Congress and destructive of the purpose of the personal holding company provisions. The District Court points out the inequity of imposing the surtax on taxpayer in this situation in 134 F. Supp. 411, at page 415:

"The overriding intent of Congress, it would seem, was, that insofar as personal holding companies are concerned, to compel such companies to distribute the funds on hand and to prevent their accumulation or to compel substantial surtaxes on such accumulation. There seems no discernible intent to discriminate against a company unsuccessful in past years as against one which had had some measure of success, when in both cases the over-riding purpose of Congress, viz., the distribution of all funds, is accomplished."

See also Pembroke Realty & Securities Corp. v. Commissioner, supra, 122 F.2d at page 254, and Piper v. United States, supra, 50 F. Supp. at page 365.

However, arguments based upon inequity are beyond judicial cognizance where the statute does not remedy the inequity, nor can we extend the meaning of the statute to embrace matters for which no provision has been made. The Supreme Court has affirmed this principle in United States v. Olympic Radio & Television, Inc., 1955, 349 U.S. 232, 236, . . . where it said:

"This taxpayer argues the inequity of the results which would follow from our construction of the Code. But as we have said before, 'general equitable considerations' do not control the question of what deductions are permissible. Deputy v. du Pont, supra, [308 U.S.] at page 493. . . . It may be that Congress granted less than some thought or less than was originally intended. We can only take the Code as we find it and give it as great an internal symmetry and consistency as its words permit." . . .

NOTES

1. See also L. C. Bohart Plumbing & Heating Co., 64 T.C. 602 (1975) (Treas. Reg. §1.316-1(b)(5) precludes amendment of filed return for liquidated corporation's final taxable year to designate liquidating distributions as §316(b)(2)(B) dividends).

2. On professional advice a corporation with a taxable year ending on July 31 declared in March a dividend to be paid in September. The purpose of the dividend was to avoid personal holding company tax for the year ended prior to the payment date through the ap-

plication of §563(b). However, since the corporation had not actually paid any dividends during that year, §563(b)(2) precluded a dividends-paid deduction. See Kenneth Farmer Darrow, 64 T.C. 217 (1975).

3. Section 545(b)(1) allows a deduction for federal income taxes in computing the base on which the personal holding company tax is imposed. If a taxpayer contests a federal income tax deficiency, however, even an accrual basis taxpayer may not deduct the deficiency until the controversy is concluded. A claim for deduction for the years to which the deficiency related was rejected in LX Cattle Co. v. United States, 629 F.2d 1096 (5th Cir. 1980).

4. Section 565 offers a "consent dividend" procedure to permit a designated portion of a corporation's earnings and profits to be treated as a deductible "dividend paid" under §§545(a) and 561 even though there is no actual distribution. The shareholders, by consenting, are deemed to have dividend income. For the question whether "consent dividends" are available when the "distributing" corporation is not subject to tax under §531 or §541, see Sheppard, Informed Consent: IRS Tries to Correct Section 565 Mistake, Tax Notes, March 28, 1988, p. 1439.

What are the implications of Treas. Reg. §1.565-3(b), Examples 1 and 2, when the "distributing" corporation is not subject to tax under §531 or §541?

FULMAN v. UNITED STATES
434 U.S. 528 (1978)

Mr. Justice Brennan delivered the opinion of the Court.

The question presented in this case is the validity of the provision of Treas. Reg. §1.562-1(a) that a personal holding company's distribution of appreciated property to its shareholders results, under sections 561 and 562 of the Internal Revenue Code of 1954, . . . in a dividends-paid deduction limited to an amount that is "the adjusted basis of the property in the hands of the distributing corporation at the time of the distribution." The Court of Appeals for the First Circuit sustained the validity of the provision in this case, 545 F.2d 268 (1976), disagreeing with the Court of Appeals for the Sixth Circuit in H. Wetter Mfg. Co. v. United States, 458 F.2d 1033 (1972) which had concluded that the limitation on the dividends-paid deduction is invalid and that a personal holding company is entitled to a deduction equal in amount to the fair market value of property distributed. We granted certiorari to resolve the conflict. 431 U.S. 928 (1977). We agree with the Court of Appeals for the First Circuit that the limitation on the dividends-paid deduction provided by the regulations is valid, and therefore affirm its judgment. . . .

II

Petitioners are the successors to Pierce Investment Corp. In 1966 the Commissioner audited Pierce and determined that it was a personal holding company for the tax years 1959, 1960, 1962, and 1963. Deficiencies in personal holding company taxes of $26,571.30 were assessed against Pierce. In response to the audit, Pierce entered an agreement with the Commissioner pursuant to §547 of the Code which provides that a corporation in Pierce's position may enter such an agreement, acknowledging its deficiency and personal holding company status, and may within 90 days thereafter make "deficiency dividend" payments that become a deduction against personal holding company income in the years for which a deficiency was determined and reduce that deficiency. Shares of stock Pierce held in other companies were promptly distributed as deficiency dividends. The fair market value of this stock at the time of distribution is agreed to have been $32,535; its adjusted tax basis, $18,725.11.

Pierce then filed a claim for a deficiency-dividend deduction, as required by §547(e), indicating that the value of dividends distributed for the tax years in question was $32,535. The Commissioner, relying on Treas. Reg. §1.562-1(a), allowed this claim only to the extent of Pierce's adjusted basis in the stock, and he determined a new deficiency after reducing Pierce's personal holding company income by the amount of the deficiency dividends allowed. Pierce paid this tax and the Commissioner denied its claim for a refund.

Petitioners as Pierce's successors thereafter brought a refund suit in the United States District Court for the District of Massachusetts, arguing that the deficiency dividends should have been valued at their fair market value. The District Court on cross-motions for summary judgment denied relief, 407 F. Supp. 1039 (1976), and the Court of Appeals for the First Circuit affirmed. Each court found the Treasury Regulation to be a reasonable interpretation of the personal holding company tax statute, and each expressly refused to follow the contrary holding of H. Wetter Mfg. Co. v. United States, supra.[7] Accordingly a refund was denied.

"[I]t is fundamental . . . that as 'contemporaneous constructions by those charged with administration of' the Code, [Treasury] Regulations 'must be sustained unless unreasonable and plainly

---

7. In *Wetter*, the Sixth Circuit, adopting a "plain meaning" rule, held that the 1954 Code required the rule of 26 U.S.C. §301 to be used in establishing the value of the dividend deduction under the personal holding company tax. The meaning of the 1954 Code is, however, anything but plain.

inconsistent with the revenue statutes,' and 'should not be overruled except for weighty reasons.' " Bingler v. Johnson, 394 U.S. 741, 749-750 (1969), quoting Commissioner v. South Texas Lumber Co., 333 U.S. 496, 501 (1948); accord, United States v. Correll, 389 U.S. 299, 306-307 (1967). This rule of deference is particularly appropriate here,[8] since, while obviously some rule of valuation must be applied, Congress, as we shall see, failed expressly to provide one. See United States v. Correll, supra; §7805(a).

Section 547(a) of the Code requires that a taxpayer who like Pierce pays dividends after a determination of liability by the Commissioner "shall be allowed" 'a deduction . . . for the amount of deficiency dividends (as defined in subsection (d)) for the purpose of determining the personal holding company tax." Subsection 547(d) in turn provides that "the term 'deficiency dividends' means the amount of the dividends paid by the corporation . . . , which would have been includible in the computation of the deduction for dividends paid under section 561 for the taxable year with respect to which the liability for personal holding company tax exists, if distributed during such taxable year."

Continuing this chain of definitions, §561(a) provides that the deduction for dividends "shall be the sum of," inter alia, dividends paid during the taxable year; and §561(b)(1) points to §562 as the source of a rule for valuing such dividends. Section 562, however, provides only exceptions to a basic rule said to be provided by §316 of the Code. But when we turn to §316, the trail of definitions finally turns cold, for that section states only that a dividend is a "distribution of property made by a corporation to its shareholders" out of current or accumulated earnings or, in the case of personal holding companies, out of its current personal holding company income. Inexplicably, moreover, the draftsmen refer us back to §562 for "[r]ules applicable in determining dividends eligible for dividends paid credit deduction." See Cross References following §316.

Petitioners suggest that the way out of this circularity is to adopt the valuation rules for distributions of property found in §301 of the Code. We cannot agree, for §301 deals not with the problem of valuing the distribution with respect to the *distributing corporation*, but establishes rules governing the valuation with respect to *distributees*. This is not to deny the logical force of petitioners' argument that, since the purpose of the personal holding company tax is to force individuals to include personal holding company income in their

---

8. Although we have said that penalty tax provisions are to be strictly construed, see Ivan Allen Co. v. United States, 422 U.S. 617, 627 (1975); Commissioner v. Acker, 361 U.S. 87, 91 (1959), this rule of construction does not apply to the personal holding company tax since any penalty can be easily avoided by following — as petitioners' predecessor did — the guidelines set out in 26 U.S.C. §547.

individual returns, the corporate distributor should get a deduction at the corporate level equal to the income generated by the distribution at the shareholder level as defined by §301, that is, the fair market value of the appreciated property in this case.[9] See §301(b)(1)(A). Indeed, *Wetter*, 458 F.2d 1033 (1972), and Gulf Inland Corp. v. United States, 75-2 U.S.T.C. ¶9620 (W.D. La.), *appeal docketed*, No. 75-3767 (C.A.5 1975), have taken the view urged by petitioners, and but for the Regulation, the argument might well prevail. But, as we have indicated, the issue before us is *not* how *we* might resolve the statutory ambiguity in the first instance, but whether there is any reasonable basis for the resolution embodied in the Commissioner's Regulation. We conclude that there is.

In the Revenue Act of 1936, Congress enacted a surtax on undistributed profits intended to supplement the 1934 enactment of the personal holding company tax. In §27(c) of the 1936 Act, 49 Stat. 1665, later codified as §27(d) of the Internal Revenue Code of 1939, 53 Stat. 20, Congress expressly provided the "adjusted basis" measure

---

9. Petitioners also argue that the valuation standard provided by §301 was expressly adopted by the House as the standard to be used in establishing the value of a dividend with respect to a corporation as well as to a distributee-shareholder. In H.R. 8300, 83d Cong., 2d Sess. (1954), the forerunner of the Internal Revenue Code of 1954, §562(a) referred to §312 which stated: "The term 'dividend' when used in this subtitle means a distribution *(as determined in section 301(a))*. . . ." (Emphasis added.) Section 301(a) defined a "distribution" as "the amount of money . . . and the fair market value of securities and property received" by a distributee. This, petitioners conclude, shows that Congress meant to use the standard of §301, now codified as 26 U.S.C. §301, as the standard for valuing distributions of property with respect to both the distributing corporation and the distributee-shareholder.

The language in §312 italicized above was deleted by the Senate, however, and does not appear in §316 of the 1954 Code — which corresponds to §312 of H.R. 8300, supra. Moreover, as explained infra, at 536-538, the House Report states that the rule of §27(c) of the Revenue Act of 1936, 49 Stat. 1665, was incorporated in the 1954 Code. If that is indeed the case, then §301 cannot be the section that governed valuation of property dividends under §562(a) of H.R. 8300, since §301 does not embody the valuation rule of §27(c) with respect to distributions to non-corporate shareholders. Instead, H.R. 8300, §301(a) mandates the use of fair market value without regard to basis when the distributee is a noncorporate shareholder, whereas §27(c) mandated the use of the *lower* of basis or fair market value. The rule of §27(c) is used in H.R. 8300 only with respect to corporate distributees, taxpayers who were *not* the target of the personal holding company tax. There is, therefore, no unambiguous inference to be drawn from the linkage between §§301, 312, and 562 of the House bill. See also nn.13-14, infra.

Finally, petitioners argue that our decision in Ivan Allen Co. v. United States, supra, supports their contention that fair market value must be the measure of property dividends. But this is not the case. As we made abundantly clear in *Ivan Allen*, the fair market value of liquid assets figures *only* in calculating whether "earnings and profits . . . [have been] permitted to accumulate beyond the reasonable needs of the business." 26 U.S.C. §533(a). Unrealized appreciation does not figure in the tax base to which the accumulated earnings tax applies. See 422 U.S., at 627, 633. Since *Ivan Allen* thus holds that appreciation does *not* figure in the accumulated earnings tax base, there is no justification for reasoning from that opinion that such appreciation must nonetheless figure in the dividends to be subtracted from that base.

for valuation with respect to the distributing corporation of dividends, paid in appreciated property rather than money: "If a dividend is paid in property other than money . . . the dividends paid credit with respect thereto shall be the adjusted basis of the property in the hands of the corporation at the time of the payment, or the fair market value of the property at the time of the payment, whichever is the lower." Although this section may not have been enacted with the personal holding company tax primarily in mind,[11] §351(b)(2)(C) of the 1936 Act nonetheless expressly provided that the dividends-paid credit for that tax would be governed by §27(c). At the same time, in contrast, the 1936 Act provided that property distributed as a dividend would be valued with respect to distributees at its fair market value. See Revenue Act of 1936, §115(j), 49 Stat. 1689.

The relevant provisions of the 1936 Revenue Act were carried over without material change into the Internal Revenue Code of 1939. See §§27(d), 115(j), of that Code, 53 Stat. 20, 48. Thus, the logical symmetry between the gain recognized at the shareholder level and the dividend credit allowed at the corporate level, which petitioners argue should be the touchstone for our decision, was not part of the scheme of the Internal Revenue Code from 1936 to 1954.

Nor can Congress' failure to re-enact a counterpart to §27(c) in the 1954 Code be read unambiguously to indicate that Congress had abandoned the "adjusted basis" measure in favor of the "fair market value" measure. In describing the purpose of §562(a), which defines dividends eligible for deduction for personal holding company tax purposes, the Senate Finance Committee explained: "Subsection (a) provides that the term 'dividend' for purposes of this part shall include, except as otherwise provided in this section, only those dividends described in section 316. . . . The requirements of sections 27(d), (e), (f), and (i) of existing law [Internal Revenue Code of 1939, as amended] are contained in the definition of 'dividend' in section 312, and accordingly are not restated in section 562." S. Rep. No. 1622, 83d Cong., 2d Sess., 325 (1954). The Report of the House Ways and Means Committee is in haec verba, except that it says that the requirements of §§27(d), (e), (f), and (i) are contained in what is now §316 of the 1954 Code.[13] See H.R. Rep. No. 1337, 83d Cong.,

11. Section 27 was added as part of a general revision of the undistributed profits and accumulated earnings taxes. See S. Rep. No. 2156, 74th Cong., 2d Sess., 12-13, 16-18 (1936). There is no discussion in the legislative history of the 1936 Act of the reason for applying §27 to personal holding companies.

13. The Court of Appeals theorized that this discrepancy may have been due to a typographical error in the Senate Report. As the bill which was to become the 1954 Code was passed by the House, the provisions of §316 of the Code were set out as §312. The Senate renumbered the bill, but adopted the discussion of the House Report essentially verbatim, possibly failing to correct all instances where section numbers had changed. . . .

2d Sess., A181 (1954). The discrepancy between the House and Senate Reports is not material, however, since, as we have explained, there is no way to reach the result of §27(c) by following *any* path through the language of the 1954 Code.[14] In light of the failure of the language of the Code to create the result of §27(c), the statement in the House and Senate Reports could be read to indicate that Congress meant to incorporate only so much of §27 as was actually enacted — that is, none of it. But this meaning is not compelled, and we cannot say that the language of the reports cannot be read to evince Congress' intention, albeit erroneously abandoned in execution, to retain the "adjusted basis" valuation rule of §27(c).

At the least, it is not unreasonable for the Commissioner to have assumed that Congress intended to carry forward the law existing prior to the 1954 Code with respect to the measure of valuation. As we said in United States v. Ryder, 110 U.S. 729, 740 (1884): "It will not be inferred that the legislature, in revising and consolidating the laws, intended to change their policy, unless such intention be clearly expressed." . . . If we will not read legislation to abandon previously prevailing law when, as here, a recodification of law is incomplete or departs substantially and without explanation from prior law, we cannot conclude that the Commissioner may not adopt a similar rationale in drafting his rule.[15] In any case, given the law under the 1939 Code and the ambiguity surrounding the House and Senate Reports on §562, it is impossible to identify in this case any "weighty reasons" that would justify setting aside the Treasury Regulation.

Affirmed.

Mr. Justice Blackmun took no part in the consideration or decision of this case.

Mr. Justice STEVENS, concurring in the judgment and concurring in part.

14. If one assumes that S. Rep. No. 1622, supra, is correct in stating that Congress re-enacted §27(c) of the Revenue Act of 1936 as §312 of the 1954 Code, 26 U.S.C. §312, but see n.13, supra, then Treas. Reg. 1.562-1(a), 26 CFR §1.562-1(a), must be upheld because §312(a)(3) provides a dividend valuation rule identical to that of §27(c). But §312 is on its face addressed only to the narrow issue of the effect of dividends on corporate earnings and profits, an issue unrelated to the personal holding company tax. Therefore §312 is no more likely to be the correct locus of the re-enactment of §27(c) than §301 of the Code. Moreover, even if the Senate did intend §312 to be the locus of the rule of §27(c), ambiguity remains because the House, if it put §27(c) anywhere, put it in §§301 and 316 of the Code. See n.9, supra.

15. Treas. Reg. 1.562-1(a), 26 CFR §1.562-1(a), does not, of course, correspond to §27(c) of the Revenue Act of 1936 in valuing *depreciated* property. The Treasury Regulation requires adjusted basis to be used in valuing all distributions of property; §27(c) provided that the *lower* of adjusted basis or fair market value would be used. . . . However, we have no occasion to pass on the validity of §1.562-1(a) as applied to depreciated property since, even if it should be invalid in that circumstance, this would not help petitioners in this case.

The only portion of the Court's opinion which I am unable to join is that quoted by Mr. Justice Powell in dissent. I do not see the ineluctable logical need to equate the amount of income received by the shareholder distributee with the amount of the deduction allowed the corporate distributor. In my judgment market value is the appropriate measure of the recipient's income, and adjusted basis is the appropriate debit on the corporation's books.

Mr. Justice POWELL, dissenting.

The Court's opinion, with commendable candor, recognizes that logic supports petitioners' position: "[We do] not . . . deny the logical force of petitioners' argument that, since the purpose of the personal holding company tax is to force individuals to include personal holding company income in their individual returns, the corporate distributor should get a deduction at the corporate level equal to the income generated by the distribution at the shareholder level as defined by §301, that is, the fair market value of the appreciated property in this case." See §301(b)(1)(A). Ante, at 534-535.

The Court also recognized the "circularity," ante, at 534, and the "ambiguity," ante, at 536, of the relevant provisions of the Internal Revenue Code, as well as the absence of any clarification thereof in the legislative history. The Court simply resolves the statutory jumble in favor of the Treasury Regulation.

It is virtually conceded that this result cannot be squared with the acknowledged purpose of the personal holding company tax. Where statutory ambiguity exists without clarification in the legislative history, a court should read the statute to accord with its manifest purpose. A regulation that defies logic, as well as the statutory purpose, merits little weight.

I find no answer in the Court's opinion to the arguments advanced by Professor Drake. See Drake, Distributions in Kind and Dividends Paid Deduction — Conflict in the Circuits, 1977 B.Y.U. L. Rev. 45. . . .*

I respectfully dissent.

---

*I do not view this as a case that, under the Court's holding today, the Government "wins" and personal holding company taxpayers (other than petitioners) "lose." It is not at all clear to me that the Court's resolution of the statutory ambiguity will in the end increase the Government's "take." The personal holding company device is used by a limited number of sophisticated taxpayers. Under the "adjusted basis" rule upheld by this decision, many of them will be able to schedule the distribution of appreciated and depreciated property in an advantageous manner. Cf. General Securities Co. v. Commissioner, 42 B.T.A. 754 (1940), aff'd, 123 F.2d 192 (C.A.10 1941). I simply would have preferred a resolution that advanced the symmetry of the relevant Code's provisions, see, e.g., 26 U.S.C. §§301, 311, and one compatible with the plain purpose of the personal holding company tax.

NOTES

1. In Rev. Rul. 86-27, 1986-1 C.B. 608, the Service ruled that a personal holding company, a subsidiary that was liquidated into its parent, could claim a dividends paid deduction to the extent the amount distributed to the parent represented undistributed personal holding company income. If P Corp. purchases all of the stock of T Corp., a personal holding company, and files a §338 election, can T Corp. avoid the personal holding company tax for its final (short) period as "old" T?

2. Prior to 1984, a corporation receiving a dividend distribution that would be within §302(b)(4) if the recipient were an individual was not thereby in receipt of "personal holding company income." The 1984 Act eliminated this anomaly by repealing the former §543(a)(1)(C).

FLETCHER v. UNITED STATES
674 F.2d 1308 (4th Cir. 1982)

Before Browning, C.J.; Skopil and Norris, JJ.
Norris, Circuit Judge.

The Fletchers appeal from a district court judgment awarding them only a partial refund for personal holding company (PHC) taxes for tax years 1971-76. We affirm in part and reverse in part.

I

The Fletchers were the sole shareholders of Fletcher Enterprises, Inc. In 1976, the corporation adopted a 12-month plan of liquidation, and in January 1977, made a final distribution of $50,000 to the Fletchers.

In May 1977, the IRS notified the Fletchers that the liquidated corporation had been a personal holding company and that it had $32,800 of undistributed and untaxed PHC income for tax years 1971-76. In January 1978, as sole directors of the liquidated corporation, the Fletchers retroactively designated $32,800 of the corporation's final distribution as a dividend pursuant to §316(b)(2)(B)(ii). The Fletchers hoped thereby to avoid the PHC tax, which is applied to undistributed PHC income.

The Commissioner assessed a deficiency of $29,855 against the Fletchers as transferees of the corporation. That amount represents a 70% PHC tax on the $32,800 PHC income, plus interest and penalties. The Fletchers paid the deficiency and sued for a refund. On summary judgment, the district court awarded a partial refund of

$2,268, holding that the January 1977 dividend could be deducted only against PHC income earned in that year.

II

A

In determining the amount of its taxable PHC income, a PHC may deduct dividends paid to shareholders. §§545, 561. "Dividends" paid by a PHC include distributions made *during* the tax year in which PHC income is earned and, in certain limited circumstances, distributions made *in respect of* the tax year in which PHC income is earned. I.R.C. §316(b)(2)(A). The term "distribution" includes a property distribution made within 24 months of the adoption of a plan of liquidation to the extent the distribution is designated as a dividend. §316(b)(2)(B).

The Fletchers argue that the January 1977 distribution, made within 24 months of the adoption of a plan of liquidation and designated in part as a dividend, is deductible against undistributed PHC income earned from 1971 to 1976. The argument is not persuasive. Dividends paid against income earned in a past year are dividends paid "in respect of" a past year. See §316(b)(2)(A)(ii). A PHC may deduct dividends paid "in respect of a past year" only: (1) when the dividend is paid within two and one-half months of the close of the tax year in which the income is earned, pursuant to §563(b); or (2) when the dividend constitutes a "deficiency dividend" under section 547. §§545, 316(b)(2)(A)(ii). The Fletchers do not contend that dividends were paid within two and one-half months of the close of the tax years in which PHC income was earned, and we conclude that the 1977 distribution does not qualify as a "deficiency dividend" under section 547.

B

Section 547 is a relief provision, designed to give PHCs a final opportunity to avoid the PHC tax by distributing PHC income after a deficiency has been determined. It permits a PHC to deduct a post-determination distribution against any year for which the corporation had undistributed PHC income, provided that the distribution is made within ninety days *after* a "determination" of the amount of deficiency. A section 547 determination is a final determination by a court, a closing agreement made under §7121, or a final agreement between the IRS and the taxpayer. §547(c). There was no agreement here, and the January 1978 dividend was paid before any final determination by a court.

The Fletchers argue that Congress did not intend the final determination requirement to apply to distributions by liquidating corporations. As a practical matter, they reason, no liquidating corporation assessed a deficiency could obtain a final determination within the 24 months allowed by section 316(b)(2)(B) for a complete liquidation; thus, the final determination requirement deprives liquidating corporations of the benefit of section 547. . . .

By its clear terms, section 547 permits deduction of a deficiency dividend *only* if the dividend is paid after a final determination. We find no basis for departing from the plain language of the statute.

The timing requirements for the distribution of PHC income are designed to ensure that PHC income is taxed to the corporation's shareholders at the time the income is earned. See Callan v. Commissioner, 54 T.C. 1514, 1518-19 (1970), *aff'd,* 426 F.2d 509 (9th Cir. 1973). To avoid the PHC tax, a corporation must ordinarily distribute its PHC income within two and one-half months of the close of the tax year in which the income is received. Section 547 provides a limited exception to that rule, permitting distribution within 90 days after a deficiency determination. If a PHC could claim a section 547 deduction for dividends distributed at any time, however, it could ignore the two and one-half month rule. The PHC could then select favorable tax years to distribute its PHC income, thereby minimizing the personal income tax liability of its shareholders while still avoiding the PHC tax. The final determination requirement of section 547 forecloses this avenue of tax avoidance. Although liquidating corporations may have difficulty complying with that requirement, we find no statutory or policy ground for exempting them from it. Cf. Leck Co. v. United States, ¶9694 (D. Minn. 1973) (denying section 547 relief to a corporation that declared a dividend after signing an agreement with the Commissioner, but before the agreement became final under section 547(c), although the corporation's action was an "apparently unwitting, good faith, harmless departure from a highly technical statutory scheme").

The Fletchers contend that liquidating corporations should be exempt from the final determination rule because Congress enacted section 316(b)(2)(B) to extend the benefits of section 547 to liquidating corporations. The argument has no merit. Section 316(b)(2)(B) permits a PHC to designate a liquidation distribution as a dividend, and thus deduct it from PHC income, if the distributee also declares the distribution as a dividend. In so providing, Congress intended to ensure that when a PHC deducts a liquidation distribution from PHC income, the distributee will be taxed at ordinary, not capital gains, rates. L. C. Bohart Plumbing & Heating Co. v. Commissioner, 64 T.C. 602, 609-12 (1975). Moreover, section 316(b)(2)(B) expressly limits liquidation dividends to the amount of undistributed PHC income "for such year"; thus, there is no reason to believe that Congress intended section 316(b)(2)(B) to broaden the timing rules for claiming a dividend deduction.

Nor is there reason to believe that Congress anticipated that section 547 would routinely be useful to liquidating corporations. Section 547 relief is available to all non-liquidating PHCs and to PHCs that adopt a plan of liquidation after a deficiency determination. It may be desirable to create a narrow exception to the final determination rule, extending the benefits of section 547 to PHCs that have liquidated before a deficiency is assessed. The current statute contains no such exception, however, and the task of statutory revision is one for Congress, not the courts. . . .

NOTE

In Rev. Rul. 86-104, 1986-2 C.B. 80, the IRS ruled that it is powerless to extend the time for distribution of dividends to qualify as "deficiency dividends" under §547(d).

VI. ONE MAN'S POISON ...

Usually a shareholder who owns a personal holding company has come into that situation unwittingly. It is not entirely uncommon, however, that a shareholder will own a personal holding company as a matter of choice. The following describes a situation in which a shareholder might choose to have his corporation become a personal holding company.

At age 65 the sole shareholder of a manufacturing corporation decides to accept a $1 million offer for the business. The basis of his stock is $200,000. The corporation's aggregate basis for its assets is $800,000. The shareholder wishes to avoid all further active business dealings and to invest his money exclusively in income-producing marketable securities. A sale of stock will produce a taxable gain to the shareholder of $800,000 and no gain to the corporation. A corporate sale of assets will produce taxable gain at the corporate level of only $200,000, but no shareholder gain if the corporation remains alive. If the latter approach is adopted, there will be substantially more aftertax funds for investment than otherwise. If the corporation invests in marketable stocks and bonds alone, it will be a personal holding company. Nevertheless, if it invests in bonds that are tax-exempt under §103, it will not have to distribute the interest income to avoid §541. If it invests in stocks whose dividends are subject to the §243 dividends received deduction, distribution of the net (after-tax) dividend income will be required. The corporate tax will be very small, however, and the shareholder will receive substantially all the income he would have received if he had invested in stocks directly and personally. (The personal holding company will avoid investing in corporate bonds because the interest income would be fully taxable to the corporation, and distribution would be required to avoid the §541 tax.)

Because no sum equivalent to the individual shareholder tax was paid, there will be more for the corporation to invest than the shareholder would have had if he had sold the corporation's stock. Moreover, if he keeps the personal holding company alive until his death, his estate can effect liquidation of the corporation under §331 without incurring any tax at the shareholder level because of the step-up in the basis of the stock provided by §1014. In the last year of its manufacturing activities, however, when the corporation is not yet a personal holding company, it bears a risk under §531 as to a tax on its undistributed "accumulated taxable income" of that year.

NOTE

With the maximum rate of tax on a shareholder's income set at 28 percent, significantly less than the 34 percent maximum rate on a corporation's income, what call is there to perpetuate the personal holding company tax? Would the elimination of the dividends received deduction in the case of closely held corporations and all "mere investment companies" (cf. §533(b)) be an appropriate and adequate substitute? See Wolfman, Subchapter C and the 100th Congress, Tax Notes, Nov. 17, 1986, p. 669, excerpted page 862 supra.

GENERAL REFERENCES

See generally B. Bittker and J. Eustice, Federal Income Taxation of Corporations and Shareholders, 8-34 to 8-50 (5th ed. 1987); Apelbaum, The Accumulated Earnings Tax and the Personal Holding Company Tax: Problems and Proposals, 3 Boston U.J. Tax L. 53 (1985); Kwall, Subchapter G of the Internal Revenue Code: Crusade Without a Cause?, 5 Va. Tax Rev. 223 (1985).

8

Subchapter S—§§1361-1379

I. INTRODUCTION

Subchapter S was added to the Code in 1958. The following excerpt from the Report of the Senate Finance Committee* describes its purpose and general scheme:

Section 68 — election of certain small-business corporations
In 1954, . . . the Senate passed, but the Congress did not enact, a provision which would, at the election of the stockholders, permit corporations to forego the payment of any tax and require their shareholders to report the corporate income (whether or not distributed) as their own for tax purposes.

Your committee believes that the enactment of a provision of this type is desirable because it permits businesses to select the form of business organization desired, without the necessity of taking into account major differences in tax consequence. In this respect, a provision to tax the income at the shareholder, rather than the corporate, level will complement the provision enacted in 1954 permitting proprietorships and partnerships to be taxed like corporations. Also, permitting shareholders to report their proportionate share of the corporate income, in lieu of a corporate tax, will be a substantial aid to small business. It will be primarily beneficial to those individuals who have marginal tax rates below the 52-percent corporate rate (or 30-percent rate in the case of the smaller corporations) where the earnings are left in the business. Where the earnings are distributed (and are in excess of what may properly be classified as salary payments), the benefit will extend to individuals with somewhat higher rates since in this case a "double" tax is removed. The provision will also be of substantial benefit to small corporations realizing losses for a period of years where there is no way of offsetting these losses against taxable income at the corporate level, but the shareholders involved have other income which can be offset against these losses. In this connection it should be noted that the President's Cabinet Committee on Small Business and the President in his budget message this last January recommended a general provision of this type for the benefit of small business.

*S. Rep. No. 1983, 85th Cong., 2d Sess. 68, 1958-3 C.B. 1008.

To permit shareholders in small-business corporations, in lieu of payment of the corporate tax, to elect to be taxed directly on the corporation's earnings, your committee has added a new sub-chapter . . .* to the code. Where the tax treatment provided by this subchapter is elected, the shareholders include in their own income for tax purposes the current taxable income of the cor-poration, both the portion which is distributed and that which is not. Neither type of income in this case is eligible for a dividend received credit or exclusion, since it has been subject to no tax at the corporate level. Generally, this income is treated as ordinary income to the shareholder without the retention of any special characteristics it might have had in the hands of the corporation. This rule has been adopted so that this provision can operate in as simple a manner as possible. Long-term capital gains, however, are an exception to this general rule. In the case of these long-term capital gains the character carries over to the shareholder level.

Where a shareholder has been taxed on corporate earnings which were not at that time distributed, and then the corporation in a subsequent year distributes these earnings to such sharehold-ers no further tax is required from the shareholder at that time, since these earnings have already been taxed to him in a prior year. Once all such earnings have been distributed, if further dis-tributions are then made, and the corporation had earnings and profits before it elected this special tax treatment, then such dis-tributions are to be taxed to the shareholders in the same manner as ordinary dividends from corporations.

Under this provision the net operating losses of the corpo-ration currently also are passed through to the shareholder. Thus, at the corporate level where this special treatment is elected, there is no carryover or carryback of operating losses to or from a year with respect to which this special treatment has been elected. At the individual level these "distributed" corporate losses are to be treated in the same manner as any loss which the individual might have from a proprietorship; that is, they first offset income of the individual, in that year (whether or not derived from another business) and then any excess of these losses may be carried back and offset against the individual's income in prior years and, if any losses still remain, they may be carried forward and offset against his income in subsequent years.

Where this special treatment has been elected the basis of a shareholder's stock is increased for any of the corporate earnings taxed to him which are not then distributed, although this basis is subsequently reduced if these taxpaid corporate earnings are dis-tributed. The basis of the stock of a shareholder is also reduced for any corporate losses which are passed through to him. The losses that he may take, however, are limited to the basis he has

*Sections 1361-1379 of the 1986 Code. — Ed.

for the stock. Thus, his basis for the stock cannot be reduced below zero.

The right to elect the treatment provided under this new subchapter is limited to what are defined as small business corporations. These corporations must be domestic corporations which are not eligible to file a consolidated return with any other corporation. Also, they must not have more than 10 shareholders,* their shareholders must all be individuals (or an estate), no nonresident aliens may be shareholders, and the corporation may not have more than one class of stock.

An election may be made to apply the tax treatment provided by this new subchapter only if all of the shareholders consent to this election. For this purpose the shareholders are those of record as of the first day of the taxable year in question, or if the election is made after that time, shareholders of record when the election is made. An election to come under this provision must be made in a two months interval, either in the first month before the beginning of the taxable year for which the election is to be made or in the first month of that year. (A longer period of time, up to 90 days after the date of enactment of this bill, is allowed for the first taxable year beginning after December 31, 1957.) Once this provision is elected it is effective not only for the taxable year but also for all subsequent years although this election may be terminated.

The election to the tax treatment provided by this subchapter can be terminated in any one of several ways. First, the election is terminated if a new person becomes a shareholder of the corporation and he does not consent to the election. Second, the election can be terminated if all of the shareholders consent to its revocation. A revocation, however, is effective only with respect to subsequent years unless it is made in the first month of the taxable year. Third, the election as to the treatment under this new subchapter is to be terminated if the corporation ceases to qualify as a small-business corporation; that is, if the corporation no longer meets the requirements of a small business corporation, such as having not more than 10 shareholders or having no nonresident alien as a shareholder. Fourth, the election to be taxed under this new subchapter terminates if the corporation derives more than 80 percent of its gross receipts from sources outside the United States and, fifth, the election terminates if more than 20 percent of the corporation's gross receipts are derived from interest, dividends, rents, royalties, or other forms of passive income.**

In order to prevent a corporation from electing in and out of the application of the provisions of this new subchapter, a limitation has been added providing that if a corporation has made an election under this subchapter, and if this election has been

*This number was increased to 35 in 1982. See page 1182 infra. — Ed.
**These provisions were repealed by the 1982 Act. — Ed.

terminated or revoked, the corporation (or any successor) is not to be eligible to elect this treatment until its fifth year after the beginning of the year in which the determination or revocation is effective. However, the Secretary or his delegate is given the authority to make exceptions to this limitation. . . .*

In 1982 Congress made substantial changes in Subchapter S, for the most part liberalizing, simplifying, and sensible. A nonsubstantive change dubs a corporation that has elected Subchapter S an "S" corporation; all others, "C" corporations. The following report describes the 1982 changes.

STAFF OF THE JOINT COMMITTEE ON TAXATION, SUMMARY OF THE SUBCHAPTER S REVISION ACT OF 1982
Aug. 24, 1982

In general, H.R. 6055 (the Subchapter S Revision Act of 1982) is intended to simplify and modify the tax rules relating to eligibility for subchapter S status and the operation of subchapter S corporations. This is accomplished by removing eligibility restrictions that appear unnecessary and by revising the rules relating to income, distributions, etc., that tend to create traps for the unwary. The principal changes from present law made by the Act are summarized below.

ELIGIBILITY

With respect to initial and continued eligibility of a corporation for subchapter S treatment, the Act makes the following changes:

(1) The number of permitted shareholders will be increased from 25 to 35;

(2) Differences in voting rights in common stock will not violate the one-class-of-stock requirement;

(3) The present law rule which results in the termination of an election if the corporation derives more than 80 percent of its gross receipts from sources outside the United States will be repealed;

(4) The present law rule which automatically terminates a corporation's subchapter S election if more than 20 percent of a corporation's gross receipts for any taxable year is passive investment income will be eliminated for corporations which do not have sub-

---

*The 1986 Act made important changes with respect to the taxable year of S corporations. See Note 2, page 1186 infra. — ED.

chapter C accumulated earnings and profits at the close of the taxable year, and will be modified for corporations with subchapter C accumulated earnings and profits by raising the 20 percent test to 25 percent, by imposing a corporate level tax on the excess passive income, and by terminating the election only where the corporation has excess passive income for three consecutive taxable years;

(5) A person who becomes a shareholder of a subchapter S corporation after the initial election of subchapter S status will not have the power to terminate the election by affirmatively refusing to consent to the election. Accordingly, the new shareholder will be bound by the initial election until the election is otherwise terminated; and

(6) A safe harbor will be provided for a debt instrument which is not convertible into stock and which consists of an unconditional promise to pay on demand or on a specified date a sum certain in money with respect to which the interest rate and payment date are fixed (straight debt). Straight debt will not be classified as a second class of stock when held by a person eligible to hold subchapter S stock. The classification of instruments outside the safe harbor rule as stock or debt will be made under usual tax law classification principles applicable to subchapter C corporations.

ELECTIONS, REVOCATIONS, AND TERMINATIONS

The Act provides that an election made on or before the fifteenth day of the third month of the taxable year will be effective for the entire taxable year if all persons who held stock in the corporation during the pre-election portion of that year were individuals, estates, and qualified trusts, and if all persons who held stock in the corporation at any time during the year up to the time the election is made consent to the election. If these requirements are not met, or if the election is made later than the fifteenth day of the third month of the taxable year, it will not be effective until the subsequent taxable year.

An event occurring during the taxable year which causes a corporation to fail to meet the definition of an eligible corporation will terminate the election as of the day on which the event occurred (rather than as of the first day of the taxable year in which the event occurred, as under present law). To minimize the effect of an inadvertent termination, the Act provides that the Internal Revenue Service may waive the terminating event so that the corporation may continue to be a subchapter S corporation notwithstanding that event.

The Act provides that an election can be revoked by those shareholders holding a majority of the corporation's voting stock (as contrasted with the current rule which requires all shareholders to consent to a revocation). The present law rule allowing a revocation filed during the first month of the taxable year to be effective for that entire taxable year is modified so that such a retroactive revocation may be filed on or before the fifteenth day of the third month of the taxable year.

PASSTHROUGH OF INCOME, ETC.

The Act provides that the character of items of income, deduction, loss, and credits of the corporation will pass through to the shareholders in the same general manner as the character of such items of a partnership passes through to partners. Thus, for example, such items as tax-exempt interest, capital gains and losses, percentage depletion, the source or allocation of foreign income or loss, and foreign income taxes will pass through and retain their character in the hands of shareholders.

As is the case under present law with respect to losses, income will be passed through and allocated to shareholders on a per-share, per-day basis.

SELECTION OF TAXABLE YEAR

Under the Act, rules generally similar to those applicable to partnerships will apply to the selection of a taxable year for a subchapter S corporation. . . .

CARRYFORWARD OF LOSS

Under the Act, a subchapter S shareholder will be entitled to carry forward a loss to the extent that the amount of the loss passed through for the year exceeds the aggregate amount of the basis in this subchapter S stock and loans to the corporation. The loss carried forward can be deducted only by that shareholder if and when the basis in his or her stock of, or loans to, the corporation is restored.

DISTRIBUTIONS

The rules relating to distributions from subchapter S corporations are substantially revised by the Act.

Under the new rules, a corporation will not have earnings and profits attributable to any taxable year beginning after the date of enactment if a subchapter S election is in effect for that year. For corporations with no earnings and profits, the amount of the distribution (generally cash plus the fair market value of property) will be tax-free and will reduce the shareholder's basis in his or her stock. To the extent that the amount of the distribution exceeds the amount of the basis in the stock, capital gains generally will result.

For corporations with accumulated earnings and profits, the distribution will be treated as a distribution by a corporation without earnings and profits to the extent of the shareholder's portion of the undistributed amount of subchapter S gross income less deductible expenses (an "accumulated adjustment account"). Any amount in excess of the accumulated adjustment account will be treated under the usual corporate rules, first as a distribution out of accumulated earnings and profits to the extent thereof.

Under the Act, both taxable and nontaxable income and deductible and nondeductible expenses will serve, respectively, to increase and decrease the subchapter S shareholder's basis in his or her stock of, and loans to, the corporation. These rules are generally analogous to those provided for partnerships. Also, unlike present law, basis will be restored to debt obligations as well as stock. Restoration of basis will be made first to debt (to the extent of prior reductions) and then to stock. Under the Act, gain will be recognized by a subchapter S corporation upon nonliquidating distributions of appreciated property.*

Fringe Benefits

Under the Act, rules similar to the partnership tax rules will apply to employee fringe benefits. For this purpose, persons owning two percent or more of the corporate stock will be treated as partners.

Treatment of Transactions Between Corporations and Related Parties

Under the Act, amounts accruing to any cash-basis shareholder owning two percent or more of the corporation's stock will be deductible only when paid.**

Administrative Provisions

The Act provides that the items of subchapter S income, deductions, and credits will be determined in audit and judicial proceedings at the corporate level rather than separately with each shareholder. Shareholders are to be given notice of, and the opportunity to participate in, Internal Revenue Service proceedings with the corporation. . . .

---

*The 1986 Act, with its repeal of the *General Utilities* doctrine, expanded the scope of the recognition principle. See Note 1, page 1186 infra. — Ed.
**This rule now applies to amounts accruing to *any* cash basis shareholder. See §267(e). — Ed.

NOTES

1. Important amendments were made to §1363(d) in 1984 and 1986. Now, reflecting the repeal of the *General Utilities* doctrine, the Code requires that an S corporation recognize gain when it distributes appreciated property unless the distribution is pursuant to a tax-free transaction embraced by §§354, 355, or 356. There is special treatment, however, for so-called built-in gains under §1374. The Conference Report explains:

> Conversion from C Corporation to S Corporation Status
>   The conference agreement modifies the treatment of an S corporation that was formerly a C corporation. A corporate-level tax is imposed on any gain that arose prior to the conversion ("built-in" gain) and is recognized by the S corporation, through sale or distribution, within ten years after the date on which the S election took effect. The total amount of gain that must be recognized by the corporation, however, will be limited to the aggregate net built-in gain of the corporation at the time of conversion to S corporation status. Gains on sales or distributions of assets by the S corporation will be presumed to be built-in gains, except to the extent the taxpayer can establish that the appreciation accrued after the conversion, such as where the asset was acquired by the corporation in a taxable acquisition after the conversion. . . .

H.R. Conf. Rep. No. 841, 99th Cong., 2d Sess., II-203 (Sept. 18, 1986).

The Act provides further that the built-in gains will be taxed at the maximum corporate rate for the year in which the disposition occurs, and that certain losses and credits can be carried forward from C corporation years to offset the recognized built-in gains.

For a discussion of the treatment of built-in gains under the 1986 Act, see Smith, S Corporation Built-in Gains: An Analysis of Section 1374 After the Tax Reform Act of 1986, 39 U. Fla. L. Rev. 1117 (1987).

2. In keeping with its effort to restrict the deferral opportunities that come about when pass-through entities have taxable years that differ from those of the taxpayers to whom the income passes, Congress amended §1378 so that *all* S corporations (including existing S corporations that have reported in the past on a fiscal year basis) must use the calendar year as the taxable year unless they establish a satisfactory business purpose, but "any deferral of income to shareholders shall not be treated as a business purpose."

3. Early in 1987 the Treasury issued temporary regulations covering a number of the administrative provisions of the Subchapter S Revision Act of 1982: Temp. Reg. §§51.6245-1T and 301.6245-1T. These temporary regulations are also proposed as final regulations.

4. In 1984, Congress provided that for purposes of attribution under §318 generally, an S corporation will be treated as a partnership and an S corporation shareholder will be treated as a partner, but not for the purpose of determining whether stock in the S corporation is constructively owned by anyone. See §318(a)(5)(E).

5. Although written before the 1986 Act, see generally August and Schwimmer, Integration of Subchapter C with Subchapter S after the Subchapter S Revision Act — Part I, 12 J. Corp. Taxn. 107 (1985); Part II, 12 J. Corp. Taxn. 269 (1985); Part III, 12 J. Corp. Taxn. 323 (1986); Coven, Making Subchapter C Work, Tax Notes, July 21, 1986, p. 271; Coven and Hess, The Subchapter S Revision Act: An Analysis and Approach, 50 Tenn. L. Rev. 569 (1983).

6. Consider also the criteria for deciding whether the preferable business format for a client is a partnership, an S corporation, or a C corporation. See generally B. Bittker and J. Eustice, Federal Income Taxation of Corporations and Shareholders 6-1 to 6-30 (5th ed. 1987).

II. ELIGIBILITY

REVENUE RULING 77-220
1977-1 C.B. 263

Advice has been requested whether elections under section [1362(a)] of the Internal Revenue Code of 1954 by the corporations described below to be treated as small business corporations will not be valid because the ten shareholder limitation of [pre-1978] section 1371* will have been violated.

Thirty unrelated individuals combined their capital and skills and entered into the joint operation of a single business. In order to take advantage of the income tax benefits of operating as small business corporations under section 1371 of the Code, the individuals divided into three groups, each consisting of ten individuals. Each group organized a separate corporation and the same amount of capital was contributed to each corporation in exchange for its stock. The three corporations, in turn, organized a partnership for the joint operation of the business. The corporations otherwise meet the definition of small business corporations as defined in section 1371.

The principal purpose of the thirty individuals for organizing three separate corporations to become partners in a single business, instead of organizing one corporation for that purpose, was to avoid

---

*Section 1371 in this Revenue Ruling is the counterpart to §1361 in the 1986 Code. As discussed at page 1181 supra, §1361(b)(1)(A) now permits corporations to have as many as 35 shareholders.—ED.

the tax liability that would occur if they operated as one corporation, since if the business was operated by one corporation it would have more than ten shareholders and thus would not qualify as a small business corporation under section 1371 of the Code. . . .

In Gregory v. Helvering, 293 U.S. 465 (1935), it was contended on behalf of the taxpayer that since every element required by the statute involved was to be found in what was done, the tax result sought by the taxpayer had been effected, and that the motive of the taxpayer thereby to escape payment of a tax would not alter the result or make unlawful what the statute allowed. The Supreme Court of the United States pointed out that the whole undertaking, though conducted according to the terms of the statute, was in fact an elaborate and devious form of conveyance consummated solely for the purpose of tax avoidance. Accordingly, the Court ruled adversely to the taxpayer.

In Higgins v. Smith, 308 U.S. 473 (1940), the Supreme Court of the United States stated that the United States Government may look at actualities in tax cases and, upon determination that the form employed for doing business or carrying out the challenged tax event is unreal or a sham, may sustain or disregard the effect of the fiction as best serves the purposes of the tax statute. To hold otherwise would permit schemes of taxpayers to supersede legislation in the determination of the time and manner of taxation.

Accordingly, in the instant case, since organizing three separate corporations instead of one corporation was for the principal purpose of being able to make the election under section [1362(a)] of the Code, solely for the purpose of making such election the three corporations will be considered to be a single corporation. As a single corporation there will be thirty shareholders and, therefore, any elections made by them will not be valid because the ten shareholder limitation of section 1371 will be considered to have been violated.

NOTE

Cf. Rev. Rul. 77-470, 1977-2 C.B. 317 (Subchapter S corporation formed to acquire and lease personal automobiles to its shareholders disregarded for tax purposes; investment credit and operating loss pass-throughs unavailable to shareholders).

PAIGE v. UNITED STATES
580 F.2d 960 (9th Cir. 1978)

Before Judges Trask and Sneed, Circuit Judges, and Skopil, District Judge.

Skopil, District Judge. Plaintiff-taxpayers appeal from the denial of their claim for a tax refund. The issue involved is whether tax-payers' corporation qualified for the subchapter S election. . . . We hold that it did not. We affirm.

Tackmer made the subchapter S election in 1965. The government now contends that Tackmer Corporation had more than one class of stock.

Tackmer is a small California company that was first incorporated in 1965. When Tackmer first issued stock, it received two different kinds of consideration. Plaintiffs and another party assigned their rights to an exclusive license agreement in exchange for Tackmer stock ("property shareholders"). Eight other parties paid cash ("cash shareholders").

The Articles of Incorporation state that "No distinction shall exist between the shares of the corporation [or] the holders thereof." . . . The applicable California Corporation Code, §304 (West 1949), stated that there could be no distinction between shares unless specified in the Articles.

Before Tackmer could issue any stock, it was required to obtain a permit from the California Department of Corporations. The California Corporation Code gave the Department authority to impose conditions on corporations for the protection of the public. Pursuant to this authority the Department had a policy of imposing certain conditions on small corporations such as Tackmer which were capitalized with both cash and property that had an indeterminate value. The purpose of the conditions was to protect the shareholders who paid with cash from having their interests diluted by overissue of stock to the shareholders who paid with property.

The conditions imposed by the Department of Corporations were as follows:

(a) The stock had to be deposited in escrow and could not be sold without the Department's consent;

(b) If the company defaulted on dividend payments for two years, the cash shareholders would have irrevocable power of attorney to vote the property shareholders' shares for the board of directors;

(c) On dissolution, the property shareholders had to waive their rights to the distribution of assets until the cash shareholders had received the full amount of their purchase price plus any unpaid accumulated dividends at 5% per year;

(d) The property shareholders had to waive their rights to any dividends until the cash shareholders annually received cumulative dividends equal to 5% of the purchase price per share;

(e) The conditions were to remain in effect until the shares were released from escrow. . . . The conditions were in effect from 1965 to 1970.

The property shareholders signed an agreement with the company stating that they would abide by the conditions. The taxpayers admit that the conditions could have been waived by the cash shareholders. . . . Notwithstanding the conditions, the differences between the two kinds of shareholders were never taken into account and all dividends were distributed on a pro rata basis. . . .

The taxpayers filed a timely joint tax return in 1970. The return claimed their proportionate share of Tackmer's investment credit and an income averaging tax reduction relating to Tackmer's income and losses for the years before 1970. On January 14, 1973, the Commissioner of Internal Revenue disallowed these claims and assessed additional taxes of $244.64 plus $37.30 interest (total: $281.94). The reason stated for the disallowance was that the conditions imposed by the California Department of Corporations created more than one class of stock, disqualifying Tackmer for subchapter S treatment. . . .

The taxpayers contend that because the Articles and state law authorized only one class of stock, there can be only one class for subchapter S purposes. We hold, however, that the interpretation of subchapter S qualifications is a federal question. . . .

Treas. Reg. §1.1371-1(g) provides that "If the outstanding shares of stock of the corporation are not identical with respect to the *rights* and interests which they convey in the control, profits, and assets of the corporation, then the corporation is considered to have more than one class of stock" [emphasis added]. The cash shareholders had preferred rights over property shareholders, notwithstanding that the cash shareholders chose not to exercise those rights. The possibility of the exercise of differing rights is enough to disqualify a corporation for subchapter S tax treatment.

Taxpayers' assertion that Tackmer in fact made all distributions on a pro rata basis is irrelevant. A corporation's qualifications for subchapter S status [are] judged at the date of election. . . . The court may not consider Tackmer's actual distributions after its election. The language in the statute is clear. Tax planners must be able to assume that the court will give it its plain meaning.

Taxpayers assert that the Treas. Reg. §1.1371-1(g) has been overturned as applied to them by Parker Oil Company, 58 T.C. 985 (1972) and the Service's acquiescence in Rev. Rul. 73-611, 1973-2 C.B. 312. Taxpayers contend that the Regulation was found to be inconsistent with the basic purpose of the requirement that there be one class of stock. We disagree. *Parker Oil* involved only voting rights arising out of shareholder agreements. It did not involve distributions from the corporations. Control of distributions is at the heart of the one class of stock requirement. This aspect of Treas. Reg. §1.1371-1(g) was untouched by *Parker Oil*.

The taxpayers also cite Portage Plastics Co. v. United States, 486 F.2d 632 (7th Cir. 1973); Shores Realty Co. v. United States, 468

F.2d 572 (5th Cir. 1972); and Amory Cotton Oil Co. v. United States, 468 F.2d 1046 (5th Cir. 1972). The taxpayers assert that these cases undercut the Treasury Department Regulations. However, these cases hold only that the Regulations may not create a presumption that all debt which is reclassified as equity automatically creates a second class of stock. In that situation the former debt could be identical to the original equity. That is distinguishable from the case here.

There is a strong policy behind the requirement that subchapter S corporations have only one class of stock. The corporations themselves pay no corporate income tax. The shareholders pay individual income tax on a pro rata share of all corporate income, regardless of whether any money or property has actually been distributed to the shareholder. If the statute allowed more than one class of stock, complicated allocation problems could arise.

The example given in the government's brief illustrates the potential problems. Assume that during its first taxable year Tackmer had earnings and profits of $5,500 and had declared and paid a preference dividend to the cash shareholders only. Pursuant to Condition (d) of the California Department of Corporations requirements, the minimum dividend would be $2,575. This would leave the corporation with an undistributed taxable income of $2,925. This sum would be taxed pro rata to all the shareholders:

To the cash shareholders (who have 5,100 of the 14,300 shares)	$1,043
To the property shareholders (who have 9,200 of 14,300 shares)	$1,882
	$2,925

If Tackmer had no earnings and profits its second year, it would still be obligated to pay $2,575 under Condition (d). It would pay the distribution out of funds generated during its first year. That is, it would pay to the cash shareholders money that had been taxed to, but not received by, both cash and property shareholders. In computing the proper liability of cash shareholders with respect to this distribution, it would be necessary to attribute in an equitable manner to cash shareholders taxes paid by property shareholders. This would introduce substantial complexity in the administration of subchapter S. It was this type of *potential* difficulty which Congress sought to avoid by limiting subchapter S corporations to one class of stock.

We agree with the taxpayers that the purpose of subchapter S is to benefit small corporations such as the one here. It is unfortunate that a requirement of state law has caused a result that no one intended. However, the taxpayers' subjective intent to create one class of stock cannot be allowed to override statutory requirements. Cf. Gamman v. Commissioner of Internal Revenue, 46 T.C. 1 (1966). Congress has set forth specific objective requirements for subchapter S qualification, and we must follow the mandate of the statute.

We affirm.

NOTES

1. In Parker Oil Co., 58 T.C. 985 (1972), the court determined that the "overriding purpose" of the one-class-of-stock requirement is "to avoid complexities in taxing income to shareholders with different preferences as to the distribution of profits." Consistent with this view, Congress in 1982 enacted §1361(c)(4), which permits differences in *voting rights* within a single class of common stock of an S corporation. In similar vein, the Service has held that employee-incentive "phantom stock" does not constitute a second class of stock. See G.C.M. 39750 (1988).

2. Consider the following excerpt from a 1980 staff report to the Congressional Joint Committee on Taxation, recommending changes in Subchapter S:

> Treasury has recommended that a specific type of preferred security be permitted. In general, the permitted preferred securities would be required to bear a fixed or determinable rate of return, and the owners of the preferred securities would be treated as shareholders for all subchapter S purposes. In determining the amount of losses allowed as a deduction to a shareholder, the shareholder's adjusted basis in preferred securities would be included in the limitation on losses. Payment of the return on preferred securities generally would be treated as ordinary income to the owner of the preferred securities and as an ordinary deduction to the corporation. However, such a deduction would be disallowed to the extent it would create a loss. The treatment of these preferred securities as a permitted second class of stock would supersede the existing case law as to when the one class of stock rule has been violated.

House Committee on Ways and Means and Senate Committee on Finance, Staff Recommendations for Simplification of Tax Rules Relating to Subchapter S Corporations (Joint Publication), 96th Cong., 2d Sess. (Comm. Print 1980).

3. Prior to 1966 the Service asserted that debt obligations that "actually represent equity capital" would be deemed to violate the one-class-of-stock requirement. In W. C. Gamman, 46 T.C. 1 (1966), the Tax Court held that this construction of an existing regulation was beyond the Treasury's authority. The regulations then in force

were accordingly amended, condemning only equity-equivalent debt that is *not* held by shareholders in "substantially the same proportion" as their stock. This pro rata standard was invalidated in James L. Stinnet, 54 T.C. 221 (1970). Portage Plastics Co. v. United States, 470 F.2d 308 (7th Cir. 1972), held, contrary to *Stinnet*, that the debt vs. equity standard was correctly applied to determine whether purported debt in fact represented a second class of stock. The Seventh Circuit granted a petition for rehearing en banc. Meanwhile, two panels of the Fifth Circuit decided this issue against the Government. See Amory Cotton Oil Co. v. United States, 468 F.2d 1046 (5th Cir. 1972) ("debt" was equity but not second class of stock; might find second class of stock in case of abuse); Shores Realty Co. v. United States, 468 F.2d 572 (5th Cir. 1972) ("debt" can never be second class of stock for Subchapter S purposes). In Portage Plastics Co. v. United States, 486 F.2d 632 (7th Cir. 1973) (en banc), the court adhered to the *Stinnet* line of cases and held that advances denominated as debt would not be considered a second class of stock unless their classification as debt was a tax-avoidance "sham."

Section 1361(c)(5), added to the Code in 1982, now provides a safe-harbor exemption for certain types of "straight debt" in applying the one-class-of-stock requirement. Debt that is not "straight debt" as defined in §1361(c)(5)(B) will continue to expose the corporation to the danger of losing its S status if the debt is classified as a second class of stock.

III.   PASS-THROUGH OF CORPORATE INCOME

A.   IN GENERAL

SPECA v. COMMISSIONER
630 F.2d 554 (7th Cir. 1980)

Before Bauer, Circuit Judge, Cudahy, Circuit Judge, and Noland, District Judge.

NOLAND, District Judge. This is an appeal from a finding by the Tax Court of a deficiency in income taxes by appellants Gino A. Speca and Joseph F. Madrigrano for the year 1971. The sole issue for review is whether the Tax Court erred in holding that certain transfers of stock by appellants to their children lacked sufficient economic reality to permit income from the stock to be taxed to the transferee-children rather than the transferor-parents. A review of the record reveals the following undisputed facts.

   Appellants are executives of Triangle Wholesale Company, Inc. (Triangle), a beer wholesaler and distributor operating in Wisconsin. Since 1969, Triangle has operated as a Subchapter S corporation. As of 1968, stock ownership in Triangle was completely within the Speca and Madrigrano families in the following amounts and percentages:

Name	Shares	Percentages
Joseph Madrigrano (Sr.)	376	18
Joseph Madrigrano (Jr.)	170	8
Glenn Madrigrano	170	8
Mary Madrigrano	170	8
Karen Madrigrano	170	8
Gino Speca	376	18
Armand Speca	170	8
Rosalyn Speca	170	8
Gene Speca	170	8
Peter Speca	170	8

   At all times relevant to these proceedings, Madrigrano was president, secretary, and a director of Triangle. Speca was also a director of Triangle in addition to serving in the capacity of vice-president and treasurer. Both Madrigrano and Speca received salaries of approximately $42,000 for each of the years 1971 through 1975.

   On March 31, 1971, the date of the transfer at issue, Madrigrano conveyed all of his remaining 376 shares of Triangle stock to his sons, Joseph and Glenn. In exchange for the stock, Joseph and Glenn each executed a non-interest bearing promissory note in the amount of $7,110.97. The notes were made payable on March 31, 1972.

   At the time of the above transfer, Joseph was 23 years of age and a full-time, second-year law student who worked part-time during the school year and during summer vacations as an employee of Triangle. Glenn was 21 years of age, and a full-time undergraduate student. Like Joseph, Glenn also worked on weekends and during summer vacations for Triangle.

   On March 31, 1971, appellant Speca also conveyed all of his remaining shares of Triangle stock to his sons, Peter and Gene, who were 10 and 7 years of age, respectively, at the time. Speca's sons were also expected to pay $7,110.97 in exchange for the stock received from their father. However, unlike the Madrigrano transfer, there were no sale documents or notes evidencing a stock sale between Speca and his children. Speca expected payment of the $7,110.97 due from each child to be made from Triangle's profits. Although minors, Peter and Gene received Triangle stock certificates without benefit of a named custodian, guardian, or trustee. The minutes of Triangle's January, 1972, shareholders' meeting note that Speca appeared on behalf of Gene and Peter and that he signed a "notice of waiver" on their behalf.

Upon completion of the above transfers, the shareholders of record held the following amounts of Triangle stock:

Name	Shares
Joseph Madrigrano (Jr.)	358
Glenn Madrigrano	358
Mary Madrigrano	170
Karen Madrigrano	170
Armand Speca	170
Rosalyn Speca	170
Gene Speca	358
Peter Speca	358

In a subsequent audit of appellants' federal income tax returns for the year 1971, respondent determined that the transfers of stock on March 31, 1971, were not bona fide and lacked economic substance. Therefore, that income from the transferred stock was included in the taxpayers-appellants' gross income. Respondent's position was upheld by the Tax Court and this appeal followed.

The first issue raised by appellants is the question of the proper standard of review. In a case such as this, this court must inquire into who has true "shareholder" status. The mere record of stock ownership is not necessarily conclusive, for the true beneficial owner must be determined. "The issue of the appropriate standards for determining beneficial ownership is a question of law . . . , however, the question of whether an individual meets them and qualifies as a beneficial shareholder is one of fact." Wilson v. Commissioner, 560 F.2d 687 (5th Cir. 1977). It is quite apparent from the record that the trial judge used appropriate standards in making his decision, which leaves open the question of whether those standards were correctly applied to the facts of this case. Thus, the issue of shareholder status is a question of fact for purposes of review, and the trial court's determination should not be reversed unless his findings are clearly erroneous.

The issue of shareholder status in subchapter S corporations is not a new one. Examination of prior decisions reveals a consistent pattern of analysis involving the use of four specific factors. Those factors include: (1) Are the transferees within the family able to effectively exercise ownership rights of their shares; (2) Did the transferor continue to exercise complete dominion and control over the transferred stock; (3) Did the transferor continue to enjoy economic benefits of ownership after conveyance of the stock; and (4) Did the transferor deal at arm's length with the corporation involved. See

Duarte v. Commissioner, 44 T.C. 193 (1965); Beirne v. Commissioner, 52 T.C. 210 (1969); Beirne v. Commissioner, 61 T.C. 268 (1973); and Kirkpatrick v. Commissioner, 36 T.C.M. (CCH) 1122 (1971).

In addition to the foregoing factors, Section 1.1373(a)(2), Income Tax Regulations, provides as follows:

> A donee or purchaser of stock in the corporation is not considered a shareholder unless such stock is acquired in a bona fide transaction and the donee or purchaser is the real owner of such stock. The circumstances, not only as of the time of the purported transfer but also during the periods preceding and following it, will be taken into consideration in determining the bona fides of the transfer. Transactions between members of a family will be closely scrutinized.

For the purpose of determining federal income tax, "command over property or enjoyment of its economic benefits marks the real owners." Anderson v. Commissioner, 164 F.2d 870, 873 (7th Cir. 1947), *cert. den.* 334 U.S. 819 (1948). Any decision with respect to an intrafamily transfer need be examined in light of these guidelines and the four factors mentioned previously.

For purposes of analysis, the instant case invites comparison to the decision rendered in *Kirkpatrick*, supra. In that case, petitioners Donald D. and Carolyn Kirkpatrick owned 52 percent of the outstanding shares of Quality Poultry and Egg Co., Inc., an Arkansas subchapter S corporation. The remaining 48 percent of Quality's shares were owned by the four Kirkpatrick children. After making use of the four factor analysis, the Tax Court determined that the ownership of 48 percent of the stock of Quality by the children did not lack economic reality and, for tax purposes, each child owned 12 percent of the common stock of Quality.

As in *Kirkpatrick*, the present case propounds the question of true shareholder status. Appellants contend that the Madrigrano and Speca factual findings are on all fours with the facts in the Kirkpatrick case, therefore requiring a similar outcome. We agree, that if upon comparison, the facts and circumstances surrounding both disputes are substantially the same, then appellants' position would be viewed favorably.

I. First to be considered is whether appellants' transfer of stock on March 31, 1971, gave the intended transferees the ability to effectively exercise their ownership rights. Appellant Speca transferred his remaining eighteen percent share ownership equally to his sons, Gene and Peter, ages ten and seven. As minors, neither child exercised any influence in the operation of Triangle. The Tax Court found no evidence that a custodian, guardian, or legally designated representative was ever appointed to represent the children's interests. These facts differ substantially from those in *Kirkpatrick*. There, the wife was named custodian for the children and was present at all corporate meetings. She fully participated in corporate decisions, acted independently, and exercised considerable influence over the affairs of "Quality." See Kirkpatrick v. Commissioner, 36 T.C.M. (CCH) at 1126. This was unlike the present situation where no independent person represented the interests of the minor transferee-children who were too young to adequately represent themselves. Duarte v. Commissioner, 44 T.C. at 197. Therefore, we conclude that stock transferees Gene and Peter Speca were unable to effectively exercise their ownership rights.

Likewise, we find that stock transferees Glenn and Joseph Madrigrano were unable to exercise their ownership rights. Although adults, both Glenn and Joseph were full-time students. In 1971, their contact with Triangle was limited to part-time employment during summers and on weekends. The record reflects no specific instance in which either Glenn or Joseph actually exercised their judgment with respect to a corporate decision. The absence of any corporate activity by either Glenn or Joseph in addition to the circumstances detailed below, lead us to believe that they also possessed no effective ownership rights.

II. The next factor for consideration involves the extent to which the transferor continues to exercise dominion and control over the transferred stock. The actions of appellant Speca evidence a retention of control in the transferred stock to the detriment of the transferees' supposed rights. Acting for his sons, Peter and Gene, Speca signed a waiver of notice as to the 1972 shareholders' meeting and also approved the minutes of said meeting. The minutes of the 1974 shareholder meeting indicate that Peter and Gene were present by "proxy" without stating who the proxy was. However, Speca's signature again appears approving the minutes even though he was not on record as a shareholder. In contrast to *Kirkpatrick*, the presence of a custodian or legal representative acting on behalf of the Speca children is noticeably absent. Instead, we find appellant Speca in "control" of those shares purportedly sold.

The "control" exercised by appellant Madrigrano was accomplished through different means. Since its formation, Triangle operated as a beer distributor and wholesaler for the Joseph Schlitz Brewing Company (Schlitz). The relationship between Triangle and Schlitz consisted of an unwritten declaration of terms by which each party was free to buy or sell on an order-to-order basis. In October of 1972, Schlitz first learned that Madrigrano was no longer a shareholder of Triangle. Subsequently, Schlitz requested a meeting with Madrigrano to insure his continued participation in Triangle operations. Schlitz, through its sales manager Donald Hucko, informed

Madrigrano that it wanted him to enter into an employment contract of at least a 5- or 10-year duration to insure his continued direction of Triangle's day-to-day operations. This request was based upon the fact that Mr. Madrigrano was no longer a Triangle shareholder.

In a memorandum sent to his superior at Schlitz, Hucko described his meeting with Madrigrano. The memorandum stated in part:

> He (Madrigrano) stated that these changes had been made in order to save a considerable sum of money for himself and Mr. Speca, ... At my request, Mr. Madrigrano wrote me the attached letter,[2] outlining what money had been saved by the current stock arrangement. He assured me that he has always been in complete control of Triangle Wholesale Company, Inc., and will continue to do so. At my suggestion, an employment contract has been entered into which insures Mr. Madrigrano's leadership for at least ten more years.

The provisions of the resulting employment contract between Madrigrano and Triangle expressly stated that Madrigrano was hired "for a period beginning October 1, 1972 and ending September 30, 1982 as general manager, advisor, and consultant to management on all matters pertaining to the business of the Company." The contract itself was discussed at the January 11, 1972 shareholders' meeting. The minutes of the meeting stated that: "Schlitz made it emphatic since he (Madrigrano) was not a stockholder he must have a five year employment contract. Without this Triangle would be a shell and worthless corporation."

Based upon the record before us, we are convinced that Madrigrano's "presence" within Triangle was greater than that which normally flows from occupying an executive position. Madrigrano was the dominant figure who controlled corporate policy. As far as Schlitz was concerned, Madrigrano himself was the distributor of Schlitz products.

The March 31, 1971, transfer of stock was simply a paper transaction. It is evident that because Triangle depended for its business existence upon Schlitz, and Schlitz dealt with Triangle only because of Madrigrano's presence, neither Glenn nor Joseph could effectively challenge their father's judgment. As noted earlier, no specific instances can be found where either son exercised their judgment as shareholders with respect to a corporate decision. Thus, it is apparent that Madrigrano continued to effectively exercise complete dominion and control over the transferred stock as well as the corporation.

---

2. The "attached letter" specifically detailed the tax savings resulting from appellants' "sale" of their remaining interests in Triangle. In closing, the letter stated, "Don, this was only done for this reason (tax savings), all [these] figures can be substantiated and I also enclosed a work agreement so that you know I'll be here for ten more years."

III.   We now turn to the question of whether appellants retained economic enjoyment of the benefits of ownership in the transferred shares of Triangle stock, and whether they dealt at arm's length with the corporation. To answer the first part of the above question is to determine whether the transferee-children were deprived of the economic incidents of ownership in their Triangle stock. In the case of the Speca children, the dividends distributed in cash were approximately equal to the increase in their tax liability due to the inclusion of Triangle's income on their returns. The same was true as to cash dividends distributed to Glenn and Joseph Madrigrano. In fact, an examination of the business records of Triangle reveals that the dividends actually received were in no way commensurate to the profits being made by Triangle. Moreover, the record reflects the failure of appellants to adequately explain the retention of large amounts of corporate income in the year 1971 and thereafter.

Further analysis reveals that during the same time period appellants were the recipients of sizeable unsecured, interest-free loans from Triangle. These loans remained outstanding long after appellants ceased ownership in Triangle. The payment of the loans was accomplished in part by appellants' use of their children's non-cash dividends. The non-cash dividends were taken by appellants as part payment for the stock "sold" to their children in March of 1971. The dividends were then applied by appellants against the balance owing Triangle on their loans.

The situation in the instant case is again clearly distinguishable from *Kirkpatrick*. In that case, the transferee-children also received insignificant corporate distribution amounts. However, the undistributed corporate income was eventually used for legitimate investment and expansion purposes. Any explanation proffered in the present case lacked such legitimacy. Although in both instances the children's dividends were tapped by a transferor-parent, only the *Kirkpatrick* children enjoyed the benefit of a custodian to insure a legitimate transaction. Taking these facts into consideration, it is our opinion that appellants retained the economic benefits of Triangle stock ownership to the detriment of their children. We also find that appellants failed to "deal at arm's length . . . either in obtaining [their loans] or paying them back." Beirne v. Commissioner, 61 T.C. at 277.

IV.   The four-prong analysis reveals a consistent pattern of appellants' continued involvement with the stock purportedly sold. The transferee-children were unable to effectively exercise the ownership rights of their shares. Appellants continued to exercise complete dominion and control over the transferred stock. Moreover, appellants failed to deal at arm's length with the corporation and continued to enjoy the economic benefits of stock ownership although no longer shareholders of record. When compared to the facts of *Kirkpatrick*, any suggested similarity disappears. Thus, the Court's conclusion in

Kirkpatrick that the children's ownership of stock was bona fide and had economic reality is not warranted here. Unlike *Kirkpatrick*, the Tax Court in this instance found, and we agree, that the transferee-children were not the true owners of the stock conveyed in March of 1971. Appellants continued as the beneficial owners of the stock purportedly sold and must be treated as such for income tax purposes.

V.   Nonetheless, various points of contention raised by appellants remain for consideration. Appellants initially seek to discredit the trial court's partial reliance on the "control" factor. It is argued that the court below confused appellants' status as executives of Triangle and their resulting responsibility for operation of the corporation with control of the transferred stock. We find no merit in such a contention, however. The evidence clearly showed that after their final conveyance of stock, Madrigrano and Speca "continued to completely control the policies and operation of the corporation." Duarte v. Commissioner, 44 T.C. at 197. Standing alone, this fact is relatively unimportant. However, the presence of the additional factors discussed previously refutes appellants' claim. Appellants' children were unable to effectively exercise their stock ownership rights. Furthermore, appellants retained the economic benefits of stock ownership although supposedly no longer shareholders. The combination of these factors evidences "control" far beyond the normal relationship of a salaried executive to his corporation. Management of corporate affairs needlessly encompassed the control of shareholder rights as well.

Appellants also argue that the Tax Court reallocated income in violation of the specific provisions of §1375(c)*. . . . Because §1375(c) only allows reallocation between members of a family who are all shareholders of a Subchapter S corporation, appellants assert that they are not within the scope of said section for the reason that they are no longer shareholders. However, such an argument assumes appellants' shareholder status. That status is precisely the issue litigated below. The Tax Court concluded that appellants remained the owners of the transferred stock for income tax purposes because the disputed transaction lacked economic substance. Thus, the statutory directive of §1375(c) was not violated.

Appellants' final point of contention centers upon the Tax Court's alleged reliance on appellants' tax avoidance motives. It is argued that the Tax Court placed undue emphasis on this factor in disallowing the purported transfer of stock. We cannot agree. While it is true that the trial court partially relied on appellants' apparent tax motives in reaching its conclusion, we note that it was but one factor in the lower court's overall analysis. The Tax Court specifically

---

*Section 1366(e) of the 1986 Code. — ED.

recognized that, "While the desire to legitimately save taxes does not taint an otherwise bona fide transaction, it is also true

> [T]hat mere passage of title to income-producing property through devices which are valid under state law will not insulate the transferor against federal income tax liability unless the passage of title is accompanied by a complete shift of the economic benefits of ownership, direct and indirect.

Anderson v. Commissioner, 164 F.2d at 873. In first determining whether there was a shift of economic benefits, the Tax Court correctly applied the four-prong analysis in reaching its conclusion. Thereafter, regardless of whether or not the trial court was influenced by appellants' tax avoidance motives, the whole subject of tax avoidance was merely ancillary to the central question of true shareholder status. Thus, any undue influence accorded this factor was of little import in light of other factors present.

VI. Having reviewed the evidence in its entirety, we necessarily conclude that the decision of the Tax Court is not clearly erroneous. Substantial evidence exists to support the Tax Court's finding that appellants' purported transfer of stock lacked sufficient economic substance and therefore appellants are the beneficial owners of the transferred stock for income tax purposes. Accordingly, the judgment appealed from is affirmed.

NOTES

1. The Service has ruled that "investment interest" must be computed separately by an S corporation and passed through to shareholders with the characteristic retained, this for the purpose of determining the shareholder's §163(d)(1) deduction limitation. See Rev. Rul. 84-131, 1984-2 C.B. 37.

2. For an example of a reallocation of income from a C corporation to an S corporation, see Crane & Tractor Parts v. Commissioner, 48 T.C.M. (CCH) 1207 (19840.

3. In E. Keith Owens, 64 T.C. 1 (1975), *aff'd on this issue and rev'd in part*, 568 F.2d 1233 (6th Cir. 1977), the taxpayer "sold" the stock of his S corporation after the corporation had realized large gains but before the end of the corporation's taxable year. The corporation's sole asset was cash in excess of the "sale" price, and the buyers had large unused net operating loss carryovers. The corporation was liquidated three days after the sale. The Tax Court held that no bona fide sale occurred prior to the liquidation and that the taxpayer would be taxed on the corporation's undistributed taxable income.

4. See Coven, Subchapter S Distributions and Pseudodistribu-

tions: Proposals for Revising the Defective Blend of Entity and Conduit Concepts, 42 Tax L. Rev. 381 (1987).

B. SUBCHAPTER S AND PASSIVE LOSSES

The 1986 Act added §469. Its primary role is to disallow so-called *passive activity losses*, except against *passive activity income*.* A "passive activity" is one in which the taxpayer does not "materially participate." For pass-through entities such as S corporations, the passive loss rules are tested at the shareholder level. As a result, if one owns stock in an S corporation, to be treated as "materially participating" the shareholder must be involved personally in the conduct of the corporate business on a "regular, continuous, and substantial" basis.

Portfolio income (including interest, dividends, and royalties) is not "passive," and so it cannot be offset by losses from passive activities. If, however, an S corporation is engaged in business, its income, when it passes through to its stockholders, is not treated as portfolio income. Therefore, if an S corporation produces "passive activity" income (because the shareholder has not participated materially in the corporation's business activity), that income will pass through to the shareholder as "passive activity" income and will be available generally as an offset to the shareholder's unrelated passive activity losses. The Treasury, however, has been given regulatory authority to prevent the sheltering of business income through the use of tax losses derived from passive business activities.**

It should be noted that if an S corporation has portfolio income, that income characteristic will pass through to the shareholders. Thus, portfolio income of an S corporation is nonpassive income to the shareholder, effectively denying the shareholder any opportunity to use that income as an offset against his passive losses. Gains on the sale of a shareholder's S stock will not be treated as portfolio income, except to the extent the gains are attributable to portfolio

---

*In reaching agreement on this provision, the House-Senate Conference Committee followed the Senate's lead, and so the report of the Senate Finance Committee is particularly helpful in gaining an understanding of §469. See S. Rep. No. 313, 99th Cong., 2d Sess. (May 29, 1986). For the relevant portion of the Conference Report, see H.R. Conf. Rep. No. 841, 99th Cong., 2d Sess., II-137 et seq. (Sept. 18, 1986). Juxtaposed with the pertinent statutory provisions, excerpts from the reports appear in CCH, Tax Reform Act of 1986, Law and Controlling Committee Reports, ¶7501 (Oct. 25, 1986).

**". . . exercise of such authority may . . . be appropriate . . . [where there were] activities previously generating active business losses that the taxpayer intentionally seeks to treat as passive at a time when they generate net income, with the purpose of circumventing the rule." H.R. Conf. Rep. No. 841, 99th Cong., 2d Sess., II-147 (Sept. 18, 1986).

type assets held by the S corporation. If, in a taxable transaction, a shareholder disposes of his entire stock interest in an S corporation, he can recognize his previously disallowed ("suspended") losses from that activity. Section 469(g).

IV. DISQUALIFICATION

FEINGOLD v. COMMISSIONER
49 T.C. 461 (1968)

SIMPSON, Judge. The respondent determined deficiencies in the petitioner's income tax for the calendar year 1961 in the amount of $1,509.91 and for the calendar year 1962 of $3,937.45. The principal question in this case is whether an election by a small business corporation under subchapter S of the Internal Revenue Code of 1954 terminated by reason of its having derived more than 20 percent of its gross receipts from "rents." . . .

FINDINGS OF FACT

The petitioners Max and Gertrude Feingold are husband and wife, who maintain their legal residence at Rockaway Beach, New York, at the time the petition was filed in this case. . . .

In 1961, the petitioners formed the Germac Realty Corporation (Germac) under the laws of the State of New York. During 1961 and 1962, they owned all of its outstanding stock and were its only officers. Max was president and Gertrude was secretary-treasurer. Germac filed its corporate tax returns for 1961 and 1962 with the district director of internal revenue, Brooklyn, New York. Germac filed a timely election to be taxed as a small business corporation under subchapter S for the years 1961 and following.

During the years 1961 and 1962, Germac operated a colony of 95 rental bungalows located in a 3-block area near the beach in Far Rockaway, New York. These bungalows were rented from Memorial Day to Labor Day to vacationers and their families, for whom the colony's major attraction was its proximity to the beach. During the rest of the year, the colony was closed and repairs were made during that time. Most of the bungalows were single-family units, although a few held two families. They were furnished with tables, chairs, refrigerators, stoves, beds, mattresses, and mattress covers. Germac paid the taxes on the property and performed the repairs. Max, who had had experience in renting bungalows prior to 1961, supervised Germac's operations.

In 1960 or 1961, Max and Germac paved, fenced, and provided

lighting for a patio on the premises measuring 30 by 115 feet. This patio was provided as a common recreation area for the tenants and was restricted to their use. Here, during the day, children played ball, and tenants played cards and bingo, with tables, chairs, and cards provided by Germac. It occasionally gave parties for the children, providing hats and small prizes.

Two or three times during the summer of each of the years 1961 and 1962, Germac sponsored parties for the tenants. Max, who was usually on the premises and who saw the tenants frequently, notified them when a party was to be given. At each of these parties, approximately $25 of food and beverages was provided by Germac. . . .

For 1961, the first year of Germac's operations, it reported gross income of $49,212.00, consisting entirely of rentals from the bungalows, and reported a loss of $9,929.73. For 1962, it reported gross income of $49,587.42, of which $49,274.50 constituted rentals from the bungalows and $312.92 was "other income." It reported a loss in that year of $15,290.59.

OPINION

The issue in this case is whether net operating losses sustained by Germac during the years 1961 and 1962 are deductible from the income of its shareholders, the petitioners, under section 1374. Under that section, the shareholders of an electing small business corporation are allowed to deduct the losses of the corporation. Since Germac made a timely election under section 1372 to be taxed as a small business corporation under subchapter S, the only question is whether that election terminated under section 1372(e)(5) because 100 per cent of the corporation's receipts in 1961 and more than 99 per cent of its receipts in 1962 were derived from the rental of vacation bungalows.

Section 1372(e)(5), as applicable to the years in controversy, provided:

. . . Sec. 1372. *Election by Small Business Corporation.*
(e) Termination. — . . .
(5) Personal holding company income. — An election under subsection (a) made by a small business corporation shall terminate if, for any taxable year of the corporation for which the election is in effect, such corporation has gross receipts more than 20 per cent of which is derived from royalties, rents, dividends, interest, annuities, and sales or exchanges of stock or securities (gross receipts from such sales or exchanges being taken into account for purposes of this paragraph only to the extent of gains therefrom). Such termination shall be effective for the taxable year of the corporation in which it has gross receipts of such amount, and for all succeeding taxable years of the corporation. . . .

Shortly after the enactment of subchapter S, the question arose whether section 1372(e)(5) would prevent a corporation engaged in the operation of a hotel or motel, where the major source of receipts was "rent" paid by guests for their rooms, from making an effective subchapter S election. This question was answered by section 1.1372-4(b)(5)(iv), Income Tax Regs., which provides:

> (iv) *Rents.* The term "rents" as used in section 1372(e)(5) means amounts received for the use of, or right to use, property (whether real or personal) of the corporation, whether or not such amounts constitute 50 per cent or more of the gross income of the corporation for the taxable year. The term "rents" does not include payments for the use or occupancy of rooms or other space where significant services are also rendered to the occupant, such as for the use of occupancy of rooms or other quarters in hotels, boarding houses, or apartment houses furnishing hotel services. . . .

In this case, no issue has been raised as to the correctness or validity of the regulations. The case turns on how they are to be interpreted and applied.

Germac's receipts indisputably arose from tenants' payments for the use of or right to use its property — the bungalows, the furniture, and the common recreation area. However, the petitioners contend that such receipts are not rents within the regulations because Germac rendered significant services which were primarily for the convenience of its tenants and which were other than those usually rendered in connection with the rental of space for occupancy only.[3] In support of this contention, the petitioners state that Germac provided the following services: It provided furniture for the bungalows and a recreation area maintained by the corporation, as well as tables and cards for use in that area; it sponsored bingo games for the adults and parties for the children at which small prizes were given; and it sponsored parties for the adults, providing food and entertainment.

We have found that Germac did provide furniture, a patio, and some recreational equipment for its tenants' use, but we do not believe that this constitutes the providing of services within the meaning of the regulations, significant or otherwise. Insofar as the corporation simply offered its tenants the right to use its property, payment by the tenant for that right constituted "rent" in its classic form and as specifically defined in the regulations. There was no proof that Germac rendered any services at all to the tenants in connection with

---

3. The proper interpretation of "rents" as used in the statute and regulations is a case of first impression. The respondent has, however, published several statements of his position in the form of revenue rulings. See Rev. Rul. 65-91, 1965-1 C.B. 431; Rev. Rul. 65-83, 1965-1 C.B. 430; Rev. Rul. 65-40, 1965-1 C.B. 429; Rev. Rul. 64-232, 1964-2 C.B. 334; Rev. Rul. 61-112, 1961-1 C.B. 399.

the use of the furniture or recreation equipment. As to the patio, the only evidence of corporate activity in connection therewith was that the corporation paid the light bill and taxes for the patio area. Such activity does not constitute the performance of services to the occupant within the meaning of the regulations. We need not therefore determine whether such activity would fulfill the requirement of "significance."

The petitioners rely primarily upon their contention that Germac provided recreation and entertainment to the tenants. The petitioners point to Max's testimony that the corporation held bingo games for the adults and gave small parties for the children. We find this evidence unsatisfactory to sustain the petitioners' contention. Although uncontradicted, the testimony was unsupported by any documentary evidence, and it was completely unexplained. There was no attempt to show how many such games and parties were given in 1961 and 1962, or any other year; no indication as to what the corporation or its officers did to promote or supervise these activities except for the testimony that "we run games" and "run the parties"; no showing as to whether such activities were a significant part of the tenants' activities in terms of time, effort, or enjoyment, or were a significant part of the corporation's operations in terms of money or employee's efforts. Indeed, the tense in which the question eliciting this testimony was asked and answered at trial suggests that Max may have been testifying as to the corporation's activities and practices at the time of the hearing rather than during the years in controversy. In short, although the testimony supports our bare finding that bingo games and children's parties did take place, it does not enable us to find that these activities constituted significant services rendered by the corporation to its tenants.

The petitioners also contend that Germac gave or sponsored weekend parties for the adults. Most of the evidence at trial concerned this contention, but it was all vague, and often contradictory, as to the number of parties given during the taxable years in controversy, the nature of those parties, and the entertainment provided. The record shows little evidence as to the role played by the corporation in sponsoring these parties and is completely silent as to the degree or nature of the participation by the tenants. Thus, when Max testified that six or seven parties were given during each summer, the respondent introduced into evidence for purposes of impeachment, without objection from the petitioners, an affidavit signed by Max and Gertrude Feingold on November 4, 1966, which had been submitted to the Internal Revenue Service in an effort to settle this case. According to that affidavit, only two or three parties were given each year. The petitioners did not attempt to explain away this affidavit, although it flatly contradicts Max's testimony. We therefore have found that the corporation gave no more than two or three parties during each of the taxable years in controversy, rather than the six or seven claimed, but that it did sponsor those two or three parties. . . .

The regulations include no standard for interpreting the term "significant," except as can be inferred from the examples contained therein. Clearly, the services supplied by Germac were not comparable to the services furnished by the operator of a hotel or motel. In those businesses, guests come and go frequently, and maids service the rooms daily. From what appears of record in this case, the occupants of the bungalows neither required nor received any such frequent or extensive services. By any test of "significance," no significant services were rendered by Germac to the tenants other than those usually rendered in connection with the rental of space or other property for occupancy only, and its income from the bungalows was "rent" within the meaning of section 1.1372-4(b)(5)(iv), Income Tax Regs.

Since more than 20 per cent of Germac's gross receipts in 1961 were such "rents," Germac's election was therefore terminated for that taxable year and subsequent taxable years under section 1372(e)(5). Consequently, its shareholders may not deduct Germac's loss from their individual income on their returns for 1961 and 1962. Our holding makes it unnecessary to consider the respondent's alternative contention that the loss suffered by Germac in 1962 was less than that claimed by the petitioners on their return for 1962.

Decision will be entered for the respondent.

NOTES

1. Section 1362(d)(3)(A) eliminates the passive investment income limitation for corporations that do not have Subchapter C accumulated earnings and profits. Section 1375 imposes a corporate level tax on passive income in excess of 25 percent of the corporation's "gross receipts" for an S corporation with Subchapter C accumulated earnings and profits, and §1362(d)(3) terminates such corporation's S status if its passive investment income exceeds 25 percent for three consecutive years. Thus, the importance of determining whether an item of income is passive has been reduced but not eliminated. For a justification of the change, consider this excerpt from a 1980 staff report to the Congressional Joint Committee on Taxation, recommending changes in Subchapter S:

> The proposal would eliminate the provision under which an election would be terminated if more than 20 percent of a corporation's gross receipts is passive investment income.

Perhaps the principal reason for the inclusion of this restriction in 1958 was to reduce the incentive to incorporate one's investment activities for the primary purpose of obtaining tax deferral benefits accorded to pension, profit-sharing, and other similar qualified plans. However, this reason appears to have been substantially reduced with the imposition by the Tax Reform Act of 1969 of the H.R. 10-type of limitation on contributions made for an employee holding more than 5 percent of the subchapter S corporation's stock. Because subchapter S income is taxed currently to the shareholders, the allowance of passive investment income does not subvert the purposes of the personal holding company provisions.

Furthermore, the passive investment income limitation has caused a number of inadvertent terminations of elections, as well as a substantial amount of litigation as to what constitutes passive investment income. Controversy exists as to whether the term passive investment income includes interest and rents which are earned in the active conduct of a trade or business (e.g., interest of a small loan company or produced film rents of an active production company). Elimination of this restriction would remove much uncertainty, reduce litigation, and prevent retroactive terminations of subchapter S elections.

House Committee on Ways and Means and Senate Committee on Finance, Staff Recommendations for Simplification of Tax Rules Relating to Subchapter S Corporations (Joint Publication), 96th Cong., 2d Sess. (Comm. Print 1980).

2. Income from a wide variety of activities has been considered passive. See, e.g., I. J. Marshall, 60 T.C. 242 (1973), *aff'd*, 510 F.2d 259 (10th Cir. 1975) (interest income); Joseph B. Zychinski, 60 T.C. 950 (1973), *aff'd*, 506 F.2d 637 (8th Cir. 1974), *cert. denied*, 421 U.S. 999 (income from active conduct of securities business is passive investment income); see also New Mexico Timber Co. v. Commissioner, 84 T.C. 1290 (1985) ("gross receipts" as used to determine the passive investment income limitation included the full amount realized by trading in commodity futures). Cf. Bradshaw v. United States, 683 F.2d 365 (Ct. Cl. 1982) (receipt of payments on installment note arising from sale of land is not passive investment income); William B. Howell, 57 T.C. 546 (1972) (*acq.*) (corporation that had no trade or business but derived capital gain from occasional sales of land did not have passive investment income and qualified for Subchapter S election); Rev. Rul. 72-457, 1972-2 C.B. 510 (income from trading in commodity futures is not passive investment income because futures are not "stock or securities").

REVENUE RULING 64-94
1964-1 C.B. 317

Advice has been requested whether an election under section [1362] of the Internal Revenue Code of 1954 is terminated with respect to the taxable year when an electing small business corporation is merged into another corporation in a statutory merger within the meaning of section 368(a)(1)(A) of the Code.

A small business corporation, as defined in section [1361(a)] of the Code, made a timely election under section [1362] of the Code which was not terminated prior to the taxable year when it was merged into another corporation in a statutory merger within the meaning of section 368(a)(1)(A) of the Code. The final taxable year of the electing small business corporation ended on the date of the merger, under section 381(b)(1) of the Code, and the surviving corporation was not an electing small business corporation.

None of the [conditions] specified in section [1362(d)] of the Code occurred in the final taxable year of the electing small business corporation which would terminate its election under section [1362] of the Code for such year, unless it is determined that the merger falls within the intendment of section [1362(d)(2)] of the Code.

Section [1362(d)(2)] of the Code provides, in effect, that an election under section [1362(a)] of the Code made by a small business corporation shall terminate if at any time the corporation ceases to be a small business corporation as defined in section [1361(a)] of the Code. Such termination shall be effective for the taxable year of the corporation in which it ceases to be a small business corporation and for all succeeding taxable years of the corporation.

Section [1362(b)] of the Code provides that an election under section [1362(a)] of the Code shall be effective for the taxable year of the corporation for which it is made and for all succeeding taxable years of the corporation, unless it is terminated with respect to any such taxable year under section [1362(d)] of the Code.

Section [1362(d)(2)] of the Code applies to a corporation which ceases to be a small business corporation by virtue of an event which does not terminate its taxable year. Where, as in the instant case, the event which causes the corporation to be disqualified as a small business corporation also terminates its taxable year, the corporation remains a small business corporation, as defined in section [1361], throughout the entire taxable year so terminated.

On the basis of the foregoing, it is held that the election, under section [1362] of the Code, of the small business corporation in the instant case was not terminated with respect to its final taxable year ending with the date of the merger.

NOTES

1. The acquisition of the stock of an S corporation by a parent corporation in a "B" reorganization, with consolidated returns filed thereafter, did not terminate the Subchapter S election for the elapsed period of its current tax year. See Rev. Rul. 80-169, 1980-1 C.B. 188. A short tax year was held to end a moment prior to the parent corporation's acquisition of the stock of the Subchapter S company. Rev. Rul. 80-169 revoked Rev. Rul. 72-201, 1972-1 C.B. 271, under which there was a retroactive termination to the beginning of the tax year.

2. Involuntary terminations under §1362(d)(2) result in the application of the short taxable year rules of §1362(e). Inadvertent terminations may be waived by the Secretary under §1362(f). See Rev. Rul. 86-110, 1986-2 C.B. 150 (inadvertent termination waived where stock was transferred to ineligible shareholder on advice of counsel); Note, When Can Inadvertent Termination of S Corporation Be Waived?, 65 J. Taxn. 116 (1986).

V. OPERATING LOSSES

SELFE v. UNITED STATES
778 F.2d 769 (11th Cir. 1985)

Before Tjoflat and Kravitch, Circuit Judges, and Dumbauld,* District Judge.

KRAVITCH, Circuit Judge.

This appeal requires us to determine whether a shareholder in a Subchapter S corporation, who personally guarantees and secures a corporate debt, may increase the adjusted basis of her stock by the full amount of the debt in order to maximize her loss deductions under §1374. . . .

The district court granted summary judgment in favor of the government and dismissed taxpayers' suit for refund of $24,287 in federal income taxes and interest paid. The district court also denied appellants' motion for summary judgment. We reverse and remand.

Taxpayer, Jane B. Selfe, formerly Jane Simon, entered into a retail clothing business in 1977 under the name of Jane Simon, Inc. She applied to the First National Bank of Birmingham for financing.

---

*Honorable Edward Dumbauld, U.S. District Judge for the Western District of Pennsylvania, sitting by designation.

In consideration of her pledge of 4,500 shares of stock in Avondale Mills owned by her and close family members, the bank agreed to extend a line of credit to her in the amount of $120,000 for use in the business. Shortly thereafter, the business was incorporated. Taxpayer and her former husband were issued all of the stock, which was subsequently conveyed to Jane upon their divorce. The shareholders of the corporation elected to have the corporation taxed pursuant to Subchapter S of the Internal Revenue Code of 1954. At the request of the bank, all loans made to the taxpayer individually pursuant to the line of credit, except $10,000 initially advanced, were converted to corporate loans. Taxpayer executed an agreement guaranteeing the corporation's indebtedness to the bank. The loan officer testified that the bank wanted the assurance of having the corporation primarily liable to repay the loan, but that the conversion did not abridge the stock pledged as collateral, or the bank's rights against the taxpayer as guarantor, in the event of the corporation's default. Subsequently, the corporation granted the bank a security interest in its receivables, inventory and contract rights in order to obtain a renewal of its loans. The business began operations on August 4, 1977 and suffered losses for each year through 1980. It never, however, defaulted on its loan payments and the bank never was required to proceed against either the Avondale Mills stock or the taxpayer. On June 30, 1980, the outstanding balance of the corporation's indebtedness to the bank exceeded $130,000.

The net operating loss of Jane Simon, Inc. for the fiscal year ending June 30, 1980 was $33,824. Taxpayer and her new husband, Edward Selfe, deducted the entire loss from gross income on their joint income tax return for the year 1980. The government, however, determined that the allowable portion of the loss was limited to $4,946, the amount it determined was the taxpayer's adjusted basis in the corporation, and accordingly disallowed $28,878 of the claimed deduction, giving rise to an income tax deficiency in the amount of $16,839.42 plus interest in the amount of $7,648.64. Taxpayer paid the claim and then filed a claim for refund of the tax and interest. The government disallowed the claim and the taxpayer instituted a refund suit in the district court. The district court judge denied the taxpayer's motion for summary judgment, but granted summary judgment to the government.

Section 1374 permits a shareholder in a Subchapter S corporation to deduct his portion of the corporation's net operating loss from his personal income. Section 1374 limits the amount of the deduction, however, to the sum of the adjusted basis of the shareholder's stock in the corporation, plus the adjusted basis of any indebtedness of the corporation to the shareholder. Relying upon the principles of Plantation Patterns, Inc. v. Commissioner, 462 F.2d 712 (5th Cir.), *cert. denied*, 409 U.S. 1076 (1972), the appellant argues that the bank is deemed to have made the loan directly to her and that she then contributed the loan proceeds to Jane Simon, Inc., thereby increasing her basis in the stock of the corporation. In *Plantation Patterns*, the Fifth Circuit held that a loan is deemed to be made to a stockholder who has guaranteed a corporate note when the facts indicate that the lender is looking primarily to the stockholder for repayment. *Plantation Patterns*, however, did not involve §1372 as the corporation in that case was not a Subchapter S corporation. Rather, in *Plantation Patterns*, the former Fifth Circuit affirmed as not clearly erroneous a Tax Court finding that a transaction structured as a loan by an independent third party to a corporation, and guaranteed by a shareholder, was in substance a loan to the shareholder followed by his contribution of the loan proceeds to the capital of the corporation, and that as a result, the corporation's payments of principal and interest on the debt constituted constructive dividends to the shareholder. The taxpayer here does not argue that the cases are identical; rather, she argues that the principles announced in *Plantation Patterns* should apply here and points to the testimony of her bank officer that the loan to Jane Simon, Inc. was secured by the taxpayer's Avondale stock and that the bank was primarily looking to the taxpayer and her pledged stock for repayment of the loan.[6]

Taxpayer's position is supported further by Peter Blum, 59 T.C. 436 (1972) and In re Lane, 742 F.2d 1311 (11th Cir. 1984). In dicta, in the *Blum* case, the Tax Court stated it could see no distinction in principle between a situation such as Selfe's and *Plantation Patterns*. In *Lane* we observed that "we pay close heed to the dictates set forth by . . . *Plantation Patterns*," when determining whether a shareholder's capital infusion is a loan or equity investment. 742 F.2d at 1320 (citations omitted). The taxpayer also points to proposed regulations, §1.385-9, under section 385 of the code, which apply the principles of *Plantation Patterns*.[7] These regulations, however, were withdrawn in 1983.

---

6. It is not clear from the bank officer's deposition testimony that the bank was primarily looking to the taxpayer for repayment. Mr. Anthony, the bank officer, testified that the loans originally advanced to the taxpayer were converted to corporate loans because "it just made more sense to have the company primarily liable and then the individuals would be just as liable as they were when the loans were direct to them." Mr. Anthony also testified, however, that the taxpayer's collateral and personal guaranty were "primarily" why the bank renewed the corporation's loans. On remand, the court will have to determine what the bank's intentions were.

7. . . . Although this proposed regulation was withdrawn, this court has never "withdrawn" the principles set forth in *Plantation Patterns*. Indeed we recently reaffirmed those principles in In re Lane, 742 F.2d at 1320.

The district court, primarily relying upon Brown v. Commissioner, 706 F.2d 755 (6th Cir. 1983), held that an economic outlay resulting in an increase in a shareholder's basis in a Subchapter S corporation occurs only when the shareholder-guarantor is called upon to pay the corporation's debt. Here, although the corporation each year had suffered losses, it did not default on the payments due the bank on the loan. Furthermore, the bank had renewed the loan to the corporation upon assignment of its accounts receivable. The government points out that taxpayer has cited no decision in which a court has held that a shareholder's guarantee of a loan made to a Subchapter S corporation increased his basis in the corporation and states that similar attempts to circumvent the limitations of section 1374(c)(2) repeatedly have been rejected by the courts. [Citations omitted.]

We find the Sixth Circuit's reasoning in *Brown* only partially persuasive. We agree with *Brown* inasmuch as that court reaffirms that economic outlay is required before a stockholder in a Subchapter S corporation may increase her basis. . . . We disagree, however, with the proposition that a stockholder/taxpayer must, in all cases, absolve a corporation's debt before she may recognize an increased basis as a guarantor of a loan to a corporation.[8] Instead, we conclude that under the principles of *Plantation Patterns*, a shareholder who has guaranteed a loan to a Subchapter S corporation may increase her basis where the facts demonstrate that, in substance, the shareholder has borrowed funds and subsequently advanced them to her corporation.

The government correctly argues that generally taxpayers are liable for the tax consequences of the transaction they actually execute and may not reap the benefit of some other transaction that they might have made. In other words, taxpayers ordinarily are bound by the "form" of their transaction and may not argue that the "substance" of their transaction triggers different tax consequences. . . .

It is equally well settled that the Commissioner need not always determine the tax effect of transactions based on the form of the transaction. . . . This principle is particularly evident where characterization of capital as debt or equity will have different tax consequences. Thus in *Plantation Patterns* the court held that interest payments by a corporation on debentures were constructive stockholder dividends and could not be deducted by the corporation as

8. For example, a guarantor who has pledged stock to secure a loan has experienced an economic outlay to the extent that the pledged stock is not available as collateral for other investments. The guarantor in this example has lost the time value or use of its collateral.

interest payments. There, the former Fifth Circuit recharacterized debt as equity at the insistence of the Commissioner. These principles, however, are not solely for the government's benefit. Section 385(b) sets forth five factors which are available to determine "whether a debtor-creditor relationship exists or a corporation-shareholder relationship exists." . . . Similarly this circuit applies a thirteen factor analysis to characterize a taxpayer's interest in a corporation. . . .

Although the question of whether a stockholder's advances to a corporation constitute debt or capital contributions is usually raised by the government, nothing in the Internal Revenue Code or our decisions suggests that the factors used to determine the substantive character of a taxpayer's interest in a corporation are available only to the government. . . . Cf. Peter E. Blum, 59 T.C. 436, 439 (1972) (principles for resolving debt-equity determinations are consistent regardless of the context in which such determinations arise); J. A. Maurer, Inc., 30 T.C. 1273 (1958). Accordingly, where the nature of a taxpayer's interest in a corporation is in issue, courts may look beyond the form of the interest and investigate the substance of the transaction. These situations present an exception to the general proposition that a shareholder/taxpayer is bound by the form of her transaction. See Georgia-Pacific Corp. v. Commissioner, 63 T.C. 790, 795-96 (1975).

At issue here, however, is not whether the taxpayer's contribution was either a loan to or an equity investment in Jane Simon, Inc. The issue is whether the taxpayer's guarantee of the corporate loan was in itself a contribution to the corporation sufficient to increase the taxpayer's basis in the corporation. In most cases, a mere guarantee of a corporate loan is insufficient, absent subrogation, to increase a taxpayer's basis. . . . Rev. Rul. 75-144 (increase basis where shareholder substitutes his promise to pay for corporation's promise). Thus arguments similar to Selfe's — that the taxpayer's guarantee is in reality a loan made to the shareholder/taxpayer that is subsequently advanced to the corporation — usually meet with little success because the taxpayer is unable to demonstrate that the substance of his transaction is different than its form. Indeed, the *Brown* court refused "to accept petitioners" contorted view of the transaction in furtherance of their "substance over form" argument when as the court below observed, "the substance matched the form." 706 F.2d at 756. Similarly, in Blum v. Commissioner, the court determined that although guaranteed loans might constitute contributions to capital, the taxpayer there was not entitled to an increased basis because the bank expected repayment of its loan from the corporation and not the taxpayer. Blum, 59 T.C. at 440. That taxpayers rarely, if ever, have demonstrated that a guarantee was in reality a loan to the corporation from the shareholder/taxpayer does not mean that this argument is legally inadequate per se. As noted in In re Breit, 460 F. Supp. 873, 875 (E.D. Va. 1978), "[t]he issue is a mixed question of law and fact ... [and] [n]o single factor determines whether the loans were in fact by the bank to appellants followed by a capital contribution on their part."

Under the principles of *Plantation Patterns*, a shareholder guarantee of a loan may be treated for tax purposes as an equity investment in the corporation where the lender looks to the shareholder as the primary obligor. Essential to the *Plantation Patterns* court's analysis was that the notes guaranteed by the shareholder were issued by a thinly capitalized corporation and had more equity characteristics than debt. The *Plantation Patterns* court stressed that its inquiry focused on highly complex issues of fact and that similar inquiries must be carefully evaluated on their own facts. 462 F.2d at 719. ... Here, the taxpayer has presented the deposition testimony of her loan officer stating that the bank primarily looked to the taxpayer and not the corporation for repayment of the loan. Moreover, the taxpayer also has elicited testimony indicating that Jane Simon, Inc. was thinly capitalized. The taxpayer argues that it is highly unlikely that the bank would have advanced funds directly to Jane Simon, Inc. — a fledgling enterprise operated by a novice in a highly competitive field. This argument is further supported by the fact that the bank previously had approved a line of credit consistent with the credit enjoyed by Jane Simon, Inc. to Jane Selfe, nee Simon, based upon her pledge of Avondale stock. The government, however, notes that it was at the bank's insistence that the line of credit originally approved for the taxpayer was converted to loans to the corporation guaranteed by the taxpayer.

Accordingly, we conclude that there are material facts still in issue and therefore summary judgment was inappropriate. We remand for a determination of whether or not the bank primarily looked to Jane Selfe for repayment and for the court to apply the factors set out in *In re Lane* and §385 to determine if the taxpayer's guarantee amounted to either an equity investment in or shareholder loan to Jane Simon, Inc. In short, we remand for the district court to apply *Plantation Patterns* and determine if the bank loan to Jane Simon, Inc. was in reality a loan to the taxpayer.

Reversed and Remanded.

NOTES

1. In Estate of Daniel Leavitt v. Commissioner, 875 F.2d 420

(4th Cir. 1989), *aff'g* 90 T.C. 206 (1988), the court held contrary to *Selfe*. That court believes that basis should be unaffected when the shareholder has made no economic outlay. See Bogdanski, Shareholder Debt: Lessons from *Leavitt* and *Lessinger*, 16 J. Corp. Taxn. 348 (1990).

2. A shareholder-guarantor who actually pays a corporate debt is subrogated to the creditor's claim and thereby acquires corporate debt with a basis equal to the amount paid. See Rev. Rul. 70-50, 1970-1 C.B. 178, clarified by Rev. Rul. 71-288, 1971-2 C.B. 319. The same rule was applied to a shareholder who discharged his corporation's bank indebtedness simply by issuing his own note. See Rev. Rul. 75-144, 1975-1 C.B. 277.

3. In Rev. Rul. 81-187, 1981-2 C.B. 167, the Service held that a shareholder with a zero basis in the stock of an S corporation may not deduct a net operating loss suffered by the corporation for a year in which the shareholder issued an unsecured, demand promissory note to the corporation that was not paid by the end of that taxable year of the corporation.

4. Section 1367(b)(3) now gives precedence to net operating losses over worthless stock and worthless debts, adopting the taxpayer's unsuccessful position in Abdalla v. Commissioner, 647 F.2d 487 (5th Cir. 1984). Cf. Sam W. Klein, 75 T.C. 298 (1980).

5. Once a shareholder's basis in his S corporation stock is reduced to zero, any amount that would have further reduced that basis reduces his basis in any debt of the S corporation that he holds. Later, if he has any increase in basis, he must restore the basis in the debt before allocating any basis restoration to the equity. See §1362(b)(2).

6. Although Subchapter S was intended to reduce the extent to which tax considerations affect the choice of form of a business organization, there remain important differences in the tax rules applicable to Subchapter S corporations and partnerships. The treatment of operating losses provides an example. Both Subchapter S shareholders and partners are subject to investment limits on the deduction of passed-through operating losses, but the "at risk" rules for the two types of enterprise are different. Compare §§465, 704(d), and 752. The investment limit for Subchapter S shareholders includes personal (shareholder) debt only, while a partner's investment includes a share of certain debts of the partnership. See §752.

7. As a result of recent changes, Subchapter S shareholders, like partners, may carry forward an excess operating loss which exceeds current basis. Section 1366(d)(2) allows a taxpayer to carry over disallowed losses and deductions indefinitely so that they may be used

in subsequent years if basis is later restored. Additionally, §1366(d)(3) allows the carryover to be extended to the corporation's "post-termination transition period" as defined in §1377(b).

Table of Cases

Table of Rulings

Revenue Ruling	Cum. Bull. Citation	
71-288	1971-2, 319	1215
71-364	1971-2, 182	822
71-426	1971-2, 173	176
71-593	1971-2, 181	720
72-264	1972-1, 131	533
72-265	1972-1, 222	533
72-327	1972-2, 197	655
72-380	1972-2, 201	176
72-457	1972-2, 510	1208
73-54	1973-1, 187	647
73-122	1973-1, 66	78
73-236	1973-1, 183	693, 694
73-237	1973-1, 185	693, 694
73-423	1973-2, 161	358
73-427	1973-2, 301	675
73-472	1973-2, 114	1062
73-473	1973-2, 115	1062
73-552	1973-2, 116	822
73-611	1973-2, 312	1190
74-5	1974-1, 82	707
74-35	1974-1, 85	651
74-36	1974-1, 85	639
74-164	1974-1, 74	120
74-296	1974-1, 80	300
74-502	*1974-2, 116*	*342*
74-503	1974-2, 117	85, 674, 677
74-515	1974-2, 118	672
74-516	1974-2, 121	672
74-544	1974-2, 108	300
74-565	*1974-2, 125*	*630*
74-598	1974-2, 287	1061, 1062
74-610	*1974-2, 288*	*1039*
75-2	1975-1, 99	176
75-3	1975-1, 108	300
75-19	1975-1, 382	907
75-67	*1975-1, 169*	*1153*
75-83	1975-1, 112	673
75-94	1975-1, 111	646
75-123	1975-1, 115	642
75-144	1975-1, 277	1215
75-160	1975-1, 112	703
75-161	1975-1, 114	654
75-223	1975-1, 109	300, 574
75-247	1975-1, 104	467
75-305	1975-2, 228	1079
75-320	1975-2, 105	161
75-321	1975-2, 123	741
75-337	1975-2, 124	686
75-383	1975-2, 127	1061
75-406	1975-2, 125	717
75-421	1975-2, 108	647
75-447	1975-2, 113	262, 672, 673
75-450	1975-2, 166	655
75-456	1975-2, 128	646
75-468	1975-2, 115	506
75-469	1975-2, 469	741
75-493	1975-2, 108	26, 258
75-502	1975-2, 111	208, 210, 212, 214, 672
75-512	1975-2, 112	210, 212

Revenue Ruling	Cum. Bull. Citation	
78-251	1978-1, 89	718
78-286	1978-2, 145	616
78-294	*1978-2, 141*	*330*
78-330	1978-2, 147	654
78-375	*1978-2, 130*	*496*
78-376	1978-2, 149	646
78-401	1978-2, 127	207, 212
78-435	1978-2, 181	1108
78-441	1978-2, 152	799
78-442	*1978-2, 143*	655, *705*
79-2	1979-1, —	1029
79-4	*1979-1, 150*	*634*
79-8	1979-1, 92	83
79-9	1979-1, 125	83, 145
79-10	1979-1, 140	148
79-50	1979-1, 138	144
79-68	1979-1, 133	123
79-70	1979-1, 144	336
79-89	1979-1, 152	636
79-106	1979-1, 448	898
79-155	1979-1, 153	533
79-163	1979-1, 131	473
79-184	1979-1, 143	300
79-194	*1979-1, 145*	*333*
79-250	1979-2, 156	567
79-257	1979-2, 136	300
79-258	1979-2, 143	395
79-274	*1979-2, 131*	*474*
79-287	1979-2, 130	473
79-289	1979-2, 145	654
79-334	1972-2, 127	176
79-394	1979-2, 141	693
79-434	1979-2, 155	573
80-26	1980-1, 66	225
80-33	1980-1, 6	467
80-46	1980-1, 62	861
80-76	1980-1, 15	86
80-105	1980-1, 78	616
80-169	1980-1, 188	1210
80-181	1980-2, 121	694
80-189	1980-2, 106	277
80-196	1980-2, 32	86
80-198	*1980-2, 113*	*408*
80-199	*1980-2, 122*	*399*
80-228	1980-2, 115	398
80-284	1981-2, 117	616
80-285	1980-2, 119	617
81-3	1981-1 I.R.B. 11	300
81-25	1981-4 I.R.B. 11	574
81-41	*1981-6 I.R.B. 5*	*177*
81-81	1981-11 I.R.B. 37	473, 639
81-91	*1981-12 I.R.B. 5*	*470*
81-92	1981-1, 133	574
81-169	1981-25 I.R.B. 17	533
81-187	1981-2, 167	1215
81-233	1981-2, 83	176
81-247	1981-2, 87	575
81-289	*1981-2, 82*	*208*, 212
82-11	1982-1, 51	27

Revenue Ruling	Cum. Bull. Citation	
82-43	1982-1, 89	976
82-118	1982-1, 56	473
82-135	1982-2, 104	963
82-187	*1982-2, 80*	*290*
82-191	1982-2, 78	473
83-42	1983-1, 76	506
83-68	1983-1, 75	489
83-73	1983-1, 84	837
83-98	*1983-2, 40*	*76*
83-114	1983-2, 66	718
84-30	1984-1, 115	617
84-71	*1984-1, 106*	*616*
84-79	1984-1, 190	1030
84-104	1984-2, 94	630
84-111	*1984-2, 88*	*336*
84-114	*1984-2, 90*	*671*
84-131	1984-2, 37	1201
84-137	1984-1, 116	1149
84-141	1984-2, 80	506
85-14	1985-1, 92	181
85-19	1985-1, 94	176
85-48	1985-1, 126	151
85-106	*1985-2, 116*	*210*
85-107	1985-2, 121	650
85-138	*1985-2, 122*	*639, 643*
85-139	*1985-2, 123*	*641*
85-164	1985-2, 117	383
85-198	1985-2, 120	575
86-4	1986-1, 174	719
86-27	1986-1, 608	1174
86-104	1986-2, 80	1177
86-110	1986-2, 150	1210
86-125	1986-2, 57	694
86-126	1986-2, 58	694
87-9	*1987-1, 133*	*353*
87-75	1987-2, 152	1046
87-76	1987-2, 84	574
87-88	*1987-2, 81*	*179*
88-38	1988-21, 17	1001
88-48	1988-1, 531	567, 652
88-55	1988-2, 45	271
88-66	1988-2, 34	15

	I.R.B. Citation	
88-76	1988-38, 1	898
89-37	*1989-11, 4*	*707*
89-46	*1989-14, 16*	*1060*
89-57	1989-17, 4	277
89-63	*1989-18, 4*	*467*

Letter Ruling	CCH Citation	
7921075	**IRS Letter Rulings** (1979)	632
8022017	**IRS Letter Rulings** (1980)	1022
8027027	**IRS Letter Rulings** (1980)	269
8428006	**IRS Letter Rulings** (1984)	556

Table of Revenue Procedures

Miscellaneous Authorities

Italic numbers indicate pages in this volume.

Index